THE WORKS

OF

BEN JONSON

WITH

CRITICAL AND EXPLANATORY NOTES

AND A MEMOIR BY

WILLIAM GIFFORD

EDITED BY LIEUT.-COL.

FRANCIS CUNNINGHAM

A NEW IMPRESSION
IN THREE VOLUMES—VOL. I

LONDON
CHATTO & WINDUS
1912

Printing Statement:

Due to the very old age and scarcity of this book, many of the pages may be hard to read due to the blurring of the original text, possible missing pages, missing text, dark backgrounds and other issues beyond our control.

Because this is such an important and rare work, we believe it is best to reproduce this book regardless of its original condition.

Thank you for your understanding.

CONTENTS

OF

THE FIRST VOLUME.

[Gifford's Dedication.]

TO

THE RIGHT HONOURABLE

GEORGE CANNING,

PRESIDENT OF THE BOARD OF CONTROL FOR INDIA, ETC. ETC.,

THIS EDITION OF THE

WORKS OF BEN JONSON,

IN TESTIMONY OF THE SINCEREST ADMIRATION OF HIS TRANSCENDENT TALENTS,

OF THE HIGHEST RESPECT FOR HIS PUBLIC PRINCIPLES AND PRIVATE VIRTUES,

AND IN GRATEFUL ACKNOWLEDGMENT OF THE FRIENDSHIP

WITH WHICH FOR A LONG SERIES OF YEARS HE HAS HONOURED THE EDITOR,

is

WITH PRIDE AND PLEASURE MOST AFFECTIONATELY

Inscribed.

July 3rd, 1816.

Memoirs of Ben Jonson.

By William Gifford.

To write the Life of Jonson as it has been usually written, would be neither a very long nor a very difficult task ; since I should have only to transcribe from former biographers the vague accounts which each, in succession, has taken from his predecessor ; and to season the whole with the captious and splenetic insinuations of the critics, and commentators on our dramatic poetry. A due respect for the public seemed to require something more. It was fully time to examine into the authenticity of the charges incessantly urged against this eminent man ; and this has been, at least, attempted. The result has not accorded with the general persuasion concerning him. The reader, therefore, who has the courage to follow me through these pages, must be prepared to see many of his prejudices overthrown, to hear that he has been imposed upon by the grossest fabrications, and (however mortifying the discovery may prove)[1] that many of those who have practised on his integrity and surprised his judgment, are weak at once and worthless, with few pretensions to talents and none to honesty.

BENJAMIN, or (as the name is usually abbreviated by himself) BEN JONSON,[1] was born in the early part of the year 1574[2] [1573]. His grandfather was a man of some family and fortune, and originally settled at Annandale, in Scotland, from which place he removed to Carlisle, and was subsequently taken into the service of Henry VIII. His father, who was probably about the court, suffered a long imprisonment under

---

[1] JONSON.] The attacks on our author begin at a pretty early period. He knew his own name, it seems, and persisted in writing it correctly, though "some of his best friends " misspelt it ! This is produced, in the "*Biographia Britannica,*" as "an instance of that *affectation* which so strongly marks the poet's character." But this perseverance in the right was a family failing, for his mother (as it appears) wrote it in the same manner. His "singularity" in this respect (these writers think) "would have been discovered, had he been more communicative—but it is observable, that though his descent was very far from being a discredit to him, yet we *never find him once* mentioning his family upon any occasion." From critics so disposed, Jonson must have had unusual good fortune to escape with justice. The fact, however, is that he is *once* found mentioning his family. He talked of it to Drummond, and had it pleased that worthy gentleman to be less sparing of his malice, and somewhat more liberal of his information, we might have obtained enough on this head to satisfy the most ardent curiosity.

[2] *The year* 1574.] The writers of the *Bio. Brit.* are somewhat embarrassed here, by a line in the Poem *left in Scotland,* in which Jonson says that he had then

"Told seven and forty years."

Now this, say they, as the poet was there in 1619, fixes his birth to the year 1572, and makes him two years older than is commonly supposed. But these critics should have looked into Drummond, instead of reasoning upon a fact which is not to be found there. In Drummond the line stands,

"Told *six and forty* years ;"

and the date subjoined is January, 1619-20. Jonson was then in his forty-sixth year : in short, there seems no plea for questioning the received opinion. The second folio is of various dates, and of little authority. That Jonson was born on the eleventh of June, which is also affirmed by those writers, is taken on the credit of another blunder in this volume, where, in the verses on Sir Kenelm Digby, "*my* birthday" is printed for "*his* birthday," &c. In the 12mo. edit., 1640, both the lines stand as here given. [The date is January, 1619, which, had it been written *in England,* would have meant 1620, but in *Scotland,* after 1600, the year commenced on the first of January. Gifford was not aware of this.—F. C.]

Queen Mary, and was finally deprived of his estate.[1] If religion was the cause, as is universally supposed, persecution only served to increase his zeal ; for he entered, some time afterwards, into holy orders, and became, as Antony Wood informs us, "a grave minister of the gospel."

Jonson was a posthumous child, and "made his first entry (the Oxford Antiquary says) on the stage of this vain world about a month after his father's death, within the city of Westminster." Fuller observes that though he could not, with all his inquiry, find him in his cradle, he could fetch him from his *long coats*. It would seem from this, that the residence of his father was unknown. Mr. Malone supposes, and on very good grounds,[2] that his mother married again in somewhat less than two years after the death of her first husband, and it was at this period, perhaps, that Fuller's researches found him, "a little child, in Hartshorn Lane, near Charing Cross," [now Northumberland Street].

His father-in-law was a master bricklayer by profession ; and there is no cause for believing that he was either unable or unwilling to bestow on his new charge such a portion of education as then commonly fell to the children of respectable craftsmen ; and Jonson was accordingly sent, when of a proper age, to a private school in the church of St. Martin in the Fields.

From this school it was natural to suppose that he would be taken to follow the occupation of his step-father ; but this was not the case. Respect for the memory of Mr. Jonson, or what is equally probable, a remarkable aptitude in the child for learning, raised him up a friend, who sent him, at his own expense, to Westminster school. Camden, a name dear to literature, was then the second master of this celebrated establishment ; young Jonson naturally fell under his care, and he was not slow in discovering, nor negligent in cultivating, the extraordinary talents of his pupil.

No record enables us to state how long he continued with this great man. Mr. Malone supposes that he was taken from him, when he had reached his thirteenth year ; but "Lord Winton" (G. Morley, Bishop of Winchester, who, as Izaak Walton tells us, knew Ben Jonson very well) "says he was in the sixth, *i. e.*, the uppermost form in the school,"[3] when he was removed ; and he could scarcely have attained this situation, as schools were then constituted, at thirteen.

---

[1] This is our author's own account ; it is therefore worse than folly to repeat from book to book, after Aubrey, that "Ben Jonson was a Warwickshire man." Mr. Malone says, that "a collection of poems by Ben Jonson, jun. (the son of our author), was published in 1672, with some lines addressed to all the ancient family of the Lucys, in which the writer describes himself as a 'little stream from their clear spring ;' a fact (continues he) which adds support to Dr. Bathurst's account" (the impossible story just quoted from Aubrey) "of his father's birth-place."—*Shak.* vol. ii. p. 311.* This is a strange passage. Young Jonson died before his father, in 1635, and the collection of which Mr. Malone speaks contains several pieces written after the Restoration. The very first poem in the book is addressed *by the author* to John, Earl of Rutland, and his son, Lord Roos, who was not born till both young Jonson and his father were dead! Had Mr. Malone even looked at the title-page of this little volume, he must have seen that the name of Ben Jonson, jun., was a mere catch-word ; for the poems are there expressly said to be "composed by W. S., gent." [Jonson's own words, as reported by Drummond, were, "His father came from Car-

lisle, and, he thought, from Annandale to It. He served King Henry VIII., and was a gentleman. His father losed all his estate under Queen Marie, having been cast in prisson and forfaitted ; at last turned minister ; so he was a minister's son."—*Conversations with Drummond.* Coming from Annandale, the family name must have been *Johnstone*. When Samuel Johnson was in the Hebrides, a certain Laird of Lochbuy asked him, "Are you of the Johnstons of Glencoe, or of Ardnamurchan?" To which Sir Walter Scott appends a note : "The Johnstons are a clan distinguished in Scottish *border* history, and as brave as any *Highland* clan that ever wore brogues."—*Croker's Boswell's Johnson*, p. 383.—F. C.]

[2] *On very good grounds.*] "I found, in the Register of St. Martin's, that a Mrs. Margaret Jonson was married in November, 1575, to Mr. Thomas Fowler."—MALONE. *Shak.*, vol. i. p. 622. There cannot, I think, be a reasonable doubt on the person here named ; unquestionably she was the poet's mother.—GIFFORD. [This conjecture has been shown to be altogether fallacious by Peter Cunningham (COLLIER's Shakspeare, 1st edit., vol. i. p. clxvi.). This Mrs. Thomas Fowler was buried in St. Martin's on the 2nd April, 1590.—F. C.]

[3] *Letters by Eminent Persons*, &c. 1813, vol. iii. p. 416. There is yet a difficulty. Grant was head master from 1572 to 1593, so that if Jonson was in the sixth form, and if the business of th.

---

* The edition of Shakspeare referred to here, and elsewhere, is uniformly that in fifteen vols. 8vo, published in 1793.

Jonson, who had a warm and affectionate heart, and ever retained an extraordinary degree of respect for his old master, thus addresses him in his Epigrams :—

> "Camden, most reverend head, to whom I owe
> All that I am in arts, and all I know——"

and in the dedication of *Every Man in his Humour*, he tells his "most learned and honoured friend," that he "is not one of those who can suffer the benefit conferred upon his youth to perish with his age;" and he adds that, in accepting the comedy, he will find no occasion to repent of having been his instructor. All this appears to argue greater maturity, and deeper studies than are usually allowed ; and I should therefore incline to refer the period of his leaving Westminster to his sixteenth year.·

From school Jonson seems to have gone at once to the University. The person who had hitherto befriended him, and whose name is unfortunately lost, gave a farther proof of kindness on this occasion, and, if we may trust Aubrey, procured him an exhibition at Cambridge, where, according to Fuller, "he was statutably admitted into St. John's College."[1] No note of his matriculation is to be found. By some accident there is an omission of names in the University Register, from June 1589 (when Jonson was in his sixteenth year), to June 1602 ; this may serve to corroborate the opinion given above, that the period fixed upon by Malone for our author's removal to the University is some-what too early.

The exhibition, whatever might be its value, was found inadequate to his support ; and as his parents were evidently unable to assist him, Jonson was compelled to relinquish his situation at Cambridge, and return to the house of his father.[2] How long he continued at college cannot be known. Fuller says "a few weeks ;" it was more probably many months : he had unquestionably a longer connexion with Cambridge than is usually supposed ; and he speaks of his obligations to the members of that University in terms which cannot be justified by a slight acquaintance.[3]

On returning to his parents, he was immediately taken into the business of his father-in-law. These good people have not been kindly treated. Wood terms the mother a silly woman ; and the father is perpetually reflected on for calling his son home, to work at his own profession. The mother, however, was not "silly ;" on the contrary, she was a high-spirited woman, fully sensible of the rank of her first husband in life, and of the extraordinary merits of her son ; but she was not apparently in circumstances to main-tain him without labour ; and as his father-in-law had readily acquiesced for many years in a mode of his education which must have occasioned some expense, there seems little cause for the ill humour with which the mention of their names is sure to be ac-companied.

Jonson, however, who both from birth and education had probably been encouraged to look to the church for an establishment, was exceedingly mortified at his new destina-tion. That he worked with a trowel in one hand, and a Horace or a Homer in the other; that he was admired, pitied, and relieved by Sutton, as Chetwood says, or by Camden, as others say,[4] and sent back to his studies, are figments pleasing enough to merit to be

---

school was conducted then as it is at present (which, however, does not appear), he must have been under him ; yet of Grant he says nothing. It is probable that Camden, who had a great affection for our author, continued to assist his studies.

[1] Aubrey says "Trinity College ;" and indeed if Jonson had been on the foundation at West-minster, and went, regularly, to Cambridge, this must have been the College : but his name does not appear among the candidates.

[2] In how many circumstances may not a re-semblance be traced between Jonson and his great namesake !

[3] In the Drummond Conversations, Jonson says "He was Master of Arts in both the Uni-versities, *by their favour not his studies;*" and Mr. David Laing remarks "there is no evidence

that he ever had the benefit of an academical education." Had he conceived himself to be-long to one University more than to the other, it seems strange that he should made no allu-sion to the circumstance in 1607, in his highly elaborated Dedication of *Volpone* to "The Most Noble and Most Equal Sisters, the Two Famous Universities." In the next age there was another illustrious poet and "old Westminster" who, under somewhat similar circumstances, left the question in no doubt.

> "Oxford to him a dearer name shall be
> Than his own mother university.
> Thebes did his green unknowing youth engage ;
> He chooses Athens in his riper age."—F. C.]

[4] Fuller tells us that "some gentlemen, pity-ing that his parts should be buried under the

believed; but, unfortunately, they have no foundation in truth. Neither friend nor admirer followed him to his humble employment; and he certainly experienced at this time no tokens of kindness. His own account is, that he "could not endure the occupation of a bricklayer; and, as his aversion increased, he made one desperate effort to escape from it altogether, not by returning to Cambridge, but by withdrawing to the Continent, and entering as a volunteer into the army then employed in Flanders. Such is the simple narrative of Jonson's life till he arrived at the age of eighteen. It is chiefly extracted from his own conversations, and has the merit of being at once probable and consistent.

How long our author had continued with his father-in-law is nowhere mentioned. It could not be a twelvemonth (though Mr. Malone strangely supposes it to have been five years);[1] but it was yet long enough to furnish a theme for illiberal sarcasm while he lived. "Let not those blush," says the worthy Fuller, "that have, but those that have not, a lawful calling;" a piece of advice which was wholly lost upon the poet's contemporaries, who recur perpetually to what Mr. A. Chalmers calls his "degrading occupation." Decker and others, who were at that very moment pledging their future labours for the magnificent loan of "five shillings," or writing "penny books" in spunging-houses, are high in mirth at the expense of the "bricklayer," and ring the changes on the "hod and trowel," the "lime-and-mortar poet," very successfully, and apparently very much to their own satisfaction.

Jonson's stay in the Low Countries did not extend much beyond one campaign: he had, however, an opportunity of signalizing his courage; having, as he told Drummond,

---

rubbish of so mean a calling, did by their bounty manumise him freely to follow his own ingenious inclination."—*Worthies of England*, vol. ii. p. 112. This, however, is no better founded than the rest. Another story is told by Wood (probably, on Aubrey's authority), that Jonson was taken from his father's business to accompany young Raleigh in his travels. Young Raleigh was at this time unborn—at any rate, he was "mewling and puking in his nurse's arms:" this, however, signifies nothing—the story is too good to be lost, as it tends to degrade Jonson, and it is therefore served up in every account of his life. "Mr. Camden recommended him to Sir W. Raleigh, who intrusted him with the education of his eldest son, a gay spark, who could not brook Ben's rigorous treatment; but perceiving one foible in his disposition, made use of that to throw off the yoke of his government, and that was an unlucky habit Ben had contracted, through his love of jovial company, of being overtaken with liquor, which Sir Walter did of all vices most abominate." And yet Sir Walter, who undoubtedly knew Jonson as well as his son, trusted this habitual drunkard with his education! and yet Camden, who never lost sight of him from his youth, recommended him!—"One day, when Ben had taken a plentiful dose, and was fallen into a profound sleep, young Raleigh got a great basket, and a couple of men, who laid Ben in it, and then with a pole carried him between their shoulders to Sir Walter, telling him their young master had sent home his tutor."—*Oldys's MS. Notes to Langbaine.* This absurd tale, which is merely calculated for the meridian of Mr. Joseph Miller, Mr. Malone quotes at full as an irrefragable proof that "Jonson was, at some period, tutor to this hopeful youth."

As young Raleigh was not born till 1595, Jonson could not well be tutor to him in 1593,

the period usually assigned. In 1603, when the child had barely attained his eighth year, Sir Walter was committed close prisoner to the Tower, where he remained under sentence of death till March, 1615, a few months before he sailed for Guiana. Of this the story-teller was probably ignorant; and he therefore talks as familiarly of Raleigh's *home*, as if he had been always living at large. The "shouldering" of Jonson, in a basket, through the streets of London, the triumphant entrance of the "porters" (with a train of boys at their heels) into the Tower, then guarded with the most jealous vigilance, and the facility with which they penetrate into the interior apartments, and lay their precious burden at the feet of the state prisoner—all these, and a hundred other improbabilities, awaken no suspicion in the commentators, nor, as far as I can find, in the reader!

Mr. A. Chalmers (*General Biography*) rejects Wood's account: yet he adds—"*So many* of Jonson's contemporaries have mentioned his connexion with the Raleigh family, that it is probable he was in some shape befriended by them." *Not one* of Jonson's contemporaries has a syllable on the subject! In fact, Jonson never much admired the moral character of Sir Walter Raleigh; his talents, indeed, he held in great respect, and he was well able to appreciate them, for he was personally acquainted with Sir Walter, and assisted him in writing his *History of the World;* he also wrote some good lines explanatory of the grave frontispiece to that celebrated work. [It is, however, quite certain that at a considerably later date Sir Walter did so employ him. In a portion of the Drummond Conversations, not known to Gifford, is the following:—"S. W. Raulighe sent him governour with his son, anno 1613, to France." The whole passage will be found in the *Conversations.*—F. C.]

[1] From 1588 to 1593.—*Shak.* vol. i. p. 624.

encountered and killed an enemy (whose spoils he carried off), in the sight of both armies.[1] This achievement is undoubtedly dwelt upon with too much complacency by the writers of the *Bio. Brit.*, for which they are properly checked by Mr. A. Chalmers, who is not himself altogether free from blame. "One man's killing and stripping another," he says, " is a degree of military prowess of no very extraordinary kind." Mr. Chalmers does not see that this was not a general action in which, as he justly observes, such circumstances are sufficiently common ; but a single combat, decided in the presence of both armies. In those days, when great battles were rarely fought, and armies lay for half a campaign in sight of each other, it was not unusual for champions to advance into the midst and challenge their adversaries. In a bravado of this nature, Jonson fought and conquered ; and though we may question the wisdom of the exploit, we may surely venture, without much violation of candour, to admit its gallantry. Jonson himself always talked with complacency of his military career. He loved, he says, the profession of arms ; and he boldly affirms, in an appeal to "the true soldier," (Epigram CVIII.) that while he followed it, he "did not shame it by his actions."[2]

Jonson brought little from Flanders (whence he was probably induced to return by the death of his father), but the reputation of a brave man, a smattering of Dutch, and an empty purse. Nothing, in fact, could be more hopeless than his situation. In the occupation of a bricklayer he had evidently attained no skill ; at all events, having already sacrificed so much to his aversion for it, he was not likely to recur to it a second time, and he had no visible means of subsistence. His biographers say, that he now went to Cambridge ; but without money, this was not in his power ; and indeed the circumstance appears altogether improbable. His father-in-law might perhaps be no more ; but his mother was still alive, and in London, and in her house he appears to have taken up his abode. He was not of a humour, however, to profit, in long inactivity, of her scanty resources, and he therefore adopted the resolution of turning his education to what account he could, and, like most of the poets, his contemporaries, seeking a subsistence from the stage. He was now about nineteen.

"Jonson began his theatrical career," Mr. Malone says, and he is followed by all who have since written on the subject, "as a strolling player, and after having rambled for some time by a play-waggon in the country, repaired to London, and endeavoured, at the Curtain, to obtain a livelihood among the actors, till, not being able to set a *good face upon't*, he could not get a service among the mimics." Although Mr. Malone gives this, and much more, from the *Satiromastix*, as if he really believed it, yet nothing is so questionable. What Decker means by "not setting a good face upon't," is easily understood :[3] Jonson was of a scorbutic habit, and his face might be affected with it at the period of Decker's writing ; but it had not been always so, and Aubrey expressly mentions that he was in his youth "of a clear and fair skin :" nor is it easy to be believed that he could not get a service among the wretched mimics in the skirts of the town. "I never," says the Duchess of Newcastle, whom Mr. Malone (upon another occasion indeed,) allows to be a good judge, "I never heard any man read well but my husband ; and I have heard him say, he never heard any man read well but Ben Jonson; and yet he hath heard many in his time."[4] With the advantages, therefore, of

---

[1] Jonson's words are, "In his service in the Low Countries, he had, in the face of both the campes, killed an enemie, and taken *opima spolia* from him."—F. C.]

[2] It is not improbable that these daring feats were encouraged by the English general. Stanley had delivered up a fort, which disgraced, as well as dispirited the army ; and Vere, who now commanded, made extraordinary efforts of gallantry to revive the ancient ardour. He stormed Daventer, and seemed to court danger. In 1591-2, large reinforcements were sent to Ostend, then held by an English garrison, and with these, I doubt not, Jonson went.

[3] It would be ridiculous to adopt this clumsy piece of wit, and argue from it that Jonson was a bad actor. Capell, who also quotes the passage, says, "This is meant of Jonson's *ugliness*, which is frequently played upon in this satire."—*School of Shakspeare*, vol. iii. p. 232. That Jonson was *ugly* is the dream of Capell ; his features were good. Decker adds that he had "a *very bad face* for a soldier." Now he certainly did not play this part amiss ; his courage was never doubted : but the quotation may serve to show the absurdity of founding positive charges upon such vague expressions. To do the commentators justice, they were ignorant of the existence of this last passage ; for they never examine their way, but boldly and blindly follow one another.

[4] His house was open to every man of genius and learning for more than half a century.—*Letters of the Duchess of Newcastle*, fol. 1664, p. 467.

youth, person, voice, and somewhat more of literature than commonly fell to the share of every obscure actor in a strolling company, Jonson could scarcely fail to get a service among the mimics, notwithstanding the grave authority of Captain Tucca.[1] That our author ever ambled by the side of a waggon, and *took mad Jeronymo's part*, though Mr. Malone repeats it with full conviction,[2] is also very questionable, or rather false altogether. It cannot have failed to strike every one who has read this production of Kyd (among whom I do not reckon Mr. Malone), that the author trusted for a great part of the effect of his tragedy to the contrast between the diminutive size of the marshal (Jeronymo) and the strutting of his language and action :

> "I'll not be long away,
> As *short my body*, short shall be my stay."
>
> "My mind's a *giant*, though my *bulk be small*."
>
> "I had need *wax* too ;
> Our foes will stride else over me and you."

He is thus addressed by Belthazar :

> "Thou *inch* of Spain,
> Thou man, from thy hose downward, scarce so much :
> Thou very little longer than thy beard,
> Speak not such big words, they will throw thee down,
> Little Jeronymo, words greater than thyself."[3]

And he signs himself " *little* Jeronymo, marshal." In a word, so many allusions of the most direct kind are made to this circumstance in every part of the play, that no tall or bulky figure could attempt the character without devoting it to utter ridicule. The fact is, that Jonson was employed by the manager to "write adycions" for this popular drama ; and that was sufficient for Decker's purpose.

Wood rejects the story of his ambling after a waggon, and tells us that upon his return from Cambridge (where he assuredly had not then been), "he did recede to a nursery or obscure playhouse, called the Green Curtain ;[4] but that his first action and writing there were both ill." Wood's authority, unfortunately, is of little weight in this case, being wholly derived from a vague report picked up by Aubrey from one John Greenhill. It is not too lightly to be credited that Jonson should be singled out for his incapacity amongst the unfledged nestlings of the "Green Curtain in Shoreditch."—But the matter is of little moment ; since wherever he acted or wherever he wrote, his labours were abruptly terminated by an event of a very serious nature, which took place almost immediately after his return from Flanders. It appears that he had some kind of

---

[1] Tucca is the creation of Jonson. He is described as a general railer, a man whose whole conversation is made up of scurrilous exaggerations and impossible falsehoods : yet he is the sole authority for this part of Jonson's life. The captain says in another place, "When thou rann'st mad for the death of Horatio, thou borrowedst a gown of Roscius, the stager, and sent'st it home lowsy ;" upon which the editor (Hawkins) wisely remarks—" Ben Jonson played the part of Jeronymo, as appears from this passage."

[2] "The first observation which I shall make on Aubrey's account is, that the latter part of it, which informs us that Ben Jonson was a bad actor," (*not a good one*, is Aubrey's expression), "is *incontestibly confirmed* by Decker," (in the passage just quoted).—*Shak.* vol. ii. p. 322. It seems to have escaped Mr. Malone, that to repeat a story after another is not to *confirm* it. Aubrey merely copies Decker.

[3] Mr. Collier in his *History of the Stage*, vol. iii. p. 208, says, "It is evident that if there be any truth in Dekker's assertion (controverted by Gifford) that Ben Jonson originally performed the part of Jeronimo, he must allude, not to the tragedy now under consideration [*The First Part of Jeronimo*], but to *The Spanish Tragedy*, where nothing is said regarding the personal appearance of the hero or his representative." Mr. Dyce remarks on the above, " Gifford's reasoning, however, still holds good. *The Spanish Tragedy* forms a *Second Part* to *The First Part of Jeronimo* ; and surely an audience to whom the diminutive hero of the *First Part* was so familiar, would hardly have tolerated such an absurdity as the personation of that character in the *Second Part* by a tall or bulky actor."— F. C.]

[4] Oldys, in his MS. notes to Langbaine, says that Jonson was himself the master of a playhouse in the Barbican. He adds that the poet speaks of his theatre ; and Mr. A. Chalmers repeats from this idle authority, that " in his writings mention is made of *his theatre* !" So the blind lead the blind ! Jonson's *theatre* is his book of Epigrams.

dispute with a person whose rank or condition in life is not known, but who is commonly supposed to be a player.[1] In consequence of this he was called out, or, as he says, "appealed to a duel." He was not of a humour to decline the invitation. They met, and he killed his antagonist,[2] who seems to have acted with little honour ; having brought to the field, as our author told Drummond, a sword ten inches longer than his own. His victory, however, left him little cause for exultation : he was severely wounded in the arm, thrown into prison for murder, and, as he says himself, "brought near the gallows."

Here he was visited by a popish priest, who took advantage of the unsettled state of his religious opinions,[3] to subvert his mind, and induce him to renounce the faith in which he had been bred, for the errors of the Romish Church. This has been attributed by some to his fears. "His tough spirit," say the authors of his life, in the *Bio. Brit.* "sank into some degrees of melancholy, so that he became a fit object to be subdued by the crafty attacks of a popish priest." Others, following the opinion of Drummond, attribute the change to an indifference about all religions. It is probable that neither was the cause. Such conversions were among the daily occurrences of the time ; even among those who had more years than Jonson, and far more skill in controversy than he could possibly have. His own account of the matter is very concise : he took, he says, the priest's word : he did not however always continue in this state of ignorance ; and it is to his praise that, at a more mature age he endeavoured to understand the ground of his belief, and diligently studied the fathers, and *those wiser guides* who preached the words of truth in simplicity.[4]

While he was in prison, there were (as he told Drummond) spies set to catch him ;[5] but he was put upon his guard by the gaoler, to whose friendly warning he probably owed his life ; as he was the most incautious of men in his conversation. These spies could have nothing to do with the cause of his imprisonment, and must therefore have been employed about him solely on account of his connexion with the popish priest. The years 1593 and 1594 were years of singular disquietude and alarm. The Catholics, who despaired of effecting anything against the Queen by open force, engaged in petty conspiracies to take her off by sudden violence. The nation was agitated by these plots,

---

[1] I know of no authority for this but Captain Tucca. "Art not famous enough yet, my mad Harostratus, for killing a *player*, but thou must eat men alive."—*Satiromastix.*

[2] "He killed," Aubrey says, "Mr. Marlow the poet, on Bunhill, coming from the Green Curtain playhouse." Mr. Marlowe the poet, whose memory Jonson held in high estimation, was killed at least two years before this period in a brothel squabble. But whoever expects a rational account of any fact, however trite, from Aubrey, will meet with disappointment. Had any one told this "maggoty-pated" man that Jonson had killed "Mr. Shakspeare the poet," he would have received the tale with equal facility, and recorded it with as little doubt of its truth. In short, Aubrey thought little, believed much, and confused everything. [Jonson's words are "Since his coming to England, being appealed to the Fields, he had killed his adversarie, which had hurt him in the arme, and whose sword was 10 inches longer than his ; to the which he was emprissoned, and almost at the gallowes." Mr. Collier among his innumerable services to our literary history, has printed (*Life of Alleyn*, p. 50) a letter from Henslowe, which makes it certain that this "appeal to the Fields" did not take place till 1598, and that the "adversarie" was an actor named Gabriel Spenser. "Since you weare with me, I have lost one of my company which hurteth me greatly, that is Gabrell, for he is slayen in

Hogesden fylldes by the hands of bergemen Jonson, bricklayer." Mr. Collier thinks it strange that the man who two years before had written *Every Man in his Humour*, should still be called *Bricklayer*, but Henslowe was writing in bitterness of spirit for the loss of a useful servant and friend, and gives him a title which we can well imagine was often enough employed behind his back, perhaps sometimes thrown in his teeth, in the horseplay and coarse raillery of a sixteenth century green-room. In this way it is quite probable that the mis-spelling *bergemen* (*quasi* bargeman) may be intentional, and that the cause of the "appeal to the Fields" may be thus shadowed forth by Henslowe.—F.C.]

[3 Drummond's words are "Then took he his religion by trust, of a priest who visited him in prison."—F.C.]

[4] I know not why Jonson should be reproached for this change, as he frequently is : far from arguing a total carelessness, as they say, it would seem rather a proof of the return of a serious mind. The great and good Jeremy Taylor was a convert to popery for a short time : so was Chillingworth, and so were a thousand more of the same description. In fact, young men (and Jonson was at this time a very young man) of a serious way of thinking, of warm imaginations, and of ill-digested studies, are not among the most unfavourable subjects for proselytism.

[5 We know that a spy reported the incautious talk of Marlowe.—F.C.]

which were multiplied by fear ; and several seminaries, as the popish priests educated abroad were then called, were actually convicted of attempts to poison the Queen, and executed. Jonson revenged himself for the insidious attacks made on his life, by an epigram which he afterwards printed, and which is not one of his best :—

> " Spies, you are lights in state, but of base stuff,
> Who, when you've burnt yourselves down to the snuff,
> Stink, and are thrown aside :—End fair enough !"

It is not known to what, or whom, Jonson finally owed his deliverance from prison. Circumstances were undoubtedly in his favour, for he had received a challenge, and he had been unfairly opposed in the field ; as criminal causes were then conducted, these considerations might not, however, have been sufficient to save him. The prosecution was probably dropt by his enemies.

On his release, he naturally returned to his former pursuits, unpromising as they are represented to be. With that happy mode of extricating himself from a part of his difficulties which men of genius sometimes adopt, he now appears to have taken a wife.[1] She was young and a Catholic like himself ; in no respect, indeed, does his choice seem to have discredited his judgement ; which is more, perhaps, than can fairly be said for his partner : but she was a woman of domestic habits, and content, perhaps, to struggle with poverty for the sake of her children.[2] She was dead when Jonson visited Scotland in 1618, and in the costive and splenetic abridgment of his conversations with Drummond, she is shortly mentioned as having been shrewish, but honest (i.e., faithfully attached) to her husband.[3]

But what were the pursuits by which Jonson had hitherto been enabled to procure a precarious subsistence ?—Assuredly not ambling by a waggon, nor "acting and writing ill" at the Green Curtain. The fortunate preservation of Mr. Henslowe's memorandums, amidst the wreck of so much valuable matter through the sloth and ignorance of the

---

[1] Jonson was now in his 20th year. I have followed the writers of the *Bio. Brit.*, who suppose that his first child was a daughter. In the beautiful Epitaph on her, beginning,—

> " Here lies, to each her parents' ruth,
> Mary, the daughter of their youth :"

she is said, by the poet, to be "his first daughter ;" she might not, however, have been his first child : yet, I believe, from other circumstances, that the biographers are correct. In this case, Jonson's marriage must have taken place at latest in 1594, as we know that he had a son born in 1596. This date is the first of which we can speak decidedly ; it is therefore of some moment in our author's life. From 1596 the years are sufficiently marked : antecedently to this period some latitude must be allowed. [Since Gifford wrote, the parish registers of London have been very narrowly examined, but as far as I am aware no record has been discovered which can determine the date of Ben Jonson's marriage. Gifford, however, is certainly wrong in saying that it took place *after* instead of *before* his imprisonment. We know that he killed Gabriel Spencer in 1598, and that his "first son" was seven in 1603, (see Epigram XLV.). In the register of St. Martin's-in-the-Fields is an entry :—

1593, November 17th. Septla fuit Maria
        Johnson peste :

which, if it applies to Mary the daughter of his youth," (see Epigram XXII.), would make him a father in his teens, for, being six months old when she died, her parents must have been married in the middle of 1592. Mr. Collier summarily rejects this entry as applying to the poet. I suppose on account of extreme improbability ; but Edward III. was not eighteen years older than the Black Prince, and Warren Hastings and his father must have been still more nearly of an age. Of other children of Jonson's the registers mention :—

1. A son, named Joseph, buried on 9th December, 1599, at St. Giles's, Cripplegate.
2. An "infant" son, named Benjamin, buried 1st October, 1600, at St. Botolph, Bishopsgate.
3. Benjamin Johnson, sonne to Benjamin, baptized 20th February, 1607, (i.e., 1608), in St. Anne's, Blackfriars, and buried in the same parish, 18th November, 1611.
4. Benjamin Johnson fil.: Ben. bapt. fuit Aprilis 6th, 1610. St. Martin's-in-the-Fields.

The learned members of the Shakspeare Society, from whose publications these facts are derived, make no attempt to explain how these two Benjamin-ben-Benjamins could have been alive at the same time. From the register of St Giles's, Cripplegate, Mr. Collier has extracted the following entry, which he thinks may probably record a second marriage of the poet's :—

"Married Ben Johnson and Hester Hopkins.
              27th July, 1623."—F.C.]

[2] He must have been married some years before his duel and imprisonment.
[3] The words are "He maried a wyfe who was a shrew, yet honest : 5 yeers he had not bedded with her, but remayned with my Lord Aulbanie."—F.C.]

members of Dulwich College, has given a sort of precision to this period of dramatic history, which no one was sanguine enough to expect. From the extracts made by Mr. Malone, and introduced into his excellent *History of the English Stage*, we are enabled to trace the early part of Jonson's dramatic career with some degree of accuracy ; and we find him, as might be expected, following the example of contemporary poets, and writing in conjunction with those who were already in possession of the stage : a practice encouraged by the managers, whose chance of loss it diminished.[1]

The notices which Mr. Malone has copied from the MS. respecting the dramatic writers, begin with 1597 ; but he has given a curious account of the pieces performed by Mr. Henslowe's companies, which commences at an earlier period. As we know not the titles of Jonson's first dramas, it is not possible to discover whether any of those mentioned previously to 1596, belong to him. *Every Man in his Humour* is the first piece in the list which we can appropriate ; and this was then a popular play ; having been acted, as Mr. Henslowe says, eleven times between the 25th of November 1596, and the 10th of May in the succeeding year. Before this period, however, he must have written for the stage both alone and with others ; and with such success as to induce Henslowe and his son-in-law, the celebrated Alleyn, to advance money upon several of his plots in embryo ; a sufficient confutation of the oft-repeated tale of his "ill-writing," &c. In this year his wife brought him a son ;[2] so that he had occasion for all his exertions.

In *Every Man in his Humour*, and in the Prologue to it, which breathes a similar spirit, we find strong traces of the ennobling idea, which Jonson had already formed of poetry in general, and of the true and dignified office of the Dramatic Muse,

> " Indeed, if you will look on Poesie,
> As she appears in many, poor and lame,
> Patch'd up in remnants, and old worn-out rags,
> Half-starv'd for want of her peculiar food,
> Sacred Invention ; then I must confirm
> Both your conceit and censure of her merit.
> But view her in her glorious ornaments,
> Attired in the majesty of art,
> Set high in spirit with the precious taste
> Of sweet philosophy, and, which is most,
> Crown'd with the rich traditions of a soul
> That hates to have her dignity profaned
> With any relish of an earthly thought ;
> Oh then how proud a presence does she bear !
> Then is she like herself ; fit to be seen
> Of none but grave and consecrated eyes !"

[1] They usually hired the writers, and advanced them money upon the credit of their talents, and the progress of their work, which was shown or reported to them from time to time.

[2] To this child, perhaps, the players stood god-fathers. A foolish story is told in some old jest-book, which would scarcely be worth repeating here, were it not for the notable use which is made of it by the commentators on Shakspeare. "Shakspeare was god-father to one of Ben Jonson's children, and after the christening, being in deep study, Jonson came to cheer him up ; and asked him why he was so melancholy ? No, faith, Ben, says he, not I ; but I have been considering a great while what should be the fittest gift for me to bestow upon my god-child, and I have resolved at last. I prithee what ? says he. I'faith, Ben, I'll e'en give her a dozen good Latin (latten) spoons, and thou shalt *translate* them. This *jest* (it is Capell who speaks) will stand in need of no comment with those who are at all acquainted with Jonson ; it must have out to the quick : and endangered the opening some old sores about the latter's *Sejanus*, whose latinity produced its damnation : this play was brought upon Shakspeare's stage in 1603, (the first year of his management,) and he performed in it himself : and the miscarriage sour'd Jonson, and he broke with the manager : venting his spleen against him in some of his prefaces, in terms oblique but intelligible, and breathing *malice* and *envy* : the breach was healed at this time ; but with *some remembrance* of it on the part of Shakspeare." *Notes on Shak.*, vol. i. p. 94. It would be a mere loss of time to strive to fix a period for an event which never took place ; though it may not be irrelevant to observe upon it, that in every occurrence between Jonson and Shakspeare which has crept into the story-books of those times, the latter is invariably represented as the aggressor. Had the foregoing anecdote been founded on fact, it would only have proved that the wit and good manners of Shakspeare's return to Ben's civility were pretty nearly equal. As the story appears in Capell, (who thought of nothing less than serving Jonson), it has yet a worse aspect.

These lines, which were probably written before he had attained his twenty-second year, do not discredit him ; and let it be added, to his honour, that he invariably supported, through every period of his chequered life, the lofty character with which his youthful fancy had invested the Muse.

Some judgment of Jonson's situation at this time may be formed from a memorandum of Mr. Henslowe's, recording an advance of "five shillings ;" yet even this could not induce him to have recourse for success to the popular expedients of bustle, and warlike show, which he believed, with his classic masters, to outrage probability, and violate the decorum of the stage. In the Prologue, he says—

> "Though NEED make many poets, and some, such
> As art and nature have not better'd much ;
> Yet OUR'S, *for want* hath *not so lov'd* the stage
> As he dare serve th' ill customs of the age ;
> Or purchase your delight at such a rate,
> As, for it, he himself must justly hate."[1]

From a resolution thus early formed, he never deviated, and when it is considered that in consequence of it he braved want and obloquy, whatever may be thought of his

---

[1] This Prologue assumes a considerable degree of importance from its being made the principal basis of the calumny against Jonson ; and the reader must therefore indulge me in some remarks on it. "All Shakspeare's plays are ridiculed in it," cry the commentators ; and a thousand voices re-echo, "all Shakspeare's plays are ridiculed in it." It might puzzle a man of plain sense (indeed, Mr. Malone confesses that it puzzled himself at first,) to comprehend how what was written in 1596 could possibly "ridicule" what was not in existence till nearly twenty years afterwards : but the difficulty is thus solved. The Prologue was not published with the 4to edition of *Every Man in his Humour ; — therefore* it was not written till some time before the appearance of the folio ;— *therefore* it ridicules all Shakspeare's plays ! That any rational being should persuade himself, or hope to persuade another, that the lines were composed and spoken at this late period, can only be accounted for by the singular power of self-delusion. For many years before and after 1616 (the date of the folio), Jonson was in a state of the highest prosperity : the favourite of princes, the companion of nobles, the pride and delight of the theatre, yet he is supposed to say that "though *poverty* made many poets, and himself, among the rest, *it* should not compel him to disgrace his judgment," &c.!—*Every Man in his Humour* had been a stock-play for nearly twenty years, during which it had probably been represented a hundred times, yet the author is imagined to beseech the audience that they would be *pleased*, TO-DAY, to see *one such a play*, &c.! As if all this was not sufficient to fool the credulous reader to *the top of his bent*, he is further required to believe that after the *Fox*, the *Silent Woman*, the *Alchemist*, in a word, after eleven of his best pieces had obtained full possession of the stage, Jonson came forward, *for the first* time, to tell the public on what principles he proposed to construct his dramas—concluding with a hope that the spectators would like the specimen which he was now about to offer them ! And why is the public called upon to swallow these monstrous absurdities ? Because the commentators cannot otherwise prove that the great object of "Jonson's life was to persecute Shakspeare." "If the Prologue was not written about 1614," says one of the most furious of them, very ingenuously, "my speculations fall to the ground !"

If it be asked why the author did not print the Prologue with the play for which it was written, it may be demanded in return, why many other things which appear in the folio were not printed in the 4tos and why much that appears in the 4tos is not found in the folio ? No better reason, I believe, can be given, than that such was the publisher's pleasure.

It is more than time to advert to the proofs produced by the commentators to show how the Prologue bears on all Shakspeare's plays.

> "To make a child new swaddled, to proceed
> *Man*, and then shoot up, in *one beard and weed*,
> To *fourscore* years."

"This is a *sneer* at the *Winter's Tale*, written in 1604," in which Perdita, as all the world knows, undergoes these various changes!*

> "with three rusty swords
> And help of some few foot-and-half-foot words,
> Fight over York's and Lancaster's long jars"—

"This is a *sneer* at Shakspeare's three parts of *Henry VI.*!" "I have endeavoured," Mr. Malone says, *Shak.* vol. I. p. 492, "to prove that *two* of

---

* Mr. Malone also proves that the *Duchess of Malfy* was written in 1616, simply because Jonson sneers at it in these lines. *Shak.* vol. xi. p. 545. Mr. Steevens, still more *mal-à-droit*, in a moment of heedlessness, informs us "that in Lily's *Endymion*, which comprises nearly half a century, all the personages of the drama, with one exception, continue *unchanged*, wearing the same *beard and weed* for more than *forty* years." These discoveries are unluckily made—as they may lead those who think at all, to suspect that Jonson might have other persons in view than Perdita.

prudence, the praise of consistency must, at least, be awarded to him. What else he wrote in 1597 is not known: two sums of "fower pounds," and "twenty shillings," were advanced to him by Mr. Henslowe, upon the credit of two plays,[1] which he had then in hand: but their titles do not occur, at least with his name. The "book of

these three parts were not written originally by Shakspeare." *Papæ!* Again: "There were *two* preceding dramas, one of which was called the contention of *York* and *Lancaster*." Why then might not this be the drama meant? But were there not *two score* old plays on this subject on the stage? Undoubtedly there were: and I could produce numerous passages in which plays on the long jars between the two houses are mentioned, all anterior to this period.

"With *three* rusty swords."*

This, however, with the rest of the quotation, is merely a versification, as Mr. Gilchrist has well observed, of what Sir Philip Sidney had written many years before on the poverty and ignorance of the old stage. Sir Philip, indeed, says "*four* swords:" of their "rustiness" he takes no notice, and so far Jonson has shown his spite to Shakspeare. But how happens it that a yet stronger passage than this escaped the vigilant malice of the commentators?

"to disgrace
With *four* or five most vile and ragged foils,
Right ill-disposed, in brawl ridiculous,
The name of Agincourt."

Here the *sneer* is evident! Here, indeed, as Mr. Malone says, "old Ben speaks out!" Here everything is changed for the worse: the *rusty sword* for "a most vile and ragged foil;" and the *long jars* of York and Lancaster, for "a ridiculous brawl!" *Ecquid, Jupiter, tam lente, audis!*—"Not to keep the reader in suspense," however, this atrocious attack on Shakspeare was made—by Shakspeare himself! It is found in one of his most beautiful choruses to *Henry V.* One curious circumstance is yet to be noticed: although the commentators dwell upon every trifling expression on which they can possibly raise a note, yet this striking passage is slipped over by them all in solemn silence; *Shak.* vol. ix. p. 401. "There's method in this madness!"

The "foot-and-half words" are "a sneer at *Richard III.*, where we find such epithets as *childish-foolish, senseless-obstinate*," &c. It is not Jonson's fault if his persecutors prove as ignorant as they are malicious. Before the date of this Prologue (1596) he had probably translated the *Art of Poetry:* there, the lines

Telephus, et Peleus cum pauper et exul uterque,
Projicit ampullas et sesquipedalia verba;

* It is observed by Mr. Malone, *Shak.* vol. ii. p. 220, that "such was the poverty of the old stage, that the same person played two or three parts, and battles, on which the fate of an empire was supposed to depend, were decided by three combatants on a side." Though this be true, yet I hardly expected to find the critic joining our author in *sneering* at Shakspeare.

are thus rendered:—

"Peleus and Telephus,
When they are poor and banish'd, must throw by
Their bombard phrase, and foot-and-half-foot words."

Here the poet, with his wonted accuracy, uses "foot-and-half-foot words"—not for feeble epithets linked together by hyphens, but for swelling, vaunting, bombast language.

"Where neither chorus wafts you o'er the seas,
Nor creaking throne comes down the boys to please,
——nor tempestuous drum."

There was scarcely a play on the stage when Jonson first came to it, which did not avail itself of a *chorus* to waft its audience over sea and land, or over wide intervals of time. Enough of both may be found in *Pericles, Faustus, Fortunatus,* and other dramas which yet remain; to say nothing of those to which allusions are made by the old critics, and which have long since worthily perished. "The *creaking throne* is a sneer at *Cymbeline*," in which Jupiter, it seems, "descends on an eagle!" "The *tempestuous* drum is a *ridicule* of the *Tempest;*" and as that comedy was not written till 1611-12-13, it ascertains the date of the Prologue to a nicety.

It is to be regretted that Mr. Malone never read Jonson, as he might have saved himself and Mr. G. Chalmers a world of trouble in dandling this play backwards and forwards, on account of the last-quoted passage. In a *Speech according to Horace* (*Underwoods,* lxiii.), undoubtedly subsequent to the *Tempest,* we find the words "*tempestuous grandlings*." Here the allusion is not only to the *title* of the play, but most palpably to Gonzalo, Adrian, Francisco, and, perhaps, to Prospero himself!

After such overwhelming proofs it cannot but surprise the reader to hear one of Jonson's critics speak thus doubtingly: "Perhaps Shakspeare himself, *by the help of a proper application,* was designed to be included!" O the power of candour! But far better is the writer's amended judgment. "Other dramatists had indeed written on the jars of York and Lancaster, but Jonson doth not appear to have thought *them* worthy of his notice"! And best of all is the liberal conclusion of Steevens: "The *whole of Ben Jonson's Prologue to Every Man in his Humour* is a *malicious sneer* at Shakspeare," vol. xiii. p. 249.

[1] "The following curious notices" (says Mr. Malone, *Shak.* vol. ii. p. 484) "occur relative to Shakspeare's *old antagonist,* Ben Jonson."—When it is considered that Jonson was at this time scarcely 22, (Shakspeare was 32,) that by Mr. Malone's own account, he was not known

which he shewed the company the plotte," might have been the *Case is Altered*.[1] He was now recent from the Roman writers of comedy, and in this pleasant piece, both Plautus and Terence are laid under frequent contribution.

The success of *Every Man in his Humour* appears to have encouraged the author to attempt to render it yet more popular: accordingly he transferred the scene, which in the former play lay in the neighbourhood of Florence, to London, changed the Italian names for English ones, and introduced such appropriate circumstances as the place of action seemed to require. In fact, the attempt was to be expected, from the improvement which was visibly taking place in his mind. Young[2] as he was, when he wrote this drama, it is scarcely to be wondered that he should fall into the common practice, and while he placed his scene in Italy, draw all his incidents from his own country. It must be added to his praise, that he did not entirely neglect the decorum of place, even in this performance: but there was yet too much of English manners, and the reformation of the piece was therefore well-timed and judicious. Jonson fell into no subsequent incongruities of this kind, for *The Fox* is without any tincture of foreign customs, and his two tragedies are chastely Roman.

"But notwithstanding" (Whalley says) "the art and care of Jonson to redress the incongruities taken notice of, a remarkable instance of Italian manners is still preserved, which, in transferring the scene he forgot to change. It is an allusion to the custom of poisoning, of which we have instances of various kinds, in the dark and fatal revenges of Italian jealousy. Kitely is blaming Well-bred for promoting the quarrel between Bobadil and Downright, and Well-bred offers to excuse himself by saying that no harm had happened from it. Kitely's wife then objects to him: 'But what harm might have come of it, brother?' to whom Well-bred replies, '*Might*, sister? so might the good warm clothes your husband wears be poisoned for anything he knows, or the wholesome wine he drank even now at table.' Kitely's jealous apprehension is immediately alarmed, and he breaks out in a passionate exclamation:—

> ' Now God forbid. O me I now I remember
> My wife drank to me last, and changed the cup ;
> And bade me wear *this cursed suit* to-day.'

And thus he goes on, imagining that he feels the poison begin to operate upon him.

---

to Shakspeare, whom he could in no possible way have offended, the justice of calling him the *old antagonist* of our great poet is not a little questionable. The notices are: " Lent unto Benjemen Johnson player, the 22nd of July 1597, in ready money, the some of fower poundes, to be payed yt agen whensoever either I or my sonne (Alleyn) shall demand yt."

" Lent unto Benjemen Johnsone the 3rd of december 1597, upon a book which he was to writte for us before crysmas nexte after the date here of, which he showed the plotte unto the company : I say lent unto hime in redy money, the some of xxs.

[1] This Comedy is usually assigned to 1598, principally because of its allusion to Antony Munday, which appeared in the *Wit's Treasurie*, published in that year. But Antony might have been called "our best plotter" before Meares wrote his pedantic conundrums ; and, indeed, the words have to me the air of a quotation. I am almost inclined to set down this as the earliest of our author's dramas; in 1598 it was already a popular piece, and it bears about it the marks of juvenility.

It is doubted in the *Bio. Dram.* whether Jonson be the author of this piece, because, says the writer, it is printed without a dedication, which is commonly prefixed to his early plays, &c. I cannot stoop to contend with sheer ignorance ; but in the first place, the play was not published by Jonson ; and in the second, his dedications are more frequent in the folio than in the 4tos.

[2] The reader of the present day, who has been accustomed to hear of nothing but " *old* Ben," will start, perhaps to find that he once was *young*. The appellation was first given to him by Sir John Suckling, a gay, careless, good-humoured wit of the court, in 1637 :

" The next that approached was *good old Ben*."

" Good," the commentators are careful to omit ; but " *old* Ben" they are never weary of repeating. Mr. Malone says that this title was not familiarly given to him during his life. In fact, it was *never* familiarly given to him, till he and his friend Steevens took it up, and applied it as a term of ridicule and contempt in every page. That Ben was termed *old* on one occasion shortly after his death is scarcely a sufficient plea for making the appellation perpetual, or we might confer it on all the writers of his time. We hear of *old* Massinger, and *old* Shirley ; and the publishers of Beaumont and Fletcher advertise their reader, " that after they shall have reprinted Jonson's two volumes, they hope to reprint *old* Shakspeare." See the Booksellers' *address*, fol. 1679. What would Mr. Malone have said if the editors of any of our old dramatists had nauseated their readers from page to page (on this authority) with a repetition of *old* Shakspeare ?

Nothing could be more in character than this surmise, supposing the persons, as was the case at first, to have been natives of Italy. But had Jonson recollected, it is probable he would have varied the thought to adapt it more consistently to the genius and manners of the speaker."—*Preface*, p. xii.

I have given this tedious passage at large because the happy discovery which it holds forth has been received with vast applause by the critics. In Hurd's letter to Mason *On the Marks of Imitation*, it is said, "The late editor of Jonson's works observes *very well* the impropriety of leaving a trait of Italian manners in his *Every Man in his Humour*, when he fitted up that play with English characters. Had the scene been originally laid in England, and that trait been given us, it had convicted the poet of *imitation*," p. 18. Such solemn absurdity is intolerable. The truth is, that Jonson could not have devised a more characteristic "trait" of the times in which he wrote. Poisoning was unfortunately too well understood and too common in this country. Elizabeth had a favourite, who, if he is not greatly belied, did not yield to the subtlest poisoner that Italy ever produced. Osborn says that "he had *frequently heard Elizabeth* blamed for not removing Mary, Queen of Scots, in the Italian fashion, by poisoning her garments," &c., p. 231. And, in fact, Elizabeth herself lived from 1594 to 1598 in constant dread of being taken off in this way; and many attempts, which kept the people in a state of agitation, were actually made to effect it. Two men were hanged in 1598 for poisoning the queen's saddle; the arm-chair of Essex was found to be rubbed with some deleterious mixture; and several poisoned articles of dress (among others, a girdle) and pieces of furniture were publicly burned in Smithfield.

According to the custom of the times, Jonson regained the property of his comedy by these numerous alterations: it was thus acted for the first time in 1598 at the Black Friars, and Shakspeare's name stands at the head of the principal performers in it.[1] The commentators appear to consider this as a mark of peculiar condescension on the part of our great poet, choosing to forget that he was an actor by profession, and that he derived his fortune from the theatre. He was not yet so independent of wealth but that he continued on the stage at least sixteen years longer; and, in the course of that time, probably played a part in more than one piece not greatly superior to the present comedy, without suspecting that he was conferring any very particular obligation on the authors.

To this period (1598) is commonly assigned the commencement of our author's acquaintance with Shakspeare. "Ben Jonson presented *Every Man in his Humour* to one of the leading players in that company of which Shakspeare was a member. After casting his eye over it superficially, the comedian was on the point of returning it with a peremptory refusal, when Shakspeare, who perhaps *had never till that instant seen* Jonson,[2] desired he might look into the play. He was so well pleased with it on perusal that he recommended the work and the author to his fellows. Notwithstanding this kindness, the prologue to his play is nothing less than a satirical picture of the *Tempest, Lear, Henry V.,* &c."—*Dram. Miscel.* vol. ii. p. 56.

"*Every Man in his Humour*" (says Mr. Malone in twenty places), "was acted in 1598: it appears to be Jonson's first performance, and we may presume that *it was the very play* which was brought on the stage by the good offices of Shakspeare, who himself acted in it. *Malignant* and *envious* as Jonson was," &c.—*Shak.* vol. i. p. 540. And the writers of our author's life in the *Bio. Brit.*, after giving us the same story a little embellished, are pleased to subjoin: "This *goodness* of Shakspeare was the more remarkable, as 'Jonson was, in his personal character, the very reverse of Shakspeare,

---

[1] The old play probably remained at the Rose, where it had been brought out.

[2] Mr. Davies is subject to little fits of inconsistency. He seems to think, and not indeed without cause, that provided he indulges his malignity towards Jonson, the public will readily forgive the want of truth and sense. "At this time," he says, i.e. 1597, a year before Shakspeare (according to his own statement) had seen or known anything of our poet, "to have observed Ben Jonson with an *assumed* countenance of gaiety, and with *envy* in his heart, join the group of laughers and applauders of *Henry IV.*, must have added to the pleasure of Shakspeare's real friends," vol. i. p. 278. This is forthwith taken for proved; and the passage is boldly referred to in the Index under the head of Jonson. "Ben Jonson *envious* of Shakspeare!" But thus the life of our great poet is written; and his admirers are not ashamed of it!

as surly, ill-natured, proud, and disagreeable, as Shakspeare was gentle, good-natured, easy, and amiable.'"[1]

Jonson was at this period struggling for a mere subsistence. When his persevering pursuit of knowledge, therefore, amidst difficulties of every kind, when his lofty ideas of poësy, his moral purpose in dramatic satire, his scorn of the popularity procured by sacrificing to what he deemed the vicious habits of the stage, are taken into consideration, it may almost be wondered why such singular pleasure should be found in combining to overwhelm him with obloquy.

With respect to the story just quoted, no words, I presume, are needed to prove it an arrant fable. Nor is the variation of it which is found in Rowe anything better. "Shakspeare's acquaintance with Ben Jonson began with a remarkable piece of humanity. Mr. Jonson, who was at that time *altogether unknown to the world*, had offered one of his plays to the players to have it acted ; and the person into whose hands it was put, after having turned it carelessly and superciliously over, was just upon the point of returning it to him with an ill-natured answer, that it would be of no service to their company, when Shakspeare luckily cast his eye upon it, and found something so well in it as to engage him to read it through, and afterwards to recommend Mr. Jonson and his writings to the public favour."[2]—*Shak.* vol. i. p. 12.

That Jonson was altogether "unknown to the world," is a palpable untruth. At this period (1598) Jonson was as well known as Shakspeare, and perhaps better. He was poor indeed, and very poor,[3] and a mere retainer of the theatres ; but he was intimately acquainted with Henslowe and Alleyn, and with all the performers at their houses. He was familiar with Drayton, and Chapman, and Rowley, and Middleton, and Fletcher ; he had been writing for three years, in conjunction with Marston, and Decker, and Chettle, and Porter, and Bird, and with most of the poets of the day : he was celebrated by Meares as one of the principal writers of tragedy ;[4]

---

[1] This exquisite character of Jonson is quoted by the biographers, with great precision, from the "Works of his *friend* Drummond, Edin. 1711, fol. p. 222." It is given on the same authority in the enlarged edition of the *Theatrum Poetarum* ; and more recently, by Mr. A. Chalmers, in the *Gen. Dict.*, who, after repeating the poet's conversation with that hospitable gentleman, breaks out : "In short, Drummond *adds*, Jonson was," &c., vol. xix. p. 156. What will the reader say, what will he think, when he is assured that not one syllable of this quotation is to be found in any part of Drummond? It is the fabrication of one Shiels, a Scotchman, who compiled, for the booksellers, the Collection called *Cibber's Lives of the Poets*, and who, not finding his countryman's character of Jonson quite to his taste, interpolated, with kindred rancour, the abusive paragraph in question. This work was published in 1753 ; the *Bio. Brit.* in 1757 ; the others later. It thus appears that of all who have so confidently quoted this passage "from Drummond," not one ever looked into him ; and thus has the scurrility of an obscure and hackney scribbler, who lived two centuries after Jonson, been palmed upon the public as the express testimony of one "who spoke of the poet from personal knowledge."

The detection of this flagrant imposture, "this innocent *jeu d'esprit*," will be ill-received. A calumny against Jonson is precious in the eyes of the commentators. I shall be quite satisfied, however, if, when they repeat this ribaldry, which they will be sure to do, they give it on the authority of Mr. Robert Shiels, and not on that of "Jonson's *friend*, Drummond of Hawthornden."

[2] In the first edition of his *Life of Shakspeare*, Rowe inserted the usual charges against Jonson of ingratitude, jealousy, &c. Subsequent inquiry proved the injustice of this attack, and he therefore, with a proper sense of what was due to truth, to his own character, and to the public, omitted the whole in the next edition. This exploded falsehood Mr. Malone, with an intrepid defiance of all that Rowe respected, brings insultingly back to him, because, as he says, "he *believes* it"! In a subsequent page Mr. Malone notices a paragraph respecting Shakspeare which also appeared in the first edition :— "But," says he, "as Mr. Rowe *suppressed the passage* in his second edition, it may be presumed *that he found reason* to change his opinion." *Shak.* vol. i. p. 482. It is a pity that this was not thought of in the former instance !

[3] "Lent the 18 of agust 1598, to bye a boocke called *Hoate anger sone cowld*, of Mr. Porter, Mr. Cheattell and Bengemen Johnson, in full payment the some of vilb." *Shak.* vol. ii. p. 484.

"Lent unto Robert Shawe, and Jewbey the 23 of Octob. 1598, to lend unto Mr. Chapman one his playboocke and ij actes of a tragedie of *Benjemen's* plotte, the sum of iij lb." *Ibid.*

[4] Mr. Malone wonders why Meares should say this of Jonson, who had only written the *Comedy* of *Every Man in his Humour*: and he concludes that *tragedy* was used for both species of dramatic writing. But Meares expressly distinguishes them, and gives the names of the chief writers in comedy, in the next paragraph. It does not follow, because we have no tragedies extant of this early date, that Jonson had written none. In the page just quoted mention is made of severa tragedies in which our poet

and he had long been rising in reputation as a scholar and poet among the most distinguished characters of the age. At this moment he was employed on *Every Man out of his Humour*, which was acted in 1599, and in the elegant Dedication of that comedy to the "Gentlemen of the Inns of Court," he says, "When I wrote this poem, I had *friendship with divers* in your Societies, who, as they were *great names* in learning, so were they no less examples of living. Of them and *then*, that I say no more, it was not despised." And yet Jonson was at this time "altogether unknown to the world!" and offered a virgin comedy (which had already been three years on the stage) to a player in the humble hope that it might be accepted! And this player discovered that *Every Man in his Humour* "would not do for the theatre" at a time when *Locrine* and old *Jeronymo*, and *Titus Andronicus*, and the worthless *Pericles*, were daily exhibiting with applause! This is but a small portion of the absurdities which the world is contented to take on trust in its eagerness to criminate Jonson ; for this notable tissue of falsehood and folly is introduced solely to prove "the baseness and malignity of our poet's conduct towards Shakspeare."

It would be an abuse of the reader's patience to add another word on the imaginary introduction of this play to the stage. It was brought out, as we have seen, at the Rose, a rival theatre with which Shakspeare had not the slightest concern. To be plain, whoever introduced Jonson to the notice of the players, we may be quite sure that it was not Shakspeare, whose merit in this case, as far as appears, must be confined to procuring for his own theatre (in Blackfriars) an improved copy of a popular performance.[2]

Every Man in his Humour, though it did not, even in its altered state, much improve the finances of the author, yet brought him what he valued more. From this period he perceptibly grew into acquaintance and familiarity with the first characters among the wise and great. This was not seen with equanimity by his dramatic associates, and the envy which it provoked pursued him to the end of his career. The writers on whom the theatres conducted by Henslowe and Alleyn principally relied at this time were, besides our author, Chettle, Heywood, and Decker, men of very considerable talents, but who wrote on the spur of the occasion, and were perhaps in little better circumstances than Jonson himself. Marston and Decker, who had frequently laboured in conjunction with our poet, appear to have viewed his success with peculiar mortification, and to have lent themselves to the cabal already raised against him. What ground of offence they chose, or what motive they alleged, cannot now be told ; but Jonson affirms that at this period they began "to provoke him on every stage with their petulant styles, as if they wished to single him out for their adversary."

His next piece was the comic satire of *Every Man out of his Humour*, in the Induction to which he addresses the audience in a strain that would not have disgraced the Grecian stage when Aristophanes was in his soberest, severest vein :

> " I fear no mood stamp'd in a private brow,
>   When I am pleas'd t' unmask a public vice.

---

was concerned, and in which, probably, "having departed with his right," he retained no property. Add to this that, in the dedication of *Catiline* to the Earl of Pembroke, he calls it "the best of his tragedies," an expression that he would scarcely have used had he written none but *Sejanus* before it.

Rowe knew little of the dramatic history of that age. There was no such thing as writing plays, and then taking them to the players for acceptance. Rowe was thinking of the practice of his own times.

[1] The critics have already forgotten that Jonson "had ambled by a waggon and played old Jeronymo ;" that "he acted and wrote, but both ill, at several theatres ;" that "he was, himself, the proprietor of a theatre in the Barbican ;" that "he had killed Mr. Marlow, the poet," and been "tutor to young Raleigh," long before he produced this comedy—these are falsehoods in which they all believe ; though, with the same consistent absurdity, they hold that he was at this time wholly unknown !

[2] The play, as we have it in the folio, was acted, Jonson informs us, in 1598. In the prologues to our ancient dramas care is usually taken to notice the variations which they had undergone since their first appearance, if at all important. The present comedy has been radically changed ; the names, the place of action, the circumstances, materially altered since it was first exhibited at the Rose, yet not the slightest allusion is made to it in any part of the prologue ; a circumstance sufficient of itself to prove that it was written and spoken previously to the re-modelling of the play, and, indeed, on its first appearance, for which it was expressly and exclusively calculated.

> I fear no strumpet's drugs, nor ruffian's stab
> Should I detect their hateful luxuries :
> No broker's, usurer's, or lawyer's gripe,
> Were I disposed to say they're all corrupt."

After more of this, Asper (the author) turns from his friends to the stage :

> " I not observed this thronged round till now.
> Gracious and kind spectators, you are welcome !
> Apollo and the Muses feast your eyes
> With graceful objects, and may our Minerva
> Answer your hopes unto their largest strain !
> Yet here, judicious friends, mistake me not ;
> I do not this to beg your patience,
> Or servilely to fawn on your applause,
> Like some dry brain, despairing in his merit.
> Let me be censured by the austerest brow ;
> When I want art or judgment, tax me freely :
> Let envious censors, with their broadest eyes,
> Look through and through me, I pursue no favour."

This was not language calculated to win the audiences of those days, nor did Jonson, on any occasion, stoop to court their favour by unworthy condescensions to their prejudices. He had nobler aims in view ; to correct their taste, to inform their judgment, to improve their morals ; and to these he steadily adhered through good and evil report, and through all the exigents of his chequered life. It cannot therefore be wondered that he was no favourite with the vulgar, and that those who trusted for a part of their success to the expedients thus openly condemned, should eagerly raise and zealously perpetuate a clamour against him : they could not, indeed, prevent his plays from being received, but they constituted a party sufficiently numerous to be heard even amidst the applause which followed his most popular pieces.

Every Man out of his Humour was, however, well received. "Queen Elizabeth" (Davies says) " drawn by its fame, honoured the play with her presence ; and Jonson, to pay a respectful compliment to his sovereign, altered the conclusion of his play into an elegant panegyric. Mr. Collins, the poet, first pointed out to me the peculiar beauty of this address." *Dram. Miscel.* vol. ii. p. 77. That Elizabeth was pleased cannot be doubted ; she was, indeed, among the first encouragers of the youthful poet, and her kindness towards him is thus noticed by Lord Falkland :

> " How great ELIZA, the retreat of those
> Who, weak and injured, her protection chose,
> Her subjects' joy, the strength of her allies,
> The fear and wonder of her enemies,
> With her judicious favours, did infuse
> Courage and strength into his younger muse."

Hurd calls this a comedy founded upon "abstract passions ;" and bids us notice " the absurdity of the attempt :" but Hurd is more than usually unfortunate when he meddles with Jonson, of whose works, in fact, he knows nothing. In the poet's days a very different opinion prevailed, namely, that the piece was merely personal, and that he had filled the stage with real characters. Though this was not the case, yet we may collect, from the charge, that the satire was felt, and that he had touched the foibles of the time with no unskilful hand. " He did gather humours " (the old critic says) "wherever he went :" and a judgment more quick to perceive, or more dextrous to embody whatever was extravagant or ridiculous, will not readily be found. To confess the truth, however, the dramatic poet had not far to go at this period for his materials. The middle aisle of St. Paul's swarmed with new and eccentric characters ; every tavern lent its aid, and even the theatres supplied a description of people whose fantastic affectations a poet even less observant than Jonson might turn to excellent account for the purposes of mirth or reproof. From these and similar sources our author undoubtedly derived the substance of his dramas : the characters themselves are not personal, though traits of real life may be occasionally involved in them : [1] these were

---

[1] Thus Tucca is said by Decker to speak the language of Captain Hannam ; and Aubrey tells us that Carlo Buffone was taken from one Charles Chester, "a bold impertinent fellow."

readily recognised, and eagerly appropriated by his enemies, who thus artfully raised the cry of personality against him of which the echo is yet heard.

Three distinct notices of Jonson appear in Mr. Henslowe's memorandum-book for the year 1599. The sum of forty shillings was advanced to him and Decker for a play which they were writing in conjunction; a like sum for another in which Chettle was joined with them; and a third sum of twenty shillings for a tragedy which he was probably writing alone.[1] None of these are now extant; but *Cynthia's Revels*, on which he was at this time employed, was brought out in the following year.

This Comical Satire (for so Jonson properly terms it) was evidently directed at the grave and formal manners of the court, to which indeed it was subsequently dedicated. After the atrocious execution[2] of Mary, Whitehall appears to have grown extremely dull. Elizabeth herself lost her spirits, and became fretful and morose. The courtiers who could not be gay became affected, and exchanged their former fashions for fantastic and apish refinements; *Euphuisme* was now in the full tide of prosperity, and the manners were as absurdly pedantic as the language. As Jonson lived much with the great, this could not altogether escape him; and it is not improbable that he was encouraged by some of those about the queen to direct his satire against the reigning follies.

Cynthia's Revels was acted in 1600 "by the Children of the Queen's Chapel."[3] It was at first, as the title-page to the 4to expresses it, "privately acted." The puerile games, the ceremonious fopperies conducted with such inflexible gravity, might, to those who probably comprehended both the motive and the objects of the drama, be sufficiently entertaining: for its subsequent success, it must have been indebted to the delight which the good citizens took in seeing the fantastic tricks of the courtiers exposed

who kept company with Sir Walter *in his youth.*[*] *Letters*, vol. iii. p. 514. But besides that there is no similarity between the two characters, as may be seen by turning to the Dramatis Personæ of this comedy, the incident of which Aubrey speaks probably took place before Jonson was born, though he might have heard of it, and adopted it; if, after all, the story was not rather made up from the play. The only personal allusion which I can discover, is to Marston. Puntarvolo says to Carlo Buffone, "What, Carlo! now by the sincerity of my soul, welcome: and how dost thou, thou grand *Scourge*, or second Untruss of the time?" The reference, which *seems* very innocent, is evidently to the title of Marston's *Satires* (*the Scourge of Villainie*), but this goes no further than a name, for Carlo and Marston do not possess any one feature in common. With respect to Captain Hannam, he might talk extravagantly and beg impudently, without possessing the other qualities of that undaunted yet entertaining railer, Captain Tucca.

[1] *The Scotts Tragedy.* The piece in which he joined with Chettle and Decker is called *Robert, the Second King of Scottes.*

[2 What would Gifford have said to Mr. Froude's eloquent and convincing justification of this deed?—F.C.]

[3] The commentators, who turn every circumstance of Jonson's life into accusations against him, have here discovered a notable proof of his "ferocious temper." He must have quarrelled with the "established comedians," they

say, (meaning Shakspeare, Burbage, &c.) or he would not have taken his play from their stage to give it to the "Children," &c. These lynx-eyed critics do not perceive that "the Children" were as popular, and as well "established" as any other company, and that they shared the Blackfriars, at which this play was performed, with the lord chamberlain's servants. Having gratuitously supposed a quarrel, the next step is to make it up. "By the mediation of friends, and most likely by the *good offices of our gentle Shakspeare*, a reconciliation was effected between this *surly* writer and the comedians." *Dram. Mis.* vol. ii. p. 83.—But the "reconciliation," it seems, did not last long: "some new quarrel with the established comedians, I *suppose*, caused him to have recourse again to the Children of the Revels," p. 105. There is not a word of sense in all this. It was no more necessary that Jonson should offer all he wrote to the same company, than any other person: he had not, like Shakspeare, an interest or a property in the theatre, and he naturally carried his talents wherever they were likely to prove acceptable. The critics who insult over his slowness, and affirm that he was a year or two "about every play," must have excellent notions of economy, if they suppose that a family could be supported on the sale of it. He wrote, like his contemporaries, for many theatres, and probably mended many plays. The theatre, however, with which he was most closely connected at this time, was Henslowe's; and while his enemies are pleased to *suppose* a succession of quarrels with this and that theatre, he was evidently living on terms of friendship with them all; writing, at one and the same time, for the Rose and the Blackfriars, for the Fortune and the Globe.

* Raleigh was born in 1552; in *his youth*, therefore, our author must have been in his cradle.

to ridicule.   The prologue to this play is beautifully written : and would seem to have been originally addressed to a select audience (perhaps at Whitehall) : the epilogue is in a different strain, and its arrogant conclusion was long remembered to the author's annoyance.[1]

That this drama should give offence to those whose grotesque humours it exposed, was perhaps to be expected ; but it does not very clearly appear why the little knot of critics, headed by Marston and Decker, should take any part of it to themselves ; as they manifestly affected to do.   The characters which the majority fixed upon, cannot be known ; but the leaders seem to have appropriated to themselves those of Hedon and Anaides.   The resemblance is not obvious to us, and could not, one would think, be very perceptible to the keener optics of those days ; but Marston and Decker were eager to revenge the imaginary insult, and readily consented to lead the attack now meditated against him.   Of this Jonson obtained full information ; for the secret was ill kept by the poets ; and as they persisted in ridiculing him on the stage, he found it necessary to draw up the *Poetaster*, in which, together with the untrussing, the whipping, and the stinging, he anticipated and answered many of the accusations subsequently brought against him in the *Satiromastix*.   The high and magisterial language which our author held in the prologue to the first of his acknowledged pieces, has been already noticed ; the same language (but in a loftier tone) is repeated in *Cynthia's Revels*, where, in imitation of the parabasis of the old comedy, the poet appears to speak in his own person ; this novelty on the English stage was probably viewed with peculiar impatience, since much of the spleen of his enemies was directed against the speeches of Asper and Crites **in** the last of his comic satires.

The *Poetaster* was brought out at the Blackfriars, by the Children of the Queen's Chapel, in 1601 ;[2] its object cannot be better given than in his own words :

> "Three years
> They did provoke me with their petulant styles
> On every stage ; and I at last, unwilling,
> But weary, I confess, of so much trouble,
> Thought I would try if shame could win upon 'em,
> And therefore chose Augustus Cæsar's times,
> When wit and arts were at their height in Rome,
> To show that Virgil, Horace, and the rest
> Of those great master spirits, did not want
> Detractors then, or practicers against them :
> And by this line, although no parallel,
> I hoped at last they would sit down and blush."

As Marston and Decker had headed the cabal against him, he introduced them under the respective names of Crispinus and Demetrius ; Marston is very distinctly marked ; Decker might perhaps have "sat still unquestioned," at least with posterity, had

---

[1] It is alluded to by the anonymous author of *Par Pari*, in his address to the reader.

> "Yet be not proud, though thou their praise
>   dost gaine ;
> 'Tis for a better pen than mine to say,
> By —— 'tis good, and if you lik't you may."

To bully critics in similar terms was then the mode.   There is enough of it in Decker alone to prove that Jonson was far from singular in this indecent defiance.   But he was probably inflated for the moment with the favourable reception of the Court ; and would not allow the city to question its infallibility

In this year *Every Man out of his Humour* was given to the press : it is dedicated to the gentlemen of the Inns of Court, and seems to be the first of our author's works that was printed.

[2] In this year "*Bengemy*" was employed by Mr. Henslowe in "writing *adycions* for Jero-

nymo."   They were so much to the manager's taste, that Mr. Alleyn was authorized to advance xxxxs. on them.   Had the records of any other theatres been preserved, we should probably have found the name of our poet among their supporters, for he must have produced much more at this time than has reached us.   *Every Man in his Humour*, as first written, and performed at the Rose, was printed this year.   I do not believe that it was given to the press by Jonson, who must rather have wished for its suppression, as the improved play had now been four years before the public.   It is evident that whatever he wrote for Mr. Henslowe was purchased outright :—the present copy, therefore, must have stolen into the world from the prompter's book, as was not unfrequently the case.   It is observable that our author's name is misspelt in the title page.   There is not a single instance, I am well persuaded, in which **he** writes his name Johnson.

not the justice of the satire filled him with rage, and induced him to appropriate the character of Demetrius to himself in an angry recrimination.

The *Poetaster* was written (Jonson says) in fifteen weeks, and it is certainly as creditable to his talents as his industry. It was favourably received by the public, though it gave offence to some of the military and the law. This could only arise from the slavish condition of the stage, which was then at the mercy of every captious officer who chose to complain to the master of the revels ; for the satire, if such it be, is put into the mouths of such speakers as would almost convince an impartial spectator that it was designed for a compliment.[1] Of the soldiers, Jonson got quit without much difficulty ; but the lawyers were not so easily shaken off ; and he was indebted, in some degree, for his escape, to the kindness of one of his earliest friends, "the worthy Master Richard Martin," who undertook for the innocency of his intentions to the lord chief-justice, and to whom he subsequently dedicated the play.

But there was yet a party which could neither be silenced nor shamed. The players, who had so long provoked him with their petulance on the stage, felt the bitterness of his reproof, and had address enough to persuade their fellows that all were included in his satire. Jonson readily admits that he taxed some of the players, as indeed he had a just right to do ; but he adds, that he touched but a few of them, and even those few he forbore to name. He treats their clamours, however, with supreme contempt, and only regrets the hostility of *some better natures*, whom they had drawn over to their side, and induced to *run in the same vile line with themselves*. By *better natures*, the commentators assure us that Shakspeare was meant ; and Mr. Malone quotes the passage in more than one place to evince the *malignity* of Jonson—as if it were a crime in him to be unjustly calumniated ! I trust that Jonson was not exhibited in a ridiculous light at the Blackfriars ; and, in any case, it is quite certain that the players on whom he retorts were to be found in the companies of the Swan, the Hope, the Fortune, and other houses situated on the river, or, as he expresses himself, "on the other side the Tiber." It would not redound greatly to the honour of Shakspeare's humanity, if he should be found to have used his "weight and credit in the scene" to depress a young writer dependent on it for subsistence. I do not, however, think that Shakspeare was meant.[2]

---

[1] Nothing can more clearly mark the tone of hostility with which every act of Jonson is pursued, than the obloquy which is *still* heaped on him for these speeches. It would be far more just, as well as generous, in us to applaud the intrepid spirit with which he dared, in slavish times, to vent his thoughts, than to join in a silly clamour against his "arrogance and ill-nature." He stood forward as a moral satirist, and the abuses, both of the law and the military service, were legitimate objects of reprehension.

[2] There is yet a charge from which it will not be so easy to exculpate Shakspeare. In the *Return from Parnassus*, written about this time (1602), Kempe and Burbage are introduced, and the former is made to say,—"Few of the University pen plays well ; they smell too much of that writer Ovid, and that writer *Metamorphosis*, and talk too much of Proserpine and Jupiter. Why, here's our fellow Shakspeare puts them all down : ay, and Ben Jonson too. O that Ben Jonson is a pestilent fellow, he brought up Horace giving the poets a pill ; but our fellow Shakspeare hath given him a purge that made him bewray his credit." To this Burbage, who seems somewhat ashamed of his associate, merely replies, "It's a shrewd fellow, indeed :" and changes the subject. "In what manner," Mr. Malone says, "Shakspeare put Jonson down, does not appear." I should think it clear enough. He put him down as he put down every other dramatic writer. "Nor does it appear," he continues, "how he made him *bewray his credit*." His retaliation, we may be well assured, contained no gross or illiberal attack, and perhaps did not go beyond a ballad or an epigram." But with Mr. Malone's leave, if it went as far as either, Shakspeare was greatly to be blamed, for Jonson had given him no offence whatever. I will take upon myself to affirm that the *Poetaster* does not contain a single passage that can be tortured, by the utmost ingenuity of malice, into a reflection on our great poet. It will scarcely be credited, that the sentence last quoted should be immediately followed by these words : "Shakspeare has, *however*," (i.e., notwithstanding he had written a ballad against Jonson) "marked his disregard for the *calumniator* of his fame" (i.e., for the unoffending object of his ridicule) "by not leaving him any memorial by his Will."—*Shak.* vol. i. p. 541. Let Mr. Malone answer for the unforgiving temper with which he has dishonoured Shakspeare :—I believe nothing of it. Kempe is brought forward as the type of ignorance in this old drama ; but a darker quality than ignorance must possess those who draw from his language any indications of Jonson's "malignity" to Shakspeare. And again, with Mr. Malone's permission, how can we be *so sure* that the *ballad* or the *epigram* which is here supposed to be written against Jonson contained

Be this as it may, Jonson was induced, after a few representations, to add to it, what he calls an Apologetical Dialogue, in which he bore the chief part. It was spoken only once, and then laid aside by command.[1] It is remarkable, the critic says, for nothing but arrogance. It is certainly not wanting in self-confidence; but it has something besides—a vein of high-toned indignation, springing from conscious innocence and worth; and a generous burst of pathos and poetry in the concluding speech, to which an equal will not easily be found.

If Jonson expected to silence his enemies by giving them "a brave defiance," or even by proving his own innocence, he speedily discovered his mistake. Decker, who had sustained the part of Demetrius, was (apparently to his own satisfaction) put forward by the rest,[2] and as he was not only a rapid but a popular writer, the choice of a champion was not injudicious. The *Satiromastix* was produced in 1602. Jonson had played with his subject; but Decker writes in downright passion, and foams through every page. He makes no pretensions to invention, but takes up the characters of his predecessor, turns them the *seamy side without*, and produces a coarse and ill-wrought caricature. Tucca, who in Jonson's hands is amusing with all his insolence and rapacity, degenerates with Decker into a mere candidate for Tyburn.[3] Nor is this the worst. In transferring the scene from the court of Augustus to England, Decker has the inconceivable folly to fix on William Rufus, a rude and ignorant soldier, whom he ridiculously terms "learning's true Mæcenas, poesy's king," for the champion of literature, when his brother, Henry I., who aspired to the reputation of a scholar, would have entered into his plot with equal facility.[4]

In the concluding lines of the Apologetical Dialogue, Jonson announces that, "since the comic muse had been so ominous to him, he would try if tragedy had a kinder aspect."[5] He had two subjects at this time in view. The first, which was written for Mr. Henslowe's[6] theatre, does not appear; the second, *Sejanus*, was brought out at

---

nothing gross or illiberal? Time has spared two specimens of Shakspeare's mode of "attack." It so happens that one of them is a *ballad*, and the other an *epigram*; the first written on a person whose park he had robbed, and the second on a friend who left him a legacy. If there be nothing "gross or illiberal" in either of these, the "assurance" may be trusted. [The Lucies had no park, but were in a position to present an occasional "bribe-buck."—F. C.]

[1] Not in consequence of the interference of the town, as Mr. Disraeli thinks; the town would probably have heard it with pleasure. Jonson's own account is, that "he was restrained from repeating it *by authority*." These words are found only in the 4to edit., and Mr. Disraeli probably consulted the fol.—*Quar. of Authors*, vol. iii. p. 135.

[2] Jonson must have been aware of this; for he makes one of the players say of Decker, "his doublet's a little decayed, otherwise he is a very simple honest fellow, sir, one Demetrius, a dresser of plays about the town here: we have hired him to abuse Horace, and bring him in, in a play;" p. 234. And, a few lines lower, he makes Tucca promise that "Crispinus (Marston) shall help him." It might have been expected that Marston, who is, in fact, the *Poetaster*, would have been the principal in the meditated plan of revenge; but he was, perhaps, too slow for the wrath of his associates: it is also possible that he might not be equally exasperated with them; for it is observable that he is treated with some kind of deference as compared with his "hanger-on," and that more than one allusion is made to the respectability of his birth.

[3] Although I cannot avoid thinking that Decker has failed altogether in the *Untrussing of the Humorous Poet*, I do not deem lightly of his *general* powers. He was a slovenly and hasty writer (perhaps from necessity), but he was a keen and vigorous observer; and he has occasional flights of poetry, which would do honour to any talents. We have, I believe, but the smallest part of what he wrote, for, with the exception of Heywood, none of our old dramatists were more prolific.

[4] Hawkins, who, like the rest of his tribe, can see no fault in any one but Jonson, observes on this parody,—"We cannot help being inclined to favour Decker, who only meant to retaliate the insults of his rival," then follows the usual raving about Jonson's *envy*, &c. But Hawkins chooses to forget, as indeed they all do, that Decker was the aggressor, and that, in conjunction with others, he had been ridiculing Jonson on every stage for *three years* before he sat down to write the *Poetaster*. Yet this is your "*harmless*" fairy!

[5] Jonson does not mean by this, as Upton and others insinuate, that his comedies had been ill received, for the contrary was the fact; but that the present one (the *Poetaster*) had subjected him to the censure of the Law, the Army, &c.

[6] The following notice is taken from Henslowe's memorandum-book:—"Lent unto Bengemy Johnsone at the appoyntment of E. Alleyn and Wm. Birde the 22 June 1602, in earnest of a boocke called *Richard Crookback*, and for new adycions for Jeronymo, the some of x lb." "This article," Mr. Malone observes, "ascertains that Jonson had the *audacity* to write a play after our author (Shakspeare) on the

the Globe, 1603. This tragedy, in which Shakspeare played a part, met with great opposition on its first presentation, and was withdrawn for a short time from the stage. The author, however, suffered neither in his reputation, nor his peace on the occasion; his fame was too well established to be affected by the fury of a party, and he proceeded, at leisure, to re-model his play.

About this time Jonson probably began to acquire that turn for conviviality for which he was afterwards noted. Sir Walter Ralelgh, previously to his unfortunate engagement with the wretched Cobham and others, had instituted a meeting of *beaux esprits* at the Mermaid, a celebrated tavern in Friday Street. Of this club, which combined more talent and genius, perhaps, than ever met together before or since, our author was a member; and here, for many years, he regularly repaired with Shakspeare, Beaumont, Fletcher, Selden, Cotton, Carew, Martin, Donne, and many others, whose names, even at this distant period, call up a mingled feeling of reverence and respect. Here, in the full flow and confidence of friendship, the lively and interesting "wit-combats" took place between Shakspeare and our author; and hither, in probable allusion to them, Beaumont fondly lets his thoughts wander, in his letter to Jonson, from the country.

> "What things have we seen,
> Done at the MERMAID! heard words that have been
> So nimble, and so full of subtle flame,
> As if that every one from whom they came,
> Had meant to put his whole wit in a jest," &c.

Fairer prospects now began to open on Jonson; Elizabeth was frugal, and paid as grudgingly for her amusements as for her more serious business; little, besides honour, was therefore derived from her patronage, and the poets were still left to the resources of their own talents; but James, who acceded to the crown at this period, was liberal to men of merit, and Jonson had the good fortune to be quickly received into his favour.

The court and city prepared to receive their new sovereign, in the taste of those times, with a magnificent display of scenery, speeches, &c., and our author was applied to for the design and execution of the pageant. Those who have been told so often of his "vindictiveness," &c. will be surprised, perhaps, to hear that his associate in this employment was Decker, the person by whom he had been so grossly treated a few months before. Jonson took to himself two-fifths of this splendid "Entertainment;" the rest was allotted to his coadjutor. Both seem to have exerted themselves greatly, and both printed an account of their respective parts : our author's description, which is equally learned and elegant, bears no marks of resentment against his late antagonist, who, in his publication, shows himself, in more than one place, yet a little sore of the *Poetaster.* The truth is, with deference to his "friend" Drummond,[1] that Jonson, far from being vindictive, was one of the most placable of mankind: he blustered, indeed, and talked angrily; but his heart was turned to affection, and his enmities appear to have been short-lived, while his friendships were durable and sincere.

James was something of a poet, and more of a scholar; what he cultivated in himself, he loved in others: he had discrimination enough to distinguish the pure and

---

subject of *King Richard III." Shak.* vol. ii. p. 484. If there be any "audacity" in this matter, which I am not inclined to dispute, it will not, I suspect, be found on the part of Jonson. I cannot discover on what grounds Mr. Malone takes upon himself to question the right of those who never acknowledged his authority, to use their own judgment, and dispose of their own property as they pleased. It might have been supposed that Henslowe and Alleyn, the one a very shrewd and the other a very sensible man, could be trusted with providing pieces for their own stage. It does not seem a necessary consequence that Shakspeare's selecting a particular part of our history should preclude the rest of the world from touching it ; and he, "who never," as Mr. Malone says,

"took up a subject which had not been previously dramatized by others," had surely the least right to complain of those who acted, or those who wrote on the same theme with himself. From the sum advanced on this play, the managers must have thought well of it. It has perished, like most of the pieces brought out at their theatre, because they endeavoured to keep them in their own hands as long as possible.

[1] His *friend* Drummond. So the commentators delight to call him on all occasions. The term is artfully chosen : it is meant to characterize the superlative infamy of Jonson, which could compel even this generous spirit, in despite of his tender regard for the poet, to blazon his vices, and bequeath them to posterity.

classical construction of the pageantry which had been displayed before him;[1] as well as the extraordinary merits of the spirited "*Panegyre* on the first meeting of his Parliament;" and he appears, from that period, to have taken the poet under his especial protection. In this opinion of his genius as well as learning, he must have been strengthened by the next publicatiom of Jonson, who had been summoned to Althorpe, to prepare a poetical compliment for the reception of the Queen and Prince Henry, when expected there on their journey from Scotland to London. He must have been well acquainted with this family: he terms Sir Robert Spencer his noble friend, and observes that "his principal object" in suffering the *Entertainment* (4to, 1603) to come abroad was to do that serviceable right to him which his affection owed, and his lordship's merits challenged." The Spencers have been well-advised to cherish the name of the author of the *Fairy Queen*, as one of the chief honours of their family. It will not greatly derogate from them to acknowledge, at the same time, that Ben Jonson, in his early days, was among their friends and clients.

His next work, as far as any memorial of the date of his writings has reached us, was still for the gratification of the royal family. May-day had been, from the earliest times, a city holyday of high account, in the celebration of which our monarchs had often joined. James, who loved, above them all, to mingle in sociable converse with his people, had accepted for himself, his queen, and his court, an invitation to keep the festival at the seat of Sir W. Cornwallis, near Highgate, and Jonson was engaged to give grace and elegance to the "Entertainment," by a complimentary effusion.[2] He did not discredit his employer, and his Majesty must have found still further reason to be satisfied with his selection. This year also Jonson revised his *Sejanus*.[3] As it was first acted, *a second pen had good share in it*,[4] on its failure, he, with equal delicacy and integrity, determined not to expose his coadjutor to the chance of a second defeat; but to make himself responsible for the whole. The tragedy, thus recast, was received with applause, and kept possession of the stage till long after the Restoration. "It hath outlived," the author says, in the dedication of his play to Lord Aubigny, "the malice of the people, and begot itself a greater favour than the subject of it lost, *the love of good* men."

Sejanus was ushered into the world by several commendatory poems, to which Jonson refers the reader as explanatory of some points relative to its reception: among these voluntary vouchers for the merits of the tragedy is Marston, who had long since repented of the part which he took against the author, and resumed his old habits of kindness.

---

[1] "The king" (say the writers of the *Bio. Brit.*) "was no less pedant than pageant wise; and therefore Jonson showed particular address in flattering him by the introduction of several copies of Latin verse;" for this, they proceed to ridicule him. The real fact is, that Jonson was *very sparing* of his "Latin verses" on this occasion, and that Decker has, at least, *three for his one!* Where Decker got them, I cannot tell—perhaps from his own stores; for he had a smattering of Latin, which he is somewhat too fond of showing; but thus every act of Jonson is perverted by the malice or ignorance of his biographers!

[2] See *The Penates*.

[3] [The late George Daniel possessed an unique copy, on large paper, of the *Sejanus*, 4to, 1605, which contained the following inscription, in Jonson's autograph:—

"To my perfect Friend, Mr. Francis Crane, I erect this Altar of Friendship, And leave it as the Eternall Witnesse of my Love.—BEN JONSON."—F.C.]

[4] Who this "second pen" was, is not known. I have supposed it (vol. i. p. 273) to be Fletcher (Shakspeare is entirely out of the question), but, if Beaumont's age would admit of it (he was in his nineteenth year), I should more willingly lean to him. Be he who he may, however, he has no reason to be displeased with the liberal acknowledgment of his merits. "I have rather chosen" (Jonson says) "to put *weaker, and no doubt, less pleasing* of mine own, than to defraud so *happy a genius* of his right by my loathed usurpation."—*Ibid.* The brutal scurrility with which Jonson is assailed on this point, has been noticed elsewhere. "Shakspeare" (says Capell) "was the happy genius whose pen 'had so good a share in this play;' for which assistance he is here *sneered* at by the person he gave it to, was quarrelled with at the time, and opposed and illtreated ever after!"—*School of Shak.* p. 479. It is excellently observed by Davies, after much abuse of Jonson: "As this play was *universally* exploded, I have a suspicion that the only parts *which escaped censure* were those written by Shakspeare," vol. ii. p. 85. The only saving part of this universally exploded play being removed, the whole became popular. Such is the logic of Mr. Davies, who adds however—with a face like Ancient Pistol's at his leek—"Jonson's name stood so high that, at the Restoration, the king's comedians, claiming a prior right to those of the Duke of York, seized upon *Sejanus* and *Catiline*."

The *Satiromastix* appeared in 1602; the *Malecontent* was probably written in the following year, as two editions of it were printed so early as 1604. This play Marston dedicated to Jonson in terms that do the highest honour to his friend, as they seem to be expressly selected for the purpose of confuting the calumnies of Decker.[1]

BENJAMIN JONSONIO
POETÆ
ELEGANTISSIMO
GRAVISSIMO
AMICO
SUO CANDIDO ET CORDATO
JOHANNES MARSTON
MUSARUM ALUMNUS
ASPERAM HANC SUAM THALIAM
D. D.

Nor was this all; for, in the epilogue to this play, he thus adverts to his "liberal and cordial friend," and his meditated tragedy:

> " Then, till another's happier muse appears,
> Till his Thalia feast your *learned* ears,
> To whose *desertful lamps*, pleas'd fates impart,
> *Art* above nature, *judgment* above art,
> Receive this piece, which hope nor fear yet daunteth,
> He that knows most, knows most how much he wanteth."

In the succeeding year (1605), Marston again addresses his "most worthy friend," as one whose work (*Sejanus*) would "even force applause from despairful envy;" yet the critics affirm that in 1606, when this poet published his *Sophonisba*,[2] he attacks him upon the score of this very tragedy, which is here declared to be unrivalled. Not a shadow of offence appears on the side of Jonson; yet because Marston changed his language, therefore, say the commentators, "it is probable that Ben's natural arrogance and self-sufficiency[3] had lessened their friendship, since we find Marston casting some very severe glances at his *Sejanus* and *Catiline*." As *Catiline* was not in being till 1611, no glances could be cast at it in 1606; for the rest, if Marston did not know his own mind, it seems hard to blame Jonson for it; since whatever might be the demerits of *Sejanus*, they could not be greater in 1606, than when he praised it two years before. In a word, if this play be meant (which is no care of mine), it will be difficult to acquit Marston of the basest flattery, or the meanest revenge; the commentators, however, can descry no fault but in Jonson.

Prior to this publication an event had taken place, which involved Marston in serious difficulties. In conjunction with Chapman, he had brought out a comedy called *Eastward Hoe!* The play was well received, as, indeed, it deserved to be, for it is exceedingly pleasant; but there was a passage in it reflecting on the Scotch, which gave offence to Sir James Murray, who represented it in so strong a light to the king, that orders were given to arrest the authors. It does not appear that Jonson had any considerable share in the composition of this piece; but as he was undoubtedly privy to its writing, and an "accessary before the fact," he justly considered himself as equally implicated with the rest. He stood in such favour, however, that he was not molested; but this did not satisfy him; and he therefore, with a high sense of honour, "VOLUNTARILY" accompanied his two friends to prison, determined to share their fate. As usual, the whole blame is thrown upon Jonson, though, in the only record which remains of this transaction, he expressly declares that he had nothing to do with the offensive passage, "Chapman and Marston (as he told Drummond) having written it amongst them." "He indulged (say the writers of the *Bio. Brit.*) the *sourness of his disposition*, in a satirical comedy, written against the Scots."[4] And Mr. A. Chalmers

---

[1] Both Demetrius and Crispinus made their peace with Horace almost immediately after the appearance of this piece. It is simple dotage, therefore, to talk of this fray, as if it had embroiled the combatants for life. Jonson appears to have had no subsequent dispute with Decker; whatever might be the case with Marston, who was exceedingly wayward.

[2] It is not very probable that Mr. M. Lewis ever looked into Marston; yet some of the most loathsome parts of the *Monk* are to be found in this detestable play.

[3] This is, no doubt, a translation of Marston's *candido et cordato!*

[4] Written *against the Scots!*—would not this lead one to suppose that the Scotch were the

adds that "it was indeed a foolish ebullition for a man in his circumstances to ridicule the Scotch nation in the court of a Scottish king." The steady friendship, the generous devotement of Jonson, are studiously kept out of sight, while Marston and Chapman are held up as sacrifices to the "sourness of his disposition."

They were not released, the biographers say, without much interest; and Camden and Selden are supposed to have supplicated the throne in favour of Jonson. This is a mere guess, and, at best, an unlucky one. Had such been needed, our author had far more powerful intercessors at court than either of those, whose influence with the sovereign was by no means equal to his own. It is probable that no very serious punishment was ever meditated; or if there were, that the desire to spare Jonson operated in their favour, and procured an unconditional pardon.

When they were first committed, a report had been propagated, Jonson says, that they should have their ears and noses cut, *i.e.* slit.[1] This had reached his mother; and, at an entertainment[2] which he made on his deliverance, "she drank to him, and shewed him a paper which she designed, if the sentence had taken effect, to have mixed with his drink, and it was strong and lusty poison. To shew that she was no churl, Jonson adds, she designed to have first drank of it herself." From such a mother he must have derived no small part of his unconquerable spirit.

Having obtained a pardon,[3] Mr. A. Chalmers says, Jonson endeavoured to conciliate his offended sovereign by taxing his genius to produce a double portion of flattery. He had, in the opening of this very paragraph, accused him of a rough and savage disposition which nothing could tame! The charge of "redoubled flattery," on this account, is also brought against him, but with much more virulence, by the writers of the *Bio. Brit.* It happens, however, somewhat unluckily for these ingenious speculators, that the Masque which he produced on his release was not written at all to flatter the king. The fact is, that there were at this period (1605), several noble and royal foreigners in this country; and to receive them in a manner worthy of the splendour and magnificence of the English court, the Queen, who had not forgotten the exquisite entertainments of Althorpe and Highgate, "expressly injoined" the poet to prepare a Masque in which

---

principal objects of the piece? Yet the only mention which is made of them occurs in the following passage.* "You shall live freely there" (*i. e.*, the new settlement of Virginia) "without serjeants, or courtiers, or lawyers, or intelligencers: only a few industrious Scots perhaps, who indeed are dispersed over the face of the whole earth. But as for them, there are no greater friends to Englishmen and England, when they are out on't, in the world, than they are: and, for my part, I would a hundred thousand of them were there, for we are all one countrymen now, ye know, and we should find ten times more comfort of them there than here." —*Old Plays*, vol. iv. p. 250. This little burst of satire (which is not found in Chetwood's edition), was probably heard with applause. The times were well inclined to apply it; and so far its suppression might be expedient. With respect to the "*sourness*" of Jonson, it would be somewhat difficult to discover any signs of it in *Eastward Hoe!* which is uncommonly sprightly and good-humoured. But the critics never looked into it.

[1] It is amusing to read the different versions of this passage. "His Majesty (says the *Bio. Brit.*) ordered that their ears and noses should be *cut off in the pillory.*" And Chetwood, more

bloody still, adds, "that it was with the greatest difficulty, and incessant solicitations of the prime nobility, Jonson" (no other culprit is named, or even hinted at) "escaped a severe punishment, that is to say, having his ears nailed to the pillory, and cut off by the common hangman, and perpetual banishment!"—*Life of B. Jonson*, p. iv. All this is raised upon the simple passage in the text, for there is no other! What is yet more ridiculous—it is highly probable that most of those who have maligned Jonson for "writing a satire against the Scotch," had, like Chetwood and the *Bio. Brit.*, an edition of this comedy before them, in which the Scotch are not once named, or even hinted at!

[2] At this entertainment "Camden, Selden, and others were present." This is the sole authority for their names being selected as intercessors for Jonson's pardon. And thus his Life is written!

[3] [On this passage Mr. Dyce remarks:—"If Gifford had lived to reprint the present essay, he would have noticed here a second imprisonment, which, soon after his release, Jonson underwent with Chapman, in consequence, it would seem, of supposed reflections cast upon some individual in a play of which they were the joint-authors. The letter from Jonson to the Earl of Salisbury, which mentions these particulars, will be found at the end of a note on a later part of this memoir, having been put into Gifford's hands by Mr. D'Israeli, 'since that note has gone to press.'"]

---

* The words of Drummond are, "he was accused by Sir James Murray to the king for writing *something* against the Scots *in a play* called *Eastward Hoe!*"

she and the prime beauties of the land might bear a part. This gave rise to the *Masque of Blackness*, in which the king is scarcely noticed, and which those who accuse the writer of "taxing his genius for a double portion of flattery to soothe his offended sovereign," will do well to read before they proceed to belie his character a second time.

"Jonson employed a year or two in composing a play."[1] This judicious remark, which Mr. Malone has introduced among the striking proofs of our author's "malevolence" to Shakspeare, is yet capable of some qualification. We have seen that this had been rather a busy year with Jonson; yet he found time to produce the comedy of the *Fox*, one of the dramas of which the nation may be justly proud. It was written, he says, "in five weeks," and we cannot doubt the truth of his assertion, which was openly made on the stage. No human powers, however, could have completed such a work in such a time, unless the author's mind had been previously stored with all the treasure of ancient and modern learning, on which he might draw at pleasure.[2] The triumph of Mr. Malone and others, therefore, over his slowness is somewhat like that of Mr. Thomas Thumb over the giants—"he made them first of all, and then he kill'd them!" Before Jonson was three-and-twenty, he had mastered the Greek and Roman classics, and was, at the period of which we are now speaking, among the first scholars of the age. Did Mr. Malone think that his "studies lay in Green's works?" He had written several of his Masques and Entertainments, and almost the whole of his Epigrams; he had translated Horace, and, as it would seem, Aristotle's Poetics, and prepared a voluminous body of notes to illustrate them; he had made prodigious collections in theology, history, and poetry, from the best writers, and perhaps drawn up his Grammar; yet the charge is still repeated, as if it were entitled to full credit. To be just, however, it was first brought forward by the poet's contemporaries,[3] and almost as soon as he began to write: it gave him, however, no concern; indeed, he rather falls in with it.[4] When the heroes of the *Poetaster*, which was written in fifteen weeks, maintained that he scarcely brought forth a play a year, he replied,

> "'Tis true:
> I would they could not say that I did that:
> There's all the joy that I take in their trade!"

---

[1] *Shak.* vol. i. p. 542.

[2] Jonson was in the laudable habit of making large extracts from the striking passages, and writing notes, and observations of a critical nature on all the books which he read. His common-place book, therefore, was a repository of everything valuable. Lord Falkland seems to have been astonished at the extent and variety of his collections. He says:

"His learning such, no author, old or new,
Escaped his reading that deserved his view;
And such his judgment, so exact his taste,
Of what was best in books, or what books best,
That had he joined those notes his labours took,
From each most praised and praise-deserving book;
And could the world of that choice treasure boast,
It need not care though all the rest were lost."

[3] "Mr. Ben Jonson and Mr. Wm. Shakspeare being merrie at a tavern, Mr. Jonson begins this for his epitaph:

Here lies Ben Jonson
Who was once one ———

he gives it to Mr. Shakspeare to make up, who presently writte:

That, while he liv'd was a *slow* thing,
And now, being dead, is *no*-thing."

This stuff is copied from the Ashmole papers,

MS. 38. It is only an additional instance of what has been already observed, that the fabricators of these things invariably make Shakspeare the most severe.

It is said by Mr. Malone that the *slowness* of Jonson is admitted by his friends; but they do not mean by this word what he does;—Mr. Malone applies it to a dulness of imagination, a want of power to bring forth without long and difficult labour; they use it of the patient revision of his productions. They speak of him as a prolific and rapid writer—whose respect for the public made him nicely weigh every word:

"And suffer nought to pass,
But what could be no better than it was."

Or, as another has it:

"Venture no syllable unto the ear,
Until the file would not make *smooth* but *wear*."

He was, in truth, too fastidious; and this couplet of Cartwright furnishes the key to that bareness and rigidity which we have so frequently to regret in some of his writings.

[4] "Jonson justly spurns," Mr. Cumberland says, "at the critics and detractors of his day, who thought to convict him of dulness by testifying in fact to his diligence. But when he *subsequently* boasted of his poetical dispatch, he forgot that he *had* noted Shakspeare with something less than friendly censure for the very

The *Fox* was received, as it well deserved to be, with general applause. The author's enemies however were not inactive : they could not venture to question his talents ; they therefore turned, as usual, their attacks against his character, and asserted that, under the person of Volpone, he had satirized Sutton, the founder of the Charterhouse, his friend and benefactor.[1] It is not a little amusing to see the calumniators of our poet in that age, driven to the same absurdities as those of the present day. Two characters more opposite in every respect than those of Sutton and Volpone are not to be found in the history of mankind. Sutton inherited a large estate ; he was one of the greatest traders of his time, he had agents in every country, and ships on every sea : he had contracts, mines, mills, ploughs ; he was a naval commissioner, and master of the ordnance in the north ; in a word, one of the most active characters of an active period. Now mark the description of Volpone, as given by himself, in the opening of the play :

> "I glory
> More in the *cunning purchase* of my wealth
> Than in the glad possession ; since I gain
> No *common* way. I *use no trade*, no *venture*,
> I wound no earth with *ploughshares*, fat *no beasts*
> To feed the shambles ; have no *mills* for iron,
> Oil, corn, or men, to grind them into powder ;
> I blow no subtle glass, expose no *ships*
> To threatenings of the furrow-faced seas ;
> I turn no monies," &c. &c.

Sutton was a meek and pious man, Volpone is a daring infidel ; Sutton was abstemious, but kind and charitable ; Volpone is painted as the most selfish and unfeeling of voluptuaries :

> "Prepare
> Me music, dances, banquets, all delights :
> The Turk is not more sensual in his pleasure
> Than will Volpone be."

Again : Volpone is a creature of ungovernable lust, a monster of seduction ; Sutton was the husband of one wife, to whose memory he was so tenderly attached, that upon her death, which took place about two years before the date of this piece, he had retired from the world, to a life of strictness and reserve ; he was, at this time, nearly fourscore, and bowed down to the grave with sorrow for his loss, while Volpone, in the full vigour of manhood, exclaims :

> "What should I do
> But cocker up my genius and live free
> To all delights?—See, I am now as fresh,
> As hot, as high, and in as jovial plight,
> As when, in that so celebrated scene,
> For entertainment of the great Valois
> I acted young Antinous?"

---

quality he is vaunting himself upon."—*Observer,* No. lxxv. What Mr. Cumberland had *forgotten,* it is hard to say : but this *vaunt* of Jonson was first made in 1601, while the allusion to Shakspeare occurs in the *Discoveries,* and is probably thirty years posterior to the passage which is here placed before it in point of time ! Besides, it is *not* of the rapidity of Shakspeare's composition that Jonson speaks, but the carelessness. A man may write fast, and yet not wreck a vessel on the coast of Bohemia. The *Fox* was rapidly written ; but it is not therefore incorrect ; and what Mr. Cumberland adds of it is as creditable to his taste as learning. "It must on all hands be considered as the masterpiece of a very capital artist ; a work that bears the stamp of elaborate design, a strong, and frequently a sublime vein of poetry, much sterling wit, comic humour, happy character, moral satire, and unrivalled erudition ; a work

Quod nec imber edax, aut Aquilo impotens Possit diruere," &c.

[1] "Sutton's biographer (S. Herne) after noticing this report, says—' It is probable the poet never intended what they think : for in that age several other men were pointed at, and who was the true person, was *then* a matter of doubt !' *Dom. Carthus.* p. 42. It is no longer so—we are better judges of these matters than the contemporaries of Sutton, and decide without difficulty." I regret to find Mr. Disraeli among the poet's accusers ; for he is an anxious inquirer after truth, and brings, as far as I have been able to discover, an unprejudiced mind to his investigations. His fault is too great a deference for names unworthy of his trust. This is an evil which every day will contribute to abate. Twice in one page (*Quarrels of Authors,* vol. iii. 134) he charges Jonson with bringing Sutton on the stage.

In a word, the contrast is so glaring, that if the commentators on Shakspeare had not afforded us a specimen of what ignorance grafted on malevolence can do, we should be lost in wonder at the obliquity of intellect which could detect the slightest resemblance of Sutton in the features of Volpone.

The *Fox* is dedicated, in a strain of unparalleled elegance and vigour, to the two Universities, before whom it had been represented with all the applause which might be anticipated from such distinguished and competent judges of its worth.[1] The English stage had hitherto seen nothing so truly classical, so learned, so correct, and so chaste.

About this time our author, who had deeply studied the grounds of the controversy between the reformed and Catholic Churches, and convinced himself, by the aid of those *wiser guides* who followed truth alone, of the delusions of Popery, made a solemn recantation of his errors, and was re-admitted into the bosom of the Church, which he had abandoned twelve years before.[2] Drummond tells us that "he drank out the full cup of wine, at his first communion, in token of his true reconciliation." Jonson's feelings were always strong; and the energy of his character was impressed upon every act of his life; but this story is foisted into his conversations by his "friend," and has perhaps no better foundation than many others wantonly invented to discredit him. It may not, however, be irrelevant to observe, that more wine was drunk at the altar in the poet's days than in ours; and that the vestiges of this custom are not yet entirely obliterated in remote situations.

Jonson had not been inactive between the first representation of the *Fox* and its publication. The Queen's brother (Christian of Denmark) paid her a visit in the summer of 1606, and our poet was called upon to furnish some of the pageantries prepared for his amusement. Of these we have little remaining but a few epigrams in Latin verse, which were displayed round the walls of the inner court "at Theobald's," when the Earl of Salisbury received the royal brothers there on the 24th of July. In the subsequent summer (1607) Theobald's was delivered up to the Queen in exchange for Hatfield Chase. A magnificent entertainment was prepared on the occasion, at which James and his Queen, the two princes, the Duke of Lorraine, and all the principal nobility were present; and the house was transferred to the new possessor in an elegant poetical apologue composed by Jonson, and distinguished by his usual felicity of appropriate character and language. Cecil had done himself honour by his early patronage of our author; and he, who was one of the most grateful and affectionate of mankind, embalmed the ashes of his benefactor in strains that yet live.[3]

Previously to this, however, Jonson had written his beautiful *Masque and Barriers* for the marriage of the Earl of Essex, which was celebrated at Whitehall with extraordinary magnificence, in the Christmas of 1606. The poet has entered with some complacency into the richness and variety of this exhibition, which seems to have astonished the beholders:[4] he drops a word too in justification of the strict regard to the pure models of antiquity, after which he usually constructed his fables.

---

[1] There is an allusion to this circumstance in the verse of Jonson's friend E. S. (Edward Scorey?)

"Now he (the *Fox*) hath run his train and shown
His subtile body, where he best was known,
In both Minerva's cities, he doth yield
His well-form'd limbs upon this open field," &c.

[2] Among the works of our author, Wood inserts one printed in 1622, 8vo, and called *His Motives*. If Jonson really wrote such a book, it might be supposed to relate to this circumstance: but the probability is, that this industrious antiquary mistook the writer's name; of the work itself I have no knowledge whatever.

[3] [Jonson told Drummond "Salisbury never cared for any man longer nor he could make use of him."—*Conversations*. F. C.]

[4] We have other evidence than the poet's for this splendid display. The kindness of Mr. Disraeli has furnished me with the following curious and interesting extract from a MS. letter of Mr. Pory to Sir Robert Cotton. Sir Robert, like most of the great men at this time, when absent from court, had a correspondent (generally some secretary) there, who furnished them with regular accounts of the various occurrences of the day. Sir Robert was fortunate in his informant.*

"Inigo, Ben, and the actors, men and women,

---

* Pory is mentioned with great respect by Hackluyt. He had travelled much, and seen a good deal of courts and public affairs; he was also an excellent scholar. As he was a Member of Parliament, he must have been a person of some property.

c

Hitherto the "flattery to which Jonson betook himself immediately after his release," has not appeared so "gross" as his biographers choose to represent it. Unfortunately for them, his next Masque, which he calls the *Queen's*, is still less to their purpose. "*Two years* (he says) being now passed that her majesty had intermitted those delights, it was her pleasure again to glorify the court, and command that I should think on some fit presentment," &c. This produced the *Masque of Beauty*, (a counterpart to that of "Blackness,") which was performed at court during the Christmas of 1608. In this, as in the preceding one, the performers were the queen, the prince, and the prime nobility of both sexes. At present, we are only told of the rudeness and barbarity of Whitehall; and Hume is so strangely ignorant of the manners of those times, as to assert that "James affected a rustic contempt of the fair sex, and banished them from his court."¹ Of his contempt I know nothing; but that the ladies were not banished from his court, is proved beyond all possibility of doubt by the records of their names in the pages of our author. Year after year, and many times in the course of the same year, (for these masques were often repeated,) the court of James was thronged with all that was distinguished for birth and beauty, for rank and worth, for grace and elegance, and every female accomplishment.

The reputation of Jonson stood so high at this time, that few public solemnities were thought perfect without his assistance. The King had expressed a wish to dine with the Company of Merchant Tailors, who accordingly met to consult on the most honourable mode of receiving him. Stow has preserved the *minutes* of the court, which are not a little amusing: Whereas the Company are informed that the King's most excellent majestie with our gratious Queene, and the noble prince and diuers honourable lords and others, determyne to dyne on the day of the eleccion of M. and Wardens, therefore the meeting was appointed to advise and consult how everie thinge may be performde for the reputacion and credit of the company, to his Majesties best lyking and content-ment. And Sir John Swynnerton" (afterwards lord mayor) "is intreated to confer with Master Benjamin Jonson, the poet, about a speech to be made to welcome his Majestie, and about music and other invencions which may give lyking and delight; by reason that the company doubt that their schoolmaster and scholleres be not acquainted with

---

did their parts with great commendation. The conceit or soul of the Mask was Hymen bring-ing in a bride, and Juno Pronuba's priest a bride-groom, proclaiming that those two should be sacrificed to Union; and here the poet made an apostrophe to the Union of the Kingdoms. But before the sacrifice could be performed, Ben Jonson turned the globe of the earth standing behind the altar, and within the concave sat the eight men-maskers, representing the four Humours and the four Affections, who leaped forth to disturb the sacrifice to Union. But amidst their fury, Reason, that sat above them all crowned with burning tapers, came down and silenced them. These eight, with Reason their mediator, sat somewhat like the ladies in the Scollop-shell of the last year. About the globe hovered a middle region of clouds, in the centre whereof stood a grand concert of musicians, and upon the cantons sat the ladies, four at one corner and four at another, who descended upon the stage, not in the downright perpendicular fashion, like a bucket in a well, but came gently sloping down.* These eight after the sacrifice was ended, represented the Eight Nuptial Powers of Juno Pronuba, who came down to confirm their Union. The men were

* Here Milton found his "smooth sliding without step;" in truth, he found much more in Jonson's Masques than his editors appear to suspect, or are willing to acknowledge.

clad in crimson, and the women in white. They had every one a white plume of the richest hern's feathers, and were so rich in jewels upon their heads as was most glorious. I think they hired and borrowed all the principal jewels and ropes of pearls both in court and city. The Spanish ambassador seemed but poor to the meanest of them.† They danced all variety of dances, both severally and *promiscuè*, and then the women took the men as named by the Prince (Henry) who danced with as great perfection, and as settled a majesty as could be devised. The Spanish ambassador, the Archduke's ambas-sador, the Duke, &c. led out the Queen, the bride, and the greatest of the ladies."—*Cott. Lib. Julii.* c. iii. It appears that Mr. Pory was present at the performance of this Masque on Twelfth-night, 1605-6.

   ¹ Hist. of England, vol. vi. p. 283.

† This was not wanted to prove the unac-countable folly of Hurd in maintaining that the Masque in the *Tempest*, which Capell, the mere idolater of Shakspeare, affirms to be "weak throughout, faulty in rimes, and faulty in mythology," &c., *Notes on Temp.* p. 68, and which was danced and sung by the ordinary performers, to a couple of fiddles, perhaps, in the balcony of the stage, "*put to shame* all the masques of Jonson not only in its construction, but in the splendour of its show."

such kinde of entertaynments." This was done ; and Stow tells us that the "Speeches" were delivered on the 16th of July 1607,[1] in a chamber called "The King's Chamber."

It is well known that our author received periodical sums not only from public bodies, but from several of the nobility and gentry :[2] these, it has been said, were not bestowed as free gifts, or as honourable testimonies of his superior talents, but extorted from reluctant hands by the dread of his satire.[3] This is *mera ærugo*. The ever active malice of his most determined enemies has hitherto been unable to discover, either in his own works, or in those of others, a single syllable to justify the infamous calumny. The truth is, that the monarchs of those times, though approached with more awe, and served with more respect than at present, yet lived more among their people. A year seldom passed without some royal progress, and corporate bodies were frequently encouraged to feast their sovereign. On all these occasions, the custom of the time,

> " And pity 'tis, so good a time had wings
> To fly away,"—

called for something more than a bare treat, some introductory compliment that might, as it were, ennoble the entertainment, and gratify at once the judgment and the taste. As these visits were irregular, and without much previous notice, it became an object of no small importance with those who were to receive them, to have a person always at command on whose abilities they could rely for an Entertainment that should neither disgrace themselves, nor their guests. Hence sprung the several pensions said to have been paid to Jonson, and which should rather be considered in the light of *retaining fees* than gratuitous donations, and still less, forced tributes to malevolence. Great and generous spirits like Sutton might, indeed, think their wealth not misemployed in supplying the deficiencies of fortune ; but that most of what he received *was hire and salary,* scarcely admits of a reasonable doubt.

Be this as it may, he was now called upon for a *Masque* to celebrate the marriage of Lord Haddington. This, which was probably the most costly and magnificent ever exhibited in this or any other country, was first performed at Whitehall on Shrove Tuesday, 1608. The Scotch and English nobility vied with each other in splendour of apparel, and the king and queen bore a part in it.

Jonson was now busily employed on the *Silent Woman,* and the *Masque of Queens,* both of which appeared in 1609 ; the former written, it seems, to *ridicule Antony and Cleopatra,* and the latter to *rival Macbeth,* "of the success of whose witches he was jealous, as he fancied himself to be Shakspeare's superior !"[4] It will be time enough to

---

[1] [Stow died 1605.— F.C.]

[2] [Jonson told Drummond, " Every first day of the new year he had 20 lb. sent to him from the Earl of Pembrok to buy bookes."*Conversations.*—F.C.]

[3] This is boldly advanced by Mr. A. Chalmers, and in the most offensive terms. "Disappointed (he says) in the hopes of wealth and independence which his high opinion of himself led him to form, Jonson degenerated even to the resources of a libeller, who extorts from fear what is denied to genius." To require from this calumniator of the poet's memory a proof of his assertion, would be to no purpose—FOR HE HAS NONE. He who produced in the page immediately preceding this, a wicked interpolation by Shiels, and fathered it, in direct terms, on Drummond, cannot be complimented with the supposition of recurring to original documents. But the *whole* of the charge is false. Jonson was not disappointed in his hopes of riches. He gave himself no concern about them. Even his "friend" Drummond admits that he was "careless to gain."—Wealth, in short, he heeded not, titles he rejected, and the only ambition which he ever felt was that of which Mr. Chalmers seeks to deprive him, an honest fame.

As to independence, Jonson relied on his talents for it.—His story indeed furnishes another melancholy proof of the instability of all human things. At the age of fifty-one, he probably felt neither doubts nor fears of his sufficiency ; yet at this period, he was struck with the malady that finally carried him off. In the twelve sad years that followed, during which he did little more than move from his bed to his grave, he felt the evils of dependence ; and let it not be charged on him as a crime that he sought to alleviate them—not by "libels," but by humble supplications for relief. Of these several are found, of the others NOT ONE WORD was ever in existence.

[4] To omit the rest at present, Mr. Davies begins one of his chapters thus, (c. xxxiii.) "Ben Jonson's ridicule on *Antony and Cleopatra.*—Ben Jonson in his *Silent Woman* has treated this tragedy as a play full of nothing but fights at sea !" This good man is a humble follower of Mr. Malone. The sea-fights in *Antony and Cleopatra* are confined to a stage direction. "Alarum *afar off, as* at a sea-fight," *i.e.* a cracker was let off, so as to make a *faint noise,* just to signify that there was a *fight at a distance ;* and therefore, when Morose, after

exonerate Jonson from his charge when the commentators shall have ascertained the date of *Macbeth*, which is very far from being the case at present; meanwhile, we may venture to observe that the production of two such pieces in one year, is no less creditable to his industry than to his talents and learning. The Masque was published, with an ample commentary, at the request of Prince Henry, who was curious to learn the authorities from which the author had derived his incantations, &c. The critics of our days have been pleased to sneer at Jonson for the attire of his witches. They are always unlucky. "The device of their attire (Jonson says), was Master Inigo Jones's;" whom, still more to confound them, he proceeds to compliment in the warmest terms that the sincerity of friendship could select. See *Masque of Queens*, vol. iii.

The year 1610, not less prolific than the preceding one, produced the beautiful *Masque of Oberon*, and the *Barriers*, written to celebrate the creation of Henry Prince of Wales, which took place on the 4th of June. The *Alchemist*, the noblest effort of Jonson's genius, appeared about the same time. This comedy he dedicated to Lady Wroth, the niece of Sir Philip Sidney, with whose family he maintained a constant intercourse of friendship; and, as if he meant to show his detractors that his obligations to the ancients were those of choice, not of necessity, he constructed the whole of this wonderful drama on the vices and follies of the age, and trusted to the extent and variety of his reading, for such apt allusions and illustrations as appear to spring spontaneously from the subject.[1]

Catiline, which followed the *Alchemist*, was brought out in 1611. "It was deservedly damned," Mr. Malone says; but Mr. Malone's *aye and no, too, are no good divinity*, when applied to Jonson. Without questioning the accuracy of the term *deservedly*, it will be sufficient to state that it was not "damned" at all. It met, indeed, with opposition (like most of his plays) from the persevering enmity which pursued him through life; but *Catiline* continued on the stage till driven from it, with every other drama, by the prevailing power of puritanism. The author inscribed it to his great patron, the Earl of Pembroke, as being, in his opinion, the best of the tragedies which he had hitherto produced. He calls it "a legitimate poem," and we may venture, notwithstanding the decision of Hurd,[2] (who appears not to have read it,) to confirm his judgment. But "we know," says Davies, "from the author's own testimony that the play was condemned." Assuredly, we *know* no such thing. Jonson evidently took a strange kind of pleasure in exaggerating the opposition which he experienced from his persecutors; and we are therefore in danger of misleading ourselves, if we adopt his expressions in all their force. It is not necessary to praise his conduct in this instance, which, to say the least of it, savours of a haughty and inflexible spirit; though it may not be improper to advert to it occasionally.

Besides publishing his play, Jonson found leisure this year to amuse himself with arranging that immense farrago of burlesque "testimonies to the author's merit," which accompanied the first appearance of *Coryat's Crudities*. In this, he seems to have engaged at the desire of Prince Henry, who found entertainment in laughing at the simple

---

enumerating a variety of the most horrid dins, adds, that he would even sit out a play *that was nothing but fights at sea*, he must mean to ridicule Shakspeare, for one that has *none!* At that very time, too, be it observed, there were scores of plays on the stage in which such fights were really exhibited: Heywood has more than one comedy with sea-fights in almost every act; and in Decker's *Whore of Babylon* there is a sea-fight that occupies the whole of a long scene; yet Jonson, who knew all this far better than ourselves, and who had been stunned a hundred times with rude representations of the *Spanish Armada* on every stage, could not speak of a sea-fight without being accused of directing the whole of his ridicule against a stage direction in Shakspeare! It is hard to say whether the propagators of these despicable calumnies, or the believers in them, are best entitled to our scorn.

[1] "Were the ancients," Mr. Headley says, "to reclaim their property, Jonson would not have a rag to cover his nakedness." With deference to this *wise young judge*, I am inclined to think that enough would remain to him of the *Alchemist* alone to obviate the danger of any indecent exposure. It is not a little singular that all the enemies of Jonson, from Dryden downwards, when they have to particularise his obligations to the ancients, refer to his two tragedies, as if he had written nothing besides, or as if they would have had him form a *Catiline* and *Sejanus* out of his own imagination!

[2] "*Catiline*," he says, "is a specimen of all the errors of tragedy." Mr. A. Chalmers, who quotes the passage, joins his suffrage to that of the bishop, and speaks of it with very edifying contempt.

vanity of " the Odcombian Traveller." Tom, it is probable, laughed more than any of them. His taste in matters of praise was not very delicate ; and he had cunning enough to discern that, at the expense of some extravagant ridicule, which could not much affect him in his absence, he was amusing his princely patron, spreading the knowledge of his book, and filling his pockets for another course of adventures. Jonson wrote the distichs, and the introductory character of *Thomas the Coryate*, in the person of " a charitable friend," to which he added some lines on the author's name. He procured verses from all his friends, and, among the rest, from Inigo Jones, whom he seems to have regarded with peculiar kindness, and to have recommended to notice with a degree of affection which deserved a better return from the growing fortunes of the architect than he was doomed to experience.

In the succeeding year our author was probably engaged on some of those exquisite Masques which appear in the folio of 1616, and to which no dates are prefixed. The death of Prince Henry threw a gloom over the nation, and saddened, for a short period, the gaiety of the court. Jonson seems to have taken advantage of the temporary cessation of festivity (for he bore no part in the celebration of the marriage of the princess) to make a second trip to the Continent.[1] How long he resided abroad, or what countries he visited, is nowhere told ; we only know, from an incidental remark in his conversations with Drummond, that he was at Paris in 1613. As he was connected with the court, and in habits of intercourse with all the literary characters of his time, he must have been amply provided with recommendations to the most distinguished personages abroad. He was introduced to the Cardinal du Perron, who, in compliment to his learning, showed him his translation of Virgil, which Jonson did not approve. "He treated the Cardinal with all that bluntness which was so much his nature." Drummond merely says that he told him "it was naught ;" but this might be done without any bluntness of language, were it not a point agreed upon by his biographers, that he must be always "brutal and ferocious." His integrity, however, merits praise. Du Perron was a confirmed bigot, and, at this period, actively engaged in undermining the liberties of the Gallican church ; he had, therefore, little leisure for poetry, and that little was misemployed.

In 1614 Jonson produced his *Bartholomew Fair*, a popular piece, but chiefly remarkable for the obloquy to which it has given birth. "About this time," Mr. A. Chalmers says, "he commenced a quarrel with Inigo Jones, and made him the subject of his ridicule." It is not so much the business of Mr. Chalmers to inquire as to write :—but, indeed, he only repeats what has been said by Steevens and others :

> *ast alii sex*
> *Et plures uno conclamant ore sophistæ.*

With the exception of Ferabosco, Jonson has spoken with more kindness of Inigo Jones than of any of his coadjutors, as the reader may see by turning to his Masques. He notices him for the fifth or sixth time, with unusual warmth, in the *Masque of Queens*, and we have just seen them playing the fool together in *Coryat's Crudities*. In the winter of 1612, Jones left this country for Italy, where he resided several years. What quarrel therefore could Jonson possibly *commence* with him in 1614? In what year Inigo returned from his travels, is not said, but, according to his biographer, (who was also his relation,) it must have been long after the appearance of *Bartholomew Fair*.[2] In the notes to that comedy, (written before I had read the life of the architect,) I was induced, from internal evidence, to express my doubts as to the identity of Lanthorn Leatherhead and Inigo Jones ; at present, I disbelieve it altogether.[3] That some traits of personality are to be found in the character of Leatherhead I do not mean to deny ; but from a few obscure hints scattered up and down our author's works, I am almost inclined to think that they point at the master of the revels (whoever he was) or his

---

[1] [This was when he accompanied Sir Walter Raleigh's son.—See *Conversations.*—F. C.]

[2] "After the death of Prince Henry in 1612, our architect made a second tour, to Italy, and continued there some years, improving himself in his favourite art, till he was recalled by the death of the surveyor-general."—*Life of Jones.* [Simon Basil, the surveyor-general, of whose office James had given Inigo the reversion, died in 1615.—F.C.]

[3] The loose reports of the time weigh nothing with me : and those who have noticed the remarks on the imaginary resemblance of Sutton and Volpone will, I flatter myself, be inclined to think as lightly of them as myself.

deputy. Mr. A. Chalmers, however, is so confident of his man, that he rakes into the scurrility of Walpole for fit language to express his sense of the poet's delinquency. "Whoever (says Lord Orford) was the aggressor, the *turbulent* temper of Jonson took care to be most in the wrong.—In his verses he fully exerted all that brutal abuse which his contemporaries were willing to think wit, and which only serves to show the arrogance of the man who presumed to satirize Jones and rival Shakspeare."—It must be confessed that Shakspeare makes his appearance here somewhat unexpectedly :—much, however, to the satisfaction of the biographer, who subjoins, "If Jonson was the rival of Shakspeare he deserves all this (abuse :)—but with no other claims than this *Cataline* and *Sejanus*, how could he for a moment fancy himself the *rival* of Shakspeare?" How indeed ! but when Mr. Chalmers shall find leisure to read what he prints, he will discover, 1st, that Jonson had other "claims ;" and 2ndly, that he did not fancy himself the "rival of Shakspeare."

As no date is affixed to his minor pieces, we know not how he was employed after the production of *Bartholomew Fair*,[1] till 1616, when he brought out his excellent comedy of *The Devil's an Ass*. A considerable time must be allotted for the preparation of the folio volume which was published this year, and contained, besides comedies and tragedies, the first book of his Epigrams, several Masques and Entertainments, and a collection of poems called the *Forest*. He seems to have meditated a complete edition of all his works ; but he apparently grew weary towards the conclusion of the volume, and never (unless peculiarly called upon) had recourse to the press afterwards. The second folio is a wretched continuation of the first, printed from MSS. surreptitiously obtained, during his life, or ignorantly hurried through the press after his death. It bears a variety of dates from 1631 to 1641 inclusive. It is probable that he looked forward to a period of retirement and ease, when he might be enabled to collect, revise, and publish his works at leisure ; but the loss of all his MSS. by fire, and the fatal illness which almost immediately afterwards seized him, rendered all such views abortive. It is remarkable that he calls his Epigrams "Book the first:" he had, therefore, others in his hand ; but they have perished.

Shakspeare died this year : what the world lost by that event need not be told ; Jonson (the commentators assure us) was freed by it from a man whom he "hated and feared through life." He had not, however, much leisure to enjoy his good fortune ; for "such was the *enviousness* of his disposition, that he immediately became jealous of Chapman, who *now began to grow* into reputation, and being, by the death of Shakspeare, left without a rival, strove to continue so, and endeavoured to suppress as much as possible the rising fame of his friend !" This medley of malice and stupidity is taken from the *Bio. Dram.* At the period of Shakspeare's death, Chapman had nearly reached his grand climacteric, and with the exception of one or two pieces, had written the *whole* of his dramatic works ; yet this is the reverend youth who "now began to grow into fame," and to excite the jealousy of Jonson ! The reader supposes, perhaps,

---

[1] It may be safely assumed, however, that he was engaged either in seeking or imparting useful knowledge. While his enemies dream of nothing but his "envy" of some dramatic writer, I find his name, whenever it occurs in the writings of his contemporaries, incessantly connected with subjects of general literature. He appears, about this time, (1615,) to have carried on some correspondence with Selden, respecting the precise import of that passage in Deuteronomy, "The woman shall not wear that which pertaineth unto a man, neither shall a man put on a woman's garment, for all that do so are an abomination to the Lord ;" c. xxii. 5. In conclusion, he desires his friend to put together what he had collected on the subject, and send it to him. Selden's answer is dated on the last day of February. It contains nearly eight folio pages full of the most curious and recondite reading—being desirous, he says, "to shew how ambitious he was

not only of Jonson's love, but also of his judgment."

Nothing is more remarkable than the respect which this prodigy of learning constantly shows for the attainments of his friend.—"With regard, (Selden says,) to what the Greeks and Latins have of Adargatis, Derceto, Atargata, Derce (all one name) &c. you *best* know, being *most* conversant in the recondite parts of human learning," &c. ; and he concludes, after a variety of extracts from the Hebrew, Syriac, Greek, &c.: "In the connexion of these *no vulgar* observations, if they had been to a *common learned* reader, there had been often room for divers pieces of theology dispersed in Latin and Greek authors, and fathers of the Church, but *your own most choice* and able store cannot but furnish you with whatever is fit that way to be thought. Whatever I have here collected, I consecrate to your love, and end with hope of your *instructing judgment.*" Vol. iv. fol. p. 1691.

that I have discovered these facts in some "rare MS. *penes me;*" to the disgrace of literature,[1] they are to be found on *the very page* which furnished the abuse of Jonson ! But we have not yet done with this momentous period. Shakspeare, as we know from the authority of Mr. Malone (enforced in a hundred places,) was persecuted by Jonson during his life with unceasing malevolence. While I was engaged on these pages, a letter of that gentleman to the Rev. Mr. Whalley, was put into my hands by Mr. Waldron, of which the following is a copy.

"SIR,—Having been out of town for some days ; I did not receive your favour till last night. I shall with great pleasure add my mite of contribution to your new edition of Ben Jonson, though I have very little hopes of being able to throw any light on what has eluded your researches. At the same time I must honestly own to you that I have never read old Ben's plays with any degree of attention, and that he is an author so little to my taste that I have no pleasure in perusing him. However, as I have just said, you may command, sir, my best services, whenever the volumes are put into my hands : they are at present, I believe, in the possession of Mr. Reed. I agree with you entirely that no ridicule was intended against Shakspeare in the *Poetaster* for the use of the word *clutch*, or in the *Case is Altered*, for the *white of an egg ;* nor against his *hot and moist* in *Othello*. Before I was honoured with your letter, I had observed in a little work of mine that is now in the press (A Second Appendix to my Supplement to Shakspeare,) that the dates of the respective pieces refute the idea of his sneering at Shakspeare, in these places. And, indeed, I believe that even in those plays of his or Fletcher's, where a direct parody appears, no ridicule may possibly have been intended. But notwithstanding this, I think I have brought together decisive proofs of Jonson's malignity and jealousy of Shakspeare. The *Return from Parnassus* shows they were at variance so early as 1602, three years only after Shakspeare had patronized him by bringing *Every Man in his Humour* on the stage. In the prologue to that piece his *Winter Tale* is, I think, evidently ridiculed. This had always puzzled me, and I conjectured that this prologue was not spoken originally, but added at a subsequent period. On looking into the 4to edit. which has lately fallen into my hands, I find my conjecture confirmed. *This* certainly, as well as the torrent of ridicule thrown out in *B. Fair* in 1614, adds great strength to your supposition that old Ben's jealousy did not display itself with full force till Shakspeare retired from the stage.
"*Queen Anne Street East, Dec.* 28, 1782."

The case of our author is thus rendered worse than ever ! it now appears that so far from being relieved by the retirement of Shakspeare, his *jealousy* did not break out in full force till that event took place ; and as he was besides tormented by the "rising fame of a new competitor," his situation can scarcely be contemplated without dismay. The reader, who has seen that he was of a disposition to stem the torrent of ill-fortune, will be naturally anxious to learn by what extraordinary exertions of dramatic power he was enabled to overcome at once his "jealousy" of Shakspeare, and his "fear" of Chapman. Comedy after comedy, he will imagine, was now brought forward with a rapidity unknown before, teeming, in every act, with the most pointed ridicule, the most envenomed malignity. I anticipate his surprise, therefore, when he hears from me the simple fact—that for the long period of ten years from the "death" of Shakspeare, and the "rise" of Chapman, Jonson DID NOT WRITE ONE LINE FOR THE STAGE ! But this surprise will be converted into scorn and indignation against his base calumniators when he further hears that during the same period, in which he is accused of such active malevolence against both, the only memorials of it to be found, are, 1st, the pleasing lines under the print of Shakspeare, and the generous burst of affection on his death; and 2ndly, a viva voce declaration to Drummond that "he *loved* Chapman," and a most kind and complimentary address to him on the completion of his translation of Hesiod ![2]

---

[1] I have said nothing of the biographers :—to suppose, indeed, that Mr. Stephen Jones should notice an error *though as wide as a church door,* would be to equal him in folly. Better optics than his, (see the *Theatrum Poetarum,* p. 052,)

when Jonson is concerned, "don't" (as Bustapha well observes,) "know a lie when they see it."
[2] As there is not a word of our author respecting Chapman that does not breathe love and esteem for him, the reader may be pleased to

A date is the spear of Ithuriel to the enemies of Jonson. Touch their "facts" with it, and they start up in loathsome and revolting deformity.

The kindness of James for our poet, which seems to have progressively increased, was this year manifested by a very substantial act of beneficence. In consideration of his services, he conferred on him, by letters patent, a pension for life of a hundred marks. In courtesy, this has been termed creating him Poet Laureat; and perhaps it was so.[1] Hitherto, the laureatship appears to have been a mere title, adopted at pleasure by those who were employed to write for the court, but conveying no privileges, and establishing no claim to a salary.[2] Occasional gratuities were undoubtedly bestowed on occasional services; but an annual and determinate sum seems to have been issued, for the first time, in favour of Jonson. The nominal laureat or court poet, when our author first came into notice, was Daniel, who was long the favourite of Elizabeth and her ladies, and who did not witness the growing popularity of the youthful bard, or hear of his being called upon for those Entertainments which he probably considered as within his province, with very commendable fortitude. It is a subject of sincere regret that many of the latter days of this amiable poet and virtuous man, should be overcast with unavailing gloom on this account, and that he should indulge any feeling of resent-

---

see the return to it. "An Invective against Ben Jonson by Mr. George Chapman:"

"Greate-learned wittie Ben, be pleasde to light
The world with that three-forked fire; nor fright
All us, the sublearn'd with luciferous boast
That thou art most great, learnd—of all the earth
As being a thing betwixt a humane birth
And an infernall; no humanytie
Of the divine soul shewing man in thee," &c.
                                        Ashmole MSS.

Chapman (whom I am unwilling to believe guilty of this malicious trash) died, I fear, poor and neglected. In another poem among the Ashmole papers, inscribed "The Genius of the Stage deploring the death of Ben Jonson;" after noticing the general sorrow, the writer says,

"Why do Apollo's sons
Meet in such throngs, and whisper as they go?—
There are no more by sad affliction hurl'd,
And friends' neglect, from this inconstant world!
Chapman alone went so; He that's now gone,
Commands his tomb; he, scarce a grave or stone."

[1] The attachment of James to our author, is thus noticed by Lord Falkland, in an allusion to the circumstance before us. Dorus, he says, would tell

"How learned James,
Who favoured quiet, and the arts of peace,
Which, in his halcyon days found large increase,
Friend to the humblest, if deserving, swain,
Who was himself a part of Phœbus' train,
Declared great JONSON worthiest to receive
The garland which the Muses' hands did weave;
And though his bounty did sustain his days,
Gave a more welcome pension in his praise."

"Of all literary tastes (says Mr. Dibdin) James had the most strange and sterile." He probably thought that there was something more valuable in *literature* than an uncut catalogue on large paper, and thus far, perhaps, differed from the critic: in other respects, James cannot be said

to evince much singularity of taste; but it is with this poor prince, as with Falstaff, "men of all sorts take a pride to gird at him." There seems no necessity for this. If James was not a wise man, he was very far indeed from being a fool; which is more, perhaps, than can be said of some of his persecutors. "James," says Mr. D'Israeli, who had just risen from an examination of his works, "was no more a pedant than the ablest of his contemporaries; nor abhorred the taste of tobacco, nor feared witches, more than they did; he was a great wit, a most acute disputant," &c. *Calam. of Authors*, vol. ii. 245. All this is simple truth; and it is mere dotage to re-echo, at this day, the senseless and savage yell of the nonconformists of James's time. They thirsted for blood, and their rage was kindled against him because his good fortune or his good sense kept him from rushing into a continental war, for which he had neither men nor money; and which, therefore, by involving him in difficulties, would, as they well knew, leave him at their mercy, and thus accelerate that overthrow of the Church and State, for which they so eagerly panted.

[2] Jonson, who was never satisfied without procuring all possible information upon every subject in which he was interested, appears, on this occasion, to have applied to Selden for assistance in his researches; and Selden, who always found a singular pleasure in gratifying him, drew up expressly, and introduced into the second part of his learned work, *Titles of Honour*, a long chapter (the forty-third) "on the custom of giving crowns of laurel to poets." At the conclusion of which he says, "Thus have I, by no unseasonable digression, performed a promise to you, my beloved Ben Jonson. Your curious learning and judgment may correct where I have erred, and add where my notes and memory have left me short. You are

omnia carmina doctus,
Et calles mython plasmata et historiam.

And so you both fully know what concerns it, and your singular excellency in the art most eminently deserves it."

ment against one who took no undue course to secure the favour from which he had apparently fallen. On the regular appointment of Jonson, Daniel withdrew himself entirely from court. He died about three years afterwards, beloved, honoured, and lamented.[1]

We now approach the most unfortunate period of our author's life. In consequence of a warm invitation to Scotland, where he had many friends, especially among the connexions of the Duke of Lenox, he determined in the summer of this year (1618) to pay a visit to this country. His journey was made on foot, and he appears to have spent several months with the nobility and gentry in the neighbourhood of Edinburgh. "At Leith," says Taylor, the Water-poet, "I found my long-approved and assured good friend, Master Benjamin Jonson, at one Master John Stuart's house. I thank him for his great kindness towards me; for at my taking leave of me, he gave me a piece of gold of two and twenty shillings to drink his health in England;[2] and withall willed me to remem-

---

[1] That Jonson's conduct towards Daniel had always been perfectly honourable, may be collected from many quarters. The celebrated John Florio (author of the *Dict. Ital.*) was brother-in-law to Daniel, and apparently much attached to his interests; yet he always lived on terms of great friendship with our author. In his Majesty's Library is a very beautiful copy of *The Fox*, which once belonged to Florio, with the following autograph of the poet: "To his loving Father and worthy friend, Master John Florio, Ben Jonson seals this testimony of his friendship and love."

Sir Tobie Mathews has preserved a letter of Jonson's:—It is an answer to Donne, who had besought him (doubtless on prudential motives) to abstain from justifying himself against some false charge. No name is given; but I am inclined to think that the person alluded to in the letter was Lucy, Countess of Bedford. She had certainly been, at one time, ill disposed towards our author; and, as it would appear, by the unhappy jealousy of Daniel, whom, as well as Donne, she warmly patronized. In the Epistle to the Countess of Rutland (vol. iii. *The Forest*, No. 12), there is an allusion to something of this kind; but whatever be the cause, the letter is honourable to the poet's feelings.

If this lady was meant, she was not long in discovering that Jonson had been calumniated. A steady friendship grew between them; she showed him many marks of favour, and he wrote some beautiful verses in her praise.

SIR,—You cannot but believe how dear and reverend your friendship is to me, (though all testimony on my part hath been too short to express me,) and therefore would I meet it with all obedience. My mind is not yet so deafened by injuries, but it hath an ear for counsel. Yet in this point that you presently dissuade, I wonder how I am misunderstood; or that you should call that an imaginary right, which is the proper justice that every clear man owes to his innocency. Exasperations I intend none, for truth cannot be sharp but to ill natures, or such weak ones whom the ill spirits, suspicion or credulity still possess. My lady may believe whisperings, receive tales, suspect and condemn my honesty, and I may not answer, on the pain of losing her! as if she, who had this prejudice of me were not already lost!—O no, she will do me no hurt, she will think and speak well of my faculties.—She

cannot there judge me; or if she could, I would exchange all glory (if I had all men's abilities) which could come that way, for honest simplicity.—But there is a greater penalty threatened, the loss of you, my true friend; for others I reckon not, who were never had. You have so subscribed yourself. Alas! how easy is a man accused that is forsaken of defence!—Well, my modesty shall sit down, and (let the world call it guilt or what it will) I will yet thank you that counsel me to a silence in these oppressures, when confidence in my right, and friends may abandon me. And lest yourself may undergo some hazard, for my questioned reputation, and draw jealousies or hatred upon you, I desire to be left to mine own innocence, which shall acquit me, or heaven shall be guilty.

Your ever true lover,
BEN JONSON.

[2] This was a considerable present: but Jonson's hand and heart were ever open to his acquaintance. All his pleasures were social; and while health and fortune smiled upon him, he was no niggard either of his time or his talents to those who needed them. There is something striking in Taylor's concluding sentence, when the result of the visit to Drummond is considered:—but there is one *evil that walks*, which keener eyes than John's have often failed to discover.

Taylor's "Pennyless Pilgrimage" to Scotland gave rise to some ridiculous reports, and it is curious to see with what a serious air he sets about refuting them. "Many shallow-brained critics (he says) do lay an aspersion on me—that I was set on by others, or did undergo this project, either in malice or mockage of Master Benjamin Jonson. I vow, by the faith of a Christian, that their imaginations are all wide; for He is a gentleman to whom I am so much obliged for many undeserved courtesies that I have received from him, and from others, *by his favour*, that I durst never be so impudent or ingrateful as to suffer any man's persuasions or mine own instigation, to incite me to make so bad a requital for so much goodness."

I have only to add, in justice to this honest man, that his gratitude outlived the subject of it. He paid the tribute of a verse to his benefactor's memory;—the verse, indeed, was mean; but poor Taylor had nothing better to give.

ber his kind commendations to all his friends. So with a friendly farewell, I left him as well as I hope never to see him in a worse estate ; for he is among noblemen and gentlemen that know his true worth and their own honours, where with much respective (respectful) love he is entertained." This was about the 20th of September. Jonson probably paid many other visits ; but he reserved the last of them for Mr. William Drummond, the poet of Hawthornden, with whom he passed the greater part of the month of April, 1619.[1]

It is not known at what period or in what manner Jonson's acquaintance with Drummond began ; but the ardour with which he cherished his friendship is almost un-exampled : he seems upon every occasion to labour for language to express his grateful sense of it ; and very depraved must have been the mind that could witness such effusions of tenderness with a determination to watch the softest moment, and betray the confidence of his guest. For this perfidious purpose no one ever afforded greater facilities than Jonson. He *wore his heart upon his sleeve for daws to peck at :* a bird of prey, therefore, like Drummond, had a noble quarry before him ; and he could strike at it without stooping.

It is much to be lamented that our author did not fall into kindly hands. His learn-ing, his judgment, his love of anecdote, his extensive acquaintance with the poets, statesmen, and eminent characters of the age, of whom he talked without reserve, would have rendered his conversations, had they been recorded with such a decent respect for the characters of the living as courtesy demanded, the most valuable body of contem-porary criticism that had ever appeared. Such was not Drummond's object. He only sought to injure the man whom he had decoyed under his roof ; and he therefore gave his remarks in rude and naked deformity. Even thus, however, without one qualifying word, without one introductory or explanatory line, there is little in them that can be dis-puted ; while the vigour, perspicuity, and integrity of judgment which they uniformly display are certainly worthy of commendation. As these "Conversations" form the text from which our author's enemies draw their topics of abuse, as they have hitherto been unfairly quoted,[2] I subjoin a faithful copy of the criticisms, from the old folio. What relates to our author's personal history, has been already given.

"HEADS OF A CONVERSATION, &C.

"Ben Jonson used to say, that many Epigrams were ill, because they expressed in the end what should have been understood by what was said before, as that of Sir John Davies. That he had a pastoral entitled the *May Lord ;* his own name is Alkin, Ethra the Countess of Bedford, Mogbel Overbury, the old Countess of Suffolk an enchan-tress ; other names are given to Somerset, his lady, Pembroke, the Countess of Rutland, Lady Wroth. In his first scene Alkin comes in mending his broken pipe. [*He bringeth in,* says our author (Drummond) *clowns making mirth and foolish sports, contrary to all other pastorals.*] He had also a design to write a Fisher or Pastoral (Piscatory?) play, and make the stage of it in the Lomond lake ; and also to write his foot-pil-grimage hither, and to call it a Discovery. In a poem he called Edinburgh

"The Heart of Scotland, Britain's other Eye."

That he had an intention to have made a play like Plautus's *Amphytruo,* but left it off, for that he could never find two so like one to the other, that he could persuade the spectator that they were one.

"That he had a design to write an epic poem, and was to call it *Chorologia,* of the Worthies of his country, raised by Fame, and was to dedicate it to his country : it is all in couplets, for he detested all other rhymes. He said, he had written a *Discourse of Poetry,* both against Campion and Daniel, especially the last, where he proves couplets to be the best sort of verses, especially when they are broke like hexameters, and that

---

[1] [The only way to combat Gifford's perpetual misrepresentation of the character of Drummond is to reprint in full the 'Notes of Conversations' in the most accurate version remaining. These will be found at the end of vol. iii. Jonson's visit to him certainly took place before the 17th January, 1619, but its exact date does not appear.—F. C.]

[2] They have, without any exception, been taken from Cibber's Lives of the Poets.

cross rhymes and stanzas, because the purpose would lead beyond eight lines, were all forced.

"His censure (judgment) of the English poets was this : that Sidney did not keep a decorum in making every one speak as well as himself. Spenser's stanza pleased him not, nor his matter ; the meaning of the Allegory of his *Faëry Queen* he had delivered in writing to Sir Walter Raleigh, which was, that by the bleating (blatant) beast he understood the Puritans, and by the false Duessa, the Queen of Scots. He told, that Spenser's goods were robbed by the Irish, and his house and a little child burnt, he and his wife escaped, and after died for want of bread in King-street ; he refused twenty pieces sent him by my Lord Essex, and said he was sure he had no time to spend them. Samuel Daniel was a good, honest man, had no children, and was no poet ;[1] and that he had wrote the *Civil Wars*, and yet had not one battle in all his book. That Michael Drayton's *Polyolbion*, if he had performed what he promised, to write the deeds of all the Worthies, had been excellent. That he was challenged for intituling one book *Mortimeriades;* that Sir John Davies played on Drayton in an epigram, who, in his sonnet, concluded his mistress might have been the ninth Worthy, and said he used a phrase like Dametas in *Arcadia*, who said his mistress for wit might be a giant.

"That Silvester's translation of Du Bartas was not well done ; and that he wrote his verses before he understood to confer ; and these of Fairfax were not good. That the translations of Homer and Virgil in long Alexandrines were but prose.[2] That Sir John Harington's *Ariosto*, under all translations, was the worst : that when Sir John desired him to tell the truth of his Epigrams, he answered him that he loved not the truth, for they were narrations, not epigrams. He said Donne was originally a poet, his grandfather on the mother side was Heywood the epigrammatist ; that Donne for want of being understood would perish. He esteemed him the first poet in the world for some things ; his verses of the *Lost Orchadine* he had by heart, and that passage of the Calm, 'that dust and feathers did not stir, all was so quiet.' He affirmed that Donne wrote all his best pieces before he was twenty-five years of age : the conceit of Donne's *Transformation*, or Μετεμψυχωσις, was that he sought the soul of that apple which Eve pulled, and thereafter made it the soul of a bitch, then of a she-wolf, and so of a woman : his general purpose was to have brought it into all the bodies of the heretics from the soul of Cain, and at last left it in the body of Calvin. He only wrote one sheet of this, and since he was made a Doctor, repented hugely, and resolved to destroy all his poems. He told Donne that his *Anniversary* was profane and full of blasphemies ; that if it had been written on the Virgin Mary it had been tolerable : to which Donne answered, that he described the idea of a woman, and not as she was. He said Shakspeare wanted art, and sometimes sense, for in one of his plays he brought in a number of men, saying they had suffered shipwreck in Bohemia, where is no sea near by a hundred miles.[3] That Sir Walter Raleigh esteemed more fame than conscience. The best wits in England were employed in making his History ; Ben himself had written a piece to him of the Punick War, which he altered and set in his book.

"He said there was no such ground for an Heroic Poem as King Arthur's fiction, and that Sir P. Sidney had an intention to have transformed all his *Arcadia* to the stories of King Arthur. He said Owen was a poor pedantic schoolmaster, sweeping his living from the posteriors of little children, and had nothing good in him, his epigrams being bare narrations. Francis Beaumont died before he was thirty years of age, who, he

---

[1] Jonson explains himself in what he says below of Du Bartas—"He was no poet, but a verser, *because he wrote not fiction.*" The allusion is to Daniel's narrative poem of the *Civil Wars*. He elsewhere expressly styles Daniel a *verser* in this sense.

[2] So Daniel in his answer to Campion :—"I find my Homer-Lucan, as if he gloried to seem to have no bounds, passing over the rhyme, albeit he were confined within his measure, to be therein, in my conceit, most happy ; for so thereby they who care not for verse or rhyme may pass it over without taking notice thereof, and please themselves with a well-measured *prose.*" This is pretty nearly what Jonson means ; and, indeed, had his remarks been given to us by any but an enemy, we should, I am convinced, have found little to qualify or correct in them.

[3] This is the tritest of all our author's observations. No one ever read the play without noticing the "absurdity," as Dr. Johnson calls it : yet for this simple *truism*, for this casual remark in the freedom of conversation, Jonson is held up to the indignation of the world, as if the blunder was invisible to all but himself, or as if he had uttered the most deliberate and spiteful calumny !

said, was a good poet, as were Fletcher and Chapman, whom he loved. That Sir William Alexander was not half kind to him, and neglected him, because a friend to Drayton: that Sir R. Ayton loved him dearly.[1] He fought several times with Marston; and says that Marston wrote his father-in-law's preachings, and his father-in-law his comedies."[2]

Such are the remarks of Jonson on his contemporaries: set down in malice, abridged without judgment, and published without shame, what is there yet in them to justify the obloquy with which they are constantly assailed, or to support the malicious conclusions drawn from them by Drummond? Or who, that leaned with such confidence on the bosom of a beloved friend, who treacherously encouraged the credulous affection, would have passed the ordeal with more honour than Jonson?—But to proceed.

"His judgment of stranger poets was, that he thought not Bartas a poet, but a verser, because he wrote not fiction. He cursed Petrarch for redacting verses into sonnets, which he said was like that tyrant's bed, where some who were too short were racked, others too long cut short. That Guarini in his *Pastor Fido* kept no decorum in making shepherds speak as well as himself. That he told Cardinal du Perron (when he was in France, 1613), who showed him his translation of Virgil, that it was naught: that the best pieces of Ronsard were his *Odes.* [*But all this was to no purpose* (says our author), *for he never understood the French or Italian languages.*[3]] He said Petronius, Plinius Secundus, and Plautus spoke best Latin; and that Tacitus wrote the secrets of the council and senate as Suetonius did those of the cabinet and court; that Lucan, taken in parts, was excellent, but altogether, naught: that Quintilian's 6, 7, and 8 books were not only to be read, but altogether digested: that Juvenal, Horace, and Martial were to be read for delight, and so was Pindar; but Hippocrates for health.

Of the English nation he said that Hooker's *Ecclesiastical Polity* was best for church-matters, and Selden's *Titles of Honour* for antiquities. Here our author relates that the "censure (judgment) of his verses was, that they were all good, especially his Epitaph on Prince Henry,[4] save that they smelled too much of the schools, and were not after the fancy of the times: for a child, says he, may write after the fashion of the Greek and Latin verse in running; yet that he wished, for pleasing the king, that piece of *Forth Feasting* had been his own."

"As Ben Jonson (say the collectors of Drummond's works) has been very liberal of his censures (opinions) on all his contemporaries, so our author *does not spare him.*"—

---

[1] "He was (Aubrey says), according to Mr. J. Dryden, who had seen his verses in MS., one of the best poets of his time. He was acquainted with all the witts (learned men) of his time in England. Mr. Thomas Hobbes of Malmsbury told me he made use of him, together with Ben Jonson, for an Aristarchus, when he drew up the Epistle Dedicatory for his translation of Thucydides."—*Letters,* &c. vol. ii. p. 200.

[2] The petty contentions in which Jonson was involved by the captiousness of Marston have been already noticed. What follows seems a humorous allusion to the sombre air of Marston's comedies, as contrasted with the cheerful tone of his father-in-law's discourses. But who was this father-in-law? Nay, who was Marston? None of his biographers know anything of either; and yet it appears to me that something on the subject of both has been, unconsciously, delivered by Wood. William Wilkes, he tells us, was chaplain to King James, before whom he often preached to his great content. This person "died at Barford S. Martin in Wiltshire, of which he was rector, leaving a daughter named Mary, who was married to John Marston, of the city of Coventry, gentleman. Which John dying 25 June 1634, was buried in the church belonging to the Temple in London, near to the body of John Marston his father, sometimes a counsellor of the Middle Temple." I flatter myself that I have here recovered both father and son, since all that is known of the latter corresponds with these particulars.

[3] It is observable that every addition by Drummond is tinctured with spleen. What a tissue of malevolence must the original record of these conversations have been! When Jonson says that he wrote his praise of Sylvester before he was able to compare the translation with the original, and, fifteen years afterwards, declares that he was wrong, I should conceive, without more authority, that he had made himself master of French in the interval. There can indeed be no doubt of it (Drummond's assertion goes for nothing), for he hardly conversed with Cardinal du Perron on the merits of French poetry without understanding the language. In fact, so common an acquirement was not a matter of boast, especially in one so much about the court as Jonson, and in the habit of hearing it spoken by almost every one around him.

[4] *Tears on the Death of Meliades.—Drum. Poems,* folio, p. 15.

But Jonson's censures are merely critical, or, if the reader pleases, hypercritical; and with the exception of Raleigh, who is simply charged with taking credit to himself for the labours of others, he belies no man's reputation, blasts no man's moral character; the apology for the slander of his host, therefore,

> " Who should against his murderer shut the door,
> Not bear the knife himself,"—

is weaker than water.

"—For he says, Ben Johnson was a great lover and praiser of himself, a contemner and scorner of others, given rather to lose a friend than a jest, jealous of every word and action of those about him, especially after drink, which is one of the elements in which he lived; a dissembler of the parts which reign in him; a bragger of some good that he wanted; thinketh nothing well done but what either he himself or some of his friends have said or done. He is passionately kind and angry, careless either to gain or keep; vindictive, but if he be well answered at himself; interprets best sayings and deeds often to the worst. He was for any religion, as being versed in both;[1] oppressed with fancy which hath overmastered his reason, a *general* disease in *many* poets: his inventions are smooth and easy, but above all he excelleth in a translation.[2] When the play of the *Silent Woman* was first acted, there were found verses after on the stage against him, concluding that that play was well named the *Silent Woman*, because there was never one *man* to say Plaudite to him."—*Drum. Works*, folio, 1711, pp. 224-6.

The writers of Jonson's life in the *Bio. Brit.*, after selecting the most envenomed passages of the *Conversations* (always, however, with due admiration of the exemplary friendship of Drummond), proceed thus: " In short (adds Drummond, folio, 1711, p. 222), Jonson was," &c. Overcome by the tender enthusiasm of this exquisite burst of friendship, the biographers indulge in a beatific vision of our author's happiness. " He passed," they say, " some months[3] with this favourite brother-poet, this *ingenuous friend*, to whom he opened his heart with a most unreserved freedom and confidence,

---

[1] To attempt a refutation of the absurd abuse poured on Jonson by this cankered hypocrite would be useless, as the history of the poet's whole life is a refutation of it; but it may not be amiss to call the attention of the reader to this passage, of which the logic is only to be equalled by the candour—" He was well versed in theology, *therefore* he was without religion !" What religion Drummond was "versed" in I know not; certainly not in that which says, "Thou shalt not bear false witness against thy neighbour."

[2] In this place Shiels interpolated the scurrilous passage already given (p. xx). I am not sure that Drummond himself is not indebted for some of his popularity to this forged panegyric on Shakspeare at the cost of Jonson, which is quoted with such delight by all that poet's biographers.

It may not be amiss, however, to observe that Drummond appears to have known or thought as little of Shakspeare as of any writer of the time. He never mentions him but once. To afford an opportunity of contrasting the "censures" of Ben with those of a master hand, his editors kindly subjoin to the passage quoted above, "Mr. Drummond's character of several authors."

"The authors I have seen," saith he, " on the subject of love are—Sidney, Daniel, Drayton, Spenser; the last we have are Sir W. Alexander and Shakspeare, who have lately published their works."—folio, p. 226. Not a word more of the latter, though he recurs to Alexander (whom he places next to Petrarch), to Daniel, Drayton, Donne, Sylvester, and others. Such is his "character" of Shakspeare ! In his letters several poets are mentioned, and notices of plays occasionally occur; but of Shakspeare's not a syllable. I much question whether Drummond ever read a play of our great poet. That he had no esteem for his writings is tolerably clear; as it is that he preferred the dull and lifeless Alexander to him.

About the year 1627 Drummond gave "a noble present of books and manuscripts to the college of Edinburgh."—So say the editors of his works (folio 1711), or I should have termed it, generally speaking, a collection of rubbish not worth the hire of the cart that took it away. Of this rare present a catalogue was published, in which the books are carefully arranged under the names of their respective authors. Under that of "William Shakspeare" there appears—what, does the reader think ?—*Love's Labour's Lost*.

[3] *He passed some months.*] This is for ever repeated; although the persons who had the care of Drummond's papers and who drew up the account of his life, expressly say that Jonson stayed with him about *three weeks* ! He arrived (p. 34) at Hawthornden in the beginning of April, 1619, and left it, on his return to London, about the end of the same month.

the *sweetest gift* of friendship!" It would appear that in the case of Jonson words and actions lost their usual import, and that the blackest perfidy, when directed against him, suddenly changed into kindness and liberality.

The words put into Drummond's mouth do not indeed belong to him. Of this, however, the critics, who trusted merely to Shiels, and quote a work which they never saw, were ignorant. No matter: there is still enough to justify the rhapsody on the "sweets of friendship!" It must not be concealed, however, that there have been persons free enough to question the purity of Drummond's conduct, and that even the wretched scribbler who interpolated the passage cannot avoid saying, "We have inserted Ben's conversations; though, perhaps, it was not altogether fair of Mr. Drummond to commit to writing things that passed over a bottle, and which perhaps were heedlessly advanced. As few people are so wise as not to speak imprudently sometimes, it is not the part of a man who invites another to his table to expose what may drop inadvertently."—*Cib. Lives*, vol. i. p. 310. This gentle reproof from Lauder the second is extremely pleasant!—perhaps it was a *compunctious visiting*. Mr. A. Chalmers, too, has an awkward observation: Drummond's return (he says) to the unreserved conduct of Jonson "has been thought *not very liberal*."[1] Is it possible! Fie, fie!—"Not *very* liberal!" To do Mr. Chalmers justice, he has no doubts of this kind himself; in tenderness, however, to those who have, he suggests "that this *suspicion* of illiberality is considerably lessened when we reflect that Drummond appears not to have intended to publish his remarks,"&c.[2] Mr. Chalmers never heard, perhaps, of a legacy of half-a-crown left to a hungry Scotsman to fire off a pistol which the ruffian who loaded and levelled it had not the courage to discharge. At any rate, he seems to think that there is nothing unusual or improper in framing a libellous attack on the character and reputation of a friend, keeping it carefully in store for thirty years, and finally bequeathing it, fairly engrossed, to the caprice or cupidity of an executor!

The parting scene at Hawthornden was undoubtedly tender; for Drummond, who had hitherto concealed his malice, was too practised an *artificer of fraud* to pull off the mask at such a moment. Ben, therefore, who saw no more than his enemies were pleased to expose to his view, went on his way with a heart overflowing with respect and gratitude, while his host, with a hand yet warm from the pressure of affection, retired to his closet, and having thanked God that he was not a "drunkard," a "dissembler," a "braggard," *as other men* were, or even one "that interpreted best deeds and sayings to the worst," *like this Jonson*, sat complacently down to destroy his character (as he fondly hoped) for ever.

Jonson reached London in the beginning of May, and soon after despatched the following letter :—

"*To my worthy, honoured, and beloved friend, Mr. W. Drummond.*

"Most loving" (poor Jonson!) "and beloved sir, against which titles I should most knowingly offend, if I made you not at length some account of myself, to come even with your friendship. I am arrived safely, with a most catholic welcome, and my reports not unacceptable to his Majesty. He professed (I thank God) some joy to see me, and is pleased to hear of the purpose of my book:[3] to which I most earnestly solicit you for your promise of the inscriptions at Pinky, some things concerning the

---

[1] Full justice will not be done to the niceness of Mr. Chalmers's feelings on this point unless we call to mind that he expressly includes the ribaldry of Shiels in Drummond's sketch of Jonson's character.

[2] I will help Mr. Chalmers to Chetwood's opinion on the subject: "This false friend (Drummond) durst not have declared his vile sentiments had our author been alive to answer him; I look, therefore, upon all that he has brought against him as the malice and envy of a bad heart."—*Life of Jonson*, p. 55.

[3] The *Discovery* (p. 35), which was to contain the Description of Scotland, with the Episode of his "Journey thither," &c. This passage is worthy of notice, as it incidentally shows the estimation in which Jonson was held by James. Those who so readily condemn him to poverty and obscurity are little aware, perhaps, that for the space of twenty years he was associated with all that was noble, or great, or virtuous, or wise. The implicit believers in the commentators on our great poet are in too forlorn a state of imbecility to encourage any hopes of returning reason; but there are others who may one day be expected to discover that there are better authorities for a Life of Jonson than Captain Tucca, Will Kempe, and Shiels, the Scotsman.

Loch of Lomond, touching the government of Edinburgh, to urge Mr. James Scot, and what else you can procure for me with all speed, [especially I make it my request that you will enquire for me whether the Students method at St. Andrews be the same with that at Edinburgh, and so to assure me, or wherein they differ.] Though these requests be full of trouble, I hope they shall neither burthen nor weary such a friendship, whose commands to me, I will ever interpret a pleasure. News we have none here, but what is making against the Queen's funeral,[1] whereof I have somewhat in hand which shall look upon you with the next. Salute the beloved Fentons, the Nisbets, the Scots, the Levingstons, and all the honest and honoured names with you, especially Mr. James Writh, his wife, your sister, &c. And if you forget yourself, you believe not in

"Your most true friend and lover,

"*London, May* 10*th*, 1619."   "BEN JONSON.

The answer to this does not appear; but a second letter which Drummond sent in consequence of another application from our author, begins thus:

"WORTHY FRIEND,

"The uncertainty of your abode was a cause of my silence this time past—I have adventured this packet upon hopes that a man so famous cannot be in any place either of the City or Court,[2] where he shall not be found out. In my last (the missing letter) I sent you a description of Loch Lomond, with a map of Inch-merionach, which may, by your book, be made most famous," &c.

"*July* 1, 1619."

We hear nothing further of Drummond till the end of this year, when he addressed another letter[3] "to his worthy friend, Master Ben Jonson."

"SIR,—Here you have that Epigram which you desired (vol. iii. *Underwoods*, No. vi.) with another of the like argument. If there be any other thing in this country (unto which my power can reach,) command it; there *is nothing I wish more than to be in the calendar of them who love you.*[4] I have heard from Court that the late Masque[5] was not so approved of the King, as in former times, and that your absence was regretted. Such applause *hath true worth* even of those who otherwise are not for it. Thus, to the next occasion, taking my leave, I remain

"Your *loving friend,*

"*Jan.* 17, 1619."   "W. D.

Enough of Drummond, with whose "friendship" for our author, the common sense of the reader will, I trust, be no longer insulted, except from the lips of hopeless idiotism —*longa manantia labra saliva.*

"Crowned with the favour of his sovereign, Jonson saw (say the writers of the *Bio. Brit.*) the most distinguished wits of his time crowding his train, and courting his acquaintance; and in this spirit he was invited to Christ Church by Dr. Corbet, then

---

[1] Ann died in March. The poem which Jonson wrote on the occasion is lost.

[2] Jonson had left London towards the end of May, and was at this time residing at Christ Church, Oxford, with his true friend, Corbet (afterwards bishop of Norwich), and others of that College.

[3] [Gifford either did not know that the date of this letter was January 17, 1619: or that *in Scotland,* January 1619 was not January 1620. The letter in fact was written *in Edinburgh,* and at the very commencement of their acquaintance.—F. C.]

[4] Hypocrite to the last! What, the "liar,"

the "drunkard," the "atheist"! This is almost too much. A voluntary plunge in infamy was by no means necessary here; it was not your credulous correspondent (whoever else it might be) that "interpreted best sayings and deeds to the worst."

[5] I know not who was called in to supply the place of Jonson during his northern tour. The king was grown somewhat fastidious, perhaps, after those exquisite Entertainments, the *Vision of Delight,* and *Pleasure reconciled to Virtue;* and talents of no ordinary kind might have fallen short of their excellencies, without much injury to the possessor's reputation.

senior student of that college."[1] Here, Wood tells us, he continued some time writing and composing of plays, and was created Master of Arts (July 19) 1619. The historian is wrong in the first part of his assertion. Jonson certainly "composed" no plays at Oxford or elsewhere: this was a labour from which he always delighted to escape, and he was now in such a comparative state of affluence as to justify his indulging in pursuits more congenial to his feelings.[2] Several of his most beautiful Masques were,

---

[1] "Thus," exclaims Mr. Headley, "Jonson was rescued from the arms of a sister University who had long treated the Muses with indignity. We do not find that Ben expressed any regret at the *change of situation:* companions whose minds and pursuits were similar to his own were not always to be found in the gross atmosphere of the muddy Cam, though easily met with on the more genial banks of the Isis." *Beauties of English Poetry,* p. xxxviii. Mr. Headley was an ingenious young man ; but like other ingenious young men, talked sometimes of what he did not understand. He is so ignorant of Jonson's history as to suppose that he was then resident at Cambridge—this, however, may be easily overlooked ; but his attempt to implicate the poet in his personal quarrels, in his splenetic and vulgar abuse of Cambridge, merits castigation. Jonson neither felt nor expressed any disrespect to Cambridge.—In the Dedication of the *Fox* to both Universities, he calls them "most noble and most equal sisters ;" and mentions, in terms of respectful gratitude, his obligations to their "favour and affection." From this language he never varied ; and, unfortunately for Mr. Headley, Cambridge, which had also conferred on him a Master of Arts degree, was fondly remembered by him to the last.*

This critic, as might reasonably be expected, entertains a supreme contempt for Jonson's writings, of which he manifests a surprising knowledge ! "While Drayton," he says, "was adopting a style that the present age may peruse, &c. Jonson" (who is always the victim) "unable to digest the mass of his reading, peopled his pages with the heathen mythology." p. lii. Mr. Headley had evidently heard "of Jonson's learning ;" the rest followed of course. But how stands the fact? That of all the writers for the stage, from old Heywood to Sir Aston Cockayne inclusive, there is not one whose pages are so free from fable as Jonson's. I will venture to affirm that more of the *heathen mythology* may be found in a single scene, nay, in a single speech, of Shakspeare, Fletcher, Massinger, and Shirley, than in the whole of Jonson's thirteen comedies. Nothing is so remarkable as his rigid exclusion of the deities of Greece and Rome. Neither as embellishments nor illustrations do they appear in his pages, yet Mr. Headley (and he is not singular, or I should have left him to his folly) assumes, as the distinguishing characteristic of the author, that *they are peopled with them !*

But Mr. Headley's candour is as conspicuous as his knowledge. "A strong and original vein of humour," he says, "is Ben's *peculiar forte ;* take away that, and he is undeserving of the fame he has attained"! *Ibid.* It was well observed by the French tailor, upon the magnificent view from Richmond Hill—"All this is very fine, to be sure ;—but take away the river and the trees, and it will be nothing"!

[2] "Both inclination and ambition (say the writers of the *Bio. Brit.*) concurred in prompting Jonson to turn from Masques and Entertainments to the graver and weightier works of the drama." This, (which is re-echoed by all his biographers,) like everything else respecting him, is said at random. "Ambition" was on the side of the Masques—and with regard to his "inclination for the drama," he expressly declares that he had it not. These gentlemen, however, are so pleased with their observation, that they repeat it on the production of the *New Inn ;* to the writing of which he was driven by absolute want. So much is said of our author, and so little known !

I have, on several occasions, noted the little pleasure which Jonson apparently took in writing for the stage ; but I hardly expected so decisive a proof of it as has reached me since this note was put to the press. The ever active kindness of Mr. D'Israeli has just furnished me with the following letter. It was found among the Hatfield state papers by Dr. Birch, who was preparing a selection of them for the press, when he was interrupted by his last illness.

The letter is inscribed—"Ben Jonson to the Earl of Salisbury, praying his lordship's protection against some evil reports." It shows (what indeed every circumstance of his life proves) that he was high-spirited, dauntless ; confident in his worth, more confident in his innocence ; complaining when wronged, with dignity, and soliciting when afflicted, with decorum.

The theatrical records of these times are so imperfect, that the circumstance and the play to which our author alludes, are equally obscure. It would seem that not long after his release, (in

---

* When Dr. Birch was writing the life of Jonson for the *Gen. Dict.* folio, 1738, he applied to a member of St. John's College for information respecting the residence of the poet, &c. This person procured several memoranda for his use, from the learned T. Baker, one of the fellows. The last of them runs thus : "Mr. Baker adds that there has always been a tradition handed down, that he was of our college—The Registrar tells me that there are several books in our Library with Ben Jonson's name, given by him to the college ; particularly an ancient edition of Aristotle's Works."

It is observable that this life of Jonson is entirely free from the deplorable raving about the poet's *envy,* &c. which disgraces all the subsequent accounts. Birch could not forge, and he would not calumniate.

however, composed about this period, both for the nobility and the Court, as well as some of those pieces which are mentioned in the *Execration on Vulcan*, and which were destroyed together with his study. There perished his *Commentary on the Poetics*, his *Grammar* complete, of which we have now but the fragments, his *Journey into Scotland*, his *May Lord*, and several other dramas. There too were lost the unfinished *Life of Henry V.*,[1] the *Rape of Proserpine*, the poem in celebration of the Ladies of Great Britain, to which he more than once alludes, and what perhaps, we ought to regret more than all, a vast body of philological collections, with notes from the classics, the fruit of twenty years' laborious study.

It is probable that Jonson spent much of his time at the country seats of the nobility and gentry, as he has allusions to several visits of this kind; and we know that he attended on the Court in some of the royal progresses.[2] He was at Burleigh on the

the beginning of 1605,) he was accused of reflecting on some one in a play written by Chapman and himself, and again imprisoned with his friend. It would be vain to indulge in farther conjecture. There are many points of similarity between the letter and the dedication of the *Fox*, which may be consulted with advantage. The letter itself is truly admirable, and well deserved the success which, we know, from collateral circumstances, it instantly found. I rejoice in its preservation, and transcribe it with pleasure.

"MOST TRULY HONOURABLE, 1605.

"It hath still been the tyranny of my fortune so to oppress my endeavours that before I can shew myself grateful in the least for former benefits, I am enforced to provoke your bounties for more. May it not seem grievous to your lordship, that now my innocence calls upon you (next the Deity) to her defence. God himself is not averted at just men's cries; and you that approach that divine goodness and supply it here on earth in your places and honours, cannot employ your aid more worthily than to the common succour of honesty and virtue, how humbly soever it be placed.

"I am here, my most honoured lord, unexamined and unheard, committed to a vile prison, and with me a gentleman, (whose name may, perhaps, have come to your lordship) one Mr. George Chapman, a learned and honest man. The cause (would I could name some worthier, though I wish we had known none worthy our imprisonment,) is (the words irk me that our fortune hath necessitated us to so despised a course,) a play, my lord; whereof we hope there is no man can justly complain that hath the virtue to think but favourably of himself, if our judge bring an equal ear; marry, if with prejudice we be made guilty afore our time, we must embrace the asinine virtue, patience. My noble lord, they deal not charitably who are witty in another man's works, and utter sometimes their own malicious meanings under our words. I protest to your honour, and call God to testimony, (since my first error,* which, yet, is punished in me more with my shame than it was then with my bondage,) I have so attempered my style, that I have given no cause to any good man of grief; and if to any ill, by touching at any gene-

ral vice, it hath always been with a regard and sparing of particular persons. I may be otherwise reported; but if all that be accused should be presently guilty, there are few men would stand in the state of innocence.

"I beseech your most honourable lordship, suffer not other men's errors or faults past to be made my crimes; but let me be examined both by all my works past and this present; and not trust to rumour but my books (for she is an unjust deliverer both of great and of small actions) whether I have ever (many things I have written private or public) given offence to a nation, to a public order or state, or any person of honour or authority; but have equally laboured to keep their dignity as mine own person, safe. If others have transgressed, let me not be entitled to their follies. But lest in being too diligent for my excuse, I may incur the suspicion of being guilty, I become a most humble suitor to your lordship that with the honourable Lord Chamberlain,* (to whom I have in like manner petitioned) you will be pleased to be the grateful means of our coming to answer; or if in your wisdoms it shall be thought necessary, that your lordship will be the most honoured cause of our liberty, where freeing us from one prison you will remove us to another; which is eternally to bind us and our muses to the thankful honouring of you and yours to posterity, as your own virtues have by many descents of ancestors ennobled you to time.

Your honour's
Most devoted in heart as words,
BEN JONSON.

"To the most nobly virtuous and thrice honoured Earl of Salisbury. 1605."

[1] *Henry V.*] In this history, Jonson tells us in one of his most popular poems, he was assisted by Cotton, Carew, and Selden: yet Mr. A. Chalmers gives this rare intelligence solely on the authority of Oldys! "See," he says, "Oldys's manuscript notes to Langbaine in *Brit. Mus.*"

[2] On one of these occasions he had an opportunity of serving Selden, who had grievously offended James by the indirect tendency of his arguments on the divine right of tythes. "The storm was blown over," his biographer says, "by

---

* In *Eastward Hoe!* See p. xxix.

* Thomas Earl of Suffolk. Jonson was not unmindful of his kindness. See vol. iii. *Epigrams*, No. lxvii. d

Hill, and at Belvoir Castle, and at Windsor when his Masque of the *Gipsies Metamor-phosed* was performed at these places, respectively, and introduced several little com-pliments into the piece, as new candidates arrived, and claimed admission into the list of the *Dramatis Personæ*. He must also have been at Newmarket with the Court, where his Masques were occasionally represented.

While he was on these progresses, he obtained from his Majesty, who seems to have been unusually pleased with the *Masque of Gipsies*, in which he bore a part, a rever-sionary grant of the office of Master of the Revels. The king, by letters patent dated Oct. 5, 1621, granted him, by the style and addition of "our beloved servant Benjamin Jonson, gentleman, the said office to be held and enjoyed by him and his assigns, during his life, from and after the death of Sir George Buc, and Sir John Astley, or as soon as the office should become vacant by resignation, forfeiture, or surrender."[1] In contem-plation, perhaps, of his speedy accession to this office, James was desirous of conferring upon him the honour of knighthood. Jonson, for whom wealth and title had no charms, and who was well aware that a distinction of this nature would exasperate the envy which pursued him from his earliest years, shrunk from the meditated kindness of his sovereign, and prevailed on some of his friends about the court to dissuade his royal master from his purpose.[2]

Jonson received no advantage from the grant specified above, as Sir J. Astley sur-vived him: it appears, however, that, finding himself incapable, during his last illness, of performing the duties of the office, supposing it to devolve upon him, he had been graciously permitted by Charles to transfer the patent to his son, who died in 1635. Why Mr. Malone should suppose (*Shak.* vol. ii. p. 311) that he was not on good terms with his father, I cannot tell. Fuller only says that Jonson "was not very happy in his children:" but an indulgent and tender parent like Jonson may be sensibly afflicted by the conduct of a child, without much diminution of affection, or interruption of kindness.

From 1621, when the *Gipsies Metamorphosed* was performed at Windsor, Jonson continued, apparently, to pass his time greatly to his satisfaction. Every Twelfth-night produced a Masque; and visits to his friends, correspondence with the literati of this and other countries, and occasional pieces of poetry, filled up the rest of his time.[3] Mr. Malone, who, from his crazy tripod, pronounces that Jonson had "stalked, for two centuries, on the stilts of artificial reputation," was little aware, perhaps, of the extent of his acquaintance with the learned, and of the estimation in which they held his talents; at any rate, the following passage from the Geneva edit. of Farnaby's Martial (and I could produce many such) must have escaped his knowledge :

"*Martialem solum à clariss. viro Petro Scriverio emendatum editumque de-*

the interest of his friend Ben Jonson with the king." Fresh offence, however, was taken soon afterwards, and Selden was summoned to Theo-balds, where his Majesty then was, on his return from Newmarket. "Not being as yet acquainted with the court or with the king, he got Master Ben Jonson, who was then at Theobalds, to in-troduce him."—*Life of Selden.* The steadiness of our author's friendship calls for no remark: it was a part of his character; but it should not be omitted that Selden, who is expressly declared by his biographers, "to be, in 1618, *yet* unac-quainted with the court," is said by all the writers of Jonson's life, to have procured the poet's release from imprisonment by his interest there, in 1605!

[1] *Shak.* vol. i. p. 626. Mr. Malone observes that "it would appear from a passage in the *Satiromastix* that Ben had made some attempts to procure the reversion of this place before the death of Elizabeth." Mr. Malone is unques-tionably right; though he has failed to draw from it the only proper conclusion—namely, that at this period, Jonson was neither so ob-scure nor so unfriended as he would have us believe.

[2] "A friend told me this Faire time (Stour-bridge) that Ben Jonson was not knighted, but scaped it narrowly, for that his majestie would have done it, had there not been means made (himself not unwilling) to avoyd it. Sep. 15, 1621." Extracted from a letter of the celebrated Joseph Mead of C. Col. Cambridge to Sir Martin Stuteville. *Baker's MSS.* vol. xxxii. p. 355. Sir M. Stuteville was a friend and admirer of Jonson. One of his family has some verses on the poet's death, preserved among the Ashmole papers. They are kind and laudatory; but merit no particular notice.

[3] He is said to have assisted Middleton and Fletcher in writing *The Widow*, which must have appeared about this time. This comedy was very popular, and, not undeservedly, for it has a considerable degree of merit. I cannot, however, discover many traces of Jonson in it. The authors' names rest, I believe, on the au-thority of the editor, A Gough, who sent the play to the press in 1652.

*siderabam, quem nulla mea aut amicorum cura parare potuit; cujus tamen vicem non
ı arò supplevit amica opera* BEN JONSONII *viri (quod quæ ille per ludum scripserit,
serio legentibus liquido apparebit) in poetis omnibus versatissimi, historiarum, morum,
rituum, antiquitatum indagatoris exquisitissimi, et (quod semper in illo adverti) non
contenti brachio levi tesqua et dignos vindice nodos transmittere, sed penitissimos usque
sensus ratione, lectione, ingenio eruere desudantis; digni denique (utcunque à probatis
merito probetur suo) meliori theatro quam* quo malevolorum invidiam pascat,[1] *quanquam et hoc regium est posse invidium cùm mereri tum pati. Ille, inquam, mihi
emendationes aliquot suppeditavit ex C. V. Scriverii Martiale, cujus copia illi facta
Lugduni Bat. a viro non sine doctrinæ et humanitatis honorifica præfatione nomi-
nando Dan. Heinsio," &c.*[2]

It has not been hitherto observed that Jonson was in possession of a most excellent
library, which, assisted by a readiness of memory altogether surprising, facilitated the
acquirement of that information for which he was so frequently solicited by his own
countrymen, as well as strangers. He began to collect the best editions of the classics
at an early period, and it may be doubted whether any private library in the kingdom
was at that time so rich in scarce and valuable books as his own. He was ever ready
to communicate them to his friends : not only was his study open to their researches ;[3]
but its contents were always at their disposal. It cannot be too often repeated that this
writer, who has been described as a mere mass of spleen and ill-nature, was, in fact, the
frankest and most liberal of mankind. I am fully warranted in saying that more valuable books given to individuals by Jonson are yet to be met with than by any person of
that age. Scores of them have fallen under my own inspection, and I have heard of
abundance of others.[4] The following passage may amuse the reader from the exquisite
absurdity of its conclusion. "In the Upper Library of Trinity College" (it is Warton
who speaks), "is a Vossius's *Greek Historians*, with a series of MS. notes. It appears,
by a Latin mem. in Dr. Bathurst's handwriting, that this book originally belonged to
BEN JONSON, who gave it to Dr. Langbaine. Jonson's name being mentioned, I cannot
forbear adding"—(Here I verily expected some compliment to his learning or liberality)
—"that in the character of Volpone, Aubrey tells us, Jonson intended Sutton, the

[1] This learned man, we see, notices the malevolence which incessantly pursued Jonson on
the stage. We now hear of nothing but Jonson's
envy:—those who lived and conversed with him,
speak of the *envy* of others :—It was *then* the
lowest description of scribblers which persecuted
him ; and I should wrong the modesty of those
who abuse him *now*, if I termed them the lights
of the age.

[2] Jonson presented a copy of this edit. to Mr.
Briggs (probably a relation of the celebrated ma-
thematician), with the following letter written on
a blank leaf :

"AMICO SUMMO
D.
R. BRIGGESIO.

*Eccum, tibi librum, mi Briggesie, quem heri,
pene cum convitio, a me efflagitasti, mitto.
Voluit ad ti afferri etiam hodie, ne diutiùs
moratus, me læsi officii reum apud te faceret.
Est Farnabii mei Martialis. Non ille Jesuita-
rum castratus, eviratus, et prorsus sine Mar-
tiali Martialis. Iste illum integrum tibi
virumque præbet, nec minus castum sed magis
virilem. Annotationes etiam suas apposuit,
tales autem ut videri possit sine commentario,
commentator. Tu fac ut illam perlegas,
protegas, et faveas homini in tanto sale,
epulisque Mart. nec insulso nec jejuno. Dig-
nus enim est, qui Virgiliis suis mereatur, ut
foret*

Toto notus in orbe Martialis,

*quod de se ingeniosissimus poeta prædicare
ausus sit, et vere; suffragante etiam*

JONSONIO TUO.
Qui x° Aug. M.DCXXIII.
*amicitia et studii ergo
hoc levidense*
D. D."

[3] The learned Selden, in speaking of a book
which he had occasion to examine, and which was
not in his extensive collection, says—"I presume that I have sufficiently manifested this out
of Euripides his Orestes, which when I was to
use, not having the scholiast, out of whom I
hoped some aid, I went for this purpose to see
it in the well furnisht librarie of my beloved
friend, that singular best in literature, MASTER BEN JON-
SON, whose special worth in literature, accurate
judgment, and performance, known only to that
FEW which are truly able to know him, hath had
from me, ever since I began to learn, an increasing admiration."—*Titles of Honour*, 1614,
fol. p. 93.

[4] I have great pleasure in copying the following
passage from Mr. D'Israeli, because it is the result of conviction acting on a liberal mind. "No
poet has left behind him in MS. so many testimonies of personal fondness as Jonson, by inscriptions and addresses, in the copies of his works,
which he presented to his friends. Of these I have
seen more than one fervent and impressive."—
Quar. of Authors, vol. iii. p. 25.

founder of the Charterhouse !"—*Life of Bathurst*, 8vo, p. 148.　It seems as if it were indispensable that the name of Jonson must always be followed by some stupid calumny.[1]

We have long lost sight of Inigo Jones ; he now reappears as Jonson's coadjutor in the Masque of *Time Vindicated*, 1623.[2] As none of those pieces which appear in the folio of 1641 were given to the press by Jonson, it is not possible to say whether he shared in any produced previously to the present one.　At all events, no symptoms of ill-will are to be found ; and there is good reason to suppose that hitherto nothing had occurred to interrupt their friendship.　In *Pan's Anniversary* (1625), Inigo again assisted Jonson, and his name is duly mentioned in the title-page, where it takes place of the Poet's, a circumstance, as it appears, of some moment.　This little piece was the last which Jonson had the good fortune to write for James I., who died on the 27th of March in this year, and in whom he lost the most indulgent of masters, and most benevolent of sovereigns.　Charles, indeed, both knew and valued Jonson ; but he was not so competent a judge of literary talents, nor was he, either by nature or habit, so familiar with his servants, or so condescending to their affairs, as the easy and good-natured James.

A long series of years had now elapsed since our author turned his thoughts to the theatre.　From 1616 to 1625, he appears to have forgotten that there was such a place ;[3] he was now, however, forcibly reminded of it, and wrote the *Staple of News*, a comedy of no ordinary merit.　Two evils were at this time rapidly gaining upon the poet, want and disease.　The first he certainly might have warded off, at least for some time, had he been gifted with the slightest portion of economy ; but he was altogether thoughtless and profuse, and his long sickness therefore overtook him totally unprovided.　From the accession to the death of James, nothing is to be found respecting his necessities ; not a complaint, not a murmur—but other times were at hand, and we shall soon hear of petitionary poems and supplications for relief.

The disease which attacked him about the end of this year was the palsy.　He seems to have laboured from his youth under a scorbutic affection (derived probably from his parents), and which assailed him with increasing virulence as his constitution gave way : to this must be added a tendency to dropsy, not the least of his evils.

From the first stroke of the palsy he gradually recovered, so far at least as to be able in some measure to pursue his usual avocations ; and, in 1626, produced the pleasant Antimasque of *Jophiel*, to vary a preceding Entertainment.　The Masques for the three following years do not appear ; nor is it known that any were written by our author : indeed, from a hint in the Epilogue to his next play, it seems as if the Court had ceased to call on him for the customary contribution.　Meanwhile his infirmities rapidly increased, and with them his wants ; he was no longer able to leave his room, or to move in it without assistance ; and in this condition he applied again to the theatre, and produced the comedy of the *New Inn*, which was brought out Jan. 19, 1629-30.　The fate of this drama is well known : it was driven from the stage, and pursued with brutal hostility by his ungenerous and unrelenting enemies.[4] The epilogue

---

[1] It may be added here, that Warton appears to have known about as much of Jonson and his writings as Mr. Headley.　In his notes on Milton's *Arcades*, he says (but with no friendly voice) that " Echo *frequently* appears in the masques of Jonson."　Frequently !　In *Pan's Anniversary* (as I think) a musical close is directed to be repeated :—and this is all the Echo.　[In the *Masque of Blackness* First Echo and Second Echo take very effective parts.—F.C.] Again : " Jonson was too proud to assist or to be assisted," a sentiment quoted for its justice by Mr. Chalmers.　Now Jonson solicited and accepted assistance, or, as he calls it, "succour," from Selden, Cotton, Carew, and many others ; and he undoubtedly assisted, or joined with, more writers than any person of the age in which he lived !

[2] The mention of this Masque gives me an opportunity of noticing a well-known song by G. Wither, "Shall I, wasting in despair," &c., published in a little vol. 1625, with an "Answere to each verse by Master Johnson."　If the reader will turn to the Masque of *Time Vindicated* (vol. iii. *post*), where I have pointed out, for the first time, the object of the poet's satire, he will need no farther proof that Jonson was little likely to busy himself with parodying the verses of Wither, however popular.　He was not prone at any time to mix his *heels with other men's heads*; and least of all would he have joined in *this kind of chase* with a declared enemy. That the "Song" is printed with his name signifies nothing.　It was current with the public ; and he gave himself no concern about the matter.

[3] See p. xxxix.

[4] *Censure of the New Inn*,

"Thou sayst no palsye doth thy braine-pan vex,

forms a melancholy contrast to some of his earlier productions, and cannot indeed be contemplated without a feeling of pity:

> " If you expect more than you had to-night:
> The maker is sick and sad:[1]—
>   He sent things fit
> In all the numbers both of verse and wit.
> If they have not miscarried: if they have,
> All that his faint and faltering tongue doth crave,
> Is that you not impute it to his brain;
> That's not unhurt, although, set round with pain,
> It cannot long hold out: all strength must yield;
> Yet judgment would the last be in the field,
> With the true poet."

An allusion to the King and Queen which follows this extract, awoke the slumbering kindness of Charles, and he instantly sent him a hundred pounds (a truly royal present), for which the poet, with an overflowing heart, returned him thanks in three poems, written at short intervals, and all labouring for adequate language to express the fulness of gratitude, respect, and duty.[2]

This timely relief appears to have produced a favourable change in the poet's mind, and encouraged him to apply to the benevolence of his sovereign for an extension of kindness. There is a flow of gaiety and good humour in the little poem which he wrote, and called a humble *Petition to the best of Monarchs, Masters, Men*, that contrasts very happily with the gloomy and desponding tone of the passage in the preceding page. It is to the honour of Charles, that he not only granted the prayer of the petition ("that he would be pleased to make the 100 marks of his father 100 pounds"), but liberally added of himself a tierce of canary[3] (Jonson's favourite wine), which has been continued to his successors, and of which the first glass should, in gratitude, be offered by them to the poet's memory. The warrant is given below.[4]

I praye the tell me what an apoplex
Thy Pegasus can stirr, yett thy best care
Makes him but shuffle like the parson's mare,
Who from his own side witt sayes thus by mee,
He hath bequeathed his bellye unto thee;
To hold that little learning which is fled
Into thy gutts from out thy emptye head," &c.
Ashmole MSS.

These are the softest lines which I could pick out from about fourscore; and these, with the verses of Gill (see *Magnetic Lady, post*) and Chapman (p. xl) furnish a correct sample of the disposition of those who attacked our author in his own times. Of all the libels on him which have fallen in my way, I do not recollect one that possessed common humanity or common sense: they never speak of any injury or provocation received from the poet; but claim to be the mere effusions of wanton malice; yet the Walpoles, *et id genus omne*, dream of nothing but "the overpowering brutality of Jonson."

[1] It should be recorded to his praise, that nothing could suppress his ardour for improvement. It is in the midst of these afflicting circumstances that he writes a poetical epistle to Howell, earnestly soliciting his aid to procure Davies's Welsh Grammar, for which he was unable to seek himself. Jonson's lines are lost: but Howell has given his reply to them. Howell notices the extensive collection of grammars of which Jonson was already possessed.

[2] This transaction is thus wilfully perverted by Shiels. "In 1629 Ben fell sick, Charles I. was supplicated in his favour, and sent him *ten guineas*. When the messenger delivered the sum, Ben said, His majesty has sent me ten guineas *because I am poor, and live in an alley: go and tell him that his soul lives in an alley.*" This impudent falsehood is still repeated, even by those who have the poet's own acknowledgments for a hundred pounds before them; and Smollett was eager to insert it in his *History of England*, because it bore hard upon Charles. The writers of the *Bio. Brit.* have given one of Jonson's grateful poems to the King—"not so much," they properly say, "to confute as to *shame* the story."—But who shames a slanderer!

[3] Milton has been unjustly charged with reflecting on Charles for his attachment to the drama. But though Milton did not urge this as a crime against the King, other writers of that disastrous period did. "Had King Charles (says one of them) but studied Scripture half so much as BEN JONSON or SHAKSPEARE, he would have learned that when Amaziah," &c.—*Appeal to all Rational Men on King Charles's Trial*, by J. Cooke, 1649.

[4] CHARLES R.
Charles, by the grace of God, Kinge of England, Scotland, Fraunce, and Ireland, defender of the faith, &c. to the Theasurer, Chancellour, under Theasurer, Chamberlens, and Barons of the Exchequer of vs, our heirs and successours, now beinge, and that hereafter shall be, and to all other the officers and ministers of the said court, and of the receipt, there now beinge, and that hereafter shall be; and to all others to whom these presents shall come, or to whom it shall

From 1627, the date of the *Fortunate Isles*, no masque appears to have been written by our author : at this period, however, the King, whose kindness had revived in all its force, commanded him, in conjunction with Inigo Jones, to prepare the usual entertainments for the festivity of the new year.   The first piece was *Love's Triumph through Callipolis*, which seems to have been well received ; the second, which was produced about

or may apperteyn, greeting. Whereas our late most deare father King James of happy memorie, by his letters pattents under the great seale of England, bearing date at Westminster, the first day of February, in the thirteenth year of his reign of England (for the considerations therein expressed) did give and graunt unto our well-beloved servaunt, Benjamin Jonson, one annuitie or yearly pension of one hundred marks of lawful money of Englande, during his life, to be paid out of the said Exchequer, at the feast of the Anunciation of the blessed Virgin Mary, the Nativity of St. John Baptist, St. Michael the Archangel, and the birth of our Lord God, quarterly, as by the said letters patents more at large may appear. Which annuity or pension, together with the said letters patents, the said Benjamin Jonson hath lately surrendered vnto vs. Know yee nowe, that wee, for divers good considerations vs at this present especially movinge, and in consideration of the good and acceptable service done vnto vs and our said father by the said Benjamin Johnson, and especially to encourage him to proceede in those services of his witt and penn, which wee have enjoined vnto him, and which we expect from him, are graciously pleased to augment and encrease the said annuitie or pension of one hundred marks, vnto an annuitie of one hundred pounds of lawful money of England for his life. And for the better effecting thereof, of our especial grace, certen knowledge and meer motion, we have given and graunted, and by these presents for vs, our heirs and successors, upon the surrender aforesaid, do give and graunt unto the said Benjamin Johnson, one annuitie or yearly pension of one hundred pounds of England by the year, to have, hold, and yearly to receive the said annuitie or yearly pension of one hundred pounds of lawful money of England, by the year, unto the said Benjamin Johnson or his assignes, from the feast of ovr Lord God last past, before the date hereof, for and during the natural life of him the said Benjamin Johnson, at the receipt of the Exchequer of vs, our heirs and successours, out of the treasure of vs, our heirs and successours, from time to time here remayning, by the Theasurer and Chamberlens of vs, our heirs, and successours there, for the time beinge, at the foresaid four usual terms of the year (that is to say) at the feast of the Annuntiation of the blessed Virgin Mary, the Nativity of St. John the Baptist, St. Michael the Archangel, and the birth of our Lord God, by even and equal portions quarterly to be paid. The first payment thereof to begin at the feast of the Annuntiation of the blessed Virgin Mary, next before the date of these presents. Wherefore our will and pleasure is, and we do by these presents for vs, our heirs and successours, require, command, and authorize the said Theasurer, Chancellour, under Theasurer, Chamberlens,

and Barons, and other officers and ministers of the said Exchequer, now and for the time being, not only to paie or cause to be paide vnto the said Benjamin Johnson, or his assignes, the said annuitie or yearly pension of one hundred pounds of lawful money of England according to our pleasure before expressed : and also from time to time to give full allowance of the same, according to the true meaning of these presents. And these presents, and the enrollment thereof, shall be unto all men whom it shall concern, sufficient warrant and discharge for the payinge and allowinge of the same accordingly, without any farther or other warrant to be in that behalf procured or obtained. And further know yee, that wee of our more especial grace, certen knowledge and meer motion, have given and granted, and by these presents for us, our heires and successors, do give and graunt unto the said Benjamin Johnson and his assigns, one terse of Canary Spanish wine yearly : to have, hold, perceive, receive, and take the said terse of Canary Spanish wine unto the said Benjamin Jonson and his assigns during the term of his natural life out of our store of wines yearly, and from time to time remayninge at or in our cellers within or belonging to our palace of Whitehall. And for the better effecting of our will and pleasure herein, we do hereby require and command all and singular officers and ministers whom it shall or may concerne, or who shall have the care or charge of our said wines, that they or some one of them do deliver or cause to be delivered the said terse of wine yearly, and once in every year vnto the said Benjamin Johnson or his assignes, during the terme of his natural life, at such time and times as he or they shall demand or desire the same. And these presents or the inrollment thereof shall be unto all men whom it shall concerne a sufficient warrant and discharge in that behalf, although express mention, &c. In witness, &c.

                            Ex. per Ro. Heath.

Witness, &c.

Maie it please your most excellent Majestie,

   This conteyneth your Majestie's graunte unto Benjamin Johnson, your majestie's servaunte, during his life, of a pension of 100*l. per annum*, and of a terse of Spanish wine yearly out of your majestie's store remaining at Whitehall.

   And is done upon surrender of a former letters patents granted unto him by your late royal father, of a pension of 100 marks *per annum*.

   Signified to be your Majestie's pleasure by the Lord Theasurer,

                                    RO. HEATH.

Endorsed thus   *March* 1630.
Expl. apud Westm' vicesimo sexto die Martii anno R Ris Caroli quinto.

                            per WINDEBANK.

two months after it, was *Chloridia*, better known by its having given birth to the dispute between these ancient friends, than by any merit of its own.   Both masques were printed before the end of the year, and the " Inventors" were said, in the title-page, to be Ben Jonson and Inigo Jones ; a fatal collocation of names for the declining poet.   His complaints, meanwhile, increased ; and, with them, his necessities. He rarely went abroad, and as his helpless state made assistance absolutely necessary, he seems about this time to have taken into his service a respectable woman, who managed his little household, and continued with him till he died.   It has been already observed that Jonson was utterly devoid of worldly prudence ; what was liberally given was lavishly spent, and he was seldom free from want.   He was indeed, like his mother, "no churl ;" his table was ever free to his friends ; and we learn from Howell that he gave repasts even in those evil days which an epicure might have shared with delight.   Wine he always considered as necessary—and perhaps it was so—to counteract the occasional influence of that morbid tendency to melancholy generated by a constitutional affection of the scurvy ; which also rendered society desirable, and, in some measure, indispensable to him.

Jonson was not called on for a masque in the following year ; and this source of emolument, which he could ill forego, was therefore lost to him.   Those who have been accustomed to hear of nothing but his unprovoked persecution of Inigo Jones, will be somewhat startled to find that this person, forgetful of old attachments, made use of his growing favour at court to depress and ruin a bedridden and necessitous friend. For the knowledge of his ungenerous conduct, in this instance not a little important in the history of our calumniated poet, I am again indebted to the kindness of Mr. D'Israeli.

Extract of a Letter from Mr. Pory to Sir Thomas Puckering, Bart.

" The last Sunday at night, the king's Mask was acted in the banquetting house, the queen's being suspended till another time, by reason of a soreness which fell into one of her delicate eyes.

"The inventor or poet of this Mask was Mr. Aurelian Townshend, sometime toward (steward) to the Lord Treasurer Salisbury; Ben Jonson being, for this time, discarded by reason of the *predominant power of his antagonist*, Inigo Jones, who, this time twelve-month, was angry with him *for putting his own name before his* in the title-page ; which Ben Jonson has made the subject of a bitter satire or two against Inigo.

" *Jan.* 12, 163½."

"Whoever was the aggressor," says Walpole, "the turbulence and brutality of Jonson were sure to place him most in the wrong." This assertion is not quite clear in the present case, in which the magnanimity of Jones is as disputable as his humanity.   He seems, indeed, to have persecuted Jonson with implacable malice :—not only *for this time* was the poet laid aside by his influence, but for the residue of his melancholy existence.   His conduct, for the rest, fully justifies the strongest lines in *The Expostulation*, vol. iii. *post :*

> " O shows, shows, mighty shows !
> The eloquence of masques ! what need of prose—
> Or verse, or prose, to express, immortal you ?"

since it cannot be denied that whatever ravages disease had made on the faculties of Jonson, he was yet many degrees above Master Aurelian Townshend, of whom no one, I believe, ever heard before.   The truth is, that Jones wanted, as Jonson has it, to be the *Dominus Do-all of the work*, and to engross all the praise.   This avarice of credit is not unpleasantly touched in the ridiculous interlude annexed to the *Tale of a Tub :*

> "*Med.* I have a little knowledge in design,
> Which I can vary, sir, to *infinito*.
> *Tub. Ad infinitum*, sir, you mean.
> *Med.* I do ;
> I stand not on my Latin : I'll invent ;
> But I must be alone then, join'd with no man."

In fact, Jones had no taste for poetry, and an obscure ballad-maker, who could string together a few rhymes to explain the scenery, was more acceptable to him than a man of talent, who might aspire to a share of the praise given to the Entertainment.

The cruelty of Jones in depriving our author of the court patronage had an unfavourable effect upon his circumstances in many respects. The city, from whom he had been accustomed to receive an annual sum by way of securing his services, when occasion called for them, seem to have watched the moment of declining favour, and withdrawn their bounty.[1] The example was probably followed by many who would not have introduced it, and as his salary was at all times irregularly paid, he was once more reduced to extremities, and driven to address a pathetic epistle to the Lord Treasurer Weston, for relief.[2] In this he says that disease and want, with their associates, had beset him for five years, and that his muse

> " Now lay blocked up and straitened, narrowed in,
> Fixed to the bed and boards, unlike to win
> Health, or scarce breath, as she had never been !"[3]

This appears to be his last "mendicant epistle," and it was not written in vain. Assistance reached him from various quarters ; and some alleviating circumstances of

---

[1] Of this Jonson complains with great indignation to the Earl of Newcastle, in a petitionary letter, written with some humour as well as spirit. He calls it their *chandlerly pension.* It deserved a better name, for it was a hundred nobles per ann., a sum which could ill be spared by him at such a time. The Court of Aldermen withdrew it December 19th, 1631. It appears from this letter that Jonson had somewhat recovered from the first stroke of the palsy ; the second, the fatal stroke, he places in 1628.
[Mr. Dyce, in his *Life of Middleton* (1840), has pointed out that Jonson succeeded Middleton as "Cities Chronologer," and has given the following very interesting extracts from the City Records. The friendly and potential intercession of the King is a most pleasing circumstance. Mr. Dyce says, " Jonson no doubt continued to hold this office till his death. He was succeeded in it by Francis Quarles."

Hamersly Mayor. Rep. No. 42. f. 271.

" Martis Secundo die Septembris 1628 Annoque R Rs Caroli Angliæ &c quarto. "Item: this daie Beniamyn Johnson Gent is by this Court admitted to be the Cities Chronologer in place of Mr. Thomas Middleton deceased, to have hold exercise and enioye the same place and to have and receive for that his service out of the Chamber of London the some of one hundred Nobles per Annum to contynue duringe the pleasure of this Court and the First quarters payment to begin att Michaelmas next."

Whitmore Mayor. Rep. N. 46. f. 8.

" Jovis decimo die Novembris 1631 Annoque Regni Regis Caroli Angliæ &c septimo. " Item: it is ordered by this Court that Mr. Chamberlen shall forbeare to pay any more fee or wages unto Beniamine Johnson the Cities Chronologer until he shall haue presented unto this Court some fruits of his labours in that his place."

" Jovis xviij° die Septembris 1634 Annoque R Rs Caroli Angliæ &c decimo.

Mowlson Mayor. Rep. N. 48, f. 433.

" Item : this day Mr. Recorder and Sir James Hamersley Knight and Alderman declared unto this Court His Majesty's pleasure signified unto them by the right honble. the Earle of Dorsett for and in the behalfe of Beniamine Johnson the Cittyes Chronologer, Whereupon it is ordered by this Court that his yearely pencion of one hundred nobles out of the Chamber of London shalbe continued and that Mr. Chamberlen shall satisfie and pay unto him his arrerages thereof."—F. C.]

[2] The following letter was probably written at this period :

" MY NOBLEST LORD AND BEST PATRON,
" I send no borrowing epistle to provoke your lordship, for I have neither fortune to repay, nor security to engage, that will be taken : but I make a most humble petition to your lordship's bounty to succour my present necessities this good time [festival] of Easter, and it shall conclude all begging requests hereafter on the behalf

" Of your truest beadsman and
" most thankful servant,
" B.J.
" *To the Earl of Newcastle*" [no date].
[*Harl. MSS.* 4955.]

[3] About this time Randolph, whom he had adopted, addressed to him, with filial reverence, " a gratulatory poem," in which he thus refers to his disease :

" And here, as piety bids me, I intreat
Phœbus to lend thee some of his own heat,
To cure thy *palsie,* else I will complain
He has no skill in herbs, and we in vain
Style him the god of physic : 'twere his praise
To make thee as immortal as thy lays," &c.

another kind contributed at the same time to smooth the bed of pain, and heal his wounded spirit. He received several copies of complimentary verses from the admirers of his talents ; and his munificent patron, the Earl of Newcastle, who had incidentally heard of it, applied to him for a transcript of some of them. Jonson's answer follows :

" MY NOBLE LORD, AND MY PATRON BY EXCELLENCE,
  " I have here obeyed your commands, and sent you a packet of my own praises ; which I should not have done if I had any stock of modesty in store :—but ' obedience is better than sacrifice,'—and you command it. I am now like an old bankrupt in wit that am driven to pay debts on my friends' credit ; and, for want of satisfying letters, to subscribe bills of exchange.

" Your devoted

" *4th February*, 1632.   " BEN JONSON.
" To the Right Hon. the Earl of Newcastle."

This letter enclosed several poems ; among which were two by the celebrated Lord Falkland, never printed ; a third, printed without a name in *Wit Restored*, but here signed Nic. Oldisworth ; and a fourth of considerable length by R. Goodwin,[1] of which this is the concluding couplet :

> " Other oblivion, BEN, thou ne'er wilt find
> Than that, which, with thee, puts out all mankind."

Lord Falkland, who is insulted by Walpole for the meanness of his poetry (which yet is superior to his own), speaks of it with a modesty which must take away all inclination to censure. I know, he says,

> " That what I here have writ
> May praise my friendship, but condemn my wit."

Our author was now employed upon the *Magnetic Lady*, which was brought out in the October term of this year. " It was generally esteemed," Langbaine tells us, "an excellent play, though in the poet's days it found some enemies ;"[2] among whom he specifies the younger Gill, of whose ribaldry a specimen will be found in the notes to that production. I have elsewhere noticed the inaccuracy of the dates prefixed to Howell's *Letters*. He speaks of this drama as in existence in 1629 ; but if the licenser's authority were not sufficient (which it is) for assigning it to the present year, there is an incidental passage in a letter from Mr. Pory to Sir Thos. Puckering (Sept. 20th, 1632) which would put it out of dispute. " Ben Jonson, who I thought had been dead, has written a play against the next term, called the *Magnetic Lady*."—*Harl. MSS*.vol. 7000. We may collect from this that Jonson had ceased to appear abroad, and was entirely lost to those who looked for him only at Whitehall and the theatres. Indeed, his maladies had recently increased, and left him as little leisure as power for literary exertions of any kind. Dryden calls his last plays his " dotages"[3]—they want indeed much of the freedom and vigour of his early performances ; but they exhibit no signs of mental imbecility, and one of them, the *New Inn*, has more than one passage of merit.[4] There

---

[1] Of this person I know no more than is found in Aubrey. " He was" (he says) " a general scholar and had a delicate witt ; was a great historian and an excellent poet."—*Letters*, vol. iii. 360. The Editors of these letters are at a loss for the meaning of the next sentence. " The journey into France crept in. Bishop Corbet's poems was made by him." Read it thus, and the difficulty will vanish. " The Journey into France, crept into Bishop Corbet's poems, was made by him." But can this be so ?

[2] There is an amiable trait recorded of Inigo Jones. He was present at the first representation of this play, and made himself remarkable by his boisterous ridicule of it. " He grew fat," Gill says, " with laughing !" " Whoever was the aggressor, Jonson always took care to be most in the wrong : such was his BRUTALITY," &c.

[3] Meaning, it may be presumed, the *New Inn*, the *Magnetic Lady*, and the *Tale of a Tub*.

[4] The good taste of Mr. Lamb has led him to make considerable extracts from this play, which is so unfeelingly ridiculed by the commentators on Shakspeare, who never condescended to open it. He concludes with a remark that does equal credit to his liberality and his judgment. " These, and the preceding extracts (from the *Case is Altered* and the *Poetaster*), may serve to show the poetical fancy and elegance of mind of the supposed rugged old bard. A thousand beautiful passages might be added from those numerous court-masques and entertainments which he was in the daily habit of producing, to prove the same thing ; but they do not fall within my plan."—*Specimens of the English Dramatic Poets*.

is, however, a want of generosity in this triumph over the poet's declining years.   His
perseverance in writing was, in truth, a misfortune ; but it was forced upon him by the
urgent calls of his situation.   There were, indeed, intervals of ease and comfort, and in
these he wrote with his usual happiness ; but he was unable to wait for them, and his
"bedridden and afflicted muse" was frequently urged to exertions of which she was manifestly incapable.

A few trifling pieces of poetry close the melancholy account of this year.   It is evident,
however, that we have but a small part of what was written.   Something was probably
lost in the confusion which followed his death, and more in the wreck of his patron's
fortunes ; but exclusively of these, it appears that we have not all our author's printed
works.   The following letter, which (though undated) appears to be written about
this period, alludes to a work of which nothing is now to be found.

"MY LORD,
"The faith of a fast friend with the duties of an humble servant, and the hearty prayers
of a religious beadsman, all kindled upon this altar to your honour, my honourable lady,
your hopeful issue, and your right noble brother, be ever my sacrifice !

" It is the lewd printer's fault that I can send your lordship no more of my book.   I
sent you one piece before the fair by Mr. Witherington, and now I send you this other
morsel.   The fine gentleman that walks the town ; the Fiend ; but before he will
perfect the rest I fear he will come himself to be a part under the title of the absolute
knave, which he hath played with me.

"My printer and I shall afford subject enough for a tragi-comedy ; for with his
delays and vexation I am almost become blind ; and if heaven be so just, in the metamorphosis, to turn him into that creature which he most resembles, a dog with a bell to
lead me between Whitehall and my lodging, I may bid the world good night.
                                                                  "And so I do.
" To the Earl of Newcastle."   " BEN JONSON.
    [*Harl. MS.* 4955.]

The *Tale of a Tub*, the last work of Jonson that was submitted to the stage, appeared
in 1633.   It makes no great pretensions to notice ; yet it is correctly and even characteristically written : but though there may be something to amuse, there is little to interest;
and it was probably not often called for.   In the last scene of this comedy Jonson had
introduced a ridiculous piece of machinery, at the expense of his powerful enemy, Inigo
Jones, who had, however (as may be easily supposed) sufficient influence with the
Master of the Revels to prevent its appearance.

In the spring of this year Charles visited his native kingdom.   He was splendidly entertained on the road by the nobility and gentry ; but by none of them with such lavish
magnificence as by the Earl of Newcastle.   Jonson was applied to on the occasion for
one of those little congratulatory interludes which usually made a part of the royal
entertainments : and the following letter from the grateful poet probably accompanied
Love's Welcome at Welbeck.[1]

"MY NOBLE LORD AND MY BEST PATRON,
" I have done the business your lordship trusted me with ; and the morning after I
received by my beloved friend, Master Payne, your lordship's timely gratuity—I style it
such, for it fell like the dew of heaven on my necessities—I pray to God my work may
have deserved it ; I meant it should in the working it, and I have hope the performance
will conclude it.   In the meantime I tell your lordship what I seriously think—God
sends you these chargeable and magnificent honours of making feasts, to mix with your
charitable succours, dropt upon me your servant ; who have nothing to claim of merit
but a cheerful undertaking whatsoever your lordship's judgment thinks me able to
perform.[2] I am in the number of your humblest servants, my lord, and the most willing;

---

[1] There was, indeed, another public occasion unpublished) some account will be found in the
on which our author was employed to write; Introduction to No. lxxxviii. of the *Underwoods.*
namely, the christening of a son of the Earl of   [2] In this humble and thankful style is con-
Newcastle, to whom some of the royal family ceived all that has reached us of Jonson's cor-
stood sponsors. Of this little interlude (hitherto respondence with his patrons. Gratitude, indeed,

and do joy in the good friendship and fellowship of my right learned friend, Master Payne, than whom your lordship could not have employed a more diligent and judicious man, or that hath treated me with more humanity ; which makes me cheerfully to insert myself into your lordship's commands, and so sure a clientele.

" Wholly and only your lordship's,

" To the Earl of Newcastle." " BEN JONSON.

It would be a heartrending task minutely to trace the progress of our author's decline from the period at which we are arrived. He continued, while his *faint and faltering tongue* could articulate, to pay his annual duty to his royal master, and he wrote, at the request of the Earl of Newcastle, another little interlude to grace the reception of the King and Queen at Bolsover, called also *Love's Welcome;* but this appears to be almost the last of his works, if we except the satires on Inigo Jones, which, according to the dates assigned by Howell, were not written till 1635.[1]

One bright and sunny ray yet broke through the gloom which hung over his closing hours. In this he produced the *Sad Shepherd*, a pastoral drama of exquisite beauty, which may not only be safely opposed to the most perfect of his early works, but to any similar performance in any age or country. The better half of this drama was unfortunately lost in the confusion that followed his death ; for, that he had put the last hand to it I see no reason to doubt.[2] This was apparently the close of his labours. Among his papers were found the plot and opening of a domestic tragedy on the story of *Mortimer, Earl of March*, together with the *Discoveries* and the *Grammar of the English Language*, on both of which he probably continued to write while he could hold a pen. The minute accuracy of the Grammar, and the spirit and elegance, the judgment and learning displayed in every part of the *Discoveries*, are worthy of all praise. It may, indeed, be said, that they are the recollections of better days ; and, in some measure, this is undoubtedly the case : but no difference of style or manner is anywhere apparent, and it is certain, from internal evidence, that a considerable portion of the latter work must have been written a short time before his dissolution.

That event was now rapidly approaching. He had evidently received a religious education from his parents, and his works sufficiently show that he was not without serious impressions of his duty towards his Maker ; these grew more frequent and strong perhaps in his affliction, and it is gratifying to learn from the Bishop of Winchester, who often visited him during his long confinement, that he expressed the deepest sorrow and contrition for " profaning the Scripture in his plays." It is proper to observe, however, that the memory of the good Isaac Walton (who gives us this part of the bishop's conversation) must have deceived him in this place. Jonson has no profanations of Scripture in his plays : he has, indeed, profanations of the sacred name (like all his contemporaries), and of these he did well to repent "with horror." In this instance, it *was good for him to have been afflicted ;* and, as his remorse was poignant, it is a part of Christian charity to hope that it was not in vain. He died on the 6th of August, 1637, and was buried on the 9th in Westminster Abbey, "in the north aisle, in the path of square stone opposite to the scutcheon of Robertus de Ros." A common pavement stone, Mr. A. Chalmers says, was laid over his grave, with the short and irreverent inscription of *O rare Ben Jonson !* There was nothing *irreverent* however intended by this brief epiphonema. His friends designed to raise a noble monument to his memory, by subscription, and till this was ready nothing more was required than to cover his ashes decently with the stone which had been removed. While this was doing, Aubrey tells us, Sir John Young, of Great Milton, Oxfordshire,

---

was one of the feelings which peculiarly marked his character. " I know," says Eliot (Jonson's personal enemy), in an epistle to the Earl of Montgomery,

" I know
That Jonson much of what he has, does owe
To you, and to your family, and is never
Slow to profess it," &c.—*Poems*, p. 108.

[1] Since I have had an opportunity of examining the Museum MSS. I have less confidence in

these *dates* than before. Oldys is completely justified in his doubts of their accuracy.

[2] It is not altogether improbable that we owe the loss of this pastoral drama to the circumstance of shutting up the theatres this year (1636). There is an allusion to this circumstance in Habington's Elegy on our author's death :

" Heaven, before thy fate,
That thou thyself mightst thine own dirges hear,
Made the sad stage close mourner for a year," &c.

whom he familiarly calls Jack Young, chanced to pass through the abbey, and, not enduring that the remains of so great a man should lie at all without a memorial, " gave one of the workmen eighteenpence to cut the words in question." The sub-scription was fully successful ; but the troubles which were hourly becoming more serious, and which not long after broke out into open rebellion, prevented the execution of the monument, and the money was returned to the subscribers.

Although Jonson had probably experienced some neglect towards the termination of his days, yet the respect for his memory was very general, and his death was long lamented as a public loss. Many of the elegies written on the occasion were collected by Dr. Duppa, Bishop of Winchester, and tutor to the Prince of Wales, and published a few months after the poet's death,[1] under the title of JONSONUS VIRBIUS. For this act of pious friendship Duppa received the thanks of his contemporaries ; and, among the rest, of Davenant, who compliments him on the occasion in a poem of some merit. As the collection is of rare occurrence, and contains several pieces by the most cele-brated names of the time, it is reprinted at the end of Jonson's Works, together with short notices of the respective authors, furnished by the kindness of my liberal and ingenious friend, Octavius Gilchrist, at a moment when kindness is doubly felt, when I was overwhelmed with affliction for an irreparable loss, and incapable of the slightest exertion.

Jonson left no family. His wife appears to have died some time before his journey into Scotland, and he never married again. Most of his children died young, and none survived him.

His person was large and corpulent. He had, Aubrey says, been fair and smooth-skinned, but a scorbutic humour appears to have fallen, at an early period, into his face, and to have scarred it in a very perceptible degree ; still, however, he must have been, while young, a personable man. Decker, as we have seen, describes him as a mere monster in the *Satiromastix;* but this is a scenical picture, the distorted repre-sentation of an exasperated enemy. Randolph and others of his friends and admirers, who could only have known him in his advanced age, trace a resemblance in him to the head of Menander, as exhibited on ancient medals. We are not left, however, to contending reports, as many portraits of him were taken in his own time, several of which are come down to us sufficiently perfect to show that his features were neither irregular nor unpleasing. After he had attained the age of forty, an unfavourable change took place in his figure, to which we find frequent allusions in his writings. He speaks of his "mountain belly, and his ungracious gait," and is always foremost to jest at what did not, perhaps, escape the pleasantry of his companions.

Whalley, who sometimes sacrifices his better judgment to the opinions of others, tells us that "his disposition was reserved and saturnine." This is contradicted by the whole tenor of his life. "He was, moreover (he adds), not a little oppressed with the gloom of a splenetic imagination, and, as an instance of it, he told Drummond that he had lain a whole night fancying he saw the Carthaginians and Romans fighting on his great toe."[2] Who does not see that Jonson was giving, in the friendly flow of conversation, an account of some casual aberration of reason, produced by a passing fever, and which no one but his perfidious entertainer would have treasured up, or sought to pervert to an unworthy purpose ! That he had occasional fits of gloom may be readily granted ; and we know whence they sprung :—apart from these, he was frank and unreserved, and it is impossible to read the accounts of the meetings at the Mermaid and the Apollo without amazement at the perversity which could thus mis-state his character.

Lord Clarendon tells us that "his conversation was very good, and with men of most note ;" and the excellent Lord Falkland observes that, upon a near acquaintance with him, he was doubtful whether his candour or his talents were the greater. No

---

[1] The *imprimatur* to this little volume is dated Jan. 23, 163⅞. Gataker told Aubrey that the title of *Jonsonus Virbius* was given to it by Lord Falkland.
[2] He told Drummond no such thing "as an instance," &c. Whalley, like the rest, looked only to Shiels, who has again interpolated his own ribaldry, and joined two passages together, which, in his author, are perfectly distinct, and relate to different qualities. But enough of this despicable scribbler, whom I gladly abandon to the admiration of those who, with Mr. Malone, think forgery, when employed in the ruin of Jonson's reputation, "*an innocent jeu-d'esprit.*" —*Shak.* vol. i. p. 619.

man, in fact, had lived more in the world than Jonson, conversed with a greater variety of characters, was quicker to remark, or abler to retain, the peculiarities of each : this, with his habitual frankness of communication, rendered his society as delightful as it was instructive. The testimony of Lord Clarendon is of the highest authority. He lived, he says, " many years on terms of the most friendly intercourse with our author," and he was, in consequence, no ill judge of the society in which he was to be found : it is therefore not without equal surprise and sorrow that I find the editor of Dryden's Works repeatedly accusing him of "delighting *in low company*[1] and *profane* conversation." Would the exemplary Earl of Clarendon have termed this conversation *very good ?* or such company, *men of most note ?* Were Camden and Selden, and Hawkins and Martin, and Cary and Morrison, were Corbet, and Hacket, and Duppa, and Morley, and King (all bishops), low company ? Were the Digbys, the Spensers, the Ogles, the Cecils, the Sidneys, the Sackvilles, low company ? Were Coke and Egerton, and Pembroke and Portland and Aubigny, low company ? Yet with these Jonson lived from youth to age ; and even his sick-chamber, and his death-bed, were consecrated by the frequent resort of the wise and good :—

> " To him how daily flock'd, what reverence gave
> All that had wit, or would be thought to have ;
> How the wise too did with mere wits agree :
> As Pembroke, Portland, and grave D'Aubigny ;
> Nor thought the rigid'st senator a shame
> To add his praise to so deserv'd a fame !"
>
> *Falkland's Ecl.*

Such is the language of one who cherished his acquaintance to the last ; and yet we are required to believe, on the word of a writer of the present day, that Jonson delighted in " gross and vulgar society !"[2] The charge of " profane conversation" is contradicted

---

[1] This contradicts even the reports of the poet's enemies. The charge against him during his life is not that he delighted in low company, but that he aspired to society far above his rank.

[2] With the contempt expressed for the poet's talents I have nothing to do : but I must not suffer his moral character to be defamed, in silence. The object is to debase Jonson by assimilating him to Shadwell. "Huge corpulence, much coarseness of manners, and an ungentlemanly vulgarity of dialect[*] seem to have distinguished both." Again : "Shadwell seems to have imitated Ben Jonson in gross and coarse sensual indulgence and profane conversation." vol. x. 445. Again : "Shadwell resembled Jonson in the brutal coarseness of his conversation, and his vulgar and intemperate pleasures."

[*] Vulgarity of dialect ! If this be meant of Jonson's conversation, it is contradicted by the testimony of all his acquaintance : if, of his compositions, it is sufficient to answer that Jonson was by far the most correct and elegant prose writer of his time. The last of his works, the *Discoveries*, may be produced not to confute, as the writers of the *Bio. Brit.* say, but to shame, such accusations. One of Decker's earliest charges against our author is the scrupulous accuracy of his language ; and the good Bishop of Chichester, (Dr. H. King,) says of him—

" It is but truth ; thou taught'st the ruder age
To speak by grammar, and reform'dst the stage."

To these may be added the testimony of

Again : "Shadwell followed Jonson as *closely as possible ;* he was brutal in his conversation, and much addicted *to the use of opium*," &c. This is the wantonness of injustice. If the elevation of Dryden made it necessary to overwhelm Shadwell with contempt, there seems to be no absolute necessity for dragging Jonson forward at every turn. Jonson never injured Dryden. If he was praised and loved by Shadwell, it ought not to be attributed to him as a crime, for he had long been in his grave.

"Jonson is described as wearing a loose coachman's coat, frequenting the Mermaid Tavern, where *he drunk seas of Canary*, then reeling home to bed, and after a profuse perspiration, arising to his dramatic studies."—*Life of Dryden*, p. 265. The passage from which the above is taken stands thus in Mr. Malone : "I E. Bolton (whom Warton calls " that sensible old English critic," and Ritson, " that man of learning"), who, after stating his opinion of the most celebrated writers down to his own times (1600), says, " But if I should declare mine own rudeness rudely, I should then confess that I never tasted English more to my liking, nor more smart, and put to the height of use in poetry, than in that vital, judicious, and most practicable language of Master Benjamin Jonson." *Hypercritica.* It is true that Jonson had not at this period written the *Silent Woman*, the *Fox*, or the *Alchemist* ; and therefore as much of " an ungentlemanly vulgarity of dialect" as these pieces afford must be subtracted from the commendations of Edmund Bolton.

by the whole tenor of his life. "For my own part," he says, in his manly appeal to the two Universities, "I can affirm, and from a *most clear conscience*, that I have ever trembled to *think towards the least profaneness ;*" and he is borne out by all that remains of his works.[1] But his enemies rely on the authority of the infamous Shiels, who, not content with the scurrility which he has put into the mouth of Drummond, adds from himself, that "Jonson took every occasion to ridicule religion in his plays, and make it his sport in conversation!" (*Cibber's Lives*, &c. vol. i. p. 236). His plays have been for two centuries before the public, and may be confidently appealed to on the present occasion. There is not a single passage in them which can be construed by the most inveterate of his persecutors into any "ridicule of religion ;" but I will not disgrace the poet any further by defending him against a convicted liar ; though I must be permitted, for the last time, to express my sincere regret that a blind hatred of Jonson should lead so many "better natures" to build their accusations on such authority. The poet's fortunes, like Marc Antony's, have "corrupted honest men."[2]

---

have heard (Aubrey says) Mr. Lacy the player say that Ben Jonson was wont to wear a coat, like a coachman's coat, with slits under the arm-pit." Lacy has good authority for this circumstance ; but to what period does it refer? To the last year of Jonson's life ; when the poet with that respect for the public which he always cherished, sent for him to his sick-chamber, to give him a list of words in the Yorkshire dialect for the *Sad Shepherd*, on which he was then employed. Lacy, who did not leave Yorkshire till 1631 or 1632, could know little of Jonson but the form of his coat, which truly seems very well adapted to one who could barely move from his bed to his "studying chair, which was of straw such as old women use, and such as Aulus Gellius is drawn in." But, continues Aubrey, "he would many times exceed in drink [this is not quite fairly translated, *he drank seas of Canary*], then he would tumble home to bed, and when he had thoroughly perspired, then to study." That Jonson was fond, too fond, if the reader pleases, of good wine and good company, we know ; but there is yet a word to be said on this passage. Aubrey leaps at once over forty years of Jonson's life : from 1596 to 1636 all that he tells us, with the exception of the passage just quoted, is that he died in Westminster, and was buried there ! Yet this is the foundation of the endless attacks upon him for *brutality* and *swinish licentiousness*. Aubrey knew nothing of our author but what he gathered from conversation, and Kent himself had not a better gift at *marring a plain tale in the telling.* Even in the short report of Lacy he confounds the *Sad Shepherd* with the *Tale of a Tub*, though he had only to open it. And what does the reader imagine to be the origin of this charge of Jonson's "exceeding in drink, tumbling home to study," &c.? Simply, a character of himself, put (in sport) into the mouth of Carlo Buffone, whom he expressly warns us against, as "a scurrilous and profane jester, as a violent railer, an immeasurable liar, and one that, swifter than Circe, transformed every person to deformity," &c. This is his speech : *Carlo.* "When the poet comes abroad (once in a fortnight) and makes a good meal among players, he has *caninum appetitum* (marry, at home he keeps a good philosophical diet, beans and buttermilk), and will take you off three, four, five of these (draughts of Canary) one after another, and look villainously the

while, like a one-headed Cerberus, and then when his belly is well-balanced, and his brains rigged a little, he sails away, as if he would work wonders when he came home."—*Every Man out of his Humour.* And this scurrility, which is given by Jonson as a striking example of the propensity of the speaker to defame "every honourable or revered person who came within the reach of his eye, by adulterate similes" (see p. 71 *a*), is taken by Aubrey as a genuine delineation of character, and made, by the poet's enemies, the distinguishing feature of his whole life ! Aubrey's addition to this precious story is too curious to be omitted. "Ben Jonson had one eie lower than t'other, like Clun the player. Perhaps he begott Clun !"—*Letters*, &c. vol. iii. p. 415. Had this passage been quoted with the rest we should have had incontinency added to "brutality and impiety."

[1] And in his *Underwoods*, after adjuring his friend Colby, in a high strain of moral philosophy, to shun the usual vices of the army, he adds, as the most momentous charge of all—

"And last, *blaspheme not.* I did never hear
Man thought the valianter, for he durst
swear," &c.

It should be observed that Antony Wood's *Life of Jonson* is incorrect in almost every part. He formed it on two documents : the MSS. of Aubrey, and the letter of Isaac Walton, which contains the passage already quoted, and which Aubrey also procured for him. Aubrey's authority is seldom to be relied on. A greater blunderer never existed, as Wood himself discovered when it was too late—he calls him "a roving magotty-pated man ;" and such he truly was. Isaac Walton cannot be mentioned without respect ; but his letter was written nearly half a century after Jonson's death, and when the writer was in his eighty-seventh year. It is made up of the common stories of the time, and a few anecdotes procured while he was writing, from the Bishop of Winchester, who must himself, at the date of Isaac's letter, have been verging on ninety. It is not easy to discover what was the bishop's and what was Walton's ; but on these Wood constructed his *Life of Jonson.* He brings little of his own but a few dates.

[2] [Sir Walter Scott is the editor here referred to   Had he not been a Quarterly Reviewer, the

I have already expressed my satisfaction at his repentance. "He had undoubtedly," as Whalley says, "a deep sense of religion, and was under its influence." His *Epigrams, Underwoods*, and other collections of poetry, bear abundant testimony of his serious disposition : sometimes his feelings of duty are rational, solemn, and pathetic ; at other times they partake of his constitutional infirmity, and become gloomy and terrific.

> " Great and good GOD ; can I not think of Thee,
> But it must straight my melancholy be?—
> I know my state, both full of shame and scorn,
> Conceived in sin, and unto labour born ;
> Standing with fear, and must with horror fall,
> And destined unto judgment after all," &c.

" It may be offered too (Whalley adds) in his favour, that his offences against piety and good manners are very few. Were authority or example an excuse for vice, there are more indecencies in a single play of the poet's contemporaries than in all the comedies which he ever wrote ; and even Shakspeare, whose *modesty is so remarkable*, has his peccant redundancies not less in number than those of Jonson." (*Life*, &c. p. liv). Where Whalley discovered the "remarkable modesty of Shakspeare,"[1] as he has not told us, it would, perhaps, be useless to inquire. Was he aware of the opinion of the poet's contemporaries on this head ? His *peccant redundancies*, too, are delicately contrasted with our author's "daring profanation of the Scriptures." The fact is, that the crime which is falsely charged on the one, falls with dreadful effect upon the other. Shakspeare is, in truth, the coryphæus of profanation. Texts of Scripture are adduced by him with the most wanton levity ; and, like his own Hal, he has led to *damnable iteration*. He too, let us hope, regarded his conduct in this respect "with horror," though no record of it be found on earth.

Jonson's guilt was of a different degree :—

> " He turned no Scripture phrases to a jest,
> And was inspired with rapture, not possest !"

It consisted, as is already observed, of an abuse of the sacred name in idle exclamations. Profane swearing was unhappily the vice of the time ; from the monarch on the throne to the peasant in his shed, all were familiarised to oaths of fearful import. Catholicism had introduced (as it everywhere does) expressions not to be repeated with impunity ; adjurations by limbs, wounds, sufferings ; by attributes, mysteries, &c., which, when they lost the reverence once attached to them—all, in short, that concealed their inherent turpitude—presented features of peculiar deformity. The most offensive of Jonson's dramas, in this respect, are the early 4tos, and of these, the first sketch of *Every Man in his Humour* ;—this, however, was not given to the press by him :—the folio edition, the only one which appears to have experienced his care, is free from many of the blemishes which deform the others. His most usual oath in the latter was an unmeaning exclamation, "by G—d so !" from this, when his works were reprinted, he withdrew the G, and thus rendered the nonsense harmless. I am not afraid to confess that, in a few instances, where there was reason to suppose that he had overlooked it, I have surreptitiously abstracted the same letter. I know the importance of fidelity ; but no considerations on earth can tempt me to the wanton or heedless propagation of impiety. I have always regarded with feelings of peculiar horror that fool-hardy accuracy which with blind and bold irreverence ferrets out every blasphemous word which the author's better feelings had thrown aside, and felicitates the reader on the pernicious discovery. More than one editor of our old poets might be named—but *ignoti alta jaceant nocte !*[2]

"cankered carle" (as he calls Gifford), would have handled him still more roughly.—F.C.]

[1] Steevens observes on a note of Warburton, in which he speaks of Shakspeare's delicacy somewhat in the style of Whalley—"Dr. Warburton's recollection must have been weak, or his zeal for his author extravagant : otherwise he could not have ventured to countenance him on the score of delicacy ; his offensive metaphors and allusions being undoubtedly more frequent than those of all his dramatic predecessors or contemporaries." *Shak.* vol. vi. p. 351.

[2] It may yet be observed that the whole of Jonson's later works (*i. e.* all the dramatic pieces

Jonson's love of conviviality has been already noticed.[1] His attachment to wine is never denied ; indeed, in this case, as in many others, he seems to have pleased himself with exaggerating his foibles, and playing into the hands of his enemies. I know not his motives for this conduct : pride was, perhaps, at the bottom of it ; and he appears to act as if he would have it thought that the accusations of such characters as were banded against him could neither disturb nor disgrace him. With all this, however, it is not true, as Drummond says, that "drink was one of the elements in which he lived," or, as has been more recently asserted, that he was "an habitual sot." The immensity of his literary acquisitions,[2] and the number and extent of his productions, refute the slander, no less than the gravity, dignity, wisdom, and piety of those with whom he passed his life from manhood to extreme old age. That he was frequently found at the Mermaid, in his earlier years, and at his own club (St. Dunstan's) in his declining age, we know ; but so were many of the most wise and virtuous of his contemporaries. Domestic entertainments were, at that time, rare : the accommodations of a private house were ill-calculated for the purposes of a social meeting ; and taverns and ordinaries are therefore almost the only places in which we hear of such assemblies. This, undoubtedly, gives an appearance of licentiousness to the age, which, in strictness, does not belong to it. Long after the period of which we are now speaking we seldom hear of the eminent characters of the day in their domestic circles ; they constantly appear at coffee-houses, which had usurped the place of ordinaries ; and it was not till the accession of the present royal family, which brought with it the stability of internal peace, that the mansions of the middle class received those advantages which made home the centre of social as well as of individual happiness and comfort.

"Jonson hath been often represented as of an envious, arrogant, overbearing temper, and insolent and haughty in his converse ; but these ungracious drawings were the performance of his enemies, who certainly were not solicitous to give a flattering likeness of the original. But considering the provocations he received, with the mean and contemptible talents of those who opposed him, what we condemn as vanity or conceit might be only the exertions of conscious and insulted merit."[3] It may be so, but instead of endeavouring to account for the origin of some of those ill qualities, or to apologise for them, it would have been more judicious to deny the existence of them altogether. It is not true that Jonson was envious of his contemporaries ;[4] he was liberal of commen-

---

produced during the last twenty-three years of his life), are remarkably free from rash ejaculations. The office-book of Sir Henry Herbert, however, supplies us with a very curious instance of the danger which he ran, notwithstanding his innocence, of being again charged with "blasphemy." The *Magnetic Lady* is void of all offence : yet for the profane language of this play the author, then sick in bed, was questioned by the Master of the Revels : and it was not till the performers were confronted with him, that they confessed themselves "to have introduced the oaths complained of into their respective parts, without his authority or even knowledge."

[1] It should be observed, however, that most of what we have on this subject was written after Jonson's death. The celebrity of his name made the *Apollo* famous, and those who belonged to the club when he died, or were successively admitted into it, *and who looked on themselves as

* Even this conferred distinction. One of Shadwell's characters in *Bury Fair* makes it his peculiar boast that "he was made Ben Jonson's son in the Apollo." It was not suspected in those days that the founder of this convivial society would be regarded hereafter as a "sullen" and "repulsive" misanthrope.

his "sons," seem to have thought it an act of filial duty to exaggerate the jovial propensities of their "father." Hence a thousand songs and invocations of this kind—

"Fetch me BEN JONSON'S skull, and fill't with sack,
Rich as the wine he drank, when the whole pack
Of jolly Sisters pledged, and did agree
It was no sin to be as gay as he :—
If there be any weakness in the wine,
There's virtue in the cup to mak't divine," &c.
           Preparations to Study, 1641.

[3] While Jonson puts a ridiculous account of himself into the mouth of an "immeasurable liar," for the purpose of dramatic satire, he thus describes, in his own person, the real nature of his employment :

"I that spend half my nights, and all my days,
Here in a cell, to get a dark pale face,
To come forth worth the ivy and the bays ;
And, in this age, can hope no other grace."

Yet his enemies persist in taking his character from Carlo Buffone !
[3] Whalley. *Life of Jonson*, p. lv.
[4] Every act of Jonson's life is perverted. He told Drummond that he could have wished the *Feasting of the Forth* had been his own. This was evidently meant to convey the most cordial

dation ; and more than enough remains to prove that he rejoiced in their merits, and forwarded their success ; he assisted Selden, and Hacket, and Raleigh, and Hobbes, and many others ; in a word, his advice, his skill, his pen were always at the command of his friends, and they were not sparingly employed by them. Neither is it true that he was "insolent and haughty in his converse." His conversation (Lord Clarendon says) was very good ; and it must, in fact, have been so, since he had the faculty of endearing himself to all who approached him. To say nothing of the distinguished characters of both sexes with whom he had grown old in a constant intercourse of friendship and familiarity, the men of genius and talents who succeeded them, the hope and pride of the coming age,[1] all flocked to Jonson, all aspired to become his "sons," all looked up to him for encouragement and advice, and all boasted of the pleasure and advantage derived from his society. Innumerable proofs of this might be accumulated without difficulty, for such was the rank of Jonson, such the space which he occupied in the literary sphere, that his name is found in contact with almost every eminent character of the day.

That he had a lofty opinion of himself may be allowed ; indeed, he never affected to conceal it ; but this did not lead to any undue contempt of others, as may be seen by what he says of Camden, Selden, and an infinite number besides, whose names occur in his *Underwoods, Epigrams,* and smaller pieces. In truth, this self-complacency frequently attends great learning ; and our author's learning was of gigantic bulk. The degree of genius and fancy which a man possesses he can scarcely be said to ascertain by comparison :—he may, indeed, over-rate it ; but he may also set it too low : and there are instances in which these qualities have been unconsciously possessed. But no man can be profoundly learned without knowing it : he cannot conceal from himself that the acquisition has been made with infinite labour ; and he can form no very inadequate judgment of its degree, compared with that of others. This will account, in some measure, for that overweening pride in which many of the most celebrated literary characters have indulged, and which, when unsupported by taste and judgment, and the better qualities of the mind, is, in truth, sufficiently offensive.

" In his studies Jonson was laborious and indefatigable : his reading was copious and extensive ; his memory so tenacious and strong that when turned of forty he could have repeated all that he ever wrote : his judgment was accurate and solid ; and often consulted by those who knew him well, in branches of very curious learning, and far remote from the flowery paths loved and frequented by the muses."[2] But, however widely diverged his occasional excursions might be, he always returned with renovated ardour to the companions of his youth, the classics of Greece and Rome, with whom his acquaintance was most familiar. "When I was in Oxon (Aubrey says) Bishop Skinner, who lay at our college (Trinity), was wont to say that Ben Jonson understood an author as well as any man in England." Of this there is no doubt ; and it may be fairly questioned whether "England" ever possessed a better scholar than this extraordinary man, whose name is become a bye-word in our time for "dulness," and whose character is thought to be of no further importance than as it serves to form a parallel with the "brutality," "sottishness," and "impiety" of Shadwell !

" In his friendships he was cautious and sincere, yet accused of levity and ingratitude to his friends ; but his accusers were the criminals, insensible of the charms, and strangers to the privileges of friendship ; for the powers of friendship, not the least of virtues, can only be experienced by the virtuous and the good." This is not one of my predecessor's happiest passages ; but it contains some truths among a few errors.

---

approbation ; yet Lord Woodhouselee cannot advert to the words without attempting to give them a malicious turn. The poem was so beautiful, it seems, that it "attracted the *envy* of Ben Jonson." Beautiful, indeed, it is :—but if Jonson *envied* Drummond, so he did "his beloved" Beaumont :

"What fate is mine, that when thou praisest me
For writing better, I must *envy* thee !"

so he did Fletcher :

"Most knowing Jonson, proud to call him son,

In friendly *envy* swore he had outdone
His very self,"&c.

so he did Cartwright and many others ; and it is for this peculiar strain of generous applause that he is taxed with hatred of all merit !

[1] The Duke of Buckingham (Sheffield) used to talk with great satisfaction of his being taken to see Jonson, then in his decline, when he was a boy. He always retained a veneration for the aged poet, which probably did him no service with Dryden.

[2] Whal. *Life,* &c. p. lv. *e*

Caution and Jonson should never be coupled together; the quality, whatever be its value, was unfortunately unknown to him: his whole history proves that he was open and unsuspecting; eager to trust, and confident no less of the sincerity than of the affection of his associates. Whalley add that "Jonson was sparing in his commendations of the works of others; but that when he commends, he commends with warmth and sincerity, and that a man of sense is cautious of giving characters," &c. But here again he should have ascertained the existence of the fact, before he proceeded to account for it. It is by no means "true," as he expresses it, that Jonson was sparing of his commendations:[1] on the contrary, as has been more than once observed, he was lavish of them; and there are *far more* laudatory poems by him than by any writer of the age. Sufficient proofs of this will be found in the succeeding volumes, and Whalley must have studied his author with little attention not to discover that too great a promptitude to praise was one of his besetting faults.

"This sparingness (continues the biographer) probably gave occasion to accuse him of envy." The *sparingness*, as we have just seen, exists only in the imagination of the critics; but (suppose it to be real) why should a canon of this nature be enforced against Jonson which was never applied to any other person? If silence be a proof of envy, what becomes of Shakspeare! With a single exception,[2] I cannot discover that he ever mentioned one of his contemporaries with commendation, or bestowed a line of praise on any publication of his time. Yet he is spoken of (and no doubt justly) as the soul of liberality; while our author, who found something to approve in every work that appeared, and praised almost every writer by name, is constantly described as envious of all around him, and sedulously engaged in decrying their merits.

"In conclusion," says Whalley, "he is accused of jealousy and ill-nature." It is well that we are arrived at the last of his bad qualities; but in sober truth they seem to be charged on him with as little justice as the rest. Of what or of whom could he be "jealous?" From the accession to the death of James, which comprehends almost the whole period of his active life, he was, as has already appeared, the "beloved servant" of his prince, the companion and friend of the nobility and gentry, and the acknowledged head of the learned part of society. None but those who have looked into the literary memoirs of his age, published as well as unpublished, can form a correct idea of the frequency with which he is named and the intimacy of his connection with the most esteemed writers of the time. Of "ill-nature," he does not appear to have had a spark in him: a constitutional warmth of temper and great quickness of feeling gave indeed a tone of bluntness to his language: but it went no further; and while many proofs of the fervour of his friendship may be cited, his whole life does not furnish an instance of one unkind act.[3] He adopted a proud and overbearing tone when speaking of his enemies; but has it ever been inquired who these enemies were? As far as we are enabled to judge, they consisted principally of obscure actors and writers, who attacked him at his entrance into public life with a degree of wanton hostility which his subsequent success embittered and envenomed: add to this, that they are spoken of in the mass, and can seldom be recognised but when, in their impatience for truth, they start forward, individually, and claim the resemblance. Opposed to these, he was not likely to be nice in his selection of terms; and a more temperate and modest person than our author might have felt a little spleen at being called from the studies which he loved to defend himself against such antagonists; but his general deportment was open; his fits of anger, if violent, were momentary, and his disposition placable and kind.

---

[1] Whalley found this in Langbaine; but when the facts are at hand it is worse than folly to copy the mistakes of former writers. Langbaine has, unfortunately, too many of these blunders: he observes, for instance, from Marston's publisher, that this poet "is free from all ribaldry, obscenity," &c., and he is followed by the editors of the *Bio. Dram.*, the *Theatrum Poetarum*, the *Gen. Dict.*, &c.; whereas, we have but to open his works to be convinced that Marston was the most scurrilous, filthy, and obscene writer of his time. Such is the negligence or ignorance of those who undertake to treat of our dramatic history!

[2] He joined with Jonson in some commendatory verses printed at the end of a little volume of poetry by Robert Chester.

[3] After what has been said of his "ill-nature," it will scarcely be believed that, in all his writings, while hundreds of contemporary names are introduced with praise, there are not half a dozen to be found accompanied by any mark of reprobation: indeed I recollect no person of any note but Inigo Jones, whom he has satirized by name.

Age and infirmity had little effect upon the general bent of his temper. Though his prevailing complaint, which was of a paralytic nature, must have occasionally affected his mind and debilitated his understanding, yet he continued frank and sociable to the end. The last circumstance recorded of him, is to be found in a letter of Howell to Sir Tho. Hawkins,[1] from which it appears that at a "solemn supper given by the poet, when good company, excellent cheer, choice wine, and jovial welcome, had opened his heart and loosened his tongue, he began to raise himself at the expense of others." This incidental trait in the closing scene of his life, is, with the usual candour of his biographers, eagerly seized upon as "the leading feature of his character." It was not thus, however, that Howell thought and acted :—"For my part," he says, "I am content to dispense with this Roman infirmity of Ben, now time hath snowed upon his pericranium." He nowhere hints that this was the ordinary conduct of Jonson ; much less that it had been the practice of his better days. And if, (as Mr. Gilchrist justly observes), "when he was old and bed-ridden, and his former vigour fled, he dwelt with some degree of fondness on his early efforts ; if he experienced some fears, lest

> ' fickle fame
> Should twine round some new minion's head,
> The fading wreath for which he bled,'—

it will not be necessary to have attained his eminence to admit, that these were apprehensions which might be entertained by him without any violent impeachment of his moral character."

From a retrospect of what has been said, an opinion may be formed of the frailties and defects, as well as of the excellencies of this eminent man, without much hazard of error :—and I must have made a bad estimate of the human powers as well as of the human heart, if the latter be not found to preponderate ; and if some degree of regret be not expressed by many of those whom the ignorance or malice of his enemies has hitherto encouraged to calumniate his name.

It yet remains to say a few words on his poetical character : which may, perhaps, be more correctly appreciated if we take a cursory view of the state of dramatic literature at the period of his first appearance as a writer.

The long reign of Elizabeth, though sufficiently agitated to keep the mind alert, was yet a season of comparative stability and peace. The nobility, who had been nursed in domestic turbulence, for which there was now no place, and the more active spirits among the gentry, for whom entertainment could no longer be found in feudal grandeur and hospitality, took advantage of the diversity of employment happily opened, and spread themselves in every direction. They put forth, in the language of Shakspeare,

> " Some to the wars, to try their fortunes there ;
> Some to discover islands far away ;
> Some to the studious universities ;"—

and the effect of these various pursuits was speedily discernible. The feelings, narrowed and embittered in household feuds, expanded and purified themselves in distant warfare, and a high sense of honour and generosity, and chivalrous valour, ran with electric speed from bosom to bosom, on the return of the first adventurers in the Flemish campaigns : while the wonderful reports of discoveries, by the intrepid mariners who opened the route since so successfully pursued, faithfully committed to writing, and acting at once upon the cupidity and curiosity of the times, produced an inconceivable effect in diffusing a thirst for novelties among a people, who, no longer driven in hostile array to destroy one another, and combat for interests in which they took little concern, had leisure for looking around them, and consulting their own amusement.

The fluctuating state of religion, from the incoherent Reformation of Henry VIII. to the Protestantism of Edward, the relapse into Popery under Mary, and the return to a purer faith with Elizabeth, interested the hopes and fears of the nation in an extra-

---

[1] The date is April 1636; but it should probably be corrected, as should the next letter respecting Jonson, also dated 1636, to 1637, for it speaks of his death.

ordinary degree, and while it invigorated the fancy, improved the understanding, by making a certain portion of literature necessary to those who contended on either side of this important question. About the middle of Elizabeth's reign, the ardour of theological controversy appears to have suffered a considerable abatement, in consequence, perhaps, of the marked preponderancy of the Protestant cause : the impulse which had been communicated, however, continued to act upon the public mind, and a craving for mental enjoyment was very widely diffused. The *Mysteries*, which were indissolubly connected with the old superstitions ; and even the *Moralities* (many of which were not without merit), were yet of too rude a nature, in the present improved state of information, to afford much rational delight.—But this "craving" was most sensibly felt in the metropolis, which began about this time to increase rapidly in population and interest. England, in fact, had been improving from the time of Henry VII. ; the middle class of society had, in almost every county, acquired wealth by trade and commerce, and with it that propensity to dissipation and amusement, and that love of litigation, which always attend the first steps to consequence among a rising people. This brought numbers to the capital at particular seasons of the year, for whom it was desirable to provide entertainment ; and happily caterers of every description were at hand. Many of those who had probably entered on a learned education, with a view of being received into the munificent establishments of the old religion, were, by the destruction of monasteries, &c. abandoned to their fortunes, and compelled to seek other modes of subsistence. The taste for reading was sufficiently general to warrant a reliance, in some degree, on the profits of the press ; and London possessed allurements of a powerful nature for the literary adventurer. Many young men of abilities, therefore, deserted the colleges and flocked to the metropolis, to procure the means of enjoying its advantages by their talents, now first become a source of regular profit. Translation was the great resource, and Spain and Italy supplied the principal part of the materials. The romances, novels, and poems of both countries, more especially those of the latter, at first *done* into English, and, when practice had given somewhat of hardihood, imitated and varied in every possible form, were poured forth with a rapidity which it would be difficult to describe or credit. Meanwhile, a humbler class of writers, or rather of performers, for it is more than probable that both professions were united in the same person, were insensibly gaining upon the public attention by rude attempts at the drama, which they exhibited to admiring crowds in the galleries of inn-yards, halls, and such vacant rooms as they could most readily procure.

The popularity of these entertainments quickly attracted the notice of those who were already in some degree of credit with the town for their writings, and opened to view a source of emolument superior to that of their present occupation : they turned their thoughts therefore to the stage, and though their plays were yet unformed and rude, they boasted an evident superiority over those of their immediate predecessors. Small theatres now rose in various parts of the city. Greene, Nash, Lyly, Peele, Marlowe, Kyd, Lodge, and others, all wrote for them, and irritated and gratified the public curiosity by an endless succession of pieces, of which few perhaps were wholly destitute of merit. Compared with the unlettered and ignorant race which they supplanted, these men must have appeared to their contemporaries as very extraordinary writers, and hence we may account for the lavish praise which they received in their own times, and which, with respect to some of them, was more fairly obtained than we now seem inclined to allow. Be they what they may, however, they left in the tiring-rooms of the several theatres a countless number of dramas which those who came immediately after them, Munday, Chettle, Hathaway, &c. who, with more knowledge of the stage, fell beneath them in genius and learning, found sufficient encouragement in adapting to the improved state of the times.

It was soon after this period that Shakspeare reached London ; and his first employ, like that of most of the poets his contemporaries, was the amending of the productions of others. Jonson followed at no long interval of time, and had recourse to the same means of procuring a subsistence. Shakspeare happily formed a permanent connexion with one company, for whom he wrote and acted ; while Jonson was compelled to carry his talents from theatre to theatre, as they were required, and had perhaps as seldom the choice as the conduct of his subject.

"From whatever cause it may have arisen, (Mr. Malone says) dramatic poetry a little before Shakspeare appeared, certainly assumed a better though still an exceptionable form." The cause is sufficiently apparent in the education which Peele, Marlowe, and others whom he names, had received at the two Universities, and in the acknowledged genius which they possessed. Peele and Marlowe had exquisite feelings for poetry ; both excelled in description, to which the former lent beauty, and the latter sublimity, though they occasionally fell into meanness or bombast. Greene abounded in narrative, Lodge had humour, and Nash an inexhaustible vein of caustic raillery, never yet surpassed. Even the quaint pedantry of Lyly was not without merit, and we are indebted to it for many of the pleasantest parodies of Shakspeare. It was impossible that such men should write in vain, or that those who had witnessed the effect of their productions should return to the former puerilities. The form of their dramas, as Mr. Malone says, was "exceptionable ;" but much was done, and master spirits were now at hand to set the seal of perfection to what had been so auspiciously begun. The wonderful powers of Shakspeare, though then but carelessly displayed, must have attracted notice, and prompted the rival theatres to exertions of the most strenuous kind. The demand for novelty was incessant, and the race of dramatic writers was thus multiplied beyond credibility.

It is not easy to ascertain with any precision how long Shakspeare had been in possession of the stage when Jonson commenced his dramatic career. Mr. Malone and Mr. G. Chalmers differ as to the period of his first essay, which is placed by the former in 1589, and by the latter two years later. The latter is of no great moment, for the production of such a drama as the *First Part of Henry VI.* (which is the point in dispute) can confer no distinction on any abilities whatever ; but in 1593, when Jonson, then in his nineteenth year, had begun to write for the theatres, he was rapidly advancing to pre-eminence.

It is somewhat singular that the literary characters who immediately preceded Jonson, should have made no improvement in the construction of their fables ; but the plot of *Tamburlaine* is not a whit more regular, or skilful than that of *Gorboduc* or *Locrine*. Beyond Seneca, these writers seldom appear to have looked ; and from him they drew little but the tameness of his dialogue, and the inflation of his sentiments : their serious scenes were still histories, and sometimes lives ; and their comic ones, though replete with grotesque humour, were without dependence, object, or end. To reform this seemed worthy of Jonson, and to this his earliest as well as his latest efforts were directed. However great might be the talents and genius now employed on the stage, he could not but see that an opening was still left for the introduction of a more regular drama than had hitherto appeared. The superiority of the ancients in this respect was forcibly impressed on his young and ardent mind ; and though his admiration of their productions might be occasionally carried too far, it led to beneficial results. "The poets (Whalley says) when Jonson first appeared, generally drew their plots from some romance, or novel," (or from the rude annals of domestic warfare,) "and from thence also they derived the different incidents of the various scenes, and the resemblance between the copy and the original was every way exact. The same wildness and extravagance of fable prevailed in both, all the absurdities of the story being faithfully transcribed into the play."[1] Anomalies like these, our author, to whom the truth and simplicity of the ancient stage were already familiar, must have regarded with no very favourable eye, and he had no sooner acquired a little credit with the managers, than he resolved to embody his own conceptions, and model his future pieces upon the plan of his classic masters. For this purpose it was necessary that he should invent his own plots.—We are not acquainted with his earliest essays ; but the piece which stands at the head of his printed works exhibited no unfavourable specimen of his judgment, taste, and learning ; and was, in fact, the first regular comedy in the English language.

So much has been incidentally said of our author's dramatic powers, in various parts of these volumes, that a very cursory notice of them is required here ; little more in fact, appears necessary, than a brief mention of those qualities by which he was chiefly distinguished.

To do Jonson full justice, we must regard him in the light in which he evidently

[1] Life of Jonson, p. vii.

viewed himself, that of a moral satirist. If the comedies of the contemporaries of his early days effected any beneficial purpose; if they led to the exposure and detestation of any evil quality, or the correction of any prevalent folly, it was by accident not design; but with Jonson this was the primary object. We see it in the first play which he is known to have written ; and he has himself called our attention to the same circumstance in that which he produced at " the close and shutting up of his circle."

With this aim in view, Jonson came to the theatre possessed of many advantages. We may collect from *The Case is Altered*, and *Every Man in his Humour*, that he was recent from the study of Plautus and Terence : but this was little ; all the stores of ancient literature were open to him, and he was familiar not only with the perfect productions of the Greek dramatists, but with the fragments which lie scattered among the works of the sophists and grammarians, and which, in his days, were not to be found without much cost and labour. Nor was he merely learned ; for he appears to have entered with the same ardour into the productions of his own times, and to have acquired a very considerable degree of information on every topic connected with the arts then known and cultivated. Nature had besides given him a quick and almost intuitive faculty of discerning the ridiculous, a powerful and original vein of humour, and a genius, if not sublime, yet occasionally so raised by intense contemplation of the sublimest models, as to bear no very distant resemblance of it.

It has been the practice of the poet's biographers to institute a comparison between him and Shakspeare. These parallels have not been always " after the manner of Plutarch ;" but indeed, their utility in any case will not be very apparent ; unless it should be admitted, that Shakspeare is best set off by throwing every object brought near him into shade. Shakspeare wants no light but his own. As he never has been equalled, and in all human probability never will be equalled, it seems an invidious employ, at best, to speculate minutely on the precise degree in which others fell short of him. Let him with his own Julius Cæsar *bestride the narrow world like a colossus ;* that is his due ; but let not the rest be compelled to *walk under his huge legs, and peep about to find themselves dishonourable graves.*—" Putting aside, therefore, (as Cumberland says,) any further mention of Shakspeare, who was a poet out of all rule, and beyond all compass of criticism, one whose excellencies are above comparison, and whose errors beyond number,"[1] I return to our author.

The judgment of Jonson was correct and severe, and his knowledge of human nature extensive and profound. He was familiar with the various combinations of the humours and affections, and with the nice and evanescent tints by which the extremes of opposing qualities melt into one another, and are lost to the vulgar eye : but the art which he possessed in perfection, was that of marking in the happiest manner the different shades of the same quality, in different minds, so as to discriminate the voluptuous from the voluptuous, the covetous from the covetous, &c.

In what Hurd calls " picturing" he was excellent. His characters are delineated with a breadth and vigour as well as truth that display a master hand ; his figures stand prominent on the canvas, bold and muscular, though not elegant : his attitudes though sometimes ungraceful, are always just, while his strict observation of proportion (in which he was eminently skilled,) occasionally mellowed the hard and rigid tone of his colouring, and by the mere force of symmetry gave a warmth to the whole, as pleasing as it was unexpected. Such, in a word, was his success, that it may be doubted whether he has been surpassed or even equalled by any of those who have attempted to tread in his steps. The striking failure of Decker in Captain Tucca has been already noticed : that of Congreve in Noll Bluff, is still more marked. Congreve designed it, Whalley says, for an imitation of Bobadil : but Noll is a beaten idiot, a character too contemptible for farce, and fit only to amuse the rabble round the stage of a mountebank. Even Ford, if we can suppose for a moment that Shakspeare had Kitely in view, will scarcely be allowed to be either so just, so natural, or so respectable a character as his prototype.

In the plots of his comedies, which were constructed from his own materials, he is deserving of undisputed praise. Without violence, without, indeed, any visible effort, the various events of the story are so linked together, that they have the appearance of

---

[1] *Observ.* No. lxxv.

accidental introduction ; yet they all contribute to the main design, and support that just harmony which alone constitutes a perfect fable. Such, in fact, is the rigid accuracy of his plans, that it requires a constant and almost painful attention to trace out their various bearings and dependencies. Nothing is left to chance ; before he sat down to write, he had evidently arranged every circumstance in his mind ; preparations are made for incidents which do not immediately occur, and hints are dropped which can only be comprehended at the unravelling of the piece. The play does not end, with Jonson, because the fifth act is come to a conclusion ; nor are the most important events precipitated, and the most violent revolutions of character suddenly effected, because the progress of the story has involved the poet in difficulties from which he cannot otherwise extricate himself. This praise, whatever be its worth, is enhanced by the rigid attention paid to the unities ; to say nothing of those of place and character, that of time is so well observed in most of his comedies, that the representation occupies scarcely an hour more on the stage than the action would require in real life.

With such extraordinary requisites for the stage, joined to a strain of poetry always manly, frequently lofty, and sometimes almost sublime, it may at first appear strange that his dramas are not more in vogue ; but a little attention to his peculiar modes and habits of thinking will perhaps enable us in some measure to account for it. The grace and urbanity which mark his lighter pieces he laid aside whenever he approached the stage, and put on the censor with the sock. This system (whether wise or unwise) naturally led to circumstances which affect his popularity as a writer ; he was obliged, as one of his critics justly observes, " to hunt down his own characters," and, to continue the metaphor, he was frequently carried too far in the chase.

But there are other causes which render his comedies less amusing than the masterly skill employed upon them would seem to warrant our expecting. Jonson was the painter of humours, not of passions. It was not his object (supposing it to have been in his power) to assume a leading passion, and so mix and qualify it with others incidental to our common nature, as to produce a being instantly recognised as one of our kind. Generally speaking, his characters have but one predominating quality : his merit (whatever it be) consists in the felicity with which he combines a certain number of such personages, distinct from one another, into a well ordered and regular plot, dexterously preserving the unities of time and place, and exhibiting all the probabilities which the most rigid admirer of the ancient models could possibly demand. Passions indeed, like humours, may be unamiable ; but they can scarcely be uninteresting. There is a natural loftiness and swelling in ambition, love, hatred, &c. which fills the mind, and, when tempered with the gentler feelings, interests while it agitates. Humours are far less tractable. If they fortunately happen to contain in themselves the seeds of ridicule ; then indeed, like the solemn vanity of Bobadil and the fantastic gravity of Puntarvolo, they become the source of infinite amusement ; but this must not always be looked for : nor should we degrade Jonson by considering him in the light of a dramatic writer, bound, like the miserable hirelings of the modern stage, to produce a certain *quantum* of laughter. Many humours and modes of common life are neither amusing in themselves, nor capable of being made so by any extraneous ingenuity whatever : the vapourers in *Bartholomew Fair*, and the jeerers in *The Staple of News*, are instances in point. But further, Jonson would have defeated his own purpose if he had attempted to elicit entertainment from them : he wished to exhibit them in an odious and disgusting light, and thus to extirpate what he considered as pests from the commerce of real life. It was in the character of the poet to bring forward such nuisances as interrupted the peace, or disturbed the happiness of private society ; and he is therefore careful to warn the audience, in his occasional addresses, that it is less his aim to *make their cheeks red* with laughter than to feast their understanding, and minister to their rational improvement. " At all the theatres," says Mr. Malone (*Shak.* vol. ii. p. 177), " it appears that noise and show were what chiefly attracted an audience." Of these Jonson had little ; indeed, he always speaks of them with dislike : and he was so sensible that he must be heard with attention to effect that *profit* which he professed to mingle with *delight*, that his prologues are invariably directed to this end.

There is yet another obstacle to the poet's popularity, besides the unamiable and uninteresting nature of some of his characters—namely, a want of just discrimination. He seems to have been deficient in that true tact or feeling of propriety which Shakspeare possessed in full excellence. He appears to have had an equal value for all his characters, and he labours upon the most unimportant, and even disagreeable of them, with the same fond and paternal assiduity which accompanies his happiest efforts. He seldom appears to think that he has said enough ; he does not perceive that he has wearied his audience, and that all attention is withdrawn from his exertions : and he continues, like the unfortunate lutanist of Dryden, to finger his instrument long after it has ceased to make music to any ear but his own.

What has been said applies chiefly to his comedies. His tragedies, of which two only are come down to us, do not call for much additional remark. Both are taken from the Roman story, and he has apparently succeeded in his principal object, which was to exhibit the characters of the drama to the spectators of his days precisely as they appeared to those of their own. The plan was scholastic, but it was not judicious. The difference between the dramatis personæ and the spectators was too wide ; and the very accuracy to which he aspired would seem to take away much of the power of pleasing. Had he drawn men instead of Romans, his success might have been more assured : but the ideas, the language, the allusions could only be readily caught by the contemporaries of Augustus and Tiberius ; and it redounds not a little to the author's praise, that he has familiarized us, in some measure, to the living features of an age so distant from our own.

Hurd, who is seldom just to our author, has entered into an elaborate examination of his *Catiline* and *Sejanus ;* both of which he condemns. It would be tedious to repeat his observations ; but the object of them is to show that as the laws of the drama confine the poet to a particular action, it is wrong to dwell on its concomitant circumstances. The critic has totally mistaken the nature of these pieces. He appears to be thinking of the Athenian, instead of the English stage. Jonson's tragedies are not confined to one great event ; they are, in fact, like those of Shakspeare, whom he probably had in view, histories, embracing an indefinite period of time, and shifting, with the action, from place to place. Why, with his profound knowledge of the ancient models, and with that respect for them which on other occasions he appears so forward to enforce, he deviated from them so widely in these instances, it is perhaps vain to inquire. He had adverted to this, and probably accounted for it, in his *Observations on the Art of Poetry ;*[1] but these are unfortunately lost ; and we can only discover that the motives which influenced him in the conduct of his earliest tragedies remained in force when, at the close of life, he drew out the plot of his *Mortimer*, which has all the irregularity of *Catiline* and *Sejanus.*

Hurd has justly objected to the protracted conclusion of *Sejanus.* Undoubtedly the curtain should have dropped before the entrance of Terentius. Jonson was so sensible of his error in this respect, that he never lingered over the catastrophe of any of his subsequent pieces. In his censure of the chorus, the critic is not so correct. Jonson expressly disclaims all intention of imitating the chorus of the ancient tragedy, for which, as he says, the English stage could neither afford "state nor splendour ;" the remarks therefore do not apply. The chorus of *Catiline* (for *Sejanus* has none) was never sung, nor intended to be sung, on the stage : it is, in fact, a simple string of moral reflections arising from the subject, as contemplated in the closet ; appropriated to no character, but appended to the play, in mere conformity with the practice of his times.

The Masques and Entertainments of Jonson must not be overlooked. In the composition of these he greatly delighted, and was, as he justly says of himself, an artificer. With him they began, and with him they may be said to have ended ; for I recollect but few after his time, entitled to any particular degree of praise, with the exception of *Comus*, of whose poetical excellence (for as a masque it is defective) it is scarcely possible to speak too highly.

Pageants and masquerades had long been sufficiently familiar to the people of this country. The latter were somewhat more grotesque perhaps than those of the present day ; but they had no distinguishing feature, and existed in much the same form here

---

[1] See p. 272.

as in every other part of Catholic Europe : having in fact one common origin, that of the Processions, which, though seriously, and even piously set on foot, were too commonly tumultuous, farcical, and profane.   Pageants (I do not speak of those proud displays of pasteboard giants and monsters which amazed the good citizens on holidays) were the relics of knight-errantry. The shows were costly and magnificent, but tasteless and laborious, consisting principally of a triumph, i.e., a grand entry of knights decorated with all the pomp of those gaudy days ; broken by an interlude taken from some tender adventure of Arthur and his knights, or some pedantic allegory in that storehouse of grave absurdity, the *Romance of the Rose*, in which the pains and pleasures of a love-suit were personified, and Hope and Fear, and Jealousy and Joy, fiercely assailed in castles and towers with fantastic names. In these boisterous amusements the ladies bore no great part, though they were sometimes called upon to advance "in measure" to the storm of some refractory Passion or Affection.

Warton says that these shows, which he improperly terms masques, attained their greatest height under Henry VIII. Certain it is that during the earlier years of this licentious tyrant the court exhibited an unusual degree of splendour, but neither then, nor during the life of Elizabeth, did the masque acquire that unity of design, that exclusive character which it assumed on the accession of James. With the diffusion of knowledge and taste came the desire of something more worthy the name of courtly entertainment than the dull and unnatural allegories of the metaphysical romance, or the simple introduction of an interlude of "baboons and satyrs."

James had more literature than taste or elegance ; but he was frank and sociable ; and inclined to expensive shows. What he wanted, however, his Queen possessed in full excellence. She was, Sully says, "a bold and enterprising woman ;" she loved pomp and understood it, and, above all, she was fond of masques and revels. She aspired to convert Whitehall, which had lately been another cave of Trophonius, into a temple of delight ; for this purpose she called around her the most accomplished of the nobility, and associated them with her in those splendid amusements which she proposed to create, and which alone she could fully enjoy, as she never was familiar with the language. The poetical powers of our author were not unknown to her, for she had witnessed them at Althorpe and elsewhere, and she seems to have engaged him to embody her conceptions shortly after she arrived at Whitehall.

The masque, as it attained its highest degree of excellence in the hands of Jonson, admitted of dialogue, singing, and dancing—these were not independent of one another, as in the entertainments of the old court, but combined, by the introduction of some ingenious fable, into an harmonious whole. The groundwork was assumed at will ; but our author, to whom the whole mythology of Greece and Rome lay open, generally drew his personages from that inexhaustible treasury of elegance and beauty : having formed the plan, he called in the aid of the sister arts ; for the essence of the masque was pomp and glory, and it could only breathe in the atmosphere of a court. Thus, while the stage was in a state of absolute nudity, moveable scenery of the most costly and splendid kind was lavished on the masque, the most celebrated masters were employed on the songs and dances, and all that the kingdom afforded of vocal and instrumental excellence was employed to embellish the exhibition.

Thus magnificently constructed, the masque was not committed to ordinary performers. It was composed, as Lord Bacon says, for princes, and by princes it was played. The prime nobility of both sexes, led on by James and his Queen, took upon themselves the respective characters ; and it may be justly questioned whether a nobler display of grace and elegance and beauty was ever beheld than appeared in the masques of Jonson. The songs in these entertainments were probably entrusted to professional men ; but the dialogue, and, above all, the dances, which were adapted to the fable, and not acquire without much study and practice, were executed by the court themselves. The skill with which these ornaments were designed, and the inexpressible grace with which they were executed, appear to have left a vivid impression on the poet's mind ; and there is, accordingly, no part of his description in which he seems to labour so much for adequate language to mark his admiration as that of the dances.

> " In curious knots and mazes so,
> The Spring, at first, was taught to go ;

> And Zephyr, when he came to woo
> His Flora, had their motions too:
> And thus did Venus learn to lead
> The Idalian brawls, and so to tread,
> As if the wind, not she, did walk,
> Nor pressed a flower, nor bowed a stalk."

It is after witnessing the "measures" here so beautifully delineated that Aurora thus interrupts the performers—

> " I was not wearier where I lay,
>   By frozen Tithon's side to-night,
> Than I am willing now to stay,
>   And be a part of your delight:
> But I am urged by the Day,
>   Against my will to bid you come away."

While Jonson thus laboured to perfect the more elegant parts of these gay fancies, he did not forget to provide amusements of another kind, which he called Antimasques (parodies or opposites of the main masque), borrowed, it would seem, from the old masquerade, and already familiar to the people. These were calculated to diversify the entertainment, and to afford a breathing-time to the principal performers. The poet was here tied to no rules : he might be as wild and extravagant as he pleased : the whole world of fancy was before him : "Satyres, Fooles, Wildemen, Antiques, Ethiopes, Pigmies, and Beastes," as Lord Bacon has it (with an eye perhaps to our author), came trooping at his call. These were probably played by the menials of the palace, assisted by actors from the regular theatres. In this part of the plot Jonson stands almost alone : his antimasques are not, like those of his contemporaries, mere extravagances, independent of the main story ; generally speaking they serve to promote or illustrate it, however fantastic they appear, and are not unfrequently the vehicle of useful satire, conveyed with equal freedom and humour. Whatever they were, however, they were the occasions of much mirth : they were eagerly "hearkened after," as the cook says in *Neptune's Triumph,* and always received with pleasure.

In these devices, as has been already observed, our author took great delight, and during the life of his royal patron never failed to exert his best faculties on the composition of them. "Had nature (says Cumberland) been as liberal in her gifts to Jonson as learning was in opening her stores to his acquirements, the world might have seen a poet to whom there had been nothing since the days of Homer, *aut simile, aut secundum.*"[1] But nature had been no step-mother to Jonson ; and when the critic adds, that the poet "stocked his mind with such a mass of other men's thoughts that his imagination had not power to struggle through the crowd," he does not perceive that he has taken up a different question, and proved no part of what he supposed himself to have decided. But omitting the consideration of this, whatever may be the case of the poet in his severer studies, in his masques his imagination is neither oppressed nor obscured. In these he makes his appearance, like his own DELIGHT, "accompanied with Grace, Love, Harmony, Revel, Sport, and Laughter." If, as the critic will have it, he was a "literary behemoth," it must be granted that here at least he *writhed his lithe proboscis* with playfulness and ease. His unbounded learning is merely an adjunct to his fancy. His mythological personages, amidst the most scrupulous preservation of their respective attributes, move with elasticity and vigour ; and while the dialogue is distinguished by a masculine strength and freedom, the lyrical part of these gay pastimes is clothed with all the richness and luxuriance of poetry. Araspes, the friend and confident of Cyrus, could only account for his perfidy to the man whom he loved and revered, by supposing that he had two souls, one prompting him to evil, the other to good. A notion of a similar kind will sometimes suggest itself to the reader of Jonson. In his tragedies he was cautious and strict, tremblingly apprehensive of starting from the bounds of regularity, and constantly rejecting every idea which was not supplied by the authorities before him ; in some of his comedies too, and in several of his longer poems, the same hardness and severity are displayed ; he perseveres in the ungrateful task of compression till the finer parts of his machinery are

---

[1] Critique on *Every Man in his Humour,* p. lii.

deprived of play, and the whole stiffened, cramped, and impaired ; but no sooner has he taken down his lyre, no sooner touched on his lighter pieces, than all is changed as if by magic, and he seems a new person. His genius awakes at once, his imagination becomes fertile, ardent, versatile, and excursive ; his taste pure and elegant ; and all his faculties attuned to sprightliness and pleasure.

Such were the Masques of Jonson, in which, as Mr. Malone says, "the wretched taste of those times found amusement." That James and his court delighted in them cannot be doubted, and we have only to open the Memoirs of Winwood and others to discover with what interest they were followed by the nobility of both sexes. Can we wonder at this ? There were few entertainments of a public kind at which they could appear, and none in which they could participate. Here all was worthy of their hours of relaxation.[1] Mythologues of classic purity, in which, as Hurd observes, the soundest moral lessons came recommended by the charm of numbers, were set forth with all the splendour of royalty, while Jones and Lanier, and Lawes and Ferrabosco, lavished all the grace and elegance of their respective arts on the embellishment of the entertainment.

But in what was " the taste of the times wretched ?" In poetry, painting, architecture, they have not since been equalled ; in theology, moral philosophy, they are not even now surpassed ; and it ill becomes us, who live in an age which can scarcely produce a Bartholomew Fair farce, to arraign the taste of a period which possessed a cluster of writers of whom the meanest would now be esteemed a prodigy. And why is it assumed that the followers of the court of James were deficient in what Mr. Malone is pleased to call taste ? To say nothing of the men, (who were trained to a high sense of decorum and intellectual discernment under Elizabeth,) the Veres, the Wroths, the Derbys, the Bedfords, the Rutlands, the Cliffords and the Arundels, who danced in the fairy rings, in the gay and gallant circles of these enchanting devices, of which our most splendid shows are at best but beggarly parodies, were fully as accomplished in every internal and external grace as those who, in our days, have succeeded to their names and honours.

Mr. Malone sets down the masques of James, (probably because they were written by Jonson,) as " bungling shows ;" when he has to speak of one produced by Heywood in 1636, he is then disposed to admit that the "art of scenery" was somewhat improved ! This is merely absurd. The art had attained its utmost degree of excellence at the death of this monarch ; it declined under his successor ; and, notwithstanding all the efforts of Inigo Jones, and his poet, Master Aurelian Townshend, it gradually lost its distinguishing characteristics, and fell back into the pageant and masquerade from which the genius and learning of our author had so happily reclaimed it.

A few years after the Restoration, an attempt was made by Charles II. to revive this species of entertainment. The daughter of James II. (then Duke of York), and many of the young nobility of both sexes, appeared in a masque written by Crowne, called Calisto : but the passion did not spread ; nor was it possible that it should. Crowne, though not altogether illiterate, was devoid of fancy, and the court itself was too frivolous, too ignorant, and too licentious for the enjoyment of elegant and rational pleasures. We hear of the masque no more.

Some time elapsed, after the death of our author, before any of his later productions appeared ; two small editions of his minor pieces were at length sent to the press in 1640, and in the subsequent year a wretched reprint of the first folio, and a second volume of the same size, containing his dramatic pieces from 1612, several masques and all that could be found of his occasional poetry, were published together. Several of the comedies appear to have been taken from the prompter's book, and surreptitiously printed (but not published) during the author's life ; how the rest were procured I know not.

Such of his dramas as were revived at the Restoration were printed separately ; and in 1692 the whole of his writings were again collected, and published in one huge folio volume. The demand for his works must have been considerable for those days, since

---

[1] "Masques (says one of the completest gentlemen of that age), the courtly recreations of gallant gentlemen and ladies of honour, striving to exceed one the other in their measures and changes, and in their repasts of wit, have been beyond the power of envy to disgrace."—Higford's Institution of a Gentleman.

in 1715 the booksellers were encouraged to prepare another edition, which they gave the world in six volumes 8vo. This publication was merely a reprint of the old copy, and with this, defective as it was, the town was content till the year 1756, when a more complete edition, in seven volumes 8vo, was published by the Rev. Peter Whalley, LL.B.

Mr. Whalley had received an academical education, and he was competent in some measure to the undertaking. He did little, however, for the poet; the form of the old editions was rigidly observed, and though a few notes were subjoined, they were seldom of material import, and never explanatory of the author's general views, though they occasionally touched on his language. It is not a little remarkable that this gentleman, who was master of the Grammar School of Christ's Hospital, and must naturally have been somewhat conversant with the ancient writers, should not have ventured on one remark of a literary nature, everything of this kind, which occurs in his edition, being, as I discovered with some surprise, taken from Upton and others.

Whether Whalley was diffident of himself, or the gentlemen volunteered their assistance, I have no means of knowing, but he availed himself occasionally of the aid of Sympson and Seward, (the editors of Beaumont and Fletcher,) who led him astray, and where he would have been simply wrong, if left to himself, rendered him absurd. In one pleasant way of making notes, and swelling the bulk of the book, they all agreed. None of them printed from the earliest editions;[1] they took up the latest which they could find, and went smoothly on till they were stopped by some palpable error of the press. This, as the clown says, *was meat and drink to them;* they immediately set themselves to conjecture what the word should be, and after a little burst of vanity, at which it is impossible to forbear a smile, they turned for the first time to the old copy, and invited the public to witness their sagacity, and partake in their triumph. An example or two taken at random from Whalley, will make this clear.

> " Long may he round about him see
> His roses and his lilies *bloom!*
> Long may his only love and he
> Joy in ideas of their own!"

" I have no objection to *bloom*, but only as it does not rhyme very exactly with *own,* I conjectured that it should be *blown;* and found my conjecture authorized by the old folio." vol. vii. p. 16.

> " Valour wins applause,
> That dares but to *mention* the weaker cause."

" No great applause of valour can be due to any one merely for *mentioning* the weaker side. This led me to conjecture that *maintain* was the word designed by the poet, and upon consulting the first folio, I found it so to be!" vol. v. 297.

> " Your *fortress* who hath bred you to this hour."

" Fortress is an error. Mr. Sympson likewise saw the mistake, and ingeniously sent me *fautress,* which I should have made use of, had not the old folio prevented me, and read *fostress!*"

Whalley prefixed to his edition a Life of the author; not injudicious in the main, but composed in a style so uncouth and antiquated, that I could not prevail on myself to reprint it, though I have thought it my duty to make a few extracts from it; chiefly, however, for the purpose of correcting the mistakes into which the writer had been led by too implicit a reliance on his authorities.

The reception of this work was sufficiently favourable to encourage the author to undertake a revision of it preparatory to a second edition. I cannot discover, however, that any substantial improvement was meditated, none at least was introduced, and the text remained in every instance as it stood before. The bulk of the work, indeed, was materially increased by the admission of an immense farrago of parallel

---

[1] Whalley's text was that of the Booksellers' edition, in 8vo. This had been in Theobald's hands, and an incidental remark by him, of no moment whatever, here and there appeared in the margin.

passages, taken, for the most part, from the numerous republications of Shakspeare, to which the last century had given birth. He did not proceed with this revision much beyond the comedies ; circumstances, with which I am but imperfectly acquainted, interrupted his literary pursuits, and this among the rest. It is said that the extravagance of a young wife involved him in pecuniary difficulties of a serious kind, and obliged him to leave his home. In this distress he was received into the house of Mr. Waldron, where he lay concealed for some time ; when the place of his retreat was at length discovered, he took refuge in Flanders, where he died after a few months' residence, in the summer of 1791.

Under the hospitable roof of this worthy and amiable man, Whalley resumed the care of Jonson ; but want of books, and, perhaps, of sufficient composure of mind, rendered his attempts ineffectual, and the manuscript was finally abandoned to his friend ; who, in the year 1792, commenced the publication of it in numbers. The success apparently fell short of the expectations of the editor, as the work was not continued beyond the second number.

Mr. Waldron neither possessed, nor pretended to be possessed of, scholastic learning : but he was laborious, accurate, conversant with the stage, and imbued with a rational love of the ancient drama, which he had studied with success. He appears to have collated Whalley's copy with the early editions ; and, on attentively retracing his steps, previously to the arrangement of the text for the present publication, I found much to approve in the caution and judgment with which he had uniformly proceeded. His friendship for Whalley, however, had led him to form far too high an estimate of that gentleman's qualifications ; and beyond the revision which I have just mentioned, he seems to have contemplated no alteration of the papers left in his hands.

Many years had elapsed since the failure last mentioned, when the republication of Jonson was proposed to me by Mr. George Nichol, to whom Whalley's corrected copy had been consigned by Mr. Waldron. I was well aware of the labour and difficulty of the task ; but my objections were overcome by the encouragement of my friend, and I undertook the edition, confident that I was not about to encumber the public with a superfluous work, for Jonson had now been long out of the booksellers' hands. One motive there yet was, which had some influence on my determination,—a desire, though late, to render justice to the moral character of the author, and rescue him from the calumnies of his inveterate persecutors. My mind had been prejudiced at an early period, by the commentators on our old dramas, and I verily believed, as they repeatedly assured me, that "the great object of Jonson's life was the persecution of Shakspeare," nor was it until I became acquainted with the dates of his respective performances, that I ventured to question the accuracy of the critics, or to entertain a suspicion that they were actuated by unworthy motives, and could only be relieved from the charge of wanton malevolence, by the plea of incorrigible folly.

Previously to the arrangement of the text, it became necessary to collate the old editions. In the execution of this part of the work, the mode adopted in the revision of Massinger was carefully followed : if the approbation of the public may be trusted, no change was required.

Had any standard of orthoëpy obtained among our old writers, it might not be improper to preserve it ; but to copy the vagaries of a careless press, would be an affectation of accuracy at once impertinent and unprofitable. Our author appears, indeed, to affect a derivative mode of spelling ; but his attention frequently relaxes, and the variations of his text are considerable ; the first folio differs from the quarto, and the second folio from both. In general, writers trusted entirely to the printers, who, on their parts, piqued themselves but little on justifying this confidence. "I never (says the author of *Father Hubbard's Tales*) wisht myself a better fortune than to fall into the hands of a true-spelling printer,"—and he was not so lucky. There seems no plausible reason for continuing to present Jonson alone to the public in the uncouth and antiquated garb of his age : the barbarous contractions, therefore, the syncopes and apocopes, which deformed the old folios, (for the quartos are remarkably free from them), have been regulated, and, in some cases removed, and the appearance of the poet's page assimilated, in a great degree, to that of his contemporaries, who spoke and wrote the same language as himself. Whalley, as has been just observed, though the modernized impressions of Shakspeare and others were before him, contented himself with simply reprinting the former text, with all its archaisms and anomalies; the same word was differently spelt in the same page, and sometimes in the same line; the pointing was seldom disturbed, the scenes were divided as the old books divided them, and not an *exit* or *entrance* was superadded; yet it could not have escaped him that no part of this arrangement made the slightest claim to uniformity or even truth. In fact, the object of the old division would almost appear to be that of throwing every obstacle in the way of the reader, and making that which could, in no case, be easy, a matter of extreme difficulty. A certain number of the dramatis personæ are set down at long intervals, but no hint is given when they appear or disappear, individually, and much time has been expended in the obscure and humble labour of inserting a name which, after all, may not be found correctly placed. Jonson, probably, adopted this costive mode from the ancient drama, but it seems to have escaped him that the Greek and Roman stage seldom permitted more than four characters to be present at the same time; whereas he has frequently introduced (especially in his *Catiline* and *Sejanus*), double, and sometimes treble that number. The scenery too, (by which nothing more is intended than the supposed place of action), was everywhere obscure, and, in the tragedies, perplexed and involved above measure. Our author, like his contemporaries, seems, in these, to have taken advantage of the poverty of the stage, and the easy faith of the audience, to represent events in the same spot, which must, in fact, have occurred in different places. Be this as it may, an attempt has been made to specify the scene in every action; and it is necessary to entreat the indulgence of the public towards this first effort to give a *local habitation and a name*, to what before had neither. In this, I have consulted the ease of the reader, who could scarcely be expected to turn the page forward and backward to ascertain the site of every event, especially as the difficulty occurs, for the most part, in those pieces which possess the fewest charms of sentiment, action, or language, to lure him on through doubt and obscurity to the point of elucidation. That the poet will be more read on this account, I dare not flatter myself; but I venture to hope that he will be comprehended with more facility; and, in this, I have already found my reward. Slight, however, as the effect may appear, it has not been produced without some pains; nor should I have been able to complete it entirely to my own satisfaction, or greatly to the advantage of the reader, had I not fortunately found in Mr. Thomas Turner,[1] (of Mr. Bulmer's office), a friend whose readiness to oblige was only equalled by his professional skill; and whose acquaintance with various parts of literature, far removed from the common track of reading, has been beneficially exerted through the course of this undertaking.

It appears from Mr. Whalley's correspondence, that his enlarged copy had been in the hands of Steevens, Reed, and Malone. What they took, or what they gave, I am unable to say; but my first care was to throw it all aside: my objection to an idle accumulation of examples upon every trite or indecorous expression, is by no means weakened since the publication of Massinger, though I have been openly reproved for the nakedness of my pages, and the obstinate refusal to illustrate "after the manner of Mr. Collins," the admired colloquies of Hircius and Spungius![2] What I could find of utility in my predecessor's observations, is retained, though with occasional variations of his language: my own notes have run to a greater length than was originally intended; but the ground was, in a manner unbeaten. They are chiefly illustrative of obsolete phrases and customs, of personal and historical notices connected with the subject, together with such incidental touches on the character and conduct of the

---

[1] [The father of my old friend and schoolfellow, Thomas Hudson Turner, whose work on the *Domestic Architecture of the Middle Ages*, incomplete though it be, will long preserve its author's name from oblivion.—F. C.]

[2] After explaining myself so fully, as I thought, on this subject, it is with pain that I find myself compelled to return to it. I should think no sacrifice on my part too great, if I could but convince the grovelling editors of our old dramatists that the filth and obscenity which they so sedulously toil to explain, is better understood by ninety-nine out of every hundred readers than by themselves, and that the turpitude of corrupting the remaining one is a crime for which their ignorance offers no adequate excuse. A plodding cold-blooded Aretine is despicable; a sprightly one is detestable; and both are among the worst pests of society.

respective pieces, as the occasion seemed to demand. There will also be found some explanatory remarks on the language of Shakspeare, a part of the work which should have been extended, (as there is nothing which I so much desire as to see him relieved from the ponderous ignorance of his commentators), had I not once flattered myself that an opportunity might hereafter occur of serving him more effectually :—that day-dream is passed ; and I am left to regret that I was so chary of my observations.

There is little to add. Assuredly, I anticipated more gratification from the termination of this undertaking than I seem to experience. I cannot give pleasure where I once hoped to give it ; and fame, or if it must be so, vanity, appears, I know not how, in colours of less seductive brightness :—the fairy vision has receded as I advanced; and the toilsome way is terminated amidst prospects of no cheering kind : I cannot conceal from myself how little has been done for an author of such exalted claims, nor how greatly I have fallen short of the justice which I once hoped to render to him. The work is now before the public. It is not exempt from errors, as will easily be discovered ; and the origin of some of them may be found in the lights (all favourable to the poet) which have broken in upon me since its commencement; such as it is, however, it is given with a free and independent spirit. No difficulty has been evaded, no labour shunned: neither hopes nor fears of a personal nature have had the slightest influence upon the conduct of the undertaking ; what has been strongly felt has been strongly expressed ; and if, before the occasional warmth of my language be challenged, the violence and injustice which I have had to repel be examined, I shall not, in this instance at least, be alarmed at the result.

What remains is pleasure. The generosity by which I was enabled to furnish so correct a text of Massinger has accompanied me with a double portion of frankness on the present occasion. Every early edition of these dramas, and almost every copy, has been tendered to my use. Mr. Kemble, whose kindness is perpetual, opened his vast collection to me with unbounded liberality. Mr. Waldron, who has taken the warmest interest in my success, not only supplied me with much valuable matter, collected from various sources during the long period that his attention was fixed on our author, but procured from Mr. Parke and other gentlemen, notices of scattered poems, plays, &c. which have been used with advantage. Of my friend Octavius Gilchrist, no particular mention is required here ; his name will be found in various parts of these volumes, in connection with information that will always be received with satisfaction. The Rev. Mr. Bandinell has been already noticed ; and I have now to add the name of Mr. Philip Bliss, who forwarded my researches at the Bodleian with all the alacrity of friendship ; nor must I forget Mr. Petrie, to whose kindness I have been singularly obliged, and to whom I am indebted for the knowledge of many useful MSS. in our public repositories. I forbear to mention more—but I should do violence to my own feelings, in closing this part of the work without adding that, if the reader has derived either amusement or information from the explanatory notes diffused over these volumes, it is to the unprecedented kindness of Richard Heber, Esq. that he is mainly indebted. The liberality with which this gentleman communicates the literary treasures of his extensive collection is too well known to be particularly insisted on here ; but he has claims to my thankfulness which must not be passed in silence. To open his library to all my requests was not sufficient in his eyes, he therefore spontaneously furnished me with a number of rare and valuable pieces material to my success, and with several of which I was not acquainted even by name. In diligently availing myself of these aids, I have constantly borne in mind that I was making the return most pleasing to my generous friend, though scarcely full enough to satisfy myself.

I have yet to mention the Very Reverend the Dean of Westminster. Avocations of a nature far removed from studies of this kind engross his leisure ; yet no one acquainted with any publication of mine, can require to be told that no part of the present work has passed the press without his anxious revision.—But with what feelings do I trace the words—*the Dean of Westminster !*—Five-and-forty springs have now passed over my head, since I first found Dr. Ireland, some years my junior, in our little school, at his spelling-book. During this long period, our friendship has been without a cloud my delight in youth, my pride and consolation in age. I have followed, with an interest that few can feel and none can know, the progress of my friend from the humble state of a curate to the elevated situation which he has now reached, and in every successive change have seen, with inexpressible delight, his reputation and the wishes of the public precede his advancement. His piety, his learning, his conscientious discharge of his sacred duties, his unwearied zeal to promote the interests of all around him, will be the theme of other times and other pens : it is sufficient for my happiness to have witnessed at the close of a career, prolonged by Infinite Goodness far beyond my expectations, the friend and companion of my heart in that dignified place, which while it renders his talents and his virtues more conspicuous, derives every advantage from their wider influence and exertion.

Proofs of Ben Jonson's Malignity,

From the Commentators on Shakspeare.

NOTWITHSTANDING the remarks which will be found scattered over the succeeding volumes, respecting the alleged hostility of Jonson to Shakspeare, it appears to me that I should but imperfectly discharge my duty unless I presented the reader with a concentrated view of a part of the proofs by which the accusation is supposed to be made good. Our dramatic literature has been absolutely poisoned by the malice of Jonson's persecutors. Whoever brought forward an old poet offered up a victim to his fame, and this victim was invariably our author : but while it was generously admitted that the rest of his contemporaries felt his malignity only at intervals, it was universally affirmed that his abuse of Shakspeare was unremitted. Neither writer nor reader ever dreamed of questioning the accuracy of this statement ; and nothing could be more amusing than the complacent simplicity with which it was handed down from Mr. Malone to Mr. Weber, from Mr. G. Chalmers to Mr. Stephen Jones.

It is to the praise of Mr. Gilchrist that he was the first person who, amidst the general outcry against Jonson, evinced sufficient honesty to investigate the truth, and sufficient courage to declare it. His little Publication[1] startled the critics, though it could not silence them. His triumph, however, was complete ; for he had justice on his side ; and there is something ludicrous in the half-concessions which the force of his facts occasionally elicits from his opponents. I should have reprinted his Essay, of which I have made a liberal use, had I not hoped that he would one day give it to the world himself with the additional matter of which I know him to be possessed.

The attack on Jonson for his supposed hostility to Shakspeare appears to have commenced with Dryden. Every word that the commentators on our great poet advance respecting the mention of this hostility by contemporary writers is, in unqualified terms, A POSITIVE FALSEHOOD. Not one of the enemies of Jonson, not one of the friends of Shakspeare, drops the slightest hint of such a circumstance during the lives of these poets ; on the contrary, they speak of Jonson's esteem for Shakspeare :

> " It is not fit each humble muse should make,
> Thy worth his subject—
> Let learned Jonson sing a dirge for thee,
> And fill our orb with mournful harmony," &c.

Not a word of hatred, envy, jealousy, and those other amiable passions, which now make so conspicuous a figure ; these were the figments of a later period : but my present business is with the last editors of Shakspeare. Before I proceed, however, it may not be inexpedient to state my own sense of the question. It is my fixed persuasion, then, (not lightly adopted, but deduced from a wide examination of the subject,) that Jonson never received either patronage, favour, or assistance of any kind from Shakspeare. I am further persuaded that they were friends and associates till the latter finally retired ; that no feud, no jealousy ever disturbed their connexion ; that Shakspeare was pleased with Jonson, and that Jonson loved and admired Shakspeare. What else I have to say will be found as the reader proceeds.

---

[1] *Examination of the charges maintained by Malone, Chalmers, and others, of Jonson's enmity, &c. towards Shakspeare*, 1808.

f

Shak. vol. i. p. 12. Mr. Malone is so eager to begin his attack on our author, that he enters upon it ere he has well opened the book. His first "labour of love" is to bring back the scurrilous falsehoods which Rowe had rejected on conviction, because he (Mr. Malone) "believes them to be strictly true," except that they are of too favourable a nature !

"Dryden, we are told by Pope, concurred with Mr. Rowe, in thinking" (observe that Rowe had cancelled the expression, and no longer thought so) "Jonson's post-humous verses on Shakspeare *sparing* and *invidious.*"—p. 12.

Mr. Malone's language is not very accurate. But leaving this,—Mr. Rowe does not allude to *any verses;* his opinion of Jonson's therefore is not quite so clear as the critic supposes. Rowe speaks (in the rejected paragraph) of the *Discoveries,* not of the Poem on Shakspeare's death, as Mr. Malone must have seen, if he had read either of them. And where does Pope say "that Dryden concurred with Mr. Rowe in thinking the verses on Shakspeare *sparing* and *invidious ?*" For the reader's satisfaction, I will transcribe what Mr. Pope really does say—"I cannot, for my own part, find any thing invidious or sparing in these verses ; but *wonder* Mr. Dryden was of that opinion. Jonson exalts Shakspeare not only above all his contemporaries, but above Chaucer and Spenser, whom he will not allow to be ranked with him : and challenges the name of Sophocles, Euripides, and Æschylus, nay all Greece and Rome at once to equal him," &c.—*Shak.* vol. i. p. 116. It must be confessed that this is an excellent passage to prove "old Ben's *envy* of Shakspeare !" Let us say that Mr. Malone was out of luck in referring to it : and yet, not quite so much as in referring to the next authority, which he does in the same line. "See also (he says) Mr. Steevens's *note* on those verses."—With pain I have *seen* it ; and with disgust will the reader learn, that this "note of Mr. Steevens" is neither more nor less than the identical letter of Macklin's which Mr. Malone had previously employed nearly thirty pages in proving to be a forgery from end to end ! The exposure occurs in the first volume, the "note" at the end of the second ; so that Mr. Malone intrepidly hurries past his own refutation in quest of a known falsehood to bolster up a recorded lie.

"Before Shakspeare's death Ben's envious disposition is mentioned by one of his own friends.

> " Thou'rt sound in body ; but some say thy mind
> Envy doth ulcer ; yet *corrupted hearts*
> *Such censurers must have.*"—p. 12.

This is excellent. Does Mr. Malone suppose that the most innocent man on earth is exempt from calumny? But the line which notices the calumny, also refutes it. It is the unjust attack of Decker and others in the *Satiromastix,* brought forward merely for the sake of exposing its malice. Those who accuse you of envy, says the writer to Jonson, must *have corrupted hearts !* Is Mr. Malone content to abide by this criterion ? "The mind (as Mr. Gilchrist well observes on this passage) can picture to itself no case more mortifying than that of Mr. Malone, who after having with unwearied industry turned up the ample dunghill of defamation, meets at last with this palpable and severe reproof of his labours."

The "friend" of our author is John Davies, the writing-master, who amused himself with composing little pieces of doggrel verse on every man within the circle of his know-ledge. Mr. Malone never read Jonson, and may therefore be excused for not dis-covering that he disclaims this "friendship." But how is it that he has forgotten to observe that Davies was also Shakspeare's "own friend," and that he informs his "good Wil." in the following page, that people "railed at him also ?" Would Mr. Malone think it just to adopt his own mode of argument, and conclude, from this passage, that Shakspeare deserved to be *railed* at ?

"The following verses by one of Jonson's admirers support Mr. Rowe in what he says," (still copying what Mr. Rowe had thrown aside as unfounded,) "relative to his slowness."

> "*Scorn then their censures* who give out thy wit
> As long upon a comedy did sit
> As elephants bring forth," &c.—p. 12.

And this too is excellent. The writer, (Jasper Mayne,) in a poem on Jonson's death, recommends a contempt of such censures; therefore they are called in to support a charge disclaimed by the author! But Mr. Malone proceeds with his quotation:—

> " That the king's yearly butt wrote, and his wine
> Had more right than thou to thy *Catiline.*"

Catiline was written in 1611, and the yearly butt was not conferred on Jonson till 1630, so that Mayne could not have produced a more striking proof of the absurd malice of the poet's enemies: but Mr. Malone sees nothing of this.

" The *Return from Parnassus* furnishes us with the earliest intimation of the *quarrel* between Jonson and Shakspeare:[1] and Fuller, who lived near enough the time to be well informed, *confirms* this account."—p. 13.

I will give Fuller's words. " Many were the wit-combates between Shakspeare and Ben Jonson. I behold them like a Spanish great galleon, and an English man-of-war. Master Jonson, like the former, was built far higher in learning, solid but slow in his performances; Shakspeare, like the latter, lesser in bulk, but lighter in sailing, could turn with all tides, tack about, and take advantage of all winds by the quickness of his wit and invention."—*Fuller,* vol. ii. p. 415.

These " wit-combates " then (on which Mr. Malone founds a charge of hostility,) turn out after all to be those sprightly repartees which so delighted their common friends. The solid attacks on Jonson repelled by the quick and lively sallies of Shakspeare (great masters, as both were, of conversation,) must, indeed, have been a mental treat of the highest kind, and could have given to no one, but one commentator, an idea of malice or ill-will on either side. There is nothing visible to ordinary eyes, but the fulness of friendship, enlivened by a social meeting, and tending to hilarity and festive delight. Yet this is produced to prove Jonson's *enmity!* What idea of friendship Mr. Malone had formed, I know not; but it seems as if he thought that the conversation of all but deadly foes must, like trade winds, *tend all one way.* Our author had other notions of friendship, and, I believe, correcter ones: he says,

> " It is an act of tyranny, not love,
> In practised friendship, wholly to approve."

Again:

> " Little know they that profess amity,
> And seek to scant her *comely liberty,*
> How much they lame her in her property."
> Vol. iii. *Underwoods* No. lvi.

" It is a singular circumstance that old Ben should for near two centuries have stalked on the stilts of *artificial* reputation."—p. 13.

If Jonson's reputation be " artificial," then, as the poet says, is " earth's base built on stubble." And who is it that presumes to oppose his private opinion to the universal award of " two centuries," and ridicule the attainments of Jonson? *Sanguinis in facie—!*

---

[1] See p. xxv, where this quarrel is noticed. In the recent edition of Beaumont and Fletcher too, it is referred to "as a proof of Jonson's *enmity,*" and called "that *strong* passage." When will this folly end?—But, true; it is a STRONG passage, a very STRONG one—but against whom? Frankly, I speak it, against Shakspeare, who, if Will Kempe be worthy of credit, wantonly interfered in a contest with which he had no concern, and ridiculed a man whose only crime (as far as related to himself,) was an unbounded regard for his persecutor.

Now I am on the subject of this old play, I will just venture to inform those egregious critics that the heroes of it are laughing both at Wil. Kempe and Shakspeare. Of Shakspeare's plays they neither know nor say anything: when they have to mention him in their own character, they speak merely of his *Lucrece* and his *Venus and Adonis.* Yet Shakspeare had then written several of his best pieces, and Jonson not one of his. I suspect that Mr. Malone would not have been much pleased with Ingenioso and Judicio, (who are, it must be confessed, a couple of pedantic coxcombs,) if he had read what they say of our author.

" *Jud.* Ben Jonson. The wittiest fellow of a bricklayer in England.

" *Ingen.* A mere empiric: one that gets what he hath by observation, and makes only *nature* privy to what he indites."—This is not altogether the critic's creed.

We shall now, I suppose, hear little more of Wil. Kempe—who was probably brought on the stage in a fool's cap to make mirth for the University wits; and who is dismissed, together with his associate, in a most contemptuous manner, as " a *mere leaden spout,*" &c.

"Ben, however, did not trust to the praises of others. One of his admirers honestly confesses

> " He
> Of whom I write this, has prevented me,
> And boldly said so much in his own praise,
> No other pen need any trophy raise.'—p. 13.

This *admirer*, whom Mr. Malone, when he next mentions him, calls "Ben's *old antagonist* " (p. 640), is Owen Feltham. But what shall be said of Mr. Malone? A judicial blindness appears to have fallen upon him the instant that he approached Jonson. Deprive him of this plea, and no terms will be strong enough to describe the excess of ignorance or his malice. The *praise* refers to our author's works. It is in the composition of his *Sejanus, Catiline*, and other poems mentioned by Feltham that he pronounces Jonson to have said so much in his own praise as to make the applause of his friends superfluous : and the critic expressly contrasts his conduct, in this respect, with that of the "trivial poets, whose chatterings live and fall at once."

"In vain, however, did Jonson endeavour to bully the town—by pouring out against those who preferred Shakspeare to him, *a torrent of illiberal* abuse."—p. 14. To this atrocious charge there is but one answer which occurs to me ; and though that be usually wrapped up in the courtesy of a learned language, I shall not make use of it.

All this, and much more, is produced in support of a passage which the author of it had deliberately cancelled on account of its falsity ; though he had every one of Mr. Malone's "proofs" before him ! We now come to another rejected paragraph, also brought back by Mr. Malone : and the history of it is not a little amusing.

Hales of Eton was reported to have said (though the matter was not much in Hales of Eton's way,) " that there was no subject of which any person ever writ, but he would produce it much better done by Shakspeare."—p. 16. This is told by Dryden, 1667. The next version is by Tate, 1680. "Our learned Hales was wont to assert that since the time of Orpheus, no commonplace has been touched upon, where Shakspeare has not performed as well." Next comes the illustrious Gildon (of Dunciad memory), and he models the story thus, from Dryden, as he says, with a salvo for the accuracy of his recollection ! "Mr. Hales of Eton affirmed that he would show all the poets of antiquity outdone by Shakspeare. The *enemies* of Shakspeare would by no means yield to this ; so it came to a trial of skill. The place agreed on for the dispute was Mr. Hales's chamber at Eton.[1] A great many *books were sent down* by the enemies of this poet, and on the appointed day my Lord Falkland, Sir John Suckling, and *all the persons of quality* that had wit and learning met there, and upon a thorough disquisition of the point, the judges chosen out of this assembly unanimously gave the preference to Shakspeare, and the Greek and Roman poets were adjudged to vail at least their glory in that to the English poet."—p. 17.

This stuff, which is merely worthy of Gildon—this flocking of persons of quality to Eton, with satchels of school-books, doubled down, it may be presumed, at the proper places—as if they could read in no books but their own, or as if Hales[2] could not supply them—is too despicable for further notice. But what, the reader will say, has all this to do with Jonson? We find no mention of him whatever. A moment's patience, and he will make his appearance ; for Mr. Malone has him in full view. The story now reached Rowe ; and as it was discovered about this time that the praise of Shakspeare was worth nothing unless coupled with the abuse of Jonson, it puts on this form: "Mr. Hales, who had sat still some time, hearing Ben reproach Shakspeare with the want of learning, and ignorance of the ancients, told him at last," &c. Thus it stood in the first edition : but Mr. Rowe was an honest man, and having found occasion

---

[1] "To this *chamber* (say his biographers) Mr. Hales retired from the College in 1644," that is, seven years after Jonson's death !

[2] Hales, who was one of the first scholars of his time, is celebrated by Wood for the extensiveness of his library, and Lord Clarendon says,

"that Hales had a greater and better collection of books than were to be found in any private library that he ever saw :"—yet Sir John Suckling, who probably never read a word of Greek in his life, must take down his own book !

to change his mind before the appearance of the second edition, he struck the passage out, and inserted in its stead, "Sir John Suckling, who was a professed admirer of Shakspeare,[1] had undertaken, with some warmth, his defence against Ben Jonson, when Mr. Hales," &c.

Thus we have the fable of the *Three Black Crows!* and thus a simple observation of Mr. Hales (which, in all probability he never made), is dramatized at length into a scene of obloquy against our author! A tissue of mere dotage scarcely deserves unravelling ; but it may be just observed that when Jonson was seized with his last illness, (after which he certainly never went "to Mr. Hales's chamber, at Eton" or elsewhere) the two grave judges, Suckling and Falkland, who sat on the merits of all the Greek and Roman poets, and decided with such convincing effect, were, the first in the twelfth and the second in the fifteenth year of their ages ! But the chief mistake lies with Dryden, whose memory was always subservient to the passion of the day ; the words which he has put into the mouth of Mr. Hales being, in fact, the property of Jonson. Long before Suckling and Falkland were out of leading strings, he had told the world that Shakspeare surpassed not only all his contemporary poets, but even those of Greece and Rome ;[2] and if Mr. Hales used these words, without giving the credit of them to Jonson, he was, to say the least of it, a bold plagiarist.

This stupid anecdote is thus concluded by Mr. Malone : " Let ever-memorable Hales, if all his other merits be forgotten, be ever mentioned with honour for his taste and admiration of Shakspeare ;" and let Jonson, who taught him both, and who went farther in both than himself, be for ever held up to the world as the reviler, hater, and persecutor of Shakspeare alive and dead. These last words seem to have been dropped at the press ; at least, I do not find them in Mr. Malone's edition, though he has everywhere acted upon them.

"Antony Munday is *ridiculed* here by Ben Jonson ; but he might notwithstanding be *deservedly eminent ;* that *malignity* which endeavoured to *tear a wreath from the brow of Shakspeare,* would certainly not spare inferior writers."—p. 481. Mr. Malone is no great logician—but let that pass. The passage to which he refers was probably written before Jonson knew Shakspeare ; for it occurs in one of his earliest pieces. With respect to the *eminence* of Antony, it is somewhat scurvily treated by Decker, Chapman, and Middleton ; it is not therefore a necessary consequence that the wreath of Shakspeare was endangered by this ridicule.

"*Every Man in his Humour,* said to be acted in 1598, appears to be Jonson's first performance, and we may presume that it was the very play which we are told was brought on the stage by the good offices of Shakspeare. *Malignant* and *envious* as Jonson appears to be, he hardly would have *ridiculed* his benefactor at the very time he was so essentially obliged to him.[3] *Some* years afterwards his *jealousy* broke out ; and vented itself in this Prologue which first appeared in 1616. It is *certain* that not long after the year 1600,[3] (again referring to the *Return from Parnassus!*) a coldness arose between Shakspeare and him, which, however he may talk of his almost idolatrous affection, produced, *on his part,*" (what is become of Shakspeare's "ballad against Jonson"?) from that time, 1600,[4] " to the death of Shakspeare, and for many years afterwards, much *clumsy sarcasm,* and many *malevolent* reflections."—p. 481.

<hr>

[1] Where does this appear?—the only authority for the assertion is, I am confident, Suckling's *Session of the Poets.* To censure Jonson with good-humoured wit for an unlucky play, is sufficient, in the eyes of the critics, to constitute an admirer of Shakspeare. But Suckling passed his days with the admirers of Jonson. Endymion Porter too, who was also present at this congress of sages, was an especial admirer of Jonson, though Mr. Malone and his *sportive* forger, Macklin, were not aware of it ; and befriended him much in his last illness.

[2] See p. 5.

[3] This is generous : for Mr. Malone had, in the very last quotation, accused Jonson of attempting *to tear the wreath* from Shakspeare's brow at the precise moment (1598) that he now affirms he would not do it ! But, one word more : as Mr. Malone affirms this to be Jonson's *first* performance, and the very occasion of his becoming acquainted with Shakspeare, where, with his permission, is that *malignity* and *envy,* so *apparent,* (as he says,) to be met with ? In Jonson's school-exercises ? or in his MS. scenes left at the Green Curtain ? Of all calumniators, Mr. Malone is the most headlong.

[4] Mr. Malone had just said that this jealousy broke out in the Prologue, written, by his own account, thirteen years afterwards !

The critic had already forgotten his unfortunate letter, p. 108, in which he admits that "old Ben's jealousy did not fully display itself till Shakspeare retired from the stage." This goblin Prologue haunts Mr. Malone so incessantly, that it absolutely confounds his faculties. He remembers neither what he would say, nor what he actually does say ; but blunders on from one absurdity to another in a manner truly pitiable : but the reader must be weary of this interminable folly.

Mr. Malone now gives us over again the old quotation from Master Kempe ; which, instead of proving Jonson's *jealousy*, bears hard upon the justice and humanity of Shakspeare ; and, as if determined to empty the whole quiver of his fury upon our great poet, he thus proceeds : "Shakspeare has, however, *marked* his disregard for the *calumniator* of his fame [in the *Poetaster*, where he is not even alluded to !] by not leaving him any memorial by his will."—*Ibid.*

Now mark the contrast. Shakspeare (it is always Mr. Malone who supplies the argument) *ridicules* Jonson in 1600, without a shadow of provocation, maintains a *coldness* towards him for sixteen years, dies with *malice* in his heart, and, *to make it as public as possible*, leaves him no legacy ! Jonson, instead of manifesting any resentment at this contemptuous treatment, openly professes his affection for Shakspeare, and pours forth the most cordial and honourable testimony to his talents and virtues that ever dropped from the tongue of man !

Mr. Malone has rendered much the same sort of kind office to Shakspeare in his account of the transaction with "John-o-Combe," where the poet appears at once malevolent and ungrateful ! Thank heaven ! the character of Shakspeare is too well established by Jonson to be shaken by the blows dealt around him in blind fury by Mr. Malone : but this mode of *backing a friend*, though well meant, is not, after all, to be much commended.

> " I am sorry for
> Some better natures, by the rest drawn in
> To run in that vile line."

"By the words *better natures* there can, I think, be *little doubt* that Shakspeare was meant."—p. 541.

I hope, on the contrary, that there are *very great doubts*, or Shakspeare must again fall under the suspicion of unprovoked hostility to our author. What had Shakspeare to do with the wretched set of actors who burlesqued Jonson ? What charm could he find in associating with "the lean Poluphagus," the "fat fool who begged scarves," or even with the furious Decker, to persecute a young writer, at the Rose, the Hope, the Green Curtain, and other theatres, with which he had no concern ! If Jonson regretted that some honest men among them were "drawn in" by the misrepresentations of the rest, it is so far to the credit of his good nature. Shakspeare, I presume, may in future be relieved from the obloquy thus *thrust upon him* by the unlucky kindness of his friends.

"In the *Silent Woman*, 1609, Jonson perhaps pointed at Shakspeare as one whom he viewed with *scornful* yet *jealous* eyes : 'So they may censure poets, and compare Jonson with t'other youth.'—p. 415 a. Decker however may be meant !—p. 541.

"Again, in the same play : 'You two shall be the chorus behind the arras, and whip out between the acts, and speak.'"—p. 444 a. Ibid.

What is there of *scorn* and *jealousy* in this ? The reader will find some remarks on these and other passages adduced by Mr. Malone, in their respective places. I cannot stop here to notice malice in its dotage ; and this is nothing better.

"In the Induction to *Bartholomew Fair* (1614) three of Shakspeare's plays, and in the piece itself two others are *ridiculed*."—p. 542. Omitting the *three* for the present, the *two* ridiculed in the piece itself are *Julius Cæsar* in that important remark, "Come, there's no malice in these fat folks."—vol. ii. p. 162 a ; and *Lear*, in that equally interesting passage, "'Tis but a blister ; I'll take it away with the *white of an egg*, a little honey, and hog's grease."—vol. ii. p. 168 a.

About twelve years before this charge was made, Mr. Malone had written to Whalley : "I *agree with you entirely*, that *no ridicule* was intended against Shakspeare for the *white of an egg*." Very good.

"In the *Devil's an Ass*, all Shakspeare's *historical plays* are obliquely *censured*.'—p. 542.

"They are again attacked in the Induction to *Bartholomew Fair*"—p. 542. I thought that we had done with *Bartholomew Fair:* but the reader shall have the "attack on *all* Shakspeare's historical plays," as established by Mr. Malone.[1] "An some writer that I know had the penning of this matter, he would have made you such a jig-a-jog in the booth, you should have thought an earthquake had been in the Fair : but these master poets" (meaning Jonson himself, whom the bookholder had just been ridiculing for not introducing the usual feats of apes, jugglers, &c.) "will have their own courses, they will be informed of nothing." This is the passage—and now what does the reader think of the critic's assertion that *all the historical plays of Shakspeare are attacked in it!* What is more to the purpose, what does he think of his own simplicity in trusting to such a guide !

"The following passage in *Cynthia's Revels*, 1601, was, I think, likewise *pointed against Shakspeare*."—p. 542.

This charge is so utterly frantic, that I must content myself with referring to the words on which it is founded, vol. i. p. 146 a.[2]

"The Induction to the *Staple of News*, 1625, contains a *sneer* at *Julius Cæsar*."

"Other passages in Jonson might be mentioned in support of his *ridiculing* Shakspeare, but being quoted hereafter they are here omitted."—p. 542. This is kind ! but why were all these produced ? Nothing led to it but an overflowing of rancour, for the subject was the date of *Henry V.*, with which none of them have anything to do. "But," continues Mr. Malone, "notwithstanding these proofs" (so he calls this medley of absurdity and falsehood), "Jonson's *malevolence* to Shakspeare has been doubted by Mr. Pope and others." Full of amazement at such want of faith, he proceeds to overwhelm their incredulity by the aid of another " proof ;" and we have, once more, " the character of Jonson by his intimate friend Mr. Drummond of Hawthornden !" Assurance is thus made doubly sure, and Mr. Malone turns the page.

" Ben Jonson has in many places endeavoured to *ridicule* Shakspeare for representing battles on the stage."—p. 561.

"Again : he *ridicules* him in his *Silent Woman*. 'I would sit out a play that was nothing but fights at sea, drum, trumpet, and *target*.' "—(vol. i. p. 440 a), p. 562. Well ! but the prologue to *Henry VIII.* mentions the *noise of targets*. How is this ! Did Shakspeare *ridicule* himself? By no means, exclaim the commentators ; "for this prologue must have been written after Shakspeare's departure from the stage, by Ben Jonson." This point being once agreed on, the abuse of our author follows as a matter of course.

"It may seem extraordinary," continues Mr. Malone, "that Jonson should *presume* to prefix this covert *censure* of Shakspeare to one of his own plays." True, it may. "But he appears to have *eagerly embraced* every opportunity of *depreciating* him. Had Shakspeare been concerned in the theatre in 1613 he would scarcely have suffered the lines to have been spoken, but he had retired from the stage some years before his death, careless to the fate of his writings, inattentive to the *illiberal* attacks of his contemporaries, and negligent alike of his present and posthumous fame." The ink was not out of Mr. Malone's pen, the note was not finished, when he thus checks himself : "Since the above was written, I have seen a mortgage which was executed by Shakspeare in March 1613 : from this Deed we find that Shakspeare was *still* in *London !*" Yet Mr. Malone has not the liberality to cancel his slander ; but meanly attempts to bolster up what he had just given as a *fact*, by a *gratuitous supposition :* "Shakspeare *might*, however, have parted with his property !"—p. 561.

Now observe : "It has generally been believed" (it is still Mr. Malone who speaks,) " that Shakspeare ceased to write for the stage about three years before his death ; this

---

[1] The speaker is an ignorant stage-keeper at one of the puppet-show booths in Bartholomew Fair ; and all that he says has reference to the farces and drolls exhibited there : beyond these he never looks ; and the *writer* of whom he speaks was some popular composer of them.

[2] One word, however, may be subjoined. Jonson says "They would wish *your poets*, &c." —Now Shakspeare, who is said by Mr. Malone to be distinctly pointed at in this passage, happens to be the *only* writer whom we can positively affirm *not* to be pointed at. So far from being one of *the poets* of the Children of the Revels, he was in the most decided opposition to them, and in his *Hamlet*, written not long before this play appeared, had ridiculed them with equal wit and severity. Such is Mr Malone's constant good luck !

must now be considered as extremely doubtful. It is *improbable* that such an excursive genius should have been immediately reconciled to a state of mental inactivity. It is *more natural* to conceive that he should have occasionally turned his thoughts towards the theatre which his muse had supported, and the *interest* of his associates whom he had left behind—and whom his last will shows us he had not forgotten."—p. 612.

Every syllable of this is in direct opposition to what Mr. Malone had just advanced, that he might have an occasion to criminate Jonson. But this is not all. The prologue to *Henry VIII.*, it seems, was written by our author " to *ridicule* Shakspeare ;" and the whole weight of the commentators' fury is directed against him, and him alone. "Jonson," says one of them, "in all probability maliciously stole this opportunity to throw in his *envious* and *spiteful invective* before the representation of his rival's play." *Henry VIII.* p. 348. But what influence had Jonson at the Globe, of which Shakspeare or his "associates" Heminge, Burbage, and Condell, were, at this time, the sole managers and proprietors ? Who employed Jonson to write this Prologue ? Shakspeare's associates. Who spoke it ? Shakspeare's associates. Who preserved it ? Shakspeare's associates. Who, finally, gave it to the world ? Shakspeare's associates ! the very men whom, as Mr. Malone has just observed, "the muse of Shakspeare had supported, and whom his last will shewed that he had not forgotten !" However great may be the obligations of Jonson to Shakspeare, (of which, I believe, the reader has here had a full account,) it will scarcely be denied that these men, who had so long profited by his wonderful talents, who were, at that very moment, profiting by them, were, at least, equally indebted to him. Yet of their ingratitude not a word is said, not a hint is dropped, while the collected fury of Mr. Malone and his followers is levelled against a person who, at the worst, was only a simple agent, and wrought as they directed !

I have entered into these details merely to shew what inconsistencies it is necessary for those to swallow who put their faith in Mr. Malone—for, after all, the whole of this tedious story is an absolute fable. The Prologue was not written by Jonson, and the play was not written by Shakspeare. The piece acted in 1613 was " A NEW PLAY, called ALL IS TRUTH,"[1] constructed, indeed, on the history of Henry VIII., and, like that, full of shows ; but giving probably a different view of some of the leading incidents of that monarch's life. Shakspeare's *Henry VIII.*, as Mr. Malone affirms, was written in 1601 ; if it had been merely revived, the Prologue would have adverted to the circumstance : but it speaks of the play as one which *had not yet appeared ;* it calls the attention of the audience *to a novelty ;* it supposes, in every line, that they *were unacquainted with its plan ;* and it finally tells them that, if they came to hear a bawdy play, a noise of targets,[2] or to see a fellow in a fool's coat, they would be deceived. Could the audience expect anything of this kind ? or was it necessary to guard them against it, in a favourite comedy, with which they had all been perfectly familiar for twelve years ?

" It appears from the *Execration of Vulcan* that Ben Jonson was at the play-house (the Globe) when it was burnt ; which in some measure strengthens the conjecture that he was employed on the revival of *Henry VIII.*, for this "—and let the words be noted— " for this was *not the theatre* at which his pieces were usually represented !"—p. 563.

He had but little interest or influence there :—for the rest, it appears that Jonson could not stir out of doors to see a fire in his neighbourhood—but that he must needs

---

[1] " But," says Mr. Malone, " *All is Truth* must be Shakspeare's *Henry VIII.*, for the titles of many of his plays were changed in 1613 : thus *Henry IV.* was called Hotspur; *Much Ado about Nothing*, Benedict and Beatrice," &c. What is this to the purpose ? If other titles were given to those plays in familiar conversation, they were still named after the principal characters or the leading events, and no mistake was likely to arise : but who would have recognised *Henry VIII.* under the name of *All is Truth* ? Besides, it is expressly termed a *new play*. Could Sir Henry Wotton, and those who notice it, be so ignorant of Shakspeare, as to call one of his most popular dramas a NEW play after it had been familiarized to the stage for so many years !

[2] On this Dr. Johnson observes—"This is *not* the only passage in which Shakspeare has discovered his conviction of the *impropriety* of battles represented on the stage," &c. Certainly not ; nor of many other improprieties, for which the poverty of the old stage furnished some plea. But the Doctor's remark, and the poet's own apologies in *Henry V.* and elsewhere, are all conveniently forgotten, that Mr. Malone may have one opportunity more of calumniating Jonson !

be at the play-house when it was burnt, for the sake of writing a malicious prologue against Shakspeare!

But did he see it? He says, indeed, in his poem (vol. iii. *Underwoods*, No. lxii), "I *was*," &c.; but this is a mere form of speech—a poetical licence; briefly, for too much has been said on the subject already, I do not believe that Jonson was in England at this time. He was at Leyden in 1613, and we know from Drummond (whose authority is paramount with Mr. Malone) that he was also at Paris in this year; he scarcely hastened home, on being told by Heminge, Burbage, and Condell that Shakspeare had stepped across the way to sign a mortgage, to take possession of his theatre, and, in conjunction with his "associates," to write a prologue against him!

"I had observed in a note that Ben Jonson had *ridiculed* the *Winter's Tale* in 1614," p. 514. Mr. Malone had first fixed the date of this play in 1594, then in 1604, afterwards in 1613, and, as far as I can understand him (for his text and his notes confound each other), ends with placing it in 1601 or 1602. Still, however, the main ground for all these dates respectively is its having been sneered at by Ben Jonson.

"*Antony and Cleopatra* is *ridiculed* in the *Silent Woman*, 1609." This clearly proves it to have been written in 1608! p. 559. "In the same play I formerly thought Shakspeare was *sneered* at in the expression, 'You have lurched your friends of the garland,' but I have since found the phrase elsewhere," p. 602. "Again: Mr. Steevens thinks *Othello* was *sneered* at in the *Alchemist*;" but as the *Alchemist* was prior in date to *Othello*, Mr. Malone differs from his coadjutor; and very opportunely observes that "when old Ben meant to *sneer* at Shakspeare he generally *spoke out* and took care that his meaning should not be missed," p. 606; as in the words chorus, arras, target, and a hundred others of the like decisive nature, on which Mr. Malone has established his charges of envy, &c.!

"Ben Jonson probably meant to *sneer* at the *Tempest* in the prologue to *Every Man in his Humour*—'nor *tempestuous* drum ;' and he has endeavoured to *depreciate* this beautiful comedy by calling it a *foolery*," p. 611. For some remarks on this audacious falsehood, see vol. ii. p. 146 *b*.

"It has been thought that Ben Jonson intended to *ridicule* *Twelfth Night* (which was written in 1614) in his *Every Man out of his Humour* (written in 1599); I do not, however, believe this comedy was meant ;"—such liberality is above all praise—" but," continues Mr. Malone, "if it were, it would ascertain *Twelfth Night* to have been written in 1598 :" and he then proceeds to prove that it was the *last* of Shakspeare's plays !—p. 613.

Thus every drama which is mentioned is made the vehicle of some new charge against Jonson ; and with this medley of spleen and folly have the readers of Shakspeare been long entertained and enlightened.

We are now arrived at Macklin's forgery. In this, almost every crime in the black catalogue of sin is heaped upon Jonson. "He was splenetic, sour, over-run with envy, —the tyrant of the theatre—perpetually uttering slights and malignities against the lowly Shakspeare, whose fame was grown too great for his envy to bear," &c.; "the contempts and invectives which he uttered against Shakspeare would *exceed* all *limits;* but they are produced in this pamphlet " (the one imagined by Macklin as the foundation of his forgery) "as unanswerable and shaming evidences to prove his ill-nature and ingratitude to Shakspeare."—*Shak.* vol. ii. p. 503. I will not nauseate the reader with more of this vile trash, which is extended through several pages, rising one above the other in baseness. In this, however, Mr. Malone revels. He proves, indeed (what was probably learned from Whalley),[1] that the whole was an impudent falsehood ; but he nevertheless maintains the justice of every abusive epithet applied to Jonson, and seems to think that Macklin has rather shown too much tenderness for the poet's character.

Mr. Malone observes that "he always thought with indignation of the tastelessness of the scholars of that age in preferring Jonson to Shakspeare after the death of the latter, and he therefore did not feel much inclined to doubt the authenticity of a story

---

[1] I observed (vol. v. p. 315) that Mr. Malone had made no acknowledgment of his obligation to Whalley. Perhaps the following words, which I had not then noticed, may refer to it : "Some additional information on this subject which I have lately obtained."—*Shak.* vol. ii. p 618. No name, however, is mentioned.

so *conformable* to his own notions," p. 618. This is very well said ; but I must beg leave to protest in this place, once for all, against the despicable trick of bringing our great poet forward in *formâ pauperis*, and bespeaking commiseration for the wrongs which he is affirmed to have sustained from the neglect of his contemporaries. The commentators seem to run about like Jack, in the *Tale of a Tub*, with Shakspeare in their hand, and to solicit persecution for him—"Pray, gentlemen, lend Mr. Shakspeare a blow ! Pray, good people, have the charity to bestow a kick upon Mr. Shakspeare !" The object of this is sufficiently obvious and sufficiently wicked. But Shakspeare was not "persecuted." No man had ever fewer enemies, alive or dead ; and this is the more remarkable as he was himself prone to parody, and must, therefore, have morti-fied many of his contemporaries, who had some reputation on the stage, until—*he drove them out of date*. It is not true that Jonson was preferred to him by the scholars of that age.[1] What was said after the death of both neither of them is accountable for ; but while they lived Shakspeare had his proportion of fame : his plays were more frequently acted than Jonson's, and, if they were not, it was the fault of himself and his brother managers, for they were performed at his own house : in fact, the person who was envied, reviled, and persecuted was our author. But to Macklin.

When Mr. Malone had discovered that the libel on Jonson, such as we have seen it, "was an *innocent forgery*," he very laudably strove to induce Macklin to own the fact, "assuring him (as he says) in the *strongest terms* that no *kind of disgrace* could attend the confession ; that his story was a *mere jeu d'esprit*, written for a harmless purpose," &c. Macklin, however, who seems to have formed a more correct view of the nature of moral turpitude than his father confessor, remained inflexible. He would *lie damnably*, as Shakspeare says, "to put off a few box-tickets ;" but he could not be brought to believe that *forgery was harmless*, or a tissue of malicious falsehood, fabri-cated to blast the character of an innocent man, a *mere jeu d'esprit :* he chose rather there-fore to persist in his story than encounter the general abhorrence which, with *one* exception, must have attended the acknowledgment of his crime.

"The *Comedy of Humours* played eleven times between 25 Nov. 1596 and 11th May, 1597." "Perhaps," says Mr. Malone (on this extract from Henslowe's memorandum-book), "*Every Man in his Humour*. It will appear that Ben Jonson had money-deal-ings with Mr. Henslowe, the manager of this theatre (the Rose), and that he wrote for him. The play might *afterwards* have been purchased *from this company* by the Lord Chamberlain's servants (Shakspeare, Burbage, Heminge, Condell, &c.), by whom it was acted in 1598."—*Shak.* vol. ii. p. 457.

Would the reader believe, on any authority but the writer's own, that the Mr. Malone who drew up this plain paragraph could be the same Mr. Malone who, not merely in one or two, but in a hundred places, has grossly reviled Jonson on the score of *in-gratitude* to Shakspeare for *introducing* him to the stage, and bringing out this very play !

> "Yet must I not give nature all ; thy *art*,
> My gentle Shakspeare, must enjoy a part."—P. 560.

Though Steevens and Malone could not avoid giving Jonson's poem *On the Memory of his Beloved Shakspeare*, they make no other use of it than to abuse the writer for his "envy, hatred, and jealousy of him." "Though he allows the poet *art* here," says Mr. Malone, "yet he told Drummond he wanted *art*,"[2] p. 500. But, with Mr. Malone's leave, the word is used in different senses. By *art* in the latter of these quotations Jon-son meant knowledge, information of a geographical or historical kind in the construc-tion of a plot ; for, says he, "in one of his plays" (which Drummond had evidently

---

[1] Yet Mr. Malone recurs to it again and again : just below he says, "that Jonson was *extrava-gantly extolled* by the scholars of that age as *much superior* to Shakspeare," p. 628. And again and again I pronounce it an unqualified falsehood.

[2] **Dryden** is subsequently appealed to on this point :

> "Shakspeare, who taught by none, did first impart
> To Fletcher wit, to labouring Jonson *art*."
> P. 519.

As if Dryden cared what he said, or ever ad-vanced a single tenet which he did not subse-quently contradict ! In his *Essay on Dramatic Poesy*, he says, "Wit and language, and, in

never seen or heard of), "he brings in a number of men, saying they had suffered shipwreck in Bohemia." In the former passage *art* is opposed to nature. But I am weary
of justifying Jonson from a charge of "malice" founded on a heartfelt effusion which
none but the most prejudiced can read without agreeing, as Farmer says, "that it is the
warmest that ever was written, and carries Shakspeare's acquirements rather *above* than
below the truth."—*Shak.* vol. ii. p. 11.

"The beauties of the *Tempest* could not secure it from the *criticism* of Ben Jonson,
whose *malignity* appears to have been more than equal to his wit."—Steevens, *Shak.*
vol. iii. p. 1.

"The *Tempest* *must* have been written before 1614, since Ben Jonson *sneers* at it in
that year," p. 2.[1]

"Ben Jonson, who takes *every opportunity* to *find fault* with Shakspeare, seems to
ridicule Twelfth Night in *Every Man out of his Humour.*—"Steevens, *Shak.* vol. iv. p. 2.

Mr. Malone had previously employed several pages (vol. i. pp. 611-15) in proving
Twelfth Night to be written in 1614, that is, sixteen years before the appearance of
Every Man out of his Humour; he had also positively affirmed (p. 275) that he "*did
not believe Twelfth Night* was meant ;" yet he subjoins to the note of Steevens (who
knew that he had been delivering a falsehood), "if the foregoing passage *was* levelled
at *Twelfth Night,* my speculation falls to the ground." He has not the integrity to support his own facts, lest he should remove one absurd and wretched calumny from Jonson.
But the best is yet to come. Steevens, who attacks Jonson (p. 2) for ridiculing *Twelfth
Night* in 1598, informs us (p. 129) that Shakspeare copied the behaviour of two of its
characters from the *Silent Woman,* which was not in being till 1609 ! Can impudence
go beyond this ! What opinion must these vile calumniators have formed of the capacity of their readers ! But they were right !

"Ben Jonson appears to have *ridiculed* this scene (of the constables) in *Bart. Fair.*"
—Steevens, p. 480.

"Mr. Steevens *justly* observes that Ben Jonson intended to ridicule this scene in
Bart. Fair, yet, in his *Tale of a Tub,* he makes his constables speak in the same style
and blunder in the same manner without any such intention," *ib.* Malone. No doubt
of it. And so did hundreds besides, both before and after Shakspeare's time ; but Mr.
Malone need not have travelled forward to the *Tale of a Tub;* had he only turned back
to *Cynthia's Revels* he would have found constables *ridiculed* by Jonson twelve years, at
least, before *Twelfth Night* was in being.

"The *Winter's Tale* is *sneered* at by B. Jonson in the *Induction to Bart. Fair.*"
—*Shak.* vol. vii. p. 2. In his Conversation with Mr. Drummond of Hawthornden he has
another *stroke* at his *beloved* friend : he said that Shakspeare wanted art,[2] &c. ; but we
have already had this over and over.

---

some measure, humour, we had before Jonson,
but *something of art was wanting to the Drama
till he came !*"—*Dry.* vol. xv. p. 355.

[1] Mr. G. Chalmers is so delighted with this
"proof," that he condescends to lend all the
strength of his reasoning faculties to enforce it.
The *Tempest,* he says, in a little Essay just
printed, must "have been written about the end
of 1613, *because* we perceive, from these *great*
authorities (those given above) that Ben Jonson
attempted, in 1614, to *depreciate* it by scattering
his *sarcasms* among the million ; and it is *obviously certain*" (I beseech the reader to attend
to this clencher) "that such *sarcasms* could only
have been thrown out against a comedy *which
had recently appeared; his sarcasms* would not
have been understood by the multitude had they
been made against a drama which had been
written some years before," p. 42. Now observe :
in this very page Mr. Chalmers charges Jonson,
with equal vehemence, with uttering his sarcasms
in the same line ("tales and tempests" are the
words) against the *Winter's Tale,* which he

himself labours to prove, and affirms that he has
proved, to be written in 1601, thirteen years
before the appearance of *Bartholomew Fair !*
He had already forgotten (such is the fatality
attendant on our author's calumniators), though
no more than six lines intervened, that it is
obviously certain that such *sarcasms could* only
be thrown out against a *comedy which had then
recently appeared !*

[2] How did Dryden escape the censure of Mr.
Malone? "Let any man" (he says) "who understands English read diligently the works of
Shakspeare, and Fletcher, and I dare undertake
that he will find *in every page* either some solecism, or some notorious flaw of *sense.*" Or
Philips? who, the commentators tell us. was assisted by Milton in his character of Shakspeare,
and who yet says of him that "his unfiled expressions, his rambling and indigested fancies
are the laughter of the critical." Jonson is the
most tender of all Shakspeare's critics, and yet
he is the only person who is taxed with malice
towards him !

"We are told by Dryden that Ben Jonson in reading some bombast speeches of *Macbeth* which were not to be understood,' used to say that it was horror. Any person but this *envious detractor* would have dwelt with pleasure," &c., p. 387. This is very good. For these speeches which, as the critic observes, are *not to be understood*, our author had liberally apologized, "they were *horror*," one of the chief properties of which is to be dark and indistinct. Mr. Malone falls furiously upon Jonson, who had justified Shakspeare, while Dryden, who had actually condemned him, is thus gently dismissed: "That there are some *bombast speeches* in *Macbeth* which are *not to be understood*, as Dryden asserts, will not very readily be granted to him." Not a word of *envy* and *detraction:* these choice terms are reserved for the judicious and friendly apology of "old Ben."

"'Clutch'—this word, though *reprobated* by Ben Jonson, who *sneers* at Decker for using it, was used by other writers (besides him and Shakspeare)."—Malone, p. 406. Now Decker does *not* use the word; and Jonson does *not* reprobate the use of it by Shakspeare. I have shown (vol. ii. p. 520) that the whole line (not merely the word) "reprobated" by Jonson, is taken from Marston.

"These words, *hold hook and line*, are *ridiculed* by Ben Jonson in the *Case is Altered*, 1609."—Steevens, *Shak.* vol. ix. p. 251. It so happens, and Steevens knew it well, that the *Case is Altered* was produced, at latest, in 1598, so that the *ridicule* (if that be the term) is Shakspeare's. Such stuff would be too contemptible for notice were it not for the malicious motive of the commentator in bringing it forward.

"'Why then lament therefore;' this was perhaps intended to be *ridiculed* by Ben Jonson in the *Poetaster*," p. 253. It is a great pity that Mr. Malone forgot to tell us whom Shakspeare intended to *ridicule* by the expression. Or was he ignorant that it was taken from Marlowe, the great but undeserving butt of Shakspeare's wit? With respect to Jonson, who admired Marlowe, he merely puts it into the mouth of Tucca's boy, who is rehearsing before a player, to procure an engagement.

"'Charming the narrow seas.'[1] Though Ben Jonson was *indebted to the kindness* of Shakspeare for the introduction of *his first piece* (*Every Man in his Humour*) to the stage" (see p. xc.), "yet in the Prologue to that play, and in *many other* places, he has endeavoured to *ridicule* and *depreciate* him."—Malone, p. 305.

"When the Prologue was written is unknown, but the *envious author of it* did not publish it till the year of Shakspeare's death."—Malone, *ibid.*

"Perhaps Ben Jonson was thinking of the *Second Part of Henry VI.* when he made Morose say, 'Nay, I would even sit out a play that *was nothing but fights* at sea.'"—Steevens, vol. x. p. 121.

Just before, Steevens had accused Jonson of *sneering* at *Antony and Cleopatra* in this passage! There, as here, the whole of the "fights at sea" are confined to one solitary stage direction of three words.

"The *malignant* Ben, in his *Devil's an Ass, sneers* at all Shakspeare's historical pieces."—Malone, p. 451. All this scurrility, and much more, is heaped upon Jonson at the conclusion of a long Essay, tending to show that these *historical pieces* were *not* Shakspeare's! The *First Part of Henry VI.*, Mr. Malone says, was *not* written at all by Shakspeare, and of the remaining two parts, not quite a third. It cannot indeed be proved that a thirtieth of this "third" was written by him; for besides what are come down to us, scores of historical dramas, among which Shakspeare might forage for the supply of his house, are utterly lost. Yet an incessant attack is maintained against Jonson for his *malignity* to Shakspeare on this head; as if Shakspeare were the only person who ever wrote an historical play, or our author the only critic who ever noticed them!

Shak. vol. xi. p. 6. Mr. Malone here repeats the old ribaldry against Jonson for the Prologue to *Henry VIII.;* which brings up Steevens: "Were it *necessary*," he says, "to prove that old Ben was the author, we might observe that *happy* is used in it in the Roman sense of *propitious* or *favourable—sis bonus O felixque tuis*—a sense which

---

[1] "This passage shows that Shakspeare was fully sensible of the *absurdity* of showing battles on the stage, which always turns | tragedy into farce."—Dr. Johnson, *Shak.* vol. ix. 266.
"Other authors of that age seem to have been

must have been unknown to Shakspeare,[1] but was familiar to Jonson." Mr. Malone
was properly grateful, I trust, for this most learned prop of his argument, which proves,
besides, that no one but Jonson understood Latin, and that none but Jonson and Shakspeare could write a prologue ! But with deference to such profundity it so chances
that in all the places in which Jonson has used *happy* in the Roman sense, it does not
even *once* occur in that of propitious, &c. Happy, in Jonson (the translation of *beatus*),
is invariably *rich, fortunate*. The reputation of the commentators must "to the barber," I fear, with Polonius's beard.

P. 187. Mr. Malone here gives us again the silly story about the dozen laten spoons
(p. xxv), and observes upon it that, "it shows Shakspeare and Ben Jonson to be once
on terms of friendship and familiarity, however *cold* and *jealous* the *latter* (always the
latter !) might have been at a subsequent period."

"Ben Jonson *unjustly sneers* at *Julius Cæsar* in his *Bart. Fair.* 'Come, there's no
malice in these fat folks.'"—*Shak.* vol. xii. p. 257. See vol. iv. p. 412.

"Ben Jonson *ridicules* this line, which he quotes unfaithfully," &c.—Steevens,
p. 314.

"It may be doubted whether Jonson quoted it unfaithfully ; but what are we to think
of his *malignity ?*" &c., *ibid.*

Shak. vol. xiii. p. 248. Percy cites an expression of Jonson to show that the wretched
Titus Andronicus was *not* written by Shakspeare ; upon which Steevens bristles up and
remarks, that "this ought to have no weight at all, as Jonson has not *very sparingly*
censured the *Tempest* and others of Shakspeare's most finished pieces : indeed (adds he)
the *whole* of Ben's prologue to *Every Man in his Humour* is a *malicious sneer* upon
him." Having thus vented his rancour, Steevens turns short round, and pronounces the
play *not* to be Shakspeare's !

"The *contemptuous* manner in which Ben Jonson (in 1631) has mentioned *Pericles*"
(he calls it a mouldy tale[2]) "is, *in my opinion*, a proof that *it was* written by Shakspeare. In his *Ode*, written *soon after*[3] his *New Inn* was damned, he *naturally* chose to
point at what he esteemed a weak play of a rival whom he *envied* and *hated* merely because the splendour of his genius had eclipsed his own, and rendered the reception of
those *tame* and *disgusting* imitations of antiquity which he boastingly called the *only
legitimate* English dramas, as *cold* as the performances themselves !"—P. 611.

Bravo ! Mr. Malone. I might perhaps reply that you have been insulting the
times through all the former volumes for preferring Jonson to Shakspeare ; but I am
nearly weary of you.

"'I'll fetch some *whites of eggs*'—this passage is *ridiculed* by Ben Jonson in the *Case
is Altered*, 1609."—Steevens, *Shak.* vol. xiv. p. 196. "The *Case is Altered* was written
before the year 1599 ; but Ben Jonson might *have inserted this sneer at Shakspeare* between the time of *Lear's* appearance (in 1605) and the publication of his own play in
1609."—*Ibid.* Malone.

O that letter ! This paragraph appeared in 1793, and in 1782, just eleven years before, Mr. Malone had thus written to Whalley, "*I entirely agree* with you that *no ridicule was intended against Shakspeare* in the *Case is Altered* for 'the white of an egg.'"
What ! not honest either ?

In a subsequent passage (vol. xv. p. 557) Steevens accuses Jonson of *ridiculing
Othello* in *Every Man out of his Humour.* On which Mr. Malone observes—"Ben
Jonson was *ready enough on all occasions* to *depreciate* and *ridicule* Shakspeare ; but, in

---

sensible of the same *absurdities ;* thus Heywood,"
&c.—Steevens, *ibid.*

[1] That Shakspeare should not know that happy
was propitious, the sense in which he and every
English scholar perpetually use it, is an assertion
worthy of Steevens.

[2] Mr. Malone forgets himself sadly—"When
Ben Jonson (he says) calls *Pericles* a *mouldy
tale*, he alludes, I apprehend, not to the *remote
date* of the play, but to the *antiquity* of the
story on which it is founded," p. 633. Where then
is the *contempt* on which, to the credit of his

liberality, he has just raised so notable an argument !

[3] Soon after ! "If (says Mr. Malone, *Shak.*
vol. i. p. 629) Mr. Macklin means that Jonson
wrote his *Ode immediately after* his play was
damned, the assertion is made at random." The
distinction between *soon after* and *immediately
after* is worthy of the critic. The fact is that
Mr. Malone did not foresee at this time that, as
he was in pursuit of the same object as Macklin,
he might have occasion hereafter for the same
argument.

the present instance he must, I *believe*, be acquitted ; for his comedy was written in 1599, at which time we are *almost* certain *Othello* had not appeared."—*Ibid.*

I *believe*, and we are *almost certain*—very cautiously put ; but Mr. Malone had again forgotten his letter, and what is more, himself. "I have," he says (vol. i. p. 606), "however, *persuaded myself* that *Othello* was one of Shakspeare's *latest* performances ;" and he accordingly places it in 1611.

There are yet two volumes, charged with the same malevolence and folly ; but I can go no further. If the reader should be as weary as myself, let him, in justice, call to mind that I have given him here but a small part of what is contained in one work only ; and that he has been in the habit of listening without a murmur, without a symptom of dissatisfaction to the same cuckoo-strain in a hundred : for I am warranted in affirming that none of our old poets, especially our dramatic ones, have been republished within the last fifty years without teeming with the same vile ribaldry against Jonson. The editors follow one another, and boldly repeat the most absurd and improbable charges with a secure reliance on the credulity of their readers, and a happy confidence in the merit of their slanderous falsehoods. For the pages of the minor dramatists I am little solicitous, but I cannot avoid thinking it more than time to disencumber those of our GREAT POET from the wretched obloquy with which they are everywhere surcharged, and to present him, at length, to the world, undefiled and undebased by a disgusting repetition of absurd and rancorous abuse on the sincerest of his admirers, the warmest of his panegyrists and the most constant and affectionate of his friends, BEN JONSON.

Characters of Jonson

" . . . HE [Lord Clarendon, speaking of himself] owed all the little he knew, and the little good that was in him, to the friendships and conversation he had still been used to, of the most excellent men in their several kinds that lived in that age ; by whose learning and information, and instruction, he formed his studies, and mended his understanding, and by whose gentleness and sweetness of behaviour, and justice, and virtue, and example, he formed his manners, subdued that pride, and suppressed that heat and passion he was naturally inclined to be transported with. Whilst he was only a student of the law, and stood at gaze, and irresolute what corner of life to take, his chief acquaintance were BEN JOHNSON, John Selden, Charles Cotton, John Vaughan, Sir Kenelm Digby, Thomas May, and Thomas Carew, and some others of eminent faculties in their several ways. BEN JOHNSON'S name can never be forgotten, having by his very good learning, and the severity of his nature and manners, very much reformed the Stage, and indeed the English poetry itself ; his natural advantages were, judgment to order and govern fancy, rather than excess of fancy, his productions being slow and upon deliberation, yet then abounding with great wit and fancy, and will live accordingly ; and surely as he did exceedingly exalt the English language in eloquence, propriety, and masculine expressions, so he was the best judge of, and fittest to prescribe rules to Poetry and Poets of any man who had lived with, or before him, or since : if Mr. Cowley had not made a flight beyond all men, with that modesty yet to ascribe much of this to the example and learning of Ben Johnson. HIS CONVERSATION WAS VERY GOOD, AND WITH THE MEN OF MOST NOTE ; and he had for many years an extraordinary kindness for Mr. Hyde, till he found he betook himself to business, which he believed ought never to be preferred before his company : he lived to be very old, and till the palsy made a deep impression upon his body and his mind."—*Life of Edward Lord Clarendon*, vol. i. 34, *ed.* 1827.

" If we look upon JONSON while he was himself (for his last plays were but his dotages), I think him the most learned and judicious writer which any theatre ever had. He was a most severe judge of himself as well as others. One cannot say he wanted wit, but rather that he was frugal of it. In his works you find little to retrench or alter. Wit and language, and humour also in some measure, we had before him ; but something of art was wanting to the drama till he came. He managed his strength to more advantage than any who preceded him. You seldom find him making love in any of his scenes, or endeavouring to move the passions ; his genius was too sullen and saturnine to do it gracefully, especially when he knew he came after those who had performed both to such a height. Humour was his proper sphere, and in that he delighted most to represent mechanic people. He was deeply conversant in the ancients, both Greek and Latin, and he borrowed boldly from them : there is scarce a poet or historian among the Roman authors of those times whom he has not translated in *Sejanus* and *Catiline*. But he has done his robberies so openly that one may see he fears not to be taxed by any law. He invades authors like a monarch, and what would be theft in other poets is only victory in him. With the spoils of these writers he so represents old Rome to us in its rites, ceremonies, and customs, that if one of their poets had written either of his tragedies, we had seen less of it than in him. If there was any fault in his language it was that he weaved it too closely and laboriously, in his comedies especially : perhaps too he did a little too much Romanize our tongue, leaving the words which he translated almost as much Latin as he found them ; wherein, though he learnedly followed their language, he did not enough comply with the idiom of ours. . . . . To conclude of him, as he has given us the most correct plays, so in the precepts which he has laid down in his *Discoveries*, we have as many and as profitable rules for perfecting the stage as any wherewith the French can furnish us." —*Dryden: Essay on Dram. Poetry.*

" BENJAMIN JOHNSON, the most learned, judicious, and correct, generally so accounted, of our English comedians, and the more to be admired for being so for that neither the height of natural parts, for he was no Shakspeare, nor the cost of extraordinary education, for he is reported but a bricklayer's son, but his own proper industry and addiction to books, advanced him to this perfection : in three of his comedies, namely, the *Fox*, *Alchemist*, and *Silent Woman*, he may be compared, in the judgment of learned men, for decorum, language, and well-humouring of the parts, as well with the chief of the ancient Greek and Latin comedians, as the prime of modern Italians, who have been judged the best of Europe for a happy vein in comedies ; nor is his *Bartholomew Fair* much short of them. As for his other comedies, *Cynthia's Revels*, *Poetaster*, and the rest, let the name of Ben Johnson protect them against whoever shall think fit to be severe in censure against them : the truth is, his tragedies, *Sejanus* and *Catiline*, seem to have in them more of an artificial and inflate than of a pathetical and naturally tragic height : in the rest of his poetry, for he is not wholly dramatic, as his *Underwoods*, *Epigrams*, &c., he is sometimes bold and strenuous, sometimes magisterial, sometimes lepid and full enough of conceit (wit), and sometimes a man as other men are."—*Theatrum Poetarum, ed.* 1675, pp. 19, 20.

" It will not perhaps be held altogether inadmissible if, before we close a volume which is consecrated to the name of Milton, a few thoughts are here thrown together on the tastes and partialities of our great poet, and the sort of author among his predecessors that he chiefly had in his eye, and whom he seems principally to resemble in his style of composition. . . . . The author to whom I allude is BEN JONSON. And a principal reason why I thus invite the public consideration to his writings is that they do not seem at this moment to possess that degree of popular favour to which in my judgment they are well entitled. It is somewhat singular that at the time when Addison dared to talk of Spenser as a writer who 'with ancient tales amused a barbarous age,' but who now 'can charm an understanding age no more,' and when Pope inquired, ' Who now reads Cowley ?' the laurels of Ben Jonson were unwithered ; and that at the present day, when fifty illustrious authors are restored to our love, whom the folly of our immediate ancestors consigned to the tomb of the Capulets, Jonson alone seems to have fallen off in the general esteem. . . . . He is admitted to have had talents ; but he is judged harsh, repulsive, and unamiable. He is too deeply entrenched in the fortifications of his learning. He is thought to have dealt perpetually in idioms imported from the classical writers, wholly alien to the genius of our language. The mind of man shrinks with conscious independence from an author who bids us censure him at our peril, and daringly assures us that the composition we are about to read is the abstract of all excellence, a work over which the corroding tooth of time shall have no power.[1] Jonson often seems to aspire to be the poet of good sense, rather than of fancy. On many occasions he has little sacrificed to the Graces. And in several of his longer poems, and *Speeches according to Horace*, as he calls them, he is flat, heavy, and tedious ; and having in a small degree won upon our attention in the beginning, brings us, after a lapse of thirty or forty lines, into a state of utter listlessness.
" Much of this is certainly true. But these are scattered features, and do not constitute the literary character of Jonson.
" It is not to the purpose of this Essay to treat of the merits of this eminent author as a comic writer, though these perhaps compose his strongest claim to the admiration of all posterity. He excels every writer that ever existed in the article of humour ; and it is a sort of identical proposition to say that humour is the soul of comedy Even the caustic severity of his turn of mind aided him in this. He seized with the

---

[1] Yet we continue to read Horace, Ovid, and a number of other writers who preceded Jonson in this boastful language.

utmost precision the weaknesses of human character, and painted them with a truth that is altogether irresistible. Shakspeare has some characters of humour marvellously felicitous. But the difference between these two great supporters of the English drama, in the point of view we are considering, lies here. Humour is not Shakspeare's mansion, the palace wherein he dwells ; there are many of his comedies where the humorous characters rather form the episode of the piece ; poetry, the manifestation of that lovely medium through which all creation appeared to his eye, and the quick sallies of repartee, are the objects with which his comic muse more usually delights herself. But Ben Jonson is all humour; and the fertility of his muse in characters of this sort is wholly inexhaustible.

"Yet out of his very excellence the ill-nature of imaginative criticism has drawn the ingredients with which to demolish the better part of his fame. Many have concluded, because he had a manly severity and steadiness of judgment, that he had a cold and unsusceptible spirit, that his writings are uniformly rugged and harsh, and that he was devoured with malice and envy towards his illustrious contemporaries. This is no bad specimen of the way in which mankind is apt, from a few scattered hints, to fill up a portrait. It must be confessed there is some keeping in the design ; its fault is, that it has no pretensions to likeness. Whether Ben Jonson was a man of cold conceptions and feelings, or his writings on all occasions rugged and harsh, we shall presently have occasion to inquire. But that he was envious, and sparing in commendation to his contemporaries, may as well immediately be denied. His Commendatory Verses on Shakspeare, Drayton, Donne, Fletcher, Sir John Beaumont, and others, may easily be consulted ; and he that finds in them any penury of praise, any malicious ambiguity, or concealed detraction, may safely be affirmed to have brought a mind already poisoned to their perusal. Let me produce an example from the fervent generosity with which he replies to the friendly epistle of Beaumont, the dramatist.

> ' How I doe loue thee, Beaumont, and thy Muse,
> That vnto me dost such religion vse !
> How I doe feare my selfe, that am not worth
> The least indulgent thought thy pen drops forth !'[1]

" A great deal of the injustice which Ben Jonson has suffered under this head has proceeded from the misfortune of his visit to Drummond of Hawthornden, and therefore on that subject I beg to be allowed to say a few words. Jonson was already fortyseven years of age, and had finished all his great works, ... when he conceived the design, struck with some beautiful effusions of the Scottish poet, of journeying on foot from London to Hawthornden to pay him a visit. Heroical and generous was certainly the sentiment that soothed his uneasy steps, and beguiled the weariness of the way. He was received no doubt with hospitality and the semblance of affection ; and when he came home again the first thing done by the illustrious votary of the English Muse, was at Drummond's request to send him a most beautiful madrigal, *On a Lover's Dust made Sand for an Hour-Glass*, with this Inscription :

> ' To the Honouring Respect
> Born
> To the Friendship contracted with
> The Right Virtuous and Learned
> Mr. William Drummond,
> And the Perpetuating the Same by all offices of Love Hereafter,
> I, Benjamin Jonson,
> Whom he hath honoured with the leave to be called His,
> Have with mine own Hand, to satisfy his Request,
> Written this imperfect Song.'

---

[1] I quote these and the succeeding remarks with great pleasure, not only because they accord with what I had long since observed on the subject, but because they seem to prove that the career of malevolence and folly is drawing to a shameful close, and that the character as well as the talents of Jonson are at length about to be judged with truth, and appreciated with candour.

I have not thought it necessary to quote the extracts given in this valuable Essay, nor any of the numerous passages in prose and verse which Milton is shown to have borrowed from our author ; suffice it to say, that Mr. Godwin has completely proved his point, and evinced at once his judgment, his taste, and his liberality.

Drummond also did his part, and has, after his fashion, consecrated the memory of this extraordinary visit by putting down the 'Heads of Certain Conversations' between them, every word of which is a libel on the man whom he made to believe that he was regarded by him with sentiments of the sincerest friendship. The question that remains is, how far a libeller and a treacherous ally is to be admitted for a competent witness ; and the incompetence may as infallibly be produced by a diseased vision in the observer (such as led Drummond in this paper to affirm generally of his guest that he was 'a great lover and praiser of himself, a contemner and scorner of others,') as by the most resolute spirit of deliberate falsehood. . . . .

"In the catalogue of poets in the age of which we speak the name of Ben Jonson will occupy no inglorious place ; and Milton will certainly be found to have studied his compositions in this kind more assiduously than those of any of his contemporaries. The following *Verses to Celia*, unfortunately founded on the faulty ethical system of Sir Philip Sidney, are entitled to be inserted here on account of the use which Milton has made of them.[1]

'Come, my Celia, let us proue,' &c.

The following *Song of Hesperus*, addressed to the Moon, in the fifth act of *Cynthia's Revels*, appears to me exquisitely simple and majestic :

'Qveene and huntresse, chaste and faire,' &c.

*   *   *   *   *   *   *

"Of the unsuccessful event of his love for Charis he speaks, in a short copy of verses, accompanying the madrigal which has already been mentioned, sent by him to the unworthy Drummond. It begins :

'I doubte that love is rather deafe then blind,
For else it could not be that she
Whom I adore so much, should so slight me,
And cast my love behind.'

The disappointed lover proceeds with conscious worth :

'I'm sure my language to her was as sweet,
And very close did meet
In sentence of as subtile feet,
As hath the youngest hee
That sits in shadow of Apollo's tree.'

*   *   *   *   *   *   *

"The following may serve as an example whether the poet spoke with too presumptuous a confidence when he asserted the smoothness of his language and the melody of his versification :

'Charis one day in discourse
Had of Love, and of his force,
Lightly promised she would tell
What a man she could love well ;
And that promise set on fire
All that heard her with desire.
With the rest I long expected
When the worke would be effected,' &c.

*   *   *   *   *   *   *

"The genius of this venerable author was particularly suited to that species of dramatical composition, at this time greatly in vogue, known by the appellation of Mask ; and his poetical vein, together with the splendid taste and invention of Inigo Jones, who superintended the decorations to it, carried it to an extraordinary degree of perfection. I may refer for some of the most finished specimens to the Satyrs in *Oberon*, and the Witches in the *Mask of Queens*. It would be strange indeed if the poet who in early

---

[1] *The Forest*, No. 5.

youth composed the *Mask of Comus*, had not diligently studied the writings of Ben Jonson.

" One conspicuous feature in the productions of Jonson, of Fletcher, and many of the most eminent poets of this age, is the fervent strains in which they deliver themselves concerning purity, moral elevation, and virtue. Fletcher occasionally is wanton, and Jonson is coarse ; this was the vice of their age. But they were men of sound and erect thinking ; they were entirely strangers to that heart-withering scepticism which I have so often heard reverend gray-beards enforce in a later age ; they believed that the good upon record were good, and the morally great were great ; and when they had occasion to express the sentiments of virtuous enthusiasm, they did not fear the imputation of having encroached on the office of the pulpit. They knew that a well-prepared mind, pouring forth from lips of fire conceptions worthy of an angelic nature, would never be mistaken for a proser or a hypocrite. It would extend my Essay too far to give examples of this ; they will readily present themselves to every one who will look for them.

" One or two passages of a moral cast, but which, if possible, are still more eminent for the poetry that prevades them, I will venture upon. The following occurs in an *Ode Pindaric, to the Memory of Sir H. Morison*, who died in the flower of his youth :

> ' It is not growing, like a tree,
>   In bulke, doth make man better be :
> Or standing long an oake, three hundred yeare,
> To fall a logge at last, dry, bald and seare :
>   A lillie of a day
>   Is fairer farre in May,
>   Although it fall and die that night :—
>   It was the plant and flowre of light.
> In small proportions we just beauties see,
> And in short measures life may perfect bee,' &c.

" The following is part of Lord Lovel's discourse, when impleaded before his mistress, in the admirable comedy of the *New Inn*, Act the Third :

> ' They are the earthly, lower form of lovers,
>   Are only taken with what strikes the senses,
>   And love by that loose scale,' &c.

" It is not however in lighter and incidental matters only that Milton studied the great model afforded him by Jonson : we may find in him much that would almost tempt us ' to hold opinion with Pythagoras,' and to believe that the very spirit and souls of some men became transfused into their poetical successors. The address of our earlier poet to the Two Universities, prefixed to his most consummate performance, the comedy of the *Fox*, will strike every reader familiar with the happiest passages of Milton's prose, with its wonderful resemblance.

*   *   *   *   *   *   *   *   *

" The resemblance between Milton and our elder bard is in many respects conspicuous. They were both of them emphatically poets who had sounded the depths, and formed themselves in the school of classic lore. . . . .

" The difference between the two poets may perhaps best be illustrated from the topic of religion. They had neither of them one spark of libertine and latitudinarian unbelief. But Jonson was not, like Milton, penetrated with his religion. It is to him a sort of servitude. . . . it is not the principle that actuates, but the check that controls him. But in Milton it is the element in which he breathes, a part of his nature. He acts 'as ever in his great Taskmaster's eye ;' and this is not his misfortune ; but he rejoices in his condition, that he has so great, so wise, and so sublime a being to whom to render his audit."—*Appendix to the Lives of E. and J. Philips*, p. 387.

Ancient Commendatory Verses on Jonson.

[It is merely necessary to observe that the greater number of these poems are taken from the earlier editions. Whalley seems not to have looked much beyond the folio, 1616, where he found the few which he prefixed to his editions of our author's works.]

ON SEJANUS.

So brings the wealth-contracting jeweller
  Pearls and dear stones from richest stores
    and streams,
As thy accomplished travail doth confer
  From skill enriched souls their wealthier
    gems ;
So doth his hand enchase inammelled gold,
  Cut, and adorned beyond their native
    merits,
His solid flames, as thine hath here inrolled
  In more than golden verse, those bettered
    spirits ;
So he entreasures princes' cabinets,
  As thy wealth will their wished libraries ;
So, on the throat of the rude sea, he sets
  His vent'rous foot, for his illustrious prize;
And through wild desarts, armed with
    wilder beasts ;
  As thou adventur'st on the multitude,
Upon the boggy, and engulfed breasts
  Of hirelings, sworn to find most right,
    most rude:
And he, in storms at sea, doth not endure,
  Nor in vast deserts amongst wolves, more
    danger;
Than we, that would with virtue live secure,
  Sustain for her in every vice's anger.
Nor is this Allegory unjustly rackt
  To this strange length : only, that jewels
    are,
In estimation merely, so exact :
  And thy work, in itself, is dear and rare;
Wherein Minerva had been vanquished,
  Had she, by it, her sacred looms advanced,
And through thy subject woven her graphic
    thread,
  Contending therein, to be more entranced;
For, though thy hand was scarce addrest to
    draw
  The semicircle of SEJANUS' life,

Thy muse yet makes it the whole sphere,
    and law
  To all state-lives; and bounds ambition's
    strife,
And as a little brook creeps from his
    spring,
  With shallow tremblings, through the
    lowest vales,
As if he feared his stream abroad to bring,
  Lest prophane feet should wrong it, and
    rude gales ;
But finding happy channels, and supplies
  Of other fords mixt with his modest
    course,
He grows a goodly river, and descries
  The strength that manned him, since he
    left his source;
Then takes he in delightsome meads and
    groves,
  And, with his two-edged waters,flourishes
Before great palaces, and all men's loves
  Build by his shores, to greet his pas-
    sages :
So thy chaste muse, by virtuous self-mis-
    trust,
  Which is a true mark of the truest merit;
In virgin fear of men's illiterate lust,
  Shut her soft wings, and durst not shew
    her spirit;
Till, nobly cherisht, now thou let'st her fly,
  Singing the sable Orgies of the Muses,
And in the highest pitch of Tragedy,
  Mak'st her command all things thy
    ground produces.
Besides, thy poem hath this due respect,
  That it lets nothing pass without ob-
    serving
Worthy instruction, or that might correct
  Rude manners, and renown the well de-
    serving:
Performing such a lively evidence
  In thy narrations, that thy hearers still

Thou turn'st to thy spectators; and the
sense
That thy spectators have of good or ill,
Thou inject'st jointly to thy readers' souls.
    So dear is held, so deckt thy numerous
        task,
As thou putt'st handles to the Thespian
    bowls,
    Or stuck'st rich plumes in the Palladian
        cask.
All thy worth, yet, thyself must patronize,
    By quaffing more of the Castalian head;
In expiscation of whose mysteries,
    Our nets must still be clogged with heavy
        lead,
To make them sink, and catch: for cheerful
    gold
Was never found in the Pierian streams,
But wants, and scorns, and shames for
    silver sold.
What, what shall we elect in these ex-
    tremes?
Now by the shafts of the great Cyrrhan
    poet,
    That bear all light, that is, about the
        world;
I would have all dull poet-haters know it,
    They shall be soul-bound, and in dark-
        ness hurled,
A thousand years (as Satan was, their sire)
    Ere any, worthy the poetic name,
(Might I, that warm but at the Muses' fire,
    Presume to guard it) should let death-
        less Fame
Light half a beam of all her hundred eyes,
    At his dim taper, in their memories.
Fly, fly, you are too near; so odorous
    flowers,
    Being held too near the sensor of our
        sense,
Render not pure, nor so sincere their powers,
    As being held a little distance thence.
O could the world but feel how sweet a
    touch
    The knowledge hath, which is in love
        with goodness,
(If Poesy were not ravished so much,
    And her composed rage, held the simplest
        woodness,
Though of all heats, that temper human
    brains,
    Hers ever was most subtle, high, and
        holy,
First binding savage lives in civil chains,
    Solely religious, and adored solely):
If men felt this, they would not think a
    love,
    That gives itself, in her, did vanities
        give;

Who is (in earth, though low) in worth
    above,
    Most able t' honour life, though least to
        live.
And so, good friend, safe passage to
    thy freight,
    To thee a long peace, through a
        virtuous strife,
In which let's both contend to virtue's
    height,
    Not making fame our object, but
        good life.

GEORGE CHAPMAN.

There is much more of this in the 4to, 1605,
which is not worth recalling. The present copy
is from the folio, 1616. Chapman has another
complimentary poem on *Sejanus*, which is only
found in the 4to; where it may be left, without
much injury to his fame.

TO HIS WORTHY FRIEND, BEN JONSON, UPON HIS SEJANUS.

In that this book doth deign SEJANUS
    name,
    Him unto more than Cæsar's love it
        brings:
For where he could not with ambition's
    wings,
    One quill doth heave him to the height
        of fame.
Ye great ones though (whose ends may be
    the same)
    Know that, however we do flatter kings,
    Their favours (like themselves) are fading
        things,
    With no less envy had, than lost with
        shame.
Nor make yourselves less honest than you
    are,
    To make our author wiser than he is;
Ne of such crimes accuse him, which I
    dare
By all his muses swear be none of his.
    The men are not, some faults may be
        these times:
    He acts those men, and they did act these
        crimes.

HUGH HOLLAND.[1]

[1] He was bred at Westminster school under
Camden, and thence elected fellow of Trinity
College, Cambridge. He is said by Dr. Fuller
to have been no bad English, but an excellent
Latin poet. He wrote several things, amongst
which is the Life of Camden; but none of them,
I believe, have been ever published. See an
account of him in *Athen. Oxon.* I. vol. col. 583.
WHAL.

ON SEJANUS.

When I respect thy argument, I see
An image of those times: but when I view
The wit, the workmanship, so rich, so true,
The times themselves do seem retrieved to
   me.
And as SEJANUS, in thy tragedy,
Falleth from Cæsar's grace; even so the
   crew
Of common playwrights, whom opinion
   blew
Big with false greatness, are disgraced by
   thee
Thus, in one tragedy, thou makest twain:
And, since fair works of justice fit the part
Of tragic writers, Muses do ordain
That all tragedians, ministers of their art,
Who shall hereafter follow on this tract,
In writing well, thy Tragedy shall act.

       —————   CYGNUS.

ON SEJANUS.

SEJANUS, great, and eminent in Rome,
Raised above all the senate, both in grace
Of princes' favour, authority, and place,
And popular dependence; yet how soon,
Even with the instant of his overthrow,
Is all this pride and greatness now forgot,
By them which did his state not treason
   know!
His very flatterers, that did adorn
Their necks with his rich medals, now in
   flame
Consume them, and would lose even his
   name,
Or else recite it with reproach, or scorn!
This was his Roman fate. But now thy
   Muse
To us that neither knew his height, nor
   fall,
Hath raised him up with such memorial,
All future states and times his name shall
   use.
What, not his good, nor ill could once
   extend
To the next age, thy verse, industrious,
And learned friend, hath made illustrious
To this. Nor shall his, or thy fame have
   end.
                        TH. R.[1]

AMICIS, AMICI NOSTRI DIGNISSIMI, B. J. DIGNISSIMIS, EPIGRAMMA. D. JOHANNES MARSTONIUS.

Ye ready friends, spare your unneedful
   bays,
This work despairful envy must even praise:
Phœbus hath voiced it loud through echoing
   skies,
SEJANUS' fall shall force thy merit rise;
For never English shall, or hath before
Spoke fuller graced. He could say much,
   not more.

ON SEJANUS.

How high a poor man shows in low estate
Whose base is firm, and whole frame com-
   petent,
That sees this cedar, made the shrub of
   fate,
Th' one's little, lasting; th' others con-
   fluence spent.
And as the lightning comes behind the
   thunder
From the torn cloud, yet first invades our
   sense:
So every violent fortune, that to wonder
Hoists men aloft, is a clear evidence
Of a vaunt-courring blow the fates have
   given
To his forced state: swift lightning blinds
   his eyes,
While thunder, from comparison-hating
   heaven,
Dischargeth on his height, and there it lies!
If men will shun swol'n fortune's ruinous
   blasts,
Let them use temperance: nothing violent
   lasts.
            WILLIAM STRACHEY.[2]

       —————

ON SEJANUS.

Thy poem (pardon me) is mere deceit,
Yet such deceit, as thou that dost beguile,
Art juster far than they who use no wile;
And they who are deceived by this feat,
More wise, than such who can eschew thy
   cheat:
For thou hast given each part so just a
   style,
That men suppose the action now on file;

---

[1] As I cannot appropriate these and some of the following signatures with any degree of satisfaction to myself, I am unwilling to perplex the reader with conjectures on them to no purpose

[2] There is a William Strachey, who published what he called *Laws, Divine, Moral, &c. for Virginia,* 4to, 1612. But I know nothing more of him, nor whether he be the author of this rugged sonnet.

(And men suppose, who are of best conceit).
Yet some there be, that are not moved
    hereby,
And others are so quick, that they will spy
Where later times are in some speech un-
    weaved,
Those, wary simples ; and these, simple
    elves;
They are so dull, they cannot be deceived,
These so unjust, they will deceive them-
    selves.   ΦΙΛΟΣ.

ON SEJANUS.

When in the Globe's fair ring, our world's
    best stage,
I saw SEJANUS set with that rich foil,
I looked the author should have born the
    spoil
Of conquest, from the writers of the age:
But when I viewed the people's beastly rage,
Bent to confound thy grave, and learned
    toil,
That cost thee so much sweat, and so much
    oil,
My indignation I could hardly assuage.
And many there (in passion) scarce could tell
Whether thy fault, or theirs deserved most
    blame ;
Thine, for so showing, theirs, to wrong the
    same :
But both they left within that doubtful hell,
From whence, this publication sets thee free:
They, for their ignorance, still damned be.

                                         EV. B.

AMICISSIMO, ET MERITISSIMO BEN. JONSON, IN VOLPONEM.

Quod arte ausus es hic tuâ, Poeta,
Si auderent hominum deique juris
Consulti, veteres sequi æmulariérque,
O omnes saperemus ad salutem.
His sed sunt v   es araneosi ;
Tam nemo veterum est sequutor, ut tu
Illos quòd sequeris novator audis.
Fac tamen quod agis ; tuique primâ
Libri canitie induantur horâ :
Nam chartis pueritia est neganda,
Nascuntúrque senes, oportet, illi
Libri, queis dare vis perennitatem.
Priscis, ingenium facit, labórque
Te parem ; hos superes, ut et futuros,
Ex nostrâ vitiositate sumas,
Quâ priscos superamus, et futuros.

                                    J. DONNE.

AD UTRAMQUE ACADEMIAM, DE BEN-JAMIN JONSONIO, IN VOLPONEM.

Hic ille est primus, qui doctum drama
    Britannis,
Graiorum antiqua, et Latii monimenta
    theatri,
Tanquam explorator versans, · fœlicibus
    ausis
Præbrebit : magnis cœptis, gemina astra,
    favete.
Alterutrâ veteres contenti laude : Cothur-
    num hic,
Atque pari soccum tractat Sol scenicus arte;
Das Volpone jocos, fletus Sejane dedisti.
At si Jonsonias mulctatas limite musas
Angusto plangent quiquam : Vos, dicite,
    contrâ,
O nimiùm miseros quibus Anglis Anglica
    lingua,
Aut non sat nota est ; aut queis (seu trans
    mare natis)
Haud nota omnino ! Vegetet cum tempore
    vates,
Mutabit patrium, fiêtque ipse Anglus
    Apollo.

                              E. BOLTON.

TO MY DEAR FRIEND, MASTER BEN. JONSON, UPON HIS FOX.

If it might stand with justice, to allow
The swift conversion of all follies ; now,
Such is my mercy, that I could admit
All sorts should equally approve the wit
Of this thy even work : whose growing
    fame
Shall raise thee high, and thou it, with thy
    name.
And did not manners, and my love com-
    mand
Me to forbear to make those understand,
Whom thou, perhaps, hast in thy wiser
    doom
Long since, firmly resolved, shall never
    come
To know more than they do ; I would have
    shewn
To all the world, the art, which thou
    alone
Hast taught our tongue, the rules of time,
    of place,
And other rites, delivered with the grace
Of comic style, which only, is far more
Than any English stage hath known before.
But since our subtle gallants think it good
To like of nought that may be understood,
Lest they should be disproved : or have, at
    best,

Stomachs so raw, that nothing can digest
But what's obscene, or barks : let us desire
They may continue, simply to admire
Fine cloaths, and strange words ; and may
   live, in age,
To see themselves ill brought upon the
   stage,
And like it.   Whilst thy bold and knowing
   Muse
Contemns all praise, but such as thou
   wouldst choose.

                    FRANCIS BEAUMONT.

ON VOLPONE.

If thou dar'st bite this Fox, then read my
   rhymes ;
Thou guilty art of some of these foul
   crimes :
Which else, are neither his nor thine, but
   Time's.

If thou dost like it, well ; it will imply
Thou lik'st with judgment, or best com-
   pany :
And he, that doth not so, doth yet envy

The ancient forms reduced, as in this age
The vices are ; and bare-faced on the
   stage :
So boys were taught to abhor seen drunkards rage.   T. R.

TO MY GOOD FRIEND MASTER
JONSON.

The strange new follies of this idle age,
In strange new forms, presented on the
   stage
By thy quick muse, so pleased judicious
   eyes ;
That th' once admired ancient comedies'
Fashions, like clothes grown out of fashion,
   lay
Locked up from use : until thy Fox' birth-
   day,
In an old garb, showed so much art, and wit,
As they the laurel gave to thee, and it.

                                   D. D.

ON VOLPONE.

The Fox, that eased thee of thy modest
   fears,
And earthed himself, alive, into our ears
Will so, in death, commend his worth, and
   thee
As neither can, by praises, mended be :

'Tis friendly folly, thou may'st thank, and
   blame,
To praise a book, whose forehead bears thy
   name.
Then JONSON, only this (among the rest,)
I, ever, have observed, thy last work's best :
Pace, gently on ; thy worth, yet higher,
   raise ;
Till thou write best, as well as the best
   plays.
                           ———   J. C.

ON VOLPONE.

Come, yet, more forth, Volpone, and thy
   ' chase
Perform to all length, for thy breath will
   serve thee ;
The usurer shall, never wear thy case :
Men do not hunt to kill, but to preserve
   thee ;
Before the best hounds, thou dost, still, but
   play ;
And, for our whelps, alas, they yelp in
   vain :
Thou hast no earth ; thou hunt'st the milk-
   white way ;
And, through th' Elysian fields, dost make
   thy train.
And as the symbol of life's guard, the
   hare,
That, sleeping, wakes ; and, for her fear
   was saf't :
So, thou shalt be advanced, and make a
   star,
Pole to all wits, believed in, for thy craft.
In which the scenes both mark, and mystery
Is hit, and sounded, to please best, and
   worst ;
To all which, since thou mak'st so sweet a
   cry,
Take all thy best fare, and be nothing
   curst.
                           ———   G. C.[1]

ON VOLPONE.

Volpone now is dead indeed, and lies
Exposed to the censure of all eyes,
And mouths ; now he hath run his train,
   and shewn
His subtle body, where he best was known ;
In both Minerva's cities : he doth yield,
His well-formed limbs upon this open
   field.

---

[1] These lines may be set down without scruple
to Chapman's account.

Who, if they now appear so fair in sight,
How did they, when they were endowed
  with spright
Of action ? In thy praise let this be read,
The Fox will live when all his hounds be
  dead.
                                         E. S.

——

TO BEN JONSON, ON VOLPONE.

Forgive thy friends ; they would, but cannot
  praise,
Enough the wit, art, language of thy plays :
Forgive thy foes ; they will not praise thee.
  Why ?
Thy fate hath thought it best, they should
  envy.
Faith, for thy Fox's sake, forgive then
  those
Who are nor worthy to be friends, nor
  foes.
Or, for their own brave sake, let them be
  still
Fools at thy mercy, and like what they will.
                                        J. F.[1]

——

ON THE SILENT WOMAN.

Hear, you bad writers, and though you not
  see,
I will inform you where you happy be :
Provide the most malicious thoughts you
  can,
And bend them all against some private
  man,
To bring him, not his vices, on the stage ;
Your envy shall be clad in some poor rage,
And your expressing of him shall be such,
That he himself shall think he hath no
  touch.
Where he that strongly writes, although he
  mean
To scourge but vices in a laboured scene,
Yet private faults shall be so well exprest,
As men do act 'em, that each private breast,
That finds these errors in itself, shall say,
He meant me, not my vices, in the play.
                            FRANCIS BEAUMONT.

——

TO MY FRIEND BEN JONSON, UPON
HIS ALCHEMIST.

A master, read in flattery's great skill,
Could not pass truth, though he would
  force his will,

——

[1] These lines are entirely in Fletcher's manner,
to whom I believe we may safely ascribe them.
The preceding are probably by Edward Scory.

By praising this too much, to get more
  praise
In his art, than you out of yours do raise.
Nor can full truth be uttered of your worth,
Unless you your own praises do set forth :
None else can write so skilfully, to shew
Your praise : Ages shall pay, yet still must
  owe.
All I dare say, is, you have written well ;
In what exceeding height, I dare not tell.
                                 GEORGE LUCY.

——

ON THE ALCHEMIST.

The Alchemist, a play for strength of wit,
And true art, made to shame what hath
  been writ
In former ages ; I except no worth
Of what or Greeks or Latins have brought
  forth ;
Is now to be presented to your ear,
For which I would each man were a Muse
  here
To know, and in his soul be fit to be
Judge of this master-piece of comedy ;
That when we hear but once of JONSON'S
  name,
Whose mention shall make proud the
  breath of fame,
We may agree, and crowns of laurel bring
A justice unto him the poet's king.
But he is dead : time, envious of that
  bliss
Which we possest in that great brain of
  his,
By putting out this light hath dark'ned all
The sphere of Poesy, and we let fall
At best unworthy elegies on his hearse,
A tribute that we owe his living verse ;
Which, though some men that never reached
  him may
Decry, that love all folly in a play.
THE WISER FEW SHALL THIS DISTINC-
  TION HAVE,
TO KNEEL, NOT TREAD, UPON HIS
  HONOURED GRAVE.
                               JAMES SHIRLEY.

——

Jonson, t' whose name wise art did bow,
  and wit
Is only justified by honouring it :
To hear whose touch, how would the
  learned quire
With silence stoop ? and when he took
  his lyre,

Apollo stopt his lute, ashamed to see
A rival to the god of harmony, &c.

SHIRLEY'S POEMS, p. 159.[1]

**TO MY FRIEND BEN JONSON, UPON
HIS CATILINE.**

If thou had'st itched after the wild applause
Of common people, and had'st made thy
　laws
In writing, such, as catched at present voice,
I should commend the thing, but not thy
　choice.
But thou hast squared thy rules by what is
　good,
And art three ages, yet, from understood ;
And (I dare say) in it there lies much wit
Lost, till the readers can grow up to it.
Which they can ne'er out-grow, to find it
　ill,
But must fall back again, or like it still.

FRANCIS BEAUMONT.

**TO MY WORTHY FRIEND, BEN JON-
SON, ON HIS CATILINE.**

He, that dares wrong this play, it should
　appear
Dares utter more than other men dare hear,
That have their wits about them: yet such
　men,
Dear friend, must see your book, and read;
　and then
Out of their learned ignorance, cry ill,
And lay you by, calling for mad Pasquil,
Or Green's dear Groatsworth, or Tom
　Coryate,
Or the new Lexicon, with the errant pate :
And pick away, from all these several ends,
And dirty ones, to make their as-wise
　friends
Believe they are translators.　Of this, pity!
There is a great plague hanging o'er the
　city ;
Unless she purge her judgment presently.
But, O thou happy man, that must not
　die,
As these things shall ; leaving no more
　behind
But a thin memory, like a passing wind
That blows, and is forgotten, ere they are
　cold.

---

[1] This is the person singled out by Steevens
and others, with such exquisite propriety, as the
most scurrilous of Jonson's enemies.—*Shak.* vol.
ii. p. 208.

Thy labours shall outlive thee; and, like
　gold
Stampt for continuance, shall be current
　where
There is a sun, a people, or a year.

JOHN FLETCHER.

**TO HIS WORTHY AND BELOVED
FRIEND, MASTER BEN JONSON,
ON HIS CATILINE.**

Had the great thoughts of Catiline been
　good,
The memory of his name, stream of his blood,
His plots past into acts (which would have
　turned
His infamy to fame, though Rome had
　burned),
Had not begot him equal grace with men,
As this, that he is writ by such a pen:
Whose inspirations, if great Rome had had,
Her good things had been bettered, and
　her bad
Undone; the first for joy, the last for fear,
That such a Muse should spread them to
　our ear.
But woe to us then ! for thy laureat brow
If Rome enjoyed had, we had wanted now.
But in this age, where jigs and dances move,
How few there are that this pure work
　approve.
Yet better than I rail at, thou canst scorn
Censures that die ere they be thoroughly
　born.
Each subject, thou, still thee each subject
　raises,
And whosoe'er thy book, himself dispraises.

NAT. FIELD.

**AD V. CL. BEN. JONSONIUM, CARMEN
PROTREPTICON.**

Raptam Threicii lyram Neanthus
Pulset; carmina circulis Palæmon
Scribat; qui manibus facit deabus
Illotis, metuat Probum.　Placere
Te doctis juvat auribus, placere
Te raris juvat auribus.　Camænas
Cùm totus legerem tuas (Camænæ
Nam totum rogitant tuæ, nec ullam
Qui pigrè trahat oscitationem,
Lectorem) et numeros, acumen, artem.
Mirum judicium, quod ipse censor,
JONSONI, nimium licèt malignus,
Si doctus simùl, exigat, viderem,
Sermonem et nitidum, facetiásque

Dignas Mercurio, novásque gnomas
Morum sed veterum, tuique juris
Quicquid dramaticum tui legebam,
Tam semper fore, támque te loquutum,
Ut nec Lemnia notior sigillo
Tellus, nec maculâ sacrandus Apis,
Non cesto Venus, aut comis Apollo,
Quàm musâ fueris sciente notus,
Quàm musâ fueris tuâ notatus,
Illâ, quæ unica, sidus ut refulgens,
Stricturas, superat comis, minorum:
In mentem subiit Stolonis illud,
Lingua Pieridas fuisse Plauti
Usuras, Ciceronis atque dictum,
Saturno genitum phrasi Platonis,
Musæ si Latio, Jovisque Athenis
Dixissent. Fore jam sed hunc et illas
Ionsoni numeros puto loquutos,
Anglis si fuerint utrique fati.
Tam, mi, tu sophiam doces amœnê
Sparslm tamque sophos amœna sternisl
Sed, tot delicias, minùs placebat,
Sparsis distraherent tot in libellis
Cerdoi caculæ. Volumen unum,
Quod seri Britonum terant nepotes,
Optabam, et thyasus chorúsque amantum
Musas hoc cupiunt, tui laborum
Et quicquid reliquum est, adhuc tuisque
Servatum pluteis. Tibi at videmur
Non tàm quærere quàm parare nobis
Laudem, dum volumus palàm merentis
Tot laurus cupidi reposta scripta;
Dum secernere te tuasque musas
Audemus numero ungulæ liquorem
Gustante, et veteres novem sorores
Et Sirenibus et solent cicadis:
Dum et secernere posse te videmur,
Efflictum petimus novúmque librum,
Qui nullo sacer haut petatur ævo,
Qui nullo sacer exolescat ævo,
Qui curis niteat tuis secundis ;
Ut nos scire aliquid simul putetur.
Atqui hoc macte sies, velutque calpar,
Quod diis inferium, tibi sacremus,
Ut nobis benè sit; tuámque frontem
Perfundant ederæ recentiores
Et splendor novus. Invident coronam
Hanc tantam patriæ tibique (quantâ
Æternùm à merito tuo superbum
Anglorum genus esse possit olim)
Tantùm qui penitùs volunt amænas
Sublatas literas, timéntve lucem
Ionsoni nimiam tenebriones.

J. SELDEN.

TO BEN JONSON, ON HIS WORKS.
May I subscribe a name? dares my bold quill
Write that or good or ill,

Whose fame is that of height, that, to mine
eye,
Its head is in the sky ?
Yes. Since the most censures, believes, and
saith
By an implicit faith :
Lest their misfortune make them chance
amiss,
I'll waft them right by this.
Of all I know thou only art the man
That dares but what he can :
Yet by performance shows he can do more
Than hath been done before,
Or will be after ; (such assurance gives
Perfection where it lives,)
Words speak thy matter ; matter fills thy
words :
And choice that grace affords,
That both are best : and both most fitly
placed,
Are with new Venus graced
From artful method. All in this point
meet,
With good to mingle sweet.
These are thy lower parts. What stands
above
Who sees not yet must love,
When on the base he reads Ben Jonson's
name,
And hears the rest from fame.
This from my love of truth : which pays
this due
To your just worth, not you.

ED. HEYWARD.[1]

ON THE AUTHOR OF THIS VOLUME,
THE POET LAUREAT, BEN JON-
SON.

Here is a poet ! whose unmuddled strains
Shew that he held all Helicon in's brains.
What here is writ, is sterling ; every line
Was well allowed of by the Muses nine.
When for the stage a drama he did lay,
Tragic or comic, he still bore away
The sock and buskin ; clearer notes than
his
No swan e'er sung upon our Thamesis ;
For lyric sweetness in an ode, or sonnet,
To BEN the best of wits might veil their
bonnet.

[1] This gentleman was by profession a lawyer,
and an intimate friend of our author, and of the
great Selden. The regard which the latter had
for him appears from his addressing to him his
book on *The Titles of Honour.*—WHAL.

His genius justly, in an entheat rage,
Oft lashed the dull-sworn factors for the
   stage :
For Alchymy, though 't make a glorious
   gloss,
Compared with Gold is bullion and base
   dross.

             WILL. HODGSON.

ON HIS ELABORATE PLAYS.—
EPIGRAM.

Each like an Indian ship or hull appears,
That took a voyage for some certain years,
To plough the sea, and furrow up the main,
And brought rich ingots from his loaded
   brain.
His art the sun ; his labours were the lines;
His solid stuff the treasure of his mines.

             WILL. HODGSON.

IN BENJAMINUM JONSONUM, POE-
TAM LAUREATUM, ET DRAMATI-
CORUM SUI SECULI FACILE PRIN-
CIPEM.

Jonsone, Angliacæ decus immortale
   Camænæ,
Magne pater vatum, Aoniæ Coryphæe
   catervæ,
Benjamine, (tibi nec vanum nominis omen,)
Cui tam dextera Pallas adest, tam dexter
   Apollo ;
Laurigeros egit quoties tuaMusa triumphos!
Laudibus en quantis, quanto evehit Anglia
   plausu
Jonsonum, pleni moderantem fræna theatri !
Per te scena loqui didicit : tibi candida vena,
Et jocus innocuus ; nec quem tua fabula
   mordet
Dente Theonino, sed pravis aspera tantum
Moribus, insanum multo sale defricat
   ævum.
Nec fescennino ludit tua carmine Musa ;
Nec petulans aures amat incestare theatri,
Aut fœdare oculos obscœnis improba nugis :
Sunt tibi tam castæ veneres, plenæque
   pudoris.
Scenam nulla tuam perfrictâ fronte puella
Intrat, nec quenquam teneræ capit illice
   vocis,
Nec spectatorem patranti frangit ocello,
Dramate tu recto, tu linguæ idiomate puro,
Exornas soccósque leves, grandésque
   cothurnos.
Si Lyricus, tu jam Flaccus ; si comicus,
   alter

Plautus es ingenio, tersivè Terentius oris
Anglicus, aut, Græcos si fortè imitere,
   Menander,
Cujus versu usus, ceu sacro emblemate,
   Paulus :
Sin Tragicus, magni jam præceptore
   Neronis
Altiùs eloqueris, Senecâ et prædivite major,
(Ingenii at tantùm dives tu divite venâ,)
Grandiùs ore tonas, verborum et fulmina
   vibras.
Tu captatores, locupleti hamata, seníque,
Munera mittentes, Vulpino decipis astu
Callidus incautos, et fraudem fraude retexis :
Atque hæredipetas corvos deludis hiantes,
Vanâ spe lactans, cera nec scribis in ima.
Per te nec leno aut meretrix impunê perurbem
Grassatur, stolidæ et tendit sua retia pubi.
Nec mœchus, nec fur, incastigatus oberrat,
Illæstsve, tuæ prudenti verbere scenæ.
Sic vitium omne vafer tuus ipse ut
   Horatius olim,
Tangis, et admissus circum præcordia ludis.
Per te audax Catilina, nefas horrendus
   Alastor
Dum struit infandum, cædésque et funera
   passim
Molitur Romæ, facundi consulis ore
Ingenióque perit ; patriæ et dum perfidus
   enses
Intentat jugulo, franguntur colla Cethegi ;
Quicquid Sylla minax, ipsis è faucibus Orci,
Et fortunati demurmuret umbra tyranni :
Nempe faces flammásque extinguit flumine
   lactis
Tullius, Angliaco meliùs sic ore locutus.
Culmine tu rapiens magnum devolvis ab alto
Sejanum ; ille potens populum, pavidúmque
   senatum
Rexerat imperio nuper, dum solus habenas
Tractaret Romæ, nutu et tremefecerat
   orbem,
Cæsare confisus ; nunc verso cardine rerum
Mole suâ miser ipse cadens, et pondere
   pressus,
Concutit attonitum lapsu graviore thea-
   trum,
Ingentémque trahit turbâ plaudente ruinam.
Sic nullum exemplo crimen tu linquis in-
   ultum,
Sive et avarities, et amor vesanus habendi,
Sive sit ambitio, et dominandi cæca libido.
Crimina sic hominum versu tortore flagellas,
Et vitia exponis toti ludibria plebi;
Protinus illa tuo sordent explosa theatro,
Dramáque virtutis schola fit, prælectio
   scena,
Histrio philosophus, morum vel denique
   censor,

Et ludi, Jonsone, tui sic seria ducunt.
Ergo tuā effigies, nostris spectanda plateis,
(Quam meliùs toti ostendit tua Pagina
 mundo)
Non hominis, sed viva Poesios extat imago;
Benjamini icon, capitísque insigne poetæ;
Nomen et ingenii, Jonsoni nomen habetur.[1]

SIR EDWARD HERBERT, UPON HIS
 FRIEND MR. BEN JONSON, AND
 HIS TRANSLATION.

'Twas not enough, Ben Jonson, to be
 thought
Of English poets best, but to have
 brought
In greater state, to their acquaintance, one
Made equal to himself and thee; that
 none
Might be thy second; while thy glory is
To be the Horace of our times, and his.[2]

TO BEN JONSON.

'Tis dangerous to praise ; besides the task
 Which to do't well, will ask
An age of time and judgment; who can
 then
 Be praised, and by what pen?
Yet, I know both, whilst thee I safely chuse
 My subject and my Muse.
For sure, henceforth our poets shall implore
 Thy aid, which lends them more,
Than can their tired Apollo, or the Nine
 She wits, or mighty wine.
The deities are bankrupts, and must be
 Glad to beg art of thee.
Some they might once perchance on thee
 bestow:
 But now to thee they owe :
Who dost in daily bounty more wit spend,
 Than they could ever lend.
Thus thou didst build the Globe, which,
 but for thee,
 Should want its axle-tree ;
And, like a careful founder, thou dost now
 Leave rules for ever, how
To keep't in reparations, which will do
 More good than to build two.
It was an able stock thou gav'st before ;
 Yet, lo, a richer store !

Which doth, by a prevention, make us quit
 With a dear year of wit :
Come when it will, by this thy name shall
 last
 Until Fame's utmost blast, &c.
 BARTON HOLYDAY.[3]

TO MASTER JONSON.
Ben,
The world is much in debt, and though it
 may
Some petty reck'nings to small poets pay:
Pardon if at thy glorious sum they stick,
Being too large for their arithmetic.
If they could prize the genius of a scene,
The learned sweat that makes a language
 clean,
Or understand the faith of ancient skill,
Drawn from the tragic, comic, lyric quill ;
The Greek and Roman denizened by thee,
And both made richer in thy poetry ;
This they may know, and knowing this
 still grudge,
That yet they are not fit of thee to judge.
I prophesy more strength to after time,
Whose joy shall call this isle the poets'
 clime,
Because 'twas thine, and unto thee return
The borrowed flames with which thy Muse
 shall burn.
Then when the stock of other's fame is
 spent,
Thy poetry shall keep its own old rent.
 ZOUCH TOWNLEY.[4]

AD BENJAMINUM JONSONUM.

In jus te voco, JONSONI venito:
Adsum, qui plagii et malæ rapinæ
Te ad Phœbi peragam reum tribunal,
Assidente choro novem dearum.
Quædam dramata scilicet diserta,
Nuper quæ Elysii roseti in umbrâ,
Fæstivissimus omnium poeta,
Plautus composuit, diisque tandem
Stellato exhibuit poli in theatro,
Movendo superis leves cachinnos,
Et risos tetrico Jovi ciendo,
Axe plausibus intonante utroque ;
Hæc tu dramata scilicet diserta,

---

[1] *Musæ Subsecivæ* J. Duporti, *Cantabrigiæ,*
8vo, 1676, p. 8.
[2] From the minor edition of Jonson's Poems,
1640.
[3] From the minor edition of Jonson's Poems,
1640.

1640. There is much more of it; but as Barton
began to grow outrageously witty, it seemed
best to stop short.
[4] From the minor edition of Jonson's Poems,
1640.

Clepsisti superis negotiosis,
Quæ tu nunc tua venditare pergis :
  In jus te voco, Jonsoni venito.
  En pro te pater ipse, Rexque Phœbus
Assurgit modò, Jonsoni, palamque
Testatur, tua serio fuisse
Illa dramata, teque condidisse
Sese non modò conscio, at juvante :
Unde ergò sibi Plautus illa tandem
Nactus exhibuit, Jovi Deisque ?
Maiæ Filius, et Nepos Atlantis,
Pennatus celeres pedes, at ungues
Viscatus, volucer puer, vaferque,
Furto condere quidlibet jocoso,
Ut quondam facibus suis Amorem
Per ludos viduavit, et pharetrâ,
Sic nuper (siquidem solet frequenter
Tecum ludere, plaudere, et jocari)
Neglectas tibi clepsit has papyrus
Secumque ad superos abire jussit :
  Jam victus taceo pudore, vincis
  Phœbo Judice, JONSONI, et Patrono.[1]

ON BEN JONSON.

Mirror of poets, mirror of our age !
Which her whole face beholding on thy
  stage,
Pleased and displeased with her own faults,
  endures
A remedy like those whom music cures.
Thou hast alone those various inclinations,
Which Nature gives to ages, sexes, nations,
So traced with thy all-resembling pen,
That whate'er custom has imposed on men,
Or ill-got habit, which deforms them so,
That scarce a brother can his brother know,
Is represented to the wond'ring eyes
Of all that see or read thy comedies ;
Whoever in those glasses looks, may find
The spots returned, or graces of his mind:
And by the help of so divine an art,
At leisure view, and dress his nobler part.
Narcissus cozened by that flatt'ring well,
Which nothing could but of his beauty tell,
Had here, discovering the deformed estate
Of his fond mind, preserved himself with
  hate ;
But virtue too, as well as vice, is clad
In flesh and blood so well, that Plato had
Beheld what his high fancy once embraced
Virtue with colours, speech, and motion
  graced
The sundry postures of thy copious Muse,
Who would express a thousand tongues
  . must use :

---

[1] *Caroli Fitzgeofridi Affan. Oxoniæ*, 1601.

Whose fate's no less peculiar than thy
  art,
For as thou couldst all characters im-
  part :
So none could render thine, who still
  escapes
Like Proteus in variety of shapes :
Who was nor this, nor that, but all we
  find,
And all we can imagine in mankind.

                 E. WALLER.

ON MASTER BENJAMIN JONSON.

After the rare arch-poet JONSON died,
The sock grew loathsome, and the buskin's
  pride,
Together with the stage's glory, stood
Each like a poor and pitied widowhood.
The cirque prophaned was ; and all pos-
  tures rackt:
For men did strut, and stride, and stare,
  not act.
Then temper flew from words : and men
  did squeak,
Look red, and blow, and bluster, but not
  speak:
No holy rage, or frantic fires did stir,
Or flash about the spacious theatre.
No clap of hands, or shout, or praises-
  proof
Did crack the play-house sides, or cleave
  her roof.
Artless the scene was ; and that monstrous
  sin
Of deep and arrant ignorance came in ;
Such ignorance as theirs was, who once
  hist
At thy unequalled play, the Alchemist:
Oh fie upon 'em ! Lastly too, all wit
In utter darkness did, and still will sit ;
Sleeping the luckless age out, till that
  she
Her resurrection has again with thee.

    HERRICK'S *Hesperides*, 1648, p. 173.

ON BEN JONSON.

Here lies JONSON with the rest
Of the poets ; but the best.
Reader, wouldst thou more have known ?
Ask his story, not this stone ;
That will speak what this can't tell,
Of his glory. So farewell !

                 Ibid. p. 342.

AN ODE FOR BEN JONSON.

Ah BEN !
  Say how, or when
  Shall we thy guests
Meet at those lyric feasts,
  Made at the Sun,
The Dog,[1] the Triple Tun ?
Where we such clusters had,
As made us nobly wild, not mad ;
  And yet each verse of thine
Outdid the meat, outdid the frolic wine.

My BEN
  Or come agen ;
  Or send to us
Thy wits great over-plus :
  But teach us yet
Wisely to husband it ;
Lest we that talent spend :
  And having once brought to an end
  That precious stock ; the store
Of such a wit : the world should have
  no more.   *Ibid.* p. 342.

TO BEN JONSON.

As Martial's Muse by Cæsar's ripening rays
Was sometimes cherished, so thy happier days
Joy'd in the sunshine of thy royal JAMES,
Whose crown shed lustre on thy Epigrams :
But I, remote from favour's fostering heat,
O'er snowy hills my Muses' passage beat,
Where weeping rocks my harder fates
  lament,
And shuddering woods whisper my discon-
  tent.
What wonder then my numbers, that have
  rolled
Like streams of Tigris, run so slow and
  cold ![2]

TO THE SAME.

Let Ignorance with Envy chat,
In spite of both, thou fame shalt win ;
Whose mass of learning seems like that,
Which Joseph gave to BENJAMIN. *Ibid.*

I do not wonder that great JONSON's play
Was scorn'd so by the ignorant that day

It did appear in its most glorious shine,
And comely acting graced each learned
  line :
There was some reason for it, 'twas above
Their reach, their envy, their applause, or
  love :
When as the wiser few did it admire,
And warmed their fancies at his genuine
  fire, &c.   C. G.[3]

A. COCKAYNE TO MR. RICHARD BROME.

"Then"—(That is, when the dull zealots
  shall give way, which yet Sir Aston did
  not live to see)—

"Then shall learned Jonson reassume his
  seat,
Revive the *Phœnix* by a second heat ;
Create the *Globe* anew, and people it
By those that flock to surfeit on his wit."—

Again, apologizing "to his worthy
friend," Marmaduke Wevil, for attempting
an epigram, he says—

"When I bethink me that great Jonson,
  (he,
Who all the ancient wit of Italy
And learned Greece, by his industrious
  pen
Transplanted hath, for his own country-
  men,
And made our English tongue so swell
  that now
We scarce an equal unto it allow)
Writ epigrams, I tremble ; and instead
Of praise, beseech a pardon when I'm
  read."

Cernitur hic, nulla Famæ dignata tabella
JONSONII effigies ; omni memorabilis ævo!
Qui mores hominum tenui depinxit avena
Stultitiam vulgi, curas, et inania vota—
Comicus ipse labor ridenti Dramata nomen
Efferat, et laudes *Mulier Taciturna*
  loquatur.
Exuberat docili vafer *Alchymista* lepore
Et *Vulpes* fallax, salo non parcente, place-
  bit,[4] &c.

---

[1] The *Dog* is mentioned by Lord Falkland, in one of his letters to our author. "If there be anything tolerable in my poem, it is somewhat you dropt negligently one day at the *Dog*, and I took up."
[2] From *Two Books of Epigrams*, by T. Bancroft, 4to, 1639.

[3] The lines are prefixed with others to Nabbes's *Unfortunate Mother*, 1640. I know not the author.
[4] From a poem on the monuments in Westminster Abbey, printed about the beginning of the last century.

AD BEN. JONSON.

Filius Hebræis Ben est : Son filius Anglis :
  Filii es ergo duo : quot tibi quæso patres ?
Si scio, disperiam : scio quod sit magnus
  Apollo
Unus de patribus, magne poeta, tuis.
            J. DUNBAR, *Epig.* 1616.

BEN JONSON.

—" The coin must sure for current sterling
    pass,
Stamped with old Chaucer's venerable face.
But JONSON found it of a gross allay,
Melted it down, and flung the scum away.
He dug pure silver from a Roman mine,
And prest his sacred image on the coin.
We all rejoiced to see the pillaged ore ;
Our tongue inriched, which was so poor
    before.
Fear not, learned poet, our impartial blame,
Such thefts as these add lustre to thy
    name.
All yield, consenting to sustain the yoke,
And learn the language which the victor
    spoke.
So Macedon's imperial hero threw
His wings abroad, and conquered as he
    flew.
Great Jonson's deeds stand parallel with his,
Are noble thefts, successful piracies,"[1] &c.

UPON THE WORKS OF BEN JONSON.

ODE.[2]

I.

Great thou ! whom 'tis a crime almost to
    dare to praise,
Whose firm established and unshaken glo-
    ries stand,
      And proudly their own fame com-
        mand,
  Above our power to lessen or to raise,
And all, but the few heirs of thy brave
      genius, and thy bays ;
Hail, mighty founder of our stage ! for so
    I dare
Entitle thee, nor any modern censures fear,
  Nor care what thy unjust detractors say ;

They'll say, perhaps, that others did
    materials bring,
  That others did the first foundations
    lay.
  And glorious 'twas (we grant) but to
    begin :
  But thou alone couldst finish the design,
All the fair model and the workmanship
    was thine :
Some bold advent'rers might have been
    before,
  Who durst the unknown world explore ;
By them it was surveyed at distant view,
And here and there a cape, and line they
    drew,
  Which only served as hints and marks
    to thee,
Who wast reserved to make the full dis-
    covery :
  Art's compass to thy painful search we
    owe,
Whereby thou went'st so far, and we may
    after go,
By that we may wit's vast and trackless
    ocean try,
    Content no longer, as before,
    Dully to coast along the shore,
But steer a course more unconfined, and free,
Beyond the narrow bounds, that pent anti-
    quity.

     *   *   *   *

IV.

Nature and Art together met, and joined,
Made up the character of thy great mind.
  That like a bright and glorious sphere,
  Appeared with numerous stars embellished
    o'er.
And much of light to thee, and much of
    influence bore.
This was the strong intelligence, whose
    power
Turned it about, and did the unerring
    motions steer :
  Concurring both like vital seed and heat,
  The noble births they jointly did beget,
    And hard 'twas to be thought,
  Which most of force to the great genera-
    tion brought :
So mingling elements compose our bodies
    frame,

---

[1] From a spirited *Poem on the British Poets*, of which I neglected to note the date.

[2] This Ode, written in the irregular and extravagant fashion of those days, is by Oldham ; it contains, like all his pieces, amidst much harshness, many passages of elegance and vigour. If the judgment of the poet be impeached, it may soften censure to recollect that he was now a mere youth, being, I believe, not above twenty-three or four when it appeared. I have borrowed but a few stanzas from it, and those, perhaps, not the best. With these the list of *Ancient Commendatory Verses on Jonson* must close : it might easily have been extended to twice its length ; but—*satis, quod sufficit.*

Fire, water, earth, and air,
Alike their just proportions share,
Each undistinguished still remains the
    same,
Yet can't we say that either's here or there,
But all, we know not how, are scattered
    ev'ry where.

* * * * *

IX.

Beshrew those envious tongues, who seek
    to blast thy bays,
Who spots in thy bright fame would find,
    or raise,
And say it only shines with borrowed rays;
Rich in thyself, to whose unbounded store
Exhausted Nature could vouchsafe no
    more :
Thou couldst alone the empire of the stage
    maintain,
Couldst all its grandeur and its port
    sustain,
Nor needest others subsidies to pay,
Needest no tax on foreign, or thy native
    country lay,
To bear the charges of thy purchased
    fame,
But thy own stock could raise the same,
Thy sole revenue all the vast expense defray:
Yet like some mighty conqueror in poetry,
    Designed by fate of choice to be
Founder of its new universal monarchy,
    Boldly thou didst the learned world in-
    vade,
    Whilst all around thy pow'rful genius
    swayed,
Soon vanquished Rome and Greece were
    made submit,
Both were thy humble tributaries made,
And thou return'dst in triumph with her
    captive wit.

X.

Unjust, and more ill-natured those,
Thy spiteful and malicious foes,
Who on thy happiest talent fix a lye,
And call that slowness which was care and
    industry.
Let me (with pride so to be guilty thought)
Share all thy wished reproach, and share
    thy shame,
If diligence be deemed a fault,
If to be faultless must deserve their blame :
Judge of thyself alone (for none there were
Could be so just, or could be so severe)
    Thou thine own works didst strictly
    try
By known and uncontested rules of poetry,
    And gavest thy sentence still impartially :

With rigour thou arraign'st each guilty line,
    And spar'dst no criminal sense, because
    'twas thine :
Unbribed with labour, love, or self-conceit,
    (For never, or too seldom we,
Objects too near us, our own blemishes can
    see)
    Thou didst not small'st delinquencies
    acquit,
    But saw'st them to correction all submit,
Saw'st execution done on all convicted
    crimes of wit.

* * * * *

XIII.

Let meaner spirits stoop to low precarious
    fame,
    Content on gross and coarse applause to
    live,
And what the dull and senseless rabble give,
Thou didst it still with noble scorn con-
    temn ;
Nor wouldst that wretched alms receive,
The poor subsistence of some bankrupt,
    sordid name :
    Thine was no empty vapour, raised
    beneath,
    And formed of common breath,
The false and foolish fire that whisked
    about
By popular air, and glares awhile, and then
    goes out ;
But 'twas a solid, whole, and perfect globe
    of light,
    That shone all over, was all over bright,
And dared all sullying clouds, and feared
    no dark'ning night ;
    Like the gay monarch of the stars and sky,
    Who wheresoe'er he does display
    His sovereign lustre, and majestic ray,
    Straight all the less, and petty glories nigh
        Vanish, and shrink away,
O'erwhelmed, and swallowed by the greater
    blaze of day ;
With such a strong, an awful and vic-
    torious beam
    Appeared, and ever shall appear, thy fame,
Viewed, and adored by all the undoubted
    race of wit,
    Who only can endure to look on it.
    The rest o'ercame with too much light,
With too much brightness dazzled, or ex-
    tinguished quite :
Restless and uncontrolled it now shall pass
As wide a course about the world as he,
And when his long-repeated travels cease
    Begin a new and vaster race,
And still tread round the endless circle of
    eternity.
                                    b

[I cannot understand why Gifford has nowhere given at length the famous *Letter from Beaumont*, to which he makes such frequent reference. It ought certainly to have been included either among the *Characters*, or the *Commendatory Verses*; and appears with peculiar propriety in a volume of the Series, which derives its name from one of its couplets.]

MASTER FRANCIS BEAUMONT'S LETTER TO BEN JONSON,

WRITTEN BEFORE HE AND MASTER FLETCHER CAME TO LONDON, WITH TWO OF THE PRECEDENT COMEDIES, THEN NOT FINISHED, WHICH DEFERRED THEIR MERRY MEETINGS AT THE MERMAID.

The sun (which doth the greatest comfort
   bring
To absent friends, because the self same
   thing
They know, they see, however absent) is
Here our best hay-maker (forgive me this ;
It is our country's style :) in this warm
   shine
I lie, and dream of your full Mermaid wine.
Oh, we have water mixed with claret lees,
Drink apt to bring in drier heresies
Than beer, good only for the sonnet's
   strain,
With fustian metaphors to stuff the brain ;
So mixed that, given to the thirstiest one,
'Twill not prove alms, unless he have the
   stone :
I think with one draught man's invention
   fades,
Two cups had quite spoiled Homer's Iliads ;
'Tis liquor that will find out Sutcliffe's wit ;
Lie where he will, and make him write
   worse yet :
Filled with such moisture, in most grievous
   qualms,
Did Robert Wisdom write his singing
   psalms ;
And so must I do this ; and yet I think
It is a potion sent us down to drink
By special Providence, keeps us from fights,
Make us not laugh when we make legs to
   knights ;
'Tis this that keeps our minds fit for our
   states,
A medicine to obey our magistrates ;

For we do live more free than you ; no
   hate,
No envy at one another's happy state,
Moves us ; we are all equal every whit :
Of land, that God gives men here is their
   wit,
If we consider fully ; for our best
And gravest man will with his main house-
   jest
Scarce please you ; we want subtilty to do
The city tricks, lie, hate, and flatter too :
Here are none that can bear a painted
   show,
Strike when you wince, and then lament
   the blow :
Who, like mills set the right way for to
   grind,
Can make their gains alike with every wind ;
Only some fellows, with the subtlest pate
Amongst us, may perchance equivocate
At selling of a horse, and that's the most.
Methinks the little wit I had is lost
Since I saw you ; for wit is like a rest
Held up at tennis, which men do the best
With the best gamesters. What things have
   we seen
Done at the Mermaid ! heard words that
   have been
So nimble, and so full of subtle flame,
As if that every one from whence they came
Had meant to put his whole wit in a jest,
And had resolved to live a fool the rest
Of his dull life ; then where there hath
   been thrown
Wit able enough to justify the town
For three days past : wit that might war-
   rant be
For the whole city to talk foolishly,
Till that were cancelled ; and when that
   was gone,
We left an air behind us, which alone
Was able to make the two next companies
Right witty ; though but downright fools,
   mere wise :[1]

---

[1] [Mr. Dyce prints this couplet :

Was able to make the two next companies
(Right witty, though but downright fools) more
   wise.

And appends a note to say, "The brackets which

I have added will render the meaning of this passage clear. Seward printed :

Was able to make the two next companies
Right witty ; though but downright fools, meer
   wise,

And so his successors." And surely they were

When I remember this, and see that now
The country gentlemen begin to allow
My wit for dry bobs, then I needs must
    cry,
I see my days of ballating grow nigh ;
I can already riddle, and can sing
Catches, sell bargains, and I fear shall
    bring
Myself to speak the hardest words I find
Over as oft as any, with one wind
That takes no medicines. But one thought
    of thee
Makes me remember all these things to
    be
The wit of our young men, fellows that
    shew
No part of good, yet utter all they know ;

Who, like trees of the gard, have growing
    souls.
Only strong Destiny, which all controls,
I hope hath left a better fate in store
For me, thy friend, than to live ever poor,
Banished unto this home. Fate once again
Bring me to thee, who canst make smooth
    and plain
The way of knowledge for me, and then I,
Who have no good but in thy company,
Protest it will my greatest comfort be
To acknowledge all I have to flow from
    thee.
Ben, when these scenes are perfect, we'll
    taste wine ;
I'll drink thy Muse's health, thou shalt
    quaff mine.

---

right. " Mere " in the sense of *absolute, decided*, is familiar to every reader. What Beaumont meant to say, is that Jonson and his friends left behind them such an aroma of wit that it was sufficient to render the two next ordinary companies " right witty," and, even supposing these companies to be composed of " downright fools," it sufficed to make them for the time being " mere wise ;" *i.e.*, models of wisdom. Mr. Dyce, on the contrary, makes Beaumont say that the two companies were " right witty, though downright fools " (a combination not easily imagined), and that under the influence of the aroma, they became " more wise than downright fools" are, (which would leave them worse *company* than before.) Still the second line is very probably corrupt. The meaning would be a trifle more clear if the couplet were printed :

Was able to make the two next companies
Right witty ; and, though downright fools, mere
    wise.—F. C.]

Every Man in his Humour.

EVERY MAN IN HIS HUMOUR.] This Comedy (as here given) was first presented in 1598, at the Globe, and, as the title says, by the Lord Chamberlain's Servants. It was not printed till 1616.

The first appearance of *Every Man in his Humour* on the stage, was either in 1595 or in 1596, when it was brought out at the Rose Theatre, by Henslowe and Alleyn, and proved exceedingly popular. Before it was purchased by the company at the Globe, it had undergone a variety of alterations ; the names, the place of action, were radically altered ; some of the dialogue was remodelled, and the incidents accommodated to the changes of the scene, which was brought from Italy to England. It has always been a favourite, and is still in possession of the stage.[1]

The 4to edition appeared in 1601: there is not the least probability of its having been given to the press by Jonson, whose name is misspelt in the title-page, and who indeed, if the property of the play had been in his own hands, would naturally be inclined to suppress it altogether. It had neither dedication nor prologue, and was probably printed from the bookholder's copy at the *Rose*.

Jonson has subjoined the names of "the principal comedians ;" these were "Will. Shakspeare, Aug. Philips, Hen. Condel, Will. Slye, Will. Kempe, Ric. Burbage, J. Hemings, Tho. Pope, Chr. Beeston, and John Duke :" this arrangement, however, does not enable us to appropriate the characters to the names, respectively.

TO THE

MOST LEARNED, AND MY HONOURED FRIEND,

MASTER CAMDEN, CLARENCIEUX.

"SIR,—There are, no doubt, a supercilious race in the world, who will esteem all office, done you in this kind, an injury ; so solemn a vice it is with them to use the authority of their ignorance, to the crying down of *Poetry*, or the professors : but my gratitude must not leave to correct their error ; since I am none of those that can suffer the benefits conferred upon my youth to perish with my age. It is a frail memory that remembers but present things : and, had the favour of the times so conspired with my disposition, as it could have brought forth other, or better, you had had the same proportion, and number of the fruits, the first. Now, I pray you to accept this ; such wherein neither the confession of my manners shall make you blush ; nor of my studies, repent you to have been the instructer : and for the profession of my thankfulness, I am sure it will, with good men, find either praise or excuse.
"Your True Lover, BEN JONSON."[2]

---

[1] "Of Jonson's fifty dramas" (as Mr. A. Chalmers informs us) "there are not above three which preserve his name on the stage." Mr. Malone, too, talks of Jonson's fifty dramas, as if he were speaking of those of Shakspeare, or Beaumont and Fletcher. Did neither of these critics know, that of those *fifty* pieces, absurdly called *dramas* by them, four-and-thirty, at least, were never intended for the stage ! But thus it ever is in the case of our author :—deception walks hand in hand with ignorance. "His first *play* (says the *Theatrum Poetarum*, 1800,) was *Every Man in his Humour*, 1598, 4to." (there is no such edition), "his *sixth, Part of King James's Entertainment in passing to his Coronation*" (an excellent *play*), "his *forty-ninth*" (more excellent still) "the *King and Queen's Entertainment at Bolsover !*" p. 243. The fiftieth *play* is not specified ; but, from its position, was probably the *Grammar*.

[2] This Dedication was not printed until Jonson collected his works, in 1616 ; Camden was made king at arms in 1597, about which time it was probably written.

VOL. I. B

PROLOGUE.

Though need make many poets, and some
    such
As art and nature have not bettered much;
Yet ours for want hath not so loved the
    stage,
As he dare serve the ill customs of the age,
Or purchase your delight at such a rate,
As, for it, he himself must justly hate:
To make a child now swaddled, to proceed
Man, and then shoot up, in one beard and
    weed,
Past threescore years; or, with three rusty
    swords,
And help of some few foot and half-foot
    words,
Fight over York and Lancaster's long jars,
And in the tyring-house bring wounds to
    scars.
He rather prays you will be pleased to see
One such to-day, as other plays should be;
Where neither chorus wafts you o'er the
    seas,

Nor creaking throne comes down the boys
    to please:
Nor nimble squib is seen to make afeard
The gentlewomen; nor rolled bullet heard
To say, it thunders; nor tempestuous drum
Rumbles, to tell you when the storm doth
    come;
But deeds, and language, such as men do
    use,
And persons, such as comedy would choose,
When she would shew an image of the
    times,
And sport with human follies, not with
    crimes,[1]
Except we make them such, by loving still
Our popular errors, when we know they're ill.
I mean such errors as you'll all confess
By laughing at them, they deserve no less:
Which when you heartily do, there's hope
    left then,
You, that have so graced monsters, may
    like men.[2]

DRAMATIS PERSONÆ.

Knowell, *an Old Gentleman.*
Edward Knowell, *his Son.*
Brainworm, *the Father's Man.*
George Downright, *a plain Squire.*
Wellbred, *his half Brother.*
Kitely, *a Merchant.*
Captain Bobadill, *a Paul's Man.*[3]
Master Stephen, *a Country Gull.*
Master Mathew, *the Town Gull.*

Thomas Cash, *Kitely's Cashier.*
Oliver Cob, *a Water-bearer.*
Justice Clement, *an old merry Magistrate.*
Roger Formal, *his Clerk.*
Wellbred's *Servant.*
Dame Kitely, *Kitely's Wife.*
Mistress Bridget, *his Sister.*
Tib, *Cob's Wife.*
Servants, &c.

SCENE,—London.

---

[1] This Prologue, which was probably written in 1596 (see Life), does not appear to have been given to the press till 1616, when the author collected and published his works in a folio volume. It makes a manly appeal to the good sense of the people, and touches with spirit as well as humour on the defects and absurdities of the old stage. Lyly, Kyd, and above all, the rude dramatisers of our ancient chronicles, are evidently pointed at; writers who had already fallen under the ridicule of Sir Philip Sidney and others in terms still stronger than these. "Squibs," "battles," "fights over sea and land, in choruses," "drums," "trumpets," "targets," "creaking thrones," and all the woful machinery of a poor stage had been the merry burden of many a prologue and epilogue from the first dawning of good taste under Shakspeare. Of this a hundred examples lie before me; but enough perhaps, and more than enough, has been already produced on the subject.

The only allusion which it is not in my power to appropriate, is that to the "descending throne;" yet that some such marvellous piece of machinery was displayed to the admiring audience, is certain, as I have found it mentioned in several places: one I have preserved:

  "First for the gallery—in which the *throne,*
  To their amazement, *shall descend alone;*
  The rosin lightning flash, the monster spire
  Squibs, and ev'n words far hotter than his
    fire."—*Epilogue to the Scholar.*

[2] *And sport with human follies, not with crimes.*] This distinction is made expressly from the precept of Aristotle; who assigns the τὸ γελοῖον, or the ridiculous, as the immediate subject of comedy, Poetic. Sect. 5; but makes the crimes of men, as being of a more serious nature, the particular object of the tragic poet.—WHAL.

[3] *A Paul's man.*] i.e., a frequenter of the middle aisle of St. Paul's cathedral, the common resort of cast captains, sharpers, gulls, and gossipers of every description.

Every Man in his Humour.

ACT I.

SCENE I.—*A Street.*

Enter Knowell *at the door of his House.*

Know. A goodly day toward, and a
fresh morning.—Brainworm!

Enter Brainworm.

Call up your young master: bid him rise,
sir.
Tell him, I have some business to employ
him.
Brai. I will, sir, presently.
Know. But hear you, sirrah,
If he be at his book, disturb him not.
Brai. Very good, sir.[1]   [*Exit.*
Know. How happy yet should I esteem
myself,
Could I, by any practice, wean the boy
From one vain course of study he affects.
He is a scholar, if a man may trust
The liberal voice of fame in her report,
Of good account in both our Universities,
Either of which hath favoured him with
graces:
But their indulgence must not spring in me
A fond opinion that he cannot err.
Myself was once a student,[2] and indeed,
Fed with the self-same humour he is now,
Dreaming on nought but idle poetry,
That fruitless and unprofitable art,
Good unto none, but least to the pro-
fessors;
Which then, I thought the mistress of all
knowledge:
But since, time and the truth have waked
my judgment,
And reason taught me better to distinguish
The vain from the useful learnings.

Enter Master Stephen.

                              Cousin Stephen!
What news with you, that you are here so
early?
Step. Nothing, but e'en come to see how
you do, uncle.
Know. That's kindly done; you are welcome, coz.
Step. Ay, I know that, sir; I would not
have come else. How does my cousin
Edward, uncle?
Know. O, well, coz; go in and see: I
doubt he be scarce stirring yet.
Step. Uncle, afore I go in, can you tell
me, an he have e'er a book of the sciences
of hawking and hunting; I would fain
borrow it.
Know. Why, I hope you will not a
hawking now, will you?
Step. No, wusse; but I'll practise against
next year, uncle. I have bought me a
hawk, and a hood, and bells, and all; I
lack nothing but a book to keep it by.[3]

[1] *Very good, sir.*] So the quarto. The answer in the folio is, *Well, sir.* It signifies little
which is taken, though it may be just necessary
to note the variation.
[2] *Myself was once, &c.*] This is taken, with
no great variation, from the eternal butt of ridicule to the wits of Jonson's days, the *Spanish
Tragedy.* It is spoken by old Jeronimo, who,
if we may believe Decker, was personated by
our poet: so that the lines probably dwelt upon
his memory:

"When I was young, I gave my mind,
  And 'plied myself to fruitless poetry:
  Which, though it profit the possessor nought,
  Yet is it passing pleasing to the world."

[3] *I lack nothing but a book to keep it by.*]
Master Stephen certainly began at the wrong
end: he had not far to seek, however, for the information which he wanted, as treatises on the
"noble science" of hawking were to be found on
every stall, and particularly in St. Paul's Churchyard. Here, among many others on the subject,
the Gentleman's Academie, or the *Book of St.
Albans,* was printed and sold by Humphrey
Lownds, 1595; and from its celebrity, might not
improbably be the book which Master Stephen
had in view. I have expressed my detestation
of this pursuit in the notes to the *Picture,* (act v.
sc. 1), Massinger, vol. iii.
  As some corroboration of what is there stated,
it may not be amiss to subjoin a few words
quoted by Whalley from Sir T. Eliot's *Governor,*
1542. "I would our falcons might be satisfied
with the division of their prey, as the falcons in
Thracia were, that they needed not to devour
the hens of this realm in such number, that unless it be shortly considered, our familiar poultry
shall be as scarce, as now partridge and
pheasant. I speak not this in dispraise of the
falcons, but of them which keepeth them like
cockneys. The mean gentlemen and honest

Know. O, most ridiculous !

Step. Nay, look you now, you are angry,
uncle :—Why, you know an a man have
not skill in the hawking and hunting languages now-a-days, I'll not give a rush for
him : they are more studied than the Greek,
or the Latin. He is for no gallants company without them ; and by gads-lid I
scorn it,[1] I, so I do, to be a consort for
every hum-drum : hang them, scroyles ![2]
there's nothing in them i' the world. What
do you talk on it ? Because I dwell at
Hogsden, I shall keep company with none
but the archers of Finsbury,[3] or the citizens
that come a ducking to Islington ponds !
A fine jest, i' faith ! 'Slid, a gentleman mun
show himself like a gentleman. Uncle, I
pray you be not angry ; I know what I
have to do, I trow, I am no novice.

Know. You are a prodigal, absurd cox-
comb, go to !
Nay, never look at me, 'tis I that speak ;
Take 't as you will, sir, I'll not flatter you.
Have you not yet found means enow to
waste
That which your friends have left you, but
you must
Go cast away your money on a buzzard,[4]
And know not how to keep it, when you
have done ?
O, it is comely ! this will make you a
gentleman !
Well, cousin, well, I see you are e'en past
hope
Of all reclaim :—ay, so ; now you are told
on't,
You look another way.

Step. What would you ha' me do ?

Know. What would I have you do ? I'll
tell you, kinsman ;
Learn to be wise, and practise how to
thrive ;
That would I have you do : and not to
spend
Your coin on every bauble that you fancy,
Or every foolish brain that humours you.
I would not have you to invade each place,
Nor thrust yourself on all societies,
Till men's affections, or your own desert,
Should worthily invite you to your rank.
He that is so respectless in his courses,
Oft sells his reputation at cheap market.
Nor would I, you should melt away your-
self
In flashing bravery,[5] lest, while you affect
To make a blaze of gentry to the world,
A little puff of scorn extinguish it ;
And you be left like an unsavoury snuff,
Whose property is only to offend.
I'd have you sober, and contain yourself,
Not that your sail be bigger than your boat ;
But moderate your expenses now, at first,
As you may keep the same proportion still :
Nor stand so much on your gentility,
Which is an airy, and mere borrowed thing,
From dead men's dust, and bones ; and
none of yours,
Except you make, or hold it.

Enter a Servant.

Who comes here ?

Serv. Save you, gentlemen !

Step. Nay, we do not stand much on

---

householders which care for the gentle entertainment of their friends, do find in their dish that I
say truth, and noblemen shall right shortly espy
it, when they come suddenly to their friend's
house unpurveyed for lack of long warning."

[1] *And by gads-lid I scorn it, I,*] I take the
earliest opportunity of remarking, that the
quarto is shockingly profane. What other vices
the poet brought from Flanders I do not wish to
inquire ; but it is to be feared, that our armies
there, as Uncle Toby says of those in his time,
"swore terribly," and that Jonson was too apt a
scholar. Better knowledge, or the dread of a
licenser, subsequently taught him to correct this
dangerous propensity, or at least to indulge it
with more caution, as a very visible improvement in this respect is manifested in the folio
copies of this and every other play.

[2] *Hang 'em, scroyles !*] Scrophulous, scabby
fellows. The word is used by Shakspeare :

By heaven, the scroyles of Angiers flout you,
kings.—*King John.*—WHALLEY.

[3] —— *the archers of Finsbury.*] In 1498, all
the gardens which had continued time out of
mind without Moorgate, to wit, about and beyond
the lordship of Finsbury, were destroyed, and of
them was made a plain field to shoot in. It was
called *Finsbury* field, in which there were three
windmills, and here they usually shoot at twelve
score. Stow, 1633, p. 913. In Jonson's time this
was the usual resort of the plainer citizens. People
of fashion, or who aspired to be thought so, probably mixed but little in those parties ; and hence
we may account for the indignation of Master
Stephen at being suspected of such vulgarity.
An idea of a similar kind occurs in Shakspeare :
"As if thou never walk'dst further than Finsbury."—*Henry IV. First Part*, act iii. sc. 2.

[4] *Go cast away your money on a* buzzard,] I
prefer this to *kite*, which is the reading of the
folio.

[5] In flashing *bravery*,] Extravagant gaiety of
apparel ; in this sense *bravery* occurs so frequently in our old authors, that it seems scarcely
necessary to notice it, unless when some ambiguity is created by a recollection of its modern
sense.

our gentility, friend ;[1] yet you are welcome :
and I assure you mine uncle here is a man
of a thousand a year, Middlesex land. He
has but one son in all the world, I am his
next heir, at the common law, Master
Stephen, as simple as I stand here, if my
cousin die, as there's hope he will : I have
a pretty living o' mine own too, beside,
hard by here.

Serv. In good time, sir.

Step. In good time, sir ! why, and in
very good time, sir ! You do not flout,
friend, do you ?

Serv. Not I, sir.

Step. Not you, sir ! you were not best,
sir ; an you should, here be them can perceive it, and that quickly too ; go to : and
they can give it again soundly too, an need
be.

Serv. Why, sir, let this satisfy you ; good
faith, I had no such intent.

Step. Sir, an I thought you had, I
would talk with you, and that presently.

Serv. Good Master Stephen, so you may,
sir, at your pleasure.

Step. And so I would, sir, good my
saucy companion ! an you were out o'
mine uncle's ground, I can tell you ;

though I do not stand upon my gentility
neither, in't.

Know. Cousin, cousin, will this ne'er be
left ?

Step. Whoreson, base fellow ! a me-
chanical serving-man ! By this cudgel, an
'twere not for shame, I would——

Know. What would you do, you pe-
remptory gull ?[2]
If you cannot be quiet, get you hence.
You see, the honest man demeans him-
self
Modestly tow'rds you, giving no reply
To your unseasoned, quarrelling, rude fa-
shion ;
And still you huff it, with a kind of carriage
As void of wit, as of humanity.
Go, get you in ; 'fore heaven, I am a-
shamed
Thou hast a kinsman's interest in me.
[*Exit* Master Stephen.

Serv. I pray, sir, is this Master Knowell's
house ?

Know. Yes, marry is it, sir.

Serv. I should enquire for a gentleman
here, one Master Edward Knowell ; do you
know any such, sir, I pray you ?

Know. I should forget myself else, sir.

Serv. Are you the gentleman ? cry you

---

[1] *We do not stand much on our gentility,
friend ;*] This answer is made with exquisite
humour. Stephen piques himself on being a
gentleman : Knowell had just reproved him for
a rough, illiberal behaviour, and cautions him not
to presume upon his birth and fortune. Master
Stephen does not seem to relish this advice, but
at the entrance of the servant, he discovers his
regard for what his uncle had been saying, by
the repetition of his last words.—WHAL.

I am doubtful whether Whalley has entered
much into the poet's drift. The answer is, indeed,
exquisitely humorous ; but it seems to be levelled
at the little effect which salutary counsel has on
such compounds of imbecility and vanity as
Master Stephen. Of all the instructions delivered in this admirable speech, he avails himself but of one, and that one affects his self-im-
portance !—Cervantes has touched this foible of
little minds with his usual felicity. While the
knight of La Mancha is delivering the most grave
and weighty instructions to Sancho respecting
his conduct in his new government, the squire
listens with inflexible apathy ; but when he proceeds to recommend humility to him, on account
of his low estate, when " he kept hogs," Sancho
interrupts him with unusual vivacity: True, quoth
the squire, but that was while I was a boy ; for
when I grew older, I kept geese, and not hogs !
"*Asi es verdad,*" *respondió Sancho,* "*pero fué
quando era muchacho; pero despues algo
hombrecillo, gansos fuéron los que guardé, que
no puercos !*"

[2] —— *you peremptory* gull ?] Master Stephen

does not escape quite so well in the quarto,
where he is termed a peremptory *ass*. As the
former word occurs frequently in Jonson, and
as, in the Dramatis Personæ of the present play,
the two witlings, Mathew and Stephen, are
characterized as the town and country gulls, it
may not be amiss, in this place, to give the admirable definition of them, by Sir J. Davis,
Epig. II.

" Oft in my laughing rimes I name a gull,
  But this new terme will many questions
     breede,
Therefore at first I will expresse at full
  Who is a true and perfect gull indeede :
A gull is he which fears a velvet gowne,
  And when a wench is brave, dares not speak
     to her ;
A gull is he which traverses the towne,
  And is for marriage known a common wooer.
A gull is he which, while he proudly weares
  A silver hilted rapier by his side,
Indures the lyes, and knocks about the eares,
  While in his sheath his sleeping sword doth
     bide ;
A gull is he which weares good handsome
     cloathes,
  And stands in presence stroaking up his
     hayre,
And fills up his unperfect speech with oathes,
  But speaks not one wise word throughout
     the yeare,
But, to define a gull in terms precise,
  A gull is he which seems, and is not, wise."

mercy, sir: I was required by a gentleman in the city, as I rode out at this end o' the town, to deliver you this letter, sir.

Know. To me, sir! What do you mean? pray you remember your oourt'sy. [*Reads.*] *To his most selected friend, Master Edward Knowell.* What might the gentleman's name be, sir, that sent it? Nay, pray you be covered.

Serv. One Master Wellbred, sir.

Know. Master Wellbred! A young gentleman, is he not?

Serv. The same, sir; Master Kitely married his sister; the rich merchant in the Old Jewry.

Know. You say very true.—Brainworm!

Enter Brainworm.

Brai. Sir.

Know. Make this honest friend drink here: pray you, go in.

[*Exeunt* Brainworm *and* Servant.

This letter is directed to my son:
Yet I am Edward Knowell too, and may,
With the safe conscience of good manners,
    use
The fellow's error to my satisfaction.
Well, I will break it ope, (old men are
    curious,)
Be it but for the style's sake and the phrase;
To see if both do answer my son's praises,
Who is almost grown the idolater
Of this young Wellbred. What have we
    here? What's this?   [*Reads.*

" Why, Ned, I beseech thee,[1] hast thou forsworn all thy friends in the Old Jewry? or dost thou think us all Jews that inhabit there? yet, if thou dost, come over, and but see our frippery;[2] change an old shirt for a whole smock with us: do not conceive that antipathy between us and Hogsden, as was between Jews and hogs-flesh. Leave thy vigilant father alone, to number over his green apricots, evening and morning, on the north-west wall: an I had been his son, I had saved him the labour long since, if taking in all the young wenches that pass by at the back-door, and codling every kernel of the fruit for them, would have served. But, prithee, come over to me quickly, this morning; I have such a present for thee!—our Turkey company never sent the like to the Grand Signior. One is a rimer, sir, of your own batch, your own leaven; but doth think himself poet-major of the town, willing to be shown, and worthy to be seen. The other—I will not venture his description with you, till you come, because I would have you make hither with an appetite. If the worst of 'em be not worth your journey, draw your bill of charges, as unconscionable as any Guildhall verdict will give it you, and you shall be allowed your viaticum.

" From the Windmill."[3]

From the Bordello it might come as well,
The Spittle, or Pict-hatch.[4] Is this the man
My son hath sung so, for the happiest wit,

[1] *Why, Ned, I beseech thee, &c.*] Jonson has shown his judgment in rewriting this letter. As it stands in the quarto, it is pert, silly, and intolerably affected.

[2] —— *and but see our* frippery;] *Fripperie,* Fr. a place where old clothes are exposed for sale. So Massinger of Luke:—

" He shews like a walking *frippery.*"

And Shakspeare:—

" —— O worthy Stephano, what a *wardrobe*
is here for thee!

Cal. Let it alone, it is but trash.

Trin. O, ho, monster; we know what belongs to a *frippery.*"—*Tempest.*

[3] *From the Windmill.*] This house then stood at the corner of the Old Jewry, towards Lothbury, and was remarkable for the various changes it had successively undergone. The Jews used it at first for a synagogue; afterwards it came into the possession of a certain order of friars called *Frotres de Sacco,* from their being clothed in sackcloth. In process of time, it was converted into a private house, wherein several mayors resided, and kept their mayoralty. In the days

of *Stow,* from whom this account is taken, it was a tavern, and had for the sign a *Windmill.*—WHAL.

[4] *From the* Bordello, *it might come as well, The* Spittle, *or* Pict-hatch.] From the brothel or stews, for which the Bankside in Southwark was at this time noted.

The *Spittle,* Whalley says, means in general an hospital; but the fact is not so; it had with our ancestors an appropriate signification, as I have proved in the notes to Massinger (vol. iv. p. 52), and meant a house for lazars, &c. Here the allusion is local, and without doubt applies to the *Loke* or *Lock,* a spittle for venereal patients, situated, as Whalley observes, at Kingsland, in the neighbourhood of *Hogsden.* *Pict-hatch* was a famous receptacle of prostitutes and pickpockets: it is mentioned with other places of equal notoriety, in our author's twelfth Epigram:—

" Squires
That haunt *Pict-hatch,* Marsh Lambeth, and Whitefryers,"

and is generally supposed to have been in Turn-mill, or, as Stow calls it, Tremill-street, near

The choicest brain, the times have sent us
    forth !
I know not what he may be in the arts,
Nor what in schools; but, surely, for his
    manners,
I judge him a profane and dissolute wretch;
Worse by possession of such great good
    gifts,
Being the master of so loose a spirit.
Why, what unhallowed ruffian would have
    writ
In such a scurrilous manner to a friend !
Why should he think I tell my apricots,
Or play the Hesperian dragon with my
    fruit,
To watch it? Well, my son, I had thought
    you
Had had more judgment to have made
    election
Of your companions, than t' have ta'en on
    trust
Such petulant, jeering gamesters, that can
    spare
No argument or subject from their jest.
But I perceive affection makes a fool
Of any man too much the father.[1]—Brain-
    worm !

Enter Brainworm.

Brai. Sir.
Know. Is the fellow gone that brought
this letter?
Brai. Yes, sir, a pretty while since.
Know. And where is your young master?
Brai. In his chamber, sir.
Know. He spake not with the fellow, did
he ?
Brai. No, sir, he saw him not.
Know. Take you this letter, and deliver
it my son; but with no notice that I have
opened it, on your life.

Brai. O lord, sir ! that were a jest in-
    deed.   [*Exit.*
Know. I am resolved I will not stop his
journey,
Nor practise any violent means to stay
The unbridled course of youth in him; for
    that
Restrained, grows more impatient; and in
    kind
Like to the eager, but the generous grey-
    hound,
Who ne'er so little from his game withheld,
Turns head, and leaps up at his holder's
    throat.
There is a way[2] of winning more by love,
And urging of the modesty, than fear:
Force works on servile natures, not the free.
He that's compelled to goodness, may be
    good,
But 'tis but for that fit; where others, drawn
By softness and example, get a habit.
Then, if they stray, but warn them, and
    the same
They should for virtue have done, they'll
    do for shame.   [*Exit.*

SCENE II.—*A Room in* Knowell's *House.*

Enter E. Knowell, *with a Letter in his
    hand, followed by* Brainworm.

E. Know. Did he open it, sayst thou?
Brai. Yes, o' my word, sir, and read the
contents.
E. Know. That scarce contents me.
What countenance, prithee, made he in the
reading of it? was he angry, or pleased?
Brai. Nay, sir, I saw him not read it,
nor open it, I assure your worship.
E. Know. No! how knowst thou then,
that he did either?

Clerkenwell Green; which, in the words of Mrs.
Quickly, lay anciently "under an ill name." So
in the *Blacksmith's Song*, by J. Smith :—

    " Smithfield he did free from dirt,
        And he had sure good reason for 't,
    It stood very near to *Venus' court.*"

Here a note by the author tells us, that "the
place meant is *Turnmill-street.*" — *Wit Restored.*
[1] *Of any man too much the father.*] Hitherto
every change of moment has been for the better;
yet the concluding lines of this soliloquy, as they
stand in the quarto, have merit :—

"Well, I had thought my son could not have
    strayed
So far from judgment, as to mart himself
Thus cheaply, in the open trade of scorn,
To jeering folly, and fantastic humour:

But now I see Opinion is a fool,
And hath abused my senses."

[2] *There is a way, &c.*] This, as Whalley
observes, is from *the Adelphi* of Terence : it is
very happily adapted to the sentiments of the
speaker ; and, with great spirit, has more than
the usual degree of freedom :—

"*Pudore, et liberalitate liberos
    Retinere, satius esse credo, quàm metu.
Malo coactus qui suum officium facit,
Dum id rescitum iri credit, tantisper cavet
Hoc patrium est, potius consuefacere filium
    Suâ sponte recte facere, quam alieno metu.*"

The whole of this fine speech is much improved
from the quarto, which, for the eight last lines,
only gives us this tame couplet :—

    "Therefore I'll study by some milder drift
    To call my son unto a happier shrift."

Brai. Marry, sir, because he charged me, on my life, to tell nobody that he opened it; which, unless he had done, he would never fear to have it revealed.

E. Know. That's true: well, I thank thee, Brainworm.

Enter Stephen.

Step. O, Brainworm, didst thou not see a fellow here in what-sha-call-him doublet? he brought mine uncle a letter e'en now.

Brai. Yes, Master Stephen; what of him?

Step. O, I have such a mind to beat him——where is he, canst thou tell?

Brai. Faith, he is not of that mind: he is gone, Master Stephen.

Step. Gone! which way? when went he? how long since?

Brai. He is rid hence; he took horse at the street-door.

Step. And I staid in the fields! Whore-son Scanderbag rogue![1] O that I had but a horse to fetch him back again!

Brai. Why, you may have my master's gelding, to save your longing, sir.

Step. But I have no boots, that's the spight on't.

Brai. Why, a fine wisp of hay rolled hard, Master Stephen.

Step. No, faith, it's no boot to follow him now:[2] let him e'en go and hang. Prithee, help to truss me a little: he does so vex me——

Brai. You'll be worse vexed when you are trussed, Master Stephen. Best keep unbraced, and walk yourself till you be cold; your choler may founder you else.

Step. By my faith, and so I will, now thou tell'st me on't: how dost thou like my leg, Brainworm?

Brai. A very good leg, Master Stephen; but the woollen stocking does not commend it so well.

Step. Foh! the stockings be good enough, now summer is coming on, for the dust; I'll have a pair of silk against winter, that I go to dwell in the town. I think my leg would shew in a silk hose——[3]

Brai. Believe me, Master Stephen, rarely well.

Step. In sadness, I think it would: I have a reasonable good leg.

Brai. You have an excellent good leg, Master Stephen; but I cannot stay to praise it longer now, and I am very sorry for it.
                                                [*Exit.*

Step. Another time will serve, Brainworm. Gramercy for this.

E. Know. Ha, ha, ha!

Step. 'Slid, I hope he laughs not at me; an he do——

E. Know. Here was a letter indeed, to be intercepted by a man's father, and do him good with him! He cannot but think most virtuously, both of me, and the sender, sure, that make the careful costermonger of him in our familiar epistles. Well, if he read this with patience I'll be gelt, and troll[4] ballads for Master John Trundle

---

[1] *Whoreson* Scanderbag *rogue!*] Scanderbeg is the name which the Turks (in allusion to Alexander the Great,) gave to the brave Castriot, chief of Albania, with whom they had continued wars. His life had been just translated from the French, by I. Gentleman (1596), and was sufficiently romantic to attract the notice of the public.

[2] *Step. No, faith, it's no* boot *to follow him now:*] The rage of punning has seized all the actors in this scene. It may tend, perhaps, to humble the pride of those who plume themselves on their dexterity in this notable art, to observe that Master Stephen is by far the most successful of the party in his attempts.

[3] *I think my leg would shew in a silk hose*——] The humour of these half-witted gallants, with relation to the furniture of their legs, is taken notice of by Shakspeare:—

"*Sir Tob.* I did think by the excellent constitution of thy leg, it was formed under the star of a galliard.

Sir And. Aye, 'tis strong; and it does indifferent well in a flame-coloured stock."—*Twelfth Night*, act i. sc. 3.

This passion for *silk stockings* is glanced at by other dramatic writers. So, in the *Miseries of Inforced Marriage:* "This town craves maintenance, *silk stockings* must be had." And, in *The Hog hath lost his Pearl*, 1614: "Good parts without habiliments of gallantry, are no more set by in these times, than a good leg in a *woollen* stocking."—WHAL.

Bobadill, who is the mirror of fashion in this play, is furnished with silk stockings; and it is not one of the least evils, with which the humorous malice of the poet has pursued his disgrace, to make him pawn this favourite article of gallantry, to procure a warrant for binding over the turbulent Downright to keep the peace. See act iv.

[4] *And* troll *ballads for Master John Trundle.*

"—— Will you *troul* the catch
You taught me but while-ere?"
                                        The Tempest.

And Milton,

"To dress, to *troll* the tongue, and roll the eye."
                                        WHAL.

With respect to *Master John Trundle*, he

yonder, the rest of my mortality. It is true, and likely, my father may have as much patience as another man, for he takes much physic; and oft taking physic makes a man very patient. But would your packet, Master Wellbred, had arrived at him in such a minute of his patience! then we had known the end of it, which now is doubtful, and threatens—— [*sees* Master Stephen.] What, my wise cousin! nay, then I'll furnish our feast with one gull more toward the mess. He writes to me of a brace, and here's one, that's three: oh, for a fourth, Fortune, if ever thou'lt use thine eyes, I entreat thee——

Step. Oh, now I see who he laughed at: he laughed at somebody in that letter. By this good light, an he had laughed at me——

E. Know. How now, Cousin Stephen, melancholy?

Step. Yes, a little: I thought you had laughed at me, cousin.

E. Know. Why, what an I had, coz? what would you have done?

Step. By this light, I would have told mine uncle.

E. Know. Nay, if you would have told your uncle, I did laugh at you, coz.

Step. Did you, indeed?

E. Know. Yes, indeed.

Step. Why then——

E. Know. What then?

Step. I am satisfied; it is sufficient.

E. Know. Why, be so, gentle coz: and, I pray you, let me intreat a courtesy of you. I am sent for this morning by a

friend in the Old Jewry, to come to him; it is but crossing over the fields to Moorgate: Will you bear me company? I protest, it is not to draw you into bond, or any plot against the state, coz.

Step. Sir, that's all one an it were; you shall command me twice so far as Moorgate, to do you good in such a matter. Do you think I would leave you? I protest——[1]

E. Know. No, no, you shall not protest, coz.

Step. By my fackings, but I will, by your leave:——I'll protest more to my friend, than I'll speak of at this time.

E. Know. You speak very well, coz.

Step. Nay, not so neither, you shall pardon me: but I speak to serve my turn.

E. Know. Your turn, coz! do you know what you say? A gentleman of your sort,[2] parts, carriage, and estimation, to talk of your turn in this company, and to me alone, like a tankard-bearer at a conduit![3] fie! A wight that, hitherto, his every step hath left the stamp of a great foot behind him, as every word the savour of a strong spirit, and he! this man! so graced, gilded, or, to use a more fit metaphor, so tin-foiled by nature, as not ten housewives pewter, again a good time,[4] shews more bright to the world than he! and he! (as I said last, so I say again, and still shall say it) this man! to conceal such real ornaments as these, and shadow their glory, as a milliner's wife does her wrought stomacher, with a smoaky lawn, or a black cyprus![5]

was a printer, who lived at the sign of the "Nobody" (a very humble designation), in Barbican. It appears, however, that he dealt in something better than *ballads,* having published Green's *Tu Quoque, Westward for Smelts,* and other fugitive and popular pieces of the day.

[1] *I protest——*] There appears to have been something affected or ridiculous, at this time, in using the word *protest.* Thus the Nurse in *Romeo and Juliet,* act ii. sc. 4: "I will tell her, sir, that you do *protest;* which, as I take it, is a gentleman-like offer." And in the old comedy of *Sir Giles Goosecap,* 1606, as cited by Mr. Steevens, "There is not the best duke's son in France dares say, *I protest,* till he be one and thirty years old at least; for the inheritance of that word is not to be possessed before."—WHAL.

[2] *A gentleman of your* sort,] That is, rank or degree in life. So Shakspeare:—

"—— none of nobler *sort*
Would so offend a virgin."
        Midsum. Night's Dream.

And Drayton—

"Men most select, of special worth and *sort.*"
        Barons' Wars. WHAL.

[3] *like a* tankard-bearer *at a conduit!*] Before the New River was brought to London, the city was chiefly supplied with water from conduits, which the patriotism of the wealthier citizens had erected in considerable numbers. From these it was fetched by a particular class of men called *tankard-bearers* (of which *Cob,* who makes his appearance in this play, was one), and sold to the citizens at so much a turn. Where a professed tankard-bearer was not employed, it was the business of the servant, and junior apprentices, to fetch water for the use of the family; and to this there are innumerable allusions in our old writers. "I had rather," says Sir J. Harrington, in his treatise on Play, "one of my sonnes were a *tankard-bearer* that weares sometymes his silke sleaves at the church on Sunday, than a cosener."

[4] —*again a* good time,] i.e., against some festival, such as Christmas, &c., when housewives are careful to set out their furniture to the best advantage.—WHAL.

[5] *or a black* cyprus!] A kind of thin, transparent crape, so called from being originally manufactured in the island of that name.—WHAL.

O, coz! it cannot be answered; go not about it: Drake's old ship[1] at Deptford may sooner circle the world again. Come, wrong not the quality of your desert, with looking downward, coz; but hold up your head, so: and let the idea of what you are be pourtrayed in your face, that men may read in your physnomy, "here within this place is to be seen the true, rare, and accomplished monster, or miracle of nature," which is all one. What think you of this, coz?

Step. Why, I do think of it; and I will be more proud, and melancholy, and gentleman-like than I have been, I'll insure you.

E. Know. Why, that's resolute, Master Stephen!—Now, if I can but hold him up to his height, as it is happily begun, it will do well for a suburb humour:[2] we may hap have a match with the city, and play him for forty pound.—Come, coz.

Step. I'll follow you.

E. Know. Follow me! you must go before.

Step. Nay, an I must, I will. Pray you, shew me, good cousin.   [*Exeunt.*

SCENE III.—*The Lane before* Cob's House.[3]

Enter Master Mathew.

Mat. I think this be the house: what, ho!

Enter Cob.

Cob. Who's there? O, Master Mathew! give your worship good morrow.

Mat. What, Cob! how dost thou, good Cob? dost thou inhabit here, Cob?

Cob. Ay, sir, I and my lineage have kept a poor house here, in our days.

Mat. Thy lineage, Monsieur Cob! what lineage? what lineage?

Cob. Why, sir, an ancient lineage, and a princely. Mine ance'try came from a king's belly, no worse man; and yet no man neither, by your worship's leave, I did lie in that, but herring, the king of fish,[4] (from his belly I proceed,) one of the monarchs of the world, I assure you. The first red herring that was broiled in Adam and Eve's kitchen, do I fetch my pedigree from, by the harrot's book.[5] His

---

It is mentioned by Shakspeare:—
    "*Cyprus, black* as any crow."
                                Winter's Tale.
And again by our author,
    "— one half drawn
    In *solemn cyprus*, th' other cobweb lawn."

[1] *Drake's old ship*] After the return of this celebrated navigator from his voyage round the world, his ship was laid up at Deptford, by Queen Elizabeth, where it was long visited as a singular curiosity, and regarded, as appears from the verses of Cowley and others, with no small degree of national pride and veneration. Much of the fondness with which Elizabeth is yet viewed by the common people, is due to her happy dexterity in flattering the prejudices of the nation, and perhaps her own (for Bess, to use her proper words, *had an English heart*), by exalting every circumstance, and perpetuating every memorial, that tended to the glory, or brought to mind its success in arts or arms. An object which has been greatly overlooked by almost every government since her time, who have abandoned to individual patriotism those tributes to national honour, which are only effective when paid by the State. I regret to say that Barrow found the ship in which Cook had twice circumnavigated the globe, at Rio Janeiro, whither she was carried by the Portuguese, who had purchased her for an inconsiderable sum! His feelings on the occasion are just and proper.

[2] *It will do well for a* suburb humour:] A low humour, not tinctured with urbanity; fitted to the tastes of the inferior people who usually reside in the suburbs.—WHAL.

[3] *The lane before Cob's House.*] Mr. Waldron observes that in a part of *Black Friars* called Broad Way, there is an avenue still called *Cob's Court*; and not improbably from its having formerly been inhabited by water-bearers; to which class of people Jonson's character of *Cob* seems to have given a sort of celebrity. Not to deprive any part of the city, however, of its due share of honour, it should be mentioned that "Cob's house stood by the Wall" at the bottom of Coleman-street.

[4] *herring, the king of fish,*] If the reader wishes to know how the herring arrived at this dignity, he may consult Nashe's "*Lenten Stuffe,*" where he will find more than enough on the subject. Briefly, a quarrel having arisen between the "land fowls and the fishes, the latter assembled to elect a king that might lead them into battle." On canvassing the respective claims of the competitors, "none woone the day but the *herring,* whom all their clamorous suffrages, &c., saluted with *Vive le roy! God save the king!*—and from that time to this he hath gone abroad with an army, and never stirs without it." 4to. 1599. It is not improbable that this title was fondly conferred on the herring by the Northern nations, in conseque nce of the immense advantages which they derived from the fishery; and in which our rivals the Dutch were at this time known to be very largely participating.

[5] *By the* harrot's *book.*] The old and obsolete mode of spelling *herald,* of which it is a corruption: herald (*here held*) is, or rather was, the champion of an army; what it is now I cannot tell.

cob[1] was my great, great, mighty great grandfather.

Mat. Why mighty, why mighty, I pray thee?

Cob. O, it was a mighty while ago, sir, and a mighty great cob.

Mat. How know'st thou that?

Cob. How know I! why, I smell his ghost ever and anon.

Mat. Smell a ghost! O unsavoury jest! and the ghost of a herring cob?

Cob. Ay, sir: With favour of your worship's nose, Master Mathew, why not the ghost of a herring cob, as well as the ghost of Rasher Bacon?

Mat. Roger Bacon, thou wouldst say.

Cob. I say Rasher Bacon. They were both broiled on the coals; and a man may smell broiled meat, I hope! you are a scholar, upsolve me that, now.

Mat. O raw ignorance!—Cob, canst thou shew me of a gentleman, one Captain Bobadill, where his lodging is?

Cob. O, my guest, sir, you mean.

Mat. Thy guest! alas, ha, ha, ha!

Cob. Why do you laugh, sir? Do you not mean Captain Bobadill?

Mat. Cob, pray thee advise thyself well; do not wrong the gentleman, and thyself too. I dare be sworn, he scorns thy house, he! he lodge in such a base obscure place as thy house! Tut, I know his disposition so well, he would not lie in thy bed if thou'dst give it him.

Cob. I will not give it him though, sir. Mass, I thought somewhat was in it, we could not get him to bed all night. Well, sir, though he lie not on my bed, he lies on my bench: an't please you to go up, sir, you shall find him with two cushions under his head, and his cloke wrapt about him, as though he had neither won nor lost, and yet, I warrant, he ne'er cast better in his life,[2] than he has done to-night.

Mat. Why, was he drunk?

Cob. Drunk, sir! you hear not me say so: perhaps he swallowed a tavern-token,[3] or some such device, sir, I have nothing to do withal. I deal with water and not with wine.—Give me my tankard there, ho!—God be wi' you, sir. It's six a clock: I should have carried two turns, by this.—What ho! my stopple; come.

Enter Tib *with a water-tankard.*

Mat. Lie in a water-bearer's house! a gentleman of his havings! Well, I'll tell him my mind![4]

Cob. What, Tib; shew this gentleman up to the captain. [*Exit* Tib *with* Master Mathew.] Oh, an my house were the Brazen-head now! faith it would e'en speak *Moe fools yet.* You should have some now would take this Master Mathew to be a gentleman, at the least. His father's an honest man, a worshipful fishmonger, and so forth; and now does he creep, and wriggle into acquaintance with all the brave gallants about the town, such as my guest is (O, my guest is a fine man!) and they flout him invincibly.[5] He useth every

---

[1] *His* Cob, *&c.*] Cob (*kop,* Belg.) is head. Our old writers used the word as a distinctive mark of bulk; thus *cob*-loaf was the largest loaf of the batch, *cob*-apple, *cob*-nut, &c., were respectively the largest apples and nuts of the crop, &c. But *cob* was more commonly applied to fishes, and of these chiefly to the red and white herring, whence it became a cant term for the whole fish. Jonson is here in his "old lunes:" he is never weary of playing with names, though no sport can well be "more flat and unprofitable."

[2] *He ne'er cast better in his life.*] A quibble, very worthy of Cob, between casting dice and vomiting. It is found in Shakspeare, and in all our old dramatists.

[3] *Perhaps he swallowed a tavern-*token.] This, as Reed observes, was a cant term for getting drunk. *Tokens* were promissory pieces of brass or copper, which tradesmen, in a scarcity of small money, were sometimes permitted to coin for themselves; a practice which has lately been revived. That most of them would travel to the *tavern,* may be easily supposed; and hence perhaps the name. Their usual value seems to have been a farthing.

[4] *Lie in a water-bearer's house! a gentleman of his* havings! *Well, I'll tell him my mind.*] This, Master Mathew forgets to do, though Bobadill seems to lead the way to it. *Havings* are possessions: it is thus used by Shakspeare, "the gentleman is of no *havings.*"—*Merry Wives of Windsor.* And by our author's imitator, Randolph:—

"One of your *havings,* thus cark and care!"
Muses' Looking Glass.

Instead of *havings,* the quarto reads *note,* which seems the better word, as Bobadill is less boastful of his fortune, than of his distinguished reputation.

[5] *And they flout him* invincibly.] I have some doubt whether we rightly comprehend this word, as understood by our ancestors. Here, and elsewhere, it is used where we should now write *invisibly.* "He was so forlorn," says Falstaff of Justice Shallow, "that his dimensions to any thick sight were *invincible.*" This reading Steevens pronounces to be absolutely spurious; and adopts, with great applause, *invisible,* "the *correction* of Rowe." The correction, as it is termed, is sufficiently obvious to

day to a merchant's house where I serve water, one Master Kitely's, in the Old Jewry; and here's the jest, he is in love with my master's sister, Mrs. Bridget, and calls her mistress; and there he will sit you a whole afternoon sometimes, reading of these same abominable, vile (a pox on 'em! I cannot abide them), rascally verses, poetrie, poetrie, and speaking of interludes; 'twill make a man burst to hear him. And the wenches, they do so jeer, and ti-he at him——Well, should they do so much to me, I'd forswear them all, by the foot of Pharaoh! There's an oath! How many water-bearers shall you hear swear such an oath? O, I have a guest—he teaches me —he does swear the legiblest of any man christened: *By St. George! the foot of Pharaoh! the body of me! as I am a gentleman and a soldier!* such dainty oaths! and withal, he does take this same filthy roguish tobacco, the finest and cleanliest! it would do a man good to see the fume come forth at's tonnels.——Well, he owes me forty shillings, my wife lent him out of her purse, by sixpence at a time, besides his lodging: I would I had it![1] I shall have it, he says, the next action. Helter skelter, hang sorrow, care'll kill a cat, up-tails all, and a louse for the hangman!   [*Exit.*

SCENE IV.—*A Room in* Cob's *House.*

Bobadill *discovered lying on a bench.*

Bob. Hostess, hostess!

Enter Tib.

Tib. What say you, sir?

Bob. A cup of thy small beer, sweet hostess.

Tib. Sir, there's a gentleman below would speak with you.

Bob. A gentleman! 'odso, I am not within.

Tib. My husband told him you were, sir.

Bob. What a plague——what meant he?

Mat. [*below.*] Captain Bobadill!

Bob. Who's there?——Take away the bason, good hostess![2]——Come up, sir.

Tib. He would desire you to come up, sir. You come into a cleanly house, here!

Enter Mathew.

Mat. Save you, sir, save you, captain!

Bob. Gentle Master Mathew! Is it you, sir? please you to sit down.

Mat. Thank you, good captain; you may see I am somewhat audacious.

Bob. Not so, sir. I was requested to supper last night by a sort[3] of gallants, where you were wished for, and drunk to, I assure you.

Mat. Vouchsafe me, by whom, good captain?

Bob. Marry, by young Wellbred, and others.——Why, hostess, a stool here for this gentleman.

Mat. No haste, sir, 'tis very well.

Bob. Body o' me! it was so late ere we parted last night, I can scarce open my eyes yet; I was but new risen, as you came: how passes the day abroad, sir? you can tell.

Mat. Faith, some half hour to seven: Now trust me, you have an exceeding fine lodging here, very neat and private.

Bob. Ay, sir: sit down, I pray you. Master Mathew, in any case, possess[4] no

---

those who are not conversant with our old writers; but not so, I should have thought, to Steevens. However this may be, I have met with the expression so frequently, that I incline to the opinion of the judicious Crites, and think "there is need of more deliberation," before it be utterly proscribed.

[1] *I would I had it, &c.*] Rude and illiterate as the author has drawn Cob, he has yet made him enter into the characters of Bobadill and Master Mathew with a shrewdness which is frequently found in people of his condition, and which evinces Jonson's strict observance of nature. The hortatory exclamations with which Cob concludes his soliloquy are either proverbial vulgarisms, or the burden of popular songs. *Up-tails-all* occurs in the *Fleire*, act iii. " She every day sings *John for the King*, and is perfect at *Up-tails-all*;" and in the *Coxcomb*, act i. where Silvio sings, "Then set your foot to my foot, and *Up-tails-all*."

[2] *Bob. Take away the bason, good hostess.* Tib. *He would desire you to come up, sir.*

You come into a cleanly house, here!] Our facetious neighbours have attempted to translate this comedy into French, and succeeded, as might be expected, to a nicety. The version of what is quoted above, may serve, as well as any other passage, for a specimen :—

Bob. *Emportez le basin, ma chère hotesse.*
Tib. *Ne craignez rien, monsieur, la chambre est propre.*

And it is from such exquisite blundering as this, that their critics presume to decide upon the taste and humour of the English stage!

[3] *By a* sort *of gallants.*] A *company.* "Yet how a *sort* of fugitives, who had quitted without stroke their own country, should so soon win another, appears not."—Milton's *Hist. of Brit.* The word occurs so frequently in this sense, that no further notice of it seems necessary.

[4] Possess *no gentlemen of our acquaintance with notice of my lodging.*] i.e., *inform no* gentlemen, &c.

gentlemen of our acquaintance with notice of my lodging.

Mat. Who, I, sir? no.

Bob. Not that I need to care who know it, for the cabbin is convenient; but in regard I would not be too popular, and generally visited, as some are.

Mat. True, captain, I conceive you.

Bob. For, do you see, sir, by the heart of valour in me, except it be to some peculiar and choice spirits, to whom I am extraordinarily engaged, as yourself, or so, I could not extend thus far.

Mat. O Lord, sir! I resolve[1] so.

Bob. I confess I love a cleanly and quiet privacy, above all the tumult and roar of fortune. What new book have you there? What! Go by, Hieronymo?[2]

Mat. Ay; did you ever see it acted? Is't not well penned?

Bob. Well penned! I would fain see all the poets of these times pen such another play as that was:[3] they'll prate and swagger, and keep a stir of art and devices, when, as I am a gentleman, read 'em, they are the most shallow, pitiful, barren fellows, that live upon the face of the earth again.

[*While* Master Mathew *reads*, Bobadill *makes himself ready*.[4]

Mat. Indeed here are a number of fine speeches in this book. *O eyes, no eyes,*[5] *but fountains fraught with tears!* there's

a conceit! *fountains fraught with tears! O life, no life, but lively form of death!* another. *O world, no world, but mass of public wrongs!* a third. *Confused and filled with murder and misdeeds!* a fourth. O, the muses! Is't not excellent? Is't not simply the best that ever you heard, captain? Ha! how do you like it?

Bob. 'Tis good.

Mat. "To thee, the purest object to my sense,

The most refined essence heaven covers,

Send I these lines, wherein I do commence

The happy state of turtle-billing lovers.

If they prove rough, unpolished, harsh, and rude,

Haste made the waste: thus mildly, I conclude."

Bob. Nay, proceed, proceed. Where's this?

Mat. This, sir! a toy of mine own, in my nonage; the infancy of my muses: But when will you come and see my study? good faith, I can shew you some very good things I have done of late—That boot becomes your leg passing well, captain, methinks.

Bob. So, so; it's the fashion gentlemen now use.[6]

Mat. Troth, captain, and now you speak of the fashion, Master Wellbred's elder brother and I are fallen out exceedingly: This other day, I happened to enter into some discourse of a hanger,[7] which, I assure

---

[1] *I resolve so.*] I am *convinced* of it. See Massinger, vol. i. 275.

[2] *What! Go by, Hieronymo?*] This alludes to the following passage in the *Spanish Tragedy*:

"*Hiero.* Justice, O justice to Hieronymo!

Loren. Back; seest thou not the king is busy?

Hiero. O, is he so!

King. Who is he that interrupts our business?

Hiero. Not I: Hieronymo beware, *go by, go by!*"

[3] *Well penned! I would fain see all the poets of these times pen such another play as that was:*] Jonson has here contrived to pay an indirect compliment to himself; for, it appears from the MS. of Mr. Henslow, the proprietor of the Rose Theatre, that he had been employed on more than one occasion to improve old Jeronymo. The article, as copied by Mr. Malone, runs thus, "Lent unto Mr. Alleyn, the 25 of September, 1601, to lend unto Bengemen Johnson, upon 'his *writing of his adycions* in Jeronymo, xxxxs." In the following year, "Bengemen wrote more adycions;" and in *Cynthia's Revels*, 1602, has not forgotten to advert again to the circumstance.

[4] *Bobadill* makes himself ready.] This was the phrase then in use for *dressing* oneself:—

"I have seen little girls that yesterday had scarce a band to *make them ready*, the next day weare wedding rings on their fingers."—*Patient Grissell*, 1603. More instances of so common an expression are not required.

[5] *O eyes, no eyes, &c.*] These lines occur in the third act of the *Spanish Tragedy*: they are, it must be confessed, sufficiently ridiculous, and the poets of those days were never weary of parodying and burlesquing them: they are, however, in the taste of the times, and may be found, with some slight variations, in writers of higher name than the author of *Hieronymo*.

[6] *Bob. So, so; it's the fashion gentlemen now use.*] Bobadill probably alludes to some particular form of the boot, which, in that capricious age, was continually varying its appearance. If, as Mr. Whalley supposes, he is sufficiently modest, for not only "gentlemen," but "citizens, plowmen, and artisans of every description walked in their boots."—*Old Plays*, vol. x. p. 118. The bon-mot of Gondemar, the Spanish Ambassador, is well known. I shall amaze my countrymen, said he to James I. by letting them know, at my return, that all London is booted, and apparently ready to walk out of town!

[7] *I happened to enter into some discourse of a hanger.*] See *the Poetaster*.

you, both for fashion and workmanship, was most peremptory beautiful, and gentleman-like : yet he condemned, and cried it down for the most pied and ridiculous that ever he saw.

Bob. Squire Downright, the half-brother, was't not?

Mat. Ay, sir, he.

Bob. Hang him, rook! he! why he has no more judgment than a malt-horse : By St. George, I wonder you'd lose a thought upon such an animal; the most peremptory absurd clown of Christendom, this day, he is holden. I protest to you, as I am a gentleman and a soldier, I ne'er changed words with his like. By his discourse, he should eat nothing but hay : he was born for the manger, pannier, or pack-saddle. He has not so much as a good phrase in his belly, but all old iron, and rusty proverbs : a good commodity for some smith to make hobnails of.

Mat. Ay, and he thinks to carry it away with his manhood still, where he comes : he brags he will give me the bastinado, as I hear.

Bob. How! he the bastinado! how came he by that word, trow?

Mat. Nay, indeed, he said, cudgel me; I termed it so, for my more grace.

Bob. That may be; for I was sure it was none of his word : but when, when said he so?

Mat. Faith, yesterday, they say; a young gallant, a friend of mine, told me so.

Bob. By the foot of Pharaoh, and 'twere my case now, I should send him a chartel[1] presently. The bastinado! a most proper and sufficient dependance,[2] warranted by the great Caranza. Come hither, you shall chartel him; I'll shew you a trick or two, you shall kill him with, at pleasure; the first stoccata, if you will, by this air.

Mat. Indeed, you have absolute knowledge in the mystery, I have heard, sir.

Bob. Of whom, of whom have you heard it, I beseech you?

Mat. Troth, I have heard it spoken **of** divers, that you have very rare, and un-in-one-breath-utterable skill, sir.

Bob. By heaven, no, not **I**; no skill in the earth; some small rudiments in the science, as to know my time, distance, or so. I have professed it more for noblemen and gentlemen's use, than mine own practice, I assure you.—Hostess, accommodate us with another bed-staff here quickly. Lend us another bed-staff—the woman does not understand the words of action.[3]—Look you, sir : exalt not your point above this state, at any hand, and let your poniard maintain your defence, thus :—give it the gentleman, and leave us. [*Exit* Tib.] So, sir. Come on : O, twine your body more about, that you may fall to a more sweet, comely, gentleman-like guard; so! indifferent : hollow your body more, sir, thus : now, stand fast o' your left leg, note your distance, keep your due proportion of time—oh, you disorder your point most irregularly.

Mat. How is the bearing of it now, sir?

Bob. O, out of measure ill : a well experienced hand would pass upon you at pleasure.

Mat. How mean you, sir, pass upon me?

Bob. Why, thus, sir,—make a thrust at me—[*Master Mathew pushes at Bobadill*] come in upon the answer, control your point, and make a full career at the body : The best practised gallants of the time name it the passado; a most desperate thrust, believe it.

Mat. Well, come, sir.

Bob. Why, you do not manage your weapon with any facility or grace to invite

---

[1] *You shall send him a* chartel *presently.*] This word, which now means a paper of stipulations or conditions, anciently signified a *challenge,* and is used in that sense by all the writers of Jonson's age :—"You had better," says Lord Roos, in his reply to the Marquis of Dorchester's challenge, "have been drunk, and set in the stocks for it, than sent the post with a whole packet of *chartels* for me."

[2] *A most proper and sufficient* dependance.] *Dependance,* in the language of the *Duello,* then in vogue, meant the ground or cause of quarrel. It is explained more at large, as Whalley observes, in *The Devil's an Ass,* act iii. and with some humour. The reader who wishes for more on the subject, may refer to Massinger, vol. iii. p. 9. The great Caranza, to whom

Bobadill appeals, is mentioned again in the *New Inn,* where he appears somewhat fallen from his dignity.

[3] *The woman does not understand the* words of action.] That *accommodate* was a *word of action,* appears from Corporal Bardolph's exquisite dissertation on it :—"Pardon me, sir, I have heard the word. Phrase, call you it? By this day, I know not the phrase : but I will maintain the word with my sword to be a *soldier-like word,* and a word of exceeding good command."—*2nd Part of Hen. IV.* act iii. sc. 4.

Accommodation, as the poet tells us in his *Discoveries,* was at this time a modish expression, and what he calls one of the perfumed terms of the age.

me. I have no spirit to play with you ; your dearth of judgment renders you tedious.

Mat. But one venue,[1] sir.

Bob. Venue ! fie ; most gross denomination, as ever I heard : O, the stoccata, while you live, sir, note that.—Come, put on your cloke, and we'll go to some private place where you are acquainted, some tavern, or so—and have a bit—I'll send for one of these fencers, and he shall breathe you, by my direction ; and then I will teach you your trick ; you shall kill him with it at the first, if you please. Why, I will learn you by the true judgment of the eye, hand, and foot, to control any enemy's point in the world. Should your adversary confront you with a pistol, 'twere nothing, by this hand ! you should, by the same rule, control his bullet, in a line, except it were hailshot, and spread. What money have you about you, Master Mathew ?

Mat. Faith, I have not past a two shillings, or so.

Bob. 'Tis somewhat with the least ; but come ; we will have a bunch of radish and salt to taste our wine, and a pipe of tobacco to close the orifice of the stomach ; and then we'll call upon young Wellbred : perhaps we shall meet the Corydon[2] his brother there, and put him to the question.

ACT II.

SCENE I.—*The* Old Jewry. *A Hall in* Kitely's *House.*

Enter Kitely, Cash, *and* Downright.

Kit. Thomas, come hither.
There lies a note within upon my desk ;
Here take my key : it is no matter,
　　neither.—
Where is the boy ?

Cash. Within, sir, in the warehouse.

Kit. Let him tell over straight that
　　Spanish gold,
And weigh it, with the pieces of eight. Do
　　you
See the delivery of those silver stuffs
To Master Lucar : Tell him, if he will,
He shall have the grograns, at the rate I
　　told him,
And I will meet him on the Exchange
　　anon.

Cash. Good, sir.　　　　　　　　[*Exit.*

Kit. Do you see that fellow, Brother
Downright.

Dow. Ay, what of him ?

Kit. He is a jewel, brother.
I took him of a child up at my door,
And christened him, gave him mine own
　　name, Thomas ;
Since bred him at the Hospital ;[3] where
　　proving
A toward imp, I called him home, and
　　taught him
So much, as I have made him my cashier,
And giv'n him, who had none, a surname,
　　Cash :
And find him in his place so full of faith,
That I durst trust my life into his hands.

Dow. So would not I in any bastard's,
　　brother,
As it is like he is, although I knew
Myself his father. But you said you had
　　somewhat
To tell me, gentle brother ; what is't, what
　　is't ?

Kit. Faith, I am very loth to utter it,
As fearing it may hurt your patience :
But that I know your judgment is of
　　strength,
Against the nearness of affection——

Dow. What need this circumstance ?
　　pray you, be direct.

Kit. I will not say how much I do ascribe
Unto your friendship, nor in what regard
I hold your love ; but let my past behaviour,

---

[1] *But one* venue, *sir.*] Few terms have had more unprofitable pains wasted on them than this, which Bobadill despatches in an instant. It means, he says, the *stoccata ;* and the stoccata is neither more nor less than the *thrust.* May we not hope, that the opinion of so competent a judge will be considered as decisive, and finally operate to the disburthenment of some of our ancient poets, who groan under the weight of discordant commentaries on this trivial word ! The only circumstance worthy of notice here, is the preference which Bobadill manifests for the Italian. This was the prevailing fashion of the day ; and is therefore judiciously attributed to him.

[2] *The Corydon his brother*] Meaning Downright, who was half brother to Wellbred.—WHAL.

The name of this unfortunate shepherd of Virgil seems to have suggested to our old writers a certain mixture of rusticity and folly. So, in the *Parson's Wedding,* "He has not so much as the family jest which these *Corydons* are to inherit," act i. sc. 3.

[3] *Since bred him at the* Hospital :] i.e., at Christ's Hospital, whither, at its first establishment, the foundlings taken up in the city were sent for maintenance and education. In the *Widow,* by Jonson, Middleton, and Massinger, the same allusion occurs :—

"—I have no child of mine own,
But two I got once of a scowering woman,
And they're both well provided for—in the
　　Hospital," act ii. sc. 1.

And usage of your sister, [both][1] confirm
How well I have been affected to your——
 Dow. You are too tedious ; come to the
matter, the matter.
 Kit. Then, without further ceremony,
thus.
My brother Wellbred, sir, I know not how,
Of late is much declined in what he
was,
And greatly altered in his disposition.
When he came first to lodge here in my
house,
Ne'er trust me if I were not proud of him :
Methought he bare himself in such a
fashion,
So full of man, and sweetness in his car-
riage,
And what was chief, it shewed not borrowed
in him,
But all he did became him as his own,
And seemed as perfect, proper, and possest,
As breath with life, or colour with the
blood.
But now his course is so irregular,
So loose, affected, and deprived of grace,
And he himself withal so far fallen off
From that first place, as scarce no note re-
mains,
To tell men's judgments where he lately
stood.

He's grown a stranger to all due respect,
Forgetful of his friends ; and not content
To stale[2] himself in all societies,
He makes my house here common as a
mart,
A theatre, a public receptacle
For giddy humour, and diseased riot ;
And here, as in a tavern or a stews,[3]
He and his wild associates spend their
hours,
In repetition of lascivious jests,
Swear, leap, drink, dance, and revel night
by night,
Control my servants, and, indeed, what
not ?
 Dow. 'Sdeins, I know not what I should
say to him, in the whole world ! He values me
at a cracked three-farthings, for aught I see.[4]
It will never out of the flesh that's bred in
the bone. I have told him enough, one would
think, if that would serve ; but counsel
to him is as good as a shoulder of mutton
to a sick horse. Well, he knows what to
trust to, for George : let him spend, and
spend, and domineer till his heart ake ; an
he think to be relieved by me, when he is
got into one o' your city pounds, the counters, he has the wrong sow by the ear, i'
faith ; and claps his dish at the wrong
man's door :[5] I'll lay my hand on my half-

---

[1] *And usage of your sister,* [both] *confirm*]
For *both,* the folio reads *but,* which appears to
have been erroneously copied from the word in
the preceding line. I am the more inclined to
this opinion by the quarto, which gives the passage thus :—
  "——let my continued zeal,
 The constant and religious regard
 That I have ever carried to your name,
 My carriage with your sister, *all* content
 How much I stand affected to your house."

[2] *To* stale *himself in all societies,*] To make
himself cheap and common.—So the word is
used by Shakspeare, and, indeed, by every
writer of his age. By a very common oversight,
it is printed *scale* in *Coriolanus,* which has
happily furnished an occasion for much perverse
ingenuity, to justify the poet's adoption of a
word which he would steadily have rejected.

[3] *or* a stews,] This was the mode of expression
then in use ; so Withers,
 "Turn his own house into *a* loathsome *stewes.'*
    Abuses Stript and Whipt, 1617.

And T. Heywood, very prettily,
   " At his departure
Was it the old man's charge to have his windowes
Glisten all night with starres ? his modest house
Turned to *a* common *stewes ?* his beds to pallats
Of lusts and prostitutions ?"
   The English Traveller, act i. sc. 2.

[4] *He values me at a cracked* three-farthings,
for aught I see.] The three-farthing pieces
current in the reign of Queen Elizabeth were
made of silver ; consequently very thin, and
much cracked by public use :—
  " My face so thin,
That in mine ear I durst not stick a rose,
Lest men should say, Look where three-farthings
 goes." Shakspeare's *King John,* act i. sc. 2.
        WHAL.

[5] *He has the wrong sow by the ear—and claps
his dish at the wrong man's door :*] The reader
is prepared for the language of Downright, by
the previous observation of Bobadill, that "his
discourse was nothing but old iron and *rusty
proverbs.*" In justice to Jonson, it should be
observed that none of our dramatic poets equal
him in the dexterity or frequency of these preparatory hints, which are scattered through all
his plays, and evince a close and judicious study
of the ancients. To *clap your dish at a wrong
man's door,* is a proverb to be found in Ray : it
alludes to the custom which prevailed in this
country, two or three centuries ago, and, not
improbably, even so late as Jonson's time, when
diseased or infectious wretches wandered up
and down with a *clap-dish,* a wooden vessel
with a moveable cover, to give the charitable
warning at once of their necessities and their
infectious condition. To this mode of begging,
our old writers frequently advert, and, among

penny, ere I part with it to fetch him out,
I'll assure him.

Kit. Nay, good brother, let it not trouble
you thus.

Dow. 'Sdeath! he mads me; I could
eat my very spur-leathers for anger! But,
why are you so tame? why do not you
speak to him, and tell him how he dis-
quiets your house?

Kit. O, there are divers reasons to dissuade me.

But, would yourself vouchsafe to travail
　in it,
(Though but with plain and easy circum-
　stance),
It would both come much better to his
　sense,
And savour less of stomach, or of passion.
You are his elder brother, and that title
Both gives and warrants your authority,
Which, by your presence seconded, must
　breed
A kind of duty in him, and regard :
Whereas, if I should intimate the least,
It would but add contempt to his neglect,
Heap worse on ill, make up a pile of hatred,
That in the rearing world come tottering
　down,
And in the ruin bury all our love.
Nay, more than this, brother; if I should
　speak,

He would be ready, from his heat of
　humour,
And overflowing of the vapour in him,
To blow the ears of his familiars,
With the false breath of telling what dis-
　graces,
And low disparagements, I had put upon
　him.
Whilst they, sir, to relieve him in the
　fable,
Make their loose comments upon every
　word,
Gesture, or look, I use ; mock me all over,
From my flat cap unto my shining shoes ;[1]
And, out of their impetuous rioting phan-
　t'sies,
Beget some slander that shall dwell with me.
And what would that be, think you ? marry,
　this :
They would give out, because my wife is
　fair,
Myself but lately married, and my sister
Here sojourning a virgin in my house,
That I were jealous!—nay, as sure as
　death,
That they would say : and how that I had
　quarrelled
My brother purposely, thereby to find
An apt pretext to banish them my house.

Dow. Mass, perhaps so : they're like
enough to do it.

---

the rest, Churchyard, in a passage of picturesque
merit.　It is Jane Shore who speaks.

" Where I was wont the golden chaines to wear,
　A payre of beads about my necke was wound,
A linnen cloth was lapt about my heare ;
　A ragged gowne that trailed on the ground,
　A dish that clapt, and gave a heavy sound,
A staying staffe, and wallet therewithall,
I bear about, as witnesse of my fall."
　　　　　　　　　　　　　Challenge, 143.

It was once also the practice for beadles and
other inferior parish officers, to go from door to
door with a clap-dish, soliciting charity for those
unhappy sufferers who are now better relieved
by voluntary subscriptions. Thus Matheo in
the second part of the *Honest Whore,* " Must I
be fed with chippings? you were best get a
clap-dish, and say you are proctor to some
spittle-house." As they naturally experienced
many repulses, it may be that the text has some
remote reference to this practice, as well as to
the former.

In the *Caveat for Cursetors,* 1567, a variety
of knavish impostors are described, and among
them *fraters:* "These men," says the writer,
"counterfeit proctors to spittle-houses. Some
of them will carry black boxes at their gyrdel,
wherein they have a brief of the Queen's
Majesty's letters patentes geven to such a poore
spittle-house for the relief of the poor there," &c.

This is probably a remnant of Popery.
Many of the religious communities of Italy have
their *Questuanti* (their proctors) going about
for alms, at this day, for particular saints,
madonnas, &c.

[1] ―――――――― *mock me all over,*
　　　　From my flat cap *unto my* shining shoes ;]
Howe says, that, in the times of Mary and
Elizabeth, "apprentices wore *flat-caps,* and
others under threescore years of age, as well
journeymen as masters, both at home and abroad,
whom the pages of the court, in derision, called
flat-caps." The derision, however, was not
confined to the pages of the court. Quicksilver
says to his master, " Marry, pho! goodman
flat-cap." And again, "Let's be no longer
fools to this *flat-cap,* Touchstone."—*Eastward Hoe.* But it is needless to multiply instances. *Shining shoes* occur frequently, and
with the same contemptuous meaning ; thus
Shirley :

" *Capt.* Will you to your shop again ?
Cit. I have no mind to woollen stockings now,
And *shoes that shine."—Doubtful Heir.*

And Massinger,

" *Bond.* How shall we know the vintners?
Claud. If they walk on foot, by their rat-
coloured stockings, and *shining shoes."*
　　　　　　　　　　　　　Guardian.

Kit. Brother, they would, believe it; so
     should I,
Like one of these penurious quack-salvers,
But set the bills up to mine own disgrace,
And try experiments upon myself ;
Lend scorn and envy opportunity
To stab my reputation, and good name——

Enter Master Mathew *struggling with*
     Bobadill.

Mat. I will speak to him.
Bob. Speak to him ! away ! By the foot
of Pharaoh, you shall not ! you shall not
do him that grace.—The time of day to you,
gentleman o' the house. Is Master Well-
bred stirring ?
Dow. How then ? what should he do ?
Bob. Gentleman of the house, it is to
you : is he within, sir ?
Kit. He came not to his lodging to-
night, sir, I assure you.
Dow. Why, do you hear ? you !
Bob. The gentleman citizen hath satisfied
me ; I'll take to no scavenger.
            [*Exeunt* Bob *and* Mat.
Dow. How ! scavenger ! stay, sir, stay !
Kit. Nay, Brother Downright.
Dow. 'Heart ! stand you away, an you
love me.
Kit. You shall not follow him now, I
pray you, brother, good faith you shall not ;
I will over-rule you.
Dow. Ha ! scavenger ! well, go to, I say
little : but, by this good day (God forgive
me I should swear), if I put it up so, say
I am the rankest cow that ever pist.
'Sdeins, an I swallow this, I'll ne'er draw
my sword in the sight of Fleet-street again
while I live ; I'll sit in a barn with madge-
howlet, and catch mice first. Scavenger !
heart !—and I'll go near to fill that huge
tumbrel-slop of yours with somewhat, an I
have good luck : your Garagantua breech
cannot carry it away so.
Kit. Oh, do not fret yourself thus ; never
think on't.
Dow. These are my brother's consorts,
these ! these are his camerades, his walking
mates ! he's a gallant, a cavaliero too, right
hangman cut ! Let me not live, an I could
not find in my heart to swinge the whole
gang of 'em, one after another, and begin
with him first. I am grieved it should be
said he is my brother, and take these
courses : Well, as he brews, so shall he
drink, for George, again. Yet he shall
hear on't, and that tightly too, an I live, i'
faith.

Kit. But, brother, let your reprehension,
     then,
Run in an easy current, not o'er high
Carried with rashness, or devouring choler,
But rather use the soft persuading way,
Whose powers will work more gently and
     compose
The imperfect thoughts you labour to re-
     claim ;
More winning, than enforcing the consent.
Dow. Ay, ay, let me alone for that, I
warrant you.
Kit. How now ! [*Bell rings.*] Oh, the
bell rings to breakfast. Brother, I pray
you go in, and bear my wife company till
I come ; I'll but give order for some dis-
patch of business to my servants.
            [*Exit* Downright.

Enter Cob *with his tankard.*

Kit. What, Cob ! our maids will have
you by the back, i' faith, for coming so late
this morning.
Cob. Perhaps so, sir ; take heed some-
body have not them by the belly, for walk-
ing so late in the evening.   [*Exit.*
Kit. Well ; yet my troubled spirit's some-
     what eased,
Though not reposed in that security
As I could wish : but I must be content,
Howe'er I set a face on't to the world.
Would I had lost this finger at a venture,
So Wellbred had ne'er lodged within my
     house.
Why't cannot be, where there is such re-
     sort
Of wanton gallants, and young revellers,
That any woman should be honest long.
Is't like, that factious beauty will preserve
The public weal of chastity unshaken,
When such strong motives muster, and
     make head
Against her single peace ? No, no : be-
     ware.
When mutual appetite doth meet to treat,
And spirits of one kind and quality
Come once to parley in the pride of blood,
It is no slow conspiracy that follows.
Well, to be plain, if I but thought the time
Had answered their affections, all the world
Should not persuade me but I were a
     cuckold.
Marry, I hope they have not got that start ;
For opportunity hath baulked them yet,
And shall do still, while I have eyes and
     ears
To attend the impositions of my heart.
My presence shall be as an iron bar,

'Twixt the conspiring motions of desire:
Yea, every look or glance mine eye ejects,
Shall check occasion, as one doth his slave,
When he forgets the limits of prescription.

Enter Dame Kitely *and* Bridget.

Dame K. Sister Bridget, pray you fetch
down the rose-water above in the closet.
[*Exit* Bridget.]—Sweetheart, will you come
in to breakfast?
Kit. An she have overheard me now!—
Dame K. I pray thee, good muss,[1] we
stay for you.
Kit. By heaven, I would not for a
thousand angels.
Dame K. What ail you, sweetheart? are
you not well? speak, good muss.
Kit. Troth my head akes extremely on
a sudden.
Dame K. [*putting her hand to his forehead.*] O, the lord!
Kit. How now! What?
Dame K. Alas, how it burns! Muss,
keep you warm; good truth it is this new
disease,[2] there's a number are troubled
withal. For love's sake, sweetheart, come
in, out of the air.
Kit. How simple, and how subtle are
her answers!
A new disease, and many troubled with it?
Why true; she heard me, all the world to
　　nothing.
Dame K. I pray thee, good sweetheart,
come in; the air will do you harm, in
troth.
Kit. The air! she has me in the wind.—

Sweetheart, I'll come to you presently;
'twill away, I hope.
Dame K. Pray heaven it do.　　[*Exit.*
Kit. A new disease! I know not, new
　　or old,
But it may well be called poor mortals plague,
For, like a pestilence, it doth infect
The houses of the brain. First it begins
Solely to work upon the phantasy,
Filling her seat with such pestiferous air,
As soon corrupts the judgment; and from
　　thence,
Sends like contagion to the memory:
Still each to other giving the infection,
Which as a subtle vapour spreads itself
Confusedly through every sensive part,
Till not a thought or motion in the mind
Be free from the black poison of suspect.
Ah! but what misery is it to know this?
Or, knowing it, to want the mind's erection
In such extremes? Well, I will once more
　　strive,
In spite of this black cloud, myself to be,
And shake the fever off that thus shakes
　　me.　　　　　　　　　　　　[*Exit.*

SCENE II.—*Moorfields.*

Enter Brainworm *disguised like a maimed
Soldier.*

Brain. 'Slid, I cannot choose but laugh
to see myself translated thus, from a poor
creature to a creator; for now must I
create an intolerable sort of lies, or my
present profession loses the grace: and yet
the lie, to a man of my coat, is as ominous
a fruit as the fico.[3] O, sir, it holds for

---

[1] Dame K. *I pray thee, good muss,*] *Muss*
(mouse) was a familiar term of endearment between married people. Thus Shakspeare:—

"Pinch wanton on your cheek, call you his
　　mouse."—*Hamlet.*

And Warner:—

"God bless thee, *mouse,* the bridegroom said."
　　　　　　　　　　Albion's Eng. WHAL.

[2] Dame K. *It is this* new disease.] Jonson
is exact in his description. Violent pains in the
head were the diagnostics of a disorder which
made its first appearance about this time, and
bore the appellation which the poet gives it. So
the author of *Anticus Coquinariæ, &c.* mentioning the illness of which Prince Henry died:
"Returned to Richmond in the fall of the leaf,
he complained afresh of his pain in the head,
with increase of a meagre complexion, inclining
to feverish; and then for the rareness thereof
called the *new disease.*"—WHAL.

[3] —— *as ominous a fruit as the* fico.]
Ominous is used by Shakspeare and others for

fatal or deadly; perhaps this is the sense of it
here; and then Brainworm means, For a soldier
to bear the imputation of lying is as fatal as the
fico, or poisoned fig of Spain and Italy, to
which our old dramatists are fond of alluding.
Thus Shirley:—

"I could soon pay him with a *fig;*
But that's not honest."—*Court Secret.*

And Webster:—

"I do now look for a *Spanish fig,* or an Italian
sallad daily."—*White Devil.*

If this be not the sense, the expression refers
to that particular mode of insult which is generally followed by blood in Italy, of thrusting out
the thumb betwixt two fingers, and forming a
coarse representation of a disease to which the
name of ficus has always been given. This is
the true import of the act, and I hope that what
is here said on the disgusting subject will have
a tendency to abridge the tedious disquisitions
into which the mass of commentators, with far
more zeal than knowledge, are always too ready
to enter.

good polity ever, to have that outwardly in vilest estimation, that inwardly is most dear to us: so much for my borrowed shape. Well, the troth is, my old master intends to follow my young master, dry-foot,[1] over Moorfields to London, this morning; now I knowing of this hunting-match, or rather conspiracy, and to insinuate with my young master (for so must we that are blue waiters, and men of hope and service do, or perhaps we may wear motley at the year's end, and who wears motley,[2] you know), have got me afore in this disguise, determining here to lie in ambuscado, and intercept him in the midway. If I can but get his cloke, his purse, his hat, nay, any thing to cut him off, that is, to stay his journey, *Veni, vidi, vici,* I may say with Captain Cæsar, I am made for ever, i' faith. Well, now must I practise to get the true garb of one of these lance-knights,[3] my arm here, and my——Odso! my young master, and his cousin, Master Stephen, as I am true counterfeit man of war, and no soldier!

Enter E. Knowell *and* Stephen.

E. Know. So, sir! and how then, coz?

Step. 'Sfoot! I have lost my purse, I think.

E. Know. How! lost your purse? where? when had you it?

Step. I cannot tell; stay.

Brai. 'Slid, I am afeard they will know me: would I could get by them!

E. Know. What, have you it?

Step. No; I think I was bewitched, I——   [*Cries.*

E. Know. Nay, do not weep the loss; hang it, let it go.

Step. Oh, it's here: No, an it had been lost, I had not cared, but for a jet ring Mistress Mary sent me.

E. Know. A jet ring! Oh, the poesie, the poesie?

Step. Fine, i' faith.—

> "Though Fancy sleep,
> My love is deep."

Meaning, that though I did not fancy her, yet she loved me dearly.

E. Know. Most excellent!

Step. And then I sent her another, and my poesie was,

> "The deeper the sweeter,
> I'll be judged by St. Peter."

E. Know. How, by St. Peter? I do not conceive that.

Step. Marry, St. Peter, to make up the metre.

E. Know. Well, there the saint was your good patron, he helped you at your need; thank him, thank him.

Brai. I cannot take leave on 'em so; I will venture, come what will. [*Comes forward.*] Gentlemen, please you change a few crowns for a very excellent good blade here? I am a poor gentleman, a soldier; one that, in the better state of my fortune, scorned so mean a refuge; but now it is the humour of necessity to have it so. You seem to be gentlemen well affected to martial men, else I should rather die with silence, than live with shame: however, vouchsafe to remember it is my want speaks, not myself; this condition agrees not with my spirit——

E. Know. Where hast thou served?

Brai. May it please you, sir, in all the late wars of Bohemia, Hungary, Dalmatia, Poland,[4] where not, sir? I have been a poor servitor by sea and land any time this fourteen years, and followed the fortunes of the best commanders in Christendom. I was twice shot at the taking of Aleppo, once at the relief of Vienna; I have been

---

[1] *To follow my young master,* dry-foot,] This is a term of the chase, and means, to follow the game by the scent of the foot. It occurs in Shakspeare, and in most of our old poets. "Nay, if he *smell* nothing but papers, I care not for his *dry-foot* hunting."—The *Dumb Knight,* 1608.

[2] —— *and who wears motley,* you know,] Servants, here called *blue* waiters, because *blue* was the colour which they usually wore; and who in Jonson's time, were somewhat more under the control of their masters, than at present, were, by way of punishment for notorious faults, stripped of their liveries and compelled to appear in a parti-coloured coat, the common habiliment of domestic fools. But *who knew this!* The audience, to whom

Brainworm improperly addresses himself. This violation of decorum was not uncommon on our stage; but Jonson, probably, thought himself justified by the example of the ancients, who practise it without scruple. In a drama which owes so little to them, it is to be regretted that he should have introduced one of their principal incongruities.

[3] —— *one of these* lance-knights,] i.e., common soldiers, men of the ranks. It is a Flemish term.

[4] In the French version of this play, we are told that this, and what follows, is an account of the campaigns really made by Jonson! It is a pity that the editors stopped here: a life of Jonson, on the authority of Quarter-master Brainworm, would have been a great curiosity.

at Marseilles, Naples, and the Adriatic gulph, a gentleman-slave in the gallies, thrice; where I was most dangerously shot in the head, through both the thighs; and yet, being thus maimed, I am void of maintenance, nothing left me but my scars, the noted marks of my resolution.

Step. How will you sell this rapier, friend?

Brai. Generous sir, I refer it to your own judgment; you are a gentleman, give me what you please.

Step. True, I am a gentleman, I know that, friend; but what though! I pray you say, what would you ask?

Brai. I assure you, the blade may become the side or thigh of the best prince in Europe.

E. Know. Ay, with a velvet scabbard, I think.

Step. Nay, an 't be mine, it shall have a velvet scabbard, coz, that's flat; I'd not wear it as it is, an you would give me an angel.

Brai. At your worship's pleasure, sir: nay, 'tis a most pure Toledo.

Step. I had rather it were a Spaniard.[1] But tell me, what shall I give you for it? An it had a silver hilt——

E. Know. Come, come, you shall not buy it; hold, there's a shilling, fellow; take thy rapier.

Step. Why, but I will buy it now, because you say so; and there's another shilling, fellow; I scorn to be outbidden. What, shall I walk with a cudgel, like Higginbottom,[2] and may have a rapier for money!

E. Know. You may buy one in the city.

Step. Tut! I'll buy this i' the field, so I will; I have a mind to't because 'tis a field rapier. Tell me your lowest price.

E. Know. You shall not buy it, I say.

Step. By this money, but I will, though I give more than 'tis worth.

E. Know. Come away, you are a fool.

Step. Friend, I am a fool, that's granted; but I'll have it, for that word's sake. Follow me for your money.

Brai. At your service, sir.   [*Exeunt.*

SCENE III.—*Another Part of* Moorfields.

Enter Knowell.

Know. I cannot lose the thought[3] yet of this letter,
Sent to my son; nor leave t' admire the change
Of manners, and the breeding of our youth
Within the kingdom, since myself was one.—
When I was young,[4] he lived not in the stews
Durst have conceived a scorn, and uttered it,
On a gray head: age was authority
Against a buffoon, and a man had then
A certain reverence paid unto his years,
That had none due unto his life: so much
The sanctity of some prevailed for others.
But now we all are fallen; youth, from their fear,
And age, from that which bred it, good example.
Nay, would ourselves were not the first,[5] even parents,

---

1 Step. *I had rather it were a* Spaniard.] Master Stephen had heard of the excellence of the Spanish blades, though his proficiency in geography did not enable him to discover in what country Toledo was situated. It is well known, that the swords manufactured in Castile were anciently much in request; they were said to owe their excellence to some peculiar quality of the water in which the metal was plunged, while glowing from the forge.

2 *Shall I walk with a cudgel, like Higginbottom,*] I have no knowledge of this Higginbottom. It appears from the Earl of Shrewsbury's Letters (see *Lodge's Illustrations*), that a country fellow of this name had been somewhat active in exciting disturbances among his lordship's tenants, and had been summoned more than once before the Privy Council, to answer the charge. But he was probably too early for Master Stephen's acquaintance; unless the allusion be to some picture of him: this, however, is mere trifling. I find a kindred expression in *Eastward Hoe.* "Methinks I see thee already walking in Moorfields, with a *cudgel under*

thine arm, borrowing and begging three pence," act i. sc. 1. Perhaps this was the *costume* of those sturdy vagrants, half footpads and half beggars, who then infested the outskirts of the metropolis.

3 Know. *I cannot lose the thought,* &c.] This most admirable soliloquy is only found in the folio; the quarto gives us, instead of it, a tame, and rather uninteresting homily, in rhyme. Jonson has made somewhat free with the ancients, it must be confessed; yet the spirit, pathos, and moral dignity of the speech are very impressive.

4 *When I was young,* &c.] This is a beautiful allusion to the *Credebant hoc grande nefas* of Juvenal. In the Notes on that passage, the reader may find my early thoughts of Jonson: to offer him my more mature opinion would be only to repeat them.

5 *Nay, would ourselves were not the first,* &c.] *Utinam liberorum nostrorum mores non ipsi perderemus! Infantiam statim deliciis solvimus;—Quid non adultus concupiscet, qui in purpuris repit? Ante palatum eorum quam*

That did destroy the hopes in our own
  children ;
Or they not learned our vices in their cradles,
And sucked in our ill customs with their
  milk !
Ere all their teeth be born, or they can
  speak,
We make their palates cunning ; the first
  words
We form their tongues with, are licentious
  jests :
Can it call whore? cry bastard? O, then,
  kiss it !
A witty child ! can't swear? the father's
  darling !
Give it two plums. Nay, rather than't
  shall learn
No bawdy song, the mother herself will
  teach it !—
But this is in the infancy, the days
Of the long coat ; when it puts on the
  breeches,
It will put off all this. Ay, it is like,
When it is gone into the bone already !
No, no, this dye goes deeper than the coat,
Or shirt, or skin ; it stains into the liver,
And heart, in some : and rather than it
  should not,
Note what we fathers do ! look how we live !
What mistresses we keep ! at what expense,
In our sons' eyes ! where they may handle
  our gifts,
Hear our lascivious courtships, see our
  dalliance,
Taste of the same provoking meats with us,
To ruin of our states ! Nay, when our own
Portion is fled, to prey on the remainder,
We call them into fellowship of vice ;
Bait 'em with the young chamber-maid, to
  seal,[1]
And teach 'em all bad ways to buy afflic-
  tion.[2]

This is one path : but there are millions
  more,
In which we spoil our own, with leading
  them.
Well, I thank heaven, I never yet was he
That travelled with my son before sixteen,
To shew him the Venetian courtezans :
Nor read the grammar of cheating I had
  made,
To my sharp boy, at twelve, repeating still
The rule, *Get money ; still get money, boy;
No matter by what means ; money will do
More, boy, than my lord's letter.* Neither
  have I
Drest snails or mushrooms[3] curiously before
  him,
Perfumed my sauces, and taught him to
  make them ;
Preceding still, with my gray gluttony,
At all the ord'naries, and only feared
His palate should degenerate, not his man-
  ners.
These are the trade of fathers now ; how-
  ever,
My son, I hope, hath met within my
  threshold
None of these household precedents, which
  are strong,
And swift, to rape youth to their precipice.
But let the house at home be ne'er so
  clean
Swept, or kept sweet from filth, nay dust
  and cobwebs,
If he will live abroad with his companions,
In dung and leystals,[4] it is worth a fear :
Nor is the danger of conversing less
Than all that I have mentioned of example.

Enter Brainworm, *disguised as before.*

Brai. My master ! nay, faith, have at
you ; I am fleshed now, I have sped so well

---

*os instituimus. Gaudemus si quid licentius
dixerint: verba, ne Alexandrinis quidem per-
mittenda deliciis, visu et osculo excipimus ; nec
mirum: nos docuimus, ex nobis audierunt !
Nostras amicas, nostros concubinos vident;
omne convivium obscenis canticis strepit; pu-
denda dictu spectantur : fit ex his consuetudo,
deinde natura.*—Quin. Inst. lib. i. c. 2.
  [1] *Bait 'em with the young chambermaid, to
seal,*] That is, tempt them by this means to
give up under their hands a part of their future
fortune, for the present enjoyment of the rest.—
WHAL.
  Is it not rather to induce them to give up their
right, and thus enable their profligate parents to
dispose of the family estates?
  [2] *And teach 'em all bad ways to buy* affliction.] The first fol. 1616, by an evident misprint,
reads *affiction.* Whalley unfortunately followed

the second, 1640, or rather the booksellers'
edition of 1716, which corrupted it into *affection,* and thus marred the sense of a very exquisite passage.
  [3] "——————— *Neither have I
    Drest snails or mushrooms, &c.*]

" *Nec de se melius cuiquam sperare propinquo
  Concedet juvenis, qui radere tubera terræ,
  Boletum condire, et eodem jure natantes
  Mergere ficedulas didicit, nebulone parente,
  Et cana monstrante gula.*"
              Juv. Sat. xiv. WHAL.

  Much of what follows is from the same satire.
In the "Grammar of cheating" above, Horace
was in the poet's thoughts.
  [4] *Leystals,*] i.e., receptacles of filth: the word
is still in use

[*aside*]. Worshipful sir, I beseech you, respect the estate of a poor soldier; I am ashamed of this base course of life.—God's my comfort, but extremity provokes me to't: what remedy?

Know. I have not for you, now.

Brai. By the faith I bear unto truth, gentleman, it is no ordinary custom in me, but only to preserve manhood. I protest to you, a man I have been; a man I may be, by your sweet bounty.

Know. Pray thee, good friend, be satisfied.

Brai. Good sir, by that hand, you may do the part of a kind gentleman, in lending a poor soldier the price of two cans of beer, a matter of small value; the king of heaven shall pay you, and I shall rest thankful: Sweet worship——

Know. Nay, an you be so importunate——

Brai. Oh, tender sir, need will have its course: I was not made to this vile use. Well, the edge of the enemy could not have abated me so much: it's hard when a man hath served in his prince's cause, and be thus—[*weeps*]. Honourable worship, let me derive a small piece of silver from you, it shall not be given in the course of time.[1] By this good ground, I was fain to pawn my rapier last night for a poor supper; I had sucked the hilts long before, I am a pagan else: Sweet honour.——

Know. Believe me, I am taken with some wonder,
To think a fellow of thy outward presence,
Should, in the frame and fashion of his mind,
Be so degenerate, and sordid-base.
Art thou a man? and sham'st thou not to beg,
To practise such a servile kind of life?
Why, were thy education ne'er so mean,
Having thy limbs, a thousand fairer courses
Offer themselves to thy election.
Either the wars might still supply thy wants,
Or service of some virtuous gentleman,
Or honest labour; nay, what can I name,
But would become thee better than to beg:
But men of thy condition feed on sloth,
As doth the beetle on the dung she breeds in;

Not caring how the metal of your minds
Is eaten with the rust of idleness.
Now, afore me, whate'er he be, that should
Relieve a person of thy quality,
While thou insist'st in this loose desperate course,
I would esteem the sin not thine, but his.

Brai. Faith, sir, I would gladly find some other course, if so——

Know. Ay,
You'd gladly find it, but you will not seek it.

Brai. Alas, sir, where should a man seek? in the wars, there's no ascent by desert in these days; but——and for service, would it were as soon purchased, as wished for! the air's my comfort [*sighs*].—I know what I would say.

Know. What's thy name?

Brai. Please you, Fitz-Sword, sir.

Know. Fitz-Sword!
Say that a man should entertain thee now,
Wouldst thou be honest, humble, just, and true?

Brai. Sir, by the place and honour of a soldier——

Know. Nay, nay, I like not these affected oaths;
Speak plainly, man, what think'st thou of my words?

Brai. Nothing, sir, but wish my fortunes were as happy as my service should be honest.

Know. Well, follow me, I'll prove thee, if thy deeds
Will carry a proportion to thy words.
[*Exit.*

Brai. Yes, sir, straight; I'll but garter my hose.—Oh, that my belly were hooped now, for I am ready to burst with laughing! never was bottle or bagpipe fuller. 'Slid, was there ever seen a fox in years to betray himself thus! now shall I be possest of all his counsels; and, by that conduit, my young master. Well, he is resolved to prove my honesty; faith, and I'm resolved to prove his patience: Oh, I shall abuse him intolerably. This small piece of service will bring him clean out of love with the soldier for ever. He will never come within the sign of it, the sight of a cassock,[2]

---

[1] *It shall not be given in the course of time.*] The meaning is, that in the course of time he should receive some recompense or other for his gift. It should not be given without any hope of return.—WHAL.
  Surely, it is an allusion (somewhat too free) to the text of Scripture. "He that giveth to the poor lendeth to the Lord."
[2] *The sight of a* cassock *or* musket-rest *again,*] A cassock, as Whalley observes, "is a soldier's loose outward coat." With respect to the *rest*, it is so well described in the *Soldier's Accidence*, a book of undoubted authority, that nothing further need be required on the subject: " Lastly, for their right hands, they (the musqueteers) shall have *rests* of ashwood, or other tough wood, with iron pikes in the nether end (to fix in the ground), and half hoops of iron above, to

or a musket-rest again. He will hate the musters at Mile-end for it, to his dying day. It's no matter, let the world think me a bad counterfeit,[1] if I cannot give him the slip at an instant: why, this is better than to have staid his journey: well, I'll follow him. Oh, how I long to be employed! [*Exit.*

ACT III.

SCENE I.—*The* Old Jewry. *A Room in the Windmill Tavern.*

Enter Master Mathew, Wellbred, *and* Bobadill.

Mat. Yes, faith, sir, we were at your lodging to seek you too.
Wel. Oh, I came not there to-night.
Bob. Your brother delivered us as much.
Wel. Who, my brother Downright?
Bob. He. Mr. Wellbred, I know not in what kind you hold me; but let me say to you this: as sure as honour, I esteem it so much out of the sunshine of reputation, to throw the least beam of regard upon such a——
Wel. Sir, I must hear no ill words of my brother.
Bob. I protest to you, as I have a thing to be saved about me, I never saw any gentleman-like part——
Wel. Good captain, faces about[2] to some other discourse.
Bob. With your leave, sir, an there were no more men living upon the face of the earth, I should not fancy him, by St. George!
Mat. Troth, nor I; he is of a rustical cut, I know not how: he doth not carry himself like a gentleman of fashion.
Wel. Oh, Master Mathew, that's a grace peculiar but to a few, *Quos æquus amavit Jupiter.*
Mat. I understand you, sir.
Wel. No question, you do,—or you do not, sir.

Enter E. Knowell *and* Master Stephen.

Ned Knowell! by my soul, welcome; how dost thou, sweet spirit, my genius? 'Slid, I shall love Apollo and the mad Thespian girls the better, while I live, for this, my dear Fury; now, I see there's some love in thee. Sirrah, these be the two I writ to thee of: nay, what a drowsy humour is this now! why dost thou not speak?
E. Know. Oh, you are a fine gallant, you sent me a rare letter.
Wel. Why, was't not rare?
E. Know. Yes, I'll be sworn, I was ne'er guilty of reading the like; match it in all Pliny, or Symmachus' epistles, and I'll have my judgment burned in the ear for a rogue: make much of thy vein, for it is inimitable. But I marle what camel it was, that had the carriage of it; for, doubtless, he was no ordinary beast that brought it.
Wel. Why?
E. Know. Why, sayst thou! why dost thou think that any reasonable creature, especially in the morning, the sober time of the day too, could have mistaken my father for me?
Wel. 'Slid, you jest, I hope.
E. Know. Indeed, the best use we can turn it to, is to make a jest on't, now: but I'll assure you, my father had the full view of your flourishing style, some hour before I saw it.
Wel. What a dull slave was this! but, sirrah, what said he to it, i' faith?
E. Know. Nay, I know not what he said; but I have a shrewd guess what he thought.
Wel. What, what?
E. Know. Marry, that thou art some strange, dissolute young fellow, and I—a grain or two better, for keeping thee company.
Wel. Tut! that thought is like the moon in her last quarter, 'twill change shortly: but, sirrah, I pray thee be acquainted with my two hang-by's here; thou wilt take exceeding pleasure in them, if thou hear'st

---

rest the musket on; and double strong stringes fastened near thereunto, to hang about the arme of the soldier, when at any time he shall have occasion to trail the same."—p. 4.

[1] *Let the world think me a bad* counterfeit, *if I cannot give him the* slip] *Counterfeit* and *slip* were synonymous, and both used indifferently for a piece of false money. Our old writers take advantage of this, to play upon the words, of which several instances will be found in the Notes to the *Magnetic Lady.*

[2] "*Faces about*" *to some other discourse.*] This simple expression, which occurs in almost every writer of the age, seems to have occasioned the commentators some trouble; for I find several elaborate notes upon it. It is merely a military phrase, equivalent to our *face* or *wheel*. In the *Soldier's Accidence*, the officers are directed to give the word of command in these terms, "used," says the author, "both here and in the Netherlands."

> *Faces* to the right,
> Faces to the left,
> *Faces about,* or } which is all one.
> Faces to the reare.

'em once go; my wind-instruments; I'll
wind them up——but what strange piece of
silence is this, the sign of the dumb man?

E. Know. Oh, sir, a kinsman of mine,
one that may make your music the fuller,
an he please; he has his humour, sir.

Wel. Oh, what is't, what is't?

E. Know. Nay, I'll neither do your judgment nor his folly that wrong, as to prepare
your apprehension: I'll leave him to the
mercy of your search; if you can take him,
so!

Wel. Well, Captain Bobadill, Master
Mathew, pray you know this gentleman
here; he is a friend of mine, and one that
will deserve your affection. I know not
your name, sir [*to* Stephen], but I shall be
glad of any occasion to render me more
familiar to you.

Step. My name is Master Stephen, sir;
I am this gentleman's own cousin, sir, his
father is mine uncle, sir; I am somewhat
melancholy, but you shall command me,
sir, in whatsoever is incident to a gentleman.

Bob. Sir, I must tell you this, I am no
general man; but for Master Wellbred's
sake (you may embrace it at what height of
favour you please), I do communicate with
you, and conceive you to be a gentleman
of some parts; I love few words.

E. Know. And I fewer, sir; I have
scarce enough to thank you.

Mat. But are you, indeed, sir, so given to it?

Step. Ay, truly, sir, I am mightily given
to melancholy.

Mat. Oh, it's your only fine humour, sir;
your true melancholy breeds your perfect
fine wit, sir.[1] I am melancholy myself,
divers times, sir, and then do I no more but

take pen and paper, presently, and overflow
you half a score, or a dozen of sonnets at a
sitting.

E. Know. Sure he utters them then by
the gross. 　　　　　　　　　　　[*Aside.*

Step. Truly, sir, and I love such things
out of measure.

E. Know. I' faith, better than in measure,
I'll undertake.

Mat. Why, I pray you, sir, make use of
my study, it's at your service.

Step. I thank you, sir, I shall be bold, I
warrant you; have you a stool there, to be
melancholy upon?

Mat. That I have, sir, and some papers
there of mine own doing, at idle hours,
that you'll say there's some sparks of wit in
'em, when you see them.

Wel. Would the sparks would kindle
once, and become a fire amongst them! I
might see self-love burnt for her heresy.
　　　　　　　　　　　　　　　[*Aside.*

Step. Cousin, is it well? am I melancholy enough?

E. Know. Oh ay, excellent.

Wel. Captain Bobadill, why muse you so?

E. Know. He is melancholy too.

Bob. Faith, sir, I was thinking of a most
honourable piece of service, was performed
to-morrow, being St. Mark's day, shall be
some ten years, now.

E. Know. In what place, captain?

Bob. Why, at the beleaguering of Strigonium,[2] where, in less than two hours,
seven hundred resolute gentlemen, as any
were in Europe, lost their lives upon the
breach. I'll tell you, gentlemen, it was the
first, but the best leaguer that ever I beheld
with these eyes, except the taking in of[3]——

---

[1] *Your true melancholy breeds your perfect
fine wit, sir.*] A sneer upon the fantastic behaviour of the gallants in that age, who affected
to appear melancholy, and abstracted from common objects. The reason assigned, its being the
physical cause of wit, which is as old as Aristotle
himself, was likewise generally received by those
who had no other pretence to genius.—WHAL.
I suppose this is the passage to which Whalley
alludes:

Δια τι παντες, ὁσοι περιττοι γεγονασιν ανδρες,
η κατα φιλοσοφιαν, η πολιτικην, η ποιησιν, η τεχ-
νας, φαινονται μελαγχολικοι οντες.—Prob. 30. 1.

Shakspeare seems to derive the fashion from
France: he makes young Arthur say—

"I do remember when I was in France,
Young gentlemen would be as sad as night,
Only for wantonness."—*King John.*

It is, however, of English growth: the French
have been frequently mad (both with joy and
grief), but never melancholy.

[2] *Strigonium,*] Graan in Hungary, which was
retaken from the Turks in the year 1597, after
having been in their possession near half a century. It should be observed, that the inroads
which the Turks made into the Emperor's do-
minions, had made it fashionable to go a volun-
teering in his service; and we find that Thomas
Lord Arundel of Wardour was created at this
very time a Count of the Empire, as a reward
of his signal valour; and because in forcing
the water tower near Strigonium, he took a
banner from the Turks with his own hand.—
WHAL.

[3] *Except the taking in of*—] To *take in* is to
capture, to subdue. Thus Shakspeare:

"Is it not strange
He should so quickly cut the Ionian sea,
And *take in* Toryne?"
　　　　　　　　　Ant. and Cleopatra.

The quarto gives the name of the place to which
Bobadill alludes, *Tortosa.*

what do you call it? last year, by the Genoways; but that, of all other, was the most fatal and dangerous exploit that ever I was ranged 'in, since I first bore arms before the face of the enemy, as I am a gentleman and a soldier!

Step. So! I had as lief as an angel I could swear as well as that gentleman.

E. Know. Then, you were a servitor at both, it seems; at Strigonium, and what do you call't?

Bob. O lord, sir! By St. George, I was the first man that entered the breach; and, had I not effected it with resolution, I had been slain if I had had a million of lives.

E. Know. 'Twas pity you had not ten; a cat's and your own, i' faith. But, was it possible?

Mat. Pray you mark this discourse, sir.

Step. So I do.

Bob. I assure you, upon my reputation, 'tis true, and yourself shall confess.

E. Know. You must bring me to the rack, first.   [*Aside.*

Bob. Observe me judicially, sweet sir; they had planted me three demi-culverius just in the mouth of the breach; now, sir, as we were to give on, their master-gunner (a man of no mean skill and mark, you must think), confronts me with his linstock, ready to give fire; I, spying his intendment, discharged my petronel in his bosom, and with these single arms, my poor rapier, ran violently upon the Moors that guarded the ordnance, and put 'em pell-mell to the sword.

Wel. To the sword! To the rapier, captain.

E. Know. Oh, it was a good figure observed, sir: but did you all this, captain, without hurting your blade?

Bob. Without any impeach o' the earth: you shall perceive, sir. [*Shews his rapier.*]

It is the most fortunate weapon that ever rid on poor gentleman's thigh. Shall I tell you, sir? You talk of Morglay, Excalibur, Durindana, or so;[1] tut! I lend no credit to that is fabled of 'em: I know the virtue of mine own, and therefore I dare the boldlier maintain it.

Step. I marle whether it be a Toledo or no.

Bob. A most perfect Toledo, I assure you, sir.

Step. I have a countryman of his here.

Mat. Pray you, let's see, sir; yes, faith, it is.

Bob. This a Toledo! Pish!

Step. Why do you pish, captain?

Bob. A Fleming, by heaven! I'll buy them for a guilder apiece, an I would have a thousand of them.

E. Know. How say you, cousin? I told you thus much.

Wel. Where bought you it, Master Stephen?

Step. Of a scurvy rogue soldier: a hundred of lice go with him! He swore it was a Toledo.

Bob. A poor provant rapier, no better.[2]

Mat. Mass, I think it be indeed, now I look on't better.

E. Know. Nay, the longer you look on't, the worse. Put it up, put it up.

Step. Well, I will put it up; but by—I have forgot the captain's oath, I thought to have sworn by it—an e'er I meet him——

Wel. O, it is past help now, sir, you must have patience.

Step. Whoreson, coney-catching rascal![3] I could eat the very hilts for anger.

E. Know. A sign of good digestion; you have an ostrich stomach, cousin.

Step. A stomach! would I had him here, you should see an I had a stomach.

Wel. It's better as it is.—Come, gentlemen, shall we go?

---

[1] *You talk of Morglay, Excalibur, Durindana, or so;*] These blades make a figure in romance: *Morglay* was the sword of Bevis of Southampton; *Durindana* of Orlando, and *Excalibur* of the renowned King Arthur. Mr. Congreve, who was a great admirer and imitator of Jonson, has formed the character of Bluff, in the *Old Batchelor*, upon this of Bobadill, as will easily appear by comparing them together.—WHAL. I do not think so, but of this elsewhere.

[2] *A poor* provant *rapier, no better.*] Properly speaking, *provant* means provisions; but it is here, and, indeed, in many other places, extended to arms, ammunition, &c. A *provant* rapier, therefore, is such a one as the common men wore; such in short, as was supplied to the

soldiers from the magazines of the army. Thus Massinger:—

"A knave with half a breech there; if you bear not Yourselves both in and upright, with a *provant* sword,

Will slash your scarlets."—*Maid of Honour.*

[3] *Whoreson* coney-catching *rascal!*] As this opprobrious term frequently occurs in our old writers, it may not be amiss, once for all, to give its meaning: "A *conie-catcher*, a name given to *deceivers*, by a metaphor taken from those that rob warrens, and conie grounds, using all means, sleights, and cunning to deceive them, as pitching of haies before their holes, fetching them in by tumblers, &c."—*Minsh. Dict.* 1617.

Enter Brainworm, *disguised as before.*

E. Know. A miracle, cousin ; look here, look here !

Step. Oh—od's lid ! By your leave, do you know me, sir?

Brai. Ay, sir, I know you by sight.

Step. You sold me a rapier, did you not ?

Brai. Yes, marry did I, sir.

Step. You said it was a Toledo, ha ?

Brai. True, I did so.

Step. But it is none.

Brai. No, sir, I confess it ; it is none.

Step. Do you confess it ? Gentlemen, bear witness, he has confest it :—Od's will, an you had not confest it——

E. Know. Oh, cousin, forbear, forbear !

Step. Nay, I have done, cousin.

Wel. Why, you have done like a gentleman ; he has confest it, what would you more ?

Step. Yet, by his leave, he is a rascal, under his favour, do you see.

E. Know. Ay, by his leave, he is, and under favour: a pretty piece of civility ! Sirrah, how dost thou like him ?

Wel. Oh, it's a most precious fool, make much on him : I can compare him to nothing more happily, than a drum ; for every one may play upon him.

E. Know. No, no, a child's whistle were far the fitter.

Brai. Sir, shall I intreat a word with you ?

E. Know. With me, sir ? you have not another Toledo to sell, have you ?

Brai. You are conceited, sir :[1] Your name is Master Knowell, as I take it ?

E. Know. You are in the right ; you mean not to proceed in the catechism, do you ?

Brai. No, sir, I am none of that coat.

E. Know. Of as bare a coat, though : well, say sir.

Brai. [*taking* E. Know. *aside.*] Faith, sir, I am but servant to the drum extraordinary, and indeed, this smoky varnish being washed off, and three or four patches removed, I appear your worship's in reversion, after the decease of your good father, Brainworm.

E. Know. Brainworm ! 'Slight, what breath of a conjurer hath blown thee hither in this shape ?

Brai. The breath of your letter, sir,

this morning ; the same that blew you to the Windmill, and your father after you.

E. Know. My father !

Brai. Nay, never start, 'tis true ; he has followed you over the fields by the foot, as you would do a hare in the snow.

E. Know. Sirrah Wellbred, what shall we do, sirrah? my father is come over after me.

Wel. Thy father ! Where is he ?

Brai. At Justice Clement's house, in Coleman-street, where he but stays my return ; and then——

Wel. Who's this? Brainworm !

Brai. The same, sir.

Wel. Why how, in the name of wit, com'st thou transmuted thus ?

Brai. Faith, a device, a device ; nay, for the love of reason, gentlemen, and avoiding the danger, stand not here ; withdraw, and I'll tell you all.

Wel. But art thou sure he will stay thy return ?

Brai. Do I live, sir? what a question is that !

Wel. We'll prorogue his expectation, then, a little : Brainworm, thou shalt go with us.—Come on, gentlemen.—Nay, I pray thee, sweet Ned, droop not : 'heart, an our wits be so wretchedly dull, that one old plodding brain can outstrip us all, would we were e'en prest to make porters of, and serve out the remnant of our days in Thames-street, or at Custom-house key, in a civil war against the carmen !

Brai. Amen, amen, amen, say I.

[*Exeunt.*

SCENE II.—*The* Old Jewry. Kitely's
Warehouse.

Enter Kitely *and* Cash.

Kit. What says he, Thomas ? did you speak with him ?

Cash. He will expect you, sir, within this half-hour.

Kit. Has he the money ready, can you tell ?

Cash. Yes, sir, the money was brought in last night.

Kit. O, that is well ; fetch me my cloak, my cloak !——   [*Exit* Cash.
Stay, let me see, an hour to go and come ;
Ay, that will be the least ; and then 'twill be
An hour before I can dispatch with him,
Or very near ; well, I will say two hours.
Two hours ! ha ! things never dreamt of yet,
May be contrived, ay, and effected too,
In two hours absence ; well, I will not go.

---

[1] *You are conceited, sir.*] Witty, disposed to jest ; or, as the quarto has it, *pleasant.* In this sense the word occurs in *Sejanus.* " Your lordship is *conceited*," act i.

Two hours ! No, fleering Opportunity,
I will not give your subtilty that scope.
Who will not judge him worthy to be
    robbed,
That sets his doors wide open to a thief,
And shews the felon where his treasure lies?
Again, what earthy spirit but will attempt
To taste the fruit of beauty's golden tree,
When leaden sleep seals up the dragon's
    eyes?
I will not go.   Business, *go by* for once.
No, beauty, no ; you are of too good
    caract,[1]
To be left so, without a guard, or open.
Your lustre, too, 'll inflame at any distance,
Draw courtship to you, as a jet doth straws ;
Put motion in a stone, strike fire from ice,
Nay, make a porter leap you with his
    burden.
You must be then kept up, close, and well
    watched,
For, give you opportunity, no quick-sand
Devours or swallows swifter ! He that lends
His wife, if she be fair, or time or place,
Compels her to be false.   I will not go ;
The dangers are too many :—and then the
    dressing
Is a most main attractive ! Our great heads,
Within this city, never were in safety,
Since our wives wore these little caps :[2] I'll
    change 'em ;
I'll change 'em straight in mine : mine shall
    no more
Wear three-piled acorns,[3] to make my
    horns ake.
Nor will I go ; I am resolved for that.

Re-enter Cash *with a cloak.*

Carry in my cloak again.   Yet stay.   Yet
    do, too :
I will defer going, on all occasions.
    Cash. Sir, Snare, your scrivener, will be
    there with the bonds.
    Kit. That's true : fool on me ! I had
    clean forgot it ;
I must go.   What's a clock ?
    Cash. Exchange-time, sir.[4]
    Kit. 'Heart, then will Wellbred pre-
    sently be here too,
With one or other of his loose consorts.
I am a knave, if I know what to say,
What course to take, or which way to re-
    solve.
My brain, methinks, is like an hour-glass,
Wherein my imaginations run like sands,
Filling up time ;[5] but then are turned and
    turned :
So that I know not what to stay upon,
And less, to put in act.—It shall be so.
Nay, I dare build upon his secrecy,
He knows not to deceive me.—Thomas !
    Cash. Sir.
    Kit. Yet now I have bethought me too,
    I will not.—
Thomas, is Cob within ?
    Cash. I think he be, sir.
    Kit. But he'll prate too, there is no
    speech of him.
No, there were no man on the earth to
    Thomas,[6]
If I durst trust him ; there is all the
    doubt.

---

[1] *No, beauty, no ; you are of too good* caract,
&c.] That is, you are of too intrinsic a value to
be left thus exposed and public, without any to
preserve and guard you. The metaphor is taken
from the finest gold, which hath the least mixture of alloy in it ; or from the value of pearls,
which are most precious when they contain more
caracts in weight.—WHAL.
[2] ——— *Our great heads,*
    Within this city, never were in safety,
    Since our wives wore these little *caps :*]
Velvet caps, of a diminutive size, were worn at
this time by citizens' wives and daughters : the
fashion indeed must have prevailed for some
years, for it is mentioned in the comedy of
Taming the Shrew, which Shakspeare afterwards remodelled. The writer of the old play
merely notices it ; but Shakspeare wantons on
the subject :—

"*Pet.* Why this was moulded on a porringer ;
A velvet dish ;—fie, fie ! 'tis lewd and filthy !
Why, 'tis a cockle, or a walnut shell,
A knack, a toy, a trick, a baby's cap ;
Away with it ! come, let me have a bigger.

Kath. I have no bigger ; this doth fit the time,
And gentlewomen *wear such caps as these.*"
Three-piled, which occurs in the next line,
means velvet of the strongest and richest quality.
The expression is very common.
[3] ——— *mine shall no more*
Wear three-piled acorns, *to make my* horns
ake.] This is about the worst pun that was ever
produced, and would scarcely pass muster in
the columns of a modern newspaper. Jonson
is nearly as fond of a pun as Shakspeare is of a
quibble.
[4] *Cash.* Exchange-time, *sir.*] The merchants
of these days may not, perhaps, be without curiosity to know at what hour their ancestors met
for the despatch of business. It appears from the
quarto to have been at "ten o'clock."
[5] *Wherein my imaginations run like sands*
    Filling up time.] These lines run smoother
and better in the quarto :—

And my imaginations, like the sands,
Run dribbling forth to fill the mouth of time.

[6] *No, there were* no *man on the earth to*
Thomas,] None to be *compared* to him. So in

But should he have a chink in him, I were
   gone,
Lost in my fame for ever, talk for th' Ex-
   change !
The manner he hath stood with, till this
   present,
Doth promise no such change; what should
   I fear then?
Well, come what will, I'll tempt my for-
   tune once.
Thomas—you may deceive me, but, I
   hope—
Your love to me is more——
   Cash. Sir, if a servant's
Duty, with faith, may be called love, you
   are
More than in hope, you are possessed of it.
   Kit. I thank you heartily, Thomas: give
me your hand :
With all my heart, good Thomas. I have,
   Thomas,
A secret to impart unto you—but,
When once you have it, I must seal your
   lips up ;
So far I tell you, Thomas.
   Cash. Sir, for that——
   Kit. Nay, hear me out. Think I esteem
you, Thomas,

When I will let you in thus to my private.
It is a thing sits nearer to my crest,
Than thou art 'ware of, Thomas; if thou
   shouldst
Reveal it, but——
   Cash. How ! I reveal it?
   Kit. Nay,
I do not think thou wouldst; but if thou
   shouldst,
'Twere a great weakness.
   Cash. A great treachery;
Give it no other name.
   Kit. Thou wilt not do't, then?
   Cash. Sir, if I do, mankind disclaim me
   ever !
   Kit. He will not swear, he has some re-
servation,
Some concealed purpose, and close mean-
   ing sure ;
Else, being urged so much, how should he
   choose
But lend an oath to all this protestation ?
He's no precisian, that I'm certain of,
Nor rigid Roman Catholic: he'll play
At fayles, and tick-tack; I have heard him
   swear.[1]
What should I think of it ? urge him again,
And by some other way ! I will do so.

---

the *Return from Parnassus:* "Well, let others
complain, but I think there is *no* felicity *to* the
serving of a fool." And in the *Jew of Malta :—*

  "There is *no* musick *to* a Christian's knell."
                                WHAL.

[1] *At* fayles, *and* tick-tack; *I have heard him
swear.*] From these instances, he concludes that
Cash is no precisian, or, as the quarto has it,
Puritan ; as from some others, he is convinced
that he is no Roman Catholic. The Puritans
were at this time remarkable for scrupulously
abstaining from diversions, and from affirmations
of every kind in their common discourse.
                                  WHAL.

Tick-tack is a complicated species of backgammon. It is played both with men and pegs,
which renders it somewhat difficult, as two kinds
of calculation are carried on at the same time.
It is not much in use with us, but is found everywhere on the Continent : when Jonson wrote,
however, the game was sufficiently common here,
and rules for playing it are to be found in the
Complete Gamester, and other vade-mecums of
the time. I have suppressed Whalley's note on
the subject, as it was evidently written at random—"a malady most incident to" the editors
of our old dramatists. In *Taming the Shrew,*
Tranio boasts that he had "faced his antagonist
with a *card of ten;*" i. e., says Warburton, "with
the highest card in the *simple* games of our ancestors." But the "*simple* games of our ancestors" were far more intricate and involved
than the most complicated ones of the present
day. To understand Gleek alone, as they played

it, would employ all the time, and more than all
the wits of a dozen modern professors. In a
word, most of their games were very difficult, and
only to be mastered by hard study. Gambling
was then a science ; and a young man could not
well be ruined by it, without an attempt, at
least, to exercise his faculties : it is now simplified ; and so dexterously "adapted to the meanest capacity," that the veriest blockhead in the
kingdom may get rid of a fortune, to any
amount, with a promptitude altogether surprising.
  Warburton's note, which is thus palpably
false, and which would explain nothing if it
were true, keeps its place, however, in all the
editions of our great poet : not less to the credit
of his commentators, than to the edification of
his readers.
  Of *fayles* I know nothing. It does not occur
in the quarto, nor have I found it anywhere else.
The word which comes nearest to it is *fayalle,*
"a kind of counter, used," as the *Dict. de Tre-
voux* says, "to cast up money in Japan :" if
this (which I much doubt) be the origin of the
term, *fayles* may be some game of chance in
which these pieces are employed. In Jonson's
days a great number of petty curiosities were
brought into this country from the Japanese
islands, and fayalles might be among them.
  I had written thus far when I received the
following explanation of *fayles* from Francis
Douce, Esq., of the British Museum.
  "It is a very old table game, and one of the
numerous varieties of backgammon that were
formerly used in this country. It was played

Well, Thomas, thou hast sworn not to dis-
close :—
Yes, you did swear ?
   Cash. Not yet, sir, but I will,
Please you——
   Kit. No, Thomas, I dare take thy word,
But, if thou wilt swear, do as thou think'st
good ;
I am resolved without it ;[1] at thy pleasure.
   Cash. By my soul's safety then, sir, I
protest,
My tongue shall ne'er take knowledge of a
word
Delivered me in nature of your trust.
   Kit. It is too much ; these ceremonies
need not :
I know thy faith to be as firm as rock.
Thomas, come hither, near ; we cannot be
Too private in this business.   So it is,
—Now he has sworn, I dare the safelier
venture.   [*Aside.*
I have of late, by divers observations——
But whether his oath can bind him, yea, or no,
Being not taken lawfully ?[2] ha ! say you ?
I will ask counsel ere I do proceed :—
                   [*Aside.*
Thomas, it will be now too long to stay,
I'll spy some fitter time soon, or to-morrow.
   Cash. Sir, at your pleasure.
   Kit. I will think :—and, Thomas,
I pray you search the books 'gainst my re-
turn,
For the receipts 'twixt me and Traps.
   Cash. I will, sir.
   Kit. And hear you, if your mistress's
brother, Wellbred,
Chance to bring hither any gentleman,

Ere I come back, let one straight bring me
word.
   Cash. Very well, sir.
   Kit. To the Exchange, do you hear ?
Or here in Coleman-street,   to Justice
Clement's.
Forget it not, nor be not out of the way.
   Cash. I will not, sir.
   Kit. I pray you have a care on't.
Or, whether he come or no, if any other,
Stranger, or else ; fail not to send me word.
   Cash. I shall not, sir.
   Kit. Be it your special business
Now to remember it.
   Cash. Sir, I warrant you.
   Kit. But, Thomas, this is not the secret,
Thomas,
I told you of.
   Cash. No, sir ; I do suppose it.
   Kit. Believe me, it is not.
   Cash. Sir, I do believe you.
   Kit. By heaven it is not, that's enough :
but, Thomas,
I would not you should utter it, do you see,
To any creature living ; yet I care not.
Well, I must hence.   Thomas, conceive
thus much ;
It was a trial of you, when I meant
So deep a secret to you, I mean not this,
But that I have to tell you ; this is nothing,
this.
But, Thomas, keep this from my wife, I
charge you,
Locked up in silence, midnight, buried
here.—
No greater hell than to be slave to fear.[3]
                   [*Exit.*

---

with three dice and the usual number of men or
pieces.   The peculiarity of the game depended
on the mode of first placing the men on the
points.   If one of the players threw some particular throw of the dice he was disabled from
bearing off any of his men, and therefore *fayled*
in winning the game, and hence the appellation
of it.   The above particulars are gathered from
a manuscript in the Royal Collection, containing, among other things, some account of the
table-games made use of in the 14th century.
In the English translation of Rabelais, by Sir
Thomas Urquhart, the *failie* is mentioned among
Gargantua's games.   The original is *barignin,*
which the Dutch editor calls 'a sort of tric-trac.'"
  I ought, perhaps, in consequence of this account, which is perfectly satisfactory, to have
suppressed my own wanderings on the subject :
but I feel no shame in avowing my ignorance,
especially as Mr. Douce supports me in thinking that the term is nearly an ἅπαξ λεγομενον.
Perhaps I have had the good fortune to apply to
the only person who could furnish me with any
information on this long-forgotten game.

[1] *I am* resolved *without it ;*] i.e., convinced.
See p. 13.
  [2] *But whether his oath can bind him, yea, or no,
Being not taken lawfully ?*] The character of
Kitely is extremely well imagined, and supported
with great propriety.   His jealousy is constantly
returning, and creates him fresh scruples in everything he sets about.   It was a question in ca-
suistry, whether an oath was of any force, unless
taken in form before a legal magistrate : the
poet therefore brings this to his imagination, to
fill him with groundless objections, and throw
him into the greater perplexity.—WHAL.
  Whalley's observation, which is very pertinent, is confirmed by Shakspeare.

  "An oath is of no moment, being not took
    Before a true and lawful magistrate."
           Hen. VI., 3rd part, act i. sc. 2.

  [3] This is a masterly scene.   Jonson had in
view, perhaps, a more masterly one, between
Hubert and King John ; and I trust that the
eternal detractors of his character as well as
talents, will not attribute to envy of Shakspeare's

Cash. Locked up in silence, midnight,
    buried here!
Whence should this flood of passion, trow,
    take head? ha!
Best dream no longer of this running
    humour,
For fear I sink; the violence of the stream
Already hath transported me so far,
That I can feel no ground at all: but soft,
Oh, 'tis our water-bearer; somewhat has
    crost him now.

Enter Cob, *hastily.*

Cob. Fasting-days! what tell you me of
fasting-days? 'Slid, would they were all on
a light fire for me! they say the whole
world shall be consumed with fire one day,
but would I had these Ember-weeks and
villanous Fridays burnt in the mean time,
and then——
Cash. Why, how now, Cob? what
moves thee to this choler, ha?
Cob. Collar, Master Thomas! I scorn
your collar, I, sir; I am none o' your cart-
horse, though I carry and draw water. An
you offer to ride me with your collar or
halter either, I may hap shew you a jade's
trick, sir.
Cash. O, you'll slip your head out of the
collar? why, goodman Cob, you mistake
me.
Cob. Nay, I have my rheum, and I can
be angry as well as another, sir.
Cash. Thy rheum, Cob, thy humour,
thy humour—thou mistak'st.[1]
Cob. Humour! mack, I think it be so,
indeed; what is that humour?[2] some rare
thing, I warrant.
Cash. Marry I'll tell thee, Cob: it is a
gentleman-like monster, bred in the special

gallantry of our time, by affectation; and
fed by folly.
Cob. How! must it be fed?
Cash. Oh ay, humour is nothing if it be
not fed: didst thou never hear that? it's a
common phrase, *feed my humour.*
Cob. I'll none on it: humour avaunt! I
know you not, be gone! let who will make
hungry meals for your monstership, it shall
not be I. Feed you, quoth he! 'slid, I have
much ado to feed myself; especially on these
lean rascally days too; an't had been any
other day but a fasting-day—a plague on
them all for me! By this light, one might have
done the commonwealth good service, and
have drowned them all in the flood, two or
three hundred thousand years ago. O, I
do stomach them hugely. I have a maw
now, an 'twere for Sir Bevis his horse,
against them.[3]
Cash. I pray thee, good Cob, what
makes thee so out of love with fasting-days?
Cob. Marry, that which will make any
man out of love with 'em, I think; their
bad conditions, an you will needs know.
First, they are of a Flemish breed, I'm sure
on't, for they raven up more butter than all
the days of the week beside; next, they
stink of fish and leek-porridge miserably;
thirdly, they'll keep a man devoutly hungry
all day, and at night send him supperless to
bed.
Cash. Indeed, these are faults, Cob.
Cob. Nay, an this were all, 'twere something; but they are the only known enemies
to my generation. A fasting-day no sooner
comes, but my lineage goes to wrack; poor
cobs! they smoke for it, they are made
martyrs o' the gridiron, they melt in passion: and your maids too know this, and yet
would have me turn Hannibal, and eat my

---

success, an honourable effort to emulate him in his
high career. "The field of glory is a field for all;"
fair contention is the fruitful source of excellence, and though Jonson must be confessed to
be outstripped in the race, yet, let it be remembered to his honour, that it is only by Shakspeare, to whom he approaches much nearer than
any third competitor ever approached to himself.
[1] Cash. *Thy rheum, Cob! thy humour—thou
mistak'st.*] Not much, however, for *rheum,*
also, appears to have been a cant term for
spleen, caprice, or fretful resentment. Thus
Daniel, in the *Queen's Arcadia,* act iii. sc. 1:—

" But now, in faith, I have found out a trick,
    That will perpetually so feed their *rheums*—"

Cob's misfortune seems to be, that he came,
like "Justice Shallow," in the rear-ward of the
fashion, and was not aware that his term had
been recently superseded.

[2] *What is that* humour?] Every oddity
which a man affected was called his humour, a
word that seems to have been first used in this
sense about the age of Jonson. But we shall
have occasion to say more of this in the notes on
the first act of *Every Man out of his Humour.*—
WHAL.
[3] *I have a maw now, an 'twere for Sir Bevis
his horse, against them.*] This horse, the gift
of the fair Josyan, and little less celebrated than
Sir Bevis himself, was named Arundel. He appears to have been of a most pugnacious disposition, and is described, in the old romance, as
rendering his master very effectual assistance in
battle, biting, kicking, and dispersing his enemies
on every side. It is to this particular trait in
his character, I suppose, that Cob alludes, by
way of illustrating the fierceness of his hostility
to fasting-days.

own flesh and blood. My princely coz,
[*pulls out a red herring*] fear nothing ; I
have not the heart to devour you, an I might
be made as rich as King Cophetua.[1] O
that I had room for my tears, I could weep
salt-water enough now to preserve the lives
of ten thousand thousand of my kin ! But
I may curse none but these filthy almanacks;
for an't were not for them, these days of
persecution would never be known. I'll be
hanged an some fishmonger's son do not
make of 'em,[2] and puts in more fasting-days
than he should do, because he would utter
his father's dried stock-fish and stinking
conger.

Cash. 'Slight, peace ! thou'lt be beaten
like a stock-fish else ; here's Master
Mathew.

Enter Wellbred, E. Knowell, Brainworm,
Mathew, Bobadill, *and* Stephen.

Now must I look out for a messenger to
my master.   [*Exit with* Cob.

Wel. Beshrew me, but it was an absolute good jest, and exceedingly well carried!

E. Know. Ay, and our ignorance maintained it as well, did it not ?

Wel. Yes, faith ; but was it possible thou
shouldst not know him ? I forgive Master
Stephen, for he is stupidity itself.

E. Know. 'Fore God, not I, an I might
have been joined patten with one of the
seven wise masters for knowing him. He
had so writhen himself into the habit of one
of your poor infantry, your decayed, ruinous, worm-eaten gentlemen of the round;[3]
such as have vowed to sit on the skirts of
the city, let your provost and his half-dozen
of halberdiers do what they can ; and have
translated begging out of the old hackney-
pace to a fine easy amble, and made it run
as smooth off the tongue as a shove-groat
shilling.[4] Into the likeness of one of these
reformados[5] had he moulded himself so perfectly, observing every trick of their action,
as, varying the accent, swearing with an
emphasis, indeed, all with so special and
exquisite a grace, that, hadst thou seen
him, thou wouldst have sworn he might
have been serjeant-major, if not lieutenant-
coronel to the regiment.

Wel. Why, Brainworm, who would have
thought thou hadst been such an artificer?

E. Know. An artificer ! an architect.
Except a man had studied begging all his
life time, and been a weaver of language
from his infancy for the cloathing of it, I
never saw his rival.

Wel. Where got'st thou this coat, I
marle?

---

[1] *An I might be made as rich as King Cophetua.*] King Cophetua is better known for
his marriage with "a beggar maid," than for his
riches : but kings, in the opinion of the Cobs of
every age, are always rich.

[2] *I'll be hanged an some fishmonger's son do
not make of 'em,*] For the support and encouragement of the fishing towns in the time of
Queen Elizabeth, Wednesdays and Fridays
were constantly observed as fast-days, or days of
abstinence from flesh. This was by the advice
of her Minister Cecil ; and by the vulgar it was
generally called Cecil's fast. See WARBURTON'S
note on *King Lear*, act i.—WHAL.

[3] *Your decayed, ruinous, worm-eaten gentlemen of the round ;*] Invalids, or disbanded men,
who, to procure themselves a livelihood, had
taken up the trade of begging. A *gentleman of
the round* was a soldier of inferior rank, but in
a station above that of a common man. This
appears from a pamphlet published in that
age, in which the several military degrees are
thus enumerated :—"The general, high mar-
shall with his provosts, serjeant-general, serjeant of a regiment, corownel, captayne, lieu-
tenant, auncient, serjeant of a company, corpo-
rall, gentleman in a company or of the rounde,
launce-passado. These," says the author, "are
special ; the other that remain, private or common soldiers."—*The Castle or Picture of Policy,
&c.*, 1581. The duty of these gentlemen was to
visit the centinels, watches, and advanced guards;
and from their office of going their rounds, they
derive their name.—WHAL.

[4] *A shove-groat shilling.*] This expression
occurs in Shakspeare :—"Quoit him down, Bardolph, like a shove-groat shilling." The thing
meant, I suppose, is the piece of metal or money,
as they term it. made use of in the play of shovel-
board.—WHAL.

Edw. VI.'s shillings were generally employed
for this purpose ; this appears from Taylor's
Travels of Twelve-pence :

" For why, with me the unthrifts every day,
  With my face downward, do at shove-board
      play."

And also from the valuables of which Master
Slender's pocket was picked, among which he
enumerates, "two Edward shovel-boards, that
cost him two and two-pence a piece,"—probably,
because they were *lucky* ones ; or, not to disparage Master Slender's talents for driving a
bargain, because they were much worn, and
therefore slid smoothly and easily. I presume
the reader knows that at *shuffle-board* the shilling is placed on the extreme edge of the table,
and propelled towards the mark, by a smart
stroke with the palm of the hand.

[5] *one of these* reformados) i.e., broken or
disbanded soldiers. Boyer translates *officier* re-
formé, a *reformado.*

Brai. Of a Houndsditch man, sir, one of the devil's near kinsmen, a broker.

Wel. That cannot be, if the proverb hold ; for *a crafty knave needs no broker.*[1]

Brai. True, sir ; but I did *need a broker, ergo——*

Wel. Well put off :—*no crafty knave,* you'll say.

E. Know. Tut, he has more of these shifts.

Brai. And yet, where I have one the broker has ten, sir.

Re-enter Cash.

Cash. Francis ! Martin ![2] ne'er a one to be found now ? what a spite's this !

Wel. How now, Thomas ? Is my brother Kitely within ?

Cash. No, sir, my master went forth e'en now ; but Master Downright *is within.*— Cob ! what, Cob ! Is he gone, too ?

Wel. Whither went your master, Thomas, canst thou tell ?

Cash. I know not ; to Justice Clement's, I think, sir.—Cob !   [*Exit.*

E. Know. Justice Clement ! what's h..?

Wel. Why, dost thou not know him ? He is a city magistrate, a justice here, an excellent good lawyer, and a great scholar, but the only mad, merry old fellow in Europe. I shewed him you the other day.

E. Know. Oh, is that he ? I remember him now. Good faith, and he is a very strange presence, methinks ; it shews as if he stood out of the rank from other men : I have heard many of his jests in the University. They say he will commit a man for taking the wall of his horse.

Wel. Ay, or wearing his cloak on one shoulder, or serving of God ; anything, indeed, if it come in the way of his humour

Re-enter Cash.

Cash. Gasper ! Martin ! Cob ! 'Heart, where should they be, trow ?

Bob. Master Kitely's man, pray thee vouchsafe us the lighting of this match.

Cash. Fire on your match ! no time but now to *vouchsafe ?*—Francis ! Cob ! [*Exit.*

Bob. Body o' me ! here's the remainder of seven pound since yesterday was sevennight. 'Tis your right Trinidado :[3] did you never take any, Master Stephen ?

Step. No, truly, sir ; but I'll learn to take it now, since you commend it so.

Bob. Sir, believe me, upon my relation, for what I tell you, the world shall not reprove.[4] I have been in the Indies, where this herb grows, where neither myself, nor a dozen gentlemen more of my knowledge, have received the taste of any other nutriment in the world, for the space of one and twenty weeks, but the fume of this simple only : therefore, it cannot be, but 'tis most divine.[5] Further, take it in the nature, in the true kind : so, it makes an antidote, that had you taken the most deadly poisonous plant in all Italy, it should expel it, and clarify you, with as much ease as I speak. And for your green wound,— your Balsamum and your St. John's wort are all mere gulleries and trash to it, especially your Trinidado : your Nicotian is good too.[6] I could say what I know of the virtue of it, for the expulsion of rheums,

---

[1] *A crafty knave needs no broker.*] This is one of Ray's proverbs ; it is also the title of an old black lettered pamphlet, by A. Nixon.

[2] *Francis ! Martin !*] Cash is impatient for a servant to send after Kitely, according to his promise, p. 30 *b.*

[3] *'Tis your right* Trinidado :] The product of that island was at this time much in request : our old cosmographer, no incompetent judge, perhaps, of this matter, tells us, it abounds with the best kind of tobacco, much celebrated formerly by the name of a *Pipe of Trinidado.* Heylin's *Cosmog.* L. iv. p. 114.—WHAL.

[4] *For what I tell you, the world shall not* reprove.] In the quarto it is *improve,* which has the same sense. The commentators on Shakspeare do not understand this word. In *Hamlet,* Horatio says of young Fortinbras, that he **was**

" Of *unimproved* mettle, hot and full,"

which is interpreted, " full of spirit not regulated by knowledge." It means just the contrary.

VOL. I.

[5] *Therefore, it cannot be, but 'tis most* divine.] Bobadill had good authority for his epithet ; and, indeed, for the whole of his panegyric :

" There, whether it *divine tobacco* were, Or panachæa," &c.

Fai. Queen, iii. c. v. 32.

Warton conjectures that Spenser meant by this to compliment Sir Walter Raleigh, (foreigners say it was Sir Francis Drake) who first introduced tobacco into England : it may be so ; but both Spenser and Jonson speak the language of the times. Many grave treatises were now extant (particularly on the Continent), which celebrated the virtues of this plant in the most extravagant terms. To listen to them, the grand elixir was scarcely more restorative and infallible.

[6] *Your* Nicotian *is good too.*] I know not what kind of tobacco is here meant. Nicotian was originally a generic name. "*Nicotiana appellata est (scil. tabacum) a Joanne Nicotio Regis Galliarum legato in Lusitania anno* 1559, *qui*

D

raw humours, crudities, obstructions, with a thousand of this kind ; but I profess myself no quacksalver. Only thus much ; by Hercules I do hold it, and will affirm it before any prince in Europe, to be the most sovereign and precious weed that ever the earth tendered to the use of man.

E. Know. This speech would have done decently in a tobacco-trader's mouth.

Re-enter Cash *with* Cob.

Cash. At Justice Clement's he is, in the middle of Coleman-street.

Cob. Oh, oh!

Bob. Where's the match I gave thee, Master Kitely's man?

Cash. Would his match and he, and pipe and all, were at Sancto Domingo! I had forgot it.   [*Exit.*

Cob. Ods me, I marle what pleasure or felicity they have in taking this roguish tobacco. It's good for nothing but to choke a man, and fill him full of smoke and embers: there were four died out of one house last week with taking of it, and two more the bell went for yesternight ; one of them, they say, will never scape it : he voided a bushel of soot yesterday,

upward and downward.[1] By the stocks, an there were no wiser men than I, I'd have it present whipping, man or woman, that should but deal with a tobacco-pipe : why, it will stifle them all in the end, as many as use it ; it's little better than ratsbane or rosaker.[2]   [Bobadill *beats him.*

All. Oh, good captain, hold, hold !

Bob. You base cullion, you !

Re-enter Cash.

Cash. Sir, here's your match.—Come, thou must needs be talking too, thou'rt well enough served.

Cob. Nay, he will not meddle with his match, I warrant you : well, it shall be a dear beating, an I live.

Bob. Do you prate, do you murmur?

E. Know. Nay, good captain, will you regard the humour of a fool? Away, knave.

Wel. Thomas, get him away.

     [*Exit* Cash *with* Cob.

Bob. A whoreson filthy slave, a dungworm, an excrement ! Body o' Cæsar, but that I scorn to let forth so mean a spirit, I'd have stabbed him to the earth.

Wel. Marry, the law forbid, sir !

---

primus hanc plantam Galliis transmisit, &c. Chrys. Magnen. Exercit. The character which Nicot gives it in his Dictionary answers the description of the poet : Nicotiane *est une espèce d'herbe, de virtu admirable pour guerir toutes navrures, playes, ulceres, chancres, dartes, et autres tels accidents au corps humain.* It is strange that Daniel (in his *Arcadia*) should say that it derived its name "from the *island* of Nicotia ;" and still more strange, that all these derivative appellations should be finally swallowed up and lost in one taken from the insignificant settlement of Tobago. The time was not far distant, when the virtues of "your Nicotian" were to be discussed before one of those "princes"—I allude to the solemn farce which took place during James's visit to Oxford, in 1605, i.e., the disputation in one of the colleges, "*Utrum frequens suffitus Nicotianæ exotica sit sanis salutaris?*" at which His Majesty graciously condescended to act the part of a moderator.

[1] *He voided a bushel of soot yesterday, upward and downward.*] We may easily imagine that tales of this kind were common enough amongst the vulgar, when tobacco first came into use. The poet may probably allude to some recent story, which was currently believed by the people ; and the joke is not destitute of humour, when considered in this light. Yet we meet with it very gravely introduced in a serious essay, as a terrible memento to all smokers, and from no less authority than a royal pen. "Surely smoke becomes a kitchen, far better than a din

ing chamber, and yet it makes a kitchen oftentimes in the inward parts of men ; soiling and infecting them with an unctuous and oily kind of soot, as hath been found in some great tobaccotakers, that after their death were opened." King James's *Counterblast to Tobacco,* in his Works in folio, p. 221.—WHAL.

The reader will think, I suspect, that enough has been said on this subject : otherwise a volume might easily be filled with quotations for and against the general introduction of this "Indian weed !" Poor James had the mortification to find his *Counterblast* puffed away without much ceremony ; he therefore revenged himself by laying a duty on tobacco ; which, as it was not very heavy, even for those times, his loving subjects regarded no more than his advice, and smoked on very composedly. Shakspeare is the only one of the dramatic writers of the age of James, who does not condescend to notice tobacco : all the others abound in allusions to it. This is a singularity for which I cannot account, as he is generally sufficiently ready to invest his characters with the prevailing fashion of the times.

It may not be amiss to add, that much of what occurs in Jonson, on the subject of tobacco, was written before the death of Elizabeth, who had no objection, good lady, to this or anything else which promoted the commerce, and assisted the revenues of her kingdom.

[2] *Ratsbane or rosaker.*] These, I believe, are pretty nearly the same things ; preparations of corrosive sublimate.

Bob. By Pharaoh's foot, I would have done it.

Step. Oh, he swears most admirably! By Pharaoh's foot! Body o' Cæsar!—I shall never do it, sure. Upon mine honour, and by St. George!—No, I have not the right grace.

Mat. Master Stephen, will you any? By this air, the most divine tobacco that ever I drunk.[1]

Step. None, I thank you, sir. O, this gentleman does it rarely too: but nothing like the other. By this air! [*practises at the post.*] As I am a gentleman! By——
　　　　　　　　[*Exeunt* Bob. *and* Mat.

Brai. [*pointing to* Master Stephen.] Master, glance, glance! Master Wellbred!

Step. As I have somewhat to be saved, I protest——

Wel. You are a fool; it needs no affidavit.

E. Know. Cousin, will you any tobacco?

Step. I, sir! Upon my reputation——

E. Know. How now, cousin!

Step. I protest, as I am a gentleman, but no soldier, indeed——

Wel. No, Master Stephen? As I remember, your name is entered in the artillery-garden.[2]

Step. Ay, sir, that's true. Cousin, may I swear, as I am a soldier, by that?

E. Know. O yes, that you may; it is all you have for your money.

Step. Then, as I am a gentleman, and a soldier, it is "divine tobacco!"

Wel. But soft, where's Master Mathew? Gone?

Brai. No, sir; they went in here.

Wel. O, let's follow them: Master Mathew is gone to salute his mistress in verse; we shall have the happiness to hear some of his poetry now; he never comes unfurnished.—Brainworm!

Step. Brainworm! Where? Is this Brainworm?

E. Know. Ay, cousin; no words of it, upon your gentility.

Step. Not I, body of me! By this air! St. George! and the foot of Pharaoh!

Wel. Rare! Your cousin's discourse is simply drawn out with oaths.

E. Know. 'Tis larded with them; a kind of French dressing, if you love it.[3]
　　　　　　　　　　　　　[*Exeunt.*

SCENE III.—Coleman-street. *A Room in* Justice Clement's *House.*

Enter Kitely *and* Cob.

Kit. Ha! how many are there, say'st thou?

Cob. Marry, sir, your brother, Master Wellbred——

Kit. Tut, beside him: what strangers are there, man?

Cob. Strangers? let me see, one, two; mass, I know not well, there are so many.

Kit. How! so many?

Cob. Ay, there's some five or six of them at the most.

Kit. A swarm, a swarm!
Spite of the devil, how they sting my head
With forked stings, thus wide and large!
　　　But, Cob,
How long hast thou been coming hither,
　　　Cob?

Cob. A little while, sir.

Kit. Didst thou come running?

Cob. No, sir.

Kit. Nay, then I am familiar with thy haste.
Bane to my fortunes! what meant I to marry?
I, that before was ranked in such content,
My mind at rest too, in so soft a peace,
Being free master of mine own free thoughts,

---

[1] *By this air, the most divine tobacco that ever I* drunk.] This affected expression for smoking tobacco, is found in many of our old writers: "Thou can'st not live on this side of the world, feed well, and *drink tobacco.*"—*Miseries of Inforced Marriage.* Again in Davies's *Scourge of Folly:*—

　"Fumosus cannot eat a bit, but he
　　Must *drink tobacco,* so to drive it down."
　　　　　　　　　　　　　　Epig. 148.

And in Donne:—

　"He drooped; we went, till one, which did excel
Th' Indians in *drinking his tobacco* well," &c.
　　　　　　　　　　　　　　Sat. 1.

[2] In the quarto it is, "As I remember, you served on a great horse, last general muster."

[3] *A kind* of French dressing, *if you love it.*] A satire on our continental neighbours for profaneness in conversation, to which, it seems, they were *then* addicted.—WHAL.
They are not, even *now,* it is thought, much reformed in this respect. It is to be wished that we had contented ourselves with taking the dressing of meat from them; but our travelled coxcombs seldom shewed much reserve in the quantity, or care in the quality of the objects of their importation. If a folly or a vice lay on the surface, they seldom failed to pick it up, and bring it home, and this more constantly, perhaps, in Jonson's time than at any subsequent period.

And now become a slave? What! never
    sigh;
Be of good cheer, man; for thou art a
    cuckold:
'Tis done, 'tis done! Nay, when such
    flowing store,
Plenty itself, falls into my wife's lap,
The cornucopiæ will be mine, I know.—
But, Cob,
What entertainment had they? I am sure
My sister and my wife would bid them wel-
    come: ha?

Cob. Like enough, sir; yet I heard not a
word of it.

Kit. No;
Their lips were sealed with kisses, and the
    voice,
Drowned in a flood of joy at their arrival,
Had lost her motion, state, and faculty.—
Cob,
Which of them was it that first kissed my
    wife,
My sister, I should say?—My wife, alas!
I fear not her: ha! who was it, sayst thou?

Cob. By my troth, sir, will you have the
truth of it?

Kit. Oh, ay, good Cob, I pray thee
heartily.

Cob. Then I am a vagabond, and fitter
for Bridewell than your worship's company,
if I saw anybody to be kissed, unless they
would have kissed the post in the middle of
the warehouse; for there I left them all at
their tobacco, with a pox!

Kit. How! were they not gone in then
    ere thou cam'st?

Cob. O no, sir.

Kit. Spite of the devil! what do I stay
    here then?
Cob, follow me.   [*Exit.*

Cob. Nay, soft and fair;[1] I have eggs on
the spit; I cannot go yet, sir. Now am I,
for some five and fifty reasons, hammering,
hammering revenge: oh for three or four
gallons of vinegar, to sharpen my wits!
Revenge, vinegar revenge, vinegar and

mustard revenge! Nay, an he had not
lien in my house, 'twould never have
grieved me; but being my guest, one that,
I'll be sworn, my wife has lent him her
smock off her back, while his own shirt
has been at washing; pawned her necker-
chers for clean bands for him; sold almost
all my platters, to buy him tobacco; and
he to turn monster of ingratitude, and
strike his lawful host! Well, I hope to
raise up an host of fury for't: here comes
Justice Clement.

Enter Justice Clement, Knowell, *and*
                    Formal.

Clem. What's Master Kitely gone,
Roger?

Form. Ay, sir.

Clem. 'Heart o' me! what made him
leave us so abruptly?—How now, sirrah!
what make you here? what would you
have, ha?

Cob. An't please your worship, I am a
poor neighbour of your worship's——

Clem. A poor neighbour of mine! Why,
speak, poor neighbour.

Cob. I dwell, sir, at the sign of the Water-
tankard, hard by the Green Lattice: I have
paid scot and lot there any time this eighteen years.

Clem. To the Green Lattice?

Cob. No, sir, to the parish: Marry, I
have seldom scaped scot-free at the Lattice.[2]

Clem. O, well! What business has my
poor neighbour with me?

Cob. An't like your worship, I am come
to crave the peace of your worship.

Clem. Of me, knave! Peace of me,
knave! Did I ever hurt thee, or threaten
thee, or wrong thee, ha?

Cob. No, sir; but your worship's warrant for one that has wronged me, sir; his
arms are at too much liberty, I would
fain have them bound to a treaty of peace,
an my credit could compass it with your
worship.

---

[1] *Nay, soft and fair; I have* eggs on the
spit;] This proverbial expression (employed
when a person is occupied on affairs which require his constant attention) occurs again in
Bartholomew Fair: "I have both *eggs on the
spit,* and iron in the fire." It is still in use. "I
write short journals now," says Swift to Stella,
"I have *eggs on the spit.*"

[2] *Marry, I have seldom scaped scot-free at
the* Lattice]. In our author's time, the windows
of alehouses were furnished with lattices of
various colours (glass, probably, was too costly
and too brittle for the kind of guests which fre-

quented them); thus we hear of the *red,* the *blue,*
and, as in this place, of the *Green Lattice.* There
is a lane in the City yet called *Green-*lettuce
(lattice) Lane, from an alehouse which once stood
in it; and Serjeant Hall, in the *Tatler,* directs
a letter to his brother, "at the *Red* Lettace (lattice) in Butcher Row." It was through one of
these that Bardolph spied Falstaff's boy. "He
called me even now, my lord, through a *red lattice.*"—*Henry IV., Part II.* act ii. sc. 2. *Lattices* of various colours or chequers as they were
sometimes called, formed also a very common
alehouse sign at this period.

Clem. Thou goest far enough about for't, I am sure.

Know. Why, dost thou go in danger of thy life for him, friend?

Cob. No, sir; but I go in danger of my death every hour, by his means; an I die within a twelvemonth and a day,[1] I may swear by the law of the land that he killed me.

Clem. How, how, knave, swear he killed thee, and by the law? What pretence, what colour hast thou for that?

Cob. Marry, an't please your worship, both black and blue; colour enough, I warrant you. I have it here to shew your worship.

Clem. What is he that gave you this, sirrah?

Cob. A gentleman and a soldier, he says he is, of the city here.

Clem. A soldier of the city! What call you him?

Cob. Captain Bobadill.

Clem. Bobadill! and why did he bob and beat you, sirrah? How began the quarrel betwixt you, ha? speak truly, knave, I advise you.

Cob. Marry, indeed, an't please your worship, only because I spake against their vagrant tobacco, as I came by them when they were taking on't; for nothing else.

Clem. Ha! you speak against tobacco? Formal, his name.

Form. What's your name, sirrah?

Cob. Oliver, sir, Oliver Cob, sir.

Clem. Tell Oliver Cob he shall go to the jail, Formal.

Form. Oliver Cob, my master, Justice Clement, says you shall go to the jail.

Cob. O, I beseech your worship, for God's sake, dear master justice!

Clem. 'Sprecious! an such drunkards and tankards as you are, come to dispute of tobacco once, I have done: Away with him!

Cob. O, good master justice! Sweet old gentleman!   [*To* Knowell.

Know. "Sweet Oliver,"[2] would I could do thee any good!—Justice Clement, let me intreat you, sir.

Clem. What! a thread-bare rascal, a beggar, a slave that never drunk out of better than piss-pot metal in his life! and he to deprave and abuse the virtue of an herb so generally received in the courts of princes, the chambers of nobles, the bowers of sweet ladies, the cabins of soldiers!— Roger, away with him! Od's precious— I say, go to.

Cob. Dear master justice, let me be beaten again, I have deserved it; but not the prison, I beseech you.

Know. Alas, poor Oliver!

Clem. Roger, make him a warrant:—he shall not go, I but fear the knave.[3]

Form. Do not stink, sweet Oliver, you shall not go; my master will give you a warrant.

Cob. O, the lord maintain his worship, his worthy worship!

Clem. Away, dispatch him. [*Ex.* Form. *and* Cob.]—How now, Master Knowell, in dumps, in dumps! Come, this becomes not.

Know. Sir, would I could not feel my cares.

Clem. Your cares are nothing: they are like my cap, soon put on, and as soon put off. What! your son is old enough to govern himself; let him run his course, it's the only way to make him a staid man. If he were an unthrift, a ruffian, a drunkard, or a licentious liver, then you had reason;

---

[1] *An I die within a* twelvemonth and a day, &c.] This is the period of time required in the construction of the common law, to determine on the cause of the death of a man bruised or wounded by another. Thus Shirley: "Ay, but I will not hurt her, I warrant thee; an she die *within a twelvemonth and a day,* I'll be hanged for her." —*Witty Fair One.*

[2] "Sweet *Oliver,*"] It may be just worth noticing that this epithet almost always accompanies the mention of this gentle rival of the mad Orlando in fame: thus Decker, "This *sweet* Oliver will eat mutton till he be ready to burst." —*Honest Whore.* And Jonson again, in his *Execration upon Vulcan:*

"All the mad Rolands and *sweet* Olivers."

[3] *I but* fear *the knave.*] The verb *fear* is used

by our old writers in the sense of *frighten* or *terrify.* Thus Shakspeare:

"I tell thee, lady, this aspect of mine,
Hath *feared* the valiant."
                    Merchant of Venice.

And Middleton:

"Art not ashamed that any flesh should
fear thee?"
    A Mad World my Masters.—WHAL.

As a proof how little our old dramatists were understood at the Restoration, it may be sufficient to mention that Dryden censures Jonson for an improper use of this word (the sense of which he altogether mistakes) in a subsequent passage. Dryden had "prayed his pible ill" at this time, or he could not have fallen into such an error.

you had reason to take care : but being
none of these, mirth's my witness, an I had
twice so many cares as you have, I'd drown
them all in a cup of sack. Come, come,
let's try it : I muse your parcel of a soldier
returns not all this while.   [*Exeunt.*

ACT IV.

SCENE I.—*A Room in* Kitely's *House.*

Enter Downright *and* Dame Kitely.

Down. Well, sister, I tell you true ; and
you'll find it so in the end.
Dame K. Alas, brother, what would you
have me do? I cannot help it ; you see my
brother brings them in here ; they are his
friends.
Down. His friends ! his fiends. 'Slud !
they do nothing but haunt him up and
down like a sort of unlucky spirits, and
tempt him to all manner of villainy that
can be thought of. Well, by this light, a
little thing would make me play the devil
with some of them : an 'twere not more
for your husband's sake than anything else,
I'd make the house too hot for the best on
'em : they should say, and swear, hell were
broken loose, ere they went hence. But,
by God's will, 'tis nobody's fault but yours ;
for an you had done as you might have
done, they should have been parboiled,
and baked too, every mother's son, ere
they should have come in, e'er a one of
them.
Dame K. God's my life ! did you ever hear

the like ? what a strange man is this ? Could
I keep out all them, think you ? I should
put myself against half a dozen men, should
I ? Good faith, you'd mad the patient'st
body in the world,[1] to hear you talk so,
without any sense or reason.

Enter Mistress Bridget, Master Mathew,
and Bobadill : *followed, at a distance,
by* Wellbred, E. Knowell, Stephen,
and Brainworm.

Brid. Servant,[2] in troth you are too pro-
digal
Of your wit's treasure, thus to pour it forth
Upon so mean a subject as my worth.
Mat. You say well, mistress, and I mean
as well.
Down. Hoy-day, here is stuff !
Well. O, now stand close ; pray heaven,
she can get him to read ! he should do it
of his own natural impudency.
Brid. Servant, what is this same, I pray
you !
Mat. Marry, an elegy, an elegy, an odd
toy—
Down. To mock an ape withal ![3] O, I
could sew up his mouth now.
Dame K. Sister, I pray you let's hear it.
Down. Are you rhime-given too?
Mat. Mistress, I'll read it, if you please.
Brid. Pray you do, servant.
Down. O, here's no foppery ! Death !
I can indure the stocks better.   [*Exit.*
E. Know. What ails my brother ? can
he not hold his water at reading of a bal-
lad ?
Well. O, no ; a rhime to him is worse

---

[1] *You'd mad the patient'st body in the world,*
&c.] Mr. Whalley has here thought it necessary to obviate, at great length, an objection,
which no man in his senses would think of making, to his printing this and other speeches as
prose.   Prose, he truly says, he found them, and
prose he has properly left them ; "though
aware," he adds, "that a *very little alteration*
would have reduced them to a hobbling kind of
measure."   It must be confessed that this is a
notable mode of improving upon an author ; and
wonderful must be the advantage derived from
it, both to his sense and his language ! luckily,
however, the experiment has been seldom tried
on Jonson ; but on Beaumont and Fletcher it
has been practised, Mr. Whalley thinks, with
great success.   Their "humorous speeches," by
the plain and simple process of a "little alteration," (such as lopping off words and phrases here,
foisting them in there, together with other ingenious contrivances of a similar kind,) "have
been happily rescued from the deformity in
which they once appeared, by their late very ingenious editors !"

Unfortunately, the laws of poetry are a mere
brutum fulmen, and Apollo and the Muses, in
these days, have less power than a parish beadle ;
otherwise Seward and Sympson, with all their
ingenuity, would have found some difficulty in
escaping a serious whipping at the cart's-tail of
Parnassus.   Whole scenes, nay whole acts, of the
most exquisite prose, have those miserable
bunglers, whose dulness is scarcely surpassed by
their temerity, transmuted by their unwarrant-
able corruptions, into a kind of jargon (metre it
is not), which "would mad the patient'st body
in the world" to hobble through it.
[2] Servant, *in troth, &c.*] *Servant* was the title
which, in Jonson's days, every lady bestowed
upon her professed lover.   To have noticed this
once is sufficient.
[3] ——— *an odd toy*
To mock an ape withal.] This expression was
proverbial. So, in the title to one of Marston's
satires,

"Here is a toy to mock an ape indeed."
                                            WHAL.

than cheese, or a bagpipe : but mark ; you lose the protestation.

Mat. Faith, I did it in a humour ; I know not how it is ; but please you come near, sir. This gentleman has judgment, he knows how to censure of a —— pray you, sir, you can judge?

Step. Not I, sir ; upon my reputation, and by the foot of Pharaoh !

Well. O, chide your cousin for swearing.

E. Know. Not I, so long as he does not forswear himself.

Bob. Master Mathew, you abuse the expectation of your dear mistress, and her fair sister : fie ! while you live avoid this prolixity.

Mat. I shall, sir ; well, *incipere dulce.*

E. Know. How ! *insipere dulce!* a sweet thing to be a fool, indeed !

Well. What, do you take *incipere* in that sense ?

E. Know. You do not, you ! This was your villainy, to gull him with a motte.[1]

Well. O, the benchers' phrase ; *pauca verba,*[2] *pauca verba!*

Mat. "Rare creature, let me speak without offence,
Would God my rude words had the influence
To rule thy thoughts, as thy fair looks do mine,
Then shouldst thou be his prisoner, who is thine."

E. Know. This is in Hero and Leander.[3]

Well. O, ay ; peace ! we shall have more of this.

Mat. "Be not unkind and fair : misshapen stuff
Is of behaviour boisterous and rough."

Well. How like you that, sir?

　　　　[*Master Stephen shakes his head.*

E. Know. 'Slight, he shakes his head like a bottle, to feel an there be any brain in it.[4]

Mat. But observe the catastrophe, now :
" And I in duty will exceed all other,
As you in beauty do excel Love's mother."

E. Know. Well, I'll have him free of the wit-brokers, for he utters nothing but stolen remnants.

Wel. O, forgive it him.

---

[1] *This was your villainy, to gull him with a motte.*] This is the reading of the quarto as well as of the folio ; it should not therefore have been changed by Mr. Whalley into *motto.* Mot or motte was the word then in use.

[2] *O, the* benchers' *phrase ; pauca verba,*] *Benchers* were idle sots who spent their time, sleeping and waking, upon alehouse benches. Thus, in *Sir John Oldcastle,* Part I. :

"When the vulgar sort
Sit on their ale-*bench* with their cups and cans."

Prince Henry declares of Falstaff, that he is grown fat with "*sleeping* out his afternoons upon *benches*;" and the parson of Wrotham, in the play quoted above, boasts of himself, that he is become "a drinker, a *bencher,* and a wencher," act ii. sc. 1.

Why *pauca verba* should be the benchers' phrase I cannot pretend to say, any more than why "dun's the mouse" should be the constable's ; it is however given to persons of this description in many of our old plays ; and Christophero Sly, a *bencher* of the first order, is furnished with a similar expression—*pocas palabras!* Perhaps it was an authoritative injunction to casual guests, not to disturb them in their serious occupations of drinking and sleeping ; or it might be a kind of cabalistical watchword among themselves, intimating that the proper business of a drunkard was to drink and not to talk. But this, as Spenser says,

"Is matter all too high for me."

[3] *This is in* Hero and Leander.] A translation or imitation of the Greek poem by Musæus, on the story of these unfortunate lovers, was begun by Christopher Marlow ; who dying before he had finished the whole, it was completed by George Chapman, and published by him, as both A. Wood and Langbaine tell us, in the year 1606. I *suspect,* however, that there was an earlier edition, or that part of it had got abroad in manuscript ; for the lines above are taken from it ; and it was in high reputation at this time. Alluding to the circumstance of Marlow's death, young Knowell accuses Master Mathew of filching from the dead.—WHAL.

Whalley is right ; among the entries at Stationers' Hall, is the following, by John Wolfe, 1593, "A booke entitled Hero and Leander, being an amorous poem, by C. Marlow :" and there appears to have been another entry in 1597. [The first ed. is 1598.] See Prol. to Malone's Shaksp. The version is also twice mentioned in Nash's *Lenten Stuff,* which appeared in 1599 ; and which Whalley must have seen. The character of Marlow is not ill drawn by the author of the *Return from Parnassus.*

" Marlowe was happy in his buskined muse,
Alas, unhappy in his life and end !
Pity it is that wit so ill should dwell,
Wit lost from heaven, but vices sent from hell."

He was a man of impious principles, and flagitious life, and perished in a drunken brawl. Jonson thought very highly of his talents.

[4] *'Slight, he shakes his head, &c.*] The writer of Junius's Letters has been poaching here : he has taken this poor witticism, which, after all, is not Jonson's, and applied it to Sir W. Blackstone ! This may serve to console Master Stephen.

E. Know. A filching rogue, hang him! and from the dead! it's worse than sacrilege.

Wellbred, E. Knowell, *and* Master Stephen *come forward.*

Wel. Sister, what have you here, verses? pray you let's see : who made these verses? they are excellent good.

Mat. O, Master Wellbred, 'tis your disposition to say so, sir. They were good in the morning ; I made them *ex tempore*, this morning.

Wel. How! *ex tempore?*

Mat. Ay, would I might be hanged else ; ask Captain Bobadill : he saw me write them, at the—pox on it!—the Star, yonder.

Brai. Can he find in his heart to curse the stars so?

E. Know. Faith, his are even with him ; they have curst him enough already.

Step. Cousin, how do you like this gentleman's verses?

E. Know. O, admirable! the best that ever I heard, coz.

Step. Body o' Cæsar, they are admirable! The best that I ever heard, as I am a soldier!

Re-enter Downright.

Down. I am vext, I can hold ne'er a bone of me still : Heart, I think they mean to build and breed here!

Wel. Sister, you have a simple servant here, that crowns your beauty with such encomiums and devices ; you may see what it is to be the mistress of a wit, that can make your perfections so transparent, that every blear eye may look through them, and see him drowned over head and ears in the deep well of desire : Sister Kitely, I marvel you get you not a servant that can rhime, and do tricks too.

Down. O, monster! impudence itself! tricks!

Dame K. Tricks, brother! what tricks?

Brid. Nay, speak, I pray you, what tricks?

Dame K. Ay, never spare anybody here ; but say, what tricks.

Brid. Passion of my heart, do tricks!

Wel. 'Slight, here's a trick vied and revied![1] Why, you monkies you, what a caterwauling do you keep? has he not given you rhimes and verses and tricks?

Down. O, the fiend!

Wel. Nay, you lamp of virginity, that take it in snuff so, come, and cherish this tame poetical fury in your servant ; you'll be begged else shortly for a concealment :[2] go to, reward his muse. You cannot give him less than a shilling in conscience, for the book he had it out of cost him a teston at least.[3] How now, gallants! Master

---

[1] *Here's a trick* vied *and* revied!] Terms in the old game at cards, called Gleek.—WHAL.
  What is explained by this? but thus, too frequently, notes are written. Neither *trick* nor *vie* was peculiar to Gleek, as it would be easy to mention a dozen old games, in which the terms perpetually recur. To *vie* was to hazard, to put down a certain sum upon a hand of cards ; to *revie*, was to cover it with a larger sum, by which the challenged became the challenger, and was to be *revied* in his turn, with a proportionate increase of stake. This vying and revying upon each other continued till one of the party lost courage, and gave up the whole ; or obtained, for a stipulated sum, a discovery of his antagonist's cards ; when the best hand swept the table. It may be worth observing here, that the final stake, *i.e.*, the largest sum which a gamester would adventure, was called his *rest*. This is the unfortunate term which the commentators on our old poets are for ever confounding with the *rest* of a musquet.

[2] *Come and cherish this tame poetical fury in your servant ; you'll be* begged *else shortly for a* concealment :] Alluding to the practice in Queen Elizabeth's time of begging lands, which had formerly been appropriated to superstitious uses. But the account of it by Strype, to whom Whalley contents himself with referring, is so explicit that I shall give it in his own words : "This year (viz. 1572) a command from the queen

went forth, for the withdrawing the commissions for *concealments*, from all to whom she had granted them, which gave a great quieting to her subjects, who were excessively plagued with these commissioners. When monasteries were dissolved, and the lands thereof, and afterwards colleges, chantries, and fraternities were all given to the crown, some demeans here and there pertaining thereunto were still privily retained, and possessed by certain private persons or corporations, or churches. This caused the queen, when she understood it, to grant commissions to some persons to search after these *concealments*, and to retrieve them to the crown (or, rather, Strype should have added, to the hungry courtiers who *begged* them) ; "but it was a world to consider what unjust oppressions of the people and the poor this occasioned by some griping men that were concerned therein."—*Annals of Elizabeth*, vol. ii. 209.

[3] *The book he had it out of cost him a* teston *at least.*] "*Testons* (or, as we commonly call them, testers, from a head that was upon them) were coined 34 Hen. VIII. Sir H. Spelman says they are a French coin of the value of 18*d.*, and he does not know but they might have gone for as much in England. He says it was brass, and covered over with silver, and went in Hen. VIII.'s time for 12*d.*, but 1 Ed. VI. it was brought down to 9*d.* and then to 6*d.*, which name it still retains."—Fleetwood's *Chron. Pretios.*

Mathew! Captain! what, all sons of silence, no spirit!

Down. Come, you might practise your ruffian tricks somewhere else, and not here, I wuss;[1] this is no tavern nor drinking-school, to vent your exploits in.

Wel. How now! whose cow has calved?

Down. Marry, that has mine, sir. Nay, boy, never look askance at me for the matter; I'll tell you of it, I, sir; you and your companions mend yourselves when I have done.

Wel. My companions!

Down. Yes, sir, your companions, so I say; I am not afraid of you, nor them neither; your hang-byes here. You must have your poets and your potlings, your soldados and foolados to follow you up and down the city; and here they must come to domineer and swagger. Sirrah you ballad-singer, and Slops your fellow there,[2] get you out, get you home; or by this steel, I'll cut off your ears, and that presently.

Wel. 'Slight, stay, let's see what he dare do; cut off his ears! cut a whetstone. You are an ass, do you see; touch any man here, and by this hand I'll run my rapier to the hilts in you.

Down. Yea that would I fain see, boy.
                    [*They all draw.*

Dame K. O Jesu! Murder! Thomas! Gasper!

Brid. Help, help! Thomas!

Enter Cash *and some of the house to part them.*

E. Know. Gentlemen, forbear, I pray you.

Bob. Well, sirrah you Holofernes; by my hand, I will pink your flesh full of holes with my rapier for this; I will, by this good heaven! nay, let him come, let him come, gentlemen; by the body of St. George, I'll not kill him.

[*Offer to fight again, and are parted.*

Cash. Hold, hold, good gentlemen.

Down. You whoreson, bragging coystril![3]

Enter Kitely.

Kit. Why, how now! what's the matter, what's the stir here?

Whence springs the quarrel? Thomas! where is he?

Put up your weapons, and put off this rage:

My wife and sister, they are cause of this.

What, Thomas! where is this knave?

Cash. Here, sir.

Wel. Come, let's go: this is one of my brother's ancient humours, this.

Step. I am glad no body was hurt by his ancient humour.

            [*Exeunt* Wel. Step. E. Know.
                        Bob. and Brai.

Kit. Why, how now, brother, who enforced this brawl?

Down. A sort of lewd rake-hells, that care neither for God nor the devil. And they must come here to read ballads, and roguery, and trash! I'll mar the knot of 'em ere I sleep, perhaps; especially Bob there, he that's all manner of shapes; and songs and sonnets, his fellow.

Brid. Brother, indeed you are too violent,

Too sudden in your humour; and you know

My brother Wellbred's temper will not bear

Any reproof, chiefly in such a presence,

Where every slight disgrace he should receive

Might wound him in opinion and respect.

Down. Respect! what talk you of respect among such as have no spark of manhood nor good manners? 'Sdeins, I am ashamed to hear you! respect!
                        [*Exit.*

Brid. Yes, there was one a civil gentleman,

And very worthily demeaned himself.

Kit. O, that was some love of yours, sister.

Brid. A love of mine! I would it were no worse, brother;

---

c. iii. This, though not rigidly correct as to dates, is, I presume, sufficiently so for the present purpose.

[1] *Not here, I* wuss;] I omitted to observe (p. 3 *b*) that *wusse* was merely a vulgarism for *wis*, to know. Our old poets use the term as a familiar and petty interjection. I wis, or *wusse*, i.e., I trow, truly, &c.

[2] *And* Slops *your fellow there,*] Downright had already noticed the "Gargantua breech" of Bobadill. *Slops* were the large loose breeches so fashionable during the greater part of Elizabeth's reign: they are often mentioned by our old dramatists, who seem about the period in which this play appeared, to have laughed them out of countenance, or, at least, to have materially reduced their bulk.

[3] *You whoreson, bragging* coystril!] A mean, dastardly wretch. The etymology of this word is uncertain; to bring it from *coustillier* (a knight's attendant), as Whalley and Tollet do, is to confound the properties of language. The term, whatever be its origin, is undoubtedly taken from the *Falconer's Vocabulary*, where a worthless and degenerate breed of hawks are called *kestrils.*

You'd pay my portion sooner than you
think for.

Dame K. Indeed he seemed to be a gentleman of an exceeding fair disposition,
and of very excellent good parts.

    [*Exeunt* Dame Kitely *and* Bridget.

Kit. Her love, by heaven! my wife's
minion.
"Fair disposition! excellent good parts!"
Death! these phrases are intolerable.
Good parts! how should she know his
parts?
His parts! Well, well, well, well, well,
well ;
It is too plain, too clear : Thomas, come
hither.
What, are they gone?

Cash. Ay, sir, they went in.
My mistress, and your sister——

Kit. Are any of the gallants within?

Cash. No, sir, they are all gone.

Kit. Art thou sure of it?

Cash. I can assure you, sir.

Kit. What gentleman was that they
praised so, Thomas?

Cash. One, they call him Master
Knowell, a handsome young gentleman, sir.

Kit. Ay, I thought so ; my mind gave
me as much :
I'll die but they have hid him in the house,
Somewhere ; I'll go and search ; go with
me, Thomas :
Be true to me, and thou shalt find me a
master.   [*Exeunt.*

SCENE II.—*The Lane before* Cob's
House.

Enter Cob.

Cob. [*knocks at the door.*] What, Tib, Tib,
I say !

Tib. [*within.*] How now, what cuckold
is that knocks so hard?

Enter Tib.

O, husband, is it you ! what's the news?

Cob. Nay, you have stunned me, i' faith ;
you have given me a knock o' the forehead will stick by me. Cuckold ! 'Slid,
cuckold !

Tib. Away, you fool! did I know it
was you that knocked? Come, come, you
may call me as bad when you list.

Cob. May I? Tib, you are a whore.

Tib. You lie in your throat, husband.

Cob. How, the lie! and in my throat
too ! do you long to be stabbed, ha?

Tib. Why, you are no soldier, I hope.

Cob. O, must you be stabbed by a
soldier? Mass, that's true! when was
Bobadill here, your captain? that rogue,
that foist, that fencing Burgullian?[1] I'll
tickle him, i' faith.

Tib. Why, what's the matter, trow !

Cob. O, he has basted me rarely, sump-
tuously ! but I have it here in black and
white, [*pulls out the warrant,*] for his
black and blue shall pay him. O, the
justice, the honestest old brave Trojan in
London ; I do honour the very flea of his
dog. A plague on him though, he put
me once in a villainous filthy fear ; marry,
it vanished away like the smoke of tobacco ;
but I was smoked soundly first. I thank
the devil, and his good angel, my guest.
Well, wife, or Tib, which you will, get you
in, and lock the door, I charge you let
no body in to you, wife ; no body in to you ;
those are my words : not Captain Bob himself, nor the fiend in his likeness. You are
a woman, you have flesh and blood enough
in you to be tempted ; therefore keep the
door shut upon all comers.

Tib. I warrant you, there shall nobody
enter here without my consent.

Cob. Nor with your consent, sweet Tib ;
and so I leave you.

Tib. It's more than you know, whether
you leave me so.

Cob. How?

Tib. Why, *sweet.*

Cob. Tut, sweet or sour, thou art a flower.
Keep close thy door, I ask no more.

    [*Exeunt.*

SCENE III.—*A Room in the Windmill
Tavern.*

Enter E. Knowell, Wellbred, Stephen, *and*
Brainworm, *disguised as before.*

E. Know. Well, Brainworm, perform

---

[1] *That* foist, *that fencing* Burgullian ?] *Foist*
was one of the thousand cant terms for a cut-
purse. *Burgullian,* or Burgonian, means a
bully, a braggadocio ; in allusion, Hawkins
says (*Origin of the English Drama,* vol. iii.
91), to the Bastard of Burgundy, who was
overthrown in Smithfield by Anthony Wood-
ville, 1467. This is by no means unlikely : for
our ancestors, who were not very delicate, nor,
generally speaking, much overburthened with
respect for the feelings of foreigners, had a
number of vituperative appellations derived
from their real or supposed ill-qualities, of many
of which the precise import cannot now be
ascertained.

this business happily, and thou makest a purchase of my love for ever.

Wel. I' faith, now let thy spirits use their best faculties : but, at any hand, remember the message to my brother; for there's no other means to start him.

Brai. I warrant you, sir; fear nothing ; I have a nimble soul has waked all forces of my phant'sie by this time, and put them in true motion. What you have possest me withal, I'll discharge it amply, sir ; make it no question.[1]　　　　　　[*Exit.*

Wel. Forth and prosper, Brainworm. Faith, Ned, how dost thou approve of my abilities in this device ?

E. Know. Troth, well, howsoever ; but it will come excellent, if it take.

Wel. Take, man ! why it cannot choose but take, if the circumstances miscarry not ; but, tell me ingenuously, dost thou affect my sister Bridget as thou pretend'st ?

E. Know. Friend, am I worth belief ?

Wel. Come, do not protest. In faith, she is a maid of good ornament, and much modesty ; and, except I conceived very worthily of her, thou should'st not have her.

E. Know. Nay, that, I am afraid, will be a question yet, whether I shall have her, or no.

Wel. 'Slid, thou shalt have her ; by this light thou shalt.

E. Know. Nay, do not swear.

Wel. By this hand thou shalt have her ; I'll go fetch her presently. 'Point but where to meet, and as I am an honest man I'll bring her.

E. Know. Hold, hold, be temperate.

Wel. Why, by —— what shall I swear by ? thou shalt have her, as I am——

E. Know. Pray thee, be at peace, I am satisfied ; and do believe thou wilt omit no offered occasion to make my desires complete.

Wel. Thou shalt see, and know, I will not.　　　　　　　　　　[*Exeunt.*

SCENE IV.—*The* Old Jewry.

Enter Formal *and* Knowell.

Form. Was your man a soldier, sir?

Know. Ay, a knave,

I took him begging o' the way, this morning, As I came over Moorfields.

Enter Brainworm, *disguised as before.*

O, here he is !—You've made fair speed, believe me :
Where, in the name of sloth, could you be thus ?

Brai. Marry, peace be my comfort, where I thought I should have had little comfort of your worship's service.

Know. How so?

Brai. O, sir, your coming to the city, your entertainment of me, and your sending me to watch—indeed, all the circumstances either of your charge, or my employment, are as open to your son, as to yourself.

Know. How should that be, unless that villain, Brainworm,

Have told him of the letter, and discovered All that I strictly charged him to conceal?
'Tis so.

Brai. I am partly o' the faith 'tis so, indeed.

Know. But, how should he know thee to be my man?

Brai. Nay, sir, I cannot tell ; unless it be by the black art. Is not your son a scholar, sir?

Know. Yes, but I hope his soul is not allied

Unto such hellish practice : if it were, I had just cause to weep my part in him, And curse the time of his creation. But, where didst thou find them, Fitz-Sword ?

Brai. You should rather ask where they found me, sir ; for, I'll be sworn, I was going along in the street, thinking nothing, when, of a sudden, a voice calls, *Mr. Knowell's man !* another cries, *Soldier !* and thus half a dozen of them, till they had called me within a house, where I no sooner came, but they seemed men,[2] and out flew all their rapiers at my bosom, with some three or four score oaths to accompany them ; and all to tell me, I was but a dead man, if I did not confess where you were, and how I was employed, and about what ; which when they could not get out of me (as, I protest, they must have dissected,

---

[1] *What you have* possest *me withal,* &c.] i e., what you have *informed* me of. Thus Davenport, "Having *possessed him with* the passages which passed upon his sister."—*City Night Cap,* act iii. sc. 1. And see page 12 b.

[2] *Where I no sooner came, but they seemed* men,] I suppose he thought them so, before he

saw them. The sentence is dark ; but there seems to be an antithesis designed between *voice* and *man.* He only tells his master, that he heard several voices calling him ; and when he entered the house, these voices were personified, and turned to men. If this is not the meaning of the author, there is a word omit-

and made an anatomy of me first, and so I told them), they locked me up into a room in the top of a high house, whence by great miracle (having a light heart) I slid down by a bottom of packthread into the street, and so 'scaped. But, sir, thus much I can assure you, for I heard it while I was locked up, there were a great many rich merchants and brave citizen's wives with them at a feast; and your son, Master Edward, withdrew with one of them, and has 'pointed to meet her anon at one Cob's house, a waterbearer, that dwells by the Wall. Now, there your worship shall be sure to take him, for there he preys, and fail he will not.

Know. Nor will I fail to break his match, I doubt not.
Go thou along with Justice Clement's man, And stay there for me. At one Cob's house, say'st thou?

Brai. Ay, sir, there you shall have him. [*Exit* Know.] Yes—invisible![1] Much wench, or much son! 'Slight, when he has staid there three or four hours, travailing with the expectation of wonders, and at length be delivered of air! O the sport that I should then take to look on him, if I durst! But now I mean to appear no more afore him in this shape: I have another trick to act yet. O that I were so happy as to light on a nupson[2] now of this justice's novice!—Sir, I make you stay somewhat long.

Form. Not a whit, sir. Pray you what do you mean, sir?

Brai. I was putting up some papers.

Form. You have been lately in the wars, sir, it seems.

Brai. Marry have I, sir, to my loss, and expense of all, almost.

Form. Troth, sir, I would be glad to be-

stow a pottle of wine on you, if it please you to accept it——

Brai. O, sir——

Form. But to hear the manner of your services, and your devices in the wars; they say they be very strange, and not like those a man reads in the Roman histories, or sees at Mile-end.[3]

Brai. No, I assure you, sir; why at any time when it please you, I shall be ready to discourse to you all I know;—and more too somewhat. [*Aside.*

Form. No better time than now, sir; we'll go to the Windmill: there we shall have a cup of neat grist, we call it. I pray you, sir, let me request you to the Windmill.

Brai. I'll follow you, sir;—and make grist of you, if I have good luck. [*Aside.*
[*Exeunt.*

SCENE V.—Moorfields.

Enter Mathew, E. Knowell, Bobadill, *and* Stephen.

Mat. Sir, did your eyes ever taste the like clown of him where we were to-day, Mr. Wellbred's half-brother? I think the whole earth cannot shew his parallel, by this daylight.

E. Know. We were now speaking of him: Captain Bobadill tells me he is fallen foul of you too.

Mat. O, ay, sir, he threatened me with the bastinado.

Bob. Ay, but I think I taught you prevention this morning for that. You shall kill him beyond question, if you be so generously minded.

Mat. Indeed, it is a most excellent trick.
[*Fences.*

---

ted. Their subsequent behaviour might lead us to think he called them *madmen.*—WHAL.
There is nothing of this in the quarto, which reads, "*one* calls, Soldier, till they got me within doors, where I no sooner came, but out flies their rapiers, and all bent against my breast." So that if Whalley's first conjecture be right, Jonson must have altered the passage solely for the sake of introducing this strange opposition of terms.

[1] *Yes—invisible! Much wench, or much son!*] *Yes—invisible!* That is, are you gone out of sight? What follows is proverbial; *Much* was a term of various senses, and often used as an expression of disdain and contempt. Much good may they do you, both wench, and son, if you find them.—WHAL.
I know not what to say of Whalley's note. *Invisible* seems to be a humorous addition to Brainworm's speech, after his master was out of

hearing——"there you shall have him——yes, invisible!" that is, not at all.
Much! is an ironical exclamation for *little,* or *none,* in which sense it frequently occurs in our old dramatists. Thus in Heywood's *Edward IV. :*—

   "*Much* duchess! and *much* queen, I trow!"

And in Shakspeare:—

   "Is it not past two o'clock? and here's *much* Orlando!"

[2] *To light on a* nupson,] i.e., O that I might happily find this justice's man to be a *nupson!* A nupson is an oaf, a simpleton. See the *Devil's an Ass.*

[3] *Or sees at* Mile-end.] The usual training ground of the city. This jest on the city campaigns was, doubtless, productive of mirth, for it occurs in many of our old plays.

Bob. O, you do not give spirit enough to your motion; you are too tardy, too heavy! O, it must be done like lightning, hay![1]

[*Practises at a post with his cudgel.*

Mat. Rare, captain!

Bob. Tut! 'tis nothing, an't be not done in a —— punto.

E. Know. Captain, did you ever prove yourself upon any of our masters of defence here?

Mat. O good sir! yes, I hope he has.

Bob. I will tell you, sir. Upon my first coming to the city, after my long travel for knowledge, in that mystery only, there came three or four of them to me, at a gentleman's house, where it was my chance to be resident at that time, to intreat my presence at their schools; and withal so much importuned me, that I protest to you, as I am a gentleman, I was ashamed of their rude demeanour out of all measure. Well, I told them that to come to a public school, they should pardon me, it was opposite, in diameter, to my humour; but, if so be they would give their attendance at my lodging, I protested to do them what right or favour I could, as I was a gentleman, and so forth.

E. Know. So, sir! then you tried their skill?

Bob. Alas, soon tried: you shall hear, sir. Within two or three days after, they came; and, by honesty, fair sir, believe me, I graced them exceedingly, shewed them some two or three tricks of prevention have purchased them since a credit to admiration: they cannot deny this; and yet now they hate me, and why? because I am excellent; and for no other vile reason on the earth.

E. Know. This is strange and barbarous, as ever I heard.

Bob. Nay, for a more instance of their preposterous natures; but note, sir. They have assaulted me[2] some three, four, five, six of them together, as I have walked alone in divers skirts i' the town, as Turnbull, Whitechapel, Shoreditch, which were then my quarters; and since, upon the Exchange, at my lodging, and at my ordinary: where I have driven them afore me the whole length of a street, in the open view of all our gallants, pitying to hurt them, believe me. Yet all this lenity will not overcome their spleen; they will be doing with the pismire, raising a hill a man may spurn abroad with his foot at pleasure. By myself, I could have slain them all, but I delight not in murder. I am loth to bear any other than this bastinado for them: yet I hold it good polity not to go disarmed, for though I be skilful, I may be oppressed with multitudes.

E. Know. Ay, believe me, may you, sir: and in my conceit, our whole nation should sustain the loss by it, if it were so.

Bob. Alas, no! what's a peculiar man to a nation? not seen.

E. Know. O, but your skill, sir.

Bob. Indeed, that might be some loss; but who respects it? I will tell you, sir, by the way of private, and under seal; I am a gentleman, and live here obscure, and to myself; but were I known to her majesty and the lords,—observe me,—I would undertake, upon this poor head and life, for the public benefit of the state, not only to spare the intire lives of her subjects in general; but to save the one half, nay, three parts of her yearly charge in holding war, and against what enemy soever. And how would I do it, think you?

E. Know. Nay, I know not, nor can I conceive.

Bob. Why thus, sir. I would select nineteen more, to myself, throughout the land; gentlemen they should be of good spirit, strong and able constitution; I would choose them by an instinct, a character that I have: and I would teach these nineteen the special rules, as your punto,[3] your

---

[1] *O, it must be done like lightning,* hay!] i.e., *a hit!* from the Italian *hai,* you have it. Our fencers very innocently cry *ha!* upon these occasions.

[2] *They have assaulted me,* &c.] Nothing can be more exquisitely imagined than the conduct of this scene, in which Bobadill boasts so loudly of his skill and intrepidity, just as disgrace is about to burst on his head. In the elevation of his fancy, Jonson, with genuine humour, makes him forget his usual caution, and betray his haunts, which, in his first conversation with Master Mathew, he appears so solicitous to conceal. All the places which he enumerates were the abodes of poverty and vice; and his acquaintance with them completely disproves his claims to gentility and fashion.

[3] *I would teach these nineteen the special rules, as your* punto, *&c.*] The terms that follow are adopted from the fencing schools of the author's days; and are enumerated, nearly in the same manner, by Shakspeare and others. They are, as the reader sees, pure Italian; and, being significant in that language, we may regret the perversity of fashion, which, under Charles II., discarded them for the vague, illsounding foppery of France. *Imbroccato* (the only one which requires an explanation) is a thrust in tierce.

reverso, your stoccata, your imbroccato, your passada, your montanto; till they could all play very near, or altogether as well as myself. This done, say the enemy were forty thousand strong, we twenty would come into the field the tenth of March, or thereabouts; and we would challenge twenty of the enemy; they could not in their honour refuse us. Well, we would kill them; challenge twenty more, kill them; twenty more, kill them; twenty more, kill them too; and thus would we kill every man his twenty a day, that's twenty score; twenty score, that's two hundred;[1] two hundred a day, five days a thousand; forty thousand; forty times five, five times forty, two hundred days kills them all up by computation. And this will I venture my poor gentleman-like carcase to perform, provided there be no treason practised upon us, by fair and discreet manhood; that is, civilly by the sword.

E. Know. Why, are you so sure of your hand, captain, at all times?

Bob. Tut! never miss thrust, upon my reputation with you.

E. Know. I would not stand in Downright's state then, an you meet him, for the wealth of any one street in London.

Bob. Why, sir, you mistake me: if he were here now, by this welkin, I would not draw my weapon on him. Let this gentleman do his mind: but I will bastinado him, by the bright sun, wherever I meet him.

Mat. Faith, and I'll have a fling at him, at my distance.

E. Know. Ods so, look where he is! yonder he goes.
[*Downright crosses the stage.*

Down. What peevish luck have I, I cannot meet with these bragging rascals?

Bob. It is not he, is it?

E. Know. Yes, faith, it is he.

Mat. I'll be hanged then if that were he.

E. Know. Sir, keep your hanging good for some greater matter, for I assure you that was he.

Step. Upon my reputation, it was he.

Bob. Had I thought it had been he, he must not have gone so: but I can hardly be induced to believe it was he yet.

E. Know. That I think, sir.

Re-enter Downright.

But see, he is come again.

Down. O, Pharaoh's foot, have I found you? Come, draw to your tools; draw, gipsy, or I'll thrash you.

Bob. Gentleman of valour, I do believe in thee; hear me——

Down. Draw your weapon then.

Bob. Tall man, I never thought on it till now[2]——Body of me, I had a warrant of the peace served on me, even now as I came along, by a water-bearer; this gentleman saw it, Master Mathew.

Down. 'Sdeath! you will not draw then?
[*Disarms and beats him. Mathew runs away.*

---

[1] *Twenty score, that's two hundred;*] Bobadill does not do justice to the prowess of himself and his brothers in arms. Twenty score are four hundred, so that the enemy would be killed up in half the time which he allows for it, or one hundred days. This error in computation runs through all the editions, so that it was probably intended. Indeed Bobadill is too much of a borrower to be an accurate reckoner: but I will not affirm that the author had this in his thoughts. After all, it must be admitted that our old dramatists (or their printers) were very indifferent arithmeticians in general; they seldom escape well from a calculation. On Bobadill's phrase of *killed up*, it may just be observed, that *off*, *out*, and *up*, are continually used by the purest and most excellent of our old writers, after verbs of destroying, consuming, eating, drinking, &c.: to us, who are less conversant with the power of language, they appear, indeed, somewhat like expletives; but they undoubtedly contributed something to the force, and something to the roundness of the sentence. There is much wretched criticism on a similar expression in Shakspeare. "Wo'ot *drink up* eisel?" Theobald gives the sense of the passage in a clumsy

note; Hanmer, who had more taste than judgment, and more judgment than knowledge, corrupts the language, as usual; Steevens gaily perverts the sense; and Malone, with great effort brings the reader back to the meaning which poor Theobald had long before excogitated. The grammatical construction of the phrase none of them appear to understand.

[2] *Bob.* Tall man, *I never thought on it till now*] Downright is described to be a tall man, or else the fears of Master Mathew misrepresented him as such. But the words *tall*, in this place, were not designed to give us an idea of his height or bulk. Our ancestors used *tall* in the sense of bold, or courageous: and this, I apprehend, is the meaning we must assign it here: thus the Lord Bacon tells us, "that Bishop Fox caused his castle of Norham to be fortified; and manned it likewise with a very great number of *tall* soldiers."—*Hist. of Henry VII.* WHAL.

I have abridged Whalley's elaborate note. There is scarcely a writer of Jonson's age who does not frequently use *tall* in the sense of bold or courageous; and even the next page to this affords two instances, where it can possibly have no other meaning.

Bob. Hold, hold ! under thy favour forbear !

Down. Prate again, as you like this, you whoreson foist you ! You'll control the point, you ![1] Your consort is gone ; had he staid he had shared with you, sir. [*Exit.*

Bob. Well, gentlemen, bear witness, I was bound to the peace, by this good day.

E. Know. No, faith, it's an ill day, captain, never reckon it other: but, say you were bound to the peace, the law allows you to defend yourself : that will prove but a poor excuse.

Bob. I cannot tell, sir ;[2] I desire good construction in fair sort. I never sustained the like disgrace, by heaven ! sure I was struck with a planet thence,[3] for I had no power to touch my weapon.

E. Know. Ay, like enough ; I have heard of many that have been beaten under a planet : go, get you to a surgeon. 'Slid ! an these be your tricks, your passados, and your montantos. I'll none of them. [*Exit*

Bobadill.] O, manners ! that this age should bring forth such creatures ! that nature should be at leisure to make them ! Come, coz.

Step. Mass, I'll have this cloak.

E. Know. Ods will, 'tis Downright's.

Step. Nay, it's mine now, another might have ta'en it up as well as I ; I'll wear it, so I will.

E. Know. How an he see it ? he'll challenge it, assure yourself.

Step. Ay, but he shall not have it : I'll say I bought it.

E. Know. Take heed you buy it not too dear, coz. [*Exeunt.*

SCENE VI.

A Room in Kitely's *House.*

Enter Kitely, Wellbred, Dame Kitely, *and* Bridget.

Kit. Now, trust me, brother, you were much to blame,

---

[1] *You'll* control the point, *you !*] To *control the point,* is to bear, or beat it down : Downright retorts his own words upon the poor baffled captain. But the expression is technical ; thus, the Bravo in the *Antiquary*, says, "I do it by a slight, and by that I can *control any man's point whatever.*"

[2] *I cannot tell,*] i.e., I know not what to say, or think, of it. So in *Cupid's Revenge :*

"3 *Cit. I cannot tell ;* methinks if men were men,
'Twere no great matter."

I should not have noticed this simple expression, of which I could give innumerable instances, were it not for the sake of observing that the commentators on Shakspeare have mistaken it. In *Henry IV.* Falstaff says to the chief justice, "Your ill angel is light ; but I hope he that looks upon me, will take me without weighing : and yet, in some respects, I grant, I cannot go ; *I cannot tell ;* virtue," &c. On which Johnson, with whom all the rest agree, says, "I cannot *tell ;*" i.e., I cannot be taken in a reckoning, I cannot pass current. Nothing can be more incorrect : it means, as I have already remarked, I cannot tell what to say or think of it ; and nothing more. As Beaumont and Fletcher are now before me, I will produce a decisive instance from them. "*Bessus.* As for my own part, I was dangerously hurt but three days before ; else, perhaps, we had been two to two : *I cannot tell ;* some thought we had."—*King and no King.*

[3] *Sure I was* struck with a planet *thence,*] Warton says that when Jonson makes Bobadill tamely submit to a beating, and with characteristical humour and readiness of invention, accounts for it by declaring that he was *planet-*struck, he indirectly intended to ridicule the prevailing fondness for astrology. "At least," continues he, "without considering the popular superstitions about the influence of the planets, Bobadill's pretence is forced, unnatural, and almost unintelligible."

It is, indeed, to be feared that much of the merit of Jonson is lost to us, through our ignorance of the sources of his humour and the precise objects of his satire ; but this misfortune he shares (though, perhaps, in a greater degree) with his contemporaries, who are all sufferers from the same causes. Undoubtedly the prompt excuse of Bobadill created no little mirth among those to whom the language was familiar. Warton believes that the ridicule was levelled at the professors of astrology ; but there was another profession, very obnoxious to wanton merriment in those days, and full as likely to be aimed at, I mean, that of physic. This noble art has always had its jargon, and its fashionable diseases : it seems to have escaped Warton that *planet-stricken* was then the term in vogue for any sudden attack for which the physician could not readily find a proper name. In some *Observations on the Bills of Mortality,* by Captain John Grant, (printed before the middle of the seventeenth century,) he observes, p. 26, that "it is enough if the searchers give the most predominant symptoms ; as, that one died of the headache, who was sorely tormented with it, though the disease might be in the stomach. Again, if one died *suddenly,* the matter is not great, whether it be reported in the bills, *Suddenly, apoplexy,* or *planet-strucken.*—And, a few pages afterwards, in "*An Account of the Diseases and Casualties of this year, being* 1632," he gives, "apoplex and meagrim, seventeen ; *Planet-struck,* thirteen ; suddenly, sixty-two."

T' incense his anger, and disturb the peace
Of my poor house, where there are centinels,
That every minute watch to give alarms
Of civil war, without adjection
Of your assistance or occasion.

Wel. No harm done, brother, I warrant
you: Since there is no harm done, anger
costs a man nothing; and a tall man is
never his own man till he be angry. To
keep his valour in obscurity, is to keep
himself as it were in a cloak-bag. What's
a musician, unless he play? What's a tall
man unless he fight? For, indeed, all this
my wise brother stands upon absolutely;
and that made me fall in with him so
resolutely.

Dame K. Ay, but what harm might have
come of it, brother?

Wel. Might, sister? so might the good
warm clothes your husband wears be
poisoned, for any thing he knows; or the
wholesome wine he drank, even now at
the table.

Kit. Now, God forbid! O me! now I
remember
My wife drank to me last, and changed the
cup,
And bade me wear this cursed suit to-day.
See, if Heaven suffer murder undiscovered!
I feel me ill; give me some mithridate,
Some mithridate and oil, good sister, fetch
me;
O, I am sick at heart! I burn, I burn.
If you will save my life, go, fetch it me.

Wel. O strange humour! my very breath
has poisoned him.

Brid. Good brother, be content, what do
you mean?
The strength of these extreme conceits will
kill you.

Dame K. Beshrew your heart-blood,
brother Wellbred, now,
For putting such a toy into his head!

Wel. Is a fit simile a toy? will he be
poisoned with a simile? Brother Kitely,
what a strange and idle imagination is this?
For shame, be wiser. O' my soul there's
no such matter.

Kit. Am I not sick? how am I then not
poisoned?
Am I not poisoned? how am I then so sick?

Dame K. If you be sick, your own
thoughts make you sick.

Wel. His jealousy is the poison he has
taken.

Enter Brainworm *disguised in* Formal's
clothes.

Brai. Master Kitely, my master, Justice
Clement, salutes you; and desires to speak
with you with all possible speed.

Kit. No time but now, when I think I
am sick, very sick! well, I will wait upon
his worship. Thomas! Cob! I must seek
them out, and set them centinels till I return. Thomas! Cob! Thomas!   [*Exit.*

Wel. This is perfectly rare, Brainworm;
[*takes him aside*] but how got'st thou this
apparel of the justice's man?

Brai. Marry, sir, my proper fine pen-man
would needs bestow the grist on me, at the
Windmill, to hear some martial discourse;
where I so marshalled him, that I made him
drunk with admiration: and, because too
much heat was the cause of his distemper,
I stript him stark naked as he lay along
asleep, and borrowed his suit to deliver this
counterfeit message in, leaving a rusty
armour, and an old brown bill to watch
him till my return; which shall be, when I
have pawned his apparel, and spent the
better part o' the money, perhaps.

Wel. Well, thou art a successful merry
knave, Brainworm: his absence will be a
good subject for more mirth. I pray thee
return to thy young master, and will him
to meet me and my sister Bridget at the
Tower instantly; for, here, tell him the
house is so stored with jealousy, there is no
room for love to stand upright in. We
must get our fortunes committed to some
larger prison, say; and than the Tower, I
know no better air,[1] nor where the liberty
of the house may do us more present service. Away.   [*Exit* Brai.

Re-enter Kitely, *talking aside to* Cash.

Kit. Come hither, Thomas. Now, my
secret's ripe,
And thou shalt have it: lay to both thine
ears.
Hark, what I say to thee. I must go forth,
Thomas;
Be careful of thy promise, keep good
watch,

---

[1] *And than the* Tower, *I know no better air,
&c.*] As the Tower was extra-parochial, it probably afforded some facility to private marriages.
To this Wellbred seems to allude; and indeed
the circumstance is frequently noted in our old
comedies. So in a *Match at Midnight:* "She
will go with you to your lodging, lie there all
night, and be *married* in the morning at the
Tower, as soon as you please." Act iv.
sc. 1.

Note every gallant, and observe him well,
That enters in my absence to thy mistress:
If she would shew him rooms, the jest is
　　stale,
Follow them, Thomas, or else hang on him,
And let him not go after; mark their looks;
Note if she offer but to see his band,
Or any other amorous toy about him;
P⁊ praise his leg, or foot; or if she say
The day is hot, and bid him feel her hand,
How hot it is; O, that's a monstrous thing !
Note me all this, good Thomas, mark their
　　sighs,
And, if they do but whisper, break 'em off:
I'll bear thee out in it. Wilt thou do this?
Wilt thou be true, my Thomas?
　　Cash. As truth's self, sir.
　　Kit. Why, I believe thee: Where is Cob,
　　now? Cob !　　　　　　　　　　*[Exit.*
　　Dame K. He's ever calling for Cob : I
wonder how he employs Cob so.
　　Wel. Indeed, sister, to ask how he employs Cob, is a necessary question for you
that are his wife, and a thing not very easy
for you to be satisfied in; but this I'll assure you, Cob's wife is an excellent bawd,
sister, and oftentimes your husband haunts
her house; marry, to what end? I cannot
altogether accuse him; imagine you what
you think convenient: but I have known
fair hides have foul hearts ere now, sister.
　　Dame K. Never said you truer than that,
brother, so much I can tell you for your
learning. Thomas, fetch your cloak and
go with me. *[Exit Cash.]* I'll after him
presently: I would to 'fortune I could take
him there, i' faith I'd return him his own, I
warrant him !　　　　　　　　　　*[Exit.*
　　Wel. So, let 'em go; this may make
sport anon. Now, my fair sister-in-law,
that you knew but how happy a thing it
were to be fair and beautiful.
　　Brid. That touches not me, brother.
　　Wel. That's true; that's even the fault

of it: for indeed, beauty stands a woman
in no stead, unless it procure her touching.
—But, sister, whether it touch you or no,
it touches your beauties; and I am sure,
they will abide the touch; an they do not,
a plague of all ceruse, say I !¹ and it touches
me too in part, though not in the —— Well,
there's a dear and respected friend of mine,
sister, stands very strongly and worthily
affected toward you, and hath vowed to inflame whole bonfires of zeal at his heart, in
honour of your perfections. I have already
engaged my promise to bring you, where
you shall hear him confirm much more.
Ned Knowell is the man, sister: there's no
exception against the party. You are ripe
for a husband; and a minute's loss to such
an occasion, is a great trespass in a wise
beauty. What say you, sister? On my
soul he loves you; will you give him the
meeting?
　　Brid. Faith I had very little confidence
in mine own constancy, brother, if I durst
not meet a man : but this motion of yours
savours of an old knight adventurer's servant a little too much, methinks.
　　Wel. What's that, sister?
　　Brid. Marry, of the squire.²
　　Wel. No matter if it did, I would be
such an one for my friend. But see who
is returned to hinder us !

　　　　　　　Re-enter Kitely.

　　Kit. What villainy is this? called out on
　　a false message !
This was some plot; I was not sent for.——
　　Bridget,
Where is your sister?
　　Brid. I think she be gone forth, sir.
　　Kit. How ! is my wife gone forth?
　　whither, for God's sake?
　　Brid. She's gone abroad with Thomas.
　　Kit. Abroad with Thomas ! oh, that
　　villain dors me :³

---

¹ *A plague of all* ceruse, *say I* !] *Ceruse*
(from *cerussa,* Lat.) a composition of white lead
with which the ladies painted their face and
bosom.—WHAL.
　This is certainly the *ceruse* of the Romans ;
whether that of our fair countrywomen was
equally deleterious, I cannot say. It is mentioned by them without reserve, and applied
without caution ; and appears to have been not
altogether colourless.
　² *Marry, of the* squire.] A cant term for a
pimp or procurer. Thus, in *A Mad World my
Masters:*

　　"This censure flies from one, that, from
　　　another ;

VOL. I.

　That man's her *squire,* says he ; her *pimp,*
　　the other."

　³ *Oh, that villain* dors *me :*] The *dor* is the
chaffer ; and the allusion, to which Jonson is
never weary of recurring, is to the desultory
flight of this insect, which appears to *mock,* or
play upon, the passenger, by striking him on the
face, and then flitting away preparatory, as it
were, to a fresh attack. To this Cowley alludes :
"A hundred businesses of other men fly continually about his head and ears, and strike him
in the face like *dorres.*"—*Essays of Liberty.*
Jonson always connects the idea of tricking, or
outwitting, with *dorring. Buzzing,* the prevailing term for deceiving, in Addison's days, as

He hath discovered all unto my wife.
Beast that I was, to trust him! whither, I
  pray you,
Went she?
  Brid. I know not, sir.
  Wel. I'll tell you, brother,
Whither I suspect she's gone.
  Kit. Whither, good brother?
  Wel. To Cob's house, I believe: but,
  keep my counsel.
  Kit. I will, I will: to Cob's house! doth
  she haunt Cob's?
She's gone a purpose now to cuckold me,
With that lewd rascal, who, to win her
  favour,
Hath told her all.   [*Exit.*
  Wel. Come, he is once more gone,
Sister, let's lose no time; the affair is worth
  it.   [*Exeunt.*

SCENE VII.—*A Street.*

Enter Mathew *and* Bobadill.

  Mat. I wonder, captain, what they will
say of my going away, ha?
  Bob. Why, what should they say, but
as of a discreet gentleman; quick, wary,
respectful of nature's fair lineaments? and
that's all.
  Mat. Why so! but what can they say
o fyour beating?
  Bob. A rude part, a touch with soft wood,
a kind of gross battery used, laid on strongly,
born most patiently; and that's all.
  Mat. Ay, but would any man have offered
it in Venice, as you say?
  Bob. Tut! I assure you, no: you shall
have there your nobilis, your gentilezza,
come in bravely upon your reverse, stand
you close, stand you firm, stand you fair,
save your retricato with his left leg, come to
the assalto with the right, thrust with brave
steel, defy your base wood! But wherefore do I awake this remembrance? I was
fascinated, by Jupiter; fascinated; but I
will be unwitched, and revenged by law.

  Mat. Do you hear? is it not best to get
a warrant, and have him arrested and
brought before Justice Clement?
  Bob. It were not amiss; would we had it!

Enter Brainworm, *disguised as* Formal.

  Mat. Why, here comes his man; let's
speak to him.
  Bob. Agreed, do you speak.
  Mat. Save you, sir!
  Brai. With all my heart, sir.
  Mat. Sir, there is one Downright hath
abused this gentleman and myself, and we
determine to make our amends by law;
now, if you would do us the favour to procure a warrant, to bring him afore your
master, you shall be well considered, I assure you, sir.
  Brai. Sir, you know my service is my
living; such favours as these gotten of my
master is his only preferment, and therefore
you must consider me as I may make
benefit of my place.
  Mat. How is that, sir?
  Brai. Faith, sir, the thing is extraordinary, and the gentleman may be of
great account; yet, be he what he will, if
you will lay me down a brace of angels in
my hand you shall have it, otherwise not.
  Mat. How shall we do, captain? he asks
a brace of angels, you have no money?
  Bob. Not a cross, by fortune.[1]
  Mat. Nor I, as I am a gentleman, but
twopence left of my two shillings in the
morning for wine and radish: let's find him
some pawn.
  Bob. Pawn! we have none to the value
of his demand.
  Mat. O, yes; I'll pawn this jewel in my
ear,[2] and you may pawn your silk stockings, and pull up your boots, they will
ne'er be mist: it must be done now.
  Bob. Well, an there be no remedy, I'll
step aside and pull them off.

                              [*Withdraws.*

---

well as that most hateful vulgarism, *humming,*
so fashionable in our own, derived its origin from
the same respectable source, and both refer to
this imaginary mockery in the "droning flight" of
the beetle.
  [1] *Not a cross, by fortune.*] The ancient penny,
according to Stow, had a double cross with a
crest stamped on it, so that it might easily be
broken in the midst, or in the four quarters.
Hence it became a common phrase when a person
had no money about him, to say, he had not a
single cross. As this was certainly an *unfortunate* circumstance, there is no end to the quib-
bling upon this poor word. Thus Shakspeare,

vir gregis ipse caper—"I had rather bear with
you than bear you; yet I should bear **no** *cross*
if I did bear you; for I think you have no *money*
in your purse."—*As You Like It,* act ii. sc. 4.
  [2] *I'll pawn this jewel in my ear,*] A fashion
at that time for the men to wear rings in their
ears. So in the Induction to *Every Man out of
his Humour,*

    "Hang my richest words
As polished *jewels* in their bounteous *ears.*"
And in the *Revenger's Tragedy,* act i. sc. 1:
  "That *jewel's* mine that quivers in his ear."
                                        WHAL.

Mat. Do you hear, sir? we have no store of money at this time, but you shall have good pawns; look you, sir, this jewel, and that gentleman's silk stockings; because we would have it dispatched ere we went to our chambers.

Brai. I am content, sir; I will get you the warrant presently. What's his name, say you? Downright?

Mat. Ay, ay, George Downright.

Brai. What manner of man is he?

Mat. A tall big man, sir; he goes in a cloak most commonly of silk-russet, laid about with russet lace.

Brai. 'Tis very good, sir.

Mat. Here, sir, here's my jewel.

Bob. [*returning.*] And here are my stockings.

Brai. Well, gentlemen, I'll procure you this warrant presently; but who will you have to serve it?

Mat. That's true, captain; that must be considered.

Bob. Body o' me, I know not; 'tis service of danger.

Brai. Why, you were best get one o' the varlets of the city,[1] a serjeant: I'll appoint you one, if you please.

Mat. Will you, sir? why, we can wish no better.

Bob. We'll leave it to you, sir.
[*Exeunt* Bob. *and* Mat.

Brai. This is rare! Now will I go pawn this cloak of the justice's man's at the broker's, for a varlet's suit, and be the varlet myself; and get either more pawns, or more money of Downright, for the arrest.   [*Exit.*

SCENE VIII.—*The Lane before* Cob's *House.*

Enter Knowell.

Know. Oh, here it is; I am glad I have found it now:
Ho! who is within here?

Tib. [*within*] I am within, sir; what's your pleasure?

Know. To know who is within besides yourself.

Tib. Why, sir, you are no constable, I hope?

Know. O, fear you the constable? then I doubt not

You have some guests within deserve that fear;
I'll fetch him straight.

Enter Tib.

Tib. O' God's name, sir!

Know. Go to: Come, tell me, is not young Knowell here?

Tib. Young Knowell! I know none such, sir, o' mine honesty.

Know. Your honesty, dame! it flies too lightly from you;
There is no way but fetch the constable.

Tib. The constable! The man is mad, I think.   [*Exit, and claps to the door.*

Enter Dame Kitely *and* Cash.

Cash. Ho! who keeps house here?

Know. O, this is the female copesmate of my son:
Now shall I meet him straight.

Dame K. Knock, Thomas, hard.

Cash. Ho, goodwife!

Re-enter Tib.

Tib. Why, what's the matter with you?

Dame K. Why woman, grieves it you to ope your door?
Belike you get something to keep it shut.

Tib. What mean these questions, pray ye?

Dame K. So strange you make it! is not my husband here?

Know. Her husband!

Dame K. My tried husband, Master Kitely?

Tib. I hope he needs not to be tried here.

Dame K. No, dame, he does it not for need, but pleasure.

Tib. Neither for need nor pleasure is he here.

Know. This is but a device to baulk me withal:

Enter Kitely, *muffled in his cloak.*

Soft, who is this? 'tis not my son disguised?

Dame K. [*spies her husband, and runs to him.*]
O, sir, have I forestalled your honest market,
Found your close walks? You stand amazed now, do you?

I' faith, I am glad I have smoked you yet at
 last.
What is your jewel, trow? In, come, let's
 see her ;
Fetch forth your housewife, dame ; if she
 be fairer,
In any honest judgment, than myself,
I'll be content with it : but she is change,
She feeds you fat, she soothes your appetite,
And you are well ! Your wife, an honest
 woman,
Is meat twice sod to you, sir ! O, you
 treachour?[1]
 Know. She cannot counterfeit thus pal-
 pably.
 Kit. Out on thy more than strumpet
impudence !

Steal'st thou thus to thy haunts ? and have
 I taken
Thy bawd and thee, and thy companion,
This hoary-headed letcher, this old goat,
Close at your villainy, and wouldst thou
 'scuse it
With this stale harlot's jest, accusing me?
O, old incontinent, [*to* Knowell] dost thou
 not shame,
When all thy powers in chastity are spent,
To have a mind so hot ?[2] and to entice,
And feed the enticements of a lustful
 woman ?
 Dame K. Out, I defy thee, I, dissem-
 bling wretch !
 Kit. Defy me, strumpet ! Ask thy
pander here,[3]

---

[1] *O, you* treachour !] Treachour, for traitor, is
common to our old writers; so in Chaucer's
Romance of the Rose,

 ' Of all this worlde is emperour
 Gile my father, the false *treachour.*"
        v. 7168.

And Spenser,

  " Hence shall I never rest
 Till I that *treachour's* art have heard and
  tryde."—*F. Q.* l. 1. c. ix. st. 32.

And in Shakspeare, " Knaves, thieves, and
treachours, by spherical predominance."—*Lear,*
act i. sc. 2. WHAL.

[2] ————————*dost thou not shame,
When all thy powers in chastity are spent,
To have a mind so hot?*] i.e., "when thy
powers for legitimate pleasures are exhausted,"
&c. There seems no great obscurity in this ;
yet Whalley appears to have stumbled at it: He
wishes to adopt a conjecture of Mr. Waldron.
In the quarto, the words, which stand asunder
in the folio, are joined, and appear as one, *inchastitie.* This, Mr. Waldron conceives to be a
misprint for inchastilie, " a reading," (he says,)
which "greatly improves the sense of the passage." I do not think so ;—but let the reader
judge. It may be added, however, that though
no example will readily be found of inchastilie,
the substantive from which it may be derived
(*inchastitie*) is sufficiently common. Thus in
Hannay's *Sheretine and Mariana :*

 "'Tis not the act that ties the marriage knot,
 It is the will : then must I all my life,
 Be stained with *inchastitie's* foul blot."

[3] The folio has a note here " *By Thomas,*"on
which Whalley remarks, "This marginal direction is obscure. Thomas Cash is the person
meant, he is called her pander, as Knowell is
afterwards termed the wicked elder. The words
By Thomas, mean, that *he comes up to Cash,*
when he gives him that appellation."
As Whalley has utterly mistaken the sense, I
should not have retained his observation but for
the opportunity which it affords me, of offering a
few words on this most trite but disputed mode

of expression. In the *Merchant of Venice,*
act ii. sc. 9, the Prince of Arragon says——

  "That many may be meant
  By the fool multitude."

On which Mr. Malone observes, " I have reason
to congratulate myself on having here adhered
to the ancient copies, in opposition to the other
modern editors, having, since this note was
printed, met with many examples of this kind of
phraseology." So, in Plutarch's Life of Cæsar,
as translated by North, 1575 : "—he aunswered,
that these fat long-bearded men made him not
affrayed, but the lean and whitely-faced fellows ;
meaning that by Brutus and Cassius ;" i.e.,
meaning by that, &c. Again, in Sir Thomas
Moore's Life of Edward the Fifth :—Holinshed,
p. 1374 : " —that *meant he by the lordes* of the
queenes kindred that were taken before," i.e.,
by that he meant the lordes, &c. Again, *ibidem,*
p. 1371 : " My lord, quoth Hastings, on my life,
never doubt you ; for while one man is there,—
never can there be, &c. This *meant he by*
Catesby, which was of his near secrete coun-
saile ;" i.e., by this he meant Catesby, &c.
Again, Puttenham in his *Arte of Poesie,* 1589,
p. 157, after citing some enigmatical verses,
adds, " —the good old gentleman would tell us
that were children, how *it was meant by* a
furred glove," i.e., a furred glove was meant by
it, &c.
This long string of examples is given by the
Critical Reviewers as a happy explanation of,
what they are pleased to call " this *peculiar*
expression," though the expression is very
common, and the resolution of it wrong in every
instance. The plain fact is (for it needs not
many words), that the prepositions *by* and *of* are
synonymous, and that our ancestors used them
indifferently, as they were well justified in doing :
place *of,* therefore, in the stead of *by,* and the
mighty difficulty vanishes at once. *By Thomas,*
is *of* Thomas, and nothing more. This simple
substitution answers in every case, whereas innumerable examples might be produced in which
the elaborate inversion recommended above,
would resolve the phrase into nonsense. In the
admirable speech of the poor persecuted James

Can he deny it? or that wicked elder?

Know. Why, hear you, sir.

Kit. Tut, tut, tut; never speak:
Thy guilty conscience will discover thee.

Know. What lunacy is this, that haunts
this man?

Kit. Well, good wife bawd, Cob's wife,
and you,
That make your husband such a hoddy-
doddy;
And you, young apple-squire, and old
cuckold-maker;
I'll have you every one before a justice:
Nay, you shall answer it, I charge you go.

Know. Marry, with all my heart, sir, I
go willingly;
Though I do taste this as a trick put on me,
To punish my impertinent search, and
justly,
And half forgive my son for the device.

Kit. Come, will you go?

Dame K. Go! to thy shame, believe it.

Enter Cob.

Cob. Why, what's the matter here, what's
here to do?

Kit. O, Cob, art thou come? I have
been abused,
And in thy house; was never man so
wronged!

Cob. 'Slid, in my house, my master
Kitely! who wrongs you in my house?

Kit. Marry, young lust in old, and old
in young here:

Thy wife's their bawd, here have I taken
them.

Cob. How, bawd! is my house come to
that? Am I preferred thither? Did I not
charge you to keep your doors shut, Isbel?
and—you let them lie open for all comers!
　　　　　　　　　　　　[*Beats his wife.*

Know. Friend, know some cause, before
thou beat'st thy wife.
This is madness in thee.

Cob. Why, is there no cause?

Kit. Yes, I'll shew cause before the justice, Cob:
Come, let her go with me.

Cob. Nay, she shall go.

Tib. Nay, I will go. I'll see an you may
be allowed to make a bundle of hemp of your
right and lawful wife thus, at every cuckoldy
knave's pleasure. Why do you not go?

Kit. A bitter quean! Come, we will
have you tamed.　　　　　　[*Exeunt.*

SCENE IX.—*A Street.*

Enter Brainworm, *disguised as a city
serjeant.*

Brai. Well, of all my disguises yet, now
am I most like myself, being in this serjeant's
gown. A man of my present profession
never counterfeits, till he lays hold upon a
debtor, and says, he rests him; for then he
brings him to all manner of unrest. A
kind of little kings we are, bearing the
diminutive of a mace,[1] made like a young

---

to his parliament, on the gunpowder plot, he says,
"I did apprehend some dark phrases therein,
to be meant *by* this terrible form of blowing us
up by gunpowder." On which the British Critic
remarks, "to be meant *by*," is a misprint for
"to mean." This is one of those venial slips
quas incuria, &c.: for few are so intimately acquainted with the language of our ancestors as
the editor of this work.

To return to Jonson: this whole scene, as
Whalley well observes, is very happily drawn,
and altogether in the spirit of the ancient comedy.

[1] *Bearing the diminutive of a* mace, &c.]
This was the badge of a city serjeant's office,
which he constantly carried when he arrested a
man for debt. Thus Shirley, "Are you in debt,
and fear arresting? You shall come up to the
face of a serjeant, nay, walk by a shoal of these
mankind horse-leeches, and be *mace proof*."—
Bird in a Cage, act ii. And Chapman,

> "If I write but my name in a mercer's book,
> I am as sure to have, at six months' end,
> A rascal at my elbow with a *mace*."
> 　　　　　　　　　*All Fools*, act i.

The *gown* too was a badge of the serjeant's or
varlet's office, and as well known as the mace;
indeed, he never appeared in public without it:

to this Brainworm alludes, when he says, "a man
of my present profession *never counterfeits*."

Though there is something coarse and rude in
the following remarks, yet they are not altogether
unworthy of notice. "How chances it that our
bailiffs have departed from the antient practice
in all civilized countries, of wearing the livery
or badge of their employment. The *varlets* and
serjeants, as they were called formerly, were
distinguished by their habit: they used 'no
counterfeits,' says Ben Jonson. It appears beneath the dignity of the law that they should:
no part of justice, I humbly conceive, ought to
be acted in masquerade—that would be to make
mummers of its inferior ministers; dangerous
mummers indeed! for they pass now in all
manner of disguises, and instead of the 'mace,'
the sober symbol of civil power, parade it with
bludgeons and concealed weapons. This is
notorious; yet no lawyer can be found who has
honesty enough to declare the practice illegal.
It is argued that they could not so readily
act in a known habit, as they would be liable
to interruption, and abuse. Is not the law
strong enough to support itself? Besides, who
shall dare to insult or oppose the avowed and
liveried officer of justice in the execution of his
duty."—*Speculations on Law,* 1788.

artichoke, that always carries pepper and salt in itself. Well, I know not what danger I undergo, by this exploit; pray heaven I come well off!

Enter Mathew and Bobadill.

Mat. See, I think, yonder is the varlet, by his gown.

Bob. Let's go in quest of him.

Mat. 'Save you, friend! are not you here by appointment of Justice Clement's man?

Brai. Yes, an't please you, sir; he told me two gentlemen had willed him to procure a warrant from his master, which I have about me, to be served on one Downright.

Mat. It is honestly done of you both; and see where the party comes you must arrest; serve it upon him quickly, before he be aware.

Bob. Bear back, Master Mathew.

Enter Stephen *in* Downright's *cloak.*

Brai. Master Downright, I arrest you in the queen's name, and must carry you afore a justice by virtue of this warrant.

Step. Me, friend! I am no Downright, I; I am Master Stephen: you do not well to arrest me, I tell you, truly; I am in nobody's bonds nor books, I would you should know it. A plague on you, heartily, for making me thus afraid afore my time!

Brai. Why, now you are deceived, gentlemen.

Bob. He wears such a cloak, and that deceived us: but see, here a'comes indeed; this is he, officer.

Enter Downright.

Down. Why, how now, signior gull! are you turned filcher of late? Come, deliver my cloak.

Step. Your cloak, sir! I bought it even now, in open market.

Brai. Master Downright, I have a warrant I must serve upon you, procured by these two gentlemen.

Down. These gentlemen? these rascals! [*Offers to beat them.*

Brai. Keep the peace, I charge you in her majesty's name.

Down. I obey thee. What must I do, officer?

Brai. Go before Master Justice Clement, to answer what they can object against you, sir; I will use you kindly, sir.

Mat. Come, let's before, and make the justice,[1] captain.

Bob. The varlet's a tall man, afore heaven![2]   [*Exeunt* Bob. *and* Mat.

Down. Gull, you'll give me my cloak?

Step. Sir, I bought it, and I'll keep it.

Down. You will?

Step. Ay, that I will.

Down. Officer, there's thy fee, arrest him.

Brai. Master Stephen, I must arrest you.

Step. Arrest me! I scorn it. There, take your cloak, I'll none on't.

Down. Nay, that shall not serve your turn now, sir. Officer, I'll go with thee to the justice's; bring him along.

Step. Why, is not here your cloak? what would you have?

Down. I'll have you answer it, sir.

Brai. Sir, I'll take your word, and this gentleman's too, for his appearance.

Down. I'll have no words taken: bring him along.

Brai. Sir, I may choose to do that, I may take bail.

Down. 'Tis true, you may take bail, and choose at another time; but you shall not now, varlet: bring him along, or I'll swinge you.

Brai. Sir, I pity the gentleman's case: here's your money again.

Down. 'Sdeins, tell not me of my money; bring him away, I say.

Brai. I warrant you he will go with you of himself, sir.

Down. Yet more ado?

Brai. I have made a fair mash on't.
                                        [*Aside.*

Step. Must I go?

Brai. I know no remedy, Master Stephen.

Down. Come along, afore me here; I do not love your hanging look behind.

Step. Why, sir, I hope you cannot hang me for it: can he, fellow?

Brai. I think not, sir; it is but a whipping matter, sure.

Step. Why then let him do his worst, I am resolute.   [*Exeunt.*

---

1 *Come, let's before, and* make *the justice,*] i.e., acquaint him with our business; or, as the quarto reads, in this place, *prepare* him. The same expression is found in Sejanus, "Were Lygdus *made*, that's done."

2 Bob. *The* varlet's a tall man, *afore heaven!*] There is some natural humour in making Bobadill, who had suffered from Downright's courage, celebrate the *prowess* of the *serjeant* (a legal officer) in venturing to arrest him.

ACT V.

SCENE I.—Coleman Street. *A Hall in Justice Clement's House.*

Enter Clement, Knowell, Kitely, Dame Kitely, Tib, Cash, Cob, *and Servants.*

Clem. Nay, but stay, stay, give me leave: my chair, sirrah. You, Master Knowell, say you went thither to meet your son?

Know. Ay, sir.

Clem. But who directed you thither?

Know. That did mine own man, sir.

Clem. Where is he?

Know. Nay, I know not now; I left him with your clerk, and appointed him to stay here for me.

Clem. My clerk! about what time was this?

Know. Marry, between one and two, as I take it.

Clem. And what time came my man with the false message to you, Master Kitely?

Kit. After two, sir.

Clem. Very good; but, Mistress Kitely, how chance that you were at Cob's, ha?

Dame K. An't please you, sir, I'll tell you: my brother Wellbred told me, that Cob's house was a suspected place——

Clem. So it appears, methinks; but on.

Dame K. And that my husband used thither daily.

Clem. No matter, so he used himself well, mistress.

Dame K. True, sir; but you know what grows by such haunts oftentimes.

Clem. I see rank fruits of a jealous brain, Mistress Kitely: but did you find your husband there, in that case as you suspected?

Kit. I found her there, sir.

Clem. Did you so! that alters the case. Who gave you knowledge of your wife's being there?

Kit. Marry, that did my brother Wellbred.

Clem. How, Wellbred first tell her; then tell you after! Where is Wellbred?

Kit. Gone with my sister, sir, I know not whither.

Clem. Why, this is a mere trick, a device; you are gulled in this most grossly,

all. Alas, poor wench! wert thou beaten for this?

Tib. Yes, most pitifully, an't please you.

Cob. And worthily, I hope, if it shall prove so.

Clem. Ay, that's like, and a piece of a sentence.——

Enter a Servant.

How now, sir, what's the matter?

Serv. Sir, there's a gentleman in the court without, desires to speak with your worship.

Clem. A gentleman! what is he?

Serv. A soldier, sir, he says.

Clem. A soldier! take down my armour, my sword quickly. A soldier speak with me! Why, when, knaves?[1] Come on, come on. [*Arms himself.*] Hold my cap there, so; give me my gorget, my sword: stand by, I will end your matters anon—— Let the soldier enter. [*Exit* Servant.

Enter Bobadill, *followed by* Mathew.

Now, sir, what have you to say to me?

Bob. By your worship's favour——

Clem. Nay, keep out, sir; I know not your pretence. You send me word, sir, you are a soldier: why, sir, you shall be answered here; here be them have been amongst soldiers. Sir, your pleasure.

Bob. Faith, sir, so it is, this gentleman and myself have been most uncivilly wronged and beaten by one Downright, a coarse fellow, about the town here; and for mine own part, I protest, being a man in no sort given to this filthy humour of quarrelling, he hath assaulted me in the way of my peace, despoiled me of mine honour, disarmed me of my weapons, and rudely laid me along in the open streets, when I not so much as once offered to resist him.

Clem. O, God's precious! is this the soldier? Here, take my armour off quickly, 'twill make him swoon, I fear; he is not fit to look on't, that will put up a blow.

Mat. An't please your worship, he was bound to the peace.

Clem. Why, an he were, sir, his hands were not bound, were they?

---

[1] *Why*, when, *knaves!*] This exclamatory mark of impatience is extremely common in our old dramatists; and I am, therefore, somewhat surprised to find it escape the notice of Reed. In the *Spanish Tragedy*, the viceroy exclaims,

"No more, I say; to the tortures: *when!* Bind him, and burn his body."

Dodsley, no very competent judge of language, altered *when*, to *with him!* and Reed approves and continues the corruption.

Re-enter Servant.

Serv. There's one of the varlets of the city, sir, has brought two gentlemen here; one, upon your worship's warrant.

Clem. My warrant!

Serv. Yes, sir; the officer says, procured by these two.

Clem. Bid him come in. [*Exit* Servant.] Set by this picture.

Enter Downright, Stephen, *and* Brainworm, *disguised as before.*

What, Master Downright! are you brought at Master Fresh-water's suit here?

Down. I' faith, sir: and here's another brought at my suit.

Clem. What are you, sir?

Step. A gentleman, sir. O, uncle!

Clem. Uncle! who, Master Knowell?

Know. Ay, sir; this is a wise kinsman of mine.

Step. God's my witness, uncle, I am wronged here monstrously; he charges me with stealing of his cloak, and would I might never stir, if I did not find it in the street by chance.

Down. O, did you find it now? You said you bought it erewhile.

Step. And you said, I stole it: nay, now my uncle is here, I'll do well enough with you.

Clem. Well, let this breathe a while. You that have cause to complain there, stand forth: Had you my warrant for this gentleman's apprehension?

Bob. Ay. an't please your worship.

Clem. Nay, do not speak in passion so:[1] where had you it?

Bob. Of your clerk, sir.

Clem. That's well! an my clerk can make warrants, and my hand not at them! Where is the warrant—officer, have you it?

Brai. No, sir, your worship's man, Master Formal, bid me do it for these gentlemen, and he would be my discharge.

Clem. Why, Master Downright, are you such a novice, to be served and never see the warrant?

Down. Sir, he did not serve it on me.

Clem. No! how then?

Down. Marry, sir, he came to me, and said he must serve it, and he would use me kindly, and so——

Clem. O, God's pity, was it so, sir? *He*

[1] *Nay, do not speak in* passion *so:*] i.e., in so melancholy a tone, so pathetically. Poor Bobadill has now been sufficiently humbled.

must serve it! Give me my long sword there, and help me off. So, come on, sir varlet, I *must* cut off your legs, sirrah; [Brainworm *kneels*]. Nay, stand up, *I'll use you kindly;* I *must* cut off your legs, I say.

[*Flourishes over him with his long sword.*

Brai. O, good sir, I beseech you; nay, good Master Justice!

Clem. I must do it, there is no remedy; I *must* cut off your legs, sirrah, I *must* cut off your ears, you rascal, I must do it; I *must* cut off your nose, I *must* cut off your head.

Brai. O, good your worship!

Clem. Well, rise; how dost thou do now? dost thou feel thyself well? hast thou no harm?

Brai. No, I thank your good worship, sir.

Clem. Why, so! I said I must cut off thy legs, and I must cut off thy arms, and I must cut off thy head; but I did not do it: so you said you must serve this gentleman with my warrant, but you did not serve him. You knave, you slave, you rogue, do you say you *must,* sirrah! away with him to the jail; I'll teach you a trick, for your *must,* sir.

Brai. Good sir, I beseech you, be good to me.

Clem. Tell him he shall to the jail; away with him, I say.

Brai. Nay, sir, if you will commit me, it shall be for committing more than this: I will not lose by my travail any grain of my fame, certain.

[*Throws off his serjeant's gown.*

Clem. How is this?

Know. My man Brainworm!

Step. O, yes, uncle; Brainworm has been with my cousin Edward and I all this day.

Clem. I told you all there was some device.

Brai. Nay, excellent justice, since I have laid myself thus open to you, now stand strong for me; both with your sword and your balance.

Clem. Body o' me, a merry knave! give me a bowl of sack: if he belong to you, Master Knowell, I bespeak your patience.

Brai. That is it I have most need of: Sir, if you'll pardon me only, I'll glory in all the rest of my exploits.

Know. Sir, you know I love not to have my favours come hard from me. — You have your pardon, though I suspect you shrewdly for being of counsel with my son against me.

Brai. Yes, faith, I have, sir, though you retained me doubly this morning for yourself: first, as Brainworm; after, as Fitz-Sword. I was your reformed soldier, sir. 'Twas I sent you to Cob's upon the errand without end.

Know. Is it possible? or that thou should'st disguise thy language so as I should not know thee?

Brai. O, sir, this has been the day of my metamorphosis. It is not that shape alone that I have run through to-day. I brought this gentleman, Master Kitely, a message too, in the form of Master Justice's man here, to draw him out o' the way, as well as your worship, while Master Wellbred might make a conveyance of Mistress Bridget to my young master.

Kit. How! my sister stolen away?

Know. My son is not married, I hope.

Brai. Faith, sir, they are both as sure as love, a priest, and three thousand pound, which is her portion, can make them; and by this time are ready to bespeak their wedding supper at the Windmill, except some friend here prevent them, and invite them home.

Clem. Marry, that will I; I thank thee for putting me in mind on't. Sirrah, go you and fetch them hither upon my warrant. [*Exit* Servant.] Neither's friends have cause to be sorry, if I know the young couple aright. Here, I drink to thee for thy good news. But, I pray thee, what hast thou done with my man, Formal?

Brai. Faith, sir, after some ceremony past, as making him drunk, first with story, and then with wine (but all in kindness), and stripping him to his shirt, I left him in that cool vein; departed, sold your worship's warrant to these two, pawned his livery for that varlet's gown, to serve it in; and thus have brought myself by my activity to your worship's consideration.

Clem. And I will consider thee in another cup of sack. Here's to thee, which having drunk off, this is my sentence: Pledge me. Thou hast done, or

assisted to nothing, in my judgment, but deserves to be pardoned for the wit of the offence. If thy master, or any man here, be angry with thee, I shall suspect his ingine,[1] while I know him, for't.—How now, what noise is that?

Enter Servant.

Serv. Sir, it is Roger is come home.

Clem. Bring him in, bring him in.

Enter Formal, *in a suit of armour.*

What! drunk? in arms against me? your reason, your reason for this?

Form. I beseech your worship to pardon me; I happened into ill company by chance that cast me into a sleep, and stript me of all my clothes.

Clem. Well, tell him I am Justice Clement, and do pardon him: but what is this to your armour? what may that signify?

Form. An't please you, sir, it hung up in the room where I was stript; and I borrowed it of one of the drawers to come home in, because I was loth to do penance through the street in my shirt.

Clem. Well, stand by a while.

Enter E. Knowell, Wellbred, *and* Bridget.

Who be these? O, the young company; welcome, welcome! Give you joy. Nay, Mistress Bridget, blush not; you are not so fresh a bride, but the news of it is come hither afore you. Master bridegroom, I have made your peace, give me your hand: so will I for all the rest ere you forsake my roof.

E. Know. We are the more bound to your humanity, sir.

Clem. Only these two have so little of man in them, they are no part of my care.

Wel. Yes, sir, let me pray you for this gentleman, he belongs to my sister, the bride.

Clem. In what place, sir?

Wel. Of her delight, sir, below the stairs, and in public: her poet, sir.

Clem. A poet! I will challenge him myself presently at extempore.

"Mount up thy Phlegon,[2] Muse, and testify

---

[1] *I shall suspect his* ingine, &c.] From the Latin, *ingenium*, his wit, his understanding.—WHAL.

[2] *Mount up thy Phlegon,* &c.] It is not easy to follow Jonson through the numerous authors whose bombast he has burlesqued: my own experience, indeed, would justify the use of stronger language, but I speak generally. Many ridiculous books, or "ballads," as the quarto calls them, are undoubtedly lost, and many are necessarily overlooked; so that much of his humour still remains in obscurity. In the first edition,

this absurd rant is said to be "in honour of the gods and goddesses;" and I observe in the *Zodiacke*, by Barnaby Googe, where there is certainly enough of this folly, a passage which our poet (though I do not give the conjecture for much), might possibly have had in view.

"Aloft, my Muse, raise up thyself,
    And use a better flite,
Mount up on hie, and think it scorn
    Of base affairs to write——
So up to Jove," &c.

How Saturn, sitting in an ebon cloud,
Disrobed his podex, white as ivory,
  And through the welkin thundered all
    aloud."

Wel. He is not for extempore, sir: he is
all for the pocket muse: please you command a sight of it.

Clem. Yes, yes, search him for a taste of
his vein.   [*They search* Mathew's *pockets.*

Wel. You must not deny the queen's
Justice, sir, under a writ of rebellion.

Clem. What! all this verse? body o' me,
he carries a whole realm, a commonwealth
of paper in his hose: let us see some of his
subjects.   [*Reads.*

" Unto the boundless ocean of thy face,
  Runs this poor river, charged with streams
    of eyes."

How! this is stolen.[1]

E. Know. A parody! a parody! with
a kind of miraculous gift, to make it absurder than it was.

Clem. Is all the rest of this batch?
Bring me a torch; lay it together, and give

fire. Cleanse the air. [*Sets the papers on
fire.*] Here was enough to have infected
the whole city, if it had not been taken in
time. See, see, how our poet's glory
shines! brighter and brighter! still it increases! O, now it is at the highest; and
now it declines as fast. You may see, *sic
transit gloria mundi!*

Know. There's an emblem for you, son,
and your studies.[2]

Clem. Nay, no speech or act of mine be
drawn against such as profess it worthily.
They are not born every year, as an alderman. There goes more to the making of a
good poet, than a sheriff.[3] Master Kitely,
you look upon me!—though I live in the
city here, amongst you, I will do more
reverence to him, when I meet him, than I
will to the mayor out of his year. But these
paper-pedlars, these ink-dabblers! they
cannot expect reprehension or reproach;
they have it with the fact.

E. Know. Sir, you have saved me the
labour of a defence.[4]

Clem. It shall be discourse for supper

However this may be, there is more than sufficient in the description of some of the constel-
lations, particularly in that of Sagittarius, to
shock the classical taste of Jonson, and excite
his utmost risibility.

Steevens inclined to believe that "a burlesque
was intended here on the masque in *Cymbeline:*—but as *Cymbeline* luckily was not written
till many years after this play, and the masque
in it not written at all by Shakspeare, no particular stress is laid on the "malignity" of
Jonson to our great bard in this instance. Such
is the force of candour!

[1] *How! this is stolen.*] Not altogether; but
parodied from the first stanza of Daniel's *Sonnet
to Delia:*

" Unto the boundless ocean of thy beauty
  Runs this poor river, charged with streams
    of zeal;
  Returning thee the tribute of my duty,
  Which here my youth, my plaints, my love
    reveal."

Jonson's disinclination to Daniel broke out
rather early. I am unable to account for it,
unless it arose from a difference in taste. The
chastised and vigorous mind of the former was
not likely to find pleasure in the soft and morbid
delicacy of the latter: yet Daniel must not be
too lightly depreciated; many of his poems
possess great beauty; and his virtues were not
inferior to his talents.

[2] Know. *There's an emblem for you, son, and
your studies.*] In the very opening of the play
old Knowell expresses an anxiety to warn his
son from the study "of idle poetry:" this application of the justice's *emblem* to him, therefore,
is well timed and judicious.

[3] *There goes more to the making of a good
poet, than a sheriff: they are not born every
year, as an alderman.*] Among plain citizens,
this might be thought a reflection upon men of
gravity and worship; and Master Kitely seemed
to take it so: but the merry Justice thought no
harm, when he thus gave us the sense of the old
Latin verses:

" *Consules fiunt quotannis, et proconsules:
Solus poeta non quotannis nascitur.*"

Which Taylor, the water poet, has paraphrased
with much greater honour to the bard:

" When heaven intends to do some mighty thing,
He makes a poet, or at least—a king."
                    WHAL.

The water poet seems to have found a more
correct copy of "the old Latin verses" than the
commentator, who has jumbled them out of all
order.

" *Consules fiunt quotannis, et novi proconsules,
Solus aut rex aut poeta non quotannis nascitur.*"

They are usually attributed to one Florus.

[4] E. Know. *Sir, you have saved me the
labour of a defence.*] In the quarto, however, it
is made. It would be unjust to Jonson, as well
as the reader, to suppress the passage, which is
full of noble feeling, at once rational, fervid, and
sublime. It breathes the very spirit of high antiquity, 'Ρηγμ' εσι γης αναπνεον ατμον ευθεον,
and forms one of those numerous sources from
which Milton (the unwearied though unnoticed
follower of this great poet) derived inspiration

between your father and me, if he dare undertake me. But to dispatch away these, you sign o' the soldier, and picture o' the poet, (but both so false, I will not have you hanged out at my door till midnight,) while we are at supper, you two shall penitently fast it out in my court without ; and, if you will, you may pray there that we may be so merry within as to forgive or forget you when we come out. Here's a third,[1] because we tender your safety, shall watch you, he is provided for the purpose. Look to your charge, sir.

Step. And what shall I do?

Clem. O! I had lost a sheep an he had not bleated : why, sir, you shall give Master Downright his cloak ; and I will intreat him to take it. A trencher and a napkin you shall have in the buttery, and keep Cob and his wife company here ; whom I will intreat first to be reconciled ; and you to endeavour with your wit to keep them so.

Step. I'll do my best.

Cob. Why, now I see thou art honest, Tib, I receive thee as my dear and mortal wife again.

Tib. And I you, as my loving and obedient husband.

Clem. Good compliment! It will be their bridal night too. They are married anew. Come, I conjure the rest to put off all discontent. You, Master Downright, your anger ; you, Master Knowell, your cares ; Master Kitely and his wife, their jealousy.

For, I must tell you both, while that is fed, Horns in the mind are worse than on the head.

Kit. Sir, thus they go from me ; kiss me, sweetheart :——

"See what a drove of horns fly in the air, Winged with my cleansed and my credulous breath!
Watch 'em, suspicious eyes, watch where they fall.
See, see! on heads, that think they have none at all!
O, what a plenteous world of this will come!
When air rains horns, all may be sure of some."

I have learned so much verse out of a jealous man's part in a play.

Clem. 'Tis well, 'tis well! This night we'll dedicate to friendship, love, and laughter. Master bridegroom, take your bride and lead ; every one a fellow. Here is my mistress, Brainworm! to whom all my addresses of courtship shall have their reference : whose adventures this day, when our grandchildren shall hear to be made a fable, I doubt not but it shall find both spectators and applause.   [*Exeunt.*[2]

---

and vigour. After giving Master Mathew's scraps, the quarto proceeds thus :——

Giu. Call you this poetry?

Lo. ju. Poetry! nay, then call blasphemy religion ;
Call devils, angels ; and sin, piety :
Let all things be preposterously transchanged.

Lo. se. Why, how now, son ; what! are you startled now?
Hath the brize prickt you, ha? go to ; you see How abjectly your poetry is ranked, In general opinion.

Lo. ju. I can refell opinion, and approve The state of poesy, such as it is, Blessed, eternal, and most true divine : Indeed, if you will look on poesy, As she appears in many, poor and lame, Patched up in remnants and old worn-out rags, Half-starved for want of her peculiar food, Sacred invention ; then I must confirm Both your conceit and censure of her merit : But view her in her glorious ornaments, Attired in the majesty of art, Set high in spirit with the precious taste Of sweet philosophy ; and, which is most, Crowned with the rich traditions of a soul, That hates to have her dignity prophaned With any relish of an earthly thought, Oh then how proud a presence doth she bear? Then is she like herself, fit to be seen Of none but grave and consecrated eyes.
Nor is it any blemish to her fame, That such lean, ignorant, and blasted wits, Such brainless gulls, should utter their stolen wares
With such applauses in our vulgar ears ; Or that their slubbered lines have current pass,
From the fat judgments of the multitude ; But that this barren and infected age, Should set no difference 'twixt these empty spirits,
And a true poet ; than which reverend name Nothing can more adorn humanity.

Giu. Ay, Lorenzo : but election is now governed altogether by the influence of humour, which, instead of those holy flames that should direct and light the soul to eternity, hurls forth nothing but smoke and congested vapours, that stifle her up, and bereave her of sight and motion.

[1] *Here's a third*, &c.] He means Formal, who appears in Brainworm's rusty armour.

[2] Having already entered into the merits of this comedy, I shall be brief in my present remarks. It is well known that *Every Man in his Humour* established the reputation of the author, and placed him, at once, in the foremost rank of the dramatic writers of the age : this station he still maintains ; for though many have

wished, yet none have found hardihood enough, to dispute his claims to it.

It has been invidiously urged that the characters of this drama are not original : as a general observation, this may be allowed to pass, for they were undoubtedly copied from nature, as modified by extraneous circumstances in the poet's days ; but when the enemies of Jonson descend to particulars, and specify the objects of his imitation, the absurdity and falsity of every charge become immediately manifest.

Jealousy is the *humour* of Kitely, but it is no more the jealousy of Ford than of Othello : original it neither is nor can be, for it is a passion as common as the air, and has been the property of the stage from the earliest times ; yet what but a jaundiced eye can discover any servile marks of imitation ? Kitely's alarms are natural, for his house is made the resort of young and riotous gallants ; yet he opens his suspicions with great delicacy, and when circumstances "light as air" confirm them, he does not bribe a stranger to complete his dishonour, but places a confidential spy over his wife, to give notice of the first approaches of familiarity. In a word, the feelings, the language, and the whole conduct of Kitely are totally distinct from those of Ford, or any preceding stage character whatever. The author drew from nature ; and as her varieties are infinite, a man of Jonson's keen and attentive observation, was under no necessity of borrowing from her at second hand.

Bobadill has never been well understood, and, therefore, is always too lightly estimated : because he is a boaster and a coward, he is cursorily dismissed as a mere copy of the ancient bully, or what is infinitely more ridiculous, of Pistol ; but Bobadill is a creature *sui generis*, and perfectly original. The soldier of the Greek comedy, from whom Whalley wishes to derive him, as far as we can collect from the scattered remains of it, or from its eternal copyists, Plautus and Terence, had not many traits in common with Bobadill. Pyrgapolonices, and other captains with hard names, are usually wealthy ; all of them keep a mistress, and some of them a parasite : but Bobadill is poor, as indeed are most of his profession, which, whatever it might be in Greece, has never been a gainful one in this country. They are profligate and luxurious ; but Bobadill is stained with no inordinate vice, and is besides so frugal, that "a bunch of radishes, and a pipe to close the orifice of his stomach," satisfy all his wants. Add to this, that the vanity of the ancient soldier is accompanied with such deplorable stupidity, that all temptation to mirth is taken away ; whereas Bobadill is really amusing. His gravity, which is of the most inflexible nature, contrasts admirably with the situations into which he is thrown ; and though

beaten, baffled, and disgraced, he never so far forgets himself as to aid in his own discomfiture. He has no soliloquies like Bessus and Parolles, to betray his real character, and expose himself to unnecessary contempt ; nor does he break through the decorum of the scene in a single instance. He is also an admirer of poetry, and seems to have a pretty taste for criticism, though his reading does not appear very extensive, and his decisions are usually made with somewhat too much promptitude. In a word, Bobadill has many distinguishing traits, and till a preceding braggart shall be discovered with something more than big words and beating to characterize him, it may not be amiss to allow Jonson the credit of having depended entirely on his own resources.

Knowell is a scholar and a gentleman ; his *humour* is an overstrained solicitude for the purity of his son's morals, amidst an indulgence of lighter foibles : he is an amiable and well-drawn character, and very artfully contrasted with the rude, but manly and consistent Downright.

Brainworm is evidently a favourite of the author ; he is sufficiently amusing, and his transformations contribute very naturally to the perplexity of the scene : he is most successful in the mendicant soldier, a character not uncommon in those days, either in the streets or on the stage.

The rest require little notice. The females, as is usually the case, occupy but a small part of the poet's care ; yet they are correctly drawn, and probably such as the family of a respectable merchant, in Jonson's time, would readily supply. Dame Kitely is a very natural character ; unsuspicious in herself, but, having her fears once awakened, credulous and violent in the extreme. Bridget is merely a sensible young woman ; not so vain of the attentions of her poetical lover, as not to sacrifice them to a more rational courtship ; won, as was then the case, with little wooing, and easily persuaded to follow her own inclinations. The two young gentlemen fill the parts allotted to them with perfect propriety, and play upon the vanity and imbecility of the other characters with very laughable effect : as for the two gulls, as they are called, they enhance and set off the absurdities of each other ; and, as natural deficiency cannot be supplied, are dismissed with a simple exposure, by way of punishment : indeed, nothing can be more admirable, or consonant with justice, than the winding up of this drama, and the various dispensations dealt out to the different characters. The unities of time and place are sufficiently preserved ; the action is confined to one neighbourhood, and occupies about eight hours, beginning at six and ending a little after two.

Every Man out of his Humour.

This "Comical Satire" was first acted in the year 1599, "by the Lord Chamberlain's servants," that is, by the Company who played at the Globe, on the Bank Side, and who, a few years afterwards, (in 1603,) obtained a licence from James, and in consequence of it, took the appellation of his Majesty's Servants. It was printed in quarto for Nicholas Linge, 1600, "as it was first composed," for several retrenchments had been made in it by the players; and from this edition the folio, 1616, was copied with very little variation. This Comedy, like the former, appears to have been acted by the whole strength of the house, with the exception of Shakspeare, who found perhaps no part in it suited to his "gentle conditions." Its merits are unquestionable; but I know not its success; nor whether it ever appeared on the modern stage. It was often played after the Restoration.

Jonson patched up a motto to it out of Horace, most of which is true, and all perhaps might have remained undisputed, had it been advanced by any one but the author.

Non aliena meo pressi pede—si propius stes,
Te capient magis—et decies repetita placebunt.

TO THE

NOBLEST NURSERIES OF HUMANITY AND LIBERTY IN
THE KINGDOM,

THE INNS OF COURT.[1]

"I understand you, Gentlemen, not your houses: and a worthy succession of you, to all time, as being born the judges of these studies. When I wrote this poem I had friendship with divers in your societies; who, as they were great names in learning, so they were no less examples of living. Of them, and then, that I say no more, it was not despised. Now that the printer, by a doubled charge, thinks it worthy a longer life than commonly the air of such things doth promise, I am careful to put it a servant to their pleasures, who are the inheritors of the first favour born it. Yet, I command it lie not in the way of your more noble and useful studies to the public: for so I shall suffer for it. But when the gown and cap is off, and the lord of liberty reigns,[2] then, to take it in your hands, perhaps may make some bencher, tincted with humanity, read and not repent him.

"By your True Honourer, BEN. JONSON."

---

[1] This elegant dedication was first published in the folio, 1616. The quarto has none.

[2] *And the lord of liberty reigns,*] He alludes to the custom of creating at Christmas, (the Saturnalia of the ancients), in the palace, the Inns of Court, and houses of the nobility, a *lord of misrule*, whose office it was to lead and regulate the revels presented at this season of festivity. His stately but transient sway is well described by Shirley:—

Gio. I have seen a counterfeit
With such a majesty compose himself,
And give his hand out to great lords to kiss

With as much grace, as all the royal blood
Had mustered in his veins.
Luc. Some monarch
Of *Inns o' Court* in England, sure: but when
His reign expires, and Christmas in the grave,
Cold as the turkies coffined up in crust,
That walk like ghosts, and glide to several tables,
When instruments are hoarse with sitting up,
When the gay triumph ceases, and the treasure
Divided, all the offices laid up,
And the new cloaths in lavender, what then!
The Sisters.

DRAMATIS PERSONÆ.

Asper, *the Presenter.*
Macilente.

Puntarvolo. {
His Lady.
Waiting Gent.
Huntsman.
Servingmen.
Dog and Cat.
}

Carlo Buffone.
Fastidious Brisk.   Cinedo, *his Page.*
Deliro.   { Fino, *their Servant.*
Fallace.   { *Musicians.*
Saviolina.

Sordido.   *His Hind.*
               { *Tailor.*
Fungoso.   { *Haberdasher.*
               { *Shoemaker.*

Sogliardo.
Shift.   *Rustics.*
Notary.

Clove.   { *A Groom.*
Orange.   { *Drawers.*
               { *Constable and Officers.*

Grex. { Cordatus.
    { Mitis.

THE CHARACTER OF THE PERSONS.

ASPER,

He is of an ingenious and free spirit, eager, and constant in reproof, without fear controlling the world's abuses.   One whom no servile hope of gain, or frosty apprehension of danger, can make to be a parasite, either to time, place, or opinion.

MACILENTE,

A man well parted,[1] a sufficient scholar, and travelled ; who, wanting that place in the world's account which he thinks his merit capable of, falls into such an envious apoplexy, with which his judgment is so dazzled and distasted, that he grows violently impatient of any opposite happiness in another.

PUNTARVOLO,

A vain-glorious knight, over-englishing his travels, and wholly consecrated to singularity ; the very Jacob's staff of compliment ;[2] a sir that hath lived to see the revolution of time in most of his apparel.   Of presence good enough, but so palpably affected to his own praise, that for want of flatterers he commends himself, to the floutage of his own family.   He deals upon returns,[3] and strange performances, resolving, in despite of public derision, to stick to his own particular fashion, phrase, and gesture.

CARLO BUFFONE,

A public, scurrilous, and prophane jester ; that more swift than Circe, with absurd similes will transform any person into deformity.   A good feast-hound, or banquet-beagle, that will scent you out a supper some three miles off, and swear to his patrons, damn him ! he came in oars, when he was but wafted over in a sculler.   A slave that hath an extraordinary gift in pleasing his palate, and will swill up more sack at a sitting than would make all the guard a posset.   His religion is railing, and his discourse ribaldry.   They stand highest in his respect whom he studies most to reproach.

---

[1] *A man well* parted,] A man endowed with good natural abilities. Jonson has the same expression in act iii. p. 193 *a.*
"Let him be poor and meanly clad,
Though ne'er so richly *parted,*" &c.

[2] *The very* Jacob's staff *of compliment* ;] The Jacob's staff here meant, is a mathematical instrument used by our ancestors for taking heights and distances.   It is now superseded by more accurate and efficient implements.   Jonson's application of the term is sufficiently obvious.
[3] *He deals upon* returns,] Ventures sent abroad, for the safe *return* of which he agrees by articles to receive so much money.—WHAL.

FASTIDIOUS BRISK,

A neat, spruce, affecting courtier, one that wears clothes well, and in fashion : practises by his glass how to salute ; speaks good remnants, notwithstanding the base viol and tobacco ; swears tersely, and with variety ; cares not what lady's favour he belies, or great man's familiarity : a good property to perfume the boot of a coach. He will borrow another man's horse to praise, and backs him as his own. Or, for a need, on foot can post himself into credit with his merchant, only with the gingle of his spur,[1] and the jerk of his wand.

DELIRO,

A good doting citizen, who, it is thought, might be of the Common Council for his wealth ; a fellow sincerely besotted on his own wife, and so rapt with a conceit of her perfections, that he simply holds himself unworthy of her. And, in that hood-winked humour, lives more like a suitor than a husband ; standing in as true dread of her displeasure, as when he first made love to her. He doth sacrifice two-pence in juniper to her every morning[2] before she rises, and wakes her with villainous out-of-tune music, which she out of her contempt (though not out of her judgment) is sure to dislike.

FALLACE,

Deliro's wife, and idol ; a proud, mincing peat, and as perverse as he is officious. She dotes as perfectly upon the courtier, as her husband doth on her, and only wants the face to be dishonest.

SAVIOLINA,

A court-lady, whose weightiest praise is a light wit, admired by herself, and one more, her servant Brisk.

SORDIDO,

A wretched hob-nailed chuff, whose recreation is reading of almanacks ; and felicity, foul weather. One that never prayed but for a lean dearth, and ever wept in a fat harvest.

FUNGOSO,

The son of Sordido, and a student ; one that has revelled in his time, and follows the fashion afar off, like a spy. He makes it the whole bent of his endeavours to wring sufficient means from his wretched father, to put him in the courtier's cut ; at which he earnestly aims, but so unluckily, that he still lights short a suit.

SOGLIARDO,

An essential clown, brother to Sordido, yet so enamoured of the name of a gentleman that he will have it, though he buys 'it. He comes up every term to learn to take tobacco, and see new motions.[3] He is in his kingdom when he can get himself into company where he may be well laughed at.

---

[1] *With the* gingle of his spur.] See act ii. sc. 1.

[2] *He doth sacrifice two-pence in* juniper *to her every morning*] To sweeten the room in which she is about to sit. Thus, in the *Mayor of Quinborough*:—

> " Then put fresh water into both the bough-pots,
> And *burn a little juniper* in the hall chimney." Act v. sc. 1.

And in *Cupid's Revenge :*—

> " *Burn a little juniper* in my murrin ; the maid made it her chamber-pot."—WHAL.

[3] *He comes up every* term *to learn to take tobacco, and see new* motions.] It appears from innumerable passages in our old writers, that the *law-terms* were the principal times for business and pleasure. The country gentlemen then flocked to London with their families, to settle their disputes, see plays and puppet shows (motions), and learn the fashions. It may seem strange to enumerate taking tobacco among the accomplishments to be acquired in town ; but it was then a matter of serious study, and had its professors, like the rest of the liberal arts.

SHIFT,

A thread-bare shark ; one that never was a soldier, yet lives upon lendings. His profession is skeldring and odling,[1] his bank Paul's, and his warehouse Picthatch.[2] Takes up single testons upon oaths, till doomsday. Falls under executions of three shillings, and enters into five-groat bonds. He waylays the reports of services,[3] and cons them without book, damning himself he came new from them, when all the while he was taking the diet in the bawdy-house, or lay pawned in his chamber for rent and victuals. He is of that admirable and happy memory, that he will salute one for an old acquaintance that he never saw in his life before. He usurps upon cheats, quarrels, and robberies, which he never did, only to get him a name. His chief exercises are, taking the whiff, squiring a cockatrice, and making privy searches for imparters.[4]

CLOVE AND ORANGE,

An inseparable case of coxcombs, city born ; the Gemini, or twins of foppery ; that like a pair of wooden foils, are fit for nothing but to be practised upon. Being well flattered they'll lend money, and repent when they have done. Their glory is to invite players, and make suppers. And in company of better rank, to avoid the suspect of insufficiency, will inforce their ignorance most desperately, to set upon the understanding of anything. Orange is the most humorous of the two (whose small portion of juice being squeezed out), Clove serves to stick him with commendations.

CORDATUS,

The author's friend ; a man inly acquainted with the scope and drift of his plot ; of a discrete and understanding judgment ; and has the place of a moderator.

MITIS,

Is a person of no action, and therefore we have reason to afford him no character.[5]

---

[1] *His profession is* skeldring *and* odling,] *Skeldring* was a cant term for impudent begging : it seems to be principally applied to those who, under false pretences of being wounded or disbanded soldiers, wandered about levying contributions on the public. Of *odling* I can say nothing with certainty, having never met with the word elsewhere : it seems, however, to mean, sliding and shifting about in quest of proper objects for preying upon.

[2] *His bank Paul's, and his warehouse Picthatch.*] Paul's church was the common resort of idlers at this time : here Cavalero Shift furnished himself, by skeldring and picking pockets, with the property which he afterwards disposed of among the prostitutes of Picthatch. See p. 6 *b*.

[3] *He way-lays the reports of* services, *&c.*] *Services*, in the military language of the time, were bold and daring actions. The word occurs in the same sense in Shakspeare, "Such fellows (as Pistol) are perfect in great commanders' names : and they will learn you by rote where *services* were done, &c.—*Hen. V.*, act iii. sc. 6. It is to something of this kind that Cob alludes, when he says that Bobadill promised to pay him his forty shillings at the next *action.* See p. 12 *a.*

[4] *His chief exercises are taking the* whiff, *squiring a* cockatrice, *and making privy searches for* imparters.] For taking the *whiff*, see act iii. sc. 1. *Cockatrice* is one of the thousand cant names for a strumpet : *squiring a cockatrice*, therefore, is officiating as bully to a brothel. *Imparters*, as the name signifies, were persons drawn in by artful pretences to part with their money to such impudent impostors as Shift. The word is often found in Jonson.

[5] The following notice is taken from the quarto : " It was not near his thought that hath published this, either to traduce the author ; or to make vulgar and cheap any of the peculiar and sufficient deserts of the actors ; but rather (whereas many censures flattered about it) to give all, leave and leisure to judge with distinction." This was undoubtedly written by Jonson. It is but common justice to add, that this descriptive list is drawn up with great spirit, elegance, and power of discrimination.

Every Man out-of his Humour.

The Stage.

After the second sounding.[1]

Enter Cordatus, Asper, *and* Mitis.[2]

Cor. Nay, my dear Asper.
Mit. Stay your mind.
Asp. Away!
Who is so patient[3] of this impious world,
That he can check his spirit, or rein his
    tongue?
Or who hath such a dead unfeeling sense,
That heaven's horrid thunders cannot wake?
To see the earth cracked with the weight of
    sin,
Hell gaping under us, and o'er our heads
Black, ravenous ruin, with her sail-stretched
    wings,[4]
Ready to sink us down, and cover us.
Who can behold such prodigies as these,
And have his lips sealed up? Not I: my
    soul
Was never ground into such oily colours,
To flatter vice, and daub iniquity:
But, with an armed and resolved hand,
I'll strip the ragged follies of the time
Naked as at their birth——
    Cor. Be not too bold.

Asp. You trouble me——and with a whip
    of steel,
Print wounding lashes in their iron ribs.
I fear no mood stamped in a private brow,
When I am pleased t'unmask a public vice.
I fear no strumpet's drugs, nor ruffian's
    stab,
Should I detect their hateful luxuries :
No broker's, usurer's, or lawyer's gripe,
Were I disposed to say, they are all corrupt.
I fear no courtier's frown, should I applaud
The easy flexure of his supple hams.
Tut, these are so innate and popular,
That drunken custom would not shame to
    laugh,
In scorn, at him, that should but dare to
    tax 'em :
And yet, not one of these, but knows his
    works,
Knows what damnation is, the devil, and
    hell ;
Yet hourly they persist, grow rank in sin,
Puffing their souls away in perjurous air,
To cherish their extortion, pride, or lusts.
    Mit. Forbear, good Asper ; be not like
    your name.
    Asp. O, but to such whose faces are all
    zeal,

---

[1] *After the second* sounding.] These several *soundings* are in the modern theatre termed first, second, and third music.—WHAL.
    When Whalley wrote this, the theatres opened at four o'clock ; since they adopted a later hour they have only given the public first and second music.
[2] *Enter* Asper, Mitis, *and* Cordatus.] The two latter of these Jonson calls the Grex, or Chorus. Like that of the Greeks, they remain on the stage during the whole of the action : but they perform a part not known to the ancient drama. They stand distinct from the scene, and occupy the place of critics. Under the name of Asper the poet intended to shadow out himself ; but he has afforded us no traces of Mitis and Cordatus.
[3] *Who is so patient, &c.*] This is from Juvenal :—
      " *Nam quis iniquæ*
Tam patiens urbis, tam ferreus, ut teneat se?"
[4] *Black, ravenous ruin, with her sail-stretched wings,*] There is a sublimity in this

and the preceding lines which shows us that Jonson could have reached a nobler flight in the greater kinds of poetry, had he not cramped his genius by confining it, in conformity to the prejudices of the age, to a model unworthy of himself, and even not agreeable to his own taste.—WHAL.
    Either Whalley has not expressed himself clearly, or I do not understand him. If by taste he means natural inclination, as he seems to do, he is evidently incorrect ; for Jonson was assuredly not led to Seneca (the model to whom he alludes) by " the prejudices of the age ;" but by choice, and a viciousness of judgment peculiar, at this period, to a few recluse scholars. After all, " sublimity" is not Jonson's element ; nor can his utmost effort support him in it long. Strong sense, keen satire, and a full vein of humour, less remarkable for elegance than vigour, are his distinguishing characteristics, and appear with unrivalled excellence in the piece before us. The " flights" of which Whalley speaks, have been attempted with more success by others.

And, with the words of Hercules, invade[1]
Such crimes as these ! that will not smell
  of sin,
But seem as they were made of sanctity !
Religion in their garments, and their hair
Cut shorter than their eyebrows ![2] when the
  conscience
Is vaster than the ocean, and devours
More wretches than the counters.
  Mit. Gentle Asper,
Contain your spirit in more stricter bounds,[3]
And be not thus transported with the
  violence
Of your strong thoughts.
  Cor. Unless your breath had power
To melt the world, and mould it new again,
It is in vain to spend it in these moods.
  Asp. [*turning to the stage.*] I not observed
  this thronged round till now !
Gracious and kind spectators, you are wel-
  come ;
Apollo and the Muses feast your eyes
With graceful objects, and may our Minerva
Answer your hopes, unto their largest
  strain !
Yet here mistake me not, judicious friends ;
I do not this, to beg your patience,
Or servilely to fawn on your applause,

Like some dry brain, despairing in his
  merit.
Let me be censured by the austerest brow,
Where I want art or judgment, tax me
  freely :
Let envious censors, with their broadest
  eyes,
Look through and through me, I pursue
  no favour ;
Only vouchsafe me your attentions,
And I will give you music worth your ears.
O, how I hate[4] the monstrousness of time,
Where every servile imitating spirit,
Plagued with an itching leprosy of wit,
In a mere halting fury, strives to fling
His ulcerous body in the Thespian spring,
And straight leaps forth a poet ! but as
  lame
As Vulcan, or the founder of Cripplegate.[5]
  Mit. In faith, this humour will come ill
  to some,
You will be thought to be too peremptory.
  Asp. This humour ? good ! and why this
  humour, Mitis ?
Nay, do not turn, but answer.
  Mit. Answer, what ?
  Asp. I will not stir your patience, pardon
  me,

---

[1] *And, with the* words of Hercules, *invade, &c.*] Among the ancients everything bold and undaunted was termed Herculean : thus Justin, in the preface to his *Epitome*, ascribes the intrepidity of Hercules to Trogus Pompeius : *Nonne nobis, Pompeius Herculea audacia orbem terrarum aggressus videri debet ?*—WHAL.

  Jonson, however, has taken the expression immediately from Juvenal :—

    " ——*sed pejores, qui talia* verbis
      Herculis invadunt.*"

[2]   —————— *and their hair*
Cut shorter than their eyebrows !] This too is from Juvenal, whose admirable description of the feigned Stoics Jonson evidently had in view in many parts of this dialogue. But the immediate objects of his satire, as Whalley justly observes, were the Puritans : thus, among other singularities, affected to cut their hair short, and close to their heads ; whence they had afterwards the appellation of *Roundheads.* This practice is alluded to in *Eastward Hoe*, where Wolf, describing the penitence of Quicksilver in the Counter, says, " He has *cut his hair* too ; he is so well given, and has such good gifts," act v.

[3] *Contain your spirit in* more stricter *bounds*,] This expression is blamed by Dryden, who thinks that few writers of his time would be guilty of it. This may be true ; but in Jonson's, and indeed every preceding age, nothing was more common than to join the signs of the comparative and superlative degrees to the degrees themselves. That it did not originate either in

negligence or ignorance may be learned from the poet, who thus speaks of it in his *Grammar*, a work of great skill and profundity of research :—

  " Furthermore, these adverbs *more* and *most* are added to the comparative and superlative degrees themselves, being after the positive. Thus Sir Thomas More, ' She saw the cardinal *more readier* to depart than the remnant ; for not only the high dignity of the civil magistrate, but the *most basest* handicraft are holy when they are directed to the honour of God.' And this is a certain kind of English atticism, or eloquent phrase of speech, imitating the manner of the *most* ancientest and finest Grecians, who for more emphasis and vehemency's sake, used so to speak."

[4] *How I hate, &c.*] Jonson began already to take a high tone :—but whatever may be thought of his confidence, it is impossible not to be pleased with the spirit of this nervous speech. It is altogether in the best manner of antiquity ; and, if it was spoken by Jonson, as is not very improbable, he might have informed the audience that they were unsuspectingly listening to the manly language of the Grecian stage.

[5] *Or the* founder of Cripplegate.] That *the founder of Cripplegate* was *lame*, must, if taken at all, be taken on the poet's word. Stow, somewhat better authority in a case of this nature, says, that it was so called from the number of lame persons who usually took their station there for the purpose of begging. The name (*Porta Contractorum*) is very ancient.

I urged it for some reasons, and the rather
To give these ignorant well-spoken days
Some taste of their abuse of this word
　　humour.
　　Cor. O, do not let your purpose fall,
　　　good Asper ;
It cannot but arrive most acceptable,
Chiefly to such as have the happiness
Daily to see how the poor innocent word
Is racked and tortured.
　　Mit. Ay, I pray you proceed.
　　Asp. Ha, what? what is't?
　　Cor. For the abuse of humour.
　　Asp. O, I crave pardon, I had lost my
　　　thoughts.
Why, humour, as 'tis *ens*, we thus define it,[1]
To be a quality of air, or water,
And in itself holds these two properties,
Moisture and fluxure : as, for demonstra-
　　tion,
Pour water on this floor, 'twill wet and run:
Likewise the air, forced through a horn or
　　trumpet,
Flows instantly away, and leaves behind
A kind of dew; and hence we do conclude,
That whatsoe'er hath fluxure and humidity,
As wanting power to contain itself,
Is humour. So in every human body,
The choler, melancholy, phlegm, and
　　blood,
By reason that they flow continually
In some one part, and are not continent,
Receive the name of humours. Now thus
　　far
It may, by metaphor, apply itself
Unto the general disposition :
As when some one peculiar quality
Doth so possess a man, that it doth draw
All his effects, his spirits, and his powers,
In their confluctions, all to run one way,
This may be truly said to be a humour.[2]
But that a rook, by wearing a pyed feather,
The cable hatband, or the three-piled ruff,
A yard of shoe-tye, or the Switzer's knot

On his French garters, should affect a
　　humour !
O, it is more than most ridiculous.
　　Cor. He speaks pure truth ; now if an
　　　ideot
Have but an apish or fantastic strain,
It is his humour.
　　Asp. Well, I will scourge those apes,
And to these courteous eyes oppose a
　　mirror,
As large as is the stage whereon we act ;
Where they shall see the time's deformity
Anatomized in every nerve and sinew,
With constant courage, and contempt of
　　fear.
　　Mit. Asper, (I urge it as your friend,)
　　　take heed,
The days are dangerous, full of exception,
And men are grown impatient of reproof.
　　Asp. Ha, ha !
You might as well have told me, yond' is
　　heaven,
This earth, these men, and all had moved
　　alike.—
Do not I know the time's condition ?[3]
Yes, Mitis, and their souls ; and who they
　　be
That either will or can except against me.
None but a sort of fools, so sick in taste,
That they contemn all physic of the mind,
And, like galled camels, kick at every touch.
Good men, and virtuous spirits, that loathe
　　their vices,
Will cherish my free labours, love my lines,
And with the fervor of their shining grace
Make my brain fruitful, to bring forth more
　　objects,
Worthy their serious and intentive eyes.
But why enforce I this? as fainting? no.
If any here chance to behold himself,
Let him not dare to challenge me of wrong;
For, if he shame to have his follies known,
First he should shame to act 'em : my strict
　　hand

---

[1] *As 'tis* ens, *we thus define it,*] *Ens* is a
term of the schools, and signifies a substance or
existence.—WHAL.
　　[2] *This may be truly said to be a* humour.]
What was usually called the *manners* in a play
or poem, began now to be called the *humours.*
The word was new : the use, or rather abuse of
it, was excessive. It was applied upon all occasions with as little judgment as wit. Every coxcomb had it always in his mouth ; and every
particularity he affected was denominated by
the name of *humour.* To redress this extravagance Jonson is exact in describing the true
meaning and proper application of the term. It
hath been observed that the word, in the sense
which he assigns it, is peculiar to our English

language ; but the quality intended by it is not
peculiar to the people. Our poet's great excellence was the lively copying of these humorous
characters.—WHAL.
　　The abuse of this word is well ridiculed by
Shakspeare in that amusing creature of whimsy,
Nym, *Merry Wives of Windsor.* Steevens
quotes a long epigram by way of illustrating the
subject, without remarking that it is a mere
copy, and, indeed, a very feeble one, of this
acute and pertinent disquisition. But Steevens
knew little of Jonson.
　　[3] *Do not I know the time's* condition ?] i.e.,
the temper, quality, or disposition of the times.
In this sense the word is used by Shakspeare and
all our old writers.

Was made to seize on vice, and with a gripe
Squeeze out the humour of such spongy
    souls,
As lick up every idle vanity.
  Cor. Why, this is right *furor poeticus!*
Kind gentlemen, we hope your patience
Will yet conceive the best, or entertain
This supposition, that a madman speaks.
  Asp. What, are you ready there? Mitis,
    sit down,
And my Cordatus. Sound ho! and begin.
I leave you two, as censors, to sit here:
Observe what I present, and liberally
Speak your opinions upon every scene,
As it shall pass the view of these spec-
    tators.
Nay, now y' are tedious, sirs; for shame
    begin.
And, Mitis, note me; if in all this front
You can espy a gallant of this mark,
Who, to be thought one of the judicious,
Sits with his arms thus[1] wreathed, his hat
    pulled here,
Cries mew, and nods, then shakes his
    empty head,
Will shew more several motions in his face
Than the new London, Rome, or Niniveh,[2]
And, now and then, breaks a dry biscuit
    jest,
Which, that it may more easily be chewed,
He steeps in his own laughter.
  Cor. Why, will that
Make it be sooner swallowed?
  Asp. O, assure you,
Or if it did not, yet, as Horace sings,[3]
Mean ca'es are welcome still to hungry
    guests.
  Cor. 'Tis true; but why should we
    observe them, Asper?

  Asp. O, I would know 'em; for in such
    assemblies
They are more infectious than the pes-
    tilence:
And therefore I would give them pills to
    purge,
And make them fit for fair societies.
How monstrous and detested is't to see
A fellow, that has neither art nor brain,
Sit like an Aristarchus, or stark ass,[4]
Taking men's lines, with a tobacco face,
In snuff, still spitting, using his wry'd
    looks,
In nature of a vice, to wrest and turn
The good aspect of those that shall sit
    near him,
From what they do behold! O, 'tis most
    vile.
  Mit. Nay, Asper.
  Asp. Peace, Mitis, I do know your
    thought;
You'll say, your guests here will except at
    this:
Pish! you are too timorous, and full of
    doubt.
Then he, a patient, shall reject all physick,
'Cause the physician tells him, you are
    sick:
Or, if I say, that he is vicious,
You will not hear of virtue. Come, you
    are fond.[5]
Shall I be so extravagant, to think,
That happy judgments, and composed
    spirits,
Will challenge me for taxing such as these?
I am ashamed.
  Cor. Nay, but good, pardon us;
We must not bear this peremptory sail,
But use our best endeavours how to please.

---

[1] *Sits with his arms, &c.*] These "marks of
the judicious" were very prevalent, and are
noticed as such by all the writers of Jonson's
time. Thus Shakspeare: "Your hat, penthouse like, o'er the shop of your eyes; with
your arms crossed on your thin belly doublet,
like a rabbit on a spit."—*Love's Labour Lost.*
And Shirley: "I do not despair, gentlemen;
you see I do not wear my hat in my eyes, cru-
cify my arms," &c.—*Bird in a Cage.* With
respect to *crying mew*, it appears to have been
an old and approved method of expressing dislike at the first representation of a play. Decker
has many allusions to the practice; and, what
appears somewhat strange, in his *Satiromastix*,
charges Jonson with *mewing* at the fate of his
own works. "When your plays are misliked at
court you shall not cry *mew*, like a puss, and say
you are glad you write out of the courtiers'
element," act v. Our gallery critics, perhaps,
will be pleased and proud to hear that their formidable cat-calls have so remote an origin.

[2] *Than the new* London, Rome, *or* Niniveh,]
Puppet-shews, or, as they were then styled,
motions, at that time in great vogue.—WHAL.

[3] *Jejunus raro stomachus vulgaria temnit.*—
JONSON.

[4] *Sit like an* Aristarchus, *or* stark ass, &c.]
This string of "clenches," Dryden flings in
Jonson's face with somewhat more justice than
the false grammar just above. Very little, indeed, can be said in their favour, and yet it
might be wished that Dryden had found a more
legitimate cause than spite for producing them.

[5] *Come, you are* fond.] You are foolish, simple,
injudicious. In this sense *fond* is used by our
earliest writers. Thus Chaucer:—

  "The riche man ful *fond* is, iwis,
    That weneth that he loved is."
        Rom. of the Rose, v. 5367.

  And so it is found in Spenser, Shakspeare, and
almost every dramatist and poet of this age.—
WHAL.

Asp. Why, therein I commend your careful thoughts,
And I will mix with you in industry
To please : but whom ? attentive auditors,
Such as will join their profit with their pleasure,
And come to feed their understanding parts :
For these I'll prodigally spend myself,
And speak away my spirit into air ;
For these I'll melt my brain into invention,
Coin new conceits, and hang my richest words
As polished jewels in their bounteous ears.[1]
But stay, I lose myself, and wrong their patience ;
If I dwell here they'll not begin, I see.
Friends, sit you still, and entertain this troop
With some familiar and by-conference,
I'll haste them sound. Now, gentlemen, I go
To turn an actor and a humorist,
Where, ere I do resume my present person,
We hope to make the circles of your eyes
Flow with distilled laughter : if we fail,
We must impute it to this only chance,
Art hath an enemy called ignorance.[2]
　　　　　　　　　　　　　　　[Exit.

Cor. How do you like his spirit, Mitis ?
Mit. I should like it much better, if he were less confident.
Cor. Why, do you suspect his merit ?
Mit. No ; but I fear this will procure him much envy.
Cor. O, that sets the stronger seal on his desert : if he had no enemies, I should esteem his fortunes most wretched at this instant.

Mit. You have seen his play, Cordatus : pray you, how is it ?
Cor. Faith, sir, I must refrain to judge ; only this I can say of it, 'tis strange, and of a particular kind by itself, somewhat like *Vetus Comœdia;* a work that hath bounteously pleased me ; how it will answer the general expectation, I know not.
Mit. Does he observe all the laws of comedy in it?
Cor. What laws mean you?
Mit. Why, the equal division of it into acts and scenes, according to the Terentian manner ; his true number of actors ; the furnishing of the scene with Grex or Chorus, and that the whole argument fall within compass of a day's business.
Cor. O no, these are too nice observations.
Mit. They are such as must be received by your favour, or it cannot be authentic.
Cor. Troth, I can discern no such necessity.
Mit. No!
Cor. No, I assure you, signior.[3] If those laws you speak of had been delivered us *ab initio,* and in their present virtue and perfection, there had been some reason of obeying their powers ; but 'tis extant, that that which we call *Comœdia,* was at first nothing but a simple and continued song, sung by one only person, till Susario invented a second ; after him, Epicharmus a third ; Phormus[4] and Chionides devised to have four actors, with a prologue and chorus ; to which Cratinus, long after, added a fifth and sixth : Eupolis, more ; Aristophanes, more than they ; every man in the dignity

---

[1] —— *hang my richest words*
As polished jewels in their bounteous ears.] The comparison alludes to the custom then in vogue, of men wearing rings and jewels in their ears. So Marston : "Give me those *jewels of your ears,* to receive my inforced duty."—*Malecontent,* act i. sc. 6.
And Beaumont and Fletcher :—
　　" Prithee, tell me,
Where hadst thou that same *jewel in thine ear ?*"—*King and no King,* act i.—WHAL.

[2] *Art hath an enemy, &c.*] Alluding to the old proverb, *Ars non habet inimicum nisi ignorantem.* Though this may be true, it would come with more propriety from the spectator than the actor ; but Jonson knew little of the golden curb which discretion hangs on self-opinion.

[3] Cor. *No, I assure you, signor, &c.*] I have already observed that the author has afforded no

hints to enable us to guess at the person of his friend Cordatus ; he has, however, supplied him with a considerable degree of accuracy and learning ; and I suspect that few, either on or off the stage, could have furnished, in those days, a better epitome of dramatic history than is here put into his mouth. It must, however, have been caviare to the general. The scholar knows that the first part of this narrative admits of some dispute ; a note, however, is not the place to treat of a question which occupies a considerable portion of the profound and acute *Dissertation upon Phalaris,* by the great Bentley.

[4] Upton supposes that Jonson wrote *Phormus* from a "lapse of memory," and therefore tells us to correct the text into *Phormis* ; but there is no need : Jonson had a better memory than his critic. He well recollected the spelling of Athenæus and Suidas, in whom, particularly in the former, he found most of what he here delivers.

of his spirit and judgment supplied something. And, though that in him this kind of poem appeared absolute, and fully perfected, yet how is the face of it changed since, in Menander, Philemon, Cecilius, Plautus, and the rest! who have utterly excluded the chorus, altered the property of the persons, their names, and natures, and augmented it with all liberty, according to the elegancy and disposition of those times wherein they wrote. I see not then, but we should enjoy the same licence, or free power to illustrate and heighten our invention, as they did; and not be tied to those strict and regular forms which the niceness of a few, who are nothing but form, would thrust upon us.

Mit. Well, we will not dispute of this now: but what's his scene?

Cor. Marry, *Insula Fortunata*, sir.

Mit. O, the Fortunate Island: mass, he has bound himself to a strict law there.

Cor. Why so?

Mit. He cannot lightly alter the scene, without crossing the seas.

Cor. He needs not, having a whole island to run through, I think.

Mit. No! how comes it then,[1] that in some one play we see so many seas, countries, and kingdoms, passed over with such admirable dexterity?

Cor. O, that but shows how well the authors can travel in their vocation, and outrun the apprehension of their auditory. But leaving this, I would they would begin once: this protraction is able to sour the best-settled patience in the theatre.

[*The third sounding.*

Mit. They have answered your wish, sir; they sound.

Cor. O, here comes the Prologue.

Enter Prologue.

Now, sir, if you had staid a little longer, I meant to have spoke your prologue for you, i' faith.

Prol. Marry, with all my heart, sir, you shall do it yet, and I thank you.   [*Going.*

Cor. Nay, nay, stay, stay; hear you?

Prol. You could not have studied to have done me a greater benefit at the instant; for I protest to you, I am unperfect, and, had I spoke it, I must of necessity have been out.

Cor. Why, but do you speak this seriously?

Prol. Seriously! ay, wit's my help, do I; and esteem myself indebted to your kindness for it.

Cor. For what?

Prol. Why, for undertaking the prologue for me.

Cor. How! did I undertake it for you?

Prol. Did you! I appeal to all these gentlemen, whether you did or no. Come, come, it pleases you to cast a strange look on't now;· but 'twill not serve.

Cor. 'Fore me, but it must serve; and therefore speak your prologue.

Prol. An I do, let me die poisoned with some venomous hiss, and never live to look as high as the two-penny room again?[2]

[*Exit.*

Mit. He has put you to it, sir.

Cor. 'Sdeath, what a humorous fellow is this! Gentlemen, good faith I can speak no prologue, howsoever his weak wit has had the fortune to make this strong use of me here before you: but I protest——

Enter Carlo Buffone, *followed by a* Boy *with wine.*

Car. Come, come, leave these fustian protestations; away, come, I cannot abide these gray-headed ceremonies. Boy, fetch me a glass quickly, I may bid these gentlemen welcome; give them a health here. [*Exit* Boy.] I marle whose wit it was to put a prologue in yond' sackbut's mouth; they might well think he'd be out of tune, and yet you'd play upon him too.

Cor. Hang him, dull block!

---

[1] Mit. *No! how comes it then, &c.*] Against this passage, Theobald has written in the margin of his copy, *a fiurt on Shakspeare.* This jealousy of our great poet, commenced under such respectable auspices, has since become epidemical, and infected almost all his critics. The charge, in the present case, is too absurd for serious notice, or indeed for any notice at all.

[2] *And never live to look as high as the* two-penny room *again.*] The cost of admission to the theatres (such of them, at least, as many of our early dramas were exhibited in) was at this time very moderate. The price of the "best rooms," or boxes, was a shilling; of the lowest places, two-pence; and, as Whalley says, in some play-houses, only a penny. The *two-penny room* mentioned above was the gallery. Thus Decker: "Pay your two-pence to a player, and you may sit in the *gallery*."—*Belman's Night Walk.* And Middleton: "One of them is a nip; I took him once in the *two-penny gallery*, at the Fortune." The place, however, seems to have been very discreditable, for it is commonly described as the resort of pickpockets and prostitutes.

Car. O, good words, good words; a well-timbered fellow, he would have made a good column, an he had been thought on, when the house was a building—

Re-enter Boy, *with glasses.*

O, art thou come? Well said; give me, boy; fill, so! Here's a cup of wine sparkles like a diamond. Gentlewomen (I am sworn to put them in first) and gentlemen, around, in place of a bad prologue, I drink this good draught to your health here, Canary, the very elixir and spirit of wine. [*Drinks.*] This is that our poet calls Castalian liquor,[1] when he comes abroad now and then, once in a fortnight, and makes a good meal among players, where he has *caninum appetitum;* marry, at home he keeps a good philosophical diet, beans and buttermilk; an honest pure rogue, he will take you off three, four, five of these, one after another, and look villainously when he has done, like a one-headed Cerberus.—He does not hear me, I hope.—And then, when his belly is well ballaced, and his brain rigged a little, he sails away withal, as though he would work wonders when he comes home. He has made a play here, and he calls it, *Every Man out of his Humour:* but an he get me out of the humour he has put me in, I'll trust none of his tribe again while I live. Gentles, all I can say for him is, you are welcome. I could wish my bottle here amongst you; but there's an old rule, *No pledging your own health.* Marry, if any here be thirsty for it, their best way (that I know) is, sit still, seal up their lips, and drink so much of the play in at their ears.   [*Exit.*
Mit. What may this fellow be, Cordatus?
Cor. Faith, if the time will suffer his description, I'll give it you.[2] He is one,

the author calls him Carlo Buffone, an impudent common jester, a violent railer, and an incomprehensible epicure; one whose company is desired of all men, but beloved of none; he will sooner lose his soul than a jest, and profane even the most holy things, to excite laughter; no honourable or reverend personage whatsoever can come within the reach of his eye, but is turned into all manner of variety, by his adulterate similes.
Mit. You paint forth a monster.
Cor. He will prefer all countries before his native, and thinks he can never sufficiently, or with admiration enough, deliver his affectionate conceit of foreign atheistical policies. But stay—

Enter Macilente.

Observe these: he'll appear himself anon.
Mit. O, this is your envious man, Macilente, I think.
Cor. The same, sir.

ACT I.

SCENE I.—*The Country.*

Enter Macilente, *with a book.*

Maci. Viri est, fortunæ cæcitatem facilè ferre.
'Tis true; but, Stoic, where, in the vast world,
Doth that man breathe, that can so much command
His blood and his affection? Well, I see
I strive in vain to cure my wounded soul;
For every cordial that my thoughts apply
Turns to a corsive, and doth eat it farther.
There is no taste in this philosophy;
'Tis like a potion that a man should drink,
But turns his stomach with the sight of it.
I am no such pilled Cynick to believe,

---

[1] *This* (Canary) *is that our poet calls Castalian liquor,* &c.] The poet, the critics say, here draws his own picture. Not so:—the *picture* is drawn by a licentious buffoon, against whom he takes all possible care to guard the reader. He describes him as "a scurrilous jester, that, more swiftly than Circe, will *transform any person into deformity:*" and in the speech which follows, he anxiously repeats his caution against giving any credit to his "adulterate" ribaldry. He could do no more; yet Aubrey and others perversely take it all for truth, and form their character of Jonson from what is expressly given as a malicious jest!
[2] *Cor. Faith, if the time will suffer his*

description, I'll give it you. He is one, &c.] Jonson seems unwilling to part with Carlo Buffone: he had already described him with great strength of colouring, and he now delays the opening of the drama, already too long protracted, while he darkens his character with additional shades. Whalley says that he should almost incline to think, notwithstanding the poet's asseverations, that he had some particular person in view, especially as Decker, in his *Satiromastix*, makes Jonson forswear "flinging epigrams about in taverns, under pain of being placed at the upper end of the table, at the left hand of Carlo Buffone."—See act v.

That beggary is the only happiness;
Or, with a number of these patient fools,
To sing: *My mind to me a kingdom is*,[1]
When the lank hungry belly barks for food.
I look into the world, and there I meet
With objects, that do strike my blood-shot
          eyes
Into my brain : where, when I view myself,
Having before observed this man is great,
Mighty, and feared ; that loved, and highly
          favoured ;
A third thought wise and learned ; a fourth
          rich,
And therefore honoured ; a fifth rarely
          featured ;
A sixth admired for his nuptial fortunes :
When I see these, I say, and view myself,
I wish the organs of my sight were cracked ;
And that the engine of my grief could cast
Mine eyeballs, like two globes of wildfire,
          forth,
To melt this unproportioned frame of
          nature.
Oh, they are thoughts that have transfixed
          my heart,
And often, in the strength of apprehension,
Made my cold passion stand upon my face,
Like drops of dew on a stiff cake of ice.

[*Cor.* This alludes well to that of the poet,
    Invidus suspirat, gemit, incutitque
          dentes,
    Sudat frigidus, intuens quod odit.
Mit. O, peace, you break the scene.]

Enter Sogliardo *and* Carlo Buffone.

Maci. Soft, who be these ?
I'll lay me down awhile till they be past.
          [*Lies down.*

[*Cor.* Signior, note this gallant, I pray
you.
Mit. What is he ?
Cor. A tame rook, you'll take him presently ; list.]

Sog. Nay, look you, Carlo ; this is my
humour now ! I have land and money,

my friends left me well, and I will be a
gentleman whatsoever it cost me.
Car. A most gentlemanlike resolution.
Sog. Tut ! an I take an humour of a
thing once, I am like your tailor's needle,
I go through : but, for my name, signior,
how think you ? will it not serve for a gentleman's name, when the signior is put to
it, ha ?
Car. Let me hear ; how is it ?
Sog. Signior Insulso[2] Sogliardo : methinks it sounds well.
Car. O excellent ! tut ! an all fitted to
your name, you might very well stand for
a gentleman : I know many Sogliardos
gentlemen.
Sog. Why, and for my wealth I might
be a justice of peace.
Car. Ay, and a constable for your wit.
Sog. All this is my lordship you see here,
and those farms you came by.
Car. Good steps to gentility too, marry;
but, Sogliardo, if you affect to be a gentleman indeed, you must observe all the rare
qualities, humours, and compliments[3] of a
gentleman.
Sog. I know it, signior, and if you please
to instruct, I am not too good to learn, I'll
assure you.
Car. Enough, sir.—I'll make admirable
use in the projection of my medicine upon
this lump of copper here. [*Aside.*] I'll
bethink me for you, sir.
Sog. Signior, I will both pay you, and
pray you, and thank you, and think on you.

[*Cor.* Is this not purely good ?]

Maci. 'Sblood, why should such a prick-
eared hind as this
Be rich, ha ? a fool ! such a transparent
          gull
That may be seen through ! wherefore
          should he have land,
Houses, and lordships ? O, I could eat
          my entrails,
And sink my soul into the earth with sorrow.
Car. First, to be an accomplished gen-
tleman, that is, a gentleman of the time,

[1] *My mind to me a kingdom is*,] Words of
an old ballad, the thought from Seneca.—WHAL.
Whalley alludes, I suppose, to this verse in
the *Thyestes*,
    "*Mens regnum bona possidet.*"
[2] Sog. *Signior Insulso Sogliardo:*] There
are several allusions in the instructions which
Carlo gives Sogliardo for becoming a gentleman,
to one of the Colloquies of Erasmus. The following is pointed out by Whalley: *Restat cog-*
*nomen. Hic illud imprimis cavendum, ne
plebeio more te patiaris vocari Harpalum
Comensem; sed Harpalum à Como: hoc enim
nobilium est.* 'Ιππευς ανιππος, *sive Ementita
Nobilitas.*
[3] Compliments *of a gentleman.*] This word,
in Jonson's age, had the sense which we now
give to *accomplishments.* Thus, in *Sir Giles
Goosecap*, 1606: "Adorned with the exactest
complements belonging to nobleness.*"

you must give over housekeeping in the country,[1] and live altogether in the city amongst gallants; where, at your first appearance, 'twere good you turned four or five hundred acres of your best land into two or three trunks of apparel—you may do it without going to a conjuror—and be sure you mix yourself still with such as flourish in the spring of the fashion, and are least popular:[2] study their carriage and behaviour in all; learn to play at primero and passage,[3] and ever (when you lose) have two or three peculiar oaths to swear by, that no man else swears: but, above all, protest in your play, and affirm, *Upon your credit, As you are a true gentleman*, at every cast; you may do it with a safe conscience, I warrant you.

Sog. O admirable rare! he cannot choose but be a gentleman that has these excellent gifts: more, more, I beseech you.

Car. You must endeavour to feed cleanly at your ordinary, sit melancholy, and pick your teeth when you cannot speak: and when you come to plays, be humorous, look with a good starched face, and ruffle your brow like a new boot, laugh at nothing but your own jests, or else as the noblemen laugh. That's a special grace, you must observe.

Sog. I warrant you, sir.

Car. Ay, and sit on the stage and flout, provided you have a good suit.

Sog. O, I'll have a suit only for that, sir.

Car. You must talk much of your kindred and allies.

Sog. Lies! no, signior, I shall not need to do so, I have kindred in the city to talk of: I have a niece is a merchant's wife; and a nephew, my brother Sordido's son, of the Inns of Court.

Car. O, but you must pretend alliance with courtiers and great persons: and ever when you are to dine or sup in any strange presence, hire a fellow with a great chain,[4] (though it be copper, it's no matter,) to bring you letters, feigned from such a nobleman, or such a knight,[5] or such a lady, *To their worshipful, right rare, and nobly qualified friend and kinsman, Signior Insulso Sogliardo:* give yourself style enough. And there, while you intend circumstances of news, or enquiry of their health, or so, one of your familiars, whom you must carry about you still, breaks it up, as 'twere in a jest, and reads it publicly at the table: at which you must seem to take as unpardonable offence, as if he had torn your mistress's colours, or breathed upon her picture,[6] and pursue it with that

---

[1] *You must give over housekeeping in the country*, &c.] *Primum fac procul te abducas a patria.—Ingere te in convictum juvenum vere nobilium. Eras.* 'Ιππ. αντπ.

[2] *Least* popular:] Least vulgar; most removed from the common people.—WHAL.

Much of what follows may be found, in fuller detail, in that most curious pamphlet of Decker, the *Gull's Hornbook,* printed a few years after this play. All the advantages of precision, vigour, and elegance are on the side of Jonson; his old antagonist, however, is extremely interesting and amusing.

[3] *Learn to play at* primero *and* passage,] Primero was a game on the cards, once very fashionable. It is not, however, described in the *Compleat Gamester,* and the explanation of it, in *Minsheu's Dictionary* (like many others of his) explains nothing. From a very long epigram in *Dodsley's Old Plays,* vol. i. p. 168, it may be collected that it was a very complicated amusement. Passage is a game at dice, which some perhaps may comprehend by the following description: "It is played at but by two, and it is performed with three dice. The *caster* throws continually till he hath thrown doublets under ten, and then he is out and loseth; or doublets above ten, and then he *passeth,* and wins.—*Comp. Gam.* p. 167.

[4] *Hire a fellow with a* great chain, &c.] The stewards and chief gentlemen of great families, were accustomed at this period to wear chains

about their necks, as badges of distinction: they were commonly of silver, or silver gilt; though mention is sometimes made of gold ones. Thus Middleton, "Run, sirrah, call in my chief gentleman in the chain of gold, expedite."—*A Mad World my Masters.*—WHAL.

[5] *To bring you letters, feigned from such a nobleman, or such a knight, &c.*] From Erasmus: *Fingito literas a magnatibus ad te missas, in quibus identidem appelleris, Eques Clarissimus — Curabis ut hujusmodi literæ tibi velut elapsæ, aut per oblivionem relictæ veniant aliorum manus.—Idem.*

[6] *As if he had* torn your mistress's colours, *or* breathed *upon her picture.*] For *colours,* see *Cynthia's Revels.* On the next passage, Whalley says, "*Breathed* has here the same meaning as Shakspeare (he means, his commentator,) has assigned it in *Henry IV.*" "And when you *breathe* in your watering, they cry, Hem! and bid you play it off."—1st part, act ii. sc. 4. And Theobald, in the margin of his copy, is yet more offensive. I should not notice this folly, were it not for the opportunity which it gives me, of relieving Shakspeare from some of the filth heaped upon him by his critics. By *breathing in his watering,* he meant neither more nor less than *taking breath in his draught,* as cattle sometimes do: a breach of good manners noticed by our old writers.

And this Steevens (to say nothing of the rest) might have concluded, if he had not been pos-

hot grace, as if you would advance a challenge upon it presently.

Sog. Stay, I do not like that humour of challenge, it may be accepted; but I'll tell you what's my humour now, I will do this: I will take occasion of sending one of my suits to the tailor's,[1] to have the pocket repaired, or so; and there such a letter as you talk of, broke open and all, shall be left: O, the tailor will presently give out what I am, upon the reading of it, worth twenty of your gallants.

Car. But then you must put on an extreme face of discontentment at your man's negligence.

Sog. O, so I will, and beat him too: I'll have a man for the purpose.

Mac. You may; you have land and crowns: O partial fate!

Car. Mass, well remembered, you must keep your men gallant at the first, fine pied liveries laid with good gold lace; there's no loss in it, they may rip it off and pawn it, when they lack victuals.

Sog. By 'r lady, that is chargeable, signior, 'twill bring a man in debt.

Car. Debt I why that's the more for your credit, sir: it's an excellent policy to owe much in these days, if you note it.[2]

Sog. As how, good signior? I would fain be a politician.

Car. O I look where you are indebted any great sum, your creditor observes you with no less regard, than if he were bound to you for some huge benefit, and will quake to give you the least cause of offence; lest he lose his money. I assure you, in these times, no man· has his servant more obsequious and pliant, than gentlemen their creditors: to whom, if at any time you pay but a moiety, or a fourth part, it comes more acceptably than if you gave them a new-year's gift.

Sog. I perceive you, sir: I will take up,[3] and bring myself in credit, sure.

Car. Marry this, always beware you commerce not with bankrupts, or poor needy Ludgathians:[4] they are impudent creatures, turbulent spirits, they care not what violent tragedies they stir, nor how they play fast and loose with a poor gentleman's fortunes, to get their own. Marry, these rich fellows, that have the world, or the better part of it, sleeping in their counting houses, they are ten times more placable, they; either fear, hope, or modesty restrains them from offering any outrages: but this is nothing to your followers, you shall not

---

sessed with the spirit of impurity, from the very passage adduced below: but the pleasure of alluding to a beastly line in the *School of Salerno* was not to be resisted.

> " We also do enact
> That all hold up their heads, and laugh aloud,
> *Drink much at one draught, breathe not in*
> *their drink;*
> That none go out to ———"—MS. *Timon of Athens.*

Can anything be clearer? and yet Shakspeare and his readers are still insulted with the vices of drunken porters.

To *breathe* upon, in the text, means either to sully or to speak dispraisingly of.—The picture was a miniature, which lovers sometimes wore with their mistress's colours, on their arms and breasts.

[1] *I will take occasion of sending one of my suits to the tailor's. &c.*] *Interdum insue vesti, aut relinque in crumena, ut quibus sarciendi negotium dederis illic reperiant. Illi non silebunt, et tu, simul ac resciveris, compones vultum ad iracundiam ac mæstitiam, quasi doleat casus.—Eras. Id.*

[2] *It's an excellent policy to owe much in these days, if you note it.*] This and much of what follows is from Panurge's panegyric on debtors. Jonson was a diligent reader of Rabelais, and has numberless allusions to him. In this place, however, Erasmus had been before him: *Nulla est commodior ad regnum via quam deberi*

quamplurimis: primum creditor observat te non aliter quam obligatus magno beneficio vereturque ne quam præbeat ansam amittendæ pecuniæ: Servos nemo magis habet obnoxios, quam debitor suos creditores; quibus si quid aliquando reddas, gratius est quam si dono des.—Idem.

[3] *I will take* up,] That is, goods on credit. The phrase is common in the writers of those times. So Falstaff: " If a gentleman would be thorough with 'em, in *honest taking up,* they stand upon security."

Again, in Donne,

> " There's now as great an itch of bravery,
> And heat of *taking up.*"—*Elegy* xvi. WHAL.

[4] *Always beware you commerce not with bankrupts, or poor needy* Ludgathians, *&c.*] I know not how this reflection on the poverty of the tradesmen of Ludgate crept in here; they were surely among the wealthiest of our author's time. The thought itself, though obvious enough, is from Erasmus: *Caveto, ne cum tenuibus habeas commercium; nam hi ob parvulam summulam ingentes excitant tragædias. Placabiliores sunt, quibus lautior est fortuna; cohibet illos pudor, lactat spes, deterret metus.—Idem.*

Our old writers sometimes use Ludgate for the prison there. Jonson could scarcely mean people imprisoned for debt by Ludgathians; for Sogliardo needed no caution on that head.

run a penny more in arrearage for them, an you list, yourself.

Sog. No! how should I keep 'em then?

Car. Keep 'em ! 'sblood, let them keep themselves, they are no sheep, are they? what ! you shall come in houses, where plate, apparel, jewels, and divers other pretty commodities lie negligently scattered, and I would have those Mercuries follow me, I trow, should remember they had not their fingers for nothing.[1]

Sog. That's not so good, methinks.

Car. Why, after you have kept them a fortnight, or so, and shewed them enough to the world, you may turn them away, and keep no more but a boy, it's enough.

Sog. Nay, my humour is not for boys, I'll keep men, an I keep any; and I'll give coats, that's my humour : but I lack a cullisen.[2]

Car. Why, now you ride to the city, you may buy one; I'll bring you where you shall have your choice for money.

Sog. Can you, sir?

Car. O, ay : you shall have one take measure of you, and make you a coat of arms to fit you, of what fashion you will.

Sog. By word of mouth, I thank you, signior : I'll be once a little prodigal in a humour, i' faith, and have a most prodigious coat.

Mac. Torment and death ! break head and brain at once,
To be delivered of your fighting issue.
Who can indure to see blind fortune dote thus?

To be enamoured on this dusty turf,
This clod, a whoreson puck-fist ![3] O God !
I could run wild with grief now, to behold
The rankness of her bounties, that doth breed
Such bulrushes ; these mushroom gentlemen,
That shoot up in a night to place and worship.

Car. [*seeing* Macilente.] Let him alone ; some stray, some stray.

Sog. Nay, I will examine him before I go, sure.

Car. The lord of the soil has all wefts and strays here, has he not?

Sog. Yes, sir.

Car. Faith then, I pity the poor fellow, he's fallen into a fool's hands.   [*Aside.*

Sog. Sirrah, who gave you a commission to lie in my lordship?

Mac. Your lordship !

Sog. How ! my lordship ? do you know me, sir ?

Mac. I do know you, sir.

Car. He answers him like an echo.
                [*Aside.*

Sog. Why, who am I, sir?

Mac. One of those that fortune favours.

Car. The periphrasis of a fool.[4]   I'll observe this better.   [*Aside.*

Sog. That fortune favours ! how mean you that, friend ?

Mac. I mean simply : that you are one that lives not by your wits.

Sog. By my wits ! no, sir, I scorn to live by my wits, I. I have better means, I tell thee, than to take such base courses as to

---

[1] *I would have those Mercuries follow me, I trow, should remember they had not their fingers for nothing.*] *Non ales famulos* αχρειους *et ob id* αχρειους, *mittantur huc et illuc, invenient aliquid: scis varias esse talium rerum occasiones.—Ergo famulos ale non segnes, aut etiam sanguine propinquos, qui alioqui forent alendi.—Reperient aliquid in diversoriis, aut in ædibus, incustoditum. Tenes? Meminerint non frustra datos homini digitos, &c.—Eras. Id.*

[2] *But I lack a* cullisen.] No dictionary that I can find will help us to the meaning of this word ; nor does the context lead us to discover it.—WHAL.

I had occasion to observe, in a note on Massinger, that dictionaries were but ill calculated to supply the kind of information here wanted, which must be sought in the colloquial language of contemporary poets. Happily, however, Jonson explains himself. In a subsequent scene Carlo says, "I come from Sogliardo but now, he is at the herald's office yonder; he requested me

to go before and take up a man or two for him in Paul's, against his *cognizance* was ready." Cognizance, or as Sogliardo ignorantly and corruptly terms it, *cullisen,* is the badge or mark of distinction which retainers, servants, &c. usually wore on the shoulder or sleeve of their coats, that it might be known to whom and what they belonged. It should be recollected that the livery of servants at this time was, with few exceptions, of blue, so that some note of discrimination was absolutely necessary. *Cullisen* appears again in the *Case is Altered,* and in a way that clearly determines its sense : " But what *badge* shall we give, what *cullisen* ?"—Act iv.

[3] *This clod, a whoreson* puck-fist !] A fungous excrescence of the mushroom kind, often used by our author to denote an insipid, insignificant fellow.—WHAL.

[4] *The periphrasis of a fool.*] According to the Latin adage, *Fortuna favet fatuis.* So in *Wily Beguiled,*

" Sir, you may see that fortune is your friend, But *fortune favours fools.*"—WHAL.

live by my wits. What, dost thou think I live by my wits?

Mac. Methinks, jester, you should not relish this well.

Car. Ha! does he know me?

Mac. Though yours be the worst use a man can put his wit to, of thousands, to prostitute it at every tavern and ordinary; yet, methinks, you should have turned your broadside at this, and have been ready with an apology, able to sink this hulk of ignorance into the bottom and depth of his contempt.

Car. Oh, 'tis Macilente! Signior, you are well encountered; how is it?——O, we must not regard what he says, man, a trout, a shallow fool, he has no more brain than a butterfly, a mere stuft suit; he looks like a musty bottle new wickered, his head's the cork, light, light! [*Aside to* Macilente.] I am glad to see you so well returned, signior.

Mac. You are! gramercy, good Janus.

Sog. Is he one of your acquaintance? I love him the better for that.

Car. Od's precious, come away, man, what do you mean? an you knew him as I do, you'd shun him as you would do the plague.

Sog. Why, sir?

Car. O, he's a black fellow,[1] take heed of him.

Sog. Is he a scholar, or a soldier?

Car. Both, both; a lean mungrel, he looks as if he were chop-fallen with barking at other men's good fortunes: 'ware how you offend him; he carries oil and fire in his pen, will scald where it drops: his spirit is like powder, quick, violent; he'll blow a man up with a jest: I fear him worse than a rotten wall does the cannon; shake an hour after at the report. Away, come not near him.

Sog. For God's sake let's be gone; an he be a scholar, you know I cannot abide him; I had as lieve see a cockatrice, specially as cockatrices go now.[2]

Car. What, you'll stay, signior? this gentleman Sogliardo, and I, are to visit the knight Puntarvolo, and from thence to the city; we shall meet there.

[*Exit with* Sogliardo.

Mac. Ay, when I cannot shun you, we will meet.

'Tis strange! of all the creatures I have seen,

I envy not this Buffone, for indeed

Neither his fortunes nor his parts deserve it:

But I do hate him as I hate the devil,

Or that brass-visaged monster Barbarism.

O, 'tis an open-throated, black-mouthed cur,

That bites at all, but eats on those that feed him.

A slave, that to your face will, serpent-like,

Creep on the ground, as he would eat the dust,

And to your back will turn the tail, and sting

More deadly than a scorpion: stay, who's this?

Now, for my soul, another minion

Of the old lady Chance's! I'll observe him.

Enter Sordido *with an almanack in his hand.*

Sord. O rare! good, good, good, good, good!

I thank my stars,[3] I thank my stars for it.

Mac. Said I not true? doth not his passion speak

Out of my divination? O my senses,

Why lose you not your powers, and become

Dulled, if not deaded, with this spectacle?

I know him, it is Sordido, the farmer,

A boor, and brother to that swine was here.

[*Aside.*

Sord. Excellent, excellent, excellent! as I would wish, as I would wish.

Mac. See how the strumpet fortune tickles him,

And makes him swoon with laughter, O, O, O!

---

[1] *O, he's a black fellow, &c.*] Black is mischievous, malignant. It is from Horace:—

"*Hic niger est, hunc tu, Romane, caveto.*"—Whal.

[2] *I had as lieve see a* cockatrice, *specially as cockatrices go now.*] A cockatrice, as every one knows, is a serpent, supposed to kill by the look; but Jonson plays on the cant meaning of the term, which I have already explained, p. 64.

[3] *I thank my stars, &c.*] The folio edition of this play varies so little from the quarto, that I have not always thought it necessary to call the reader's attention to the very few unimportant changes made in the present text. Not to defraud Jonson of his due praise, however, it is proper to observe, that in this, as in the preceding play, he has omitted or softened many of the profane ejaculations which deformed the first copies. To shock or nauseate the reader, by bringing back what the author, upon better consideration, flung out of his text, though unfortunately not without example, is yet a species of gratuitous mischief, for which simple stupidity scarcely forms an adequate excuse.

Sord. Ha, ha, ha! I will not sow my grounds this year. Let me see, what harvest shall we have? *June, July?*

Mac. What, is't a prognostication raps him so?

Sord. The 20, 21, 22 *days, rain and wind.* O good, good! *the 23 and 24, rain and some wind,* good! *the 25, rain;* good still! 26, 27, 28, *wind and some rain;* would it had been rain and some wind! well, 'tis good when it can be no better. 29, *inclining to rain:* inclining to rain! that's not so good now : 30 *and 31, wind and no rain:* no rain! 'slid, stay; this is worse and worse : What says he of Saint Swithin's? turn back, look, *Saint Swithin's: no rain!*

Mac. O, here's a precious, dirty, damned rogue,
That fats himself with expectation
Of rotten weather, and unseasoned hours;
And he is richer for it, an elder brother!
His barns are full, his ricks and mows well trod,
His garners crack with store! O, 'tis well; ha, ha, ha!
A plague consume thee, and thy house!
　　　　　　　　　　　　　　[Aside.

Sord. O, here, *Saint Swithin's,* the 15 *day, variable weather, for the most part rain,* good! *for the most part rain:* why, it should rain forty days after, now, more or less, it was a rule held afore I was able to hold a plough, and yet here are two days no rain; ha! it makes me muse. We'll see how the next month begins, if that be better. *August* 1, 2, 3, *and* 4, *days rainy and blustering* : this is well now : 5, 6, 7, 8, *and* 9, *rainy, with some thunder;* Ay, marry, this is excellent; the other was false printed sure : *the* 10 *and* 11, *great store of rain;* O good, good, good, good, good! *the* 12, 13, *and* 14 *days, rain;* good still : 15 *and* 16, *rain;* good still : 17 *and* 18, *rain,* good still; 19 *and* 20, good still, good still, good still, good still, good still!

21, *some rain;* some rain! well, we must be patient, and attend the heavens' pleasure, would it were more though : *the* 22, 23, *great tempests of rain, thunder, and lightning.*
O good again, past expectation good!
I thank my blessed angel; never, never
Laid I [a] penny better out[1] than this,
To purchase this dear book : not dear for price,
And yet of me as dearly prized as life,
Since in it is contained the very life,
Blood, strength, and sinews of my happiness.
Blest be the hour wherein I bought this book;
His studies happy that composed the book,
And the man fortunate that sold the book!
Sleep with this charm, and be as true to me,
As I am joyed and confident in thee.
　　　　　　　　　　　　　　[Puts it up.

Enter a Hind, *and gives* Sordido *a paper to read.*

Mac. Ha, ha, ha!
Is not this good? Is it not pleasing this?
Ha, ha, ha? God pardon me! ha, ha!
Is't possible that such a spacious villain
Should live, and not be plagued? or lies he hid
Within the wrinkled bosom of the world,
Where heaven cannot see him? 'Sblood! methinks
'Tis rare, and strange, that he should breathe and walk,
Feed with digestion, sleep, enjoy his health,
And, like a boisterous whale swallowing the poor,
Still swim in wealth and pleasure! is't not strange?
Unless his house and skin were thunderproof,
I wonder at it! Methinks, now, the hectic,

---

[1] *Laid I* [a] penny *out, &c.*] We must not be surprised at the confidence which Sordido reposes in his almanack, as persons in his station of life are to be found, even now, superstitiously attentive to its predictions. The ancient almanacks too possessed higher claims to respect, than those of our days, since besides certain assurance of the downfall of the Pope, and every potentate with whom we might happen to be at war, circumstances common to both, they contained lists of the days favourable for buying and selling : — matters of high import to the Sordidos of all ages. What appears somewhat extraordinary, is the cheapness of this miraculous information : Sordido purchases it at a *penny,* and that this was not below the stated price, appears from other authorities. Thus Beaumont and Fletcher :

　　　　　"Why all physicians,
And *penny* almanacks allow," &c.—*The Chances.*

And Massinger :

　　　　　"Stargaze! sure,
I have a *penny* almanack about me,
Inscribed to you, as to his patroness,
In his name published."—Vol. iv. p. 37.

Gout, leprosy, or some such loathed dis-
ease,
Might light upon him; or that fire from
heaven
Might fall upon his barns; or mice and
rats
Eat up his grain; or else that it might rot
Within the hoary ricks, even as it stands:
Methinks this might be well; and after all
The devil might come and fetch him. Ay,
'tis true!
Meantime he surfeits in prosperity,
And thou, in envy of him, gnaw'st thy-
self:
Peace, fool, get hence, and tell thy vexed
spirit,
Wealth in this age will scarcely look on
merit.   [*Rises and exit.*
  Sord. Who brought this same, sirrah?
  Hind. Marry, sir, one of the justice's
men; he says 'tis a precept, and all their
hands be at it.
  Sord. Ay, and the prints of them stick
in my flesh
Deeper than in their letters: they have sent
me
Pills wrapt in paper here, that, should I
take them,
Would poison all the sweetness of my
book,
And turn my honey into hemlock-juice.
But I am wiser than to serve their pre-
cepts,
Or follow their prescriptions. Here's a
device,
To charge me bring my grain unto the
markets:
Ay, much![1] when I have neither barn nor
garner,
Nor earth to hide it in, I'll bring 't; till
then,
Each corn I send shall be as big as Paul's.
O, but (say some) the poor are like to
starve.
Why, let 'em starve, what's that to me?
are bees
Bound to keep life in drones and idle
moths? no:
Why such are these that term themselves
the poor,
Only because they would be pitied,
But are indeed a sort of lazy beggars,
Licentious rogues, and sturdy vagabonds,
Bred by the sloth of a fat plenteous year,

Like snakes in heat of summer, out of
dung;
And this is all that these cheap times are
good for:
Whereas a wholesome and penurious
dearth
Purges the soil of such vile excrements,
And kills the vipers up.[2]
  Hind. O, but, master,
Take heed they hear you not.
  Sord. Why so?
  Hind. They will exclaim against you.
  Sord. Ay, their exclaims
Move me as much as thy breath moves a
mountain.
Poor worms, they hiss at me, whilst I at
home[3]
Can be contented to applaud myself,
To sit and clap my hands, and laugh, and
leap,
Knocking my head against my roof, with
joy
To see how plump my bags are, and my
barns.
Sirrah, go hie you home, and bid your
fellows
Get all their flails ready again I come.
  Hind. I will, sir.   [*Exit.*
  Sord. I'll instantly set all my hinds to
thrashing
Of a whole rick of corn, which I will hide
Under the ground; and with the straw
thereof
I'll stuff the outsides of my other mows:
That done, I'll have them empty all my
garners,
And in the friendly earth bury my store,
That, when the searchers come, they may
suppose
All's spent, and that my fortunes were
belied.
And to lend more opinion to my want,
And stop that many-mouthed vulgar dog,
Which else would still be baying at my
door,
Each market-day I will be seen to buy
Part of the purest wheat, as for my house-
hold;
Where when it comes, it shall increase my
heaps:
'Twill yield me treble gain at this dear
time,
Promised in this dear book: I have cast
all.

---

[1] *Ay, much!*] i.e., by no means; not at all.
See p. 44 *b*.
[2] *And kills the vipers* up.] See p. 46 *a*.
[3] *Poor worms, they hiss at me, whilst I at*

home, &c.] Taken from Horace, but heightened
and improved:
    "*Populus me sibilat, at mihi plaudo
Ipse domi.*"

Till then I will not sell an ear, I'll hang
    first.
O, I shall make my prices as I list;
My house and I can feed on peas and
    barley.
What though a world of wretches starve
    the while;
He that will thrive must think no courses
    vile.   [*Exit.*

[*Cor.* Now, signior, how approve you
this? have the humourists exprest themselves truly or no?

Mit. Yes, if it be well prosecuted, 'tis
hitherto happy enough: but methinks Macilente went hence too soon; he might
have been made to stay, and speak somewhat in reproof of Sordido's wretchedness
now at the last.

Cor. O, no, that had been extremely
improper; besides, he had continued the
scene too long with him as 'twas, being in
no more action.

Mit. You may inforce the length as a
necessary reason; but for propriety, the
scene would very well have borne it, in my
judgment.

Cor. O, worst of both; why, you mistake his humour utterly then.

Mit. How do I mistake it? Is it not
Envy?

Cor. Yes, but you must understand,
signior, he envies him not as he is a villain,
a wolf in the commonwealth, but as he is
rich and fortunate; for the true condition
of envy is, *dolor alienæ felicitatis*, to have
our eyes continually fixed upon another
man's prosperity, that is, his chief happiness, and to grieve at that. Whereas, if
we make his monstrous and abhorred
actions our object, the grief we take then
comes nearer the nature of hate than envy,
as being bred out of a kind of contempt
and loathing in ourselves.

Mit. So you'll infer it had been hate, not
envy in him, to reprehend the humour of
Sordido?

Cor. Right, for what a man truly envies
in another, he could always love and cherish
in himself; but no man truly reprehends in
another, what he loves in himself; therefore reprehension is out of his hate. And
this distinction hath he himself made in a
speech there, if you marked it, where he
says, *I envy not this Buffone, but I hate
him.*

Mit. Stay, sir: *I envy not this Buffone,
but I hate him.* Why might he not as well
have hated Sordido as him?

Cor. No, sir, there was subject for his
envy in Sordido, his wealth: so was there
not in the other. He stood possest of no
one eminent gift, but a most odious and
fiend-like disposition, that would turn
charity itself into hate, much more envy,
for the present.

Mit. You have satisfied me, sir. O,
here comes the fool and the jester again,
methinks.

Cor. 'Twere pity they should be parted,
sir.

Mit. What bright-shining gallant's that
with them? the knight they went to?

Cor. No, sir, this is one Monsieur Fastidious Brisk, otherwise called the fresh
Frenchified courtier.

Mit. A humourist too?

Cor. As humourous as quicksilver; do
but observe him; the scene is the country
still, remember.]

ACT II.

SCENE I.—*The* Country; *before* Puntarvolo's *House.*

Enter Fastidious Brisk, Cinedo, Carlo
    Buffone, *and* Sogliardo.

Fast. Cinedo, watch when the knight
comes, and give us word.

Cin. I will, sir.   [*Exit.*

Fast. How lik'st thou my boy, Carlo?

Car. O, well, well. He looks like a
colonel of the Pigmies horse, or one of
these motions[1] in a great antique clock; he
would shew well upon a haberdasher's stall,
at a corner shop, rarely.

Fast. 'Sheart, what a damned witty
rogue's this! How he confounds with his
similes!

---

[1] *Or one of these* motions *in a great antique clock;*] A puppet, in this age, was
called a *motion*: it here means one of those
small figures in the face of a large clock, which
was moved by the vibration of the pendulum.
We have them in clocks of the present day.—
WHAL.

There is an allusion to the figures in the
Ordinary:

    " For my good toothless countess, let us try
    To win that old emerit thing, that like
    An image in a German clock, doth move,
    Not walk; I mean that rotten antiquary "

Car. Better with similes than smiles:
and whither were you riding now, signior?

Fast. Who, I? What a silly jest's
that! Whither should I ride but to the
court?

Car. O, pardon me, sir, twenty places
more; your hot-house, or your whore-
house——[1]

Fast. By the virtue of my soul, this
knight dwells in Elisium here.

Car. He's gone now, I thought he would
fly out presently. These be our nimble-
spirited catsos,[2] that have their evasions at
pleasure, will run over a bog like your wild
Irish; no sooner started, but they'll leap
from one thing to another like a squirrel,
heigh! dance and do tricks in their discourse, from fire to water, from water to
air, from air to earth, as if their tongues

did but e'en lick the four elements over,
and away.

Fast. Sirrah Carlo, thou never saw'st
my gray hobby yet, didst thou?

Car. No; have you such a one?

Fast. The best in Europe, my good
villain, thou'lt say when thou seest him.

Car. But when shall I see him?

Fast. There was a nobleman in the court
offered me a hundred pound for him, by
this light: a fine little fiery slave, he runs
like a—oh, excellent, excellent!—with the
very sound of the spur.

Car. How! the sound of the spur?

Fast. O, it's your only humour now
extant, sir; a good gingle, a good gingle.[3]

Car. 'Sblood! you shall see him turn
morrice-dancer, he has got him bells, a
good suit, and a hobby-horse.[4]

---

[1] *Your hot-house, or your* whore-house.]
An unusual fit of reserve has visited the quarto,
which omits the last word; little, however, is
gained by it, on the score of decorum, for, as
Jonson observes in his epigrams, the terms were
"synonima."

[2] *These be our nimble-spirited* catsos, &c.]
Carlo applies this opprobrious term to the travelled and affected coxcombs of the day, whose
vapid follies he ridicules with great pleasantry.
With respect to the word itself, on which the
commentators on our old plays dilate with a
gravity truly laughable, it is a petty oath, a cant
exclamation, generally expressive, among the
Italian populace, who have it constantly in their
mouth, of defiance or contempt. Jonson points
his satire at the use of it, which was very prevalent when he wrote.

[3] *Car. How! the sound of the spur?*
*Fast. O, it's your only humour now extant,
sir; a good* gingle, *a good* gingle.] There has
been a great deal written on this "humour," but
very little to the purpose. Whalley observes
that the gallants of this age had small *rings*
(Theobald and others say *bells*) fixed to their
spurs, which made a noise when they rode or
walked. But they had neither the one nor the
other; the gingling was produced by the large
loose *rowels* then worn, which were commonly
of silver, and which every motion of the foot set
in play. Thus Shirley: "I perceive 'tis an advantage for a man to wear spurs; the *rowel* of
knighthood does so *gingle* in the ear of their
understanding."—*Love in a Maze.* We may
learn something of the offensive nature of this
fashion from a passage in Chapman's *Monsieur
d'Olive:* "You may hear them (the gallants)
half a mile ere they come at you—six or seaven
make a perfect morris-daunce; they need no
bells, their *spurs* serve their turne."—Act iii.
But a yet more convincing proof of it may be
found in some of our parish records. It is well
known that our cathedrals (and above all, St.
Paul's) were, in Jonson's time, frequented by
people of all descriptions, who, with a levity

scarcely credible, walked up and down the
aisles, and transacted business of every kind,
during divine service. To expel them was not
possible; such, however, was the noise occasioned by the incessant gingling of their spur-
rowels, that it was found expedient to punish
those who approached the body of the church,
thus indecently equipped, by a small fine, under
the name of *spur-money,* the exaction of which
was committed to the beadles and singing-boys,
who seem to have exerted their authority with
sufficient vigour, and sometimes even to the
neglect of their more important duties. About
the time when this play was written, I find the
following, "Presentment to the Visitor, 1598:
Wee think it a very necessarye thinge that
every quoirister sholde bringe with him to
church a Testament, in Englishe, and torne to
every chapter, as it is daily read, or som other
good and godly prayer-booke, rather than spend
their tyme in talk and hunting after *spurr-money,*
whereon they set their whole mindes, and do
often abuse dyvers if they doe not bestowe somewhat on them." See *post* 93, *b.*

[4] *Car. 'Sblood! you shall see him turn
morrice-dancer, he has got him* bells, *a good*
suit, *and a* hobby-horse.] Of morrice-dancers,
enough and more than enough has been already
written. When the sports of our ancestors were
rude and few, they formed a very favourite part
of their merry meetings. They were at first
undoubtedly a company of people that represented the military dances of the Moors (once
the most lively and refined people in Europe) in
their proper habits and arms, and must have
been sufficiently amusing to an untravelled
nation like the English; but by degrees they
seem to have adopted into their body all the
prominent characters of the other rustic May-
games and sports, which were now probably
declining, and to have become the most anoma-
lous collection of performers that ever appeared
at once upon the stage of the world. Besides
the hobby-horse, there were the fool (not the
driveller, as Tollet supposes, but the buffoon of

Sog. Signior, now you talk of a hobby-horse, I know where one is will not be given for a brace of angels.

Fast. How is that, sir?

Sog. Marry, sir, I am telling this gentleman of a hobby-horse, it was my father's indeed, and, though I say it——

Car. That should not say it—on, on.

Sog. He did dance in it, with as good humour and as good regard as any man of his degree whatsoever, being no gentleman: I have danced in it myself too.

Car. Not since the humour of gentility was upon you, did you?

Sog. Yes, once; marry, that was but to shew what a gentleman might do in a humour.

Car. O, very good.

————————

[*Mit.* Why, this fellow's discourse were nothing but for the word humour.

Cor. O, bear with him; an he should lack matter and words too, 'twere pitiful.]

————————

Sog. Nay, look you, sir, there's ne'er a gentleman in the country has the like humours, for the hobby-horse, as I have; I have the method for the threading of the needle and all, the——

Car. How, the method!

Sog. Ay, the leigerity for that, and the whigh-hie, and the daggers in the nose, and the travels of the egg from finger to finger, and all the humours incident to the quality. The horse hangs at home in my parlour. I'll keep it for a monument as long as I live, sure.

Car. Do so; and when you die, 'twill be an excellent trophy to hang over your tomb.

Sog. Mass, and I'll have a tomb, now I think on't; 'tis but so much charges.

Car. Best build it in your lifetime then, your heirs may hap to forget it else.

Sog. Nay, I mean so, I'll not trust to them.

Car. No, for heirs and executors are grown damnable careless, specially since the ghosts of testators left walking.—How like you him, signior?

Fast. 'Fore heavens, his humour arrides me exceedingly.[1]

Car. Arrides you!

Fast. Ay, pleases me: a pox on't! I am so haunted at the court, and at my lodging, with your refined choice spirits,

————————

the party); may, or maid, Marian, and her paramour, a friar; a serving-man; a piper, and two moriscoes. These, with their bells, rings, streamers, &c. all in motion at one time, must have, as Rabelais says, made a *tintamarre de diable!* Their dress is prettily described by Fletcher:

"*Soto.* Do you know what sports are in season?
Silvio. I hear there are some a-foot.
Soto. Where are your bells then,
Your rings, your ribbands, friend, and your clean napkins;
Your nosegay in your hat, pinned up?" &c.
Women Pleased, act iv. sc. 1.

When the right good-will with which these worthy persons capered is taken into consideration, the clean napkin, which was never omitted, will not appear the least necessary part of the apparatus. Thus Clod, in the masque of *Gipseys*, observes, "They should be morris-dancers by their *gingle*, but they have no *napkins.*" The hobby-horse (Sogliardo's choice) who once performed the principal character in the dance, and whose banishment from it is lamented with such ludicrous pathos by our old dramatists, was a light frame of wickerwork, furnished with a pasteboard head and neck of a horse. This was buckled round the waist, and covered with a foot-cloth which reached to the ground, and concealed at once the legs of the performer and his juggling apparatus. Thus equipped, he

VOL. I.

pranced and curvetted in all directions (probably to keep the ring clear), neighing, or *whigh-hie-ing*, as the author calls it, and exhibiting specimens of boisterous and burlesque horsemanship. The *whigh-hies* are mentioned by Fletcher in *Women Pleased*, where Bomby, now converted to Puritanism, renounces the hobby-horse, in which he had just been dancing:

"This beast of Babylon I'll ne'er back again,
His pace is sure profane, and his lewd *wi-hees*,
The songs of Hymyn and Gymyn in the wilderness."—Act iv. sc. 1.

The feats of *leigerity* (legerdemain), such as *threading the needle*, conveying an egg from hand to hand, which Jonson terms the *travels of the egg*; running *daggers through the nose, and other humours incident to the quality* which Sogliardo exhibited in his career, may yet be seen at country fairs. "*But O! the hobby-horse is forgot.*" We have now *Pizarro* and the *Castle Spectre* in our holiday booths. We are certainly more genteel in our rural amusements than our fathers; but I doubt whether we are quite as merry, or even as wise.

[1] *Fast. 'Fore heavens, his humour* arrides *me exceedingly.*] This Latinism is copied by Marmion: "Her form answers my expectation; it *arrides* (pleases) me exceedingly!"—*The Antiquary.* Shirley, too, has it in his *Love Tricks.* It is a most affected piece of pedantry, but it does not misbecome the characters who employ it. In the next speech there is more of it.

G

that it makes me clean of another garb, another sheaf, I know not how! I cannot frame me to your harsh vulgar phrase, 'tis against my genius.

Sog. Signior Carlo! [*Takes him aside.*

[*Cor.* This is right to that of Horace, *Dum vitant stulti vitia, in contraria currunt;* so this gallant, labouring to avoid popularity, falls into a habit of affectation ten thousand times hatefuller than the former.]

Car. [*pointing to* Fastidious.] Who, he? a gull, a fool, no salt in him i' the earth, man: he looks like a fresh salmon kept in a tub; he'll be spent shortly. His brains lighter than his feather already, and his tongue more subject to lye, than that is to wag; he sleeps with a musk-cat every night, and walks all day hanged in pomander chains[1] for penance; he has his skin tanned in civet, to make his complexion strong, and the sweetness of his youth lasting in the sense of his sweet lady; a good empty puff, he loves you well, signior.

Sog. There shall be no love lost, sir, I'll assure you.

Fast. [*advancing to them.*] Nay, Carlo, I am not happy in thy love, I see: pray thee suffer me to enjoy thy company a little, sweet mischief: by this air, I shall envy this gentleman's place in thy affections, if you be thus private, i' faith.

Enter Cinedo.

How now! Is the knight arrived?

Cin. No, sir, but 'tis guessed he will arrive presently, by his forerunners.

Fast. His hounds! by Minerva, an excellent figure; a good boy.

Car. You should give him a French crown for it;[2] the boy would find two better figures in that, and a good figure of your bounty beside.

Fast. Tut, the boy wants no crowns.

Car. No crown; speak in the singular number, and we'll believe you.

Fast. Nay, thou art so capriciously conceited now. Sirrah damnation, I have heard this knight Puntarvolo reported to be a gentleman of exceeding good humour, thou know'st him; prithee, how is his disposition? I never was so favoured of my stars as to see him yet. Boy, do you look to the hobby?

Cin. Ay, sir, the groom has set him up.

[*As* Cinedo *is going out,* Sogliardo *takes him aside.*

Fast. 'Tis well: I rid out of my way of intent to visit him, and take knowledge of his——Nay, good Wickedness, his humour, his humour.

Car. Why, he loves dogs, and hawks, and his wife well; he has a good riding face, and he can sit a great horse; he will taint a staff well at tilt;[3] when he is mounted he looks like the sign of the George, that's all I know; save, that instead of a dragon, he will brandish against a tree, and break his sword as confidently upon the knotty bark, as the other did upon the scales of the beast.

Fast. O, but this is nothing to that's delivered of him. They say he has dialogues and discourses between his horse, himself, and his dog; and that he will court his own lady, as she were a stranger never encountered before.

---

[1] *And walks all day hanged in* pomander *chains,* &c.] Pomanders were little balls of perfumed paste, worn in the pocket, or strung round the neck, as amulets, to prevent infection in times of the plague: they were also an article of luxury among people of rank and fashion, or who aspired to be thought such. Directions for making them frequently occur in our old poets, books of housewifery, &c. " A good *pomander,* a little decayed in the scent; but six grains of musk, ground with rose water, and tempered with a little civet, shall fetch her again presently."—*Malcontent,* act v. sc. 1. Another receipt, more complicated, and therefore more in the taste of the times, occurs in *Lingua,* act iv. sc. 3. This kind of amulet has lately been revived with great parade or novelty; such is our credulity, or our ignorance!

[2] Car. *You should give him a* French crown *for it;*] French crown, like the miserable word

do, is almost sure to draw from the commentators a profusion of filth and obscenity wherever it occurs. Whalley says that it means a corona veneris, a caries in the head, &c.; though how Fastidious was to give this, is not very apparent. A French crown here means neither more nor less than a piece of money so called.

[3] *He will* taint *a staff well at* tilt;] i.e., break it, but not in the most honourable and scientific manner. Such at least is the meaning it seems to have here, the only place but one (as far as I know) in which the expression occurs (see Massinger, vol. ii. p. 293), unless, from Jonson's known attachment to playing on words, it should be thought to bear a similar meaning in a subsequent passage of the present play:

Punt. There never was so witty a jest broken at the *tilt,* of all the court wits christened.
Maci. O, this applause *taints* it foully.

Car. Ay, that he will, and make fresh love to her every morning ; this gentleman has been a spectator of it, Signior Insulso.

Sog. I am resolute to keep a page.—Say you, sir ?

    [*Leaps from whispering with* Cinedo.

Car. You have seen Signior Puntarvolo accost his lady ?

Sog. O, ay, sir.

Fast. And how is the manner of it, prithee, good signior ?

Sog. Faith, sir, in every good sort ; he has his humours for it, sir ; as first (suppose he were now to come from riding or hunting, or so), he has his trumpet to sound, and then the waiting-gentlewoman, she looks out, and then he speaks, and then she speaks,——very pretty, i' faith, gentlemen.

Fast. Why, but do you remember no particulars, signior ?

Sog. O, yes, sir, first, the gentlewoman, she looks out at the window.

Car. After the trumpet has summoned a parle, not before ?

Sog. No, sir, not before ; and then says he,—ha, ha, ha, ha !

Car. What says he ? be not rapt so.

Sog. Says he,—ha, ha, ha !

Fast. Nay, speak, speak.

Sog. Ha, ha, ha !—says he, God save you, says he ;—ha, ha !

Car. Was this the ridiculous motive to all this passion ?

Sog. Nay, that, that comes after is,——ha, ha, ha, ha !

Car. Doubtless he apprehends more than he utters, this fellow ; or else——

    [*A cry of hounds within.*

Sog. List, list, they are come from hunting ; stand by, close under this terras, and you shall see it done better than I can shew it.[1]

Car. So it had need, 'twill scarce poise the observation else.

Sog. Faith, I remember all, but the manner of it is quite out of my head.

Fast. O, withdraw, withdraw, it cannot be but a most pleasing object.

    [*They stand aside.*

Enter Puntarvolo, *followed by his* Huntsman *leading a greyhound.*

Punt. Forester, give wind to thy horn.—Enough ; by this the sound hath touched the ears of the inclosed : depart, leave the dog, and take with thee what thou hast deserved, the horn, and thanks.

    [*Exit* Huntsman.

Car. Ay, marry, there is some taste in this.

Fast. Is't not good ?

Sog. Ah, peace ; now above, now above !

    [*A* Waiting-gentlewoman *appears at the window.*

Punt. Stay ; mine eye hath, on the instant, through the bounty of the window, received the form of a nymph. I will step forward three paces ; of the which, I will barely retire one ; and, after some little flexure of the knee, with an erected grace salute her ; one, two, and three ! Sweet lady, God save you !

Gent. [*above.*] No, forsooth ; I am but the waiting-gentlewoman.

Car. He knew that before.

Punt. Pardon me : *humanum est errare.*

Car. He learned that of his chaplain.[2]

Punt. To the perfection of compliment (which is the dial of the thought, and guided by the sun of your beauties) are required these three specials ; the gnomon, the puntilios, and the superficies : the superficies is that we call place ; the puntilios, circumstance ; and the gnomon, ceremony ; in either of which, for a stranger to err, 'tis easy and facile ; and such am I.

Car. True, not knowing her horizon, he must needs err ; which I fear he knows too well.

Punt. What call you the lord of the castle, sweet face ?

Gent. [*above.*] The lord of the castle is a knight, sir ; Signior Puntarvolo.

Punt. Puntarvolo ! O——

Car. Now must he ruminate.

Fast. Does the wench know him all this while, then ?

Car. O, do you know me, man ? why, therein lies the syrup of the jest ; it's a project, a designment of his own, a thing studied, and rehearst as ordinarily at his

---

[1] *You shall see it done better than I can shew it.*] It is to be regretted that this observation came so late. Certainly it does no credit to the judgment of the poet thus to destroy a part of the interest of his own scene by anticipating what it was meant to display. But Jonson excelled in strong and vigorous description ; and this is not the only place in which his consciousness of his superior talents for delineating characters has betrayed him into improprieties.

[2] *Car. He learned that of his* chaplain.] An improvement of the quarto, which reads, " He learned that of a *Puritan ;*" the only description of people, perhaps, who never made use of the expression.

coming from hawking or hunting, as a jig after a play.[1]

Sog. Ay, e'en like your jig, sir.

Punt. 'Tis a most sumptuous and stately edifice ! Of what years is the knight, fair damsel?

Gent. Faith, much about your years, sir.

Punt. What complexion, or what stature bears he?

Gent. Of your stature, and very near upon your complexion.

Punt. Mine is melancholy

Car. So is the dog's, just.

Punt. And doth argue constancy, chiefly in love. What are his endowments? is he courteous?

Gent. O, the most courteous knight in Christian land, sir.

Punt. Is he magnanimous?

Gent. As the skin between your brows, sir.

Punt. Is he bountiful?

Car. 'Slud, he takes an inventory of his own good parts.

Gent. Bountiful ! ay, sir, I would you should know it ; the poor are served at his gate, early and late, sir.

Punt. Is he learned !

Gent. O, ay, sir, he can speak the French and Italian.

Punt. Then he has travelled ?

Gent. Ay, forsooth, he hath been beyond seas once or twice.

Car. As far as Paris, to fetch over a fashion, and come back again.

Punt. Is he religious?

Gent. Religious ! I know not what you call religious, but he goes to church, I am sure.

Fast. 'Slid, methinks these answers should offend him.

Car. Tut, no; he knows they are ex-cellent, and to her capacity that speaks them.

Punt. Would I might but see his face !

Car. She should let down a glass from the window at that word, and request him to look in't.

Punt. Doubtless the gentleman is most exact, and absolutely qualified ; doth the castle contain him?

Gent. No, sir, he is from home, but his lady is within.

Punt. His lady ! what, is she fair, splen-didious, and amiable ?

Gent. O, Lord, sir !

Punt. Prithee, dear nymph, intreat her beauties to shine on this side of the building.
           [*Exit* Waiting-gentlewoman *from the window.*

Car. That he may erect a new dial of compliment, with his gnomons and his puntilios.

Fast. Nay, thou art such another Cynick now, a man had need walk uprightly be-fore thee.

Car. Heart, can any man walk more upright than he does? Look, look ; as if he went in a frame, or had a suit of wains-cot on : and the dog watching him, lest he should leap out on't.

Fast. O, villain !

Car. Well, an e'er I meet him in the city, I'll have him jointed, I'll pawn him in Eastcheap, among the butchers, else.

Fast. Peace ; who be these, Carlo ?

Enter Sordido *and* Fungoso.

Sord. Yonder's your godfather; do your duty to him, son.

Sog. This, sir? a poor elder brother of mine, sir, a yeoman, may dispend some seven or eight hundred a year; that's his son, my nephew, there.

---

[1] *As a* jig *after a play.*] In our author's days a *jig* did not always mean a dance, but frequently, as here, a ballad, or a low ludicrous dialogue, in metre. So in *The Hog hath lost his Pearl:* "Here's the player would speak with you—about the *jig* I promised him."—Act i. sc. 1. And in *Hamlet:* O ! your only *jig*-maker;" upon which Mr. Steevens cites the following lines from Shirley's *Love in a Maze:*

"Many gentlemen
Are not, as in the days of understanding,
Now satisfied without a *jig*, which since
They cannot, with their honour, call for, after
The play, they look to be served up i' th' middle."—WHAL.

The conclusion of this note affords a curious specimen of the disingenuity of Steevens, and the improper confidence of Whalley. The former quotes this passage to prove that a *jig* meant, as above, "a farcical dialogue in verse," and breaks off within a word of what expressly ascertains that Shirley meant neither more nor less by it than a *dance:*

"I' th' middle ;
Your *dance* is the best language of some comedies,
And footing runs away with all ; a scene
Exprest with life of art, and squared to nature,
Is dull and phlegmatic poetry."

Steevens, as Mr. Gilchrist justly observes, had no plea for thus garbling a quotation, since a hundred passages might be fairly produced in which *jig* is used for a scene of low buffoonery, or farce.

Punt. You are not ill come, neighbour Sordido, though I have not yet said, well-come; what, my godson is grown a great proficient by this.

Sord. I hope he will grow great one day, sir.

Fast. What does he study? the law?

Sog. Ay, sir, he is a gentleman, though his father be but a yeoman.

Car. What call you your nephew, signior?

Sog. Marry, his name is Fungoso.

Car. Fungoso! O, he looked somewhat like a sponge in that pinked yellow doublet, methought; well, make much of him; I see he was never born to ride upon a mule.[1]

Gent. [*reappears at the window.*] My lady will come presently, sir.

Sog. O, now, now!

Punt. Stand by, retire yourselves a space; nay, pray you, forget not the use of your hat; the air is piercing.

[*Sordido and Fungoso withdraw.*

Fast. What! will not their presence prevail against the current of his humour?

Car. O, no; it's a mere flood, a torrent carries all afore it.

[*Lady* Puntarvolo *appears at the window.*

Punt. What more than heavenly pulchritude is this,
What magazine, or treasury of bliss?
Dazzle, you organs to my optic sense,
To view a creature of such eminence:
O, I am planet-struck, and in yon sphere
A brighter star than Venus doth appear!

Fast. How! in verse!

Car. An extacy, an extacy, man.

Lady P. [*above.*] Is your desire to speak with me, sir knight?

Car. He will tell you that anon; neither his brain nor his body are yet moulded for an answer.

Punt. Most debonair and luculent lady, I decline me as low as the basis of your altitude.

[*Cor.* He makes congies to his wife in geometrical proportions.

Mit. Is it possible there should be any such humourist?

Cor. Very easily possible, sir, you see there is.]

Punt. I have scarce collected my spirits, but lately scattered in the admiration of your form; to which, if the bounties of your mind be any way responsible, I doubt not but my desires shall find a smooth and secure passage. I am a poor knight-errant, lady, that hunting in the adjacent forest, was by adventure, in the pursuit of a hart, brought to this place; which hart, dear madam, escaped by enchantment: the evening approaching, myself and servant wearied, my suit is, to enter your fair castle and refresh me.

Lady. Sir knight, albeit it be not usual with me, chiefly in the absence of a husband, to admit any entrance to strangers, yet in the true regard of those innated virtues, and fair parts, which so strive to express themselves, in you; I am resolved to entertain you to the best of my unworthy power; which I acknowledge to be nothing, valued with what so worthy a person may deserve. Please you but stay while I descend.

[*Exit from the window.*

Punt. Most admired lady, you astonish me.

[*Walks aside with* Sordido *and his son.*

Car. What! with speaking a speech of your own penning?

Fast. Nay, look; prithee, peace.

Car. Pox on't! I am impatient of such foppery.

Fast. O, let us hear the rest.

Car. What! a tedious chapter of courtship, after Sir Lancelot and Queen Guenever?[2] Away! I marle in what dull cold nook he found this lady out; that, being a woman, she was blest with no more copy of

---

[1] *I see he was never born to ride upon a mule,*] i.e., he was never born to be a great lawyer. It was the custom anciently for the judges or serjeants at law to go to Westminster in great state, and riding on mules. Thus Stow, describing the order of Wolsey's going to Westminster, in term-time: "And when he come at the hall door, there was *hys mule,* being trapped all in crimson velvet, wyth a saddle of the same, and guilte styrops."—Ann. ed. 1580, p. 917.—WHAL.
John Whiddon, justice of the King's Bench Court, 1 Mar. as we are informed by Dugdale, "was the first of the judges who rode to West-

minster-hall on an horse or gelding; for before that time they *rode on mules.*"—Dug. Orig. *Ju. L.* p. 38.
Jonson, or his printer, spells this word several ways, moile, moyl, and mule, I have adopted the last.
[2] *After Sir Lancelot and Queen Guenever?*] After *the manner,* &c. *Cui non dictus Hylas?* and who does not know that Guenever was the wife of King Arthur, and Lancelot her favoured and faithful lover? Their amours fill many a page of the old romance of *Prince Arthur.*

wit[1] but to serve his humour thus. 'Slud,
I think he feeds her with porridge, I; she
could never have such a thick brain else.

Sog. Why, is porridge so hurtful, signior?

Car. O, nothing under heaven more
prejudicial to those ascending subtile
powers, or doth sooner abate that which
we call *acumen ingenii*, than your gross
fare: Why, I'll make you an instance;
your city wives, but observe 'em, you have
not more perfect true fools in the world
bred than they are generally; and yet you
see, by the fineness and delicacy of their diet,
diving into the fat capons, drinking your
rich wines, feeding on larks, sparrows,
potato-pies, and such good unctuous meats,
how their wits are refined and rarified;
and sometimes a very quintessence of conceit flows from them, able to drown a
weak apprehension.

Enter Lady Puntarvolo *and her* Waiting-
woman.

Fast. Peace, here comes the lady.

Lady. Gad's me, here's company! turn
in again.   [*Exit with her* Woman.

Fast. 'Slight, our presence has cut off
the convoy of the jest.

Car. All the better, I am glad on't; for
the issue was very perspicuous. Come,
let's discover and salute the knight.
      [*They come forward.*

Punt. Stay; who be these that address
themselves towards us? What, Carlo!
Now by the sincerity of my soul, welcome;
welcome, gentlemen: and how dost thou,
thou *Grand Scourge*, or *Second Untruss of
the time?*[2]

Car. Faith, spending my metal in this
reeling world (here and there), as the sway
of my affection carries me, and perhaps
stumble upon a yeoman-feuterer,[3] as I do
now; or one of fortune's mules, laden
with treasure, and an empty cloak-bag,
following him, gaping when a bag will
untie.

Punt. Peace, you bandog, peace! What

brisk Nymphadoro is that in the white
virgin-boot there?

Car. Marry, sir, one that I must intreat
you to take a very particular knowledge of,
and with more than ordinary respect;
Monsieur Fastidious.

Punt. Sir, I could wish that for the time
of your vouchsafed abiding here, and more
real entertainment,[4] this my house stood on
the Muses' hill, and these my orchards
were those of the Hesperides.

Fast. I possess as much in your wish,
sir, as if I were made lord of the Indies;
and I pray you believe it.

Car. I have a better opinion of his faith,
than to think it will be so corrupted.

Sog. Come, brother, I'll bring you
acquainted with gentlemen, and good fellows, such as shall do you more grace
than——

Sord. Brother, I hunger not for such
acquaintance: Do you take heed, lest——
      [Carlo *comes toward them.*

Sog. Husht! My brother, sir, for want of
education, sir, somewhat nodding to the
boor, the clown; but I request you in private, sir.

Fung. [*Looking at* Fastidious Brisk.] By
heaven, it is a very fine suit of clothes.
      [*Aside.*

[*Cor.* Do you observe that, signior?
There's another humour has new-cracked
the shell.

Mit. What! he is enamoured of the
fashion, is he?

Cor. O, you forestall the jest.]

Fung. I marle what it might stand him
in.   [*Aside.*

Sog. Nephew!

Fung. 'Fore me, it's an excellent suit,
and as neatly becomes him.   [*Aside.*]
What said you, uncle?

Sog. When saw you my niece?

Fung. Marry, yesternight I supped
there.—That kind of boot does very rare
too.   [*Aside.*

---

[1] *She was blest with no more copy of wit*]
From the Latin *copia*, plenty, abundance; familiar in this sense to our author.—WHAL.
    This word was not introduced by Jonson; it
occurs in Chaucer; and even in writers anterior
to Chaucer: luckily, its uncouthness has long
since banished it from the language, which it
only served to stiffen and deform. See *post* 100 *b*.
[2] *Thou* Grand Scourge, *or* Second Untruss *of
the time?*] The allusion is here to Marston,
whose Satires, called the *Scourge of Villanie*,
in three books, were printed the year before the
first edition of this Comedy, 1599.
[3] *A yeoman*-feuterer.] Meaning Puntarvolo.
Feuterer is a dog-keeper, from the French
vautrier or *vaultrier*; one that leads a lime-
hound or greyhound for the chase.—WHAL.
    See Massinger, vol. iii. p. 213.
[4] *And more* real *entertainment.*] It may be
just worth observing that, in the affected language of Puntarvolo, *real* means regal, noble: the
word is distinguished in the quarto by a capital.

Sog. And what news hear you?

Fung. The gilt spur and all![1] Would I were hanged, but 'tis exceeding good. [*Aside.*] Say you, uncle?

Sog. Your mind is carried away with somewhat else: I ask what news you hear?

Fung. Troth, we hear none.—In good faith, [*looking at* Fastidious Brisk] I was never so pleased with a fashion, days of my life. O an I might have but my wish, I'd ask no more of heaven now but such a suit, such a hat, such a band, such a doublet, such a hose, such a boot, and such a—— [*Aside.*

Sog. They say there's a new motion of the city of Nineveh,[2] with Jonas and the whale, to be seen at Fleet-bridge. You can tell, cousin?

Fung. Here's such a world of questions with him now!—Yes, I think there be such a thing, I saw the picture.—Would he would once be satisfied! Let me see, the doublet, say fifty shillings the doublet, and between three or four pound the hose; then boots, hat, and band: some ten or eleven pound will do it all, and suit me, for the heavens![3] [*Aside.*

Sog. I'll see all those devices an I come to London once.

Fung. Ods 'slid, an I could compass it, 'twere rare. [*Aside.*] Hark you, uncle.

Sog. What says my nephew?

Fung. Faith, uncle, I would have desired you to have made a motion for me to my father, in a thing that——Walk aside, and I'll tell you, sir; no more but this: there's a parcel of law books (some twenty pounds' worth) that lie in a place for little more

---

[1] *The* gilt *spur and all*] Gilt *spurs* were one of the extravagant articles affected by the gallants of the age. Thus Fennor, in the *Compter's Commonwealth*, 1617, p. 32: "Gallants that scorned to weare any other than beaver hats, and gold bands, rich swords, and scarfes, silk stockings, and gold fringed garters, or russet bootes, and *gilt* spurs."—WHAL.

[2] *They say there's a new* motion *of the city of Nineveh, &c.*] There is no *puppet-show* of which our old writers make such frequent mention as this of Nineveh, which must have been exceedingly popular. Fleet-street appears to have been the principal place where sights of every kind were exhibited, and probably from its being the great thoroughfare of the city. This would scarcely deserve notice were it not for a passage in Butler which it serves to explain, and of which the sense has been hitherto mistaken:

"And now at length he's brought
Unto fair London city,
Where in Fleet-street
All those may see't,
That will not believe my ditty."
Ballad on Cromwell.

"Alluding," says the Editor, "to Cromwell's having lodged there at some period of his life." But the allusion is to the notoriety of this street for its exhibitions of puppet-shows, "naked Indians," "strange fishes," and "monsters" of every description. The laudable custom of hanging out a picture of what was to be seen, is still preserved in full force.

[3] *Some ten or eleven pound will do it all, and suit me,* for the heavens!] This expression occurs in *The Merchant of Venice.* "Away! says the fiend, for the heavens!" Upon which Mr. M. Mason observes, "As it is not likely that Shakspeare should make the Devil conjure Launcelot to do any thing *for the heavens,* I have no doubt but the passage is corrupt, and that we ought to read, Away! says the fiend, for the *haven*—by which Launcelot was to make

his escape, if he was determined to run away!" My old acquaintance succeeds no better in geography than in criticism: the *haven* of Venice is all his own, and it would be the height of injustice to compliment Shakspeare with the discovery of it.

Mr. Malone says that the expression means, "Begone, says the fiend, to the heavens." This appears less likely to come from the "Devil," than the "conjuration" which so scandalized Mr. M. Mason. But enough of trifling; the words are merely a petty oath; and wheresoever they occur, in this manner, and by whomsoever they are spoken, mean neither more nor less than —by heaven! Such is the sense of them in the text: Some ten or eleven pound will do it all, *by heaven!*

This ignorance of the language, if accompanied by modesty, would be no great evil; but when it emboldens the commentator to corrupt and alter it to his own conceptions, as Whalley has done in this place, it becomes a serious matter. In a subsequent scene of this play Macilente says:

"Now, *for* my soul, another minion
Of the old lady Chance's!"

On which Whalley observes, "I apprehend the words *for my soul* are corrupt, and should be read *'fore my soul.*" And accordingly the expression, thus happily corrected a second time, is made part of the text.

That no future doubts may arise on the subject, I will subjoin two or three of as many score examples which I could instantly produce: the first shall be from Jonson himself: "Come on, Sir Valentine, I'll give you a health, *for the heavens,* you mad Capricio, hold hook and line!"—*Case is Altered.* The second, from his old enemy Decker: "A lady took a pipefull or two (of tobacco) at my hands, and praised it, *for the heavens!*"—*Untrussing the Humourous Poet.* And, to conclude, Tweddle, the drunken piper, in *Pasquil and Katherine,* exclaims, "I must goe and clap my mistress' cheekes (his tabor) there, *for the heavens.*"

than half the money they cost; and I think, for some twelve pound, or twenty mark, I could go near to redeem them; there's Plowden, Dyar, Brooke, and Fitz-Herbert, divers such as I must have ere long; and you know, I were as good save five or six pound as not, uncle. I pray you, move it for me.

Sog. That I will: when would you have me do it? presently?

Fung. O, ay, I pray you, good uncle: [*Sogliardo takes Sordido aside.*]—send me good luck! Lord, an't be thy will, prosper it! O, my stars, now, now, if it take now, I am made for ever.

Fast. Shall I tell you, sir? by this air, I am the most beholden to that lord of any gentleman living; he does use me the most honourably, and with the greatest respect, more indeed than can be uttered with any opinion of truth.

Punt. Then have you the Count Gratiato?

Fast. As true noble a gentleman too as any breathes; I am exceedingly endeared to his love: By this hand, I protest to you, signior, I speak it not gloriously,[1] nor out of affectation, but there's he, and the Count Frugale, Signior Illustre, Signior Luculento, and a sort of 'em, that when I am at court, they do share me amongst them; happy is he can enjoy me most private. I do wish myself sometime an ubiquitary for their love, in good faith.

Car. There's ne'er a one of these but might lie a week on the rack, ere they could bring forth his name; and yet he pours them out as familiarly as if he had seen them stand by the fire in the presence, or ta'en tobacco with them over the stage, in the lords' room.[2]

Punt. Then you must of necessity know

our court-star there, that planet of wit, Madona Saviolina?

Fast. O Lord, sir! my mistress.

Punt. Is she your mistress?

Fast. Faith, here be some slight favours of hers, sir, that do speak it she is; as this scarf, sir, or this riband in my ear, or so; this feather grew in her sweet fan sometimes,[3] though now it be my poor fortune to wear it, as you see, sir: slight, slight, a foolish toy.

Punt. Well, she is the lady of a most exalted and ingenious spirit.

Fast. Did you ever hear any woman speak like her? or enriched with a more plentiful discourse?

Car. O villainous! nothing but sound, sound, a mere echo; she speaks as she goes tired, in cobweb-lawn, light, thin; good enough to catch flies withal.

Punt. O, manage your affections.

Fast. Well, if thou be'st not plagued for this blasphemy one day——

Punt. Come, regard not a jester: It is in the power of my purse to make him speak well or ill of me.

Fast. Sir, I affirm it to you upon my credit and judgment, she has the most harmonious and musical strain of wit that ever tempted a true ear; and yet to see!—— a rude tongue would profane heaven, if it could.

Punt. I am not ignorant of it, sir.

Fast. Oh, it flows from her like nectar, and she doth give it that sweet, quick grace, and exornation in the composure, that by this good air, as I am an honest man, would I might never stir, sir, but—— she does observe as pure a phrase, and use as choice figures in her ordinary conferences, as any be in the *Arcadia.*[4]

---

[1] *I speak it not* gloriously,] i.e., *gloriosè,* vaingloriously; a common acceptation of the word by the writers of Jonson's time.

[2] *Or ta'en tobacco with them over the stage, in* the lords' room.] The *lords' rooms* answered to the present stage-boxes. The price of admission to them appears to have been originally a shilling. Thus Decker: "At a new play you take up the *twelve-penny room,* next the stage, because the *lords* and you may seem to be hail-fellow, well met."—*Gull's Hornbook,* 1609.

[3] *This scarf, sir, or this riband in my ear, or so; this feather grew in her sweet fan sometimes,*] In those days of gallantry, it was an honourable mode for the men to wear publicly some token of their mistress, or favour she was supposed to give them. Gloves, ribands, &c. were the usual insignia of this kind. The

fans then in use were made of feathers.—WHAL.

The fashion of wearing roses, that is, knots of ribands, in the ear, is frequently mentioned by our old dramatists, and among the rest by Shakspeare:

"My face so thin,
That in my *ear* I could not stick a *rose,*
Lest men should say, Look, where three-farthings goes."—*King John.*

Theobald supposes the rose here mentioned to be the flower so called; but he is mistaken.

[4] *She does observe as pure a phrase, and use as choice figures as any be in the* Arcad'a.] An unfinished pastoral romance written by Sir P. Sidney, in compliment to his sister. It is mentioned in the *Antiquary:* "'Twere a solecism

Car. Or rather in Green's works, whence she may steal with more security.[1]

Sord. Well, if ten pound will fetch 'em, you shall have it; but I'll part with no more.

Fung. I'll try what that will do, if you please.

Sord. Do so; and when you have them, study hard.

Fung. Yes, sir. An I could study to get forty shillings more now! Well, I will put myself into the fashion, as far as this will go, presently.

Sord. I wonder it rains not: the almanack says we should have store of rain to-day.   [*Aside.*

Punt. Why, sir, to-morrow I will associate you to court myself, and from thence to the city, about a business, a project I have; I will expose it to you, sir; Carlo, I am sure, has heard of it.

Car. What's that, sir?

Punt. I do intend, this year of jubilee coming on, to travel: and because I will not altogether go upon expense, I am determined to put forth some five thousand pound,[2] to be paid me five for one, upon the return of myself and wife, and my dog, from the Turk's court in Constantinople. If all or either of us miscarry in the way, 'tis gone: if we be successful, why, there will be five and twenty thousand pound to entertain time withal. Nay, go not, neigh-

bour Sordido; stay to-night, and help to make our society the fuller. Gentlemen, frolick:[3] Carlo! what! dull now?

Car. I was thinking on your project, sir, an you call it so. Is this the dog goes with you?

Punt. This is the dog, sir.

Car. He does not go barefoot, does he?

Punt. Away, you traitor, away!

Car. Nay, afore God, I speak simply; he may prick his foot with a thorn, and be as much as the whole venture is worth. Besides, for a dog that never travelled before, it's a huge journey to Constantinople. I'll tell you now, an he were mine, I'd have some present conference with a physician, what antidotes were good to give him, preservatives against poison; for, assure you, if once your money be out, there'll be divers attempts made against the life of the poor animal.

Punt. Thou art still dangerous.

Fast. Is Signior Deliro's wife your kinswoman?

Sog. Ay, sir, she is my niece, my brother's daughter here, and my nephew's sister.

Sord. Do you know her, sir?

Fast. O lord, sir! Signior Deliro, her husband, is my merchant.[4]

Fung. Ay, I have seen this gentleman there often.

Fast. I cry you mercy, sir; let me crave your name, pray you.

---

to imagine that a young bravery, who lives where any waiting-woman speaks perfect *Arcadia*," &c. Lord Orford talks slightly of it in his *Royal and Noble Authors*, and with a certain degree of justice: for though it contains some nervous and elegant passages, yet the plan of it is poor; the incidents trite and uninteresting, and the general style pedantic and affected. It does not appear to have been meant for the public.

[1] *Whence she may steal with more security.*] Because, as Whalley says, and as Jonson certainly means to insinuate, they were less read. But the fact is not so; Robert Green was at once the most voluminous and the most popular author of his time. He was, says Wood, "a pastoral sonnet-maker" (Antony misconceives the general nature of his writings), "and author of several things which were pleasing to men and women of his time. They made much sport, and were valued among scholars, but since they have been mostly sold on ballad-mongers' stalls." Green died in great poverty, in 1592.

[2] *I am determined to put forth some five thousand pound, to be paid me five for one,* &c.] In this age, when travelling was hazardous and insecure, it seems to have been no unusual practice to put out money at going abroad, on

condition of receiving it back trebled, quadrupled, or, as here, quintupled on the completion of the expedition. To this there are innumerable allusions in our old writers. In the *Ball*, by Shirley, it forms a principal incident of the play. Barnaby Riche also mentions it, "whipsters, that having spent the greatest part of their patrimony in prodigality, will give out the rest of their stocke to be paid *two or three for one*, upon their return from Rome," &c. Thus too, Shakspeare.

Each putter out of *one for five*,—as Malone properly reads; and not as Steevens has it, "*on* five for *one*," which to the ears of Shakspeare and his audiences would have been intolerable.

As voyages became more frequent, and the dangers of them consequently better understood, the odds fell, and adventurers were content to take three to one upon their return.

"Sir Solus straight will travell, as they say,
And gives out *one for three*," &c.

(This expression justifies Malone's correction.) Davies, *Epig.* II.

[3] *Gentlemen,* frolick!] See *The Alchemist.*

[4] *Signior Deliro is my* merchant.] i.e., my broker or banker. In Jonson's days there were none who professed the trade of banking exclusively. The goldsmiths of Lombard-street were almost all bankers.

Fung. Fungoso, sir.

Fast. Good Signior Fungoso, I shall request to know you better, sir.

Fung. I am her brother, sir.

Fast. In fair time, sir.

Punt. Come, gentlemen, I will be your conduct.[1]

Fast. Nay, pray you, sir; we shall meet at Signior Deliro's often.

Sog. You shall have me at the herald's office, sir, for some week or so, at my first coming up. Come, Carlo.   [*Exeunt.*

[*Mit.* Methinks, Cordatus, he dwelt somewhat too long on this scene; it hung in the hand.

Cor. I see not where he could have insisted less, and to have made the humours perspicuous enough.

Mit. True, as his subject lies; but he might have altered the shape of his argument, and explicated them better in single scenes.

Cor. That had been single indeed.[2] Why, be they not the same persons in this, as they would have been in those? and is it not an object of more state, to behold the scene full,[3] and relieved with variety of speakers to the end, than to see a vast empty stage, and the actors come in, one by one, as if they were dropt down with a feather into the eye of the spectators?

Mit. Nay, you are better traded with these things than I, and therefore I'll subscribe to your judgment; marry, you shall give me leave to make objections.

Cor. O, what else? It is the special intent of the author you should do so; for thereby others, that are present, may as well be satisfied, who haply would object the same you would do.

Mit. So, sir; but when appears Macilente again?

Cor. Marry, he stays but till our silence give him leave: here he comes, and with

him Signior Deliro, a merchant, at whose house he is come to sojourn: make your own observation now, only transfer your thoughts to the city, with the scene; where, suppose they speak.]

SCENE II.—*The City. A Room in Deliro's House.*

Enter Deliro, Macilente, *and* Fido, *with flowers and perfumes.*

Deli. I'll tell you by and by, sir.——
Welcome, good Macilente, to my house,
To sojourn even for ever;[4] if my best
In cates, and every sort of good entreaty,
May move you stay with me.
          [*He censeth: the boy strews flowers.*

Maci. I thank you, sir.——
And yet the muffled Fates, had it pleased them,
Might have supplied me from their own full store,
Without this word *I thank you* to a fool.
I see no reason why that dog called Chance,
Should fawn upon this fellow, more than me:
I am a man, and I have limbs, flesh, blood,
Bones, sinews, and a soul, as well as he:
My parts are every way as good as his;
If I said better, why, I did not lie.
Nath'less, his wealth, but nodding on my wants,
Must make me bow, and cry, *I thank you,
sir.*   [*Aside.*

Deli. Dispatch! take heed your mistress see you not.

Fido. I warrant you, sir, I'll steal by her softly.   [*Exit.*

Deli. Nay, gentle friend, be merry; raise your looks
Out of your bosom: I protest, by heaven,
You are the man most welcome in the world.

Maci. I thank you, sir.—I know my cue, I think.   [*Aside.*

---

1 *I will be your* conduct.] Your conductor or guide. So Shakspeare:

"Come, bitter *conduct*, come unsavoury guide."
—*Rom. and Jul.*—WHAL.

2 *That had been* single *indeed.*] That had been *weak* or *silly;* in this sense *single* occurs perpetually in our old writers. This is the meaning of the term in *Macbeth* (my *single* state of man), about which so much has been written to so little purpose: and this too is the undoubted sense of it in *Henry IV.* "Is not your wit *single*?"

3 *Is it not an object of more state to behold the scene* full, &c.] Yet I see not what is

gained by this fulness of the scene. The characters are not blended into one whole; they disperse into little groups, and carry on their business distinct from one another, advancing alternately to the front of the stage, and retiring to make room for others. The acquiescence of Mitis in the reasoning of his friend Cordatus is no great proof of its accuracy or justice, for Mitis is a man of straw, and liable to be overthrown with the slightest effort.

4 *To sojourn even for ever;*] This is the reading of the quarto, and evidently right; the folio, which Whalley followed, has "To sojourn *at my house* for ever." My house was repeated by the compositor from the preceding line.

Re-enter Fido, *with more perfumes
and flowers.*

Fido. Where will you have them burn,
sir?
Deli. Here, good Fido.
What, she did not see thee?
Fido. No, sir.
Deli. That is well.
Strew, strew, good Fido, the freshest
flowers; so!
Maci. What means this, Signior Deliro?
all this censing?
Deli. Cast in more frankincense, yet
more; well said.——
O, Macilente, I have such a wife!
So passing fair! so passing-fair-unkind!
But of such worth, and right to be unkind,
Since no man can be worthy of her kind-
ness.
Maci. What, can there not?
Deli. No, that is sure as death,
No man alive. I do not say is not,
But cannot possibly be worth her kindness.
Nay, it is certain, let me do her right.
How, said I? do her right! as though I
could,
As though this dull, gross tongue of mine
could utter
The rare, the true, the pure, the infinite
rights,
That sit as high as I can look, within her!
Maci. This is such dotage as was never
heard.
Deli. Well, this must needs be granted.
Maci. Granted, quoth you?
Deli. Nay, Macilente, do not so discredit
The goodness of your judgment to deny it,
For I do speak the very least of her;
And I would crave, and beg no more of
heaven,
For all my fortunes here, but to be able
To utter first in fit terms, what she is,
And then the true joys I conceive in her.
Maci. Is't possible she should deserve so
well
As you pretend?
Deli. Ay, and she knows so well
Her own deserts, that when I strive t'enjoy
them,
She weighs the things I do with what she
merits;
And, seeing my worth outweighed so in
her graces,
She is so solemn, so precise, so froward,
That no observance I can do to her
Can make her kind to me; if she find fault,
I mend that fault; and then she says, I
faulted,

That I did mend it. Now, good friend,
advise me
How I may temper this strange spleen in
her.
Maci. You are too amorous, too obse-
quious,
And make her too assured she may com-
mand you.
When women doubt most of their hus-
bands' loves,
They are most loving. Husbands must
take heed
They give no gluts of kindness to their
wives,
But use them like their horses; whom they
feed
Not with a mangerful of meat together,
But half a peck at once; and keep them so
Still with an appetite to that they give
them.
He that desires to have a loving wife,
Must bridle all the shew of that desire:
Be kind, not amorous; nor bewraying kind-
ness,
As if love wrought it, but considerate duty.
Offer no love rites, but let wives still seek
them,
For when they come unsought, they seldom
like them.
Deli. Believe me, Macilente, this is gos-
pel.
O, that a man were his own man so much,
To rule himself thus. I will strive, i' faith,
To be more strange and careless; yet I
hope
I have now taken such a perfect course,
To make her kind to me, and live contented,
That I shall find my kindness well re-
turned,
And have no need to fight with my affec-
tions.
She late hath found much fault with every
room
Within my house; one was too big, she
said,
Another was not furnished to her mind,
And so through all; all which now I have
altered.
Then here, she hath a place, on my back-
side,
Wherein she loves to walk; and that, she
said,
Had some ill smells about it: now this walk
Have I, before she knows it, thus perfumed
With herbs and flowers, and laid in divers
places,
As 'twere on altars consecrate to her,
Perfumed gloves, and delicate chains of
amber,

To keep the air in awe of her sweet nostrils :
This have I done, and this I think will
please her.
Behold she comes.

Enter Fallace.

Fal. Here's a sweet stink indeed !
What, shall I ever be thus crost and plagued,
And sick of husband? O, my head doth
ache,
As it would cleave asunder, with these sa-
vours !
All my rooms altered, and but one poor
walk
That I delighted in, and that is made
So fulsome with perfumes, that I am feared,
My brain doth sweat so, I have caught the
plague.
Deli. Why, gentle wife, is now thy walk
too sweet ?
Thou said'st of late, it had sour airs about
it,
And found much fault that I did not cor-
rect it.
Fal. Why, an I did find fault, sir?
Deli. Nay, dear wife,
I know thou hast said thou hast loved per-
fumes,
No woman better.
Fal. Ay, long since, perhaps ;
But now that sense is altered : you would
have me,
Like to a puddle, or a standing pool,
To have no motion, nor no spirit within me.
No, I am like a pure and sprightly river,
That moves for ever, and yet still the same;
Or fire, that burns much wood, yet still one
flame.
Deli. But yesterday I saw thee at our
garden,
Smelling on roses, and on purple flowers ;
And since, I hope, the humour of thy sense
Is nothing changed.
Fal. Why, those were growing flowers,
And these within my walk are cut and
strewed.
Deli. But yet they have one scent.
Fal. Ay ! have they so?
In your gross judgment. If you make no
difference
Betwixt the scent of growing flowers and
cut ones,
You have a sense to taste lamp oil, i' faith :

And with such judgment have you changed
the chambers,
Leaving no room that I can joy to be in,
In all your house ; and now my walk, and
all,
You smoke me from, as if I were a fox,
And long, belike, to drive me quite away :
Well, walk you there, and I'll walk where
I list.
Deli. What shall I do? O, I shall never
please her.
Maci. Out on thee, dotard! what star
ruled his birth,
That brought him such a Star? blind For-
tune still
Bestows her gifts on such as cannot use
them :
How long shall I live ere I be so happy
To have a wife of this exceeding form?
                                        [*Aside.*
Deli. Away with 'em ! would I had broke
a joint
When I devised this, that should so dislike
her.
Away, bear all away.
                        [*Exit* Fido *with flowers, &c.*
Fal. Ay, do ; for fear
Aught that is there should like her.[1] O,
this man,
How cunningly he can conceal himself,
As though he loved, nay, honoured and
adored !——
Deli. Why, my sweet heart?
Fal. Sweet heart? O better still !
And asking, why? wherefore? and looking
strangely,
As if he were as white as innocence !
Alas, you're simple, you ; you cannot
change,
Look pale at pleasure, and then red with
wonder :
No, no, not you ! 'tis pity o' your naturals.
I did but cast an amorous eye, e'en
now,
Upon a pair of gloves that somewhat liked
me,
And straight he noted it, and gave com-
mand
All should be ta'en away.
Deli. Be they my bane then !
What, sirrah Fido, bring in those gloves
again
You took from hence.
Fal. 'Sbody, sir, but do not :

---

[1]   Fal. *Ay, do ; for fear*
Aught that is there should like *her.*] i.e., should
please her. So in the line just above, "that
should so *dislike*," i.e., displease her: and this is

the language of the poet's contemporaries. So
Shakspeare :
" His countenance *likes* me not."—*King Lear.*
and almost every dramatist of the age.—WHAL

Bring in no gloves to spite me ; if you
do——

Deli. Ah me, most wretched; how am I
misconstrued !

Maci. O, how she tempts my heart-
strings with her eye,
To knit them to her beauties, or to break !
What moved the heavens, that they could
not make
Me such a woman ! but a man, a beast,
That hath no bliss like others? Would to
heaven,
In wreak of my misfortunes, I were turned
To some fair water nymph, that, set upon
The deepest whirl-pit of the rav'nous seas,
My adamantine eyes might headlong hale
This iron world to me, and drown it all!
[*Aside.*

——————

[*Cor.* Behold, behold, the translated gallant.

Mit. O, he is welcome.]

——————

Enter Fungoso, *apparelled like*
Fastidious Brisk.

Fung. Save you, brother and sister; save
you, sir ! I have commendations for you
out o' the country.——I wonder they take no
knowledge of my suit : [*Aside.*] Mine
uncle Sogliardo is in town. Sister, methinks you are melancholy; why are you
so sad ? I think you took me for Master
Fastidious Brisk, sister, did you not?

Fal. Why should I take you for him ?

Fung. Nay, nothing.——I was lately in
Master Fastidious's company, and methinks we are very like.

Deli. You have a fair suit, brother, 'give
you joy on't.

Fung. Faith, good enough to ride in,
brother; I made it to ride in.

Fal. O, now I see the cause of his idle
demand was his new suit.

Deli. Pray you, good brother, try if you
can change her mood.

Fung. I warrant you, let me alone : I'll
put her out of her dumps. Sister, how like
you my suit?

Fal. O, you are a gallant in print now,
brother.[1]

Fung. Faith, how like you the fashion ?
it is the last edition, I assure you.

Fal. I cannot but like it to the desert.

Fung. Troth, sister, I was fain to borrow
these spurs, I have left my gown in gage
for them ; pray you lend me an angel.

Fal. Now, beshrew my heart then.

Fung. Good truth, I'll pay you again at
my next exhibition.[2] I had but bare ten
pound of my father, and it would not
reach to put me wholly into the fashion.

Fal. I care not.

Fung. I had spurs of mine own before,
but they were not ginglers.[3] Monsieur
Fastidious will be here anon, sister.

Fal. You jest !

Fung. Never lend me penny more while
you live then; and that I'd be loth to say,
in truth.

Fal. When did you see him?

Fung. Yesterday ; I came acquainted
with him at Sir Puntarvolo's : nay, sweet
sister.

Maci. I fain would know of heaven now,
why yond fool
Should wear a suit of satin? he? that rook,
That painted jay, with such a deal of out-
side?
What is his inside, trow? ha, ha, ha, ha,
ha !
Good heaven, give me patience, patience,
patience,
A number of these popinjays there are,
Whom, if a man confer, and but examine
Their inward merit, with such men as
want;
Lord, lord, what things they are ! [*Aside.*

——————

[1] Fal. *O, you're a gallant* in print *now,
brother.*] You are now a perfect, complete
gallant. Thus Chapman :

" 'Tis such a picked fellow, not a hair
About his whole bulk, but it stands *in print.*"
All Fools.

And Massinger :

"Is he not, madam,
A monsieur now *in print ?*"—*Guardian.*
WHAL.

[2] Fung. *Good truth, I'll pay you again at my
next* exhibition.] i.e., at the next payment of my
allowance. Thus Shakspeare :

" What maintenance he from his friends receives,
Like *exhibition* shalt thou have from me."
WHAL.

The word is used by Wycherley in the *Plain
Dealer,* " And then, widow, you must settle on
your son an *exhibition* of forty pounds a year."

[3] Fung. *I had spurs of mine own before, but
they were not* ginglers.] See p. 80 *a.* I omitted
to observe in that place that these gingling spurs
were merely an appendage of fashion, as their
rowels were perfectly blunt, and not at all calculated for riding. Thus, in the *Fleire* : " Your
swaggerer is like your *walking* spur ; he gingles
much, but he never cuts."

Fal. [*Gives him money.*] Come, when will you pay me again now?

Fung. O lord, sister!

Maci. Here comes another.

Enter Fastidious Brisk, *in a new suit.*

Fast. Save you, Signior Deliro! How dost thou, sweet lady? let me kiss thee.

Fung. How! a new suit? ah me!

Deli. And how does Master Fastidious Brisk?

Fast. Faith, live in court, Signior Deliro; in grace, I thank God, both of the noble masculine and feminine. I must speak with you in private by and by.

Deli. When you please, sir.

Fal. Why look you so pale, brother?

Fung. 'Slid, all this money is cast away now.

Maci. Ay, there's a newer edition come forth.

Fung. 'Tis but my hard fortune! well, I'll have my suit changed, I'll go fetch my tailor presently, but first I'll devise a letter to my father. Have you any pen and ink, sister?

Fal. What would you do withal?

Fung. I would use it. 'Slight, an it had come but four days sooner, the fashion.
[*Exit.*

Fast. There was a countess gave me her hand to kiss to-day, i' the presence: did me more good by that light than—— and yesternight sent her coach twice to my lodging, to intreat me accompany her, and my sweet mistress, with some two or three nameless ladies more: O, I have been graced by them beyond all aim of affection: this is her garter my dagger hangs in: and they do so commend and approve my apparel, with my judicious wearing of it, it's above wonder.

Fal. Indeed, sir, 'tis a most excellent suit, and you do wear it as extraordinary.

Fast. Why, I'll tell you now, in good faith, and by this chair, which, by the grace of God, I intend presently to sit in, I had three suits in one year made three great ladies in love with me: I had other three, undid three gentlemen in imitation: and other three gat three other gentlemen widows of three thousand pound a year.

Deli. Is't possible?

Fast. O, believe it, sir; your good face is the witch, and your apparel the spells, that bring all the pleasures of the world into their circle.

Fal. Ah, the sweet grace of a courtier!

Maci. Well, would my father had left me but a good face for my portion yet! though I had shared the unfortunate wit that goes with it, I had not cared; I might have passed for somewhat in the world then.

Fast. Why, assure you, signior, rich apparel has strange virtues: it makes him that hath it without means, esteemed for an excellent wit: he that enjoys it with means, puts the world in remembrance of his means: it helps the deformities of nature, and gives lustre to her beauties; makes continual holiday where it shines; sets the wits of ladies at work, that otherwise would be idle; furnisheth your two-shilling ordinary; takes possession of your stage at your new play; and enricheth your oars, as scorning to go with your scull.

Maci. Pray you, sir, add this; it gives respect to your fools, makes many thieves, as many strumpets, and no fewer bankrupts.

Fal. Out, out! unworthy to speak where he breatheth.

Fast. What's he, signior?

Deli. A friend of mine, sir.

Fast. By heaven I wonder at you citizens, what kind of creatures you are!

Deli. Why, sir?

Fast. That you can consort yourselves with such poor seam-rent fellows.[1]

Fal. He says true.

Deli. Sir, I will assure you, however you esteem of him, he's a man worthy of regard.

Fast. Why, what has he in him of such virtue to be regarded, ha?

Deli. Marry, he is a scholar, sir.

Fast. Nothing else!

Deli. And he is well travelled.

Fast. He should get him clothes; I would cherish those good parts of travel in him, and prefer him to some nobleman of good place.

Deli. Sir, such a benefit should bind me to you for ever, in my friend's right; and I doubt not but his desert shall more than answer my praise.

Fast. Why, an he had good clothes, I'd carry him to court with me to-morrow.

---

[1] *Fast. That you can consort yourselves with such poor seam-rent fellows.*] This contemptuous term for raggedness appears again in the *Poetas-* ter: "A lean visage 'pearing out of a seam-, rent suit."—Act i. Decker, in the *Satiromastix,* seems to twit Jonson with the frequent use of it

Deli. He shall not want for those, sir, if gold and the whole city will furnish him.

Fast. You say well, sir: faith, Signior Deliro, I am come to have you play the alchemist with me, and change the species of my land into that metal you talk of.

Deli. With all my heart, sir; what sum will serve you?

Fast. Faith, some three or four hundred.

Deli. Troth, sir, I have promised to meet a gentleman this morning in Paul's, but upon my return I'll dispatch you.

Fast. I'll accompany you thither.[1]

Deli. As you please, sir; but I go not thither directly.

Fast. 'Tis no matter, I have no other designment in hand, and therefore as good go along.

Deli. I were as good have a quartain fever follow me now, for I shall ne'er be rid of him. Bring me a cloak there, one. Still, upon his grace at court, I am sure to be visited; I was a beast to give him any hope. Well, would I were in, that I am out with him once, and ——Come, Signior Macilente, I must confer with you as we go. Nay, dear wife, I beseech thee, forsake these moods: look not like winter thus. Here, take my keys, open my counting-houses, spread all my wealth before thee, choose any object that delights thee; if thou wilt eat the spirit of gold, and drink dissolved pearl in wine,[2] 'tis for thee.

Fal. So, sir!

Deli. Nay, my sweet wife.

Fal. Good lord, how you are perfumed in your terms and all! pray you leave us.

Deli. Come, gentlemen.

Fast. Adieu, sweet lady.

[*Exeunt all but Fallace.*

Fal. Ay, ay! let thy words ever sound in mine ears, and thy graces disperse contentment through all my senses! O, how happy is that lady above other ladies, that enjoys so absolute a gentleman to her servant! *A countess gives him her hand to kiss:* ah, foolish countess! he's a man worthy, if a woman may speak of a man's worth, to kiss the lips of an empress.

Re-enter Fungoso, *with his* Tailor.

Fung. What's Master Fastidious gone, sister?

Fal. Ay, brother.—He has a face like a cherubin! [*Aside.*

Fung. 'Ods me, what luck's this? I have fetched my tailor and all: which way went he, sister, can you tell?

Fal. Not I, in good faith—and he has a body like an angel! [*Aside.*

Fung. How long is't since he went?

Fal. Why, but e'en now; did you not meet him?—and a tongue able to ravish any woman in the earth. [*Aside.*

Fung. O, for God's sake—I'll please you for your pains [*to his* Tailor.] But e'en now, say you? Come, good sir: 'slid, I had forgot it too: if any body ask for mine uncle Sogliardo, they shall have him at the herald's office yonder, by Paul's.

[*Exit with his* Tailor.

Fal. Well, I will not altogether despair: I have heard of a citizen's wife has been beloved of a courtier; and why not I? heigh, ho! well, I will into my private chamber, lock the door to me, and think over all his good parts one after another.

[*Exit.*

———

[*Mit.* Well, I doubt this last scene will endure some grievous torture.

Cor. How? you fear 'twill be racked by some hard construction?

Mit. Do not you?

Cor. No, in good faith: unless mine eyes could light me beyond sense. I see no reason why this should be more liable to the rack than the rest: you'll say, perhaps, the city will not take it well that the merchant is made here to dote so perfectly upon his wife; and she again to be so *Fastidiously* affected as she is.

Mit. You have uttered my thought, sir, indeed.

Cor. Why, by that proportion, the court might as well take offence at him we call the courtier, and with much more pretext, by how much the place transcends, and goes before in dignity and virtue: but can you imagine that any noble or true spirit in court, whose sinewy and altogether unaffected graces, very worthily express him a courtier, will make any exception at the opening of such an empty trunk as this Brisk is? or think his own worth impeached by beholding his motley inside?

Mit. No, sir, I do not.

———

[1] *Fast. I'll accompany you thither.*] In this, and some of the following speeches, Jonson had Horace in view: *Ibam forte viâ sacra,* &c.

[2] *And drink dissolved pearl in wine,*] As Cleopatra is said to have done.—WHAL.

———

Jonson recurs to this again in his *Fox*:

" See, here's a rope of *pearl,* and each more
orient
Than that the brave Egyptian queen caroused;
Dissolve and drink them."   -Act iii.

Cor. No more, assure you, will any grave, wise citizen, or modest matron, take the object of this folly in Deliro and his wife; but rather apply it as the foil to their own virtues. For that were to affirm, that a man writing of Nero, should mean all emperors; or speaking of Machiavel, comprehend all statesmen; or in our Sordido, all farmers; and so of the rest: than which nothing can be uttered more malicious or absurd. Indeed there are a sort of these narrow-eyed decypherers, I confess, that will extort strange and abstruse meanings out of any subject, be it never so conspicuous and innocently delivered. But to such, where'er they sit concealed, let them know, the author defies them and their writing-tables:[1] and hopes no sound or safe judgment will infect itself with their contagious comments, who, indeed, come here only to pervert and poison the sense of what they hear, and for nought else.

Enter Cavalier Shift, *with two* Si quisses (bills) *in his hand.*

Mit. Stay, what new mute is this, that walks so suspiciously?

Cor. O, marry, this is one for whose better illustration we must desire you to presuppose the stage the middle isle in Paul's, and that the west end of it.

Mit. So, sir, and what follows?

Cor. Faith, a whole volume of humour, and worthy the unclasping.

Mit. As how? What name do you give him first?

Cor. He hath shift of names, sir: some call him Apple-John, some Signior Whiffe; marry, his main standing name is Cavalier Shift: the rest are but as clean shirts to his natures.

Mit. And what makes he in Paul's now?

Cor. Troth, as you see, for the advancement of a *si quis* or two; wherein he has so varied himself, that if any of 'em take, he may hull up and down in the humourous world a little longer.

Mit. It seems then he bears a very changing sail?

Cor. O, as the wind, sir: here comes more.]

ACT III.

SCENE I.—*The Middle Aisle of St. Paul's.*

Shift. [*coming forward.*] This is rare, I have set up my bills without discovery.[2]

Enter Orange.

Orange. What, Signior Whiffe! what fortune has brought you into these west parts?

Shift. Troth, signior, nothing but your rheum; I have been taking an ounce of tobacco hard by here, with a gentleman,

---

[1] *The author defies them and their writing-tables.*] It was customary for the critics of Jonson's time to carry pocket-books (*tables*) to the theatres, for the purpose of writing down such passages as struck them: to this there are many allusions in our old plays. Thus, in the *Malecontent:* "I am one that hath seen this play often; I have most of the jests here in my *table-book.*" And, in the *Woman Hater:* "If there be any lurking among you in corners, with *table-books,* who have some hopes to find fit matter to feed their malice, let them clasp them up and slink away."

[2] *This is rare, I have* set up my bills *without discovery.*] i.e., his *Si quisses,* his advertisements. "It appears," says a late commentator on Shakspeare, "from *a very rare little piece,* that St. Paul's was a place in which bills were posted up." This is the very foppery of black-letter reading. The play before us, which is to be found in every library in the kingdom, and which conveys more information on the subject than can be picked out of all the *rarities* in the critic's cabinet, is not once noticed! I know that Jonson is no favourite with the idolizers of Shakspeare, who never mention him but to calumniate his name, and I do not therefore address myself to them; but I can assure those unprejudiced readers who are solicitous to become acquainted with the domestic manners and pursuits of our forefathers, that they will find more to gratify their rational curiosity in the dramas of this great poet, than in all the writers of his age. Jonson was a keen observer, and an accurate describer of the scenes before him: added to which, his idea of the true intent of comedy, and the examples of Aristophanes and Plautus, his principal models, came in aid of his natural bent, and converted what was inclination into duty.

A modern reader, Whalley says, will be surprised, perhaps, to find business of the following description transacted in St. Paul's: but the middle aisle of this church was in the poet's days, the common resort of bullies, knights of the post, and others of the like reputable professions, who carried on their various occupations here with great success: indeed, bargains of all kinds were made here as commonly as on the Exchange, and with as little feeling of impropriety. The reader who wishes for more on the subject, may turn to a very curious passage in Reed's *Old Plays,* vol. vii p. 136.

and I am come to spit private in Paul's.
'Save you, sir.

Orange. Adieu, good Signior Whiffe.
[*Passes onward.*

Enter Clove.

Clove. Master Apple-John! you are well
met: when shall we sup together, and
laugh, and be fat with those good wenches,
ha?

Shift. Faith, sir, I must now leave you,
upon a few humours and occasions; but
when you please, sir. [*Exit.*

Clove. Farewell, sweet Apple-John! I
wonder there are no more store of gallants
here.

———

[*Mit.* What be these two, signior?

Cor. Marry, a couple, sir, that are mere
strangers to the whole scope of our play;
only come to walk a turn or two in this
scene of Paul's, by chance.]

———

Orange. Save you, good Master Clove!

Clove. Sweet Master Orange.

———

[*Mit.* How! Clove and Orange?

Cor. Ay, and they are well met, for 'tis
as dry an Orange as ever grew: nothing
but salutation, and, *O lord, sir!* and, *It
pleases you to say so, sir!* one that can laugh
at a jest for company with a most plausible
and extemporal grace; and some hour after
in private ask you what it was. The other
monsieur, Clove, is a more spiced youth;
he will sit you a whole afternoon sometimes
in a bookseller's shop, reading the Greek,
Italian, and Spanish, when he understands
not a word of either; if he had the tongues
to his suits, he were an excellent linguist.]

———

Clove. Do you hear this reported for certainty?

Orange. O lord, sir.

Enter Puntarvolo *and* Carlo, *followed by
two Serving-men, one leading a dog,
the other bearing a bag.*

Punt. Sirrah, take my cloak; and you,
sir knave, follow me closer. If thou losest
my dog, thou shalt die a dog's death; I
will hang thee.

Car. Tut, fear him not, he's a good lean
slave, he loves a dog well, I warrant him;
I see by his looks, I:—Mass, he's somewhat like him. 'Slud [*to the* Servant.]
poison him, make him away with a crooked
pin, or somewhat, man; thou may'st have
more security of thy life; and—So, sir;
what! you have not put out your whole
venture yet, have you?

Punt. No, I do want yet some fifteen or
sixteen hundred pounds; but my lady, my
wife, is *Out of her Humour,*[1] she does not
now go.

Car. No! how then?

Punt. Marry, I am now enforced to give
it out, upon the return of myself, my dog,
and my cat.

Car. Your cat! where is she?

Punt. My squire has her there in the
bag; sirrah, look to her. How lik'st thou
my change, Carlo?

Car. Oh, for the better, sir; your cat
has nine lives, and your wife has but one.

Punt. Besides, she will never be sea-sick,
which will save me so much in conserves.
When saw you Signior Sogliardo?

Car. I came from him but now; he is at
the herald's office yonder; he requested me
to go afore, and take up a man or two for
him in Paul's, against his cognizance was
ready.

Punt. What, has he purchased arms,
then?

Car. Ay, and rare ones too; of as many
colours as e'er you saw any fool's coat in
your life.[2] I'll go look among yond bills,
an I can fit him with legs to his arms.

Punt. With legs to his arms! Good!
I will go with you, sir.
[*They go to read the bills.*

Enter Fastidious, Deliro, *and* Macilente.

Fast. Come, let's walk in Mediterraneo:[3]
I assure you, sir, I am not the least respected among ladies; but let that pass:
do you know how to go into the presence,
sir?

Maci. Why, on my feet, sir.

Fast. No, on your head, sir; for 'tis
that must bear you out, I assure you; as
thus, sir. You must first have an especial
care so to wear your hat, that it oppress

———

[1] *My wife is* out of her humour.] Jonson
forgot to account for this: but he has so many
characters on his hands, that the loss of one may
well be overlooked.

[2] *Of as many colours as e'er you saw any*
fool's coat *in your life.*] Jonson plays on the

word: the privileged fool of his days wore a
parti-coloured dress.

[3] *Come, let's walk in Mediterraneo:*] In the
middle aisle: the quarto reads, in the Mediterraneum.

not confusedly this your predominant, or foretop; because, when you come at the presence-door, you may with once or twice stroking up your forehead,[1] thus, enter with your predominant perfect; that is, standing up stiff.

Maci. As if one were frighted?

Fast. Ay, sir.

Maci. Which, indeed, a true fear of your mistress should do, rather than gum-water, or whites of eggs; is't not so, sir?

Fast. An ingenious observation. Give me leave to crave your name, sir?

Deli. His name is Macilente, sir.

Fast. Good Signior Macilente, if this gentleman, Signior Deliro, furnish you, as he says he will, with clothes, I will bring you, to-morrow by this time, into the presence of the most divine and acute lady in court; you shall see sweet silent rhetorick,[2] and dumb eloquence speaking in her eye; but when she speaks herself, such an anatomy of wit, so sinewized and arterized, that 'tis the goodliest model of pleasure that ever was to behold. Oh! she strikes the world into admiration of her; O, O, O! I cannot express them, believe me.

Maci. O, your only admiration is your silence, sir.

Punt. 'Fore God, Carlo, this is good! let's read them again.   [*Reads the bill.*

"If there be any lady or gentlewoman of

good carriage that is desirous to entertain to her private uses a young, straight, and upright gentleman, of the age of five or six and twenty at the most; who can serve in the nature of a gentleman-usher, and hath little legs of purpose,[3] and a black satin suit of his own, to go before her in; which suit, for the more sweetening, now lies in lavender; and can hide his face with her fan, if need require; or sit in the cold at the stairfoot for her, as well as another gentleman: let her subscribe her name and place, and diligent respect shall be given."

Punt. This is above measure excellent, ha!

Car. No, this, this! here's a fine slave.
    [*Reads.*

"If this city, or the suburbs of the same, do afford any young gentleman of the first, second, or third head, more or less, whose friends are but lately deceased, and whose lands are but new come into his hands, that, to be as exactly qualified as the best of our ordinary gallants are, is affected to entertain the most gentlemanlike use of tobacco; as first, to give it the most exquisite perfume; then, to know all the delicate sweet forms for the assumption of it; as also the rare corollary and practice of the Cuban ebolition, euripus, and whiff,[4] which he shall receive, or take in here at London, and

---

[1] *Your predominant, or* foretop—*once or twice stroking up your forehead, &c.*] This appears to have been the fashionable mode of wearing the hair at this time. Thus Rowley, "While I tie my band, prithee *stroke up my foretop a little.*"—*Match at Midnight.*

[2] *You shall see* sweet silent rhetoric, &c.] I know not what Jonson found so ridiculous in the following extract, but this is not the only place in which he laughs at it:

" Ah, Beauty, Syren, fair enchanting good,
   Sweet silent rhetoric of persuading eyes,
Dumb eloquence, whose power doth move the blood,
   More than the words or wisdom of the wise!"—Daniel's *Comp. of Rosamond.*

[3] *And hath* little legs *of purpose.*] These are mentioned as characteristic of a gentleman in many of our old plays: see Massinger, vol. iv. 280. To *lie in lavender,* which occurs just below, is also a cant term for lying in pawn. So in *Eastward Hoe,* "Good faith, rather than thou shouldst *pawn* a rag, I'd *lay* my ladyship *in lavender,* if I knew where." The expression is so common, that more examples of it are unnecessary.

[4] *As also the rare corollary and practice of the* Cuban ebolition, euripus, *and* whiff.] In p. 64, it is said that one of Cavaliero Shift's chief exer-

cises was taking the whiff; here we find that this accomplished personage was also master of the *delicate sweet forms* of taking the euripus and the Cuban ebolition. I regret my inability to furnish any precise information upon those terms, which are almost peculiar to Jonson. *Whiff,* indeed, occurs in a dull, prosing account of tobacco, in the *Queen's Arcadia,* from which, as well as from what our author says elsewhere, it would seem to be either a swallowing of the smoke, or a retaining it in the throat for a given space of time. The lines of Daniel are:

" This herb in powder made, and fired, he sucks,
   Out of a little hollow instrument
Of calcinated clay, the smoke thereof:
Which either he conveys out of his nose,
Or down into his stomach with a *whiff,*" &c.

It is also noticed in *Pasquil and Katherine,* 1601:

" Indeed young Brabant is a proper man,
   He curles his boote with judgment, takes a
      whiffe,
With graceful fashion," &c.—Act i.

And in the *Gull's Hornbook,* in a manner which proves that Shift was a professor of no vulgar arts! "Then let him shew his several tricks in taking the *whiffe,* the ring, &c., for these are compliments (accomplishments) that gain gen-

evaporate at Uxbridge, or farther, if it please him. If there be any such generous spirit, that is truly enamoured of these good faculties ; may it please him, but by a note of his hand to specify the place or ordinary where he uses to eat and lie; and most sweet attendance, with tobacco and pipes of the best sort, shall be ministered. *Stet, quæso candide Lector*."[1]

Punt. Why, this is without parallel, this.
Car. Well, I'll mark this fellow for Sógliardo's use presently.
Punt. Or rather Sogliardo for his use.
Car. Faith, either of them will serve, they are both good properties : I'll design the other a place too, that we may see him.
Punt. No better place than the Mitre, that we may be spectators with you, Carlo. Soft, behold who enters here :

Enter Sogliardo.

Signior Sogliardo ! save you.
Sog. Save you, good Sir Puntarvolo ; your dog's in health, sir, I see. How now, Carlo?
Car. We have ta'en simple pains to choose you out followers here.
    [*Shews him the bill.*
Punt. Come hither, signior.
Clove. Monsieur Orange, yon gallants observe us ; prithee let's talk fustian a little, and gull them ; make them believe we are great scholars.
Orange. O lord, sir !
Clove. Nay, prithee let us,—believe me, you have an excellent habit in discourse.

Orange. It pleases you to say so, sir.
Clove. By this church, you have, la; nay, come, begin—Aristotle, in his dæmonologia, approves Scaliger for the best navigator in his time; and in his hypercritics, he reports him to be Heautontimorumenos :—you understand the Greek, sir?
Orange. O, good sir !
Maci. For society's sake he does. O, here be a couple of fine tame parrots !
Clove. Now, sir, whereas the ingenuity[2] of the time, and the soul's synderisis are but embrions in nature, added to the panch of Esquiline, and the intervallum of the zodiac, besides the ecliptic line being optic, and not mental, but by the contemplative and theoric part thereof, doth demonstrate to us the vegetable circumference, and the ventosity of the tropics, and whereas our intellectual or mincing capreal (according to the metaphysicks) as you may read in Plato's Histriomastix—You conceive me, sir?
Orange. O lord, sir !
Clove. Then coming to the pretty animal, as reason long since is fled to animals,[3] you know, or indeed for the more modelizing, or enamelling or, rather diamondizing of your subject, you shall perceive the hypothesis, or galaxia (whereof the meteors long since had their initial inceptions and notions), to be merely Pythagorical, mathematical, and aristocratical—For, look you, sir, there is ever a kind of concinnity and species—Let us turn to our former discourse, for they mark us not.

---

tlemen no mean respect ; and for which indeed they are more worthily noticed than for any skill they have in learning."
  Cuban ebolition, or a corruption of it, appears in the *Return from Parnassus*. "Good faith," exclaims one of the pages, "Master Prodigo is an excellent fellow, he takes the *Cuban ebullitio* so excellently !" This, indeed, explains nothing ; but, from the expression itself, we may conjecture that it meant a forcible and rapid ejection of the smoke. Of the *euripus*, I can find no other example. This was the name which the ancients gave to that narrow and rapid streight between the island of Eubœa and the continent. It was proverbial for its frequent flux and reflux, and its name may therefore have been given to the trick, which we have all witnessed, of inhaling and emitting smoke in quick succession. But all this is uncertain, and must be so received. I have nothing better.
  [1] *Stet, quæso*,] The usual adjuration, I suppose, not to cover, or tear down, the advertisements.
  [2] *Now, sir, whereas the ingenuity, &c.*]

This precious nonsense is somewhat of the nature of the *Chresme Philosophale des Questions Encyclopedicques de Pantagruel*, which Jonson probably had in his thoughts.
  [3] *As reason long since is fled to animals*,] Designed as a sneer on those philosophers who, from the tractable and imitative qualities in brutes, maintained that they were reasonable creatures.—WHAL.
  This is very gravely said : but I wonder the commentators have not rather pointed out this passage as *designed to sneer* at Shakspeare :

"O judgment, thou art fled to brutish beasts,
And men have lost their reason !"
         Julius Cæsar.

  It is true that *Every Man out of his Humour* was published several years before *Julius Cæsar*, but that I find is no conclusive argument in favour of Jonson, for—"he might have seen the lines in manuscript ; or, as the manuscript was certainly not in existence at this time, he might have known that Shakspeare intended to make use of such an expression.

Fast. Mass, yonder's the knight Puntarvolo.

Deli. And my cousin Sogliardo, methinks.

Maci. Ay, and his familiar that haunts him, the devil with the shining face.

Deli. Let 'em alone, observe 'em not.

[Sogliardo, Puntarvolo, *and*
          Carlo *walk together.*

Sog. Nay, I will have him, I am resolute for that. By this parchment, gentlemen, I have been so toiled among the harrots yonder,[1] you will not believe ! they do speak in the strangest language, and give a man the hardest terms for his money, that ever you knew.

Car. But have you arms, have you arms?

Sog. I' faith, I thank them ; I can write myself gentleman now ; here's my patent, it cost me thirty pound, by this breath.

Punt. A very fair coat,[2] well charged, and full of armory.

Sog. Nay, it has as much variety of colours in it as you have seen a coat have ; how like you the crest, sir ?

Punt. I understand it not well, what is't ?

Sog. Marry, sir, it is your boar without a head, rampant. A boar without a head, that's very rare !

Car. Ay, and rampant too ! troth, I commend the herald's wit, he has decyphered him well : a swine without a head, without brain, wit, anything indeed, ramping to gentility. You can blazon the rest, signior, can you not?

Sog. O, ay, I have it in writing here of purpose ; it cost me two shillings the tricking.[3]

Car. Let's hear, let's hear.

Punt. It is the most vile, foolish, absurd, palpable, and ridiculous escutcheon that ever this eye survised.—Save you, good Monsieur Fastidious.

[*They salute as they meet in the walk.*

Car. Silence, good knight ; on, on.

Sog. [reads.] "Gyrony of eight pieces ; azure and gules ; between three plates, a chevron engrailed checquy, or, vert, and ermins ; on a chief argent, between two ann'lets sable, a boar's head, proper."

Car. How's that ! on a chief argent ?

Sog. [reads.] "On a chief argent, a boar's head proper, between two ann'lets sable.

Car. 'Slud, it's a hog's cheek and puddings in a pewter field, this.

[*Here they shift.* Fastidious *mixes
          with* Puntarvolo ; Carlo *and* Sogliardo ; Deliro *and* Macilente ; Clove *and* Orange ; *four couple.*

Sog. How like you them, signior?

Punt. Let the word be,[4] *Not without mustard :* your crest is very rare, sir.

Car. A frying-pan to the crest had had no fellow.

Fast. Intreat your poor friend to walk off a little, signior, I will salute the knight.

Car. Come, lap it up, lap it up.

Fast. You are right well encountered, sir ; how does your fair dog ?

Punt. In reasonable state, sir ; what citizen is that you were consorted with? A merchant of any worth?

Fast. 'Tis Signior Deliro, sir.

Punt. Is it he ?—Save you, sir !

[*They salute.*

Deli. Good Sir Puntarvolo !

Maci. O what copy of fool[5] would this place minister, to one endued with patience to observe it !

Car. Nay, look you, sir, now you are a gentleman, you must carry a more exalted presence, change your mood and habit to a more austere form ; be exceeding proud, stand upon your gentility, and scorn every

---

[1] *I have been so toiled among the* harrots *yonder,*] See p. 10 *b.*

[2] *A very fair coat, &c.*] In this and what follows, Jonson had evidently the *Ementita Nobilitas* again in view : *Adde clypeum cum insignibus.* Ha. *Quænam mihi suades deligam?* Ne. *Duo mulctra, si velis, et cantharum cerevisiarium.* Ha. *Ludis : age dic serio.* Ne. *Nunquam fuisti in bello ?* Ha. *Ne vidi quidem.* Ne. *At interim, opinor, decollasti anseres et capos rusticorum?* Ha. *Persæpe, et quidem fortiter.* Ne. *Pone machæram argenteam, tria anserum capita aurea.* Ha. *In quo solo?* Ne. *Quo nisi sanguinolento, monumentum fortiter effusi cruoris.—In vertice quid eminebit?* Ha. *Expecto.* Ne. *Caput canis demissis auribus.*

[3] *It cost me two shillings the* tricking.] The drawing of it out with pen and ink ; it is an heraldic term.

[4] *Punt. Let the word be, &c.*] The motto. Thus in *Albion's England :*

          " *Non mærens moriar* for the *mot.*"

And, in Webster's *White Devil,*

          "The *word, Inopem me copia fecit.*"—WHAL.

[5] *O what* copy *of fool, &c.*] What abundance. Thus Gosson (forgetting himself, poor man !) observes, that "carpers doe nowe long for *copie* of abuses." We had this vile expression before.—See p. 86 *a.*

man ; speak nothing humbly, never discourse under a nobleman, though you never
saw him but riding to the Star Chamber,
it's all one.   Love no man : trust no man :
speak ill of no man to his face ; nor well of
any man behind his back.   Salute fairly on
the front, and wish them hanged upon the
turn.   Spread yourself upon his bosom
publicly, whose heart you would eat in
private.   These be principles, think on
them ; I'll come to you again presently.
                                                [*Exit.*
Punt. [*to his* Servant.] Sirrah, keep close ;
yet not so close : thy breath will thaw my
ruff.[1]
Sog. O, good cousin, I am a little busy,
how does my niece ? I am to walk with a
knight here.

Enter Fungoso *with his* Tailor.

Fung. O, he is here ; look you, sir, that's
the gentleman.
Tai. What, be in the blush-coloured
satin ?
Fung. Ay, he, sir ; though his suit blush,
he blushes not ; look you, that's the suit,
sir : I would have mine such a suit without
difference, such stuff, such a wing,[2] such a
sleeve, such a skirt, belly and all ; therefore, pray you observe it.   Have you a pair
of tables ?[3]
Fast. Why, do you see, sir, they say I
am fantastical ; why, true, I know it, and I
pursue my humour still, in contempt of this
censorious age.   'Slight, an a man should
do nothing but what a sort of stale judgments about this town will approve in him,
he were a sweet ass : I'd beg him, i' faith.[4]
I ne'er knew any more find fault with a
fashion, than they that knew not how to
put themselves into it.   For mine own part,
so i please mine own appetite, I am care-
les; what the fusty world speaks of me.
Puh !
Fung. Do you mark how it hangs at the
knee there ?

Tai. I warrant you, sir.
Fung. For God's sake do, note all ; do
you see the collar, sir ?
Tai. Fear nothing, it shall not differ in
a stitch, sir.
Fung. Pray heaven it do not ! you'll
make these linings serve, and help me to a
chapman for the outside, will you ?
Tai. I'll do my best, sir ; you'll put it
off presently.
Fung. Ay, go with me to my chamber
you shall have it —— but make haste of it,
for the love of a customer ; for I'll sit in
my old suit, or else lie a bed, and read the
Arcadia till you have done.
                                    [*Exit with his* Tailor.

Re-enter Carlo.

Car. O, if ever you were struck with a
jest, gallants, now, now, now, I do usher
the most strange piece of military profession that ever was discovered in *Insula
Paulina.*[5]
Fast. Where ? where ?
Punt. What is he for a creature ?[6]
Car. A pimp, a pimp, that I have observed yonder, the rarest superficies of a
humour ; he comes every morning to empty
his lungs in Paul's here ; and offers up
some five or six hecatombs of faces and
sighs, and away again.   Here he comes :
nay, walk, walk, be not seen to note him,
and we shall have excellent sport.

Enter Shift ; *and walks by, using action
to his rapier.*

Punt. 'Slid, he vented a sigh e'en now,
I thought he would have blown up the
church.
Car. O, you shall have him give a
number of those false fires ere he depart.
Fast. See, now he is expostulating with
his rapier : look, look !
Car. Did you ever in your days observe
better passion over a hilt ?

---

[1] *Thy breath will* thaw my ruff.] The expression is humourous, for the ruffs then worn were
made extremely stiff with starch.—WHAL.
[2] *Such a* wing,] A lateral prominency, extending from each shoulder, which, as appears
from the portraits of the age, was a fashionable
part of the dress.—WHAL.
[3] *Have you a* pair of tables ?] i.e., a *pocket-
book,* for taking memorandums.—See p. 96 a.
[4] *I'd beg him, i' faith.*] Alluding to the common expression of *begging a man for a fool.*
Great interest was formerly made with the
Crown, to obtain the custody of a wealthy idiot,
and the profit of his lands : probably too some

cajolery was used to the poor innocent himself.
Thus in *Drum's Entertainment,* "Be my *ward,*
John. Faith, I'll give thee two coats a year, an
thou'lt be my *fool.*"
[5] *In Insula Paulina.*] This is worse than in
Mediterraneum.   But I suppose that Jonson
did not think himself responsible for Carlo's
Latin.   He spells the word aisle, indeed, *isle,*
but he must have known the meaning of it too
well to imagine that *Insula* was the proper
translation.
[6] *What is he* for a creature ?] See *The Silent
Woman.*

Punt. Except it were in the person of a cutler's boy, or that the fellow were nothing but vapour,[1] I should think it impossible.

Car. See again, he claps his sword o' the head, as who should say, well, go to.

Fast. O, violence! I wonder the blade can contain itself, being so provoked.

Car. "With that the moody squire thumpt his breast,
And reared his eyen to heaven for revenge."[2]

Sog. Troth, an you be good gentlemen, let's make them friends, and take up the matter between his rapier and him.

Car. Nay, if you intend that, you must lay down the matter; for this rapier, it seems, is in the nature of a hanger-on, and the good gentleman would happily be rid of him.

Fast. By my faith, and 'tis to be suspected; I'll ask him.

Maci. O, here's rich stuff! for life's sake, let us go:
A man would wish himself a senseless pillar,
Rather than view these monstrous prodigies:
*Nil habet infœlix paupertas durius in se,
Quam quod ridiculos homines facit——*
        [*Exit with* Deliro.

Fast. Signior!

Shift. At your service.

Fast. Will you sell your rapier?

Car. He is turned wild upon the question; he looks as he had seen a serjeant.[3]

Shift. Sell my rapier! now fate bless me!

Punt. Amen.

Shift. You asked me if I would sell my rapier, sir?

Fast. I did indeed.

Shift. Now, lord have mercy upon me!

Punt. Amen, I say still.

Shift. 'Slid, sir, what should you behold in my face, sir, that should move you, as they say, sir, to ask me, sir, if I would sell my rapier?

Fast. Nay, let me pray you, sir, be not moved: I protest I would rather have been silent than any way offensive, had I known your nature.

Shift. Sell my rapier? 'ods lid!—Nay, sir, for mine own part, as I am a man that has served in causes, or so, so I am not apt to injure any gentleman in the degree of falling foul, but—sell my rapier! I will tell you, sir, I have served with this foolish rapier where some of us dare not appear in haste; I name no man; but let that pass. Sell my rapier!—death to my lungs! This rapier, sir, has travelled by my side, sir, the best part of France, and the Low Country: I have seen Flushing, Brill, and the Hague, with this rapier, sir, in my lord of Leicester's time: and, by God's will, he that should offer to disrapier me now, I would—— Look you, sir, you presume to be a gentleman of sort, and so likewise your friends here; if you have any disposition to travel for the sight of service, or so, one, two, or all of you, I can lend you letters to divers officers and commanders in the Low Countries, that shall for my cause do you all the good offices that shall pertain or belong to gentlemen of your—— [*lowering his voice.*] Please you, to shew the bounty of your mind, sir, to impart some ten groats,[4] or half a crown to our use, till our ability be of growth to return it, and we shall think ourself—— 'Sblood! sell my rapier!

Sog. I pray you what said he, signior? he's a proper man.

Fast. Marry, he tells me, if I please to shew the bounty of my mind, to impart some ten groats to his use, or so——

Punt. Break his head, and give it him.

Car. I thought he had been playing o' the Jew's trump, I.

Shift. My rapier! no, sir; my rapier is my guard, my defence, my revenue, my honour—if you cannot impart, be secret, I beseech you—and I will maintain it, where there is a grain of dust, or a drop of water. [*sighs.*] Hard is the choice when the valiant must eat their arms, or clem.[5] Sell my rapier! no, my dear, I will not be divorced from thee yet; I have ever found thee true as steel, and—— You cannot impart, sir?—

Save you, gentlemen ;—nevertheless, if you have a fancy to it, sir——

Fast. Prithee away : Is Signior Deliro departed ?

Car. Have you seen a pimp outface his own wants better ?

Sog. I commend him that can dissemble them so well.

Punt. True, and having no better a cloak for it than he has neither.

Fast. Od's precious, what mischievous luck is this ! adieu, gentlemen.

Punt. Whither in such haste, Monsieur Fastidious ?

Fast. After my merchant, Signior Deliro, sir. [*Exit.*

Car. O, hinder him not, he may hap lose his tide ; a good flounder, i' faith.

Orange. Hark you, Signior Whiffe, a word with you.

[*Orange and* Clove *call* Shift *aside.*

Car. How ! Signior Whiffe ?

Orange. What was the difference between that gallant that's gone and you, sir ?

Shift. No difference ; he would have given me five pound for my rapier, and I refused it ; that's all.

Clove. O, was it no otherwise? we thought you had been upon some terms.

Shift. No other than you saw, sir.

Clove. Adieu, good Master Apple-John.

[*Exit with* Orange.

Car. How ! Whiffe, and Apple-John too ? Heart, what will you say if this be the appendix or label to both yon indentures ?[1]

Punt. It may be.

Car. Resolve us of it, Janus, thou that look'st every way ; or thou, Hercules, that hast travelled all countries.[2]

Punt. Nay, Carlo, spend not time in invocations now, 'tis late.

Car. Signior, here's a gentleman desirous of your name, sir.

Shift. Sir, my name is Cavalier Shift : I am known sufficiently in this walk, sir.

Car. Shift ! I heard your name varied even now, as I take it.

Shift. True, sir, it pleases the world as I am her excellent tobacconist, to give me the style of Signior Whiffe ; as I am a poor esquire about the town here, they call me Master Apple-John. Variety of good names does well, sir.

Car. Ay, and good parts, to make those good names ; out of which I imagine yon bills to be yours.

Shift. Sir, if I should deny the manuscripts, I were worthy to be banished the middle aisle for ever.

Car. I take your word, sir : this gentleman has subscribed to them, and is most desirous to become your pupil. Marry, you must use expedition. Signior Insulso Sogliardo, this is the professor.

Sog. In good time, sir ; nay, good sir, house your head :[3] do you profess these sleights in tobacco ?

Shift. I do more than profess, sir, and, if you please to be a practitioner, I will undertake in one fortnight to bring you, that you shall take it plausibly in any ordinary, theatre, or the Tilt-yard, if need be, in the most popular assembly that is.

Punt. But you cannot bring him to the whiffe so soon ?

Shift. Yes, as soon, sir ; he shall receive the first, second, and third whiffe, if it please him, and, upon the receipt, take his horse, drink his three cups of canary, and expose one at Hounslow, a second at Stains, and a third at Bagshot.

Car. Baw-waw !

Sog. You will not serve me, sir, will you ? I'll give you more than countenance.[4]

Shift. Pardon me, sir, I do scorn to serve any man.

Car. Who ! he serve ? 'sblood, he keeps

---

[1] *What will you say if this be the appendix or label to both yon indentures ?*] From the names, which Carlo overhears, he conjectures that Shift is the person meant in both the advertisements : *Whiffe*, as professor of the noble art of smoking, and *Apple-John*, as pimp and squire to "gentlewomen of good carriage."

[2] *Or thou, Hercules, that hast travelled all countries.*] Jupiter, upon the arrival of Claudius among the gods, dispatches Hercules, who had travelled all countries, to know who he was: *Tum Jupiter Herculem, quia totum orbem terrarum pererraverat, et nosse videbatur omnes nationes, jubet ire, &c.—Seneca, de morte Claudii.* The

invocation of Janus is in the same spirit of humour.—WHAL.

[3] *House your head ;*] i.e., put it under shelter, cover it. They walked, we see, with their hats on :—but no species of irreverence was omitted.

[4] *I'll give you more than countenance.*] "*Countenance* is a law term from the French *contenement*, or the Latin *contenementum*, and denotes the credit and reputation which a person hath by reason of his freehold ; and most commonly what is necessary for his support and maintenance according to his condition of life. In this sense it occurs in several old statutes." *Observations on the more Ancient Statutes*, p. 11.

high men, and low men, he ! he has a fair living at Fullam.[1]

Shift. But in the nature of a fellow, I'll be your follower, if you please.

Sog. Sir, you shall stay, and dine with me, and if we can agree, we'll not part in haste : I am very bountiful to men of quality. Where shall we go, signior ?

Punt. Your Mitre is your best house.

Shift. I can make this dog take as many whiffes as I list, and he shall retain, or effume them, at my pleasure.

Punt. By your patience, follow me, fellows.

Sog. Sir Puntarvolo !

Punt. Pardon me, my dog shall not eat in his company for a million.

[*Exit with his* Servants.

Car. Nay, be not you amazed, Signior Whiffe, whatever that stiff-necked gentleman says.

Sog. No, for you do not know the humour of the dog as we do. Where shall we dine, Carlo ? I would fain go to one of these ordinaries, now I am a gentleman.

Car. So you may ; were you never at any yet ?

Sog. No, faith ; but they say there resorts your most choice gallants. ·

Car. True, and the fashion is, when any stranger comes in amongst 'em, they all stand up and stare at him, as he were some unknown beast, brought out of Africk ; but

that will be helped with a good adventurous face. You must be impudent enough, sit down, and use no respect : when anything's propounded above your capacity, smile at it, make two or three faces, and 'tis excellent ; they'll think you have travelled ; though you argue, a whole day, in silence thus, and discourse in nothing but laughter, 'twill pass. Only, now and then, · give fire, discharge a good full oath, and offer a great wager ; 'twill be admirable.

Sog. I warrant you, I am resolute ; come, good signior, there's a poor French crown for your ordinary.

Shift. It comes well, for I had not so much as the least portcullis of coin before.[2]

———

[*Mit.* I travail with another objection,[3] signior, which I fear will be enforced against the author, ere I can be delivered of it.

Cor. What's that, sir?

Mit. That the argument of his comedy might have been of some other nature, as of a duke to be in love with a countess, and that countess to be in love with the duke's son, and the son to love the lady's waiting-maid ; some such cross wooing, with a clown to their serving-man, better than to be thus near, and familiarly allied to the time.

Cor. You say well, but I would fain hear one of these autumn-judgments define once,

———

[1] *Who! he serve ? 'sblood, he keeps* high *men, and* low *men, he! he has a fair living at* Fullam.] He is a sharper and uses false dice. The dice were loaded to run high or low ; hence they were called *high men* or *low men*, and sometimes high and low *Fullams.* The phrase is common in the writers of this age.—WHAL.

Thus Piston :

"Nay, I use not to go without a pair of false dice : here are *tall men* and *little men.*

Julio. *High men* and *low men*, thou wouldst say."—*Soliman and Perseda*, act ii.

And Pistol :

"Gourd and *fullam* holds,
And *high* and *low* beguiles the rich and poor."
Merry Wives of Windsor.

Whalley says that false dice were called *fullams*, either because Fulham was the resort of sharpers, or because they were chiefly manufactured there. The last supposition is not improbable.

[2] *I had not so much as the least* portcullis *of coin before.*] Some old coins have a *portcullis* stamped on their reverse : which I suppose gave rise to the expression. Thus Stow gives us an account of the fall of base money, in the second year of Queen Elizabeth : "It was published by

proclamation, that the teston coined for twelvepence, and in the reign of Edward VI. called down to sixpence, should now forthwith (of the best sort marked with the *portcullice*) be taken for fourpence halfpenny."—*Annals*, p. 1115.—WHAL.

[3] Mitis. *I travail with another objection*, &c.] Jonson was so sensible of the extraordinary merit of this part of his drama, that he wantons in the consciousness of his own superiority. But for this, Mitis might have spared his remarks : — they have contributed, however, to draw down the indignation of the commentators on the head of the author, who, in what follows, is accused of *sneering* (for that is the eternal phrase) at *Twelfth Night.* This is as absurd as most of the other charges brought against him. *Twelfth Night* has no countess in love with a duke's son, nor no duke's son in love with a waiting-maid ; though it is probable that some such "cross wooing" was to be found among the old trash which has long since perished. What is more to the purpose is, that this was written at least a dozen years before *Twelfth Night* appeared, since it is found in the quarto, 1600, precisely as it stands here, while the earliest date of the play which it is so wisely supposed to ridicule, was never brought lower than 1613.

Quid sit comœdia? if he cannot, let him content himself with Cicero's definition, till he have strength to propose to himself a better, who would have a comedy to be *imitatio vitæ, speculum consuetudinis, imago veritatis;* a thing throughout pleasant and ridiculous, and accommodated to the correction of manners : if the maker have failed[1] in any particle of this, they may worthily tax him; but if not, why—be you, that are for them, silent, as I will be for him ; and give way to the actors.]

SCENE II.—The Country.

Enter Sordido, *with a halter about his neck.*

Sord. Nay, God's precious, if the weather and season be so respectless, that beggars shall live as well as their betters; and that my hunger and thirst for riches shall not make them hunger and thirst with poverty; that my sleep shall be broken, and their hearts not broken ; that my coffers shall be full, and yet care; theirs empty, and yet merry;—'tis time that a cross should bear flesh and blood, since flesh and blood cannot bear this cross.

[*Mit.* What, will he hang himself?
Cor. Faith, ay; it seems his prognostication has not kept touch with him, and that makes him despair.
Mit. Beshrew me, he will be OUT OF HIS HUMOUR then indeed.]

Sord. Tut, these starmonger knaves, who would trust them? One says dark and rainy, when 'tis as clear as crystal; another says tempestuous blasts and storms, and 'twas as calm as a milk-bowl; here be sweet rascals for a man to credit his whole fortunes with! You skystaring coxcombs you, you fat-brains, out upon you; you are good for nothing but to sweat night-caps and make rug-gowns dear![2] you learned

men, and have not a legion of devils *à vostre service! à vostre service!* by heaven, I think I shall die a better scholar than they: but soft—

Enter a Hind, *with a letter.*

How now, sirrah ?
Hind. Here's a letter come from your son, sir.
Sord. From my son, sir! what would my son, sir? some good news, no doubt.
[*Reads.*

"Sweet and dear father, desiring you first to send me your blessing, which is more worth to me than gold or silver, I desire you likewise to be advertised, that this Shrove-tide, contrary to custom, we use always to have revels ;[3] which is indeed dancing, and makes an excellent shew in truth; especially if we gentlemen be well attired, which our seniors note, and think the better of our fathers, the better we are maintained, and that they shall know if they come up, and have anything to do in the law ; therefore, good father, these are, for your own sake as well as mine, to redesire you, that you let me not want that which is fit for the setting up of our name in the honourable volume of gentility, that I may say to our calumniators, with Tully, *Ego sum ortus domus meæ, tu occasus tuæ.* And thus, not doubting of your fatherly benevolence, I humbly ask your blessing and pray God to bless you.
"Yours, if his own [FUNGOSO.]"

How's this! *Yours, if his own!* Is he not my son, except he be his own son? belike this is some new kind of subscription the gallants use. Well! wherefore dost thou stay, knave? away; go. [*Exit* Hind.] Here's a letter indeed! revels? and benevolence? is this a weather to send benevolence? or is this a season to revel in? 'Slid, the devil and all takes part to vex me, I think! this letter would never have

---

[1] *If the* maker *have failed, &c.*] By the *maker,* Jonson means the *poet:* he seems peculiarly fond of this word; and not improbably considered it as a more honourable designation of the artist than the more modern term. For the rest, he might safely challenge censure here, for he has assuredly failed in no particle of "Cicero's definition." But alas! that definition is incomplete :—it overlooks simplicity of design, connexion, and mutual dependence, all, in short, that is wanting to render this exquisite *image of truth* as interesting as it is faithful.

[2] *You are good for nothing but to sweat*

night-caps *and make* rug-gowns *dear!*] This was the usual dress of mathematicians, astrologers, &c. when engaged in their sublime speculations, if we may trust the portraits of such of them as have condescended to favour us with their *veræ effigies,* in the front of their books.

[3] *That this Shrove-tide, contrary to custom, we use always to have* revels ; *&c.*] Fungoso imposes on his father ; the revels were at Christmas : but he wanted money to enable him to copy the finery of Fastidious Brisk. There is some humour in this letter, especially in the quotation from Cicero.

come now else, now, now, when the sun shines, and the air thus clear. Soul! if this hold, we shall shortly have an excellent crop of corn spring out of the highways : the streets and houses of the town will be hid with the rankness of the fruits, that grow there in spite of good husbandry. Go to, I'll prevent the sight of it, come as quickly as it can, I will prevent the sight of it. I have this remedy, heaven. [*Clambers up, and suspends the halter to a tree.*] Stay ; I'll try the pain thus a little. O, nothing, nothing. Well now! shall my son gain a benevolence by my death? or anybody be the better for my gold, or so forth? no ; alive I kept it from them, and dead, my ghost shall walk about it and preserve it. My son and daughter shall starve ere they touch it ; I have hid it as deep as hell from the sight of heaven, and to it I go now.
[*Flings himself off.*

Enter five or six Rustics, *one after another.*

1 *Rust.* Ah me, what pitiful sight is this! help, help, help !

2 *Rust.* How now ! what's the matter?

1 *Rust.* O, here's a man has hanged himself, help to get him again.

2 *Rust.* Hanged himself ! 'Slid, carry him afore a justice, 'tis chance medley, o' my word.

3 *Rust.* How now, what's here to do?

4 *Rust.* How comes this?

2 *Rust.* One has executed himself, contrary to order of law, and by my consent he shall answer it.   [*They cut him down.*

5 *Rust.* Would he were in case to answer it !

1 *Rust.* Stand by, he recovers, give him breath.

Sord. Oh !

5 *Rust.* Mass, 'twas well you went the footway, neighbour.

1 *Rust.* Ay, an I had not cut the halter——

Sord. How! cut the halter! ah me, I am undone, I am undone !

2 *Rust.* Marry, if you had not been undone, you had been hanged, I can tell you.

Sord. You thread-bare, horse-bread-eating[1] rascals, if you would needs have been meddling, could you not have untied it, but you must cut it ; and in the midst too! ah me !

1 *Rust.* Out on me, 'tis the caterpillar Sordido ! how curst are the poor, that the viper was blest with this good fortune !

2 *Rust.* Nay, how accurst art thou, that art cause to the curse of the poor?

3 *Rust.* Ay, and to save so wretched a caitiff !

4 *Rust.* Curst be thy fingers that loosed him !

2 *Rust.* Some desperate fury possess thee, that thou mayst hang thyself too !

5 *Rust.* Never mayst thou be saved, that saved so damned a monster !

Sord. What curses breathe these men ! how have my deeds
Made my looks differ from another man's,
That they should thus detest and loathe my life !
Out on my wretched humour ! it is that
Makes me thus monstrous in true humane eyes.
Pardon me, gentle friends, I'll make fair 'mends
For my foul errors past, and twenty-fold
Restore to all men, what with wrong I robbed them :
My barns and garners shall stand open still
To all the poor that come, and my best grain
Be made alms-bread to feed half-famished mouths.
Though hitherto amongst you I have lived,
Like an unsavoury muck-hill[2] to myself,

---

[1] Sord. *You thread-bare,* horse-bread-*eating rascals.*] "It appears," says Dr. Percy, "from the Earl of Northumberland's *Household Book*, that horses were not so usually fed with corn loose in the manger, in the present manner, as with their provender made into *loaves.*" This, indeed, is sufficiently clear from our old dramas, where the expressions of *horse-bread* and *horse-loaves* perpetually occur : thus, in *Gammer Gurton*, "Save this piece of dry *horse-bread*, chave byt no byt this lyvelonge daie." And in the *Little Thief*, by Beaumont and Fletcher : "Oh that I were in my oat-tub, with a *horse-loaff*" Probably, too, the coarse bread eaten by the common people of those "golden days,"

as they have been ignorantly or mischievously termed, composed principally of oats and barley, went under the same names.

[2] *Though hitherto amongst you I have lived, Like an unsavoury muck-hill,* &c.] This is not much unlike what Pope says of wealth :

" In heaps, like ambergrease, a stink it lies,
But well dispersed, is incense to the skies."

May has a feeble imitation of this character, in his *Old Couple.* Earthworm, like Sordido, undergoes a sudden change, but I think less naturally, and by means not so well calculated to produce a striking effect. Avarice may be terrified, but not flattered into liberality.

Yet now my gathered heaps being spread abroad,
Shall turn to better and more fruitful uses.
Bless then this man, curse him no more for saying
My life and soul together. O, how deeply
The bitter curses of the poor do pierce!
I am by wonder changed; come in with me
And witness my repentance: now I prove,
No life is blest that is not graced with love.
                                        [*Exit.*
2 *Rust.* O miracle! see when a man has grace!

3 *Rust.* Had it not been pity so good a man should have been cast away?

2 *Rust.* Well, I'll get our clerk put his conversion in the *Acts and Monuments.*[1]

4 *Rust.* Do, for I warrant him he's a martyr.

2 *Rust.* O God, how he wept, if you marked it! did you see how the tears trilled?

5 *Rust.* Yes, believe me, like master vicar's bowls upon the green, for all the world.

3 *Rust.* O neighbour, God's blessing o' your heart, neighbour, 'twas a good grateful deed.   [*Exeunt.*

———

[*Cor.* How now, Mitis! what's that you consider so seriously?

Mit. Troth, that which doth essentially please me, the warping condition of this green and soggy multitude;[2] but in good faith, signior, your author hath largely outstript my expectation in this scene, I will liberally confess it. For when I saw Sordido so desperately intended, I thought I had had a hand of him, then.

Cor. What! you supposed he should have hung himself indeed?

Mit. I did, and had framed my objection to it ready, which may yet be very fitly urged, and with some necessity; for though his purposed violence lost the effect, and extended not to death, yet the intent and horror of the object was more than the nature of a comedy will in any sort admit.

Cor. Ay! what think you of Plautus, in his comedy called *Cistellaria?*[3] there, where he brings in Alcesimarchus with a drawn sword ready to kill himself, and as he is e'en fixing his breast upon it, to be restrained from his resolved outrage by Silenium and the bawd? Is not his authority of power to give our scene approbation?

Mit. Sir, I have this only evasion left me, to say, I think it be so indeed;[4] your memory is happier than mine: but I wonder what engine he will use to bring the rest out of their humours!

Cor. That will appear anon, never preoccupy your imagination withal. Let your mind keep company with the scene still, which now removes itself from the country to the court. Here comes Macilente and

———

[1] The quarto reads:
"2 *Rust.* Well, I'll get our clarke put his conversion into the *Chronicle.*
4 *Rust.* Do, for I warrant he's a *virtuous man.*"
The necessity of change is not very obvious, for the *Chronicles* were as popular as the *Acts and Monuments;* unless, as Whalley thinks, there is a satirical allusion to Fox's *History of Martyrs.*

[2] *Of this green and* soggy *multitude.*] In the margin of Whalley's copy, he has written "quere *foggy?*" but the text, I presume, is right. *Soggy,* indeed, is not a very common word, nor does it appear elsewhere in Jonson, or, as I think, in any of our old dramatists; yet I have heard it applied (with what propriety I know not) to hay that has been cut too early, and "sweats" as it lies in heaps.

[3] Act iii. scene the last.

[4] Mit. *Sir, I have this only evasion left me, to say, I think it be so indeed;* &c.] Poor Mitis is a most convenient antagonist; for though he sometimes stumbles on a valid objection, any answer satisfies him. The truth is, that "the horror of the action" was too great; for Sordido had really hanged himself, and is saved by chance; whereas the spectators could be in little pain about Alcesimarchus, whose mistress is upon the stage, and ready to preserve him. It might have been urged in favour of the poet, that avarice is so odious and debasing a vice, that scarcely any degree of suffering can interest our feelings for the character tainted with it: nor is this all—for, of the ten thousand modes in which avarice may be held forth to public indignation, no one is, or ever was regarded with more abhorrence than that of the hoarder of grain. Neither was the idea of such a wretch as Sordido hanging himself at all new to the audiences of Jonson's days, when almost every term produced a "warning ballad" on the subject. "Here's a farmer that hanged himself on the expectation of plenty," says the porter in *Macbeth:* and Mr. Waldron has furnished me with an extract from a publication of that age, which undoubtedly expresses the general belief of the people, "That God hath made the curses of the poore effectuall upon such covetous corne-horders, even in recent remembrance, may appeare by this, that some of this cursed crue have become their own executioners, and in kindnesse have saved the hang-man a labour by haltering themselves, when, contrary to their expectation, the price of corne had sodainly fallen: and this both in other countries, and among us, as divines of good reputation have delivered upon their owne knowledge."—*The Curse of Corne-horders,* quarto, 1631, p. 24.

Signior Brisk freshly suited ; lose not yourself, for now the epitasis,[1] or busy part of
our subject, is in act.]

SCENE III.—An Apartment at the Court.

Enter Macilente, Fastidious, *both in a new
suit, and* Cinedo *with tobacco.*

Fast. Well, now, Signior Macilente, you
are not only welcome to the court, but also
to my mistress's withdrawing chamber.—
Boy, get me some tobacco. I 'll but go in,
and shew I am here, and come to you pre-
sently, sir.   [*Exit.*
    Maci. What's that he said ? by heaven,
I marked him not :
My thoughts and I were of another world.
I was admiring mine own outside here,
To think what privilege and palm it bears
Here in the court ! be a man ne'er so vile,
In wit, in judgment, manners, or what else;
If he can purchase but a silken cover,
He shall not only pass, but pass regarded :
Whereas let him be poor and meanly clad,
Though ne'er so richly parted,[2] you shall
have
A fellow that knows nothing but his beef,
Or how to rince his clammy guts in beer,
Will take him by the shoulders or the
throat,
And kick him down the stairs. Such is the
state
Of virtue in bad clothes !—ha, ha, ha, ha !
That raiment should be in such high re-
quest !
How long should I be ere I should put off
To the lord chancellor's tomb, or the
shrives' posts?[3]
By heaven, I think a thousand thousand
year.
His gravity, his wisdom, and his faith
To my dread sovereign, graces that survive
him,
These I could well indure to reverence,
But not his tomb ; no more than I 'd com-
mend

The chapel organ for the gilt without,
Or this base-viol for the varnished face.

Re-enter Fastidious.

    Fast. I fear I have made you stay some-
what long, sir ; but is my tobacco ready,
boy?
    Cin. Ay, sir.
    Fast. Give me ; my mistress is upon
coming, you shall see her presently, sir,
[*puffs.*] You'll say you never accosted a
more piercing wit.—This tobacco is not
dried, boy, or else the pipe is defective.—
Oh, your wits of Italy are nothing comparable to her ; her brain's a very quiver of
jests, and she does dart them abroad with
that sweet, loose, and judicial aim, that you
would—here she comes, sir.
            [*Saviolina looks in, and draws
                back again.*
    Maci. 'Twas time, his invention had been
bogged else.
    Savi. [*within.*] Give me my fan there.
    Maci. How now, Monsieur Brisk ?
    Fast. A kind of affectionate reverence
strikes me with a cold shivering, methinks.
    Maci. I like such tempers well as stand
before their mistresses with fear and trembling ; and before their Maker, like impudent mountains !
    Fast. By this hand, I'd spend twenty
pounds my vaulting-horse stood here now,
she might see me do but one trick.
    Maci. Why, does she love activity?
    Cin. Or if you had but your long stock-
ings on, to be dancing a galliard as she
comes by.
    Fast. Ay, either. O, these stirring hu-
mours make ladies mad with desire ; she
comes. My good genius embolden me :
boy, the pipe quickly.

Enter Saviolina.

    Maci. What ! will he give her music?
    Fast. A second good morrow to my fair
mistress.

---

[1] *Lose not yourself, for now the* epitasis,
&c.] The old critics assign four parts to comedy;
the *Prologue*, the *Protasis*, or proposition of the
subject ; the *Epitasis*, or busy part of it ; and
the *Catastrophe*, or conclusion.
    [2] *Though ne'er so richly* parted,] Though
possessed of the most excellent parts and natural
talents.—WHAL.
    The expression has occurred before. See p. 62.
    [3] *To the lord chancellor's tomb, or the shrives'
posts ?*] The sheriffs had posts set up before
their door, on which proclamations were fastened, which it was usual, out of respect, to
read bareheaded. —WHAL.

We meet with many allusions to these *posts* in
our old dramatists. Thus Shakspeare :

" I'll stand at your door like a *sheriff's post."*
                                    Twelfth Night.

Again, " *Worship*, I think ; for so much the
posts at his door should signify."—*Puritan,*
act iii. sc. 5. But the expression is so common,
that more examples would be tedious. The *lord
chancellor's tomb*, is the tomb of Sir Christopher
Hatton, then an object of great respect with the
country visitors of St. Paul's. See the *Entertainment at Althorpe.*

Sav. Fair servant, I'll thank you a day hence, when the date of your salutation comes forth.

Fast. How like you that answer? is't not admirable?

Maci. I were a simple courtier, if I could not admire trifles, sir.

Fast. [*Talks and takes tobacco between the breaks.*] Troth, sweet lady, I shall [*puffs*]—be prepared to give you thanks for those thanks, and—study more officious, and obsequious regards—to your fair beauties.—Mend the pipe, boy.

Maci. I never knew tobacco taken as a parenthesis before.

Fast. 'Fore God, sweet lady, believe it, I do honour the meanest rush in this chamber for.your love.[1]

Sav. Ay, you need not tell me that, sir; I do think you do prize a rush before my love.

Maci. Is this the wonder of nations!

Fast. O, by this air, pardon me, I said *for* your love, by this light; but it is the accustomed sharpness of your ingenuity, sweet mistress, to [*takes down the viol,*[2] *and plays*]—Mass, your viol's new strung, methinks.

Maci. Ingenuity! I see his ignorance will not suffer him to slander her, which he had done most notably if he had said wit for ingenuity,[3] as he meant it.

Fast. By the soul of music, lady—*hum, hum.*

Sav. Would we might hear it once.

Fast. I do more adore and admire your —*hum, hum*—predominant perfections than —*hum, hum*—ever I shall have power and faculty to express—*hum.*

Sav. Upon the viol de gambo, you mean?

Fast. It is miserably out of tune, by this hand.

Sav. Nay, rather by the fingers.

Maci. It makes good harmony with her wit.

Fast. Sweet lady, tune it. [*Saviolina tunes the viol.*]—Boy, some tobacco.

Maci. Tobacco again! he does court his mistress with very exceeding good changes.

Fast. Signior Macilente, you take none, sir?

Maci. No, unless I had a mistress, signior, it were a great indecorum for me to take tobacco.

Fast. How like you her wit?
[*Talks and takes tobacco between again.*]

Maci. Her ingenuity is excellent, sir.

Fast. You see the subject of her sweet fingers there—Oh, she tickles it so, that— She makes it laugh most divinely;—I'll tell you a good jest now, and yourself shall say it's a good one: I have wished myself to be that instrument, I think, a thousand times, and not so few, by heaven.

Maci. Not unlike, sir; but how? to be cased up and hung by on the wall?

Fast. O, no, sir, to be in use, I assure you; as your judicious eyes may testify.

Sav. Here, servant, if you will play, come.

Fast. Instantly, sweet lady.—In good faith, here's most divine tobacco!

Sav. Nay, I cannot stay to dance after your pipe.

Fast. Good! nay, dear lady, stay; by this sweet smoke, I think your wit be all fire.

---

[1] *I do honour the meanest* rush *in this chamber for your love.*] Before carpets came into use, the floors of chambers, and the stage itself, were strewed with rushes. So in the *Widow's Tears*:

" Their honours are upon coming, and the room
     not ready?
Rushes and seats instantly."—Act iii. sc. 1.

Again, in the *Coxcomb*:

" Take care my house be handsome,
And the new stools set out, and boughs, and
     rushes."—Act iv.—WHAL.

My predecessor might have added, that from the indelicate and filthy habits of our forefathers, carpets would have been a grievous nuisance; whereas rushes, which concealed the impurities with which they were charged, were, at convenient times, gathered up and thrown into the streets, where they only bred a general plague, instead of a particular one.

[2] *Takes down the* viol,] It appears, from numerous passages in our old plays, that a viol de gambo (a bass-viol, as Jonson calls it, in a subsequent passage) was an indispensable piece of furniture in every fashionable house, where it hung up in the best chamber, much as the guitar does in Spain, and the violin in Italy, to be played on at will, and to fill up the void of conversation. Whoever pretended to fashion affected an acquaintance with this instrument; and it is well known that Sir Andrew Aguecheek could play upon it, as he spoke the languages, " word for word, without book."

[3] *If he had said* wit *for* ingenuity,] Ingenuity has a twofold signification: derived from *ingenuous,* it means openness, candour, or fairness; from *ingenious,* it implies *wit,* invention, genius. In this last sense it is here to be understood; but Macilente plays upon the double meaning. Ingenious and ingenuous were often used for each other.—WHAL.

Maci. And he's the salamander belongs to it.[1]

Sav. Is your tobacco perfumed, servant, that you swear by the sweet smoke?

Fast. Still more excellent! Before heaven, and these bright lights, I think—you are made of ingenuity, I——

Maci. True, as your discourse is. O, abominable!

Fast. Will your ladyship take any?

Sav. O, peace, I pray you; I love not the breath of a woodcock's head.

Fast. Meaning my head, lady?[2]

Sav. Not altogether so, sir; but, as it were fatal to their follies that think to grace themselves with taking tobacco, when they want better entertainment, you see your pipe bears the true form of a woodcock's head.

Fast. O admirable simile!

Sav. 'Tis best leaving of you in admiration, sir.   [*Exit.*

Maci. Are these the admired lady-wits, that having so good a plain song can run no better division upon it? All her jests are of the stamp March was fifteen years ago. Is this the comet, Monsieur Fastidious, that your gallants wonder at so?

Fast. Heart of a gentleman, to neglect me afore the presence thus! Sweet sir, I beseech you be silent in my disgrace. By the muses, I was never in so vile a humour in my life, and her wit was at the flood too! Report it not for a million, good sir; let me be so far endeared to your love.

                 [*Exeunt.*

[*Mit.* What follows next, Signior Cordatus? this gallant's humour is almost spent; methinks it ebbs apace, with this contrary breath of his mistress.

Cor. O, but it will flow again for all this, till there comes a general drought of humour among all our actors, and then I fear not but his will fall as low as any. See who presents himself here!

Mit. What, in the old case?

Cor. Ay, faith, which makes it the more pitiful; you understand where the scene is?]

ACT IV.

SCENE I.—*A Room in* Deliro's *House.*

Enter Fungoso, Fallace *following him.*

Fal. Why are you so melancholy, brother?

Fung. I am not melancholy, I thank you, sister.

Fal. Why are you not merry then? there are but two of us in all the world, and if we should not be comforts one to another, God help us!

Fung. Faith, I cannot tell, sister, but if a man had any true melancholy in him, it would make him melancholy to see his yeomanly father cut his neighbours' throats, to make his son a gentleman; and yet, when he has cut them, he will see his son's throat cut too, ere he make him a true gentleman indeed, before death cut his own throat. I must be the first head of our house, and yet he will not give me the head till I be made so. Is any man termed a gentleman that is not always in the fashion? I would know but that.

Fal. If you be melancholy for that, brother, I think I have as much cause to be melancholy as any one: for I'll be sworn, I live as little in the fashion as any woman in London. By the faith of a gentlewoman, beast that I am to say it! I have not one friend in the world besides my husband. When saw you Master Fastidious Brisk, brother?

Fung. But a while since, sister, I think; I know not well in truth. By this hand I could fight with all my heart, methinks.

Fal. Nay, good brother, be not resolute.

---

[1] Maci. *And he's the salamander* belongs *to it.*] In the quarto it is—*that lives by it.* It seems scarcely worth the pains of altering, or, indeed, of noticing.

[2] Fast. *Meaning my head, lady?*] To account for the captious question of Fastidious, it should be observed that *woodcock* was a cant term for a *fool.* From the following drawing of an ancient tobacco-pipe, which was in the possession of Mr. Reed, it appears that Saviolina was not far from the truth, when she compared it to "the true form of a woodcock's head."

Fung. I sent him a letter,[1] and he writes me no answer neither.

Fal. Oh, sweet Fastidious Brisk! O fine courtier! thou art he makest me sigh, and say, how blessed is that woman that hath a courtier to her husband, and how miserable a dame she is, that hath neither husband nor friend in the court! O sweet Fastidious! O fine courtier! How comely he bows him in his courtesy! how full he hits a woman between the lips when he kisses! how upright he sits at the table! how daintily he carves! how sweetly he talks, and tells news of this lord and of that lady! how cleanly he wipes his spoon at every spoonful of any whitemeat he eats! and what a neat case of pick-tooths he carries about him still![2] O sweet Fastidious! O fine courtier!

Enter Deliro *at a distance, with* Musicians.

Deli. See yonder she is, gentlemen. Now, as ever you'll bear the name of musicians touch your instruments sweetly; she has a delicate ear, I tell you: play not a false note, I beseech you.

Musi. Fear not, Signior Deliro.

Deli. O, begin, begin, some sprightly thing: Lord, how my imagination labours with the success of it! [*they strike up a lively tune.*] Well said, good, i' faith! Heaven grant it please her. I'll not be seen, for then she'll be sure to dislike it.

Fal. Hey——da! this is excellent! I'll lay my life this is my husband's dotage. I thought so; nay, never play bo-peep with me; I know you do nothing but study how to anger me, sir.

Deli. [*coming forward.*] Anger thee, sweet wife! why, didst thou not send for musicians at supper last night thyself?

Fal. To supper, sir! now come up to supper, I beseech you: as though there were no difference between supper-time, when folks should be merry, and this time when they should be melancholy. I would never take upon me to take a wife, if I had no more judgment to please her.

Deli. Be pleased, sweet wife, and they shall have done, and would to fate my life were done, if I can never please thee!

      [*Exeunt* Musicians.

Enter Macilente.

Maci. Save you, lady; where is Master Deliro?

Deli. Here, Master Macilente: you are welcome from court, sir; no doubt you have been graced exceedingly of Master Brisk's mistress, and the rest of the ladies for his sake.

Maci. Alas, the poor fantastic! he's scarce known
To any lady there; and those that know him,
Know him the simplest man of all they know:
Deride and play upon his amorous humours,
Though he but apishly doth imitate
The gallant'st courtiers, kissing ladies' pumps,
Holding the cloth for them,[3] praising their wits,
And servilely observing every one
May do them pleasure: fearful to be seen
With any man, though he be ne'er so worthy,
That's not in grace with some that are the greatest.
Thus courtiers do, and these he counterfeits,
But sets no such a sightly carriage
Upon their vanities, as they themselves;
And therefore they despise him: for indeed
He's like the zany to a tumbler,
That tries tricks after him, to make men laugh.

Fal. Here's an unthankful spiteful wretch! the good gentleman vouchsafed to make him his companion, because my husband put him into a few rags, and now see how the unrude rascal backbites him![4]

       [*Aside.*

Deli. Is he no more graced amongst them then, say you?

---

[1] Fung. *I sent him a letter,* &c.] By *him*, Fungoso means his father, not Fastidious Brisk : he is talking to himself.

[2] *And what a neat case of pick-tooths he carries about him still!* See *The Devil's an Ass.*—Act v. sc. 1.

[3] *Holding the cloth for them.*] Lifting up the arras, or hangings, for them, as they moved from room to room, so that they might pass without disordering their dress. So in *Cynthia's Revels :* "This repeats jests, this presents gifts, this holds up the *arras.*"—Act v.

[4] *How the* unrude *rascal backbites him !*] *Un* is commonly used in composition as a negative, as *un*thankful, *un*civil, &c; here, however, it seems to be employed as an augmentative. Unless, indeed, unrude be synonymous with the primitive rude, as *un*loose probably is with *loose,* &c. It occurs again in the *Masque of Christmas :* " *Unrude* people they are, your courtiers."

Maci. Faith, like a pawn at chess: fills up a room, that's all.

Fal. O, monster of men! can the earth bear such an envious caitiff?   [*Aside.*

Deli. Well, I repent me I ever credited him so much; but now I see what he is, and that his masking vizor is off, I'll forbear him no longer. All his lands are mortgaged to me, and forfeited; besides, I have bonds of his in my hand, for the receipt of now fifty pound, now a hundred, now two hundred; still, as he has had a fan but wagged at him, he would be in a new suit. Well, I'll salute him by a serjeant the next time I see him, i' faith, I'll suit him.

Maci. Why, you may soon see him, sir, for he is to meet Signior Puntarvolo at a notary's by the Exchange, presently; where he means to take up, upon return.

Fal. Now, out upon thee, Judas! canst thou not be content to backbite thy friend, but thou must betray him! Wilt thou seek the undoing of any man? and of such a man too? and will you, sir, get your living by the counsel of traitors?

Deli. Dear wife, have patience.

Fal. The house will fall, the ground will open and swallow us: I'll not bide here for all the gold and silver in heaven.
            [*Exit with* Fungoso.

Deli. O, good Macilente, let's follow and appease her, or the peace of my life is at an end.   [*Exit.*

Maci. Now pease, and not peace, feed that life,[1] whose head hangs so heavily over a woman's manger!   [*Exit.*

SCENE II.—*Another Room in the same.*

Enter Fallace *and* Fungoso *running; she claps to the door.*

Fal. Help me, brother! Ods body, an you come here I'll do myself a mischief.

Deli. [*within.*] Nay, hear me, sweet wife; unless thou wilt have me go, I will not go.

Fal. Tut, you shall never have that vantage of me, to say, you are undone by me. I'll not bid you stay, I. Brother, sweet brother, here's four angels I'll give you towards your suit: for the love of gentry, and as ever you came of Christian creature, make haste to the water side, (you know where Master Fastidious uses to land,) give him warning of my husband's malicious intent; and tell him of that lean rascal's treachery. O, heavens, how my flesh rises at him! Nay, sweet brother, make haste: you may say, I would have writ to him, but that the necessity of the time would not permit. He cannot choose but take it extraordinarily from me: and commend me to him, good brother; say I sent you.   [*Exit.*

Fung. Let me see, these four angels, and then forty shillings more I can borrow on my gown in Fetter-lane.—Well, I will go presently, say on my suit,[2] pay as much money as I have, and swear myself into credit with my tailor for the rest.   [*Exit.*

SCENE III.—*Another Room in the same.*

Enter Deliro *and* Macilente.

Deli. O, on my soul you wrong her, Macilente. Though she be froward, yet I know she is honest.

Maci. Well, then have I no judgment. Would any woman, but one that were wild in her affections, have broke out into that immodest and violent passion against her husband? or is't possible——

Deli. If you love me, forbear; all the arguments i' the world shall never wrest my heart to believe it.   [*Exeunt.*

[*Cor.* How like you the deciphering of his dotage?

Mit. O, strangely: and of the other's envy too, that labours so seriously to set debate betwixt a man and his wife. Stay, here comes the knight adventurer.

Cor. Ay, and his scrivener with him.]

---

[1] *Now* pease *and not* peace *feed that life,* &c.] Deplorable as this attempt at a pun is, it has yet found imitators; see Fletcher's *King and no King,* act ii. For the credit of both poets, I hope that *peace* and *pease* were in their days pronounced alike.

[2] Say *on my suit,*] i.e., try it on This word is so common that I should not have noticed it, were it not to observe that the modern editors usually print it with a mark of elision, 'say: a practice which I have been reprehended for not following; (Massinger, vol. i. p. 169;) but

there is no necessity, as a few examples will prove:

     "But pray do not
Take the first *say* of her yourself."—*Chapman.*

" So good a *say* invites the eye
     A little downward to espy.—*Sir P. Sidney.*

"Wolsey makes dukes and erles to serve him of wine with a *say* taken."—*Holinshed.*

" I could cite more, but these shall suffice for a *say.*—*Old Trans. of the Andria.*

SCENE IV.—Puntarvolo's *Lodgings.*

Enter Puntarvolo, Notary, *and* Servants
with the dog and cat.

Punt. I wonder Monsieur Fastidious
comes not ! But, notary, if thou please to
draw the indentures the while, I will give
thee thy instructions.

Not. With all my heart, sir; and I'll fall
in hand with them presently.

Punt. Well then, first the sum is to be
understood.

Not. [*writes.*] Good, sir.

Punt. Next, our several appellations,
and character of my dog and cat must be
known. Shew him the cat, sirrah.

Not. So, sir.

Punt. Then, that the intended bound is
the Turk's court in Constantinople ; the
time limited for our return, a year; and
that if either of us miscarry the whole
venture is lost. These are general, con-
ceiv'st thou ? or if either of us turn Turk.

Not. Ay, sir.

Punt. Now, for particulars : that I may
make my travels by sea or land, to my best
liking ; and that hiring a coach for myself,
it shall be lawful for my dog or cat, or both,
to ride with me in the said coach.

Not. Very good, sir.

Punt. That I may choose to give my dog
or cat, fish, for fear of bones ; or any other
nutriment that, by the judgment of the most
authentical physicians[1] where I travel, shall
be thought dangerous.

Not. Well, sir.

Punt. That, after the receipt of his
money, he shall neither, in his own person,
nor any other, either by direct or indirect
means, as magic, witchcraft,[2] or other such
exotic arts, attempt, practise, or complot
anything to the prejudice of me, my dog,
or my cat: neither shall I use the help of
any such sorceries or enchantments, as unc-
tions to make our skins impenetrable, or to
travel invisible by virtue of a powder, or a
ring, or to hang any three-forked charm
about my dog's neck, secretly conveyed
into his collar ;[3] (understand you ?) but that
all be performed sincerely, without fraud or
imposture.

Not. So, sir.

Punt. That, for testimony of the performance, myself am to bring thence a
Turk's mustachio, my dog a Grecian hare's
lip, and my cat the train or tail of a Thra-
cian rat.

Not. [*writes.*] 'Tis done, sir.

Punt. 'Tis said, sir ; not done, sir. But
forward ; that upon my return, and landing on the Tower-wharf, with the aforesaid
testimony, I am to receive five for one, according to the proportion of the sums put
forth.

Not. Well, sir.

Punt. Provided, that if before our departure, or setting forth, either myself or
these be visited with sickness, or any other
casual event, so that the whole course of
the adventure be hindered thereby, that
then he is to return, and I am to receive
the prenominated proportion upon fair and
equal terms.

---

[1] *By the judgment of the most* authentical
physicians.] *Authentical* physicians are those
who are allowed to practise publicly. There is
a similar expression in Shakspeare, "*Par.* So
I say both of Galen and Paracelsus. *Laf.* Of
all the learned and *authentic* fellows."—*All's
Well that Ends Well,* act ii. sc. 3.—WHAL.

[2] *That, after the receipt of his money, he
shall neither, by direct or indirect means, as
magic, witchcraft,* &c.] The whole of this is a
solemn burlesque upon the oaths which were
taken by the combatants of romance, and indeed
of history, before they were permitted to encounter each other. The *powder,* Whalley conceives to be tern-seed, which from its minuteness,
not being itself visible, was supposed, according
to the vulgar superstition, "to make the person
invisible who carried it about him." This is
rather doubtful : but the subject is scarcely
worth pursuing. By the ring, is meant that
of Gyges, which, when the bezel was turned
towards the palm of the hand, rendered the
wearer of it invisible. Both are mentioned by
Fletcher :

"Why, did you think that you had Gyges' ring,
Or the herb that gives invisibility ?"
　　　　　Fair Maid of the Inn, act i. sc. 1.

[3] *Or to hang any three-forked charm about
my dog's neck, secretly conveyed into his collar.*]
Alluding probably to Cornelius Agrippa's dog.
Paulus Jovius gives the following account of the
master and his dog : (*Elog. doct. Viror.* edit.
Basil. 1577, p. 187.) *Excessit è vita nondum
senex apud Lugdunum, ignobili et tenebroso
in diversorio, multis eum tanquam necromantiæ
suspicione infamem execrantibus ; quod cacodæ-
monem nigri canis specie circumduceret ; ita ut
quum propinquâ morte ad pænitentiam urge-
retur, cani collare loreum magicis per clavorum
emblemata inscriptum notis exsolverit ; in hæc
suprema verba irate prorumpens, Abi, perdita
bestia, quæ me totum perdidisti ! nec usquam
familiaris ille canis, aut assiduus itinerum
omnium comes, et tum morientis domini deser-
tor postea conspectus est, quum precipiti fuga
saltu in Ararim se immersisse, nec enatasse
ab his qui id vidisse asserebant, existimetur.*
　　　　　　　　　　　　　　　　　WHAL.

Not. Very good, sir; is this all?

Punt. It is all, sir; and dispatch them, good notary.

Not. As fast as is possible, sir.   [*Exit.*

Enter Carlo.

Punt. O, Carlo! welcome: saw you Monsieur Brisk?

Car. Not I: did he appoint you to meet here?

Punt. Ay, and I muse he should be so tardy; he is to take an hundred pounds of me in venture, if he maintain his promise.

Car. Is his hour past?

Punt. Not yet, but it comes on apace.

Car. Tut, be not jealous of him; he will sooner break all the commandments than his hour; upon my life, in such a case trust him.

Punt. Methinks, Carlo, you look very smooth, ha!

Car. Why, I came but now from a hot-house; I must needs look smooth.

Punt. From a hot-house!

Car. Ay, do you make a wonder on't? why, it is your only physic. Let a man sweat once a week in a hot-house, and be well rubbed, and froted, with a good plump juicy wench and sweet linen, he shall ne'er have the pox.

Punt. What, the French pox?

Car. The French pox! our pox: we have them in as good a form as they, man; what?

Punt. Let me perish, but thou art a salt one! was your new-created gallant there with you, Sogliardo?

Car. O porpoise! hang him, no: he's a leiger at Horn's ordinary yonder;[1] his villainous Ganymede and he have been droning a tobacco-pipe[2] there ever since yesterday noon.

Punt. Who? Signior Tripartite, that would give my dog the whiffe?

Car. Ay, he. They have hired a chamber and all, private, to practise in, for the making of the patoun, the receipt reciprocal, and a number of other mysteries not yet extant.[3] I brought some dozen or twenty gallants this morning to view them, as you'd do a piece of perspective, in at a key-hole; and there we might see Sogliardo sit in a chair, holding his snout up like a sow under an apple-tree, while the other opened his nostrils with a poking-stick, to give the smoke a more free delivery. They had spit some three or four-score ounces between 'em afore we came away.

Punt. How! spit three or fourscore ounces?

Car. Ay, and preserved it in porringers, as a barber does his blood when he opens a vein.

Punt. Out, pagan! how dost thou open the vein of thy friend?

Car. Friend! is there any such foolish thing in the world, ha? 'slid, I never relished it yet.

Punt. Thy humour is the more dangerous.

Car. No, not a whit, signior. Tut, a man must keep time in all; I can oil my tongue when I meet him next, and look

---

[1] *He's a leiger at Horn's ordinary yonder;*] i.e., he has taken up his abode there : a *leiger* was a resident ambassador. Of Horn I know nothing; he was perhaps the master of the Mitre : and yet the Mitre was too respectable an inn for the haunts of Cavaliero Shift.

[2] Droning *a tobacco-pipe.*] See the *Silent Woman,* act iv. sc. I.

[3] *For the making of the* patoun, *the* receipt reciprocal, *and a number of other mysteries not yet extant.*] An editor of Jonson has to struggle with difficulties which seem to grow beneath his toil. I know no other poet of that age whose language may not be explained by reference to contemporary writers ; but with Jonson it is not so ; at least as far as my little experience enables me to judge. He has many terms which are nowhere else to be found, many allusions to customs which are not noticed by the poets of his time. I mention this to procure some indulgence for the conjectures in which I frequently find myself engaged at a venture. *Patoun* I have never met with elsewhere, nor can I pretend to determine its precise meaning here. Patons, in

French, are those small pellets of paste with which poultry are crammed : *making of the* patoun, may therefore be moulding tobacco, which was then always cut small, into some fantastic or fashionable form for the pipe. The *receipt reciprocal,* is not improbably what Decker, in the *Gull's Hornbook,* calls the *ring,* that is, as I suppose, passing the pipe from one to another, as is done now in some countries, and was once sufficiently common here ; but this, with the former term, must be left to the reader. It appears that Whalley had endeavoured to procure some information on these points, for on the margin of his copy I find the following memorandum by Steevens :

"Mr. Reed, who may be considered as the high-priest of black letter, declares no book to have been written containing instructions how to take tobacco. You have therefore not a single auxiliary on the present subject, except your own sagacity ; and must of course be content to rank the patoun, &c. among ' the mysteries not yet extant.'—Aug. 29, 1781."

This somewhat consoles me in my ignorance.

with a good sleek forehead; 'twill take away all soil of suspicion, and that's enough: what Lynceus can see my heart? Pish, the title of a friend! it's a vain, idle thing, only venerable among fools; you shall not have one that has any opinion of wit affect it.

Enter Deliro *and* Macilente.

Deli. Save you, good Sir Puntarvolo.

Punt. Signior Deliro! welcome.

Deli. Pray you, sir, did you see Master Fastidious Brisk? I heard he was to meet your worship here.

Punt. You heard no figment, sir;[1] I do expect him at every pulse of my watch.

Deli. In good time, sir.

Car. There's a fellow now looks like one of the patricians of Sparta; marry, his wit's after ten i' the hundred:[2] a good blood-hound, a close-mouthed dog, he follows the scent well; marry, he's at a fault now, methinks.

Punt. I should wonder at that creature is free from the danger of thy tongue.

Car. O, I cannot abide these limbs of satin, or rather Satan indeed, that will walk, like the children of darkness, all day in a melancholy shop, with their pockets full of blanks,[3] ready to swallow up as many poor unthrifts as come within the verge.

Punt. So! and what hast thou for him that is with him, now?

Car. O, d——n me! immortality! I'll not meddle with him; the pure element of fire, all spirit, extraction.

Punt. How, Carlo! ha, what is he, man?

Car. A scholar, Macilente; do you not know him? a rank, raw-boned anatomy, he walks up and down like a charged musket, no man dares encounter him: that's his rest there.

Punt. His rest! why, has he a forked head?[4]

Car. Pardon me, that's to be suspended you are too quick, too apprehensive.

Deli. Troth, now I think on't, I'll defer it till some other time.

Maci. Not by any means, signior, you shall not lose this opportunity, he will be here presently now.

Deli. Yes, faith, Macilente, 'tis best. For look you, sir, I shall so exceedingly offend my wife in't, that——

Maci. Your wife! now for shame lose these thoughts, and become the master of your own spirits. Should I, if I had a wife, suffer myself to be thus passionately carried to and fro with the stream of her humour, and neglect my deepest affairs, to serve her affections? 'Slight, I would geld my-self first.

Deli. O, but, signior, had you such a wife as mine is, you would——

Maci. Such a wife! Now hate me, sir, if ever I discerned any wonder in your wife yet, with all the speculation I have: I have seen some that have been thought fairer than she, in my time; and I have seen those have not been altogether so tall, esteemed properer women; and I have seen less noses grow upon sweeter faces, that have done very well too, in my judgment. But, in good faith, signior, for all this, the gentlewoman is a good, pretty, proud, hard-favoured thing, marry not so peerlessly to be doted upon, I must confess: nay, be not angry.

Deli. Well, sir, however you please to forget yourself, I have not deserved to be thus played upon; but henceforth, pray you forbear my house, for I can but faintly endure the savour of his breath, at my table, that shall thus jade me for my courtesies.

Maci. Nay, then, signior, let me tell you your wife is no proper woman,[5] and by my

---

[1] *You heard no* figment, *sir;*] See *Cynthia's Revels.* For *every pulse of my watch,* the quarto has "every minute my watch strikes."

[2] *There's a fellow now looks like one of the* patricians of Sparta; *marry, his wit's after ten i'* the hundred:] i.e., his imagination is employed in contriving how to place out his money at interest, which, by a statute of the thirteenth of Elizabeth, was fixed at *ten per cent.* What idea Carlo had of a *Spartan patrician* I know not: there is surely nothing very republican in the conduct of Deliro: but it is perhaps impossible to allot any determinate sense to such patronymic expressions of kindness or contempt, as *Grecian, Trojan, Spartan,* &c. which seem in our old plays to signify just what the speaker pleases. Sparta was famous for its breed of dogs: perhaps some recollection of this circumstance might give rise to the abusive terms which follow.

[3] *With their pockets full of* blanks, &c.] Meaning, I suppose, bonds and covenants, ready drawn, and only waiting to be filled up by such as were reduced to sell or mortgage their estates.

[4] *Punt. His* rest! *why, has he a forked head?*] Alluding to the semi-circular form of the musket rest; see p. 23 *b*.

[5] *Nay then, signior, let me tell you your wife is no proper woman,*] i.e., not *proper* or peculiar

life, I suspect her honesty, that's more,
which you may likewise suspect if you
please, do you see? I'll urge you to
nothing against your appetite, but if you
please, you may suspect it.

Deli. Good, sir.   [*Exit.*

Maci. Good sir! now horn upon horn
pursue thee, thou blind, egregious dotard!

Car. O, you shall hear him speak like
envy.—Signior Macilente, you saw Monsieur
Brisk lately: I heard you were with him at
court.

Maci. Ay, Buffone, I was with him.

Car. And how is he respected there? I
know you'll deal ingenuously with us; is
he made much of amongst the sweeter sort
of gallants?

Maci. Faith, ay; his civet and his cast-
ing-glass[1]
Have helpt him to a place amongst the
rest:
And there, his seniors give him good slight
looks,
After their garb, smile, and salute in
French
With some new compliment.

Car. What, is this all?

Maci. Why say, that they should shew
the frothy fool
Such grace as they pretend comes from the
heart,
He had a mighty windfall out of doubt!
Why, all their graces are not to do grace
To virtue or desert; but to ride both
With their gilt spurs quite breathless, from
themselves.
'Tis now esteemed precisianism in wit,[2]
And a disease in nature, to be kind

Toward desert, to love or seek good
names.
Who feeds with a good name? who thrives
with loving?
Who can provide feast for his own desires,
With serving others?—ha, ha, ha!
'Tis folly, by our wisest worldlings proved,
If not to gain by love, to be beloved.

Car. How like you him? is't not a good
spiteful slave, ha?

Punt. Shrewd, shrewd.

Car. D—n me! I could eat his flesh
now; divine, sweet villain!

Maci. Nay, prithee leave: What's he
there?

Car. Who? this in the starched beard?[3]
it's the dull, stiff knight Puntarvolo, man;
he's to travel now presently: he has a good
knotty wit; marry, he carries little on't out
of the land with him.

Maci. How then?

Car. He puts it forth in venture, as he
does his money upon the return of a dog
and cat.

Maci. Is this he?

Car. Ay, this is he: a good tough gentleman: he looks like a shield of brawn at
Shrove-tide, out of date, and ready to take
his leave; or a dry pole of ling upon Easter-
eve, that has furnished the table all Lent,
as he has done the city this last vacation.

Maci. Come, you'll never leave your
stabbing similes: I shall have you aiming
at me with 'em by and by; but——

Car. O, renounce me then I pure, honest,
good devil, I love thee above the love of
women: I could e'en melt in admiration of
thee, now. Ods so, look here, man; Sir
Dagonet and his squire![4]

---

to yourself, but common to all who solicit her.
This is Mr. Whalley's explanation; which he in-
forces by several examples of the word *proper*
thus applied. As I think him wrong, I have
omitted his quotations: *proper* is used here, as
properer is just above, for *handsome*; had it
been otherwise, Macilente would not have immediately subjoined—"and, by my life, I suspect
her honesty, *that's more.*"

[1] *His* casting-glass.] Casting-glasses, or, as
they were more generally termed *casting-bottles*,
were small bottles for holding liquid essences
and perfumes. They were in very general use,
and are mentioned in a thousand places by our
old dramatists. It may be observed here that
perfumes of all kinds were more in vogue in
the age of Elizabeth than of George III.
They were certainly more necessary; but
fashion and propriety do not always walk hand
in hand.

[2] *'Tis now esteemed* precisianism *in wit,*] i.e.,

Puritanism, the Puritans in this age being called
the *precise.*—WHAL.

[3] *Car. Who? this in the* starched *beard?*] The
precise and formal gallants of the day (such as
Puntarvolo is described to be) had their beard
stiffened with starch: thus Taylor, the water-
poet, no ill chronicler of the fashions:

"Some seem as they were starched, stiff, and
    fine,
Like to the bristles of an angry swine."

In a preceding passage Puntarvolo desires
the boy not to stand too near him, lest his breath
should thaw his ruff.—P. 101 *a.*

[4] *Sir* Dagonet *and his squire.*] Sir Dagonet
is a considerable personage in *Morte Arthur.*
He was the squire, or, as the old romance calls
him, the fool of good King Arthur, and seems to
be introduced like a Shrovetide cock, for the
sake of being buffeted and abused by every
one.

Enter Sogliardo *and* Shift.

Sog. Save you, my dear gallantos: nay, come, approach, good cavalier: prithee, sweet knight, know this gentleman, he's one that it pleases me to use as my good friend and companion; and therefore do him good offices: I beseech you, gentles, know him, I know him all over.

Punt. Sir, for Signior Sogliardo's sake, let it suffice, I know you.

Sog. Why, as I am a gentleman, I thank you, knight, and it shall suffice. Hark you, Sir Puntarvolo, you'd little think it; he's as resolute a piece of flesh as any in the world.

Punt. Indeed, sir!

Sog. Upon my gentility, sir; Carlo, a word with you; do you see that same fellow there?

Car. What, Cavalier Shift?

Sog. O, you know him; cry you mercy: before me, I think him the tallest man living¹ within the walls of Europe.

Car. The walls of Europe! take heed what you say, signior, Europe's a huge thing within the walls.

Sog. Tut, an 'twere as huge again, I'd justify what I speak. 'Slid, he swaggered even now in a place where we were—I never saw a man do it more resolute.

Car. Nay, indeed, swaggering is a good argument of resolution. Do you hear this, signior?

Maci. Ay, to my grief. O, that such muddy flags,
For every drunken flourish, should achieve
The name of manhood; whilst true perfect valour,
Hating to shew itself, goes by despised!
Heart! I do know now, in a fair just cause,
I dare do more than he, a thousand times:
Why should not they take knowledge of this, ha!

And give my worth allowance before his?
Because I cannot swagger.—Now, the pox
Light on your Pickt-hatch prowess!

Sog. Why, I tell you, sir: he has been the only *Bid-stand*² that ever kept New-market, Salisbury-plain, Hockley i' the Hole, Gads-hill, and all the high places of any request: he has had his mares and his geldings, he, have been worth forty, three-score, a hundred pound a horse, would ha' sprung you over hedge and ditch like your greyhound: he has done five hundred robberies in his time, more or less, I assure you.

Punt. What, and scaped?

Sog. Scaped! i' faith, ay: he has broken the gaol when he has been in irons and irons; and been out, and in again; and out, and in; forty times, and not so few, he.

Maci. A fit trumpet to proclaim such a person.

Car. But can this be possible?

Shift. Why, 'tis nothing, sir, when a man gives his affections to it.

Sog. Good Pylades, discourse a robbery or two, to satisfy these gentlemen of thy worth.

Shift. Pardon me, my dear Orestes: causes have their quiddits, and 'tis ill jesting with bell-ropes.

Car. How! Pylades and Orestes?

Sog. Ay, he is my Pylades, and I am his Orestes: how like you the conceit?

Car. O, 'tis an old stale interlude device: no, I'll give you names myself, look you; he shall be your Judas, and you shall be his elder-tree³ to hang on.

Maci. Nay, rather let him be Captain Pod, and this his motion;⁴ for he does nothing but shew him.

Car. Excellent: or thus; you shall be Holden, and he your camel.⁵

Shift. You do not mean to ride, gentlemen?

---

¹ *I think him the* tallest *man living,* &c.] i.e., the stoutest, the bravest: the ambiguity of this word must apologize for its being noticed a second time.

² *Why, I tell you, sir, he has been the only* Bid-stand!] A cant term for a highwayman. Thus, in the *Parson's Wedding:* "If you dare do this, I shall sing a song of one that *bade-stand,* and made a carrier pay dear for a little ground-rent upon his majesty's *highway.*"—Act i. sc. 1.

³ *And you shall be his* elder tree,] It was the tradition that Judas hung himself on an *elder tree:* thus, in Nixon's *Strange Foot-post:* "Our gardens will prosper the better, when they have in them not one of these *elders,* whereupon so many covetous *Judasses hang* themselves."

⁴ *Let him be Captain* Pod, *and this his motion;*] The celebrated owner of a puppet-shew. He is often mentioned in Jonson.
                        WHAL.

⁵ *You shall be* Holden, *and he* your *camel.*] This seems to be no bad compliment to Cavaliero Shift, for Holden's camel was a beast of parts. He is mentioned by Taylor, and in very good company:

"That for *ingenuous study* down can put
Old *Holden's camel,* or fine Banks his cut."
           Cast over the Water, p. 159.

Our camels now stalk along the street with exemplary gravity: but they appear to have intermitted their "ingenious studies" of late, which

Punt. Faith, let me end it for you, gallants: you shall be his Countenance, and he your Resolution.

Sog. Troth, that's pretty: how say you, Cavalier, shall it be so?

Car. Ay, ay, most voices.

Shift. Faith, I am easily yielding to any good impressions.

Sog. Then give hands, good Resolution.

Car. Mass, he cannot say, good Countenance, now properly to him again.

Punt. Yes, by an irony.

Maci. O, sir, the countenance of Resolution should, as he is, be altogether grim and unpleasant.

Enter Fastidious Brisk.

Fast. Good hours make music with your mirth, gentlemen, and keep time to your humours!—How now, Carlo?

Punt. Monsieur Brisk! many a long look have I extended for you, sir.

Fast. Good faith, I must crave pardon: I was invited this morning, ere I was out of my bed, by a bevy of ladies, to a banquet: whence it was almost one of Hercules's labours for me to come away, but that the respect of my promise did so prevail with me. I know they'll take it very ill, especially one that gave me this bracelet of her hair[1] but over night, and this pearl another gave me from her forehead, marry she—— what! are the writings ready?

Punt. I will send my man to know. Sirrah, go you to the notary's, and learn if he be ready: leave the dog, sir.
                                [*Exit* Servant.

Fast. And how does my rare qualified friend Sogliardo? Oh, Signior Macilente!

by these eyes, I saw you not; I had saluted you sooner else, o' my troth. I hope, sir, I may presume upon you, that you will not divulge my late check, or disgrace, indeed, sir.

Maci. You may, sir.

Car. He knows some notorious jest by this gull,[2] that he hath him so obsequious.

Sog. Monsieur Fastidious, do you see this fellow there? does he not look like a clown? would you think there were anything in him?

Fast. Anything in him! beshrew me, ay; the fellow hath a good ingenious face.

Sog. By this element he is as ingenious a tall man as ever swaggered about London: he, and I, call Countenance and Resolution; but his name is Cavalier Shift.

Punt. Cavalier, you knew Signior Clog, that was hanged for the robbery at Harrow-on-the-Hill?

Sog. Knew him, sir! why, 'twas he gave all the directions for the action.

Punt. How! was it your project, sir?

Shift. Pardon me, Countenance, you do me some wrong to make occasions public which I imparted to you in private.

Sog. God's will! here are none but friends, Resolution.

Shift. That's all one; things of consequence must have their respects; where, how, and to whom.—Yes, sir, he shewed himself a true Clog in the coherence of that affair, sir; for, if he had managed matters as they were corroborated to him, it had been better for him by a forty or fifty score of pounds, sir; and he himself might have lived, in despight of fates, to have fed on woodcocks,[3] with the rest: but it was his

---

have been zealously taken up by bears and pigs; with more advantage, it is to be feared, (as indeed has been sometimes said of students with two legs), to others than to themselves.

[1] *Especially one that gave me this* bracelet of her hair, &c.] These pretty love-tokens are frequently mentioned by our old dramatists: thus Brathwayt:

"Didst ever see a favour worn by me,
But that poor *bracelet* I received of thee,
Twined with thy faithless *hair?*"
                    Inconstant Shepheardesse.

But it was not the ladies only who bestowed them; the gentlemen appear to have been equally lavish of their lovelocks. In *The Ball,* Lucina is very pleasant with poor Sir Ambrose on this subject:

"*Luc.* Had you not
A head once?
Amb. A head! I have one still.

Luc. Of *hair,* I mean;
Favours have gleaned too much: pray, pardon me,
If it were mine, they should go look their bracelets,
Or stay till the next crop."

[2] *He knows some notorious jest* by *this gull,*] i.e., *of* this gull.—See p. 52 *a, b.* The *check* to which Fastidious alludes was the contempt expressed for him at court by Saviolina.

[3] *He might have lived to have fed on* woodcocks, &c.] A woodcock is frequently mentioned by our old dramatists, as the chief dish at ordinaries (gambling-houses), and at the best tables; but *woodcock,* as has been already noticed, was also a cant name for a fool: to *feed on woodcocks,* therefore, in the language of Shift, most probably meant, *to prey on dupes* who assembled there. This Shift is really a pleasant fellow, and Gay, in the *Beggar's Opera,* has some obligations to him.

heavy fortune to sink, poor Clog! and therefore talk no more of him.

Punt. Why, had he more aiders then?

Sog. O lord, sir! ay, there were some present there, that were the Nine Worthies to him, i' faith.

Shift. Ay, sir, I can satisfy you at more convenient conference: but for mine own part, I have now reconciled myself to other courses, and profess a living out of my other qualities.

Sog. Nay, he has left all now, I assure you, and is able to live like a gentleman, by his qualities. By this dog, he has the most rare gift in tobacco that ever you knew.

Car. He keeps more ado with this monster than ever Banks did with his horse, or the fellow with the elephant.[1]

Maci. He will hang out his picture, shortly, in a cloth, you shall see.

Sog. O, he does manage a quarrel the best that ever you saw, for terms and circumstances.

Fast. Good faith, signior, now you speak of a quarrel, I'll acquaint you with a difference that happened between a gallant and myself; Sir Puntarvolo, you know him if I should name him, Signior Luculento.

Punt. Luculento! what inauspicious chance interposed itself to your two loves?

Fast. Faith, sir, the same that sundered Agamemnon and great Thetis' son; but let the cause escape, sir: he sent me a challenge, mixt with some few braves, which I restored, and in fine we met. Now, indeed, sir, I must tell you he did offer at first very desperately, but without judgment: for, look you, sir, I cast myself into this figure;

now he comes violently on, and withal advancing his rapier to strike, I thought to have took his arm, for he had left his whole body to my election, and I was sure he could not recover his guard. Sir, I mist my purpose in his arm, rashed his doublet-sleeve,[2] ran him close by the left cheek, and through his hair. He again lights me here,—I had on a gold cable hatband, then new come up, which I wore about a murrey French hat I had,—cuts my hat-band, and yet it was massy goldsmith's work, cuts my brims, which, by good fortune, being thick embroidered with gold twist and spangles, disappointed the force of the blow: nevertheless, it grazed on my shoulder, takes me away six purls of an Italian cut-work band I wore, cost me three pound in the Exchange but three days before.

Punt. This was a strange encounter.

Fast. Nay, you shall hear, sir: with this we both fell out, and breathed. Now, upon the second sign of his assault, I betook me to the former manner of my defence; he, on the other side, abandoned his body to the same danger as before, and follows me still with blows: but I being loth to take the deadly advantage that lay before me of his left side, made a kind of stramazoun,[3] ran him up to the hilts through the doublet, through the shirt, and yet missed the skin. He, making a reverse blow,—falls upon my embossed girdle, I had thrown off the hangers a little before,[4] —strikes off a skirt of a thick-laced satin doublet I had, lined with four taffatas, cuts off two panes embroidered with pearl,

---

[1] *He keeps more ado with this monster than ever Banks did with his* horse, *or the fellow with the* elephant.] Banks's cut (curtal) has been just noticed in the quotation from Taylor; he was taught, says Sir Kenelm Digby, to shew tricks, with cards and dice, and perform several feats of art to the admiration of the virtuosos of those days, who mention him with great respect on all occasions. Not satisfied with his reputation in this country, *Morocco* (for that was the animal's name), wandered in a luckless hour to the Continent, where, if we may trust Jonson, (*Epig.* 134,) both he and his master were "burned for witches" The *elephant,* though not so well known as the "cut," was also of some celebrity in his time, and is mentioned together with him by Donne, *Sat.* i.:

" But to a grave man he doth move no more
Than the *wise politique horse* would heretofore,
Or thou, O *elephant,* or ape wilt do,
When any names the King of Spain to you."

[2] Rashed *his doublet sleeve.*] To *rash* (a verb which we have improvidently suffered to grow obsolete), is to strike obliquely with violence, as a wild boar does with his tusk. It is observable with what accuracy Shakspeare has corrected the old quarto of King Lear, which reads:

" Nor thy fierce sister
In his anointed flesh *rash* boarish fangs,"

for which he has properly given, "*stick* boarish fangs."

[3] *Made a kind of* stramazoun,] *Stramazzone,* Italian (*estramaçon,* French) is a descending blow with the edge of a sword as opposed to *stoccata,* a thrust. It frequently occurs in our old writers, with whom a duel was not so quickly dispatched as it is in our days. I am not accountable for the sense which Fastidious gives the term, for he was probably designed to blunder.

[4] *I had thrown off the* hangers *before,*] i.e., the fringed loops appended to the girdle, in which the dagger or small sword usually hung.

rends through the drawings-out of tissue, enters the linings, and skips the flesh.

Car. I wonder he speaks not of his wrought shirt.[1]

Fast. Here, in the opinion of mutual damage, we paused; but ere I proceed I must tell you, signior, that, in this last encounter, not having leisure to put off my silver spurs, one of the rowels catched hold of the ruffle of my boot, and being Spanish leather,[2] and subject to tear, overthrows me, rends me two pair of silk stockings, that I put on, being somewhat a raw morning, a peach colour and another, and strikes me some half inch deep into the side of the calf; he, seeing the blood come, presently takes horse and away; I, having bound up my wound with a piece of my wrought shirt——

Car. O! comes it in there?

Fast. Rid after him, and, lighting at the court gate both together, embraced, and marched hand in hand up into the presence. Was not this business well carried?

Maci. Well! yes, and by this we can guess what apparel the gentleman wore.

Punt. 'Fore valour, it was a designment begun with much resolution, maintained with as much prowess, and ended with more humanity.—

Re-enter Servant.

How now, what says the notary?

Serv. He says he is ready, sir; he stays but your worship's pleasure.

Punt. Come, we will go to him, monsieur. Gentlemen, shall we entreat you to be witnesses?

Sog. You shall entreat me, sir.—Come, Resolution.

Shift. I follow you, good Countenance.

Car. Come, signior, come, come.

[*Exeunt all but* Macilente.

Maci. O, that there should be fortune
To clothe these men, so naked in desert!
And that the just storm of a wretched life
Beats them not ragged, for their wretched
 souls,
And, since as fruitless, even as black as
 coals.   [*Exit.*

[*Mit.* Why, but, signior, how comes it that Fungoso appeared not with his sister's intelligence to Brisk?

Cor. Marry, long of the evil angels that she gave him, who have indeed tempted the good simple youth to follow the tail of the fashion, and neglect the imposition of his friends. Behold, here he comes, very worshipfully attended, and with good variety.]

SCENE V.—*A Room in* Deliro's *House.*

Enter Fungoso *in a new suit, followed by his* Tailor, Shoemaker, *and* Haberdasher.

Fung. Gramercy, good shoemaker, I'll put to strings myself. [*Exit* Shoemaker.] Now, sir, let me see what must you have for this hat?

Habe. Here's the bill, sir.

Fung. How does it become me, well?

Tai. Excellent, sir, as ever you had any hat in your life.

Fung. Nay, you'll say so all.

Habe. In faith, sir, the hat's as good as any man in this town can serve you, and will maintain fashion as long; never trust me for a groat else.

Fung. Does it apply well to my suit?

Tai. Exceeding well, sir.

Fung. How lik'st thou my suit, haberdasher?

Habe. By my troth, sir, 'tis very rarely well made; I never saw a suit sit better, I can tell on.

---

[1] *I wonder he speaks not of his* wrought shirt.] This was one of the fashionable extravagancies of the time. The linen, both of men and women, was either so worked as to resemble the finest lace, or was ornamented, by the needle, with representations of fruits, flowers, passages of history, &c. The Puritans, it appears, turned the mode to account, and substituted texts of Scripture for the usual embellishments. There is a pleasant allusion to this practice in the *City Match:*
" Sir, she's a Puritan at her needle too:
My smock sleeves have such holy embroideries,
And are so learned, that I fear in time
All my apparel will be quoted by
Some pure instructor."—Act ii. sc. **2.**

[2] *One of the spurs catched hold of the* ruffle *of my boot, and being* Spanish leather, *&c.*] This explains what the nature of the *ruff* or *ruffle* was, about which there have been some doubts. The tops of the boots of Jonson's time, as Whalley observes, turned down, and hung in loose folds over the leg; they were probably of a finer leather than the rest of the boot, and seem to have had their edges fringed or scolloped; the exact form of them may be seen in several of the whole length portraits of James and Charles's days, particularly in those by Vandyke; the edges of the *ruffle* in some instances were evidently laid with gold lace.

Tai. Nay, we have no art to please our friends, we !

Fung. Here, haberdasher, tell this same. [*Gives him money.*

Habe. Good faith, sir, it makes you have an excellent body.

Fung. Nay, believe me, I think I have as good a body in clothes as another.

Tai. You lack points to bring your apparel together, sir.

Fung. I'll have points anon. How now ! Is't right.

Habe. Faith, sir, 'tis too little, but upon farther hopes—— Good morrow to you, sir. [*Exit.*

Fung. Farewell, good haberdasher. Well, now, Master Snip, let me see your bill.

[*Mit.* Methinks he discharges his followers too thick.

Cor. O, therein he saucily imitates some great man. I warrant you, though he turns off them, he keeps this tailor, in place of a page, to follow him still.]

Fung. This bill is very reasonable, in faith : hark you, Master Snip——Troth, sir, I am not altogether so well furnished at this present, as I could wish I were ; but—if you'll do me the favour to take part in hand, you shall have all I have, by this hand

Tai. Sir——

Fung. And but give me credit for the rest until the beginning of the next term.

Tai. O lord, sir——

Fung. 'Fore God, and by this light, I'll pay you to the utmost, and acknowledge myself very deeply engaged to you by the courtesy.

Tai. Why, how much have you there, sir ?

Fung. Marry, I have here four angels, and fifteen shillings of white money :[1] it's all I have, as I hope to be blest.

Tai. You will not fail me at the next term with the rest ?

Fung. No, an I do, pray heaven I be hanged. Let me never breathe again upon

this mortal stage, as the philosopher calls it ! By this air, and as I am a gentleman, I'll hold.

[*Cor.* He were an iron-hearted fellow, in my judgment, that would not credit him upon this volley of oaths.]

Tai. Well, sir, I'll not stick with any gentleman for a trifle : you know what 'tis remains ?

Fung. Ay, sir, and I give you thanks in good faith. O fate, how happy am I made in this good fortune ! Well, now I'll go seek out Monsieur Brisk. 'Ods so, I have forgot riband for my shoes, and points. 'Slid, what luck's this ! how shall I do ? Master Snip, pray let me reduct some two or three shillings for points and ribands : as I am an honest man, I have utterly disfurnished myself, in the default of memory ; pray let me be beholding to you ; it shall come home in the bill, believe me.

Tai. Faith, sir, I can hardly depart with ready money ;[2] but I'll take up, and send you some by my boy presently. What coloured riband would you have ?

Fung. What you shall think meet in your judgment, sir, to my suit.

Tai. Well, I'll send you some presently.

Fung. And points too, sir ?

Tai. And points too, sir.

Fung. Good lord, how shall I study to deserve this kindness of you, sir ! Pray let your youth make haste, for I should have done a business an hour since, that I doubt I shall come too late. [*Exit* Tailor.] Now, in good faith, I am exceeding proud of my suit.

[*Cor.* Do you observe the plunges that this poor gallant is put to, signior, to purchase the fashion ?

Mit. Ay, and to be still a fashion behind with the world, that's the sport.

Cor. Stay : O, here they come from *sealed and delivered.*]

---

[1] *Four* angels, *and fifteen shillings of* white money :] An angel was a *gold* coin, worth about ten shillings ; white money was the cant term for silver specie. Thus Massinger : " If thou wert an *angel of gold*, I would not put thee into *white money.*"—*Virgin Martyr.*

[2] Tai. *Faith, sir, I can hardly* depart *with ready money ;*] To part and *depart* with any-

thing, were synonymous expressions. So our author, in the *Sad Shepherd* :

" I have *departed* it 'mong my poor neighbours."

And Shakspeare, in *King John* :

" John, to stop Arthur's title in the whole, Hath willingly *departed* with a part."--WHAL

SCENE VI.—Puntarvolo's *Lodgings*.

Enter Puntarvolo, Fastidious Brisk *in a new suit, and* Servants, *with the dog.*

Punt. Well, now my whole venture is forth, I will resolve to depart shortly.

Fast. Faith, Sir Puntarvolo, go to the court, and take leave of the ladies first.

Punt. I care not if it be this afternoon's labour. Where is Carlo?

Fast. Here he comes.

Enter Carlo, Sogliardo, Shift, *and* Macilente.

Car. Faith, gallants, I am persuading this gentleman [*points to* Sogliardo] to turn courtier. He is a man of fair revenue, and his estate will bear the charge well. Besides, for his other gifts of the mind, or so, why, they are as nature lent him them, pure, simple, without any artificial drug or mixture of these too threadbare beggarly qualities, learning and knowledge, and therefore the more accommodate and genuine. Now, for the life itself——

Fast. O, the most celestial, and full of wonder[1] and delight, that can be imagined, signior, beyond thought and apprehension of pleasure! A man lives there in that divine rapture, that he will think himself i' the ninth heaven for the time, and lose all sense of mortality whatsoever, when he shall behold such glorious and almost immortal beauties; hear such angelical and harmonious voices, discourse with such flowing and ambrosial spirits, whose wits are as sudden as lightning, and humorous as nectar; oh, it makes a man all quintessence and flame, and lifts him up, in a moment, to the very crystal crown of the sky, where, hovering in the strength of his imagination, he shall behold all the delights of the Hesperides, the Insulæ Fortunatæ, Adonis' Gardens, Tempe, or what else, confined within the amplest verge of poesy, to be mere umbræ, and imperfect figures, conferred with the most essential felicity of your court.

Maci. Well, this encomium was not extemporal, it came too perfectly off.[2]

Car. Besides, sir, you shall never need to go to a hot-house, you shall sweat there with courting your mistress, or losing your money at primero, as well as in all the stoves in Sweden. Marry, this, sir, you must ever be sure to carry a good strong perfume about you, that your mistress's dog may smell you out amongst the rest; and in making love to her, never fear to be out; for you may have a pipe of tobacco, or a bass viol shall hang o' the wall, of purpose, will put you in presently. The tricks your Resolution has taught you in tobacco, the whiffe, and those sleights, will stand you in very good ornament there.

Fast. Ay, to some, perhaps; but, an he should come to my mistress with tobacco (this gentleman knows) she'd reply upon him, i' faith. O, by this bright sun, she has the most acute, ready, and facetious wit, that ——tut, there's no spirit able to stand her. You can report it, signior, you have seen her.

Punt. Then can he report no less, out of his judgment, I assure him.

Maci. Troth, I like her well enough, but she's too self-conceited, methinks.

Fast Ay, indeed, she's a little too self-conceited; an 'twere not for that humour, she were the most-to-be-admired lady in the world.

Punt. Indeed, it is a humour that takes from her other excellencies.

Maci. Why, it may easily be made to forsake her, in my thought.

Fast. Easily, sir! then are all Impossibilities easy.

Maci. You conclude too quick upon me, signior. What will you say, if I make it so perspicuously appear now, that yourself shall confess nothing more possible?

Fast. Marry, I will say, I will both applaud and admire you for it.

Punt. And I will second him in the admiration.

Maci. Why, I'll shew you, gentlemen. —Carlo, come hither.
  [Maci. Car. Punt. *and* Fast. *whisper together.*

[1] *Fast. O, the most celestial and full of wonder,* &c.] This interruption of Brisk's is very artful in the poet: Carlo was more a man of the town, whose elysium was the inside of a tavern or an ordinary, and not the presence-chamber at court; but Brisk, whose happiness centred in the circle of courtiers, may with great propriety break out into a rapturous harangue on the pleasures of a court life.—WHAL.
[2] *This encomium was not extemporal, it* came too perfectly off.] i.e., it was too fluent and highly finished; and, indeed, it has the air of being borrowed from some pedantic rhapsodist of the day. *Adonis' Gardens,* and the *Fortunate Isles,* were not likely to be much known to Fastidious: there is, besides, an evident allusion to the elegant day-dreams of Plato in every part of the speech. Carlo plunges at once into common life and common language.

Sog. Good faith, I have a great humour to the court. What thinks my Resolution? shall I adventure?

Shift. Troth, Countenance, as you please; the place is a place of good reputation and capacity.

Sog. O, my tricks in tobacco, as Carlo says, will shew excellent there.

Shift. Why, you may go with these gentlemen now, and see fashions; and after, as you shall see correspondence.

Sog. You say true. You will go with me, Resolution?

Shift. I will meet you, Countenance, about three or four o'clock; but to say to go with you, I cannot; for, as I am Apple-John, I am to go before the cockatrice you saw this morning, and, therefore, pray, present me excused, good Countenance.

Sog. Farewell, good Resolution, but fail not to meet.

Shift. As I live.   [*Exit.*

Punt. Admirably excellent!

Maci. If you can but persuade Sogliardo to court, there's all now.

Car. O, let me alone, that's my task.
                    [*Goes to* Sogliardo.

Fast. Now, by wit, Macilente, it's above measure excellent: 'twill be the only court-exploit that ever proved courtier ingenious.

Punt. Upon my soul, it puts the lady quite out of her humour, and we shall laugh with judgment.

Car. Come, the gentleman was of himself resolved to go with you, afore I moved it.

Maci. Why, then, gallants, you two and Carlo go afore to prepare the jest; Sogliardo and I will come some while after you.

Car. Pardon me, I am not for the court.

Punt. That's true; Carlo comes not at court, indeed. Well, you shall leave it to the faculty of Monsieur Brisk and myself; upon our lives, we will manage it happily. Carlo shall bespeak supper at the Mitre, against we come back; where we will meet, and dimple our cheeks with laughter at the success.

Car. Ay, but will you promise to come?

Punt. Myself shall undertake for them; he that fails, let his reputation lie under the lash of thy tongue.

Car. Ods so, look who comes here!

Enter Fungoso.

Sog. What, nephew!

Fung. Uncle, God save you; did you see a gentleman, one Monsieur Brisk, a courtier? he goes in such a suit as I do.

Sog. Here is the gentleman, nephew, but not in such a suit.

Fung. Another suit!   [*Swoons.*

Sog. How now, nephew?

Fast. Would you speak with me, sir?

Car. Ay, when he has recovered himself, poor Poll![1]

Punt. Some rosa-solis.

Maci. How now, signior?

Fung. I am not well, sir.

Maci. Why, this it is to dog the fashion.[2]

Car. Nay, come, gentlemen, remember your affairs; his disease is nothing but the flux of apparel.

Punt. Sirs, return to the lodging, keep the cat safe; I'll be the dog's guardian myself.   [*Exeunt* Servants.

Sog. Nephew, will you go to court with us? these gentlemen and I are for the court: nay, be not so melancholy.

Fung. 'Slid, I think no man in Christendom has that rascally fortune that I have.

Maci. Faith, your suit is well enough, signior.

Fung. Nay, not for that, I protest; but I had an errand to Monsieur Fastidious, and I have forgot it.

Maci. Why, go along to court with us, and remember it; come, gentlemen, you three take one boat, and Sogliardo and I will take another: we shall be there instantly.

Fast. Content: good sir, vouchsafe us your pleasance.

Punt. Farewell, Carlo; remember.

Car. I warrant you: would I had one of Kemp's shoes to throw after you.[3]

---

[1] *Poor poll!*] He calls him parrot, from his imitating the dress, as that bird does the words, of others.—WHAL.

[2] *This it is to dog the fashion.*] I.e., to follow the fashion at a distance, as a dog follows the heels of his master.—WHAL.

[3] *Would I had one of* Kemp's *shoes to throw after you.*] "To throw an old shoe after one for luck's sake," is a proverb of very ancient standing; and Kempe, who about this time had finished his "*Nine Days' Wonder*," or his *Morrice-dance from London to Norwich*, was sufficiently popular (exclusive of his talents on the stage) to make the allusion to his shoes well received. Peradventure too, as Nic. Bottom says, "to render the jest more gracious," *Kempe* himself might be the speaker; for though his name does not appear among the performers, as

Punt. Good fortune will close the eyes of our jest, fear not ; and we shall frolick.
[*Exeunt.*

[*Mit.* This Macilente, signior, begins to be more sociable on a sudden, methinks, than he was before : there's some portent in it, I believe.

Cor. O, he's a fellow of a strange nature. Now does he, in this calm of his humour, plot, and store up a world of malicious thoughts in his brain, till he is so full with them, that you shall see the very torrent of his envy break forth like a land-flood : and, against the course of all their affections, oppose itself so violently, that you will almost have wonder to think, how 'tis possible the current of their dispositions shall receive so quick and strong an alteration.

Mit. Ay marry, sir, this is that on which my expectation has dwelt all this while : for I must tell you, signior, though I was loth to interrupt the scene, yet I made it a question in mine own private discourse, how he should properly call it *Every Man out of his Humour,* when I saw all his actors so strongly pursue, and continue their humours?

Cor. Why, therein his art appears most full of lustre,[1] and approacheth nearest the life: especially when in the flame and height of their humours, they are laid flat, it fills the eye better, and with more contentment. How tedious a sight were it to behold a proud exalted tree lopt, and cut down by degrees, when it might be felled in a moment? and to set the axe to it before it came to that pride and fullness, were, as not to have it grow.

Mit. Well, I shall long till I see this fall you talk of.

Cor. To help your longing, signior, let your imagination be swifter than a pair of oars: and by this, suppose Puntarvolo, Brisk, Fungoso, and the dog, arrived at the court-gate, and going up to the great chamber. Macilente and Sogliardo, we'll leave them on the water, till possibility and natural means may land them. Here come the gallants, now prepare your expectation.]

ACT V.

SCENE I.—*The Palace Stairs.*

Enter Puntarvolo, *with his dog, followed by* Fastidious Brisk *and* Fungoso.

Punt. Come, gentles. Signior, you are sufficiently instructed.

Fast. Who, I, sir?

Punt. No, this gentleman. But stay, I take thought how to bestow my dog; he is no competent attendant for the presence.

Fast. Mass, that's true indeed, knight; you must not carry him into the presence.

Punt. I know it, and I, like a dull beast, forgot to bring one of my cormorants to attend me.[2]

Fast. Why, you were best leave him at the porter's lodge.

Punt. Not so; his worth is too well known amongst them, to be forth-coming.

Fast. 'Slight, how will you do then?

Punt. I must leave him with one that is ignorant of his quality, if I will have him to be safe. And see! here comes one that will carry coals, ergo, will hold my dog.

Enter a Groom, *with a basket.*[3]

My honest friend, may I commit the tuition of this dog to thy prudent care?

---

in the preceding comedy, yet it is almost certain that he was in the list ; and he, not improbably, played Carlo Buffone. Kempe published the account of his singular expedition in 1600. It is a great curiosity, and, as a rude picture of national manners, extremely well worth reprinting.— [Reprinted by Mr. Dyce, *Cam. Soc.* 1840.]

[1] Cor. *Why, therein his art appears most full of lustre,* &c.] In this compliment, which Jonson pays to himself, there is a portion of sophistry and bad reasoning, of which poor Mitis, as usual, suspects nothing. A tree, whether felled in a moment or cut down by degrees, is still destroyed by *violence;* but violent changes in humours, as Jonson justly understands the word, are neither probable nor natural. He had well learned, from his beloved ancients, that, previously to a change in the tenor of the plot, the

incidents should all grow to *their pride and fulness;* but he forgot, or rather did not choose to remember, that the development should not, for that, be hasty and abrupt. This error is not of modern date, for it is noticed by Aristotle. There are many, he says, who complicate and involve their plots with much art, but who are not equally successful in the unravelling of them : Πολλοι δε, πλεξαντες ευ, λυουσι κακως. Περι Ποι. cap. 18.

[2] *Forgot to bring one of my cormorants to attend me.*] i.e., one of my servants. Menials appear to have been treated formerly with very little ceremony : they were stripped and beaten at their master's pleasure ; and *cormorants, eaters,* and *feeders,* were among the civilest names bestowed upon them.

[3] *Enter a* Groom, *with a basket.*] This stage

Groom. You may, if you please, sir.

Punt. Pray thee let me find thee here at my return; it shall not be long till I will ease thee of thy employment, and please thee. Forth, gentles.

Fast. Why, but will you leave him with so slight command, and infuse no more charge upon the fellow?

Punt. Charge! no; there were no policy in that; that were to let him know the value of the gem he holds, and so to tempt frail nature against her disposition. No, pray thee let thy honesty be sweet, as it shall be short.

Groom. Yes, sir.

Punt. But hark you, gallants, and chiefly Monsieur Brisk; when we come in eye-shot, or presence of this lady, let not other matters carry us from our project; but, if we can, single her forth to some place——

Fast. I warrant you.

Punt. And be not too sudden, but let the device induce itself with good circumstance. On.

Fung. Is this the way? good truth, here be fine hangings.

[*Exeunt* Punt. Fast. *and* Fungoso.

Groom. Honesty! *sweet*, and *short!* Marry, it shall, sir, doubt you not; for even at this instant if one would give me twenty pounds, I would not deliver him; there's for the *sweet*: but now, if any man come offer me but twopence, he shall have him; there's for the *short* now. 'Slid, what a mad humourous gentleman is this to leave his dog with me! I could run away with him now, an he were worth anything.

Enter Macilente *and* Sogliardo.

Maci. Come on, signior, now prepare to court this all-witted lady, most naturally, and like yourself.

Sog. Faith, an you say the word, I'll begin to her in tobacco.

Maci. O, fie on't! no; you shall begin with *How does my sweet lady*, or, *Why are you so melancholy, madam?* though she be very merry, it's all one. Be sure to kiss your hand often enough; pray for her health and tell her, how *more than most fair she is*.[1] Screw your face at one side thus, and protest:[2] let her fleer, and look askance, and hide her teeth with her fan, when she laughs a fit, to bring her into more matter, that's nothing; you must talk forward (though it be without sense, so it be without blushing), 'tis most court-like and well.

Sog. But shall I not use tobacco at all?

Maci. O, by no means; 'twill but make your breath suspected, and that you use it only to confound the rankness of that.

Sog. Nay, I'll be advised, sir, by my friends.

Maci. Od's my life, see where Sir Puntarvolo's dog is.

Groom. I would the gentleman would return for his follower here, I'll leave him to his fortunes else.

Maci. 'Twere the only true jest in the world to poison him now; ha! by this hand I'll do it, if I could but get him of the fellow. [*Aside.*] Signior Sogliardo, walk

---

direction is from the quarto, and it may be assumed, from Puntarvolo's observation, that the basket had coals in it. With our ancestors, *colliers*, I know not for what reason, lay, like Mrs. Quickly, *under an ill name*: Decker has a little treatise on them, full of the grossest abuse; and a *dealer in coals*, an article at that time of no great sale perhaps, seems synonymous with everything base and vile. Thus Marston, speaking of worthless people, says, that "they were born naturally for a *coal-basket*."—*Malecontent*, act iv. sc. 1. The allusion here, however, is not to the seller of this unfortunate article, but to the bearer of it. In all great houses, but particularly in the royal residences, there were a number of mean and dirty dependents, whose office it was to attend the wood-yard, sculleries, &c. Of these (for in the lowest deep there was a lower still) the most forlorn wretches seem to have been selected to carry coals to the kitchens, halls, &c. To this smutty regiment, who attended the progresses, and rode in the carts with the pots and kettles, which, with every other article of furniture,

were then moved from palace to palace, the people, in derision, gave the name of *black* guards, a term since become sufficiently familiar, and never properly explained. Mr. Pinkerton, with his usual success in etymologizing, attempts to derive them from *blaguer*, which, he tells us, is French for a soldier's trull: they were, however, what I have described; and it is to one of this degraded race, who now enters with his basket of charcoal, that Puntarvolo ventures to commit the tuition of his dog. See p. 128 *b*.

[1] *How* more than most fair she is.] Macilente speaks *pure Arcadia*, as did probably all the affected courtiers of the day:

"O teares, no teares, but raine from beauties skies,
　Making those lillies and those roses grow,
　Which ay most fair, now *more than most fair* show,
While graceful pity beauty beautifies."

[2] *Screw your face at one side thus, and protest*:] i.e., use some petty and affected oaths. See p. 9 *a*.

aside, and think upon some device to entertain the lady with.

Sog. So I do, sir.
　　　[*Walks off in a meditating posture.*
Maci. How now, mine honest friend !
whose dog-keeper art thou ?

Groom. Dog-keeper, sir ! I hope I scorn
that, i' faith.

Maci. Why, dost thou not keep a dog ?

Groom. Sir, now I do, and now I do
not : [*throws off the dog.*] I think this be
sweet and *short.* Make me his dog-keeper !
　　　　　　　　　　　　　　[*Exit.*

Maci. This is excellent, above expectation ! nay, stay, sir ; [*seizing the dog.*] you'd
be travelling ; but I'll give you a dram shall
shorten your voyage, here. [*gives him
poison.*] So, sir, I'll be bold to take my
leave of you. Now to the Turk's court in
the devil's name, for you shall never go o'
God's name. [*kicks him out.*] Sogliardo,
come.

Sog. I have it, i' faith now, will sting it.

Maci. Take heed you leese it not,[1]
signior, ere you come there ; preserve it.
　　　　　　　　　　　　　　[*Exeunt.*

[*Cor.* How like you this first exploit of
his ?

Mit. O, a piece of true envy ; but I
expect the issue of the other device.

Cor. Here they come will make it
appear.]

SCENE II.—*An Apartment in the
Palace.*

Enter Saviolina, Puntarvolo, Fastidious
Brisk, *and* Fungoso.

Sav. Why, I thought, Sir Puntarvolo,
you had been gone your voyage.

Punt. Dear and most amiable lady, your
divine beauties do bind me to those offices,
that I cannot depart when I would.

Sav. 'Tis most court-like spoken, sir ;
but how might we do to have a sight of
your dog and cat ?

Fast. His dog is in the court, lady.

Sav. And not your cat ? how dare you
trust her behind you, sir.

Punt. Troth, madam, she hath sore eyes,
and she doth keep her chamber ; marry, I
have left her under sufficient guard, there
are two of my followers to attend her.

Sav. I'll give you some water for her
eyes. When do you go, sir ?

Punt. Certes, sweet lady, I know not.

Fast. He doth stay the rather, madam,
to present your acute judgment with so
courtly and well parted a gentleman as yet
your ladyship hath never seen.

Sav. What is he, gentle Monsieur Brisk ?
not that gentleman ? [*Points to* Fungoso.

Fast. No, lady, this is a kinsman to
Justice Silence.[2]

Punt. Pray, sir, give me leave to report
him. He's a gentleman, lady, of that rare
and admirable faculty, as, I protest, I know
not his like in Europe ; he is exceedingly
valiant, an excellent scholar, and so exactly
travelled, that he is able, in discourse, to
deliver you a model of any prince's court
in the world ; speaks the languages with
that purity of phrase, and facility of accent,
that it breeds astonishment ; his wit the
most exuberant, and, above wonder, pleasant, of all that ever entered the concave of
this ear.

Fast. 'Tis most true, lady ; marry, he is
no such excellent proper man.[3]

Punt. His travels have changed his complexion, madam.

Sav. O, Sir Puntarvolo, you must think
every man was not born to have my servant
Brisk's feature.

Punt. But that which transcends all,
lady ; he doth so peerlessly imitate any
manner of person for gesture, action, passion, or whatever——

Fast. Ay, especially a rustic or a clown,
madam, that it is not possible for the
sharpest-sighted wit in the world to discern
any sparks of the gentleman in him, when
he does it.

Sav. O, Monsieur Brisk, be not so
tyrannous to confine all wits within the
compass of your own ; not find the sparks

---

[1] *Take heed you* leese *it not.*] Leese is frequently used for *lose* by the writers of Jonson's
age. Thus, in the *Spanish Tragedy :*

"To *leese* thy life ere life was new begun."
　　　　　　　　　　　　　Act ii.

And in Stow's *Annals,* "I would my uncle
would let me have my life yet, though I *leese*
my kingdom."—*Edit.* 1580, p. 827. More examples are unnecessary.

[2] *This is a kinsman to* Justice Silence.] From
this allusion, it is clear that Shakspeare's second
part of *Henry IV.* could not, as Mr. Malone
observes, be written later than 1598, the year
before the date of this comedy.—WHAL.

[3] *Marry, he is no such excellent* proper man.]
His *personal* endowments are not so extraordinary : this he says to prepare the lady for the
appearance of Sogliardo, who is described in
the Introduction as "an essential clown."

of a gentleman in him, if he be a gentleman :

Fung. No, in truth, sweet lady, I believe you cannot.

Sav. Do you believe so ? why, I can find sparks of a gentleman in you, sir.

Punt. Ay, he is a gentleman, madam, and a reveller.

Fung. Indeed, I think I have seen your ladyship at our revels.[1]

Sav. Like enough, sir; but would I might see this wonder you talk of; may one have a sight of him for any reasonable sum ?

Punt. Yes, madam, he will arrive presently.

Sav. What, and shall we see him clown it ?

Fast. I' faith, sweet lady, that you shall; see, here he comes.

Enter Macilente *and* Sogliardo.

Punt. This is he I pray observe him, lady.

Sav. Beshrew me, he clowns it properly indeed.

Punt. Nay, mark his courtship.

Sog. How does my sweet lady ? *hot and moist ?*[2] *beautiful and lusty ?* ha !

Sav. Beautiful, an it please you, sir, but not lusty.

Sog. O ho, lady, it pleases you to say so, in truth : And *how does my sweet lady ?* in health ? *Bona roba, quæso, que novelles ? que novelles ?* sweet creature !

Sav. O excellent ! why, gallants, is this[3]

he that cannot be deciphered ?[3] they were very blear-witted, i' faith, that could not discern the gentleman in him.

Punt. But you do, in earnest, lady ?

Sav. Do I, sir ! why, if you had any true court-judgment in the carriage of his eye, and that inward power that forms his countenance, you might perceive his counterfeiting as clear as the noon-day; alas ——nay, if you would have tried my wit, indeed, you should never have told me he was a gentleman, but presented him for a true clown indeed ; and then have seen if I could have deciphered him.

Fast. 'Fore God, her ladyship says true, knight : but does he not affect the clown most naturally, mistress ?

Punt. O, she cannot but affirm that, out of the bounty of her judgment.

Sav. Nay, out of doubt he does well, for a gentleman to imitate : but I warrant you, he becomes his natural carriage of the gentleman much better than his clownery.

Fast. 'Tis strange, in truth, her ladyship should see so far into him !

Punt. Ay, is it not ?

Sav. Faith, as easily as may be; not decipher him, quoth you !

Fung. Good sadness, I wonder at it.

Maci. Why, has she deciphered him, gentlemen ?

Punt. O, most miraculously, and beyond admiration.

Maci. Is it possible ?

Fast. She hath gathered most infallible signs of the gentleman in him, that's certain.

[1] *I think I have seen your ladyship at our revels.*] At the Inns of Court : see the letter to his father, p. 105 *b*. Saviolina evidently mistakes his meaning, for the *revels* of which he speaks were not calculated for the amusement of ladies of fashion : nor was she *likely* to be seen at them.

[2] Hot and moist ?] These two important words have been produced by Steevens as a striking proof of Jonson's malignity to Shakspeare, they being a manifest sneer at *hot and moist* in *Othello.* I believe Shakspeare to be the greatest parodist, or sneerer, except Aristophanes, that ever existed ; and I know that, in many instances, where Jonson has been represented as the aggressor, he is "a man more sinned against than sinning." *Every Man out of his Humour* preceded *Othello* by many years ; the sneer therefore, if any there be, must be placed to the account of the latter. But, seriously, can any folly equal that of construing every application of a written passage into an insult upon the original ? When we quote Horace or Virgil either seriously or humorously,

we do it, I suppose, to show our wit or our reading, and not to sneer at them. But Shakspeare is sacred ! Not so ; for we have recourse to him upon all occasions : yet who so honoured? ——The fact seems to be, that his expressions may be lawfully used by every one but Jonson ; upon whom, if a single word employed by Shakspeare be found, the whole cry of commentators open at once,

" With wide Cerberean mouths full loud, and ring
   A hideous peal."

After all, the trite words which gave rise to this attack upon our author, are expressly marked by himself as a quotation :—this, however, his calumniators did not know.

[3] *Why, gallants, is this he that cannot be deciphered ?*] Saviolina had been told that Sogliardo spoke the languages with purity ; from the gallimaufry of Latin, French, and Italian, with which he accosts her, she naturally concludes that he is endeavouring to impose upon her by an appearance of ignorance.

Sav. Why, gallants, let me laugh at you a little: was this your device to try my judgment in a gentleman?

Maci. Nay, lady, do not scorn us, though you have this gift of perspicacy above others. What if he should be no gentleman now, but a clown indeed, lady?

Punt. How think you of that? would not your ladyship be Out of your Humour?

Fast. O, but she knows it is not so.

Sav. What if he were not a man, ye may as well say? Nay, if your worships could gull me so, indeed, you were wiser than you are taken for.

Maci. In good faith, lady, he is a very perfect clown, both by father and mother; that I'll assure you.

Sav. O, sir, you are very pleasurable.

Maci. Nay, do but look on his hand, and that shall resolve you; look you, lady, what a palm here is.

Sog. Tut, that was with holding the plough.

Maci. The plough! did you discern any such thing in him, madam?

Fast. Faith, no, she saw the gentleman as bright as at noon-day, she; she deciphered him at first.

Maci. Troth, I am sorry your ladyship's sight should be so suddenly struck.

Sav. O, you are goodly beagles!

Fast. What, is she gone?

Sog. Nay, stay, sweet lady? *que novelles? que novelles?*

Sav. Out, you fool, you!

[*Exit in anger.*

Fung. She's Out of her Humour, i' faith.

Fast. Nay, let's follow it while 'tis hot, gentlemen.

Punt. Come, on mine honour we shall make her blush in the presence; my spleen is great with laughter.

Maci. Your laughter will be a child of a feeble life, I believe, sir. [*Aside.*] Come, signior, your looks are too dejected, methinks; why mix you not mirth with the rest?

Fung. Od's will, this suit frets me at the soul. I'll have it altered to-morrow, sure.

[*Exeunt.*

SCENE III.—*The Palace Stairs.*

Enter Shift.

Shift. I am come to the court to meet with my Countenance, Sogliardo; poor men must be glad of such countenance, when they can get no better. Well, need may insult upon a man, but it shall never make him despair of consequence. The world will say, 'tis base: tush, base! 'tis base to live under the earth, not base to live above it by any means.

Enter Fastidious, Puntarvolo, Sogliardo, Fungoso, *and* Macilente.

Fast. The poor lady is most miserably out of her humour, i' faith.

Punt. There was never so witty a jest broken, at the tilt of all the court wits christened.

Maci. O, this applause taints it foully.[1]

Sog. I think I did my part in courting,— O, Resolution!

Punt. Ah me, my dog!

Maci. Where is he?

Fast. 'Sprecious, go seek for the fellow, good signior.   [*Exit* Fungoso.

Punt. Here, here I left him.

Maci. Why none was here when we came in now but Cavalier Shift; enquire of him.

Fast. Did you see Sir Puntarvolo's dog here, Cavalier, since you came?

Shift. His dog, sir! he may look his dog, sir. I saw none of his dog, sir.

Maci. Upon my life, he has stolen your dog, sir, and been hired to it by some that have ventured with you; you may guess by his peremptory answers.

Punt. Not unlike; for he hath been a notorious thief by his own confession. Sirrah, where is my dog?

Shift. Charge me with your dog, sir! I have none of your dog, sir.

Punt. Villain, thou liest.

Shift. Lie, sir! 'sblood,—you are but a man, sir.

Punt. Rogue and thief, restore him.

Sog. Take heed, Sir Puntarvolo, what you do; he'll bear no coals, I can tell you,[2] o' my word.

---

[1] *O, this applause taints it foully.*] See p. 82 b.

[2] *Take heed what you do; he'll bear no coals, I can tell you.*] He will not be insulted; he will bear no injuries. From the mean nature of this occupation, it seems to have been somewhat hastily concluded, that a man who would *carry coals*, would submit to any indignity (see p. 125).

Hence to *carry coals*, in the sense of tamely putting up an affront, occurs perpetually in our old writers, both serious and comic. It is needless to multiply examples, but as I have one before me which does not, I think, appear in the long lists of Steevens and Malone, I will subjoin it: "It remayneth now that I take notice of

Maci. This is rare.

Sog. It's marle he stabs you not: By this light, he hath stabbed forty for forty times less matter, I can tell you of my knowledge.

Punt. I will make thee stoop, thou abject.

Sog. Make him stoop, sir! Gentlemen, pacify him, or he'll be killed.

Maci. Is he so tall a man?

Sog. Tall a man! if you love his life, stand betwixt them. Make him stoop!

Punt. My dog, villain, or I will hang thee; thou hast confest robberies and other felonious acts, to this gentleman, thy Countenance——

Sog. I'll bear no witness.

Punt. And without my dog, I will hang thee for them. [*Shift kneels.*

Sog. What! kneel to thine enemies!

Shift. Pardon me, good sir; God is my witness, I never did robbery in all my life.

Re-enter Fungoso.

Fung. O, Sir Puntarvolo, your dog lies giving up the ghost in the Wood-yard.

Maci. Heart, is he not dead yet.

[*Aside.*

Punt. O, my dog, born to disastrous fortune! pray you conduct me, sir.

[*Exit with* Fungoso.

Sog. How! did you never do any robbery in your life?

Maci. O, this is good! so he swore, sir.

Sog. Ay, I heard him: and did you swear true, sir?

Shift. Ay, as I hope to be forgiven, sir, I never robbed any man; I never stood by the highway-side, sir; but only said so because I would get myself a name, and be counted a tall man.

Sog. Now out, base viliaco![1] thou my Resolution! I thy Countenance! By this light, gentlemen, he hath confest to me the most inexorable company of robberies, and damned himself that he did 'em; you never heard the like. Out, scoundrel, out! follow me no more, I command thee; out of my sight, go, hence, speak not; I will not hear thee: away, camouccio!

[*Exit* Shift.

Maci. O, how I do feed upon this now, and fat myself! here were a couple unexpectedly dishumoured. Well, by this time, I hope, Sir Puntarvolo and his dog are both out of humour to travel. [*Aside.*] Nay, gentlemen, why do you not seek out the knight, and comfort him? our supper at the Mitre must of necessity hold to-night,[2] if you love your reputations.

Fast. 'Fore God, I am so melancholy for his dog's disaster—but I'll go.

Sog. Faith, and I may go too, but I know I shall be so melancholy.

Maci. Tush, melancholy! you must forget that now, and remember you lie at the mercy of a fury; Carlo will rack your sinews asunder, and rail you to dust, if you come not. [*Exeunt.*

[*Mit.* O, then their fear of Carlo, belike, makes them hold their meeting.

Cor. Ay, here he comes; conceive him but to be entered the Mitre, and 'tis enough.]

SCENE IV.—*A Room at the Mitre.*

Enter Carlo.

Car. Holloa! where be these shot-sharks?[3]

Jaspar's arryvall, and of those Letters with which the Queene was exceedingly well satisfied: saying, that you were too like some body in the world, to whom she is afrayde you are a little kin, *to be content to carry coales at any Frenchman's hand.*"—Secretary Cecyll to Sir Henry Neville, March 2, 1559.

[1] *Out, base* viliaco!] This word occurs in Decker: "Before they came near the great hall, the faint-hearted *villiacoes* sounded at least thrice."—*Untrussing the Humourous Poet.* In both places it means a worthless dastard: (from the Italian *vigliacco.*) *Camouccio,* which concludes this speech, is perhaps a corruption of *camoscio, a goat* or *goat's skin;* and may mean *clown,* or *flat-nose,* or any other apposite term which pleases the reader better. I cannot pretend, in fact, to fix the precise sense of those vituperative appellations, of which the purport, perhaps, was as vague as the orthography.

[2] *Our supper at the* Mitre *must of necessity hold to-night,*] And, above (p. 99 a), "No better place than the Mitre." This celebrated tavern, of which such frequent mention is made in our old plays, is described in some of them as standing in Cheapside, and in others in Bread-street: it was therefore not improbably the corner house. *In tenui labor.* It is noticed for the goodness of its entertainments by Middleton: "Why, this will be a *true feast,* a right *Mitre* supper."—*A Mad World my Masters,* act v.

[3] *Where be these* shot-sharks?] Improved from the quarto, which reads *shot-makers.* *Shot,* a tavern reckoning, is correctly rendered by Horne Tooke, *that which is thrown out,* or flung upon the table; and to hunt greedily and eagerly after this, is certainly no bad designation of a waiter.

Enter Drawer.

Draw. By and by; you are welcome, good Master Buffone.

Car. Where's George? call me George hither, quickly.

Draw. What wine please you have, sir? I'll draw you that's neat, Master Buffone.

Car. Away, neophite,[1] do as I bid thee, bring my dear George to me:—

Enter George.

Mass, here he comes.

George. Welcome, Master Carlo.

Car. What, is supper ready, George?

George. Ay, sir, almost. Will you have the cloth laid, Master Carlo?

Car. O, what else? Are none of the gallants come yet?

George. None yet, sir.

Car. Stay, take me with you, George;[2] let me have a good fat loin of pork laid to the fire presently.

George. It shall, sir.

Car. And withal, hear you, draw me the biggest shaft you have out of the butt you wot of;[3] away, you know my meaning, George; quick!

George. Done, sir.   *[Exit.*

Car. I never hungered so much for anything in my life as I do to know our gallants' success at court; now is that lean, bald-rib Maciente, that salt villain, plotting some mischievous device, and lies a soaking in their frothy humours like a dry crust, till he has drunk 'em all up. Could the pummice but hold up his eyes at other

men's happiness, in any reasonable proportion, 'slid, the slave were to be loved next heaven, above honour, wealth, rich fare, apparel, wenches, all the delights of the belly and the groin whatever.

Re-enter George, *with two jugs of wine.*

George. Here, Master Carlo.

Car. Is it right, boy?

George. Ay, sir, I assure you 'tis right.

Car. Well said, my dear George, depart; [*Exit* George.] Come, my small gimblet, you in the false scabbard, away, so! [*Puts forth the* Drawer *and shuts the door.*] Now to you, Sir Burgomaster, let's taste of your bounty.

[*Mit.* What, will he deal upon such quantities of wine alone?

Cor. You will perceive that, sir.]

Car. [*drinks.*] Ay, marry, sir, here's purity; O, George—I could bite off his nose for this now;[4] sweet rogue, he has drawn nectar, the very soul of the grape! I'll wash my temples with some on't presently, and drink some half a score draughts; 'twill heat the brain, kindle my imagination, I shall talk nothing but crackers and fireworks to-night. So, sir! please you to be here, sir, and I here: so.[5]
[*Sets the two cups asunder, drinks with the one, and pledges with the other, speaking for each of the cups, and drinking alternately.*

---

[1] *Away,* neophite,] i.e., youngster or novice: the word occurs again in *Cynthia's Revels.*

[2] *Stay,* take me with you, *George;*] i.e., understand me perfectly before you go. The phrase is very common in our old dramas; see Massinger, vol. iii. p. 488.

[3] *Draw me the biggest shaft you have out of the butt you wot of;*] I shall certainly incur the censure of poor Tibbald of "restoring lost puns;" for which, after all, I have no great respect: but I cannot avoid observing that here is a twofold allusion, 1. to *archery,* and 2. to the device of the worthy prior *Bolt ton.*

[4] *I could bite off his nose now:*] This odd mode of expressing pleasure, which seems to be taken from the practice of animals, who, in a playful mood, bite each other's ears, &c. is very common in our old dramatists. Thus Shakspeare, "I will bite thee by the ear for that jest."—*Romeo and Juliet.* And Sir John Suckling, in the *Goblins,* "Rare rogue in buckram, let me bite thee," &c.

[5] *So, sir! please you to be here, sir, and I here: so.*] The reader may possibly imagine

the following scene to be extremely ridiculous, and that the incident it contains could hardly be copied from real life. Mr. Dryden, I believe, thought otherwise. He hath given us a close imitation of it in the *Wild Gallant.* A person is represented playing by himself at backgammon, who throws first out of one dice-box, and then out of the other: just as Carlo drinks alternately out of the two cups. In the progress of the game, words arise between the players, which bring on a quarrel; and it ends in the actor's overturning the tables, and throwing the men about the floor. This may sufficiently vindicate our author from the charge of singularity.—WHAL.

Jonson does not derive much credit to his *incident,* from the circumstance of its being imitated by Dryden. The *Wild Gallant* is a first play, and a very insignificant performance; written, the author says, while he was yet "unfledged, and wanted knowledge." I suspect, however, that the poet took the scene from real life; it is sufficiently dull and uninteresting, but it is not improbable, and, unless I have been

[*Cor.* This is worth the observation, signior.]

Car. 1 *Cup.* Now, sir, here's to you; and I present you with so much of my love.

2 *Cup.* I take it kindly from you, sir [*drinks*,] and will return you the like proportion; but withal, sir, remembering the merry night we had at the countess's, you know where, sir.

1 *Cup.* By heaven, you put me in mind now of a very necessary office, which I will propose in your pledge, sir; the health of that honourable countess, and the sweet lady that sat by her, sir.

2 *Cup.* I do vail to it with reverence.[1] [*drinks.*] And now, signior, with these ladies, I'll be bold to mix the health of your divine mistress.

1 *Cup.* Do you know her, sir?

2 *Cup.* O lord, sir, ay; and in the respectful memory and mention of her, I could wish this wine were the most precious drug in the world.

1 *Cup.* Good faith, sir, you do honour me in't exceedingly. [*Drinks.*]

[*Mit.* Whom should he personate in this, signior?

Cor. Faith, I know not, sir; observe, observe him.[2]]

2 *Cup.* If it were the basest filth, or mud that runs in the channel, I am bound to pledge it respectively,[3] sir. [*drinks.*] And now, sir, here is a replenished bowl, which I will reciprocally turn upon you, to the health of the Count Frugale.

1 *Cup.* The Count Frugale's health, sir? I'll pledge it on my knees, by this light. [*Kneels.*

2 *Cup.* Will you, sir? I'll drink it on my knees then by the light.

[*Mit.* Why, this is strange.

Cor. Have you heard a better drunken dialogue?]

2 *Cup.* Nay, do me right, sir.

1 *Cup.* So I do, in faith.

2 *Cup.* Good faith you do not; mine was fuller.

1 *Cup.* Why, believe me, it was not.

2 *Cup.* Believe me it was; and you do lie.

1 *Cup.* Lie, sir!

2 *Cup.* Ay, sir.

1 *Cup.* 'Swounds! you rascal!

2 *Cup.* O, come, stab if you have a mind to it.

1 *Cup.* Stab! dost thou think I dare not?

Car. [*speaks in his own person.*] Nay, I beseech you, gentlemen, what means this? nay, look, for shame, respect your reputations.

[*Overturns wine, pot, cups, and all.*

Enter Macilente.

Maci. Why, how now Carlo! what humour's this?

Car. O, my good mischief! art thou come? where are the rest? where are the rest?

Maci. Faith, three of our ordnance are burst.

misinformed, has actually taken place in our own times. If Carlo, as Whalley wishes to suppose, and as I incline to think, was a real person, the mummery, we may be pretty confident, was characteristic of him, for, in those times, little delicacy or reserve was thought necessary, either on or off the stage.

[1] *I do vail to it with reverence,*] i.e., bow or bend submissively. The word is so common in this, its proper sense, that I shall content myself with merely referring to Massinger, vol. iii. p. 255.

[2] Mit. *Whom should he personate in this, signior?*

Cor. *Faith, I know not, sir; observe, observe him.*] The question of Mitis is natural enough, upon seeing so peculiar an extravagance: but the answer of Cordatus is not in the usual manner. It is rather an evasion of the question than a satisfactory reply: He doth not attempt to clear the poet by a parallel example, either in some ancient comic writer, or from what might be observed in common life; but puts off the inquirer's curiosity by desiring him to attend to what follows. This looks as if the matter would not bear a very nice examination, lest a discovery should be made of what the author did not choose to have publicly known. Hence one is induced to imagine that the character is personal; and that the humour exposed in it was the humour of a particular man.—WHAL.

See the Introductory Verses by Jaspar Mayne.

[3] *I am bound to pledge it respectively,*] i.e., *respectfully.* So the word is used by our author's contemporaries. Thus May:

"The modest and *respective* nothing gains."
All Fools, act i. sc. 1.

And Daniel:

"Out of the compass of *respective* awe."
Civil Wars.

And Shakspeare very frequently.—WHAL.

Car. Burst! how comes that?

Maci. Faith, overcharged, overcharged.

Car. But did not the train hold?

Maci. O, yes, and the poor lady is irrecoverably blown up.

Car. Why, but which of the munition is miscarried, ha?

Maci. Imprimis, Sir Puntarvolo; next, the Countenance and Resolution.

Car. How, how, for the love of wit?

Maci. Troth, the Resolution is proved recreant; the Countenance hath changed his copy; and the passionate knight is shedding funeral tears over his departed dog.

Car. What! is his dog dead?

Maci. Poisoned, 'tis thought; marry, how, or by whom, that's left for some cunning woman here o' the Bank-side[1] to resolve. For my part, I know nothing more than that we are like to have an exceeding melancholy supper of it.

Car. 'Slife, and I had purposed to be extraordinarily merry, I had drunk off a good preparative of old sack here; but will they come, will they come?

Maci. They will assuredly come; marry, Carlo, as thou lov'st me, run over 'em all freely to-night, and especially the knight; spare no sulphurous jest that may come out of that sweaty forge of thine; but ply them with all manner of shot, minion, saker, culverin, or anything, what thou wilt.

Car. I warrant thee, my dear case of petronels; so I stand not in dread of thee, but that thou'lt second me.

Maci. Why, my good German tapster, I will.

Car. What, George! *Lomtero, Lomtero,* &c.   [*Sings and dances.*

Re-enter George.

George. Did you call, Master Carlo?

Car. More nectar, George: *Lomtero,* &c.

George. Your meat's ready, sir, an your company were come.

Car. Is the loin of pork enough?

George. Ay, sir, it is enough.   [*Exit.*

Maci. Pork! heart, what dost thou with such a greasy dish? I think thou dost varnish thy face with the fat on't, it looks so like a glue-pot.

Car. True, my raw-boned rogue, and if thou wouldst farce[2] thy lean ribs with it too, they would not, like ragged laths, rub out so many doublets as they do; but thou know'st not a good dish, thou. O, it's the only nourishing meat in the world. No marvel though that saucy, stubborn generation, the Jews, were forbidden it; for what would they have done, well pampered with fat pork, that durst murmur at their Maker out of garlick and onions? 'Slight! fed with it, the whoreson strummel-patched, goggle-eyed grumbledories, would have gigantomachized——

Re-enter George *with wine.*

Well said, my sweet George, fill, fill.

[*Mit.* This savours too much of profanation.

Cor. O, servetur ad imum,
Qualis ab incœpto processerit, et sibi constet.
The necessity of his vain compels a toleration, for, bar this, and dash him out of humour before his time.]

Car. 'Tis an axiom in natural philosophy, what comes nearest the nature of that it feeds, converts quicker to nourishment, and doth sooner essentiate. Now nothing in flesh and entrails assimilates or resembles man more than a hog or swine. [*Drinks.*

Maci. True; and he, to requite their courtesy oftentimes doffeth his own nature, and puts on theirs; as when he becomes as churlish as a hog, or as drunk as a sow; but to your conclusion.   [*Drinks.*

Car. Marry, I say, nothing resembling man more than a swine, it follows nothing can be more nourishing; for indeed (but that it abhors from our nice nature) if we fed one upon another, we should shoot up a great deal faster, and thrive much better; I refer me to your usurous cannibals, or such like; but since it is so contrary, pork, pork, is your only feed.

Maci. I take it, your devil be of the same diet; he would never have desired to have been incorporated into swine else.—O, here comes the melancholy mess; upon 'em, Carlo, charge, charge!

---

[1] *Here, o' the Bank-side*] It should be recollected that this comedy was acted at the Globe play-house, on the Surrey side of the river.

[2] *And if thou wouldst* farce *thy lean ribs, &c.*] i.e., *stuff* or fill them out. Our old poets are fond of this culinary term. Thus Beaumont, "Whatever she's about, the name, Palamon, *lards* it; that she *farces* every business withal."—*Two Noble Kinsmen.* And Shakspeare, "Wit *larded* with malice, malice *farced* with wit."—*Troilus and Cressida.*

Enter Puntarvolo, Fastidious Brisk, Sogliardo, *and* Fungoso.

Car. 'Fore God, Sir Puntarvolo, I am sorry for your heaviness; body o' me, a shrewd mischance! why, had you no unicorn's horn, nor bezoar's stone about you,[1] ha?

Punt. Sir, I would request you be silent.

Maci. Nay, to him again.

Car. Take comfort, good knight, if your cat have recovered her catarrh,[2] fear nothing; your dog's mischance may be holpen.

Fast. Say how, sweet Carlo; for, so God mend me, the poor knight's moans draw me into fellowship of his misfortunes. But be not discouraged, good Sir Puntarvolo, I am content your adventure shall be performed upon your cat.

Maci. I believe you, musk-cod, I believe you; for rather than thou wouldst make present repayment, thou wouldst take it upon his own bare return from Calais. [*Aside.*

Car. Nay, 'slife, he'd be content so he were well rid out of his company, to pay him five for one, at his next meeting him in Paul's. [*Aside to* Macilente.] But for your dog, Sir Puntarvolo, if he be not out-right dead, there is a friend of mine, a quack-salver, shall put life in him again, that's certain.

Fung. O no, that comes too late.

Maci. 'Sprecious! knight, will you suffer this?

Punt. Drawer, get me a candle and hard wax presently. [*Exit* George.

Sog. Ay, and bring up supper; for I am so melancholy.

Car. O, signior, where's your Resolution?

Sog. Resolution! hang him, rascal: O, Carlo, if you love me, do not mention him.

Car. Why, how so?

Sog. O, the arrantest crocodile that ever Christian was acquainted with. By my gentry, I shall think the worse of tobacco while I live, for his sake: I did think him to be as tall a man——

Maci. Nay, Buffone, the knight, the knight. [*Aside to* Carlo.

Car. 'Slud, he looks like an image carved out of box, full of knots; his face is, for all the world, like a Dutch purse, with the mouth downward, his beard the tassels; and he walks—let me see—as melancholy as one o' the master's side in the Counter.[3] ——Do you hear, Sir Puntarvolo?

Punt. Sir, I do entreat you no more, but enjoin you to silence, as you affect your peace.

Car. Nay, but dear knight, understand, here are none but friends, and such as wish you well. I would have you do this now; flay me your dog presently (but in any case keep the head), and stuff his skin well with straw, as you see these dead monsters at Bartholomew fair.

Punt. I shall be sudden, I tell you.

Car. Or, if you like not that, sir, get me somewhat a less dog, and clap into the skin; here's a slave about the town here, a Jew, one Yohan: or a fellow that makes

---

[1] *Had you no* unicorn's horn, *nor* bezoar's stone *about you?*] These were supposed to be antidotes to poison, and what passed under their names was once sold at a vast price. Their virtues, it is now known, are as imaginary as their appellations; but many strange stories were formerly current of them. Both are frequently mentioned by our old dramatists. Thus Webster:

"I do not doubt,
As men, to try the precious *unicorn's horn*,
Make of the powder a preservative circle,
And in it put a spider; so," &c.*—White Devil.*

And Massinger, who indeed appears somewhat incredulous:

"His syrups, julips, *bezoar stone*, nor his
Imagined *unicorn's horn*, comes in my
    belly."
　　　　　　　　　　Roman Actor, act ii. sc. 1.

[2] *Your cat have recovered her* catarrh.] See p. 126 b. The quarto reads cat*aract*: either word will serve.

[3] *As melancholy as one o' the* master's side *in the* Counter.] See p. 138 b.

---

* Aubrey has a curious anecdote on this subject. Sir W. Davenant, in his youth, was page to the Duchess of Richmond. "I remember, (says Aubrey,) he told me, she sent him to a famous apothecary for some *unicorn's horne*, which he was resolved to try with a spyder, which he empaled in it, but without the expected success: the spyder would goe over, and through and through unconcerned."—MS. Aubrey. Mus. Ashm.

I quote this to Sir William's honour. Trying experiments was not much in vogue in his days. Our ancestors loved wonders, and believed from generation to generation, without once questioning the authenticity of what they heard and read: hence the silly and disgusting trash about raising fairies, giving men asses' heads, and I know not what, formerly detailed from book to book by Scott, Bulwer, and others, and now copied with all the complacency of parade, into the comments on our dramatic poets.

perukes will glue it on artificially, it shall
never be discerned ; besides, 'twill be so
much the warmer for the hound to travel
in, you know.

Maci. Sir Puntarvolo, death, can you be
so patient !

Car. Or thus, sir ; you may have, as you
come through Germany, a familiar[1] for
little or nothing, shall turn itself into the
shape of your dog, or anything, what you
will, for certain hours—[*Puntarvolo strikes
him*].—'Ods my life, knight, what do you
mean? you'll offer no violence, will you?
hold, hold !

Re-enter George, *with wax and a lighted
candle.*

Punt. 'Sdeath, you slave, you ban-dog,
you !

Car. As you love wit, stay the enraged
knight, gentlemen.

Punt. By my knighthood, he that stirs
in his rescue dies.—Drawer, begone !
                        [*Exit* George.

Car. Murder, murder, murder !

Punt. Ay, are you howling, you wolf?—
Gentlemen, as you tender your lives, suffer
no man to enter till my revenge be perfect.
Sirrah Buffone, lie down ; make no exclamations, but down ; down, you cur, or I
will make thy blood flow on my rapier
hilts.

Car. Sweet knight, hold in thy fury, and
'fore heaven I'll honour thee more than the
Turk does Mahomet.

Punt. Down, I say ! [*Carlo lies down.*]
—Who's there?   [*Knocking within.*

Cons. [*within.*] Here's the constable,
open the doors.

Car. Good Macilente——

Punt. Open no door ; if the Adalantado
of Spain[2] were here he should not enter :
one help me with the light, gentlemen ;
you knock in vain, sir officer.

Car. Et tu, Brute [3]

Punt. Sirrah, close your lips, or I will
drop it in thine eyes, by heaven.

Car. O ! O !

Cons. [*within.*] Open the door, or I will
break it open.

Maci. Nay, good constable, have pa-

tience a little, you shall come in presently,
we have almost done.
                        [*Puntarvolo seals up Carlo's lips.*

Punt. So now, are you Out of your
Humour, sir? Shift, gentlemen.
                [*They all draw, and run out, except
                Fungoso, who conceals himself
                beneath the table.*

Enter Constable *and* Officers, *and seize*
Fastidious *as he is rushing by.*

Cons. Lay hold upon this gallant, and
pursue the rest.

Fast. Lay hold on me, sir, for what?

Cons. Marry, for your riot here, sir, with
the rest of your companions.

Fast. My riot ! Master constable, take
heed what you do. Carlo, did I offer any
violence ?

Cons. O, sir, you see he is not in case to
answer you, and that makes you so peremptory.

Re-enter George *and* Drawer.

Fast. Peremptory ! 'Slife, I appeal to
the drawers, if I did him any hard measure.

George. They are all gone, there's none
of them will be laid any hold on.

Cons. Well, sir, you are like to answer
till the rest can be found out.

Fast. 'Slid, I appeal to George, here.

Cons. Tut, George was not here : away
with him to the Counter, sirs.—Come, sir,
you were best get yourself drest somewhere.
                [*Exeunt* Constable *and* Officers,
                with Fast. *and* Cor.

George. Good lord, that Master Carlo
could not take heed, and knowing what a
gentleman the knight is, if he be angry.

Drawer. A pox on 'em, they have left
all the meat on our hands ; would they
were choked with it for me.

Re-enter Macilente.

Maci. What, are they gone, sirs?

George. O, here's Master Macilente.

Maci. [*pointing to* Fungoso.] Sirrah
George, do you see that concealment there,
that napkin under the table?

George. 'Ods so, Signior Fungoso !

Maci. He's good pawn for the reckon-

---

[1] *You may have, as you come through Germany,
a familiar, &c.*] This alludes, probably, to the
strange stories propagated in Germany respecting the dog of Cornelius Agrippa. See p. 113 *b*.
[2] *Adalantado of Spain.*] "*Adalantado* is a
lord deputie or president of a countrie ; in *His-*
*pania unius provinciæ præses determinandis
litibus destinatus."—Minsheu.
[3] Car. *Et tu, Brute !*] This, I suppose, is
said to Macilente, who had privately instigated
his attacks on the knight, and, from his officious
malignity, probably held the candle.

ing ; be sure you keep him here, and let him not go away till I come again, though he offer to discharge all : I'll return presently.

George. Sirrah, we have a pawn for the reckoning.

Draw. What, of Macilente?

George. No ; look under the table.

Fung. [*creeping out.*] I hope all be quiet now ; if I can get but forth of this street, I care not : masters, I pray you tell me, is the constable gone?

George. What, Master Fungoso!

Fung. Was't not a good device this same of me, sirs?

George. Yes, faith ; have you been here all this while?

Fung. O lord, ay ; good sir, look an the coast be clear, I'd fain be going.

George. All's clear, sir, but the reckoning ; and that you must clear and pay before you go, I assure you.

Fung. I pay! 'Slight, I eat not a bit since I came into the house, yet.

Draw. Why, you may when you please, 'tis all ready below that was bespoken.

Fung. Bespoken! not by me, I hope?

George. By you, sir! I know not that ; but 'twas for you and your company, I am sure.

Fung. My company! 'Slid, I was an invited guest, so I was.

Draw. Faith, we have nothing to do with that, sir : they are all gone but you, and we must be answered; that's the short and the long on't.

Fung. Nay, if you will grow to extremities, my masters, then would this pot, cup, and all were in my belly, if I have a cross about me.

George. What, and have such apparel! do not say so, signior ; that mightily discredits your clothes.

Fung. As I am an honest man, my tailor had all my money this morning, and yet I must be fain to alter my suit too. Good sirs, let me go, 'tis Friday night, and in good truth I have no stomach in the world to eat anything.[1]

Draw. That's no matter, so you pay, sir.

Fung. 'Slight, with what conscience can you ask me to pay that I never drank for?

---

[1] *'Tis* Friday *night,—and I have no stomach in the world to* eat *anything.*] Friday, it should be recollected, was a *fast-day.* The allusion recurs in p. 138 *b* : "What! *Friday* night, and yet your *delicate* morsels!"

George. Yes, sir, I did see you drink once.

Fung. By this cup, which is silver, but you did not ; you do me infinite wrong : I looked in the pot once, indeed, but I did not drink.

Draw. Well, sir, if you can satisfy our master, it shall be all one to us.

[*Within.*] George!

George. By and by. [*Exeunt.*

[*Cor.* Lose not yourself now, signior.]

SCENE V.—*A Room in* Deliro's *House.*

Enter Macilente *and* Deliro.

Maci. Tut, sir, you did bear too hard a conceit of me in that ; but I will now make my love to you most transparent, in spite of any dust of suspicion that may be raised to cloud it ; and henceforth, since I see it is so against your humour, I will never labour to persuade you.

Deli. Why, I thank you, signior ; but what is that you tell me may concern my peace so much?

Maci. Faith, sir, 'tis thus. Your wife's brother, Signior Fungoso, being at supper to-night at a tavern, with a sort of gallants, there happened some division amongst them, and he is left in pawn for the reckoning. Now, if ever you look that time shall present you with an happy occasion to do your wife some gracious and acceptable service, take hold of this opportunity, and presently go and redeem him ; for, being her brother, and his credit so amply engaged as now it is, when she shall hear (as he cannot himself, but he must out of extremity report it), that you came, and offered yourself so kindly, and with that respect of his reputation, why, the benefit cannot but make her dote, and grow mad of your affections.

Deli. Now, by heaven, Macilente, I acknowledge myself exceedingly indebted to you, by this kind tender of your love ; and I am sorry to remember that I was ever so rude, to neglect a friend of your importance. —Bring me shoes and a cloak there.—I was going to bed, if you had not come. What tavern is it?

Maci. The Mitre, sir.

Deli. O! Why, Fido! my shoes.— Good faith, it cannot but please her exceedingly.

Enter Fallace.

Fal. Come, I marle what piece of night-work you have in hand now, that you call for a cloak and your shoes : What, is this your pander?

Deli. O, sweet wife, speak lower, I would not he should hear thee for a world——

Fal. Hang him, rascal, I cannot abide him for his treachery, with his wild quick-set beard there.[1] Whither go you now with him?

Deli. No whither with him, dear wife; I go alone to a place, from whence I will return instantly.—Good Macilente, acquaint not her with it by any means, it may come so much the more accepted ; frame some other answer.—I'll come back immediately.
[*Exit.*

Fal. Nay, an I be not worthy to know whither you go, stay till I take knowledge of your coming back.

Maci. Hear you, Mistress Deliro.

Fal. So, sir, and what say you?

Maci. Faith, lady, my intents will not deserve this slight respect, when you shall know them.

Fal. Your intents! why, what may your intents be, for God's sake?

Maci. Troth, the time allows no circum-stance, lady, therefore know this was but a device to remove your husband hence, and bestow him securely, whilst, with more conveniency, I might report to you a mis-fortune that hath happened to Monsieur Brisk——Nay, comfort, sweet lady. This night, being at supper, a sort of young gallants committed a riot, for the which he only is apprehended and carried to the Counter, where, if your husband, and other creditors, should but have knowledge of him, the poor gentleman were undone for ever.

Fal. Ah me! that he were.

Maci. Now, therefore, if you can think upon any present means for his delivery, do not foreslow it.[2] A bribe to the officer that committed him, will do it.

Fal. O lord, sir! he shall not want for a bribe ; pray you, will you commend me to him, and say I'll visit him presently.

Maci. No, lady, I shall do you better service, in protracting your husband's re-turn, that you may go with more safety.

Fal. Good truth, so you may; farewell, good sir. [*Exit* Maci.]—Lord, how a woman may be mistaken in a man! I would have sworn upon all the Testaments in the world he had not loved Master Brisk. Bring me my keys there, maid. Alas, good gentleman, if all I have in this earthly world will pleasure him, it shall be at his service. [*Exit.*

[*Mit.* How Macilente sweats in this business, if you mark him!

Cor. Ay, you shall see the true picture of spight anon : here comes the pawn and his redeemer.]

SCENE VI.—*A Room at the* Mitre.

Enter Deliro, Fungoso, *and* George.

Deli. Come, brother, be not discouraged for this, man; what!

Fung. No, truly, I am not discouraged; but I protest to you, brother, I have done imitating any more gallants either in purse or apparel, but as shall become a gentle-man for good carriage or so.

Deli. You say well.—This is all in the bill here, is it not?

George. Ay, sir.

Deli. There's your money, tell it : and, brother, I am glad I met with so good oc-casion to shew my love to you.

---

1 *With his wild* quickset beard *there.*] His *beard* cut like a *quick-set* hedge. The several figures into which they pruned their beards, and this among the rest, are mentioned by Taylor, the water-poet, in his *Whip of Pride:*

" And some, to set their loves' desire on edge,
Are cut and pruned like to a *quick-set hedge.*"
WHAL.

This seems to be the simplest of all the modes in vogue. Mrs. Quickly talks of a *beard* rounded "like a glover's paring-knife ;" and Taylor, in the poem just quoted by Whalley, mentions two others, "with the *hammer-cut*, or the *Roman* T." This last, from its perfect absurdity, seems to have been in high request :

" He strokes his *beard*,
Which now he puts i' th' posture of a T,
The Roman T ; your T *beard is the fashion.*"
Queen of Corinth, act iv. sc. r.

2 *Do not* foreslow *it.*] i.e., slacken or delay it. Thus Spenser:

" But by no means **my way I would** *forslow.*"

And Shakspeare :

" *Forslow* no longer, make we hence amain."

And almost every writer of the time : though Theobald pronounces the word to have been then obsolete.

Fung. I will study to deserve it in good truth, an I live.

Deli. What, is it right?

George. Ay, sir, and I thank you.

Fung. Let me have a capon's leg saved, now the reckoning is paid.

George. You shall, sir.   [*Exit.*

Enter Macilente.

Maci. Where's Signior Deliro?

Deli. Here, Macilente.

Maci. Hark you, sir, have you dispatched this same?

Deli. Ay, marry have I.

Maci. Well, then, I can tell you news; Brisk is in the Counter.

Deli. In the Counter!

Maci. 'Tis true, sir, committed for the stir here to-night. Now would I have you send your brother home afore, with the report of this your kindness done him, to his sister, which will so pleasingly possess her, and out of his mouth too, that in the mean time you may clap your action on Brisk, and your wife, being in so happy a mood, cannot entertain it ill, by any means.

Deli. 'Tis very true, she cannot, indeed, I think.

Maci. Think! why, 'tis past thought; you shall never meet the like opportunity, I assure you.

Deli. I will do it.—Brother, pray you go home afore (this gentleman and I have some private business), and tell my sweet wife I'll come presently.

Fung. I will, brother.

Maci. And, signior, acquaint your sister, how liberally, and out of his bounty, your brother has used you (do you see?) made you a man of good reckoning; redeemed that you never were possest of, credit; gave you as gentleman-like terms as might be; found no fault with your coming behind the fashion; nor nothing.

Fung. Nay, I am out of those humours now.

Maci. Well, if you be out, keep your distance, and be not made a shot-clog[1] any more.—Come, signior, let's make haste.
    [*Exeunt.*

SCENE VII.—*The Counter.*

Enter Fallace *and* Fastidious Brisk.

Fal. O, Master Fastidious, what pity is it to see so sweet a man as you are, in so sour a place!   [*Kisses him.*

[*Cor.* As upon her lips, does she mean?

Mit. O, this is to be imagined the Counter, belike.]

Fast. Troth, fair lady, 'tis first the pleasure of the fates, and next of the constable, to have it so: but I am patient, and indeed comforted the more in your kind visit.

Fal. Nay, you shall be comforted in me more than this, if you please, sir. I sent you word by my brother, sir, that my husband laid to 'rest you this morning; I know not whether you received it or no.

Fast. No, believe it, sweet creature, your brother gave me no such intelligence.

Fal. O, the lord!

Fast. But has your husband any such purpose?

Fal. O, sweet Master Brisk, yes: and therefore be presently discharged, for if he come with his actions upon you, Lord deliver you! you are in for one half-a-score year; he kept a poor man in Ludgate once twelve year for sixteen shillings. Where's your keeper? for love's sake call him, let him take a bribe, and dispatch you. Lord, how my heart trembles! here are no spies, are there?

Fast. No, sweet mistress. Why are you in this passion?

Fal. O lord, Master Fastidious, if you knew how I took up my husband to-day, when he said he would arrest you; and how I railed at him that persuaded him to it, the scholar there, (who, on my conscience loves you now,) and what care I took to send you intelligence by my brother; and how I gave him four sovereigns[2] for his pains: and now, how I came running out hither without man or boy with me, so soon as I heard on't; you'd say I were in a passion indeed. Your keeper, for God's sake! O, Master Brisk, as 'tis in *Euphues*,[3]

[1] *A* shot-clog.] i.e., an incumbrance on the reckoning, as Whalley observes. The agency of Macilente is employed with great art, in hastening the catastrophe, so long delayed. Jonson has everywhere distinguished, with matchless dexterity, the subtle and active malignity of this dangerous character, from the boisterous and sarcastic petulance of the mischievous Carlo.

[2] *I gave him four* sovereigns.] Four ten-shilling pieces, four angels. See p. 112 *b*.

[3] *As 'tis in* Euphues,] This was written by John Lilly, the author of several plays, which were once in high favour. Its title was

*Hard is the choice, when one is compelled
either by silence to die with grief, or by
speaking to live with shame.*

Fast. Fair lady, I conceive you, and
may this kiss assure you, that where adver-
sity hath, as it were, contracted, prosperity
shall not—— Od's me ! your husband.

Enter Deliro *and* Macilente.

Fal. O me !
Deli. Ay ! Is it thus ?
Maci. Why, how now, Signior Deliro !
has the wolf seen you,[1] ha ? Hath Gorgon's head made marble of you ?
Deli. Some planet strike me dead !
Maci. Why, look you, sir, I told you,
you might have suspected this long afore,
had you pleased, and have saved this
labour of admiration now, and passion,
and such extremities as this frail lump of
flesh is subject unto. Nay, why do you not
dote now, signior ? methinks you should
say it were some enchantment, *deceptio
visus,* or so, ha ! If you could persuade
yourself it were a dream now, 'twere excellent : faith, try what you can do, signior ;
it may be your imagination will be brought
to it in time ; there's nothing impossible.
Fal. Sweet husband !
Deli. Out, lascivious strumpet !   [*Exit.*
Maci. What ! did you see how ill that
stale vein became him afore, of *sweet wife,*
and *dear heart;* and are you fallen just
into the same now, with *sweet husband!*
Away, follow him, go, keep state : what !
remember you are a woman, turn impudent ; give him not the head, though you
give him the horns. Away. And yet, methinks, you should take your leave of *enfant*

perdu here, your forlorn hope.[2] [*Exit* Fal.]
How now, Monsieur Brisk ? what, Friday
night, and in affliction, too, and yet your
pulpamenta,[3] your delicate morsels ! I
perceive the affection of ladies and gentlewomen pursues you wheresoever you go,
monsieur.
Fast. Now, in good faith, and as I am
gentle, there could not have come a thing
in this world to have distracted me more
than the wrinkled fortunes of this poor
dame.
Maci. O yes, sir ; I can tell you a thing
will distract you much better, believe it :
Signior Deliro has entered three actions
against you, three actions, monsieur !
marry, one of them (I'll put you in comfort) is but three thousand, and the other
two, some five thousand pounds together :
trifles, trifles.
Fast. O, I am undone !
Maci. Nay, not altogether so, sir ; the
knight must have his hundred pound re-
paid, that will help, too ; and then six
score pounds for a diamond, you know
where. These be things will weigh, monsieur, they will weigh.
Fast. O heaven !
Maci. What ? do you sigh ? this it is to
*kiss the hand of a countess, to have her
coach sent for you, to hang poniards in
ladies' garters, to wear bracelets of their
hair,* and for every one of these great
favours, to *give some slight jewel of five
hundred crowns or so;* why, 'tis nothing.
Now, monsieur, you see the plague that
treads on the heels o' your foppery : well,
go your ways in, remove yourself to the
two-penny ward[4] quickly, to save charges,

"Euphues; the Anatomie of Wit, verie pleasant
for all gentlemen to read, and most necessarie to
remember," &c. 1580. Two years afterwards
came out, "Euphues and his England, containing his Voyage and Adventures," &c. These
notable productions were full of pedantic and
affected phraseology (as Whalley truly says),
and of high-strained antitheses of thought and
expression. Unfortunately they were well received at court, where they did incalculable
mischief, by vitiating the taste, corrupting the
language, and introducing a spurious and unnatural mode of conversation and action, which
all the ridicule in this and the following drama
could not put out of countenance.
[1] *Why, how now,—has the* wolf seen you?]
It was anciently supposed that if a *wolf* saw
any one before he was seen, that person was deprived of speech. Hence Virgil :

" *Vox quoque Mœrin
Jam fugit ipsa; lupi Mœrin videre priores.*"
Ec. ix.

[2] *And yet, methinks, you should take your
leave of* enfant perdu *here, your* forlorn hope.]
These are military terms, and denote a body of
men, placed even in the cannon's mouth, or sent
out upon any desperate service.—WHAL.
[3] *And yet your* pulpamenta,] i.e., as Jonson
well explains it, your delicacies, your nice bits.
Whalley says that the allusion is to Terence,

" *Lepus tute es, et pulpamentum quæris ?*"
Eun. act iii. sc. i.

Was he aware of the sense of this passage ? In
any case, it does not apply to Fastidious and
Fallace.
[4] *Remove yourself to the* two-penny ward *to
save charges.*] Fastidious was now in the
master's ward (see p. 133 *b*). The Counter had
four compartments, or "sides," the knight's
ward, the master's ward, the two-penny ward,
and the hole ; and it was not uncommon for the
debtors, as their means wasted, to descend
gradually from the first to the last. The rooms

and there set up your rest to spend Sir
Puntarvolo's hundred pound for him.
Away, good pomander, go !
                    [*Exit* Fastidious.
Why, here's a change ! now is my soul at
    peace :
I am as empty of all envy now,
As they of merit to be envied at.
My humour, like a flame, no longer lasts
Than it hath stuff to feed it ; and their
    folly
Being now raked up in their repentant
    ashes,
Affords no ampler subject to my spleen,
I am so far from malicing their states,
That I begin to pity them.   It grieves
    me
To think they have a being.   I could wish
They might turn wise upon it, and be
    saved now,
So heaven were pleased ; but let them
    vanish, vapours !——
Gentlemen, how like you it? has't not
    been tedious ?[1]

<hr>

[*Cor.* Nay, we have done censuring now.
Mit. Yes, faith.]

<hr>

in the knight's ward seem to have been expensive: the hole was a mere dungeon, and only
tenanted by the poorest prisoners.   See Massinger, vol. iv. p. 7, and, for a fuller account,
Fenner's *Compter's Commonwealth.*
  [1] After this line there follow in the quarto
several others, which concluded the play: as
as they are not without merit, I shall subjoin
them :
" And now with Asper's tongue, though not his
    shape,
Kind patrons of our sports, you that can judge,
And with discerning thoughts measure the
    space
Of our strange Muse in this her maze of
    humour ;
You, whose fine notions do confine the forms
And nature of sweet poesy to you,
I tender solemn, and most duteous thanks,
For your stretched patience and attentive
    grace.
We know, and we are pleased to know so
    much,
The cates that you have tasted were not
    seasoned

Maci. How so ?

<hr>

[*Cor.* Marry, because we'll imitate your
actors, and be out of our humours.   Besides, here are those round about you of
more ability in censure than we, whose
judgments can give it a more satisfying
allowance ; we'll refer you to them.
                    [*Exeunt* Cordatus *and* Mitis.]

<hr>

Maci. [*coming forward.*] Ay, is it even
so ?—Well, gentlemen, I should have gone
in, and returned to you as I was Asper at
the first ; but by reason the shift would
have been somewhat long, and we are loth
to draw your patience farther, we'll intreat
you to imagine it.   And now, that you may
see I will be out of humour for company, I
stand wholly to your kind approbation, and
indeed am nothing so peremptory as I was
in the beginning : marry, I will not do as
Plautus in his *Amphitryo*, for all this,
summi Jovis causâ, plaudite ; beg a plaudite for God's sake ; but if you, out of the
bounty of your good-liking, will bestow it,
why, you may in time make lean Macilente
as fat as Sir John Falstaff.   [*Exit.*

<hr>

For every vulgar palate, but prepared
To banquet pure and apprehensive ears :
Let then their voices speak for our desert ;
Be their applause the trumpet to proclaim
Defiance to rebelling ignorance :
And the green spirits of some tainted few,
That, spight of pity, do betray themselves
To scorn and laughter ; and, like guilty chil-
    dren,
Publish their infancy, before their time,
By their own fond exception : such as these
We pawn 'em to your *censure*, till time, wit,
Or observation, set some stronger seal
Of *judgment* on their judgments ; and entreat
The happier spirits in this fair-fitted *Globe*,
(So many as have sweet minds in their breasts
And are too wise to think themselves are taxed
In any general figure, or too virtuous
To need that wisdom's imputation :)
That with their bounteous hands they would
    confirm
This, as their pleasure's patent : which so
    signed,
Our leavened spent endeavours shall renew
Their beauties, with the spring, to smiles on
    you."

THE

EPILOGUE,

AT THE

PRESENTATION BEFORE QUEEN ELIZABETH.

BY MACILENTE.

NEVER till now did object greet mine eyes
With any light content: but in her graces
All my malicious powers have lost their
    stings.
Envy is fled my soul at sight of her,
And she hath chased all black thoughts
    from my bosom,
Like as the sun doth darkness from the
    world.
My stream of humour is run out of me,
And as our city's torrent, bent t'infect
The hallowed bowels of the silver Thames,
Is checked by strength and clearness of the
    river,
Till it hath spent itself even at the shore;
So in the ample and unmeasured flood
Of her perfections, are my passions
    drowned;
And I have now a spirit as sweet and clear
As the more rarified and subtle air :—
With which, and with a heart as pure as
    fire,
Yet humble as the earth, do I implore,
    [*Kneels.*
O heaven, that She, whose presence hath
    effected
This change in me, may suffer most late
    change
In her admired and happy government:
May still this Island be called Fortunate,
And ragged Treason tremble at the sound,
When Fame shall speak it with an em-
    phasis.
Let foreign polity be dull as lead,
And pale Invasion come with half a heart,
When he but looks upon her blessed
    soil.
The throat of War be stopt within her
    land,
And turtle-footed Peace dance fairy rings
About her court ;[1] where never may there
    come
Suspect or danger, but all trust and safety.
Let Flattery be dumb, and Envy blind

---

[1] *And turtle-footed Peace dance* fairy *rings
About her court* ;] There is a true poetical
spirit in the preceding and following verses ;
and the principal occurrences which distinguished
the reign of Queen Elizabeth are touched upon
with extreme delicacy and justice. The allusion
of this line refers to Spenser's *Fairy Queen,*
which was a compliment to the princess then on
the throne.—WHAL.

There is nothing so general, nor so deplorable
as the blunders of the commentators about
fairies. Spenser's *Fairy Queen,* which is one of
the grossest misnomers in romance or history,
bears no features of the fairy nation. She might
have been (for it is clear that Spenser himself
had no definite ideas on the subject) the Calypso
of antiquity, or the Enchantress of the Middle
Ages, but could never have possessed one attribute in common with the fairy of our simple
ancestors. I may one day, perhaps, find an
opportunity of giving the popular tradition on
this subject, which will be found as elegant as
any of the mythological fables of Greece and
Rome; meanwhile it will be sufficient to ask
where Whalley found his "reference" to Spenser,
whose knights are neither more nor less than the
knights of Arthur's Round Table ; polished indeed into the formality of his own times ; but
who neither dance *fairy rings,* nor very sedulously cultivate the acquaintance of *turtle-footed
Peace.*

This spirited and poetical Epilogue, as he
justly terms it, originally made part of Macilente's concluding speech, and was prefaced by
four lines of absurd and fulsome rant, bordering
on profaneness. It is to the praise of the
audience that, though accustomed to hear the
queen addressed in terms of the grossest adula-
tion, they yet murmured at this, and expressed
their dislike so strongly as to draw from Jonson
an awkward attempt at justification. Neither
the verses, nor the apology for them, call for
preservation ; the former were rejected by the
author, and the latter appeared only in the
quarto. Jonson was undoubtedly ashamed of
both.

In her dread presence; Death himself ad-
   mire her;
And may her virtues make him to forget
The use of his inevitable hand.

Fly from her, Age; sleep, Time, before her
   throne;
Our strongest wall falls down, when she is
   gone.[1]

---

[1] The preliminary observations of the author have left me little to say on this "Comical Satire." In vigour, in purity and elegance of style, it is perhaps superior to *Every Man in his Humour:* it is also more correspondent to its title; for we have real humours here, i.e., qualities "whose currents run all one way," while in the former we have chiefly affectations.

It is said by Hurd that Jonson has given us in this drama "an unnatural delineation of a group of passions wholly chimerical, and unlike to anything we observe in the commerce of common life:" this is hazarded without much consideration of the subject. The characters seem to be drawn from a close observation of human nature as she appeared in the poet's days; and to call them "chimerical," because the originals, after a lapse of two centuries, are not discernible, is at once illogical and unjust. No one believes that Bobadill was a mere creature of the imagination; yet what is Fastidious Brisk but a Bobadill at Whitehall? The court, like the army, had undoubtedly its boasters and pretenders, and Jonson portrayed them as they probably offered themselves to his pencil, in his intercourse with both.

Nor is Bobadill the only character of the preceding play which he has, in the present, endeavoured to heighten and improve. Sogliardo and Fungoso are Master Mathew and Master Stephen thrown into new situations, and marked with more skilful and vivid touches.

With all these excellencies, and many others—for most of the persons of the drama (and above all, Cavalier Shift), are delineated with a masterly hand, *Every Man out of his Humour* is, as a whole, very deficient in interest. The plot is progressive, but not well combined; the action awkwardly helped forward by the Chorus; and the catastrophe, though sufficiently ingenious, not altogether legitimately produced by previous occurrences. A poet, said Horace, should endeavour either to profit or delight. This is not enough: he should seek to do both, or he will but imperfectly secure his end. Like Jonson, in the present case, he may, and must, be admired in the closet; but he will not be followed to the stage.

Cynthia's Revels; or, The Fountain of Self-Love.

CYNTHIA'S REVELS.] The first edition of this "Comical Satire" was printed in quarto, 1601, with this motto,

Quod non dant proceres, dabit histrio—
Haud tamen invideas vati, quem pulpita pascunt;

which probably bore an allusion to some circumstance now unknown. When Jonson republished it, he chose a more intelligible passage: *Nasutum volo, nolo polyposum;* and transferred the last line of the former motto, to the title-page of his general works. The folio edition of this play, which appeared in 1616, differs considerably from the quarto, being increased by several new scenes, with which, to the utter discomfiture of the reader's patience, the author injudiciously swelled out the last two acts. *Cynthia's Revels* appears to have been not unfavourably received, since we are told that it was "frequently acted at the Blackfriars, by the children of Queen Elizabeth's chapel." It was also among the earliest plays revived after the Restoration, and was often performed at the New Theatre in Drury Lane, "very satisfactorily," as Downes says, "to the town:" though now laid aside. *Cynthia's Revels* was first acted in 1600, and the folio gives the names of the boys (children, as they were called) who performed the principal parts: "Nat. Field, Sal. Pavy, Tho. Day, I. Underwood, Rob. Baxter, and John Frost." Of these some lived to be eminent in their profession; and one, who died young, and who was, indeed, an actor of very extraordinary promise, was honoured by the grateful poet with an epitaph, which has not often been surpassed.

[See "Epitaph on Salathiel Pavy, a child of Queen Elizabeth's Chapel."—Post *Epigrams* cxx.]

TO

THE SPECIAL FOUNTAIN OF MANNERS,

THE COURT.

"THOU art a bountiful and brave spring, and waterest all the noble plants of this Island. In thee the whole kingdom dresseth itself, and is ambitious to use thee as her glass. Beware then thou render men's figures truly, and teach them no less to hate their deformities, than to love their forms: for to grace there should come reverence; and no man can call that lovely which is not also venerable. It is not powdering, perfuming, and every day smelling of the tailor, that converteth to a beautiful object: but a mind shining through any suit, which needs no false light, either of riches or honours, to help it. Such shalt thou find some here, even in the reign of Cynthia,[1]—a Crites and an Arete. Now, under thy Phœbus, it will be thy province to make more;[2] except thou desirest to have thy source mix with the spring of self-love, and so wilt draw upon thee as welcome a discovery of thy days, as was then made of her nights.

"Thy Servant, but not Slave,   BEN. JONSON."

DRAMATIS PERSONÆ.

Cynthia.	Echo.
Mercury.	Arete.
Hesperus.	Phantaste.
Crites.	Argurion.
Amorphus.	Philautia.
Asotus.	Moria.
Hedon.	Cos.
Anaides.	Gelaia.
Morphides.	Phronesis, ⎫
Prosaites.	Thauma, ⎬ *Mutes.*
Morus.	Time,[3] ⎭
Cupid.	

SCENE,—Gargaphie.

---

[1] *Such shalt thou find here, even in the reign of Cynthia,*] Cynthia was now dead, and this little reflection upon her memory, which might have been spared, was thrown in to cajole her successor. The quarto has no dedication. It is unnecessary to call the reader's attention to the extreme elegance of this little composition.

[2] *Now under thy Phœbus, it will be thy province to make more:*] This was intended as a compliment to James. Our poet growing into reputation by the representation of his last comedy, in the presence of the queen and court, endeavours to ingratiate himself by the following performance; which he designed, with an honest freedom, for the correction of the fantastic humour and extravagance of courtiers.—WHAL.

[3] *Time,*] Time is the Greek word for Honour, and must be pronounced as a dissyllable.

WHAL.

Cynthia's Revels.

INDUCTION.

The Stage.

After the second sounding.

Enter three of the Children *struggling.*

1 *Child.* Pray you away ; why, fellows ! Gods so, what do you mean ?

2 *Child.* Marry, that you shall not speak the prologue, sir.

3 *Child.* Why, do you hope to speak it ?

2 *Child.* Ay, and I think I have most right to it : I am sure I studied it first.

3 *Child.* That's all one, if the author think I can speak it better.

1 *Child.* I plead possession of the cloak :[1] gentles, your suffrages, I pray you.

[*Within.*] Why, Children ! are you not ashamed ? come in there !

3 *Child.* 'Slid, I'll play nothing in the play, unless I speak it.

1 *Child.* Why, will you stand to most voices of the gentlemen ? let that decide it.

3 *Child.* O, no, sir gallant ; you presume to have the start of us there, and that makes you offer so prodigally.

1 *Child.* No, would I were whipped, if I had any such thought ; try it by lots either.

2 *Child.* Faith, I dare tempt my fortune in a greater venture than this.

3 *Child.* Well said, resolute Jack ! I am content too, so we draw first. Make the cuts.

1 *Child.* But will you not snatch my cloak while I am stooping ?

3 *Child.* No, we scorn treachery.

2 *Child.* Which cut shall speak it ?

3 *Child.* The shortest.

1 *Child.* Agreed : draw. [*they draw cuts.*] The shortest is come to the shortest. Fortune was not altogether blind in this. Now, sir, I hope I shall go forward without your envy.

2 *Child.* A spite of all mischievous luck ! I was once plucking at the other.

3 *Child.* Stay, Jack : 'slid, I'll do somewhat now afore I go in, though it be nothing but to revenge myself upon the author : since I speak not his prologue. I'll go tell all the argument of his play afore-hand, and so stale his invention[2] to the auditory, before it comes forth.

1 *Child.* O, do not so.

2 *Child.* By no means.

3 *Child.* [*Advancing to the front of the Stage.*]—First, the title of his play is *Cynthia's Revels*, as any man that hath hope to be saved by his book can witness ;[3] the scene Gargaphie, which I do vehemently suspect for some fustian country ; but let that vanish. Here is the court of Cynthia, whither he brings Cupid travelling on foot, resolved to turn page. By the way Cupid meets with Mercury ; — that's a thing to be noted ; take any of our play-books without a Cupid or a Mercury in it, and burn it for an heretic in poetry. [*In these and the subsequent speeches, at every break, the other two interrupt, and endeavour to stop him.*] Pray thee let me alone. Mercury, he in the nature of a conjuror, raises up Echo, who weeps over her love, or daffodil, Narcissus, a little ; sings ; curses

---

[1] *I plead possession of the* cloak :] The usual dress of the person who spoke the prologue was a black velvet cloak.—WHAL.

So in the prologue to Heywood's *Four Prentices of London*, "Do you not know that I am the *Prologue*? Do you not see this *long black velvet cloak* upon my back?" And in that to the *Woman Hater*, "A *prologue* in verse is as stale as a *black velvet cloak*," &c. The only remaining vestige of this ancient custom is to be found in *Hamlet*, where the prologue to the tragedy played before the king still appears in his *black cloak*.

[2] *And so stale his invention*,] i.e., disclose it prematurely, make it common, so as to deprive it at once of all interest and novelty. See p. 16 a.

[3] *As any man that hath hope to be saved by his book can witness ;*] i.e., that can read : alluding, in the first place, to what is vulgarly called the neck-verse, and secondly to the title of the play, which, in those days, when scenery was unknown to the stage, was written or painted in large letters, and stuck up in some conspicuous place.

the spring wherein the pretty foolish gentleman melted himself away: and there's an end of her.—Now I am to inform you that Cupid and Mercury do both become pages. Cupid attends on Philautia, or Self-love, a court lady: Mercury follows Hedon, the Voluptuous, and a courtier; one that ranks himself even with Anaides, or the Impudent, a gallant, and that's my part; one that keeps Laughter, Gelaia, the daughter of Folly, a wench in boy's attire, to wait on him.—These, in the court, meet with Amorphus, or the Deformed, a traveller that hath drunk of the fountain, and there tells the wonders of the water. They presently dispatch away their pages with bottles to fetch of it, and themselves go to visit the ladies. But I should have told you—Look, these emmets put me out here—that with this Amorphus, there comes along a citizen's heir, Asotus, or the Prodigal, who, in imitation of the traveller, who hath the Whetstone following him,[1] entertains the Beggar, to be his attendant. Now the nymphs who are mistresses to these gallants, are Philautia, Self-love; Phantaste, a light Wittiness; Argurion, Money; and their guardian, Mother Moria, or Mistress Folly——

1 Child. Pray thee, no more.

3 Child. There Cupid strikes Money in love with the Prodigal, makes her dote upon him, give him jewels, bracelets, carcanets, &c. All which he most ingeniously departs withal to be made known to the other ladies and gallants; and in the heat of this, increases his train with the Fool to follow him as well as the Beggar. By this time, your Beggar begins to wait close, who is returned with the rest of his fellow bottlemen. There they all drink, save Argurion, who is fallen into a sudden apoplexy——

1 Child. Stop his mouth.

3 Child. And then, there's a retired scholar there, you would not wish a thing to be better contemned of a society of gallants, than it is; and he applies his service, good gentleman, to the Lady Arete, or Virtue, a poor nymph of Cynthia's train: that's scarce able to buy herself a gown; you shall see

her play in a black robe anon: a creature that, I assure you, is no less scorned than himself. Where am I now? at a stand!

2 Child. Come, leave at last, yet.

3 Child. O, the night is come, ('twas somewhat dark, methought,) and Cynthia intends to come forth; that helps it a little yet. All the courtiers must provide for revels; they conclude upon a masque, the device of which, is—What, will you ravish me?—that each of these Vices, being to appear before Cynthia, would seem other than indeed they are; and therefore assume the most neighbouring Virtues as their masking habit——I'd cry a rape, but that you are children.

2 Child. Come, we'll have no more of this anticipation ;[2] to give them the inventory of their cates aforehand, were the discipline of a tavern, and not fitting this presence.

1 Child. Tut, this was but to shew us the happiness of his memory. I thought at first he would have played the ignorant critic with everything, along as he had gone; I expected some such device.

3 Child. O, you shall see me do that[3] rarely; lend me thy cloak.

1 Child. Soft, sir, you'll speak my prologue in it.

3 Child. No, would I might never stir then.

2 Child. Lend it him, lend it him.

1 Child. Well, you have sworn.

[Gives him the cloak.

3 Child. I have. Now, sir, suppose I am one of your genteel auditors, that am come in, having paid my money at the door, with much ado, and here I take my place and sit down: I have my three sorts of tobacco in my pocket, my light by me, and thus I begin. [*At the breaks he takes his tobacco.*] By this light, I wonder that any man is so mad, to come to see these rascally tits play here. They do act like so many wrens, or pismires—not the fifth part of a good face amongst them all. And then their music is abominable—able to stretch a man's ears worse than ten—pillories, and their ditties—most lamentable things, like the pitiful fellows that make

---

[1] *Who hath the* Whetstone *following him,*] I.e., Cos.

[2] *2 Child. Come, we'll have no more of this anticipation;*] This is well thought on!

　"'Fore the beginning of this play,
　I, hapless Polydore, was found
　By fishermen, or others drowned," &c.

If Jonson had really meant to satirize the practice, he could not have done it more effectually.

[3] *3 Child. O, you shall see me do that,*] i.e., the part of an *ignorant critic;* and certainly the boy does it *rarely,* as he promises. Decker has copied much of this in his *Gull's Hornbook*

them—poets. By this vapour, an 'twere not for tobacco—I think—the very stench of 'em would poison me, I should not dare to come in at their gates. A man were better visit fifteen jails—or a dozen or two of hospitals—than once adventure to come near them. How is't? well?

  1 *Child.* Excellent ; give me my cloak.

  3 *Child.* Stay ; you shall see me do another now, but a more sober, or better-gathered gallant ; that is, as it may be thought, some friend, or well-wisher to the house : and here I enter.

  1 *Child.* What, upon the stage too?

  2 *Child.* Yes ; and I step forth like one of the children, and ask you, Would you have a stool, sir?[1]

  3 *Child.* A stool, boy!

  2 *Child.* Ay, sir, if you'll give me six-pence I'll fetch you one.

  3 *Child.* For what, I pray thee? what shall I do with it?

  2 *Child.* O lord, sir! will you betray your ignorance so much? why throne your-self in state on the stage, as other gen-tlemen use, sir.

  3 *Child.* Away, wag ; what, wouldst thou make an implement of me? 'Slid, the boy takes me for a piece of perspective, I hold my life, or some silk curtain, come to hang the stage here! Sir crack,[2] I am none of your fresh pictures, that use to beautify the decayed dead arras in a public theatre.

  2 *Child.* 'Tis a sign, sir, you put not

that confidence in your good clothes, and your better face, that a gentleman should do, sir. But I pray you, sir, let me be a suitor to you, that you will quit our stage then, and take a place, the play is instantly to begin.

  3 *Child.* Most willingly, my good wag ; but I would speak with your author, where is he?

  2 *Child.* Not this way, I assure you, sir ; we are not so officiously befriended by him, as to have his presence in the tiring-house, to prompt us aloud, stamp at the book-holder, swear for our properties, curse the poor tireman, rail the music out of tune, and sweat for every venial tres-pass we commit, as some author would, if he had such fine enghles as we.[3] Well, 'tis but our hard fortune !

  3 *Child.* Nay, crack, be not disheartened.

  2 *Child.* Not I, sir ; but if you please to confer with our author, by attorney, you may, sir ; our proper self here, stands for him.

  3 *Child.* Troth, I have no such serious affair to negotiate with him, but what may very safely be turned upon thy trust. It is in the general behalf of this fair society here that I am to speak, at least the more judi-cious part of it, which seems much dis-tasted with the immodest and obscene writing of many in their plays. Besides, they could wish your poets would leave to be promoters of other men's jests,[4] and to

---

[1] *Would you have a stool, sir?*] At the theatres in Jonson's time, spectators were ad-mitted on the stage. Here they sat on *stools*, the price of which, as the situation was more or less commodious, was *sixpence*, or a shilling : here, too, their own pages, or the boys of the house, supplied them with pipes and tobacco. Amidst such confusion and indecency were the dramatic works of Shakspeare and his contem-poraries produced, works which we,

  "With all appliances and means to boot,"

with everything that can promote the reality of the scene, and invigorate exertion, have never equalled, and very seldom indeed approached.

[2] *Sir* crack,] *Crack* is a sprightly forward boy. It frequently occurs in Jonson and his contemporaries. Thus Heyward :

  "It is a rogue, a wag, his name is Jack,
  A notable dissembling lad, a *crack*."
    Four Prentices of London.—WHAL.

[3] *If he had such fine* enghles *as we.*] See the *Poetaster.*—Act ii.

[4] *They could wish your poets would leave to be promoters of other men's jests*, &c.] This, with what follows, has, as Whalley says, been un-derstood to be pointed at Shakspeare. I am weary

of repelling such malicious absurdities, and must therefore leave them to the reader's scorn. This comedy, as the title-page tells us, was acted by the children of the queen's chapel, and the current complaint against them was, that they gave the public but little novelty. Thus in *Pasquil and Katharine* :

  " I sawe the children of Powles last night,
  And troth they pleased me prettie, prettie
    well,
  The apes in time will do it handsomely.
Pla. I' faith,
  I like the audience that frequenteth there
  With much applause : a man shall not be
    choakt
  With the (strong) stench of garlick, nor
    be pasted
  To the barmy jacket of a beer-brewer.
Bra. 'Tis a good gentle audience, and I hope
  The boys will come one day into request.
Pla. Ay, *an they had good playes, but they
    produce*
  Such musty fopperies of antiquity,
  And do not suit the humerous age's backs
  With cloathes in fashion."

This is precisely what Jonson says, and the satire, in both poets, is levelled at Lilly, Mar-

way-lay all the stale apothegms, or old books, they can hear of, in print or otherwise, to farce their scenes withal.[1] That they would not so penuriously glean wit from every laundress or hackney-man, or derive their best grace, with servile imitation, from common stages, or observation of the company they converse with ; as if their invention lived wholly upon another man's trencher. Again, that feeding their friends with nothing of their own, but what they have twice or thrice cooked, they should not wantonly give out, how soon they had drest it ;[2] nor how many coaches came to carry away the broken meat, besides hobby-horses and foot-cloth nags.

2 *Child.* So, sir, this is all the reformation you seek ?

3 *Child.* It is ; do not you think it necessary to be practised, my little wag ?

2 *Child.* Yes, where any such ill-habited custom is received.

3 *Child.* O, (I had almost forgot it too,) they say, the *umbræ* or ghosts of some three or four plays departed a dozen years since, have been seen walking on your stage here ; take heed, boy, if your house be haunted with such hobgoblins, 'twill fright away all your spectators quickly.

2 *Child.* Good, sir ; but what will you say now, if a poet, untouched with any breath of this disease, find the tokens upon you, that are of the auditory ? As some one civet-wit among you, that knows no other learning than the price of satin and velvets ; no other perfection than the wearing of a neat suit ; and yet will censure as desperately as the most professed critic in the house, presuming his clothes should bear him out in it. Another, whom it hath pleased nature to furnish with more beard than brain, prunes his mustaccio, lisps, and, with some score of affected oaths, swears down all that sit about him ; "That the old Hieronimo, as it was first acted,[3] was the only best, and judiciously penned play of Europe." A third great-bellied juggler talks of twenty years since, and when Monsieur was here,[4] and would enforce all wits to be of that fashion, because his doublet is still so. A fourth miscalls all by the name of fustian, that his grounded capacity cannot aspire to. A fifth only shakes his bottle head, and out of his corky brain squeezeth out a pitiful learned face, and is silent.

3 *Child.* By my faith, Jack, you have put me down : I would I knew how to get off with any indifferent grace ! Here, take your cloak, and promise some satisfaction in your prologue, or, I'll be sworn, we have marred all.

2 *Child.* Tut, fear not, child,[5] this will never distaste a true sense : be not out, and

---

ston, and, perhaps, Decker. Shakspeare is entirely out of the question. He manifests, indeed, in his *Hamlet*, a little managerial jealousy at the success of the "eyasses," and probably did not see new plays put into their hands with much pleasure ; but this has nothing to do with Jonson, who, for anything that appears to the contrary, was living on terms of confidence and kindness with him.

[1] *To farce their scenes withal.*] See p. 132 *a.* To live upon another man's trencher, which occurs just below, is literally from Juvenal :

  "*Aliena vivere quadra.*"—Sat. v.

[2] *They should not wantonly give out, how soon they had drest it ;*] In this speech the poet obliquely commends himself ; and in these words he retorts the accusation of his adversaries, who charged him with being a year about every play. —WHAL.

I am not altogether so certain of this, as my predecessor seems to be. Jonson has got among a new set of players, and he is distributing very wholesome satire to the comedians, who usually wrote for them. When Whalley talks of the "accusation of Jonson's enemies," had he forgotten that he had, at this time, only two plays on the stage! That the charge was subsequently made is as certain as that Jonson replied to it in the most triumphant manner ;

but I can discover no marks of a "retort," upon it here.

[3] *That the old Hieronimo, as it* was first acted, *&c.*) Here, indeed, our author palpably alludes to himself, for he had, about this time, borrowed of Mr. Henslow xxxxs. upon the credit of his *adycions* to this old favourite of the stage. *Ante,* p. 13 *a.* It is not a little singular that he should be so vain of these improvements, which, after all, possess no extraordinary degree of merit ; especially as it was not then the practice to lay open claim to the *purpurei panni* with which almost every drama of the time was patched. But Ben was unwilling that any of his labours should be confounded and lost in those of his contemporaries.

[4] *When* Monsieur *was here,*] In 1579, the Duke of Anjou, brother to Charles IX., King of France, came into England and paid his addresses to Queen Elizabeth, who cajoled him for some time, and then sent him home in disgrace. His residence here seems to have formed an era for our old dramatists, who make frequent mention of it. Thus Middleton :

" It was suspected much in *Monsieur's* days."
    Mad World my Masters.

[5] 2 Child. *Tut, fear not,* child,] In the quarto it is, "Tut, fear not, *Sall,*" from which it appears that the third child was Salathiel

good enough. I would thou hadst some sugar-candied to sweeten thy mouth.

The third sounding.

PROLOGUE.

If gracious silence, sweet attention,
Quick sight, and quicker apprehension,
The lights of judgment's throne, shine any where,
Our doubtful author hopes this is their sphere;
And therefore opens he himself to those,
To other weaker beams his labours close,
As loth to prostitute their virgin-strain,
To every vulgar and adulterate brain.
In this alone, his Muse her sweetness hath,
She shuns the print of any beaten path;
And proves new ways to come to learned ears:
Pied ignorance she neither loves nor fears.
Nor hunts she after popular applause,
Or foamy praise, that drops from common jaws:
The garland that she wears, their hands must twine,
Who can both censure, understand, define
What merit is: then cast those piercing rays,
Round as a crown, instead of honoured bays,
About his poesy; which, he knows, affords
Words, above action; matter, above words.

ACT I.

SCENE I.—*A Grove and Fountain.*

Enter Cupid, *and* Mercury *with his caduceus, on different sides.*

Cup. Who goes there?
Mer. 'Tis I, blind archer.
Cup. Who, Mercury?
Mer. Ay.
Cup. Farewell.
Mer. Stay, Cupid.
Cup. Not in your company, Hermes, except your hands were rivetted at your back.

Mer. Why so, my little rover?
Cup. Because I know you have not a finger, but is as long as my quiver, cousin Mercury, when you please to extend it.

Mer. Whence derive you this speech, boy?
Cup. O! 'tis your best polity to be ignorant. You did never steal Mars his sword out of the sheath, you! nor Neptune's trident! nor Apollo's bow! no, not you! Alas, your palms, Jupiter knows, they are as tender as the foot of a foundered nag, or a lady's face new mercuried, they'll touch nothing.

Mer. Go to, infant, you'll be daring still.
Cup. Daring! O Janus! what a word is there? why, my light feather-heeled coz, what are you any more than my uncle Jove's pander? a lacquey that runs on errands for him, and can whisper a light message to a loose wench with some round volubility? wait mannerly at a table with a trencher, warble upon a crowd a little,[1] and fill out nectar when Ganymede's away? one that sweeps the gods' drinking-room every morning, and sets the cushions in order again, which they threw one at another's head over night: can brush the carpets, call the stools again to their places, play the crier of the court with an audible voice, and take state of a president upon you at wrestlings, pleadings, negociations, &c. Here's the catalogue of your employments, now! O no, I err; you have the marshalling of all the ghosts too that pass the Stygian ferry, and I suspect you for a share with the old sculler there, if the truth were known: but let that scape. One other peculiar virtue you possess, in lifting,[2] or *leiger-du-main*, which few of the house of heaven have else besides, I must confess. But, methinks, that should not make you put that extreme distance 'twixt yourself and others, that we should be said to "over dare" in speaking to your nimble deity. So Hercules might challenge priority of us both, because he can throw the

---

Pavy, who also played Anaides. *Jack,* the second boy, was probably John Underwood, who proved a good actor, though he died young.
[1] Warble *upon a* crowd *a little,*] This seems but a scurvy compliment to the *curvæ lyræ parentem;* but Cupid is pleased to be satirical. To *warble* on a crowd is a Latinism, *canere tibia,* &c. *Crowd* is the old word for a fiddle; indeed, it is still in use in every part of the kingdom. I need not inform the learned reader, that Jonson is here trying his strength with Lucian, from whom many of the circumstances are taken; and surely prejudice itself must admit that in elegance and sprightliness of style, this dialogue is not a whit inferior to any in that lively and Attic writer. The allusions to him are too crowded and too obvious, to be pointed out.
[2] *In* lifting,] i.e., stealing; hence the modern word *shoplifter.*—WHAL.

bar farther, or lift more join'd stools at the arm's end, than we. If this might carry it, then we, who have made the whole body of divinity tremble at the twang of our bow, and enforced Saturnius himself to lay by his curled front, thunder, and three-forked fires, and put on a masking-suit, too light for a reveller of eighteen to be seen in——

Mer. How now ! my dancing braggart in *decimo sexto !*[1] charm your skipping tongue, or I'll——

Cup. What? use the virtue of your snaky tipstaff there upon us?

Mer. No, boy, but the smart vigour of my palm about your ears. You have forgot since I took your heels up into air, on the very hour I was born, in sight of all the bench of deities, when the silver roof of the Olympian palace rung again with applause of the fact.

Cup. O no, I remember it freshly, and by a particular instance ; for my mother Venus, at the same time, but stooped to embrace you, and, to speak by metaphor, you borrowed a girdle of hers, as you did Jove's sceptre while he was laughing ; and would have done his thunder too, but that 'twas too hot for your itching fingers.

Mer. 'Tis well, sir.

Cup. I heard you but looked in at Vulcan's forge the other day, and entreated a pair of his new tongs along with you for company : 'tis joy on you, i' faith, that you will keep your hooked talons in practice with anything. 'Slight, now you are on earth, we shall have you filch spoons and candlesticks rather than fail : pray Jove the perfumed courtiers keep their casting-bottles, pick-tooths, and shittle-cocks from you, or our more ordinary gallants their tobacco-boxes ; for I am strangely jealous of your nails.

Mer. Never trust me, Cupid, but you are turned a most acute gallant of late ! the edge of my wit is clean taken off with the fine and subtile stroke of your thin-ground tongue ; you fight with too poignant a phrase, for me to deal with.

Cup. O Hermes, your craft cannot make

me confident. I know my own steel to be almost spent, and therefore entreat my peace with you, in time : you are too cunning for me to encounter at length, and I think it my safest ward to close.

Mer. Well, for once, I'll suffer you to win upon me, wag ; but use not these strains too often, they'll stretch my patience. Whither might you march now ?

Cup. Faith, to recover thy good thoughts, I'll discover my whole project. The huntress and queen of these groves, Diana, in regard of some black and envious slanders hourly breathed against her, for her divine justice on Acteon, as she pretends, hath here in the vale of Gargaphie,[2] proclaimed a solemn revels, which (her godhead put off) she will descend to grace, with the full and royal expense of one of her clearest moons : in which time it shall be lawful for all sorts of ingenious persons to visit her palace, to court her nymphs, to exercise all variety of generous and noble pastimes : as well to intimate how far she treads such malicious imputations beneath her, as also to shew how clear her beauties are from the least wrinkle of austerity they may be charged with.

Mer. But what is all this to Cupid ?

Cup. Here do I mean to put off the title of a god, and take the habit of a page, in which disguise, during the interim of these revels, I will get to follow some one of Diana's maids, where, if my bow hold, and my shafts fly but with half the willingness and aim they are directed, I doubt not but I shall really redeem the minutes I have lost, by their so long and over nice proscription of my deity from their court.

Mer. Pursue it, divine Cupid, it will be rare.

Cup. But will Hermes second me?

Mer. I am now to put in act an especial designment from my father Jove ; but, that performed, I am for any fresh action that offers itself.

Cup. Well, then we part. [*Exit.*

Mer. Farewell, good wag.

---

[1] *My dancing braggart in* decimo sexto !] This expression for a youth, a stripling, occurs in many of our old writers. See Massinger, vol. iii. p. 32. *Charm* your tongue, is silence it, put a spell on its motion. Thus Shakspeare :

"*Peace*, wilful boy, or I shall *charm* your tongue."—*Hen. VI.*

And again :

"Mistress, go to ! *charm* your tongue."
Othello.

[2] *Here in the vale of* Gargaphie.] The vale where Acteon was torn to pieces by his own hounds :

"*Vallis erat piceis, et acuta densa cupresso,*
Nomine Gargaphie, &c. Ovid, Metam. l. 3.
WHAL.

Now to my charge.—Echo, fair Echo,
    speak,
'Tis Mercury that calls thee; sorrowful
    nymph,
Salute me with thy repercussive voice,
That I may know what cavern of the earth
Contains thy airy spirit, how, or where
I may direct my speech, that thou mayest
    hear.
    Echo [*below*]. Here.
    Mer. So nigh!
    Echo. Ay.
    Mer. Know, gentle soul, then, I am sent
    from Jove,
Who, pitying the sad burthen of thy woes,
Still growing on thee, in thy want of words
To vent thy passion for Narcissus' death,
Commands, that now, after three thousand
    years,
Which have been exercised in Juno's spite,
Thou take a corporal figure, and ascend,
Enriched with vocal and articulate power.
Make haste, sad nymph; thrice shall my
    winged rod
Strike the obsequious earth, to give thee
    way.
Arise, and speak thy sorrows, Echo, rise,
Here, by this fountain, where thy love did
    pine,
Whose memory lives fresh to vulgar fame,
Shrined in this yellow flower, that bears his
    name.
    Echo [*ascends*.[1]]   His name revives, and
    lifts me up from earth,
O, which way shall I first convert myself,[2]
Or in what mood shall I essay to speak,
That, in a moment, I may be delivered
Of the prodigious grief I go withal?
See, see, the mourning fount, whose springs
    weep yet
Th' untimely fate of that too beauteous boy,
That trophy of self-love, and spoil of nature,
Who, now transformed into this drooping
    flower,

Hangs the repentant head, back from the
    stream,
As if it wished, *Would I had never looked
In such a flattering mirror!* O Narcissus,
Thou that wast once, and yet art, my Nar-
    cissus,
Had Echo but been private with thy
    thoughts,
She would have dropt away herself in tears,
Till she had all turned water; that in her,
As in a truer glass, thou mightst have gazed,
And seen thy beauties by more kind reflec-
    tion,
But self-love never yet could look on truth
But with bleared beams; slick flattery and
    she
Are twin-born sisters, and so mix their eyes,
As if you sever one, the other dies.
Why did the gods give thee a heavenly
    form,
And earthly thoughts to make thee proud
    of it?
Why do I ask? 'Tis now the known disease
That beauty hath, to bear too deep a sense
Of her own self-conceived excellence.
O, hadst thou known the worth of heaven's
    rich gift,
Thou wouldst have turned it to a truer use,
And not with starved and covetous igno-
    rance,
Pined in continual eyeing that bright gem,
The glance whereof to others had been
    more,
Than to thy famished mind the wide world's
    store:
So wretched is it to be merely rich!
Witness thy youth's dear sweets here spent
    untasted,
Like a fair taper, with his own flame wasted.
    Mer. Echo be brief, Saturnia is abroad,
And if she hear, she'll storm at Jove's high
    will.
    Echo. I will, kind Mercury, be brief as
    time.

---

[1] Echo [*ascends*.] Warton affirms that Jonson meant in this place to ridicule the frequent introduction of Echo in the masques of his time; (a practice which he himself followed;) and he gives a ludicrous abridgment of the scene. It certainly requires far less ability than Warton possessed, to burlesque any mythological fable; and therefore it was the less necessary that he should misrepresent it. To say that Mercury strikes the earth twice, &c. may be very facetious; but cannot much affect the poet's reputation with those who know him. Jonson was infinitely superior to Warton as a classical scholar, and the whole of this scene is in the strictest conformity with the ancient models. It is not perhaps as poetical as some of his con-temporaries would have made it; but it is not very defective even in this respect, and is, besides, quite as serious as any other part of the play. In the song which follows, there is, indeed, as the clown says, *no great matter*; but it is not *burlesque*, as Warton asserts; nor is it true "that a song was always the sure consequence of Echo being raised." Why would Mr. Todd encumber the pages of his *Milton* with such inconsiderate attempts at criticism?

[2] *O, which way shall I first* convert *myself,*] i.e., *turn* myself. The word occurs in this sense in the old translation of the Bible: "Howbeit, after this, Jeroboam *converted* not from his wicked way."—1 Kings xiii. 33.

Vouchsafe me, I may do him these last rites,
But kiss his flower, and sing some mourning strain
Over his watery hearse.[1]
Mer. Thou dost obtain ;
I were no son to Jove should I deny thee.
Begin, and more to grace thy cunning voice,
The humourous air[2] shall mix her solemn tunes
With thy sad words: strike, music, from the spheres,
And with your golden raptures swell our ears.

Echo [*accompanied.*]

Slow, slow, fresh fount, keep time with my salt tears :
Yet slower, yet ; O faintly, gentle springs:
List to the heavy part the music bears,
Woe weeps out her division, when she sings.
    Droop herbs and flowers,
    Fall grief in showers,
    Our beauties are not ours ;
    O, I could still,
Like melting snow upon some craggy hill,
    Drop, drop, drop, drop,
Since nature's pride is now a withered daffodil. —

Mer. Now, have you done ?
Echo. Done presently, good Hermes ; bide a little:
Suffer my thirsty eye to gaze awhile,
But e'en to taste the place, and I am vanished.
Mer. Forego thy use and liberty of tongue,
And thou mayst dwell on earth, and sport thee there.
Echo. Here young Acteon fell, pursued and torn
By Cynthia's wrath, more eager than his hounds ;
And here—ah me, the place is fatal !—see
The weeping Niobe, translated hither
From Phrygian mountains ; and by Phœbe reared,

As the proud trophy of her sharp revenge.
Mer. Nay, but hear——
Echo. But here, O here, the fountain of self-love,
In which Latona, and her careless nymphs,
Regardless of my sorrows, bathe themselves
In hourly pleasures.
Mer. Stint thy babbling tongue !
Fond Echo, thou profanest the grace is done thee.
So idle worldlings merely made of voice,
Censure the Powers above them.   Come, away,
Jove calls thee hence, and his will brooks no stay.
Echo. O, stay: I have but one poor thought to clothe
In airy garments, and then, faith, I go.
Henceforth, thou treacherous and murdering spring,
Be ever called the FOUNTAIN OF SELF-LOVE :
And with thy water let this curse remain,
As an inseparate plague, that who but taste
A drop thereof, may, with the instant touch,
Grow dotingly enamoured on themselves.
Now, Hermes, I have finished.
Mer. Then thy speech
Must here forsake thee, Echo, and thy voice,
As it was wont, rebound but the last words.
Farewell.
Echo. [*retiring.*] Well.
Mer. Now, Cupid, I am for you, and your mirth,
To make me light before I leave the earth.

Enter Amorphus, *hastily.*

Amo. Dear spark of beauty, make not so fast away.
Echo. Away.
Mer. Stay, let me observe this portent yet.[3]
Amo. I am neither your Minotaur, nor

---

1   *Sing some mourning strain*
Over his watery hearse.] Beautifully imitated by Milton :

" He must not float upon his wat'ry bier
    Unwept, and welter to the parching wind,
    Without the meed of some melodious tear."

[2] *The humourous air, &c.*] *Humourous* here means moist, flaccid from humidity, flexible, &c. I merely notice this to prevent the reader, who

may chance to peruse this passage in Warton, from taking it, as he evidently does, in contrast to *sad* in the next line, for mirthful, or frolicksome.

[3] *Stay, let me observe this portent* yet.] This word is not well understood by modern critics, who seem to consider it, in such expressions as this before us, as little more than an expletive. It has, however, a meaning, and a very good one, though it may be difficult to define it pre-

your Centaur, nor your satyr, nor your hyæna, nor your babion,[1] but your mere traveller, believe me.

Echo. Leave me.

Mer. I guessed it should be some travelling motion pursued Echo so.

Amo. Know you from whom you fly? or whence?

Echo. Hence.   [*Exit.*

Amo. This is somewhat above strange: A nymph of her feature and lineament, to be so preposterously rude! well, I will but cool myself at yon spring, and follow her.

Mer. Nay, then I am familiar with the issue: I'll leave you too.   [*Exit.*

Amo. I am a rhinoceros, if I had thought a creature of her symmetry could have dared so improportionable and abrupt a digression.—Liberal and divine fount, suffer my profane hand to take of thy bounties. [*takes up some of the water.*] By the purity of my taste, here is most ambrosiac water; I will sup of it again. By thy favour, sweet fount. See, the water, a more running, subtile, and humourous nymph than she, permits me to touch and handle her. What should I infer? if my behaviours had been of a cheap or customary garb; my accent or phrase vulgar; my garments trite; my countenance illiterate, or unpractised in the encounter of a beautiful and brave attired piece; then I might with some change of colour have suspected my faculties. But, knowing myself an essence

so sublimated and refined by travel; of so studied and well exercised a gesture; so alone in fashion; able to render the face of any statesman living;[2] and to speak the mere extraction of language; one that hath now made the sixth return upon venture; and was your first that ever enriched his country with the true laws of the duello; whose optics have drunk the spirit of beauty in some eight score and eighteen princes' courts, where I have resided, and been there fortunate in the amours of three hundred forty and five ladies, all nobly, if not princely descended; whose names I have in catalogue. To conclude, in all so happy, as even admiration herself doth seem to fasten her kisses upon me:—certes, I do neither see, nor feel, nor taste, nor savour the least steam or fume of a reason, that should invite this foolish, fastidious nymph, so peevishly to abandon me. Well, let the memory of her fleet into air; my thoughts and I am for this other element, water.

Enter Crites[3] *and* Asotus.

Cri. What, the well dieted Amorphus become a water drinker! I see he means not to write verses then.

Aso. No, Crites! why?

Cri. Because—
Nulla placere diu, nec vivere carmina possunt,
Quæ scribuntur aquæ potoribus.

---

cisely. It seems to have somewhat of the power of notwithstanding, &c., and can only be felt in all its force by those who have diligently studied our old writers, far better judges of the euphony as well as the power of language than ourselves. In Todd's *Milton*, vol. v. p. 368, is this passage:

"This is mere moral babble, and direct
   Against the common laws of our foundation;
I must not suffer this; *yet* 'tis but the lees
   And settlings," &c.

"*Yet*," says Hurd, "is bad; *but*, very inaccurate." Tickell and Fenton omit *yet!* All this comes from not understanding the phrase, and the consequent vile pointing. It should be:

"I must not suffer this *yet*; 'tis but the lees," &c.

i.e., *however.* This restores the passage to sense and rhythm: as it stood, it had but little of either.

[1] *Nor your babion,*] i.e. baboon. Our old writers spell this word in many different ways; all derived, however, from *bavaan*, Dutch. We had our knowledge of this animal from the

Hollanders, who found it in great numbers at the Cape.

[2] *Able to* render *the face of any statesman living;*] To explain his looks, and guess at his intention and thoughts by them. The first folio has, *tender* the face, which seems to be corrupt.—WHAL.

I doubt, after all, whether the folio be not right: the quarto reads "to *make* the face," &c.; that is, I believe, to put on the air and gravity "of any statesman living." Whalley found his reading in the octavo of 1716, an edition of no authority, and utterly beneath his care.

[3] *Enter* Crites.] Throughout the quarto he is called Criticus. By Crites here, as well as by Asper in *Every Man out of his Humour*, and Horace in the *Poetaster*, Jonson undoubtedly meant to shadow forth himself. This sacrifice to vanity, as it involved him in personalities, naturally increased the number of his enemies, and exasperated the hostility with which he was long pursued. Decker, in his *Untrussing the humourous Poet*, does not overlook this circumstance. "You must be called *Asper*, and *Criticus*, and *Horace!* Your title's longer reading than the stile o' the big Turk's: Asper, Criticus, Quintus, Horatius, Flaccus." It appears that the boy who performed this laborious part was John Underwood.

Amo. What say you to your Helicon?

Cri. O, the Muses' well! that's ever excepted.

Amo. Sir, your Muses have no such water, I assure you; your nectar or the juice of your nepenthe, is nothing to it; 'tis above your metheglin, believe it.

Aso. Metheglin; what's that, sir? may I be so audacious to demand?

Amo. A kind of Greek wine I have met with, sir, in my travels; it is the same that Demosthenes usually drunk, in the composure of all his exquisite and mellifluous orations.

Cri. That's to be argued, Amorphus, if we may credit Lucian, who, in his *Encomio Demosthenis*, affirms he never drunk but water[1] in any of his compositions.

Amo. Lucian is absurd, he knew nothing: I will believe mine own travels before all the Lucians of Europe. He doth feed you with fittons,[2] figments, and leasings.

Cri. Indeed, I think, next a traveller, he does prettily well.

Amo. I assure you it was wine, I have tasted it, and from the hand of an Italian antiquary, who derives it authentically from the Duke of Ferrara's bottles. How name you the gentleman you are in rank with there, sir?

Cri. 'Tis Asotus, son to the late deceased Philargyrus, the citizen.

Amo. Was his father of any eminent place or means?

Cri. He was to have been prætor next year.

Amo. Ha! a pretty formal young gallant, in good sooth; pity he is not more genteelly propagated. Hark you, Crites, you may say to him what I am, if you please; though I affect not popularity, yet I would be loth to stand out to any whom you shall vouchsafe to call friend.

Cri. Sir, I fear I may do wrong to your sufficiencies in the reporting them, by forgetting or misplacing some one: yourself can best inform him of yourself, sir; except you had some catalogue or *tent* of your faculties ready drawn, which you would request me to shew him for you, and him to take notice of.

Amo. This Crites is sour; [*aside.*] I will think, sir.

Cri. Do so, sir.—O heaven! that anything in the likeness of man should suffer these racked extremities for the uttering of his sophisticate good parts. [*Aside.*

Aso. Crites, I have a suit to you; but you must not deny me: pray you make this gentleman and I friends.

Cri. Friends! why, is there any difference between you?

Aso. No; I mean acquaintance, to know one another.

Cri. O, now I apprehend you; your phrase was without me before.

Aso. In good faith, he's a most excellent rare man, I warrant him.

Cri. 'Slight, they are mutually enamoured by this time. [*Aside.*

Aso. Will you, sweet Crites?

Cri. Yes, yes.

Aso. Nay, but when? you'll defer it now, and forget it.

Cri. Why, is it a thing of such present necessity, that it requires so violent a dispatch?

Aso. No, but would I might never stir, he's a most ravishing man! Good Crites, you shall endear me to you, in good faith; la!

Cri. Well, your longing shall be satisfied, sir.

Aso. And withal, you may tell him what my father was, and how well he left me, and that I am his heir.

Cri. Leave it to me, I'll forget none of your dear graces, I warrant you.

Aso. Nay, I know you can better marshal these affairs than I can——O gods! I'd give all the world, if I had it, for abundance of such acquaintance.

---

[1] Lucian, *in his Encomio Demosthenis, affirms he never drunk but water*] These are the words of Lucian, ουκ οντως ὁ Δημοσθενης συνετιθει ὡρος μεθην τους λογους αλλ' ὑδωρ πινων.   WHAL.

[2] *He doth feed you with* fittons, figments, *and* leasings.] Perhaps the reading of the quarto is most eligible, and that is *fictions;* unless we suppose that *fittons* is an affected expression of this travelled gallant; which is not improbable.
                                                                WHAL.

The quarto has merely "fictions and leasings." It does not appear that *fitton* is an "affected expression," as it is used by some of our plainest writers. Thus old Gascoigne, "to tell a *fittone* in your landlord's eares." And North, in his Translation of Plutarch, "In many other places he commonly used to *fitton*, and to write devices of his own." It seems synonymous with feign or fabricate. *Figment is thus explained* by Fletcher:

" A figment is a candid lie,
This is an old pass."—*Four Plays in One.*

Leasing is, or ought to be, familiar to every reader. In Jonson's time, perhaps, these words had different shades of turpitude, which are no longer distinguishable.

Cri. What ridiculous circumstance might I devise now to bestow this reciprocal brace of butter ones one upon another?   [*Aside.*

Amo. Since I trod on this side the Alps,[1] I was not so frozen in my invention. Let me see: to accost him with some choice remnant of Spanish or Italian! that would indifferently express my languages now: marry, then, if he should fall out to be ignorant, it were both hard and harsh. How else? step into some *ragioni del stato*,[2] and so make my induction! that were above him too; and out of his element, I fear. Feign to have seen him in Venice or Padua! or some face near his in similitude! 'tis too pointed and open. No, it must be a more quaint and collateral device, as——stay: to frame some encomiastic speech upon this our metropolis, or the wise magistrates thereof, in which politic number, 'tis odds but his father filled up a room? descend into a particular admiration of their justice, for the due measuring of coals, burning of cans,[3] and such like? as also their religion, in pulling down a superstitious cross, and advancing a Venus, or Priapus, in place of it?[4] ha! 'twill do well. Or to talk of some hospital whose walls record his father a benefactor? or of so many buckets bestowed on his parish church in his life time, with his name at length, for want of arms, trickt upon them? any of these. Or to praise the cleanness of the street wherein he dwelt? or the provident painting of his posts, against he should have been prætor?[5] or, leaving his parent, come to some special ornament about himself, as his rapier, or some other of his accoutrements? I have it: thanks, gracious Minerva!

Aso. Would I had but once spoke to him, and then——He comes to me!

Amo. 'Tis a most curious and neatly wrought band, this same, as I have seen, sir.

Aso. O lord, sir!

Amo. You forgive the humour of mine eye, in observing it.

Cri. His eye waters after it, it seems.   [*Aside.*

Aso. O lord, sir! there needs no such apology, I assure you.

Cri. I am anticipated: they'll make a solemn deed of gift of themselves, you shall see.   [*Aside.*

Amo. Your riband too does most gracefully, in troth.

Aso. 'Tis the most genteel, and received wear now, sir.

Amo. Believe me, sir, I speak it not to humour you—I have not seen a young gentleman, generally, put on his clothes with more judgment.

Aso. O, 'tis your pleasure to say so, sir.

Amo. No, as I am virtuous, being altogether untravelled, it strikes me into wonder.

Aso. I do purpose to travel, sir, at spring.

Amo. I think I shall affect you, sir. This last speech of yours hath begun to make you dear to me.

Aso. O lord, sir! I would there were anything in me, sir, that might appear worthy the least worthiness of your worth, sir. I protest, sir, I should endeavour to shew it, sir, with more than common regard, sir.

Cri. O, here's rare motley,[6] sir.   [*Aside.*

Amo. Both your desert, and your endeavours are plentiful, suspect them not: but your sweet disposition to travel, I assure you, hath made you another myself in

---

[1] *Since I trod* on this side *the Alps,*] O bone! Was the scene laid in Bœotia for this?

[2] *Ragioni del stato,*] This "choice remnant of Italian," (which no Italian could pronounce,) or, something like it, seems to have been proverbial for the politics of different countries. It is used by Cartwright, (and many others,) "*Ragioni di stato* generally reek in all."—*Ordinary*, act i. sc. 4.

[3] Burning *of cans,*] i.e., impressing the mark of legality with a hot iron, on the wooden measures then in use.—WHAL.

[4] *As also their religion, in pulling down a superstitious cross, and advancing a Venus, or Priapus, in place of it?*] This alludes to the practices of the Puritans. Stowe tells us, that many of the lower images belonging to the cross in Cheapside were frequently broken or pulled

down, and particularly, that about the year 1596, "under the image of Christ's resurrection defaced, was set up a curious wrought tabernacle of grey marble; and in the same, an alabaster image of Diana, a woman for the most part naked, and water conveyed from the Thames prilling from her naked breast."—WHAL.

Jonson was at this time a Catholic; but the satire is not, on that account, the less ingenious and severe, if what is strictly just can be termed satire.

[5] *Or the provident painting of his posts, against he should have been prætor?*] See p. 108 *a.*

[6] *O, here's rare* motley,] i.e., simple, silly; from the parti-coloured dress worn by fools. Thus Fletcher, "What *motley* stuff is this! sirrah, speak sense."—*Maid in the Mill.*

mine eye, and struck me enamoured on your beauties.

Aso. I would I were the fairest lady of France for your sake, sir! and yet I would travel too.

Amo. O, you should digress from yourself else: for, believe it, your travel is your only thing that rectifies, or, as the Italian says, *vi rendi pronto all' attioni*, makes you fit for action.

Aso. I think it be great charge though, sir.

Amo. Charge! why, 'tis nothing for a gentleman that goes private, as yourself, or so; my intelligence shall quit my charge at all time. Good faith, this hat hath possest mine eye exceedingly; 'tis so pretty and fantastic: what! is it a beaver?

Aso. Ay, sir, I'll assure you 'tis a beaver, it cost me eight crowns but this morning.

Amo. After your French account?

Aso. Yes, sir.

Cri. And so near his head! beshrew me, dangerous.   [*Aside.*

Amo. A very pretty fashion, believe me, and a most novel kind of trim: your band is conceited too!

Aso. Sir, it is all at your service.

Amo. O, pardon me.

Aso. I beseech you, sir, if you please to wear it, you shall do me a most infinite grace.

Cri. 'Slight, will he be praised out of his clothes?

Aso. By heaven, sir, I do not offer it you after the Italian manner ;[1] I would you should conceive so of me.

Amo. Sir, I shall fear to appear rude in denying your courtesies, especially being invited by so proper a distinction. May I pray your name, sir?

Aso. My name is Asotus, sir.

Amo. I take your love, gentle Asotus; but let me win you to receive this, in exchange——   [*They exchange beavers.*

Cri. Heart! they'll change doublets anon.   [*Aside.*

Amo. And, from ... time esteem yourself in the first rank of the ... few whom I profess to love. What make you in company of this scholar here? I will bring you known to gallants, as Anaides of the ordinary, Hedon the courtier, and others, whose society shall render you graced and respected: this is a trivial fellow, too mean, too cheap, too coarse for you to converse with.

Aso. 'Slid, this is not worth a crown, and mine cost me eight but this morning.

Cri. I looked when he would repent him, he has begun to be sad a good while.

Amo. Sir, shall I say to you for that hat? Be not so sad, be not so sad. It is a relic I could not so easily have departed with, but as the hieroglyphic of my affection; you shall alter it to what form you please, it will take any block; I have received it varied on record to the three thousandth time, and not so few. It hath these virtues beside; your head shall not ache under it, nor your brain leave you, without licence; it will preserve your complexion to eternity; for no beam of the sun, should you wear it under *zona torrida*, hath power to approach it by two elis. It is proof against thunder and enchantment; and was given me by a great man in Russia, as an especial prized present; and constantly affirmed to be the hat that accompanied the politic Ulysses in his tedious and ten years travels.

Aso. By Jove, I will not depart withal, whosoever would give me a million.

Enter Cos *and* Prosaites.

Cos. Save you, sweet bloods! does any of you want a creature, or a dependent?

Cri. Beshrew me, a fine blunt slave!

Amo. A page of good timber! it will now be my grace to entertain him first, though I cashier him again in private.—— How art thou called?

Cos. Cos, sir, Cos.

Cri. Cos! how happily hath fortune furnished him with a whetstone ?[2]

---

[1] *After the Italian manner,*] i.e., with a hope to have it refused. *Beaver* hats were not common in this country. Howel sends home one from Paris (Lett. 17) as a great rarity.

[2] *Cos! how happily hath fortune furnished him with a whetstone?*] *Cos* is the Latin word for a *whetstone;* and the joke consists in the allusion of his name to his manners. A *whetstone* was a cant term of that age to denote the faculty of lying, or any incitement to tell a lie. So in the Induction, the traveller is said to have the *Whetstone* following him.—WHAL.

Whalley has said nothing of the origin of this

"joke," as he calls it: nor can I pretend to advance anything with certainty on the subject. It may have arisen from the story of the *whetstone* which was cut in two by the augur, Accius: though why the simplest miracle in all Livy should have been singled out to typify lying, it is not easy to conjecture. Amidst the elegant amusements of our ancestors at wakes and fairs, such as jumping in a sack, grinning through a collar, &c., there was one of a most extraordinary and culpable nature, which was *lying.* The clown who told the most enormous and impossible falsehood, was rewarded for his perverse

Amo. I do entertain you, Cos: conceal your quality, and we be private; if our parts be worthy of me, I will countenance you; if not, catechize you.—Gent⁻ˢ, shall we go?

Aso. Stay, sir; I'll but entertain this other fellow, and then——I have a great humour to taste of this water too, but I'll come again alone for that——mark the place.—What's your name, youth?

Pros. Prosaites, sir.

Aso. Prosaites! a very fine name; Crites, is it not?

Cri. Yes, and a very ancient one, sir, the Beggar.

Aso. Follow me, good Prosaites; let's talk.   [*Exeunt all but* Crites.

Cri. He will rank even with you, ere't be long,
If you hold on your course. O vanity,
How are thy painted beauties doted on,
By light and empty ideots! how pursued
With open and extended appetite!
How they do sweat, and run themselves from breath,
Raised on their toes, to catch thy airy forms,
Still turning giddy, till they reel like drunkards,
That buy the merry madness of one hour
With the long irksomeness of following time!
O how despised and base a thing is man,
If he not strive t'erect his grovelling thoughts
Above the strain of flesh! but how more cheap,
When, ev'n his best and understanding part,
The crown and strength of all his faculties,

Floats, like a dead drowned body, on the stream
Of vulgar humour, mixt with common'st dregs!
I suffer for their guilt now, and my soul,
Like one that looks on ill-affected eyes,
Is hurt with mere intention on their follies.[1]
Why will I view them then, my sense might ask me?
Or is't a rarity, or some new object,
That strains my strict observance to this point?
O, would it were! therein I could afford
My spirit should draw a little near to theirs,
To gaze on novelties; so vice were one.
Tut, she is stale,[2] rank, foul; and were it not
That those that woo her greet her with locked eyes,
In spight of all th' impostures, paintings, drugs,
Which her bawd, Custom, dawbs her cheeks withal,
She would betray her loathed and leprous face,
And fright the enamoured dotards from themselves:
But such is the perverseness of our nature,
That if we once but fancy levity,
How antic and ridiculous soe'er
It suit with us, yet will our muffled thought
Choose rather not to see it, than avoid it:
And if we can but banish our own sense,
We act our mimic tricks with that free licence
That lust, that pleasure, that security,
As if we practised in a paste-board case,
And no one saw the motion, but the motion.[3]

---

ingenuity with a *whetstone*, which four or five centuries ago might perhaps be somewhat more valuable than it is at present. Hence the familiar connexion between the vice and the reward. A notorious liar was said to be *lying for a whetstone;* and it was no uncommon punishment for such a one to have a whetsone tied round his neck, or fastened on the outside of his garment, and to be thus publicly exposed. I could give many instances of this; but enough perhaps has been already said.

[1] *Is hurt with mere* intention *on their follies.*] *Intention* is the act of fixed and earnest gazing on an object. In this sense the word occurs frequently in Jonson.

[2] *Tut, she is stale, &c.*] This passage is well abridged by Pope:

"Vice is a monster of so foul a mien,
    That, to be hated, needs but to be seen."

[3] *As if we practised in a pasteboard case,*

And no one saw the motion, *but the* motion.] A simile taken from the management of puppets behind the curtain, with strings and wires: the cause of whose *motion* must be kept from the eyes of the spectators. The obscurity lies in the different senses of the word *motion;* the first is taken in the common sense, the last signifies the puppet itself.—WHAL.

Whalley seems pleased with this note, for, in the margin of his copy, he has directed it to stand: it is, however, incorrect. Jonson's meaning is simply this—"As if we were without spectators, and none but the puppets saw the puppet-show." In the quarto *Motion* is in both places distinguished by italics and capitals: this, perhaps, Whalley did not know; for he seems to have generally overlooked the first copies.

There is great force and beauty in this speech of Crites; and, indeed, the whole of this act is worthy of the author in his happiest moments.

Well, check thy passion, lest it grow too
— loud :
While fools are pitied, they wax fat and
proud.

ACT II.

SCENE I.—*The Court.*

Enter Cupid *and* Mercury, *disguised
as pages.*

Cup. Why, this was most unexpectedly
followed, my divine delicate Mercury ; by
the beard of Jove, thou art a precious
deity.

Mer. Nay, Cupid, leave to speak improperly ; since we are turned cracks, let's
study to be like cracks ; practise their
language and behaviours, and not with a
dead imitation : Act freely, carelessly, and
capriciously, as if our veins ran with quicksilver, and not utter a phrase but what
shall come forth steeped in the very brine
of conceit, and sparkle like salt in fire.

Cup. That's not every one's happiness,
Hermes : Though you can presume upon
the easiness and dexterity of your wit, you
shall give me leave to be a little jealous
of mine ; and not desperately to hazard it
after your capering humour.

Mer. Nay, then, Cupid, I think we
must have you hoodwinked again ; for you
are grown too provident since your eyes
were at liberty.

Cup. Not so, Mercury, I am still blind
Cupid to thee.

Mer. And what to the lady nymph you
serve?

Cup. Troth, page, boy, and sirrah :
these are all my titles.

Mer. Then thou hast not altered thy
name, with thy disguise?

Cup. O no, that had been supereroga-
tion ; you shall never hear your courtier
call but by one of these three.

Mer. Faith, then both our fortunes are
the same.

Cup. Why, what parcel of man hast
thou lighted on for a master?

Mer. Such a one as, before I begin to
decipher him, I dare not affirm to be anything less than a courtier. So much he is
during this open time of revels, and would
be longer, but that his means are to leave
him shortly after. His name is Hedon, a
gallant wholly consecrated to his pleasures.

Cup. Hedon! he uses much to my
lady's chamber, I think.

Mer. How is she called, and then I can
shew thee?

Cup. Madam Philautia.

Mer. O ay, he affects her very particularly indeed. These are his graces.
He doth (besides me) keep a barber and a
monkey ; he has a rich wrought waistcoat
to entertain his visitants in, with a cap
almost suitable. His curtains and bedding
are thought to be his own : his bathing-
tub is not suspected.[1] He loves to have a
fencer, a pedant,[2] and a musician seen in
his lodging a-mornings.

Cup. And not a poet ?

Mer. Fie, no : himself is a rhymer, and
that's thought better than a poet. He is
not lightly within to his mercer,[3] no, though
he come when he takes physic, which is
commonly after his play. He beats a
tailor very well, but a stocking-seller admirably : and so consequently any one he
owes money to, that dares not resist him.
He never makes general invitement, but
against the publishing of a new suit ;
marry, then you shall have more drawn to
his lodging, than come to the launching of
some three ships ; especially if he be furnished with supplies for the retiring of his
old wardrobe from pawn : if not, he does
hire a stock of apparel, and some forty or
fifty pound in gold, for that forenoon, to
shew. He is thought a very necessary
perfume for the presence, and for that only
cause welcome thither : six milliners' shops
afford you not the like scent. He courts
ladies with how many great horse he hath
rid that morning, or how oft he hath done
the whole, or half the pommado[4] in a

---

[1] *His* bathing-tub *is not suspected.*] i.e., is
supposed to be used simply for a bath, and not
for the cure of any disease, as was then the
common practice.

[2] *A pedant,*] i.e., a teacher of the languages.

[3] *He is not* lightly *within to his mercer,*]
Lightly is commonly, in ordinary cases. Thus
Shakspeare :

"Short summers *lightly* have a forward spring."
    Richard III.—WHAL.

[4] *The whole or half the* pommado] It may
be just necessary to observe, that the *pommado*
is vaulting on a horse, without the aid of stir-
rups, by resting one hand on the saddle-bow.
The pommado reversa was vaulting off again.
Thus Marston :

"Room for a vaulting skip,
Room for Torquatus, that ne'er opt his lip
But in prate of pommado reversa."—*Sat.* xi.

seven-night before : and sometimes ventures so far upon the virtue of his pomander,
that he dares tell 'em how many shirts he
has sweat at tennis that week ; but wisely
conceals so many dozen of balls he is on
the score. Here he comes, that is all
this.

 Enter Hedon, Anaides, *and* Gelaia.

 Hed. Boy !
 Mer. Sir.
 Hed. Are any of the ladies in the
presence?
 Mer. None yet, sir.
 Hed. Give me some gold,—more.
 Ana. Is that thy boy, Hedon?
 Hed. Ay, what think'st thou of him?
 Ana. I'd geld him ; I warrant he has
the philosopher's stone.
 Hed. Well said, my good melancholy
devil ; sirrah, I have devised one or two of
the prettiest oaths, this morning in my
bed, as ever thou heard'st, to protest
withal in the presence.
 Ana. Prithee, let's hear them.
 Hed. Soft, thou'lt use them afore me.
 Ana. No, d—mn me then—I have
more oaths than I know how to utter, by
this air.
 Hed. Faith, one is, *By the tip of your
ear, sweet lady.* Is it not pretty, and
genteel?
 Ana. Yes, for the person 'tis applied to,
a lady. It should be light and——
 Hed. Nay, the other is better, exceeds it
much : the invention is farther fet too.
*By the white valley that lies between the
alpine hills of your bosom, I protest——*
 Ana. Well, you travelled for that,
Hedon.
 Mer. Ay, in a map, where his eyes were
but blind guides to his understanding, it
seems.
 Hed. And then I have a salutation will
nick all, by this caper : hay !

 Ana. How is that?
 Hed. You know I call madam Philautia,
my Honour ; and she calls me, her Ambition. Now, when I meet her in the presence anon, I will come to her, and say,
*Sweet Honour, I have hitherto contented
my sense with the lilies of your hand, but
now I will taste the roses of your lip ;* and
withal, kiss her : to which she cannot but
blushing answer, *Nay, now you are too
ambitious.* And then do I reply : *I cannot
be too Ambitious of Honour, sweet lady.*
Will't not be good? ha? ha?
 Ana. O, assure your soul.
 Hed. By heaven, I think 'twill be excellent ; and a very politic achievement of
a kiss.
 Ana. I have thought upon one for
Moria of a sudden too, if it take.
 Hed. What is't, my dear Invention?
 Ana. Marry, I will come to her, (and
she always wears a muff, if you be remembered,) and I will tell her, *Madam, your
whole self cannot but be perfectly wise ; for
your hands have wit enough to keep themselves warm.*[1]
 Hed. Now, before Jove, admirable !
[Gelaia *laughs.*] Look, thy page takes it
too. By Phœbus, my sweet facetious
rascal, I could eat water-gruel with thee a
month for this jest, my dear rogue.
 Ana. O, by Hercules, 'tis your only
dish ; above all your potatoes or oyster-
pies in the world.
 Hed. I have ruminated upon a most
rare wish too, and the prophecy to it ; but
I'll have some friend to be the prophet ;
as thus : I do wish myself one of my
mistress's cioppini.[2] Another demands,
Why would he be one of his mistress's
cioppini? a third answers, Because he
would make her higher : a fourth shall
say, That will make her proud ! and a fifth
shall conclude, Then do I prophesy pride
will have a fall ;—and he shall give it her.

---

[1] *Your hands have wit enough to keep themselves warm.*] This proverbial phrase is found
in most of our ancient dramas. Thus, in *The
Wise Woman of Hogsden :* "You are the wise
woman, are you? you *have wit to keep yourself
warm enough,* I warrant you." It seems unnecessary to cite more examples of so common
an expression.

[2] *I do wish myself one of my mistress's* cioppini.] A high shoe, or rather clog, worn by the
Spanish and Italian ladies. Coriat, who travelled, with a foolish face of wonder, over a great
part of Europe and Asia, gives a particular
account of the "*chapineys*" that he saw in the
Venetian territories, some of which were "half

a yard in height." Honest Tom seems to have
somewhat availed himself of the traveller's
privilege ; but that they were of a most preposterous thickness cannot be denied. Bulwer
is very angry with them : "What a prodigious"
(portentous) "affectation is that of *choppines,*
wherein our ladies imitate the Venetian and
Persian ladies !" And he expresses some concern for the ungenerous deception practised on
the Spanish husbands, whose wives, though
tall in appearance, "commonly prove no more
but half wives ; for at the wedding night it
may be perceived that halfe the bride **vx**
made of guilded corke."—*Artificial Changling,*
p. 550.

Ana. I will be your prophet. Gods so, it will be most exquisite ; thou art a fine inventious rogue, sirrah.

Hed. Nay, and I have poesies for rings too, and riddles that they dream not of.

Ana. Tut, they'll do that, when they come to sleep on them, time enough. But were thy devices never in the presence yet, Hedon ?

Hed. O no, I disdain that.

Ana. 'Twere good we went afore then, and brought them acquainted with the room where they shall act, lest the strangeness of it put them out of countenance, when they should come forth.

[*Exeunt* Hedon *and* Anaides.

Cup. Is that a courtier too ?

Mer. Troth, no ; he has two essential parts of the courtier, pride and ignorance ; marry, the rest come somewhat after the ordinary gallant. 'Tis Impudence itself, Anaides ; one that speaks all that comes in his cheeks, and will blush no more than a sackbut. He lightly occupies the jester's room at the table, and keeps laughter, Gelaia, a wench in page's attire, following him in place of a squire, whom he now and then tickles with some strange ridiculous stuff, uttered as his land came to him, by chance. He will censure or discourse of anything, but as absurdly as you would wish. His fashion is not to take knowledge of him that is beneath him in clothes. He never drinks below the salt.[1] He

does naturally admire his wit that wears gold lace or tissue ; stabs any man that speaks more contemptibly of the scholar than he. He is a great proficient in all the illiberal sciences, as cheating, drinking, swaggering, whoring, and such like : never kneels but to pledge healths, nor prays but for a pipe of pudding-tobacco.[2] He will blaspheme in his shirt. The oaths which he vomits at one supper would maintain a town of garrison in good swearing a twelvemonth. One other genuine quality he has[3] which crowns all these, and that is this : to a friend in want, he will not depart with the weight of a soldered groat, lest the world might censure him prodigal, or report him a gull : marry, to his cockatrice, or punquetto, half a dozen taffata gowns or satin kirtles[4] in a pair or two of months, why, they are nothing.

Cup. I commend him, he is one of my clients.

[*They retire to the back of the stage.*

Enter Amorphus, Asotus, *and* Cos.

Amo. Come, sir. You are now within regard of the presence, and see, the privacy of this room how sweetly it offers itself to our retired intendments.—Page, cast a vigilant and enquiring eye about, that we be not rudely surprised by the approach of some ruder stranger.

Cos. I warrant you, sir. I'll tell you when the wolf enters,[5] fear nothing.

---

[1] *He never* drinks *below the* salt.] He never *drinks* to those at the lower end of the table. It refers to the manner in which our ancestors were usually seated at their meals. The tables being long, the *salt* was commonly placed about the middle, and served as a kind of boundary to the different quality of the guests invited. Those of distinction were ranked above ; the space below was assigned to the dependents, or inferior relations of the master of the house.—WHAL.

All that remains to be added to this pertinent note is, that the *salt* (salt-cellar) was of a very large size, and easily distinguishable; so that the mortification of the humbler guests was complete. See Massinger, vol. i. p. 170: but, indeed, the allusions to this practice are so numerous, that no reader of our old poets can want any reference on the subject.

[2] *A pipe of* pudding-*tobacco*.] It appears from the Induction (p. 145 *b*) that there were "three sorts of tobacco" then in vogue ; which, from the names scattered over our old plays, seem to be leaf, *pudding*, and cane tobacco. I can give the reader no other information respecting them, than that cane tobacco appears to have been the most expensive of the whole :

" The nostrils of his chimnies are still stuffed
    With smoak, more chargeable than *cane* tobacco."—*Merry Devil of Edmonton.*

[3] *One other genuine quality he has*, &c.] This genuine quality is remarked by Juvenal :

" *Nil habet infelix Numitor quod mittat amico,*
    Quintillæ quod donet, habet," &c. &c.
                        Sat. vii.

[4] *Or satin* kirtles] Few words have occasioned such controversy among the commentators on our old plays, as this ; and all for want of knowing that it is used in a twofold sense, sometimes for the jacket merely, and sometimes for the train or upper petticoat attached to it. A full kirtle was always a jacket and petticoat, a *half kirtle* (a term which frequently occurs) was either the one or the other : but our ancestors,who wrote when this article of dress was everywhere in use, and when there was little danger of being misunderstood, most commonly contented themselves with the simple term (*kirtle*), leaving the sense to be gathered from the context. A man's jacket was also called a kirtle.

[5] *I'll tell you when the* wolf enters,] This is an allusion to a Latin proverb, and applied when the person talked of comes in unexpectedly, and puts an end to the discourse.—WHAL.

Mer. O what a mass of benefit shall we possess, in being the invisible spectators of this strange show now to be acted!

Amo. Plant yourself there, sir; and observe me. You shall now, as well be the ocular, as the ear-witness, how clearly I can refel that paradox, or rather pseudo-dox, of those, which hold the face to be the index of the mind, which, I assure you, is not so in any politic creature: for instance; I will now give you the particular and distinct face[1] of every your most noted species of persons, as your merchant, your scholar, your soldier, your lawyer, courtier, &c., and each of these so truly, as you would swear, but that your eye shall see the variation of the lineament, it were my most proper and genuine aspect. First, for your merchant, or city-face, 'tis thus; a dull, plodding face, still looking in a direct line, forward: there is no great matter in this face. Then have you your student's, or academic face, which is here an honest, simple, and methodical face; but somewhat more spread than the former. The third is your soldier's face, a menacing and astounding face, that looks broad and big: the grace of this face consisteth much in a beard. The anti-face to this is your lawyer's face a contracted, subtile, and intricate face, full of quirks and turnings, a labyrinthean face, now angularly, now circularly, every way aspected. Next is your statist's face,[2] a serious, solemn, and supercilious face, full of formal and square gravity: the eye for the most part deeply and artificially shadowed: there is great judgment required in the making of this face. But now, to come to your face of faces, or courtier's face; 'tis of three sorts, according to our subdivision of a courtier, elementary, practic,[1] and theoric. Your courtier theoric, is he that hath arrived to his farthest, and doth now know the court rather by speculation than practice; and

this is his face: a fastidious and oblique face; that looks as it went with a vice, and were screwed thus. Your courtier practic, is he that is yet in his path, his course, his way, and hath not touched the punctilio or point of his hopes; his face is here: a most promising, open, smooth, and overflowing face, that seems as it would run and pour itself into you: somewhat a northerly face. Your courtier elementary, is one but newly entered, or as it were in the alphabet, or *ut-re-mi-fa-sol-la* of courtship. Note well this face, for it is this you must practise.

Aso. I'll practise them all, if you please, sir.

Amo. Ay, hereafter you may: and it will not be altogether an ungrateful study. For, let your soul be assured of this, in any rank or profession whatever, the more general or major part of opinion goes with the face, and simply respects nothing else. Therefore, if that can be made exactly, curiously, exquisitely, thoroughly, it is enough: but for the present you shall only apply yourself to this face of the elementary courtier, a light, revelling, and protesting face, now blushing, now smiling, which you may help much with a wanton wagging of your head, thus, (a feather will teach you,) or with kissing your finger that hath the ruby, or playing with some string of your band, which is a most quaint kind of melancholy besides: or, if among ladies, laughing loud, and crying up your own wit, though perhaps borrowed, it is not amiss. Where is your page? call for your casting-bottle, and place your mirror in your hat,[3] as I told you: so! Come, look not pale, observe me, set your face, and enter.

Mer. O for some excellent painter, to have taken the copy of all these faces! [*Aside.*

Aso. Prosaites!

Amo. Fie! I premonish you of that: in the court, boy, lacquey, or sirrah.

Cos. Master, *lupus in*——O, 'tis Prosaites.

---

[1] *I will now give you the particular and distinct face*, &c.] This corroborates my explanation of the passage, p. 152 b. That "the face is the index of the mind" was "held" by Ovid, Juvenal, and others.

[2] *Next is your* statist's *face*,] i.e., your *statesman's.* Thus Marmion: "Adorned with that even mixture of fluency and grace, as are required both in a *statist* and a courtier."—*The Antiquary*, act i. sc. 1.—WHAL.

[3] *Place your* mirror *in your hat*,] "It should seem," Whalley says, "from this passage, that the finical courtiers carried a pocket-mirror about them, which they sometimes put in their hats." There can be no doubt of it: both sexes wore

them publicly; the men, as brooches or ornaments in their hats; and the women, at their girdles (see Massinger, vol. iv. p. 8), or on their breasts; nay, sometimes in the centre of their fans, which were then made of feathers, inserted into silver or ivory tubes. Lovelace has a poem on his mistress's fan, "with a looking-glass in it." This is a part of her address to it:

" My lively shade thou ever shalt retaine
    In thy inclosed *feather-framed* glasse;
And, but unto ourselves, to all remaine
    Invisible, thou feature of this face!" &c.

[4] *Master*, lupus in ——] *fabulâ*, the Latin proverb referred to, p. 159 b.

Enter Prosaites.

Aso. Sirrah, prepare my casting-bottle; I think I must be enforced to purchase me another page; you see how at hand Cos waits here.

　　　[*Exeunt* Amorphus, **Asotus, Cos,** *and* Prosaites.

Mer. So will he too, in time.

Cup. What's he, Mercury?

Mer. A notable smelt.[1] One that hath newly entertained the beggar to follow him, but cannot get him to wait near enough. 'Tis Asotus, the heir of Philargyrus; but first I'll give ye the other's character,[2] which may make his the clearer. He that is with him is Amorphus, a traveller, one so made out of the mixture of shreds of forms, that himself is truly deformed. He walks most commonly with a clove or pick-tooth in his mouth, he is the very mint of compliment, all his behaviours are printed, his face is another volume of essays, and his beard is an Aristarchus. He speaks all cream skimmed, and more affected than a dozen waiting-women. He is his own promoter in every place. The wife of the ordinary gives him his diet to maintain her table in discourse; which, indeed, is a mere tyranny over her other guests, for he will usurp all the talk: ten constables are not so tedious.[3] He is no great shifter; once a year his apparel is ready to revolt. He doth use much to arbitrate quarrels, and fights himself, exceeding well, out at a window. He will lie cheaper than any beggar, and louder than most clocks: for which he is right properly accommodated to the Whetstone, his page. The other gallant is his Zany, and doth most of these tricks after him; sweats to imitate him in every-

thing to a hair, except a beard, which is not yet extant. He doth learn to make strange sauces, to eat anchovies, macca-roni, bovoli, fagioli,[4] and caviare, because he loves them; speaks as he speaks, looks, walks, goes so in clothes and fashion: is in all as if he were moulded of him. Marry, before they met, he had other very pretty sufficiencies, which yet he retains some light impression of; as frequenting a dancing school, and grievously torturing stran-gers with inquisition after his grace in his galliard. He buys a fresh acquaintance at any rate. His eyes and his raiment confer much together as he goes in the street. He treads nicely like the fellow that walks upon ropes, especially the first Sunday of his silk stockings; and when he is most neat and new, you shall strip him with commen-dations.

Cup. Here comes another.

　　　[*Crites passes over the stage.*

Mer. Ay, but one of another strain, Cupid; this fellow weighs somewhat.

Cup. His name, Hermes?

Mer. Crites. A creature of a most per-fect and divine temper: one in whom his humours and elements are peaceably met, without emulation of precedency; he is neither too fantastically melancholy, too slowly phlegmatic, too lightly sanguine, or too rashly choleric; but in all so composed and ordered, as it is clear Nature went about some full work, she did more than make a man when she made him. His discourse is like his behaviour, uncommon, but not unpleasing; he is prodigal of neither. He strives rather to be that which men call judicious, than to be thought so; and is so truly learned, that he affects not to shew it. He will think and speak his

---

[1] *A notable* smelt.] The quarto reads *finch. Smelt*, like *gudgeon*, is used by our old writers for a gull, a simpleton. Thus Beaumont and Fletcher:

"These direct men, they are no men of fashion; Talk what you will, this is a very *smelt*."
　　　　　　Love's Pilgrimage, act v. sc. 2.

[2] *But first I'll give ye the other's character,* &c.] This is all very inartificial. The plot stands still while the author is displaying his dexterity in drawing individual and insulated characters. Undoubtedly, if keen, vigorous, and discriminating delineations of this nature were sufficient of themselves to constitute a legitimate drama, no man who ever wrote for the stage would stand in competition with Jon-son But the vivifying soul of the drama is action. Of this, unfortunately, we have but little; and that little is nearly overlooked amidst

a minute and tiresome description of what the progress of the plot alone should have unfolded.

[3] *Ten constables are not so tedious,*] This is said to be an attack on the constables in *Muc.. Ado about Nothing* and *Measure for Measure*. The last of these comedies, be it observed, was written full two years after *Cynthia's Revels!* and the first probably about as many months, for it was not brought on the stage till 1600. The prolixity, as well as the dulness, of a con-stable was proverbial; and Shakspeare, Jonson, and hundreds besides, turned it to a humourous account. This is the whole of the matter.

[4] *Bovoli, fagioli,* &c.] These were delicacies in Jonson's days, and probably for some time after; the first were snails, or rather cockles; and the latter, French beans: they were dressed after the Italian manner, which was the fashion in vogue, and which gave way to a better taste at the Restoration.

thoughts both freely; but as distant from depraving another man's merit, as proclaiming his own. For his valour, 'tis such that he dares as little to offer an injury as receive one. In sum, he hath a most ingenuous and sweet spirit, a sharp and seasoned wit, a straight judgment and a strong mind. Fortune could never break him, nor make him less. He counts it his pleasure to despise pleasures, and is more delighted with good deeds than goods. It is a competency to him that he can be virtuous. He doth neither covet nor fear; he hath too much reason to do either; and that commends all things to him.

Cup. Not better than Mercury commends him.

Mer. O, Cupid, 'tis beyond my deity to give him his due praises: I could leave my place in heaven to live among mortals, so I were sure to be no other than he.

Cup. 'Slight, I believe he is your minion, you seem to be so ravished with him.

Mer. He's one I would not have a wry thought darted against, willingly.

Cup. No, but a straight shaft in his bosom I'll promise him, if I am Cytherea's son.

Mer. Shall we go, Cupid?

Cup. Stay, and see the ladies now: they'll come presently. I'll help to paint them.

Mer. What, lay colour upon colour! that affords but an ill blazon.

Cup. Here comes metal to help it, the Lady Argurion.

[*Argurion passes over the stage.*

Mer. Money, money.

Cup. The same. A nymph of a most wandering and giddy disposition, humorous as the air, she'll run from gallant to gallant, as they sit at primero in the presence, most strangely, and seldoms stays with any. She spreads as she goes. To-day you shall have her look as clear and fresh as the morning, and to-morrow as melancholic as midnight. She takes special pleasure in a close obscure lodging, and for that cause visits the city so often, where she has many secret true concealing favourites. When she comes abroad, she's more loose and scattering than dust, and will fly from place to place, as she were wrapped

with a whirlwind. Your young student, for the most part, she affects not, only salutes him, and away: a poet, nor a philosopher, she is hardly brought to take any notice of; no, though he be some part of an alchemist. She loves a player well, and a lawyer infinitely; but your fool above all. She can do much in court for the obtaining of any suit whatsoever, no door but flies open to her, her presence is above a charm. The worst in her is want of keeping state, and too much descending into inferior and base offices; she's for any coarse employment you will put upon her, as to be your procurer, or pander.[1]

Mer. Peace, Cupid, here comes more work for you, another character or two.

Enter Phantaste, Moria, *and* Philautia.

Phan. Stay, sweet Philautia, I'll but change my fan, and go presently.

Mor. Now, in very good serious, ladies, I will have this order reversed, the presence must be better maintained from you: a quarter past eleven, and ne'er a nymph in prospective! Beshrew my hand, there must be a reformed discipline. Is that your new ruff, sweet lady-bird? By my truth, 'tis most intricately rare.

Mer. Good Jove, what reverend gentlewoman in years might this be?

Cup. 'Tis Madam Moria, guardian of the nymphs; one that is not now to be persuaded of her wit; she will think herself wise against all the judgments that come. A lady made all of voice and air, talks anything of anything. She is like one of your ignorant poetasters of the time, who, when they have got acquainted with a strange word, never rest till they have wrung it in, though it loosen the whole fabric of their sense.

Mer. That was pretty and sharply noted, Cupid.

Cup. She will tell you, Philosophy was a fine reveller, when she was young, and a gallant, and that then, though she say it, she was thought to be the dame Dido and Helen of the court: as also, what a sweet dog she had this time four years, and how it was called Fortune; and that, if the Fates had not cut his thread, he had been

---

[1] Nothing can possibly be more lively and ingenious than this description of Argurion; it partakes, however, of the defect which is so visible in many parts of the author's model, the *Plutus* of Aristophanes; where the literal and metaphorical sense is so blended as to form a very indistinct, though an amusing representation. This character Jonson subsequently expanded into the Lady Pecunia and her train, in that most singular drama, the *Staple of News*.

a dog to have given entertainment to any gallant in this kingdom; and unless she had whelped it herself, she could not have loved a thing better in this world.

Mer. O, I prithee no more, I am full of her.

Cup. Yes, I must needs tell you she composes a sack-posset well; and would court a young page sweetly, but that her breath is against it.

Mer. Now, her breath or something more strong protect me from her! The other, the other, Cupid?

Cup. O, that's my lady and mistress, Madam Philautia. She admires not herself for any one particularity, but for all: she is fair, and she knows it; she has a pretty light wit too, and she knows it; she can dance, and she knows that too: play at shuttle-cock, and that too: no quality she has, but she shall take a very particular knowledge of, and most lady-like commend it to you. You shall have her at any time read you the history of herself, and very subtilely run over another lady's sufficiencies to come to her own. She has a good superficial judgment in painting, and would seem to have so in poetry. A most complete lady in the opinion of some three beside herself.

Phi. Faith, how liked you my quip to Hedon, about the garter? Was't not witty?

Mor. Exceeding witty and integrate: you did so aggravate the jest withal.

Phi. And did I not dance movingly the last night?

Mor. Movingly! out of measure, in troth, sweet charge.

Mer. A happy commendation, to dance out of measure!

Mor. Save only you wanted the swim in the turn: O! when I was at fourteen——

Phi. Nay, that's mine own from any nymph in the court, I'm sure on't; therefore you mistake me in that, guardian: both the swim and the trip are properly mine; everybody will affirm it that has any judgment in dancing, I assure you.

Pha. Come now, Philautia. I am for you; shall we go?

Phi. Ay, good Phantaste. What! have you changed your head-tire?

Pha. Yes, faith, the other was so near the common, it had no extraordinary grace; besides, I had worn it almost a day, in good troth.

Phi. I'll be sworn, this is most excellent for the device, and rare; 'tis after the Italian print[1] we looked on t'other night.

Pha. 'Tis so: by this fan, I cannot abide anything that savours the poor over-worn cut, that has any kindred with it; I must have variety, I: this mixing in fashion, I hate it worse than to burn juniper[2] in my chamber, I protest.

Phi. And yet we cannot have a new peculiar court-tire, but these retainers will have it; these suburb Sunday-waiters; these courtiers for high days; I know not what I should call 'em——

Pha. O, ay, they do most pitifully imitate; but I have a tire a coming, i' faith, shall——

Mor. In good certain, madam, it makes you look most heavenly; but, lay your hand on your heart, you never skinned a new beauty more prosperously in your life, nor more metaphysically: look, good lady; sweet lady, look.

Phi. 'Tis very clear and well, believe me. But if you had seen mine yesterday, when 'twas young, you would have——Who's your doctor, Phantaste?

Pha. Nay, that's counsel,[3] Philautia; you shall pardon me: yet I'll assure you he's the most dainty, sweet, absolute, rare man of the whole college. O! his very looks, his discourse, his behaviour, all he does is physic, I protest.

Phi. For heaven's sake, his name, good dear Phantaste.

Pha. No, no, no, no, no, no, believe me, not for a million of heavens: I will not make him cheap. Fie——

[*Exeunt* Phantaste, Moria, *and* Philautia.

Cup. There is a nymph too of a most curious and elaborate strain, light, all motion, an ubiquitary, she is everywhere, Phantaste——

Mer. Her very name speaks her, let her pass. But are these, Cupid, the stars of Cynthia's court? Do these nymphs attend upon Diana?

---

[1] *'Tis after the Italian print,* &c.] Phantaste alludes, perhaps, to the *Habiti Antichi e Moderni di Cesare Vecellio,* published at Venice in 1589.

[2] *I hate it worse than to burn juniper in my chamber,*] I know not the cause of Phantaste's contempt. Perhaps she thought the practice too common; or, as juniper was burnt to sweeten rooms (p. 63), she might look on it as "insinuating her" of not being sufficiently fragrant in herself.

[3] *Nay, that's* counsel,] i.e., that's a secret: the expression is very common in this sense. See Massinger, vol. i. p. 281.

Cup. They are in her court, Mercury, but not as stars; these never come in the presence of Cynthia. The nymphs that make her train are the divine Arete, Timè, Phronesis, Thauma, and others of that high sort. These are privately brought in by Moria in this licentious time, against her knowledge: and, like so many meteors, will vanish when she appears.

Enter Prosaites, *singing, followed by* Gelaia *and* Cos, *with bottles.*

" Come follow me, my wags, and say, as I
    say,
There's no riches but in rags, hey day,
    hey day:
You that profess this art, come away,
    come away,
And help to bear a part. Hey day, hey
    day,"[1] *&c.*
   [Mercury *and* Cupid *come forward.*
Mer. What, those that were our fellow pages but now, so soon preferred to be yeomen of the bottles! The mystery, the mystery, good wags?
Cup. Some diet-drink they have the guard of.
Pro. No, sir, we are going in quest of a strange fountain, lately found out.
Cup. By whom?
Cos. My master, or the great discoverer, Amorphus.
Mer. Thou hast well intitled him, Cos, for he will discover all he knows.
Gel. Ay, and a little more too, when the spirit is upon him.
Pro. O, the good travelling gentleman yonder has caused such a drought in the presence, with reporting the wonders of this new water, that all the ladies and gallants lie languishing upon the rushes,[2] like so many pounded cattle in the midst of harvest, sighing one to another, and gasping, as if each of them expected a cock from the fountain to be brought into his mouth; and without we return quickly, they are all, as a youth would say, no better than a few trouts cast ashore, or a dish of eels in a sand-bag.

Mer. Well then, you were best dispatch, and have a care of them. Come, Cupid, thou and I'll go peruse this dry wonder.
                    [Exeunt.

ACT III.

SCENE I.—*An Apartment at the Court.*

Enter Amorphus *and* Asotus.

Amo. Sir, let not this discountenance or disgallant you a whit; you must not sink under the first disaster. It is with your young grammatical courtier, as with your neophyte player, a thing usual to be daunted at the first presence or interview: you saw, there was Hedon, and Anaides, far more practised gallants than yourself, who were both out, to comfort you. It is no disgrace, no more than for your adventurous reveller to fall by some inauspicious chance in his galliard, or for some subtile politic to undertake the bastinado, that the state might think worthily of him, and respect him as a man well beaten to the world. What! hath your tailor provided the property we spake of at your chamber, or no?
Aso. I think he has.
Amo. Nay, I intreat you, be not so flat and melancholic. Erect your mind: you shall redeem this with the courtship I will teach you against the afternoon. Where eat you to-day?
Aso. Where you please, sir; anywhere, I.
Amo. Come, let us go and taste some light dinner, a dish of sliced caviare, or so; and after, you shall practise an hour at your lodging some few forms that I have recalled. If you had but so far gathered your spirits to you, as to have taken up a rush when you were out, and wagged it thus, or cleansed your teeth with it; or but turned aside, and feigned some business to whisper with your page, till you had recovered yourself, or but found some slight stain in your stocking, or any other pretty invention, so it had been sudden, you might

---

[1] In the quarto there is more of this doggrel. Jonson did well in omitting it; and I shall not bring it back.
[2] *The ladies and gallants lie languishing upon the* rushes,] The chambers of palaces, as well as of noblemen and gentlemen's houses, were at this time strewed with rushes. See p. 109 *a.* "Rushes," says the old *Boke of Simples,* "that growe upon dry groundes, be good to strew in halles, chambers, and galleries, to walk upon, defending apparel, as traynes of gowns and kertles, from dust. Rushes be old courtiers; and when they be nothing worthe, then they be cast out of the doores; so be many that doe *tread* upon them."—P. 36. But they not only *trod,* but danced upon them; this was not the way to keep their "trains from dust."

" Thou *daucest* on my heart, lascivious queen,
  Even as upon these *rushes.*"
            Dumb Knight, act iv. sc. 1

have come off with a most clear and courtly grace.

Aso. A poison of all! I think I was forespoke, I.[1]

Amo. No, I must tell you, you are not audacious enough; you must frequent ordinaries a month more, to initiate yourself: in which time, it will not be amiss, if, in private, you keep good your acquaintance with Crites, or some other of his poor coat, visit his lodging secretly and often; become an earnest suitor to hear some of his labours.

Aso. O Jove! sir, I could never get him to read a line to me.

Amo. You must then wisely mix yourself in rank with such as you know can; and, as your ears do meet with a new phrase, or an acute jest, take it in: a quick nimble memory will lift it away, and, at your next public meal, it is your own.

Aso. But I shall never utter it perfectly, sir.

Amo. No matter, let it come lame. In ordinary talk you shall play it away, as you do your light crowns at primero: it will pass.

Aso. I shall attempt, sir.

Amo. Do. It is your shifting age for wit, and, I assure you, men must be prudent. After this you may to court, and there fall in, first with the waiting-woman, then with the lady. Put case they do retain you there, as a fit property, to hire coaches some pair of months, or so; or to read them asleep in afternoons upon some pretty pamphlet, to breathe you; why, it shall in time embolden you to some farther achievement: in the interim, you may fashion yourself to be careless and impudent.

Aso. How if they would have me to make verses? I heard Hedon spoke to for some.

Amo. Why, you must prove the aptitude of your genius; if you find none, you must hearken out a vein, and buy; provided you pay for the silence as for the work, then you may securely call it your own.

Aso. Yes, and I'll give out my acquaintance with all the best writers, to countenance me the more.

Amo. Rather seem not to know them, it is your best. Ay, be wise, that you never so much as mention the name of one, nor remember it mentioned; but if they be offered to you in discourse, shake your light head, make between a sad and a smiling face, pity some, rail at all, and commend yourself: 'tis your only safe and unsuspected course. Come, you shall look back upon the court again to-day, and be restored to your colours: I do now partly aim at the cause of your repulse—which was ominous indeed—for as you enter at the door, there is opposed to you the frame of a wolf in the hangings, which, surprising your eye suddenly, gave a false alarm to the heart; and that was it called your blood out of your face, and so routed the whole rank of your spirits: I beseech you labour to forget it. And remember, as I inculcated to you before, for your comfort, Hedon and Anaides.   [*Exeunt.*

SCENE II.—*Another Apartment in the same.*

Enter Hedon *and* Anaides.

Hed. Heart, was there ever so prosperous an invention thus unluckily perverted and spoiled by a whoreson bookworm, a candle-waster?[3]

Ana. Nay, be not impatient, Hedon.

Hed. 'Slight, I would fain know his name.

Ana. Hang him, poor grogran rascal! prithee think not of him: I'll send for him to my lodging, and have him blanketed when thou wilt, man.

Hed. Ods so, I would thou couldst. Look, here he comes.

---

[1] *I think I was* forespoke, *I.*] *Fore,* prefixed to a verb, is frequently taken negatively; as in Shakspeare:

"Thou hast *forespoke* my being in these wars."
    Antony and Cleopatra, act iii. sc. 7.—WHAL.

This is true; but the expression is often applied by our old writers, and with perfect propriety, to the supposed effects of a supernatural power. To *forespeak* here, like *forbid* in Macbeth, is to subject to a curse, to *bewitch.* Thus Drayton, in his Epistles:

"Or to *forespeak* whole flocks, as they did feed."

And in many other places.

What follows, to the conclusion of the scene, is not in the quarto.

[3] *A* candle-waster?] This contemptuous term for a hard student occurs in *Much Ado about Nothing;* where Whalley, though with somewhat too much parade, has set the commentators right, and settled the meaning of a disputed passage:

"Patch grief with proverbs, make misfortune drunk
    With *candle-wasters.*"

Enter Crites, *and walks in a musing posture at the back of the stage.*

Laugh at him, laugh at him; ha, ha, ha !

Ana. Fough ! he smells all lamp-oil with studying by candle-light.

Hed. How confidently he went by us, and carelessly ! Never moved, nor stirred at anything ! Did you observe him ?

Ana. Ay, a pox on him, let him go, dor-mouse : he is in a dream now. He has no other time to sleep, but thus when he walks abroad to take the air.

Hed. 'Sprecious, this afflicts me more than all the rest, that we should so par-ticularly direct our hate and contempt against him, and he to carry it thus with-out wound or passion ! 'tis insufferable.

Ana. 'Slid, my dear Envy, if thou but say'st the word now, I'll undo him eter-nally for thee.

Hed. How, sweet Anaides ?

Ana. Marry, half a score of us get him in, one night, and make him pawn his wit for a supper.

Hed. Away, thou hast such unseasonable jests ! By this heaven, I wonder at nothing more than our gentlemen ushers, that will suffer a piece of serge or perpetuana[1] to come into the presence : methinks they should, out of their experience, better dis-tinguish the silken disposition of courtiers, than to let such terrible coarse rags mix with us, able to fret any smooth or gentle society to the threads with their rubbing devices.

Ana. Unless 'twere Lent, Ember-weeks, or fasting-days, when the place is most penuriously empty of all other good out-sides. D——n me, if I should adventure on his company once more, without a suit of buff to defend my wit ! he does nothing but stab, the slave ! How mischievously he crossed thy device of the prophecy there ? and Moria, she comes without her muff too, and there my invention was lost.

Hed. Well, I am resolved what I'll do.

Ana. What, my good spirituous spark ?

Hed. Marry, speak all the venom I can of him ; and poison his reputation in every place where I come.

Ana. 'Fore God, most courtly.

Hed. And if I chance to be present where any question is made of his sufficiencies, or of anything he hath done private or public, I'll censure it slightly and ridiculously.

Ana. At any hand beware of that ; so thou mayst draw thine own judgment in suspect. No, I'll instruct thee what thou shalt do, and by a safer means : approve anything thou hearest of his, to the re-ceived opinion of it ; but if it be extraordi-nary, give it from him to some other whom thou more particularly affect'st ; that's the way to plague him, and he shall never come to defend himself. 'Slud, I'll give out all he does is dictated from other men,[2] and swear it too, if thou'lt have me, and that I know the time and place where he stole it, though my soul be guilty of no such thing ; and that I think, out of my heart, he hates such barren shifts : yet to do thee a pleasure, and him a disgrace, I'll damn myself, or do anything.

Hed. Gramercy, my dear devil ; we'll put it seriously in practice, i' faith.

             [*Exeunt* Hedon *and* Anaides.

Cri. [*coming forward.*] Do, good De-traction, do, and I the while
Shall shake thy spight off with a careless smile.
Poor piteous gallants ! what lean idle slights
Their thoughts suggest to flatter their starved hopes !
As if I knew not how to entertain
These straw-devices ; but of force must yield
To the weak stroke of their calumnious tongues.
What should I care what every dor or both buz[3]

---

[1] *A piece of serge or* perpetuana] This seems to be that glossy kind of stuff now called *ever-lasting*, and anciently worn by serjeants, and other city officers. It was also worn by the poet himself, and (whether out of modesty or arro-gance let the reader determine) he has chosen to dress his diminutive representative in it. Decker has not forgotten this circumstance, nor to twit him with being in debt even for his homely attire :

"*Tucca.* Is't not better to be out at elbows, than to be a bond-slave, and to go all in parch-ment as thou dost ?

Horace. Parchment ! Nay, 'tis *perpetuana*, I assure you."

[2] *I'll give out all he does is dictated from other men, &c.*] If Jonson really designed the character of Crites for his own picture, it will be no easy matter to acquit him of the charge of vanity, which his enemies so often brought against him ; but I will not affirm the similitude to be perfectly exact. It is only probable, that as he glanced at his ad-versaries in some passages of the play, he might have intended to sketch the outlines of his own character.—WHAL.

[3] *Why should I care what every* dor *doth* buz, *&c.*] I have already had occasion to notice the impertinent attacks of this troublesome in-

In credulous ears? It is a crown to me
That the best judgments can report me
 wronged;
Them liars, and their slanders impudent.
Perhaps, upon the rumour of their speeches,
Some grieved friend will whisper to me;
 Crites,
Men speak ill of thee. So they be ill men,
If they spake worse, 'twere better: for of
 such
To be dispraised, is the most perfect praise.
What can his censure hurt me whom the
 world
Hath censured vile before me! If good
 Chrestus,
Euthus, or Phronimus, had spoke the
 words,
They would have moved me, and I should
 have called
My thoughts and actions to a strict account
Upon the hearing: but when I remember,
'Tis Hedon and Anaides, alas, then
I think but what they are, and am not
 stirred.
The one a light voluptuous reveller,
The other, a strange arrogating puff,
Both impudent, and ignorant enough;
That talk as they are wont, not as I merit:
Traduce by custom, as most dogs do bark,
Do nothing out of judgment, but disease,
Speak ill, because they never could speak
 well.
And who'd be angry with this race of
 creatures?
What wise physician have we ever seen
Moved with a frantic man? the same
 affects[1]
That he doth bear to his sick patient,
Should a right mind carry to such as these:

And I do count it a most rare revenge,
That I can thus, with such a sweet neglect,
Pluck from them all the pleasure of their
 malice,
For that's the mark of all their enginous
 drifts,[2]
To wound my patience, howsoe'er they
 seem
To aim at other objects; which if missed,
Their envy's like an arrow shot upright,
That, in the fall, endangers their own
 heads.

Enter Arete.

Are. What, Crites! where have you
 drawn forth the day,
You have not visited your jealous friends?
Cri. Where I have seen, most honoured
 Arete,
The strangest pageant, fashioned like a
 court,
(As least I dreamt I saw it) so diffused,[3]
So painted, pied, and full of rainbow strains,
As never yet, either by time, or place,
Was made the food to my distasted sense:
Nor can my weak imperfect memory
Now render half the forms unto my tongue,
That were convolved within this thrifty
 room.
Here stalks me by a proud and spangled
 sir,
That looks three handfuls higher than his
 foretop;
Savours himself alone, is only kind
And loving to himself; one that will speak
More dark and doubtful than six oracles;
Salutes a friend, as if he had a stitch;
Is his own chronicle, and scarce can eat
For registring himself; is waited on

---

sect, of which the poet always speaks with
great contempt. It is mentioned in the same
way by Fletcher and others. Thus in the
Merry Milkmaids: "*Cal.* What was that?
Kar. What? *Cal.* Something crost my nose.
Kar. A *dor,* a *dor;* the fields are full of them.
Smirke. I'll give you the *dor* too. [*fillips*
her.]" It is singular that the editors of Beaumont and Fletcher should doubt the existence
of *dor* as a verb; it is by no means uncommon,
and an instance of it may be found in Jonson,
p. 49 *b.*
  Decker, as Whalley observes, has fastened on
many parts of this speech as proofs, perhaps, of
Jonson's personality and arrogance; it is to be
lamented that they savour of both. But Decker
also attempts to ridicule them:—in this he is, of
course, unfortunate; for the English stage does
not afford a more spirited and masterly delineation of characters than is to be found in this and
the six following pages. It is a pitch far above
the flight of the "*Untrusser.*"

[1] *The same affects,*] i.e., affections, dispositions.—WHAL.
  See Massinger, vol. ii. p. 29.
[2] *For that's the mark of all their* enginous
drifts,] So the quarto. The folio reads *in-
ginous,* which has the same sense. Whalley
printed it from the paltry edition of the booksellers, *ingenious,* and then remarked that the
line "was not very harmonious." *Engine* an-
ingine, are both used by our old poets for
craft, artifice, and sometimes in a better sense
for wit, that is, genius, or the inventive
faculty.
  [3] *So* diffused,] i.e., wild, irregular, careless,
&c. So in the *Merry Wives of Windsor:*

           "Rush at once
  With some *diffused* song."

And *Henry V.:*

  "Swearing and stern looks, *diffused* attire."
                                        WHAL.

By mimics, jesters, panders, parasites,
And other such like prodigies of men.
He past, appears some mincing marmoset
Made all of clothes and face ; his limbs so
    set
As if they had some voluntary act
Without man's motion, and must move
    just so
In spight of their creation : one that weighs
His breath between his teeth, and dares
    not smile
Beyond a point, for fear t'unstarch his look;
Hath travelled to make legs, and seen the
    cringe
Of several courts, and courtiers ; knows the
    time
Of giving titles, and of taking walls ;
Hath read court-common-places; made
    them his :
Studied the grammar of state, and all the
    rules
Each formal usher in that politic school
Can teach a man. A third comes, giving
    nods
To his repenting creditors, protests
To weeping suitors, takes the coming gold
Of insolent and base ambition,
That hourly rubs his dry and itchy palms ;
Which griped, like burning coals, he hurls
    away
Into the laps of bawds, and buffoons'
    mouths.
With him there meets some subtle Proteus,
    one
Can change, and vary with all forms he
    sees ;
Be anything but honest ; serves the time ;
Hovers betwixt two factions, and explores
The drifts of both ; which, with cross face,
    he bears
To the divided heads, and is received
With mutual grace of either: one that
    dares
Do deeds worthy the hurdle or the wheel,
To be thought somebody : and is in sooth
Such as the satirist[1] points truly forth,
That only to his crimes owes all his worth.
    Are. You tell us wonders, Crites.
    Cri. This is nothing.
There stands a neophite glazing of his face,
Pruning his clothes, perfuming of his hair,
Against his idol enters ; and repeats,
Like an unperfect prologue, at third music,
His part of speeches, and confederate jests,

In passion to himself. Another swears
His scene of courtship over; bids, believe
    him,
Twenty times ere they will; anon, doth
    seem
As he would kiss away his hand in kindness;
Then walks off melancholic, and stands
    wreathed,
As he were pinned up to the arras, thus.
A third is most in action, swims and frisks,
Plays with his mistress's paps, salutes her
    pumps,
Adores her hems, her skirts, her knots, her
    curls,
Will spend his patrimony for a garter,
Or the least feather in her bounteous fan.
A fourth, he only comes in for a mute ;
Divides the act with a dumb shew, and
    exit.
Then must the ladies laugh, straight comes
    their scene,
A sixth times worse confusion than the rest.
Where you shall hear one talk of this man's
    eye,
Another of his lip, a third, his nose,
A fourth commend his leg, a fifth, his foot,
A sixth, his hand, and every one a limb ;
That you would think the poor distorted
    gallant
Must there expire. Then fall they in dis-
    course
Of tires and fashions, how they must take
    place,
Where they may kiss, and whom, when to
    sit down,
And with what grace to rise ; if they salute,
What court'sy they must use : such cobweb
    stuff
As would enforce the common'st sense
    abhor
Th' Arachnean workers.
    Are. Patience, gentle Crites.
This knot of spiders will be soon dissolved,
And all their webs swept out of Cynthia's
    court,
When once her glorious deity appears,
And but presents itself in her full light :
Till when, go in, and spend your hours
    with us,
Your honoured friends, Time and Phronesis,
In contemplation of our goddess' name.
Think on some sweet and choice invention
    now,
Worthy her serious and illustrious eyes,

---

[1] *Such as the satirist, &c.*]
*Aude aliquid brevibus Gyaris, et carcere
    dignum,*

*Si vis esse aliquis ; probitas laudatur et alget ;
Criminibus debent hortos, prætoria, mensas,
Argentum vetus, et stantem extra pocula
    caprum.*—Juvenal, Sat. I.

That from the merit of it we may take
Desired occasion to prefer your worth,
And make your service known to Cynthia.
It is the pride of Arete to grace
Her studious lovers ; and, in scorn of time,
Envy, and ignorance, to lift their state
Above a vulgar height. True happiness
Consists not in the multitude of friends,
But in the worth and choice. Nor would
    I have
Virtue a popular regard pursue :
Let them be good that love me, though
    but few.
  Cri. I kiss thy hands, divinest Arete,
And vow myself to thee and Cynthia.
                      [Exeunt.

SCENE III.—*Another Apartment in
the same.*

Enter Amorphus, *followed by* Asotus *and
his* Tailor.

  Amo. A little more forward : so, sir.
Now go in, discloak yourself, and come
forth. [*Exit* Asotus.] Tailor, bestow thy
absence upon us ; and be not prodigal of
this secret, but to a dear customer.
                      [Exit Tailor.

Re-enter Asotus.

'Tis well entered, sir. Stay, you come on
too fast ; your pace is too impetuous.
Imagine this to be the palace of your
pleasure, or place where your lady is
pleased to be seen. First, you present
yourself, thus : and spying her, you fall off,
and walk some two turns ; in which time,
it is to be supposed, your passion hath sufficiently whited your face, then, stifling a
sigh or two, and closing your lips, with a
trembling boldness, and bold terror, you
advance yourself forward. Prove thus
much, I pray you.
  Aso. Yes, sir ;—pray Jove I can light on
it ! Here, I come in, you say, and present
myself ?
  Amo. Good.
  Aso. And then I spy her, and walk off ?
  Amo. Very good.
  Aso. Now, sir, I stifle, and advance forward ?

  Amo. Trembling.
  Aso. Yes, sir, trembling : I shall do it
better when I come to it. And what must
I speak now ?
  Amo. Marry, you shall say : " Dear
Beauty," or "Sweet Honour," (or by what
other title you please to remember her,)
" methinks you are melancholy." This is,
if she be alone now, and discompanied.
  Aso. Well, sir, I'll enter again ; her title
shall be, " My dear Lindabrides."[1]
  Amo. Lindabrides !
  Aso. Ay, sir, the Emperor Alicandroe's
daughter, and the Prince Meridian's sister,
in *The Knight of the Sun ;* she should
have been married to him, but that the
Princess Claridiana——
  Amo. O, you betray your reading.
  Aso. Nay, sir, I have read history, I am
a little humanitian. Interrupt me not,
good sir. " My dear Lindabrides,—my
dear Lindabrides,—my dear Lindabrides,
methinks you are melancholy."
  Amo. Ay, and take her by the rosy-
fingered hand.
  Aso. Must I so : O !—" My dear Lindabrides, methinks you are melancholy."
  Amo. Or thus, sir. " All variety of
divine pleasures, choice sports, sweet music,
rich fare, brave attire, soft beds, and silken
thoughts, attend this dear beauty."
  Aso. Believe me, that's pretty. " All
variety of divine pleasures, choice sports,
sweet music, rich fare, brave attire, soft
beds, and silken thoughts, attend this dear
beauty."
  Amo. And then, offering to kiss her
hand, if she shall coyly recoil, and signify
your repulse ; you are to re-enforce yourself with,

" More than most fair lady,
  Let not the rigour[2] of your just disdain
Thus coarsely censure of your servant's
  zeal."

And withal, protest her to be the only and
absolute unparalleled creature you do adore,
and admire, and respect, and reverence, in
this court, corner of the world, or kingdom.
  Aso. This is hard, by my faith. I'll
begin it all again.

---

[1] *My dear* Lindabrides.] This fair creature,
who should have been married to the Donzel del
Phebo, is often mentioned by our old writers.
So Rowley: "*Lindabrides!* slid, I have read
of her in the *Mirror of Knighthood*," &c.—
Match at Midnight. From her celebrity, she
became with them a common name for a mistress.

[2] *Let not, &c.*] These verses are probably
what Jonson just below calls "play-particles."
The prose was undoubtedly borrowed from
the absurd and fustian courtship of the times,
which was a corruption of the *Euphues* and
Arcadia.

Amo. Do so, and I will act it for your lady.

Aso. Will you vouchsafe, sir? "All variety of divine pleasures, choice sports, sweet music, rich fare, brave attire, soft beds, and silken thoughts, attend this dear beauty."

Amo. So, sir, pray you away.

Aso. "More than most fair lady, Let not the rigour of your just disdain Thus coarsely censure of your servant's zeal; I protest you are the only, and absolute, unapparelled"——

Amo. Unparalleled.

Aso. "Unparalleled creature, I do adore, and admire, and respect, and reverence, in this court, corner of the world, or kingdom."

Amo. This is, if she abide you. But now, put the case she should be passant when you enter, as thus: you are to frame your gait thereafter, and call upon her, "lady, nymph, sweet refuge, star of our court." Then, if she be guardant, here; you are to come on, and, laterally disposing yourself, swear by her blushing and well-coloured cheek, the bright dye of her hair, her ivory teeth (though they be ebony), or some such white and innocent oath, to induce you. If regardant, then maintain your station, brisk and irpe,[1] shew the supple motion of your pliant body, but in chief of your knee, and hand, which cannot but arride her proud humour exceedingly.

Aso. I conceive you, sir, I shall perform all these things in good time, I doubt not, they do so hit me.

Amo. Well, sir, I am your lady; make use of any of these beginnings, or some other out of your own invention; and prove how you can hold up, and follow it. Say, say.

Aso. Yes, sir. "My dear Lindabrides."

Amo. No, you affect that Lindabrides too much; and let me tell you it is not so courtly. Your pedant[2] should provide you some parcels of French, or some pretty commodity of Italian, to commence with, if you would be exotic and exquisite.

Aso. Yes, sir, he was at my lodging t'other morning, I gave him a doublet.

Amo. Double your benevolence, and give him the hose too; clothe you his body, he will help to apparel your mind. But now, see what your proper genius can perform alone, without adjection of any other Minerva.

Aso. I comprehend you, sir.

Amo. I do stand you, sir: fall back to your first place. Good, passing well; very properly pursued.

Aso. "Beautiful, ambiguous, and sufficient lady, what! are you all alone?"

Amo. "We would be, sir, if you would leave us."

Aso. "I am at your beauty's appointment, bright angel; but——"

Amo. "What but?"

Aso. "No harm, more than most fair feature."

Amo. That touch relished well.

Aso. "But, I protest——"

Amo. "And why should you protest?"

Aso. "For good will, dear esteemed madam, and I hope your ladyship will so conceive of it:
'And will, in time, return from your disdain,
And rue the suff'rance of our friendly pain.'"

Amo. O, that piece was excellent! If you could pick out more of these play-particles, and, as occasion shall salute you, embroider or damask your discourse with them, persuade your soul, it would most judiciously commend you. Come, this was a well-discharged and auspicious bout. Prove the second.

Aso. "Lady, I cannot ruffle it[3] in red and yellow."

Amo. "Why, if you can revel it in white, sir, 'tis sufficient."

Aso. "Say you so, sweet lady! Lan, tede, de, de, de, dant, dant, dant, dante. [*Sings and dances.*] No, in good faith, madam, whosoever told your ladyship so, abused you; but I would be glad to meet your ladyship in a measure."[4]

---

[1] *Brisk* and *irpe.*] See the *Palinode.* p. 203

[2] *Your* pedant,] See p. 157 a, and the *Poetaster.*

[3] *I cannot ruffle it,*] i.e., flaunt it, swagger, or act the part of a ruffler. A cheating bully is called a ruffler in several acts of parliament in the reign of Hen. VIII. See Old Plays, vol. i. p. 259. So in *The Roaring Girl*, 1611: "A *ruffler* is my stile, my title, my profession." A ruffler is described in Decker's *Belman of London*, 1616, Sign. D.—WHAL.

[4] *I would be glad to meet your ladyship in a measure,*] Measures (when spoken of technically) were dances of a grave and dignified kind, performed at court and at public entertainments at the Temple, Inns of Court, &c. They were not to the taste of Sir Toby, if we may trust Shakspeare; and that the knight was not singular in his dislike appears from Shirley's *Bird in a Cage*: "No, none of your dull *measures*! There's no sport but in your country figaries."

Amo. " Me, sir ! Belike you measure me by yourself, then ?"

Aso. " Would I might, fair feature."

Amo. " And what were you the better, if you might ?"

Aso. " The better it please you to ask, fair lady."

Amo. Why, this was ravishing, and most acutely continued. Well, spend not your humour too much, you have now competently exercised your conceit : this, once or twice a day, will render you an accomplished, elaborate, and well-levelled gallant. Convey in your courting-stock, we will in the heat of this go visit the nymphs' chamber.   [*Exeunt.*

ACT IV.

SCENE I.—*An Apartment in the Palace.*

Enter Phantaste, Philautia, Argurion, Moria, *and* Cupid.

Pha. I would this water would arrive once, our travelling friend so commended to us.

Arg. So would I, for he has left all us in travail with expectation of it.

Pha. Pray Jove, I never rise from this couch, if ever I thirsted more for a thing in my whole time of being a courtier.

Phi. Nor I, I'll be sworn : the very mention of it sets my lips in a worse heat, than if he had sprinkled them with mercury. Reach me the glass, sirrah.

Cup. Here, lady.

Mor. They do not peel, sweet charge, do they ?

Phi. Yes, a little, guardian.

Mor. O, 'tis an eminent good sign. Ever when my lips do so, I am sure to have some delicious good drink or other approaching.

Arg. Marry, and this may be good for us ladies ;[1] for it seems 'tis far fet by their stay.

Mor. My palate for yours, dear Honour, it shall prove most elegant, I warrant you. O, I do fancy this gear that's long a coming, with an unmeasurable strain.

Pha. Pray thee sit down, Philautia ; that rebatu becomes thee singularly.[2]

Phi. Is it not quaint ?

Pha. Yes, faith. Methinks, thy servant Hedon is nothing so obsequious to thee as he was wont to be : I know not how, he is grown out of his garb a-late, he's warped.

Mor. In trueness, and so methinks too : he is much converted.

Phi. Tut, let him be what he will, 'tis an animal I dream not of. This tire, methinks, makes me look very ingeniously, quick, and spirited ; I should be some Laura, or some Delia, methinks.

Mor. As I am wise, fair Honours, that title she gave him, to be her Ambition, spoiled him : before, he was the most propitious and observant young novice——

Pha. No, no, you are the whole heaven awry, guardian ; 'tis the swaggering coach-horse Anaides draws with him there,[3] has been the diverter of him.

Phi. For Cupid's sake speak no more of him ; would I might never dare to look in a mirror again, if I respect ever a marmoset of 'em all, otherwise than I would a feather, or my shuttlecock, to make sport with now and then.

Pha. Come, sit down ; troth, an you be good beauties, let's run over them all now. Which is the properest man amongst them ? I say, the traveller, Amorphus.

Phi. O, fie on him, he looks like a Venetian trumpeter in the battle of Lepanto,[4] in the gallery yonder ; and speaks

---

[1] *This may be good for us ladies,* &c.] Argurion alludes to the old proverb : "*Far fet* (fetched) *is good for ladies.*"

[2] *That* rebatu *becomes thee singularly.*] This was a kind of ruff or collar-band, which turned back, and lay in plaits, on the shoulders. It is frequently mentioned by our old poets, as a fashionable part of the dress both of ladies and gentlemen.

[3] *'Tis the swaggering* coach-horse *Anaides draws with him*] This contemptuous term for a companion or close associate is very common. Thus, in *Mons. d'Olive :* " Welcome, little wit ; my page Pacque here makes choice of you to be his *fellow coach-horse.*"

Again :

" He'll be an excellent coach-horse for any captain."—*Green's Tu Quoque.*

And Shakspeare : " Three reprieves for you and your coach-fellow Nym."—*Merry Wives of Windsor.* WHAL.

[4] *He looks like a Venetian trumpeter in the battle of Lepanto.*] Alluding to the famous sea-fight between the Turks and Christians in the year 1571, in which the Turks were defeated with great loss.—WHAL.

And to little purpose, Whalley might have added. The 4to reads *Dutch* trumpeter, which was well corrected in the folio.

to the tune of a country lady, that comes ever in the rearward or train of a fashion.

Mor. I should have judgment in a feature, sweet beauties.

Pha. A body would think so, at these years.

Mor. And I prefer another now, far before him, a million at least.

Pha. Who might that be, guardian?

Mor. Marry, fair charge, Anaides.

Pha. Anaides! you talked of a tune, Philautia: there's one speaks in a key, like the opening of some justice's gate, or a postboy's horn, as if his voice feared an arrest for some ill words it should give, and were loth to come forth.

Phi. Ay, and he has a very imperfect face.

Pha. Like a sea-monster, that were to ravish Andromeda from the rock.

Phi. His hands too great too, by at least a straw's breadth.

Pha. Nay, he has a worse fault than that too.

Phi. A long heel?

Pha. 'That were a fault in a lady, rather than him: no, they say he puts off the calves of his legs, with his stockings, every night.

Phi. Out upon him! Turn to another of the pictures, for love's sake. What says Argurion? Whom does she commend after the rest?

Cup. I hope I have instructed her sufficiently for an answer.   [*Aside.*

Mor. Troth, I made the motion to her ladyship for one to-day, i' the presence, but it appeared she was otherways furnished before: she would none.

Pha. Who was that, Argurion?

Mor. Marry, the poor plain gentleman in the black there.

Pha. Who, Crites?

Arg. Ay, ay, he: a fellow that nobody so much as looked upon, or regarded; and she would have had me done him particular grace.

Pha. That was a true trick of yourself, Moria, to persuade Argurion to affect the scholar.

Arg. Tut, but she shall be no chooser for me. In good faith, I like the citizen's son there, Asotus; methinks none of them all come near him.

Pha. Not Hedon?

Arg. Hedon! in troth, no. Hedon's a pretty slight courtier, and he wears his clothes well, and sometimes in fashion; marry, his face is but indifferent, and he has no such excellent body. No, the other is a most delicate youth; a sweet face, a straight body, a well-proportioned leg and foot, a white hand, a tender voice.

Phi. How now, Argurion!

Pha. O, you should have let her alone, she was bestowing a copy of him upon us. Such a nose were enough to make me love a man, now.

Phi. And then his several colours, he wears; wherein he flourisheth changeably, every day.

Pha. O, but his short hair, and his narrow eyes!

Phi. Why she doats more palpably upon him than ever his father did upon her.

Pha. Believe me, the young gentleman deserves it. If she could doat more, 'twere not amiss. He is an exceeding proper youth, and would have made a most neat barber-surgeon, if he had been put to it in time.

Phi. Say you so! Methinks he looks like a tailor already.

Pha. Ay, that had sayed on one of his customer's suits. His face is like a squeezed orange, or——

Arg. Well, ladies, jest on: the best of you both would be glad of such a servant.

Mor. Ay, I'll be sworn would they, though he be a little shame-faced.

Pha. Shame-faced, Moria! out upon him. Your shame-faced servant is your only gull.

Mor. Go to, beauties, make much of time, and place, and occasion, and opportunity, and favourites, and things that belong to them, for I'll ensure you they will all relinquish; they cannot endure above another year; I know it out of future experience; and therefore take exhibition, and warning. I was once a reveller myself, and though I speak it, as mine own trumpet, I was then esteemed——

Phi. The very march-pane of the court,[1] I warrant you.

Pha. And all the gallants came about you like flies, did they not?

Mor. Go to, they did somewhat;[2] that's no matter now.

Pha. Nay, good Moria, be not angry. Put

---

[1] *The very* march-pane *of the court.*] A confection made of pistachio nuts, almonds, sugar, &c. much esteemed in the poet's age.—WHAL.

[2] *Go to, they did somewhat,* &c.] All, from this speech to the entrance of Hedon, was first added in the folio, 1616. It is admirably written,

case, that we four now had the grant from Juno, to wish ourselves into what happy estate we could, what would you wish to be, Moria?

Mor. Who, I! let me see now. I would wish to be a wise woman, and know all the secrets of court, city, and country. I would know what were done behind the arras, what upon the stairs, what in the garden, what in the nymphs' chamber, what by barge, and what by coach. I would tell you which courtier were scabbed and which not; which lady had her own face to lie with her a-nights and which not; who put off their teeth with their clothes in court, who their hair, who their complexion; and in which box they put it. There should not a nymph, or a widow, be got with child in the Verge, but I would guess, within one or two, who was the right father, and in what month it was gotten; with what words, and which way. I would tell you which madam loved a monsieur, which a player, which a page; who slept with her husband, who with her friend, who with her gentleman-usher, who with her horse-keeper, who with her monkey, and who with all; yes, and who jigged the cock too.[1]

Pha. Fie, you'd tell all, Moria! If I should wish now, it should be to have your tongue out. But what says Philautia? Who should she be?

Phi. Troth, the very same I am. Only I would wish myself a little more command and sovereignty; that all the court were subject to my absolute beck, and all things in it depending on my look; as if there were no other heaven but in my smile, nor other hell but in my frown; that I might send for any man I list, and have his head cut off when I have done with him, or made a eunuch if he denied me; and if I saw a better face than mine own, I might have my doctor to poison it. What would you wish, Phantaste?

Pha. Faith, I cannot readily tell you what: but methinks I should wish myself all manner of creatures. Now I would be an empress, and by and by a duchess; then a great lady of state, then one of your miscellany madams, then a waiting-woman, then your citizen's wife, then a coarse country gentlewoman, then a dairy-maid, then a shepherd's lass, then an empress again, or the queen of fairies: and thus I would prove the vicissitudes and whirl of pleasures about and again. As I were a shepherdess, I would be piped and sung to; as a dairy-wench, I would dance at maypoles, and make syllabubs; as a country gentlewoman, keep a good house, and come up to term to see motions; as a citizen's wife, be troubled with a jealous husband, and put to my shifts; others' miseries should be my pleasures. As a waiting-woman I would taste my lady's delights to her; as a miscellany madam, invent new tires, and go visit courtiers; as a great lady, lie a-bed, and have courtiers visit me; as a duchess, I would keep my state; and as an empress, I would do anything. And, in all these shapes, I would ever be followed with the affections of all that see me. Marry, I myself would affect none: or if I did, it should not be heartily, but so as I might save myself in them still, and take pride in tormenting the poor wretches. Or, now I think on't, I would, for one year, wish myself one woman; but the richest, fairest, and delicatest in a kingdom, the very centre of wealth and beauty, wherein all lines of love should meet; and in that person I would prove all manner of suitors, of all humours, and of all complexions, and never have any two of a sort. I would see how love, by the power of his object, could work inwardly alike, in a choleric man and a sanguine, in a melancholic and a phlegmatic, in a fool and a wise man, in a clown and a courtier, in a valiant man and a coward; and how he could vary outward, by letting this gallant express himself in dumb gaze; another with sighing and rubbing his fingers; a third, with play-ends and pitiful verses; a fourth with stabbing himself,[2] and drink-

---

and perfectly characteristic of the several speakers; yet it might well have been spared, as it conduces nothing to the progress of the plot, (such as it is,) and the play was before sufficiently long.

[1] *Yes, and who* jigged the cock *too.*] This expression I do not understand. In canting language *jigger* is a *key*. Whether Mother Moria means to say that she knew who turned the cock clandestinely, and added *drunkenness*

to her other vices, I know not; perhaps the subject is better left in obscurity: I may, however, observe that the good old lady had been looking into Juvenal.

[2] *A fourth, with* stabbing *himself,* &c.] These appear to have been marks of heroic gallantry in this age.

" By the faith of a soldier, lady, I do reverence the ground that you walk upon. I will fight with him that dares say you are not fair, stab him

ing healths, or writing languishing letters
in his blood ; a fifth, in coloured ribands
and good clothes ; with this lord to smile,
and that lord to court, and the t'other lord
to dote, and one lord to hang himself.
And, then, I to have a book made of all
this, which I would call the *Book of
Humours*, and every night read a little
piece ere I slept, and laugh at it.—Here
comes Hedon.

Enter Hedon, Anaides, *and* Mercury,
who retires with Cupid *to the back of
the stage, where they converse together.*

Hed. Save you, sweet and clear beauties !
By the spirit that moves in me, you are all
most pleasingly bestowed, ladies. Only I
can take it for no good omen, to find mine
Honour so dejected.

Phi. You need not fear, sir; I did of
purpose humble myself against your
coming, to decline the pride of my
Ambition.

Hed. Fair Honour, Ambition dares not
stoop; but if it be your sweet pleasure I
shall lose that title, I will, as I am Hedon,
apply myself to your bounties.

Phi. That were the next way to dis-title
myself of honour. O no, rather be still
Ambitious, I pray you.

Hed. I will be anything that you please,
whilst it pleaseth you to be yourself, lady.
Sweet Phantaste, dear Moria, most beautiful Argurion——

Ana. Farewell, Hedon.

Hed. Anaides, stay, whither go you?

Ana. 'Slight, what should I do here?
an you engross them all for your own use,
'tis time for me to seek out.

Hed. I engross them ! Away, mischief ;
this is one of your extravagant jests now,
because I began to salute them by their
names.

Ana. Faith, you might have spared us
Madam Prudence, the guardian there,
though you had more covetously aimed at
the rest.

Hed. 'Sheart, take them all, man : what
speak you to me of aiming or covetous ?

Ana. Ay, say you so ! nay, then, have
at them :—Ladies, here's one hath distinguished you by your names already. It
shall only become me to ask how you do.

Hed. Ods so, was this the design you
travailed with ?

Pha. Who answers the brazen head ? it
spoke to somebody.

Ana. Lady Wisdom, do you interpret
for these puppets ?

Mor. In truth and sadness, honours,
you are in great offence for this. Go to ;
the gentleman (I'll undertake with him) is
a man of fair living, and able to maintain
a lady in her two coaches a day, besides
pages, monkeys, and paraquettoes, with
such attendants as she shall think meet for
her turn ; and therefore there is more
respect requirable, howsoe'er you seem to
connive.[1] Hark you, sir, let me discourse
a syllable with you. I am to say to you,
these ladies are not of that close-and-open
behaviour as haply you may suspend ;[2]
their carriage is well known to be such as
it should be, both gentle and extraordinary.

Mer. O, here comes the other pair.

Enter Amorphus *and* Asotus.

Amo. That was your father's love, the
nymph Argurion. I would have you direct
all your courtship thither ; if you could but
endear yourself to her affection, you were
eternally engallanted.

Aso. In truth, sir ! pray Phœbus I prove
favoursome in her fair eyes.

Amo. All divine mixture, and increase of
beauty to this bright bevy of ladies ; and to

---

that will not pledge your health, and with a
dagger open *a vein* to drink a full health to you."
                Green's Tu Quoque.

[1] *Howsoe'er you seem to* connive,] i.e., I suppose to wink or make faces at it. Decker ridicules Jonson for the use of this word in his
Satiromastix. "I was but at the barber's last day,
and when he was rincing my face, did but cry out,
Fellow, thou makest me *connive* too long ; and
says he, Master Asinius Bubo, you have e'en
Horace's words as right as if he had spit them into
your mouth." As the poet is evidently imitating
the affected jargon of the ladies of the court, it
may be questioned whether his language be a
legitimate object of satire : but, indeed, *connive*
is used by other dramatic writers without the

preposition; if it be this which offended Decker.
Thus Fletcher :
         " The truth is, ·
I must *connive* no more, no more admittance
Must I consent to."—*Martial Maid.*

And Massinger:
        "'Tis then most fit that we
Should not *connive*, and see his government
Depraved and scandalized."—*Roman Actor.*

[2] *These ladies are not of that close and* open
behaviour, as haply you may suspend.] If this be
not an *Euphuism* for a disposition in the ladies to
play *fast and loose* with their lovers, the reader,
I believe, must acquiesce in Whalley's conjecture, and for *close* read *loose*. *Suspend*, as he
observes, has the sense of *suspect*.

the male courtiers, compliment and courtesy.

Hed. In the behalf of the males, I gratify
you, Amorphus.

Pha. And I of the females.

Amo. Succinctly returned. I do vail to
both your thanks, and kiss them; but pri-
marily to yours, most ingenious, acute, and
polite lady.

Phi. Ods my life, how he does all-to-be-
qualify her! *ingenious, acute,* and *polite!*
as if there was not others in place as ingenious, acute, and polite as she.

Hed. Yes, but you must know, lady, he
cannot speak out of a dictionary method.

Pha. Sit down, sweet Amorphus. When
will this water come, think you?

Amo. It cannot now be long, fair lady.

Cup. Now observe, Mercury.

Aso. How, most ambiguous beauty!
love you? that I will by this handkerchief.

Mer. 'Slid, he draws his oaths out of his
pocket.

Arg. But will you be constant?

Aso. Constant, madam! I will not say
for constantness; but by this purse, which
I would be loth to swear by, unless it were
embroidered, I protest, more than most fair
lady, you are the only absolute and unparalleled creature, I do adore, and admire, and respect, and reverence in this
court, corner of the world, or kingdom.
Methinks you are melancholy.

Arg. Does your heart speak all this?

Aso. Say you?

Mer. O, he is groping for another
oath.

Aso. Now by this watch—I marle how
forward the day is—I do unfeignedly vow
myself—'slight, 'tis deeper than I took it,
past five—yours entirely addicted, madam.

Arg. I require no more, dearest Asotus;
henceforth let me call you mine, and in remembrance of me, vouchsafe to wear this
chain and this diamond.

Aso. O lord, sweet lady!

Cup. There are new oaths for him.

What! doth Hermes taste no alteration in
all this?

Mer. Yes, thou hast strook Argurion
enamoured on Asotus, methinks.

Cup. Alas, no; I am nobody, I; I can
do nothing in this disguise.

Mer. But thou hast not wounded any of
the rest, Cupid.

Cup. Not yet; it is enough that I have
begun so prosperously.

Arg. Nay, these are nothing to the gems
I will hourly bestow upon thee; be but
faithful and kind to me, and I will lade thee
with my richest bounties; behold, here my
bracelets from mine arms.

Aso. Not so, good lady, by this diamond.

Arg. Take 'em, wear 'em; my jewels,
chain of pearl, pendants, all I have.

Aso. Nay, then, by this pearl you make
me a wanton.

Cup. Shall she not answer for this, to
maintain him thus in swearing?

Mer. O no, there is a way to wean him
from this, the gentleman may be reclaimed.

Cup. Ay, if you had the airing of his apparel, coz, I think.

Aso. Loving! 'twere pity an I should
be living else, believe me. Save you, sir,
save you, sweet lady, save you, Monsieur
Anaides, save you, dear madam.

Ana. Dost thou know him that saluted
thee, Hedon?

Hed. No, some idle Fungoso, that hath
got above the cupboard since yesterday.[1]

Ana. 'Slud, I never saw him till this
morning, and he salutes me as familiarly
as if we had known together since the
deluge, or the first year of Troy action.

Amo. A most right-handed and auspicious encounter. Confine yourself to your
fortunes.

Phi. For sport's sake let's have some
Riddles or Purposes, ho!

Pha. No, faith, your Prophecies are best,
the t'other are stale.

Phi. Prophecies! we cannot all sit in

---

[1] *Some Fungoso that hath got* above the cupboard *since yesterday.*] Some mushroom, some
upstart servant who has been just advanced.
The cupboard (the modern sideboard) then contained the plate: near this, and above it, the
retainers and superior domestics of great families
were ranged for state, and for the service of the
nobler guests. When the numerous gradations
of servitude are considered, and the strictness
with which each of them was formerly defined
and maintained, it will not appear strange that
a rapid advancement should produce some degree
of pride, in weak minds. These *cupboards* are
often mentioned by our old writers. Thus Sir
John Harington: "I have ever been against
the opinion of some elder servitors, who will
maintain that till ii of the clocke no *gentleman*
should stand *above the cupboard.*"
　　　　　　　　　　　　　Treatise on Plays.

And Donne:

" Hear how the huishers cheques, *cupbord* and
　　fire
I passed: by which degrees young men aspire
In court," &c.—*Sat.* vi.

at them ; we shall make a confusion. No ; what called you that we had in the forenoon?

Pha. Substantives and adjectives, is it not, Hedon?

Phi. Ay, that. Who begins?

Pha. I have thought; speak your adjectives, sirs.

Phi. But do not you change then.

Pha. Not I. Who says?

Mor. Odoriferous.

Phi. Popular.

Arg. Humble.

Ana. White-livered.

Hed. Barbarous.

Amo. Pythagorical.

Hed. Yours, signior?

Aso. What must I do, sir?

Amo. Give forth your adjective with the rest ; as preposterous, good, fair, sweet, well——

Hed. Anything that hath not been spoken.

Aso. Yes, sir, well-spoken shall be mine.

Pha. What, have you all done?

All. Ay.

Pha. Then the substantive is Breeches. Why *odoriferous* breeches, guardian?

Mor. Odoriferous,——because odoriferous: that which contains most variety of savour and smell we say is most odoriferous ; now breeches, I presume, are incident to that variety, and therefore odoriferous breeches.

Pha. Well, we must take it howsoever. Who's next? Philautia?

Phi. Popular.

Pha. Why *popular* breeches?

Phi. Marry, that is, when they are not content to be generally noted in court, but will press forth on common stages and brokers' stalls, to the public view of the world.

Pha. Good. Why *humble* breeches, Argurion?

Arg. Humble! because they use to be sat upon ; besides, if you tie them not up, their property is to fall down about your heels.

Mer. She has worn the breeches, it seems, which have done so.

Pha. But why *white-livered?*

Ana. Why! are not their linings white? Besides, when they come in swaggering company, and will pocket up anything, may they not properly be said to be white-livered?

Pha. O yes, we must not deny it. And why *barbarous*, Hedon?

Hed. Barbarous! because commonly, when you have worn your breeches sufficiently, you give them to your barber.

Amo. That's good; but how *Pythagorical?*

Phi. Ay, Amorphus, why Pythagorical breeches?

Amo. O most kindly of all; 'tis a conceit of that fortune, I am bold to hug my brain for.

Pha. How is it, exquisite Amorphus?

Amo. O, I am rapt with it, 'tis so fit, so proper, so happy——

Phi. Nay, do not rack us thus.

Amo. I never truly relished myself before. Give me your ears. Breeches Pythagorical, by reason of their transmigration into several shapes.

Mor. Most rare, in sweet troth. Marry this young gentleman, for his well-spoken——

Pha. Ay, why *well-spoken* breeches?

Aso. Well-spoken! Marry, well-spoken, because—whatsoever they speak is well-taken ; and whatsoever is well-taken is well-spoken.

Mor. Excellent! believe me.

Aso. Not so, ladies, neither.

Hed. But why breeches, now?

Pha. Breeches, *quasi* bear-riches; when a gallant bears all his riches in his breeches.

Amo. Most fortunately etymologized.

Pha. [1]Nay, we have another sport afore this, of A thing done, and who did it, &c.

Phi. Ay, good Phantaste, let's have that: distribute the places.

Pha. Why, I imagine, A thing done ; Hedon thinks, who did it ; Moria, with what it was done; Anaides, where it was done; Argurion, when it was done ; Amorphus, for what cause was it done ; you, Philautia, what followed upon the doing of it ; and this

---

[1] *Pha. Nay, we have another sport afore this, &c.*] The preceding and following sport, as the author calls it, were probably the diversion of the age, and of the same stamp with our modern *cross-purposes, questions and commands,* &c.; but, trifling as it is, Jonson is not to be censured for representing his courtiers as they really were.—WHAL.

This "other sport" is not in the quarto. Jon-

son or his audiences must have found the ridicule on the state follies of Whitehall highly entertaining, to encourage such frequent interpolations in this interminable drama. "Good Queen Bess" was now growing indifferent to popular amusements; but there had been a time when such attempts to excite mirth at the expense of even her meanest servants could not be hazarded with impunity.

gentleman, who would have done it better?
What? is it conceived about?

All. Yes, yes.

Pha. Then speak you, sir, *Who would
have done it better?*

Aso. How! does it begin at me?

Pha. Yes, sir: this play is called the
Crab, it goes backward.

Aso. May I not name myself?

Phi. If you please, sir, and dare abide
the venture of it.

Aso. Then I would have done it better,
whatever it is.

Pha. No doubt on't, sir: a good confidence. *What followed upon the act*, Philautia?

Phi. A few heat drops, and a month's
mirth.

Pha. For what cause, Amorphus?

Amo. For the delight of ladies.

Pha. When, Argurion?

Arg. Last progress.

Pha. Where, Anaides?

Ana. Why, in a pair of pained slops.[1]

Pha. With what, Moria?

Mor. With a glyster.

Pha. Who, Hedon?

Hed. A traveller.

Pha. Then the thing done was, *An oration was made*. Rehearse. An oration was
made—

Hed. By a traveller—

Mor. With a glyster—

Ana. In a pair of pained slops—

Arg. Last progress—

Amo. For the delight of ladies—

Phi. A few heat drops, and a month's
mirth followed.

Pha. And, this silent **gentleman** would
have done it better.

Aso. This was not so good, now.

Phi. In good faith, these unhappy pages
would be whipped for staying thus.

Mor. Beshrew my hand and my heart
else.

Amo. I do wonder at their protraction.

Ana. Pray Venus my whore have not discovered herself to the rascally boys, and
that be the cause of their stay.

Aso. I must suit myself with another
page: this idle Prosaites will never be
brought to wait well.

Mor. Sir, I have a kinsman I could willingly wish to your service,[2] if you will
deign to accept of him.

Aso. And I shall be glad, most sweet
lady, to embrace him. Where is he?

Mor. I can fetch him, sir, but I would
be loth to make you to turn away your other
page.

Aso. You shall not, most sufficient lady;
I will keep both: pray you let's go see
him.

Arg. Whither goes my love?

Aso. I'll return presently, I go but to see
a page with this lady.

[*Exeunt* Asotus *and* Moria.

Ana. As sure as fate, 'tis so; she has
opened all: a pox of all cockatrices! D—n
me, if she have played loose with me, I'll
cut her throat, within a hair's breadth, so it
may be healed again.

Mer. What, is he jealous of his hermaphrodite?

Cup. O, ay, this will be excellent sport.

Phi. Phantaste, Argurion! what, you
are suddenly struck, methinks! For love's
sake let's have some music till they come:
Ambition, reach the lyra, I pray you.

Hed. Anything to which my Honour shall
direct me.

Phi. Come, Amorphus, cheer up Phantaste.

Amo. It shall be my pride, fair lady, to
attempt all that is in my power. But here
is an instrument that alone is able to infuse
soul into the most melancholic and dull-
disposed creature upon earth. O, let me
kiss thy fair knees. Beauteous ears, attend it.

Hed. Will you have "*the Kiss*," Honour?

Phi. Ay, good Ambition.

Hedon *sings.*

O, that joy so soon should waste!
    Or so sweet a bliss
    As a kiss
Might not for ever last!
So sugared, so melting, so soft, so delicious,
    The dew that lies on roses,

---

[1] *Pained slops.*] Large and loose breeches,
which were the fashionable dress of the age, and
seem to have been made of *panes* or partitions,
perhaps of different colours. Of this make were
the coverings for beds, which are still called
counterpanes. These slops seem to be alluded
to in *Marston's* Satires:

" Yon tissue *slop*, yon holy-crossed *pane*."
                         B. ii. Sat. 7.—WHAL.

[2] Wish *to your* service.] To *wish* is to recommend. Thus in a *Match at Midnight*:
" He says he was *wished* to a very wealthy
widow." And in *The City Night-cap*: " He is
wished to her by Madona Lussuriosa." The
word occurs again in the *Alchemist*.—WHAL.

When the morn herself discloses,
    Is not so precious.
O rather than I would it smother,
Were I to taste such another;
    It should be my wishing
    That I might die with kissing.

Hed. I made this ditty, and the note to
it, upon a kiss that my Honour gave me;
how like you it, sir?

Amo. A pretty air; in general, I like it
well: but in particular, your long die-note
did arride me most, but it was somewhat
too long. I can shew one almost of the
same nature, but much before it, and not so
long, in a composition of mine own. I think
I have both the note and ditty about me.

Hed. Pray you, sir, see.

Amo. Yes, there is the note; and all the
parts if I misthink not. I will read the
ditty to your beauties here; but first I am
to make you familiar with the occasion,
which presents itself thus. Upon a time,
going to take my leave of the emperor, and
kiss his great hands, there being then present the kings of France and Arragon, the
dukes of Savoy, Florence, Orleans, Bourbon,
Brunswick, the Landgrave, Count Palatine;
all which had severally feasted me; besides infinite more of inferior persons, as
counts and others; it was my chance (the
emperor detained by some exorbitant affair)
to wait him the fifth part of an hour, or
much near it. In which time, retiring myself into a bay-window,[1] the beauteous lady
Annabel, niece to the empress, and sister
to the king of Arragon, who having never
before eyed me, but only heard the common
report of my virtue, learning, and travel,
fell into that extremity of passion for my
love, that she there immediately swooned:
physicians were sent for, she had to her
chamber, so to her bed; where, languishing some few days, after many times calling upon me, with my name in her lips, she
expired. As that (I must mourningly say)
is the only fault of my fortune, that, as it
hath ever been my hap to be sued to, by
all ladies and beauties, where I have come;

so I never yet sojourned or rested in that
place or part of the world, where some
high-born, admirable, fair feature died not
for my love.

Mer. O, the sweet power of travel!—
Are you guilty of this, Cupid?

Cup. No, Mercury, and that his page
Cos knows, if he were here present to be
sworn.

Phi. But how doth this draw on the
ditty, sir?

Mer. O, she is too quick with him; he
hath not devised that yet.

Amo. Marry, some hour before she departed, she bequeathed to me this glove:
which golden legacy, the emperor himself
took care to send after me, in six coaches,
covered all with black velvet, attended by
the state of his empire; all which he freely
presented me with: and I reciprocally (out
of the same bounty) gave to the lords
that brought it: only reserving the gift of
the deceased lady, upon which I composed
this ode, and set it to my most affected instrument, the lyra.

Thou more than most sweet glove,
Unto my more sweet love,
Suffer me to store with kisses
This empty lodging, that now misses
The pure rosy hand, that wear thee,
Whiter than the kid that bare thee.
Thou art soft, but that was softer;
Cupid's self hath kissed it ofter
Than e'er he did his mother's doves,
Supposing her the queen of loves,
That was thy mistress, BEST OF GLOVES.

Mer. Blasphemy, blasphemy, Cupid!

Cup. I'll revenge it time enough, Hermes.

Phi. Good Amorphus, let's hear it sung.

Amo. I care not to admit that, since it
pleaseth Philautia to request it.

Hed. Here, sir.

Amo. Nay, play it, I pray you; you do
well, you do well. [*He sings it.*] How
like you it, sir?

Hed. Very well, in troth.

Amo. But very well! O, you are a mere
mammothrept[2] in judgment, then. Why,

---

[1] *A bay-window,*] This is what we call a
bow-window, and was very common in our old
houses. As these bows were sufficiently large,
they were the common retiring-places; and it is
impossible to read any of our ancient historians
without discovering that the most confidential
conversations were held in them. "It hath its
name," says Minsheu, "because it is builded in
manner like a *baie* or rode for shippes, that is,
round." He is right in his explanation; but
why a *bay* window should take its name from a

bay for shipping, does not appear: both terms,
in fact, are equally ancient, and derived, with a
variety of others, from the Anglo-Saxon verb
Bygan, signifying to bend or curve.

[2] *O, you are a mere* mammothrept] i.e., a
spoiled child, a delicate nursling, a cockney, as
Ainsworth has it. It is thus learnedly discussed
in the *Colloquies*: "*Hoc dilucide docet Mam-
metrectus vulgô corrupte dictus, cum vero
nomine dicatur* Mammothreptus, *quasi disas
avia alumnum.*"—Synod. Grammat.

do you not observe how excellently the ditty is affected in every place? that I do not marry a word of short quantity to a long note? nor an ascending syllable to a descending tone? Besides, upon the word *best* there, you see how I do enter with an odd minum, and drive it through the brief; which no intelligent musician, I know, but will affirm to be very rare, extraordinary, and pleasing.

Mer. And yet not fit to lament the death of a lady, for all this.

Cup. Tut, here be they will swallow any-thing.

Pha. Pray you, let me have a copy of it, Amorphus.

Phi. And me too; in troth, I like it exceedingly.

Amo. I have denied it to princes; never-theless, to you, the true female twins of perfection, I am won to depart withal.

Hed. I hope, I shall have my Honour's copy.

Pha. You are Ambitious in that, Hedon.

Re-enter Anaides.

Amo. How now, Anaides! what is it hath conjured up this distemperature in the circle of your face?

Ana. Why, what have you to do? A pox upon your filthy travelling face! hold your tongue.

Hed. Nay, dost hear, Mischief?

Ana. Away, musk-cat!

Amo. I say to thee thou art rude, de-bauched, impudent, coarse, unpolished, a frapler,[1] and base.

Hed. Heart of my father, what a strange alteration has half a year's haunting of or-dinaries wrought in this fellow! that came with a tufftaffata jerkin to town but the other day, and a pair of pennyless hose, and now he is turned Hercules, he wants but a club.

Ana. Sir, you with the pencil on your

chin;[2] I will garter my hose with your guts, and that shall be all.   [*Exit.*

Mer. 'Slid, what rare fireworks be here? flash, flash.

Pha. What's the matter, Hedon? can you tell?

Hed. Nothing, but that he lacks crowns, and thinks we'll lend him some to be friends.

Re-enter Asotus and Moria, with Morus.

Aso. Come, sweet lady, in good truth I'll have it, you shall not deny me, Morus, persuade your aunt I may have her picture, by any means.

Morus. Yea, sir: good aunt now, let him have it, he will use me the better; if you love me, do, good aunt.

Mor. Well, tell him he shall have it.

Morus. Master, you shall have it, she says.

Aso. Shall I? thank her, good page.

Cup. What, has he entertained the fool?

Mer. Ay, he'll wait close, you shall see, though the beggar bang off a while.

Morus. Aunt, my master thanks you.

Mor. Call him hither.

Morus. Yes; master.

Mor. Yes, in verity, and gave me this purse, and he has promised me a most fine dog; which he will have drawn with my picture, he says: and desires most vehe-mently to be known to your ladyships.

Pha. Call him hither, 'tis good groping such a gull.

Morus. Master Asotus, Master Asotus!

Aso. For love's sake, let me go: you see I am called to the ladies.

Arg. Wilt thou forsake me, then?

Aso. Od so! what would you have me do?

Mer. Come hither, Master Asotus.—I do ensure your ladyships, he is a gentleman of a very worthy desert: and of a most bountiful nature.—You must shew and in-sinuate yourself responsible, and equivalent now to my commendment.—Good honours, grace him.

---

[1] *A frapler.*] A quarreller, a bully, perhaps from the French, *frapper*; but I can produce no instance of the use of the word. *Frape* is in Bulloker's *Expositor*, and is there said to mean a rabble: this too is Coles's explanation, for he translates *frape* by *cœtus, turba*.

[2] *Sir, you with the* pencil *on your chin*;] Here again I am left to guess. Probably the allusion is to the form of Hedon's beard, which might resemble a *pencil*, or, as our old writers sometimes spell the word, *penselle*, a small flag gradually diminishing to a point. The beard of Charles I. and other persons of this age appears from their portraits to have been picked in

this manner: and that such kind of beards were not unfashionable may be learned from Greene: "Then he descends as low as his beard, and asketh whether he will be shaven or no: whether he will have his *peake cut short and sharpe, amiable like an* inamorato, or broad pendant, like a spade, to be terrible like a warrior and a soldado."—*Quip for an Upstart Courtier.* Taylor mentions "perpendicular beards," which seem to have been of the same description; but this, with many other doubtful points, must be left to the better knowledge of the reader. The passage is not in the quarto. [The term pen-ciled, applied to eyebrows, preserves this idea.]

Aso. I protest, more than most fair ladies, "I do wish all variety of divine pleasures, choice sports, sweet music, rich fare, brave attire, soft beds, and silken thoughts, attend these fair beauties." Will it please your ladyship to wear this chain of pearl, and this diamond, for my sake?

Arg. O!

Aso. And you, madam, this jewel and pendants?

Arg. O!

Pha. We know not how to deserve these bounties, out of so slight merit, Asotus.

Phi. No, in faith, but there's my glove for a favour.

Pha. And soon after the revels, I will bestow a garter on you.

Aso. O lord, ladies! it is more grace than ever I could have hoped, but that it pleaseth your ladyships to extend. I protest it is enough, that you but take knowledge of my—— if your ladyship want embroidered gowns, tires of any fashion, rebatues, jewels, or carcanets,[1] anything whatsoever, if you vouchsafe to accept——

Cup. And for it they will help you to shoe-ties and devices.

Aso. I cannot utter myself, dear beauties, but you can conceive——

Arg. O!

Pha. Sir, we will acknowledge your service, doubt not—henceforth, you shall be no more Asotus to us, but our goldfinch, and we your cages.

Aso. O Venus! madams! how shall I deserve this? if I were but made acquainted with Hedon, now,—I'll try: pray you, away.   [*To* Argurion.

Mor. How he prays money to go away from him!

Aso. Amorphus, a word with you; here's a watch I would bestow upon you, pray you make me known to that gallant.

Amo. That I will, sir.—Monsieur Hedon, I must entreat you to exchange knowledge with this gentleman.

Hed. 'Tis a thing, next to the water we expect, I thirst after, sir. Good Monsieur Asotus.

Aso. Good Monsieur Hedon, I would be glad to be loved of men of your rank and spirit, I protest. Please you to accept this pair of bracelets, sir; they are not worth the bestowing ——

---

[1] *Carcanets,*] i.e., necklaces, and sometimes bracelets for the arm; the word has occurred before, and indeed is sufficiently common in our old poets.

Mer. O Hercules, how the gentleman purchases! this must needs bring Argurion to a consumption.

Hed. Sir, I shall never stand in the merit of such bounty, I fear.

Aso. O Venus, sir; your acquaintance shall be sufficient. And, if at any time you need my bill, or my bond——

Arg. O, O!   [*Swoons.*

Amo. Help the lady there!

Mor. Gods-dear, Argurion! madam, how do you?

Arg. Sick.

Pha. Have her forth, and give her air.

Aso. I come again straight, ladies.

[*Exeunt* Asotus, Morus, *and* Argurion.

Mer. Well, I doubt all the physic he has will scarce recover her; she's too far spent.

Re-enter Anaides *with* Gelaia, Prosaites, *and* Cos, *with the bottles.*

Phi. O, here's the water come; fetch glasses, page.

Gel. Heart of my body, here's a coil, indeed, with your jealous humours! nothing but whore and bitch, and all the villainous swaggering names you can think on! 'Slid, take your bottle, and put it in your guts for me, I'll see you poxed ere I follow you any longer.

Ana. Nay, good punk, sweet rascal; d—n me, if I am jealous now.

Gel. That's true, indeed; pray let's go.

Mor. What's the matter, there?

Gel. 'Slight, he has me upon interrogatories, (nay, my mother shall know how you use me,) where I have been? and why I should stay so long, and, how is't possible? and withal calls me at his pleasure I know not how many cockatrices, and things.

Mor. In truth and sadness, these are no good epitaphs, Anaides, to bestow upon any gentlewoman; and I'll ensure you if I had known you would have dealt thus with my daughter, she should never have fancied you so deeply as she has done. Go to.

Ana. Why, do you hear, Mother Moria? heart!

Mor. Nay, I pray you, sir, do not swear.

Ana. Swear! why? 'sblood, I have sworn afore now, I hope. Both you and your daughter mistake me. I have not honoured Arete, that is held the worthiest lady in court, next to Cynthia, with half that observance and respect as I have done her in private, howsoever outwardly I have carried myself careless and negligent. Come, you are a foolish punk, and know not when you are well employed. Kiss me, come on ; do it, I say.

Mor. Nay, indeed, I must confess, she is apt to misprision. But I must have you leave it, minion.

Re-enter Asotus.

Amo. How now, Asotus ? how does the lady ?

Aso. Faith, ill. I have left my page with her, at her lodging.

Hed. O, here's the rarest water that ever was tasted : fill him some.

Pro. What ! has my master a new page?

Mer. Yes, a kinsman of the Lady Moria's : you must wait better now, or you are cashiered, Prosaites.

Ana. Come, gallants, you must pardon my foolish humour ; when I am angry, that anything crosses me, I grow impatient straight. Here, I drink to you.

Phi. O, that we had five or six bottles more of this liquor !

Pha. Now I commend your judgment, Amorphus : [*knocking within.*] Who's that knocks? look page.　　[*Exit* Cos.

Mor. O, most delicious ; a little of this would make Argurion well.

Pha. O, no, give her no cold drink by any means.

Ana. 'Sblood, this water is the spirit of wine, I'll be hanged else.

Re-enter Cos *with* Arete.

Cos. Here's the Lady Arete, madam.

Are. What, at your bever, gallants?

Mor. Will't please your ladyship to drink? 'tis of the New Fountain water.

Are. Not I, Moria, I thank you.—Gallants, you are for this night free to your peculiar delights ; Cynthia will have no sports : when she is pleased to come forth, you shall have knowledge. In the mean-time, I could wish you did provide for solemn revels, and some unlooked-for device of wit, to entertain her, against she should vouchsafe to grace your pastimes with her presence.

Amo. What say you to a masque ?

Hed. Nothing better, if the project were new and rare.

Are. Why, I'll send for Crites, and have his advice : be you ready in your endeavours : he shall discharge you of the inventive part.

Pha. But will not your ladyship stay?

Are. Not now, Phantaste.　　　[*Exit.*

Phi. Let her go, I pray you good Lady Sobriety, I am glad we are rid of her.

Pha. What a set face the gentlewoman has, as she were still going to a sacrifice !

Phi. O, she is the extraction of a dozen of Puritans, for a look.

Mor. Of all nymphs i' the court, I cannot away with her ;[1] 'tis the coarsest thing !

Phi. I wonder how Cynthia can affect her so above the rest. Here be they are every way as fair as she, and a thought fairer, I trow.

Pha. Ay, and as ingenious and conceited as she.

Mor. Ay, and as politic as she, for all she sets such a forehead on't.

Phi. Would I were dead, if I would change to be Cynthia.

Pha. Or I.

Mor. Or I.

Amo. And there's her minion, Crites : why his advice more than Amorphus ? Have not I invention afore him ? learning to better that invention above him ? and in-fanted with pleasant travel——

Ana. Death, what talk you of his learning ? he understands no more than a schoolboy ; I have put him down myself a thousand times, by this air, and yet I never talked with him but twice in my life : you never saw his like. I could never get him to argue with me but once ; and then, because I could not construe an author I quoted at first sight, he went away and laughed at me. By Hercules, I scorn him, as I do the sodden nymph that was here even now, his mistress, Arete ? and I love myself for nothing else.

Hed. I wonder the fellow does not hang himself, being thus scorned and contemned of us that are held the most accomplished society of gallants.

Mer. By yourselves, none else.

Hed. I protest, if I had no music in me, no courtship, that I were not a reveller and could dance, or had not those excellent qualities that give a man life and perfec-tion, but a mere poor scholar as he is, I think I should make some desperate way with myself ; whereas now,—would I might never breathe more, if I do know that crea-ture in this kingdom with whom I would change.

---

[1] *I cannot* away with *her* ;] I cannot endure her. See *Bartholomew Fair.*

Cup. This is excellent! Well, I must alter all this soon.

Mer. Look you do, Cupid. The bottles have wrought, it seems.

Aso. O, I am sorry the revels are crost. I should have tickled it soon. I did never appear till then. 'Slid, I am the neatliest-made gallant i' the company, and have the best presence; and my dancing—well, I know what our usher said to me last time I was at the school. Would I might have led Philautia in the measures, an it had been the gods' will! I am most worthy, I am sure.

Re-enter Morus.

Morus. Master, I can tell you news; the lady kissed me yonder, and played with me, and says she loved you once as well as she does me, but that you cast her off.

Aso. Peace, my most esteemed page.

Morus. Yes.

Aso. What luck is this, that our revels are dashed! now was I beginning to glister in the very highway of preferment. An Cynthia had but seen me dance a strain, or do but one trick, I had been kept in court, I should never have needed to look towards my friends again.

Amo. Contain yourself, you were a fortunate young man, if you knew your own good; which I have now projected, and will presently multiply upon you. Beauties and valours, your vouchsafed applause to a motion. The humorous Cynthia hath, for this night, withdrawn the light of your delight.

Pha. 'Tis true, Amorphus; what may we do to redeem it?

Amo. Redeem that we cannot, but to create a new flame is in our power. Here is a gentleman, my scholar, whom, for some private reasons me specially moving, I am covetous to gratify with title of master in the noble and subtile science of courtship: for which grace he shall this night, in court, and in the long gallery, hold his public act, by open challenge, to all masters of the mystery whatsoever, to play at the four choice and principal weapons thereof, viz. *the Bare Accost, the Better Regard, the Solemn Address,* and *the Perfect Close.* What say you?

All. Excellent, excellent, Amorphus.

Amo. Well, let us then take our time by the forehead: I will instantly have bills drawn, and advanced in every angle of the court.—Sir, betray not your too much joy.—Anaides, we must mix this gentleman

with you in acquaintance, Monsieur Asotus.

Ana. I am easily entreated to grace any of your friends, Amorphus.

Aso. Sir, and his friends shall likewise grace you, sir. Nay, I begin to know myself now.

Amo. O, you must continue your bounties.

Aso. Must I! Why, I'll give him this ruby on my finger. Do you hear, sir? I do heartily wish your acquaintance, and I partly know myself worthy of it; please you, sir, to accept this poor ruby in a ring, sir. The poesy is of my own device, *Let this blush for me,* sir.

Ana. So it must for me too, for I am not ashamed to take it.

Morus. Sweet man! By my troth, master, I love you; will you love me too, for my aunt's sake? I'll wait well, you shall see. I'll still be here. Would I might never stir, but you are a fine man in these clothes; master, shall I have them when you have done with them?

Aso. As for that, Morus, thou shalt see more hereafter, in the meantime, by this air, or by this feather, I'll do as much for thee, as any gallant shall do for his page, whatsoever, in this court, corner of the world, or kingdom.

[*Exeunt all but the* Pages.

Mer. I wonder this gentleman should affect to keep a fool: methinks he makes sport enough with himself.

Cup. Well, Prosaites, 'twere good you did wait closer.

Pro. Ay, I'll look to it; 'tis time.

Cos. The revels would have been most sumptuous to-night, if they had gone forward.   [*Exit.*

Mer. They must needs, when all the choicest singularities of the court were up in pantofles; ne'er a one of them but was able to make a whole shew of itself.

Aso. [*within.*] Sirrah, a torch, a torch!

Pro. O, what a call is there! I will have a canzonet made, with nothing in it but sirrah; and the burthen shall be, I come.   [*Exit.*

Mer. How now, Cupid, how do you like this change?

Cup. Faith, the thread of my device is cracked, I may go sleep till the revelling music awake me.

Mer. And then too, Cupid, without you had prevented the fountain. Alas, poor god, that remembers not self-love to be proof against the violence of his quiver!

Well, I have a plot upon these prizers, for which I must presently find out Crites, and with his assistance pursue it to a high strain of laughter, or Mercury hath lost of his metal.   [_Exeunt._

ACT V.

SCENE I.[1]—_The same._

Enter Mercury _and_ Crites.

Mer. It is resolved on, Crites, you must do it.

Cri. The grace divinest Mercury hath done me,
In this vouchsafed discovery of himself,
Binds my observance in the utmost term
Of satisfaction to his godly will:
Though I profess, without the affectation
Of an enforced and formed austerity,
I could be willing to enjoy no place
With so unequal natures.

Mer. We believe it.
But for our sake, and to inflict just pains
On their prodigious follies, aid us now:
No man is presently made bad with ill.[2]
And good men, like the sea, should still
  maintain
Their noble taste in midst of all fresh
  humours
That flow about them, to corrupt their
  streams,
Bearing no season, much less salt of good-
  ness.
It is our purpose, Crites, to correct,
And punish, with our laughter, this night's
  sport,
Which our court-dors so heartily intend:
And by that worthy scorn, to make them
  know
How far beneath the dignity of man
Their serious and most practised actions
  are.

Cri. Ay, but though Mercury can war-
  rant out
His undertakings, and make all things good,
Out of the powers of his divinity,
Th' offence will be returned with weight on
  me,
That am a creature so despised and poor;
When the whole court shall take itself
  abused
By our ironical confederacy.

Mer. You are deceived. The better race
  in court,
That have the true nobility called virtue,[3]
Will apprehend it, as a grateful right
Done to their separate merit; and approve
The fit rebuke of so ridiculous heads,
Who with their apish customs and forced
  garbs
Would bring the name of courtier in con-
  tempt,
Did it not live unblemished in some few,
Whom equal Jove hath loved, and Phœbus
  formed
Of better metal, and in better mould.

Cri. Well, since my leader-on is Mercury,
I shall not fear to follow. If I fall,
My proper virtue shall be my relief,
That followed such a cause, and such a
  chief.   [_Exeunt._

SCENE II.—_Another Room in the same._

Enter Asotus _and_ Amorphus.

Aso. No more, if you love me, good master; you are incompatible to live withal: send me for the ladies!

Amo. Nay, but intend me.[4]

Aso. Fear me not; I warrant you, sir.

Amo. Render not yourself a refractory on the sudden. I can allow well, you should repute highly, heartily, and to the most, of your own endowments; it gives you forth to the world the more assured: but with reservation of an eye, to be

---

[1] The whole of what follows, to the entrance of Crites and Arete (near two-thirds of this immeasurable act), was first added in the folio, 1616. It consists of "inexplicable dumb shew," which, if the reader comprehends it, may not be unamusing.

[2] _No man is presently made bad with ill._] Opus est interprete; and, luckily, we find him in Juvenal, who is perfectly intelligible: "_Nemo repente fuit turpissimus._"

[3] _The true nobility called virtue,_] Mercury acts quite in character, and lays the poets under heavy contribution. This is from Juvenal— _Nobilitas sola est atque unica virtus._ Just below he contributes, with Virgil, to furnish a couple of lines:

"_Pauci quos æquus amavit_
Jupiter."

"_Quibus arte benigna,_
Et meliore luto finxit præcordia Titan."

[4] _Nay, but_ intend _me._] Note me heedfully. Our old writers sometimes use this word in the sense of attend; and sometimes for a higher and more active degree of observation. Jonson usually adopts the latter sense, as here, and in a former passage of this play, already noted:

"My soul
Is hurt with mere _intention_ on their follies."

always turned dutifully back upon your
teacher.

Aso. Nay, good sir, leave it to me.
Trust me with trussing all the points of
this action, I pray. 'Slid, I hope we shall
find wit to perform the science as well as
another.

Amo. I confess you to be of an apted[1]
and docible humour. Yet there are certain
punctilios, or (as I may more nakedly insinuate them), certain intrinsecate strokes
and wards, to which your activity is not
yet amounted, as your gentile dor in
colours. For supposition, your mistress
appears here in prize, ribanded with green
and yellow; now, it is the part of every
obsequious servant, to be sure to have daily
about him copy and variety of colours,[2] to
be presently answerable to any hourly or
half-hourly change in his mistress's revolution——

Aso. I know it, sir.

Amo. Give leave, I pray you—which, if
your antagonist, or player against you,
shall ignorantly be without, and yourself
can produce, you give him the **dor.**

Aso. Ay, ay, sir.

Amo. Or, if you can possess your opposite, that the green your mistress wears, is
her rejoicing or exultation in his service ;
the yellow, suspicion of his truth, from her
height of affection : and that he, greenly
credulous, shall withdraw thus, in private,
and from the abundance of his pocket (to
displace her jealous conceit) steal into his
hat the colour, whose blueness doth express trueness, she being not so, nor so
affected ; you give him the dor.[3]

Aso. Do not I know it, sir?

Amo. Nay, good——swell not above
your understanding. There is yet a third
dor in colours.

Aso. I know it too, I know it.

Amo. Do you know it too? what is it?
make good your knowledge.

Aso. Why, it is——no matter for that.

Amo. Do it, on pain of the dor.

Aso. Why ; what is't, say you?

Amo. Lo, you have given yourself the
dor. But I will remonstrate to you the
third dor, which is not, as the two former
dors, indicative, but deliberative : as how?
as thus. Your rivalis, with a dutiful and
serious care, lying in his bed, meditating
how to observe his mistress, dispatcheth his
lacquey to the chamber early, to know
what her colours are for the day, with
purpose to apply his wear that day accordingly : you lay wait before, preoccupy the
chambermaid, corrupt her to return false
colours ; he follows the fallacy, comes out
accoutred to his believed instructions ; your
mistress smiles, and you give him the
dor.

Aso. Why, so I told you, sir, I knew it.

Amo. Told me ! It is a strange outrecuidance :[4] your humour too much re-
doundeth.

---

[1] *I confess you to be of an* aped *and docible
humour.*] Here appears to be a mistake in the
word *aped*, and I am glad to have Mr. Theobald's conjecture in support of my own. I
imagined that *apted* was the true word ; and
confirmed by this authority, it has now a place
in the text.—WHAL.

I confess you to be of an apted, *&c.*] I have
not disturbed Whalley's reading, because it
affords very good sense : yet the old copies may
after all be right. *Apted*, in the fantastical language of Amorphus, may mean "having the
imitative qualities of an ape," and, therefore,
prone to learn. The reader must decide for
himself.

[2] *Now it is the part of an obsequious servant
to have daily about him* copy *and variety of*
colours, *&c.*] We have had this vile Latinism
(*copy*) for plenty already : others follow to
which it scarcely appears necessary to call the
reader's attention. With respect to *colours*, on
which the most learned commentary extant is
here furnished by Amorphus, it is only necessary
to observe that the gallants of the court (and
perhaps of the city) carried about with them
different coloured ribands, that they might be
prepared to place in their hats, or on their arms,
the colour in which their respective mistresses

dressed for the day. To this custom there are
numerous allusions. Thus in the *Parson's
Wedding:* "As visible in your face, as your
mistress's *colours* in your hat."—Act ii. sc. 7.
And in the *Antiquary :*

"I was so simple, mistress,
To wear your foolish colour," &c.

To a favourite, or accepted lover, a lady
would sometimes, as a mark of especial kind
ness, present a riband or some other ornamental
article of her dress ; this was guarded with
superstitious care :

"To lose't, or give't away, was such perdition
As nothing else could match."

See Massinger, vol. ii. p. 105.

[3] *You give him the* dor,] i.e., as I must remark
for the last time, baffle him, subject him to scorn.
The reader who hopes to understand any part of
the mummery which follows, must carefully
attend to these instructions.

[4] *It is a strange* outrecuidance.] Pride, arrogance, or presumption.—WHAL.

It should be observed that this strange petulance and forwardness in the once sheepish and
timid Asotus, is the effect of the waters of the
fountain of Self-love. No man ever preserved

Aso. Why, sir, what, do you think you know more?

Amo. I know that a cook may as soon and properly be said to smell well, as you to be wise. I know these are most clear and clean strokes. But then, you have your passages and imbrocatas in courtship; as the bitter bob in wit; the reverse in face or wry-mouth; and these more subtile and secure offenders. I will example unto you: Your opponent makes entry as you are engaged with your mistress. You seeing him, close in her ear with this whisper, *Here comes your baboon, disgrace him;* and withal stepping off, fall on his bosom, and turning to her, politicly, aloud say, Lady, regard this noble gentleman, a man rarely parted, second to none in this court; and then, stooping over his shoulder, your hand on his breast, your mouth on his backside, you give him the reverse stroke, with this sanna, or stork's-bill,[1] which makes up your wit's bob most bitter.

Aso. Nay, for heaven's sake, teach me no more. I know all as well——'Slid, if I did not, why was I nominated? why did you choose me? why did the ladies prick out me? I am sure there were other gallants. But me of all the rest! By that light, and, as I am a courtier, would I might never stir, but 'tis strange. Would to the lord the ladies would come once!

Enter Morphides.

Morp. Signior, the gallants and ladies are at hand. Are you ready, sir?

Amo. Instantly. Go, accomplish your attire. [*Exit* Asotus.] Cousin Morphides, assist me to make good the door with your officious tyranny.

Citizen [*within.*] By your leave, my masters there, pray you let's come by.

Pages [*within*]. You by! why should you come by more than we?

Citizen's Wife [*within.*] Why, sir! because he is my brother that plays the prizes.

Morp. Your brother!

Citizen [*within.*] Ay, her brother, sir, and we must come in.

Tailor [*within.*] Why, what are you?

Citizen [*within.*] I am her husband, sir.

Tailor [*within.*] Then thrust forward your head.

Amo. What tumult is there?

Morp. Who's there? bear back there! Stand from the door!

Amo. Enter none but the ladies and their hang-byes.

Enter Phantaste, Philautia, Argurion, Moria, Hedon, *and* Anaides, *introducing two* Ladies.

Welcome, beauties, and your kind shadows.

Hed. This country lady, my friend, good Signior Amorphus.

Ana. And my cockatrice here.

Amo. She is welcome.

The Citizen *and his* Wife, Pages, *&c., appear at the door.*

Morp. Knock those same pages there; and, goodman coxcomb the citizen, who would you speak withal?

Wife. My brother.

Amo. With whom? Your brother!

Morp. Who is your brother?

Wife. Master Asotus.

Amo. Master Asotus! is he your brother? he is taken up with great persons; he is not to know you to-night.

Re-enter Asotus, *hastily.*

Aso. O Jove, master! an there come e'er a citizen gentlewoman in my name, let her have entrance, I pray you: it is my sister.

Wife. Brother!

Cit. [*thrusting in.*] Brother, Master Asotus!

Aso. Who's there?

Wife. 'Tis I, brother.

Aso. Gods me, there she is! good master, intrude her.

Morp. Make place! bear back there!

Enter Citizen's Wife.

Amo. Knock that simple fellow there.

Wife. Nay, good sir, it is my husband.

---

the consistency of his characters with such scrupulous, such unbending circumspection, as our great poet. If it were ever true of any English dramatic writer, that his dialogue might be correctly appropriated to the several speakers, without seeing their names, I do not hesitate to affirm that it was so of Jonson above all that ever wrote.

[1] *With this* sanna, *or* stork's-bill.] *Sanna* is

a Latin word which implies some gesture of scorn and contempt; which the poet calls *stork's-bill,* in allusion to the *ciconia* of the ancients; a manner of deriding a person, by extending the forefinger at him. See Casaubon on this verse of Persius:

"*O Jane, à tergo quem nulla ciconia pinsit.*"
                                    WHAL.

Mor. The simpler fellow he.—Away! back with your head, sir!

[*Pushes the Citizen back.*

Aso. Brother, you must pardon your non-entry: husbands are not allowed here, in truth. I'll come home soon with my sister; pray you meet us with a lantern, brother. Be merry, sister; I shall make you laugh anon.   [*Exit.*

Pha. Your prizer is not ready, Amorphus.

Amo. Apprehend your places; he shall be soon, and at all points.

Ana. Is there anybody come to answer him? shall we have any sport?

Amo. Sport of importance; howsoever, give me the gloves.

Hed. Gloves! why gloves, signior?

Phi. What's the ceremony?

Amo. [*distributing gloves.*] Beside their received fitness, at all prizes, they are here properly accommodate to the nuptials of my scholar's 'haviour to the lady Courtship. Please you apparel your hands. Madam Phantaste, Madam Philautia, guardian, Signior Hedon, Signior Anaides, gentlemen all, ladies.

All. Thanks, good Amorphus.

Amo. I will now call forth my provost, and present him.   [*Exit.*

Ana. Heart! why should not we be masters as well as he?

Hed. That's true, and play our masters' prizes as well as the t'other?

Mor. In sadness, for using your court-weapons, methinks you may.

Pha. Nay, but why should not we ladies play our prizes, I pray? I see no reason but we should take them down at their own weapons.

Phi. Troth, and so we may, if we handle them well.

Wife. Ay, indeed, forsooth, madam, if 'twere in the city, we would think foul scorn but we would, forsooth.

Pha. Pray you, what should we call your name?

Wife. My name is Downfall.

Hed. Good Mistress Downfall! I am sorry your husband could not get in.

Wife. 'Tis no matter for him, sir.

Ana. No, no, she has the more liberty for herself.   [*A flourish.*

Pha. Peace, peace! they come.

Re-enter Amorphus, *introducing* Asotus *in a full-dress suit.*

Amo. So, keep up your ruff; the tincture of your neck is not all so pure, but it will ask it. Maintain your sprig upright! your cloke on your half-shoulder falling; so: I will read your bill, advance it, and present you.—Silence!

" Be it known[1] to all that profess courtship, by these presents (from the white satin reveller, to the cloth of tissue and bodkin) that we, Ulysses-Polytropus-Amorphus, master of the noble and subtile science of courtship, do give leave and licence to our provost, Acolastus-Polypragmon-Asotus, to play his master's prize, against all masters whatsoever, in this subtile mystery, at these four, the choice and most cunning weapons of court-compliment, viz. the BARE ACCOST; the BETTER REGARD; the SOLEMN ADDRESS; and the PERFECT CLOSE. These are therefore to give notice to all comers, that he, the said Acolastus-Polypragmon-Asotus, is here present (by the help of his mercer, tailor, milliner, sempster, and so forth) at his designed hour, in this fair gallery, the present day of this present month, to perform and do his uttermost for the achievement and bearing away of the prizes, which are these: viz. For the Bare Accost, two wall-eyes in a face forced: for the Better Regard, a face favourably simpering, with a fan waving: for the Solemn Address, two lips wagging, and never a wise word: for the Perfect Close, a wring by the hand, with a banquet in a corner.   And Phœbus save Cynthia!"

Appeareth no man yet, to answer the prizer? no voice?—Music, give them their summons.   [*Music.*

Pha. The solemnity of this is excellent.

Amo. Silence! Well, I perceive your name is their terror, and keepeth them back.

Aso. I 'faith, master, let's go; nobody comes. *Victus, victa, victum; victi, victæ, victi*—let's be retrograde.

Amo. Stay. That were dispunct to the ladies. Rather ourself shall be your encounter. Take your state up to the wall;[2]

---

[1] *Be it known, &c.*] This *bill* is a parody on one of the licences formerly granted by *masters* of defence to their pupils, when they were supposed to be properly qualified for taking either of their three degrees in the fencing-school, viz., a *master's,* a *provost's,* or a *scholar's*: indeed, the whole of this scene is a burlesque imitation of these public trials of skill in the "noble science of defence."

[2] *Take your state up to the wall;*] The *state* sometimes means the raised platform and canopy under which the ornamented chair was placed,

and, lady [*leading* Moria *to the state*] may
we implore you to stand forth, as first term
or bound to our courtship.

Hed. 'Fore heaven, 'twill shew rarely.

Amo. Sound a charge.   [*A charge.*

Ana. A pox on't! Your vulgar wits
count this fabulous and impudent now! by
that candle, they'll never conceit it.

        [*They act their Accost severally to*
                                    Moria.

Pha. Excellent well! admirable!

Phi. Peace!

Hed. Most fashionably, believe it.

Phi. O, he is a well-spoken gentleman.

Pha. Now the other.

Phi. Very good.

Hed. For a scholar, Honour.

Ana. O, 'tis too Dutch. He reels too
much.   [*A flourish.*

Hed. This weapon is done.

Amo. No, we have our two bouts at
every weapon; expect.

Cri. [*within.*] Where be these gallants,
and their brave prizer here?

Morp. Who's there? bear back: keep
the door.

        Enter Crites, *introducing* Mercury,
                fantastically dressed.

Amo. What are you, sir?

Cri. By your licence, grand-master.——
Come forward, sir.   [*To* Mercury.

Ana. Heart! who let in that rag there
amongst us? Put him out, an impecunious
creature.

Hed. Out with him!

Morp. Come, sir.

Amo. You must be retrograde.

Cri. Soft, sir, I am truchman,[1] and do
flourish before this monsieur, or French-
behaved gentleman, here; who is drawn
hither by report of your chartels, advanced
in court, to prove his fortune with your
prizer, so he may have fair play shewn him,
and the liberty to choose his stickler.[2]

Amo. Is he a master?

Cri. That, sir, he has to shew here; and

confirmed under the hands of the most
skilful and cunning complimentaries alive:[3]
Please you read, sir.

                  [*Gives him a certificate.*

Amo. What shall we do?

Ana. Death! disgrace this fellow in the
black stuff, whatever you do.

Amo. Why, but he comes with the
stranger.

Hed. That's no matter: he is our own
countryman.

Ana. Ay, and he is a scholar besides.
You may disgrace him here with authority.[4]

Amo. Well, see these first.

Aso. Now shall I be observed by yon
scholar till I sweat again; I would to
Jove it were over.

Cri. [*to* Mercury.] Sir, this is the wight
of worth that dares you to the encounter.
A gentleman of so pleasing and ridiculous
a carriage; as, even standing, carries meat
in the mouth, you see; and, I assure you,
although no bred courtling, yet a most
particular man, of goodly havings, well
fashioned 'haviour, and of as hardened and
excellent a bark as the most naturally qualified amongst them, informed, reformed, and
transformed from his original cityciem; by
this elixir, or mere magazine of man. And,
for your spectators, you behold them what
they are: the most choice particulars in
court: this tells tales well; this provides
coaches; this repeats jests; this presents
gifts; this holds up the arras; this takes
down from horse; this protests by this
light; this swears by that candle; this
delighteth; this adoreth: yet all but three
men. Then, for your ladies, the most
proud, witty creatures, all things appre-
hending, nothing understanding, perpetually laughing, curious maintainers of
fools, mercers, and minstrels, costly to be
kept, miserably keeping, all disdaining but
their painter and apothecary, 'twixt whom
and them there is this reciprock commerce,
their beauties maintain their painters, and
their painters their beauties.

---

and sometimes, as here, the chair itself. Instances of both these senses are so common in
our old writers, that it seems sufficient just to
have noticed them.

  [1] *Sir, I am truchman,*] i.e., interpreter: the
word is originally Turkish.—WHAL.

  Is it not rather a miserable corruption of the
modern Greek, δραγωμανος? [Dragoman.]

  [2] *To choose his* stickler.] *Sticklers* were side-
men to fencers, or seconds in a duel; and were
so called from the *sticks*, or wands, which they
carried to part the combatants before blood was
drawn.—WHAL.

  [3] *The most cunning* complimentaries *alive*:]
Complimentaries were masters of defence, such
as Caranza, &c., who published elaborate
works on the *compliments* and ceremonies of
duelling.

  [4] *He is our own* countryman.——*Ay, and a*
scholar besides. *You may disgrace him with
authority.*] "Let us cast nothing away," says
Pandarus, "for we know not what use we may
have for it." Anaides has lately found admirers in the North, who have put his notable
maxim in practice with great perseverance and
success [Edinburgh Reviewers, to wit].

Mer. Sir, you have played the painter yourself, and limned them to the life. I desire to deserve before them.

Amo. [*returning the certificate.*] This is authentic.   We must resolve to entertain the monsieur, howsoever we neglect him.[1]

Hed. Come, let's all go together, and salute him.

Ana. Content, and not look on the other.

Amo. Well devised ; and a most punishing disgrace.

Hed. On.

Amo. Monsieur, we must not so much betray ourselves to discourtship, as to suffer you to be longer unsaluted : please you to use the state ordained for the opponent ; in which nature, without envy, we receive you.

Hed. And embrace you.

Ana. And commend us to you, sir.

Phi. Believe it, he is a man of excellent silence.

Pha. He keeps all his wit for action.

Ana. This hath discountenanced our scholaris, most richly.

Hed. Out of all emphasis. The monsieur sees we regard him not.

Amo. Hold on ; make it known how bitter a thing it is not to be looked on in court.

Hed. 'Slud, will he call him to him yet ! Does not monsieur perceive our disgrace ?

Ana. Heart ! he is a fool, I see. We have done ourselves wrong to grace him.

Hed. 'Slight, what an ass was I to embrace him !

Cri. Illustrious and fearful judges——

Hed. Turn away, turn away.

Crt. It is the suit of the strange opponent (to whom you ought not to turn your tails, and whose noses I must follow) that he may have the justice, before he encounter his respected adversary, to see some light stroke of his play, commenced with some other.

Hed. Answer not him, but the stranger ; we will not believe him.

Amo. I will demand him myself.

Cri. O dreadful disgrace, if a man were so foolish to feel it !

Amo. Is it your suit, monsieur, to see some prelude of my scholar ? Now, sure the monsieur wants language——

Hed. And take upon him to be one of the accomplished ! 'Slight, that's a good jest ; would we could take him with that nullity.—*Non sapete voi parlar' Italiano!*

Ana. 'Sfoot, the carp has no tongue.[2]

Cri. Signior, in courtship, you are to bid your abettors forbear, and satisfy the monsieur's request.

Amo. Well, I will strike him more silent with admiration, and terrify his daring hither. He shall behold my own play with my scholar. Lady, with the touch of your white hand, let me reinstate you. [*Leads* Moria *back to the state.*]   Provost, [*to* Asotus,] begin to me at the *Bare Accost.*[3] [*A charge.*] Now, for the honour of my discipline.

Hed. Signior Amorphus, reflect, reflect : what means he by that mouthed wave?

Cri. He is in some distaste of your fellow-disciple.

Mer. Signior, your scholar might have played well still, if he could have kept his seat longer : I have enough of him now. He is a mere piece of glass, I see through him by this time.

Amo. You come not to give us the scorn, monsieur?

Mer. Nor to be frighted with a face, signior. I have seen the lions. You must pardon me. I shall be loth to hazard a reputation with one that has not a reputation to lose.

Amo. How !

Cri. Meaning your pupil, sir.

Ana. This is that black devil there.

Amo. You do offer a strange affront, monsieur.

Cri. Sir, he shall yield you all the honour of a competent adversary, if you please to undertake him.

Mer. I am prest for the encounter.[4]

---

[1] *Howsoever we neglect* him,] i.e., the "impecunious fellow in the black stuff," Crites.

[2] *'Sfoot, the carp has no tongue.*] See the *Alchemist.*

[3] Provost, *begin to me at the Bare Accost.*] It appears from this term (*provost*) that Asotus had obtained his second degree in the school of courtship. Of the mummery which follows I comprehend but little ; that little, however, is more than I can pretend to make intelligible to the reader.

[4] *I am prest for the encounter.*] I am ready, I am prepared. Thus Spenser :

" Who him affronting soone to fight was readie prest :"

And Beaumont and Fletcher :

" However, stand prepared, *prest* for our journey."—*Wildegoose Chase.* WHAL.

Amo. Me! challenge me!

Aso. What, my master, sir! 'Slight, monsieur, meddle with me, do you hear: but do not meddle with my master.

Mer. Peace, good squib, go out.

Cri. And stink, he bids you.

Aso. Master!

Amo. Silence! I do accept him. Sit you down and observe. Me! he never profest a thing at more charges.——Prepare yourself, sir.—Challenge me! I will prosecute what disgrace my hatred can dictate to me.

Cri. How tender a traveller's spleen is! Comparison to men that deserve least, is ever most offensive.

Amo. You are instructed in our chartel, and know our weapons?

Mer. I appear not without their notice, sir.

Aso. But must I lose the prizes, master?

Amo. I will win them for you; be patient.—Lady, [*to* Moria.] vouchsafe the tenure of this ensign.—Who shall be your stickler?

Mer. Behold him.   [*Points to* Crites.

Amo. I would not wish you a weaker.—Sound, musics.—I provoke you at the Bare Accost.   [*A charge.*

Pha. Excellent comely!

Cri. And worthily studied. This is the exalted foretop.

Hed. O, his leg was too much produced.

Ana. And his hat was carried scurvily.

Phi. Peace; let's see the monsieur's Accost. Rare!

Pha. Sprightly and short.

Ana. True, it is the French courteau:[1] he lacks but to have his nose slit.

Hed. He does hop. He does bound too much.   [*A flourish.*

Amo. The second bout, to conclude this weapon.   [*A charge.*

Pha. Good, believe it!

Phi. An excellent offer!

Cri. This is called the solemn bandstring.

Hed. Foh, that cringe was not put home.

Ana. He makes a face like a stabbed Lucrece.[2]

Aso. Well, he would needs take it upon

him, but would I had done it for all this He makes me sit still here, like a baboon as I am.

Cri. Making villainous faces.

Phi. See, the French prepares it richly.

Cri. Ay, this is ycleped the Serious Trifle.

Ana. 'Slud, 'tis the horse-start out o' the brown study.

Cri. Rather the bird-eyed stroke, sir. Your observance is too blunt, sir.

        [*A flourish.*

Amo. Judges, award the prize. Take breath, sir. This bout hath been laborious.

Aso. And yet your critic, or your besogno,[3] will think these things foppery, and easy, now!

Cri. Or rather mere lunacy. For would any reasonable creature make these his serious studies and perfections, much less, only live to these ends? to be the false pleasure of a few, the true love of none, and the just laughter of all?

Hed. We must prefer the monsieur, we courtiers must be partial.

Ana. Speak, guardian. Name the prize, at the Bare Accost.

Mor. A pair of wall eyes in a face forced.

Ana. Give the monsieur. Amorphus hath lost his eyes.

Amo. I! Is the palate of your judgment down? Gentles, I do appeal.

Aso. Yes, master, to me: the judges be fools.

Ana. How now, sir! tie up your tongue, mungrel. He cannot appeal.

Aso. Say you, sir?

Ana. Sit you still, sir.

Aso. Why, so I do; do not I, I pray you?

Mer. Remercie, madame, and these honourable censors.

Amo. Well, to the second weapon, the Better Regard. I will encounter you better. Attempt.

Hed. Sweet Honour.

Phi. What says my good Ambition?

Hed. Which take you at this next weapon? I lay a Discretion with you on Amorphus's head.

Phi. Why, I take the French behaved gentleman.

---

[1] *It is the French* courteau:] i.e., bidet, a little active horse: whence our curtal.

[2] *He makes a face like a* stabbed *Lucrece.*] Perhaps the poet alludes to Purfoote the printer's sign of Lucretia, in St. Paul's churchyard. This lady, with the dagger at her breast and a ridiculous expression of agony in her face, formed a vignette to most of his books: the same figure was also stamped on the covers of them. Several of his books thus ornamented, Mr. Steevens says, are in the British Museum.

[3] *Or your* besogno,] i.e., your beggar, your needy wretch: he alludes to Crites. This contemptuous term is very common in our old writers. See Massinger, vol. iii. 67.

Hed. 'Tis done, a Discretion.

Cri. A Discretion ! A pretty court-wager ! Would any discreet person hazard his wit so?

Pha. I'll lay a Discretion with you, Anaides.

Ana. Hang 'em, I'll not venture a doit of Discretion on either of their heads.

Cri. No, he should venture all then.

Ana. I like none of their plays.
                                        [*A charge.*

Hed. See, see ! this is strange play !

Ana. 'Tis too full of uncertain motion. He hobbles too much.

Cri. 'Tis called your court-staggers, sir.

Hed. That same fellow talks so now he has a place !

Ana. Hang him ! neglect him.

Mer. "Your good ladyship's affectioned."

Wife. Ods so ! they speak at this weapon, brother.

Aso. They must do so, sister ; how should it be the Better Regard, else ?

Pha. Methinks he did not this respectively enough.

Phi. Why, the monsieur but dallies with him.

Hed. Dallies ! 'Slight, see ! he'll put him to 't in earnest.—Well done, Amorphus !

Ana. That puff was good indeed.

Cri. Ods me ! this is desperate play : he hits himself o' the shins.

Hed. An he make this good through, he carries it, I warrant him.

Cri. Indeed he displays his feet rarely.

Hed. See, see ! he does the respective leer damnably well.

Amo. "The true idolater of your beauties shall never pass their deities unadored: I rest your poor knight."

Hed. See, now the oblique leer, or the Janus: he satisfies all with that aspect most nobly.   [*A flourish.*

Cri. And most terribly he comes off; like your rodomontado.

Pha. How like you this play, Anaides?

Ana. Good play ; but 'tis too rough and boisterous.

Amo. I will second it with a stroke easier, wherein I will prove his language.
                                        [*A charge.*

Ana. This is filthy, and grave, now.

Hed. O, 'tis cool and wary play. We must not disgrace our own camerade too much.

Amo. "Signora, ho tanto obligo per le favore resciuto da lei ; che veramente desidero con tutto il core, à remunerarla in parte : e sicurative, signora mea cara, chè io sera sempre pronto à servirla, e honorarla. Bascio le mane de vo' signoria."

Cri. The Venetian dop this.[1]

Pha. Most unexpectedly excellent ! The French goes down certain.

Aso. "As buckets are put down into a well ;
Or as a school-boy——"

Cri. Truss up your simile, jackdaw, and observe.

Hed. Now the monsieur is moved.

Ana. Bo-peep !

Hed. O, most antick.

Cri. The French quirk, this, sir.

Ana. Heart, he will over-run her.

Mer. "Madamoyselle, Je voudroy que pouvoy monstrer mon affection, mais je suis tant malheureuse, ci froid, ci layd, ci—Je ne scay qui de dire—excuse moi, Je suis tout vostre."   [*A flourish.*

Phi. O brave and spirited ! he's a right Jovialist.

Pha. No, no : Amorphus's gravity outweighs it.

Cri. And yet your lady, or your feather, would outweigh both.

Ana. What's the prize, lady, at this Better Regard?

Mor. A face favourably simpering, and a fan waving.

Ana. They have done doubtfully. Divide. Give the favourable face to the signior, and the light wave to the monsieur.

Ana. You become the simper well, lady.

Mer. And the wag better.

Amo. Now to our *Solemn Address.* Please the well-graced Philautia to relieve the lady sentinel; she hath stood long.

Phi. With all my heart ; come, guardian, resign your place.
                [*Moria comes from the state.*

Amo. Monsieur, furnish yourself with what solemnity of ornament you think fit for this third weapon ; at which you are to shew all the cunning of stroke your devotion can possibly devise.

Mer. Let me alone, sir. I'll sufficiently decipher your amorous solemnities.—Crites, have patience. See, if I hit not all their practic observance, with which they lime twigs to catch their fantastic lady-birds.

---

[1] *The Venetian* dop this.] The *dop* is the dip, a very low bow, or curtesy. I have not attempted to correct the complimentary jargon in the preceding speech, or in that of Mercury below ; as the poet perhaps meant to display his courtier's ignorance in them.

Cri. Ay, but you should do more charitably to do it more openly, that they might
discover themselves mocked in these monstrous affections.   [*A charge.*

Mer. Lackey, where's the tailor?

Enter Tailor, Barber, Perfumer, Milliner,
Jeweller, *and* Feather-maker.

Tai. Here, sir.

Hed. See, they have their tailor, barber,
perfumer, milliner, jeweller, feather-maker,
all in common!

    [*They make themselves ready on the
    stage.*

Ana. Ay, this is pretty.

Amo. Here is a hair too much, take it off.
Where are thy mullets?[1]

Mer. Is this pink of equal proportion to
this cut, standing off this distance from it?

Tai. That it is, sir.

Mer. Is it so, sir? You impudent poltroon, you slave, you list, you shreds,
you——   [*Beats the* Tailor.

Hed. Excellent! This was the best yet.

Ana. Why, we must use our tailors thus:
this is our true magnanimity.

Mer. Come, go to, put on; we must bear
with you for the times' sake.

Amo. Is the perfume rich in this jerkin?

Per. Taste, smell; I assure you, sir, pure
benjamin,[2] the only spirited scent that ever
awaked a Neapolitan nostril. You would
wish yourself all nose for the love on't. I
frotted a jerkin for a new-revenued gentleman yielded me threescore crowns but this
morning, and the same titillation.

Amo. I savour no sampsuchine in it.[3]

Per. I am a Nulli-fidian,[4] if there be not
three-thirds of a scruple more of sampsu-
chinum in this confection than ever I put
in any. I'll tell you all the ingredients,
sir.

Amo. You shall be simple to discover
your simples.

Per. Simple! why, sir? What reck I
to whom I discover? I have in it musk,
civet, amber, Phœnicobalanus, the decoction of turmerick, sesana, nard, spikenard,

calamus odoratus, stacte, opobalsamum,
amomum, storax, ladanum, aspalathum,
opoponax, œnanthe. And what of all
these now? what are you the better? Tut,
it is the sorting, and the dividing, and the
mixing, and the tempering, and the searching, and the decocting, that makes the
fumigation and the suffumigation.

Amo. Well, indue me with it.

Per. I will, sir.

Hed. An excellent confection.

Cri. And most worthy a true voluptuary.
Jove! what a coil these musk-worms take
to purchase another's delight? for themselves, who bear the odours, have ever the
least sense of them. Yet I do like better
the prodigality of jewels and clothes, whereof
one passeth to a man's heirs; the other at
least wears out time. This presently expires, and, without continual riot in repa-
ration, is lost: which whoso strives to keep,
it is one special argument to me, that,
affecting to smell better than other men, he
doth indeed smell far worse.

Mer. I know you will say, it sits well,
sir.

Tai. Good faith, if it do not, sir, let
your mistress be judge.

Mer. By heaven, if my mistress do not
like it, I'll make no more conscience to
undo thee than to undo an oyster.

Tai. Believe it, there's ne'er a mistress
in the world can mislike it.

Mer. No, not goodwife tailor, your
mistress; that has only the judgment to
heat your pressing-tool. But for a court-
mistress that studies these decorums, and
knows the proportion of every cut to a hair,
knows why such a colour is cut upon such
a colour, and when a satin is cut upon six
taffatæs, will look that we should dive into
the depth of the cut——Give me my scarf.
Shew some ribands, sirrah. Have you the
feather?

Feat. Ay, sir.

Mer. Have you the jewel?

Jew. Yes, sir.

Mer. What must I give for the hire on't?

Jew. You shall give me six crowns, sir.

---

[1] *Where are thy* mullets?] *Mullets* are small
pincers, answering perhaps to our curling-irons.
The word is in Coles's English Dictionary: but
I can give no example of its use by Jonson's
contemporaries.

[2] *Pure* benjamin.] Benjamin or benjouin is
an aromatic gum, sent into these parts from the
East, from whence it is probable the name itself
came likewise.—WHAL.

In the next line there is an allusion to Martial:

"*Totum te cupias, Fabulle, nasum.*"

[3] *I savour no* sampsuchine *in it.*] Sampsuchine is sweet marjoram, an herb much in
repute once for its sanative virtues.

[4] *I am a* Nulli-fidian,] An unbeliever, an
atheist, or, in the modern phrase, a free-thinker:
the perfumer seems to use the word for a person
of no honour or credit, which is not much
amiss.

Mer. Six crowns! By heaven 'twere a good deed to borrow it of thee to shew, and never let thee have it again.

Jew. I hope your worship will not do so, sir.

Mer. By Jove, sir, there be such tricks stirring, I can tell you, and worthily too. Extorting knaves, that live by these court-decorums, and yet——What's your jewel worth, I pray?

Jew. A hundred crowns, sir.

Mer. A hundred crowns, and six for the loan on't an hour! what's that in the hundred for the year? These impostors would not be hanged! Your thief is not comparable to them, by Hercules. Well, put it in, and the feather; you will have it an you shall, and the pox give you good on't!

Amo. Give me my confects, my mosca-dini, and place those colours in my hat.

Mer. These are Bolognian ribands, I warrant you.

Mil. In truth, sir, if they be not right Granado silk——

Mer. A pox on you, you'll all say so.

Mil. You give me not a penny, sir.

Mer. Come, sir, perfume my devant;[1]

"May it ascend, like solemn sacrifice,
Into the nostrils of the Queen of Love!"

Hed. Your French ceremonies are the best.

Ana. Monsieur, signior, your Solemn Address is too long; the ladies long to have you come on.

Amo. Soft, sir, our coming on is not so easily prepared. Signior Fig!

Per. Ay, sir.

Amo. Can you help my complexion, here?

Per. O yes, sir, I have an excellent mineral fucus for the purpose. The gloves are right, sir; you shall bury them in a muck-hill, a draught, seven years, and take them out and wash them, they shall still retain their first scent, true Spanish. There's ambre in the umbre.[2]

Mer. Your price, sweet Fig?

Per. Give me what you will, **sir; the** signior pays me two crowns a pair; you shall give me your love, sir.

Mer. My love! with a pox to you, goodman Sassafras.

Per. I come, sir. There's an excellent diapasm in a chain too,[3] if you like it.

Amo. Stay, what are the ingredients to your fucus?

Per. Nought but sublimate and crude mercury, sir, well prepared and dulcified, with the jaw-bones of a sow, burnt, beaten, and searced.[4]

Amo. I approve it. Lay it on.

Mer. I'll have your chain of pomander, sirrah; what's your price?

Per. We'll agree, monsieur; I'll assure you it was both decocted and dried where no sun came, and kept in an onyx ever since it was balled.

Mer. Come, invert my mustachio, and we have done.

Amo. 'Tis good.

Bar. Hold still, I pray you, sir.

Per. Nay, the fucus is exorbitant, sir.

Mer. Death, dost thou burn me, harlot!

Bar. I beseech you, sir.

Mer. Beggar, varlet, poltroon.
                              [*Beats him.*

Hed. Excellent, excellent!

Ana. Your French beat is the most natural beat of the world.

Aso. O that I had played at this weapon!
                              [*A charge.*

Pha. Peace, now they come on; the second part.

Amo. "Madam, your beauties being so attractive, I muse you are left thus alone."

Phi. "Better be alone, sir, than ill ac-companied."

Amo. "Nought can be ill, lady, that can come near your goodness."

Mer. "Sweet madam, on what part of you soever a man casts his eye, he meets with perfection; you are the lively image of Venus throughout; all the graces smile in your cheeks; your beauty nourishes as well as delights; you have a tongue steeped in honey, and a breath like a panther;[5] your breasts and forehead are whiter than goat's

---

[1] *Come, sir, perfume my* devant;] Meaning, perhaps, his "predominant," his foretop: but I would not have the reader rely too securely on these and similar attempts at explanation, which, at best, are but lucky guesses.

[2] *There's* ambre *in the* umbre.] There's ambergris in the dye. The gloves, I suppose, were of a brown colour.

[3] *There's an excellent* diapasm *in a chain,*]

Diapasms are aromatic herbs dried, and reduced to powder; they were formerly made into little balls with sweet water, and strung together as here, or worn loose in the pocket. This is the "pomander chain," mentioned just below.

[4] *Searced,*] i.e., finely sifted.

[5] *A breath like a panther,*] i.e., sweet. See the *Fox.*

milk or May blossoms ; a cloud is not so soft as your skin——"

Hed. Well strook, monsieur ! He charges like a Frenchman indeed, thick and hotly.[1]

Mer. "Your cheeks are Cupid's baths, wherein he uses to steep himself in milk and nectar : he does light all his torches at your eyes, and instructs you how to shoot and wound with their beams. Yet I love nothing in you more than your innocence ; you retain so native a simplicity, so unblamed a behaviour ! Methinks, with such a love, I should find no head, nor foot of my pleasure : you are the very spirit of a lady."

Ana. Fair play, monsieur, you are too hot on the quarry ; give your competitor audience.

Amo. "Lady, how stirring soever the monsieur's tongue is, he will lie by your side more dull than your eunuch."

Ana. A good stroke ; that mouth was excellently put over.

Amo. "You are fair, lady——"

Cri. You offer foul, signior, to close ; keep your distance ; for all your bravo rampant here.

Amo. "I say you are fair, lady, let your choice be fit, as you are fair."

Mer. "I say ladies do never believe they are fair, till some fool begins to doat upon them."

Phi. You play too rough, gentlemen.

Amo. "Your Frenchified fool is your only fool, lady : I do yield to this honourable monsieur in all civil and humane courtesy.   [*A flourish.*

Mer. Buz !

Ana. Admirable. Give him the prize, give him the prize : that mouth again was most courtly hit, and rare.

Amo. I knew I should pass upon him with the bitter bob.

Hed. O, but the reverse was singular.

Pha. It was most subtile, Amorphus.

Aso. If I had done 't, it should have been better.

Mer. How heartily they applaud this, Crites !

Cri. You suffer them too long.

Mer. I'll take off their edge instantly.

Ana. Name the prize, at the *Solemn Address.*

---

[1] *He charges like a Frenchman indeed, thick and hotly.*] This, as Whalley observes, is from Florus. "*Sicut primus impetus eis major quam virorum est, ita sequens minor quam feminarum.*"—Lib. ii. c. iv.

Phi. Two lips wagging.

Cri. And never a wise word, I take it.

Ana. Give to Amorphus. And, upon him again ; let him not draw free breath.

Amo. Thanks, fair deliverer, and my honourable judges. Madam Phantaste, you are our worthy object at this next weapon.

Pha. Most covetingly ready, Amorphus.
                    [*She takes the state instead of Philautia.*

Hed. Your monsieur is crest-fallen.

Ana. So are most of them once a year.

Amo. You will see, I shall now give him the gentle Dor presently, he forgetting to shift the colours, which are now changed with alteration of the mistress. At your last weapon, sir. *The Perfect Close.* Set forward. [*A charge.*] Intend your approach, monsieur.

Mer. 'Tis yours, signior.

Amo. With your example, sir.

Mer. Not I, sir.

Amo. It is your right.

Mer. By no possible means.

Amo. You have the way.

Mer. As I am noble——

Amo. As I am virtuous——

Mer. Pardon me, sir.

Amo. I will die first.

Mer. You are a tyrant in courtesy.

Amo. He is removed. [*Stays Mercury on his moving.*] Judges, bear witness.

Mer. What of that, sir ?

Amo. You are removed, sir.

Mer. Well.

Amo. I challenge you ; you have received the Dor. Give me the prize.

Mer. Soft, sir. How, the Dor ?

Amo. The common mistress, you see, is changed.

Mer. Right, sir.

Amo. And you have still in your hat the former colours.

Mer. You lie, sir, I have none : I have pulled them out. I meant to play discoloured.   [*A flourish.*

Cri. The Dor, the Dor, the Dor, the Dor, the Dor, the palpable Dor !

Ana. Heart of my blood, Amorphus, what have you done ? stuck a disgrace upon us all, and at your last weapon !

Aso. I could have done no more.

Hed. By heaven, it was most unfortunate luck.

Ana. Luck ! by that candle, it was mere rashness, and oversight ; would any man have ventured to play so open, and forsake his ward ? D—n me, if he have not eter-

O

nally undone himself in court, and discountenanced us that were his main countenance, by it.

Amo. Forgive it now : it was the solecism of my stars.

Cri. The Wring by the hand, and the Banquet, is ours.

Mer. O, here's a lady feels like a wench of the first year; you would think her hand did melt in your touch ; and the bones of her fingers ran out at length when you prest 'em, they are so gently delicate ! He that had the grace to print a kiss on these lips, should taste wine and rose-leaves. O, she kisses as close as a cockle. Let's take them down, as deep as our hearts, wench, till our very souls mix. Adieu, signior : good faith, I shall drink to you at supper, sir.

Ana. Stay, monsieur. Who awards you the prize ?

Cri. Why, his proper merit, sir ; you see he has played down your grand garb-master here.

Ana. That's not in your logic to determine, sir : you are no courtier. This is none of your seven or nine beggarly sciences, but a certain mystery above them, wherein we that have skill must pronounce, and not such fresh men as you are.

Cri. Indeed, I must declare myself to you no profest courtling ; nor to have any excellent stroke at your subtile weapons ; yet if you please, I dare venture a hit with you, or your fellow, Sir Dagonet, here.

Ana. With me ?

Cri. Yes, sir.

Ana. Heart, I shall never have such a fortune to save myself in a fellow again, and your two reputations, gentlemen, as in this. I'll undertake him.

Hed. Do, and swinge him soundly, good Anaides.

Ana. Let me alone; I'll play other manner of play than has been seen yet. I would the prize lay on't !

Mer. It shall if you will, I forgive my right.

Ana. Are you so confident ! what's your weapon ?

Cri. At any, I, sir.

Mer. The Perfect Close, that's now the best.

Ana. Content, I'll pay your scholarity. Who offers ?

Cri. Marry, that will I : I dare give you that advantage too.

Ana. You dare ! well, look to your liberal sconce.

Amo. Make your play still, upon the answer, sir.

Ana. Hold your peace, you are a hobbyhorse.

Aso. Sit by me, master.

Mer. Now, Crites, strike home.

[*A charge.*

Cri. You shall see me undo the assured swaggerer with a trick, instantly : I will play all his own play before him ; court the wench in his garb, in his phrase, with his face ; leave him not so much as a look, an eye, a stalk, or an imperfect oath, to express himself by, after me.

[*Aside to* Mercury.

Mer. Excellent, Crites.

Ana. When begin you, sir ? have you consulted ?

Cri. To your cost, sir. Which is the piece stands forth to be courted ? O, are you she ? [*To* Philautia.] " Well, madam, or sweet lady, it is so, I do love you in some sort, do you conceive ? and though I am no monsieur, nor no signior, and do want, as they say, logic and sophistry, and good words, to tell you why it is so ; yet by this hand and by that candle it is so ; and though I be no book-worm, nor one that deals by art, to give you rhetoric and causes why it should be so, or make it good it is so ; yet d—n me, but I know it is so, and am assured it is so, and I and my sword shall make it appear it is so, and give you reason sufficient how it can be no otherwise but so——"

Hed. 'Slight, Anaides, you are mocked, and so we are all.

Mer. How now, signior ! what, suffer yourself to be cozened of your courtship before your face ?

Hed. This is plain confederacy to disgrace us : let's be gone, and plot some revenge.

Amo. " When men disgraces share,
       The lesser is the care."

Cri. Nay, stay, my dear Ambition. [*To* Hedon.] I can do you over too. You that tell your mistress, her beauty is all composed of theft ; her hair stole from Apollo's goldy-locks ; her white and red, lilies and roses stolen out of paradise ; her eyes two stars, plucked from the sky ; her nose the gnomon of Love's dial, that tells you how the clock of your heart goes : and for her other parts, as you cannot reckon them, they are so many ; so you cannot recount them, they are so manifest. Yours, if his own, unfortunate Hoyden, instead of Hedon.

[*A flourish.*

Aso. Sister, come away, I cannot endure
them longer.
    [*Exeunt all but* Mercury *and* Crites.
  Mer. Go, Dors, and you, my madam
    Courtingstocks,
Follow your scorned and derided mates;
Tell to your guilty breasts, what mere gilt
    blocks
You are, and how unworthy human states.
  Cri. Now, sacred God of Wit, if you
    can make
Those, whom our sports tax in these apish
    graces, ·
Kiss, like the fighting snakes, your peaceful
    rod;
These times shall canonize you for a god.
  Mer. Why, Crites, think you any noble
    spirit,
Or any, worth the title of a man,
Will be incensed to see the enchanted veils
Of self-conceit, and servile flattery,
Wrapt in so many folds by time and cus-
    tom,
Drawn from his wronged and bewitched
    eyes?
Who sees not now their shape and naked-
    ness,
Is blinder than the son of earth, the mole;
Crowned with no more humanity, nor soul.
  Cri. Though they may see it, yet the
    huge estate,
Fancy, and form, and sensual pride have
    gotten,
Will make them blush for anger, not for
    shame,
And turn shewn nakedness to impudence.
Humour is now the test we try things in:
All power is just: nought that delights is
    sin.
And yet the zeal of every knowing man
Opprest with hills of tyranny, cast on
    virtue
By the light fancies of fools, thus trans-
    ported,
Cannot but vent the Ætna of his fires,
T"inflame best bosoms with much worthier
    love
Than of these outward and effeminate
    shades;
That these vain joys, in which their wills
    consume
Such powers of wit and soul as are of force
To raise their beings to eternity,
May be converted on works fitting men:
And, for the practice of a forced look,
An antic gesture, or a fustian phrase,
Study the native frame of a true heart,
An inward comeliness of bounty, know-
    ledge,

And spirit that may conform them actually
To God's high figures, which they have in
    power;
Which to neglect for a self-loving neatness,
Is sacrilege of an unpardoned greatness.
  Mer. Then let the truth of these things
    strengthen thee,
In thy exempt and only man-like course;
Like it the more, the less it is respected:
Though men fail, virtue is by gods pro-
    tected.—
See, here comes Arete; I'll withdraw my-
    self.   [*Exit.*

Enter Arete.

  Are. Crites, you must provide straight
    for a masque,
'Tis Cynthia's pleasure.
  Cri. How, bright Arete!
Why, 'twere a labour more for Hercules:
Better and sooner durst I undertake
To make the different seasons of the year,
The winds or elements, to sympathize,
Than their unmeasurable vanity
Dance truly in a measure. They agree!
What though all concord's born of con-
    traries;
So many follies will confusion prove,
And like a sort of jarring instruments,
All out of tune: because, indeed, we see
There is not that analogy 'twixt discords,
As between things but merely opposite.
  Are. There is your error: for as Hermes'
    wand
Charms the disorders of tumultuous ghosts;
And as the strife of Chaos then did cease,
When better light than Nature's did arrive:
So what could never in itself agree,
Forgetteth the eccentric property,
And at her sight turns forthwith regular,
Whose sceptre guides the flowing ocean:
And though it did not, yet the most of
    them
Being either courtiers, or not wholly rude,
Respect of majesty, the place, and pre-
    sence,
Will keep them within ring, especially
When they are not presented as themselves,
But masqued like others: for, in troth, not
    so
To incorporate them, could be nothing
    else,
Than like a state ungoverned, without laws,
Or body made of nothing but diseases:
The one, through impotency, poor and
    wretched;
The other, for the anarchy, absurd.
  Cri. But, lady, for the revellers them-
    selves,

It would be better, in my poor conceit,
That others were employed ; for such as are
Unfit to be in Cynthia's court, can seem
No less unfit to be in Cynthia's sports.
   Are. That, Crites, is not purposed without
Particular knowledge of the goddess' mind ;
Who holding true intelligence, what follies
Had crept into her palace, she resolved
Of sports and triumphs, under that pretext,
To have them muster in their pomp and fulness,
That so she might more strictly, and to root,
Effect the reformation she intends.
   Cri. I now conceive her heavenly drift in all,
And will apply my spirits to serve her will.
O thou, the very power by which I am,
And but for which it were in vain to be,
Chief next Diana, virgin heavenly fair,
Admired Arete, of them admired
Whose souls are not enkindled by the sense,
Disdain not my chaste fire, but feed the flame
Devoted truly to thy gracious name.
   Are. Leave to suspect us : Crites well shall find,
As we are now most dear, we'll prove most kind.
   [*Within.*] Arete !
   Are. Hark, I'm called.   [*Exit.*
   Cri. I follow instantly.
Phœbus Apollo, if with ancient rites,
And due devotions, I have ever hung
Elaborate Pæans on thy golden shrine,
Or sung thy triumphs in a lofty strain,
Fit for a theatre of gods to hear ;
And thou, the other son of mighty Jove,
Cyllenian Mercury, sweet Maia's joy,
If in the busy tumults of the mind
My path thou ever hast illumined,
For which thine altars I have oft perfumed,
And decked thy statues with discoloured flowers :[1]
Now thrive invention in this glorious court,

That not of bounty only, but of right,
Cynthia may grace, and give it life by sight.
                   [*Exit.*

SCENE III.

Enter Hesperus, Cynthia, Arete, Time,
     Phronesis, *and* Thauma.

Music accompanied.   Hesperus *sings.*

Queen, and huntress,[2] chaste and fair,
Now the sun is laid to sleep,
Seated in thy silver chair,
State in wonted manner keep :
   Hesperus entreats thy light,
   Goddess, excellently bright.

Earth, let not thy envious shade
Dare itself to interpose ;
Cynthia's shining orb was made
Heav'n to clear, when day did close :
   Bless us then with wished sight,
   Goddess excellently bright.

Lay thy bow of pearl apart,
And thy crystal shining quiver ;
Give unto the flying hart
Space to breathe, how short soever :
   Thou that mak'st a day of night,
   Goddess excellently bright.

   Cyn. When hath Diana, like an envious wretch,
That glitters only to his soothed self,
Denying to the world the precious use
Of hoarded wealth, withheld her friendly aid?
Monthly we spend our still-repaired shine,
And not forbid our virgin-waxen torch
To burn and blaze while nutriment doth last :
That once consumed, out of Jove's treasury
A new we take, and stick it in our sphere,
To give the mutinous kind of wanting men
Their looked-for light.   Yet what is their desert ?
Bounty is wronged, interpreted as due ;
Mortals can challenge not a ray, by right,
Yet do expect the whole of Cynthia's light.
But if that deities withdrew their gifts
For human follies, what could men deserve

---

[1] *And decked thy statues with* discoloured *flowers :*] i.e., with flowers of different colours. So in *David and Bethsebe*, 1595 :
   " May that sweet plain that bears her pleasant weight
   Be still enamelled with *discoloured* flowers."
And in *Britannia's Pastorals :*
   " As are the dainty flowers which Flora spreads
   Unto the Spring in the *discoloured* meads."

Just above Jonson uses discoloured for colourless, without colours. There is, as Whalley truly observes, a noble spirit of poetry in this invocation, not unworthy of a classic author. In the quarto this scene concludes the fourth act.

[2] *Queen, and huntress,* &c.] This little hymn is delicate, both in the sentiment and expression ; the images are picturesque, and the verses easy and flowing.—WHAL.

But death and darkness? It behoves the
   high,
For their own sakes, to do things worthily.
   Are. Most true, most sacred goddess,
      for the heavens
Receive no good of all the good they do :
Nor Jove, nor you, nor other heavenly
   Powers,
Are fed with fumes which do from incense
   rise,
Or sacrifices reeking in their gore ;
Yet for the care which you of mortals have,
(Whose proper good it is that they be so,)
You well are pleased with odours redolent:
But ignorant is all the race of men,
Which still complains, not knowing why,
   or when.
   Cyn. Else, noble Arete, they would not
      blame,
And tax, or for unjust, or for as proud,
Thy Cynthia, in the things which are in-
   deed
The greatest glories in our starry crown ;
Such is our chastity, which safely scorns,
Not love, for who more fervently doth love
Immortal honour, and divine renown ?
But giddy Cupid, Venus' frantic son.
Yet, Arete, if by this veiled light
We but discovered (what we not discern)
Any the least of imputations stand
Ready to sprinkle our unspotted fame
With note of lightness, from these revels
   near;
Not, for the empire of the universe,
Should night, or court, this whatsoever
   shine,
Or grace of ours, unhappily enjoy.
Place and occasion are two privy thieves,
And from poor innocent ladies often steal
The best of things, an honourable name ;
To stay with follies, or where faults may
   be,
Infers a crime, although the party free.
   Are. How Cynthianly, that is, how wor-
      thily
And like herself, the matchless Cynthia
      speaks!
Infinite jealousies, infinite regards,
Do watch about the true virginity :
But Phœbe lives from all, not only fault,
But as from thought, so from suspicion free.
Thy presence broad-seals our delights for
   pure;
What's done in Cynthia's sight is done se-
   cure.
   Cyn. That then so answered, dearest
      Arete,
What th' argument, or of what sort our
   sports

Are like to be this night, I not demand.
Nothing which duty,[1] and desire to please,
Bears written in the forehead, comes amiss.
But unto whose invention must we owe
The complement of this night's furniture?
   Are. Excellent goddess, to a man's,
      whose worth,
Without hyperbole, I thus may praise ;
One at least studious of deserving well,
And, to speak truth, indeed deserving well.
Potential merit stands for actual,
Where only opportunity doth want,
Not will, nor power ; both which in him
   abound.
One whom the Muses and Minerva love ;
For whom should they, than Crites, more
   esteem,
Whom Phœbus, though not Fortune, hold-
   eth dear?
And, which convinceth excellence in him,
A principal admirer of yourself.
Even through the ungentle injuries of Fate,
And difficulties, which do virtue choke,
Thus much of him appears. What other
   things
Of farther note do lie unborn in him,
Them I do leave for cherishment to shew,
And for a goddess graciously to judge.
   Cyn. We have already judged him,
      Arete ;
Nor are we ignorant how noble minds
Suffer too much through those indignities
Which times and vicious persons cast on
   them.
Ourself have ever vowed to esteem
As virtue for itself, so fortune, base ;
Who's first in worth, the same be first in
   place.
Nor farther notice, Arete, we crave
Than thine approval's sovereign warranty:
Let 't be thy care to make us known to him :
Cynthia shall brighten what the world
   made dim.   [*Exit* Arete.

                 The First Masque.

Enter Cupid, *disguised as* Anteros, *followed by* Storgé, Aglaia, Euphantaste,
   and Apheleia.

   Cup. " Clear pearl of heaven, and, not

---

1 *Nothing which duty,* &c.] This sentiment of
humanity is from Shakspeare :

      " Never anything can be amiss,
   When simpleness and duty tender it."
                  Midsummer Night's Dream.

Cynthia and Theseus are exactly in the same
situation, both preparing to see a dramatic exhibition.—WHAL.

to be farther ambitious in titles, Cynthia !
the fame of this illustrious night, among
others, hath also drawn these four fair
virgins from the palace of their queen Perfection, (a word which makes no sufficient
difference betwixt hers and thine,) to visit
thy imperial court: for she, their sovereign,
not finding where to dwell among men,
before her return to heaven, advised them
wholly to consecrate themselves to thy
celestial service, as in whose clear spirit
(the proper element and sphere of virtue)
they should behold not her alone, their
ever-honoured mistress, but themselves
(more truly themselves) to live enthronized.
Herself would have commended them unto
thy favour more particularly, but that she
knows no commendation is more available
with thee than that of proper virtue. Nevertheless she willed them to present this crystal
mound,[1] a note of monarchy, and symbol of
perfection, to thy more worthy deity;
which, as here by me they most humbly do,
so amongst the rarities thereof, that is the
chief, to shew whatsoever the world hath
excellent, howsoever remote and various.
But your irradiate judgment will soon discover the secrets of this little crystal world.
Themselves, to appear more plainly, because they know nothing more odious than
false pretexts, have chosen to express their
several qualities thus in several colours.

"The first, in citron colour, is natural
affection, which, given us to procure our
good, is sometime called Storgé; and as
every one is nearest to himself, so this
handmaid of reason, allowable Self-love,
as it is without harm, so are none without
it: her place in the court of Perfection was
to quicken minds in the pursuit of honour.
Her device is a perpendicular level, upon a
cube or square; the word *se suo modulo;*
alluding to that true measure of one's self,
which, as every one ought to make, so is it
most conspicuous in thy divine example.

"The second, in green, is Aglaia, delecta-
ble and pleasant conversation, whose property is to move a kindly delight, and some-

time not without laughter: her office to entertain assemblies, and keep societies together with fair familiarity. Her device,
within a ring of clouds, a heart with shine
about it;[2] the word, *curarum nubila pello:*
an allegory of Cynthia's light, which no
less clears the sky than her fair mirth the
heart.

"The third, in the discoloured[3] mantle
spangled all over, is Euphantaste, a well-
conceited Wittiness, and employed in
honouring the court with the riches of her
pure invention. Her device, upon a Petasus, or Mercurial hat, a crescent; the
word, *sic laus ingenii;* inferring that the
praise and glory of wit doth ever increase,
as doth thy growing moon.

"The fourth, in white, is Apheleia, a
nymph as pure and simple as the soul, or
as an abrase table, and is therefore called
Simplicity; without folds, without plaits,
without colour, without counterfeit; and,
(to speak plainly) plainness itself. Her
device is no device.[4] The word under her
silver shield, *omnis abest fucus;* alluding
to thy spotless self, who art as far from
impurity as from mortality.

"Myself, celestial goddess, more fit for
the court of Cynthia than the arbours of
Cytherea, am called Anteros, or Love's
enemy; the more welcome therefore to
thy court, and the fitter to conduct this
quaternion, who, as they are thy professed votaries, and for that cause adversaries to Love, yet thee, perpetual virgin,
they both love, and vow to love eternally."

Re-enter Arete, *with* Crites.

Cyn. Not without wonder, nor without
    delight,
Mine eyes have viewed, in contemplation's
    depth,
This work of wit, divine and excellent:
What shape, what substance, or what un-
    known power,
In virgin's habit, crowned with laurel
    leaves,

---

[1] *This crystal* mound,] Mound is an orb or
globe: and by this name particularly the globe
is called which the king carries at his coronation.—WHAL.

[2] *A heart with* shine *about it;*] Shine or
sheen was anciently used for brightness, splendour, &c. Thus in the old translation of the
Psalms: "His lightening gave *shine* unto the
world." And in *Venus* and *Adonis:*

"Cynthia for shame obscures her silver *shine.*"

It is pure Saxon.

[3] *The third, in the* discoloured *mantle*] See
p. 196 *a.* *Abrase table,* which occurs just below,
is a Latinism, and means clear and smooth as
virgin wax, or paper.

[4] *Her device is no device,*] i.e., she bears a
plain shield, without any emblem portrayed
upon it.—WHAL.
Thus, in the *Arcadia,* "Whose *device* was to
come *without any device,* all in white, like a new
knight," p. 180.

And olive-branches woven in between,
On sea-girt rocks, like to a goddess shines !
O front ! O face ! O all celestial, sure,
And more than mortal ! Arete, behold
Another Cynthia, and another queen,
Whose glory, like a lasting plenilune,
Seems ignorant of what it is to wane.
Nor under heaven an object could be
　found
More fit to please.　Let Crites make ap-
　proach.
Bounty forbids to pall our thanks with stay,
Or to defer our favour, after view :
The time of grace is, when the cause is
　new.
　Are. Lo, here the man, celestial Delia,
Who (like a circle bounded in itself)
Contains as much as man in fullness may.
Lo, here the man, who not of usual earth,
But of that nobler and more precious
　mould
Which Phœbus self doth temper, is com-
　posed ;
And who, though all were wanting to
　reward,
Yet to himself he would not wanting be :
Thy favour's gain is his ambition's most,
And labour's best; who (humble in his
　height)
Stands fixed silent in thy glorious sight.
　Cyn. With no less pleasure than we
　have beheld
This precious crystal work of rarest wit,
Our eye doth read thee, now instiled, our
　Crites ;
Whom learning, virtue, and our favour last,
Exempteth from the gloomy multitude.
With common eye the Supreme should not
　see :
Henceforth be ours, the more thyself to be.
　Cri. Heaven's purest light, whose orb
　may be eclipsed,
But not thy praise ; divinest Cynthia !
How much too narrow for so high a grace,
Thine (save therein) the most unworthy
　Crites
Doth find himself ! for ever shine thy
　fame ;
Thine honours ever, as thy beauties do.
In me they must, my dark world's chiefest
　lights,
By whose propitious beams my powers are
　raised
To hope some part of those most lofty
　points,
Which blessed Arete hath pleased to name,
As marks, to which my endeavour's steps
　should bend :
Mine, as begun at thee, in thee must end.

The Second Masque.

Enter Mercury *as a page, introducing*
　Eucosmos, Eupathes, Eutolmos, *and*
　Eucolos.

Mer. "Sister of Phœbus, to whose
bright orb we owe, that we not complain
of his absence : these four brethren (for
they are brethren, and sons of Eutaxia, a
lady known, and highly beloved of your
resplendent deity) not able to be absent,
when Cynthia held a solemnity, officiously
insinuate themselves into thy presence : for
as there are four cardinal virtues, upon
which the whole frame of the court doth
move, so are these the four cardinal properties, without which the body of compliment moveth not.　With these four
silver javelins (which they bear in their
hands) they support in princes' courts the
state of the presence, as by office they are
obliged ; which, though here they may
seem superfluous, yet, for honour's sake,
they thus presume to visit thee, having
also been employed in the palace of Queen
Perfection.　And though to them that
would make themselves gracious to a
goddess, sacrifices were fitter than presents,
or impresses, yet they both hope thy
favour, and (in place of either) use several
symbols, containing the titles of thy imperial dignity.

"First, the hithermost, in the change-
able blue and green robe, is the com-
mendably-fashioned gallant, Eucosmos ;
whose courtly habit is the grace of the
presence, and delight of the surveying eye :
whom ladies understand by the names of
Neat and Elegant.　His symbol is *divæ
virgini*, in which he would express thy
deity's principal glory, which hath ever
been virginity.

"The second, in the rich accoutrement,
and robe of purple, empaled with gold, is
Eupathes ; who entertains his mind with
an harmless, but not incurious variety : all
the objects of his senses are sumptuous,
himself a gallant, that, without excess, can
make use of superfluity, go richly in embroideries, jewels, and what not, without
vanity, and fare delicately without gluttony ; and therefore (not without cause) is
universally thought to be of fine humour.
His symbol is *divæ optimæ;* an attribute
to express thy goodness, in which thou so
resemblest Jove thy father.

"The third, in the blush-coloured suit,
is Eutolmos, as duly respecting others, as

never neglecting himself; commonly known by the title of good Audacity; to courts and courtly assemblies a guest most acceptable. His symbol is *divæ viragini;* to express thy hardy courage in chase of savage beasts, which harbour in woods and wildernesses.

"The fourth, in watchet tinsel,[1] is the kind and truly benefique Eucolos, who imparteth not without respect, but yet without difficulty, and hath the happiness to make every kindness seem double, by the timely and freely bestowing thereof. He is the chief of them, who by the vulgar are said to be of good nature. His symbol is *divæ maximæ;* an adjunct to signify thy greatness, which in heaven, earth, and hell, is formidable.

Music. A Dance by the two Masques joined, during which Cupid and Mercury retire to the side of the stage.

Cup. Is not that Amorphus, the traveller?

Mer. As though it were not! do you not see how his legs are in travail with a measure?

Cup. Hedon, thy master, is next.

Mer. What, will Cupid turn nomenclator, and cry them?

Cup. No, faith, but I have a comedy toward, that would not be lost for a kingdom.

Mer. In good time, for Cupid will prove the comedy.

Cup. Mercury, I am studying how to match them.

Mer. How to mismatch them were harder.

Cup. They are the nymphs must do it; I shall sport myself with their passions above measure.

Mer. Those nymphs would be tamed a little indeed, but I fear thou hast not arrows for the purpose.

Cup. O yes, here be of all sorts—flights, rovers, and butt-shafts.[2] But I can wound with a brandish, and never draw bow for the matter.

Mer. I cannot but believe it, my invisible archer, and yet methinks you are tedious.

Cup. It behoves me to be somewhat circumspect, Mercury; for if Cynthia hear the twang of my bow, she'll go near to whip me with the string: therefore, to prevent that, I thus discharge a brandish upon——it makes no matter which of the couples. Phantaste and Amorphus, at you.
                                        [*Waves his arrow at them.*

Mer. Will the shaking of a shaft strike them into such a fever of affection?

Cup. As well as the wink of an eye: but, I pray thee, hinder me not with thy prattle.

Mer. Jove forbid I hinder thee! Marry, all that I fear is Cynthia's presence, which, with the cold of her chastity, casteth such an antiperistasis[3] about the place, that no heat of thine will tarry with the patient.

Cup. It will tarry the rather, for the antiperistasis will keep it in.

Mer. I long to see the experiment.

Cup. Why, their marrow boils already, or they are all turned eunuchs.

Mer. Nay, an't be so, I'll give over speaking, and be a spectator only.
                                        [*The first dance ends.*

Amo. Cynthia, by my bright soul, is a right exquisite and splendidious lady; yet Amorphus, I think, hath seen more fashions, I am sure more countries: but whether I have or not, what need we gaze on Cynthia, that have ourselves to admire?

Pha. O, excellent Cynthia! yet if Phantaste sat where she does, and had such attire on her head, (for attire can do much,) I say no more—but goddesses are goddesses, and Phantaste is as she is! I would the revels were done once, I might go to my school of glass again, and learn to do myself right after all this ruffling.
                                        [*Music: they begin the second dance.*

Mer. How now, Cupid? here's a wonderful change with your brandish! do you not hear how they dote?

Cup. What prodigy is this? no word of love, no mention, no motion!

---

[1] *The fourth, in* watchet *tinsel,*] i.e., in light sky-coloured blue.—*Dict.*

[2] *Here be of all sorts,* flights, rovers, *and* butt-shafts.] *Flights* were long and light-feathered arrows, which went level to the mark; *rovers* were arrows shot compass-wise, or with a certain degree of elevation; these were the all-dreaded war-weapons of the English; *butt-shafts*, as the name sufficiently intimates, were the strong unbarbed arrows used in the field exercises and amusements of the day. If the reader wishes to peruse a couple of pages on the subject, which will leave him very nearly as wise as they found him, he may turn to the first scene of *Much Ado About Nothing.*

[3] *Casteth such an* antiperistasis] "The opposition of a contrary quality, by which the quality it opposes becomes heightened or intended."
                                        Cowley, *Dict.*

Mer. Not a word, my little *ignis fatue,* not a word.

Cup. Are my darts enchanted? is their vigour gone? is their virtue——

Mer. What! Cupid turned jealous of himself? ha, ha, ha!

Cup. Laughs Mercury?

Mer. Is Cupid angry?

Cup. Hath he not cause, when his purpose is so deluded?

Mer. A rare comedy, it shall be entitled Cupid's.

Cup. Do not scorn us, Hermes.

Mer. Choler and Cupid are two fiery things; I scorn them not. But I see that come to pass, which I presaged in the beginning.

Cup. You cannot tell: perhaps the physic will not work so soon upon some as upon others. It may be the rest are not so resty.

Mer. Ex ungue; you know the old adage: as these, so are the remainder.

Cup. I'll try: this is the same shaft with which I wounded Argurion.
                           [*Waves his arrow again.*

Mer. Ay, but let me save you a labour, Cupid: there were certain bottles of water fetched, and drunk off since that time, by these gallants.

Cup. Jove strike me into earth! the Fountain of Self-love!

Mer. Nay, faint not, Cupid.

Cup. I remembered it not.

Mer. Faith, it was ominous to take the name of Anteros upon you; you know not what charm or enchantment lies in the word: you saw I durst not venture upon any device in our presentment, but was content to be no other than a simple page. Your arrows' properties (to keep decorum), Cupid, are suited, it should seem, to the nature of him you personate.

Cup. Indignity not to be born!

Mer. Nay, rather an attempt to have been forborn.   [*The second dance ends.*

Cup. How might I revenge myself on this insulting Mercury? there's Crites, his minion, he has not tasted of this water. [*Waves his arrow at* Crites.] It shall be so. Is Crites turned dotard on himself too?

Mer. That follows not, because the venom of your shafts cannot pierce him, Cupid.

Cup. As though there were one antidote for these, and another for him.

Mer. As though there were not; or, as if one effect might not arise of divers causes? What say you to Cynthia, Arete, Phronesis, Timè, and others there?

Cup. They are divine.

Mer. And Crites aspires to be so.
     [*Music: they begin the third dance.*

Cup. But that shall not serve him.

Mer. 'Tis like to do it, at this time. But Cupid is grown too covetous, that will not spare one of a multitude.

Cup. One is more than a multitude.

Mer. Arete's favour makes any one shotproof against thee, Cupid. I pray thee, light honey-bee, remember thou art not now in Adonis' garden, but in Cynthia's presence, where thorns lie in garrison about the roses. Soft, Cynthia speaks.

Cyn. Ladies and gallants of our court, to
     end
And give a timely period to our sports,
Let us conclude them with declining night;
Our empire is but of the darker half.
And if you judge it any recompense
For your fair pains, t' have earned Diana's
     thanks,
Diana grants them, and bestows their crown
To gratify your acceptable zeal.
For you are they, that not, as some have
     done,
Do censure us, as too severe and sour,
But as, more rightly, gracious to the good;
Although we not deny, unto the proud,
Or the profane, perhaps indeed austere:
For so Actæon, by presuming far,
Did, to our grief, incur a fatal doom;
And so, swoln Niobe, comparing more
Than he presumed, was trophæed into
     stone.
But are we therefore judged too extreme?
Seems it no crime to enter sacred bowers,
And hallowed places, with impure aspèct,
Most lewdly to pollute? Seems it no crime
To brave a deity? Let mortals learn
To make religion of offending heaven,[1]
And not at all to censure powers divine.
To men this argument should stand for
     firm,
A goddess did it, therefore it was good:
We are not cruel, nor delight in blood,—
But what have serious repetitions
To do with revels, and the sports of court?
We not intend to sour your late delights
With harsh expostulation. Let it suffice
That we take notice, and can take revenge
Of these calumnious and lewd blasphemies.
For we are no less Cynthia than we were,
Nor is our power, but as ourself, the same:

---

[1] *To make* religion *of offending heaven,*] This Latinism is not unfrequent in Jonson. It means to make a tender and conscientious scruple, &c.

Though we have now put on no tire of
    shine,[1]
But mortal eyes undazzled may endure.
Years are beneath the spheres, and time
    makes weak
Things under heaven, not powers which
    govern heaven.
And though ourself be in ourself secure,
Yet let not mortals challenge to themselves
Immunity from thence. Lo, this is all :
Honour hath store of spleen, but wanteth
    gall.
Once more we cast the slumber of our
    thanks
On your ta'en toil, which here let take an
    end.
And that we not mistake your several
    worths,
Nor you our favour, from yourselves re-
    move
What makes you not yourselves, those
    clouds of masque ;
Particular pains particular thanks do ask.
                    [The dancers unmask.
How ! let me view you. Ha ! are we con-
    temned?
Is there so little awe of our disdain,
That any (under trust of their disguise)
Should mix themselves with others of the
    court,
And, without forehead, boldly press so far,
As farther none? How apt is lenity
To be abused ! severity to be loathed !
And yet how much more doth the seeming
    face
Of neighbour virtues, and their borrowed
    names,
Add of lewd boldness to loose vanities !
Who would have thought that Philautia
    durst
Or have usurped noble Storgé's name,
Or with that theft have ventured on our
    eyes?
Who would have thought, that all of them
    should hope
So much of our connivance, as to come
To grace themselves with titles not their
    own?
Instead of med'cines, have we maladies?
And such imposthumes as Phantaste is
Grow in our palace? We must lance these
    sores,
Or all will putrify. Nor are these all,

---

[1] *No tire of shine*,] i.e., no attire of light. So
Whalley explains it : but tire is usually spoken
of a head-dress, and here means the glory or
rays of light that usually circled the brows of
Diana.

For we suspect a farther fraud than this :
Take off our veil, that shadows may depart,
And shapes appear, beloved Arete. So,
Another face of things presents itself,
Than did of late. What ! feathered Cupid
    masqued,
And masqued like Anteros? And stay !
    more strange !
Dear Mercury, our brother, like a page,
To countenance the ambush of the boy !
Nor endeth our discovery as yet :
Gelaia, like a nymph, that but erewhile,
In male attire, did serve Anaides?—
Cupid came hither to find sport and game,
Who heretofore hath been too conversant
Among our train, but never felt revenge ;
And Mercury bare Cupid company.
Cupid, we must confess, this time of mirth,
Proclaimed by us, gave opportunity
To thy attempts, although no privilege :
Tempt us no farther ; we cannot endure
Thy presence longer ; vanish hence, away !
                    [*Exit* Cupid.
You, Mercury, we must entreat to stay,
And hear what we determine of the rest ;
For in this plot we well perceive your hand.
But, (for we mean not a censorian task,
And yet to lance these ulcers grown so
    ripe,)
Dear Arete, and Crites, to you two
We give the charge ; impose what pains
    you please :
Th' incurable cut off, the rest reform,
Remembering ever what we first decreed,
Since revels were proclaimed, let now none
    bleed.
    Are. How well Diana can distinguish
    times,
And sort her censures, keeping to herself
The doom of gods, leaving the rest to us !
Come, cite them, Crites, first, and then
    proceed.
    Cri. First, Philautia, for she was the
    first,
Then light Gelaia in Aglaia's name,
Thirdly, Phantaste, and Moria next,
Main Follies all, and of the female crew :
Amorphus, or Eucosmos' counterfeit,
Voluptuous Hedon ta'en for Eupathes,
Brazen Anaides, and Asotus last,
With his two pages, Morus and Prosaites;
And thou, the traveller's evil, Cos, ap-
    proach,
Impostors all, and male deformities——
    Are. Nay, forward, for I delegate my
    power,
And will that at thy mercy they do stand,
Whom they so oft, so plainly scorned be-
    fore.

'Tis virtue which they want, and wanting
    it,
Honour no garment to their backs can fit.
Then Crites, practise thy discretion.
    Cri. Adored Cynthia, and bright Arete,
Another might seem fitter for this task,
Than Crites far, but that you judge not so :
For I (not to appear vindicative,
Or mindful of contempts, which I con-
    temned,
As done of impotence) must be remiss ;
Who, as I was the author, in some sort.
To work their knowledge into Cynthia's
    sight,
So should be much severer to revenge
The indignity hence issuing to her name :
But there's not one of these who are un-
    pained,
Or by themselves unpunished ; for vice
Is like a fury to the vicious mind,
And turns delight itself to punishment.
But we must forward, to define their doom.
You are offenders, that must be confessed ;
Do you confess it?
    All. We do.
    Cri. And that you merit sharp correc-
tion ?
    All. Yes.
    Cri. Then we (reserving unto Delia's
    grace
Her farther pleasure, and to Arete
What Delia granteth) thus do sentence you:
That from this place (for penance known
    of all,
Since you have drunk so deeply of Self-
    love)
You, two and two, singing a Palinode,
March to your several homes by Niobe's
    stone,
And offer up two tears apiece thereon,
That it may change the name, as you must
    change,
And of a stone be called Weeping-cross ;
Because it standeth cross of Cynthia's way,
One of whose names is sacred Trivia.

And, after penance thus performed, you
    pass
In like set order, not as Midas did,
To wash his gold off into Tagus' stream ;
But to the well of knowledge, Helicon ;
Where, purged of your present maladies,
Which are not few, nor slender, you become
Such as you fain would seem, and then
    return,
Offering your service to great Cynthia.
This is your sentence, if the goddess please
To ratify it with her high consent ;
The scope of wise mirth unto fruit is bent.
    Cyn. We do approve thy censure, be-
    loved Crites ;[1]
Which Mercury, thy true propitious friend,
(A deity next Jove beloved of us,)
Will undertake to see exactly done.
And for this service of discovery,
Performed by thee, in honour of our name,
We vow to guerdon it with such due grace
As shall become our bounty, and thy
    place.
Princes that would their people should do
    well
Must at themselves begin, as at the head ;
For men, by their example, pattern out
Their imitations, and regard of laws :
A virtuous court[2] a world to virtue draws.
    [*Exeunt* Cynthia *and her* Nymphs, *fol-
        lowed by* Arete *and* Crites :—Amor-
        phus, Phantaste, &c., go off the stage
        in pairs, singing the following*

PALINODE.

    Amo. From Spanish shrugs, French
faces, smirks, irpes,[3] and all affected humours,
    Chorus. Good Mercury defend us.
    Pha. From secret friends, sweet ser-
vants, loves, doves, and such fantastic humours,
    Chorus. Good Mercury defend us.

---

[1] *We do approve thy censure,* beloved Crites.]
The change of name has here spoiled a verse,
The quarto reads :

    "We do approve thy censure, *Criticus.*"

[2] *A virtuous court,* &c.] This and the preceding lines form an elegant amplification of the
well-known saying :

"*Regis ad exemplum totus componitur orbis.*"

[3] *Smirks,* irpes, *&c.*] This word occurred in
a former part of this play (p. 170 *a*), and I recollect
it nowhere else in our old poetry. Its meaning
must be gathered from the context, and may
probably be set down, without much deviation

from the fact, as a fantastic grimace or contor-
tion of the body. Whether the word bears any
allusion to that convulsive affection of the features
caused by the *herpes* (St. Antony's fire), or be
derived from *weörfern, werfen* (Teut.) *to warp,*
I cannot say. There is indeed a substantive in
Dutch, of which Jonson unquestionably understood something, which probably bids fairer than
either to be the parent of this strange term.
Werp, wierp, or *worp* (the *w* in Dutch is pronounced as a *v*), means a jerking, *starting,* or
bowing. From *verp* to *irp* the transition is
natural and easy ; and the sense of both words
appears to be very nearly the same. Let the
reader judge.

Amo. From stabbing of arms, flap-dragons,[1] healths, whiffs, and all such swaggering humours,

    Chorus. Good Mercury defend us.

Pha. From waving fans, coy glances, glicks, cringes, and all such simpering humours,

    Chorus. Good Mercury defend us.

Amo. From making love by attorney, courting of puppets, and paying for new acquaintance,

    Chorus. Good Mercury defend us.

Pha. From perfumed dogs, monkies, sparrows, dildoes, and paraquettoes,

    Chorus. Good Mercury defend us.

Amo. From wearing bracelets of hair, shoe-ties, gloves, garters, and rings with poesies.

    Chorus. Good Mercury defend us.

Pha. From pargetting, painting, slicking, glazing, and renewing old rivelled faces,

    Chorus. Good Mercury defend us.

Amo. From squiring to tilt-yards, play-houses, pageants, and all such public places,

    Chorus. Good Mercury defend us.

Pha. From entertaining one gallant to gull another, and making fools of either,

    Chorus. Good Mercury defend us.

Amo. From belying ladies' favours, noblemen's countenance, coining counterfeit employments, vain-glorious taking to them other men's services, and all self-loving humours,

    Chorus. Good Mercury defend us.

    Mercury *and* Crites *sing.*

Now each one dry his weeping eyes,
    And to the Well of Knowledge haste;

Where purged of your maladies,
    You may of sweeter waters taste:
And with refined voice report
    The grace of Cynthia, and her court.

                   [*Exeunt.*

THE EPILOGUE.

Gentles, be 't known to you, since I went in
I am turned rhymer, and do thus begin.
The author (jealous how your sense doth take
His travails) hath enjoined me to make
Some short and ceremonious epilogue;
But if I yet know what, I am a rogue;
He ties me to such laws as quite distract
My thoughts, and would a year of time exact.
I neither must be faint, remiss, nor sorry,
Sour, serious, confident, nor peremptory;
But betwixt these. Let's see; to lay the blame
Upon the children's action, that were lame.
To crave your favour with a begging knee,
Were to distrust the writer's faculty.
To promise better at the next we bring,
Prorogues disgrace, commends not anything.
Stiffly to stand on this, and proudly approve
The play, might tax the maker of Self-love.
I'll only speak what I have heard him say,
" By —— 'tis good, and if you like't, you may."[2]

Ecce rubet quidam, pallet, stupet, oscitat, odit.
    Hoc volo: nunc nobis carmina nostra placent.

---

[1] *From* stabbing of arms, flap-dragons, *&c.*] The first of these fashionable practices has been already noticed (p. 173 *b*); it occurs also in Decker's *Honest Whore*:
  " How many gallants have drank healths to me
    Out of *their daggered* arms !"
Flap-dragons are plums, &c. placed in a shallow dish filled with some spirituous liquor, out of which, when set on fire, they are to be dextrously snatched with the mouth. This elegant amusement was once more common in England than it is at present, and has been at all times a favourite one in Holland. Thus in *RamAlley*:
" My brother swallows it with more ease than a Dutchman does *flap-dragons.*" And in *A Christian turned Turk:* "They will devour one

another as familiarly as pikes doe gudgeons, and with as much facility as Dutchmen doe flap-dragons."—Act i. sc. 4. *Glicks,* which occurs in the next line, means ogling or leering looks. *Pargetting* (see below) is contemptuously used for painting or rather daubing the face: literally, it signifies coating a wall with plaster. The other terms are either such as have already occurred, or as do not require an explanation.

[2] *And if you like't, you may.*] "Short and ceremonious" with a witness! This is what the modest Massinger calls "strange self-love in a writer," and what might well have been dispensed with on the present occasion. This overweening confidence procured Jonson a

host of enemies, and involved him in petty warfare, unworthy of his powers. The truth is, that
he wrote above his audience, and adopted this
rude and desperate mode of overawing their
censure when he suspected that he had failed to
convince their judgment. Not that this way of
bullying the hearer (for it is no better) was new
to the stage, or peculiar to Jonson. Fletcher's
Nice Valour, not composed, like this piece, with
all the austerity of the ancient drama, but thrown
out at random, when he was either drunk or
lightheaded, or both, concludes somewhat in
the same audacious manner:

" But for the love-scenes——
He'll stand no shock of censure. *The play's
good,*
He says, *he knows it,* if well understood."

This is better perhaps than to have the Poet
enter in a mourning suit, with an axe on his
shoulders, and a piteous request to the audience,
that, "if they are determined not to like his play
they will be pleased to cut his head off." But,
in fact, both practices are reprehensible in a high
degree, and always defeat their own ends. Overstrained humiliation excites ridicule; arrogant
assumption provokes indignation: and both are
bosti'e alike to the poet's genuine object.

Little remains to be said of *Cynthia's Revels.*
The characters are well drawn, and well supported: and the influence of the Fountain of
Self-love upon their natural vanity is pleasantly
described: but they have little bearing upon one
another; while the plot of the drama is so finely
spun that no eye perhaps but Jonson's has ever
been able to trace it. The gradual decline of
interest from *Every Man in his Humour* to the
present play, is as striking as it is mortifying,
especially as the author appears to have spared
no pains, and even to have exhibited more neatness of style, and perhaps more force of expression. There is still a retrospect to the preceding
comedies. Amorphus and Asotus are Bobadill
and Master Stephen; yet without their natural
touches: the rest scarcely merit particular
attention. Cupid and Mercury, who open the
" Revels" with such pure and genuine humour,
lose all their pleasantry after the first act. As
deities they do well, as pages they have " no
more wit than ordinary men, and are scarcely
distinguishable from Cos and Prosaites. What
amusement the spectators might find in the
solemn buffoonery of the contending courtiers
I know not; but the reader, to whom it appears
unintelligible, for want of a few marginal notes,
which the author would not, and the editor cannot supply, must find it intolerably tedious. The
fulsome compliments paid to the "obdurate
virgin" of threescore and ten, the hoary-headed
Cynthia of Whitehall, must have appeared infinitely ridiculous if the frequency of the practice
had not utterly taken away the sense of derision.
Yet Jonson must not be without his peculiar
praise. The language of the time was grossly
adulatory; and from Spenser to the meanest
scribbler, our poet was almost the only one who
interspersed salutary counsels among his flatteries.

The Poetaster; or, his Arraignment.

THE POETASTER.] This "Comical Satire." as the folio terms it, was produced in 1601, and acted, like *Cynthia's Revels*, by the children of the queen's chapel. It was printed in quarto the following year, with this motto from Martial:

Et mihi de nullo fama rubore placet,

and again, in folio, in 1616. The *Poetaster* was frequently performed at the private theatre in Black Friars, where it seems to have been a favourite. The actors were the same that appeared in the preceding drama, with the exception of Wil. Ostler and Tho. Marton. Of the last I can give the reader no information; but Wil. Ostler, who probably played the part of Julia, rose to considerable eminence in his profession, and was subsequently addressed by Davies as " the Roscius of his times," in a prosing epigram which concludes in this singular manner:—

" But if thou plaist thy dying part as well
  As thy stage part, thou hast no part in hell."

VIRTUOUS, AND MY WORTHY FRIEND,

MR. RICHARD MARTIN.[1]

"SIR,—A thankful man owes a courtesy ever; the unthankful but when he needs it. To make mine own mark appear, and shew by which of these seals I am known, I send you this piece of what may live of mine; for whose innocence, as for the author's, you were once a noble and timely undertaker[2] to the greatest justice of this kingdom. Enjoy now the delight of your goodness, which is to see that prosper you preserved, and posterity to owe the reading of that, without offence, to your name, which so much ignorance and malice of the times then conspired to have supprest.

"Your True Lover,   BEN. JONSON."[3]

DRAMATIS PERSONÆ.

Augustus Cæsar.	Asinius Lupus.	Æsop.
Mecænas.	Pantilius Tucca.	Pyrgi.
Marc. Ovid.	Luscus.	Lictors, Equites, &c.
Cor. Gallus.	Ruf. Lab. Crispinus.	
Sex. Propertius.	Hermogenes Tigellius.	Julia.
Fus. Aristius.	Demetrius Fannius.	Cytheris.
Pub. Ovid.	Albius.	Plautia.
Virgil.	Minos.	Chloe.
Horace.	Histrio.	Maids.
Trebatius.		

SCENE,—Rome.

---

[1] *To the virtuous, and my worthy friend, Mr. Richard Martin.*] This gentleman, who was bred a lawyer, and who was Recorder of the City of London, was himself a man of parts, and a poet, and much respected by the learned and ingenious of his own age. See a more particular account of him in Wood's *Athenæ Oxon.* vol. i. col. 441.—WHAL.

Whalley has not said too much of Richard Martin. He was a man of great eloquence, and possessed of many virtues. He was besides pleasant and facetious in a high degree; and it is, therefore, more to be regretted than wondered at, that these sociable but dangerous qualities should sometimes lead him into excesses. Aubrey says in one of his MS. notes that he finally fell a sacrifice to the glass; in which he indulged with the wits of the age, not improbably with Shakspeare, Beaumont and Fletcher, and his admired Jonson. He died in 1618, two years after the appearance of this dedication, and was buried in the Temple Church.

[2] *For whose innocence, as for the author's, you were once a noble and timely undertaker, &c.*] It appears from the *Apologetical Dialogue* subjoined to this Drama, that Jonson was accused of having reflected in it on the professions of law and arms. By one of these he was probably threatened with a prosecution, either in the Star-chamber or the King's Bench, from which the friendly offices of Mr. Martin with the Lord Chief Justice seem to have delivered him. So, at least, I understand the passage. There was, indeed, another occasion on which the friendship of this generous man might have stood Jonson in great stead. I speak of his imprisonment, together with Chapman and Marston, for the satire against the Scots in *Eastward Hoe!* but as this was a most serious affair, and really implicated the poet's safety, he would perhaps have been more explicit had the allusion been to this circumstance.

[3] The quarto has no dedication, but merely the following address to the reader:

"*Ludimus innocuis verbis, hoc juro potentis*
Per Genium Famæ, Castalidumque gregem;
Perque tuas aures, magni mihi numinis instar,
Lector, inhumana liber ab invidia."—Mart.

The Poetaster.

After the second sounding.

Envy arises in the midst of the stage.

Light, I salute thee, but with wounded
  nerves,
Wishing thy golden splendour pitchy dark-
  ness.
What's here? THE ARRAIGNMENT![1] ay;
  this, this is it,
That our sunk eyes have waked for all this
  while:
Here will be subject for my snakes and me.
Cling to my neck and wrists, my loving
  worms,[2]
And cast you round in soft and amorous
  folds,
Till I do bid uncurl; then, break your
  knots,
Shoot out yourselves at length, as your
  forced stings
Would hide themselves within his maliced
  sides,
To whom I shall apply you. Stay! the
  shine
Of this assembly here offends my sight;
I'll darken that first, and outface their
  grace.
Wonder not, if I stare: these fifteen weeks,

So long as since the plot was but an em-
  brion,[3]
Have I, with burning lights mixt vigilant
  thoughts,
In expectation of this hated play,
To which at last I am arrived as Prologue.
Nor would I you should look for other
  looks,
Gesture, or compliment from me, than
  what
The infected bulk of Envy can afford:
For I am risse here with a covetous hope,
To blast your pleasures and destroy your
  sports,
With wrestings, comments, applications,
Spy-like suggestions, privy whisperings,
And thousand such promoting sleights as
  these.
Mark how I will begin: The scene is, ha!
Rome? Rome?[4] and Rome? Crack, eye-
  strings, and your balls
Drop into earth; let me be ever blind.
I am prevented; all my hopes are crost,
Checked, and abated; fie, a freezing sweat
Flows forth at all my pores, my entrails
  burn:
What should I do? Rome! Rome! O,
  my vext soul,
How might I force this to the present state?

---

[1] *What's here!* THE ARRAIGNMENT!] Envy says this upon discovering, as Whalley observes, the title of the play, which, as is already mentioned, was always written or painted in large letters, and fixed in some conspicuous part of the stage. To this practice there are innumerable allusions in our old dramatists.

[2] *Cling to my neck and wrists, my loving worms,]* *Worms*, the generic English word for snake, is very common in our ancient writers, though now confined to one or two of the species. Cowley seems to have had this description in view in the first book of the Davideis. Envy rises from the infernal regions, attired as she is here, and thus addresses her ministers:

  " With that she takes
One of her worst, her best *beloved snakes*,
Softly, *dear worm*, soft and unseen, she said,
Into his bosom steal," &c.

Cowley is so pleased with the management and address of Envy, that he very characteristically makes her "envy herself!"

[3] ———— *These* fifteen weeks,
So long as since the plot was but an embrion,] There is no pleasing Decker; for he twits Jonson with this confession. " What, will he be *fifteen weeks* about this cockatrice's egg too? has he not cackled yet? has he not layed yet?" Surely our Untrusser must have possessed a very extraordinary facility in writing, if such a period as this appeared too long for the production of the *Poetaster.*

[4] ———— *The scene is, ha!*
Rome! Rome! &c.] We have here a curious proof of the absolute poverty of the stage. As far as we have hitherto gone in Jonson, not the slightest notice has occurred of a moveable scene: a board, or a slip of paper, tells the audience that *Rome* is before them; and if there is any necessity for changing the place of action, as in *Catiline*, another bit of deal is thrust in to inform them that they now see Fesulæ. The rage of Envy is excited because the scene is not laid in London, and among the poet's contemporaries; a little patience, however, would have rendered her fury unnecessary.

Are there no players here? no poet apes,
That come with basilisk's eyes, whose
  forked tongues
Are steeped in venom, as their hearts in
  gall?
Either of these would help me; they could
  wrest,
Pervert, and poison all they hear, or see,
With senseless glosses, and allusions.
Now, if you be good devils, fly me not.
You know what dear and ample faculties
I have endowed you with: I'll lend you
  more.
Here, take my snakes among you, come
  and eat,
And while the squeezed juice flows in your
  black jaws,
Help me to damn the author. Spit it forth
Upon his lines, and shew your rusty teeth
At every word, or accent: or else choose
Out of my longest vipers, to stick down
In your deep throats; and let the heads
  come forth
At your rank mouths; that he may see you
  armed
With triple malice, to hiss, sting, and tear
His work and him; to forge, and then
  declaim,
Traduce, corrupt, apply, inform, suggest;
O, these are gifts wherein your souls are
  blest.
What! do you hide yourselves? will none
  appear?
None answer? what, doth this calm troop
  affright you?
Nay, then I do despair; down, sink again:
This travail is all lost with my dead hopes.
If in such bosoms spite have left to dwell,
Envy is not on earth, nor scarce in hell.
[*Descends slowly.*

The third sounding.

As she disappears, enter Prologue *hastily,
in armour.*

Stay, monster, ere thou sink—thus on thy
  head
Set we our bolder foot; with which we tread
Thy malice into earth: so Spite should die,
Despised and scorned by noble Industry.
If any muse why I salute the stage,
An armed Prologue;[1] know, 'tis a dan-
  gerous age:
Wherein who writes, had need present his
  scenes
Forty-fold proof against the conjuring
  means
Of base detractors, and illiterate apes,
That fill up rooms in fair and formal shapes.
'Gainst these, have we put on this forced
  defence:
Whereof the allegory and hid sense
Is, that a well erected confidence
Can fright their pride, and laugh their folly
  hence.
Here now, put case our author should, once
  more,
Swear that his play were good;[2] he doth
  implore,
You would not argue him of arrogance:
Howe'er that common spawn of ignorance,
Our fry of writers, may beslime his fame,
And give his action that adulterate name.
Such full-blown vanity he more doth loathe,
Than base dejection: there's a mean 'twixt
  both.
Which with a constant firmness he pursues,
As one that knows the strength of his own
  Muse.
And this he hopes all free souls will allow:

---

[1] *An armed Prologue;*] The prologue is spoken by a person in armour, to defend the author against the attacks of his adversaries and detractors. This whimsical circumstance has been imitated in the prologue to *Langartha*, a tragi-comedy by Henry Burnell, which an Amazon delivers with a battle-axe in her hand. And the prologue to *Troilus and Cressida* was so spoken:

  "And hither am I come,
A *prologue armed*—but not in confidence
Of author's pen."

Not, as the commentators observe, in confidence of the author's abilities, but in a character suited to the subject. *Troilus and Cressida* is supposed to have been written in 1602.—WHAL.

O bone, ποιον σε επος φυγεν? But for this inadvertent introduction of the date of *Troilus*

and *Cressida*, the passage in the text might have passed for a "wanton sneer" at Shakspeare: now, alas! the quotation can only be considered as a "just reflection" upon Jonson; which, as the commentators well know, is a very different thing.

[2] ——*Put case our author should, once more,*
  Swear that his play were good;] This alludes to the last line of the epilogue to *Cynthia's Revels*. It had justly scandalized the audience, and Jonson takes the first occasion to apologize for the language. His apology, however, is but awkward, and little more at best than an assumption of the very point in dispute. It is indeed true, that "there is a mean betwixt full-blown vanity and base dejection," but where is it to be found in the lines before us, or in those already noticed? It is but fair to remark that Jonson hazarded nothing equally offensive in his subsequent addresses to the theatre.

Others that take it with a rugged brow,
Their modes he rather pities than envíes:
His mind it is above their injuries.

─────

ACT I.

SCENE I.—*Scene draws, and discovers*
Ovid *in his study.*

Ovid. "Then, when this body falls in
    funeral fire,
My name shall live, and my best part aspire."
It shall go so.

Enter Luscus *with a gown and cap.*

Lus. Young master, Master Ovid, do
you hear? Gods a' me! away with your
songs and sonnets, and on with your gown
and cap quickly: here, here, your father
will be a man of this room presently. Come,
nay, nay, nay, nay, be brief. These verses
too, a poison on 'em! I cannot abide
them, they make me ready to cast, by the
banks of Helicon! Nay, look, what a
rascally untoward thing this poetry is; I
could tear them now.
Ovid. Give me; how near is my father?
Lus. Heart a' man: get a law book in
your hand, I will not answer you else.
[Ovid *puts on his cap and gown.*] Why so!
now there's some formality in you. By
Jove, and three or four of the gods more,
I am right of mine old master's humour
for that; this villainous poetry will undo
you, by the welkin.
Ovid. What, hast thou buskins on,
Luscus, that thou swearest so tragically and
high?

Lusc. No, but I have boots on, sir, and
so has your father too by this time; for he
called for them ere I came from the
lodging.
Ovid. Why, was he no readier?
Lus. O no; and there was the mad
skeldering captain,[1] with the velvet arms,
ready to lay hold on him as he comes down:
he that presses every man he meets, with
an oath to lend him money, and cries, *Thou
must do't, old boy, as thou art a man, a
man of worship.*
Ovid. Who, Pantilius Tucca?
Lus. Ay, he; and I met little Master
Lupus, the tribune, going thither too.
Ovid. Nay, an he be under their arrest,
I may with safety enough read over my
elegy before he come.
Lus. Gods a' me! what will you do?
why, young master, you are not Castalian
mad, lunatic, frantic, desperate, ha!
Ovid. What ailest thou, Luscus?
Lus. God be with you, sir; I'll leave you
to your poetical fancies and furies. I'll
not be guilty, I.   [*Exit.*
Ovid. Be not, good ignorance. I'm glad
th' art gone;
For thus alone, our ear shall better judge
The hasty errors of our morning muse.
"Envy, why twit'st thou me,[2] my time's
    spent ill,
And call'st my verse, fruits of an idle quill?
Or that, unlike the line from whence I
    sprung,
War's dusty honours I pursue not young?
Or that I study not the tedious laws,
And prostitute my voice in every cause?
Thy scope is mortal; mine, eternal fame,
Which through the world shall ever chant
    my name.

─────

[1] *The mad* skeldering *captain,*] This word,
which is explained in p. 64, is adopted by our
poet's antagonist, and applied to the same
character: "Come—if *skeldering* fall not to
decay, thou shalt flourish."—*Satiromastix.*
And by Marmion:

"Wandering abroad to *skelder* for a shilling,
    Amongst your bowling allies."
        Fine Companion, act iii. sc. 4.

[2] *Envy, why twit'st thou me, &c.*] Jonson's
translations, as Whalley somewhere observes,
"are not to be estimated by the smooth and
flowing elegance of modern paraphrasts." Con-
ciseness and a close adherence to the text were
the points at which he aimed; and in these he
rarely fails of his ends. The present version,
which is that of El. 15, Amor. Lib. i., gives us
line for line of the original, without the omission
of a single idea; nor is it altogether devoid of
ease and spirit.

This little poem does not now appear for the
first time. In 1599 was published a translation
of Ovid's *Elegies* by Christopher Marlow, and
this among them: not, indeed, precisely as it
stands here, but with such variations as may be
supposed to exist in the rough sketch of a finished
original. Marlow was now dead; but it seems
strange that the editor of his poems, who might
be Chapman, should print this under his name,
especially as it is followed by that before us;
which Jonson probably reclaimed when he wrote
the *Poetaster.*
I give this poem to Jonson, because he is well
known to be incapable of taking credit for the
talents of another; and it certainly affords a curious instance of the laxity of literary morality in
those days, when a scholar could assert his title to
a poem of forty-two lines, of which thirty at least
are literally borrowed, and the remainder only
varied for the worse. [This charge is altogether
groundless, see *Marlowe's Works,* p. 357.—F.C.]

Homer will live whilst Tenedos stands, and
   Ide,
Or, to the sea, fleet Simois doth slide:
And so shall Hesiod too, while vines do
   bear,
Or crooked sickles crop the ripened ear.
Callimachus, though in invention low,
Shall still be sung, since he in art doth flow.
No loss shall come to Sophocles' proud
   vein;
With sun and moon Aratus shall remain.
While slaves be false, fathers hard, and
   bawds be whorish,
Whilst harlots flatter, shall Menander
   flourish.
Ennius, though rude, and Accius' high-
   reared strain,
A fresh applause in every age shall gain.
Of Varro's name, what ear shall not be told,
Of Jason's Argo and the fleece of gold?
Then shall Lucretius' lofty numbers die,
When earth and seas in fire and flame shall
   fry.
Tityrus, Tillage, Ænee shall be read,
Whilst Rome of all the conquered world is
   head!
Till Cupid's fires be out, and his bow
   broken,
Thy verses, neat Tibullus, shall be spoken.
Our Gallus shall be known from east to
   west;
So shall Lycoris whom he now loves best.
The suffering plough-share or the flint may
   wear;
But heavenly Poesy no death can fear.
Kings shall give place to it, and kingly
   shows,
The banks o'er which gold-bearing Tagus
   flows.
Kneel hinds to trash: me lef bright
   Phœbus swell
With cups full flowing from the Muses' well.
Frost-fearing myrtle shall impale my head,
And of sad lovers I be often read.
Envy the living, not the dead, doth bite;
For after death all men receive their right.
Then, when this body falls in funeral fire,
My name shall live, and my best part
   aspire."

Enter Ovid *senior, followed by* Luscus,
   Tucca, *and* Lupus.

Ovid se. Your "name shall live," indeed,
sir! you say true: but how infamously,
how scorned and contemned in the eyes
and ears of the best and gravest Romans,
that you think not on; you never so much
as dream of that. Are these the fruits of
all my travail and expenses? Is this the
scope and aim of thy studies? Are these
the hopeful courses, wherewith I have so
long flattered my expectation from thee?
Verses! Poetry! Ovid, whom I thought
to see the pleader, become Ovid the play-
maker!
Ovid ju. No, sir.
Ovid se. Yes, sir; I hear of a tragedy of
yours coming forth for the common players
there, called Medea.[1] By my household
gods, if I come to the acting of it, I'll add
one tragic part more than is yet expected
to it: believe me, when I promise it.
What! shall I have my son a stager now?
an enghle for players?[2] a gull, a rook, a
shot-clog, to make suppers, and be laughed
at? Publius, I will set thee on the funeral
pile first.
Ovid ju. Sir, I beseech you to have
patience.
Lus. Nay, this 'tis to have your ears
dammed up to good counsel. I did augur
all this to him beforehand, without poring
into an ox's paunch for the matter, and yet
he would not be scrupulous.
Tuc. How now, goodman slave! what,
rowly-powly? all rivals, rascal? Why, my
master of worship,[3] dost hear? are these
thy best projects? is this thy designs and
thy discipline, to suffer knaves to be competitors with commanders and gentlemen?
Are we parallels, rascal, are we parallels?
Ovid se. Sirrah, go get my horses ready.
You'll still be prating.
Tuc. Do, you perpetual stinkard, do,
go; talk to tapsters and ostlers, you slave;
they are in your element, go: here be the
emperor's captains, you ragamuffin rascal,
and not your comrades. [*Exit* Luscus.

---

[1] *A tragedy of yours called* Medea.] Of this
tragedy all but one line is lost. It is mentioned
by Quintilian and the elder Seneca as a work of
considerable merit: indeed, Ovid himself speaks
of it with some complacency, and asserts that he
was not without talents for compositions of this
nature:

  " *Sceptra tamen sumpsi; curaque tragædia*
    nostra

    Crevit, et huic operi quamlibet aptus eram."
          Am. lib. 2, el. xviii.

[2] *An* enghle *for players.*] See p. 222.
[3] *Why, my* master *of worship, &c.*] The
quarto reads my *knight*, &c. Ovid was of the
equestrian order: there are several variations of
a similar nature in the appellations with which
this whimsical character so frequently sports;
but they are in general too unimportant for particular notice.

Lup. Indeed, Marcus Ovid, these players are an idle generation, and do much
harm in a state, corrupt young gentry very
much, I know it ; I have not been a tribune
thus long and observed nothing : besides,
they will rob us, us, that are magistrates, of
our respect, bring us upon their stages, and
make us ridiculous to the plebeians ; they
will play you or me, the wisest men they
can come by still, only to bring us in
contempt with the vulgar, and make us
cheap.

Tuc. Thou art in the right, my venerable
crop-shin, they will indeed ; the tongue of
the oracle never twanged truer.   Your
courtier cannot kiss his mistress's slippers
in quiet for them ; nor your white innocent
gallant pawn his revelling suit to make his
punk a supper.   An honest decayed commander cannot skelder, cheat, nor be seen
in a bawdy-house, but he shall be straight
in one of their wormwood comedies.   They
are grown licentious, the rogues ; libertines,
flat libertines.   They forget they are in the
statute,[1] the rascals ; they are blazoned
there ; there they are tricked,[2] they and
their pedigrees ; they need no other heralds,
I wiss.

Ovid se. Methinks, if nothing else, yet
this alone, the very reading of the public
edicts, should fright thee from commerce
with them, and give thee distaste enough
of their actions.   But this betrays what a
student you are, this argues your proficiency
in the law !

Ovid ju. They wrong me, sir, and do
  abuse you more,
That blow your ears with these untrue
  reports.
I am not known unto the open stage,
Nor do I traffic in their theatres :
Indeed, I do acknowledge, at request
Of some near friends,[3] and honourable
  Romans,
I have begun a poem of that nature.

Ovid se. You have, sir, a poem ! and
where is it ?   That's the law you study.

Ovid ju. Cornelius Gallus borrowed it
to read.

Ovid se. Cornelius Gallus ! there's another gallant too hath drunk of the same
poison, and Tibullus and Propertius.   But
these are gentlemen of means and revenues
now.   Thou art a younger brother, and
hast nothing but thy bare exhibition ;[4]
which I protest shall be bare indeed, if thou
forsake not these unprofitable by-courses,
and that timely too.   Name me a profest
poet, that his poetry did ever afford him so
much as a competency.   Ay, your god of
poets there, whom all of you admire and
reverence so much, Homer, he whose
worm-eaten statue must not be spewed
against, but with hallowed lips and grovelling adoration, what was he ? what was he ?

Tuc. Marry, I'll tell thee, old swaggerer ;
he was a poor blind, rhyming rascal, that
lived obscurely up and down in booths and
tap-houses, and scarce ever made a good
meal in his sleep, the whoreson hungry
beggar.

Ovid se. He says well :—nay, I know
this nettles you now ; but answer me, is it
not true ?   You'll tell me his name shall
live ; and that now being dead his works
have eternized him, and made him divine :
but could this divinity feed him while he
lived ? could his name feast him ?

Tuc. Or purchase him a senator's revenue, could it ?

Ovid se. Ay, or give him place in the
commonwealth ? worship, or attendants ?
make him be carried in his litter ?

Tuc. Thou speakest sentences, old Bias.[5]

Lup. All this the law will do, young sir,
if you'll follow it.

Ovid se. If he be mine, he shall follow
and observe what I will apt him to, or I
profess here openly and utterly to disclaim
him.

---

[1] *They forget they are in the* statute, *&c.*]
He alludes to the statute of the thirty-ninth of
Elizabeth, by which common players, i.e., persons not authorized to act under the hand and
seal of some nobleman, were deemed rogues and
vagabonds.

[2] *They are blazoned there; there they are*
tricked,] To *blazon*, is to set forth a coat
of arms in its proper colours ; to *trick*, as has
been before observed, is to draw it only with
a pen.

[3] *Of some near friends,*] Whalley, who took
for his text the paltry edition of the booksellers,
gave *meer* friends ; an expression not bad in
itself, but without authority.   This very corrup-

tion has been frequently produced by the commentators, as ascertaining the ancient sense of
the word *mere*.   It is seldom safe to trust a copy
of a copy ; they should have turned to the quarto
and folio editions.

[4] *Thy bare* exhibition ;] i.e., stipend, or annual
allowance from his father.   This word has been
already noticed.

[5] *Thou speakest sentences, old* Bias.]   Bias
was one of the seven sages of Greece.   Immortality was cheaply purchased in his days, for, to
speak tenderly, there is "no great matter" in
such of his "sentences" as have come down to
us.   What follows, as far as "Well, the day
grows old," is not in the quarto.

Ovid ju. Sir, let me crave you will forego these moods :
I will be anything, or study anything ;
I'll prove the unfashioned body of the law
Pure elegance, and make her rugged'st strains
Run smoothly as Propertius' elegies.

Ovid se. Propertius' elegies ? good !

Lup. Nay, you take him too quickly, Marcus.

Ovid se. Why, he cannot speak, he cannot think out of poetry ; he is bewitched with it.

Lup. Come, do not misprize him.

Ovid se. Misprize ! ay, marry, I would have him use some such words now; they have some touch, some taste of the law. He should make himself a style out of these, and let his Propertius' elegies go by.

Lup. Indeed, young Publius, he that will now hit the mark, must shoot through the law ;[1] we have no other planet reigns, and in that sphere you may sit and sing with angels. Why, the law makes a man happy,[2] without respecting any other merit ; a simple scholar, or none at all, may be a lawyer.

Tuc. He tells thee true, my noble neophyte ; my little grammaticaster, he does : it shall never put thee to thy mathematics, metaphysics, philosophy, and I know not what supposed sufficiencies ; if thou canst but have the patience to plod enough, talk, and make a noise enough, be impudent enough, and 'tis enough.

Lup. Three books will furnish you.

Tuc. And the less art the better : besides, when it shall be in the power of thy chevril conscience ;[3] to do right or wrong at thy pleasure, my pretty Alcibiades.

Lup. Ay, and to have better men than

himself, by many thousand degrees, to observe him, and stand bare.

Tuc. True, and he to carry himself proud and stately, and have the law on his side for't, old boy.

Ovid se. Well, the day grows old, gentlemen, and I must leave you. Publius, if thou wilt hold my favour, abandon these idle, fruitless studies that so bewitch thee. Send Janus home his backface again, and look only forward to the law : intend that. I will allow thee what shall suit thee in the rank of gentlemen, and maintain thy society with the best ; and under these conditions I leave thee. My blessings light upon thee, if thou respect them ; if not, mine eyes may drop for thee, but thine own heart will ache for itself; and so farewell ! What, are my horses come ?

Lus. Yes, sir, they are at the gate without.

Ovid se. That's well.—Asinius Lupus, a word. Captain, I shall take my leave of you ?

Tuc. No, my little old boy, dispatch with Cothurnus there : I'll attend thee, I——

Lus. To borrow some ten drachms: I know his project.   [*Aside.*

Ovid se. Sir, you shall make me beholding to you. Now, Captain Tucca, what say you ?

Tuc. Why, what should I say, or what can I say, my flower o' the order ? Should I say thou art rich, or that thou art honourable, or wise, or valiant, or learned, or liberal ? why, thou art all these, and thou knowest it, my noble Lucullus, thou knowest it. Come, be not ashamed of thy virtues, old stump : honour's a good brooch to wear in a man's hat[4] at all times. Thou art the man of war's Mecænas, old boy.

---

[1] *He that will now hit the mark, must shoot through the law," &c.*] These and what follow are probably the passages which gave offence to the professors of the law. Jonson's old antagonist thus alludes to them, "Thou hast entered actions of assault and battery against a company of honourable and worshipful fathers of the law, thou wrangling rascal : law is one of the pillars of the land."—*Satiromastix.*

[2] *Why, the law makes a man happy, &c.*] i.e., rich ; a Latinism ; there is something too pedantical in this ;—it is, however, more excusable than the carelessness of our modern translators, who sometimes anglicise the word (*beatus*) literally, to the utter destruction of the sense. An instance just occurs to me. *Cat.* Car. x.

"*Ego, ut puellæ*
Unum me facerem beatiorum," &c.

This is rendered,

"I answered, that the slut, I own,
Might take me for a *lucky* one," &c.

It should be, for a *wealthy* one.

[3] *Thy chevril conscience ;*] i.e., stretching : the allusion is to kid's leather, which is yielding and pliable : thus Shakspeare :

"The capacity
Of your soft *chevril* conscience would receive,
If you might please to stretch it."
Henry VIII., act ii. sc. 3. WHAL.

[4] *Honour's a good brooch to wear in a man's hat*] The fashion of wearing some kind of ornament in the front of the hat is noticed by all our old poets. These *brooches* were sometimes of great value, and formed of jewels set in gold or silver (see Massinger, vol. iv. p. 213), and some-

Why shouldst not thou be graced then by them, as well as he is by his poets?—

Enter Pyrgus *and whispers* Tucca.

How now, my carrier, what news?

Lus. The boy has stayed within for his cue this half hour.   [*Aside.*

Tuc. Come, do not whisper to me, but speak it out: what! it is no treason against the state I hope, is it?

Lus. Yes, against the state of my master's purse.   [*Aside, and exit.*

Pyr. [*aloud.*] Sir, Agrippa desires you to forbear him till the next week; his mules are not yet come up.

Tuc. His mules! now the bots, the spavin, and the glanders, and some dozen diseases more, light on him and his mules! What, have they the yellows, his mules, that they come no faster? or are they foundered, ha? his mules have the staggers belike, have they?

Pyr. O no, sir:—then your tongue might be suspected for one of his mules. [*Aside.*

Tuc. He owes me almost a talent, and he thinks to bear it away with his mules, does he? Sirrah, you nut-cracker, go your ways to him again, and tell him I must have money, I: I cannot eat stones and turfs, say. What, will he clem me and my followers?[1] ask him an he will clem me; do, go. He would have me fry my jerkin, would he? Away, setter, away. Yet, stay, my little tumbler,[2] this old boy shall supply now. I will not trouble him, I cannot be importunate, I; I cannot be impudent.

Pyr. Alas, sir, no; you are the most maidenly blushing creature upon the earth.   [*Aside.*

Tuc. Dost thou hear, my little six and fifty, or thereabouts? thou art not to learn the humours and tricks of that old bald cheater, Time; thou hast not this chain for nothing. Men of worth have their

chimeras, as well as other creatures; and they do see monsters sometimes, they do, they do, brave boy.

Pyr. Better cheap than he shall see you,[3] I warrant him.   [*Aside.*

Tuc. Thou must let me have six—six drachms, I mean, old boy: thou shalt do it; I tell thee, old boy, thou shalt, and in private too, dost thou see?—Go, walk off: [*to the Boy*]—There, there. Six is the sum. Thy son's a gallant spark, and must not be put out of a sudden. Come hither, Callimachus; thy father tells me thou art too poetical, boy: thou must not be so; thou must leave them, young novice, thou must; they are a sort of poor starved rascals, that are ever wrapt up in foul linen; and can boast of nothing but a lean visage, peering out of a seam-rent suit, the very emblems of beggary. No, dost hear, turn lawyer, thou shalt be my solicitor.—'Tis right, old boy, is 't?

Ovid se. You were best tell it, captain.

Tuc. No; fare thou well, mine honest horseman; and thou, old beaver. [*to* Lupus] —Pray thee, Roman, when thou comest to town, see me at my lodging, visit me sometimes; thou shalt be welcome, old boy. Do not balk me, good swaggerer. Jove keep thy chain from pawning; go thy ways, if thou lack money I'll lend thee some: I'll leave thee to thy horse now. Adieu.

Ovid se. Farewell, good captain.

Tuc. Boy, you can have but half a share now, boy.   [*Exit, followed by* Pyrgus.

Ovid se. 'Tis a strange boldness that accompanies this fellow.—Come.

Ovid ju. I'll give attendance on you to your horse, sir, please you——

Ovid se. No; keep your chamber, and fall to your studies; do so. The gods of Rome bless thee!   [*Exit with* Lupus.

Ovid ju. And give me stomach to digest this law:[4]

---

times of copper, lead, &c., nay, so universal was the mode, that to accommodate the poor, it was found necessary to form them like the boss of the Romans, of yet ruder materials, pasteboard and leather. The last is mentioned by Decker, "Thou shalt wear her glove in thy worshipful hat, like to a *leather brooch.*"— *Satiromastix.*

[1] *What, will he clem me and my followers?*] i.e., *starve.* It has occurred already, p. 102 *b,* "Hard is the choice, when the valiant must eat their arms or clem." See also Massinger, vol. ii. p. 362. There is some pleasantry in making Agrippa, the first man in the state, indebted to this beggarly captain.

[2] *Yet, stay, my little* tumbler,] Not one that

shews postures, but a particular kind of dog, to which our ancestors gave the name of *tumbler,* from his manner of hunting.—WHAL.

[3] *Better cheap than he shall see you,*] At a less price. *Cheap* is market, and the adjective *good,* with its comparatives, is often joined with it by our old writers; thus we have continually good cheap, *better cheap,* &c. for cheap, cheaper, and cheapest.

[4] *And give me stomach to digest this law: That should have followed,* &c.] So Gloster, in the same strain of irony:

" Amen! and make me die a good old man! That is the butt end of a mother's blessing; I marvel that her Grace did leave it out." *Rich. III.,* act ii. sc. 2. WHAL.

That should have followed sure, had I
    been he.
O, sacred Poesy, thou spirit of arts,
The soul of science, and the queen of souls ;
What profane violence, almost sacrilege,
Hath here been offered thy divinities !
That thine own guiltless poverty should
    arm
Prodigious ignorance to wound thee thus !
For thence is all their force of argument
Drawn forth against thee ; or from the
    abuse
Of thy great powers in adulterate brains :
When, would men learn but to distinguish
    spirits,
And set true difference 'twixt those jaded
    wits
That run a broken pace for common hire,
And the high raptures of a happy muse,
Born on the wings of her immortal thought,
That kicks at earth with a disdainful heel,
And beats at heaven gates with her bright
    hoofs ;
They would not then, with such distorted
    faces,
And desperate censures, stab at Poesy.
They would admire bright knowledge, and
    their minds
Should ne'er descend on so unworthy
    objects
As gold or titles ; they would dread far
    more
To be thought ignorant than be known
    poor.
The time was once,[1] when wit drowned
    wealth ; but now,
Your only barbarism is t' have wit, and
    want.
No matter now in virtue who excels,
He that hath coin, hath all perfection else.
  Tib. [*within.*] Ovid !
  Ovid. Who's there ? Come in.

Enter Tibullus.

  Tib. Good morrow, lawyer.[2]
  Ovid. Good morrow, dear Tibullus ; wel-
come : sit down.
  Tib. Not I. What, so hard at it ? Let's
see what's here ?
" Numa in decimo nono !" Nay, I will see
  it——
  Ovid. Prithee away——
  Tib. " If thrice in field a man vanquish
    his foe,
    'Tis after in his choice to serve or no."
How now, Ovid ! Law cases in verse ?
  Ovid. In troth, I know not ; they run
from my pen unwittingly, if they be verse.[3]
What's the news abroad ?
  Tib. Off with this gown ; I come to have
thee walk.
  Ovid. No, good Tibullus, I'm not now
    in case.
Pray let me alone.
  Tib. How ! not in case ?
'Slight, thou'rt in too much case, by all
    this law.
  Ovid. Troth, if I live, I will new dress
    the law
In sprightly Poesy's habiliments.
  Tib. The hell thou wilt ! What ! turn
law into verse ?
Thy father has school'd thee, I see. Here,
    read that same.
There's subject for you ; and, if I mistake
    not,
A *supersedeas* to your melancholy.
  Ovid. How ! subscribed *Julia !* O my
    life, my heaven !
  Tib. Is the mood changed ?
  Ovid. Music of wit ! note for the har-
monious spheres !
Celestial accents, how you ravish me !
  Tib. What is it, Ovid ?

---

[1] *The time was once,* &c.] This is from
Amor. lib. iii. eleg. 8.
" *Ingenium quondam fuerat pretiosius auro ;*
  At nunc barbaries grandis, habere nihil."
[2] *Good morrow, lawyer.*] It should be observed, that Ovid is still in the cap and gown
which he had assumed upon the entrance of his
father.
[3] *They run from my pen unwittingly, if they
be verse.*]
" *Sponte tamen numeros carmen veniebat ad
  aptos,*
  Et quod conabar scribere, versus erat."
The above, however, is but a poor specimen of
it ; though it serves well enough to show that
Lord Hardwicke was not the first who thought
of putting the common law into verse. As

Whalley brought back the date of this law from
the 4to, it is here retained ; though with some
little injustice perhaps to Jonson. He had discovered, I imagine, the impropriety of attri-
buting regulations of a warlike nature to Numa,
and therefore omitted the title upon a revision of
the play.
  We hear no more of Ovid's law ; yet he was
somewhat farther advanced in it than Jonson
seems to admit : he was apparently a very
respectable advocate. He tells Augustus that
he had pleaded causes in his youth with success
as one of the Centumviri ; and that, when he
heard private disputes as a judge, the losing
parties were satisfied with the equity of his
decision :
" *Nec male commissa est nobis fortuna reorum,*
  Lisque," &c.—*Trist.* lib. ii. v. 93.

Ovid. That I must meet my Julia, the
Princess Julia.
Tib. Where?
Ovid. Why, at——
Heart, I've forgot; my passion so trans-
ports me.
Tib. I'll save your pains : it is at Albius'
house,
The jeweller's, where the fair Lycoris lies.
Ovid. Who? Cytheris, Cornelius Gallus'
love?
Tib. Ay, he'll be there too, and my
Plautia.
Ovid. And why not your Delia?
Tib. Yes, and your Corinna.
Ovid. True; but, my sweet Tibullus,
keep that secret;
I would not, for all Rome, it should be
thought
I veil bright Julia underneath that name :
Julia, the gem and jewel of my soul,
That takes her honours from the golden sky,
As beauty doth all lustre from her eye.
The air respires the pure Elysian sweets
In which she breathes, and from her looks
descend
The glories of the summer. Heaven she is,
Praised in herself above all praise ; and he
Which hears her speak, would swear the
tuneful orbs
Turned in his zenith only.
Tib. Publius, thou'lt lose thyself.
Ovid. O, in no labyrinth can I safelier err,
Than when I lose myself in praising her.
Hence, law, and welcome Muses! though
not rich,
Yet are you pleasing : let's be reconciled,
And new made one. Henceforth, I pro-
mise faith,
And all my serious hours to spend with
you ;
With you, whose music striketh on my
heart,
And with bewitching tones steals forth my
spirit,
In Julia's name; fair Julia : Julia's love
Shall be a law, and that sweet law I'll
study,
The law and art of sacred Julia's love :
All other objects will but abjects prove.
Tib. Come, we shall have thee as pas-
sionate as
Propertius anon.
Ovid. O, how does my Sextus?
Tib. Faith, full of sorrow for his Cynthia's
death.
Ovid. What, still?
Tib. Still, and still more, his griefs do
grow upon him

As do his hours. Never did I know
An understanding spirit so take to heart
The common work of Fate.
Ovid. O, my Tibullus,
Let us not blame him; for against such
chances
The heartiest strife of virtue is not proof.
We may read constancy and fortitude
To other souls ; but had ourselves been
struck
With the like planet, had our loves, like
his,
Been ravished from us by injurious death,
And in the height and heat of our best
days,
It would have cracked our sinews, shrunk
our veins,
And made our **very** heart-strings jar, like
his.
Come, let's go take him forth, and prove
if mirth
Or company will but abate his passion:
Tib. Content, and I implore the gods
it may.   [*Exeunt.*

——

ACT II.

SCENE I.—*A Room in* Albius's *House.*

Enter Albius *and* Crispinus.

Alb. Master Crispinus, you are welcome :
pray use a stool, sir. Your cousin Cytheris will come down presently. We are
so busy for the receiving of these courtiers
here, that I can scarce be a minute with
myself, for thinking of them. Pray you
sit, sir ; pray you sit, sir.
Crisp. I am very well, sir. Never trust
me, but you are most delicately seated
here, full of sweet delight and blandish-
ment ! an excellent air, an excellent air !
Alb. Ay, sir, 'tis a pretty air. These
courtiers run in my mind still ; I must
look out. For Jupiter's sake, sit, sir ; or
please you walk into the garden? There's
a garden on the back-side.
Crisp. I am most strenuously well, I
thank you, sir.
Alb. Much good do you, sir.

Enter Chloe, *with two* Maids.

Chloe. Come, bring those perfumes forward a little, and strew some roses and
violets here. Fie! here be rooms savour
the most pitifully rank that ever I felt. I
cry the gods mercy, [*sees* Albius] my
husband's in the wind of us !

Alb. Why, this is good, excellent, excellent! well said, my sweet Chloe; trim up your house most obsequiously.

Chloe. For Vulcan's sake, breathe somewhere else: in troth, you overcome our perfumes exceedingly; you are too predominant.

Alb. Hear but my opinion, sweet wife.

Chloe. A pin for your pinion! In sincerity, if you be thus fulsome to me in everything, I'll be divorced. Gods my body! you know what you were before I married you; I was a gentlewoman born, I; I lost all my friends to be a citizen's wife, because I heard, indeed, they kept their wives as fine as ladies; and that we might rule our husbands like ladies, and do what we listed; do you think I would have married you else?

Alb. I acknowledge, sweet wife:—she speaks the best of any woman in Italy, and moves as mightily; which makes me, I had rather she should make bumps on my head, as big as my two fingers, than I would offend her.—But, sweet wife——

Chloe. Yet again! Is it not grace enough for you, that I call you husband, and you call me wife; but you must still be poking me, against my will, to things?

Alb. But you know, wife, here are the greatest ladies, and gallantest gentlemen of Rome, to be entertained in our house now; and I would fain advise thee to entertain them in the best sort, i' faith, wife.

Chloe. In sincerity, did you ever hear a man talk so idly? You would seem to be master! you would have your spoke in my cart! you would advise me to entertain ladies and gentlemen! Because you can marshal your pack-needles, horse-combs, hobby-horses, and wall-candlesticks in your warehouse better than I, therefore you can tell how to entertain ladies and gentlefolks better than I!

Alb. O, my sweet wife, upbraid me not with that; gain savours sweetly from any thing;[1] he that respects to get, must relish all commodities alike, and admit no difference between oade and frankincense,[2] or the most precious balsamum and a tar-barrel.

Chloe. Marry, foh! you sell snuffers too,[3] if you be remembered; but I pray you let me buy them out of your hand; for, I tell you true, I take it highly in snuff, to learn how to entertain gentlefolks of you, at these years, i' faith. Alas, man, there was not a gentleman came to your house in your t'other wife's time, I hope! nor a lady, nor music, nor masques! Nor you nor your house were so much as spoken of, before I disbased myself, from my hood and my farthingal, to these bum-rowls and your whalebone bodice.

Alb. Look here, my sweet wife; I am mum, my dear mummia, my balsamum, my spermaceti, and my very city of——She has the most best, true, feminine wit in Rome!

Cris. I have heard so, sir; and do most vehemently desire to participate the knowledge of her fair features.

Alb. Ah, peace; you shall hear more anon; be not seen yet, I pray you; not yet: observe.   [*Exit.*

Chloe. 'Sbody! give husbands the head a little more, and they'll be nothing but head shortly. What's he there?

1 Maid. I know not, forsooth.

2 Maid. Who would you speak with, sir?

Cris. I would speak with my cousin Cytheris.

2 Maid. He is one, forsooth, would speak with his cousin Cytheris.

Chloe. Is she your cousin, sir?

Cris. [*coming forward.*] Yes, in truth, forsooth, for fault of a better.

Chloe. She is a gentlewoman.

Cris. Or else she should not be my cousin, I assure you.

Chloe. Are you a gentleman born?

Cris. That I am, lady; you shall see mine arms if it please you.

Chloe. No, your legs do sufficiently shew you are a gentleman born, sir; for a man

---

[1] *Gain savours sweetly from anything;*] When Jonson thus gave us the meaning of the Latin saying, *Lucri bonus est odor ex re qualibet,* he forgot that the occasion from which it took its rise was much posterior to the age in which the persons of his drama lived.—WHAL.

Whalley alludes to the well-known anecdote of Vespasian: the words of the text, however, are a proverbial sentence as old in the world as the love of gain. The merit of Vespasian's jest consists in the practical application of them.

[2] *Admit no difference between* oade, *&c.*] i.e., "woad, a plant much cultivated in this country for the use of dyers."—*Dict.* The blue tinct with which the ancient Britons stained their bodies, is said to have been obtained from this vegetable.

[3] *Marry, foh! you sell* snuffers *too, &c.*] These, with the articles enumerated above, seem rather awkwardly placed in a jeweller's shop: but trades were fewer, and less accurately defined, in Jonson's days; hence these collections of heterogeneous wares were to be found in every street. Chloe is a confirmed punster.

borne upon little legs, is always a gentleman born.[1]

Cris. Yet, I pray you, vouchsafe the sight of my arms, mistress ; for I bear them about me to have them seen. My name is *Crispinus*, or *Cri-spinas* indeed ; which is well expressed in my arms ;[2] a face crying *in chief;* and beneath it a bloody toe, between three thorns *pungent.*

Chloe. Then you are welcome, sir ; now you are a gentleman born, I can find in my heart to welcome you ; for I am a gentlewoman born too, and will bear my head high enough, though 'twere my fortune to marry a tradesman.[3]

Cris. No doubt of that, sweet feature ; ycu carriage shews it in any man's eye, that is carried upon you with judgment.

Re-enter Albius.

Alb. Dear wife, be not angry.

Chloe. Gods my passion !

Alb. Hear me but one thing ; let not your maids set cushions in the parlour windows, nor in the dining-chamber windows ; nor upon stools, in either of them, in any case ; for 'tis tavern-like : but lay them one upon another, in some outroom or corner of the dining-chamber.

Chloe. Go, go ; meddle with your bedchamber only ; or rather with your bed in your chamber only ; or rather with your wife in your bed only ; or, on my faith, I'll not be pleased with you only.

Alb. Look here, my dear wife, entertain that gentleman kindly, I prithee——mum. [*Exit.*

Chloe. Go, I need your instructions indeed ! anger me no more, I advise you. Citi-sin, quoth'a !⁴ she's a wise gentlewoman, i' faith, will marry herself to the sin of the city.

Alb. [*re-entering.*] But this time, and no more, by heav'n, wife : hang no pictures in the hall, nor in the dining-chamber, in any case, but in the gallery only : for 'tis not courtly else, o' my word, wife.

Chloe. 'Sprecious, never have done !

Alb. Wife—— [*Exit.*

Chloe. Do I not bear a reasonable corrigible hand over him, Crispinus ?

Cris. By this hand, lady, you hold a most sweet hand over him.

Alb. [*re-entering.*] And then, for the great gilt andirons——

Chloe. Again ! Would the andirons were in your great guts for me !

Alb. I do vanish, wife. [*Exit.*

Chloe. How shall I do, Master Crispinus? here will be all the bravest ladies in court presently to see your cousin Cytheris : O the gods ! how might I behave myself now, as to entertain them most courtly?

Cris. Marry, lady, if you will entertain them most courtly, you must do thus : as soon as ever your maid or your man brings you word they are come, you must say, *A pox on 'em! what do they here?* And yet, when they come, speak them as fair, and give them the kindest welcome in words that can be.

Chloe. Is that the fashion of courtiers, Crispinus ?

[1] *A man borne upon little legs is always a gentleman born.*] To this fashionable characteristic of a fine gentleman, there are innumerable allusions in our old writers ; thus Browne :

" If *small legs* wan
Ever the title of a *gentleman,*
His did acquire it."—*Brit. Past.* lib. 2.

And Beaumont and Fletcher :

" I'll never trust long chins and *little legs* again ;
But know them, sure, for *gentlemen* hereafter."

And see Massinger, vol. iv. 278. Decker, in his *Gull's Hornbook,* evidently refers to this passage. " Now, sir, if the writer" (of the comedy) "be a fellow that hath either epigrammed you or hath had a flurt at your mistress, or hath brought either your feather or your *red* beard, or your *little legs* on the stage, you shall disgrace him worse than by tossing him in a blanket, or giving him the bastinado in a taverne, if, in the middle of his play, you rise," &c. Here Decker retorts on Jonson ; the *blanketting* alludes to the punishment inflicted on him in the *Satiromastix,* and

the *bastinadoing* to a circumstance of which (whether true or not) several hints are to be found in the same play.

[2] *My name is Crispinus, or Cri-spinas indeed; which is well expressed in my arms,* &c.] There is probably some personal allusion here, which is now lost. Whatever it was, it seems to have distressed Decker, for he strives to parry the attack by introducing a miserable witticism of his own—" as for Crispinus, that Crispineass," &c. These barbarous attempts upon names, under the title of anagrams, were among the amusements of scholars in Jonson's time : he, however, seems to have had a fixed contempt for them.

[3] *To marry a* tradesman.] The quarto reads —to marry a *flat-cap,* a term of contempt usually applied to a citizen. See p. 17 b.

⁴ Citi-sin, *quoth'a!* &c.] This exquisite pun on citizen serves very well to keep Cri-spinas [Cry-thorns] in countenance. A little false spelling, I presume, (for I am no great adept in these matters), is allowable where the effect produced by it is so very striking.

Cris. I assure you it is, lady ; I have observed it.

Chloe. For your pox, sir, it is easily hit on ; but it is not so easy to speak fair after, methinks.

Alb. [*re-entering.*] O, wife, the coaches are come, on my word ; a number of coaches and courtiers.

Chloe. A pox on them ! what do they here ?[1]

Alb. How now, wife ! wouldst thou not have them come ?

Chloe. Come ! come, you are a fool, you.—He knows not the trick on't. Call Cytheris, I pray you : and, good Master Crispinus, you can observe, you say ; let me entreat you for all the ladies' behaviours, jewels, jests, and attires, that you marking, as well as I, we may put both our marks together, when they are gone, and confer of them.

Cris. I warrant you, sweet lady ; let me alone to observe till I turn myself to nothing but observation.—

Enter Cytheris.

Good morrow, cousin Cytheris.

Cyth. Welcome, kind cousin, What ! are they come ?

Alb. Ay, your friend Cornelius Gallus, Ovid, Tibullus, Propertius, with Julia, the emperor's daughter, and the Lady Plautia, are 'lighted at the door ; and with them Hermogenes Tigellius, the excellent musician.

Cyth. Come, let us go meet them, Chloe.

Chloe. Observe, Crispinus.

Crisp. At a hair's breadth, lady, I warrant you.

As they are going out, enter Cornelius Gallus, Ovid, Tibullus, Propertius. Hermogenes, Julia, *and* Plautia.

Gal. Health to the lovely Chloe ! you must pardon me, mistress, that I prefer this fair gentlewoman.

Cyth. I pardon, and praise you for it, sir ; and I beseech your excellence, receive her beauties into your knowledge and favour.

Jul. Cytheris, she hath favour and behaviour, that commands as much of me ; and, sweet Chloe, know I do exceedingly love you, and that I will approve in any grace my father the emperor may shew you. Is this your husband ?

Alb. For fault of a better, if it please your highness.

Chloe. Gods my life, how he shames me !

Cyth. Not a whit, Chloe, they all think you politic and witty ; wise women choose not husbands for the eye, merit, or birth, but wealth and sovereignty.

Ovid. Sir, we all come to gratulate, for the good report of you.

Tib. And would be glad to deserve your love, sir.

Alb. My wife will answer you all, gentlemen ; I'll come to you again presently.
[*Exit.*

Plau. You have chosen you a most fair companion here, Cytheris, and a very fair house.

Cyth. To both which, you and all my friends are very welcome, Plautia.

Chloe. With all my heart, I assure your ladyship.

Plau. Thanks, sweet Mistress Chloe.

Jul. You must needs come to court, lady, i' faith, and there be sure your welcome shall be as great to us.

Ovid. She will deserve it, madam ; I see, even in her looks, gentry, and general worthiness.

Tib. I have not seen a more certain character of an excellent disposition.

Alb. [*re-entering.*] Wife !

Chloe. O, they do so commend me here, the courtiers ! what's the matter now ?

Alb. For the banquet, sweet wife.

Chloe. Yes ; and I must needs come to court, and be welcome, the princess says.
[*Exit with* Albius.

Gal. Ovid and Tibullus, you may be bold to welcome your mistress here.

Ovid. We find it so, sir.

Tib. And thank Cornelius Gallus.

Ovid. Nay, my sweet Sextus, in faith thou art not sociable.

Prop. In faith I am not, Publius ; nor I cannot.

Sick minds are like sick men that burn with fevers,
Who when they drink, please but a present taste,
And after bear a more impatient fit.
Pray let me leave you ; I offend you all,
And myself most.

Gal. Stay, sweet Propertius.

Tib. You yield too much unto your griefs, and fate,

---

[1] *A pox on them ! what do they here ?*] Chloe is an apt scholar :—but who would think the lesson of so old a date ! It seems as if it were delivered but yesterday.

Which never hurts, but when we say it
 hurts us.

Prop. O, peace, Tibullus; your philosophy
Lends you too rough a hand to search my
 wounds.
Speak they of griefs, that know to sigh and
 grieve;
The free and unconstrained spirit feels
No weight of my oppression.   [*Exit.*
 Ovid. Worthy Roman![1]
Methinks I taste my misery, and could
Sit down, and chide at his malignant stars.
 Jul. Methinks I love him, that he loves
 so truly.
 Cyth. This is the perfectest love, lives
 after death.
 Gal. Such is the constant ground of
 virtue still.
 Plau. It puts on an inseparable face.

Re-enter Chloe.

 Chloe. Have you marked everything,
Crispinus?
 Cris. Everything, I warrant you.
 Chloe. What gentlemen are these? do
you know them?
 Cris. Ay, they are poets, lady.
 Chloe. Poets! they did not talk of me
since I went, did they?
 Cris. O yes, and extolled your perfec-
tions to the heavens.
 Chloe. Now in sincerity they be the
finest kind of men that ever I knew:
Poets! Could not one get the emperor to
make my husband a poet, think you?
 Cris. No, lady, 'tis love and beauty
make poets: and since you like poets so
well, your love and beauties shall make me
a poet.
 Chloe. What! shall they? and such a
one as these?
 Cris. Ay, and a better than these: I
would be sorry else.
 Chloe. And shall your looks change, and
your hair change, and all, like these?[2]

 Cris. Why, a man may be a poet, and
yet not change his hair, lady.
 Chloe. Well, we shall see your cunning:
yet, if you can change your hair, I pray do.

Re-enter Albius.

 Alb. Ladies, and lordlings, there's a
slight banquet stays within for you; please
you draw near, and accost it.
 Jul. We thank you, good Albius: but
when shall we see those excellent jewels
you are commended to have?
 Alb. At your ladyship's service.—I got
that speech by seeing a play last day, and
it did me some grace now: I see, 'tis good
to collect sometimes; I'll frequent these
plays more than I have done, now I come
to be familiar with courtiers.   [*Aside.*
 Gal. Why, how now, Hermogenes?
what ailest thou, trow?
 Her. A little melancholy; let me alone,
prithee.
 Gal. Melancholy! how so?
 Her. With riding: a plague on all
coaches for me!
 Chloe. Is that hard-favoured gentleman
a poet too, Cytheris?
 Cyth. No, this is Hermogenes: as
humorous as a poet, though: he is a
musician.
 Chloe. A musician! then he can sing.
 Cyth. That he can, excellently: did you
never hear him?
 Chloe. O no: will he be entreated, think
you?
 Cyth. I know not. — Friend, Mistress
Chloe would fain hear Hermogenes sing:
are you interested in him?
 Gal. No doubt his own humanity will
command him so far, to the satisfaction of
so fair a beauty; but rather than fail, we'll
all be suitors to him.
 Her. 'Cannot sing.
 Gal. Prithee, Hermogenes.
 Her. 'Cannot sing.

---

[1] *Worthy Roman, &c.*] Ovid and his friends
seem to have taken Propertius at his word, and
given him credit for more affliction than he really
suffered. Cynthia's own opinion of the matter is
not quite so favourable to the feelings of her
quondam lover. Her "grimly ghost" comes,
like Margaret's, to his bedside, and exhibits a
fearful scroll of complaints against him:

" *Denique quis nostro curvum te funere vidit,*
   Atram quis lachrymis incaluisse togam?
 Si piguit portas ultra procedere, at illud,
   Jussisses, lectum lentius ire meum!
 Cur ventos non ipse rogis, ingrate, petisti?
   Cur nardo flammæ non oluere meæ?"—

But this is nothing to what follows. Briefly, if
half of what she says be true, her ghost is fully
justified in walking.

[2] *And shall your hair change, like these?*]
This is personal. It appears that Rufus Laberius Crispinus had red hair, which was not to
Chloe's taste: Decker adverts to the bringing of
a *red* beard on the stage, in the *Gull's Hornbook.*
See p. 218 a. *Cunning*, which occurs in Chloe's
next speech, means *skill* in poetry: in which
sense, and in its kindred one, proficiency in
music, it is often found in Jonson and his contemporaries.

Gal. For honour of this gentlewoman, to whose house I know thou mayest be ever welcome.

Chloe. That he shall, in truth, sir, if he can sing.

Ovid. What's that?

Gal. This gentlewoman is wooing Hermogenes for a song.

Ovid. A song! come, he shall not deny her. Hermogenes!

Her. 'Cannot sing.

Gal. No, the ladies must do it; he stays but to have their thanks acknowledged as a debt to his cunning.

Jul. That shall not want; ourself will be the first shall promise to pay him more than thanks, upon a favour so worthily vouchsafed.

Her. Thank you, madam; but 'will not sing.

Tib. Tut, the only way to win him is to abstain from entreating him.

Cris. Do you love singing, lady?

Chloe. O, passingly.

Cris. Entreat the ladies to entreat me to sing then, I beseech you.

Chloe. I beseech your grace, entreat this gentleman to sing.

Jul. That we will, Chloe; can he sing excellently?

Chloe. I think so, madam; for he entreated me to entreat you to entreat him to sing.

Cris. Heaven and earth! would you tell that?

Jul. Good sir, let's entreat you to use your voice.

Cris. Alas, madam, I cannot in truth.

Pla. The gentleman is modest: I warrant you he sings excellently.

Ovid. Hermogenes, clear your throat; I see by him here's a gentleman will worthily challenge you.

Cris. Not I, sir, I'll challenge no man.

Tib. That's your modesty, sir; but we, out of an assurance of your excellency, challenge him in your behalf.

Cris. I thank you, gentlemen, I'll do my best.

Her. Let that best be good, sir, you were best.

Gal. O, this contention is excellent! What is't you sing, sir?

Cris. If I freely may discover, sir; I'll sing that.

Ovid. One of your own compositions, Hermogenes. He offers you vantage enough.

Cris. Nay, truly, gentlemen, I'll challenge no man.—I can sing but one staff of the ditty neither.

Gal. The better: Hermogenes himself will be entreated to sing the other.

Crispinus *sings.*

If I freely may discover
What would please me in my lover,
I would have her fair and witty,
Savouring more of court than city;
A little proud, but full of pity:
Light and humourous in her toying,
Oft building hopes, and soon destroying,
Long, but sweet in the enjoying;
Neither too easy, nor too hard:
All extremes I would have barred.

Gal. Believe me, sir, you sing most excellently.

Ovid. If there were a praise above excellence, the gentleman highly deserves it.

Her. Sir, all this doth not yet make me envy you; for I know I sing better than you.

Tib. Attend Hermogenes, now.

Hermogenes, *accompanied.*

She should be allowed her passions,
So they were but used as fashions;
Sometimes froward, and then frowning,
Sometimes sickish, and then swowning,
Every fit with change still crowning.
Purely jealous I would have her,
Then only constant when I crave her:
'Tis a virtue should not save her.
Thus, nor her delicates would cloy me,
Neither her peevishness annoy me.

Jul. Nay, Hermogenes, your merit hath long since been both known and admired of us.

Her. You shall hear me sing another. Now will I begin.[1]

---

[1] *Now will I begin.*] The character of Hermogenes is drawn with great pleasantry by Horace, and Jonson has embodied his description very successfully: his insolence, vanity, affectation, and capriciousness are distinctly placed before the reader. The outlines, and merely the outlines, of the elegant song in the text, Ben found in Martial, as Whalley observes; the filling up is his own.

" *Qualem, Flacce, velim quæris, nolimve puellam?*
Nolo nimis facilem, difficilemve nimis:
Illud quod medium est, atque inter utrumque probamus,
Nec volo quod cruciat, nec volo quod satiat."
                                                L. i. ep. 58.

Gal. We shall do this gentleman's banquet too much wrong, that stays for us, ladies.

Jul. 'Tis true ; and well thought on, Cornelius Gallus.

Her. Why, 'tis but a short air, 'twill be done presently, pray stay : strike, music.

Ovid. No, good Hermogenes ; we'll end this difference within.

Jul. 'Tis the common disease[1] of all your musicians, that they know no mean, to be entreated either to begin or end.

Alb. Please you lead the way, gentles.

All. Thanks, good Albius.

[*Exeunt all but* Albius.

Alb. O, what a charm of thanks was here put upon me ! O Jove, what a setting forth it is to a man to have many courtiers come to his house ! Sweetly was it said of a good old housekeeper, *I had rather want meat, than want guests ;* especially if they be courtly guests. For, never trust me, if one of their good legs made in a house be not worth all the good cheer a man can make them. He that would have fine guests, let him have a fine wife ; he that would have a fine wife, let him come to me.

Re-enter Crispinus.

Cris. By your kind leave, Master Albius.

Alb. What, you are not gone, Master Crispinus ?

Cris. Yes, faith, I have a design draws me hence : pray, sir, fashion me an excuse to the ladies.

Alb. Will you not stay and see the jewels, sir ? I pray you stay.

Cris. Not for a million, sir, now. Let it suffice, I must relinquish ; and so, in a word, please you to expiate this compliment.

Alb. Mum.   [*Exit.*

Cris. I'll presently go and enghle some broker for a poet's gown,[2] and bespeak a garland : and then, jeweller, look to your best jewel, i' faith.   [*Exit,*

---

[1] *'Tis the common disease,* &c.] With this observation Horace introduces his character of Hermogenes :

"*Omnibus hoc vitium est cantoribus, inter amicos*
Ut nunquam inducant animum cantare, rogati,
Injussi, nunquam desistant."—Lib. i. sat. iii.

[2] *I'll presently go and* enghle *some broker for a poet's gown,*] This word, the modern *angle,* is used with some latitude by our old poets ; in general, however, it means to cheat, to impose upon, to draw in, as here—the substantive is always taken in a bad sense, sometimes for a *bait thrown out,* and sometimes for a *person deceived by it :* simply for a dupe, a gull, a Master Stephen. Hanmer derives enghle from the Fr. *engluer,* and Steevens from inveigle : both are mistaken, however : it comes from a Saxon, or, if the reader likes it better, an old English word, signifying to suspend or *hang,* which is but another mode of spelling it.

Now I am advanced thus far, I will just observe that the commentators have made strange work of a passage in Shakspeare, for want of understanding the import of this term :

"O, master, master, I have watched so long,
That I'm dog weary ; but at last I spied
An ancient *angel* coming down the hill
Will serve our turn."—*Taming the Shrew.*

Angel can have no sense here, for if a *messenger* be meant by it, as the critics say, this ancient personage could never be mistaken for one, by anybody. Theobald and Warburton read Engle, meaning, perhaps, a native of the North of Europe ; Steevens writes about it, and about it, and says nothing ; and Malone leaves the passage in obscurity. Hanmer, however, reads *enghle,* and this, I have no doubt, was the very word which Shakspeare, amidst all the uncertainty of his orthography, meant to use. What Tranio wanted was a simpleton, a man fit to be imposed upon, by a feigned tale ; such a one Biondello, after a tedious search, presumes that he has discovered. But why does he form this conclusion ? This is not even guessed at by the critics. It is pretty clearly hinted at, however, in the old comedy of the *Supposes,* from which Shakspeare took this part of his plot. There Erostrato, the Biondello of Shakspeare, looks out for a person to gull by an idle story, judges from *appearances,* that he has found him, and is not deceived : "At the foot of the hill I met a gentleman, and, as *methought, by his habits and his looks, he should be none of the wisest.*" Again : "this gentleman being, *as I guessed at first,* a man of small sapientia." And Dulippo (the Lucentio of Shakspeare) as soon as he spies him coming, exclaims, "Is this he ? go meet him : by my troth, *he looks like a good soul,* he that fisheth for him *might be sure to catch a codshead,*" act ii. sc. 1. These are the passages which our great poet had in view : and these, I trust, are more than sufficient to explain why Biondello concludes at first sight that this "ancient piece of formality" *will serve his turn.* From his being constantly termed a *pedant,* it is probable that he was dressed in a long stuff gown, which is the invariable *costume* of a schoolmaster ; the object of incessant ridicule in the old Italian comedy, from whom we borrowed him. "I was often," says Montaigne, "when a boy, wonderfully concerned to see, in the Italian farces, a *pedant* always brought in as the *fool of the play.*"—*Essays,* vol. i. p. 190.

ACT III.

SCENE I.—*The Via Sacra,*[1] *(or Holy Street.)*

Enter Horace, Crispinus *following.*

Hor. Umph! yes, I will begin an ode so; and it shall be to Mecænas.

Cris. 'Slid, yonder's Horace! they say he's an excellent poet: Mecænas loves him. I'll fall into his acquaintance, if I can; I think he be composing as he goes in the street! ha! 'tis a good humour, if he be: I'll compose too.

Hor. "Swell me a bowl with lusty wine,[2] Till I may see the plump Lyæus swim
Above the brim:
I drink as I would write,
In flowing measure filled with flame and sprite."

Cris. Sweet Horace, Minerva and the Muses stand auspicious to thy designs! How farest thou, sweet man? frolic? rich? gallant? ha!

Hor. Not greatly gallant, sir; like my fortunes, well: I am bold to take my leave, sir; you'll nought else, sir, would you?

Cris. Troth, no, but I could wish thou didst know us, Horace; we are a scholar, I assure thee.

Hor. A scholar, sir! I shall be covetous of your fair knowledge.

Cris. Gramercy, good Horace. Nay, we are new turned poet too, which is more; and a satirist too, which is more than that: I write just in thy vein, I. I am for your odes, or your sermons,[3] or anything indeed; we are a gentleman besides; our name is Rufus Laberius Crispinus; we are a pretty Stoic too.

Hor. To the proportion of your beard, I think it, sir.

Cris. By Phœbus, here's a most neat, fine street, is't not? I protest to thee, I am enamoured of this street now, more than of half the streets of Rome again; 'tis so polite, and terse! there's the front of a building now! I study architecture too: if ever I should build, I'd have a house just of that prospective.

Hor. Doubtless this gallant's tongue has a good turn, when he sleeps. [*Aside.*

Cris. I do make verses, when I come in such a street as this: O, your city ladies, you shall have them sit in every shop like the Muses—offering you the Castalian dews, and the Thespian liquors, to as many as have but the sweet grace and audacity to —sip of their lips. Did you never hear any of my verses?

Hor. No, sir;—but I am in some fear I must now. [*Aside.*

Cris. I'll tell thee some, if I can but recover them, I composed even now of a dressing I saw a jeweller's wife wear, who indeed was a jewel herself: I prefer that kind of tire now;[4] what's thy opinion, Horace?

Hor. With your silver bodkin, it does well, sir.

Cris. I cannot tell;[5] but it stirs me more than all your court-curls, or your spangles, or your tricks: I affect not these high gable ends, these Tuscan tops, nor your coronets, nor your arches, nor your pyramids; give me a fine, sweet—little delicate dressing with a bodkin, as you say; and a mushroom for all your other ornatures!

Hor. Is it not possible to make an escape from him? [*Aside.*

Cris. I have remitted my verses all this while; I think I have forgot them.

Hor. Here's he could wish you had else. [*Aside.*

Cris. Pray Jove I can entreat them of my memory!

Hor. You put your memory to too much trouble, sir.

---

[1] *The Via Sacra, &c.*] This scene is little more than a translation of Hor. Lib. I. Sat. ix. It is far from ill done; and yet, methinks, Jonson might have found a happier method of introducing himself.

[2] *Swell me a bowl with lusty wine,*] Decker attempts to ridicule this little ode, but without success. It is easy to parody anything into nonsense; but to make the public believe that it comes from such men as Jonson, when it is done, exceeds the powers of a hundred Deckers. This is some consolation.

[3] *I am for your odes or your* sermons,] This is a barbarous version of *sermones,* which Horace modestly applies to his *Satires,* on account of the approaches which the diction of them makes to familiar discourse.

[4] *I prefer that kind of* tire *now;*] i.e., headdress. Crispinus shows his taste here: the hair neatly twisted and confined at the top by a pearl brooch or a silver bodkin, is certainly a more becoming fashion than any of the fantastic modes which he enumerates. The *jeweller's wife* is Chloe, who had expressed a desire to see Crispinus a poet, p. 220.

[5] *I cannot tell,*] I know not what to say of it. Another example of that mode of speech which the commentators have so unaccountably overlooked.—See p. 47 *n.*

Cris. No, sweet Horace, we must not have thee think so.

Hor. I cry you mercy; then they are my ears
That must be tortured: well, you must have patience, ears.

Cris. Pray thee, Horace, observe.

Hor. Yes, sir; your satin sleeve begins to fret[1] at the rug that is underneath it, I do observe; and your ample velvet bases[2] are not without evident stains of a hot disposition naturally.

Cris. O——I'll dye them into another colour, at pleasure. How many yards of velvet dost thou think they contain?

Hor. 'Heart! I have put him now in a fresh way
To vex me more :—faith, sir, your mercer's book
Will tell you with more patience than I can :——
For I am crost, and so's not that, I think.[3]

Cris. 'Slight, these verses have lost me again !
I shall not invite them to mind, now.

Hor. Rack not your thoughts, good sir ; rather defer it
To a new time; I'll meet you at your lodging,
Or where you please: till then, Jove keep you, sir !

Cris. Nay, gentle Horace, stay; I have it now.

Hor. Yes, sir. Apollo, Hermes, Jupiter, Look down upon me ! 　　　　　[*Aside.*

Cris.

"　Rich was thy hap, sweet dainty cap,
　　There to be placed ;
　Where thy smooth black, sleek white
　　may smack,
　And both be graced."

White is there usurped for her brow; her forehead? and then sleek, as the parallel to smooth, that went before. A kind of paranomasie, or agnomination: do you conceive, sir?

Hor. Excellent. Troth, sir, I must be abrupt, and leave you.

Cris. Why, what haste hast thou? prithee, stay a little ; thou shalt not go yet, by Phœbus.

Hor. I shall not ! what remedy? fie, how I sweat with suffering !

Cris. And then——

Hor. Pray, sir, give me leave to wipe my face a little.

Cris. Yes, do, good Horace.

Hor. Thank you, sir.
Death ! I must crave his leave to p——anon ;
Or that I may go hence with half my teeth :
I am in some such fear. This tyranny
Is strange, to take mine ears up by commission,
(Whether I will or no,) and make them stalls
To his lewd solecisms, and worded trash.
Happy thou, bold Bolanus,[4] now I say ;

---

[1] *Your* satin sleeve begins to fret, &c.] Decker appears to have been extremely mortified at these reflections on his own and his friend's dress, and adverts to them with great bitterness. *Tucca.* "Thou wrongest here a good honest rascal, Crispinus, and a poor varlet Demetrius, brethren in thine own trade of poetry : thou say'st Crispinus' *satin doublet is ravelled out here;* and that this penurious sneaker is out at elbows."—*Satiro.* And again : "They have sewn up that seam-rent lie of thine, that Demetrius is out at elbows and Crispinus is *fallen out with satin* here."—*Ib.* The audience before whom these illiberal scenes were played must have had singular notions of delicacy if they found pleasure in them. Decker, however, is far more gross and scurrilous than Jonson : this, indeed, does not justify our author ; but it serves to show that the people were not scandalized by such conduct ; and consequently, that little or no restraint was laid on the coarsest expressions of vulgar feeling.

[2] *Your ample velvet* bases] In the quarto it is velvet *hose*; from which it appears that Jonson, as was sometimes the case with the writers of his age, uses the word for breeches. Strictly speaking, however, *bases* were a kind of short petticoat, somewhat like the phillibegs of the Highlanders, and were probably suggested by the military dress of the Romans. Thus, in the *Picture :*

"You, minion,
Had a hand in it, too, as it appears ;
Your *petticoat* serves for *bases* to this warrior."

[3] *For I am crost, and so's not that, I think.*] A play on the word cross. Decker does not forget this sneer. "Thou art great in somebody's books for thy parchment suit, (the *perpetuana* which Jonson usually wore, p. 166,) thou knowest where : thou wouldst be *out at elbows* and *out at heels*, too, but thou layest about thee with a *bill* for this."—*Satiromastix.*

[4] *Happy thou, bold Bolanus,* &c.] This is the sense usually given, I believe, to these words :

"*O te, Bolane, cerebri
Felicem !*"

But no one could shew more fretfulness and impatience than Horace himself does. Surely the *felicity* of Bolanus must have consisted in an impenetrable, rather than a ticklish and tender skull: a comfortable indifference to all attacks ; a good humoured stupidity that dozed over all impertinence ; this, indeed, was to be envied.
In this speech Horace has taken a line, by anticipation, from Juvenal :

"*Ut liceat paucis cum dentibus inde reverti.*"

Whose freedom, and impatience of this
    fellow,
Would, long ere this, have call'd him fool,
    and fool,
And rank and tedious fool! and have flung
    jests
As hard as stones, till thou hadst pelted
    him
Out of the place; whilst my tame modesty
Suffers my wit be made a solemn ass,
To bear his fopperies——   [*Aside.*
    Cris. Horace, thou art miserably affected
to be gone, I see. But—prithee let's prove
to enjoy thee awhile. Thou hast no business,
I assure me. Whither is thy journey directed, ha?
    Hor. Sir, I am going to visit a friend
that's sick.
    Cris. A friend! what is he; do not I
know him?
    Hor. No, sir, you do not know him;
and 'tis not the worse for him.
    Cris. What's his name? where is he
lodged?
    Hor. Where I shall be fearful to draw
you out of your way, sir; a great way
hence; pray, sir, let's part.
    Cris. Nay, but where is't? I prithee say.
    Hor. On the far side of all Tyber yonder,
by Cæsar's gardens.[1]
    Cris. O, that's my course directly; I am
for you. Come, go; why stand'st thou?
    Hor. Yes, sir: marry, the plague is in
that part of the city; I had almost forgot
to tell you, sir.
    Cris. Foh! it is no matter, I fear no
pestilence; I have not offended Phœbus.[2]
    Hor. I have, it seems, or else this heavy
    scourge
Could ne'er have lighted on me.
    Cris. Come along.
    Hor. I am to go down some half mile
this way, sir, first, to speak with his physician; and from thence to his apothecary,
where I shall stay the mixing of divers
drugs.
    Cris. Why, it's all one, I have nothing

to do, and I love not to be idle; I'll bear
thee company. How call'st thou the apothecary?
    Hor. O that I knew a name would fright
    him now!——
Sir, Rhadamanthus, Rhadamanthus, sir.
There's one so call'd, is a just judge in
    hell,
And doth inflict strange vengance on all
    those
That here on earth torment poor patient
    spirits.
    Cris. He dwells at the Three Furies, by
Janus's temple.
    Hor. Your pothecary does, sir.
    Cris. Heart, I owe him money for sweet-
meats, and he has laid to arrest me, I hear:
but——
    Hor. Sir, I have made a most solemn
vow, I will never bail any man.
    Cris. Well then, I'll swear, and speak
him fair, if the worst come. But his name
is Minos, not Rhadamanthus, Horace.
    Hor. That may be, sir, I but guessed at
his name by his sign. But your Minos is
a judge too, sir.
    Cris. I protest to thee, Horace (do but
taste me once), if I do know myself, and
mine own virtues truly, thou wilt not make
that esteem of Varius, or Virgil, or Tibullus,
or any of 'em indeed, as now in thy ignorance thou dost; which I am content to
forgive. I would fain see which of these
could pen more verses in a day, or with
more facility, than I; or that could court
his mistress, kiss her hand, make better
sport with her fan or her dog——
    Hor. I cannot bail you yet, sir.
    Cris. Or that could move his body more
gracefully, or dance better; you should see
me, were it not in the street——
    Hor. Nor yet.
    Cris. Why, I have been a reveller, and
at my cloth of silver suit, and my long
stocking,[3] in my time, and will be again——
    Hor. If you may be trusted, sir.
    Cris. And then, for my singing, Hermo-

---

[1] *On the* far side *of all Tyber yonder, by*
Cæsar's gardens. Had Shakspeare forgotten
this when, in *Julius Cæsar,* he placed the gardens *on this side Tyber!* or did he prefer the
authority of North to that of his old acquaintance.
[2] *I fear no* pestilence; *I have not offended
Phœbus.*] Alluding to the *plague* sent by
Apollo among the Grecians, on account of the
insult offered to his priest.—Hom. Il. lib. i.
        WHAL.
[3] *My* long stocking,] In this age the breeches,
    VOL. I.

or, more properly, the drawers, with men of
fashion, fell short of the knees, and the defect
was supplied by *long stockings,* the tops of which
were fastened under the drawers. This may be
seen in most of the portraits of the times.
    This is Whalley's note: he could scarcely be
mistaken in what he represents as so common to
be seen; and yet, before I read it, I always supposed the allusion to be to that kind of stocking
which was drawn up very high, and then rolled
back over the breeches, till it nearly touched the
knee.

Q

genes himself envies me, that is your only
master of music you have in Rome.

Hor. Is your mother living, sir?

Cris. Au! convert thy thoughts to somewhat else, I pray thee.

Hor. You have much of the mother in
you, sir. Your father is dead?

Cris. Ay, I thank Jove, and my grandfather too, and all my kinsfolks, and well
composed in their urns.

Hor. The more their happiness, that rest
in peace,
Free from the abundant torture of thy
tongue:
Would I were with them too!

Cris. What's that, Horace?

Hor. I now remember me, sir, of a sad
fate
A cunning woman, one Sabella, sung,[1]
When in her urn she cast my destiny,
I being but a child.

Cris. What was it, I pray thee?

Hor. She told me I should surely never
perish
By famine, poison, or the enemy's sword;
The hectic fever, cough, or pleurisy,[2]
Should never hurt me, nor the tardy gout:
But in my time I should be once surprised
By a strong tedious talker, that should vex
And almost bring me to consumption:
Therefore, if I were wise, she warned me
shun
All such long-winded monsters as my bane;
For if I could but scape that one discourser,
I might no doubt prove an old aged man.—
By your leave, sir.   [*Going.*

Cris. Tut, tut; abandon this idle humour,
'tis nothing but melancholy. 'Fore Jove,
now I think on't, I am to appear in court
here, to answer to one that has me in suit:
sweet Horace, go with me, this is my hour;
if I neglect it, the law proceeds against me.
Thou art familiar with these things: prithee, if thou lov'st me, go.

Hor. Now, let me die, sir, if I know
your laws,

Or have the power to stand still half so
long
In their loud courts, as while a case is
argued.
Besides, you know, sir, where I am to go,
And the necessity——

Cris. 'Tis true.

Hor. I hope the hour of my release be
come: he will, upon this consideration, discharge me, sure.

Cris. Troth, I am doubtful what I may
best do, whether to leave thee or my affairs,
Horace.

Hor. O Jupiter! me, sir, me, by any
means; I beseech you, me, sir.

Cris. No, faith, I'll venture those now;
thou shalt see I love thee: come, Horace.

Hor. Nay, then I am desperate: I follow
you, sir. 'Tis hard contending with a man
that overcomes thus.

Cris. And how deals Mecænas with
thee? liberally, ha? is he open-handed?
bountiful?

Hor. He's still himself, sir.

Cris. Troth, Horace, thou art exceeding
happy in thy friends and acquaintance;
they are all most choice spirits, and of the
first rank of Romans: I do not know that
poet, I protest, has used his fortune more
prosperously than thou hast.   If thou
wouldst bring me known to Mecænas, I
should second thy desert well; thou shouldst
find a good sure assistant of me, one that
would speak all good of thee in thy absence,
and be content with the next place, not
envying thy reputation with thy patron.
Let me not live, but I think thou and I, in
a small time, should lift them all out of
favour, both Virgil, Varius, and the best
of them, and enjoy him wholly to ourselves.

Hor. Gods, you do know it, I can hold
no longer;
This brize has pricked my patience.[3] Sir,
your silkness
Clearly mistakes Mecænas and his house,

---

[1] *One Sabella, sung,* &c.] Jonson has followed Horace in his Epodes, and made a proper name of this adjective:

   "*Instat mihi fatum triste,* Sabella
   Quod puero cecinit divina mota anus urna.

What follows is translated with considerable
pleasantry and spirit.

[2] *The hectic fever, cough, or pleurisy.*] These
were disorders most incident to the climate of
Italy: the pleurisy, or *laterum dolor,* we meet
with frequently in classic authors; and it is now
the most reigning disorder, during the summer
months.—WHAL.

[3] *This brize has pricked my patience.*] The
brize is the gad-fly, the constant persecutor of
cattle in the summer. The use of this word is
so common, that an example of it seems scarcely
necessary; the following, however, from Dryden,
is entirely to the purpose:

"This flying plague, to mark its quality,
Oestros, the Grecians call; asylus we:
A fierce loud buzzing *breeze;*—their stings
        draw blood,
And drive the cattle madding through the
        wood."—*Georg.* iii.

To think there breathes a spirit beneath his roof,
Subject unto those poor affections
Of undermining envy and detraction,
Moods only proper to base grovelling minds.
That place is not in Rome, I dare affirm,
More pure or free from such low common evils.
There's no man grieved that this is thought more rich,
Or this more learned; each man hath his place,
And to his merit his reward of grace,
Which, with a mutual love, they all embrace.

Cris. You report a wonder ; 'tis scarce credible, this.

Hor. I am no torturer to enforce you to believe it ; but it is so.

Cris. Why, this inflames me with a more ardent desire to be his, than before ; but I doubt I shall find the entrance to his familiarity somewhat more than difficult, Horace.

Hor. Tut, you'll conquer him, as you have done me ; there's no standing out against you, sir, I see that : either your importunity, or the intimation of your good parts, or——

Cris. Nay, I'll bribe his porter, and the grooms of his chamber ; make his doors open to me that way first, and then I'll observe my times. Say he should extrude me his house to-day, shall I therefore desist, or let fall my suit to-morrow ? No ; I'll attend him, follow him, meet him in the street, the highways, run by his coach, never leave him. What ! man hath nothing given him in this life without much labour——

Hor. And impudence.
Archer of heaven, Phœbus, take thy bow,
And with a full-drawn shaft nail to the earth
This Python, that I may yet run hence and live :
Or, brawny Hercules, do thou come down,
And, tho' thou mak'st it up thy thirteenth labour,

Rescue me from this hydra of discourse here.

Enter Fuscus Aristius.

Ari. Horace, well met.
Hor. O welcome, my reliever ;
Aristius, as thou lov'st me, ransom me.
Ari. What ail'st thou, man ?
Hor. 'Death, I am seized on here
By a land remora ;[1] I cannot stir,
Nor move, but as he pleases.
Cris. Wilt thou go, Horace ?
Hor. Heart ! he cleaves to me like Alcides' shirt,
Tearing my flesh and sinews : O, I've been vexed
And tortured with him beyond forty fevers.
For Jove's sake, find some means to take me from him.
Ari. Yes, I will ;—but I'll go first and tell Mecænas.   [*Aside.*
Cris. Come, shall we go ?
Ari. The jest will make his eyes run, i' faith.   [*Aside.*
Hor. Nay, Aristius !
Ari. Farewell, Horace.   [*Going.*
Hor. 'Death ! will he leave me ? Fuscus Aristius ! do you hear ? Gods of Rome ! You said you had somewhat to say to me in private.
Ari. Ay, but I see you are now employed with that gentleman ; 'twere offence to trouble you ; I'll take some fitter opportunity :[2] farewell.   [*Exit.*
Hor. Mischief and torment ! O my soul and heart,
How are you cramped with anguish ! Death itself
Brings not the like convulsions. O, this day !
That ever I should view thy tedious face.——
Cris. Horace, what passion, what humour is this ?
Hor. Away, good prodigy, afflict me not.—
A friend, and mock me thus ! Never was man
So left under the axe.——

---

[1] *By a land* remora :] *Remora* is the Latin name of a fish that adheres to the sides and keels of ships, and retards their way. Thus Mayne :

" No *remora* that stops your fleet,
Like serjeants gallants in the street."
        City Match.

Figuratively it is taken for any impediment or obstacle whatever.—WHAL.

[2] *I'll take some fitter opportunity,* &c.] Aristius has not full justice done him. There is nothing in Horace more amusing than the manner in which this person, who must have been a very sprightly, humourous, and agreeable gentleman, plays on the visible impatience of his friend. Here he takes his leave very tamely.

Enter Minos, *with two* Lictors.

How now?

Min. That's he in the embroidered hat there, with the ash-coloured feather ;[1] his name is Laberius Crispinus.

Lict. Laberius Crispinus, I arrest you in the Emperor's name.

Cris. Me, sir! do you arrest me?

Lict. Ay, sir, at the suit of Master Minos the apothecary.

Hor. Thanks, great Apollo, I will not slip thy favour offered me in my escape, for my fortunes. [*Exit hastily.*

Cris. Master Minos! I know no Master Minos. Where's Horace? Horace! Horace!

Min. Sir, do not you know me?

Cris. O yes, I know you, Master Minos; cry you mercy. But Horace? Gods me, is he gone?

Min. Ay, and so would you too, if you knew how.—Officer, look to him.

Cris. Do you hear, Master Minos? pray let us be used like a man of our own fashion. By Janus and Jupiter, I meant to have paid you next week every drachm. Seek not to eclipse my reputation thus vulgarly.

Min. Sir, your oaths cannot serve you; you know I have forborne you long.

Cris. I am conscious of it, sir. Nay, I beseech you, gentlemen, do not exhale me thus ;[2] remember 'tis but for sweetmeats——

Lict. Sweet meat must have sour sauce, sir. Come along.

Cris. Sweet Master Minos, I am for-

feited to eternal disgrace, if you do not commiserate. Good officer, be not so officious.

Enter Tucca *and* Pyrgi.[3]

Tuc. Why, how now, my good brace of bloodhounds, whither do you drag the gentleman? You mungrels, you curs, you ban-dogs! we are Captain Tucca that talk to you, you inhuman pilchers.[4]

Min. Sir, he is their prisoner.

Tuc. Their pestilence! What are you, sir.

Min. A citizen of Rome, sir.

Tuc. Then you are not far distant from a fool, sir.

Min. A pothecary, sir.

Tuc. I knew thou wast not a physician: foh! out of my nostrils, thou stink'st of lotium and the syringe; away, quack-salver!—Follower, my sword.

1 *Pyr.* Here, noble leader; you'll do no harm with it, I'll trust you. [*Aside.*

Tuc. Do you hear, you, goodman slave? Hook, ram, rogue, catchpole, loose the gentleman, or by my velvet arms——

Lict. What will you do, sir?

[*Strikes up his heels, and seizes his sword.*

Tuc. Kiss thy hand, my honourable active varlet, and embrace thee thus.

1 *Pyr.* O patient metamorphosis!

Tuc. My sword, my tall rascal.

Lict. Nay, soft, sir; some wiser than some.

Tuc. What! and a wit too? By Pluto,

---

[1] *That's he, with the* ash-coloured *feather* there,] Which Decker (or whoever is meant by Crispinus) probably wore:—at least he seems to resent the mention of it in his *Gull's Hornbook:* "Now, sir, if the writer hath brought *your feather* on the stage," &c. See p. 25.

[2] *Do not exhale me thus ;*] i.e., drag me out. This is the language of ancient Pistol, and corroborates the conjecture of Malone on the meaning of the expression in *Henry V.*, act ii. sc. 1. It is strange that Steevens should reject this explanation; and it is still more strange that neither of these distinguished commentators should be aware of the application of the word by Jonson.

[3] *Enter* Tucca *and* Pyrgi.] It appears that Tucca has now two boys in his train. It would be as well if Jonson had anglicised his dramatis personæ, here and elsewhere. I should give them the common appellations, if the frequent recurrence of their Latin names in the dialogue did not forbid it. The reader will therefore please to recollect that *Histrio* stands for player, and *Pyrgus* for page. I presume that the author gave this ironical appellation (*pyrgus* is

a tower) to the latter on account of their diminutive size.

[4] *You inhuman* pilchers.] So he calls the serjeants of the Counter, either from the glossy everlasting, or leather coats, which they usually wore. Pilches or pilchers are skins (from *pellis*), and, in a more general sense, coverings of fur, woollen, &c. Shakspeare uses the word for the sheath of a sword; and his contemporaries, for that "most sweet robe of durance, a *buff jerkin.*" Nash speaks of a carman in a *leather pilche;* and Decker twits Jonson more than once with wearing it: "Thou hast forgot how thou ambled'st in a *leather pilche* by a playwaggon, and took'st mad Jeronimo's part to get service amongst the mimicks." "Whence it appears," says Steevens, with unusual glee, "that Ben Jonson acted Hieronimo in the Spanish Tragedy; the speech being addressed to Horace, under which name *old* Ben is ridiculed." At the time alluded to, *old* Ben might probably be about twenty years of age : but Steevens is too ready to trust the calumnies of any of Jonson's enemies. There are reasons for thinking that Ben never played Hieronimo.

thou must be cherished, slave; here's three drachms for thee; hold.

2 Pyr. There's half his lendings gone.

Tuc. Give me.

Lict. No, sir, your first word shall stand; I'll hold all.

Tuc. Nay, but, rogue——

Lict. You would make a rescue of our prisoner, sir, you.

Tuc. I a rescue! Away, inhuman varlet. Come, come, I never relish above one jest at most; do not disgust me, sirrah; do not, rogue! I tell thee, rogue, do not.

Lict. How, sir? rogue?

Tuc. Ay; why, thou art not angry, rascal, art thou?

Lict. I cannot tell, sir; I am little better upon these terms.

Tuc. Ha, gods and fiends! why, dost hear, rogue thou? give me thy hand; I say unto thee, thy hand, rogue. What, dost not thou know me? not me, rogue? not Captain Tucca, rogue?

Min. Come, pray surrender the gentleman his sword, officer; we'll have no fighting here.

Tuc. What's thy name?

Min. Minos, an't please you.

Tuc. Minos! Come hither, Minos; thou art a wise fellow, it seems; let me talk with thee.

Cris. Was ever wretch so wretched as unfortunate I !

Tuc. Thou art one of the centumviri, old boy, art not?[1]

Min. No indeed, master captain.

Tuc. Go to, thou shalt be then; I'll have

thee one, Minos. Take my sword from these rascals, dost thou see I go, do it; I cannot attempt with patience. What does this gentleman owe thee, little Minos?

Min. Fourscore sesterties, sir.[2]

Tuc. What, no more! Come, thou shalt release him, Minos: what, I'll be his bail, thou shalt take my word, old boy, and cashier these furies: thou shalt do't, I say, thou shalt, little Minos, thou shalt.

Cris. Yes; and as I am a gentleman and a reveller, I'll make a piece of poetry, and absolve all, within these five days.

Tuc. Come, Minos is not to learn how to use a gentleman of quality, I know.—— My sword. If he pay thee not, I will, and I must, old boy. Thou shalt be my pothecary too. Hast good eringos, Minos?

Min. The best in Rome, sir.

Tuc. Go to, then——Vermin, know the house.

1 Pyr. I warrant you, colonel.

Tuc. For this gentleman, Minos——

Min. I'll take your word, captain.

Tuc. Thou hast it. My sword.

Min. Yes, sir. But you must discharge the arrest, Master Crispinus.

Tuc. How, Minos! Look in the gentleman's face, and but read his silence. Pay, pay; 'tis honour, Minos.

Cris. By Jove, sweet captain, you do most infinitely endear and oblige me to you.

Tuc. Tut, I cannot compliment, by Mars; but, Jupiter love me, as I love good words and good clothes, and there's an end. Thou shalt give my boy that girdle and hangers,[3] when thou hast worn them a little more.

---

[1] *Thou art one of the* centumviri, *old boy, art not ?*] The *centumviri* were a body of men, chosen three out of every tribe, for the judgment of such matters as the prætors committed to their decision. This office was one of the first steps to public preferment.—WHAL.

[2] *Fourscore* sesterties, *sir.*] A sesterce was worth about two-pence of our money; so that the whole of Crispinus' debt did not much exceed twelve shillings.

[3] *Thou shalt give my boy that* girdle *and* hangers,] Previously to noticing the text, I wish to introduce a few words, which were inadvertently omitted in their proper place, respecting the dress of our ancestors. Over the shirt they wore a tight *vest*, or waistcoat, to the skirts of which were appended a number of tagged strings, or, as they were then called, *points:* these were designed to support the hose or large *slops*, also furnished with points, by which they were tied or *trussed* to the vest. This awkward mode of supplying the place of buttons, rendered assistance at all times desirable, and, in some cases, absolutely necessary. Every man

had a page, whose office it was to *truss his points;* in plain language, to tie up his breeches : Master Stephen (ante, p. 8 *a*) entreats Brainworm to "help to *truss* him a little :" and, indeed, it is scarcely possible to mention an old comedy in which some allusion to this practice is not to be found. The vest was fastened by a *girdle*, furnished with a pair of loops, i.e., *hangers*, in which the dagger was constantly worn. This article of finery was adorned with fringes and tassels of needlework; and a lady would sometimes condescend to embroider a girdle and hangers for a favourite lover, or a relation. Joice tells her brother that "since he came to the Inns o' Court, she had wrought him a *faire pair of hangers*."— Green's *Tu Quoque*. They were often very costly. Thus, in that rare old song of *Jockie is grown a gentleman :*

"Thy *belt* was made of a white leather thonge,
　Which thou and thy father wore so longe,
Is turned to *hangers* of velvet stronge,
　With gold and pearle embroydered amonge."

If a hat and feather, a satin cloak, and a pair of

Cris. O Jupiter! captain, he shall have them now, presently :—Please you to be acceptive, young gentleman.

1 *Pyr.* Yes, sir, fear not; I shall accept; I have a pretty foolish humour of taking, if you knew all. [*Aside.*

Tuc. Not now, you shall not take, boy.

Cris. By my truth and earnest, but he shall, captain, by your leave.

Tuc. Nay, an he swear by his truth and earnest, take it, boy; do not make a gentleman forsworn.

Lict. Well, sir, there's your sword; but thank Master Minos; you had not carried it as you do else.

Tuc. Minos is just, and you are knaves, and——

Lict. What say you, sir?

Tuc. Pass on, my good scoundrel, pass on, I honour thee : [*Exeunt* Lictors.] But that I hate to have action with such base rogues as these, you should have seen me unrip their noses now, and have sent them to the next barber's to stitching ;[1] for do you see—I am a man of humour, and I do love the varlets, the honest varlets, they have wit and valour, and are indeed good profitable, —— errant rogues,[2] as any live in an empire. Dost thou hear, poetaster? [*to* Crispinus.] second me. Stand up, Minos, close, gather, yet, so! Sir, (thou shalt have a quarter share, be resolute) you shall, at my request, take Minos by the hand here, little Minos, I will have it so; all friends, and a health : be not inexo-

rable. And thou shalt impart the wine, old boy, thou shalt do it, little Minos, thou shalt ; make us pay it in our physic. What! we must live, and honour the Gods sometimes ; now Bacchus, now Comus, now Priapus; every god a little. [Histrio *passes by.*] What's he that stalks by there, boy, Pyrgus? You were best let him pass, sirrah; do, ferret, let him pass, do——

2 *Pyr.* 'Tis a player, sir.

Tuc. A player! call him, call the lousy slave hither; what, will he sail by, and not once strike, or vail to a man of war?[3] ha!—Do you hear, you player, rogue, stalker, come back here ;—

Enter Histrio.

No respect to men of worship, you slave! what, you are proud, you rascal, are you proud, ha? you grow rich, do you, and purchase, you two-penny tear-mouth?[4] you have FORTUNE,[5] and the good year on your side, you stinkard, you have, you have!

Hist. Nay, sweet captain, be confined to some reason; I protest I saw you not, sir.

Tuc. You did not! where was your sight, Œdipus? you walk with hare's eyes, do you? I'll have them glazed, rogue; an you say the word, they shall be glazed for you : come, we must have you turn fiddler, again, slave, get a base viol at your back, and march in a tawney coat, with one sleeve, to Goose-fair ;[6] then you'll know us, you'll

---

boots were added to these, the *costume* was complete, and the gallant was equipped in the most fashionable mode during the early part of the seventeenth century.

[1] *And have sent them to the next barber's to stitching, &c.*] The barbers in Jonson's days practised many inferior parts of surgery.—WHAL.

[2] *And are, indeed, good, profitable—errant rogues, &c.*] This is the σχημα παρ' ὑπονοιαν, in which Jonson and his master, Aristophanes, so much delight :

Αλλ' ου σε κρυψω' των εμων γαρ οικετων
Πιστοτατον ηγουμαι σε, και—κλεπτισατον.
                              Plut. v. 2ᵃ.

[3] *And not strike or* vail *to a* man-of-war?] i.e., to himself. The allusion is to merchant vessels *vailing*, or lowering their topsails or their colours to a king's ship. To *vail*, as I have already observed, p. 131 *a*, occurs incessantly in our old dramatists, and always in the same sense, viz. as a mark of inferiority or submission.

[4] *You two-penny tear-mouth ?*] So he calls the players, from the *two-penny* gallery in the theatres of that age.—WHAL.

[5] *You have* FORTUNE, *&c.*] He alludes to the

Fortune playhouse, one of the earliest theatres in London, and situate somewhere about White-cross-street. [In Golden-lane, Barbican.—F.C.]

[6] *March in a* tawney-coat, with one sleeve, to Goose-fair.] This is the colour still most affected by such as grind music at the vestibule of the palace of King Solomon, or the royal tiger from Bengal, at races and country fairs. "The widow, and two of her gallants, being *at the fair*, entered a tavern, where they had not sitten long, but in comes a noise (a company) of *musicians in tawney coats*, who, putting off their cappes, asked *if they would have any music*."—*Hist. of John Newchombe.* Goose-fair, or, as it is usually called, *Green-goose fair*, is mentioned by many of Jonson's contemporaries. Thus Glapthorne, in that excellent old comedy, *Wit in a Constable :*

"And you,
That are the precious paragons of the city
And scorn our country sports, can have your
        meetings
At Islington and *Green-goose* fair, and sip
A zealous glass of wine."

It is still held (as in the poet's days) on Whitsunmonday, at Bow, near Stratford, in Essex; and

see us then, you will, gulch,[1] you will.
Then, *Will't please your worship to have
any music, captain ?*
　Hist. Nay, good captain.
　Tuc. What, do you laught, Howleglas !²
death, you perstemptuous varlet, I am
none of your fellows ; I have commanded
a hundred and fifty such rogues, I.
　2 *Pyr.* Ay, and most of that hundred
and fifty have been leaders of a legion.
　　　　　　　　　　　　　　[*Aside.*
　Hist. If I have exhibited wrong, I'll
tender satisfaction, captain.
　Tuc. Say'st thou so, honest vermin !
Give me thy hand ; thou shalt make us a
supper one of these nights.
　Hist. When you please, by Jove, captain, most willingly.
　Tuc. Dost thou swear ! To-morrow then ;
say and hold, slave. There are some of
you players honest gentlemen-like scoundrels, and suspected to have some wit, as
well as your poets, both at drinking and
breaking of jests, and are companions for
gallants. A man may skelder ye, now and
then, of half a dozen shillings, or so. Dost
thou not know that Pantalabus there ?³

　Hist. No, I assure you, captain.
　Tuc. Go ; and be acquainted with him
then ; he is a gentleman, parcel poet, you
slave ; his father was a man of worship, I
tell thee. Go, he pens high, lofty, in a
new stalking strain, bigger than half the
rhymers in the town again : he was born to
fill thy mouth, Minotaurus, he was, he will
teach thee to tear and rand. Rascal, to
him, cherish his muse, go ; thou hast forty—
forty shillings, I mean, stinkard ; give him
in earnest, do, he shall write for thee,
slave !⁴ If he pen for thee once, thou shalt
not need to travel with thy pumps full of
gravel any more, after a blind jade and a
hamper, and stalk upon boards and barrel
heads to an old cracked trumpet.
　Hist. Troth, I think I have not so much
about me, captain.
　Tuc. It's no matter ; give him what thou
hast, stiff-toe, I'll give my word for the
rest ; though it lack a shilling or two, it
skills not ; go, thou art an honest shifter ;
I'll have the statute repealed for thee.⁵—
Minos, I must tell thee, Minos, thou hast
dejected yon gentleman's spirit exceedingly ; dost observe, dost note, little Minos ?

takes its name from young or *green geese*, which
form the principal part of the entertainment. In
Jonson's time, probably, itinerant companies of
players resorted there : but all this seems very
strange at Rome !
　¹ *You will*, gulch,] Gulch is a stupid, fat-
headed fellow. The word occurs in the old
comedy of *Lingua*. "You muddy *gulch*, dare
you look me in the face ?"—See *Old Plays*.
　　　　　　　　　　　　　　　WHAL.
　² *What, do you laugh*, Howleglas !] There
is an allusion to this person in the Latin poem
called *Grobianus :*

"*Fecit idem quondam vir famigeratus ubique,
　Nomina cui speculo noctua juncta dedit.*"

On which the English translator has the following note ! "Here the author alludes to a book
written in Dutch, intituled, *The Life of Uyle-
spegel, or Owl-glass*, an hero of equal rank with
Tom Tram in English."—WHAL. See the *Alchemist.*
　³ *Dost thou not know that Pantalabus there ?*]
In the quarto it is, that *Caprichio* there. Perhaps
it should be Pantalabus, as in Horace, unless
Jonson thought Pantalabus more agreeable to
etymology. The real appellation of this person
was Mallius : his nickname he acquired from
borrowing money of every one he met. It does
not appear in what Crispinus resembled Pantalabus ; the "skeldering captain" himself was
much more like him.—But difficulties increase at
every step ; Langbaine, who probably spoke the
language of his time, roundly asserts that
Decker is lashed under the character of Crispinus ; and his assertion has been repeated by

every writer on the subject, without a single exception, to the present day. But is this the fact ?
Nothing of what follows can be applied to
Decker ; his father was not "a man of worship,"
nor did he "pen high, lofty, in a new stalking
strain." Briefly, "I do now," like Stephano,
"let loose my opinion," the Crispinus of
Jonson is Marston, to whom every word of
this directly points. This will derange much
confident criticism ; but I shall be found even-
tually in the right. Decker I take to be the
Demetrius of the present play. He is treated
with far more contempt than Crispinus, who, on
the other hand, is persecuted with more
severity. I know not the origin of our poet's
quarrel with either : but he denies, and I believe with truth, that he made the first attack.
　⁴ *Give him in earnest, do, he shall write for
thee, slave !*] This was not an uncommon practice : and time and the diligence of Mr. Malone
have brought to light many memorandums of Mr.
Henslowe, the proprietor of several of our old
theatres, which prove that Jonson himself was
often obliged to have recourse to it. Had Ben forgotten this ? or were his circumstances so much
changed for the better in a few months, that he had
no apprehensions of a similar necessity in future ?
　⁵ *Go, thou art an honest shifter ; I'll have the
statute repealed for thee.*] Meaning that by
which unauthorized players were declared rogues
and vagabonds, see p. 212 a. In the quarto Tucca
addresses himself to Minos, "Thou art an honest
twenty i' the hundred, I'll have," &c. Here the
allusion is to the statute of 13th Eliz. confirming
that passed in 3rd Henry V., which reduced all
legal interest to *ten per cent.*

Min. Yes, sir.

Tuc. Go to then, raise, recover, do; suffer him not to droop in prospect of a player, a rogue, a stager: put twenty into his hand, twenty sesterces I mean, and let nobody see; go, do it, the work shall commend itself; be Minos,[1] I'll pay.

Min. Yes, forsooth, captain.

2 *Pyr.* Do not we serve a notable shark?
                                        [*Aside.*

Tuc. And what new matters have you now afoot, sirrah, ha? I would fain come with my cockatrice one day, and see a play, if I knew when there were a good bawdy one; but they say you have nothing but HUMOURS, REVELS, and SATIRES,[2] that gird and f——t at the time, you slave.

Hist. No, I assure you, captain, not we. They are on the other side of Tyber: we have as much ribaldry in our plays as can be, as you would wish, captain: all the sinners in the suburbs come and applaud our action daily.

Tuc. I hear you'll bring me o' the stage there; you'll play me, they say; I shall be presented by a sort of copper-laced scoundrels of you: life of Pluto! an you stage me, stinkard, your mansions shall sweat for't, your tabernacles, varlets, your Globes, and your Triumphs.[3]

Hist. Not we, by Phœbus, captain; do not do us imputation without desert.

Tuc. I will not, my good two-penny rascal; reach me thy neuf.[4] Dost hear? what wilt thou give me a week for my brace of beagles here, my little point-trussers? you shall have them act among ye.—Sirrah, you, pronounce.—Thou shalt hear him speak in King Darius' doleful strain.

1 *Pyr.* "O doleful days![5] O direful deadly dump!
O wicked world, and worldly wickedness!
How can I hold my fist from crying, thump,
In rue of this right rascal wretchedness?"

Tuc. In an amorous vein now, sirrah: peace!

1 *Pyr.* "O, she is wilder,[6] and more hard, withal,
Than beast, or bird, or tree, or stony wall.
Yet might she love me, to uprear her state:
Ay, but perhaps she hopes some nobler mate.
Yet might she love me, to content her fire:
Ay, but her reason masters her desire.
Yet might she love me as her beauty's thrall:
Ay, but I fear she cannot love at all."

Tuc. Now the horrible, fierce soldier, you, sirrah.

2 *Pyr.* "What! will I brave thee? ay, and beard thee too;
A Roman spirit scorns to bear a brain
So full of base pusillanimity."

Hist. Excellent!

Tuc. Nay, thou shalt see that shall ravish thee anon; prick up thine ears, stinkard.—The ghost, boys?

1 *Pyr.* "Vindicta!"[7]

2 *Pyr.* "Timoria!"

---

[1] *Be Minos,*] Be *just,* I suppose; but it is not easy to explain all the extravagances of this whimsical character.

[2] *You have nothing but* HUMOURS, REVELS, *and* SATIRES,] A compliment paid by the author to his own plays.—WHAL.

[3] *Your* Globes *and your* Triumphs.] Alluding to playhouses of those names. By those on the other side of Tyber, mentioned in the preceding speech, are meant the Globe, the Swan, and the Hope playhouses, which were situated on the Bankside in Southwark. Of the Triumph, there is no mention in the list of playhouses which subsisted about this time.—WHAL.

[4] *Reach me thy neuf.*] *Neuf,* or *nief,* is a north-country word for hand or fist. It frequently occurs in Shakspeare.—WHAL.

[5] *O doleful days, &c.*] I suspect that Shakspeare (First Part of *Henry IV.*) confounded *King Cambyses* with this King Darius. Falstaff's solemn fustian bears not the slightest resemblance, either in metre or in matter, to the *vein of King Cambyses. Kyng Daryus,* whose "doleful strain" is here burlesqued, was a *pithie and pleasant Enterlude,* printed about the middle of the sixteenth century.

[6] *O she is wilder, &c.*] This is from the poor persecuted play of old *Jeronimo:* certainly it must have been much in vogue, to make these eternal allusions to it so popular.

[7] *The* ghost, boys.

1 Pyr. *Vindicta!*] Here again Jonson is accused of sneering at Shakspeare! Nay, so determined are the commentators to find enemies to this great poet (who probably had none), that they even charge the anonymous author of *A Warning for Fair Women* with a hostile attack upon him, in the following lines:

"A filthie whining ghost,
Lapt in some foule sheet, or a leather pilch,
Comes screaming like a pigge half stickt,
And cries, *Vindicta, revenge, revenge!*"

Though the words are not in *Hamlet,* but, like Jonson's, literally taken from the ghost of Albanactus, in the old tragedy of *Locrine.*

This absurd piece of fustian seems to have shared with *Jeronimo* (to which it is infinitely inferior) the ridicule of the wits of James's days: allusions to it frequently occur, and particularly to the "whining of this filthie ghost." Thus Fletcher: "In despite of thee, my master, and thy master, the grand devil himself, *Vindicta!*

1 *Pyr.* " Vindicta !"

2 *Pyr.* " Timoria !"

1 *Pyr.* " Veni !"

2 *Pyr.* " Veni !"

Tuc. Now, thunder, sirrah, you the rumbling player.

2 *Pyr.* Ay, but somebody must cry *Murder !* then, in a small voice.[1]

Tuc. Your fellow-sharer there shall do't : Cry, sirrah, cry.

1 *Pyr.* " Murder, murder !"

2 *Pyr.* " Who calls out murder? lady, was it you?"

Hist. O, admirable good, I protest.

Tuc. Sirrah boy, brace your drum a little straiter, and do the t'other fellow there, he in the—what sha' call him—and yet stay too.

2 *Pyr.* " Nay, an thou dalliest, then I am thy foe,

And fear shall force what friendship cannot win ;

Thy death shall bury what thy life conceals.

Villain ! thou diest for more respecting her——"

1 *Pyr.* " O stay, my lord."

2 *Pyr.* "Than me :

Yet speak the truth, and I will guerdon thee ;

But if thou dally once again, thou diest."

Tuc. Enough of this, boy.

2 *Pyr.* " Why then lament therefore : d—ned be thy guts

Unto King Pluto's hell, and princely Erebus,[2]

For sparrows must have food——"

Hist. Pray, sweet captain, let one of them do a little of a lady.

Tuc. O, he will make thee eternally enamoured of him, there : do, sirrah, do ; 'twill allay your fellow's fury a little.

1 *Pyr.* " Master, mock on ; the scorn thou givest me,

Pray Jove some lady may return on thee."

2 *Pyr.* Now you shall see me do the Moor :[3] master, lend me your scarf a little.

Tuc. Here, 'tis at thy service, boy.

2 *Pyr.* You, Master Minos, hark hither a little.

[*Exit with* Minos, *to make himself ready.*

Tuc. How dost like him? art not rapt, art not tickled now? dost not applaud, rascal? dost not applaud ?

Hist. Yes: what will you ask for them a week, captain ?

Tuc. No, you mangonizing slave,[4] I

---

vindicta !"—*Fair Maid of the Inn*. And Crispinus himself :

" *Ant.* Vindicta !
    Alb. Mellida !
    Ant. Vindicta !
    Alb. Antonio !"—*Antonio's Revenge.*

[1] *In a* small *voice,*] i.e., a feminine voice, like that of Mrs. Anne Page. The allusion again is to *Jeronimo,* where Belimperia exclaims, on the seizure of Horatio :

"*Murder! murder!* help, Hieronimo."

[2] " *D—ned be thy guts,*" &c.] This absurd rant, which is ridiculed by so many of our old dramatists, is parodied from *The Battle of Alcazar*. In *Eastward Hoe!* written by Jonson, Chapman, and Marston in conjunction, Quicksilver, a profligate apprentice, whose language, like Pistol's, is made up of burlesque scraps from old plays, introduces two or three words of this parody ; upon which Mr. Steevens observes : "This is a fragment from *Pistol!* I should not hesitate to pronounce such parts of this play as are written in ridicule of Shakspeare to be Jonson's." It requires no common assurance in the authors of such wanton and outrageous calumny, to talk of the malignity of Jonson. It was surely the prototype of Steevens who sat for Macilente.

[3] *Now you shall see me do the* Moor :] Not Othello, as it luckily falls out, but Muley, a character in the old play mentioned in the preceding note.

[4] *No, you* mangonizing *slave,*] From *mango,* Lat. a slave-merchant.—WHAL.

It is impossible to say who is meant by Histrio : but it may be conjectured, from this reproachful term, that he had been accessary in seducing some of the "children of the revels" to join the company at his own theatre. The remainder of this act is merely personal ; indeed the author makes no scruple of avowing it :

" Now, for the *players,* it is true I taxed them, And yet but some," &c.

It is to no purpose that he endeavours to save himself by saying that he "used no names," for Poluphagus, Ænobarbus, Frisker, and *father* Æsop, the *politician,* as the quarto calls him, are so characteristically described as to make the discovery of their real names a task of no great difficulty to their contemporaries. When a staunch hound opens, it is curious to note with what eagerness the yelping curs, "Tray, Blanche, and Sweetheart," rush headlong in and swell the cry. Messrs. Steevens and Malone content their spleen, in general, with harping on the "malignity of Jonson to *Shakspeare :*" their zany, Mr. Thomas Davies, takes up the idle calumny, and embellishes it with ingenious additions of his own. Jonson, it seems, not only abused and insulted Shakspeare, but all the actors of his theatre. The " lean Poluphagus " is Burbage : this is clear ; for Tucca says, " he will eat a leg of mutton while he is in his porridge !" Whether Burbage could do this, Davies

will not part from them ; you'll sell them for enghles, you ; let's have good cheer to-morrow night at supper, stalker, and then we'll talk ; good capon and plover, do you hear, sirrah ? and do not bring your eating player with you there ; I cannot away with him : he will eat a leg of mutton while I am in my porridge, the lean Poluphagus, his belly is like Barathrum ; he looks like a midwife in man's apparel, the slave : nor the villainous out-of-tune fidler, Æno-barbus, bring not him. What hast thou there ? six and thirty, ha ?

Hist. No, here's all I have, captain, some five and twenty : pray, sir, will you present and accommodate it unto the gentleman ? for mine own part, I am a mere stranger to his humour ; besides, I have some business invites me hence, with Master Asinius Lupus, the tribune.

Tuc. Well, go thy ways, pursue thy projects, let me alone with this design ; my Poetaster shall make thee a play, and thou shalt be a man of good parts in it. But stay, let me see : do not bring your Æsop, your politician,[1] unless you can ram up his mouth with cloves ; the slave smells ranker than some sixteen dunghills, and is seventeen times more rotten. Marry, you may bring Frisker, my zany ; he's a good skipping swaggerer ; and your fat fool there, my mango, bring him too ; but let him not beg rapiers nor scarfs, in his over-familiar playing face, nor roar out his barren bold jests with a tormenting laughter, between drunk and dry. Do

you hear, stiff-toe ? give him warning, admonition, to forsake his saucy glavering grace, and his goggle eye ; it does not become him, sirrah ; tell him so. I have stood up and defended you, I, to gentlemen when you have been said to prey upon puisnes, and honest citizens for socks or buskins ; or when they have called you usurers or brokers, or said you were able to help to a piece of flesh—I have sworn I did not think so, nor that you were the common retreats for punks decayed in their practice ; I cannot believe it of you.

Hist. Thank you, captain. Jupiter and the rest of the gods confine your modern delights without disgust !

Tuc. Stay, thou shalt see the Moor ere thou goest.——

Enter Demetrius *at a distance.*

What's he with the half arms there, that salutes us out of his cloak, like a motion, ha ?

Hist. O, sir, his doublet's a little decayed ; he is otherwise a very simple honest fellow, sir, one Demetrius, a dresser of plays about the town[1] here ; we have hired him to abuse Horace, and bring him in, in a play, with all his gallants, as Tibullus, Mecænas, Cornelius Gallus, and the rest.

Tuc. And why so, stinkard ?

Hist. O, it will get us a huge deal of money, captain, and we have need on't ; for this winter has made us all poorer than

---

never thought of inquiring : but thus the first point is made out. "Frisker" is Kempe, who, continues our egregious critic, was celebrated for his ready wit and facetiousness. This also is clear. The "fat fool that begged rapiers and scarfs," is Lowin, the original Falstaff, who played all parts of humour and pleasantry. Mr. Davies now grows generous, and forbears to affirm that the "rotten Æsop" is Shakspeare ; though it is quite as demonstrable as any of his other conjectures. However, as he triumphantly adds, " we have leave to guess anybody, since he spares nobody."—*Dram. Misc.* vol. ii. p. 82. But enough of such deplorable folly ; all the players here satirized are expressly said to belong to the Fortune company, with which none of our great poet's "fellows" had the slightest concern.

[1] *One* Demetrius, *a dresser of plays about the town,* &c.] Here the allusion is too plain to be mistaken, except by those who can see nothing with their own eyes. *Demetrius* is unquestionably *Decker ;* who seems to have derived no small part of his sustenance from *altering* and *amending* the old dramas then on the stage. No one occurs half so frequently in Mr. Hen-

slowe's books as a "dresser of plays ;" Decker must therefore be content, however reluctantly, to resign all claim to the title of Crispinus, and descend from the "bad eminence" which he has so long usurped, as the *Poetaster* of Jonson.

It seems from what follows that our poet's enemies made no secret of their determination to *untruss* him ; he appears here well informed of their design, and of the names of the chief agents who had already volunteered their services against him. It is certain, therefore, that the quarrel between him and Decker did not break out for the first time in the *Poetaster,* as is generally asserted : and it is no less clear that Jonson gives his opponents credit for more good sense than they actually possessed ; since, instead of bringing him in with Mecænas, Tibullus, &c., they introduced him with Wat Terill, Sir Adam Prickshaft, and Sir Rice ap Vaughan, a sputtering Welsh knight of the meanest order. These, with William Rufus, Asinius Bubo, Demetrius, and Crispinus, form a plot that can scarcely be equalled in absurdity by the worst of the plays which Decker was ever employed to "dress."

so many starved snakes : nobody comes at us, not a gentleman, nor a——

Tuc. But you know nothing by him, do you, to make a play of?

Hist. Faith, not much, captain ; but our author will devise that that shall serve in some sort.

Tuc. Why, my Parnassus here shall help him, if thou wilt. Can thy author do it impudently enough?

Hist. O, I warrant you, captain, and spitefully enough too : he has one of the most overflowing rank wits in Rome ; he will slander any man that breathes, if he disgust him.

Tuc. I'll know the poor, egregious, nitty rascal ; an he have these commendable qualities, I'll cherish him—stay, here comes the Tartar—I'll make a gathering for him, I, a purse, and put the poor slave in fresh rags ; tell him so to comfort him.

[*Demetrius comes forward.*

Re-enter Minos, *with* 2 Pyrgus *on his shoulders, and stalks backward and forward, as the boy acts.*

Well said, boy.

2 *Pyr.* "Where art thou, boy?[1] where is Calipolis?

Fight earthquakes in the entrails of the earth,

And eastern whirlwinds in the hellish shades ;

Some foul contagion of the infected heavens

Blast all the trees, and in their cursed tops

The dismal night-raven and tragic owl

Breed and become forerunners of my fall !"

Tuc. Well, now fare thee well, my honest penny-biter : commend me to seven shares and a half, and remember to-morrow. If you lack a service, you shall play in my name, rascals ; but you shall buy your own cloth, and I'll have two shares for my countenance.[2] Let thy author stay with me. [*Exit* Histrio.

Dem. Yes, sir.

Tuc. 'Twas well done, little Minos, thou didst stalk well : forgive me that I said thou stink'st, Minos ; 'twas the savour of a poet I met sweating in the street, hangs yet in my nostrils.

Cris. Who, Horace?

Tuc. Ay, he ; dost thou know him?

Cris. O, he forsook me most barbarously, I protest.

Tuc. Hang him, fusty satyr, he smells all goat ; he carries a ram under his arm-holes,[3] the slave : I am the worse when I see him.—Did not Minos impart?

[*Aside to* Crispinus.

Cris. Yes, here are twenty drachms he did convey.

Tuc. Well said, keep them, we'll share anon ; come, little Minos.

Cris. Faith, captain, I'll be bold to shew you a mistress of mine, a jeweller's wife, a gallant, as we go along.

Tuc. There spoke my genius. Minos, some of thy eringos, little Minos ; send.

---

[1] *Where art thou, boy?* &c.] These lines are taken from the part of the Moor, in the old play of the *Battle of Alcazar*, already mentioned. This second introduction of the Moor offended Decker, who seems to advert to it with some ill humour, but in a way which I do not clearly understand. "As for Crispinus, and Demetrius his *play-dresser*, who, to make the Muses believe that there was a dearth of poesy, *cut an innocent Moor in the middle, to serve him in twice ;* and when he had done made *Paul's work* of it :" (Here Decker retorts on Jonson's actors:) "as for these twins,

"These *poet-apes,* their mimic tricks shall serve
　With mirth to feast our Muse, while their own
　　starve."

If Mr. Chalmers, who stoutly maintains that Shakspeare is the *poet-ape* of our author, should ever condescend to open this volume, he will learn from Decker's own confession that Crispinus and Demetrius were the *poet-apes* of Jonson ; and that our great poet was never yet supposed to be characterized under either of these names. The blundering alacrity with which Jonson's supposed hostility to Shakspeare is pointed out is at once mortifying and amusing.

"In his *Poetaster,*" says Oldys (MS. notes to Langbaine), "some play is touched that has a Moor in it, perhaps Titus Andronicus : I should hope that he did not *dare to mean* Othello." Oldys had pored for half a century over our old plays, and was generally reputed an accurate man ; yet with the fatality of those who in our days find a malicious gratification in injuring Jonson, he has selected as the object of his ridicule two dramas, the one not written by Shakspeare at all, the other produced many years after the present piece, and neither of them containing a syllable to which it bears the slightest reference : while the passage to which he alludes must have stared him in the face as a transcript, verbatim et literatim, from the speech of the Moorish prince in the *Battle of Alcazar :* "Fie on't, oh, fie !"

[2] *I'll have two shares for my* countenance.] See p. 103 *b.*

[3] *He carries a ram under his arm-holes.*] The poet is truly classical here ;

　　　"*Fertur*
　Valle sub alarum trux habitare caper."
　　　　　　　　　　　　　WHAL.

And truly coarse and disgusting.

Come hither, Parnassus, I must have thee
familiar with my little locust here; 'tis a
good vermin, they say.[1] [Horace *and* Trebatius *pass over the stage.*]   See, here's
Horace and old Trebatius, the great
lawyer, in his company; let's avoid him
now, he is too well seconded.   [*Exeunt.*

ACT IV.

SCENE I.—*A Room in* Albius's *House.*

Enter Chloe, Cytheris, *and* Attendants.

Chloe. But, sweet lady, say; am I well
enough attired for the court, in sadness?[2]

Cyth. Well enough! excellent well, sweet
Mistress Chloe; this strait-bodied city
attire, I can tell you, will stir a courtier's
blood more than the finest loose sacks the
ladies use to be put in; and then you are
as well jewelled as any of them, your ruff
and linen about you is much more pure
than theirs; and for your beauty, I can
tell you there's many of them would defy
the painter, if they could change with you.
Marry, the worst is, you must look to be
envied, and endure a few court-frumps for
it.

Chloe. O Jove, madam, I shall buy them
too cheap!—Give me my muff, and my

dog there.—And will the ladies be anything familiar with me, think you?

Cyth. O Juno! why, you shall see them
flock about you with their puff-wings,[3] and
ask you where you bought your lawn, and
what you paid for it? who starches you?
and entreat you to help 'em to some pure
laundresses[4] out of the city.

Chloe. O Cupid!—Give me my fan, and
my mask too.   And will the lords, and the
poets there, use one well too, lady?

Cyth. Doubt not of that; you shall have
kisses from them, go pit-pat, pit-pat, pit-
pat, upon your lips, as thick as stones out
of slings at the assault of a city.   And then
your ears will be so furred with the breath
of their compliments, that you cannot catch
cold of your head, if you would, in three
winters after.

Chloe. Thank you, sweet lady.   O heaven! and how must one behave herself
amongst 'em?   You know all.

Cyth. Faith, impudently enough, Mistress Chloe, and well enough.   Carry not
too much under thought betwixt yourself
and them; nor your city-mannerly word,
forsooth,[5] use it not too often in any case;
but plain *Ay, madam,* and *no, mad.m:*
nor never say, *your lordship,* nor *your
honour;* but *you,* and *you, my lord,* and
my lady: the other they count too simple
and minsitive.   And though they desire to

---

[1] *'Tis a good vermin, they say.*] Here the
third act ends in the 4to.   In the folio, Jonson,
as if this play had not a sufficient number of
translations in it, bad added a literal version of
Horace, lib. ii. sat. 1; which, as the reader
knows, is an exculpatory dialogue between the
poet and Trebatius.   As it is awkwardly introduced, tends to no particular object, interrupts
the progress of the story, and spins out an act
already too long, I have ventured to avail myself
of the authority of the 4to so far as to remove it
to the end of the piece.   The reader will not
regret the short delay in arriving at it, for it has
no very prominent excellencies; being, like most
of Jonson's longer translations, merely vigorous
and faithful, without pretending to any of the
higher graces of poetry.

[2] *In sadness,*] i.e., in *seriousness* or *earnest.*
Sad is used by all our old writers for grave,
sober, staid, also for dark-coloured, &c.   Thus
Stowe says of Fitz-William, the Recorder, "He
was a *sad* man and an honest," p. 817.   And
Walton of the great and good Bishop Sanderson,
"About the time of printing the excellent preface
to his Sermons (in Cromwell's usurpation), I met
him accidentally in London, in *sad*-coloured
cloathes, and, God knows, far from being costly."
—*Walton's Lives.*

[3] *With their puff-wings,*] That part of their
dress which sprung from the shoulders, and had

the appearance of a wing, inflated or blown up.
See p. 101 *a.*

[4] *And help 'em to some* pure laundresses, *&c.*]
This is a hit at the Puritans, many of whom followed the business of tire-women, clear-starchers,
feather-makers, &c.   It is not a little singular
that while they declaimed most vehemently
against the idol, Fashion, they should be
among the most zealous in administering to
its caprice.   Jonson notices this with good
effect in his *Bartholomew Fair;* and Randolph ridicules it no less successfully in the
commencement of his *Muses' Looking-Glass:*
"Enter Bird and Mrs. Flowerdale, two of the
sanctified fraternity, the one having brought
feathers to the play-house to sell, the other pins
and looking-glasses."   The opening of the dialogue is excellent.   Fraud and hypocrisy have
seldom been more humorously exposed.

"*Mrs. Flowerdale.* See, brother, how the
                wicked throng and crowd
To works of vanity!   Not a nook or corner,
In all this house of sin, this cave of filthiness,
This den of spiritual thieves, but it is stuffed,
Stuffed, and stuffed full, as is a cushion,
With the lewd reprobate!"

[5] *Your city-mannerly word,* forsooth,] See
the *Entertainment of the Queen and Prince at
Althorpe.*

kiss heaven with their titles, yet they will count them fools that give them too humbly.

Chloe. O intolerable, Jupiter! by my troth, lady, I would not for a world but you had lain in my house; and, i' faith, you shall not pay a farthing for your board, nor your chambers.

Cyth. O, sweet Mistress Chloe!

Chloe. I' faith you shall not, lady; nay, good lady, do not offer it.

Enter Gallus *and* Tibullus.

Gal. Come, where be these ladies? By your leave, bright stars, this gentleman and I are come to man you to court; where your late kind entertainment is now to be requited with a heavenly banquet.

Cyth. A heavenly banquet, Gallus!

Gal. No less, my dear Cytheris.

Tib. That were not strange, lady, if the epithet were only given for the company invited thither; yourself, and this fair gentlewoman.

Chloe. Are we invited to court, sir?

Tib. You are, lady, by the great Princess Julia; who longs to greet you with any favours that may worthily make you an often courtier.

Chloe. In sincerity, I thank her, sir. You have a coach, have you not?

Tib. The princess hath sent her own, lady.

Chloe. O Venus! that's well: I do long to ride in a coach most vehemently.

Cyth. But, sweet Gallus, pray you resolve me why you give that heavenly praise to this earthly banquet?

Gal. Because, Cytheris, it must be celebrated by the heavenly powers; all the gods and goddesses will be there; to two of which you two must be exalted.

Chloe. A pretty fiction, in truth.

Cyth. A fiction indeed, Chloe, and fit for the fit of a poet.

Gal. Why, Cytheris, may not poets (from whose divine spirits all the honours of the gods have been deduced) entreat so much honour of the gods, to have their divine presence at a poetical banquet?

Cyth. Suppose that no fiction; yet, where are your habilities to make us two goddesses at your feast?

Gal. Who knows not, Cytheris, that the sacred breath of a true poet can blow any virtuous humanity up to deity?

Tib. To tell you the female truth, which is the simple truth, ladies, and to shew that poets in spite of the world, are able to deify

themselves; at this banquet, to which you are invited, we intend to assume the figures of the gods; and to give our several loves the forms of goddesses. Ovid will be Jupiter; the Princess Julia, Juno; Gallus here, Apollo; you, Cytheris, Pallas; I will be Bacchus; and my love Plautia, Ceres; and to install you and your husband, fair Chloe, in honours equal with ours, you shall be a goddess, and your husband a god.

Chloe. A god!—O my gods!

Tib. A god, but a lame god, lady; for he shall be Vulcan, and you Venus: and this will make our banquet no less than heavenly.

Chloe. In sincerity, it will be sugared. Good Jove, what a pretty foolish thing it is to be a poet! but hark you, sweet Cytheris, could they not possibly leave out my husband? methinks a body's husband does not so well at court; a body's friend, or so—but, husband! 'tis like your clog to your marmoset, for all the world, and the heavens.

Cyth. Tut, never fear, Chloe; your husband will be left without in the lobby, or the great chamber, when you shall be put in, i' the closet, by this lord, and by that lady.

Chloe. Nay, then I am certified; he shall go.

Enter Horace.

Gal. Horace! welcome.

Hor. Gentlemen, hear you the news?

Tib. What news, my Quintus?

Hor. Our melancholic friend, Propertius, Hath closed himself up in his Cynthia's tomb;
And will by no entreaties be drawn thence.

Enter Albius, *introducing* Crispinus *and* Demetrius, *followed by* Tucca.

Alb. Nay, good Master Crispinus, pray you bring near the gentleman.

Hor. Crispinus! Hide me, good Gallus; Tibullus, shelter me. [*Going.*

Cris. Make your approach, sweet captain.

Tib. What means this, Horace?

Hor. I am surprised again; farewell.

Gal. Stay, Horace.

Hor. What, and be tired on by yond vulture![1] No:
Phœbus defend me! [*Exit hastily.*

---

[1] *What, and be* tired *on by yond* vulture!] Horace alludes to the story of Prometheus, or rather, perhaps, of Tityus:

"*Incontinentis nec Tityi jecur*
Relinquit ales."—

To *tire* is to peck eagerly, to feed on, as a hawk

Tib. 'Slight, I hold my life
This same is he met him in Holy-street.

Gal. Troth, 'tis like enough.—This act of Propertius relisheth very strange with me.

Tuc. By thy leave, my neat scoundrel: what, is this the mad boy you talked on?

Cris. Ay, this is Master Albius, captain.

Tuc. Give me thy hand, Agamemnon; we hear abroad thou art the Hector of citizens. What sayest thou? are we welcome to thee, noble Neoptolemus?

Albi. Welcome, captain, by Jove and all the gods in the Capitol——

Tuc. No more, we conceive thee. Which of these is thy wedlock,[1] Menelaus? thy Helen, thy Lucrece? that we may do her honour, mad boy.

Cris. She in the little fine dressing, sir,[2] is my mistress.

Alb. For fault of a better, sir.

Tuc. A better! profane rascal: I cry thee mercy, my good scroyle,[3] was't thou?

Alb. No harm, captain.

Tuc. She is a Venus, a Vesta, a Melpomene: come hither Penelope; what's thy name, Iris?

Chloe. My name is Chloe, sir; I am a gentlewoman.

Tuc. Thou art in merit to be an empress, Chloe, for an eye and a lip; thou hast an emperor's nose: kiss me again; 'tis a virtuous punk; so! Before Jove, the gods were a sort of goslings, when they suffered so sweet a breath to perfume the bed of a stinkard: thou hadst ill fortune, Thisbe; the Fates were infatuate, they were, punk, they were.

Chloe. That's sure, sir; let me crave your name, I pray you, sir.

Tuc. I am known by the name of Captain Tucca, punk; the noble Roman,

punk; a gentleman, and a commander, punk.

Chloe. In good time: a gentleman, and a commander! that's as good as a poet, methinks.   [*Walks aside.*

Cris. A pretty instrument![4] It's my cousin Cytheris' viol this, is it not?

Cyth. Nay, play, cousin; it wants but such a voice and hand to grace it as yours is.

Cris. Alas, cousin, you are merrily inspired.

Cyth. Pray you play, if you love me.

Cris. Yes, cousin; you know I do not hate you.

Tib. A most subtile wench! how she hath baited him with a viol yonder, for a song!

Cris. Cousin, pray you call Mistress Chloe; she shall hear an essay of my poetry.

Tuc. I'll call her.—Come hither, cockatrice: here's one will set thee up, my sweet punk, set thee up.

Chloe. Are you a poet so soon, sir?

Alb. Wife, mum.

Crispinus *plays and sings.*

Love is blind, and a wanton;
In the whole world there is scant one
——Such another:
    No, not his mother.
He hath plucked her doves and sparrows,
To feather his sharp arrows,
    And alone prevaileth,
    While sick Venus waileth.
But if Cypris once recover
The wag; it shall behove her
    To look better to him:
    Or she will undo him.

Alb. O, most odoriferous music!

Tuc. Aha, stinkard! Another Orpheus,

---

does on the quarry, or game, which is thrown to her. "Look, my masters, what a bone Sir Richard Bulkeley hath cast into the court for you to *tire* upon."—Pennant's *Tour in Wales*, vol. ii. p. 467. The word occurs perpetually in this sense, in all our old writers, who draw most of their allusions from the amusements of hawking and hunting.

[1] *Which of these is thy* wedlock?] i.e., thy wife. So Beaumont and Fletcher use it:

"'Tis sacrilege to violate a *wedlock*,
   You rob two temples."
                    Rule a Wife and have a Wife.

And, *matrimony*, in the same sense:

"Restore my matrimony undefiled."
                    Little French Lawyer.

So *matrimonium* is used for *uxor* more than once by Justin: "*Ut severius viri matrimonia sua coercerent.*—Lib. 3, c. iv.   WHAL.

[2] *She in the little* fine dressing, *sir.*] In the quarto it is, "In the *velvet cap.*" This is judiciously altered, for the velvet cap was the ensign of a citizen's wife, which Chloe, by the advice of her hopeful tutor, Cytheris, had now laid aside.

[3] Scroyle.] For this contemptuous term, see p. 4 *a*.

[4] *A pretty* instrument, &c.] I have already observed, p. 109 *a*, that every fashionable house in Jonson's time was furnished with a viol de gambo: whether it stood in the Via Sacra, or the Strand, made little difference to our old poets.

you slave, another Orpheus! an Arion riding on the back of a dolphin, rascal!

Gal. Have you a copy of this ditty, sir?

Cris. Master Albius has.

Alb. Ay, but in truth they are my wife's verses, I must not shew them.

Tuc. Shew them, bankrupt, shew them; they have salt in them, and will brook the air, stinkard.

Gal. How! "To his bright mistress Canidia!"

Cris. Ay, sir, that's but a borrowed name; as Ovid's Corinna, or Propertius his Cynthia, or your Nemesis, or Delia, Tibullus.

Gal. It's the name of Horace his witch, as I remember.

Tib. Why, the ditty's all borrowed; 'tis Horace's: hang him, plagiary!

Tuc. How! he borrow of Horace? he shall pawn himself to ten brokers first. Do you hear, Poetasters? I know you to be men of worship——He shall write with Horace, for a talent; and let Mecænas and his whole college of critics take his part: thou shalt do't, young Phœbus; thou shalt, Phæton, thou shalt.

Dem. Alas, sir, Horace! he is a mere sponge; nothing but Humours and observation; he goes up and down sucking from every society, and when he comes home squeezes himself dry again. I know him, I.

Tuc. Thou say'st true, my poor poetical fury, he will pen all he knows. A sharp thorny-toothed satirical rascal, fly him; he carries hay in his horn;[1] he will sooner lose his best friend than his least jest. What he once drops upon paper against a man, lives eternally to upbraid him in the mouth of every slave, tankard-bearer, or waterman; not a bawd, or a boy that comes from the bakehouse, but shall point at him: 'tis all dog and scorpion; he carries poison in his teeth, and a sting in his tail.

Fough! body of Jove! I'll have the slave whipt one of these days for his Satires and his Humours, by one cashiered clerk or another.

Cris. We'll undertake him, captain.

Dem. Ay, and tickle him, i' faith, for his arrogancy and his impudence, in commending his own things; and for his translating,[2] I can trace him, i' faith. O, he is the most open fellow living; I had as lieve as a new suit I were at it.

Tuc. Say no more then, but do it; 'tis the only way to get thee a new suit; sting him, my little neufts; I'll give you instructions: I'll be your intelligencer; we'll all join, and hang upon him like so many horse-leeches, the players and all. We shall sup together soon; and then we'll conspire, i' faith.

Gal. O that Horace had stayed still here!

Tib. So would not I; for both these would have turned Pythagoreans then.

Gal. What, mute?

Tib. Ay, as fishes, i' faith; come, ladies, shall we go?

Cyth. We wait you, sir. But Mistress Chloe asks, if you have not a god to spare for this gentleman.

Gal. Who, Captain Tucca?

Cyth. Ay, he.

Gal. Yes, if we can invite him along, he shall be Mars.

Chloe. Has Mars anything to do with Venus?

Tib. O, most of all, lady.

Chloe. Nay, then I pray let him be invited. And what shall Crispinus be?

Tib. Mercury, Mistress Chloe.

Chloe. Mercury! that's a poet, is it?

Gal. No, lady, but somewhat inclining that way; he is a herald at arms.

Chloe. A herald at arms! good; and Mercury! pretty: he has to do with Venus too?

---

[1] *He carries* hay in his horn, &c.] As a mark of a petulant or dangerous person: this is well explained by the old scholiast: *Romæ, videmus hodieque fænum velut ansulam factum, in cornulo bovis, quo signum datur transeuntibus, ut eum vitent.* The whole of what follows is from Horace:

" *Fænum habet in cornu, longe fuge! dummodo risum*
Excutiat sibi, non hic cuiquam parcet amico:
Et quodcunque semel chartis illeverit, omnes
Gestiet a furno redeuntes scire lacuque,
Et pueros et anus."—Lib. 1. sat. iv.

[2] *For his impudence in commending his own things, and for his translating.*] These were the objections commonly urged against Jonson: and to these he replies in several places, particularly in the last scene of the present play: how satisfactorily, must be left to the reader's judgment. He seems to justify his boldness of self-commendation, by an appeal to his talents, which he well knew to appreciate; and to the practice of his beloved ancients, in whom he never saw anything absurd or indelicate. As for his translations——be was perfectly incorrigible there; for he maintained to the last that they were the best part of his works: in which heresy he was countenanced not only by many of his friends, but also of his enemies! The conclusion of this speech is a sneer at the ignorance and vanity of Decker: it is full of bitterness.

Tib. A little with her face,[1] lady, or so.

Chloe. 'Tis very well; pray let us go, I long to be at it.

Cyth. Gentlemen, shall we pray your companies along?

Cris. You shall not only pray, but prevail, lady.—Come, sweet captain.

Tuc. Yes, I follow: but thou must not talk of this now, my little bankrupt.

Alb. Captain, look here, mum.[2]

Dem. I'll go write, sir.

Tuc. Do, do; stay, there's a drachm to purchase gingerbread for thy muse.

[*Exeunt.*

SCENE II.—*A Room in* Lupus's *House.*

Enter Lupus, Histrio, *and* Lictors.

Lup. Come, let us talk here; here we may be private; shut the door, lictor. You are a player, you say.

Hist. Ay, an't please your worship.

Lup. Good; and how are you able to give this intelligence?

Hist. Marry, sir, they directed a letter to me and my fellow-sharers.

Lup. Speak lower, you are not now in your theatre, stager:—my sword, knave. They directed a letter to you, and your fellow-sharers: forward.

Hist. Yes, sir, to hire some of our properties; as a sceptre and crown for Jove; and a caduceus for Mercury; and a petasus——

Lup. Caduceus and petasus! let me see your letter. This is a conjuration; a conspiracy, this. Quickly, on with my buskins: I'll act a tragedy, i' faith. Will nothing but our gods serve these poets to profane? dispatch! Player, I thank thee. The emperor shall take knowledge of thy good service. [*A knocking within.*] Who's there now? Look, knave. [*Exit* Lictor.] *A crown and a sceptre!* this is good rebellion now.

Re-enter Lictor.

Lic. 'Tis your pothecary, sir, Master Minos.

Lup. What tell'st thou me of pothecaries, knave! Tell him I have affairs of state in hand; I can talk to no pothecaries now. Heart of me! Stay the pothecary there. [*Walks in a musing posture.*] You shall see, I have fished out a cunning piece of plot now: they have had some intelligence that their project is discovered, and now have they dealt with my pothecary to poison me; tis so; knowing that I meant to take physic to-day: as sure as death, 'tis there. Jupiter, I thank thee, that thou hast yet made me so much of a politician.

Enter Minos.

You are welcome, sir; take the potion from him there; I have an antidote more than you wot of sir; throw it on the ground there: so! Now fetch in the dog; and yet we cannot tarry to try experiments now: arrest him; you shall go with me, sir; I'll tickle you, pothecary; I'll give you a glister, i' faith. Have I the letter? ay, 'tis here.—Come, your fasces, lictors: the half pikes and the halberds, take them down from the Lares there.[3] Player, assist me.

As they are going out, enter Mecænas *and* Horace.

Mec. Whither now, Asinius Lupus, with this armory?

Lup. I cannot talk now; I charge you assist me: treason! treason!

Hor. How! treason?

Lup. Ay: if you love the emperor, and the state, follow me.   [*Exeunt.*

SCENE III.—*An Apartment in the Palace.*

Enter Ovid, Julia, Gallus, Cytheris, Tibullus, Plautia, Albius, Chloe, Tucca, Crispinus, Hermogenes, Pyrgus, *characteristically habited, as gods and goddesses.*

Ovid. Gods and goddesses, take your several seats. Now, Mercury, move your caduceus, and, in Jupiter's name, command silence.

Cris. In the name of Jupiter, silence!

Her. The crier of the court hath too clarified a voice.

---

[1] *A little with her face,*] Alluding, I believe, to the deleterious washes then in use.

[2] *Captain, look here, mum.*] While he speaks this, he must be supposed to lay his finger on his lip, as a sign of secrecy.

[3] *Take them down from the* Lares *there.*] The Lares were the domestic tutelary deities of the Romans: their images seem to have been placed near the hearth of the grand entrance room, or hall, where a fire was constantly kept up by the *servus atriensis,* or janitor. This room was adorned with the statues of the possessor's ancestors; and here, too, either for ornament or preservation, were suspended, along the sides of the wall, the bucklers, swords, and javelins of the family.

Gal. Peace, Momus.

Ovid. Oh, he is the god of reprehension; let him alone: 'tis his office. Mercury, go forward, and proclaim, after Phœbus, our high pleasure, to all the deities that shall partake this high banquet.

Cris. Yes, sir.

Gal. "The great god, Jupiter,"—[Here, and at every break in the line, Crispinus repeats aloud the words of Gallus.]—"Of his licentious goodness,—Willing to make this feast no fast—From any manner of pleasure;—Nor to bind any god or goddess—To be anything the more god or goddess, for their names:—He gives them all free licence—To speak no wiser than persons of baser titles ;—And to be nothing better than common men, or women— And therefore no god—Shall need to keep himself more strictly to his goddess—Than any man does to his wife :—Nor any goddess—Shall need to keep herself more strictly to her god—Than any woman does to her husband.—But, since it is no part of wisdom,—In these days, to come into bonds ;—It shall be lawful for every lover —To break loving oaths,—To change their lovers, and make love to others,—As the heat of every one's blood,—And the spirit of our nectar, shall inspire.—And Jupiter save Jupiter !"

Tib. So: now we may play the fools by authority.

Her. To play the fool by authority is wisdom.

Jul. Away with your mattery sentences, Momus ; they are too grave and wise for this meeting.

Ovid. Mercury, give our jester a stool, let him sit by; and reach him one of our cates.

Tuc. Dost hear, mad Jupiter? we'll have it enacted, he that speaks the first wise word, shall be made cuckold. What say'st thou ? Is it not a good motion?

Ovid. Deities, are you all agreed?

All. Agreed, great Jupiter.

Alb. I have read in a book, that to play the fool wisely, is high wisdom.

Gal. How now, Vulcan ! will you be the first wizard ?

Ovid. Take his wife, Mars, and make him cuckold quickly.

Tuc. Come, cockatrice.

Chloe. No, let me alone with him, Jupiter: I'll make you take heed, sir, while you live again, if there be twelve in a company, that you be not the wisest of 'em.

Alb. No more; I will not indeed, wife, hereafter; I'll be here: mum.

Ovid. Fill us a bowl of nectar, Ganymede: we will drink to our daughter Venus.

Gal. Look to your wife, Vulcan: Jupiter begins to court her.

Tib. Nay, let Mars look to it: Vulcan must do as Venus does, bear.

Tuc. Sirrah, boy; catamite. Look you play Ganymede well now, you slave. Do not spill your nectar; carry your cup even: so! You should have rubbed your face with whites of eggs, you rascal, till your brows had shone like our sooty brother's here, as sleek as a horn-book: or have steept your lips in wine till you made them so plump that Juno might have been jealous of them. Punk, kiss me, punk.

Ovid. Here, daughter Venus, I drink to thee.

Chloe. Thank you, good father Jupiter.

Tuc. Why, mother Juno ! gods and fiends ! what, wilt thou suffer this ocular temptation ?

Tib. Mars is enraged, he looks big, and begins to stut¹ for anger.

Her. Well played, Captain Mars.

Tuc. Well said, minstrel Momus: I must put you in, must I? when will you be in good fooling of yourself, fiddler, never?

Her. O, 'tis our fashion to be silent when there is a better fool in place ever.

Tuc. Thank you, rascal.

Ovid. Fill to our daughter Venus, Ganymede, who fills her father with affection.

Jul. Wilt thou be ranging, Jupiter, before my face ?

Ovid. Why not, Juno? why should Jupiter stand in awe of thy face, Juno ?

Jul. Because it is thy wife's face, Jupiter.

Ovid. What, shall a husband be afraid of his wife's face? will she paint it so horribly ? we are a king, cotquean; and we will reign in our pleasures; and we will cudgel thee to death if thou find fault with us.

Jul. I will find fault with thee, king cuckold-maker. What, shall the king of gods turn the king of good-fellows, and have no fellow in wickedness? This makes our poets, that know our profaneness, live as profane as we. By my godhead, Jupiter,

---

¹ *To* stut] i.e., to stutter ; the word is used by Marston :

"He hath Albano's imperfection too,
And *stuts* when he is vehemently moved."
What you Will.

I will join with all the other gods here,
bind thee hand and foot, throw thee down
into the earth, and make a poor poet of
thee, if thou abuse me thus.

Gal. A good smart-tongued goddess, a
tight Juno!

Ovid. Juno, we will cudgel thee, Juno;
we told thee so yesterday, when thou wert
jealous of us for Thetis.

Pyr. Nay, to-day she had me in inquisition too.

Tuc. Well said, my fine Phrygian fry;
inform, inform. Give me some wine, king
of heralds, I may drink to my cockatrice.

Ovid. No more, Ganymede; we will
cudgel thee, Juno; by Styx, we will.

Jul. Ay, 'tis well; gods may grow impudent in iniquity, and they must not be
told of it——

Ovid. Yea, we will knock our chin against
our breast, and shake thee out of Olympus
into an oyster-boat for thy scolding.

Jul. Your nose is not long enough to do
it, Jupiter, if all thy strumpets thou hast
among the stars took thy part. And there
is never a star in thy forehead but shall be
a horn, if thou persist to abuse me.

Cris. A good jest, i' faith.

Ovid. We tell thee thou angerest us,
cotquean;[1] and we will thunder thee in
pieces for thy cotqueanity.

Cris. Another good jest.

Alb. O, my hammers and my Cyclops!
This boy fills not wine enough to make us
kind enough to one another.

Tuc. Nor thou hast not collied thy face
enough, stinkard.

Alb. I'll ply the table with nectar, and
make them friends.

Her. Heaven is like to have but a lame
skinker, then.

Alb. Wine and good livers make true
lovers: I'll sentence them together. Here,
father, here, mother, for shame, drink yourselves drunk,[2] and forget this dissension;
you two should cling together before our
faces, and give us example of unity.

Gal. O, excellently spoken, Vulcan, on
the sudden!

Tib. Jupiter may do well to prefer his
tongue to some office for his eloquence.

Tuc. His tongue shall be gentleman-
usher to his wit, and still go before it.

Alb. An excellent fit office!

Cris. Ay, and an excellent good jest besides.

Her. What, have you hired Mercury to
cry your jests you make?

Ovid. Momus, you are envious.

Tuc. Why, ay, you whoreson blockhead,
'tis your only block of wit in fashion now-
a-days, to applaud other folks' jests.

Her. True; with those that are not artificers themselves. Vulcan, you nod, and
the mirth of the jest droops.

Pyr. He has filled nectar so long, till his
brain swims in it.

Gal. What, do we nod, fellow-gods!
Sound music, and let us startle our spirits
with a song.

Tuc. Do, Apollo, thou art a good
musician.

Gal. What says Jupiter?

Ovid. Ha! ha!

Gal. A song.

Ovid. Why, do, do, sing.

Pla. Bacchus, what say you?

Tib. Ceres?

Pla. But, to this song?

Tib. Sing, for my part.

Jul. Your belly weighs down your head,
Bacchus; here's a song toward.

Tib. Begin, Vulcan.

Alb. What else, what else?

---

[1] *Thou angerest us,* cotquean.] This word is
strangely explained in Johnson's *Dictionary.*
Cotquean, a corruption of cuckquean, is a woman
whose husband is unfaithful to her bed, which
Juno's manifestly was. The word is used by
Warner, and applied as here:

"Queen Juno, not a little wroth, against her
    husband's crime,
By whom she was a *cuckqueane* made," &c.
                              Albion's Eng. c. iv.

This speech is lengthened in the quarto with
some strange unintelligible stuff: the author
did well to throw it out. *Collied,* which occurs
just below, means blackened, begrimed with
soot, &c.

[2] *Here, father, here, mother, for shame,
drink yourselves drunk,* &c.] Albius, who represents Vulcan, does not act out of character:
the poet had Homer in his eye, who reconciles
the quarrelsome deities by the buffoonery and
archness of Vulcan, who takes on himself the
office of skinker to the celestial assembly.
                                          WHAL.

That Vulcan "does not act out of character"
may be granted. After all, the poet acquits
himself but poorly. When the brightest wits of
the court of Augustus took on themselves the
characters of deities, we may be pretty confident
that it was not to doze and get drunk, nor to
bandy round vulgar ribaldry, and such miserable abortions of wit as would scarcely do honour
to the "Vapourers" of *Bartholomew Fair.* It
is indeed very possible that Jonson might mean
to ridicule the gods: even in that case, he has
only disgraced the men.

Tuc. Say, Jupiter——
Ovid. Mercury——
Cris. Ay, say, say.　　　　　[*Music.*
Alb.
"Wake ! our mirth begins to die ;
　　Quicken it with tunes and wine.
Raise your notes ; you're out: fie, fie !
　　This drowsiness is an ill sign.
We banish him the quire of gods,
　　That droops agen ;
　　　　Then all are men,
For here's not one but nods. "

Ovid. I like not this sudden and general
heaviness amongst our godheads; 'tis some-
what ominous. Apollo, command us louder
music, and let Mercury and Momus con-
tend to please and revive our senses.
　　　　　　　　　　　　　　　[*Music.*
Herm.
"Then, in a free and lofty strain,
　　Our broken tunes we thus repair ;
Cris.
　And we answer them again,
　　Running division on the panting
　　　　air ;
Ambo.
　To celebrate this feast of sense,
　　As free from scandal as offence.
Herm.
　Here is beauty for the eye ;
Cris.
　For the ear sweet melody.
Herm.
　Ambrosiac odours for the smell ;

Cris.
　Delicious nectar for the taste ;
Ambo.
　For the touch, a lady's waist ;
　　Which doth all the rest excel."

Ovid. Ay, this has waked us. Mercury
our herald ; go from ourself, the great god
Jupiter, to the great Emperor Augustus
Cæsar, and command him, from us, of
whose bounty he hath received the sirname
of Augustus, that, for a thank-offering to
our beneficence, he presently sacrifice, as
a dish to this banquet, his beautiful and
wanton daughter Julia : she's a curst quean,
tell him, and plays the scold behind his
back ; therefore let her be sacrificed. Command him this, Mercury, in our high name
of Jupiter Altitonans.
Jul. Stay, feather-footed Mercury, and
tell Augustus, from us, the great Juno
Saturnia ; if he think it hard to do as
Jupiter hath commanded him, and sacrifice
his daughter, that he had better do so ten
times than suffer her to love the well-nosed
poet, Ovid ; whom he shall do well to whip,
or cause to be whipped, about the capitol,
for soothing her in her follies.

Enter Augustus Cæsar, Mecænas, Horace,
　　Lupus, Histrio, Minos, *and* Lictors.

Cæs. What sight is this? Mecænas !
　　Horace ! say ?
Have we our senses ? do we hear and see ?[1]

---

[1] *What sight is this?* &c.] The friends of
Ovid may have much to object to the justice of
Jonson, in his design of the preceding scene.
Ovid had faults enough to answer for without
being charged with others of mere invention.
It is generally supposed that he was banished by
Augustus for an amour with his daughter Julia :
and this circumstance our poet mentions with
propriety : and he fancied, I presume, that an
entertainment of the kind represented was not
inconsistent with the luxuriance of Ovid's imagination. But the truth is, that Jonson is partial ;
and Ovid does not appear to have had any share
in the contrivance. Let us transfer then the
infamy of this feast to its real author, who is no
other than the emperor himself. The account is
preserved in Suetonius, who tells us, that on
this occasion Augustus assumed the dress and
character of Apollo : "*Cæna quoque ejus se-
cretior in fabulis fuit, quæ vulgo* Δωδεκαθεος
*vocabatur: in quâ deorum dearumque habitu
discubuisse convivas, et ipsum pro Apolline
ornatum, non Antonii modo epistolæ singu-
lorum nomina amarissime enumerantis expro-
brant, sed et sine auctore notissimi versus :*

*Cum primum istorum conduxit mensa Cho-
　　ragum,*

*Sexque deos vidit Mallia, sexque deas :
Impia dum Phœbi Cæsar mendacia ludit,
Dum nova divorum cœnat adulteria ;
Omnia se à terris tunc numina declinârunt,
Fugit et auratos Jupiter ipse thronos.*

*Auxit cœnæ rumorem summa tunc in civitate
penuria ac fames : acclamatumque est post-
ridie, frumentum omne deos comedisse, et
Cæsarem plane esse Apollinem, sed tortorem :
quo cognomine is deus quadam in parte urbis
colebatur.*—Sueton. *August.* c. lxx. WHAL.
Whalley is perfectly right in transferring the
odium of this feast to the emperor : but he mistakes Jonson, and confounds events very distant
in time. Our author was too well acquainted
with the history of Ovid not to know that his
amour with Corinna (whoever she was) took place
in his youth :

"*Carmina cum primum populo juvenilia legi,
　Barba resecta mihi bisve semelve fuit :
　Moverat ingenium, totam cantata per urbem
　Nomine non vero dicta Corinna mihi.*"
　　　　　　　　　　Trist. l. 4, el. x.

Whereas, he was not banished till he was up-
wards of fifty. Jonson, however, speaks not of
his banishment, but simply of his exile from

Or are these but imaginary objects
Drawn by our fantasy! Why speak you not?
Let us do sacrifice. Are they the gods?
                [*Ovid and the rest kneel.*
Reverence, amaze, and fury fight in me.
What, do they kneel! Nay, then I see 'tis
        true
I thought impossible: O, impious sight!
Let me divert mine eyes; the very thought
Everts my soul with passion. Look not,
        man,
There is a panther, whose unnatural eyes
Will strike thee dead: turn, then, and die
        on her
With her own death.
                [*Offers to kill his daughter.*
  Mec. Hor. What means imperial Cæsar?
  Cæs. What! would you have me let the
        strumpet live,
That, for this pageant, earns so many deaths?
  Tuc. Boy, slink, boy.
  Pyr. Pray Jupiter we be not followed by
the scent, master.
                [*Exeunt* Tucca *and* Pyrgus.
  Cæs. Say, sir, what are you?
  Alb. I play Vulcan, sir.
  Cæs. But what are you, sir?
  Alb. Your citizen and jeweller, sir.
  Cæs. And what are you, dame?
  Chloe. I play Venus, forsooth.
  Cæs. I ask not what you play, but what
        you are.
  Chloe. Your citizen and jeweller's wife,
        sir.
  Cæs. And you, good sir?
  Cris. Your gentleman parcel-poet, sir.
                [*Exit.*
  Cæs. O, that profaned name?—
And are these seemly company for thee,
                [*To* Julia.
Degenerate monster? All the rest I know,
And hate all knowledge for their hateful
        sakes.
Are you, that first the deities inspired
With skill of their high natures and their
        powers,
The first abusers of their useful light;
Profaning thus their dignities in their forms,
And making them, like you, but counter-
        feits?
O, who shall follow Virtue and embrace
        her,
When her false bosom is found nought but
        air?
And yet of those embraces centaurs spring,[1]
That war with human peace, and poison
        men.—
Who shall, with greater comforts compre-
        hend
Her unseen being and her excellence;
When you, that teach, and should eternize
        her,
Live as she were no law unto your lives,
Nor lived herself but with your idle breaths?
If you think gods but feigned, and virtue
        painted,
Know we sustain an actual residence,
And with the title of an emperor,
Retain his spirit and imperial power;
By which, in imposition too remiss,
Licentious Naso, for thy violent wrong,
In soothing the declined affections
Of our base daughter, we exile thy feet
From all approach to our imperial court,
On pain of death; and thy misgotten love
Commit to patronage of iron doors,
Since her soft-hearted sire cannot contain
        her.
  Mec. O, good my lord, forgive! be like
        the gods.
  Hor. Let royal bounty, Cæsar, mediate.
  Cæs. There is no bounty to be shewed to
        such
As have no real goodness: bounty is
A spice of virtue; and what virtuous act
Can take effect on them, that have no power
Of equal habitude to apprehend it,
But live in worship of that idol, vice,

---

court, as Whalley might have seen in the next
page. The Julia here mentioned (the daughter
of Augustus) was banished for her licentiousness
thirteen years before this event took place.
There is indeed another Julia, cousin to the
former (Augustus's niece), who was banished at
the same time with Ovid; but Augustus was at
that period somewhat too old for love, being
turned of seventy. Besides, if Ovid had de-
bauched the emperor's daughter, he would
scarcely have recurred to the subject so frequently. He was evidently conscious of some
impurities in the imperial family. He pretends,
indeed, that what he saw was not meant to be
seen by him; but as he was not over nice in his
morality, he might have furthered the niece's
amours, and been more officious than he is
willing to allow. After all, he attributes his
banishment in a great degree to his indecent
verses; and perhaps justly. He seems to think
this hard upon him. Other poets, it is true, had
written grosser lines with impunity; but the
express purpose of Ovid, whether avowed or not,
was to reduce licentiousness to an art, and facilitate the corruption of innocence: he was,
therefore, infinitely more dangerous than the
coarse and disgusting writers who preceded
him.
  [1] *And yet of those embraces centaurs spring,*]
Alluding to the fable of Ixion's embracing Juno
in the shape of a cloud; from which conjunction
arose the centaurs.—WHAL.

As if there were no virtue, but in shade
Of strong imagination, merely enforced?
This shews their knowledge is mere igno-
    rance,
Their far-fetched dignity of soul a fancy,
And all their square pretext of gravity
A mere vain-glory: hence, away with
    them!
I will prefer for knowledge, none but such
As rule their lives by it, and can becalm
All sea of Humour with the marble trident
Of their strong spirits: others fight below
With gnats and shadows; others nothing
    know.   [*Exeunt.*

SCENE IV.—*A Street before the Palace.*

Enter Tucca, Crispinus, *and* Pyrgus.

Tuc. What's become of my little punk,
Venus, and the poult-foot stinkard,[1] her
husband, ha?
  Cris. O, they are rid home in the coach,
as fast as the wheels can run.
  Tuc. God Jupiter is banished, I hear,
and his cockatrice Juno locked up. 'Heart,
an all the poetry in Parnassus get me to
be a player again, I'll sell 'em my share for
a sesterce. But this is Humours, Horace,
that goat-footed envious slave; he's turned
faun now;[2] an informer, the rogue! 'tis he
has betrayed us all. Did you not see him
with the emperor crouching?
  Cris. Yes.
  Tuc. Well, follow me. Thou shalt
libel, and I'll cudgel the rascal. Boy,
provide me a truncheon. Revenge shall
gratulate him, *tam Marti, quam Mercurio.*
  Pyr. Ay, but, master, take heed how

you give this out; Horace is a man of the
sword.
  Cris. 'Tis true, in troth; they say he's
valiant.[3]
  Tuc. Valiant? so is mine a—. Gods
and fiends! I'll blow him into air when I
meet him next; he dares not fight with a
puck-fist.
             [Horace *passes over the stage.*
  Pyr. Master, he comes!
  Tuc. Where? Jupiter save thee, my
good poet, my noble prophet, my little fat
Horace.—I scorn to beat the rogue in the
court; and I saluted him thus fair, because he should suspect nothing, the
rascal. Come, we'll go see how far forward our journeyman is toward the untrussing of him.[4]
  Cris. Do your hear, captain? I'll write
nothing in it but innocence, because I may
swear I am innocent.   [*Exeunt.*

SCENE V.

Enter Horace, Mecænas, Lupus, Histrio,
and Lictors.

Hor. Nay, why pursue you not the
  emperor
For your reward now, Lupus?
  Mec. Stay, Asinius;
You and your stager, and your band of
  lictors:
I hope your service merits more respect,
Than thus, without a thanks, to be sent
  hence.
  His. Well, well, jest on, jest on.
  Hor. Thou base, unworthy groom!
  Lup. Ay, ay, 'tis good.

---

[1] *The* poult-foot *stinkard,*] i.e., lame, or club-
foot. See *Mercury vindicated from the Alche-
mists.*

[2] *He's turned* faun *now;*] The writers of
Jonson's days seem to have connected, I know
not why, the idea of a spy, or splenetic observer,
with that of a *faun.* Marston calls one of his
plays *The Fawne,* in allusion to a character in
disguise, who watches and exposes all the persons of the drama in succession.

[3] *In troth, they say he's* valiant.] It would
seem from this as if Jonson did not join in the
general outcry against the *cowardice* of Horace.
I confess myself to be of his opinion. If Horace
fled at the battle of Philippi, it was not till
courage was become unavailable, and the best
and bravest troops of the army had fallen on the
spot. How beautifully does he paint all this!

  " *Tecum Philippos et celerem fugam
    Sensi, relicta non bene parmula;
    Cum fracta virtus, et minaces,
    Turpe ! solum tetigere mento.*"

Was Pompeius Varus a coward? yet he too fled.
Surely the *non bene,* the *fracta virtus,* and the
turpe, all bear the same meaning, and allude to
the decisive defeat, not to the ill-conduct of the
patriotic army. It argues as little good sense as
liberality, to take advantage of a poetical expression, and, without considering the circumstances under which it was used, to stigmatize
the writer to all ages.
  As for Ben, the Horace of the *Poetaster,* he
was undoubtedly *valiant.* He had given fatal
proofs of courage in a duel, in which he killed
his antagonist; and he had acquitted himself
with honour in his Flemish campaigns.

  [4] *Come, we'll go see how far forward our
journeyman is toward the untrussing of him.*]
More proof that Demetrius is Decker; for Crispinus is now on the stage!—A man " with the
spleen of a wren," might be gratified at seeing
how the critics, like Ding-dong's sheep, blindly
leap after one another.

Hor. Was this the treason, this the
  dangerous plot,
Thy clamorous tongue so bellowed
  through the court?
Hadst thou no other project to encrease
Thy grace with Cæsar but this wolfish
  train,
To prey upon the life of innocent mirth
And harmless pleasures, bred of noble wit?
Away! I loathe thy presence; such as
  thou,
They are the moths and scarabs of a state,[1]
The bane of empires, and the dregs of
  courts;
Who, to endear themselves to an em-
  ployment,
Care not whose fame they blast, whose life
  they endanger;
And, under a disguised and cobweb mask
Of love unto their sovereign, vomit forth
Their own prodigious malice; and pre-
  tending
To be the props and columns of their
  safety,
The guards unto his person and his peace,
Disturb it most, with their false, lapwing-
  cries.[2]
  Lup. Good! Cæsar shall know of this,
  believe it.
  Mec. Cæsar doth know it, wolf, and to
  his knowledge,
He will, I hope, reward your base en-
  deavours.
Princes that will but hear, or give access
To such officious spies, can ne'er be safe:
They take in poison with an open ear,
And, free from danger, become slaves to
  fear.   *[Exeunt.*

SCENE VI.—*An open Space before the
  Palace.*

Enter Ovid.

Banished the court! Let me be banished
  life,
Since the chief end of life is there con-
  cluded:[3]
Within the court is all the kingdom
  bounded,
And as her sacred sphere doth comprehend
Ten thousand times so much, as so much
  place
In any part of all the empire else;

So every body, moving in her sphere,
Contains ten thousand times as much in
  him,
As any other her choice orb excludes.
As in a circle, a magician then
Is safe against the spirit he excites;
But, out of it, is subject to his rage,
And loseth all the virtue of his art:
So I, exiled the circle of the court,
Lose all the good gifts that in it I 'joyed.
No virtue current is, but with her stamp,
And no vice vicious, blanched with her
  white hand.
The court's the abstract of all Rome's
  desert,
And my dear Julia the abstract of the
  court.
Methinks, now I come near her, I respire
Some air of that late comfort I received;
And while the evening, with her modest
  veil,
Gives leave to such poor shadows as myself
To steal abroad, I, like a heartless ghost,
Without the living body of my love,
Will here walk and attend her: for I know
Not far from hence she is imprisoned,
And hopes of her strict guardian, to bribe
So much admittance, as to speak to me,
And cheer my fainting spirits with her
  breath.
  Julia. [*appears above at her chamber
  window.*]
  Ovid? my love?
  Ovid. Here, heavenly Julia.
  Jul. Here! and not here! O, how that
  word doth play
With both our fortunes, differing, like our-
  selves,
Both one; and yet divided, as opposed!
I high, thou low: O, this our plight of
  place
Doubly presents the two lets of our love,
Local and ceremonial height, and lowness:
Both ways, I am too high, and thou too
  low.
Our minds are even yet; O, why should
  our bodies,
That are their slaves, be so without their
  rule?
I'll cast myself down to thee; if I die,
I'll ever live with thee: no height of birth,
Of place, of duty, or of cruel power,
Shall keep me from thee; should my
  father lock

---

[1] *They are the* moths *and* scarabs *of a state.*]
"*Moths* are small winged insects that eat
clothes." *Scarabs* are beetles. I mention this
because I am told that the information may be
useful to some readers. [*E. Rev. of Massinger.*]

[2] *With their false,* lapwing *cries.*] See
Sejanus, p. 325 a.
[3] *Is there* concluded:] i.e., included or confined: there is a terrible number of Latinisms in
this play.

This body up within a tomb of brass,
Yet I'll be with thee.   If the forms I hold
Now in my soul, be made one substance
    with it ;
That soul immortal, and the same 'tis now ;
Death cannot raze the affects she now re-
    taineth :
And then, may she be anywhere she will.
The souls of parents rule not children's
    souls,
When death sets both in their dissolved
    estates ;
Then is no child nor father ; then eternity
Frees all from any temporal respect.
I come, my Ovid, take me in thine arms,
And let me breathe my soul into thy breast.
    Ovid. O stay, my love ; the hopes thou
        dost conceive
Of thy quick death, and of thy future life,
Art not authentical.   Thou choosest death,
So thou might'st 'joy thy love in the other
    life :
But know, my princely love, when thou
    art dead,
Thou only must survive in perfect soul ;
And in the soul are no affections.
We pour out our affections with our blood,
And, with our blood's affections, fade our
    loves.
No life hath love in such sweet state as
    this ;
No essence is so dear to moody sense
As flesh and blood, whose quintessence is
    sense.
Beauty, composed of blood and flesh,
    moves more,
And is more plausible to blood and flesh,
Than spiritual beauty can be to the spirit.
Such apprehension as we have in dreams,
When, sleep, the bond of senses, locks
    them up,
Such shall we have, when death destroys
    them quite.
If love be then thy object, change not life ;
Live high and happy still : I still below,
Close with my fortunes, in thy height shall
    joy.
    Jul. Ah me, that virtue, whose brave
        eagle's wings
With every stroke blow stars in burning
    heaven,
Should, like a swallow, preying towards
    storms,
Fly close to earth, and with an eager
    plume,
Pursue those objects which none else can
    see,
But seem to all the world the empty air !
Thus thou, poor Ovid, and all virtuous men,

Must prey, like swallows, on invisible food,
Pursuing flies, or nothing : and thus love,
And every worldly fancy, is transposed
By worldly tyranny to what plight it list.
O father, since thou gav'st me not my
    mind,
Strive not to rule it ; take but what thou
    gav'st
To thy disposure : thy affections
Rule not in me ; I must bear all my griefs,
Let me use all my pleasures ; virtuous love
Was never scandal to a goddess' state.—
But he's inflexible ! and, my dear love,
Thy life may chance be shortened by the
    length
Of my unwilling speeches to depart.
Farewell, sweet life ; though thou be yet
    exiled
The officious court, enjoy me amply still :
My soul, in this my breath, enters thine
    ears,
And on this turret's floor will I lie dead,
Till we may meet again.   In this proud
    height,
I kneel beneath thee in my prostrate love,
And kiss the happy sands that kiss thy
    feet.
Great Jove submits a sceptre to a cell,
And lovers, ere they part, will meet in hell.
    Ovid. Farewell all company, and, if I
        could,
All light with thee ! hell's shade should
    hide my brows,
Till thy dear beauty's beams redeemed my
    vows.   [*Going.*
    Jul. Ovid, my love ; alas ! may we not
        stay
A little longer, think'st thou, undiscerned ?
    Ovid. For thine own good, fair goddess,
        do not stay.
Who would engage a firmament of fires
Shining in thee, for me, a falling star ?
Begone, sweet life-blood ; if I should
    discern
Thyself but touched for my sake, I should
    die.
    Jul. I will begone, then ; and not
        heaven itself
Shall draw me back.   [*Going.*
    Ovid. Yet, Julia, if thou wilt,
A little longer stay.
    Jul. I am content.
    Ovid. O, mighty Ovid ! what the sway
        of heaven
Could not retire, my breath hath turned
    back.
    Jul. Who shall go first, my love ? my
        passionate eyes
Will not endure to see thee turn from me.

Ovid. If thou go first, my soul will
    follow thee.
Jul. Then we must stay.
Ovid. Ah me, there is no stay
In amorous pleasures ; if both stay, both
    die.
I hear thy father ; hence, my deity.
            [Julia *retires from the window.*
Fear forgeth sounds in my deluded ears ;
I did not hear him : I am mad with love.
There is no spirit under heaven, that
    works
With such illusion ; yet such witchcraft
    kill me,
Ere a sound mind, without it, save my
    life !
Here, on my knees, I worship the blest
    place
That held my goddess ; and the loving air,
That closed her body in his silken arms.
Vain Ovid ! kneel not to the place, nor air ;
She's in thy heart ; rise then, and worship
    there.
The truest wisdom silly men can have,
Is dotage on the follies of their flesh:[1]
                                    [*Exit.*

ACT V.

SCENE I.—*An Apartment in the Palace.*

Enter Cæsar, Mecænas, Gallus, Tibullus,
    Horace, *and* Equites Romani.

Cæs. We, that have conquered still, to
    save the conquered,
And loved to make inflictions feared, not
    felt ;
Grieved to reprove, and joyful to reward ;
More proud of reconcilement than revenge ;
Resume into the late state of our love,
Worthy Cornelius Gallus, and Tibullus ;
You both are gentlemen : and you, Cor-
    nelius,
A soldier of renown, and the first provost
That ever let our Roman eagles fly
On swarthy Ægypt, quarried with her
    spoils,
Yet (not to bear cold forms, nor men's
    out-terms,[2]
Without the inward fires, and lives of men)

You both have virtues, shining through
    your shapes ;
To shew your titles are not writ on posts,
Or hollow statues which the best men are,
Without Promethean stuffings reached from
    heaven !
Sweet poesy's sacred garlands crown your
    gentry :
Which is, of all the faculties on earth,
The most abstract and perfect ; if she be
True-born, and nursed with all the
    sciences,
She can so mould Rome, and her monu-
    ments,
Within the liquid marble of her lines,
That they shall stand fresh and miraculous,
Even when they mix with innovating
    dust ;
In her sweet streams shall our brave Roman
    spirits
Chase, and swim after death, with their
    choice deeds
Shining on their white shoulders ; and
    therein
Shall Tyber, and our famous rivers fall
With such attraction, that the ambitious
    line
Of the round world shall to her center
    shrink,
To hear their music : and, for these high
    parts,
Cæsar shall reverence the Pierian arts.
    Mec. Your majesty's high grace to poesy,
Shall stand 'gainst all the dull detractions
Of leaden souls ; who, for the vain assum-
    ings
Of some, quite worthless of her sovereign
    wreaths,
Contain her worthiest prophets in con-
    tempt.
    Gal. Happy is Rome of all earth's other
    states,
To have so true and great a president,
For her inferior spirits to imitate,
As Cæsar is ; who addeth to the sun
Influence and lustre ; in increasing thus
His inspirations, kindling fire in us.
    Hor. Phœbus himself shall kneel at
    Cæsar's shrine,
And deck it with bay garlands dewed with
    wine,
To quit the worship Cæsar does to him :

---

[1] I am afraid that this ridiculous love scene
will not strike the reader as much in the manner
of Ovid : there is neither pathos nor passion, nor
interest in it, but a kind of metaphysical hurly-
burly, of which it is not easy to discover the
purport or end.

[2] *Yet not to bear cold forms, nor men's* out-
terms,] Merely the figures and outlines of men.
A metaphor from painting.—WHAL.
    Is it not rather from sculpture ? Jonson has
adhered closely to history in the character which
he gives of these eminent writers.

Where other princes, hoisted to their
   thrones
By Fortune's passionate and disordered
   power,
Sit in their height, like clouds before the
   sun,
Hindering his comforts; and, by their
   excess
Of cold in virtue, and cross heat in vice,
Thunder and tempest on those learned
   heads,[1]
Whom Cæsar with such honour doth ad-
   vance.
   Tib. All human business fortune doth
      command
Without all order; and with her blind hand,
She, blind, bestows blind gifts, that still
   have nurst,
They see not who, nor how, but still, the
   worst.
   Cæs. Cæsar, for his rule, and for so
      much stuff
As Fortune puts in his hand, shall dispose
   it,
As if his hand had eyes and soul in it,
With worth and judgment.   Hands, that
   part with gifts,
Or will restrain their use, without desert,
Or with a misery numbed to virtue's right,
Work, as they had no soul to govern them,
And quite reject her; severing their estates
From human order.   Whosoever can,
And will not cherish virtue, is no man.

   Enter some of the Equestrian order.

   Eques. Virgil is now at hand, imperial
      Cæsar.
   Cæs. Rome's honour is at hand then.
      Fetch a chair,
And set it on our right hand, where 'tis fit
Rome's honour and our own should ever sit.
Now he is come out of Campania,
I doubt not he hath finished all his Æneids,
Which, like another soul, I long to enjoy.
What think you three of Virgil, gentlemen,
That are of his profession, though ranked
   higher;

Or, Horace, what say'st thou, that art the
   poorest,
And likeliest to envy, or to detract?
   Hor. Cæsar speaks after common men
      in this,
To make a difference of me for my poorness;
As if the filth of poverty sunk as deep
Into a knowing spirit, as the bane
Of riches doth into an ignorant soul.
No, Cæsar, they be pathless, moorish
   minds,
That being once made rotten with the dung
Of damned riches, ever after sink
Beneath the steps of any villainy.
But knowledge is the nectar that keeps
   sweet
A perfect soul, even in this grave of sin;
And for my soul, it is as free as Cæsar's,
For what I know is due I'll give to all.
He that detracts or envies virtuous merit,
Is still the covetous and the ignorant spirit.
   Cæs. Thanks, Horace, for thy free and
      wholesome sharpness,
Which pleaseth Cæsar more than servile
   fawns.
A flattered prince soon turns the prince of
   fools.
And for thy sake, we'll put no difference
   more
Between the great and good, for being poor.
Say then, loved Horace, thy true thought
   of Virgil.
   Hor. I judge him of a rectified spirit,
By many revolutions of discourse,
(In his bright reason's influence,) refined
From all the tartarous moods of common
   men;
Bearing the nature and similitude
Of a right heavenly body; most severe
In fashion and collection of himself;
And, then, as clear and confident as Jove.
   Gal. And yet so chaste and tender is his
      ear,
In suffering any syllable to pass,
That he thinks may become the honoured
   name
Of issue to his so examined self,
That all the lasting fruits of his full merit,

---

[1] *Thunder and* tempest *on those learned heads,*] This expression is adopted by Milton:

> " Part, huge of bulk,
> Wallowing unwieldy, enormous in their gait,
> *Tempests* the ocean."

And one of his commentators compliments him on the service rendered to the English language by the introduction of such a verb from the Italian. With submission to so much erudition, the word was introduced into our language long before Milton was born: though Jonson, to whom none of the critics refer, was the first, I believe, who used it in poetry:—and, now I am on the subject, I will just hint to those who may undertake hereafter the unprofitable drudgery of tracing out the property of every word and phrase and idea in Milton, that, next to the translators of the *Bible*, Jonson will be found more to their purpose than all the writers of the age put together.

In his own poems, he doth still distaste;
As if his mind's piece, which he strove to
   paint,
Could not with fleshly pencils have her
   right.
   Tib. But to approve his works of sove-
   reign worth,[1]
This observation, methinks, more than
   serves,
And is not vulgar. That which he hath
   writ
Is with such judgment laboured, and dis-
   tilled
Through all the needful uses of our lives,
That could a man remember but his lines,
He should not touch at any serious point,
But he might breathe his spirit out of him.
   Cæs. You mean, he might repeat part of
   his works,
As fit for any conference he can use?
   Tib. True, royal Cæsar.
   Cæs. Worthily observed;
And a most worthy virtue in his works.
What thinks material Horace of his learn-
   ing?[2]
   Hor. His learning savours not the school-
   like gloss,
That most consists in echoing words and
   terms,
And soonest wins a man an empty name;
Nor any long or far-fetched circumstance
Wrapped in the curious generalties of arts;
But a direct and analytic sum
Of all the worth and first effects of arts.
And for his poesy, 'tis so rammed with life,
That it shall gather strength of life with
   being,
And live hereafter more admired than now.
   Cæs. This one consent in all your dooms
   of him,
And mutual loves of all your several merits,
Argues a truth of merit in you all.

Enter Virgil.

See, here comes Virgil; we will rise and
   greet him.
Welcome to Cæsar, Virgil! Cæsar and
   Virgil
Shall differ but in sound; to Cæsar, Virgil,
Of his expressed greatness, shall be made
A second sirname, and to Virgil, Cæsar.
Where are thy famous Æneids? do us grace
To let us see, and surfeit on their sight.
   Virg. Worthless they are of Cæsar's
   gracious eyes,
If they were perfect ; much more with their
   wants,
Which are yet more than my time could
   supply.
And, could great Cæsar's expectation
Be satisfied with any other service,
I would not shew them.
   Cæs. Virgil is too modest ;
Or seeks, in vain, to make our longings
   more :
Shew them, sweet Virgil.
   Virg. Then, in such due fear
As fits presenters of great works to Cæsar,
I humbly shew them.
   Cæs. Let us now behold
A human soul made visible in life;
And more refulgent in a senseless paper
Than in the sensual complement of kings.
Read, read thyself, dear Virgil; let not me
Profane one accent with an untuned
   tongue:
Best matter, badly shewn, shews worse
   than bad.
See then this chair, of purpose set for thee
To read thy poem in ; refuse it not.
Virtue, without presumption, place may
   take
Above best kings, whom only she should
   make.

---

[1] *But to approve his works of sovereign
worth*, &c.] The great and glorious character
of Virgil, given in the two preceding speeches,
is at once discriminative and just. What follows,
however, is of a different description, and can by
no means be applied to him.   It is evident that
throughout the whole of this drama Jonson
maintains a constant allusion to himself and his
contemporaries : and were it not that it is fully
settled by the critics, from Theobald to Chalmers,
that the whole purport of his writings was to
"malign" Shakspeare, I should incline to believe
that this speech, and that of Horace, which immediately follows, were both intended for him.
Jonson could not think that Virgil was the poet
of common life, as Tibullus affirms ; or, as
Horace, that he was unostentatious of literature, and averse from *echoing* the terms of others :
whereas all this is as undoubtedly true of Shakspeare, as if it were pointedly written to describe
him. Indeed, the speech of Tibullus is so characteristic of our great poet, that I am persuaded
nothing but the ignorance of his numerous
editors of the existence of such a passage has
prevented its being taken for the motto to his
works.
   [2] *What thinks* material *Horace of his learning*?] *Material*, i.e., full of solid sense and
observation. "I love," says the Duke, speaking
of Jaques,

   " I love to cope him in these sullen fits,
   For then he's full of *matter*."

And Jaques himself calls Touchstone "a *material* fool ;" i.e., as Jonson explains it, a fool
stocked with notions.

Virg. It will be thought a thing ridiculous
To present eyes, and to all future times
A gross untruth, that any poet, void
Of birth, or wealth, or temporal dignity,
Should, with decorum, transcend Cæsar's
　　chair.
Poor virtue raised, high birth and wealth
　　set under,
Crosseth heaven's courses, and makes
　　worldlings wonder.
　　Cæs. The course of heaven, and fate
　　　　itself, in this,
Will Cæsar cross ; much more all worldly
　　custom.
　　Hor. Custom, in course of honour, ever
　　　　errs ;
And they are best whom fortune least pre-
　　fers.
　　Cæs. Horace hath but more strictly
　　　　spoke our thoughts.
The vast rude swing of general confluence
Is, in particular ends, exempt from sense :
And therefore reason (which in right should
　　be
The special rector of all harmony)
Shall shew we are a man distinct by it,
From those, whom custom rapteth in her
　　press.
Ascend then, Virgil ; and where first by
　　chance
We here have turned thy book, do thou
　　first read.
　　Virg. Great Cæsar hath his will ; I will
　　　　ascend.
'Twere simple injury to his free hand,
That sweeps the cobwebs from unused
　　virtue,
And makes her shine proportioned to her
　　worth,
To be more nice to entertain his grace,
Than he is choice, and liberal to afford it.[1]
　　Cæs. Gentlemen of our chamber, guard
　　　　the doors,
And let none enter ; [*Exeunt* Equites.]
　　peace.　Begin, good Virgil.
　　Virg. "Meanwhile the skies 'gan thun-
　　　　der, and in tail
Of that, fell pouring storms of sleet and
　　hail :

The Tyrian lords and Trojan youth, each
　　where
With Venus' Dardane nephew, now, in fear,
Seek out for several shelter[2] through the
　　plain,
Whilst floods come rolling from the hills
　　amain.
Dido a cave, the Trojan prince the same
Lighted upon.　There earth and heaven's
　　great dame,
That hath the charge of marriage, first gave
　　sign
Unto his contract ; fire and air did shine,
As guilty of the match ; and from the hill
The nymphs with shriekings do the region
　　fill.
Here first began their bane ; this day was
　　ground
Of all their ills ; for now, nor rumour's
　　sound,
Nor nice respect of state, moves Dido
　　ought ;
Her love no longer now by stealth is sought :
She calls this wedlock, and with that fair
　　name
Covers her fault.　Forthwith the bruit and
　　fame,
Through all the greatest Libyan towns is
　　gone ;
Fame, a fleet evil, than which is swifter
　　none,
That moving grows, and flying gathers
　　strength ;
Little at first, and fearful ; but at length
She dares attempt the skies, and stalking
　　proud
With feet on ground, her head doth pierce
　　a cloud !
This child, our parent earth, stirred up
　　with spite
Of all the gods, brought forth ; and, as
　　some write,
She was last sister of that giant race,
That thought to scale Jove's court ; right
　　swift of pace,
And swifter far of wing ; a monster vast,
And dreadful.　Look, how many plumes
　　are placed
On her huge corps, so many waking eyes

---

[1] This is expressed with great beauty and
propriety, and shows Virgil to be a man of perfect good breeding.
[2] *Seek out for* several *shelter*, &c.] i.e., for
separate places of shelter.　I have little to
observe on this version : it probably cost Jonson
some trouble ; and, according to the ancient
notion of what translation should be, must be
allowed some merit.　It was not a general view
of an author's sense which contented the writers

of those times : they aspired to give his precise
words, without addition or diminution ; and unfortunately attempted to do it within the compass
of the original.　It is to Jonson's praise perhaps
that he moves in his awkward trammels with
more facility than his rivals ; still, however,
there is little grace in his steps, and he more
frequently excites wonder than communicates pleasure.　The text is from the *Æneid*,
lib. iv.

Stick underneath ; and, which may stranger
rise
In the report, as many tongues she bears,
As many mouths, as many listening ears.
Nightly in midst of all the heaven, she flies,
And through the earth's dark shadow
  shrieking cries ;
Nor do her eyes once bend to taste sweet
  sleep;
By day on tops of houses she doth keep,
Or on high towers ; and doth thence
  affright
Cities and towns of most conspicuous site :
As covetous she is of tales and lies,
As prodigal of truth : this monster——"

Lup. [*within.*] Come, follow me, assist
me, second me ! Where's the emperor?

1 *Eques.* [*within.*] Sir, you must pardon
us.

2 *Eques.* [*within.*] Cæsar is private now ;
you may not enter.

Tuc. [*within.*] Not enter ! Charge them
upon their allegiance, cropshin.

1 *Eques.* [*within.*] We have a charge to
the contrary, sir.

Lup. [*within.*] I pronounce you all
traitors, horrible traitors. What, do you
know my affairs ? I have matter of danger
and state to impart to Cæsar.

Cæs. What noise is there? who's that
names Cæsar ?

Lup. [*within.*] A friend to Cæsar.
One that, for Cæsar's good, would speak
with Cæsar.

Cæs. Who is it ? look, Cornelius.

1 *Eques.* [*within.*] Asinius Lupus.

Cæs. O, bid the turbulent informer
hence ;
We have no vacant ear now, to receive
The unseasoned fruits of his officious tongue.

Mec. You must avoid him there.

Lup. [*within.*] I conjure thee, as thou
art Cæsar, or respectest thine own safety,
or the safety of the state, Cæsar, hear me,
speak with me, Cæsar ; 'tis no common
business I come about, but such, as being
neglected, may concern the life of Cæsar.

Cæs. The life of Cæsar ! Let him enter.
Virgil, keep thy seat.

Equites. [*within.*] Bear back, there :
whither will you ? keep back !

Enter Lupus, Tucca, *and* Lictors.

Tuc. By thy leave, goodman usher :
mend thy peruke ; so.

Lup. Lay hold on Horace there; and on
Mecænas, lictors. Romans, offer no
rescue, upon your allegiance : read, royal
Cæsar. [*Gives a paper.*] I'll tickle you,
Satyr.

Tuc. He will, Humours, he will ; he will
squeeze you, poet puck-fist.[1]

Lup. I'll lop you off for an unprofitable
branch, you satirical varlet.

Tuc. Ay, and Epaminondas your patron
here, with his flagon chain ; come, resign :
[*takes off* Mecænas' *chain*] though 'twere
your great-grandfather's, the law has made
it mine now, sir. Look to him, my party-
coloured rascals ; look to him.

Cæs. What is this, Asinius Lupus? I
understand it not.

Lup. Not understand it ! A libel, Cæsar;
a dangerous, seditious libel ; a libel in picture.

Cæs. A libel !

Lup. Ay ; I found it in this Horace his
study, in Mecænas his house, here ; I
challenge the penalty of the laws against
them.

Tuc. Ay, and remember to beg their
land betimes ;[2] before some of these hungry
court hounds scent it out.

Cæs. Shew it to Horace : ask him if he
know it.

Lup. Know it ! his hand is at it, Cæsar.

Cæs. Then 'tis no libel.

Hor. It is the imperfect body of an emblem, Cæsar, I began for Mecænas.

Lup. An emblem ! right : that's Greek
for a libel. Do but mark how confident
he is.

Hor. A just man cannot fear, thou foolish
tribune ;
Not though the malice of traducing
  tongues,
The open vastness of a tyrant's ear,[3]
The senseless rigour of the wrested laws,

[1] *He will squeeze you, poet* puck-fist.] See
p. 75 *b.*

[2] *Remember to beg their land betimes,* &c.]
It was the practice of the greedy courtiers at
the Reformation to scent out such lands as
became forfeited to the crown, and beg the
grant of them. Thus, in *Jack Drum's Entertainment:* "I have followed ordinaries this
twelvemonth, onely to find a foole that had
landes, or a fellow that woulde *talke treason,*

that I might *beg him."* Some remarkable instances are mentioned in history. This practice
was not worn out in Elizabeth's days, particularly with respect to what were called *concealed
lands.* See p. 40 *a.*

[3] *The open vastness of a tyrant's ear,*] I
know not where Jonson got this idea; perhaps
he has some allusion to the auriform cavity of
the Syracusian dungeon : the expression, however, is very noble.

Or the red eyes of strained authority,
Should, in a point, meet all to take his life:
His innocence is armour 'gainst all these.

Lup. Innocence! O impudence! let me
see, let me see. Is not here an eagle! and
is not that eagle meant by Cæsar, ha?[1]
Does not Cæsar give the eagle? answer
me; what sayest thou?

Tuc. Hast thou any evasion, stinkard?

Lup. Now he's turned dumb. I'll tickle
you, Satyr.

Hor. Pish: ha, ha!

Lup. Dost thou pish me? Give me my
long sword.

Hor. With reverence to great Cæsar,
worthy Romans,
Observe but this ridiculous commenter;
The soul to my device was in this distich:
" Thus oft, the base and ravenous multi-
tude
Survive, to share the spoils of fortitude."
Which in this body I have figured here,
A vulture——

Lup. A vulture! Ay, now, 'tis a vulture.
O abominable! monstrous! monstrous!
Has not your vulture a beak? has it not
legs, and talons, and wings, and feathers?

Tuc. Touch him, old buskins.

Hor. And therefore must it be an eagle?

Mec. Respect him not, good Horace:
say your device.

Hor. A vulture and a wolf——

Lup. A wolf! good: that's I; I am the
wolf: my name's Lupus; I am meant by
the wolf. On, on; a vulture and a wolf.

Hor. Preying upon the carcass of an
ass——

Lup. An ass! good still: that's I too; I
am the ass.[2] You mean me by the ass.

Mec. Prithee leave braying then.

Hor. If you will needs take it, I cannot
with modesty give it from you.

Mec. But, by that beast, the old Egyp-
tians
Were wont to figure, in their hieroglyphics,
Patience, frugality, and fortitude;
For none of which we can suspect you,
tribune.

Cæs. Who was it, Lupus, that informed
you first,
This should be meant by us? Or was't
your comment?

Lup. No, Cæsar; a player gave me the
first light of it indeed.

Tuc. Ay, an honest sycophant-like slave,
and a politician besides.[3]

Cæs. Where is that player?

Tuc. He is without here.

Cæs. Call him in.

Tuc. Call in the player there, Master
Æsop; call him.

Equites. [*within.*] Player! where is the
player? bear back: none but the player
enter.

Enter Æsop, followed by Crispinus *and*
Demetrius.

Tuc. Yes, this gentleman and his Achates
must.

Cris. Pray you, master usher:—we'll
stand close here.

Tuc. 'Tis a gentleman of quality, this;[4]
though he be somewhat out of clothes, I
tell ye.—Come, Æsop, hast a bay-leaf in
thy mouth?[5] Well said; be not out, stin-

---

[1] *And is not that eagle meant by Cæsar?*]
i.e., *of* Cæsar. See p. 52 a.

" Stewart tharwith all bolnyt in to baill,
Wallace, he sed, *be* the I tell a taill;
Say furth, quoth he, &c.——
That taill ful meit thou has tald *be* thi sell."
Wallace, lib. x. 130, 149.

The excellent compiler of the Scottish Dict. says
that *be* (by) is used here rather in an uncommon
sense. It is used simply for *of;* a sense perfectly
familiar to the old writers of both countries.
Give is a term in heraldry; in common language
it means, to take or assume, as a particular *bearing,* in the escutcheon.

[3] *I am the ass, &c.*] Here and above the
honest tribune alludes to his name, Asinius
Lupus.

[3] *Ay, an honest sycophant-like slave, and a
politician besides.*] This is beyond question an
allusion to a piece of private history. Perhaps
Æsop, the politician here meant, and who is
charged with the discovery of this notable piece

of treason, had actually framed some plot or laid
some information against Jonson. He was an
actor at the Fortune play-house, which is all
that I can say of him. Our author treats him
with marked dislike: he merely allows him to
make his appearance, and then hurries him off
the stage to undergo a servile punishment.

[4] *'Tis a* gentleman of quality, *this;*] This is
Marston (Crispinus), who was born and educated
a gentleman. Jonson carefully distinguishes
him from Decker (Demetrius) throughout the
whole of this drama.

[5] *Come, Æsop, hast a* bay-leaf *in thy mouth?*]
The bay was sacred to Apollo; hence perhaps
the notion of the ancients, that a bay-leaf placed
under the tongue was conducive to eloquence.
But, indeed, the *bay-leaf* in all ages has been
subservient to a number of petty superstitions.
Absolon, in the *Milleres Tale,* among other
amatory artifices to captivate the affections of
the carpenter's wife,

" Under his tonge a *trewe love* bere,
For therby wend he to ben gracious."

kard. Thou shalt have a monopoly of playing confirmed to thee and thy covey,[1] under the emperor's broad seal, for this service.

Cæs. Is this he?

Lup. Ay, Cæsar, this is he.

Cæs. Let him be whipped. Lictors, go take him hence.

And, Lupus, for your fierce credulity,[2] One fit him with a pair of larger ears: 'Tis Cæsar's doom, and must not be revoked.

We hate to have our court and peace disturbed

With these quotidian clamours. See it done.

Lup. Cæsar!

    [*Exeunt some of the* Lictors, *with* Lupus *and* Æsop.

Cæs. Gag him, [that] we may have his silence.

Virg. Cæsar hath done like Cæsar. Fair and just

Is his award against these brainless creatures.

'Tis not the wholesome sharp morality, Or modest anger of a satiric spirit, That hurts or wounds the body of the state; But the sinister application Of the malicious, ignorant, and base Interpreter; who will distort, and strain The general scope and purpose of an author To his particular and private spleen.

Cæs. We know it, our dear Virgil, and esteem it

A most dishonest practice in that man, Will seem too witty in another's work. What would Cornelius Gallus, and Tibullus?   [*They whisper* Cæsar.

Tuc. [*to* Mecænas.] Nay, but as thou art a man, dost hear? a man of worship and honourable: hold, here, take thy chain again. Resume, mad Mecænas. What! dost thou think I meant to have kept it, old boy? no: I did it but to fright thee, I,

to try how thou wouldst take it. What! will I turn shark upon my friends, or my friends' friends? I scorn it with my three souls.[3] Come, I love bully Horace as well as thou dost, I: 'tis an honest hieroglyphic. Give me thy wrist, Helicon. Dost thou think I'll second e'er a rhinoceros of them all against thee, ha? or thy noble Hippocrene, here? I'll turn stager first, and be whipt too: dost thou see, bully?

Cæs. You have your will of Cæsar: use it, Romans.

Virgil shall be your prætor; and ourself Will here sit by, spectator of your sports; And think it no impeach of royalty. Our ear is now too much profaned, grave Maro,

With these distastes, to take thy sacred lines:

Put up thy book, till both the time and we Be fitted with more hallowed circumstance For the receiving so divine a work. Proceed with your design.

Mec. Gal. Tib. Thanks to great Cæsar.

Gal. Tibullus, draw you the indictment then, whilst Horace arrests them on the statute of Calumny. Mecænas and I will take our places here. Lictors, assist him.

Hor. I am the worst accuser under heaven.

Gal. Tut, you must do it; 'twill be noble mirth.

Hor. I take no knowledge that they do malign me.

Tib. Ay, but the world takes knowledge.

Hor. Would the world knew, How heartily I wish a fool should hate me!

Tuc. Body of Jupiter! what! will they arraign my brisk Poetaster and his poor journeyman, ha? Would I were abroad skeldering for a drachm, so I were out of this labyrinth again! I do feel myself turn

---

Of this passage Tyrwhitt says that he can make nothing. I have little doubt but that it was a *bay leaf* which Absolon *bere* in his mouth, of which the imaginary virtue was to render his language at once bold and persuasive. Cartwright, a close follower of Jonson, alludes to this circumstance in his *Lady-Errant*, where Philænis describes the mode in which she proposes to humanize the pigmies:

    " Teach them good language by cleft sticks and   bay-leaves,
    And civilize them finally by puppet-plays."

I do not suppose that Voltaire ever looked into Cartwright: but this is nearly the way in which

he recommended us to treat the revolted Caraibs. "There is nothing new under the sun."

[1] *Thou shalt have a monopoly of playing confirmed to thee and thy* covey,] Here is a slight gird at the practice of *monopolies*, now growing into fashion.—WHAL.

Growing! It had attained a pretty considerable bulk long before this was written.

[2] *And, Lupus, for your* fierce *credulity.*] Fierce is rash, inconsiderate, and violent: the word occurs again in *Sejanus.*—WHAL.

[3] *Will I turn shark upon my friends, or my friends' friends? I scorn it with my* three souls.] The Peripatetic philosophy gave every man three souls; a plastic, an animal, and a rational soul.—WHAL.

stinkard already: but I must set the best face I have upon't now. [*Aside.*] Well said, my divine, deft Horace, bring the whoreson detracting slaves to the bar, do; make them hold up their spread golls:[1] I'll give in evidence for thee, if thou wilt. Take courage, Crispinus; would thy man had a clean band!

Cris. What must we do, captain?

Tuc. Thou shalt see anon: do not make division with thy legs so.

Cæs. What's he, Horace?

Hor. I only know him for a motion, Cæsar.

Tuc. I am one of thy commanders, Cæsar; a man of service and action: my name is Pantilius Tucca; I have served in thy wars against Mark Antony, I.

Cæs. Do you know him, Cornelius?

Gal. He's one that hath had the mustering, or convoy of a company now and then: I never noted him by any other employment.

Cæs. We will observe him better.

Tib. Lictor, proclaim silence in the court.

Lict. In the name of Cæsar, silence!

Tib. Let the parties, the accuser and the accused, present themselves.

Lict. The accuser and the accused, present yourselves in court.

Cris. Dem. Here.

Virg. Read the indictment.

Tib. "Rufus Laberius Crispinus, and Demetrius Fannius, hold up your hands. You are, before this time, jointly and severally indicted, and here presently to be arraigned upon the statute of calumny, or *Lex Remmia*,[2] the one by the name of Rufus Laberius Crispinus, alias Cri-spinas, poetaster and plagiary; the other by the name of Demetrius Fannius, play-dresser and plagiary. That you (not having the fear of Phœbus, or his shafts, before your eyes) contrary to the peace of our liege lord, Augustus Cæsar, his crown and dignity, and against the form of a statute, in that case made and provided, have most ignorantly, foolishly, and, more like yourselves, maliciously, gone about to deprave and calumniate the person and writings of Quintus Horatius Flaccus, here present, poet, and priest to the Muses; and to that end have mutually conspired and plotted,

at sundry times, as by several means, and in sundry places, for the better accomplishing your base and envious purpose; taxing him falsely, of self-love, arrogancy, impudence, railing, filching by translation, &c. Of all which calumnies, and every of them, in manner and form aforesaid; what answer you? Are you guilty, or not guilty?"

Tuc. Not guilty, say.

Cris. Dem. Not guilty.

Tib. How will you be tried?

Tuc. By the Roman gods, and the noblest Romans.　　　　[*Aside to* Cris.

Cris. Dem. By the Roman gods, and the noblest Romans.

Virg. Here sits Mecænas, and Cornelius Gallus.

Are you contented to be tried by these?

Tuc. Ay, so the noble captain may be joined with them in commission, say.
　　　　　　　　　　　　　　[*Aside.*

Cris. Dem. Ay, so the noble captain may be joined with them in commission.

Virg. What says the plaintiff?

Hor. I am content.

Virg. Captain, then take your place.

Tuc. Alas, my worshipful prætor! 'tis more of thy gentleness than of my deserving, I wusse. But since it hath pleased the court to make choice of my wisdom and gravity, come, my calumnious varlets; let's hear you talk for yourselves, now, an hour or two. What can you say? Make a noise. Act, act!

Vir. Stay, turn, and take an oath first.
　　"You shall swear,
By thunder-darting Jove, the king of gods,
And by the genius of Augustus Cæsar;
By your own white and uncorrupted souls,
And the deep reverence of our Roman
　　justice;
To judge this case with truth and equity:
As bound, by your religion, and your
　　laws."
Now read the evidence: but first demand
Of either prisoner, if that writ be theirs.
　　　　　　　　[*Gives him two papers.*

Tib. Shew this unto Crispinus. Is it yours?

Tuc. Say ay: [*Aside.*] What! dost thou stand upon it, pimp? Do not deny thine own Minerva, thy Pallas, the issue of thy brain.

---

[1] *Make them hold up their spread* golls:] Their hands. Thus Decker: "Hold up thy *hands*: I have seen the time thou didst not scorn to hold up thy *golls.*"—*Satirom. Deft,* which occurs just before, is adroit, clever, handy.

[2] *On the statute of calumny, or* Lex Remmia.] By this *Law* persons convicted of calumny were to be branded on the forehead with the letter C.
　　　　　　　　　　　　　　　　WHAL.

Cris. Yes, it is mine.

Tib. Shew that unto Demetrius.   Is it yours?

Dem. It is.

Tuc. There's a father will not deny his own bastard now, I warrant thee.

Virg. Read them aloud.[1]

Tib. "Ramp up my genius,[2] be not retrograde;
But boldly nominate a spade a spade.
What, shall thy lubrical and glibbery muse[3]

Live, as she were defunct, like punk in stews!"

Tuc. Excellent!

"Alas! that were no modern consequence,
To have cothurnal buskins[4] frighted hence.
No, teach thy Incubus to poetize;[5]
And throw abroad thy spurious snotteries,[6]
Upon that puft-up lump of balmy froth,"

Tuc. Ah, ha!

"Or clumsy chilblained judgment;[7] that with oath

---

[1] *Read them aloud, &c.*] I have already observed, in opposition to the whole string of commentators, that Crispinus is Marston: if any doubts of it should remain after what has been advanced, the lines which follow will be more than sufficient to remove them. In these, Jonson has accumulated many of the uncouth and barbarous terms which characterize Marston's poetry. Such of them as I could readily call to mind, are here thrown together: an attentive perusal of his works might probably furnish others; but the labour would be neither pleasant nor profitable. As Holofernes justly observes, *satis quod sufficit.*

The works which our author had chiefly in view, were the *Scourge of Villainie,* and the two parts of *Antonio and Mellida.* In the former of these Jonson is ridiculed under the name of Torquatus, for his affected use of "new-minted words, such as *real, intriusicate,* and *delphicke,*" which are all found in his earliest comedies: so that we have here, in fact, little more than "the retort courteous."

"*Cædimus, inque vicem præbemus crura sagittis.*"

But, indeed, Marston deserved some reprehension. He boasts, and his boasts have been repeated by the commentators who generally take all upon trust, that he is "free from licentiousness of language." The fact is not so; he is extremely gross and impure. This is what Jonson means, when he makes him "boldly nominate a spade a spade:" and this too is the just object of the attack upon him, in the old play of the *Return from Parnassus:*

"Tut! what cares he for modest, close-couched terms,
Cleanly to gird our looser libertines?
Give him plain naked words, stripped of their shirts,
That might beseem plain-dealing Aretine."

I will not affirm that Marston's manner is very correctly imitated in this collection of his words and phrases; yet those who read his *Satires* cannot fail to be struck with the arrogance, pedantry, and harshness (qualities here attempted to be caricatured) which pervade every part of them: while his dramatic works, more particularly those noticed by Jonson, are distinguished by nothing so much as a perpetual bluster, an overstrained reaching after sublimity of expression, which ends in abrupt and unintelligible starts, and bombast anomalies of language. It

is but fair to add, that whatever Marston might think of the present castigation, he had the good sense to profit by it, since his latter works exhibit but few of the terms here ridiculed.

[2] Ramp *up my genius, &c.*]

"The rawish danke of clumzie winter *rampes*
The fluent summer's vein," &c.

This is taken from the Prologue to the Second Part of *Antonio,* which is very much in the style of this burlesque.

[3] *What, shall thy lubrical and* glibbery *muse*] There is no word of which Marston seems more fond than of this; he introduces it on all occasions:

"His love is *glibbery,* there's no hold on't, wench."—*Antonio and Mellida.*

Again:

"Milke, milke, you *glibbery* urchin,
Is food for infants."—*Id.*

[4] *Alas! that were no* modern *consequence,
To have* cothurnal buskins, *&c.*] *Modern* is slight, trivial : this word, though much affected by Marston, is not peculiar to him. *Cothurnal buskins* is parodied from an absurd expression in *Antonio and Mellida,* part 2, act ii. sc. 5.

"O now *tragedia cothurnata* mounts!"

[5] *No, teach thy* incubus *to poetize.*]

"I would have told you of the *incubus*
That rides your bosom."
    Antonio and Mellida, 2nd part.

"Then death, like to a stifling *incubus,*
Lie on my bosom."—*Id.*

[6] *And throw abroad thy* spurious snotteries,]

"To purge the *snotterie* of our slimie time."
    Scourge of Villainie.

[7] *Upon that puft-up lump of* barmy froth,
Or clumzie chilblained judgment.]

"Shall each odde puisne of the Lawyers Inne,
Each *barmy froth,* that last day did beginne
To read his *nere a whit,*" &c.
    Scourge of Villainie.

Again: "That, like some rotten stick in troubled water, hath gott a great deal of *barmie froth* to stick to his sides."—*Preface to Satires.*

The rawish danke of *clumzie* winter, &c. This absurd fustian has been already quoted: from the forced application of this epithet, well might Jonson observe (as he does below) "that *clumzie* stuck terribly."

Magnificates his merit;[1] and bespawls
The conscious time with humourous foam
   and brawls,
As if his organons of sense would crack
The sinews of my patience.   Break his
   back,
O poets all and some ! for now we list
Of strenuous vengeance to clutch the fist.[2]
                   CRISPINUS."

  Tuc. Ay, marry, this was written like a
Hercules in poetry, now.
  Cæs. Excellently well threatened !
  Virg. And as strangely worded, Cæsar.
  Cæs. We observe it.
  Virg. The other now.[3]
  Tuc. This is a fellow of a good prodigal
tongue too ; this will do well.

  Tib. "Our Muse is in mind for th' un-
   trussing a poet ;
I slip by his name, for most men do know it:
A critic that all the world bescumbers[4]
With satirical humours and lyrical numbers:
  Tuc. Art thou there, boy?
"And for the most part, himself doth ad-
   vance
With much self-love, and more arrogance."
  Tuc. Good again !
"And, but that I would not be thought a
   prater,
I could tell you he were a translator.
I know the authors from whence he has
   stole,
And could trace him too, but that I under-
   stand them not full and whole."[5]

---

[1] Magnificates *his merit*;] This, like *barmie froth*, is a favourite expression with Marston :

"I cannot with swoln lines *magnificate*
  Mine owne poor worth."—*Sat.*

Again :

   " Shall a trencher slave extenuate
Some Lucrece rape, and straight *magnificate*
Lewd Jovian lust," &c.—*Id.*

[2]   *For now we* list
Of strenuous vengeance *to* clutch *the* fist.] Steevens, with his customary disregard of truth in everything which relates to our author, declares, in his final remarks on *Hamlet*, that Jonson has more than once, in the *Poetaster*, pointed his ridicule at some of Shakspeare's descriptions and characters, and frequently sneered at his choice of words, of which he instances *clutch*. I will take upon me to affirm that the play does not contain a single allusion to any character that Shakspeare ever drew, nor an expression that can, by any ingenuity, however malicious, be tortured into a sneer at his language. *Clutch*, indeed, is used by him (as well as others), and with strict propriety ; which can scarcely be said of it, as employed by Marston : let the reader judge :

" 'Tis yet dead night, yet all the earth is *clutched*
  In the dull leaden hand of snoring sleepe."
        Antonio's Revenge, act i. sc. 1.

" Seize on revenge, graspe the sterne-bended
   front
Of frowning *vengeance* with unpaized *clutch*."
        Id. act iii. sc. 1.

Is it yet clear ? To come to the point, however, at once,—not only this word, but the whole line, is taken literatim from a bombastic speech in *Antonio's Revenge*, act v. sc. 1 :

" *The fist of strenuous vengeance is clutcht.*"

[3] *The other now.*] The lines which follow, and which are signed Demetrius, are most assuredly meant to ridicule the loose and desultory style of Decker ; though here too something of Marston is suffered to appear. Indeed it is more than probable that other poets besides

" Crispinus and his Achates" are included in the ARRAIGNMENT.
[4] *A critic that all the world* bescumbers.] This word is also in Marston's *Satires*, and is deservedly stigmatized. Yet I should not have noticed it but for the opportunity which it gives me of setting right the learned and ingenious author of that stupendous monument of successful industry, the *Etymological Dictionary* of the Scottish Language :

" Better thou gains to leid a dog *to skomer*
  Pynd pyck-purse pelour, than wi' thy master
   pingle."

This seems to mean "to cater for thee," or to " smell where there is provision." Voce *Scomer*. Very different is the sense :—but a passage from Massinger will explain it sufficiently :

" *Hil.* How do you like
Your airing ? Is it not a favour ?
  Ric. Yes ;
Just such a one as you use to a brace of grey-
   hounds,
When they are led out of their kennels to
   scumber,
But our case is ten times harder, we have
   nothing
In our bellies to be vented."
        The Picture, act v. sc. 1.

If Dr. Jamieson will turn to his witty countryman's translation of Rabelais, he will find more than one instance of the use of this word in its proper sense. *To leid a dog to skomer*, to submit to the lowest and most degrading offices.

[5] *But that I understand them not full and whole.*] This could in no sense be said of Marston, who had received an University education, and was, indeed, a very considerable scholar ; but was probably true of Decker, who seems to have no great stock of literature, and whose history, as far at least as it is known, is little more than a hopeless struggle with poverty. Much of his life was spent in confinement for debt, though he had talents sufficient, in ordinary times, to have secured not only freedom, but independence.

                                8

Tuc. That line is broke loose from all his fellows: chain him up shorter, do.

"The best note I can give you to know him by,
Is, that he keeps gallants' company;
Whom I could wish, in time should him fear,
‿est after they buy repentance too dear.
                    DEME. FANNIUS."

Tuc. Well said! this carries palm with it.[1]

Hor. And why, thou motley gull, why should they fear?
When hast thou known us wrong or tax a friend?
I dare thy malice to betray it.   Speak.
Now thou curl'st up, thou poor and nasty snake,
And shrink'st thy poisonous head into thy bosom:
Out, viper! thou that eat'st thy parents, hence!
Rather such speckled creatures as thyself,
Should be eschewed,[2] and shunned: such as will bite
And gnaw their absent friends, not cure their fame;
Catch at the loosest laughters, and affect
To be thought jesters; such as can devise
Things never seen, or heard, t'impair men's names,
And gratify their credulous adversaries;
Will carry tales, do basest offices,
Cherish divided fires, and still encrease
New flames out of old embers; will reveal
Each secret that's committed to their trust:
These be black slaves; Romans, take heed of these.

Tuc. Thou twang'st right, little Horace: they be indeed a couple of chap-fallen curs. Come, we of the bench,[3] let's rise to the urn, and condemn them quickly.

Virg. Before you go together, worthy Romans,

We are to tender our opinion;
And give you those instructions that may add
Unto your even judgment in the cause:
Which thus we do commence.   First, you must know,
That where there is a true and perfect merit,
There can be no dejection; and the scorn
Of humble baseness, oftentimes so works
In a high soul, upon the grosser spirit,
That to his bleared and offended sense,
There seems a hideous fault blazed in the object;
When only the disease is in his eyes.
Here-hence it comes our Horace now stands taxed
Of impudence, self-love, and arrogance,
By those who share no merit in themselves,
And therefore think his portion is as small.
For they, from their own guilt, assure their souls,
If they should confidently praise their works,
In them it would appear inflation:
Which, in a full and well digested man,
Cannot receive that foul abusive name,
But the fair title of erection.
And, for his true use of translating men,
It still hath been a work of as much palm,
In clearest judgments, as to invent or make.
His sharpness,—that is most excusable;
As being forced out of a suffering virtue,
Oppressed with the licence of the time:
And howsoever fools or jerking pedants,
Players, or such like buffoon barking wits,[4]
May with their beggarly and barren trash,
Tickle base vulgar ears, in their despite;
This, like Jove's thunder, shall their pride control,
"The honest satire hath the happiest soul."
Now, Romans, you have heard our thoughts; withdraw when you please.

Tib. Remove the accused from the bar.

Tuc. Who holds the urn to us, ha?

---

[1] *This carries palm with it.*] A Latin form of speaking, equivalent to our English phrase, "This bears the bell."—WHAL.
It is so, though the one expression be as mean as the other is elegant and noble; both, however, mean *victory.*   The word is used with great beauty in *Julius Cæsar:*

"In the most high and *palmy* state of Rome."

And again, in *Troilus and Cressida:*

'No; this thrice worthy and right valiant lord
Must not so stale his *palm,* nobly acquired."

[2] *Rather such speckled creatures as thyself
Should be eschewed, &c.*]

" *Absentem qui rodit amicum,*
Qui non defendit, alio culpante, solutos
Qui captat risus hominum, famamque dicacis,
Fingere qui non visa potest, commissa tacere
Qui nequit, hic niger est, hunc tu, Romane,
caveto."—Lib. i. Sat. 4.

[3] *Come, we of the bench, let's rise to the urn, &c.*] See my translation of Juvenal, Sat. xiv. v. 6.

[4] *Players, or such like* buffoon barking wits.] This is from the folio, the quarto reads *buffoonary* wits, which is just as good.

Fear nothing, I'll quit you, mine honest pitiful stinkards; I'll do't.

Cris. Captain, you shall eternally girt me to you, as I am generous.

Tuc. Go to.

Cæs. Tibullus, let there be a case of vizards privately provided;[1] we have found a subject to bestow them on.

Tib. It shall be done, Cæsar.

Cæs. Here be words, Horace, able to bastinado a man's ears.

Hor. Ay.
Please it great Cæsar, I have pills about me,
Mixt with the whitest kind of hellebore,
Would give him a light vomit[2] that should purge
His brain and stomach of those tumorous heats:
Might I have leave to minister unto him.

Cæs. O, be his Æsculapius, gentle Horace!
You shall have leave, and he shall be your patient.
Virgil,
Use your authority, command him forth.

Virg. Cæsar is careful of your health, Crispinus;
And hath himself chose a physician
To minister unto you: take his pills.

Hor. They are somewhat bitter, sir, but very wholesome.
Take yet another; so; stand by, they'll work anon.

Tib. Romans, return to your several seats: lictors, bring forward the urn; and set the accused to the bar.

Tuc. Quickly, you whoreson egregious varlets; come forward. What! shall we sit all day upon you? You make no more haste now than a beggar upon pattens; or a physician to a patient that has no money, you pilchers.

Tib. "Rufus Laberius Crispinus, and Demetrius Fannius, hold up your hands. You have, according to the Roman custom,

put yourselves upon trial to the urn, for divers and sundry calumnies, whereof you have, before this time, been indicted, and are now presently arraigned: prepare yourselves to hearken to the verdict of your tryers. Caius Cilnius Mecænas pronounceth you, by this hand-writing, guilty. Cornelius Gallus, guilty. Pantilius Tucca——"

Tuc. Parcel-guilty, I.[3]

Dem. He means himself; for it was he indeed
Suborned us to the calumny.

Tuc. I, you whoreson cantharides! was it I?

Dem. I appeal to your conscience, captain.

Tib. Then you confess it now?

Dem. I do, and crave the mercy of the court.

Tib. What saith Crispinus?

Cris. O, the captain, the captain——

Hor. My physic begins to work with my patient, I see.

Virg. Captain, stand forth and answer.

Tuc. Hold thy peace, poet prætor: I appeal from thee to Cæsar, I. Do me right, royal Cæsar.

Cæs. Marry, and I will, sir.—Lictors, gag him; do.
And put a case of vizards o'er his head,
That he may look bifronted, as he speaks.

Tuc. Gods and fiends! Cæsar! thou wilt not, Cæsar, wilt thou? Away, you whoreson vultures; away. You think I am a dead corps now, because Cæsar is disposed to jest with a man of mark, or so. Hold your hooked talons out of my flesh, you inhuman harpies. Go to, do't. What! will the royal Augustus cast away a gentleman of worship, a captain and a commander, for a couple of condemned caitiff calumnious cargos?[4]

Cæs. Dispatch, lictors.

Tuc. Cæsar!

[*The vizards are put upon him.*

---

[1] *Let there be a case of vizards privately provided;*] A *case* is a pair: so in *Ram Alley*:

    "What, my *case* of justices!
What, are you eavesdropping?"—WHAL.

[2] Hor. *Please it, great Cæsar, I have pills about me,*
Would give him a light vomit, &c.] What follows is an imitation of the *Lexiphanes* of Lucian, as Whalley has observed. It might have been omitted without much injury to the plot, as most of the words about to be noticed have already been stigmatized; and the poetasters tried and condemned on a separate indictment. The management of the patient,

however, is ingenious; and certainly well calculated to provoke mirth among a people not over-delicate in their notions of humour.

[3] Parcel-*guilty, I.*] i.e., *partly* guilty: *non liquet*.

[4] *A couple of calumnious cargos?*] i.e., bullies, bravoes, or whatever the reader pleases, of a kindred import. It is useless to attempt to assign a precise meaning to such cant vulgarisms. *Cargo* is used by our old poets as an interjection. Reed pronounces it to be a corruption of *coragio*. His word will not go far in Italian; but it may be as he says. What is more certain, is that it was a military term, and signified *charge!*

Cæs. Forward, Tibullus.

Virg. Demand what cause they had to malign Horace.

Dem. In troth, no great cause, not I, I must confess ; but that he kept better company, for the most part, than I ; and that better men loved him than loved me ; and that his writings thrived better than mine, and were better liked and graced : nothing else.

Virg. Thus envious souls repine at others' good.

Hor. If this be all,[1] faith, I forgive thee freely.

Envy me still, so long as Virgil loves me, Gallus, Tibullus, and the best-best Cæsar, My dear Mecænas ; while these, with many more,
Whose names I wisely slip, shall think me worthy
Their honoured and adored society,
And read and love, prove and applaud my poems ;
I would not wish but such as you should spite them.

Cris. O———!

Tib. How now, Crispinus?

Cris. O, I am sick———!

Hor. A bason, a bason, quickly ; our physic works. Faint not, man.

Cris. O—*retrograde* — *reciprocal* — *incubus.*

Cæs. What's that, Horace?

Hor. *Retrograde, reciprocal,* and *incubus,* are come up.

Gal. Thanks be to Jupiter !

Cris. O———*glibbery*—*lubrical*—*defunct* —O—!

Hor. Well said ; here's some store.

Virg. What are they ?

Hor. *Glibbery, lubrical,* and *defunct.*

Gal. O, they came up easy.

Cris. O———O——— |

Tib. What's that?

Hor. Nothing yet.

Cris. *Magnificate———*

Mec. Magnificate ! That came up somewhat hard.

Hor. Ay. What cheer, Crispinus?

Cris. O ! I shall cast up my—*spurious*— *snotteries*—

Hor. Good. Again.

Cris. Chilblained —O — O —*clumsie*—

Hor. That *clumsie* stuck terribly.

Mec. What's all that, Horace?

Hor. Spurious, snotteries, chilblained, clumsie.

Tib. O Jupiter !

Gal. Who would have thought there should have been such a deal of filth in a poet ?

Cris. O—*barmy froth*———

Cæs. What's that ?

Cris. Puffie — inflate — turgidous—ventosity.

Hor. Barmy froth, puffie, inflate, turgidous, and *ventosity* are come up.

Tib. O terrible windy words.

Gal. A sign of a windy brain.

Cris. O — *oblatrant—furibund—fatuate —strenuous.*

Hor. Here's a deal : *oblatrant, furibund, fatuate, strenuous.*

Cæs. Now all's come up, I trow. What a tumult he had in his belly ?[2]

Hor. No, there's the often *conscious damp* behind still.

Cris. O—*conscious—damp.*

Hor. It is come up, thanks to Apollo and Æsculapius : yet there's another ; you were best take a pill more.

Cris. O, no ; O –O–O–O–O |

Hor. Force yourself then a little with your finger.[3]

Cris. O—O—*prorumped.*

Tib. Prorumped ! What a noise it made ! as if his spirit would have prorumpt with it.[4]

Cris. O–O–O |

Virg. Help him, it sticks strangely, whatever it is.

Cris. O—*clutcht.*

Hor. Now it is come ; *clutcht.*

Cæs. Clutcht ! it is well that's come up ; it had but a narrow passage.

Cris. O——— !

Virg. Again ! hold him, hold his head there.

Cris. Snarling gusts—quaking custard.[5]

---

[1] *If this be all, &c.*] Immediately from Horace:

" *Fannius Hermoginis lædat conviva Tigelli ? Plotius et Varius, Mæcenas, Virgiliusque Valgius, et probet hæc Octavius optimus— Complures alios, doctos ego quos et amicos Prudens prætereo,*" *&c.*—Lib. i. Sat. x.

[2] *What a tumult he had in his belly.*] Φευ, τι τουτο; πολυς Βορβορυγμος.—*Lex.*

[3] *Force yourself a little with your finger.*]

βιασαι δ' ὁμως, και καθες εις την φαρυγγα τους δακτυλους.—*Lex.*

[4] *Prorumped ! What a noise it made ! as if his spirit would have prorumpt with it.*] Η γουν σιληπορδια, μεγαν τον ψοφον εργασεται συνεκπεσουσα μετα του πνευματος.—*Lex.*

[5] *Cris. ——— quaking custard.*] A ridicule of this line in Marston :

" *Let custards quake, my rage must freely runne.*"—Lib. i. Sat. 2.

Hor. How now, Crispinus?
Cris. O—*obstupefact.*
Tib. Nay, that are all we, I assure you.
Hor. How do you feel yourself?
Cris. Pretty and well, I thank you.
Virg. These pills[1] can but restore him for a time,
Not cure him quite of such a malady,
Caught by so many surfeits, which have filled
His blood and brain thus full of crudities:
'Tis necessary therefore he observe
A strict and wholesome diet. Look you take
Each morning of old Cato's principles
A good draught next your heart; that walk upon,
Till it be well digested: then come home,
And taste a piece of Terence, suck his phrase
Instead of liquorice; and, at any hand,
Shun Plautus and old Ennius; they are meats
Too harsh for a weak stomach. Use to read
(But not without a tutor) the best Greeks,
As Orpheus, Musæus, Pindarus,
Hesiod, Callimachus, and Theocrite,
High Homer; but beware of Lycophron,
He is too dark and dangerous a dish.
You must not hunt for wild outlandish terms,
To stuff out a peculiar dialect;
But let your matter run before your words.
And if at any time you chance to meet
Some Gallo-Belgic phrase,[2] you shall not straight
Rack your poor verse to give it entertainment,
But let it pass; and do not think yourself
Much damnified, if you do leave it out,
When nor your understanding, nor the sense
Could well receive it. This fair abstinence,
In time, will render you more sound and clear:

And this have I prescribed to you, in place
Of a strict sentence; which till he perform,
Attire him in that robe. And henceforth learn
To bear yourself more humbly; not to swell,
Or breathe your insolent and idle spite
On him whose laughter can your worst affright.
Tib. Take him away.
Cris. Jupiter guard Cæsar!
Virg. And for a week or two see him locked up
In some dark place, removed from company;
He will talk idly else after his physic.
Now to you, sir. [*To* Demetrius.] The extremity of law
Awards you to be branded in the front,
For this your calumny: but since it pleaseth
Horace, the party wronged, t' intreat of Cæsar
A mitigation of that juster doom,
With Cæsar's tongue thus we pronounce your sentence.
Demetrius Fannius, thou shalt here put on
That coat and cap, and henceforth think thyself
No other than they make thee; vow to wear them
In every fair and generous assembly,
Till the best sort of minds shall take to knowledge
As well thy satisfaction, as thy wrongs.
Hor. Only, grave prætor, here, in open court,
I crave the oath for good behaviour
May be administered unto them both.
Virg. Horace, it shall: Tibullus, give it them.
Tib. "Rufus Laberius Crispinus, and Demetrius Fannius, lay your hands on your hearts. You shall here solemnly attest and swear, that never, after this instant, either at booksellers' stalls, in taverns, two-penny rooms,[3] tyring-houses, noblemen's but-

---

[1] *Virg. These pills,* &c.] The whole of this speech, *mutatis mutandis,* is taken from the very excellent advice which Lycinus gives to Lexiphanes. It will not be an unprofitable amusement to the learned reader to follow our author through this part of Lucian, and observe with what happy dexterity he has contrived to avail himself of his sentiments and exemplify his precepts.
[2] *Some* Gallo-Belgic *phrase.*] This alludes to the Latinity of this celebrated political "Register," as Mr. Chalmers aptly terms it, which was now much read. Mention of it is made by almost all the writers of Jonson's age. As it

treated of contemporary events, treaties, sieges, &c. in a dead language, it was necessarily driven to the use of awkward and unwarranted terms, which Crispinus is here judiciously advised to "let pass." This is all levelled at Marston, who has too many of these *Gallo-Belgic phrases* in his Plays and Satires. Affectation of wild outlandish terms cannot be charged on Decker, whose crying sins are roughness and vulgarity.
[3] Two-penny *rooms, tyring-houses,* noblemen's butteries, *puisnts chambers, the* best and farthest places where you are admitted to come.] Mr. Malone thinks the observation of Pope, namely, that "players in Shakspeare's time were led

teries, puisnés chambers (the best and farthest places where you are admitted to come), you shall once offer or dare (thereby to endear yourself the more to any player, enghle, or guilty gull in your company) to malign, traduce, or detract the person or writings of Quintus Horatius Flaccus, or any other eminent man, transcending you in merit, whom your envy shall find cause to work upon, either for that, or for keeping himself in better acquaintance, or enjoying better friends ; or if, transported by any sudden and desperate resolution, you do, that then you shall not under the batoon, or in the next presence, being an honourable assembly of his favourers, be brought as voluntary gentlemen to undertake the forswearing of it. Neither shall you, at any time, ambitiously affecting the title of the Untrussers or Whippers of the age, suffer the itch of writing to over-run your performance in libel, upon pain of being taken up for lepers in wit, and, losing both your time and your papers, be irrecoverably forfeited to the hospital of fools. So help you our Roman gods, and the Genius of great Cæsar !"

Virg. So ! now dissolve the court.

Hor. Tib. Gal. Mec. And thanks to Cæsar,

That thus hath exercised his patience.

Cæs. We have, indeed, you worthiest friends of Cæsar.

It is the bane and torment of our ears,
To hear the discords of those jangling rhymers,
That with their bad and scandalous practices

Bring all true arts and learning in contempt.
But let not your high thoughts descend so low
As these despised objects ; let them fall.
With their flat grovelling souls : be you yourselves ;
And as with our best favours you stand crowned,
So let your mutual loves be still renowned.
Envy will dwell where there is want of merit,
Though the deserving man should crack his spirit.

" Blush, folly, blush : here's none that fears
The wagging of an ass's ears,
Although a wolfish case he wears.
Detraction is but baseness' varlet ;
And apes are apes, though clothed in scarlet." ———— [*Exeunt.*

Rumpatur, quisquis rumpitur invidiâ.

"Here, reader, in place of the epilogue, was meant to thee an apology from the author, with his reasons for the publishing of this book : but, since he is no less restrained, than thou deprived of it by authority, he prays thee to think charitably of what thou hast read, till thou mayest hear him speak what he hath written."[1]

HORACE *and* TREBATIUS.

A Dialogue.[2]

Sat. I. Lib. 2.

Hor. There are to whom I seem excessive sour,
And past a satire's law t' extend my power :

into the *buttery* by the steward, not placed at the lord's table," originated from an expression in the *Taming of the Shrew :*

"Go, sirrah, take them to the buttery," &c.

But there can, I think, be little doubt that Pope had this very passage of Jonson, which has so strangely escaped the commentators, in his thoughts ; at any rate, it is fully sufficient to justify the assertion. With great deference to Mr. Malone, I conceive that even the respectable names which he mentions, Heminge, Burbage, and Lowin, were seldom to be found at "my lord's table or my ladie's toilette." Shakspeare and, above all, Jonson were, it is to be presumed, free of both ; not, however, as players, but as distinguished writers : indeed Jonson's familiar friends are well known to have been among the first for rank and talents in the state. This is overlooked or forgotten by the calumniators of the present day, who enjoy a malignant pleasure in talking of this great poet, as if, like Master Stephen, he had "kept company

with none but the archers of Finsbury." His contemporaries, however, were well acquainted with the fact ; to which they have many envious allusions. It is for this reason that Crispinus is made to say (p. 226 *b*) : "Troth, Horace, thou art exceeding happy in thy friends, they are all most choice spirits, and of the first rank of Romans ;" and that he and Demetrius are in the "oath" below compelled to abjure "maligning him for keeping better acquaintance than themselves." Decker, however, often returned to the charge in the *Satiromastix ;* which, as Jonson had anticipated it in the present piece, argues no great felicity of invention.

[1] This was subjoined to the first edition of the *Poetaster.* It does not appear why the restraint of which Jonson complains was imposed ; but such was then the servile and dependent state of the stage, that the actors were at the mercy of any man of fashion who thought it worth his while to complain of them.

[2] This Dialogue, which is **not in the quarto**

Others, that think whatever I have writ
Wants pith and matter to eternize it;
And that they could, in one day's light,
    disclose
A thousand verses, such as I compose.
What shall I do, Trebatius? say.
    Treb. Surcease.
    Hor. And shall my muse admit no more
    increase?
    Treb. So I advise.
    Hor. An ill death let me die,
If 'twere not best; but sleep avoids mine
    eye,
And I use these, lest nights should tedious
    seem.
    Treb. Rather, contend to sleep, and live
    like them,
That, holding golden sleep in special price,
Rubbed with sweet oils, swim silver Tyber
    thrice,
And every even with neat wine steeped be:
Or, if such love of writing ravish thee,
Then dare to sing unconquered Cæsar's
    deeds;
Who cheers such actions with abundant
    meeds.
    Hor. That, father, I desire; but, when
    I try,
I feel defects in every faculty:
Nor is't a labour fit for every pen,
To paint the horrid troops of armed men,
The lances burst, in Gallia's slaughtered
    forces;
Or wounded Parthians, tumbled from their
    horses;
Great Cæsar's wars cannot be fought with
    words.
    Treb. Yet, what his virtue in his peace
    affords,
His fortitude and justice thou canst show,
As wise Lucilius honoured Scipio.
    Hor. Of that, my powers shall suffer no
    neglect,
When such slight labours may aspire re-
    spect:
But, if I watch not a most chosen time,
The humble words of Flaccus cannot climb
Th' attentive ear of Cæsar; nor must I
With less observance shun gross flattery:
For he, reposed safe in his own merit,
Spurns back the gloses of a fawning spirit.
    Treb. But how much better would such
    accents sound

Than with a sad and serious verse to wound
Pantolabus, railing in his saucy jests,
Or Nomentanus spent in riotous feasts?
In satires, each man, though untouched,
    complains
As he were hurt; and hates such biting
    strains.
    Hor. What shall I do? Milonius shakes
    his heels
In ceaseless dances, when his brain once
    feels
The stirring fervour of the wine ascend;
And that his eyes false numbers apprehend.
Castor his horse, Pollux loves handy-fights:
A thousand heads, a thousand choice de-
    lights.
My pleasure is in feet my words to close,
As, both our better, old Lucilius does:
He, as his trusty friends, his books did trust
With all his secrets; nor, in things unjust,
Or actions lawful, ran to other men:
So that the old man's life described, was
    seen
As in a votive table in his lines:
And to his steps my genius inclines;
Lucanian, or Apulian, I know not whether,
For the Venusian colony ploughs either;
Sent thither, when the Sabines were forced
    thence,
As old Fame sings, to give the place de-
    fence
'Gainst such as, seeing it empty, might
    make road
Upon the empire; or there fix abode:
Whether the Apulian borderer it were,
Or the Lucanian violence they fear.—
But this my style no living man shall touch,
If first I be not forced by base reproach;
But like a sheathed sword it shall defend
My innocent life; for why should I con-
    tend
To draw it out, when no malicious thief
Robs my good name, the treasure of my
    life?
O Jupiter, let it with rust be eaten,
Before it touch, or insolently threaten
The life of any with the least disease;
So much I love, and woo a general peace.
But, he that wrongs me, better, I proclaim,
He never had assayed to touch my fame.
For he shall weep, and walk with every
    tongue
Throughout the city, infamously sung.
Servius the prætor threats the laws, and
    urn,
If any at his deeds repine or spurn;
The witch Canidia, that Albutius got,
Denounceth witchcraft, where she loveth
    not:

(see p. 236 *a*,) bears no appearance of having been spoken on the stage; though it stands in the folio as the concluding scene of the third act. I have nothing to add on its merits; nor does it seem to call for any particular notice.

Thurius, the judge, doth thunder worlds of
    ill,
To such as strive with his judicial will.
All men affright their foes in what they
    may,
Nature commands it, and men must obey.
    Observe with me: The wolf his tooth
        doth use,
The bull his horn ; and who doth this in-
    fuse,
But nature?   There's luxurious Scæva ;
    trust
His long-lived mother with him ; his so
    just
And scrupulous right-hand no mischief will;
No more than with his heel a wolf will kill,
Or ox with jaw : marry, let him alone
With tempered poison to remove the croan.
But briefly, if to age I destined be,
Or that quick death's black wings environ
    me ;
If rich, or poor ; at Rome ; or fate com-
    mand
I shall be banished to some other land ;
What hue soever my whole state shall bear,
I will write satires still, in spite of fear.
    Treb. Horace, I fear thou draw'st no
        lasting breath ;
And that some great man's friend will be
    thy death.
    Hor. What ! when the man that first did
        satirize
Durst pull the skin over the ears of vice,
And make, who stood in outward fashion
    clear,
Give place, as foul within ; shall I forbear?
Did Lælius, or the man so great with fame,
That from sacked Carthage fetched his
    worthy name,
Storm that Lucilius did Metellus pierce,
Or bury Lupus quick in famous verse ?
Rulers and subjects, by whole tribes he
    checkt,
But virtue and her friends did still protect :
And when from sight, or from the judg-
    ment seat,
The virtuous Scipio and wise Lælius met,
Unbraced, with him in all light sports they
    shared,
Till their most frugal suppers were pre-
    pared.

Whate'er I am, though both for wealth
    and wit
Beneath Lucilius I am pleased to sit ;
Yet Envy, spite of her empoisoned breast,
Shall say, I lived in grace here with the
    best ;
And seeking in weak trash to make her
    wound,
Shall find me solid, and her teeth unsound:
'Less learned Trebatius' censure disagree.
    Treb. No, Horace, I of force must yield
        to thee ;
Only take heed, as being advised by me,
Lest thou incur some danger : better pause,
Than rue thy ignorance of the sacred laws;
There's justice, and great action may be
    sued
'Gainst such as wrong men's fames with
    verses lewd.
    Hor. Ay, with lewd verses, such as libels
        be,
And aimed at persons of good quality :
I reverence and adore that just decree.
But if they shall be sharp, yet modest
    rhimes,
That spare men's persons, and but tax their
    crimes,
Such shall in open court find current pass,
Were Cæsar judge, and with the maker's
    grace.
    Treb. Nay, I'll add more ; if thou thy-
        self, being clear,
Shall tax in person a man fit to bear
Shame and reproach, his suit shall quickly
    be
Dissolved in laughter, and thou thence set
    free.

TO THE READER.

IF, by looking on what is past, thou hast
deserved that name, I am willing thou
shouldst yet know more, by that which
follows, an APOLOGETICAL DIALOGUE ;
which was only once spoken upon the
stage,[1] and all the answer I ever gave to
sundry impotent libels then cast out (and
some yet remaining) against me, and this
play.   Wherein I take no pleasure to revive
the times ; but that posterity may make a

---

[1] *Only once spoken upon the stage,*] This
Apology was first printed in 1616 ; so that we
have no means of ascertaining how long the
injunction mentioned above continued in force ;
it could not, however, be many weeks. It
appears that Jonson himself took the part of
"the Author ;" and no one could do it more
justice, for he was a most excellent declaimer.

But how little did he know of himself !   He
talks of *neglecting* his enemies at the very
moment that he is pouring out his utmost indignation upon them.   There is, however, much
merit in this little piece.   What credit was given
to the author's declarations, I know not ; but if
he expected to silence his detractors by them, he
was evidently disappointed.

difference between their manners that provoked me then, and mine that neglected
them ever. For, in these strifes, and on
such persons, were as wretched to affect a
victory, as it is unhappy to be committed
with them. *Non annorum canities est
laudanda, sed morum.*

SCENE, *The* Author's *Lodgings.*

Enter Nasutus *and* Polyposus.

Nas. I pray you, let's go see him, how
he looks
After these libels.
  Pol. O, vexed, vexed, I warrant you.
  Nas. Do you think so? I should be sorry
for him,
If I found that.
  Pol. O, they are such bitter things,
He cannot choose.
  Nas. But is he guilty of them?
  Pol. Fuh! that's no matter.
  Nas. No!
  Pol. No. Here's his lodging.
We'll steal upon him: or, let's listen; stay.
He has a humour oft to talk t' himself.
  Nas. They are your manners lead me,
not mine own.
    [*They come forward: the scene opens,
    and discovers the* Author *in his
    study.*
  Aut. The fates have not spun him the
coarsest thread,
That (free from knots of perturbation)
Doth yet so live, although but to himself,
As he can safely scorn the tongues of slaves,
And neglect fortune, more than she can
him.
It is the happiest thing this, not to be
Within the reach of malice; it provides
A man so well, to laugh off injuries;
And never sends him farther for his ven-
geance,
Than the vexed bosom of his enemy.
I, now, but think how poor their spite sets
off,
Who, after all their waste of sulphurous
terms,
And burst-out thunder of their charged
mouths,
Have nothing left but the unsavoury smoke
Of their black vomit, to upbraid them-
selves:

Whilst I, at whom they shot, sit here shot-
free,
And as unhurt of envy, as unhit.
    [Pol. *and* Nas. *discover themselves.*
  Pol. Ay, but the multitude they think
not so, sir;
They think you hit, and hurt: and dare
give out,
Your silence argues it, in not rejoining
To this or that late libel.
  Aut. 'Las, good rout!
I can afford them leave to err so still;
And, like the barking students of Bears-
college,[1]
To swallow up the garbage of the time
With greedy gullets, whilst myself sit by,
Pleased, and yet tortured, with their beastly
feeding.
'Tis a sweet madness runs along with them,
To think, all that are aimed at still are
struck;
Then, where the shaft still lights, make
that the mark:
And so, each fear or fever-shaken fool
May challenge Teucer's hand in archery.
Good troth, if I knew any man so vile,
To act the crimes these Whippers repre-
hend,
Or what their servile apes gesticulate,
I should not then much muse their shreds
were liked;
Since ill men have a lust t' hear others' sins,
And good men have a zeal to hear sin
shamed.
But when it is all excrement they vent,
Base filth and offal; or thefts, notable
As ocean-piracies, or highway-stands;
And not a crime there taxed but is their
own,
Or what their own foul thoughts suggested
to them;
And that, in all their heat of taxing others.
Not one of them but lives himself, if known,
Improbior satiram scribente cinædo,[2]
What should I say more, than turn stone
with wonder!
  Nas. I never saw this play bred all this
tumult:
What was there in it could so deeply offend,
And stir so many hornets?
  Aut. Shall I tell you?
  Nas. Yes, and ingenuously.
  Aut. Then, by the hope
Which I prefer unto all other objects,

---

[1] *Students of Bears-college.*] The dogs at the
bear-garden.—WHAL.
[2] This is from Juvenal, as are several other
passages in this bitter satire, which need not be
pointed out: the names of the speakers have a
reference to a line in Martial. A more contemptuous one than Polyposus he could not easily
have found.

I can profess, I never writ that piece
More innocent or empty of offence.
Some salt it had, but neither tooth nor
gall,
Nor was there in it any circumstance
Which, in the setting down, I could sus-
pect
Might be perverted by an enemy's tongue;
Only it had the fault to be called mine ;
That was the crime.
Pol. No ! why, they say you taxed
The law and lawyers, captains and the
players,
By their particular names.
Aut. It is not so.
I used no name. My books have still been
taught
To spare the persons and to speak the
vices.[1]
These are mere slanders, and enforced by
such
As have no safer ways to men's disgraces,
But their own lies and loss of honesty:
Fellows of practised and most laxative
tongues,
Whose empty and eager bellies, in the
year,
Compel their brains to many desperate
shifts,
(I spare to name them, for their wretched-
ness
Fury itself would pardon.) These, or such,
Whether of malice, or of ignorance,
Or itch t' have me their adversary, I know
not,
Or all these mixt ; but sure I am, three
years
They did provoke me with their petulant
styles
On every stage : and I at last, unwilling,
But weary, I confess, of so much trouble,
Thought I would try if shame could win
upon 'em ;
And therefore chose Augustus Cæsar's
times,
When wit and arts were at their height in
Rome,
To shew that Virgil, Horace, and the rest
Of those great master-spirits, did not want
Detractors then, or practicers against them :

And by this line, although no parallel,
I hoped at last they would sit down and
blush ;
But nothing I could find more contrary.
And though the impudence of flies be
great,
Yet this hath so provoked the angry wasps,
Or, as you said, of the next nest, the
hornets,
That they fly buzzing, mad, about my
nostrils,
And, like so many screaming grasshoppers[2]
Held by the wings, fill every ear with
noise.
And what ? those former calumnies you
mentioned.
First, of the law : indeed I brought in
Ovid
Chid by his angry father for neglecting
The study of their laws for poetry :
And I am warranted by his own words :

*Sæpe pater dixit, studium quid inutile
tentas ?
Mæonides nullas ipse reliquit opes.*[3]

And in far harsher terms elsewhere, as
these :

*Non me verbosas leges ediscere, non me
Ingrato voces prostituisse foro.*[4]

But how this should relate unto our laws,
Or the just ministers, with least abuse,
I reverence both too much to understand !
Then, for the captain, I will only speak
An epigram I here have made : it is

Unto true Soldiers. That's the
lemma :[5] mark it.
"Strength of my country, whilst I bring to
view
Such as are mis-called captains, and wrong
you,
And your high names ; I do desire, that
thence,
Be nor put on you, nor you take, offence :
I swear by your true friend, my muse, I
love
Your great profession which I once did
prove ;[6]
And did not shame it with my actions then,

---

[1] *Parcere personis, dicere de vitiis.*—Mart.
Whal.

[2] *And like so many screaming grasshoppers,
&c.*] See the *Fox*, p. 365 a.

[3] Renounce this thriftless trade, my father
cried :
Mæonides himself—a beggar died.
Trist. lib. iv. eleg 10.

[4] To learn the wrangling law was ne'er my choice,
Nor, at the hateful bar, to sell my voice.
Amor. lib. i. eleg. 15.

[5] *That's the* lemma.] The subject proposed,
or title of the epigram.—Whal.

[6] *I love
Your great profession ; which I once did
prove ;*] Jonson bore arms in Flanders, where
he acquitted himself with reputation.—Whal.

No more than I dare now do with my pen.
He that not trusts me, having vowed thus much,
But's angry for the captain, still : is such."[1]
Now for the players, it is true, I taxed them,
And yet but some; and those so sparingly,
As all the rest might have sat still unquestioned,
Had they but had the wit or conscience
To think well of themselves. But, impotent, they
Thought each man's vice belonged to their whole tribe;[2]
And much good do't them ! What they have done 'gainst me,
I am not moved with : if it gave them meat,
Or got them clothes, 'tis well; that was their end.
Only amongst them, I am sorry for
Some better natures, by the rest so drawn,
To run in that vile line.[3]

Pol. And is this all !
Will you not answer then the libels?

Aut. No.

Pol. Nor the Untrussers?

Aut. Neither.

Pol. Y'are undone then.

Aut. With whom ?

Pol. The world.

Aut. The bawd !

Pol. It will be taken
To be stupidity or tameness in you.

Aut. But they that have incensed me, can in soul
Acquit me of that guilt. They know I dare
To spurn or baffle them, or squirt their eyes
With ink or urine; or I could do worse,
Armed with Archilochus' fury, write lambics,
Should make the desperate lashers hang themselves,
Rhime them to death, as they do Irish rats[1]
In drumming tunes. Or, living, I could stamp
Their foreheads with those deep and public brands,
That the whole company of barber-surgeons
Should not take off,[5] with all their art and plasters.

---

[1] *Is such.*] i.e., such as are miscalled captains. —WHAL.
This little piece Jonson afterwards reprinted among his Epigrams. [No. CVIII.]

[2] *But impotent they, &c.*] One might almost suspect that Gay had this passage in his thoughts when he wrote the *Beggar's Opera:*

" If you mention gift or bribe,
'Tis so pat to all the tribe,
Each cries—*that* was levelled at me !"

[3]   *I am sorry for*
Some better natures, by the rest so drawn
To run in that vile line,] It has been *thought* that Shakspeare was here alluded to, under the expression of *better natures.* But I see no reason to confine the phrase to so particular a restriction. It makes good sense to take it in the most obvious meaning : nor does it appear there was any difference now subsisting between Shakspeare and our author.—WHAL.
Thus far Whalley is right. He might have added, to the confusion of the *thinkers,* that if their ingenious supposition were true, it would go near to prove—not that Jonson was hostile to Shakspeare, but that Shakspeare was captiously disinclined to Jonson. But, in fact, there is no allusion whatever to Shakspeare, or to the company with which he was connected. The commentators are absolutely mad : they will allow Jonson neither to compliment nor criticize any one but our great poet; and this merely for the pleasure of taxing him with hypocrisy in the one case and envy in the other. I have already observed that the actors ridiculed belonged to the Fortune playhouse ; and the critics must have discovered, if their judgment had been half as active as their enmity, a very frequent recurrence throughout the *Poetaster,* and the Apology, to the poverty and low estimation of this unfortunate company.

" If it gave them *meat,*
Or got them *clothes,* 'tis well ; that was their end."

Could this be said of Allen and Shakspeare, of Burbage, Lowin, and Taylor ? Without question the Fortune possessed more actors than the "lean Poluphagus" and the "politic Æsop," and to some of those the poet might allude : "the better natures" were not confined, I trust, in Jonson's days any more than in our own, to a single person, or even a single theatre.

[4] *Rhime them to death, as they do Irish rats, &c.*] The fatal effects of poetry on these Opici, these Hibernian vermin, are noticed by many of our old dramatists. Thus Shakspeare : "I was never so *be-rhimed* since Pythagoras' time, that I was an *Irish rat.*"—*As You Like It.* And Randolph :

                    "My poets
Shall with a satire, steeped in vinegar,
Rhime them to death, as they do *rats in Ireland.*"

[5] *That the whole company of barber-surgeons Should not take off, &c.*] This sentiment, which Jonson repeats in his dedication of the *Fox,* is from Martial :

" At si quid nostræ tibi bilis inusserit ardor,
Vivet, et hærebit, totoque legetur in urbe ;
Stigmata nec vafra delebit Cinnamus arte."
                              Lib. vi. 6.

And these my prints should last, still to be
   read
In their pale fronts; when, what they write
   'gainst me   .
Shall, like a figure drawn in water, fleet,
And the poor wretched papers be em-
   ployed
To clothe tobacco, or some cheaper
   drug:
This I could do, and make them infa-
   mous.
But, to what end? when their own deeds
   have marked 'em;
And that I know, within his guilty breast
Each slanderer bears a whip that shall tor-
   ment him
Worse than a million of these temporal
   plagues:
Which to pursue, were but a feminine hu-
   mour,
And far beneath the dignity of man.
   Nas. 'Tis true; for to revenge their in-
   juries,
Were to confess you felt them. Let them
   go,
And use the treasure of the fool, their
   tongues,
Who makes his gain by speaking worst of
   best.
   Pol. O, but they lay particular impu-
   tations——
   Aut. As what?
   Pol. That all your writing is mere
   railing.
   Aut. Ha?
If all the salt in the old comedy
Should be so censured, or the sharper wit
Of the bold satire termed scolding rage,
What age could then compare with those
   for buffoons?
What should be said of Aristophanes,
Persius, or Juvenal, whose names we now
So glorify in schools, at least pretend it?—
Have they no other?
   Pol. Yes; they say you are slow,
And scarce bring forth a play a year.
   Aut. 'Tis true.
I would they could not say that I did
   that!

There's all the joy that I take in their
   trade,
Unless such scribes as these might be pro-
   scribed
Th' abused theatres. They would think it
   strange, now,
A man should take but colts-foot for one
   day,
And, between whiles, spit out a better
   poem
Than e'er the master of art,[1] or giver of
   wit,
Their belly, made. Yet, this is possible,
If a free mind had but the patience,
To think so much together, and so vile.
But that these base and beggarly conceits
Should carry it, by the multitude of voices,
Against the most abstracted work, opposed
To the stuffed nostrils of the drunken
   rout!
O, this would make a learned and liberal
   soul
To rive his stained quill up to the back,
And damn his long-watched labours to the
   fire;
Things that were born when none but the
   still night
And his dumb candle, saw his pinching
   throes;
Were not his own free merit a more crown
Unto his travails than their reeling claps.
This 'tis that strikes me silent, seals my
   lips,
And apts me rather to sleep out my time,
Than I would waste it in contemned
   strifes
With these vile Ibides, these unclean birds,
That make their mouths their clysters, and
   still purge
From their hot entrails. But I leave the
   monsters
To their own fate. And, since the Comic
   Muse
Hath proved so ominous to me, I will try
If TRAGEDY have a more kind aspect;
Her favours in my next I will pursue,
Where, if I prove the pleasure but of
   one,
So he judicious be, he shall be alone

What follows is from Juvenal:

         " *Diri conscia facti*
Mens habet attonitos, et surdo verbere cædit,
Occultum quatiente animo tortore flagellum."
                    Sat. xiv.

Again:

    " *Continuò sic collige, quod vindicta*
Nemo magis gaudet quam fæmina."—*Ibid.*

[1] *Than e'er the master of art, &c.*] Our
industrious bee is ever on the search after
stores: just above he lighted on Horace; here
he visits Persius:

    " *Magister artis, ingenique largitor*
     Venter."—Prol. v. 10.

And finally he settles on Juvenal. See his
seventh *Satire.*

A theatre unto me.[1] Once I'll say[2]
To strike the ear of time in those fresh
strains,
  As shall, beside the cunning of their
   ground,
Give cause to some of wonder, some de-
spite,
And more despair, to imitate their sound.
I, that spend[3] half my nights, and all my
days,
  Here in a cell, to get a dark pale face,

To come forth worth the ivy or the bays,
  And in this age can hope no other
   grace——
Leave me! There's something come into
my thought,
That must and shall be sung high and
aloof,
Safe from the wolf's black jaw, and the dull
ass's hoof.
    Nas. I reverence these raptures, and
    obey them.   [*The scene closes.*[4]

[1] *Where, if I prove the pleasure but of one,*
So be judicious be, he shall be alone
A theatre unto me ;] This passage, says Mr.
Malone, Jonson imitated from Shakspeare,—the
censure of " which one (judicious) must, in your
allowance, o'erweigh a whole theatre of others."
—*Hamlet.* The thought is not so deep but that
it might have occurred to less inventive faculties
than either of those great poets possessed. If,
however, one of them must borrow from the
other, I should incline to set down Shakspeare
as the obliged person ; for though we do not
know the exact date of the Apologetical Dialogue, yet we are sure that it cannot be later
than 1602, since it alludes to the design of composing a tragedy on the fall of *Sejanus,* which
was effected in that year, or in the beginning of
the next. After all, Jonson's words are little
more than a translation from Cicero, to whom
he was much more likely to be indebted than to
any contemporary whatever : " *Hæc ego non*
multis, sed tibi satis magnum alter alteri
theatrum sumus." Cicero himself alludes to a
story told of Plato.

[2] *Once I'll say.*] i.e., try. Once is used here
in a sense in which it frequently occurs with our
old writers—that is, emphatically, *Once for all.*

[3] *I, that spend, &c.*] These are truly noble
lines ; and cannot be read without exciting feelings of respect and tenderness for the author.
Let it never be forgotten that in every condition
of life, in poverty and neglect, in competence
and ease, in sickness and in sorrow, in youth
and in age, Jonson steadily maintained the high
character of the poet. If he failed to exemplify it in himself, it must be attributed to
natural deficiencies ; for he was fully sensible of
what was required, and declined no toil which
promised to facilitate its attainment. There is a
lofty moral tone which constantly accompanies
all his definitions and descriptions of true poetry,
and which may be sought in vain in any other
writer in the English language, except perhaps
Milton, who sanctified what he borrowed from
Jonson, by inspiration from a source not to be
named here without irreverence.

[4] Nothing can so strikingly manifest the vast
superiority of Jonson, as a comparison of this
lively and interesting comedy with that of
Decker, which was meant to rival and eclipse it.
The plot is well arranged, and the *dramatis*
personæ admirably supported. Augustus and the
eminent men of his court maintain, on all serious
occasions, a dignity of thought and expression
highly decorous, and in strict consonance with

their established characters. Amidst all the encomiums bestowed on the poets, his friends, a
perceptible advantage is adroitly given to
Horace, which is farther heightened by the
absurd malice of his persecutors. The comic
part of the play is pleasantly conducted, and
the conspirators happily set off the defects of
one another. Mr. Davies, with whose perspi-
cacity the reader is already acquainted, is
pleased to affirm that the *Poetaster* is one of the
lowest productions, and that Tucca is a wretched
copy of Falstaff. This stuff would not be worth
repeating, if the grovelling malice of the poet's
enemies had not led them to stoop to it. We
have seen that the author has interwoven an ingenious satire of Lucian in his scenes ; but the
chief object of his imitation was the *Frogs* of
Aristophanes. That ancient comedy was the
Rehearsal of Athens, as this undoubtedly was
of the age of Jonson ; and though much of the
praise to which, perhaps, it is entitled, is lost
from our imperfect knowledge of the precise objects of ridicule, we can still discover that its
satire was at once ingenious and powerful, and
its justice sufficiently obvious to some of those for
whom it was meant. That Tucca is a *wretched*
copy, or indeed any copy at all of Falstaff, could
be maintained by none but Davies, or those who
affirmed (as he tells us) " Sir Epicure Mammon
also to be a copy of Falstaff ;" and who, perhaps, were equally prepared to swear that *Cap-*
tain Otter was stolen from the same inimitable
personage. That this extraordinary character,
this compound of impudence and artifice, of
meanness and arrogance, this importunate
beggar, who insults the charity which feeds him,
and whose quaint versatility of style and manner
is at once so repulsive and so amusing, is not
original must be granted ; and Decker (though
Davies was ignorant of it) has pointed out the
archetype ; " I wonder," says he, " what language *Tucca* would have spoken, if honest
Captain Hannam had been born without a
tongue." Decker, however, confesses that Tucca
was received with decided approbation ; and he
expresses great anxiety to ensure to himself
some portion of the popular favour. " It cannot be much improper," he adds, " to set the
same dog upon Horace whom Horace had set
to worry others ;" and the unfortunate captain,
in consequence of this happy thought, is again
brought forward. But Decker had overrated
his own powers. Tucca, in his hands, becomes
absolutely disgusting ; his impudent familiarity
degenerates into low scurrility, and he is thrown

into situations, which, from his utter unfitness for them, alternately subject him to displeasure and contempt. Nor is this the only instance of Decker's want of judgment in borrowing his characters from the *Poetaster*. He ought to have considered that the demerits of Crispinus and Demetrius have been so universally acknowledged, and so strongly fixed in the mind of every reader, since Horace first recorded them, that no efforts can raise their names to respectability, or redeem their poetry from the ridicule under which it has so long suffered. But, indeed, the whole plot of the *Satiromastix* is absurd.

This, as Jonson says, was the only answer which he gave to his libellers. He was hourly growing in reputation with the wise and good ; and in his three succeeding comedies soared to a height which his persecutors never reached, and where he consequently suffered but little molestation from their hostility. We hear no more of Decker ; Marston probably acknowledged the justice of the poet's recrimination, for he joined in the applause of his next piece : and the " soldiers, lawyers, and players," who at first took umbrage, seem to have discovered that their resentment was unjustifiable, and to have been cordially reconciled.

Sejanus, his Fall.

SEJANUS.] This "Tragedy" was first acted in 1603, by the company at the Globe; and Shakspeare, Burbage, Lowin, Hemings, Condel, Philips, Cooke, and Sly, had parts in it. Though much applauded by the fashionable part of the audience, it proved "caviare to the general," and experienced considerable opposition. *Sejanus* was not published till 1605; when it appeared in quarto, without a dedication, but accompanied by several copies of commendatory verses. Subsequently it seems to have acquired some degree of popularity. Jonson says that it had outlived the malice of its enemies, when he republished it in folio, in 1616; and it was one of the first plays revived after the Restoration. *Sejanus* is not divided into scenes in any of the editions; it has neither exits or entrances; and is, upon the whole, the most involved and puzzling drama, in its internal arrangement, that was ever produced. The motto both to the quarto and folio is the same:—

Non hîc centauros, non gorgonas, harpyiasque
Invenies: hominem pagina nostra sapit.

It is taken from Martial, and had already furnished the groundwork for the admirable prologue to *Every Man in his Humour.*

TO THE

NO LESS NOBLE BY VIRTUE THAN BLOOD,

ESME, LORD AUBIGNE.[1]

"MY LORD,—If ever any ruin were so great as to survive, I think this be one I send you, The Fall of Sejanus. It is a poem, that, if I well remember, in your lordship's sight, suffered no less violence from our people here,[2] than the subject of it did from the rage of the people of Rome; but with a different fate, as, I hope, merit; for this hath outlived their malice, and begot itself a greater favour than he lost, the love of good men. Amongst whom, if I make your lordship the first it thanks, it is not without a just confession of the bond your benefits have, and ever shall hold upon me,
" Your Lordship's most faithful honourer, BEN. JONSON."

---

[1] See Epig. 127. [He was afterwards Duke of Lenox.]
[2] *Suffered no less violence from our people, &c.*] The opposition made to *Sejanus* (of which Jonson here puts his patron in mind) is noticed in a poem by Fennor, which appeared about the time of this Dedication, 1616.

" Sweet poesie
Is oft convict, condemned, and judged to die
Without just triall by a *multitude,*
Whose judgments are illiterate and rude.
Witnesse *Sejanus,* whose *approved* worth
Sounds from the calme South to the freezing North.
With more than human art it was bedewd,
Yet to the *multitude* it nothing shewd.
They screwed their scurvy jawes, and lookt awry,
Like hissing snakes adjudging it to die;
When wits of *gentry* did *applaud.*" &c.

TO THE

READERS.

THE following and voluntary labours[1] of my friends, prefixed to my book, have relieved me in much whereat, without them, I should necessarily have touched. Now I will only use three or four short and need'ul notes, and so rest.

First, if it be objected, that what I publish is no true poem, in the strict laws of time, I confess it : as also in the want of a proper chorus ; whose habit and moods are such and so difficult, as not any, whom I have seen, since the ancients, no, not they who have most presently affected laws, have yet come in the way of. Nor is it needful, or almost possible in these our times, and to such auditors as commonly things are presented, to observe the old state and splendor of dramatic poems, with preservation of any popular delight. But of this I shall take more seasonable cause to speak, in my observations upon Horace his Art of Poetry, which, with the text translated, I intend shortly to publish.[2] In the meantime, if in truth of argument, dignity of persons, gravity and height of elocution, fulness and frequency of sentence, I have discharged the other offices of a tragic writer, let not the absence of these forms be imputed to me, wherein I shall give you occasion hereafter, and without my boast, to think I could better prescribe, than omit the due use for want of a convenient knowledge.

The next is, lest in some nice nostril the quotations might savour affected, I do let you know, that I abhor nothing more ; and I have only done it to shew my integrity in the story, and save myself in those common torturers that bring all wit to the rack ; whose noses are ever like swine spoiling and rooting up the Muses' gardens ; and their whole bodies like moles, as blindly working under earth, to cast any, the least, hills upon virtue.

Whereas they are in Latin, and the work in English, it was presupposed none but the learned would take the pains to confer them ; the authors themselves being all in the learned tongues, save one, with whose English side I have had little to do. To which it may be required, since I have quoted the page, to name what editions I followed : *Tacit. Lips. in quarto, Antwerp. edit.* 1600 *Dio. folio, Hen. Steph.* 1592. For the rest, as *Sueton. Seneca,* &c., the chapter doth sufficiently direct, or the edition is not varied.

Lastly, I would inform you, that this book, in all numbers, is not the same with that which was acted on the public stage ; wherein a second pen had good share : in place of which, I have rather chosen to put weaker, and, no doubt, less pleasing, of mine own, than to defraud so happy a genius of his right by my loathed usurpation.[3]

---

[1] *The following and voluntary labours of my friends.*] Commendatory copies of verses, which the reader will find in the beginning of this volume : they amount to eight, of which Whalley reprinted but two. This address is only in the quarto, 1605.

[2] The learned world has reason to regret the loss of those *observations* to which Jonson frequently alludes. They were burnt in the fire which consumed his study, as appears from the *Execration upon Vulcan :*

> "All the old Venusine in poetry
> And lighted by the Stagyrite, could spy,
> Was there made English," &c.

[3] *Defraud so happy a genius of his right by my loathed usurpation.*] The genius here alluded to undoubtedly was Shakspeare, who was also a performer in the play : but, I believe, posterity wishes that Jonson had rather have let them stood with some note of distinction than have substituted his own in their room, from a false point of modesty, or to render the whole more uniform and of a piece.—WHAL.

In evil hour did Jonson write the manly passage to which Whalley's note refers. It has drawn upon him a world of obloquy from the commentators of Shakspeare, couched in language which the vocabulary of Billingsgate must have been narrowly ransacked to supply. "Mean," "haughty," "malignant," "envious," "ungrateful," "treacherous," &c. &c. are among the gentlest epithets which the righteous indignation of these gentlemen can afford. "He affirms, *with a sneer,*" (says

Fare you well, and if you read farther of me, and like, I shall not be afraid of it, though you praise me out.

Neque enim mihi cornea fibra est.[1]

But that I should plant my felicity in your general saying, *good*, or *well*, &c., were a weakness which the better sort of you might worthily contemn, if not absolutely hate me for.

BEN. JONSON ;

and no such,

Quem
Palma negata macrum, donata reducit opimum.

one of them), "that he would not join his inferior matter to that of the great poet ; but wrote over again those *scenes* which had been wrought into the piece by his pen. Who does not wish that Shakspeare had put as high a value upon his true brilliants as Ben upon his jewels of paste, and preserved the rejected scenes? I have had some little suspicion that Shakspeare's part might possibly be that alone which *escaped* public censure ; as the play was *universally* exploded." And thus Shakspeare is honoured !

Whalley wishes that Jonson had marked the lines furnished by Shakspeare : but this, besides being a most invidious mode of distinction, was directly contrary to the established practice of the times. But why must the poet's assistant be Shakspeare ? I know that all the critics are positive on the subject : but of this I make no great account ; having had frequent opportunities of observing that where Jonson is to be condemned, it is not thought at all necessary to establish the validity of whatever tends to criminate him.

Why might not Chapman or Middleton be intended here? they, like Shakspeare, were living in habits of kindness with the poet : they wrote in conjunction with him : they were both men of learning : and no great violation seems offered to language (at least no greater than courtesy would excuse) in terming them *happy geniuses*. Beaumont was perhaps too young ; but Fletcher, who loved Jonson, and was greatly beloved in his turn, was extremely well qualified to assist him ; and, not to keep the reader in suspense, was in my opinion the person actually meant.—Shakspeare seems to be almost the last eminent writer to whom our author would look for assistance on the present occasion. *Sejanus* is entirely founded on the Greek and Latin historians, who are carefully quoted in the margin of the first copy : and the author values himself on the closeness with which he has followed his originals. Shakspeare, as Jonson well knew, derived all his knowledge of Roman story from translations, and this was scarcely sufficiently accurate or extensive to induce our author to solicit his aid in the production of his meditated Tragedy, which he certainly intended to be "a palmarian work," as to its fidelity. The author to whom Jonson alludes as being "in English," is Tacitus, whose Annals (the only work from which an unlearned reader could derive any knowledge of the subject of this tragedy) were translated by one Grenaway a few years before.

Enough perhaps on the subject—yet I am still inclined to ask, What is Jonson's offence? and (even supposing, for the sake of argument, that Shakspeare was really the person meant) why has he been visited with such severity? He speaks of his coadjutor with respect, and of himself with modesty ; he addresses those who were well acquainted with the play as it was acted, and who, if the cause of poetry had sustained any very serious loss by his alterations, were not unlikely to have reproached him with it. That he should be anxious to render a drama which seemed condemned by its want of popularity to the closet of the learned, uniform and of a piece, is by no means singular ; and it may be fairly questioned, whether it was not altogether as honourable in the author to take on himself the demerits of the whole, thus made his own, as to purloin a portion of fame from the secret appropriation of what the critics are now pleased to assure us was the only valuable part of the piece.

As Jonson is very profuse in his explanatory references, I have contented myself with bringing them back (for Whalley omitted them altogether), and again left the play, as the author left it, to the "judgment of the learned." I can much easier excuse Whalley for suppressing Jonson's notes and taking the merit of his quotations, than for introducing the names of Simpson, Seward, and Grey, the opprobrium of criticism, with fulsome compliments to their ingenuity, for discovering allusions which Jonson himself had pointed out more than a century before. The whole of this officious impertinence is now removed.

[1] This is from Persius, as are the allusions in the following line : the conclusion is from Horace.

THE ARGUMENT.

ÆLIUS SEJANUS, son to Seius Strabo, a gentleman of Rome, and born at Vulsinium; after his long service in court, first under Augustus; afterward, Tiberius; grew into that favour with the latter, and won him by those arts, as there wanted nothing but the name to make him a co-partner of the empire. Which greatness of his, Drusus, the Emperor's son, not brooking; after many smothered dislikes, it one day breaking out, the prince struck him publicly on the face. To revenge which disgrace, Livia, the wife of Drusus (being before corrupted by him to her dishonour, and the discovery of her husband's counsels) Sejanus practiseth with, together with her physician, called Eudemus, and one Lygdus, an eunuch, to poison Drusus. This their inhuman act having successful and unsuspected passage, it emboldeneth Sejanus to further and more insolent projects, even the ambition of the empire; where finding the lets he must encounter to be many and hard, in respect of the issue of Germanicus, who were next in hope for the succession,[1] he deviseth to make Tiberius' self his means, and instils into his ears many doubts and suspicions, both against the princes, and their mother Agrippina; which Cæsar jealously hearkening to, as covetously consenteth to their ruin, and their friends. In this time, the better to mature and strengthen his design, Sejanus labours to marry Livia, and worketh with all his ingine, to remove Tiberius from the knowledge of public business, with allurements of a quiet and retired life; the latter of which, Tiberius, out of a proneness to lust, and a desire to hide those unnatural pleasures which he could not so publicly practise, embraceth: the former enkindleth his fears, and there gives him first cause of doubt or suspect towards Sejanus: against whom he raiseth in private a new instrument, one Sertorius Macro, and by him underworketh, discovers the other's counsels, his means, his ends, sounds the affections of the senators, divides, distracts them: at last, when Sejanus least looketh, and is most secure; with pretext of doing him an unwonted honour in the senate, he trains him from his guards, and with a long doubtful letter, in one day hath him suspected, accused, condemned, and torn in pieces by the rage of the people.[2]

DRAMATIS PERSONÆ.

Tiberius.	Terentius.	Sanquinius.	Flamen.
Drusus senior.	Gracinus Laco.	Pomponius.	Tubicines.
Nero.	Eudemus.	Julius Posthumus.	Nuntius.
Drusus junior.	Rufus.	Fulcinius Trio.	Lictores.
Caligula.	Sejanus.	Minutius.	Ministri.
Lucius Arruntius.[3]	Latiaris.	Satrius Secundus.	Tibicines.
Caius Silius.	Varro.	Pinnarius Natta.	Servi, &c.
Titius Sabinus.	Sertorius Macro.	Opsius.	
Marcus Lepidus.	Cotta.		Agrippina.
Cremutius Cordus.	Domitius Afer.	Tribuni.	Livia.
Asinius Gallus.	Haterius.	Præcones.	Sosia.
Regulus.			

The SCENE,—Rome.

---

[1] *For the succession.*] These words, wanting in the quarto of 1605, were added in the folio, 1616, to complete the sense.—WHAL.

[2] *By the rage of the people.*] After this the quarto has the following: "This do we advance, as a mark of terror to all traitors, and treasons; to shew how just the heavens are, in pouring and thundering down a weighty vengeance on their unnatural intents, even to the worst princes; much more to those, for guard of whose piety and virtue the angels are in continual watch, and GOD himself miraculously working."

This seems to have been added, in compliment to K. James, on the discovery of the *powder-plot.*—WHAL.

[3] Lucius *Arruntius, &c.*] I have added the cognomen or pronomen to many of the characters as a necessary help for the English reader, since Jonson, without noticing the circumstance, sometimes uses the one and sometimes the other, as suits the convenience of his verse.

Sejanus.

ACT I.

SCENE I.—*A State Room in the Palace.*

Enter Sabinus *and* Silius, *followed by*
Latiaris.

Sab. Hail, Caius Silius !*
Sil. Titius Sabinus,† hail !
You're rarely met in court.
Sab. Therefore, well met.
Sil. 'Tis true : indeed, this place is not
our sphere.
Sab. No, Silius, we are no good in-
giners.
We want their fine arts, and their thriving
use
Should make us graced, or favoured of the
times :
We have no shift of faces, no cleft tongues,
No soft and glutinous bodies, that can
stick,
Like snails on painted walls ; or, on our
breasts,
Creep up, to fall from that proud height,
to which
We did by slavery,‡ not by service climb.
We are no guilty men, and then no great ;
We have no place in court, office in state,
That we can say,§ we owe unto our
crimes :
We burn with no black secrets,‖ which can
make
Us dear to the pale authors ; or live feared
Of their still waking jealousies, to raise
Ourselves a fortune, by subverting theirs.
We stand not in the lines, that do advance
To that so courted point.

Enter Satrius *and* Natta *at a distance.*

Sil. But yonder lean
A pair that do.
Sab. [*salutes* Latiaris.] Good cousin
Latiaris.¶
Sil. Satrius Secundus,** and Pinnarius
Natta,††
The great Sejanus' clients : there be two,
Know more than honest counsels ; whose
close breasts,
Were they ripped up to light, it would be
found
A poor and idle sin,¹ to which their
trunks
Had not been made fit organs. These can
lie,
Flatter, and swear, forswear, deprave,‡‡ in-
form,
Smile, and betray ; make guilty men ; then
beg
The forfeit lives, to get their livings ; cut
Men's throats with whisperings ; sell to
gaping suitors

---

¹ *A poor and* idle *sin,*] That is, barren, unprofitable. The word is so used by Shakspeare :

"Of antres vast, and desarts idle."—*Othello.*

So, in the first chapter of *Genesis* : " The earth
was without form, and *void,*" is rendered in the
Saxon, "The earth was ydæl."—WHAL.
Mr. Pope changed idle for *wild,* at which Dr.
Johnson expresses his surprise. Mr. Malone
taxes the editor of the second folio (where Pope
found the word) with ignorance of Shakspeare's
meaning ; and *idle* is triumphantly reinstated in
the text. It does not seem to have occurred to
the commentators that *wild* might add a feature
of some import, event to a desert ; whereas
sterile leaves it just as it found it, and is (without a pun) the *idlest* epithet which could be
applied. Mr. Pope too had an ear for rhythm ;
and as his reading has some touch of Shakspeare,
which the other has not, and is besides better
poetry, I should hope that it will one day
resume its proper place in the text. *Idle* in the
line above quoted signifies, not " barren, unprofitable," but trifling, insignificant. It would
be a sin of a very paltry nature indeed, which had
not engaged their attention, and been deemed
worthy of their practice. In other words, no
vice has escaped them.

---

* *De Caio Silio, vid. Tacit.* Lips. edit. quarto.
Ann. Lib. i. pag. 11, Lib. ii. p. 28 *et* 33. This,
together with every succeeding note not distin-
guished by a numeral, is from the pen of Jonson.
† *De Titio Sabino, vid. Tacit.* Lib. iv. p. 79.
‡ *Tacit. Ann.* Lib. i. p. 2.
§ *Juv. Sat.* i. v. 75.
‖ *Juv. Sat.* iii. v. 49, &c.
¶ *De Latiari, cons. Tacit. Ann.* Lib. iv.
p. 94, *et Dion.* Step. edit. fol. Lib. lviii. p. 711.
** *De Satrio Secundo, et* (††) *Pinnario Natta,*
leg. Tacit. Ann. Lib. iv. p. 83. *Et de Satrio*
cons. Senec. Consol. ad Marciam.
‡‡ *Vid. Sen. de Benef.* Lib. iii. cap. 26.

The empty smoke, that flies about the
    palace;
Laugh when their patron laughs; sweat
    when he sweats;
Be hot and cold with him; change every
    mood,
Habit, and garb, as often as he varies;
Observe him, as his watch observes his
    clock;[1]
And, true as turquoise in the dear lord's
    ring,[2]
Look well or ill with him:[4] ready to praise
His lordship, if he spit, or but p— fair,
Have an indifferent stool, or break wind
    well;
Nothing can scape their catch.
    Sab. Alas! these things
Deserve no note, conferred with other vile
And filthier flatteries,† that corrupt the
    times;
When, not alone our gentrics chief are
    fain
To make their safety from such sordid acts;
But all our consuls,‡ and no little part
Of such as have been prætors, yea, the
    most
Of senators,§ that else not use their voices,[3]
Start up in public senate, and there strive
Who shall propound most abject things,
    and base.
So much, as oft Tiberius hath been heard,
Leaving the court, to cry,‖ O race of men,

Prepared for servitude!—which shewed
    that he,
Who least the public liberty could like,
As lothly brooked their flat servility.
    Sil. Well, all is worthy of us, were it more,
Who with our riots, pride, and civil hate,
Have so provoked the justice of the gods:
We, that, within these fourscore years, were
    born
Free, equal lords of the triúmphed world,[4]
And knew no masters but affections;
To which betraying first our liberties,
We since became the slaves to one man's
    lusts;
And now to many:¶ every minist'ring spy
That will accuse and swear, is lord of you,
Of me, of all our fortunes and our lives.
Our looks are called to question,** and our
    words,
How innocent soever, are made crimes;
We shall not shortly dare to tell our
    dreams,
Or think, but 'twill be treason.
    Sab. Tyrants' arts
Are to give flatterers grace; accusers, power;
That those may seem to kill whom they
    devour.

                Enter Cordus *and* Arruntius.

Now, good Cremutius Cordus.††
    Cor. [*salutes* Sabinus.] Hail to your
        lordship!

---

[1] *Observe him as his* watch *observes his clock.*] Steevens, who is supported by Whalley, maintains that this line refers to the figure of a *watchman*, which was placed on the dial-plate of our ancient clocks, with a lantern and pole to point out the hour. I have many doubts whether such a personage was ever so employed; but none as to the fallacy of the explanation. The speaker alludes to the pocket-watch, which in Jonson's days was not so independent of correction as at present, but was constantly regulated by the motion of the clock, at that time the more accurate machine of the two.

[2] *And true, as turquoise in the dear lord's ring,*
Look well or ill with him:] Alluding to the fable of the turquoise, which is said to change its colour as the wearer is in good or bad health. To this supposed quality of the stone, our old writers have innumerable allusions: "*Turcois* is a compassionate stone—if the wearer of it be not well it changeth colour and looketh pale and dim; but increaseth to his perfectnesse as the wearer recovereth to his health."—Swan's *Speculum mundi.*
    Again:
"Or *faithful turquoises,* which heaven sent
    For a discovery not a punishment;

To show the ill, not make it, and to tell,
By their pale looks, *the bearer was not well.*"
                                    Cartwright.
[3] *Senators, that else not use their voices.*] The poet has here added the word *Pedarii.* It is the classical expression for those who never spoke in the senate, but only went over to the side for which they voted: hence they were said *pedibus ire in sententiam.*—WHAL.
[4] *Equal lords of the triúmphed world,*] i.e., the Roman empire. The expression is fine, and gives us an admirable idea of what every private citizen of Rome esteemed himself in the times of the republic.—WHAL.

* *Juv. Sat.* iii. ver. 105, &c.
† *Vid. Tacit. Ann.* Lib. i. p. 3.
‡ *Tacit. Ann.* Lib. iii. p. 69.   § *Pedarii.*
‖ *Tacit. Ann.* Lib. iii. p. 69.
¶ *Lege Tacit. Ann.* Lib. i. p. 24. *de Romano, Hispano, et cæteris, ibid. et* Lib. iii. *Ann.* p. 61 *et* 62. *Juv. Sat.* x. v. 87.   *Suet. Tib.* cap. 61.
** *Vid. Tacit. Ann.* i. p. 4, *et* Lib. iii. p. 62. *Suet. Tib.* cap. 61. *Senec. de Benef.* Lib. iii. cap. 26.
†† *De Crem. Cordo, vid. Tacit. Ann.* Lib. iv. p. 83, 84.   *Senec. Cons. ad Marciam. Dio.* Lib. lvii. p. 710.   *Suet. Aug.* c. 35.   *Tib.* c. 61. *Cal.* c. 16.

Nat. [*whispers* Latiaris.] Who's that
salutes your cousin?
Lat. 'Tis one Cordus,
A gentleman of Rome: one that has writ
Annals of late, they say, and very well.
Nat. Annals! of what times?
Lat. I think of Pompey's,*
And Caius Cæsar's; and so down to these.
Nat. How stands he affected to the pre-
sent state?
Is he or Drusian,† or Germanican,
Or ours, or neutral?
Lat. I know him not so far.
Nat. Those times are somewhat queasy
to be touched.[1]
Have you or seen, or heard part of his work?
Lat. Not I; he means they shall be public
shortly.
Nat. O, Cordus do you call him?
Lat. Ay. [*Exeunt* Natta *and* Satrius.
Sab. But these our times
Are not the same, Arruntius.‡
Arr. Times! the men,
The men are not the same! 'tis we are
base,
Poor, and degenerate from the exalted
strain
Of our great fathers. Where is now the
soul
Of god-like Cato? he, that durst be good,
When Cæsar durst be evil; and had power,
As not to live his slave, to die his master?
Or where's the constant Brutus, that being
proof
Against all charm of benefits, did strike
So brave a blow into the monster's heart
That sought unkindly[2] to captive his
country?
O, they are fled the light! Those mighty
spirits
Lie raked up with their ashes in their urns,

And not a spark of their eternal fire
Glows in a present bosom. All's but blaze,
Flashes and smoke, wherewith we labour so,
There's nothing Roman in us; nothing
good,
Gallant, or great: 'tis true that Cordus says,
" Brave Cassius was the last of all that
race."
[Drusus *passes over the stage, at-
tended by* Haterius, &c.
Sab. Stand by! Lord Drusus.§
Hat. The emperor's son! give place.
Sil. I like the prince well.
Arr. A riotous youth;∥
There's little hope of him.
Sab. That fault his age
Will, as it grows, correct. Methinks he
bears
Himself each day more nobly than other;
And wins no less on men's affections,
Than doth his father lose. Believe me, I
love him;
And chiefly for opposing to Sejanus.¶
Sil. And I, for gracing his young kins-
men so,**
The sons†† of prince Germanicus:‡‡ it shews
A gallant clearness in him, a straight mind,
That envies not, in them, their father's
name.
Arr. His name was, while he lived,
above all envy;
And, being dead, without it. O, that man!
If there were seeds of the old virtue left,
They lived in him.
Sil. He had the fruits, Arruntius,
More than the seeds:§§ Sabinus, and myself
Had means to know him within; and can
report him.
We were his followers, he would call us
friends;
He was a man[3] most like to virtue; in all,

---

[1] Queasy *to be touched.*] Nice, tender, delicate. Thus Shakspeare:

"And I have one thing of a *queasy* question."
King Lear, act ii. sc. 1.

[2] Unkindly *to captive his country!*] i.e., *un-*
naturally; for the word *kind* signifying nature,
with its compounds and derivatives, was thus
used by the writers of that age.—WHAL.
    "Let any *candid judge,*" says one of the com-
mentators, "compare *Sejanus* with the third-rate
tragedies of Shakspeare, and he will find it *far*
inferior to the worst of them." The critic had
probably just got up from this speech of Arruntius, when he exhibited so notable a specimen of
his own *candour* and *judgment.*
[3] *He was a man, &c.*] Jonson has borrowed
the noble character which Paterculus hath given
Cato, and applies it with great propriety to Ger-

manicus. *Homo virtuti simillimus, et per*
omnia ingenio diis quam hominibus propior,

* *Suet. Aug.* cap. 35.
† *Vid. de faction. Tacit. Ann.* Lib. ii. p. 39
et Lib. iv. p. 79.
‡ *De Lu. Arrun. isto vid. Tacit. Ann.* Lib. i.
p. 6, *et* Lib. iii. p. 60, *et Dion. Rom. Hist.*
Lib. 58.
§ *Lege de Druso Tacit. Ann.* Lib. i. p. 9. *Suet.*
Tib. c. 52. *Dio. Rom. Hist.* Lib. lvii. p. 699.
∥ *Tacit. Ann.* Lib. iii. p. 62.
¶ *Vid. Tacit. Ann.* Lib. iv. p. 74.
** *Ann.* Lib. iv. p. 75, 76.
†† *Nero, Drusus, Caius, qui in castris genitus,*
et Caligula nominatus. Tacit. Ann. Lib. i.
‡‡ *De Germanico cons. Tacit. Ann.* Lib. i.
p. 14, *et Dion. Rom. Hist.* Lib. lvii. p. 694.
§§ *Vid. Tacit. Ann.* Lib. iv. p. 79.

And every action, nearer to the gods,
Than men, in nature; of a body as fair
As was his mind; and no less reverend
In face than fame:* he could so use his
state,
Tempering his greatness with his gravity,
As it avoided all self-love in him,
And spite in others.   What his funerals
lacked
In images and pomp, they had supplied
With honourable sorrow, soldiers' sadness,
A kind of silent mourning, such as men,
Who know no tears but from their cap-
tives, use
To shew in so great losses.
    Cor. I thought once,
Considering their forms, age, manner of
deaths,
The nearness of the places where they fell,
To have paralleled him with great
Alexander :[1]
For both were of best feature, of high race,
Yeared but to thirty, and, in foreign
lands,
By their own people alike made away.
    Sab. I know not, for his death, how you
might wrest it :
But, for his life, it did as much disdain
Comparison with that voluptuous, rash,
Giddy, and drunken Macedon's, as mine
Doth with my bondman's. All the good
in him,
His valour, and his fortune, he made his ;
But he had other touches of late Romans,
That more did speak him :† Pompey's
dignity,
The innocence of Cato, Cæsar's spirit,
Wise Brutus' temperance : and every
virtue,
Which, parted unto others, gave them
name,

Flowed mixed in him. He was the soul
of goodness ;
And all our praises of him are like streams
Drawn from a spring, that still rise full,
and leave
The part remaining greatest.
    Arr. I am sure
He was too great for us,‡ and that they
knew
Who did remove him hence.
    Sab. When men grow fast
Honoured and loved, there is a trick in
state,
Which jealous princes never fail to use,
How to decline that growth, with fair
pretext,
And honourable colours of employment,
Either by embassy, the war, or such,
To shift them forth into another air,
Where they may purge, and lessen ; so was
he :§
And had his seconds there, sent by Ti-
berius,
And his more subtile dam, to discontent
him ;
To breed and cherish mutinies ; detract
His greatest actions ; give audacious check
To his commands ; and work to put him
out
In open act of treason. All which snares
When his wise cares prevented,‖ a fine
poison
Was thought on, to mature their practices.

Enter Sejanus, *talking to* Terentius ;
    followed by Satrius, Natta, &c.

    Cor. Here comes Sejanus.¶
    Sil. Now observe the stoops,
The bendings, and the falls.
    Arr. Most creeping base !

---

l. ii. c. 35. His references to the Roman historians are chiefly brought as vouchers for the
facts alluded to, or the descriptions which he
gives of the persons concerned. When he
borrows the sentiment or thought, he is frequently silent; and particularly, he takes no
notice of being here indebted to Paterculus.—
WHAL.
    Whalley should have read a few lines farther.
Jonson refers expressly to the passage.

[1] *I thought once—*
    *To have paralleled him with great Alexan-
der* :] This observation comes with great decorum
of character from the mouth of Cordus: but
Tacitus, from whom it is taken, assigns no particular person as the author of the parallel : *Erant
qui formam, ætatem, genus mortis, ob pro-
pinquitatem etiam locorum in quibus interiit,*

magni Alexandri fatis adequarent, Annal. l. ii.
c. 73.—WHAL.

---

* *Tacit. Ann.* Lib. ii. p. 47, *et Dion. Rom.
Hist.* Lib. lvii. p. 705.
    † *Vid. apud Vell. Paterc.* Lips. 4to. p. 35—47,
istorum hominum characteres.
    ‡ *Vid. Tacit.* Lib. ii, *Ann.* p. 28 *et* p. 34.
Dio. Rom. Hist. Lib. lvii. p. 705.
    § *Con. Tacit. Ann.* Lib. ii. p. 39, *de occultis
mandatis Pisoni, et postea,* p. 42, 43, 48. *Orat.
D. Celeris. Est Tibi Augustæ conscientia, est
Cæsaris favor, sed in occulto, &c. Leg. Suet.
Tib.* c. 52. *Dio.* p. 706.
    ‖ *Vid. Tacit. Ann.* Lib. ii. p. 46, 47, Lib. iii.
p. 54, *et Suet. Cal.* c. 1 *et* 2.
    ¶ *De Sejano vid. Tacit. Ann.* Lib. i. p. 9.
Lib. iv. *princip. et per tot. Suet. Tib. Dio.*
Lib. lvii. lviii. *et Plin. et Senec.*

Sej. [*to* Natta.] I note them well : no more.
Say you?
Sat. My lord,
There is a gentleman of Rome would buy——
Sej. How call you him you talked with?
Sat. Please your lordship,
It is Eudemus,* the physician
To Livia, Drusus' wife.
Sej. On with your suit.
Would buy, you said——
Sat. A tribune's place, my lord.
Sej. What will he give?
Sat. Fifty sestertia.†
Sej. Livia's physician, say you, is that fellow?
Sat. It is, my lord.　Your lordship's answer.
Sej. To what?
Sat. The place, my lord.　'Tis for a gentleman
Your lordship will well like of, when you see him ;
And one that you may make yours, by the grant.
Sej. Well, let him bring his money, and his name.
Sat. 'Thank your lordship.　He shall, my lord.
Sej. Come hither.
Know you this same Eudemus? is he learned?
Sat. Reputed so, my lord, and of deep practice.
Sej. Bring him in to me, in the gallery ;
And take you cause to leave us there together :
I would confer with him, about a grief——
On.
[*Exeunt* Sejanus, Satrius, Terentius, &c.
Arr. So! yet another? yet? O desperate state
Of grovelling honour! seest thou this, O sun,
And do we see thee after? Methinks, day
Should lose his light, when men do lose their shames,
And for the empty circumstance of life,[1]
Betray their cause of living.
Sil. Nothing so.‡

Sejanus can repair, if Jove should ruin.
He is now the court god ; and well applied
With sacrifice of knees, of crooks, and cringes ;
He will do more than all the house of heaven
Can for a thousand hecatombs.　'Tis he
Makes us our day, or night ; hell and elysium
Are in his look : we talk of Rhadamanth,
Furies, and firebrands ; but it is his frown
That is all these ; where, on the adverse part,
His smile is more than e'er yet poets feigned
Of bliss, and shades, nectar——
Arr. A serving boy!
I knew him, at Caius' trencher,§ when for hire
He prostituted his abused body
To that great gormond, fat Apicius :
And was the noted pathic of the time.
Sab. And, now, the second face of the whole world!
The partner of the empire, hath his image
Reared equal with Tiberius, born in ensigns ;
Commands, disposes every dignity,
Centurions, tribunes, heads of provinces,
Prætors, and consuls ; all that heretofore
Rome's general suffrage gave, is now his sale.
The gain, or rather spoil of all the earth,
One, and his house, receives.
Sil. He hath of late
Made him a strength too, strangely, by reducing
All the prætorian bands into one camp,
Which he commands : pretending that the soldiers,
By living loose and scattered, fell to riot ;
And that if any sudden enterprise
Should be attempted, their united strength
Would be far more than severed ; and their life
More strict, if from the city more removed.
Sab. Where now he builds what kind of forts he please,
Is heard to court the soldier by his name,
Woos, feasts the chiefest men of action,

---

[1] *And for the empty circumstance of life,*
Betray their cause of living.]

"*Et propter vitam, vivendi perdere causam.*"
Juv. Sat. viii. v. 84.

* *De Eudemo isto vid. Tacit. Ann.* Lib. iv.
p. 74.

† *Monetæ nostræ* 375 *lib. vid. Budæum de asse,* Lib. ii. p. 64.
‡ *De ingenio, moribus, et potentia Sejani. leg. Tacit. Ann.* Lib. iv. p. 74.　*Dio. Rom. Hist.* Lib. lvii. p. 708.
§ *Caius divi Augusti nepos. Cons. Tacit. Ann.* Lib. iv. p. 74, *et Dio.* Lib. lvii. p. 706.
‖ *Juv. Sat.* x. v. 63, &c.　*Tacit. ibid. Dion. ibid. et sic passim.*

Whose wants, not loves, compel them to
    be his.
And though he ne'er were liberal by kind,[1]
Yet to his own dark ends, he's most pro-
    fuse,
Lavish, and letting fly, he cares not what
To his ambition.
    Arr. Yet, hath he ambition?
Is there that step in state can make him
    higher,
Or more, or anything he is, but less?
    Sil. Nothing but emperor.
    Arr. The name Tiberius,
I hope, will keep, howe'er he hath fore-
    gone
The dignity and power.
    Sil. Sure, while he lives.
    Arr. And dead, it comes to Drusus.
    Should he fail,
To the brave issue of Germanicus ;
And they are three :* too many—ha? for
    him
To have a plot upon?
    Sab. I do not know
The heart of his designs ; but sure their
    face
Looks farther than the present.
    Arr. By the gods,
If I could guess he had but such a thought,
My sword should cleave him down from
    head to heart,
But I would find it out : and with my
    hand
I'd hurl his panting brain about the air
In mites as small as atomi, to undo
The knotted bed——
    Sab. You are observed, Arruntius.
    Arr. [*Turns to* Natta, Terentius, *&c.*]
Death ! I dare tell him so ; and all his
    spies :
You, sir, I would, do you look? and you.
    Sab. Forbear.

    SCENE II.—(*The former Scene
        continued.*)

*A Gallery discovered opening into the
    State Room.*

    Enter Satrius *with* Eudemus.

    Sat. Here he will instant be ; let's walk
    a turn ;

You're in a muse, Eudemus?
    Eud. Not I, sir.
I wonder he should mark me out so ! well,
Jove and Apollo form it for the best.
                     [*Aside.*
    Sat. Your† fortune's made unto you now,
    Eudemus,
If you can but lay hold upon the means ;
Do but observe his humour, and—believe
    it—
He is the noblest Roman, where he takes—

        Enter Sejanus.

Here comes his lordship.
    Sej. Now, good Satrius.
    Sat. This is the gentleman, my lord.
    Sej. Is this?
Give me your hand, we must be more ac-
    quainted.
Report, sir, hath spoke out your art and
    learning :
And I am glad I have so needful cause,
However in itself painful and hard,
To make me known to so great virtue.—
    Look,
Who is that, Satrius? [*Exit* Sat.] I have
    a grief, sir,
That will desire your help. Your name's
    Eudemus?
    Eud. Yes.
    Sej. Sir?
    Eud. It is, my lord.
    Sej. I hear you are
Physician to Livia,‡ the princess.
    Eud. I minister unto her, my good lord.
    Sej. You minister to a royal lady, then.
    Eud. She is, my lord, and fair.
    Sej. That's understood
Of all their sex, who are or would be so ;
And those that would be, physic soon can
    make them :
For those that are, their beauties fear no
    colours.
    Eud. Your lordship is conceited.[2]
    Sej. Sir, you know it,
And can, if need be, read a learned lec-
    ture
On this, and other secrets. 'Pray you, tell
    me,
What more of ladies, besides Livia,
Have you your patients?
    Eud. Many, my good lord.

---

[1] *He ne'er were liberal* by kind.] By nature.
See p. 277 a.—WHAL.
[2] *Your lordship is conceited.*] Merry, disposed to joke. So in *Every Man in his Humour,*
"You are conceited, sir."—WHAL.

* *Nero, Drusus, et Caligula.*—Tacit. ibid.
† *Lege Terentii defensionem.* Tacit. Ann.
Lib. vi. p. 102.
‡ *Germanici soror, uxor Drusi. Vid. Tacit.
Ann.* Lib. iv. p. 74.

The great Augusta,* Urgulania,†
Mutilia Prisca,‡ and Plancina:§ divers—
  Sej. And, all these tell you the particu-
    lars
Of every several grief? how first it grew,
And then increased ; what action caused
    that ;
What passion that ; and answer to each
    point
That you will put them?
  Eud. Else, my lord, we know not
How to prescribe the remedies.
  Sej. Go to,
You are a subtile nation, you physicians !
And grown the only cabinets in court,‖
To ladies' privacies. Faith, which of these
Is the most pleasant lady in her physic ?
Come, you are modest now.
  Eud. 'Tis fit, my lord.
  Sej. Why, sir, I do not ask you of their
    urines,
Whose smell's most violet, or whose siege is
    best,[1]
Or who makes hardest faces on her stool?
Which lady sleeps with her own face a
    nights ?
Which puts her teeth off, with her clothes,
    in court ?
Or, which her hair, which her complexion,
And, in which box she puts it ? These
    were questions,
That might, perhaps, have put your gravity
To some defence of blush. But, I en-
    quired,
Which was the wittiest, merriest, wanton-
    est?
Harmless interrogatories, but conceits.——
Methinks Augusta should be most per-
    verse,
And froward in her fit.
  Eud. She's so, my lord.
  Sej. I knew it : and Mutilia the most
    jocund.
  Eud. 'Tis very true, my lord.
  Sej. And why would you
Conceal this from me, now ? Come, what
    is Livia?
I know she's quick and quaintly spirited,

And will have strange thoughts, when she
    is at leisure :
She tells them all to you.
  Eud. My noblest lord,
He breathes not in the empire, or on earth,
Whom I would be ambitious to serve
In any act, that may preserve mine honour,
Before your lordship.
  Sej. Sir, you can lose no honour,
By trusting aught to me. The coarsest act
Done to my service, I can so requite,
As all the world shall style it honourable :
Your idle, virtuous definitions,
Keep honour poor, and are as scorned as
    vain :
Those deeds breathe honour that do suck
    in gain.
  Eud. But, good my lord, if I should
    thus betray
The counsels of my patient, and a lady's
Of her high place and worth ; what might
    your lordship,
Who presently are to trust me with your
    own,
Judge of my faith ?
  Sej. Only the best, I swear.
Say now that I should utter you my grief,
And with it the true cause; that it were
    love,
And love to Livia ;¶ you should tell her
    this :
Should she suspect your faith ? I would
    you could
Tell me as much from her; see if my brain
Could be turned jealous.
  Eud. Happily, my lord,
I could in time tell you as much and more ;
So I might safely promise but the first
To her from you.
  Sej. As safely, my Eudemus,
I now dare call thee so, as I have put
The secret into thee.
  Eud. My lord——
  Sej. Protest not,
Thy looks are vows to me ; use only speed,
And but affect her with Sejanus' love,**
Thou art a man, made to make consuls.
  Go.

---

[1] *Whose siege is best,*] This word, which was
growing out of use in Jonson's time, is found in
Barclay's *Eclogues :*

  " For sure the lord's *siege* and the rural man's
    Is of like savour."

It is also used by Shakspeare, *Tempest*, act ii.
sc. 2, where it is well explained by Steevens.

  * *Mater Tiberii. vid. Tacit. Ann.* 1, 2, 3, 4,

moritur 5. *Suet. Tib. Dio. Rom. Hist.*
57, 58.
  † *Delicium Augustæ. Tacit. Ann.* Lib. ii.
et iv.
  ‡ *Adultera Julii Posthumi. Tacit. Ann.*
Lib. iv. p. 77.
  § *Pisonis uxor Tacit. Ann.* Lib. ii iii. iv.
  ‖ *Via. Tacit. Ann.* Lib. iv. p. 74, *et Plin.
Nat. Hist.* Lib. xxix. c. 1.
  ¶ *Cons. Tacit. Ann.* Lib. iv. p. 74.
  ** *Tacit. ibid.*

Eud. My lord, I'll promise you a private
　　meeting
This day together.
　Sej. Canst thou?
　Eud. Yes.
　Sej. The place?
　Eud. My gardens, whither I shall fetch
　　your lordship.
　Sej. Let me adore my Æsculapius.
Why, this indeed is physic! and outspeaks
The knowledge of cheap drugs, or any use
Can be made out of it! more comforting
Than all your opiates, juleps, apozems,
Magistral syrups, or——Begone, my friend,
Not barely styled, but created so;
Expect things greater than thy largest hopes,
To overtake thee: Fortune shall be taught
To know how ill she hath deserved thus
　　long,
To come behind thy wishes.　Go, and
　　speed.　　　　　　[*Exit* Eudemus.[1]
Ambition makes more trusty slaves than
　　need.
These fellows,[*] by the favour of their art,
Have still the means to tempt; oft-times
　　the power.
If Livia will be now corrupted, then
Thou hast the way, Sejanus, to work out
His secrets, who, thou know'st, endures
　　thee not,
Her husband, Drusus: and to work against
　　them.
Prosper it, Pallas, thou that betterest wit;
For Venus hath the smallest share in it.

　Enter Tiberius *and* Drusus, *attended.*

　Tib. [*to* Haterius, *who kneels to him.*]
　　We not† endure these flatteries; let
　　him stand;
Our empire, ensigns, axes, rods, and state
Take not away our human nature from us:
Look up on us, and fall into the gods.
　Sej. How like a god speaks Cæsar!
　Arr. There, observe!
He can endure that second, that's no
　flattery.

O, what is it, proud slime[2] will not believe
Of his own worth, to hear it equal praised
Thus with the gods!
　Cor. He did not hear it, sir.
　Arr. He did not! Tut, he must not,
　we think meanly.
'Tis your most courtly known confederacy,
To have your private parasite redeem
What he, in public, subtiley will lose,
To making him a name.
　Hat. Right mighty lord——
　　　　　　　　　　[*Gives him letters.*
　Tib. We must make up our ears 'gainst
　　these assaults
Of charming tongues;‡ we pray you use no
　more
These contumelies to us; style not us
Or lord, or mighty, who profess ourself
The servant of the senate, and are proud
T' enjoy them our good, just, and favouring
　lords.
　Cor. Rarely§ dissembled!
　Arr. Prince-like to the life.
　Sab. When power that may command,
　so much descends,
Their bondage, whom it stoops to, it in-
　tends.
　Tib. Whence are these letters?
　Hat. From the senate.
　Tib. So.　　　[Lat. *gives him letters.*
Whence these?
　Lat. From thence too.
　Tib. Are they sitting now?
　Lat. They stay thy answer, Cæsar.
　Sil. If this man
Had but a mind allied unto his words,
How blest a fate were it to us, and Rome!
We could not think that state for which to
　change,
Although the aim were our old liberty:
The ghosts‖ of those that fell for that,
　would grieve
Their bodies lived not, now, again to serve.
Men are deceived, who think there can be
　thrall
Beneath a virtuous prince.　Wished liberty[3]

---

[1] *Exit* Eudemus.] Sejanus plays on the
vanity of this man with singular cunning and
dexterity.
　[2] *O, what is it, proud slime, &c.*]

　　"*Nihil est quod credere de se*
Non possit, cum laudatur Diis æqua potestas?"
　　　　　　　　　　　　Juv. Sat. iv.
　[3] *Wished liberty, &c.*]

　　"*Nunquam libertas gratior exstat,*
Quam sub rege pio."
　　　　　　Claud de laud. Stil. Lib. iii.

[*] *Eud. specie artis frequens secretis. Tacit.
ibid. Vid. Plin. Nat. Hist. Lib. xxix. c. 1. in
criminat. medicorum.*
　† *De initio Tiberii principatus vid. Tacit.
Ann. Lib. i. p. 23, Lib. iv. p. 75, et Suet. Tib.
c. 27. De Haterio vid. Tacit. Ann. Lib. i.
p. 6.*
　‡ *Cons. Tacit. Ann. Lib. ii. p. 50, et Suet.
Tib. c. 27 et 29.*
　§ *Nullam æque Tiberius ex virtutibus suis
quam dissimulationem diligebat. Tacit. Ann.
Lib. iv. p. 95.*
　‖ *Bruti, Cassii, Catonis, &c.*

Ne'er lovelier looks, than under such a
    crown.
But, when his grace* is merely but lip-good,
And that, no longer than he airs himself
Abroad in public, there, to seem to shun
The strokes and stripes of flatterers, which
    within
Are lechery unto him, and so feed
His brutish sense with their afflicting sound,
As, dead to virtue, he permits himself
Be carried like a pitcher by the ears,
To every act of vice: this is a case
Deserves our fear, and doth presage the
    nigh
And close approach of blood and tyranny.
Flattery is midwife† unto prince's rage:
And nothing sooner doth help forth a
    tyrant,
Than that and whisperers' grace, who have
    the time,
The place, the power, to make all men
    offenders.
    Arr. He should be told this; and be bid
    dissemble
With fools and blind men: we that know
    the evil,
Should hunt the palace-rats,‡ or give them
    bane;
Fright hence these worse than ravens, that
    devour
The quick, where they but prey upon the
    dead:
He shall be told it.
    Sab. Stay, Arruntius,
We must abide our opportunity;
And practise what is fit, as what is needful.
It is not safe t' enforce a sovereign's ear:
Princes hear well, if they at all will hear.
    Arr. Ha, say you so? well! In the
    mean time, Jove,
(Say not but I do call upon thee now,)
Of all wild beasts preserve me from a
    tyrant;
And of all tame, a flatterer.
    Sil. 'Tis well prayed.
    Tib. [*having read the letters.*] Return
    the lords this voice, We are their
    creature,
And it is fit a good and honest prince,
Whom they, out of their bounty, have in-
    structed§

With so dilate and absolute a power,
Should owe the office of it to their service,
And good of all and every citizen.
Nor shall it e'er repent us to have wished
The senate just, and favouring lords unto
    us,
Since their free loves do yield no less de-
    fence
To a prince's state, than his own innocence.
Say then, there can be nothing in their
    thought
Shall want to please us, that hath pleased
    them;
Our suffrage rather shall prevent, than stay
Behind their wills: 'tis empire to obey,
Where such, so great, so grave, so good
    determine.
Yet, for the suit of Spain,‖ to erect a temple
In honour of our mother and our self,
We must, with pardon of the senate, not
Assent thereto. Their lordships may object
Our not denying the same late request
Unto the Asian cities: we desire
That our defence for suffering that be
    known
In these brief reasons, with our after pur-
    pose.
Since deified Augustus hindered not
A temple to be built at Pergamum,
In honour of himself and sacred Rome;
We, that have all his deeds¶ and words
    observed
Ever, in place of laws, the rather followed
That pleasing precedent, because with ours,
The senate's reverence, also, there was
    joined.
But as, t' have once received it, may de-
    serve
The gain of pardon; so, to be adored
With the continued style, and note of gods,
Through all the provinces, were wild am-
    bition,
And no less pride: yea, even Augustus'
    name
Would early vanish, should it be profaned
With such promiscuous flatteries. For our
    part,
We here protest it, and are covetous
Posterity should know it, we are mortal;
And can but deeds of men: 'twere glory
    enough,

---

* *Vid. Dio. Hist.* Lib. lvii. *de moribus Tiberii.*
† *Tyrannis fere oritur ex nimia procerum adulatione in principem. Arist. Pol.* Lib. v. c. 10, 11, *et delatorum auctoritate. Leg. Tacit. Dio. Suet. Tib. per totum. Sub quo decreta accusatoribus præcipua præmia. Vid. Suet. Tib.* c. 61, *et Sen. Benef.* Lib. iii. c. 6.

‡ *Tineas soricesque Palatii vocat istos Sex. Aurel. Vict. et Tacit. Hist.* Lib. i. p. 233, *qui secretis criminat. infamant ignarum, et quo incautior deciperetur, palam laudatum, &c.*
§ *Vid. Suet. Tib.* c. 20, *et Dio. Hist.* Lib. lvii. p. 696.
‖ *Tacit. Ann.* Lib. iv. p. 84 *et* 85.
¶ *Cons. Strab.* Lib. vi. *de Tib.*

Could we be truly a prince. And, they
   shall add
Abounding grace unto our memory,
That shall report us worthy our fore-
   fathers,
Careful of your affairs, constant in dangers,
And not afraid of any private frown
For public good. These things shall be
   to us
Temples and statues, reared in your minds,
The fairest, and most during imagery:
For those of stone or brass, if they become
Odious in judgment of posterity,
Are more contemned as dying sepulchres,
Than ta'en for living monuments. We
   then
Make here our suit, alike to gods and men;
The one, until the period of our race,
To inspire us with a free and quiet mind,
Discerning both divine and human laws;
The other, to vouchsafe us after death,
An honourable mention, and fair praise,
To accompany our actions and our name:
The rest of greatness princes may com-
   mand,
And, therefore, may neglect; only, a long,
A lasting, high, and happy memory
They should, without being satisfied,
   pursue:
Contempt of fame begets contempt of
   virtue.
   Nat. Rare!
   Sat. Most divine!
   Sej. The oracles are ceased,
That only Cæsar, with their tongue, might
   speak.
   Arr. Let me be gone: most felt and
   open this!
   Cor. Stay.
   Arr. What! to hear more cunning and
   fine words,
With their sound flattered ere their sense
   be meant?
   Tib. Their choice of Antium,* there to
   place the gift
Vowed to the goddess† for our mother's
   health,
We will the senate know, we fairly like;
As also of their grant‡ to Lepidus,
For his repairing the Æmilian place,
And restoration of those monuments:
Their grace§ too in confining of Silanus
To the other isle Cithera, at the suit

Of his religious‖ sister, much commends
Their policy, so tempered with their mercy.
But for the honours which they have de-
   creed
To our Sejanus,¶ to advance his statue
In Pompey's theatre, (whose ruining fire
His vigilance and labour kept restrained
In that one loss,) they have therein out-
   gone
Their own great wisdoms, by their skilful
   choice,
And placing of their bounties on a man,
Whose merit more adorns the dignity,
Than that can him; and gives a benefit,
In taking, greater than it can receive.
Blush not, Sejanus,** thou great aid of
   Rome,
Associate of our labours, our chief helper;
Let us not force thy simple modesty
With offering at thy praise, for more we
   cannot,
Since there's no voice can take it. No man
   here
Receive our speeches as hyperboles:
For we are far from flattering our friend,
Let envy know, as from the need to flatter.
Nor let them ask the causes of our praise:
Princes have still their grounds reared with
   'themselves,
Above the poor low flats of common
   men;
And who will search the reasons of their
   acts,
Must stand on equal bases. Lead, away:
Our loves unto the senate.
   [*Exeunt* Tib. Sejan. Natta, Hat. Lat.
     Officers, &c.
   Arr. Cæsar! ·
   Sab. Peace.
   Cor. Great Pompey's theatre†† was never
   ruined
Till now, that proud Sejanus hath a statue
Reared on his ashes.
   Arr. Place the shame of soldiers
Above the best of generals? crack the
   world,
And bruise the name of Romans into dust,
Ere we behold it!
   Sil. Check your passion;
Lord Drusus tarries.
   Dru. Is my father mad,‡‡
Weary of life, and rule, lords? thus to
   heave

---

  * *Tacit.* Lib. iii. p. 71.
  † *Fortuna equestris, ibid.*
  ‡ *Tacit. ibid.*
  § *Tacit. Ann.* Lib. iii. p. 170.
  ‖ *Torquata virgo vestalis, cujus memoriam*

*servat marmor Romæ, vid. Lips. comment. in
Tacit.*
  ¶ *Tacit. Ann.* Lib. iii. p. 71.
  ** *Tacit. Ann.* Lib. iv. p. 74-76.
  †† *Vid. Sen. Cons. ad. Marc.* c. 22.
  ‡‡ *Tacit. Ann.* Lib. iv. p. 76.

An idol up with praise! make him his mate,
His rival in the empire!
Arr. O, good prince.
Dru. Allow him statues,* titles, honours, such
As he himself refuseth!
Arr. Brave, brave Drusus!
Dru. The first ascents to sovereignty are hard;
But, entered once, there never wants or means,
Or ministers, to help the aspirer on.
Arr. True, gallant Drusus.
Dru. We must shortly pray
To Modesty, that he will rest contented—
Arr. Ay, where he is, and not write emperor.

    Re-enter Sejanus, Satrius, Latiaris,
        Clients, &c.

Sej. There is your bill, and yours; bring you your man. [*To* Satrius.]
I have moved for you, too, Latiaris.
Dru. What!
Is your vast greatness grown so blindly bold,
That you will over us?
Sej. Why then give way.
Dru. Give way, Colossus! do you lift? advance you?
Take that!†   [*Strikes him.*
Arr. Good! brave! excellent, brave prince!
Dru. Nay, come, approach. [*Draws his sword.*] What, stand you off? at gaze?
It looks too full of death for thy cold spirits.
Avoid mine eye, dull camel, or my sword
Shall make thy bravery fitter for a grave,
Than for a triumph. I'll advance a statue
O' your own bulk; but 't shall be on the cross;‡
Where I will nail your pride at breadth and length,
And crack those sinews, which are yet but stretched
With your swoln fortune's rage.
Arr. A noble prince!
All. A Castor,§ a Castor, a Castor, a Castor.   [*Exeunt all but Sejanus.*

Sej. He that, with such wrong moved,
    can bear it through
With patience, and an even mind, knows how
To turn it back. Wrath covered carries fate:
Revenge is lost, if I profess my hate.
What was my practice late, I'll now pursue,
As my fell justice: this hath styled it new.[1]
                [*Exit.*

ACT II.

SCENE I.—*The Garden of* Eudemus.

    Enter Sejanus, Livia, *and* Eudemus.

Sej. Physician, thou art worthy of a province,
For the great favours done unto our loves;
And, but that greatest Livia bears a part
In the requital of thy services,
I should alone despair of aught, like means,
To give them worthy satisfaction.
Liv. Eudemus, I will see it, shall receive
A fit and full reward for his large merit.—
But for this potion‖ we intend to Drusus,
No more our husband now, whom shall we choose
As the most apt and abled instrument,
To minister it to him?
Eud. I say, Lygdus.¶
Sej. Lygdus? what's he?
Liv. An eunuch Drusus loves.
Eud. Ay, and his cup-bearer.
Sej. Name not a second.
If Drusus love him, and he have that place,
We cannot think a fitter.
Eud. True, my lord.
For free access and trust are two main aids.
Sej. Skilful physician!
Liv. But he must be wrought
To the undertaking, with some laboured art.
Sej. Is he ambitious?
Liv. No.
Sej. Or covetous?
Liv. Neither.

-----

[1] There is something very striking in the silence of Sejanus. After this speech the quarto has, Mu. Chorus, which is repeated at the end of every succeeding act. As it seems to mean, in plain English, merely the music between the acts, I have not thought it worth preserving.

* *Tacit. ibid.*
† *Tacit. sequimur Ann. Lib. iv. p. 74, quanquam apud Dionem et Zonaram aliter legitur.*

‡ *Servile, apud Romanos, et ignominiosissimum mortis genus erat supplicium crucis, ut ex Liv. ipso. Tacit. Dio. et omnibus fere antiquis, præsertim historicis constet. vid. Plaut. in Mil. Amph. Aulii. Hor. Lib. i. Ser. 3, et Juv. Sat. vi. Pone crucem servo, &c.*

§ *Sic Drusus ob violentiam cognominatus, vid. Dion. Rom. Hist. Lib. lvii. p. 701.*

‖ *Vid. Tacit. Ann. Lib. iv. p. 74-76.*

¶ *Tacit. ibidem.*

Eud. Yet, gold is a good general charm.
Sej. What is he, then?
Liv. Faith, only wanton, light.
Sej. How! is he young and fair?
Eud. A delicate youth.
Sej. Send him to me,* I'll work him.—
  Royal lady,
'Though I have loved you long, and with
  that height
Of zeal and duty, like the fire, which more
It mounts it trembles, thinking nought
  could add
Unto the fervour which your eye had
  kindled;
Yet, now I see your wisdom, judgment,
  strength,
Quickness, and will, to apprehend the
  means
To your own good and greatness, I protest
Myself through rarified, and turned all
  flame
In your affection: such a spirit as yours,
Was not created for the idle second
To a poor flash, as Drusus; but to shine
Bright as the moon among the lesser lights,
And share the sov'reignty of all the world.
Then Livia triumphs in her proper sphere,
When she and her Sejanus shall divide
The name of Cæsar, and Augusta's star
Be dimmed with glory of a brighter beam;
When Agrippina's† fires are quite extinct,
And the scarce-seen Tiberius borrows all
His little light from us, whose folded arms
Shall make one perfect orb. [*Knocking
  within.*] Who's that? Eudemus.
Look. [*Exit* Eudemus.] 'Tis not Drusus,
  lady, do not fear.
Liv. Not I, my lord: my fear and love
  of him
Left me at once.
Sej. Illustrious lady, stay——
Eud. [*within.*] I'll tell his lordship.

Re-enter Eudemus.

Sej. Who is it, Eudemus?
Eud. One of your lordship's servants
  brings you word
The emperor hath sent for you.
Sej. O! where is he?
With your fair leave, dear princess, I'll but
  ask
A question, and return.   [*Exit.*

Eud. Fortunate princess!
How are you blest in the fruition
Of this unequalled man, the soul of Rome,
The empire's life, and voice of Cæsar's
  world!
Liv. So blessed, my Eudemus, as to
  know
The bliss I have, with what I ought to owe
The means that wrought it. How do I
  look to-day?
Eud. Excellent clear, believe it. This
  same fucus
Was well laid on.
Liv. Methinks 'tis here not white.
Eud. Lend me your scarlet, lady. 'Tis
  the sun,
Hath giv'n some little taint unto the
  ceruse;‡
You should have used of the white oil I
  gave you.
Sejanus, for your love! his very name
Commandeth above Cupid or his shafts——
      [*Paints her cheeks.*
Liv. Nay, now you've made it worse.
Eud. I'll help it straight——
And but pronounced, is a sufficient charm
Against all rumour; and of absolute power
To satisfy for any lady's honour.
Liv. What do you now, Eudemus?
Eud. Make a light fucus,
To touch you o'er withal. Honoured
  Sejanus!
What act, though ne'er so strange and in-
  solent,
But that addition will at least bear out,
If 't do not expiate?
Liv. Here, good physician.
Eud. I like this study to preserve the love
Of such a man, that comes not every hour
To greet the world.—'Tis now well, lady,
  you should
Use of the dentrifice I prescribed you too,
To clear your teeth, and the prepared
  pomatum,
To smooth the skin:—A lady cannot be
Too curious of her form, that still would
  hold
The heart of such a person, made her
  captive,
As you have his: who, to endear him more
In your clear eye, hath put away his wife,§
The trouble of his bed, and your delights,

---

* *Spadonis animum stupro devinxit. Tacit.*
ibid.
† *Germanici vidua.*
‡ *Cerussa (apud Romanos) inter fictitiores
colores erat et quæ solem ob calorem timebat.
vid. Mart.* Lib. ii. Epig. 41:

*Quæ cretata timet Fabulla nimbum,
Cerussata timet Sabellà solem.*

§ *Ex qua tres liberos genuerat, ne pel-
lici suspectaretur. Tacit. Ann.* Lib. iv.
p. 76.

Fair Apicata, and made spacious room
To your new pleasures.
   Liv. Have not we returned
That with our hate to Drusus, and dis-
   covery*
Of all his counsels?
   Eud. Yes, and wisely, lady.
The ages that succeed, and stand far off
To gaze at your high prudence, shall ad-
   mire,
And reckon it an act without your sex:[1]
It hath that rare appearance. Some will
   think
Your fortune could not yield a deeper sound,
Than mixed with Drusus; but, when they
   shall hear
That, and the thunder of Sejanus meet,
Sejanus, whose high name doth strike the
   stars,
And rings about the concave; great Sejanus,
Whose glories, style, and titles are himself,
The often iterating of Sejanus:
They then will lose their thoughts, and be
   ashamed
To take acquaintance of them.

        Re-enter Sejanus.

   Sej. I must make
A rude departure, lady; Cæsar sends
With all his haste both of command and
   prayer.
Be resolute in our plot; you have my soul,
As certain yours as it is my body's.
And, wise physician,† so prepare the poison,
As you may lay the subtile operation
Upon some natural disease of his:
Your eunuch send to me. I kiss your hands,
Glory of ladies, and commend my love
To your best faith and memory.
   Liv. My lord,
I shall but change your words. Farewell.
   Yet, this
Remember for your heed, he loves you not;
You know what I have told you; his designs
Are full of grudge and danger; we must use
More than a common speed.
   Sej. Excellent lady,
How you do fire my blood!
   Liv. Well, you must go?
The thoughts be best, are least set forth to
   show: *[Exit Sejanus.*
   Eud. When will you take some physic,
   lady?

   Liv. When
I shall, Eudemus: but let Drusus' drug
Be first prepared.
   Eud. Were Lygdus made,[2] that's done;
I have it ready. And to-morrow morning
I'll send you a perfume, first to resolve
And procure sweat, and then prepare a
   bath
To cleanse and clear the cutis; against
   when
I'll have an excellent new fucus made,
Resistive 'gainst the sun, the rain, or wind,
Which you shall lay on with a breath, or
   oil,
As you best like, and last some fourteen
   hours.
This change came timely, lady, for your
   health,
And the restoring your complexion,
Which Drusus' choler had almost burnt up;
Wherein your fortune hath prescribed you
   better
Than art could do.
   Liv. Thanks, good physician,
I'll use my fortune, you shall see, with re-
   verence.
Is my coach ready?
   Eud. It attends your highness.
                   [Exeunt.

   SCENE II.—*An Apartment in the
            Palace.*

        Enter Sejanus.

If this be not revenge, when I have done
And made it perfect, let Egyptian slaves,‡
Parthians, and barefoot Hebrews brand my
   face,
And print my body full of injuries.
Thou lost thyself, child Drusus, when thou
   thoughtst
Thou couldst outskip my vengeance, or
   outstand
The power I had to crush thee into air.
Thy follies now shall taste what kind of
   man
They have provoked, and this thy father's
   house
Crack in the flame of my incensed rage,
Whose fury shall admit no shame or
   mean.—
Adultery! it is the lightest ill
I will commit. A race of wicked acts

   An act without *your sex:*] i.e., an act beyond the weakness or fears of your sex.
                      WHAL.
   [2] *Were Lygdus* made, &c.] i.e., prepared for
the business. See p. 54 a.

   * *Leg. Tacit. Ann.* Lib. iv. p. 76.
   † *Tacit. ibid. et Dion. Rom. Hist.* Lib. lvii.
p. 709.
   ‡ *Hi apud Romanos barbari et vilissimi esti-
mab. Juv. Mart. &c.*

Shall flow out of my anger, and o'erspread
The world's wide face, which no posterity[1]
Shall e'er approve, nor yet keep silent :
    things
That for their cunning, close, and cruel
    mark,
Thy father would wish his, and shall, per-
    haps,
Carry the empty name, but we the prize.
On, then, my soul, and start not in thy
    course ;
Though heaven drop sulphur, and hell
    belch out fire,
Laugh at the idle terrors : tell proud Jove,
Between his power and thine there is no
    odds :
'Twas only fear first in the world made
    gods.*

Enter Tiberius *attended.*

Tib. Is yet Sejanus come?
Sej. He's here, dread Cæsar.
Tib. Let all depart that chamber, and
    the next.   [*Exeunt* Attendants.
Sit down, my comfort.† When the master
    prince
Of all the world, Sejanus, saith he fears,
Is it not fatal?
Sej. Yes, to those are feared.
Tib. And not to him ?
Sej. Not if he wisely turn
That part of fate he holdeth, first on them.
Tib. That nature, blood, and laws of
    kind forbid.
Sej. Do policy and state forbid it ?
Tib. No.
Sej. The rest of poor respects, then let
    go by ;
State is enough to make the act just, them
    guilty.
Tib. Long hate pursues such acts.
Sej. Whom hatred frights,
Let him not dream of sovereignty.

Tib. Are rites
Of faith, love, piety, to be trod down
Forgotten, and made vain ?
Sej. All for a crown.
The prince who shames a tyrant's name to
    bear,
Shall never dare do anything but fear ;
All the command of sceptres quite doth
    perish,
If it begin religious thoughts to cherish :
Whole empires fall, swayed by those nice
    respects ;
It is the licence of dark deeds protects
Even states most hated, when no laws
    resist
The sword, but that it acteth what it list.
Tib. Yet so, we may do all things cruelly,
Not safely.
Sej. Yes, and do them thoroughly.
Tib. Knows yet Sejanus whom we point
    at ?
Sej. Ay,
Or else my thought, my sense, or both do
    err :
'Tis Agrippina.‡
Tib. She, and her proud race.
Sej. Proud ! dangerous,§ Cæsar : for in
    them apace
The father's spirit shoots up. Germanicus‖
Lives in their looks, their gait, their form,
    t' upbraid us
With his close death, if not revenge the
    same.
Tib. The act's not known.
Sej. Not proved ; but whispering Fame
Knowledge and proof doth to the jealous
    give,
Who, than to fail, would their own thought
    believe.[2]
It is not safe, the children draw long breath,
That are provoked by a parent's death.
Tib. It is as dangerous to make them
    hence,
If nothing but their birth be their offence.

---

[1]   *Which no posterity*
    Shall e'er approve, nor yet keep silent :]
This sentiment, with what precedes and follows
it, is from the *Thyestes* of Seneca :

" *Age, anime, fac quod nulla posteritas probet,*
    Sed nulla taceat : aliquod audendum est
        nefas
    Atrox, cruentum ; tale quod frater meus
    Suum esse malit," act ii. v. 192.—WHAL.

[2] *Who, than to fail, would their own thought
believe.*] i.e., who, rather than fail of proof,
would believe the mere evidence of their own
thoughts. Jonson affects great brevity in his

expression, and, in consequence of that, is not
always so clear as he might be.—WHAL.

---

    * *Idem, et Petro. Arbiter, Sat. et Statius,*
Lib. iii.
    † *De hac consultatione, vid. Suet. Tib.* c. 55.
    ‡ *De Agrip. vid. Dio. Rom. Hist.* Lib. lvii. p. 69.
    § *De Sejani consil. in Agrip. leg. Tacit.
Ann.* Lib. i. p. 23, *et* Lib. iv. p. 77-79, *de
Tib. susp.* Lib. iii. p. 52.
    ‖ *Gnaris omnibus lætam Tiberio Germanici
mortem male dissimulari. Tacit.* Lib. iii. *ibid.
Huc confer Tacit. narrat. de morte Pisonis,*
p. 55, *et* Lib. iv. p. 74. *Germanici mortem inter
prospera ducebat.*

Sej. Stay, till they strike at Cæsar; then
  their crime
Will be enough; but late and out of time
For him to punish.
  Tib. Do they purpose it?
  Sej. You know, sir, thunder speaks not
  till it hit.
Be not secure; none swiftlier are opprest,
Than they whom confidence betrays to
  rest.
Let not your daring make your danger
  such:
All power is to be feared, where 'tis too
  much.
The youths are of themselves hot, violent,
Full of great thought; and that male-
  spirited dame,*
Their mother, slacks no means to put them
  on,
By large allowance, popular presentings,
Increase of train and state, suing for titles;
Hath them commended with like prayers,†
  like vows,
To the same gods, with Cæsar: days and
  nights
She spends in banquets and ambitious
  feasts
For the nobility; where Caius Silius,
Titius Sabinus, old Arruntius,
Asinius Gallus, Furnius, Regulus,
And others of that discontented list,
Are the prime guests. There, and to these,
  she tells
Whose niece she was,‡ whose daughter,
  and whose wife.
And then must they compare her with
  Augusta,
Ay, and prefer her too; commend her form,
Extol her§ fruitfulness, at which a shower
Falls for the memory of Germanicus.
Which they blow over straight with windy
  praise
And puffing hopes of her aspiring sons;
Who, with these hourly ticklings, grow so
  pleased,
And wantonly conceited of themselves,
As now they stick not to believe they're
  such
As these do give them out; and would be
  thought

More than competitors, immediate heirs.
Whilst to their thirst of rule, they win the
  rout
(That's still the friend of novelty),‖ with
  hope
Of future freedom, which on every change
That greedily, though emptily expects.
Cæsar, 'tis age in all things breeds neglects,
And princes that will keep old dignity
Must not admit too youthful heirs stand
  by;
Not their own issue; but so darkly set
As shadows are in picture, to give height
And lustre to themselves.
  Tib. We will command¶
Their rank thoughts down, and with a
  stricter hand
Than we have yet put forth; their trains
  must bate,
Their titles, feasts, and factions.
  Sej. Or your state.
But how, sir, will you work?
  Tib. Confine them.
  Sej. No.
They are too great, and that too faint a
  blow
To give them now; it would have served
  at first,
When with the weakest touch their knot
  had burst.
But now, your care must be, not to detect
The smallest cord, or line of your suspect;
For such, who know the weight of princes'
  fear,
Will, when they find themselves discovered,
  rear
Their forces, like seen snakes, that else
  would lie
Rolled in their circles, close: nought is
  more high,
Daring, or desperate, than offenders
  found;
Where guilt is,[1] rage and courage both
  abound.
The course must be, to let them still swell
  up,
Riot, and surfeit on blind fortune's cup;
Give them more place, more dignities,
  more style,
Call them to court, to senate; in the while,

---

[1] *Where guilt is, &c.*]
  "*Nihil est audacius illis*
Deprensis: iram et animos a crimine sumunt."
——————————— Juv. Sat. vi.

* *De anim. virili Agrip. cons. Tacit. Ann.*
Lib. i. p. 12 *et* 22. Lib. ii. p. 47.
† *Tacit. Ann.* Lib. iv. p. 79.
‡ *Erat enim neptis Augusti, Agrippæ et*
  VOL. I.

Juliæ filia, Germanici uxor. Suet. Aug.
c. 64.
§ *De fæcund. ejus. vid. Tacit. Ann.* Lib. ii.
p. 39, *et* Lib. iv. p. 77.
‖ *Displicere regnantibus civilia filiorum
ingenia: neque ob aliud interceptos quam quia
Pop. Rom. æquo jure complecti, reddita liber-
tate, agitaverint. Nat. Tacit.* Lib. ii. *Ann.* p. 49
¶ *Vid. Suet. Tib.* c. 54.

Take from their strength some one or
    twain or more,
Of the main fautors, (it will fright the store,)
And, by some by-occasion. Thus, with
    slight
You shall disarm them first ; and they, in
    night
Of their ambition, not perceive the train,
Till in the engine they are caught and slain.
  Tib. We would not kill, if we knew how
    to save ;
Yet, than a throne, 'tis cheaper give a grave.
Is there no way to bind them by deserts ?
  Sej. Sir, wolves do change their hair, but
    not their hearts.
While thus your thought unto a mean is
    tied,
You neither dare enough, nor do provide.
All modesty is fond, and chiefly where
The subject is no less compelled to bear,
Than praise his sovereign's acts.
  Tib. We can no longer*
Keep on our mask to thee, our dear
    Sejanus ;
Thy thoughts are ours, in all, and we but
    proved
Their voice, in our designs, which by
    assenting
Hath more confirmed us, than if hearten-
    ing Jove
Had, from his hundred statues, bid us
    strike,
And at the stroke clicked all his marble
    thumbs.†
But who shall first be struck ?
  Sej. First, Caius Silius ;
He is the most of mark, and most of
    danger :
In power and reputation equal strong,
Having commanded‡ an imperial army
Seven years together, vanquished Sacrovir
In Germany, and thence obtained to wear
The ornaments triumphal. His steep fall,
By how much it doth give the weightier
    crack,
Will send more wounding terror to the rest,
Command them stand aloof, and give more
    way
To our surprising of the principal.

  Tib. But what,§ Sabinus?
  Sej. Let him grow awhile,
His fate is not yet ripe : we must not pluck
At all together, lest we catch ourselves.
And there's Arruntius too, he only talks.
But Sosia,‖ Silius' wife, would be wound in
Now, for she hath a fury in her breast,
More than hell ever knew ; and would be
    sent
Thither in time. Then is there one Cremu-
    tius¶
Cordus, a writing fellow, they have got
To gather notes of the precedent times,
And make them into Annals ; a most tart
And bitter spirit, I hear : who, under colour
Of praising those, doth tax the present
    state,
Censures the men, the actions, leaves no
    trick,
No practice unexamined, parallels
The times, the governments ; a profest
    champion
For the old liberty——
  Tib. A perishing wretch !
As if there were that chaos bred in things,
That laws and liberty would not rather
    choose
To be quite broken, and ta'en hence by us,
Than have the stain to be preserved by
    such.
Have we the means to make these guilty
    first ?
  Sej. Trust that to me : let Cæsar, by his
    power,
But cause a formal meeting of the senate,
I will have matter and accusers ready.
  Tib. But how ? let us consult.
  Sej. We shall misspend
The time of action. Counsels are unfit
In business, where all rest is more perni-
    cious
Than rashness can be. Acts of this close
    kind
Thrive more by execution than advice.
There is no lingering in that work begun,
Which cannot praised be, until through
    done.
  Tib. Our edict shall forthwith command
    a court.**

---

  * *Tiberium variis artibus devinxit adeo Sejanus, ut obscurum adversum alios, sibi uni incautum, intectumque efficeret. Tacit. Ann.* Lib. iv. p. 74. *Vid. Dio. Hist. Rom.* Lib. lvii. p. 707.
  † *Premere pollicem, apud Romanos, maximi favoris erat signum. Horat. Epist. ad Lollium. Fautor utroque horum laudabit pollice ludum. Et Plin. Nat. Hist.* Lib. xxviii. cap. 2. *Pollices, cum faveamus, premere etiam proverbio jubemur. De interp. loci, vid. Aug. Pol. Miscell.* cap. xlii. *et Turn. Adver.* Lib. xi. cap. 6.
  ‡ *Tacit. Lib. Ann.* iii. p. 63, *et* Lib. iv. p. 79.
  § *Tacit. ibid.*   ‖ *Tacit. ibid.*
  ¶ *Vid. Tacit. Ann.* Lib. iv. p. 83. *Dio. Hist. Rom.* Lib. lvii. p. 710, *et Sen. Cons. ad Marc.* cap. 1, *et fusius,* cap. 22.
  ** *Edicto ut plurimum Senatores in curiam vocatos constat. Tacit. Ann.* Lib. i. p. 3.

While I can live, I will prevent earth's fury:
'Εμοῦ θανόντος γαῖα μιχθήτω πυρί.*   [*Exit.*

Enter Julius Posthumus.

Pos. My lord Sejanus——
Sej. Juliust Posthumus !
Come with my wish ! What news from
    Agrippina's ?
Pos. Faith, none. They all lock up them-
    selves a' late,
Or talk in character ; I have not seen
A company so changed.   Except they had
Intelligence by augury of our practice.
Sej. When were you there ?
Pos. Last night.
Sej. And what guests found you ?
Pos. Sabinus, Silius, the old list, Ar-
    runtius,
Furnius, and Gallus.
Sej. Would not these talk ?
Pos. Little.
And yet we offered choice of argument.
Satrius was with me.
Sej. Well : 'tis guilt enough
Their often meeting.   You forgot to extol‡
The hospitable lady ?
Pos. No ; that trick
Was well put home, and had succeeded
    too,
But that Sabinus coughed a caution out ;
For she began to swell.
Sej. And may she burst !
Julius, I would have you go instantly
Unto the palace of the great Augusta,
And, by your§ kindest friend, get swift
    access ;
Acquaint her with these meetings : tell the
    words‖
You brought me the other day, of Silius,
Add somewhat to them.   Make her under-
    stand
The danger of Sabinus, and the times,
Out of his closeness. Give Arruntius' words
Of malice against Cæsar ; so, to Gallus ;
But, above all, to Agrippina.   Say,
As you may truly, that her infinite pride, ¶
Propt with the hopes of her too fruitful
    womb,
With popular studies gapes for sovereignty,

And threatens Cæsar.   Pray Augusta then,
That for her own, great Cæsar's, and the
    pub-
Lic safety, she be pleased to urge these
    dangers.
Cæsar is too secure, he must be told,
And best he'll take it from a mother's
    tongue.
Alas ! what is't for us to sound, to explore,
To watch, oppose, plot, practise, or pre-
    vent,
If he, for whom it is so strongly laboured,
Shall, out of greatness and free spirit, be
Supinely negligent ? our city's now**
Divided as in time o' the civil war,
And men forbear not to declare them-
    selves
Of Agrippina's party.   Every day
The faction multiplies ; and will do more,
If not resisted : you can best enlarge it,
As you find audience.   Noble Posthumus,
Commend me to your Prisca : and pray
    her,
She will solicit this great business,
To earnest and most present execution,
With all her utmost credit with Augusta.
Pos. I shall not fail in my instructions.
                                         [*Exit.*
Sej. This second, from his mother, will
    well urge
Our late design, and spur on Cæsar's rage ;
Which else might grow remiss.   The way
    to put
A prince in blood, is to present the shapes
Of dangers greater than they are, like late
Or early shadows ; and, sometimes, to
    feign
Where there are none, only to make him
    fear ;
His fear will make him cruel : and once
    entered,
He doth not easily learn to stop, or spare
Where he may doubt.   This have I made
    my rule,
To thrust Tiberius into tyranny,
And make him toil, to turn aside those
    blocks,
Which I alone could not remove with
    safety.
Drusus once gone, Germanicus' three sons††

---

* *Vulgaris quidam versus, quem sæpe Tiber.
recitasse memoratur.   Dion. Hist. Rom. Lib.
lviii. p. 729.*—[Equivalent to *Après moi le dé-
luge.*—F. C.]
    † *De Julio Posthumo, vid. Tacit. Ann.
Lib. iv. p. 77.*
    ‡ *Proximi Agrip. inliciebantur pravis ser-
monibus tumidos spiritus perstimulare. Tacit.
ibid.*

§ *Mutilia Prisca, quæ in animum Augustæ
valida.   Tacit. ibid.*
    ‖ *Verba Silii inmodice jactata, vid. apud
Tac. Ann. Lib. iv. p. 79.*
    ¶ *Tacit. Ann. Lib. iv. p. 77.*
    ** *Hæc apud Tacit. leg. Ann. Lib. iv. p. 79.*
    †† *Quorum non dubia successio, neque spargi
venenum in tres poterat, &c. vid. Tacit. Ann.
Lib. iv. p. 77.*

Would clog my way; whose guards have
    too much faith
To be corrupted: and their mother known
Of too too unreproved a chastity,
To be attempted, as light Livia was.
Work then, my art, on Cæsar's fears, as
    they
On those they fear, till all my lets be
    cleared,
And he in ruins of his house, and hate
Of all his subjects, bury his own state;
When with my peace, and safety, I will rise,
By making him the public sacrifice.
                          [Exit.

SCENE III.—*A Room in* Agrippina's *House.*

Enter Satrius *and* Natta.

Sat. They're grown exceeding circum-
    spect, and wary.
Nat. They have us in the wind: and yet
    Arruntius
Cannot contain himself.
Sat. Tut, he's not yet
Looked after; there are others more de-
    sired,*
That are more silent.
Nat. Here he comes. Away.
                          [Exeunt.

Enter Sabinus, Arruntius, *and* Cordus.

Sab. How is it, that these beagles haunt
    the house
Of Agrippina?
Arr. O, they hunt,† they hunt!
There is some game here lodged, which
    they must rouse,
To make the great ones sport.
Cor. Did you observe
How they inveighed 'gainst Cæsar?
Arr. Ay, baits, baits,
For us to bite at: would I have my flesh
Torn by the public hook, these qualified
    hangmen
Should be my company.
Cor. Here comes another.
    [Dom. Afer *passes over the stage.*
Arr. Ay, there's a man,‡ Afer the orator!
One that hath phrases, figures, and fine
    flowers,

To strew his rhetoric with,§ and doth make
    haste,
To get him note, or name by any offer
Where blood or gain be objects; steeps his
    words,
When he would kill, in artificial tears:
The crocodile of Tyber! him I love,
That man is mine; he hath my heart and
    voice
When I would curse! he, he.
Sab. Contemn the slaves,
Their present lives will be their future
    graves.   *[Exeunt.*

SCENE IV.—*Another Apartment in the same.*

Enter Silius, Agrippina, Nero, *and* Sosia.

Sil. May't please your highness not for-
    get yourself;
I dare not, with my manners, to attempt
Your trouble farther.
Agr. Farewell, noble Silius!
Sil. Most royal princess.
Agr. Sosia stays with us?
Sil. She is your servant, and doth owe
    your grace
An honest, but unprofitable love.
Agr. How can that be, when there's no
    gain but virtue's?
Sil. You take the moral, not the politic
    sense.
I meant, as she is bold, and free of speech,
Earnest‖ to utter what her zealous thought
Travails withal, in honour of your house;
Which act, as it is simply born in her,
Partakes of love and honesty; but may,
By the over-often, and unseasoned use,
Turn to your loss and danger:¶ for your
    state
Is waited on by envies, as by eyes;
And every second guest your tables take
Is a fee'd spy, to observe who goes, who
    comes;
What conference you have, with whom,
    where, when,
What the discourse is, what the looks, the
    thoughts
Of every person there, they do extract,
And make into a substance.
Agr. Hear me, Silius.

---

* *Silius, Sabinus, de quibus supra.*
† *Tib. tempor. delatores genus hominum publico exitio repertum, et pœnis quidem nunquam satis coërcitum, per præmia eliciebantur. Tac. Ann.* Lib. iv. p. 82.
‡ *De Domit. Af. vid. Tac. Ann.* Lib. iv. p. 89-93.

§ *Quoquo facinore properus clarescere. Tacit. ibid. Et infra. prosperiore eloquentiæ quam morum famâ fuit. Et p.* 93. *diu egens, et parto nuper præmio male usus, plura ad flagitia accingeretur.*
‖ *Vid. Tac. Ann.* Lib. iv. p. 79.
¶ *Ibid.* p. 77.

Were all Tiberius' body stuck with eyes,
And every wall and hanging in my house
Transparent, as this lawn I wear, or air;
Yea, had Sejanus both his ears as long
As to my inmost closet, I would have
To whisper any thought, or change an
    act,
To be made Juno's rival.   Virtue's forces
Shew ever noblest in conspicuous courses.
    Sil. 'Tis great, and bravely spoken, like
        the spirit
Of Agrippina: yet, your highness knows,
There is nor loss nor shame in provi-
    dence;
Few can, what all should do, beware
    enough.
You may perceive* with what officious
    face,
Satrius, and Natta, Afer, and the rest
Visit your house, of late, to enquire the
    secrets;
And with what bold and privileged art,
    they rail
Against Augusta, yea, and at Tiberius;
Tell tricks of Livia, and Sejanus; all
To excite, and call your indignation on,
That they might hear it at more liberty.
    Agr. You're too suspicious, Silius.
    Sil. Pray the gods,
I be so, Agrippina; but I fear
Some subtile practice.† They that durst
    to strike
At so examples, and unblamed a life,[1]
As that of the renowned Germanicus,
Will not sit down with that exploit alone:
He threatens many that hath injured
    one.[2]
    Nero. 'Twere best rip forth their tongues,
        sear out their eyes,
When next they come.
    Sos. A fit reward for spies.

Enter Drusus jun.

    Dru. jun. Hear you the rumour?
    Agr. What?

    Dru. jun. Drusus is dying.‡
    Agr. Dying!
    Nero. That's strange!
    Agr. You were with him yesternight.
    Dru. jun. One met Eudemus the phy-
        sician,
Sent for, but now; who thinks he cannot
    live.
    Sil. Thinks! if it be arrived at that, he
        knows,
Or none.
    Agr. 'Tis quick! what should be his
        disease?
    Sil. Poison, poison——
    Agr. How, Silius!
    Nero. What's that?
    Sil. Nay, nothing.   There was late a
        certain blow
Given o' the face.
    Nero. Ay, to Sejanus.
    Sil. True.
    Dru. jun. And what of that?
    Sil. I'm glad I gave it not.
    Nero. But there is somewhat else?
    Sil. Yes, private meetings,
With a great lady—at a physician's,
And a wife turned away.
    Nero. Ha!
    Sil. Toys, mere toys:
What wisdom's now in th' streets, in the
    common mouth?
    Dru. jun. Fears, whisperings, tumults,
        noise, I know not what:
They say the Senate sit.§
    Sil. I'll thither straight;
And see what's in the forge.
    Agr. Good Silius, do;
Sosia and I will in.
    Sil. Haste you, my lords,
To visit the sick prince; tender your
    loves,
And sorrows to the people.   This Se-
    janus,
Trust my divining soul, hath plots on all:
No tree, that stops his prospect, but must
    fall.   [*Exeunt.*

---

[1] *At so* examples, *and unblamed a life.*] At
a life that had no parallel; was beyond all example, or imitation. *Examples* is a term of
the author's coining: and by the same poetical
prerogative, Chapman, in his verses on this
tragedy, uses the word *exampling.*

"Our Phœbus may with his exampling beams."
                                    WHAL.

[2] *He threatens many that hath injured one.*]

"*Multis minatur, qui uni facit injuriam.*"
                              PUB. SYRUS.

In this fulness and frequency of sentence, as he
calls it in his preface, Jonson placeth one part of
the office of a tragic poet: and the learned reader
will perceive, from the brevity and number of
these maxims, that instead of copying after the
models of ancient Greece, he hath conformed to
the practice of Seneca the tragedian.—WHAL.

* *Tacit. ibid. et* pp. 90 *et* 92.
† *Suet. Tib.* c. 2, *Dion. Rom. Hist.* Lib. lvii
p. 705.
‡ *Tac. Ann.* Lib. iv. pp. 74, 75, 76, 77.
§ *Vid. Tac. Ann.* Lib. iv. p. 76.

ACT III.

SCENE I.—*The Senate House.*

Enter Præcones, Lictores, Sejanus, Varro, Latiaris, Cotta, *and* Afer.

Sej. 'Tis only* you must urge against him, Varro ;
Nor I, nor Cæsar may appear therein,
Except in your defence, who are the consul;
And, under colour of late enmity
Between your father and his, may better do it,
As free from all suspicion of a practice.
Here be your notes, what points to touch at ; read:
Be cunning in them. Afer has them too.
Var. But is he summoned?
Sej. No. It was debated
By Cæsar, and concluded as most fit
To take him unprepared.
Afer. And prosecute
All under name of treason.†
Var. I conceive.

Enter Sabinus, Gallus, Lepidus, *and* Arruntius.

Sab. Drusus being dead, Cæsar will not be here.
Gal. What should the business of this senate be?
Arr. That can my subtle whisperers tell you: we
That are the good-dull-noble lookers on,
Are only called to keep the marble warm.
What should we do with those deep mysteries,
Proper to these fine heads? let them alone.
Our ignorance may, perchance, help us be saved
From whips and furies.
Gal. See, see, see their action!
Arr. Ay, now their heads do travail, now they work;
Their faces run like shittles; they are weaving
Some curious cobweb to catch flies.
Sab. Observe,
They take their places.

Arr. What,‡ so low !
Gal. O yes,
They must be seen to flatter Cæsar's grief,
Though but in sitting.
Var. Bid us silence.
Præ. Silence !
Var. " Fathers conscript,§ may this our present meeting
Turn fair, and fortunate to the commonwealth !"

Enter Silius, *and other* Senators.

Sej. See, Silius enters.
Sil. Hail, grave fathers !
Lic. Stand.
Silius, forbear thy place.
Sen. How !
Præ. Silius, stand forth,
The consul hath to charge thee.
Lic. Room for Cæsar.
Arr. Is he come too ! nay then expect a trick.
Sab. Silius accused ! sure he will answer nobly.

Enter Tiberius *attended.*

Tib. We stand amazed, fathers, to behold
This general dejection. Wherefore sit
Rome's consuls thus dissolved,‖ as they had lost
All the remembrance both of style and place?
It not becomes. No woes are of fit weight,
To make the honour of the empire stoop:
Though I, in my peculiar self may meet
Just reprehension, that so suddenly,
And, in so fresh a grief, would greet the senate,
When private tongues, of kinsmen and allies,
Inspired with comforts, lothly are endured,
The face of men not seen, and scarce the day,
To thousands that communicate our loss.[1]
Nor can I argue these of weakness; since
They take but natural ways ; yet I must seek

For stronger aids, and those fair helps draw
    out
From warm embraces of the common-
    wealth.
Our mother, great Augusta, 's struck with
    time,
Our self imprest with aged characters,
Drusus is gone, his children young and
    babes;
Our aims must now reflect on those that
    may
Give timely succour to these present ills,
And are our only glad-surviving hopes,
The noble issue of Germanicus,
Nero and Drusus: might it please the
    consul
Honour them in, they both attend without.
I would present them to the senate's care,
And raise those suns of joy that should
    drink up[1]
These floods of sorrow in your drowned
    eyes.
    Arr. By Jove, I am not Œdipus enough
To understand this Sphinx.
    Sab. The princes come.

    Enter Nero *and* Drusus *junior.*

    Tib. Approach you, noble Nero, noble
    Drusus.
These princes, fathers, when their parent
    died,
I gave unto their uncle, with this prayer,
That though he had proper issue of his
    own,
He would no less bring up, and foster
    these,
Than that self-blood; and by that act con-
    firm
Their worths to him, and to posterity.
Drusus ta'en hence, I turn my prayers to
    you,
And 'fore our country and our gods, be-
    seech
You take, and rule Augustus' nephew's
    sons,
Sprung of the noblest ancestors; and so
Accomplish both my duty, and your own.
Nero, and Drusus, these shall be to you

In place of parents, these your fathers,
    these;
And not unfitly: for you are so born,
As all your good, or ill's the common-
    wealth's.
Receive them, you strong guardians; and
    blest gods,
Make all their actions answer to their
    bloods:
Let their great titles find increase by them,
Not they by titles. Set them, as in place,
So in example, above all the Romans:
And may they know no rivals but them-
    selves.[2]
Let Fortune give them nothing; but attend
Upon their virtue: and that still come forth
Greater than hope, and better than their
    fame.
Relieve me, fathers, with your general
    voice.
    Senators. "May all the gods consent to
    Cæsar's wish,
And add to any honours that may crown
The hopeful issue of Germanicus!"
    Tib. We thank you, reverend fathers, in
    their right.
    Arr. If this were true now! but the space,
    the space
Between the breast and lips — Tiberius'
    heart
Lies a thought farther than another man's.
                                              [*Aside.*
    Tib. My comforts are so flowing in my
    joys,
As, in them, all my streams of grief are lost,
No less than are land waters in the sea,
Or showers in rivers; though their cause
    was such,
As might have sprinkled ev'n the gods with
    tears:
Yet, since the greater doth embrace the
    less,
We covetously obey.
    Arr. Well acted, Cæsar.   [*Aside.*
    Tib. And now I am the happy witness
    made
Of your so much desired affections
To this great issue, I could wish, the Fates
Would here set peaceful period to my days;

---

[1] *And raise those* suns *of joy that should
drink up, &c.*] The quarto reads:

"And raise those *springs* of joy that should *ex-
    haust*," &c.

[2] *And may they know no rivals but themselves.*] In the *Double Falsehood*, brought out
by Mr. Theobald as written by Shakspeare, is
this line:—

"None but himself can be his parallel,"

a mode of expression which drew on him the
ridicule of wits and critics. In vindication of
himself he produced many similar passages from
the classics, &c., and against this verse of Jonson,
in the margin of his copy, he hath written *parallel*,
as an instance of the like kind. I will add
another from the *Dumb Knight*, 1608, act i. sc. 1:

"She is herself, compared with herself,
    For but herself she hath no companion."
                                                WHAL.

However to my labours, I entreat,
And beg it of this senate, some fit ease.
   Arr. Laugh, fathers, laugh:* have you
     no spleens about you?   [*Aside.*
   Tib. The burden is too heavy I sustain
On my unwilling shoulders; and I pray
It may be taken off, and reconferred
Upon the consuls, or some other Roman,
More able, and more worthy.
   Arr. Laugh on still   [*Aside.*
   Sab. Why, this doth render all the rest
     suspected!
   Gal. It poisons all.
   Arr. O, do you taste it then?
   Sab. It takes away my faith to anything
He shall hereafter speak.
   Arr. Ay, to pray that,
Which would be to his head as hot as
     thunder,
'Gainst which he wears that charm,† should
     but the court
Receive him at his word.
   Gal. Hear!
   Tib. For myself
I know my weakness, and so little covet,
Like some gone past, the weight that will
     oppress me,
As my ambition is the counter-point.
   Arr. Finely maintained; good still!
   Sej. But Rome, whose blood,
Whose nerves, whose life, whose very frame
     relies
On Cæsar's strength, no less than heaven
     on Atlas,
Cannot admit it but with general ruin.
   Arr. Ah! are you there to bring him off?
     [*Aside.*
   Sej. Let Cæsar
No more then urge a point so contrary
To Cæsar's greatness, the grieved senate's
    vows,
Or Rome's necessity.
   Gal. He comes about——
   Arr. More nimbly than Vertumnus.
   Tib. For the public,
I may be drawn to shew I can neglect

All private aims, though I affect my rest;
But if the senate still command me serve,
I must be glad to practise my obedience.‡
   Arr. You must and will, sir. We do
     know it.   [*Aside.*
   Senators. "Cæsar,
Live long and happy, great and royal
     Cæsar;
The gods preserve thee and thy modesty,
Thy wisdom and thy innocence!"
   Arr. Where is't?
The prayer is made before the subject.
     [*Aside.*
   Senators. "Guard
His meekness, Jove, his piety, his care,
His bounty——"
   Arr. And his subtilty, I'll put in:
Yet he'll keep that himself, without the gods.
All prayers are vain for him.   [*Aside.*
   Tib. We will not hold
Your patience, fathers, with long answer;
     but
Shall still contend to be what you desire,
And work to satisfy so great a hope.
Proceed to your affairs.
   Arr. Now, Silius, guard thee;
The curtain's drawing. Afer advanceth.
     [*Aside.*

   Præ. Silence!
   Afer. Cite Caius Silius.
   Præ. Caius Silius!
   Sil. Here.
   Afer. The triumph that thou hadst in
     Germany
For thy late victory on Sacrovir,
Thou hast enjoyed so freely, Caius Silius,
As no man it envied thee; nor would
     Cæsar,
Or Rome admit, that thou wert then
     defrauded
Of any honours thy deserts could claim
In the fair service of the common-wealth;
But now, if after all their loves and graces,
(Thy actions, and their courses being
     discovered)
It shall appear to Cæsar and this senate,

---

  * *Tac. Lib. iv. p. 76. Ad vana et toties inrisa revolutus de reddenda Rep. utque consules, seu quis alius regimen susciperent.*
  [It may be added that Jonson is perfectly justified in putting this language into the mouth of Arruntius; as both he and his friend Asinius Gallus, were well known to be hostile to the new order of things, and indeed had been pointed out as determined republicans by Augustus, in one of his last conversations with Tiberius. They had also detected the hypocrisy of the latter, when, on another occasion, he had expressed a wish, as here, to share the burden of the empire with the senate, and bluntly demanded what part he

would choose to take on himself: a question which completely silenced Tiberius, and which, though he openly expressed no displeasure at it, he neither forgot nor forgave.—GIFFORD.]
  † *'Gainst which he wears that charm.*] *Tonitrua præter modum expavescebat; et turbatiore cælo nunquam non coronam lauream capite gestavit, quod fulmine afflari negetur id genus frondis.* Suet. Tib. c. 69. Plin. Nat. Hist. Lib. xv. c. 20.
  ‡ *Semper perplexa et obscura orat. Tib. vid. Tacit. Ann. Lib. i. p. 5.*
  § *Citabatur reus è tribunali voce præconis. vid. Bar. Brisson. Lib. 5, de form.*

Thou hast defiled those glories with thy
   crimes——
  Sil. Crimes !
  Afer. Patience, Silius.
  Sil. Tell thy mule of patience ;
I am a Roman. What are my crimes ?
   proclaim them.
Am I too rich, too honest for the times ?
Have I or treasure, jewels, land, or houses
That some informer gapes for ? is my
   strength
Too much to be admitted, or my know-
   ledge ?
These now are crimes.*
  Afer. Nay, Silius, if the name
Of crime so touch thee, with what impotence
Wilt thou endure the matter to be searched ?
  Sil. I tell thee, Afer, with more scorn
   than fear :
Employ your mercenary tongue and art.
Where's my accuser?
  Var. Here.
  Arr. Varro, the consul !
Is he thrust in ?   [*Aside.*
  Var. 'Tis I accuse thee, Silius.
Against the majesty of Rome, and Cæsar,
I do pronounce thee here a guilty cause,
First of beginning† and occasioning,
Next, drawing out the war in‡ Gallia,
For which thou late triúmph'st ; dissembling
   long
That Sacrovir to be an enemy,
Only to make thy entertainment more.
Whilst thou, and thy wife Sosia, polled the
   province :
Wherein, with sordid, base desire of gain,
Thou hast discredited thy actions' worth,
And been a traitor to the state.
  Sil. Thou liest.
  Arr. I thank thee, Silius, speak so still
   and often.
  Var. If I not prove it, Cæsar,§ but un-
   justly
Have called him into trial ; here I bind
Myself to suffer, what I claim against him;
And yield to have what I have spoke, con-
   firmed
By judgment of the court, and all good men.
  Sil. Cæsar, I crave to have my cause
   deferred,
Till this man's consulship be out.

  Tib. We cannot,
Nor may we grant it.
  Sil. Why ? shall he design
My day of trial ? Is he my accuser,
And must he be my judge ?
  Tib. It hath been usual,
And is a right that custom hath allowed
The magistrate,‖ to call forth private men ;
And to appoint their day : which privilege
We may not in the consul see infringed,
By whose deep watches, and industrious
   care
It is so laboured, as the common-wealth
Receive no loss, by any oblique course.
  Sil. Cæsar, thy fraud is worse than vio-
   lence.
  Tib. Silius, mistake us not, we dare not
   use
The credit of the consul to thy wrong ;
But only do preserve his place and power,
So far as it concerns the dignity
And honour of the state.
  Arr. Believe him, Silius.
  Cot. Why, so he may, Arruntius.
  Arr. I say so.
And he may choose too.
  Tib. By the Capitol,
And all our gods, but that the dear re-
   public,
Our sacred laws, and just authority
Are interessed therein,[1] I should be silent.
  Afer. 'Please Cæsar to give way unto his
   trial,
He shall have justice.
  Sil. Nay, I shall have law;
Shall I not, Afer ? speak.
  Afer. Would you have more ?
  Sil. No, my well-spoken man, I would
   no more ;
Nor less : might I enjoy it natural,
Not taught to speak unto your present
   ends,
Free from thine, his, and all your unkind
   handling,
Furious enforcing, most unjust presuming,
Malicious, and manifold applying,
Foul wresting, and impossible construction.
  Afer. He raves, he raves.
  Sil. Thou durst not tell me so,
Hadst thou not Cæsar's warrant. I can see
Whose power condemns me.

---

[1] *Are* interested *therein,*] i.e., deeply implicated. See Massinger, vol. i. p. 239.

* *Vid. Suet. Tib. Tacit. Dio. Senec.*
† *Tacit.* Lib. iv. p. 79. *Conscientiâ belli,
Sacrovir diu dissimulatus, victoria per avari-
tiam fœdata, et uxor Sosia arguebantur.*
‡ *Bellum Sacrovirianum in Gall. erat.*

Triumph. in Germ. vid. Tacit. Ann. Lib. iii.
p. 63.
§ *Vid. accusandi formulam apud Brisson.*
Lib. v. *de form.*
‖ *Tacit. Ann.* Lib. iv. p. 79. *Adversatus est
Cæsar, solitum quippe magistratibus diem pri-
vatis dicere, nec infringendum Consulis jus,
cujus vigiliis, &c.*

Var. This betrays his spirit:
This doth enough declare him what he is.
Sil. What am I? speak.
Var. An enemy to the state.
Sil. Because I am an enemy to thee,
And such corrupted ministers o' the state,
That here art made a present instrument
To* gratify it with thine own disgrace.
Sej. This, to the consul, is most insolent,
And impious!
Sil. Ay, take part.   Reveal yourselves,
Alas! I scent not your confederacies,
Your plots, and combinations! I not know
Minion Sejanus hates me; and that all
This boast of law, and law, is but a form,
A net of Vulcan's filing, a mere ingine,
To take that life by a pretext of justice,
Which you pursue in malice! I want brain,
Or nostril to persuade me, that your ends
And purposes are made to what they are,
Before my answer! O, you equal gods,
Whose justice not a world of wolf-turned
   men
Shall make me to accuse, howe'er pro-
   voked;
Have I for this so oft engaged myself?
Stood in the heat and fervour of a fight,
When Phœbus sooner hath forsook the day
Than I the field, against the blue-eyed
   Gauls,
And crisped Germans? when our Roman
   eagles
Have fanned the fire with their labouring
   wings,
And no blow dealt, that left not death be-
   hind it?
When I have charged, alone, into the troops
Of curled Sicambrians,† routed them, and
   came
Not off with backward ensigns of a slave;
But forward marks, wounds on my breast
   and face,
Were meant to thee, O Cæsar, and thy
   Rome?
And have I this return! did I, for this,
Perform so noble, and so brave defeat,
On Sacrovir! O Jove, let it become me
To boast my deeds, when he, whom they
   concern,
Shall thus forget them.

Afer. Silius, Silius,
These are the common customs of thy
   blood,
When it is high with wine, as now with
   rage:
This well agrees with that intemperate
   vaunt,
Thou lately mad'st‡ at Agrippina's table,
That, when all other of the troops were
   prone
To fall into rebellion, only thine
Remained in their obedience. Thou wert he
That saved the empire, which had then
   been lost
Had but thy legions there rebelled, or
   mutined;
Thy virtue met, and fronted every peril.
Thou gav'st to Cæsar, and to Rome their
   surety;
Their name, their strength, their spirit, and
   their state,
Their being was a donative from thee.
   Arr. Well worded, and most like an
      orator.
   Tib. Is this true, Silius?
   Sil. Save thy question, Cæsar,
Thy spy of famous credit hath affirmed it.
   Arr. Excellent Roman!
   Sab. He doth answer stoutly.
   Sej. If this be so, there needs no farther
      cause
Of crime against him.
   Var. What can more impeach
The royal dignity and state of Cæsar,
Than to be urged with a benefit
He cannot pay.
   Cot. In this, all Cæsar's fortune
Is made unequal to the courtesy.
   Lat. His means are clean destroyed that
      should require.
   Gal. Nothing is great enough for Silius'
      merit.
   Arr. Gallus on that side too!   [*Aside.*
   Sil. Come, do not hunt,
And labour so about for circumstance,
To make him guilty, whom you have fore-
   doomed:
Take shorter ways, I'll meet your purposes.
The words were mine, and more I now will
   say:

---

* *Tacit. Ann.* Lib. iv. p. 79. *Immissusque
Varro consul qui paternas inimicitias obten-
dens, odiis Sejani per dedecus suum gratifi-
cabatur.*
   † *Populi Germ. hodie Geldri in Belgica sunt
inter Mosam et Rhenum, quos celebrat Mart.
Spect.* 3:
   "*Crinibus in nodum tortis venere Sicambri.*"

[The blue eyes and crisped locks of the Germans, mentioned above, are from Juvenal:

" *Cærula quis stupuit Germani lumina, flavam
   Cæsariem, et madido torquantem cornua
   cirro.*"—Sat. 13, 164.—GIFFORD.]

   ‡ *Tacit. Ann.* Lib. iv. p. 79.

Since I have done thee that great service,
   Cæsar,
Thou still hast feared me; and, in place of
   grace,
Returned me hatred: so soon all best turns,
With doubtful princes, turn deep injuries
In estimation, when they greater rise
Than can be answered. Benefits, with you,
Are of no longer pleasure, than you can
With ease restore them; that transcended
   once,
Your studies are not how to thank, but kill.
It is your nature, to have all men slaves
To you, but you acknowledging to none.
The means that make your greatness, must
   not come
In mention of it; if it do, it takes
So much away, you think: and that which
   helped,
Shall soonest perish, if it stand in eye,
Where it may front, or but upbraid the
   high.
Cot. Suffer him speak no more.
Var. Note but his spirit.
Afer. This shews him in the rest.
Lat. Let him be censured.
Sej. He hath spoke enough to prove him
   Cæsar's foe.
Cot. His thoughts look through his words.
Sej. A censure.
Sil. Stay,
Stay, most officious senate, I shall straight
Delude thy fury. Silius hath not placed
His guards within him, against fortune's
   spite,
So weakly but he can escape your gripe
That are but hands of fortune: she herself,
When virtue doth oppose, must lose her
   threats.
All that can happen in humanity,
The frown of Cæsar, proud Sejanus'
   hatred,
Base Varro's spleen, and Afer's bloodying
   tongue,
The senate's servile flattery, and these
Mustered to kill, I'm fortified against;
And can look down upon: they are beneath
   me.

It is not life whereof I stand enamoured
Nor shall my end make me accuse my
   fate.
The coward and the valiant man must fall,
Only the cause, and manner how, discerns
   them:
Which then are gladdest, when they cost
   us dearest.
Romans, if any here be in this senate,
Would know to mock Tiberius' tyranny,
Look upon Silius, and so learn to die.[1]
               [*Stabs himself.*
Var. O desperate act!
Arr. An honourable hand!
Tib. Look, is he dead?
Sab. 'Twas nobly struck, and home.
Arr. My thought did prompt him to it.
   Farewell, Silius.
Be famous ever for thy great example.
Tib. We are not pleased in this sad
   accident,
That thus hath stalled, and abused our
   mercy,
Intended to preserve thee, noble Roman,
And to prevent thy hopes.
Arr. Excellent wolf!
Now he is full he howls.   [*Aside.*
Sej. Cæsar doth wrong
His dignity and safety thus to mourn
The deserved end of so profest a traitor
And doth, by this his lenity, instruct
Others as factious to the like offence.
Tib. The confiscation merely of his state
Had been enough.
Arr. O, that was gaped for then? [*Aside.*
Var. Remove the body.
Sej. Let citation
Go out for Sosia.
Gal. Let her be proscribed:
And for the goods, I think it fit that half
Go to the treasure, half unto the children.
Lep. With leave of Cæsar, I would think
   that fourth,
The which the law doth cast on the in-
   formers,
Should be enough; the rest go to the chil-
   dren.
Wherein the prince shall shew humanity,

---

[1] *Look upon Silius, and so learn to die.*] *Silius* (says the historian) *imminentem damnationem voluntario fine prævertit.* Ann. l. iv. c. 19. It doth not appear, however, that this happened in the senate-house, or at the immediate time of his accusation: yet the liberty which the poet hath taken is easily allowable. Afer has a part in this transaction not assigned him by Tacitus: but it is given him with the utmost probability, and with the exactest preservation of character. For we may remark, to the honour of Jonson's judgment, that whenever he departs from the thread of the narration, it is always with an improvement of the subject, and upon the strongest grounds of presumption. Thus, by introducing Afer as a manager of the impeachment against Silius, he hath a proper opportunity of displaying the mercenary oratory and art of the informers, prevalent in the reign of Tiberius, which are finely contrasted by the truly honest and spirited replies of Silius.—WHAL.

And bounty; not to force them by their
want,
Which in their parent's trespass they de-
served,
To take ill courses.
   Tib. It shall please us.
   Arr. Ay,
Out of necessity. This Lepidus*
Is grave and honest, and I have observed
A moderation still in all his censures.
   Sab. And bending to the better——Stay,
who's this?

Enter Satrius *and* Natta, *with* Cremutius
Cordus, *guarded.*

Cremutius Cordus! What! is he brought
in?
   Arr. More blood into the banquet!
Noble Cordus,†
I wish thee good: be as thy writings, free
And honest.
   Tib. What is he?
   Sej. For the Annals, Cæsar.
   Præ. Cremutius Cordus!
   Cor. Here.
   Præ. Satrius Secundus,
Pinnarius Natta, you are his accusers.
   Arr. Two of Sejanus' blood-hounds,
whom he breeds
With human flesh, to bay at citizens.
   Afer. Stand forth before the Senate, and
confront him.
   Sat. I do accuse thee here, Cremutius
Cordus,
To be a man factious and dangerous.
A sower of sedition in the state,
A turbulent and discontented spirit,
Which I will prove from thine own writings,
here,
The Annals thou hast published; where
thou bit'st
The present age, and with a viper's tooth,
Being a member of it, dar'st that ill
Which never yet degenerous bastard did
Upon his parent.
   Nat. To this I subscribe;
And, forth a world of more particulars,
Instance in only one: comparing men,
And times, thou praisest Brutus, and af-
firm'st   1
That Cassius was the last of all the
Romans.¹

   Cot. How! what are we then?
   Var. What is Cæsar? nothing?
   Afer. My lords, this strikes at every
Roman's private,
In whom reigns gentry, and estate of spirit,
To have a Brutus brought in parallel,
A parricide, an enemy of his country,
Ranked, and preferred to any real worth
That Rome now holds. This is most
strangely invective,
Most full of spite, and insolent upbraiding.
Nor is 't the time alone is here disprised,
But the whole man of time, yea, Cæsar's
self
Brought in disvalue; and he aimed at most,
By oblique glance of his licentious pen.
Cæsar, if Cassius were the last of Romans,
Thou hast no name.
   Tib. Let's hear him answer. Silence!
   Cor. So innocent I am of fact, my lords,
As but my words are argued: yet those
words
Not reaching either prince or prince's
parent;
The which your law of treason compre-
hends.
Brutus and Cassius I am charged to have
praised;
Whose deeds, when many more, besides
myself,
Have writ, not one hath mentioned without
honour.
Great Titus Livius, great for eloquence,
And faith amongst us, in his History,
With so great praises Pompey did extol,
As oft Augustus called him a Pompeian:
Yet this not hurt their friendship. In his
book
He often names Scipio, Afranius,
Yea, the same Cassius, and this Brutus too,
As worthiest men; not thieves and par-
ricides,
Which notes upon their fames are now
imposed.
Asinius Pollio's writings quite throughout
Give them a noble memory; so‡ Messala
Renowned his general Cassius: yet both
these
Lived with Augustus, full of wealth and
honours.
To Cicero's book, where Cato was heaved
up

---

¹   *Thou praisest Brutus, and affirm'st*
    That Cassius was the last of all the
Romans.] *Objectum est historico* (Cremutio
Cordo. Tacit. Ann. l. iv. c. 34) *quod Brutum
Cassiumque ultimos Romanorum dixisset.*
Suet. *Tiber.* c. 61.

* *Tacit. Ann.* Lib. iv. p. 80.

† *Tacit. Ann.* Lib. iv. p. 83, 84. *Dio. Hist.
Rom.* Lib. lvii. p. 710.

‡ *Septem dec. lib. Hist. scripsit. vid. Suid.*
Suet.

Equal with heaven, what else did Cæsar
    answer,[1]
Being then dictator, but with a penned
    oration,
As if before the judges? Do but see
Antonius' letters; read but Brutus' plead-
    ings:
What vile reproach they hold against
    Augustus,
False, I confess, but with much bitterness.
The epigrams of Bibaculus and Catullus
Are read, full stuft with spite of both the
    Cæsars;
Yet deified Julius, and no less Augustus,
Both bore them, and contemned them: I
    not know,
Promptly, to speak it, whether done with
    more
Temper, or wisdom; for such obloquies
If they despised be, they die supprest;
But if with rage acknowledged, they are
    confest.
The Greeks I slip, whose licence not alone,
But also lust did scape unpunished:
Or where some one, by chance, exception
    took,
He words with words revenged. But, in
    my work,
What could be aimed more free, or farther
    off
From the time's scandal, than to write of
    those,
Whom death from grace or hatred had
    exempted?
Did I, with Brutus and with Cassius,
Armed, and possessed of the Philippi fields,
Incense the people in the civil cause,
With dangerous speeches? Or do they,
    being slain
Seventy years since, as by their images,
Which not the conqueror hath defaced,
    appears,
Retain that guilty memory with writers?
Posterity pays every man his honour:
Nor shall there want, though I condemned
    am,
That will not only Cassius well approve,
And of great Brutus' honour mindful be,
But that will also mention make of me.
    Arr. Freely and nobly spoken!
    Sab. With good temper;

I like him, that he is not moved with
    passion.
    Arr. He puts them to their whisper.
    Tib. Take him hence;*
We shall determine of him at next sitting.
              [*Exeunt* Officers *with* Cordus.
    Cot. Mean time, give order, that his
    books be burnt,
To the ædiles.
    Sej. You have well advised.
    After. It fits not such licentious things
    should live
T' upbraid the age.
    Arr. If the age were good, they might.
    Lat. Let them be burnt.
    Gal. All sought, and burnt to-day.
    Præ. The court is up; lictors, resume
    the fasces.
              [*Exeunt all but* Arruntius,
                  Sabinus, *and* Lepidus.
    Arr. Let them be burnt! O, how ridi-
    culous
Appears the senate's brainless diligence,
Who think they can, with present power,
    extinguish
The memory of all succeeding times!
    Sab. 'Tis true; when, contrary, the
    punishment
Of wit, doth make the authority increase.
Nor do they aught, that use this cruelty
Of interdiction, and this rage of burning,
But purchase to themselves rebuke and
    shame,
And to the writers† an eternal name.
    Lep. It is an argument the times are sore,
When virtue cannot safely be advanced;
Nor vice reproved.
    Arr. Ay, noble Lepidus;
Augustus well foresaw what we should suffer
Under Tiberius, when he did pronounce
The Roman race most wretched,‡ that
    should live
Between so slow jaws, and so long a
    bruising.   [*Exeunt.*

SCENE II.—*A Room in the Palace.*

Enter Tiberius *and* Sejanus.

    Tib. This business hath succeeded well,
Sejanus;
And quite removed all jealousy of practice

---

[1] *To Cicero's book, where Cato was heaved up
    Equal with heaven, what else did Cæsar
answer, &c.*] Cicero published an essay upon
the character of Cato; and Cæsar, who perhaps
might be reflected upon in it, wrote an answer,
which he called *Anti-Cato:* both these pieces
are lost.—WHAL.

* *Egressus dein senatu vitam abstinentiâ
finivit. Tacit. ibid. Generosam ejus mortem
vid. apud Sen. Cons. ad Marc. cap.* 22.
† *Manserunt ejus libri occultati et editi.
Tacit. ibid. Scripserat his Cremut. bella civilia,
et res Aug. extantque fragmenta in Suasoriâ
sextâ Senec.*
‡ *Vid. Suet. Tib.* c. 21.

'Gainst Agrippina, and our nephews.
　Now,
We must bethink us how to plant our
　ingines
For th' other pair, Sabinus and Arruntius,
And Gallus* too ; howe'er he flatter us,
His heart we know.
　Sej. Give it some respite, Cæsar.
Time shall mature, and bring to perfect
　crown,
What we, with so good vultures have
　begun :[1]
Sabinus shall be next.
　Tib. Rather Arruntius.
　Sej. By any means, preserve him. His
　frank tongue
Being lent the reins, would take away all
　thought
Of malice, in your course against the rest :
We must keep him to stalk with.[2]
　Tib. Dearest head,
To thy most fortunate design I yield it.
　Sej. Sir,† I have been so long trained up
　in grace,
First with your father, great Augustus ;
　since,
With your most happy bounties so fa-
　miliar ;[3]
As I not sooner would commit my hopes
Or wishes to the Gods, than to your ears.
Nor have I ever yet been covetous
Of over-bright and dazzling honours ;
　rather
To watch and travail in great Cæsar's
　safety,
With the most common soldier.
　Tib. 'Tis confest.
　Sej. The only gain, and which I count
　most fair
Of all my fortunes, is, that mighty Cæsar
Has thought me worthy his alliance.‡
　Hence
Begin my hopes.
　Tib. Umph !
　Sej. I have heard, Augustus,
In the bestowing of his daughter, thought
But even of gentlemen of Rome : if so,—

I know not how to hope so great a favour—
But if a husband should be sought for
　Livia,
And I be had in mind, as Cæsar's friend,
I would but use the glory of the kindred :
It should not make me slothful, or less
　caring
For Cæsar's state ; it were enough to me
It did confirm, and strengthen my weak
　house,
Against the now unequal opposition
Of Agrippina ; and for dear regard
Unto my children, this I wish : myself
Have no ambition farther than to end
My days in service of so dear a master.
　Tib. We cannot but commend thy piety ;
Most loved Sejanus, in acknowledging
Those bounties ; which we, faintly, such
　remember—
But to thy suit. The rest of mortal men,
In all their drifts and counsels, pursue
　profit ;
Princes alone are of a different sort,
Directing their main actions still to fame :
We therefore will take time to think and
　answer.
For Livia she can best, herself, resolve
If she will marry, after Drusus, or
Continue in the family ; besides,
She hath a mother, and a grandam yet,
Whose nearer counsels she may guide
　her by:
But I will simply deal. That enmity
Thou fear'st in Agrippina, would burn
　more,
If Livia's marriage should, as 'twere in
　parts,
Divide the imperial house ; an emulation
Between the women might break forth ;
　and discord
Ruin the sons and nephews on both hands.
What if it cause some present difference ?
Thou art not safe, Sejanus, if thou prove it.
Canst thou believe, that Livia, first the
　wife
To Caius Cæsar,§ then my Drusus, now
Will be contented to grow old with thee,

---

[1] *What we with so* good vultures *have begun :*]
The expression is ambiguous and satirical. The
Roman phrase, *bonis avibus*, signified prosperously, or with a good omen : he uses the word
vultures in reference to the bloodthirsty nature
of the informers, whom he represents as so many
birds of prey.—WHAL.
　Whalley is, I believe, mistaken ; the expression seems rather pedantic than satirical. However, I have retained his note.
　[2] *We must keep him to stalk with.*] i.e., as a
stalking horse, under cover of which we may
securely aim at our game.

[3] *With your most happy bounties, &c.*] the
quarto reads:

" To your most happy bounties so *inured.*"

　The skill and judgment displayed in this
scene, where two mighty artificers of fraud seek
to circumvent each other, are above all praise.

---

* *Vid. Tacit. Ann.* Lib. i. p. 6, Lib. ii. p. 85.
† *Tacit. Ann.* Lib. iv. p. 85.
‡ *Filia ejus Claudii filio desponsa.*
§ *August. neboti et M. Vopsanii Agrippæ
filio ex Julia.*

Born but a private gentleman of Rome,
And raise thee with her loss, if not her
    shame?
Or say that I should wish it, canst thou
    think
The senate, or the people (who have seen
Her brother, father, and our ancestors,
In highest place of empire) will endure it?
The state thou hold'st already, is in talk;
Men murmur at thy greatness; and the
    nobles
Stick not, in public, to upbraid thy climbing
Above our father's favours, or thy scale:
And dare accuse me, from their hate to
    thee.
Be wise, dear friend. We would not hide
    these things,
For friendship's dear respect: nor will we
    stand
Adverse to thine, or Livia's designments.
What we have purposed to thee, in our
    thought,
And with what near degrees of love to
    bind thee,
And make thee equal to us; for the
    present,
We will forbear to speak.   Only, thus
    much
Believe, our loved Sejanus, we not know
That height in blood or honour, which thy
    virtue
And mind to us, may not aspire with
    merit.
And this we'll publish, on all watched
    occasion
The senate or the people shall present.
    Sej. I am restored, and to my sense
    again,
Which I had lost in this so blinding suit.
Cæsar hath taught me better to refuse,
Than I knew how to ask.   How pleaseth*
    Cæsar
T' embrace my late advice for leaving
    Rome?
    Tib. We are resolved.
    Sej. Here are some motives more,
                    [*Gives him a paper.*
Which I have thought on since, may more
    confirm.
    Tib. Careful Sejanus! we will straight
    peruse them:
Go forward in our main design, and
    prosper.   [*Exit.*
    Sej. If those but take, I shall.   Dull,
    heavy Cæsar!
Wouldst thou tell me, thy favours were
    made crimes,
And that my fortunes were esteemed thy
    faults,

That thou for me wert hated, and not
    think
I would with winged haste prevent that
    change,
When thou might'st win all to thyself
    again,
By forfeiture of me? Did those fond
    words
Fly swifter from thy lips, than this my
    brain,
This sparkling forge, created me an ar-
    mour
T' encounter chance and thee? Well, read
    my charms,
And may they lay that hold upon thy
    senses,
As thou hadst snuft up hemlock, or ta'en
    down
The juice of poppy and of mandrakes.
    Sleep,
Voluptuous Cæsar, and security
Seize on thy stupid powers, and leave them
    dead
To public cares; awake but to thy lusts,
The strength of which makes thy libidinous
    soul
Itch to leave Rome! and I have thrust
    it on;
With blaming of the city business,
The multitude of suits, the confluence
Of suitors: then their importunacies,
The manifold distractions he must suffer,
Besides ill-rumours, envies, and reproaches,
All which a quiet and retired life,
Larded with ease and pleasure,† did
    avoid:
And yet for any weighty and great affair,
The fittest place to give the soundest
    counsels.
By this I shall remove him both from
    thought
And knowledge of his own most dear
    affairs;
Draw all dispatches through my private
    hands;
Know his designments, and pursue mine
    own;
Make mine own strengths by giving suits
    and places,
Conferring dignities and offices;
And these that hate me now, wanting
    access
To him, will make their envy none, or less:
For when they see me arbiter of all,
They must observe; or else with Cæsar
    fall.   [*Exit.*

* *Tacit. Ann.* Lib. iv. p. 85, *Dio.* Lib. lviii.
† *Tacit. ibid.*

SCENE III.—*Another Room in the same.*

Enter Tiberius.

Tib. To marry Livia! will no less, Se-
janus,
Content thy aims? no lower object? well!
Thou know'st how thou art wrought into
     our trust;
Woven in our design; and think'st we
     must
Now use thee, whatsoe'er thy projects are:
'Tis true. But yet with caution and fit care.
And, now we better think—who's there
     within?

Enter an Officer.

Off. Cæsar!
Tib. To leave our journey off, were sin
'Gainst our decreed delights; and would
     appear
Doubt; or, what less becomes a prince,
     low fear.
Yet doubt hath law, and fears have their
     excuse,
Where princes' states plead necessary use;
As ours doth now: more in Sejanus' pride,
Than all fell Agrippina's hates beside.
Those are the dreadful enemies, we raise
With favours, and make dangerous with
     praise;
The injured by us may have will alike,
But 'tis the favourite hath the power to
     strike;
And fury ever boils more high and strong,
Heat with ambition, than revenge of wrong.
'Tis then a part of supreme skill, to grace
No man too much; but hold a certain
     space
Between the ascender's rise and thine own
     flat,
Lest, when all rounds be reached, his aim
     be that.
'Tis thought [*Aside*]. Is Macro* in the
     palace? see:
If not, go seek him, to come to us. [*Exit
     Officer.*] He
Must be the organ we must work by now;
Though none less apt for trust: need doth
     allow
What choice would not. I have heard that
     aconite,

Being timely taken, hath a healing might[1]
Against the scorpion's stroke; the proof
     we'll give:
That, while two poisons wrestle, we may
     live.
He hath a spirit too working to be used
But to the encounter of his like; excused
Are wiser sov'reigns then, that raise one ill
Against another, and both safely kill:
The prince that feeds great natures, they
     will sway him;
Who nourisheth a lion, must obey him.—

Re-enter Officer *with* Macro.

Macro, we sent for you.
Mac. I heard so, Cæsar.
Tib. Leave us a while. [*Exit* Officer.]
     When you shall know, good Macro,
The causes of our sending, and the ends,
You will then hearken nearer; and be
     pleased
You stand so high both in our choice and
     trust.
Mac. The humblest place in Cæsar's
     choice or trust,
May make glad Macro proud; without
     ambition,
Save to do Cæsar service.
Tib. Leave your courtings.
We are in purpose, Macro,† to depart
The city for a time, and see Campania;
Not for our pleasures, but to dedicate
A pair of temples, one to Jupiter
At Capua; th' other at Nola,‡ to Augus-
     tus:
In which great work, perhaps our stay will
     be
Beyond our will produced. Now, since we
     are
Not ignorant what danger may be born
Out of our shortest absence in a state
So subject unto envy, and embroiled
With hate and faction; we have thought on
     thee,
Amongst a field of Romans, worthiest
     Macro,
To be our eye and ear: to keep strict
     watch
On Agrippina, Nero, Drusus; ay,
And on Sejanus: not that we distrust
His loyalty, or do repent one grace,

---

1   *I have heard that aconite,
Being timely taken, hath a healing might
Against the scorpion's stroke;] Hoc quoque
tamen in usus humanæ salutis vertere; scor-
pionum ictibus adversari experiendo, datum in
vino calido. Plin. Nat. Hist. l. xxvii. c. 2.—*
WHAL.

* *De Macrone isto, vid. Dio. Rom. Hist.*
Lib. lii. p. 718, *et Tacit. Ann.* Lib. vi. p. 109,
&c.
† *Suet. Tib.* c. 4. *Dio. Rom. Hist.* Lib. lviii.
p. 711.
‡ *Suet. Tib.* c. 43. *Tacit. Ann.* Lib. iv.
p. 91.

Of all that heap we have conferred on
  him ;
For that were to disparage our election,
And call that judgment now in doubt, which
  then
Seemed as unquestioned as an oracle—
But greatness hath his cankers. Worms
  and moths
Breed out of too much humour,[1] in the
  things
Which after they consume, transferring
  quite
The substance of their makers into them-
  selves.
Macro is sharp, and apprehends: besides,
I know him subtle, close, wise, and well
  read
In man, and his large nature; he hath
  studied
Affections, passions, knows their springs,
  their ends,
Which way, and whether they will work:
  'tis proof
Enough of his great merit that we trust him.
Then to a point, because our conference
Cannot be long without suspicion—
Here, Macro, we assign thee both to spy,
Inform, and chastise; think, and use thy
  means,
Thy ministers, what, where, on whom thou
  wilt;
Explore, plot, practise: all thou dost in this
Shall be, as if the senate or the laws
Had given it privilege, and thou thence
  styled
The saviour both of Cæsar and of Rome.
We will not take thy answer but in act:
Whereto, as thou proceed'st, we hope to
  hear
By trusted messengers. If 't be enquired
Wherefore we called you, say you have in
  charge
To see our chariots ready, and our horse.
Be still our loved and, shortly, honoured
  Macro.   [*Exit*.
  Mac. I will not ask why Cæsar bids do
  this;
But joy, that he bids me.* It is the bliss
Of courts to be employed, no matter how;

A prince's power makes all his actions
  virtue.
We, whom he works by, are dumb instru-
  ments,
To do, but not enquire: his great intents
Are to be served, not searched. Yet, as
  that bow
Is most in hand whose owner best doth
  know
To affect his aims; so let that statesman hope
Most use, most price, can hit his prince's
  scope.
Nor must he look at what or whom to
  strike,
But loose at all; each mark must be alike.
Were it to plot against the fame, the life
Of one with whom I twinned; remove a
  wife
From my warm side, as loved as is the air;
Practise away each parent; draw mine heir
In compass, though but one; work all my
  kin
To swift perdition ; leave no untrained
  engin,
For friendship, or for innocence; nay, make
The gods all guilty; I would undertake
This, being imposed me, both with gain
  and ease:
The way to rise is to obey and please.
He that will thrive in state, he must neglect
The trodden paths that truth and right re-
  spect;
And prove new, wilder ways: for virtue there
Is not that narrow thing, she is elsewhere;
Men's fortune there is virtue; reason their
  will;
Their licence, law; and their observance,
  skill.
Occasion is their foil; conscience, their
  stain;
Profit their lustre; and what else is, vain.
If then it be the lust of Cæsar's power,[†]
To have raised Sejanus up, and in an hour
O'erturn him, tumbling down, from height
  of all;
We are his ready engine: and his fall
May be our rise. It is no uncouth thing[2]
To see fresh buildings from old ruins spring.
                         [*Exit*.

---

[1] *Breed out of too much* humour, &c.] This
is agreeable to the notion of equivocal generation received in that age.—WHAL.
[2] *It is no* uncouth *thing, &c.*] i.e., strange,
unknown, unproved. Thus Spenser, *F. Q.*,
B. 1, c. ii. 20:

    " The percing steele there wrought a wound
      full wyde,
    That with the *uncouth* smart the monster
      loudly cryde."
      VOL. I.

And Milton, the constant follower of our poet:

  " And through the palpable obscure find out
    His *uncouth* way."—*Par. Lost*, B. 2, 404.

---

* *De Macrone et ingenio ejus, cons. Tacit.
Ann.* Lib. vi. pp. 114, 115.

† *Vide Dio. Rom. Hist.* Lib. lviii. p. 718, &c.

                                        x

ACT IV.

SCENE I.—*An Apartment in* Agrippina's *House.*

Enter Gallus *and* Agrippina.

Gal. You must have patience,* royal
Agrippina.
Agr. I must have vengeance first; and
that were nectar
Unto my famished spirits. O, my fortune,
Let it be sudden thou prepar'st against me;
Strike all my powers of understanding
blind,
And ignorant of destiny to come!
Let me not fear, that cannot hope.
Gal. Dear princess,
These tyrannies on yourself are worse than
Cæsar's.
Agr. Is this the happiness of being born
great?
Still to be aimed at? still to be suspected?
To live the subject of all jealousies?
At least the colour made, if not the ground
To every painted danger? who would not
Choose once to fall, than thus to hang for
ever?
Gal. You might be safe if you would——
Agr. What, my Gallus!
Be lewd Sejanus' strumpet, or the bawd
To Cæsar's lusts, he now is gone to prac-
tise?
Not these are safe, where nothing is. Your-
self,
While thus you stand but by me, are not
safe.
Was Silius safe? or the good Sosia safe?
Or was my niece, dear Claudia Pulchra,†
safe,
Or innocent Furnius? they that latest have
(By being made guilty) added reputation‡
To Afer's eloquence? O, foolish friends,
Could not so fresh example warn your
loves,
But you must buy my favours with that
loss
Unto yourselves; and when you might per-
ceive
That Cæsar's cause of raging must forsake
him,
Before his will! Away, good Gallus, leave
me.

Here to be seen, is danger; to speak, trea-
son:
To do me least observance, is called fac-
tion.
You are unhappy in me, and I in all.
Where are my sons Nero and Drusus? We
Are they be shot at; let us fall apart;
Not in our ruins, sepulchre our friends,
Or shall we do some action like offence,
To mock their studies that would make us
faulty,
And frustrate practice by preventing it?
The danger's like: for what they can con-
trive,
They will make good. No innocence is
safe,
When power contests: nor can they tres-
pass more,
Whose only being was all crime before.

Enter Nero, Drusus, *and* Caligula.

Ner. You hear Sejanus is come back
from Cæsar?
Gal. No. How? disgraced?
Dru. More graced now than ever.
Gal. By what mischance?
Cal. A fortune like enough
Once to be bad.
Dru. But turned too good to both.
Gal. What was't?
Ner. Tiberius§ sitting at his meat,
In a farm-house they call Spelunca,‖ sited
By the sea-side, among the Fundane hills,
Within a natural cave; part of the grot,
About the entry, fell, and overwhelmed
Some of the waiters; others ran away:
Only Sejanus with his knees, hands, face,
O'erhanging Cæsar, did oppose himself
To the remaining ruins, and was found
In that so labouring posture by the soldiers
That came to succour him. With which
adventure,
He hath¶ so fixed himself in Cæsar's trust,
As thunder cannot move him, and is come
With all the height of Cæsar's praise to
Rome.
Agr. And power to turn those ruins all
on us;
And bury whole posterities beneath them.
Nero, and Drusus, and Caligula,
Your places are the next, and therefore
most

---

* *Agrippina semper atrox, tum et periculo
propinquæ accensa. Tacit. Ann. Lib. iv. p. 89.*
† *Pulchra et Furnius damnat. Tacit. Ann.
ibid.*
‡ *Afer primoribus oratorum additus, divul-
gato ingenio, &c. Tacit. Ann. Lib. iv. p. 89.*

§ *Tacit. Ann. Lib. iv. p. 91.*
‖ *Prætorium Suet. appellat. Tib. c. 39.*
¶ *Præbuitque ipsi materiem cur amicitiæ
constantiæque Sejani magis fideret. Tacit.
Ann. Lib. iv. p. 91.*

In their offence. Think on your birth and
  blood,
Awake your spirits, meet their violence;
'Tis princely when a tyrant doth oppose,
And is a fortune sent to exercise
Your virtue, as the wind doth try strong
  trees,
Who by vexation grow more sound and
  firm.
After your father's fall, and uncle's fate,
What can you hope, but all the change of
  stroke
That force or sleight can give? then stand
  upright;
And though you do not act, yet suffer
  nobly:
Be worthy of my womb, and take strong
  cheer;
What we do know will come, we should
  not fear.   [*Exeunt.*

SCENE II.—*The Street.*

Enter Macro.

Mac. Returned so soon! renewed in
  trust and grace!
Is Cæsar then so weak, or hath the place
But wrought this alteration with the air;
And he, on next remove, will all repair?
Macro, thou art engaged: and what before
Was public; now, must be thy private,
  more.
The weal of Cæsar, fitness did imply;
But thine own fate confers necessity
On thy employment; and the thoughts born
  nearest
Unto ourselves, move swiftest still, and
  dearest.
If he recover, thou art lost; yea, all
The weight of preparation to his fall
Will turn on thee, and crush thee: there-
  fore strike
Before he settle, to prevent the like
Upon thyself. He doth his vantage know,
That makes it home, and gives the fore-
  most blow.   [*Exit.*

SCENE III.—*An Upper Room of* Agrippina's *House.*

Enter Latiaris, Rufus, *and* Opsius.

Lat. It is a service Lord Sejanus* will
See well requited, and accept of nobly.

Here place yourselves between the roof and
  cieling;
And when I bring him to his words of
  danger,
Reveal yourselves, and take him.
  Ruf. Is he come?
  Lat. I'll now go fetch him.   [*Exit.*
  Ops. With good speed.—I long
To merit from the state in such an action.
  Ruf. I hope it will obtain the consulship
For one of us.
  Ops. We cannot think of less,
To bring in one so dangerous as Sabinus.
  Ruf. He was a follower of Germanicus,
And still is an observer of his wife
And children,† though they be declined in
  grace;
A daily visitant, keeps them company
In private and in public, and is noted
To be the only client of the house:
Pray Jove, he will be free to Latiaris.
  Ops. He's allied to him, and doth trust
  him well.
  Ruf. And he'll requite his trust!
  Ops. To do an office
So grateful to the state, I know no man
But would strain nearer bands than kin-
  dred——
  Ruf. List!
I hear them come.
  Ops. Shift to our holes‡ with silence.
                      [*They retire.*

Re-enter Latiaris *with* Sabinus.

Lat. It is a noble constancy you shew
To this afflicted house; that not like others,
The friends of season, you do follow for-
  tune,
And, in the winter of their fate, forsake
The place whose glories warmed you. You
  are just,
And worthy such a princely patron's love,
As was the world's renowned Germanicus,
Whose ample merit when I call to thought,
And see his wife and issue, objects made
To so much envy, jealousy, and hate;
It makes me ready to accuse the gods
Of negligence, as men of tyranny.
  Sab. They must be patient, so must we.
  Lat. O Jove,
What will become of us or of the times,
When, to be high or noble, are made
  crimes,

---

* *Sabinum aggrediuntur cupidine consula-*
tus, ad quem non nisi per Sejanum aditus,
neque Sejani voluntas nisi scelere quærebatur.
Tacit. Lib. iv. p. 94. *Dio. Hist. Rom.* Lib.
lviii. p. 711.

† *Eoque apud bonos laudatus, et gravis*
iniquis. Tacit. Lib. iv. p. 94.
‡ *Haud minus turpi latebrâ quam detestandâ*
fraude, sese abstrudunt; foraminibus et rimis
aurem admovent. Tacit. Ann. Lib. iv. c. 69.

When land and treasure are most dangerous
　　faults?
　　Sab. Nay, when our table, yea our bed,[*]
　　assaults
Our peace and safety? when our writings
　　are,
By any envious instruments, that dare
Apply them to the guilty, made to speak
What they will have to fit their tyrannous
　　wreak?
When ignorance is scarcely innocence;
And knowledge made a capital offence?
When not so much, but the bare empty shade
Of liberty is reft us; and we made
The prey to greedy vultures and vile spies,
That first transfix us with their murdering
　　eyes?
　　Lat. Methinks the genius of the Roman
　　race
Should not be so extinct, but that bright
　　flame
Of liberty might be revived again,
(Which no good man but with his life should
　　lose)
And we not sit like spent and patient fools,
Still puffing in the dark at one poor coal,
Held on by hope till the last spark is out.
The cause is public, and the honour, name,
The immortality of every soul,
That is not bastard or a slave in Rome,
Therein concerned: whereto, if men would
　　change
The wearied arm, and for the weighty shield
So long sustained, employ the facile sword,
We might have soon assurance of our vows.
This ass's fortitude doth tire us all:
It must be active valour must redeem
Our loss, or none. The rock and our hard
　　steel
Should meet to enforce those glorious fires
　　again,
Whose splendour cheered the world, and
　　heat gave life,
No less than doth the sun's.

　　Sab. 'Twere better stay
In lasting darkness, and despair of day.
No ill should force the subject under-
　　take
Against the sovereign, more than hell
　　should make
The gods do wrong. A good man should
　　and must
Sit rather down with loss than rise unjust.
Though, when the Romans first did yield
　　themselves
To one man's power, they did not mean
　　their lives,
Their fortunes and their liberties should be
His absolute spoil, as purchased by the
　　sword.
　　Lat. Why, we are worse, if to be slaves,
　　and bond
To Cæsar's slave, be such, the proud
　　Sejanus!
He that is all, does all, gives Cæsar leave
To hide his ulcerous[†] and anointed face,
With his bald crown at Rhodes,[‡] while he
　　here stalks
Upon the heads of Romans, and their
　　princes,
Familiarly to empire.
　　Sab. Now you touch
A point indeed, wherein he shews his art,
As well as power.
　　Lat. And villainy in both.
Do you observe where Livia lodges? how
Drusus came dead? what men have been
　　cut off?
　　Sab. Yes, those are things removed. I
　　nearer looked
Into his later practice, where he stands
Declared a master in his mystery.
First, ere Tiberius went, he wrought his
　　fear
To think that Agrippina sought his death.
Then put those doubts in her; sent her oft
　　word,
Under the show of friendship, to beware

---

* *Ne nox quidem secura, cum uxor (Neronis)
vigilias, somnos, suspiria matri Liviæ, atque
illa Sejano patefaceret. Tacit. Ann.* Lib. iv.
p. 92.
　† *Facies ulcerosa ac plerumque medicamini-
b::s interstincta. Tacit. Ann.* Lib. iv. p. 91.
　‡ *Tacit. ibid. Et Rhodi secreto, vitare
cœtus, recondere voluptates insuerat.*
　[Whalley observes that Jonson has confounded
two events very distinct in time. The residence
of Tiberius at Rhodes took place during the life
of Augustus, and he was now at Capua, as the
author well knew, and indeed expressly mentions
just below. Either this is one of the inadver-
tencies to which the correctest minds are occasionally subject; or, as I rather think, a line has

dropped out, and been subsequently overlooked.
Perhaps the passage might originally have stood
somewhat in this way:

　　　　　　　"Gives Cæsar leave
　　To hide his ulcerous and anointed face,
　　With his bald crown, *and ply his secret lusts,*
　　As once he did, at Rhodes," *&c.*

Whalley adds that Tacitus, from whom Jonson
derived most of his facts, is prejudiced against
Tiberius. It cannot be denied; but, after full
allowance is made for this, more than enough
will remain to prove that at this period of his
life he was one of the most detestable and dangerous characters with which the old world was
acquainted.—GIFFORD.]

Of Cæsar, for he laid to poison* her:
Drave them to frowns, to mutual jealousies,
Which, now, in visible hatred are burst
    out.
Since, he hath had his hired instruments
To work† on Nero, and to heave him up;
To tell him Cæsar's old, that all the
    people,
Yea, all the army have their eyes on him;
That both do long to have him undertake
Something of worth, to give the world a
    hope;
Bids him to court their grace: the easy
    youth
Perhaps gives ear, which straight he writes
    to Cæsar;
And with this comment: "See yon dan-
    gerous boy;
Note but the practice of the mother, there ;
She's tying him for purposes at hand,
With men of sword." Here's Cæsar put in
    fright
'Gainst son and mother. Yet he leaves
    not thus.
The second brother, Drusus, a fierce
    nature,
And fitter for his snares, because ambi-
    tious
And full of envy, him‡ he clasps and
    hugs,
Poisons with praise, tells him what hearts
    he wears,
How bright he stands in popular expec-
    tance;
That Rome doth suffer with him in the
    wrong
His mother does him, by preferring Nero:
Thus sets he them asunder, each 'gainst
    other,
Projects the course that serves him to con-
    demn,
Keeps in opinion of a friend to all,
And all drives on to ruin.
    Lat. Cæsar sleeps,
And nods at this.
    Sab. Would he might ever sleep,
Bogged in his filthy lusts !
        [Opsius *and* Rufus *rush in.*
    Ops. Treason to Cæsar !
    Ruf. Lay hands upon the traitor,
    Latiaris,
Or take the name thyself.

    Lat. I am for Cæsar.
    Sab. Am I then catched ?
    Ruf. How think you, sir? you are.
    Sab. Spies of this head, so white, so full
    of years !
Well, my most reverend monsters, you may
    live
To see yourselves thus snared.
    Ops. Away with him !
    Lat. Hale him away.
    Ruf. To be a spy for traitors,
Is honourable vigilance.
    Sab. You do well,§
My most officious instruments of state;
Men of all uses: drag me hence, away.
The year is well begun, and I fall fit
To be an offering to Sejanus. Go !
    Ops. Cover him with his garments, hide
    his face.[1]
    Sab. It shall not need. Forbear your
    rude assault.
The fault's not shameful, villainy makes a
    fault.   [*Exeunt.*

    SCENE IV.—*The Street before*
        Agrippina's *House.*

    Enter Macro *and* Caligula.

    Mac. Sir, but observe how thick your
    dangers meet
In his clear drifts ! your mother‖ and your
    brothers,
Now cited to the senate; their friend Gal-
    lus,¶
Feasted to-day by Cæsar, since com-
    mitted !
Sabinus here we meet, hurried to fetters:
The senators all strook with fear and
    silence,
Save those whose hopes depend not on
    good means,
But force their private prey from public
    spoil.
And you must know, if here you stay, your
    state
Is sure to be the subject of his hate,
As now the object.
    Cal. What would you advise me?
    Mac. To go for Capreæ presently; and
    there
Give up yourself entirely to your uncle.

---

[1] *Cover him with his garments,* &c.] Alluding to the form by which a criminal was condemned to death: "*I, lictor, colliga manus,
caput obnubito,*" &c.

* *Tacit. Ann.* Lib. iv. p. 90.

† *Tacit.* Lib. eod. pp. 91, 92.
‡ *Tacit. Ann.* Lib. iv. pp. 91, 92.
§ *Tacit. Ann.* Lib. iv. pp. 94, 95.
‖ *Tacit. Ann.* Lib. iv. p. 98.
¶ *Asinium Gal. eodem die et convivam Ti-
berii fuisse et eo subornante damnatum narrat
Dio.* Lib. lviii. p. 713.

Tell Cæsar (since your mother* is accused
To fly for succours to Augustus' statue,
And to the army, with your brethren) you
Have rather chose to place your aids in
    him,
Than live suspected; or in hourly fear
To be thrust out, by bold Sejanus' plots:
Which you shall confidently urge to be
Most full of peril to the state, and Cæsar,
As being laid to his peculiar ends,
And not to be let run with common safety.
All which, upon the second, I'll make plain,
So both shall love and trust with Cæsar
    gain.
    Cal. Away then, let's prepare us for our
    journey.   [*Exeunt.*

SCENE V.—*Another Part of the Street.*

Enter Arruntius.

    Arr. Still dost thou suffer, heaven! will
    no flame,
No heat of sin, make thy just wrath to
    boil
In thy distempered bosom, and o'erflow
The pitchy blazes of impiety,
Kindled beneath thy throne! Still canst
    thou sleep,
Patient, while vice doth make an antick
    face
At thy dread power, and blow dust and
    smoke
Into thy nostrils! Jove, will nothing wake
    thee?
Must vile Sejanus pull thee by the beard,[1]
Ere thou wilt open thy black-lidded eye,
And look him dead? Well! snore on,
    dreaming gods;
And let this last of that proud giant-race
Heave mountain upon mountain 'gainst
    your state—
Be good unto me, Fortune and you powers,
Whom I, expostulating, have profaned;
I see, what's equal with a prodigy,
A great, a noble Roman, and an honest,
Live an old man!—

Enter Lepidus.

            O Marcus Lepidus,[†]
When is our turn to bleed? Thyself and I,
Without our boast, are almost all the few
Left to be honest in these impious times.
    Lep. What we are left to be, we will be,
        Lucius;
Though tyranny did stare as wide as death,
To fright us from it.
    Arr. 'T hath so on Sabinus.
    Lep. I saw him now drawn from the
        Gemonies,[‡]
And what increased the direness of the
    fact,
His faithful dog,[§] upbraiding all us Ro-
    mans,
Never forsook the corps, but, seeing it
    thrown
Into the stream, leaped in, and drowned
    with it.
    Arr. O act, to be envied him of us men!
We are the next the hook lays hold on,
    Marcus:
What are thy arts, good patriot, teach
    them me,
That have preserved thy hair to this white
    dye,
And kept so reverend and so dear a head
Safe on his comely shoulders?
    Lep. Arts, Arruntius!
None,[‖] but the plain and passive fortitude,
To suffer and be silent; never stretch
These arms against the torrent;[2] live at
    home,
With my own thoughts and innocence
    about me,
Not tempting the wolves' jaws: these are my
    arts.
    Arr. I would begin to study 'em, if I
        thought
They would secure me. May I pray to
    Jove
In secret and be safe? ay, or aloud,
With open wishes, so I do not mention
Tiberius or Sejanus? yes I must,

---

[1] *Must vile Sejanus pull thee by the beard?*]
*Idcirco stolidam præbet tibi vellere barbam
Jupiter?*—Pers. Sat. ii. v. 28. WHAL.
[2]   *Never stretch
These arms against the torrent, &c.*] This
is from Juvenal, as are many other short passages in this scene; to which Persius also contributes. Jonson seems almost afraid to trust
himself out of the classics.

* *Vid. Tacit.* Lib. v. p. 94. *Suet. Tib.* c. 53.

[†] *De Lepido isto vid. Tacit. Ann.* Lib. i.
p. 6, Lib. iii. pp. 60, 65, *et* Lib. iv. p. 81.
[‡] *Scalæ Gemoniæ fuerunt in Aventino, prope
templum Junonis reginæ a Camillo captis Veiis
dicatum: a planctu et gemitu dictas vult
Rhodig. In quas contumeliæ causâ cadavera
projecta; aliquando a carnifice unco trahe-
bantur. Vid. Tac. Suet. Dio. Senec. Juvenal.*
[§] *Dio. Rom. Hist.* Lib. lviii. p. 714. *Et
Tacit. Ann.* Lib. iv. p. 94.
[‖] *Tacit. Ann.* Lib. iv. p. 80.

If I speak out. 'Tis hard that. May I
  think,
And not be racked? What danger is't to
  dream,
Talk in one's sleep, or cough? Who knows
  the law?
May I shake my head without a comment?
  say
It rains, or it holds up, and not be thrown
Upon the Gemonies? These now are
  things,
Whereon men's fortune, yea, their fate
  depends.
Nothing hath privilege 'gainst the violent
  ear.
No place, no day, no hour, we see, is free,
Not our religious and most sacred times,[1]
From some one kind of cruelty: all matter,
Nay, all occasion pleaseth. Madmen's
  rage,
The idleness of drunkards, women's no-
  thing,
Jester's simplicity, all, all is good
That can be catcht at. Nor is now the
  event
Of any person, or for any crime,
To be expected; for 'tis always one:
Death, with some little difference of place,
Or time——What's this? Prince Nero,
  guarded!

Enter Laco[*] *and* Nero, *with* Guards.

  Lac. On, lictors, keep your way. My
  lords, forbear.
On pain of Cæsar's wrath, no man attempt
Speech with the prisoner.
  Ner. Noble friends, be safe;
To lose yourselves for words, were as vain
  hazard,
As unto me small comfort: fare you well.
Would all Rome's sufferings in my fate did
  dwell!
  Lac. Lictors, away.
  Lep. Where goes he, Laco?
  Lac. Sir,
He's banished into Pontia[†] by the senate.
  Arr. Do I see, hear, and feel? May I
  trust sense,
Or doth my phant'sie form it?
  Lep. Where's his brother?

  Lac. Drusus[‡] is prisoner in the palace.
  Arr. Ha!
I smell it now: 'tis rank. Where's Agrip-
  pina?
  Lac. The princess is confined to Pan-
  dataria.[§]
  Arr. Bolts, Vulcan; bolts for Jove!
  Phœbus, thy bow;
Stern Mars, thy sword; and, blue-eyed
  maid, thy spear;
Thy club, Alcides: all the armoury
Of heaven is too little!—Ha! to guard
The gods, I meant. Fine, rare dispatch!
  this same
Was swiftly born! Confined, imprisoned,
  banished?
Most tripartite! the cause, sir?
  Lac. Treason.
  Arr. O!
The[‖] complement of all accusings! that
Will hit, when all else fails.
  Lep. This turn is strange!
But yesterday the people would not hear,
Far less objected, but cried[¶] Cæsar's letters
Were false and forged; that all these plots
  were malice;
And that the ruin of the prince's house
Was practised 'gainst his knowledge.
  Where are now
Their voices, now that they behold his heirs
Locked up, disgraced, led into exile?
  Arr. Hushed,
Drowned in their bellies. Wild Sejanus'
  breath
Hath, like a whirlwind, scattered that poor
  dust,
With this rude blast.—We'll talk no trea-
  son, sir, [*Turns to* Laco *and the rest.*
If that be it you stand for. Fare you well.
We have no need of horse-leeches. Good
  spy,
Now you are spied, be gone.
      [*Exeunt* Laco, Nero, *and* Guards.
  Lep. I fear you wrong him:
He has the voice to be an honest Roman.
  Arr. And trusted to this office! Lepidus,
I'd sooner trust Greek Sinon than a man
Our state employs. He's gone: and being
  gone,
I dare tell you, whom I dare better trust,
That our night-eyed[**] Tiberius doth not see

---

[1] *Not our religious and most sacred times,*]
Alluding to the fate of Sabinus, who was accused
upon the calends of January, and suffered death
soon after.—WHAL.

---

[*] *Le, Lacon. vid. Dio. Rom. Hist.* Lib. lviii.
p. 718.

[†] *Suet. Tib.* c. 54.
[‡] *Suet. ibid.*
[§] *Suet. ibid.*
[‖] *Tacit. Ann.* Lib. iii. p. 62.
[¶] *Tacit.* Lib. v. p. 98.
[**] *Tiberius in tenebris videret: testibus Dio.
Hist. Rom.* Lib. lvii. p. 691. *Et Plin. Nat.
Hist.* Lib. ii. c. 37.

His minion's drifts; or, if he do, he's not
So arrant subtile, as we fools do take him;
To breed a mongrel up, in his own house,
With his own blood, and, if the good gods
     please,
At his own throat flesh him to take a leap.
I do not beg it, heaven; but if the fates
Grant it these eyes, they must not wink.
     Lep. They must
Not see it, Lucius.
     Arr. Who should let them?
     Lep. Zeal,
And duty; with the thought he is our
     prince.
     Arr. He is our monster: forfeited to vice
So far, as no racked virtue can redeem
     him.
His loathed person* fouler than all crimes:
An emperor only in his lusts.   Retired,
From all regard of his own fame, or Rome's,
Into an obscure island;† where he lives
Acting his tragedies with a comic face,
Amidst his rout of Chaldees:‡ spending
     hours,
Days, weeks, and months, in the unkind
     abuse
Of grave astrology, to the bane of men,
Casting the scope of men's nativities,
And having found aught worthy in their
     fortune,
Kill, or precipitate them in the sea,
And boast he can mock fate.   Nay, muse
     not: these
Are far from ends of evil, scarce degrees.
He hath his slaughter-house at Capreæ;
Where he doth study murder as an art;
And they are dearest in his grace, that can
Devise the deepest tortures.   Thither, too,
He hath his boys, and beauteous girls
     ta'en up
Out of our noblest houses, the best formed,
Best nurtured, and most modest; what's
     their good,
Serves to provoke his bad.   Some are§
     allured,
Some threatened; others, by their friends
     detained,
Are ravished hence, like captives, and, in
     sight
Of their most grieved parents, dealt away
Unto his spintries, sellaries, and slaves,

Masters of strange and new commented
     lusts,
For which wise nature hath not left a name.
To this (what most strikes us, and bleeding
     Rome)
He is, with all his craft, become‖ the ward
To his own vassal, a stale catamite:
Whom he, upon our low and suffering
     necks,
Hath raised from excrement to side the
     gods,
And have his proper sacrifice in Rome:
Which Jove beholds, and yet will sooner
     rive
A senseless oak with thunder than his
     trunk!

     Re-enter Laco,¶ *with* Pomponius *and*
                    Minutius.

     Lac. These** letters make men doubtful
     what t' expect,
Whether his coming, or his death.
     Pom. Troth, both:
And which comes soonest, thank the gods
     for.
     Arr. List!
Their talk is Cæsar; I would hear all voices.
           [Arrunt. *and* Lepidus *stand aside.*
     Min. One day,†† he's well; and will re-
     turn to Rome;
The next day, sick; and knows not when
     to hope it.
     Lac. True; and to-day, one of Sejanus'
     friends
Honoured by special writ; and on the
     morrow
Another punished——
     Pom. By more special writ.
     Min. This man‡‡ receives his praises of
     Sejanus,
A second but slight mention, a third none,
A fourth rebukes: and thus he leaves the
     senate
Divided and suspended, all uncertain.
     Lac. These forked tricks, I understand
     them not:
Would he would tell us whom he loves or
     hates,
That we might follow, without fear or
     doubt.

---

* *Cons. Tacit. Ann.* Lib. iv. p. 91. (*Juv.
Sat.* 4.)
† *Vid. Suet. Tib. de secessu Caprensi,* c. 43.
Dio. p. 715. *Juv. Sat.* 10.
‡ *Tacit. Ann.* Lib. vi. p. 106. *Dio. Rom.
Hist.* Lib. lvii. p. 706. *Suet. Tib.* c. 62,
&c. 44.

§ *Tacit. Ann.* Lib. iv. p. 100. *Suet. Tib.* c. 43.
‖ *Leg. Dio. Rom. Hist.* Lib. lviii. p. 714.
¶ *De Pomponio et Minutio vid. Tacit. Ann.*
Lib. vi.
** *Dio. Rom. Hist.* Lib. lviii. p. 716.
†† *Dio. Rom. Hist.* Lib. lviii. p. 716.
‡‡ *Dio. ibid.*

Arr. Good Heliotrope! Is this your
honest man?
Let him be yours so still; he is my knave.
Pom. I cannot tell,[1] Sejanus still goes on,
And mounts, we see;* new statues are ad-
vanced,
Fresh leaves of titles, large inscriptions
read,
His fortune sworn by,† himself new gone
out
Cæsar's‡ colleague in the fifth consulship;
More altars smoke to him than all the gods:
What would we more?
Arr. That the dear smoke would choke
him,
That would I more.
Lep. Peace, good Arruntius.
Lat. But there are§ letters come, they
say, ev'n now,
Which do forbid that last.
Min. Do you hear so?
Lac. Yes.
Pom. By Castor that's the worst.
Arr. By Pollux, best.
Min. I did not like the sign, when∥
Regulus,
Whom all we know no friend unto Sejanus,
Did, by Tiberius' so precise command,
Succeed a fellow in the consulship:
It boded somewhat.
Pom. Not a mote. His¶ partner,
Fulcinius Trio, is his own, and sure.—
Here comes Terentius.

Enter Terentius.

He can give us more.
[*They whisper with* Terentius.
Lep. I'll ne'er believe but Cæsar hath
some scent
Of bold Sejanus' footing.** These cross
points
Of varying letters, and opposing consuls,
Mingling his honours and his punishments,
Feigning now ill, now well,†† raising Se-
janus,
And then depressing him, as now of late
In all reports we have it, cannot be
Empty of practise: 'tis Tiberius' art.
For having found his favourite grown too
great,

And with his greatness‡‡ strong; that all the
soldiers
Are, with their leaders, made at his devo-
tion;
That almost all the senate are his creatures,
Or hold on him their main dependencies,
Either for benefit, or hope, or fear;
And that himself hath lost much of his own,
By parting unto him; and, by th' increase
Of his rank lusts and rages, quite disarmed
Himself of love, or other public means,
To dare an open contestation;
His subtilty hath chose this doubling line,
To hold him even in: not so to fear him,
As wholly put him out, and yet give check
Unto his farther boldness. In mean time,
By his employments, makes him odious
Unto the staggering rout, whose aid in fine
He hopes to use, as sure, who, when they
sway,
Bear down, o'erturn all objects in their way.
Arr. You may be a Lynceus, Lepidus:
yet I
See no such cause, but that a politic tyrant,
Who can so well disguise it, should have
ta'en
A nearer way: feigned honest, and come
home
To cut his throat, by law.
Lep. Ay, but his fear
Would ne'er be masked, allbe his vices
were.
Pom. His lordship then is still in grace?
Ter. Assure you,
Never in more, either of grace or power.
Pom. The gods are wise and just.
Arr. The fiends they are,
To suffer thee belie 'em.
Ter. I have here
His last and present letters, where he writes
him,
"The partner of his cares," and "his
Sejanus."—
Lac. But is that true,§§ it is prohibited
To sacrifice unto him?
Ter. Some such thing
Cæsar makes scruple of, but forbids it not;
No more than to himself: says he could
wish
It were forborn to all.

---

[1] *I cannot tell,*] i.e., I know not what to
think of it. See p. 47 *a*. This phrase, of which
the sense is now, I presume, sufficiently established, is here noticed for the last time.

* *Leg. Tacit, Ann.* Lib. iv. p. 96.
† *Adulationis pleni omnes ejus Fortunam
jurabant. Dio. Hist. Rom.* Lib. lviii. p. 714.

‡ *Dio.* p. 714. *Suet. Tib.* c. 65.
§ *Dio.* Lib. lviii. p. 718.
∥ *De Regulo cons. Dio. ibid.*
¶ *Dio. ibid.*
** *Suet. Tib.* c. 65.
†† *Dio.* p. 726.
‡‡ *Dio.* p. 714.
§§ *Dio. Hist. Rom.* Lib. lviii. p. 718.

Lac. Is it no other?

Ter. No other, on my trust. For your more surety,

Here is that letter too.

Arr. How easily

Do wretched men believe what they would have!

Looks this like plot?

Lep. Noble Arruntius, stay.

Lac. He names him here* without his titles.

Lep. Note!

Arr Yes, and come off your notable fool. 1 will.

Lac. No other than Sejanus.

Pom. That's but haste

In him that writes: here he gives large amends.

Mar. And with his own hand written?

Pom. Yes.

Lac. Indeed?

Ter. Believe it, gentlemen, Sejanus' breast

Never received more full contentments in, Than at this present.

Pom. Takes he well† the escape

Of young Caligula, with Macro?

Ter. Faith,

At the first air it somewhat troubled him.

Lep. Observe you?

Arr. Nothing; riddles. Till I see

Sejanus struck, no sound thereof strikes me.

[*Exeunt* Arrun. *and* Lepidus.

Pom. I like it not. I muse he would not attempt

Somewhat against him in the consulship,‡

Seeing the people 'gin to favour him.

Ter. He doth repent it now; but he has employed

Pagonianus after him :§ and he holds

That correspondence there, with all that are

Near about Cæsar, as no thought can pass

Without his knowledge, thence in act to front him.

Pom. I gratulate the news.

Lac. But how comes Maero

So in trust and favour with Caligula?

Pom. O, sir, he has a wife ;|| and the young prince

An appetite : he can look up and spy

Flies in the roof, when there are fleas i' the bed ;

And hath a learned nose to assure his sleeps.

Who to be favoured of the rising sun,

Would not lend little of his waning moon?

It is the saf'st ambition. Noble Terentius!

Ter. The night grows fast upon us. At your service.   [*Exeunt.*

ACT V.

SCENE I.—*An Apartment in* Sejanus's *House.*

Enter Sejanus.

Sej. Swell, swell, my joys ; and faint not to declare

Yourselves as ample as your causes are.

I did not live till now : this my first hour ;

Wherein I see my thoughts reached by my power.

But this, and gripe my wishes.¶ Great and high,

The world knows only two, that's Rome and I.

My roof receives me not ; 'tis air I tread ;

And, at each step, I feel my advanced head

Knock out a star in heaven ! reared to this height,

All my desires seem modest, poor, and slight,

That did before sound impudent : 'tis place,

Not blood, discerns the noble and the base.

Is there not something more than to be Cæsar?

Must we rest there? it irks t' have come so far,

To be so near a stay. Caligula,

Would thou stood'st stiff, and many in our way !

Winds lose their strength, when they do empty fly,

Unmet of woods or buildings ; great fires die,

That want their matter to withstand them : so,

It is our grief, and will be our loss, to know

Our power shall want opposites ; unless

The gods, by mixing in the cause, would bless

Our fortune with their conquest. That were worth

---

* *Dio. ibid.*   † *Dio.* p. 717.
‡ *Dio.* p. 717.
§ *De Pagoniano,* vid. *Tacit. Ann.* Lib. vi. p. 101, *alibi Paconiano.*

|| *Tacit. cons. Ann.* Lib. vi. p. 114.
¶ *De fastu Sejani leg. Dio. Hist. Rom.* Lib. lviii. p. 715, *et Tacit. Ann.* Lib. iv. p. 96.

Sejanus' strife; durst fates but bring it
    forth.
                Enter Terentius.
Ter. Safety to great Sejanus !
Sej. Now, Terentius?
Ter. Hears not my lord the wonder?
Sej. Speak it ; no.
Ter. I meet it violent in the people's
    mouths,
Who run in routs to Pompey's theatre,
To view your statue,* which, they say,
    sends forth
A smoke, as from a furnace, black and
    dreadful.
    Sej. Some traitor hath put fire in : you,
    go see,
And let the head be taken off, to look
What 'tis. [*Exit* Terentius.[Some slave
    hath practised an imposture
To stir the people.—How now ! why re-
    turn you?
        Re-enter Terentius, *with* Satrius
                and Natta.
    Sat. The head,† my lord, already is
    ta'en off,
I saw it ; and, at opening, there leapt out
A great and monstrous serpent.
    Sej. Monstrous ! why?
Had it a beard, and horns? no heart? a
    tongue
Forked as flattery? looked it of the hue,
To such as live in great men's bosoms?
    was
The spirit of it Macro's?
    Nat. May it please
The most divine Sejanus, in my days,
(And by his sacred fortune, I affirm it,)
I have not seen a more extended, grown,
Foul, spotted, venomous, ugly——
    Sej. O, the fates !
What a wild muster's here of attributes,
T'' express a worm, a snake !
    Ter. But how that should
Come there, my lord !
    Sej. What, and you too, Terentius !
I think you mean to make 't a prodigy
In your reporting.
    Ter. Can the wise Sejanus
Think heaven hath meant it less ?
    Sej. O, superstition !

Why, then the falling‡ of our bed, that
    brake
This morning, burdened with the populous
    weight
Of our expecting clients, to salute us ;
Or running of the cats§ betwixt our legs,
As we set forth unto the Capitol,
Were prodigies.
    Ter. I think them ominous :
And would they had not happened ! As, to-
    day,
The fate of some your servants :‖ who
    declining
Their way,[1] not able, for the throng, to
    follow,
Slipt down the Gemonies, and brake their
    necks !
Besides, in taking your last augury,¶
No prosperous bird appeared ; but croak-
    ing ravens
Flagged up and down, and from the
    sacrifice
Flew to the prison, where they sat all
    night,
Beating the air with their obstreperous
    beaks !
I dare not counsel, but I could entreat,
That great Sejanus would attempt the gods
Once more with sacrifice.
    Sej. What excellent fools
Religion makes of men ! Believes Teren-
    tius,
If these were dangers, as I shame to think
    them,
The gods could change the certain course
    of fate ?
Or, if they could they would, now in a
    moment,
For a beeve's fat, or less, be bribed to
    invert
Those long decrees ? Then think the gods,
    like flies,
Are to be taken with the steam of flesh,
Or blood, diffused about their altars :
    think
Their power as cheap as I esteem it
    small.
Of all the throng that fill th' Olympian
    hall,
And, without pity, lade poor Atlas' back,
I know not that one deity, but Fortune,

[1] *Who,* declining their way,] Turning out of
the way. This is from the folio, 1616: the
quarto reads *diverting;* but as *declining* seems
to have been the poet's own choice, and the
language of that age, I have given it the preference. So the author of *Aulicus Coquinariæ,*
speaking of Sir Walter Raleigh, when out of
place, says that, " when it fell out to be so, he

would wisely decline himself out of the court-
road."—WHAL.

* *Dio. Hist. Rom.* Lib. lviii. p. 717.
† *Dio. ibid.*   ‡ *Dio. ibid.* p. 715.
§ *Dio. ibid.* p. 716.   ‖ *Dio. ibid.*
¶ *Dio ibid.*

To whom I would throw up, in begging
    smoke,
One grain of incense ;* or whose ear I'd buy
With thus much oil. Her I indeed adore ;
And keep her grateful image† in my house,
Sometime belonging to a Roman king,
But now called mine, as by the better style :
To her I care not, if, for satisfying
Your scrupulous phant'sies, I go offer. Bid
Our priest prepare us honey,‡ milk, and
    poppy,
His masculine odours, and night-vest-
    ments : say
Our rites are instant ; which performed,
    you'll see
How vain, and worthy laughter, your fears
be.   [Exeunt.

SCENE II.—Another Room in the same.

Enter Cotta and Pomponius.

Cot. Pomponius, whither in such speed?
Pom. I go
To give my lord Sejanus notice——
Cot. What ?
Pom. Of Macro.
Cot. Is he come?
Pom. Entered but now
The house of Regulus.§
Cot. The opposite consul !
Pom. Some half hour since.
Cot. And by night too ! Stay, sir ;
I'll bear you company.
Pom. Along then.   [Exeunt.

SCENE III.—A Room in Regulus's
House.

Enter Macro, Regulus, and Attendant.

Mac. 'Tis Cæsar's will to have a frequent
    senate ;
And therefore must your edict‖ lay deep
    mulct
On such as shall be absent.
Reg. So it doth.
Bear it my fellow consul to adscribe.
Mac. And tell him it must early be pro-
    claimed :
The place Apollo's temple.¶
                            [Exit Attendant.

Reg. That's remembered.
Mac. And at what hour?
Reg. Yes.
Mac. You do** forget
To send one for the provost of the watch.
Reg. I have not : here he comes.

Enter Laco.

Mac. Gracinus Laco,
You are a friend most welcome . by and by,
I'll speak with you. You must procure
    this list
Of the prætorian cohorts, with the names
Of the centurions, and their tribunes.
Reg. Ay.
Mac. I bring you letters,†† and a health
    from Cæsar.
Lac. Sir, both come well.
Mac. And hear you? with your note,
Which are the eminent men, and most of
    action.
Reg. That shall be done you too.
Mac. Most worthy Laco,
Cæsar salutes you. [Exit Regulus.] Con-
    sul ! death and furies !
Gone now ! The argument will please you,
    sir,
Ho ! Regulus ! The anger of the gods
Follow your diligent legs, and overtake
    'em,
In likeness of the gout !

Re-enter Regulus.

                        O, my good lord,
We lacked you present ; I would pray you
    send
Another to Fulcinius Trio, straight,
To tell him you will come, and speak with
    him :
The matter we'll devise, to stay him there,
While I with Laco do survey the watch.
                            [Exit Regulus.
What are your strengths, Gracinus ?
Lac. Seven cohorts.‡‡
Mac. You see what Cæsar writes ; and—
    Gone again !
H' has sure a vein of mercury in his feet.
Know you what store of the prætorian
    soldiers
Sejanus holds about him, for his guard ?

---

* Grani turis. Plaut. Pænu. act i. sc. 1, et
Ovid. Fast. Lib. iv.
† Dio. Hist. Rom. Lib. lviii. p. 717.
‡ De sacris Fortunæ, vid. Lil. Gre. Gyr.
Synt. 17, et Stuch. lib. de Sacrif. Gent. p. 48.
§ Dio. Hist. Rom. Lib. lviii. p. 718.
‖ Edicto ut plurimum senatores in curiam
vocatos constat, ex Tacit. Ann. Lib. i. et Liv.

Lib. ii. Fest. Pon. Lib. xv. vid. Bar. Briss. de
Form. Lib. i. et Lips. Sat. Menip.
¶ Dio. Rom. Hist. Lib. lvii. p. 718.
** Dio. ibid.
†† Dio. Rom. Hist. Lib. lviii. p. 718.
‡‡ De prefecto vigilum vid. Ros. Antiq. Rom.
Lib. vii. et Dio. Rom. Hist. Lib. lv.

Lac. I cannot the just number ; but I think
Three centuries.
Mac. Three ! good.
Lac. At most not four.
Mac. And who be those centurions ?
Lac. That the consul
Can best deliver you.
Mac. When he's away !—Gracinus,
Spite on his nimble industry—Gracinus,
You find what place you hold, there, in the trust
Of royal Cæsar ?
Lac. Ay, and I am——
Mac. Sir,
The honours there proposed are but beginnings
Of his great favours.
Lac. They are more——
Mac. I heard him
When he did study what to add.
Lac. My life,
And all I hold——
Mac. You were his own first choice !
Which doth confirm as much as you can speak ;
And will, if we succeed, make more——
Your guards
Are seven cohorts, you say ?
Lac. Yes.
Mac. Those we must
Hold still in readiness* and undischarged.
Lac. I understand so much. But how it can——
Mac. Be done without suspicion, you'll object?

Re-enter Regulus.

Reg. What's that ?
Lac. The keeping of the watch in arms,
When morning comes.
Mac. The senate shall be met, and set
So early in the temple, as all mark
Of that shall be avoided.
Reg. If we need,
We have commission to possess† the palace,
Enlarge Prince Drusus, and make him our chief.

Mac. That secret would have burnt his reverend mouth,
Had he not spit it out now : by the gods,
You carry things too——Let me borrow a man
Or two, to bear these——That of freeing Drusus,
Cæsar projected as the last and utmost ;
Not else to be remembered.

Enter Servants.

Reg. Here are servants.
Mac. These to Arruntius, these to Lepidus.
This bear to Cotta, this to Latiaris.
If they demand you of me, say I have ta'en
Fresh horse, and am departed. [*Exeunt* Servants.] You, my lord,
To your colleague, and be you sure to hold him
With long narration of the new fresh favours,
Meant to Sejanus, his great patron ; I,
With trusted Laco, here, are for the guards :
Then to divide. For night hath many eyes,
Whereof, though most do sleep, yet some are spies. [*Exeunt.*

SCENE IV.—*A Sacellum* (*or Chapel*) *in* Sejanus's *House.*

Enter Præcones,‡ Flamen,§ Tubicines, Tibicines, Ministri, Sejanus, Terentius, Satrius, Natta, &*c.*

Præ. ‖ " Be all profane far hence ; fly, fly far off :
Be absent far ; far hence be all profane !"
[Tub. *and* Tib.¶ *sound while the* Flamen *washeth.*
Fla. We have been faulty, but repent us now.
And bring pure** hands, pure vestments, and pure minds.
1 *Min.* Pure vessels.
2 *Min.* And pure offerings.
3 *Min.* Garlands pure.

---

* *Dio. Rom. Hist.* Lib. lviii. p. 718.
† *Vid. Tacit. Ann.* Lib. vi. p. 107, *et Suet. Tib.* c. 65.
‡ *Præcones, Flamen, hi omnibus sacrificiis interesse solebant. Ros. Ant. Rom.* Lib. iii. *Stuch. de Sac.* p. 72.
§ *Ex iis, qui Flamines Curiales dicerentur, vid. Lil. Greg. Gyr. Synt.* 17, *et Onup. Panvin. Rep. Rom. Comment.* 2.
‖ *Moris antiqui erat, Præcones præcedere,*
et sacris arcere profanos. Cons. Briss. Ross. Stuch. Lil. Gyr. &c.
¶ *Observatum antiquis invenimus, ut qui rem divinam facturus erat, lautus, ac mundus accederet, et ad suas levandas culpas, se imprimis reum dicere solitum, et noxæ pœnituisse. Lil. Gyr. Synt.* 17.
** *In sacris puras manus, puras vestes, pura vasa, &c. antiqui desiderabunt ; ut ex Virg. Plaut. Tibul. Ovid. &c. pluribus locis constat.*

Fla. Bestow your garlands:* and, with
   reverence, place
The vervin on the altar.
  Præ. Favour† your tongues.
    [*While they sound again,‡ the* Flamen
    takes of the honey with his finger,
    and tastes, then ministers to all the
    rest: so of the milk§ in an earthen
    vessel, he deals about ; which done,
    he sprinkleth upon the altar, milk ;
    then imposeth the honey, and
    kindleth his gums, and after cens-
    ing about the altar, placeth his
    censer thereon, into which they put
    several branches‖ of poppy, and the
    music ceasing, proceeds.
  Fla. " Great mother Fortune,¶ queen of
   human state,
Rectress of action, arbitress of fate,
To whom all sway, all power, all empire
  bows,
Be present, and propitious to our vows !"
  Præ. Favour** it with your tongues.
  Min. Be present, and propitious to our
   vows !
  Omnes. Accept our offering,†† and be
   pleased, great goddess.
  Ter. See, see, the image stirs !
  Sat. And turns away !
  Nat. Fortune‡‡ averts her face !
  Fla. Avert, you gods,
The prodigy. Still ! still ! some pious rite
We have neglected. Yet, heaven be ap-
  peased,
And be all tokens false and void, that speak
Thy present wrath !
  Sej. Be thou dumb, scrupulous priest :
And gather up thyself, with these thy wares,
Which I, in spight of thy blind mistress, or

Thy juggling mystery, religion, throw
Thus scorned on the earth.
    [*Overturns the statue and the altar.*
             Nay, hold thy look
Averted till I woo thee turn again ;
And thou shalt stand to all posterity,
The eternal game and laughter, with thy
  neck
Writhed to thy tail, like a ridiculous cat.
Avoid these fumes, these superstitious
  lights,
And all these cosening ceremonies ! you,
Your pure and spiced conscience !
    [*Exeunt all but* Sejanus, Terent.
     Satri. *and* Natta.
                I, the slave
And mock of fools, scorn on my worthy
  head !
That have been titled§§ and adored a god,
Yea sacrificed‖‖ unto, myself, in Rome,
No less than Jove : and I be brought to do¹
A peevish giglot, rites ! perhaps the thought
And shame of that, made Fortune turn her
  face,
Knowing herself the lesser deity,
And but my servant.—Bashful queen, if so,
Sejanus thanks thy modesty. Who's that ?

    Enter Pomponius *and* Minutius.¶¶

  Pom. His fortune suffers, till he hears
   my news :
I have waited here too long. Macro, my
  lord——
  Sej. Speak lower and withdraw.
               [*Takes him aside.*
  Ter. Are these things true ?
  Min. Thousands are gazing at it in the
   streets.

---

¹   *I be brought to do*
  A peevish giglot, *rites !*] *Giglot* is a wanton
girl : so Shakspeare :

    " Young Talbot was not born
  To be the pillage of a *giglot* wench."—WHAL.

* *Alius ritus sertis aras coronare, et verbe-*
nas imponere.
  † *Hujusmodi verbis silentium imperatum*
fuisse constat. Vid. Sen. in lib. de beata vita.
Serv. et Don. ad eum versum, Lib. v. *Æneid :*
" *Ore favete omnes, et cingite tempora ramis.*"
  ‡ *Vocabatur hic ritus Libatio. Lege Rosin.*
Ant. Lib. iii. *Bar. Brisson. de form.* Lib. i.
Stuchium de Sacrif. et Lil. Synt. 17.
  § *In sacris Fortunæ lacte non vino libabant.*
iisdem test. Talia sacrificia ἄοινα *et* νηφάλια
dicta. Hoc est sobria, et vino carentia.
  ‖ *Hoc reddere erat et litare, id est propitiare.*

et votum impetrare ; secundum Nonium Mar-
cellum. Litare enim Mac. Lib. iii. c. 5, *explicat,*
sacrificio facto placare numen. In quo sens.
leg. apud Plaut. Senec. Suet. *&c.*
  ¶ *His solemnibus præfationibus in sacris*
utebantur.
  ** *Quibus, in clausu, populus vel cœtus a præ-*
conibus favere jubebatur ; id est, bona verba
fari. Talis enim altera hujus formæ interpre-
tatio apud Briss. Lib. i. *extat. Ovid.* Lib. i.
Fast. Linguis animisque favete. Et Metam.
Lib. xv.
           " *Piumque*
Æneadæ præstant et mente, et voce favorem."
  †† *Solennis formula in donis cuivis nomini*
offerendis.
  ‡‡ *Leg. Dio. Rom. Hist.* Lib. lviii. p. 717, *de*
hoc sacrificio.
  §§ *Tacit. Ann.* Lib. iv. p. 96.
  ‖‖ *Dio.* Lib. lviii. p. 716.
  ¶¶ *De Minutio vid. Tacit. Ann.* Lib. vi.

Sej. What's that?

Ter. Minutius tells us here, my lord,
That a new head being set upon your statue,
A rope* is since found wreathed about it! and,
But now† a fiery meteor in the form
Of a great ball was seen to roll along
The troubled air, where yet it hangs unperfect,
The amazing wonder of the multitude!

Sej. No more. That Macro's come, is more than all!

Ter. Is Macro come?

Pom. I saw him.

Ter. Where? with whom?

Pom. With Regulus.

Sej. Terentius!

Ter. My lord.

Sej. Send for the tribunes,‡ we will straight have up
More of the soldiers for our guard. [*Exit* Ter.] Minutius,
We pray you go for Cotta, Latiaris,
Trio the consul, or what senators
You know are sure, and ours. [*Exit* Min.] You, my good Natta,
For Laco, provost of the watch. [*Exit* Nat.] Now, Satrius,
The time of proof comes on; arm all our servants,
And without tumult. [*Exit* Sat.] You, Pomponius,
Hold some good correspondence with the consul:
Attempt him, noble friend. [*Exit* Pomp.] These things begin
To look like dangers, now, worthy my fates.
Fortune, I see thy worst: let doubtful states,
And things uncertain hang upon thy will;
Me surest death shall render certain still.
Yet, why is now my thought turned toward death,

Whom fates have let go on, so far in breath,
Unchecked or unreproved? I,§ that did help
To fell the lofty cedar of the world
Germanicus; that at one stroke‖ cut down
Drusus, that upright elm; withered his vine;[1]
Laid Silius¶ and Sabinus,** two strong oaks,
Flat on the earth; besides those other shrubs,
Cordus†† and Sosia,‡‡ Claudia Pulchra,§§
Furnius and Gallus,‖‖ which I have grubbed up;
And since, have set my axe so strong and deep
Into the root of spreading Agrippine;¶¶
Lopt off and scattered her proud branches, Nero,
Drusus; and Caius*** too, although replanted.
If you will, Destinies, that after all,
I faint now ere I touch my period,
You are but cruel; and I already have done
Things great enough. All Rome hath been my slave,
The senate sate an idle looker on,
And witness of my power; when I have blushed
More to command than it to suffer: all
The fathers have sate ready and prepared,
To give me empire, temples, or their throats,
When I would ask 'em; and, what crowns the top,
Rome, senate, people, all the world have seen
Jove but my equal; Cæsar but my second.
'Tis then your malice, Fates, who, but your own,
Envy and fear to have any power long known. [*Exit.*

---

1 *That at one stroke cut down Drusus, that upright elm; withered his vine.*] As Drusus is here called an elm, his wife Livia, by a very elegant and easy metaphor, is termed *his vine.* The whole description is a beautiful allegory, animated with the most sublime spirit of true poetry.—WHAL.
Beaumont and Fletcher have closely imitated, or rather copied, this passage in the *False One.*

* *Dio. Hist. Rom.* Lib. lviii. p. 717.
† *Vid. Senec. Nat. Quest.* Lib. i. c. 1.
‡ *Dio. Hist. Rom.* Lib. lviii. p. 718.
§ *Vid. Tacit. Ann.* Lib. i. p. 23.

‖ *Tacit. Ann.* Lib. iv. pp. 74, 75, *et Dio.* Lib. lvii. p. 709.
¶ *Tacit.* Lib. iv. p. 79.
** *Ibid.* p. 94.
†† *De Cremut. Cor. vid. Dio. Rom. Hist.* Lib. lvii. p. 710. *Tacit. Ann.* Lib. iv. p. 83.
‡‡ *De Sosia. Tacit. Ann.* Lib. iv. p. 94.
§§ *De Clau. et Furnio, quære Tacit. Ann.* Lib. iv. p. 89.
‖‖ *De Gallo, Tacit.* Lib. iv. p. 95, *et Dio.* Lib. lviii. p. 713.
¶¶ *De Agr. Ner. et Dru. leg. Suet. Tib.* cap. 53, 4.
*** *De Caio. cons. Dio.* Lib. lviii. p. 727.

SCENE V.—*A Room in the same.*

Enter Terentius *and* Tribunes.

Ter. Stay here: I'll give his lordship
you are come.

Enter Minutius, *with* Cotta *and* Latiaris.

Min. Marcus Terentius, pray you tell
my lord
Here's Cotta, and Latiaris.
Ter. Sir, I shall.   [*Exit.*
Cot. My letter is the very same with
yours;
Only requires me to be present there,
And give my voice to strengthen his design.
Lat. Names he not what it is?
Cot. No, nor to you.
Lat. 'Tis strange and singular doubtful!
Cot. So it is.
It may be all is left to lord Sejanus.

Enter Natta *and* Gracinus Laco.

Nat. Gentlemen, where's my lord?
Tri. We wait him here.
Cot. The provost Laco! what's the news?
Lat. My lord——

Enter Sejanus.

Sej. Now, my right dear, noble, and
trusted friends,
How much I am a captive to your kindness!
Most worthy Cotta, Latiaris, Laco,
Your valiant hand; and, gentlemen, your
loves.
I wish I could divide myself unto you;
Or that it lay within our narrow powers,
To satisfy for so enlarged bounty.
Gracinus, we must pray you, hold your
guards
Unquit when morning comes. Saw you
the consul?
Min. Trio will presently be here, my
lord.
Cot. They are but giving order* for the
edict,
To warn the senate?
Sej. How! the senate?
Lac. Yes.
This morning in Apollo's temple——
Cot. We
Are charged by letter to be there, my lord.
Sej. By letter! pray you let's see.
Lat. Knows not his lordship?
Cot. It seems so!
Sej. A senate warned! without my know-
ledge!
And on this sudden! Senators by letters
Required to be there! who brought these?

Cot. Macro.
Sej. Mine† enemy! and when?
Cot. This midnight.
Sej. Time,
With every other circumstance, doth give
It hath some strain of engine in 't!—How
now?

Enter Satrius.

Sat. My lord, Sertorius Macro is without,
Alone, and prays t' have private con-
ference
In business of high nature with your lord-
ship,
He says to me, and which regards you
much.
Sej. Let him come here.
Sat. Better, my lord, withdraw:
You will betray what store and strength of
friends
Are now about you; which he comes to
spy.
Sej. Is he not armed?
Sat. We'll search him.
Sej. No; but take,
And lead him to some room, where you
concealed
May keep a guard upon us. [*Exit* Sat.]
Noble Laco,
You are our trust; and till our own co-
horts
Can be brought up, your strengths must
be our guard.
Now, good Minutius, honoured Latiaris,
                    [*He salutes them humbly.*
Most worthy and my most unwearied
friends;
I return instantly.   [*Exit.*
Lat. Most worthy lord!
Cot. His lordship is turned instant kind,
methinks;
I have not observed it in him heretofore.
1 *Tri.* 'Tis true, and it becomes him
nobly.
Min. I
Am wrapt withal.
2 *Tri.* By Mars, he has my lives,
Were they a million, for this only grace.
Lac. Ay, and to name a man!
Lat. As he did me!
Min. And me!
Lat. Who would not spend his life and
fortunes
To purchase but the look of such a lord?
Lac. He that would nor be lord's fool,
nor the world's.   [*Aside.*

* *Vid. Dio. Rom. Hist.* Lib. lviii. p. 718.
† *Dio.* Lib. lviii. p. 718.

SCENE VI.—*Another Room in the same.*

Enter Sejanus, Macro, *and* Satrius.

Sej. Macro !* most welcome, a most coveted friend !
Let me enjoy my longings. When arrived you ?
Mac. About† the noon of night.[1]
Sej. Satrius, give leave.　　　[*Exit* Sat.
Mac. I have been, since I came, with both the consuls,
On a particular design from Cæsar.
Sej. How fares it with our great and royal master ?
Mac. Right plentifully well ; as with a prince
That still holds out‡ the great proportion
Of his large favours, where his judgment hath
Made once divine election : like the god
That wants not, nor is wearied to bestow
Where merit meets his bounty, as it doth
In you, already the most happy, and ere
The sun shall climb the south, most high Sejanus.
Let not my lord be amused.[2] For to this end
Was I by Cæsar sent for to the isle,
With special caution to conceal my journey ;
And thence had my dispatch as privately
Again to Rome ; charged to come here by night ;
And only to the consuls make narration
Of his great purpose ; that the benefit
Might come more full, and striking, by how much
It was less.looked for, or aspired by you,
Or least informed to the common thought.
Sej. What may this be ? part of myself, dear Macro,
If good, speak out ; and share with your Sejanus.
Mac. If bad, I should for ever loathe myself
To be the messenger to so good a lord.

I do exceed my instructions to acquaint
Your lordship with thus much ; but 'tis my venture
On your retentive wisdom : and because
I would no jealous scruple should molest
Or rack your peace of thought. For I assure
My noble lord, no senator yet knows
The business meant : though all by several letters
Are warned to be there, and give their voices,
Only to add unto the state and grace
Of what is purposed.
Sej. You take pleasure, Macro,
Like a coy wench, in torturing your lover.
What can be worth this suffering ?
Mac. That which follows,
The tribunitial§ dignity and power :
Both which Sejanus is to have this day
Conferred upon him, and by public senate.
Sej. Fortune be mine again ! thou hast satisfied
For thy suspected loyalty.　　　[*Aside.*
Mac. My lord,
I have no longer time, the day approacheth,
And I must back to Cæsar.
Sej. Where's Caligula ?
Mac. That I forgot to tell your lordship. Why,
He lingers yonder about Capreæ,
Disgraced ; Tiberius hath not seen him yet :
He needs would thrust himself to go with me,
Against my wish or will ; but I have quitted
His forward trouble, with as tardy note
As my neglect or silence could afford him.
Your lordship cannot now command me aught,
Because I take no knowledge that I saw you ;
But I shall boast to live to serve your lordship :
And so take leave.
Sej. Honest and worthy Macro ;

---

[1] *About the noon of night.*] This poetical expression, though now common by general use, seems to have been first introduced into our language by Jonson. And he appears to have been diffident of the reception it might meet with, or whether the licence he had taken would be approved by custom. For he refers us in the margin of the quarto to the author of whom he borrowed it.—WHAL.

I have not, any more than Whalley, been able to find an earlier instance of the use of this phrase. It was speedily adopted, however, by Drayton, Crashaw, and Herrick. Milton, who resorted to

Jonson for poetical expressions upon all occasions, could not miss this ; though his editors, as usual, make no mention of his obligation to our author.
[2] *Let not my lord be* amused.] i.e., amazed. See the *Alchemist.*

* *Dio. Hist. Rom.* Lib. lviii. p. 78.
† *Meridies noctis, Varr. Marcipor. vid. Non. Mar.* cap. vi.
‡ *Dio.* Lib. lviii. p. 78.
§ *Dio.* Lib. lviii. p. 78, *vid. Suet. de oppress. Sejan. Tib.* c. 65.

Your love and friendship. [*Exit* Macro.]
  Who's there? Satrius,
Attend my honourable friend forth.—O !
How vain and vile a passion is this fear,
What base uncomely things it makes men
  do !
Suspect their noblest friends, as I did this,
Flatter poor enemies, entreat their servants,
Stoop, court, and catch at the benevolence
Of creatures unto whom, within this hour,
I would not have vouchsafed a quarter-
  look,
Or piece of face ! By you that fools call
  gods,
Hang all the sky with your prodigious
  signs,
Fill earth with monsters, drop the scorpion
  down,
Out of the zodiac, or the fiercer lion,
Shake off the loosened globe from her long
  hinge,
Roll all the world in darkness, and let
  loose
The enraged winds to turn up groves and
  towns !
When I do fear again, let me be struck
With forked fire, and unpitied die :
Who fears, is worthy of calamity.   [*Exit*.

SCENE VII.—*Another Room in the
          same.*

Enter Terentius, Minutius, Laco, Cotta,
  Latiaris, *and* Pomponius ; Regulus,
  Trio, *and others, on different sides.*

  Pom. Is not my lord here ?
  Ter. Sir, he will be straight.
  Cot. What news, Fulcinius Trio ?
  Tri. Good, good tidings ;
But keep it to yourself.   My lord Sejanus
Is to receive this day in open senate
The tribunitial dignity.
  Cot. Is 't true ?
  Tri. No words, not to your thought :
  but, sir, believe it.
  Lat. What says the consul ?
  Cot. Speak it not again :
He tells me that to-day my lord Sejanus——
  Tri. I must entreat you, Cotta, on your
  honour
Not to reveal it.
  Cot. On my life, sir.
  Lat. Say.
  Cot. Is to receive the tribunitial power.
But, as you are an honourable man,

Let me conjure you not to utter it ;
For it is trusted to me with that bond.
  Lat. I am Harpocrates.
  Ter. Can you assure it ?
  Pom. The consul told it me ; but keep
  it close.
  Min. Lord Latiaris, what's the news ?
  Lat. I'll tell you ;
But you must swear to keep it secret.

            Enter Sejanus.

  Sej. I knew the Fates had on their dis-
  taff left
More of our thread, than so.
  Reg. Hail, great Sejanus !
  Tri. Hail, the most* honoured !
  Cot. Happy !
  Lat. High Sejanus !
  Sej. Do you bring prodigies too ?
  Tri. May all presage
Turn to those fair effects, whereof we
  bring
Your lordship news.
  Reg. May't please my lord withdraw.
  Sej. Yes :—I will speak with you anon.
                    [*To some that stand by.*
  Ter. My lord,
What is your pleasure for the tribunes ?
  Sej. Why,
Let them be thanked and sent away.
  Min. My lord——
  Lac. Will't please your lordship to com-
  mand me——
  Sej. No :
You are troublesome.
  Min. The mood† is changed.
  Tri. Not speak,
Nor look !
  Lac. Ay, he is wise, will make him
  friends
Of such who never love but for their ends.
                            [*Exeunt.*

SCENE VIII.—*A Space before the Temple
          of Apollo.*

  Enter Arruntius *and* Lepidus, *divers
          Senators passing by them.*

  Arr. Ay, go, make haste ; take heed
      you be not last
To tender your All Hail‡ in the wide hall
Of huge Sejanus : run a lictor's pace :
Stay not to put your robes on ; but away
With the pale troubled ensigns of great
  friendship

---

* *Dio. Rom. Hist.* Lib. lviii. p. 718.
† *Dio. Rom. Hist.* Lib. lviii. p. 718.

‡ *Ave, matutina vox salutanti propria, apud
Romanos, vid. Briss. de form.* Lib. viii.

Stamped in your face!¹ Now, Marcus
 Lepidus,
You still believe your former augury !
Sejanus must go downward ! You perceive
His wane approaching fast !
 Lep. Believe me, Lucius,
I wonder at this rising.
 Arr. Ay, and that we
Must give our suffrage to it. You will say,
It is to make his fall more steep and
 grievous :
It may be so. But think it, they that can
With idle wishes 'say to bring back time :
In cases desperate, all hope is crime.
See, see ! what troops of his officious
 friends
Flock to salute my lord, and start before
My great proud lord ! to get a lord-like nod!
Attend my lord unto the senate-house !
Bring back my lord ! like servile ushers,
 make
Way for my lord ! proclaim his idol lord-
 ship,
More than ten criers, or six noise of
 trumpets !
Make legs, kiss hands, and take a scattered
 hair
From my lord's eminent shoulder ! [*San-
quinius and* Haterius *pass over the
stage.*] See, Sanquinius*
With his slow belly, and his dropsy ! look,
What toiling haste he makes ! yet here's
 another
Retarded with the gout, will be afore him.
Get thee Liburnian† porters, thou gross
 fool,
To bear thy obsequious fatness, like thy
 peers.
They are met ! the gout returns, and his
 great carriage.
  [Lictors, Regulus, Trio, Sejanus,
  Satrius, *and many other* Senators
  pass over the stage.
 Lict. Give way, make place, room for
 the consul !
 San. Hail,
Hail, great Sejanus !
 Hat. Hail, my honoured lord !

Arr. We shall be marked anon, for our
 not Hail.
Lep. That is already done.
Arr. It is a note²
Of upstart greatness, to observe and watch
For these poor trifles, which the noble mind
Neglects and scorns.
 Lep. Ay, and they think themselves
Deeply dishonoured where they are omitted,
As if they were necessities‡ that helped
To the perfection of their dignities ;
And hate the men that but refrain them.
 Arr. O !
There is a farther cause of hate. Their
 breasts
Are guilty that we know their obscure
 springs,
And base beginnings ; thence the anger
 grows.
On. Follow.   [*Exeunt.*

SCENE IX.—*Another Part of the same.*

Enter Macro *and* Laco.

Mac. When all are entered, shut§ the
 temple doors ;
And bring your guards up to the gate.
 Lac. I will.
 Mac. If you shall hear commotion in the
 senate,
Present yourself : and charge on any man
Shall offer to come forth.
 Lac. I am instructed.   [*Exeunt.*

SCENE X.—*The Temple of Apollo.*

Enter Haterius, Trio, Sanquinius, Cotta,
 Regulus, Sejanus, Pomponius, Latiaris,
 Lepidus, Arruntius, *and divers other*
 Senators ; Præcones *and* Lictores.

 Hat. How well his lordship looks to-
 day !
 Tri. As if
He had been born, or made for this hour's
 state.
 Cot. Your fellow consul's come about,
 methinks ?

---

¹ Much of this speech is copied from Juvenal :
    " *Vocantur*
*Ergo in concilium proceres, quos oderat ille,
In quorum facie misera magnæque sedebat
Pallor amicitiæ.*"—Sat. iv. v. 73. WHAL.

² *It is a note,* &c.] This excellent maxim is
expressed with great force and beauty. It
proves Jonson to be a keen observer of men and
manners.

* *De Sanquinio vid. Tacit. Ann. Lib. vi. et
de Haterio, ibid.*
† *Ex Liburnia, magnæ et proceræ staturæ
mittebantur, qui erant Rom. Lecticarii ;* test.
Juv. Sat. iii. v. 240 :

   " *Turba cedente vehetur
Dives, et ingenti curret super ora Liburno.*"

‡ *Dio. Rom. Hist.* Lib. lviii.
§ *Dio. ibid.* p. 718.

Tri. Ay, he is wise.

Sau. Sejanus trusts him well.

Tri. Sejanus is a noble, bounteous*
lord.

Hat. He is so, and most valiant.

Lat. And most wise.

1 *Sen.* He's everything.

Lat. Worthy of all, and more
Than bounty can bestow.

Tri. This dignity
Will make him worthy.

Pom. Above Cæsar.

San. Tut,
Cæsar is but the rector† of an isle,
He of the empire.

Tri. Now he will have power
More to reward than ever.

Cot. Let us look
We be not slackt‡ in giving him our voices.

Lat. Not I.

San. Nor I.

Cot. The readier we seem
To propagate his honours, will more bind
His thoughts to ours.

Hat. I think right with your lordship;
It is the way to have us hold our places.

San. Ay, and get more.

Lat. More office and more titles.

Pom. I will not lose the part I hope to
share
In these his fortunes, for my patrimony.

Lat. See how Arruntius sits, and Lepidus!

Tri. Let them alone, they will be marked
anon.

1 *Sen.* I'll do with others.

2 *Sen.* So will I.

3 *Sen.* And I.
Men grow not in the state but as they are
planted
Warm in his favours.

Cot. Noble Sejanus!

Hat. Honoured Sejanus!

Lat. Worthy and great Sejanus!

Arr. Gods! how the sponges open and
take in,
And shut again! look, look! is not he
blest
That gets a seat in eye-reach of him?
more
That comes in ear, or tongue-reach? O
but most,

Can claw his subtle elbow, or with a buz
Fly-blow his ears?

Præt. Proclaim the senate's peace,
And give last summons by the edict.

Præ. Silence!
In name of Cæsar, and the senate, silence!

"Memmius Regulus, and Fulcinius
Trio,§ consuls, these present kalends of
June, with the first light, shall hold a
senate, in the temple of Apollo Palatine:‖
all that are fathers, and are registered
fathers, that have right of entering the
senate, we warn or command you be frequently present, take knowledge the business is the commonwealth's: whosoever is
absent, his fine or mulct will be taken, his
excuse will not be taken."

Tri. Note who are absent, and record
their names.

Reg. Fathers conscript,¶ may what I am
to utter
Turn good and happy for the common-
wealth!
And thou, Apollo, in whose holy house
We here are met, inspire us all with truth,
And liberty of censure to our thought!
The majesty of great Tiberius Cæsar
Propounds to this grave senate, the be-
stowing
Upon the man he loves, honoured Sejanus,
The tribunitial** dignity and power:
Here are his letters, signed with his signet.
What pleaseth†† now the fathers to be done?

Sen. Read, read them, open, publicly
read them.

Cot. Cæsar hath honoured his own greatness much
In thinking of this act.

Tri. It was a thought
Happy, and worthy Cæsar.

Lat. And the lord
As worthy it, on whom it is directed!

Hat. Most worthy!

San. Rome did never boast the virtue
That could give envy bounds, but his: Sejanus——

1 *Sen.* Honoured and noble!

2 *Sen.* Good and great Sejanus!

Arr. O, most tame slavery, and fierce
flattery!

Præ. Silence!

---

* *Vid. acclamation. Senat. Dio. Rom. Hist.*
Lib. lviii. p. 719.
† *Dio.* p. 715.
‡ *Dio.* p. 719.
§ *Vid. Brissonium de formul.* Lib. ii. *et
Lipsium Sat. Menip.*

‖ *Palatinus, a monte Palatino dictus.*
¶ *Solemnis præfatio consulum in relationibus.
Dio.* p. 718.
** *Vid. Suet. Tib.* cap. 65.
†† *Alia formula solemnis, vid. Briss.* Lib. ii.
et Dio. p. 719.

" Tiberius Cæsar to the Senate greeting.

If you, conscript* fathers, with your
children, be in health, it is abundantly
well: we with our friends here are so. The
care of the commonwealth, howsoever we
are removed in person, cannot be absent
to our thought; although, oftentimes, even
to princes most present, the truth of their
own affairs is hid; than which nothing falls
out more miserable to a state, or makes the
art of governing more difficult. But since
it hath been our easeful happiness to enjoy
both the aids and industry of so vigilant a
senate, we profess to have been the more
indulgent to our pleasures, not as being
careless of our office, but rather secure of
the necessity. Neither do these common
rumours of many, and infamous libels published against our retirement, at all afflict us;
being born more out of men's ignorance than
their malice: and will, neglected, find their
own grave quickly; whereas, too sensibly
acknowledged, it would make their obloquy
ours. Nor do we desire their authors, though
found, be censured, since in a free† state, as
ours, all men ought to enjoy both their
minds and tongues free."

Arr. The lapwing, the lapwing![1]

" Yet in things which shall worthily and
more near concern the majesty of a prince,
we shall fear to be so unnaturally cruel to
our own fame, as to neglect them. True
it is, conscript fathers, that we have raised
Sejanus from obscure, and almost unknown
gentry,"

Sen. How, how!

" to the highest and most conspicuous point
of greatness, and, we hope, deservingly;
yet not without danger: it being a most
bold hazard in that sovereign who, by his
particular love to one, dares adventure the
hatred of all his other subjects."

Arr. This touches; the blood turns.

" But we affy in your loves and understandings, and do no way suspect the merit of
our Sejanus, to make our favours offensive
to any."

Sen. O! good, good.

" Though we could have wished his zeal
had run a calmer course against Agrippina
and our nephews, howsoever the openness
of their actions declared them delinquents;
and that he would have remembered no
innocence is so safe, but it rejoiceth to stand
in the sight of mercy: the use of which in
us he hath so quite taken away toward
them, by his loyal fury, as now our clemency would be thought but wearied
cruelty,[2] if we should offer to exercise it."

Arr. I thank him; there I looked for 't.
A good fox!

" Some there be that would‡ interpret this
his public severity to be particular ambition; and that, under a pretext of service
to us, he doth but remove his own lets:
alleging the strengths he hath made to himself, by the prætorian soldiers, by his faction in court and senate, by the offices he
holds himself, and confers on others, his
popularity and dependents, his urging and
almost driving us to this our unwilling retirement, and, lastly, his aspiring to be
our son-in-law."

Sen. This is strange!

Arr. I shall anon believe your vultures,
Marcus.[3]

" Your wisdoms, conscript fathers, are able
to examine, and censure these suggestions.
But were they left to our absolving voice,
we durst pronounce them, as we think them,
most malicious."

---

[1] *The lapwing, the lapwing l*] See p. 246.
The lapwing is said to cry out at a distance
from her nest, in order to draw the searchers
away from her young. This is what Shakspeare
calls, "crying, *tongue far from heart;*" as
Tiberius does here: and indeed our old writers
are full of allusions to the same practice. Thus,
in the *Ploughman's Tale:*

"And *lapwinges*, that wel conith lie."

Again: "You resemble the *lapwing*, who crieth
most where her nest is not."—*Lingua*, act ii.
sc. 2.
And in the *Old Law:*

" He has the *lapwing's* cunning, I'm afraid,
    That cries most when she's *farthest* from the
      nest."

[2] *Our clemency would be thought but wearied
cruelty,*] *Ego vero clementiam non voco lassam
crudelitatem.* Senec. de Clemen. Lib. i. c. 11.
—WHAL.
[3] *I shall anon believe your vultures, Marcus;*] i.e., your augury, what you conjectured.
Lepidus, in a former scene, had foretold the
downfall of Sejanus.

* *Soleune exordium epistolar. apud Romanos.
cons. Briss. de formul.* Lib. viii.
† *Firmus et patiens subinde jactabat, in
civitate libera, linguam mentemque liberas
esse debere.* Suet. Tib. c. 28.
‡ *De hac epist. vid. Dio. Rom. Hist.* Lib.
lviii. p. 719, *et Juv. Sat.* x.

Sen. O, he has restored all; list!

"Yet are they offered to be averred, and on the lives of the informers. What we should say, or rather what we should not say, lords of the senate, if this be true, our gods and goddesses confound us if we know![1] Only we must think, we have placed our benefits ill; and conclude, that in our choice, either we were wanting to the gods, or the gods to us." [*The* Senators *shift their places.*

Arr. The place grows hot; they shift.

"We have not been covetous, honourable fathers, to change; neither is it now any new lust that alters our affection, or old loathing; but those needful jealousies of state, that warn wiser princes hourly to provide their safety;[2] and do teach them how learned a thing it is to beware of the humblest enemy; much more of those great ones, whom their own employed favours have made fit for their fears."

1 Sen. Away.

2 Sen. Sit farther.

Cot. Let's remove——

Arr. Gods! how the leaves drop off, this little wind!

"We therefore desire, that the office he holds be first seized by the senate; and himself suspended from all exercise of place or power——"

Sen. How!

San. [*Thrusting by.*] By your leave.

Arr. Come, porpoise;[3] where's Haterius? His gout keeps him most miserably constant! Your dancing shews a tempest.

Sej. Read no more.

Reg. Lords of the senate, hold your seats: read on.

Sej. These letters they are forged.

Reg. A guard! sit still.

Enter Laco, *with the* Guards.

Arr. Here's change!

Reg. Bid silence, and read forward.

Præ. Silence—"and himself suspended from all exercise of place or power, but till due and mature trial be made of his innocency, which yet we can faintly apprehend the necessity to doubt. If, conscript fathers, to your more searching wisdoms, there shall appear farther cause—or of farther proceeding, either to seizure of lands, goods, or more—it is not our power that shall limit your authority, or our favour that must corrupt your justice: either were dishonourable in you, and both uncharitable to ourself. We would willingly* be

---

[1] *What we should say, or rather what we should not say, lords of the senate, if this be true, our gods and goddesses confound us if we know!*] Juvenal styles the letter which Tiberius sent to the senate, *verbosa et grandis epistola;* and this before us is agreeable to that character. So far the judgment of Jonson is evident enough: but it seems to have failed him when he inserted the words above as a part of this epistle. They are to be found, indeed, both in Tacitus and Suetonius; and are very remarkable in themselves: but they are reported, which makes them still more remarkable, to have been the beginning of a letter he once wrote to the senate; and in that connexion they are a much stronger evidence of uneasiness and perturbation of spirit in the emperor, arising from the consciousness of guilt. The poet indeed hath added something, and given a different turn to the words, that he might introduce them in this epistle with the greater propriety: "*Insigne visum est earum Cæsaris literarum initium: nam his verbis exorsus est: Quid scribam vobis, P.C. aut quomodo scribam, aut quid omnino non scribam hoc tempore, dii me deæque pejus perdant quàm perire quotidie sentio, si scio.*"—*Tacit. Ann.* Lib. vi. c. 6. WHAL.

It is with regret that I so often find myself obliged to differ from Whalley. I cannot possibly think that Jonson's judgment failed him in this instance: the words which he has adopted are extremely proper for the occasion, and might be fitly used by a Roman in any question of extraordinary doubt and difficulty. How could it escape the critic, that the only passage which gave peculiarity to the quotation from the historian (for the rest is common enough) is, "Dii me deæque *pejus perdant quàm perire quotidie sentio,*" which strongly marks the intolerable anguish of a guilty mind, and which Jonson has wholly omitted? In a word, he has shown uncommon skill in the composition of this letter, and entered with matchless dexterity into the cloudy and sanguinary character of Tiberius.

[2] *To provide their safety;*] i.e., to look to by anticipation. A Latinism, like a hundred other expressions in this play. Whalley probably overlooked this sense of the word, for he inserted *for* after it; but Jonson has it again in the dedication to *Volpone:*—"who *providing*" (foreseeing) "the hurts these licentious spirits may do in a state," &c.—See p. 334.

[3] *Come, porpoise, &c.*] Sanquinius has been already described as fat and clumsy; but the allusion is to a circumstance often mentioned by the navigators of Jonson's days, that the gambols of porpoises always portended foul weather. Thus Webster: "He lifts his nose like a *porpus before a storm.*"—*Dutchess of Malfy.* The awkward motion of this unwieldy sycophant, in hastening from the side of Sejanus, is well illustrated by the example.

* *Dio. Rom. Hist.* Lib. lviii. p. 719, *et Suet. Tib.*

present with your counsels in this business ;
but the danger of so potent a faction, if it
should prove so, forbids our attempting it :
except one of the consuls would be entreated for our safety, to undertake the
guard of us home ; then we should most
readily adventure.　In the meantime, it
shall not be fit for us to importune so
judicious a senate, who know how much
they hurt the innocent, that spare the
guilty ; and how grateful a sacrifice to the
gods is the life of an ingrateful person.
We reflect not in this on Sejanus, (notwithstanding, if you keep an eye upon
him—and there is Latiaris, a senator, and
Pinnarius Natta, two of his most trusted
ministers; and so professed, whom we
desire not to have apprehended,) but as
the necessity of the cause exacts it."

　Reg. A guard on Latiaris !
　Arr. O, the spy,
The reverend spy is caught ! who pities
　　him ?
Reward, sir, for your service : now, you
　　have done
Your property, you see what use is made !
　　　[*Exeunt* Latiaris *and* Natta *guarded.*
Hang up the instrument.
　Sej. Give leave.
　Lac. Stand, stand !
He comes upon his death, that doth ad-
　　vance
An inch toward my point.
　Sej. Have we no friends here ?
　Arr. Hushed !
Where now are all the hails and accla-
　　mations ?

　　　　　Enter Macro.

　Mac. Hail to the consuls, and this noble
　　senate !
　Sej. Is Macro here ? O, thou art lost,
　　Sejanus !　　　　　　　　　[*Aside.*
　Mac. Sit still, and unaffrighted, reverend
　　fathers ;
Macro, by Cæsar's grace, the new-made
　　provost,
And now possest of the prætorian bands,
An honour late belonged to that proud
　　man,
Bids you be safe : and to your constant
　　doom
Of his deservings, offers you the surety
Of all the soldiers, tribunes, and cen-
　　turions,
Received in our command.
　Reg. Sejanus, Sejanus,
Stand forth, Sejanus !
　Sej. Am I called !

　Mac. Ay, thou,
Thou insolent monster, art bid stand.
　Sej. Why, Macro,
It hath been otherwise between you and I ;
This court, that knows us both, hath seen
　　a difference,
And can, if it be pleased to speak, confirm
Whose insolence is most.
　Mac. Come down, Typhœus.
If mine be most, lo ! thus I make it more ;
Kick up thy heels in air, tear off thy
　　robe,
Play with thy beard and nostrils.　Thus
　　'tis fit
(And no man take compassion of thy
　　state)
To use th' ingrateful viper, tread his brains
Into the earth.
　Reg. Forbear.
　Mac. If I could lose
All my humanity now, 'twere well to
　　torture
So meriting a traitor.—Wherefore, fathers,
Sit you amazed and silent ; and not censure
This wretch, who, in the hour he first
　　rebelled
'Gainst Cæsar's bounty, did condemn him-
　　self ?
Phlegra, the field where all the sons of
　　earth
Mustered against the gods, did ne'er ac-
　　knowledge
So proud and huge a monster.
　Reg. Take him hence ;
And all the gods guard Cæsar !
　Tri. Take him hence.
　Hat. Hence.
　Cot. To the dungeon with him.
　San. He deserves it.
　Sen. Crown all our doors * with bays.
　San. And let an ox,
With gilded horns and garlands, straight
　　be led
Unto the Capitol.
　Hat. And sacrificed
To Jove, for Cæsar's safety.
　Tri. All our gods
Be present still to Cæsar !
　Cot. Phœbus.
　San. Mars.
　Hat. Diana.
　San. Pallas.
　Sen. Juno, Mercury.
All guard him !
　Mac. Forth, thou prodigy of men.
　　　　　　[*Exit* Sejanus, *guarded.*
　Cot. Let all the traitor's titles be defaced.

　　　　* *Leg. Juv. Sat. x.*

Tri. His images and statues be pulled
  down.

Hat. His chariot-wheels be broken.

Arr. And the legs
Of the poor horses, that deserved nought,
Let them be broken too ![1]

  [*Exeunt* Lictors, Præcones, Macro,
    Regulus, Trio, Haterius, and San-
    quinius: *manent* Lepidus, Arrun-
    tius, *and a few* Senators.

Lep. O violent change,
And whirl of men's affections !

Arr. Like, as both
Their bulks and souls were bound on
  Fortune's wheel,
And must act only with her motion.

Lep. Who would depend upon the
  popular air,
Or voice of men, that have to-day beheld
That which, if all the gods had fore-
  declared,
Would not have been believed, Sejanus'
  fall?
He that this morn rose proudly as the
  sun,
And, breaking through a mist of clients'
  breath,
Came on, as gazed at and admired as he,
When superstitious Moors salute his light !
That had our servile nobles waiting him
As common grooms; and hanging on his
  look,
No less than human life on destiny !
That had men's knees as frequent as the
  gods ;
And sacrifices* more than Rome had
  altars :
And this man fall ! fall? ay, without a
  look
That durst appear his friend, or lend so
  much
Of vain relief, to his changed state, as
  pity !

Arr. They that before, like gnats,
  played in his beams,
And thronged to circumscribe him, now
  not seen,

Nor deign to hold a common seat with
  him !
Others, that waited him unto the senate,
Now inhumanely ravish him to prison,
Whom but this morn they followed as
  their lord !
Guard through the streets, bound like a
  fugitive,
Instead of wreaths give fetters, strokes for
  stoops:
Blind shames for honours, and black
  taunts for titles !
Who would trust slippery chance ?

Lep. They that would make
Themselves her spoil ; and foolishly forget,
When she doth flatter, that she comes to
  prey.
Fortune, thou hadst no deity, if men
Had wisdom: we have placed thee so
  high,
By fond belief in thy felicity.

  [*Shout within.*] The gods guard Cæsar !
    All the gods guard Cæsar !

  Re-enter Macro, Regulus, *and divers*
    Senators.

Mac. Now, great Sejanus,† you that
  awed the state,
And sought to bring the nobles to your
  whip ;
That would be Cæsar's tutor, and dispose
Of dignities and offices ! that had
The public head still bare to your designs,
And made the general voice to echo
  yours !
That looked for salutations twelve score
  off,[2]
And would have pyramids, yea, temples,
  reared
To your huge greatness ; now you lie as
  flat
As was your pride advanced !

Reg. Thanks to the gods !

Sen. And praise to Macro, that hath
  saved Rome !
Liberty, liberty, liberty ! Lead on,

---

[1]   *The legs*
Of the poor horses, that deserved nought,
Let them be broken too !]

" *Ipsas deinde rotas bigarum impacta securis*
  Cædit, et immeritis franguntur crura cabal-
  lis."—*Juv. Sat.* x. v. 59.

And the subsequent description of the insults
and indignities which were offered to whatever
had the least relation to Sejanus is taken from
the same satirist.—WHAL.

This indeed Jonson himself has already told
us more than once. It may, however, be ob-

served, that what he gives to the senate Juvenal,
with more propriety, puts into the mouth of the
rabble.

[2] *That 'looked for salutations* twelve score
off.] Who expected to be saluted at the distance
of twelve score yards; it was common in that
age to omit the substantive. So Shakspeare :

" I know his death will be a march of *twelve*
  score."—WHAL.

* *Dio. Rom. Hist.* Lib. lviii. p. 719, &c.
† *Vid. Dio. Rom. Hist.* Lib. lviii. p. 720, &c.

And praise to Macro, that hath saved
　Rome !
　　　　[*Exeunt all but* Arruntius
　　　　and Lepidus.[1]
　Arr. I prophesy, out of the senate's
　　flattery,
That this new fellow, Macro, will become
A greater prodigy in Rome than he
That now is fallen.

　　　　Enter Terentius.

　Ter. O you, whose minds are good,
And have not forced all mankind from your
　breasts ;
That yet have so much stock of virtue left,
To pity guilty states, when they are
　wretched :
Lend your soft ears to hear, and eyes to
　weep,
Deeds done by men, beyond the acts of
　furies.
The eager multitude (who never yet
Knew why to love or hate, but only pleased
T' express their rage of power) no sooner
　heard
The murmur of Sejanus in decline,
But with that speed and heat of appetite,
With which they greedily devour the way
To some great sports, or a new theatre,
They filled the Capitol, and Pompey's
　Cirque
Where, like so many mastiffs, biting stones,
As if his statues now were sensitive
Of their wild fury ; first, they tear them
　down ;*
Then fastening ropes, drag them along the
　streets,
Crying in scorn, This, this was that rich
　head
Was crowned with garlands, and with
　odours, this
That was in Rome so reverenced ! Now
The furnace and the bellows shall to work,
The great Sejanus crack, and piece by
　piece
Drop in the founder's pit.
　Lep. O popular rage !

　Ter. The whilst the senate at the temple†
　of Concord
Make haste to meet again, and thronging
　cry,
Let us condemn him, tread him down in
　water,
While he doth lie upon the bank ; away !
While some more tardy, cry unto their
　bearers,
He will be censured ere we come ; run,
　knaves,
And use that furious diligence, for fear
Their bondmen should inform against
　their slackness,
And bring their quaking flesh unto the
　hook :
The rout they follow with confused voice,
Crying they're glad, say they could ne'er
　abide him ;
Enquire what man he was,[2] what kind of
　face,
What beard he had, what nose, what lips ?
　Protest
They ever did presage he'd come to this ;
They never thought him wise, nor valiant ;
　ask
After his garments, when he dies, what
　death ;
And not a beast of all the herd demands
What was his crime, or who were his
　accusers,
Under what proof or testimony he fell ?
There came, says one, a huge long-worded
　letter
From Capreæ against him.　Did there so ?
O, they are satisfied ; no more.
　Lep. Alas !
They follow Fortune,‡ and hate men con-
　demned,
Guilty or not.
　Arr. But had Sejanus thrived
In his design, and prosperously opprest
The old Tiberius ; then, in that same
　minute,
These very rascals, that now rage like
　furies,
Would have proclaimed Sejanus emperor.
　Lep. But what hath followed ?

---

[1] Here perhaps this tragedy originally ended ;
and here indeed is its proper close.　What
follows is merely tedious, and has more the
appearance of a closet exercise than a dramatic
exhibition.　All that has passed since the exit of
Sejanus is of uncommon spirit and beauty.
　[2] *Enquire what man he was,* &c.] Jonson has
repeatedly told us that all this is from Juvenal—
but he translates him very strangely in this place :
　　　　"*Quæ labra !　Quis illi*
　Vultus erat !"

is the language of contempt, not of curiosity.
The "rout" were jeering at his mangled and
distorted features.　Verbal translations, unless
taste and judgment be ever on the watch, will
lead even the learned into absurdities.

---

* *Vid. Juv. Sat.* x.
† *Dio. Rom. Hist.* Lib. lviii. p. 720.
‡ *Juv. Sat.* x.

Ter. Sentence* by the senate,
To lose his head; which was no sooner off,
But that and the unfortunate trunk were
　　seized
By the rude multitude; who not content
With what the forward justice of the state
Officiously had done, with violent rage
Have rent it limb from limb.　A thousand
　　heads,
A thousand hands, ten thousand tongues
　　and voices,
Employed at once in several acts of malice!
Old men not staid with age, virgins with
　　shame,
Late wives with loss of husbands, mothers
　　of children,
Losing all grief in joy of his sad fall,
Run quite transported with their cruelty!
These mounting at his head, these at his
　　face,
These digging out his eyes, those with his
　　brains
Sprinkling themselves, their houses and
　　their friends;
Others are met, have ravished thence an
　　arm,
And deal small pieces of the flesh for
　　favours;
These with a thigh, this hath cut off his
　　hands,
And this his feet; these fingers, and these
　　toes;
That hath his liver, he his heart: there
　　wants
Nothing but room for wrath, and place for
　　hatred!
What cannot oft be done, is now o'erdone.
The whole, and all of what was great
　　Sejanus,
And, next to Cæsar, did possess the world,
Now torn and scattered, as he needs no
　　grave;
Each little dust covers a little part:
So lies he nowhere, and yet often buried!

　　　　　Enter Nuntius.

Arr. More of Sejanus?
Nun. Yes.
Lep. What can be added?
We know him dead.
Nun. Then there begin your pity.
There is enough behind to melt ev'n Rome,

And Cæsar into tears; since never slave
Could yet so highly offend, but tyranny,
In torturing him, would make him worth
　　lamenting.
A son and daughter to the dead Sejanus,
(Of whom† there is not now so much re-
　　maining
As would give fastening to the hangman's
　　hook,)
Have they drawn forth for farther sacrifice;
Whose tenderness of knowledge, unripe
　　years,
And childish silly innocence was such,
As scarce would lend them feeling of their
　　danger:
The‡ girl so simple, as she often asked
"Where they would lead her? for what
　　cause they dragged her?"
Cried, "She would do no more:" that she
　　could take
"Warning with beating."　And because
　　our laws
Admit no virgin§ immature to die,
The wittily and strangely cruel Macro,
Delivered her to be deflowered and spoiled,
By the rude lust of the licentious hang-
　　man,
Then to be strangled with her harmless
　　brother.
　　Lep. O, act most worthy hell, and last-
　　ing night,
To hide it from the world!
　　Nun. Their bodies thrown
Into the Gemonies (I know not how,
Or by what accident returned), the mother,
The expulsed Apicata,‖ finds them there;
Whom when she saw lie spread on the
　　degrees,¶
After a world of fury on herself,
Tearing her hair, defacing of her face,
Beating her breasts and womb, kneeling
　　amazed,
Crying to heaven, then to them; at last,
Her drowned voice gat up above her woes,
And with such black and bitter execrations
As might affright the gods, and force the
　　sun
Run backward to the east; nay, make the
　　old
Deformed chaos rise again, to o'erwhelm
Them, us, and all the world, she fills the
　　air,

---

* *Dio. Rom. Hist.* Lib. lviii. p. 720.　*Senec. lib. de Tranq. Anim.* c. 11.　*Quo die illum senatus deduxerat, populus in frusta divisit,* &c.
† *Vid. Senec. lib. de Tranq. Ani.* c. xi.
‡ *Tac. Ann.* Lib. v. p. 99.　*Et Dio.* Lib. lviii. p. 720.

§ *Lex non tam virginitati ignotum cautumque voluit quam ætati.　Cons. Lips. comment. Tac.*
‖ *Dio.* Lib. lviii. c. 720.
¶ *Scalæ Gemoniæ in quas erant projecta damnator. corpora.*

Upbraids the heavens with their partial dooms,
Defies their tyrannous powers,* and demands,
What she, and those poor innocents have transgressed,
That they must suffer such a share in vengeance,
Whilst Livia, Lygdus, and Eudemus live,
Who, as she says, and firmly vows to prove it
To Cæsar and the senate, poisoned Drusus?
Lep. Confederates with her husband!
Nun. Ay.
Lep. Strange act!
Arr. And strangely opened: what says now my monster,
The multitude? they reel now, do they not?
Nun. Their gall is gone, and now they 'gin to weep
The mischief they have done.
Arr. I thank 'em, rogues.
Nun. Part are so stupid, or so flexible,
As they believe him innocent; all grieve:
And some, whose hands yet reek with his warm blood,
And gripe the part which they did tear of him,
Wish him collected and created new.

Lep. How Fortune plies her sports, when she begins
To practise them! pursues, continues, adds,
Confounds with varying her impassioned moods!
Arr. Dost thou hope, Fortune, to redeem thy crimes,
To make amend for thy ill placed favours,
With these strange punishments? Forbear, you things
That stand upon the pinnacles of state,
To boast your slippery height; when you do fall,
You pash yourselves in pieces, ne'er to rise;
And he that lends you pity, is not wise.
Ter. Let this example move the insolent man,
Not to grow proud and careless of the gods.
It is an odious wisdom to blaspheme,
Much more to slighten,[1] or deny their powers:
For whom the morning saw so great and high,
Thus low and little, 'fore the even doth lie.   [*Exeunt.*

---

[1] *Much more to* slighten, &c.] This form of the word is used by Ford and others of Jonson's contemporaries:

"Debates already 'twixt his wife and him
Thicken and run to head; she, as 'tis said,
Slightens his love, and he abandons hers."
                    'Tis Pity She's a Whore.

Propriety of sentiment and decorum of character are what we are principally to look for in the plays of Jonson; especially in those where the characters are known from history, and he is necessarily obliged to draw them like. Agreeably to this, the moral of the play hath an exact conformity to the action of the chief person in the drama. Sejanus is represented without any principle of conscience, ambitious, and a contemner of all religion, with the power and providence of the gods. His fall therefore, considered as a punishment for his neglect of the gods, must naturally insinuate that obedience to them is the only foundation of happiness; and that lawless and irregular ambition is constantly attended with destruction. This moral is inculcated in these last lines.—WHAL.

This tragedy is much too lightly estimated. It wants indeed passion and interest for the general reader: but the scholar will find in it more to admire than blame. All the *dramatis personæ*, from the high spirited and untractable Agrippina to the most subtle follower of the favourite, are marked with truth and vigour: but it is in the characters of Tiberius and Sejanus that the poet hath put forth his strength.

The profound art and deep dissimulation of the former, as contrasted with the versatile and shallow cunning of the latter, are portrayed with a most skilful and discriminating hand; so fully and happily indeed has Jonson entered into the character of this subtle and sanguinary tyrant, that his drama might have been more appositely termed the triumph of Tiberius than the *Fall of Sejanus.*

The voluntary death of Silius in the senate-house, after a defence worthy of the best times of the republic, is an incident at once affecting and dramatical: nor is the justification of Cremutius Cordus, in the same scene, to be passed without praise. The last act is particularly striking, both from the lively and picturesque representation of the sacrifice to Fortune, and the artful development of the plot against Sejanus. Had it concluded, as it ought, with the death of this personage, it might have been securely paralleled for spirit and effect with the catastrophe of many of our most celebrated pieces.

Jonson has beautifully pointed out the moral of this drama in the concluding lines: it is but justice to him to add, that no play of his own or later times abounds so much in moral and political maxims of high import as SEJANUS; and though some perhaps may incline to doubt his "height of elocution," yet all will acknowledge that "in fulness and frequency of sentence, he has discharged the offices of a tragic writer."

---

* *Dio.* Lib. lviii. p. 720.

Volpone; or, The Fox.

VOLPONE, &c.] This celebrated Comedy was first brought out at the Globe Theatre in 1605, and printed in quarto, 1607, after having been acted with great applause at both Universities. Jonson republished it in 1616, without alterations or additions, and with the former appropriate motto, from Horace,

Simul et jucunda, et idonea dicere vitæ.

The actors were the same as in *Sejanus*, with the exception, perhaps, of Shakspeare, whose name does not appear in the list. Lowin played Volpone, which was one of his favourite characters; and Cooke, who is supposed to have performed Livia in the preceding drama, probably took the part of Lady Would-be.

The Fox continued on the stage till the final dispersion of the players, and was one of the first pieces revived at the Restoration; when, as old Downes says, "it proved very satisfactory to the town." Langbaine tells us that it was "in vogue" in his time; as, indeed, it was for a century afterwards.

Its last appearance, I believe, was at the Haymarket, some time before the death of the elder Colman, who made some trifling alterations in the disposition of the scenes. That it was not successful cannot be wondered at; the age of dramatic imbecility was rapidly advancing upon us, and the stage already looked to jointed-dolls, water-spaniels, and peacocks'-tails, for its main credit and support.

MOST NOBLE AND MOST EQUAL SISTERS,

THE TWO FAMOUS UNIVERSITIES,

FOR THEIR

LOVE AND ACCEPTANCE SHOWN TO THIS POEM

IN THE PRESENTATION;

BEN JONSON,

THE GRATEFUL ACKNOWLEDGER,

DEDICATES BOTH IT AND HIMSELF.

NEVER, most equal Sisters, had any man a wit so presently excellent, as that it could raise itself; but there must come both matter, occasion, commenders, and favourers to it. If this be true, and that the fortune of all writers doth daily prove it, it behoves the careful to provide well towards these accidents; and, having acquired them, to preserve that part of reputation most tenderly, wherein the benefit of a friend is also defended. Hence is it, that I now render myself grateful, and am studious to justify the bounty of your act; to which, though your mere authority were satisfying, yet it being an age wherein poetry and the professors of it hear so ill[1] on all sides, there will a reason be looked for in the subject. It is certain, nor can it with any forehead be opposed, that the too much licence of poetasters in this time, hath much deformed their mistress; that every day their manifold and manifest ignorance doth stick unnatural reproaches upon her: but for their petulancy, it were an act of the greatest injustice, either to let the learned suffer, or so divine a skill (which indeed should not be attempted with unclean hands) to fall under the least contempt. For if men will impartially, and not asquint, look toward the offices and function of a poet, they will easily conclude to themselves the impossibility of any man's being the good poet, without first being a good man. He[2] that is said to be able to inform young men to all good disciplines, inflame grown men to all great virtues, keep old men in their best and supreme state, or, as they decline to childhood, recover them to their first strength; that comes forth the interpreter and arbiter of natue, a teacher of things divine no less than human, a master in manners; and can alone, or with a few, effect the business of mankind: this,

---

[1] *Hear so ill,*] A mere Latinism *(tam male audiunt)* for—are so ill spoken of. It is used by Spenser:

> " If old Aveugle's son *so evil hear;*"

And again by Jonson, in *Catiline:*

> " And glad me doing well, though *I hear ill.*

[2] *He that is said to be able to inform young men,* &c.] In this description of the offices and function of a good poet, our author, as Whalley observes, "seems to have had his eye on different passages in Horace." Here he alludes to the Epistle to Augustus:

> " *Recte facta refert, orientia tempora notis,*
> *Instruit exemplis, inopem solatur et ægrum,*" &c.

A ittle below, to the Art of Poetry, v. 396:

> " *Fuit hæc sapientia quondam*
> *Publica privatis secernere, sacra profanis,*" &c.

The sentence immediately preceding this, is taken almost literally from Strabo: Ἡ δε ποιητου συνεζευκται τη του ανθρωπου· και ουχ οιον τε αγαθον γενεσθαι ποιητην, μη προτερον γεννηθεντα ανδρα αγαθον.—Lib. i. p. 33.

I take him, is no subject for pride and ignorance to exercise their railing rhetoric upon. But it will here be hastily answered, that the writers of these days are other things; that not only their manners, but their natures, are inverted, and nothing remaining with them of the dignity of poet, but the abused name, which every scribe usurps; that now, especially in dramatic, or, as they term it, stage-poetry, nothing but ribaldry, profanation, blasphemy, all licence of offence to God and man is practised. I dare not deny a great part of this, and am sorry I dare not, because in some men's abortive features (and would they had never boasted the light) it is over true: but that all are embarked in this bold adventure for hell, is a most uncharitable thought, and, uttered, a more malicious slander. For my particular, I can, and from a most clear conscience, affirm, that I have ever trembled to think toward the least profaneness; have loathed the use of such foul and unwashed bawdry, as is now made the food of the scene: and, howsoever I cannot escape from some, the imputation of sharpness, but that they will say, I have taken a pride, or lust, to be bitter, and not my youngest infant but hath come into the world with all his teeth; I would ask of these supercilious politics, what nation, society, or general order or state, I have provoked? What public person? Whether I have not in all these preserved their dignity, as mine own person, safe? My works are read, allowed (I speak of those that are intirely mine,[1]) look into them, what broad reproofs have I used? where have I been particular? where personal? except to a mimic, cheater, bawd, or buffoon, creatures, for their insolencies, worthy to be taxed? yet to which of these so pointingly, as he might not either ingenuously have confest, or wisely dissembled his disease? But it is not rumour can make men guilty, much less entitle me to other men's crimes. I know that nothing can be so innocently writ or carried, but may be made obnoxious to construction; marry, whilst I bear mine innocence about me, I fear it not. Application is now grown a trade with many; and there are that profess to have a key for the decyphering of everything: but let wise and noble persons take heed how they be too credulous, or give leave to these invading interpreters to be over familiar with their fames, who cunningly, and often, utter their own virulent malice under other men's simplest meanings. As for those that will (by faults which charity hath raked up,[2] or common honesty concealed) make themselves a name with the multitude, or, to draw their rude and beastly claps, care not whose living faces they intrench with their petulant styles, may they do it without a rival, for me! I choose rather to live graved in obscurity, than share with them in so preposterous a fame. Nor can I blame the wishes of those severe and wise patriots, who providing the hurts[3] these licentious spirits may do in a state, desire rather to see fools and devils, and those antique relics of barbarism retrieved, with all other ridiculous and exploded follies, than behold the wounds of private men, of princes and nations: for, as Horace makes Trebatius speak among these,

Sibi quisque timet, quanquam est intactus, et odit.

And men may justly impute such rages, if continued, to the writer, as his sports. The increase of which last in liberty, together with the present trade of the stage, in all their miscelline interludes, what learned or liberal soul doth not already abhor? where nothing but the filth of the time is uttered, and with such impropriety of phrase, such plenty of solecisms, such dearth of sense, so bold prolepses, so racked metaphors, with brothelry able to violate the ear of a pagan, and blasphemy to turn the blood of a Christian to water. I cannot but be serious in a cause of this nature, wherein my fame, and the reputation of divers honest and learned are the question; when a name so full of authority, antiquity, and all great mark, is, through their insolence, become the

---

[1] *My works are read, allowed—(I speak of those that are intirely mine.)* This he says, because he had written in conjunction with Chettle, Decker, Chapman, and others. It appears from this judicious and learned composition, which in elegance and vigour stands yet unrivalled, that the objections subsequently urged against the stage by Prynne and Collier, were but the echoes of former complaints. It would not have been much amiss, if those who found themselves aggrieved by them had been content with referring to Jonson; for, to speak tenderly, they have, after all their exculpatory efforts, added little of moment to what is to be found in this and the preceding pages.
[2] *Which charity hath* raked up,] i.e., smothered, hidden; alluding to the practice of covering live embers, by *raking* ashes *over* them.
[3] *Who providing the hurts,*] i.e., foreseeing the hurts. See p. 326 *b*.

lowest scorn of the age ; and those men subject to the petulancy of every vernaculous orator, that were wont to be the care of kings and happiest monarchs. This it is that hath not only rapt me to present indignation, but made me studious heretofore, and by all my actions, to stand off from them ; which may most appear in this my latest work, which you, most learned Arbitresses, have seen, judged, and to my crown, approved ; wherein I have laboured for their instruction and amendment, to reduce not only the ancient forms, but manners of the scene, the easiness, the propriety, the innocence, and last, the doctrine, which is the principal end of poesie, to inform men in the best reason of living. And though my catastrophe may, in the strict rigour of comic law, meet with censure, as turning back to my promise ; I desire the learned and charitable critic to have so much faith in me, to think it was done of industry : for, with what ease I could have varied it nearer his scale (but that I fear to boast my own faculty) I could here insert. But my special aim being to put the snaffle in their mouths, that cry out, We never punish vice in our interludes, &c., I took the more liberty ; though not without some lines of example, drawn even in the ancients themselves, the goings out of whose comedies are not always joyful, but oft times the bawds, the servants, the rivals, yea, and the masters are mulcted ; and fitly, it being the office of a comic poet to imitate justice, and instruct to life, as well as purity of language, or stir up gentle affections : to which I shall take the occasion elsewhere to speak.[1]

For the present, most reverenced Sisters, as I have cared to be thankful for your affections past, and here made the understanding acquainted with some ground of your favours ; let me not despair their continuance, to the maturing of some worthier fruits : wherein, if my muses be true to me, I shall raise the despised head of poetry again, and stripping her out of those rotten and base rags wherewith the times have adulterated her form, restore her to her primitive habit, feature, and majesty, and render her worthy to be embraced and kist of all the great and master-spirits of our world. As for the vile and slothful, who never affected an act worthy of celebration, or are so inward with their own vicious natures as they worthily fear her, and think it an high point of policy to keep her in contempt with their declamatory and windy invectives ; she shall out of just rage incite her servants (who are *genus irritabile*) to spout ink in their faces that shall eat farther than their marrow, into their fames ; and not Cinnamus the barber,[2] with his art, shall be able to take out the brands ; but they shall live, and be read, till the wretches die, as things worst deserving of themselves in chief, and then of all mankind.

From my House in the Black-Friars,
   this 11th day of February, 1607.

DRAMATIS PERSONÆ.

Volpone, *a Magnifico.*
Mosca, *his Parasite.*
Voltore, *an Advocate.*
Corbaccio, *an old Gentleman.*
Corvino, *a Merchant.*
Bonario, *son to* Corbaccio.
Sir Politick Would-be, *a Knight.*
Peregrine, *a Gentleman Traveller.*
Nano, *a Dwarf.*
Castrone, *an Eunuch.*
Androgyno, *an Hermaphrodite.*

Grege (*or Mob.*)
Commandadori, Officers of justice.
Mercatori, three Merchants.
Avocatori, four Magistrates.
Notario, *the Register.*

Lady Would-be, *Sir Politick's Wife.*
Celia, *Corvino's Wife.*

Servitori, Servants, two Waiting-women,
   &c.

The SCENE,--Venice.

[1] *To which I shall take the occasion elsewhere to speak.*] In the quarto Jonson was somewhat more particular—" to which, upon my next opportunity toward the examining and digesting of my NOTES, I shall speak more wealthily, and pay the world a debt." He alludes to the promise in his former play, of publishing a translation of the Art of Poetry (p. 272). The "notes" were written, and, as I have already observed, burnt in the fire which destroyed his library.
[2] *And not Cinnamus the barber, &c.*] We have had this thought before ; see p. 267 *b.*

Volpone ; or, The Fox.

THE ARGUMENT.[1]

V olpone, childless, rich, feigns sick, de-
    spairs,
O ffers his state to hopes of several heirs,
L ies languishing: his parasite receives
P resents of all, assures, deludes; then
    weaves
O ther cross plots, which ope themselves,
    are told.
N ew tricks for safety are sought; they
    thrive : when bold,
E ach tempts the other again, and all are
    sold.

PROLOGUE.

Now, luck yet send us, and a little wit
  Will serve to make our play hit;
(According to the palates of the season)
  Here is rhyme, not empty of reason.
This we were bid to credit from our poet,
  Whose true scope,[2] if you would know it,

In all his poems still hath been this
    measure,
  To mix profit with your pleasure;
And not as some, whose throats their envy
    failing,
  Cry hoarsely, All he writes is railing:[3]
And when his plays come forth,[4] think they
    can flout them,
  With saying, he was a year about them.
To this there needs no lie, but this his
    creature,
  Which was two months since no feature ;
And though he dares give them five lives to
    mend it,
  'Tis known, five weeks fully penned it,
From his own hand, without a coadjutor,
  Novice, journeyman, or tutor.
Yet thus much I can give you as a token
  Of his play's worth, no eggs are broken,
Nor quaking custards with fierce teeth
    affrighted,[5]
  Wherewith your rout are so delighted ;
Nor hales he in a gull old ends reciting,
  To stop gaps in his loose writing ;

---

[1] *The Argument.*] It is an acrostic: and
seems to be written in imitation of those acros-
tical arguments, invented by Priscian or some
later grammarians, and prefixed to the Comedies
of Plautus.—WHAL.

[2] *Whose true scope, &c.*] Jonson never forgets to put the audience in mind of the ethical
purpose of his writings. He has adverted to
this already in *Every Man out of his Humour,*
and he returns to it again in the *Silent Woman:*
the expression itself is from Horace :

" *Omne tulit punctum qui miscuit utile dulci,*
  Lectorem delectando pariterque monendo."

[3] *Cry hoarsely, All* he writes is railing, &c.]
This alludes to the Apologetical Dialogue :

P. O, but they lay particular imputations—
A. As what?
P. That *all your writing is mere railing,*
  &c.

[4] *And when his plays come forth, &c.*]
Again :

A. Have they no other?
P. Yes, they say you're slow,
And *scarce bring forth a play a year.*—Ibid.

[5]   *No eggs are broken,*
  Nor quaking custards *with fierce teeth
affrighted.*] In the *Poetaster* Marston (not
Decker, as Whalley has it) throws up the words
quaking custard: the allusion, however, is not
to this, but to a burlesque representation of a
city feast, of which, in Jonson's days, an immense custard always made a conspicuous part.
With this custard a number of foolish tricks
were played, at the Lord Mayor's table, to the
unspeakable delight of the guests ; and some
dramatic writer, perhaps, had transferred them,
with improvements, to the stage, where they
seem to have given equal pleasure. I suspect
that Jonson's "taxing" did not always "fly like
a wild goose unclaimed of any man ;" yet I cannot pretend to guess at the objects of his present
satire. Whalley observes, in the margin of his
copy, that Marston is probably meant by the
" reciter of old ends ;" and it must be granted that
they abound, as he says, in the *Malcontent.* The
Malcontent, however, which was inscribed to
Jonson, has no "gull" amongst its characters ;
who are all equally liberal of *old ends,* and all
equally oracular. In those days the town
swarmed with writers for the stage : and we may
collect from various sources, that there was no
incident so extravagant and ridiculous which
some or other of them did not venture to adopt.

With such a deal of monstrous and forced
　　action,
　As might make Bethlem a faction :
Nor made he his play for jests stolen from
　　each table,
　But makes jests to fit his fable ;
And so presents quick comedy refined,
　As best critics have designed ;
The laws of time, place, persons he ob-
　　serveth,
　From no needful rule he swerveth.
All gall and copperas from his ink he
　　draineth,
　Only a little salt remaineth,[1]
Wherewith he'll rub your cheeks, till red
　　with laughter,
　They shall look fresh a week after.

ACT I.

SCENE I.—*A Room in* Volpone's *House.*

Enter Volpone *and* Mosca.

Volp. Good morning to the day ;[2] and
　next, my gold !
Open the shrine, that I may see my saint.
　　[Mosca *withdraws the curtain, and*
　　discovers piles of gold, plate,
　　jewels, &c.
Hail the world's soul, and mine ! more
　glad than is
The teeming earth to see the longed-for
　sun
Peep through the horns of the celestial
　Ram,
Am I, to view thy splendour darkening
　his ;
That lying here, amongst my other hoards,

Shew'st like a flame by night, or like the
　day
Struck out of chaos, when all darkness
　fled
Unto the centre.　O thou son of Sol,
But brighter than thy father, let me kiss,
With adoration, thee, and every relick
Of sacred treasure in this blessed room.
Well did wise poets, by thy glorious name,
Title that age which they would have the
　best :
Thou being the best of things,[3] and far
　transcending
All style of joy, in children, parents,
　friends,
Or any other waking dream on earth :
Thy looks when they to Venus did as-
　cribe,
They should have given her twenty thou-
　sand Cupids ;
Such are thy beauties and our loves ! Dear
　saint,
Riches, the dumb god, that giv'st all men
　tongues,
That canst do nought, and yet mak'st men
　do all things ;
The price of souls ; even hell, with thee to
　boot,
Is made worth heaven.　Thou art virtue,
　fame,
Honour, and all things else.　Who can get
　thee,
He shall be noble, valiant, honest, wise——
Mos. And what he will, sir.　Riches are
　in fortune
A greater good than wisdom is in nature.
Volp. True, my beloved Mosca.　Yet I
　glory
More in the cunning purchase of my
　wealth,

---

[1] *Only a little* salt *remaineth, &c.*] From
Horace :
　　　" At idem, quod sale multo
Urbem defricuit," &c.

[2] *Good morning to the day, &c.*] The reader
cannot but perceive, says Upton, that the diction of this opening scene rises to a tragic sublimity. This expression, *Shew'st like a flame by
night,* is from Pindar :
　　'Ο δε
Χρυσος, αιθομενον πυρ
'Ατε, διαπρεπει νυ——
κτι μεγανορος εξοχα πλουτου.

[3] *Thou being the best of things, &c.*] Upton
had reason to say that the diction of this piece
rose to a tragic sublimity : since Jonson has had
recourse for it to the tragic poets.　This most
learned man, who has " stalked for two centuries," as Mr. Malone takes upon himself to assure
us, " on the stilts of an artificial reputation," was

not only familiar with the complete dramas of
the Athenian stage, but even with the minutest
fragments of them, which have come down to
us.　The beautiful lines above are from the
Bellerophon, a lost play of Euripides.—Edit...
Beck. vol. ii. p. 432 :

Ω χρυσε, δεξιωμα καλλισον βροτοις,
'Ως ουδε μητηρ ηδονας τοιασδ' εχει,
Ου παιδες ανθρωποισιν, ου φιλος πατηρ,
Οιας συ χ'οι σε δωμασιν κεκτημενοι.
Ει δ' η Κυπρις τοιουτον οφθαλμοις ορα,
Ου θαυμ', ερωτας μυριους αυτην τρεφειν.

The concluding lines are from Horace, lib. ii.
Sat. 3 :
　　　" Omnis enim res
Virtus, fama, decus, divina humanaque, pulcris
Divitiis parent, quas qui construxerit, ille
Clarus erit, fortis, justus. — Sapiensque?
　　Etiam, et rex,
Et quicquid volet."

Than in the glad possession, since I gain
No common way; I use no trade, no
   venture;
I wound no earth with plough-shares, fat
   no beasts
To feed the shambles; have no mills for
   iron,
Oil, corn, or men, to grind them into
   powder:
I blow no subtle glass,[1] expose no ships
To threat'nings of the furrow-faced sea;
I turn no monies in the public bank,
Nor usure private.
   Mos. No, sir, nor devour
Soft prodigals. You shall have some will
   swallow
A melting heir as glibly as your Dutch
Will pills of butter, and ne'er purge for it;
Tear forth the fathers of poor families
Out of their beds, and coffin them alive
In some kind clasping prison, where their
   bones
May be forthcoming, when the flesh is
   rotten:
But your sweet nature doth abhor these
   courses;
You loathe the widow's or the orphan's tears
Should wash your pavements, or their
   piteous cries
Ring in your roofs, and beat the air for
   vengeance.
   Volp. Right, Mosca; I do loathe it.
   Mos. And, besides, sir,
You are not like the thresher[2] that doth
   stand
With a huge flail, watching a heap of
   corn,
And, hungry, dares not taste the smallest
   grain,
But feeds on mallows, and such bitter
   herbs;
Nor like the merchant, who hath filled his
   vaults
With Romagnia, and rich Candian wines,
Yet drinks the lees of Lombard's vinegar:
You will not lie in straw, whilst moths and
   worms

Feed on your sumptuous hangings and soft
   beds;
You know the use of riches, and dare give
   now
From that bright heap, to me, your poor
   observer,
Or to your dwarf, or your hermaphrodite,
Your eunuch, or what other household
   trifle
Your pleasure allows maintenance——
   Volp. Hold thee, Mosca,
                  [Gives him money.
Take of my hand; thou strik'st on truth
   in all,
And they are envious term thee parasite.
Call forth my dwarf, my eunuch, and my
   fool,
And let them make me sport. *[Exit* Mos.]
   What should I do,
But cocker up my genius, and live free
To all delights my fortune calls me to?
I have no wife, no parent, child, ally,
To give my substance to; but whom I
   make
Must be my heir; and this makes men
   observe me:
This draws new clients daily to my house,
Women and men of every sex and age,
That bring me presents, send me plate,
   coin, jewels,
With hope that when I die (which they
   expect
Each greedy minute) it shall then return
Tenfold upon them; whilst some, covetous
Above the rest, seek to engross me whole,
And counter-work the one unto the other,
Contend in gifts, as they would seem in
   love:
All which I suffer, playing with their
   hopes,
And am content to coin them into profit,
And look upon their kindness, and take
   more,
And look on that; still bearing them in
   hand,[3]
Letting the cherry knock against their
   lips,

---

[1] *I blow no subtle glass,*] Venice, where the scene is laid, and the neighbouring island of Murano, being famous for their manufacture in *glass.*—WHAL.

[2] *You are not like the thresher, &c.*] This, too, is imitated from Horace, but so obviously, as Upton truly says, as to be visible to every schoolboy. He takes this opportunity, however, of mentioning another imitation, which he thinks not quite so plain:

"Great mother Fortune, queen of human state, Rectress *of action.*" &c.—*Sej.* act v.

"Those," he adds, "who know anything of Jonson's perpetual allusions to ancient authors, *will plainly perceive* that he wrote:

"Rectress of *Antium!*—from Horace, Lib. i. Od. 35."

There is nothing in the "treatise on the Bathos" quite so good as this.

[3] *Still* bearing them in hand,] i.e., flattering their hopes, keeping them in expectation. "You may remember," says Archbishop King to Swift, "how we were *borne in hand* in my lord Pem-

And draw it by their mouths, and back
   again.—
How now !

Re-enter Mosca *with* Nano, Androgyno,
   and Castrone.

Nan.
  " Now, room for fresh gamesters, who
    do will you to know,
  They do bring you neither play nor
    university show ;[1]
  And therefore do intreat you that
    whatsoever they rehearse,
  May not fare a whit the worse, for the
    false pace of the verse.[2]

If you wonder at this, you will wonder
   more ere we pass,
For know, here is inclosed the soul of
   Pythagoras,[3]
That juggler divine, as hereafter shall
   follow ;[4]
Which soul, fast and loose, sir, came
   first from Apollo,[5]
And was breathed into Æthalides,
   Mercurius his son,[6]
Where it had the gift to remember all
   that ever was done.
From thence it fled forth, and made
   quick transmigration
To goldy-locked Euphorbus,[7] who was
   killed in good fashion,

broke's time, that the Queen had passed the
grant," &c. The phrase occurs perpetually in
our old poets. Thus in *Ram Alley*, act ii. :

  " Yet I will *bear some dozen more in hand*,
   And make them all my gulls."

In the preceding lines Jonson had Petronius
in view :—*Incidimus in turbam hæredipetarum
sciscitantium quod genus hominum, aut unde
veniremus. Ex præscripto ergo consilii com-
munis, exaggerati prudenter unde, aut qui esse-
mus, haud dubie credentibus indicavimus. Qui
statim opes suas summo cum certamine in Eu-
molpium congesserunt : et omnes ejus gratiam
sollicitant.*"

  [1] *Now, room for fresh gamesters, who do will
    you to know,
  They do bring you neither play nor* university show ;] This scene is a kind of antimasque or jig, such as is found in many of our
old plays. "It is chiefly taken," as Upton observes, "from one of Lucian's dialogues, and is
meant as a ridicule on the metempsychosis."
Both Lucian and Jonson, however, had better
objects in view, than the exposure of such
absurdities. "By *university show*, is meant
such masques and plays, as our universities used
to exhibit to our kings and queens, and which
were acted by the scholars in their halls."

  [2] *May not fare a whit the worse, for* the false
pace *of the verse*.] Upton, a man of very considerable learning, which (unaccompanied, as it
was, with an adequate portion of judgment) frequently betrayed him into absurdities ; published,
in 1749, " Remarks " on this and the two following plays ; of which, Mr. Whalley occasionally
availed himself. It seems to have been Upton's
chief object to point out Jonson's allusions to the
classics ; in this he is generally successful ; indeed, he seldom ventures beyond such as are sufficiently trite and obvious. When he attempts to
correct the text, he fails : whilst his explanations,
which are given in a tone of formal gravity highly
ludicrous, when contrasted with the subject,
usually aim beyond the poet, and perplex where
they do not mislead. Jonson apologizes for the
false pace of his doggrel. But of this Upton
will not hear : "We must not understand," he
says, " that he errs against the laws of metre ;

but that the pace of his verse may sometimes
offend the too delicate ear." Those who recollect that, when Shakspeare produced a few words
of prose, such as, "Where hast thou been,
sister?" Upton pronounced that he meant to
afford a beautiful example of the "trochaic-
dimeter-brachy-catalectic, commonly called the
ithyphallic measure" (*Observ.* p. 382), will not be
surprised to hear that the hobbling lines above
are all good metre : they are, it seems, "of the
anapestic kind, consisting of anapests, spondees,
dactyls, and sometimes the *pes proceleusmaticus*," and are to be scanned in this manner :

$$\overset{1}{\text{And therefore}} \mid \overset{2}{\text{do intreat you}} \mid \overset{3}{\text{that whatsoever}}$$
$$\overset{4}{\mid \text{they rehearse,}}$$
$$\overset{1}{\text{May not fare a}} \mid \overset{2}{\text{whit the worse}} \mid \overset{3}{\text{for the false}}$$
$$\overset{4}{\text{pace}} \mid \text{of the verse.}$$

"To this measure," exclaims Upton with great
glee, "the reader may reduce them all." There
is no doubt of it : and so he may all the lines in
the daily papers, if he pleases. Surely unlettered
sense is far more valuable than learning thus
ridiculously abused.

  [3] *For know*, here *is inclosed the soul of Pythagoras*,] δεικτικως, in *Androgyno* the hermaphrodite, of whose various transformations the
dwarf gives an account.

  [4] *That juggler divine, that hereafter shall
follow ;*] That *juggler divine*, as Upton observes,
is from Lucian, γοητα και τετρατουργον, as indeed is much of the rest.

  [5] *Which soul—came first from Apollo*.] Ὡς
μεν εξ Απολλωνος το προτον ἡ ψυχη μοι καταπτα-
μενη εις την γην ενεδυ ες ανθρωπου σωμα, &c.
                    Luc. Gall.

  [6] *And was breathed into Æthalides, Mercu-
rius his son*,]
               'Ερμειαο,
Σφωιτεροιο τακηος, ὃς δι μνηστιν πορε παντων
Αφθιτον.—*Apollon.* Lib. i. v. 644.

  [7] *To goldy-locked Euphorbus*, &c.] Πλην
αλλα επειπερ Ευφορβος εγενομην, εμαχομην εν
Ιλιῳ και αποθανων ὑπο Μενελαῳ. κ. τ. λ.
                     Luc. ibid.

At the siege of old Troy, by the
cuckold of Sparta.
Hermotimus was next (I find it in my
charta)
To whom it did pass, where no sooner
it was missing,
But with one Pyrrhus of Delos it
learned to go a fishing;
And thence did it enter the sophist of
Greece.
From Pythagore, she went into a beau-
tiful piece,[1]
Hight Aspasio, the meretrix; and the
next toss of her
Was again of a whore, she became a
philosopher,
Crates the cynick, as itself doth relate it:
Since kings, knights, and beggars,
knaves, lords, and fools gat it,
Besides ox and ass, camel, mule, goat,
and brock,
In all which it hath spoke, as in the
cobbler's cock.[2]
But I come not here to discourse of
that matter,
Or his one, two, or three, or his great
oath, BY QUATER!
His musics, his trigon, his golden thigh,[3]
Or his telling how elements shift; but I
Would ask, how of late thou hast suf-
fered translation,
And shifted thy coat in these days of
reformation.

And.
Like one of the reformed, a fool, as you
see,
Counting all old doctrine heresie.[4]

Nan.
But not on thine own forbid meats hast
thou ventured?

And.
On fish, when first a Carthusian I entered.

Nan.
Why, then thy dogmatical silence hath
left thee?

And.
Of that an obstreperous lawyer bereft
me.

Nan.
O wonderful change, when sir lawyer
forsook thee!
For Pythagore's sake, what body then
took thee?

And.
A good dull mule.

Nan.
And how! by that means
Thou wert brought to allow of the eat-
ing of beans?

And.
Yes.

Nan.
But from the mule into whom didst
thou pass?

And.
Into a very strange beast, by some
writers called an ass;
By others, a precise, pure, illuminate
brother,
Of those devour flesh, and sometimes
one another;[5]
And will drop you forth a libel, or a
sanctified lie,

---

[1] *From Pythagore, she went into a beautiful
piece,*] Αποδυσαμενος δε τον Πυθαγοραν, τινα
μετημφιασω μετ' αυτον;—Ασπασιαν την εκ
Μιλητου εταιραν. κ. τ. λ.
[2] *The* cobbler.] Mycillus, with whom the cock
carries on the dialogue, here abridged.
[3] *His* one, two, *or* three, *or his great oath,* by
quater,
His musics, his trigon, his golden thigh,]
It would perhaps have puzzled Pythagoras himself, "juggler" as he was, to explain this empty
jargon. His scholars have written innumerable
volumes upon it, more to their own satisfaction,
I believe, than the edification of their readers;
for while it was thought worth contending about,
no two of them were agreed upon any part of the
subject. The "great oath," or tetractys, as Upton
observes, "is mentioned in the *Golden Verses;*"
a little poem written by one of Pythagoras's
scholars, and containing more wisdom perhaps
than his master taught.
[4] *Counting all* old doctrine *heresie.*] By *old
doctrine* he means the doctrine commonly received before the Reformation; which was

at first opprobriously called the *new learning.*
It is not improbable that Jonson, when he wrote
this, was a convert to the church of Rome; and
might desire to sneer at the zealots of the establishment, as he does soon after at the Puritans.
WHAL.

[5] *Of those devour flesh, and sometimes one
another;*] Wonderful is the advantage of scan-
sion, aided by the occasional admission of the
pes proceleusmaticus, in detecting the errors of
copyists and printers. Upton, who measured
the harmonious line

         1   2   3   4
   Counting | all old | doctrine | heresie,
and found it perfect in all its members, immediately discovered the unmetrical pace of that
above. "There is plainly," says he, "a word
wanting which *spoils* both the measure and the
sense; we must read,

              1   2   3
Of those *that* | devour flesh | and sometimes |
              4
     one another."

Betwixt every spoonful of a nativity-
　　pie.[1]

Nan.

Now quit thee, for heaven, of that pro-
　　fane nation,
And gently report thy next transmigra-
　　tion.

And.

To the same that I am.

Nan.

A creature of delight,
And, what is more than a fool, an her-
　　maphrodite!
Now, prithee, sweet soul, in all thy
　　variation,
Which body wouldst thou choose to
　　keep up thy station?

And.

Troth, this I am in: even here would
　　I tarry.

Nan.

'Cause here the delight of each sex
　　thou canst vary?

And.

Alas, those pleasures be stale and for-
　　saken;
No, 'tis your fool wherewith I am so
　　taken,
The only one creature that I can call
　　blessed;
For all other forms I have proved most
　　distressed.

Nan.

Spoke true, as thou wert in Pythagoras
　　still.
This learned opinion we celebrate
　　will,
Fellow eunuch, as behoves us, with all
　　our wit and art,

To dignify that whereof ourselves are
　　so great and special a part."

Volp. Now, very, very pretty! Mosca,
　　this
Was thy invention?

Mos. It it please my patron,
Not else.

Volp. It doth, good Mosca.

Mos. Then it was, sir.

Nano *and* Castrone *sing.*

" Fools, they are the only nation
Worth men's envy or admiration;
Free from care or sorrow-taking,
Selves and others merry making:
All they speak or do is sterling.
Your fool he is your great man's darling,
And your ladies' sport and pleasure;
Tongue and bauble are his treasure.
E'en his face begetteth laughter,
And he speaks truth free from slaughter;[2]
He's the grace of every feast,
And sometimes the chiefest guest;
Hath his trencher and his stool,
When wit waits upon the fool.
　　O, who would not be
　　He, he, he?"　　[*Knocking without.*

Volp. Who's that? Away! [*Exeunt*
Nano *and* Castrone.] Look, Mosca.
Fool, begone!　　[*Exit* Androgyno.

Mos. 'Tis Signior Voltore, the advocate;
I know him by his knock.

Volp. Fetch me my gown,
My furs, and night-caps; say my couch is
　　changing.
And let him entertain himself awhile
Without i' the gallery. [*Exit* Mosca.] Now,
　　now my clients

Whalley subscribes to this assertion; and the verse thus happily restored to "sense and measure," is accordingly placed in his text. It is singular that neither of these critics should have adverted to the peculiarity of Jonson's style.

[1] *Betwixt every spoonful of a* nativity *pie.*] i.e., of a *Christmas*-pie. The Puritans, who are here ridiculed, affected to shrink with horror from the mention of the popish word *mass*, though in conjunction with the most sacred names. Jonson alludes to this again, with exquisite humour, in the *Alchemist*, where the Saints are about to cozen with the philosopher's stone:

"*Subtle.* And then the turning of this lawyer's pewter
To plate at Christmas——
Ananias. Christ-*tide*, I pray you."

[2] *And he speaks truth* free from slaughter;] i.e., he is indulged in speaking truth, without being punished or called to account for it. This

impunity, however, if it really existed, did not long survive the period of this song; as Mass Stone, who is mentioned in the second act, found to his sorrow.

Jonson makes slaughter rhyme to laughter; it seems, however, to have been considered as improper, and to have excited some degree of disapprobation. In the *Faune*, which appeared shortly after this comedy, Marston speaks of two critics, one of which "had lost his flesh with fishing at the measure of Plautus's verses, and the other had vowed to get the consumption of the lungs, or leave to posterity the *true pronunciation and orthography of laughing*," act iv. Shakspeare spells the word *loffe* in *Midsummer Night's Dream*, to accommodate it to *cough*, and it is not improbable but that he, as well as Jonson, might be in Marston's thoughts: not that our great bard was in much danger of a consumption from his abstruse studies for the benefit of posterity. To do him justice, few cared less about these matters than himself.

Begin their visitation! Vulture, kite,
Raven, and gorcrow, all my birds of prey,
That think me turning carcase, now they
  come;
I am not for them yet.

Re-enter Mosca, *with the gown, &c.*

                How now! the news?
Mos. A piece of plate, sir.
Volp. Of what bigness?
Mos. Huge,
Massy, and antique, with your name in-
  scribed,
And arms engraven.
Volp. Good! and not a fox
Stretched on the earth, with fine delusive
  sleights,
Mocking a gaping crow?[1] ha, Mosca!
Mos. Sharp, sir.
Volp. Give me my furs. [*Puts on his
  sick dress.*] Why dost thou laugh so,
  man?
Mos. I cannot choose, sir, when I appre-
  hend
What thoughts he has without now, as he
  walks:
That this might be the last gift he should
  give;
That this would fetch you; if you died to-
  day,
And gave him all, what he should be to-
  morrow;
What large return would come of all his
  ventures;
How he should worshipped be, and reve-
  renced;
Ride with his furs, and foot-cloths; waited
  on
By herds of fools and clients; have clear
  way
Made for his mule, as lettered as himself;
Be called the great and learned advocate:
And then concludes, there's nought impos-
  sible.
Volp. Yes, to be learned, Mosca.
Mos. O, no: rich
Implies it.   Hood an ass with reverend
  purple,

So you can hide his two ambitious ears,
And he shall pass for a cathedral doctor[2]
Volp. My caps, my caps, good Mosca.
  Fetch him in.
Mos. Stay, sir; your ointment for your
  eyes.
Volp. That's true;
Dispatch, dispatch: I long to have posses-
  sion
Of my new present.
Mos. That, and thousands more,
I hope to see you lord of.
Volp. Thanks, kind Mosca.
Mos. And that, when I am lost in blended
  dust,
And hundred such as I am, in succession—
Volp. Nay, that were too much, Mosca.
Mos. You shall live
Still to delude these harpies.
Volp. Loving Mosca!
'Tis well: my pillow now, and let him
  enter.   [*Exit* Mosca.
Now, my feigned cough,[3] my phthisic, and
  my gout,
My apoplexy, palsy, and catarrhs,
Help, with your forced functions, this my
  posture,
Wherein, this three year, I have milked
  their hopes.
He comes; I hear him—Uh! [*coughing.*]
  uh! uh! uh! O—

Re-enter Mosca, *introducing* Voltore
  with a piece of Plate.

Mos. You still are what you were, sir,
  Only you,
Of all the rest, are he commands his love,
And you do wisely to preserve it thus,
With early visitation, and kind notes
Of your good meaning to him, which, I
  know,
Cannot but come most grateful.   Patron!
  sir!
Here's Signior Voltore is come——
Volp. [*faintly.*] What say you?
Mos. Sir, Signior Voltore is come this
  morning
To visit you.

---

[1]   *And not a fox*
*Stretched on the earth, with fine delusive
  sleights,*
Mocking a gaping crow?] From Horace:
          "*Plerumque recoctus*
*Scriba ex quinqueviro corvum deludet hian-
  tem.*"
The fable is well known.
[2]   *Hood an ass with reverend purple,*

So you can hide his two ambitious *ears,
And he shall pass for a cathedral doctor.*]
This, as Upton well observes, is true satire, and
very elegantly expressed.—*Ambitious* is used
according to its original meaning in the Latin
language.
  [3] *Now my feigned cough, &c.*] "*Secundùm
hanc formulam imperamus Eumolpo, ut plurimum tussiat, ut sit modò salatiaris stomachi,*"
&c.—PETRON.

Volp. I thank him.

Mos. And hath brought
A piece of antique plate, bought of St.
    Mark,[1]
With which he here presents you.

Volp. He is welcome.
Pray him to come more often.

Mos. Yes.

Volt. What says he?

Mos. He thanks you, and desires you
    see him often.

Volp. Mosca.

Mos. My patron!

Volp. Bring him near, where is he?
I long to feel his hand.

Mos. The plate is here, sir.

Volt. How fare you, sir?

Volp. I thank you, Signior Voltore;
Where is the plate? mine eyes are bad.

Volt. [*putting it into his hands.*] I'm
    sorry,
To see you still thus weak.

Mos. That he's not weaker.   [*Aside.*

Volp. You are too munificent.

Volt. No, sir; would to heaven,
I could as well give health to you, as that
    plate!

Volp. You give, sir, what you can; I
    thank you.   Your love
Hath taste in this, and shall not be un-
    answered:
I pray you see me often.

Volt. Yes, I shall, sir.

Volp. Be not far from me.

Mos. Do you observe that, sir?

Volp. Hearken unto me still; it will
    concern you.

Mos. You are a happy man, sir; know
    your good.

Volp. I cannot now last long——

Mos. You are his heir, sir.

Volt. Am I?

Volp. I feel me going: Uh! uh! uh!
    uh!
I'm sailing to my port, Uh! uh! uh! uh!
And I am glad I am so near my haven.

Mos. Alas, kind gentleman! Well, we
    must all go——

Volt. But, Mosca——

Mos. Age will conquer.

Volt. Pray thee, hear me;
Am I inscribed his heir for certain?

Mos. Are you!
I do beseech you, sir, you will vouchsafe
To write me in your family.[2]   All my
    hopes
Depend upon your worship: I am lost
Except the rising sun do shine on me.

Volt. It shall both shine, and warm thee,
    Mosca.

Mos. Sir,
I am a man that hath not done your love
All the worst offices: here I wear your
    keys,
See all your coffers and your caskets
    locked,
Keep the poor inventory of your jewels,
Your plate, and monies; am your steward,
    sir,
Husband your goods here.

Volt. But am I sole heir?

Mos. Without a partner, sir: confirmed
    this morning:
The wax is warm yet, and the ink scarce
    dry
Upon the parchment.

Volt. Happy, happy me!
By what good chance, sweet Mosca?

Mos. Your desert, sir;
I know no second cause.

Volt. Thy modesty
Is not to know it; well, we shall requite it.

Mos. He ever liked your course, sir;
    that first took him.
I oft have heard him say how he admired
Men of your large profession, that could
    speak
To every cause, and things mere con-
    traries,
Till they were hoarse again, yet all be law;
That, with most quick agility, could turn,
And return;   make knots, and undo
    them;[3]
Give forked counsel; take provoking
    gold
On either hand, and put it up: these
    men,
He knew, would thrive with their humility.

---

[1] *Bought of St. Mark,*] The great mart of
Venice.   Whalley supposed the allusion to be to
the treasury in St. Mark's Church: he did not
know, perhaps, that this celebrated edifice was
surrounded with shops of all kinds, particularly
goldsmiths'.

[2] *To write me in your family.*] This, as
Upton says, is borrowed from Horace: *Scribe
tui gregis hunc.*   It may be so; though it is
quite as probable that it was "borrowed" from
the poet's own times; when it was customary for
the names and offices of the servants and retainers
of great families to be entered in the *Household
Book*; of this practice many proofs yet remain.
The conduct of this scene is above all praise.

[3] [Gifford altered this line to

And [re] return; [could] make knots, and undo
    them;

but surely the original is harmonious and clear
enough.   Jonson frequently lays a strong accent
on the *re* of *return.*—F. C.]

And, for his part, he thought he should be
  blest
To have his heir of such a suffering spirit,
So wise, so grave, of so perplexed a
  tongue,
And loud withal, that would not wag, nor
  scarce
Lie still, without a fee ; when every word
Your worship but lets fall, is a chequin !—
                    [*Knocking without.*
Who's that? one knocks ; I would not
  have you seen, sir.
And yet—pretend you came, and went in
  haste ;
I'll fashion an excuse—and, gentle sir,
When you do come to swim in golden
  lard,[1]
Up to the arms in honey, that your chin
Is born up stiff with fatness of the flood,
Think on your vassal ; but remember me :
I have not been your worst of clients.
Volt. Mosca!—
Mos. When will you have your inven-
  tory brought, sir?
Or see a copy of the Will?—Anon ![2]—
I'll bring them to you, sir. Away, begone,
Put business in your face. [*Exit* Voltore.
Volp. [*springing up.*] Excellent Mosca !
Come hither, let me kiss thee.
Mos. Keep you still, sir.
Here is Corbaccio.
Volp. Set the plate away :
The vulture's gone, and the old raven's
  come ![3]
Mos. Betake you to your silence, and
  your sleep.
Stand there and multiply. [*Putting the
  plate to the rest.*] Now, shall we see
A wretch who is indeed more impotent
Than this can feign to be ; yet hopes to
  hop
Over his grave.

Enter Corbaccio.

                    Signior Corbaccio !
You're very welcome, sir.
Corb. How does your patron?
Mos. Troth, as he did, sir ; no amends.
Corb. What ! mends he ?
Mos. No, sir : he's rather worse.

Corb. That's well.   Where is he ?
Mos. Upon his couch, sir, newly fall'n
  asleep.
Corb. Does he sleep well ?
Mos. No wink, sir, all this night,
Nor yesterday ; but slumbers.
Corb. Good ! he should take
Some counsel of physicians : I have
  brought him
An opiate here, from mine own doctor.
Mos. He will not hear of drugs.
Corb. Why ? I myself
Stood by while it was made, saw all the
  ingredients ;
And know it cannot but most gently
  work :
My life for his, 'tis but to make him sleep.
Volp. Ay, his last sleep, if he would
  take it.   [*Aside.*
Mos. Sir,
He has no faith in physic.
Corb. Say you, say you ?
Mos. He has no faith in physic : he does
  think
Most of your doctors are the greater
  danger,
And worse disease, to escape. I often
  have
Heard him protest that your physician
Should never be his heir.
Corb. Not I his heir ?
Mos. Not your physician, sir.
Corb. O, no, no, no,
I do not mean it.
Mos. No, sir, nor their fees
He cannot brook : he says they flay a
  man
Before they kill him.
Corb. Right, I do conceive you.
Mos. And then they do it by experiment ;
For which the law not only doth absolve
  them,
But gives them great reward : and he is loth
To hire his death so.
Corb. It is true, they kill
With as much licence as a judge.
Mos. Nay, more ;
For he but kills, sir, where the law con-
  demns,
And these can kill him too.

---

[1]   *And, gentle sir,*
When you do come to swim in golden lard,
&c.]   Upton was too busy with his trite
classical imitations to notice this bold and beautiful adoption of the eastern metaphor for a state
of prosperity.
  [2] *Anon !*]   In the margin of Whalley's copy,
a note in the handwriting of Mr. Waldron gives

this expression to *Voltore.* It belongs, however,
to *Mosca*, who pretends to speak to some one
without, in order to quicken the advocate's departure.
  [3] *The vulture's gone, and the old raven's
come !*]   In allusion to their different names.
Corbaccio, in Italian, signifies an old raven.
                                    WHAL*

Corb. Ay, or me;
Or any man.　How does his apoplex?
Is that strong on him still?
　Mos. Most violent.
His speech is broken, and his eyes are set,
His face drawn longer than 'twas wont——
　Corb. How! how!
Stronger than he was wont?
　Mos. No, sir: his face
Drawn longer than 'twas wont.
　Corb. O, good!
　Mos. His mouth
Is ever gaping, and his eyelids hang.
　Corb. Good.
　Mos. A freezing numbness stiffens all
　his joints,
And makes the colour of his flesh like lead.
　Corb. 'Tis good.
　Mos. His pulse beats slow, and dull.
　Corb. Good symptoms still.
　Mos. And from his brain——
　Corb. I conceive you; good.
　Mos. Flows a cold sweat, with a con-
　tinual rheum,
Forth the resolved corners of his eyes.
　Corb. Is't possible? Yet I am better, ha!
How does he with the swimming of his
　head?
　Mos. O, sir, 'tis past the scotomy;[1] he
　now
Hath lost his feeling, and hath left to snort:
You hardly can perceive him, that he
　breathes.
　Corb. Excellent, excellent! sure I shall
　outlast him:
This makes me young again, a score of
　years.
　Mos. I was a coming for you, sir.
　Corb. Has he made his Will?
What has he given me?
　Mos. No, sir.
　Corb. Nothing! ha?
　Mos. He has not made his Will, sir.
　Corb. Oh, oh, oh!
What then did Voltore, the lawyer, here?
　Mos. He smelt a carcase, sir, when he
　but heard
My master was about his testament;
As I did urge him to it for your good——
　Corb. He came unto him, did he? I
　thought so.
　Mos. Yes, and presented him this piece
　of plate.
　Corb. To be his heir?
　Mos. I do not know, sir.

---

[1] *O, sir, 'tis past the* scotomy;] *Scotomia* is
a dizziness or swimming in the head.　See Massinger, vol. iv. 521.

Corb. True:
I know it too.
　Mos. By your own scale, sir.　　[*Aside.*
　Corb. Well,
I shall prevent him yet.　See, Mosca,
　look,
Here I have brought a bag of bright
　chequines,
Will quite weigh down his plate.
　Mos. [*taking the bag.*] Yea, marry, sir.
This is true physic, this your sacred me-
　dicine;
No talk of opiates to this great elixir!
　Corb. 'Tis aurum palpabile, if not po-
　tabile.
　Mos. It shall be ministered to him in his
　bowl.
　Corb. Ay, do, do, do.
　Mos. Most blessed cordial!
This will recover him.
　Corb. Yes, do, do, do.
　Mos. I think it were not best, sir.
　Corb. What?
　Mos. To recover him.
　Corb. O, no, no, no; by no means.
　Mos. Why, sir, this
Will work some strange effect, if he but
　feel it.
　Corb. 'Tis true, therefore forbear; I'll
　take my venture:
Give me it again.
　Mos. At no hand; pardon me:
You shall not do yourself that wrong,
　sir.　I
Will so advise you, you shall have it all.
　Corb. How?
　Mos. All, sir; 'tis your right, your own;
　no man
Can claim a part: 'tis yours without a
　rival,
Decreed by destiny.
　Corb. How, how, good Mosca?
　Mos. I'll tell you, sir.　This fit he shall
　recover.
　Corb. I do conceive you.
　Mos. And on first advantage
Of his gained sense, will I re-importune him
Unto the making of his testament:
And shew him this.
　　　　　　　　[*Pointing to the money.*
　Corb. Good, good.
　Mos. 'Tis better yet,
If you will hear, sir.
　Corb. Yes, with all my heart.
　Mos. Now would I counsel you, make
　home with speed;
There, frame a Will; whereto you shall
　inscribe
My master your sole heir.

Corb. And disinherit
My son!
Mos. O, sir, the better: for that colour
Shall make it much more taking.
    Corb. O, but colour?
    Mos. This Will, sir, you shall send it
    unto me.
Now, when I come to inforce, as I will do,
Your cares, your watchings, and your many
    prayers,
Your more than many gifts, your this day's
    present,
And last, produce your Will; where, with-
    out thought,
Or least regard, unto your proper issue,
A son so brave, and highly meriting,
The stream of your diverted love hath
    thrown you
Upon my master, and made him your heir:
He cannot be so stupid, or stone-dead,
But out of conscience, and mere grati-
    tude——
    Corb. He must pronounce me his?
    Mos. 'Tis true.
    Corb. This plot
Did I think on before.
    Mos. I do believe it.
    Corb. Do you not believe it?
    Mos. Yes, sir.
    Corb. Mine own project.
    Mos. Which, when he hath done, sir——
    Corb. Published me his heir?
    Mos. And you so certain to survive
    him——
    Corb. Ay.
    Mos. Being so lusty a man——
    Corb. 'Tis true.
    Mos. Yes, sir——
    Corb. I thought on that too. See, how
    he should be
The very organ to express my thoughts!
    Mos. You have not only done yourself a
    good——

    Corb. But multiplied it on my son.
    Mos. 'Tis right, sir.
    Corb. Still, my invention.
    Mos. 'Las, sir! heaven knows,
It hath been all my study, all my care,
(I e'en grow gray withal,) how to work
    things——
    Corb. I do conceive, sweet Mosca.
    Mos. You are he
For whom I labour here.
    Corb. Ay, do, do, do:
I'll straight about it.   *[Going.*
    Mos. Rook go with you, raven![1] *[Aside.*
    Corb. I know thee honest.
    Mos. You do lie, sir!
    Corb. And——
    Mos. Your knowledge is no better than
    your ears, sir.
    Corb. I do not doubt to be a father to
    thee.
    Mos. Nor I to gull my brother of his
    blessing.
    Corb. I may have my youth restored to
    me, why not?
    Mos. Your worship is a precious ass!
    Corb. What sayst thou?
    Mos. I do desire your worship to make
    haste, sir.
    Corb. 'Tis done, 'tis done; I go. *[Exit.*
    Volp. [*leaping from his couch.*] O, I
    shall burst!
Let out my sides, let out my sides——
    Mos. ·Contain
Your flux of laughter, sir: you know this
    hope
Is such a bait, it covers any hook.
    Volp. O, but thy working, and thy plac-
    ing it!
I cannot hold; good rascal, let me kiss thee:
I never knew thee in so rare a humour.
    Mos. Alas, sir, I but do as I am taught;
Follow your grave instructions; give them
    words;[2]

---

[1] *Rook go with you, raven!*] May you, *raven,*
be *rooked,* or cheated! as Upton explains it.
There never was a scene of avarice in the extremity of old age better drawn than this.—
WHAL.
    Nor ever so well. Hurd (who had just been
reading Congreve's letters to Dennis) terms the
humour of it "inordinate;" and blames Jonson
for sporting so freely with the infirmities of Corbaccio. I can see no occasion for this. If
avarice be, in any case, a legitimate object of
satire, surely it is eminently so when accompanied as here with age and infirmity. Bad
passions become more odious in proportion as
the motives for them are weakened; and gratuitous vice cannot be too indignantly exposed
te reprehension.

[2] *Give them words;*] i.e., deceive or impose
on them:
        "*An ut ignotum, dare nobis*
    Verba putas?"—Horace, L. i. Sat. 3.

    This is Upton's remark. That *dare verba*
signifies to cajole, to impose upon, is certain;
such, however, is not the sense of the expression
here. By *give them words,* Mosca simply, or
rather artfully, means that he clothes the "grave
instructions" of his patron in fitting language.
He speaks of Volpone, not of Corbaccio and the
rest, who are distinctly noticed in the next line.
The glimpse of a classical allusion is a perfect
ignis fatuus to Upton, who is sure to blunder
after it at all hazards.

Pour oil into their ears, and send them
　　hence.
Volp. 'Tis true, 'tis true.　What a rare
　　punishment
Is avarice to itself!
　Mos. Ay, with our help, sir.
　Volp. So many cares, so many maladies,[1]
So many fears attending on old age,
Yea, death so often called on, as no wish
Can be more frequent with them, their
　　limbs faint,
Their senses dull, their seeing, hearing,
　　going,
All dead before them; yea, their very teeth,
Their instruments of eating, failing them:
Yet this is reckoned life! nay, here was
　　one,
Is now gone home, that wishes to live
　　longer!
Feels not his gout, nor palsy; feigns him-
　　self
Younger by scores of years, flatters his age
With confident belying it, hopes he may,
With charms like Æson, have his youth re-
　　stored:
And with these thoughts so battens, as if
　　fate
Would be as easily cheated on as he,
And all turns air! [*knocking within.*] Who's
　　that there, now? a third!
　Mos. Close, to your couch again; I hear
　　his voice:
It is Corvino, our spruce merchant.
　Volp. [*lies down as before.*] Dead.
　Mos. Another bout, sir, with your eyes.
[*anointing them.*] Who's there?

Enter Corvino.

Signior Corvino! come most wished for! O,
How happy were you, if you knew it, now!
　Corv. Why? what? wherein?
　Mos. The tardy hour is come, sir.
　Corv. He is not dead?
　Mos. Not dead, sir, but as good;
He knows no man.
　Corv. How shall I do then?
　Mos. Why, sir?

Corv. I have brought him here a pearl.
　Mos. Perhaps he has
So much remembrance left as to know you,
　　sir:
He still calls on you; nothing but your
　　name
Is in his mouth. Is your pearl orient, sir?[2]
　Corv. Venice was never owner of the like.
　Volp. [*faintly.*] Signior Corvino!
　Mos. Hark.
　Volp. Signior Corvino!
　Mos. He calls you; step and give it
　　him.—He's here, sir,
And he has brought you a rich pearl.
　Corv. How do you, sir?
Tell him it doubles the twelfth caract.[3]
　Mos. Sir,
He cannot understand, his hearing's gone;
And yet it comforts him to see you——
　Corv. Say
I have a diamond for him, too.
　Mos. Best shew it, sir;
Put it into his hand; 'tis only there
He apprehends: he has his feeling yet.
See how he grasps it!
　Corv. 'Las, good gentleman!
How pitiful the sight is!
　Mos. Tut, forget, sir.
The weeping of an heir should still be
　　laughter
Under a visor.[4]
　Corv. Why, am I his heir?
　Mos. Sir, I am sworn, I may not show
　　the Will
Till he be dead; but here has been Cor-
　　baccio,
Here has been Voltore, here were others
　　too,
I cannot number 'em, they were so many;
All gaping here for legacies: but I,
Taking the vantage of his naming you,
Signior Corvino, Signior Corvino, took
Paper, and pen, and ink, and there I asked
　　him
Whom he would have his heir!　*Corvino.*
　　Who
Should be executor?　*Corvino.*　And

---

[1] *So many cares,* &c.] In this fine speech
Jonson has again laid the fragments of the
Greek drama under contribution; Lucian and
Juvenal, however, had set him the example.
　[2] *Is your pearl* orient, *sir?*] i.e., bright,
sparkling, pellucid. Thus Shakspeare:

"Bright *orient* pearl, alack! too timely shaded."

And Milton:

　"Offering to every wearied traveller
　　His *orient* liquor in a crystal glass."
　　　　　　　　　　　　Comus, v. 64.

[3] *It doubles the twelfth* caract.] A caract is
a weight of four grains, by which jewels are
weighed.　The same expression occurs in Cartwright:

　　　　　　"Diamonds, *two whereof*
Do *double the twelfth caract.*"—*Lady Errant.*

　[4] *The weeping of an heir should still be
　　　　laughter
　　Under a visor.*]

"*Hæredis fletus sub personâ risus est.*"
　　　　　　　　　　　　P. Syrus.

To any question he was silent to,
I still interpreted the nods he made,
Through weakness, for consent: and sent
   home th' others,
Nothing bequeathed them, but to cry and
   curse.[1]
  Corv. O, my dear Mosca. [*They em-
brace.*] Does he not perceive us?
  Mos. No more than a blind harper. He
   knows no man,
No face of friend, nor name of any servant,
Who 'twas that fed him last, or gave him
   drink:
Not those he hath begotten, or brought up,
Can he remember.
  Corv. Has he children?
  Mos. Bastards,
Some dozen, or more, that he begot on
   beggars,
Gypsies,[2] and Jews, and black-moors, when
   he was drunk.
Knew you not that, sir? 'tis the common
   fable.
The dwarf, the fool, the eunuch, are all
   his ;
He's the true father of his family,
In all save me :—but he has given them
   nothing.
  Corv. That's well, that's well ! Art sure
   he does not hear us?
  Mos. Sure, sir ! why, look you, credit
   your own sense.
           [*Shouts in* Vol.'s *ear.*
The pox approach, and add to your
   diseases,
If it would send you hence the sooner, sir,
For your incontinence, it hath deserved it
Throughly and throughly, and the plague
   to boot !—
You may come near, sir. — Would you
   would once close
Those filthy eyes of yours, that flow with
   slime,
Like two frog-pits ; and those same hang-
   ing cheeks,

Covered with hide instead of skin—Nay,
   help, sir—[3]
That look like frozen dish-clouts set on end !
  Corv. [*aloud.*] Or like an old smoked
   wall, on which the rain
Ran down in streaks !
  Mos. Excellent, sir ! speak out:
You may be louder yet ; a culverin
Discharged in his ear would hardly bore it.
  Corv. His nose is like a common sewer,
   still running.
  Mos. 'Tis good ! And what his mouth?
  Corv. A very draught.
  Mos. O, stop it up——
  Corv. By no means.
  Mos. Pray you, let me:
Faith I could stifle him rarely with a pillow,
As well as any woman that should keep
   him.
  Corv. Do as you will ; but I'll begone.
  Mos. Be so ;
It is your presence makes him last so long.
  Corv. I pray you use no violence.
  Mos. No, sir ! why?
Why should you be thus scrupulous, pray
   you, sir?
  Corv. Nay, at your discretion.
  Mos. Well, good sir, be gone.
  Corv. I will not trouble him now to take
   my pearl.[4]
  Mos. Puh ! nor your diamond. What a
   needless care
Is this afflicts you? Is not all here yours?
Am not I here, whom you have made your
   creature?
That owe my being to you?
  Corv. Grateful Mosca !
Thou art my friend, my fellow, my com-
   panion,
My partner, and shalt share in all my for-
   tunes.
  Mos. Excepting one.
  Corv. What's that?
  Mos. Your gallant wife, sir.
              [*Exit* Corv.

---

[1] *Nothing bequeathed them, but to cry and
curse.*] From Horace, as Upton observes :

          "*Invenietque*
Nil sibi legatum, præter plorare, suisque."

[2] *Bastards,
Some dozen or more, that he begot on beggars,
Gypsies, &c.*] This is a playful application of
Martial's epigram on Quirinalis :

" *Uxorem habendam non putat Quirinalis,
Cum vult habere filios ; et invenit
Quo possit istud more: (amplectitur) ancillas,*

*Domumque et agros implet equitibus vernis.
Paterfamilias verus est Quirinalis.*"
             Lib. i. ep. 85.

Upton also points out the allusions to Juvenal ;
but they are too well known to call for particular
notice.

[3] *Nay, help, sir,*] i.e., to rail and abuse
Volpone. This exposure of Corvino is happily
designed : but, indeed, the whole of the act is a
masterpiece of truth and genuine comic humour.

[4] *I will not trouble him now to take my
pearl.*] i.e., to wrest it from Volpone, who in his
supposed state of insensibility had closed his
hand upon it.

Now is he gone : we had no other means
To shoot him hence but this.
　　Volp. My divine Mosca !
Thou hast to-day outgone thyself. [*Knock-
　　ing within.*] Who's there?
I will be troubled with no more.　Prepare
Me music, dances, banquets, all delights;
The Turk is not more sensual in his
　　pleasures
Than will Volpone. [*Exit* Mos.] Let me
　　see; a pearl !
A diamond ! plate ! chequines !　Good
　　morning's purchase.
Why, this is better than rob churches, yet ;
Or fat, by eating, once a month, a man—

　　　　Re-enter Mosca.

Who is 't ?
　　Mos. The beauteous Lady Would-be, sir,
Wife to the English knight, Sir Politick
　　Would-be,
(This is the style, sir, is directed me,)
Hath sent to know how you have slept to-
　　night,
And if you would be visited?
　　Volp. Not now:
Some three hours hence.
　　Mos. I told the squire so much.
　　Volp. When I am high with mirth and
　　wine ; then, then :
'Fore heaven, I wonder at the desperate
　　valour
Of the bold English, that they dare let
　　loose
Their wives to all encounters !
　　Mos. Sir, this knight
Had not his name for nothing, he is
　　politick,
And knows, howe'er his wife affect strange
　　airs,
She hath not yet the face to be dishonest :
But had she Signior Corvino's wife's
　　face——[1]
　　Volp. Has she so rare a face ?
　　Mos. O, sir, the wonder,
The blazing star of Italy ! a wench
Of the first year ! a beauty ripe as harvest !
Whose skin is whiter than a swan all over,
Than silver, snow, or lilies ! a soft lip,
Would tempt you to eternity of kissing !
And flesh that melteth in the touch to
　　blood !
Bright as your gold, and lovely as your
　　gold !

　　Volp. Why had not I known this before?
　　Mos. Alas, sir,
Myself but yesterday discovered it.
　　Volp. How might I see her?
　　Mos. O, not possible ;
She's kept as warily as is your gold :
Never does come abroad, never takes air
But at a window.　All her looks are
　　sweet,
As the first grapes or cherries, and are
　　watched
As near as they are.
　　Volp. I must see her.
　　Mos. Sir,
There is a guard of spies ten thick upon
　　her,
All his whole household ; each of which is
　　set
Upon his fellow, and have all their
　　charge,
When he goes out, when he comes in,
　　examined.
　　Volp. I will go see her, though but at
　　her window.
　　Mos. In some disguise then.
　　Volp. That is true ; I must
Maintain mine own shape still the same :
　　we'll think.　　　　　　　　[*Exeunt.*

　　　　　　　　ACT II.

SCENE I.—St. Mark's *Place; a retired
　　corner before* Corvino's *House.*

　　Enter Sir Politick Would-be, *and* Pere-
　　　　grine.

　　Sir P. Sir, to a wise man, all the world's
　　his soil :
It is not Italy, nor France, nor Europe,
That must bound me, if my fates call me
　　forth.
Yet I protest, it is no salt desire
Of seeing countries, shifting a religion,
Nor any disaffection to the state
Where I was bred, and unto which I owe
My dearest plots, hath brought me out ;
　　much less
That idle, antique, stale, gray-headed pro-
　　ject
Of knowing men's minds and manners,
　　with Ulysses !
But a peculiar humour of my wife's
Laid for this height of Venice, to observe,

---

[1] *But had she Signior Corvino's wife's face——*]
This circumstance, on which the catastrophe of
the play hinges, is very naturally introduced.

Mosca's glowing description of the lady might
inflame the imagination of a less voluptuous
sensualist than Volpone.

To quote,[1] to learn the language, and so
  forth——
I hope you travel, sir, with licence?
  Per. Yes.
  Sir P. I dare the safelier converse——
  How long, sir,
Since you left England?
  Per. Seven weeks.
  Sir P. So lately!
You have not been with my lord ambas-
  sador?[2]
  Per. Not yet, sir.
  Sir P. Pray you, what news, sir, vents
  our climate?
I heard last night a most strange thing re-
  ported
By some of my lord's followers, and I long
To hear how 'twill be seconded.
  Per. What was 't, sir?
  Sir P. Marry, sir, of a raven that should
  build
In a ship royal of the king's.
  Per. This fellow,
Does he gull me, trow? or is gulled?
  [*Aside.*] Your name, sir.
  Sir P. My name is Politick Would-be.
  Per. O, that speaks him. [*Aside.*]
A knight, sir?
  Sir P. A poor knight, sir.
  Per. Your lady
Lies here in Venice, for intelligence
Of tires and fashions, and behaviour,
Among the courtezans? the fine Lady
  Would-be?
  Sir P. Yes, sir; the spider and the bee,
  ofttimes,
Suck from one flower.

  Per. Good Sir Politick,
I cry you mercy; I have heard much of
  you:
'Tis true, sir, of your raven.
  Sir P. On your knowledge?
  Per. Yes, and your lion's whelping in
  the Tower.
  Sir P. Another whelp![3]
  Per. Another, sir.
  Sir P. Now heaven!
What prodigies be these? The fires at
  Berwick!
And the new star! these things concurring,
  strange,
And full of omen! Saw you those meteors?
  Per. I did, sir.
  Sir P. Fearful! Pray you, sir, confirm
  me,
Were there three porpoises seen above the
  bridge,[4]
As they give out?
  Per. Six, and a sturgeon, sir.
  Sir P. I am astonished.
  Per. Nay, sir, be not so;
I'll tell you a greater prodigy than these.
  Sir P. What should these things por-
  tend?
  Per. The very day
(Let me be sure) that I put forth from
  London,
There was a whale discovered in the river,
As high as Woolwich, that had waited
  there,
Few know how many months, for the sub-
  version
Of the Stode fleet.
  Sir P. Is 't possible? believe it,

---

[1] *To* quote, *&c.*] To quote is to notice, to
write down. Thus Polonius:

" I'm sorry that with better heed and judgment
  I had not *quoted* him."

And thus Webster, in the *White Devil:*

  " It is reported you possess a book
  Wherein you have *quoted* by intelligence,
  The names of all offenders."

The triumph of Sir Politick over poor Ulysses is
an excellent trait of character.
  [2] The celebrated Sir Henry Wotton. Coryat
found "his lordship" here, he says, in 1608, and
experienced "much kindness at his hands." He
was introduced to Sir Henry by Mr. Richard
Martin (the person to whom Jonson dedicated
the *Poetaster*) in a letter which plays upon the
simple vanity of our traveller in a most arch and
entertaining manner.
  [3] *Another whelp!*] The birth of the first is
thus gravely recorded by Stow: "Sunday, the
fifth of August (1604), a lionesse, named Eliza-

beth, in the Tower of London, brought foorth a
lyons whelpe, which lyons whelpe lived not
longer than till the next day." The other,
which is spoken of here, was whelped, as Stow
also carefully informs us, on the 26th of February, 1606. As the former had lived so short
a time, James ordered this to be taken from the
dam and brought up by hand; by which wise
mode of management the animal was speedily
dispatched after his brother. These were the
first whelps produced in a tame state in this
country, and perhaps in Europe.
  [4] *Were there three* porpoises *seen above the
bridge, &c.*] This prodigy and that of the
appearance of the whale at Woolwich, mentioned
just below, are duly noticed by Stow: "The
19th of January (1605), a great *porpus* was
taken alive at Westham,—and within a few days
after, a very great *whale* came up *as high as
Woolwich;* and when she tasted the fresh water
and scented the land, she returned into the sea."
—P. 881. The references to the remaining prodigies, I have (fortunately for the reader'
patience) mislaid or overlooked among my notes.

'Twas either sent from Spain, or the arch-
   duke's :
Spinola's whale, upon my life, my credit !
Will they not leave these projects ? Worthy
   sir,
Some other news.
   Per. Faith, Stone the fool is dead,
And they do lack a tavern fool extremely.
   Sir P. Is Mass Stone dead ?[1]
   Per. He's dead, sir; why, I hope
You thought him not immortal ?—O, this
   knight,
Were he well known, would be a precious
   thing
To fit our English stage: he that should
   write
But such a fellow, should be thought to
   feign
Extremely, if not maliciously.   [*Aside.*
   Sir P. Stone dead !
   Per. Dead.—Lord ! how deeply, sir,
   you apprehend it !
He was no kinsman to you?
   Sir P. That I know of.
Well ! that same fellow was an unknown
   fool.
   Per. And yet you knew him, it seems ?
   Sir P. I did so. Sir,
I knew him one of the most dangerous
   heads
Living within the state, and so I held
   him.
   Per. Indeed, sir ?
   Sir P. While he lived, in action.
He has received weekly intelligence,
Upon my knowledge, out of the Low
   Countries,
For all parts of the world, in cabbages ;[2]
And those dispensed again to ambassadors,
In oranges, musk-melons, apricocks,

Lemons, pome-citrons, and such like ;
   sometimes
In Colchester oysters, and your Selsey
   cockles.
   Per. You make me wonder.
   Sir P. Sir, upon my knowledge.
Nay, I've observed him, at your public
   ordinary,
Take his advertisement from a traveller,
A concealed statesman, in a trencher of
   meat ;
And instantly, before the meal was done,
Convey an answer in a tooth-pick.
   Per. Strange !
How could this be, sir?
   Sir P. Why, the meat was cut
So like his character, and so laid as he
Must easily read the cipher.
   Per. I have heard,
He could not read, sir.
   Sir P. So 'twas given out,
In policy, by those that did employ him :
But he could read, and had your lan-
   guages,
And to 't, as sound a noddle——
   Per. I have heard, sir,
That your baboons were spies, and that
   they were
A kind of subtle nation near to China.
   Sir P. Ay, ay, your Mamaluchi. Faith,
   they had
Their hand in a French plot or two; but
   they
Were so extremely given to women, as
They made discovery of all : yet I
Had my advices here, on Wednesday last,
From one of their own coat, they were re-
   turned,
Made their relations, as the fashion is,
And now stand fair for fresh employment.

---

1 *Is* Mass *Stone dead ?*] In the margin of his
copy, Whalley has written "*Mass,* an abridgment of Master." The thing scarcely deserved
a note ; but he is wrong : Mass is an abridgment
of Messer, an old Italian word, familiarly applied
to a priest or person above the lower rank of
life. I have already alluded to the castigation
of Mass Stone : the following passage relating
to him is curious. On the expensive preparations for the Earl of Northampton's embassy to
Spain, Sir Dudley Carleton thus writes to Mr.
Winwood : "My Lord Admiral's number is 500,
and he swears 500 oaths he will not admit of one
man more. But if he will stand to that rule, and
take in one as another will desire to be discharged, in my opinion, all men's turn will be
served. There was great execution done lately
upon Stone the fool, who was well whipped in
Bridewell for a blasphemous speech, 'that there
went sixty fools into Spain, besides my Lord
Admiral and his two sons.' But he is now at

liberty again, and for this unexpected release
gives his lordship the praise of a very pittiful
lord. His comfort is, that the news of El Senor
Piedra (i.e. Seignior Stone) will be in Spaine
before our ambassador."—Winwood's Memorials,
vol. ii. p. 52.
   2 *He has received weekly intelligence,*
   Out of the Low Countries, in cabbages ;]
This is not an expression thrown out at random.
Cabbages were not originally the growth of
England ; but about this time were sent to us
from Holland, and so became the product of our
kitchen-gardens. I mention this circumstance,
trifling as it seems, because it serves to point out
that propriety and decorum which so strongly
mark the character of Jonson.—WHAL.
   "'Tis scarce an hundred years," says Evelyn,
in his *Discourse of Sallets,* 1706, "since we first
had *cabbages* out of Holland. Sir Anth. Ashley,
of Wimborne St. Giles, in Dorsetshire, being, as I
m told, the first who planted them in England.

Per. Heart !
This Sir Pol will be ignorant of nothing.
                                                    [*Aside.*
It seems, sir, you know all.
    Sir P. Not all, sir; but
I have some general notions.   I do love
To note and to observe: though I live
    out,
Free from the active torrent, yet I'd mark
The currents and the passages of things.
For mine own private use; and know the
    ebbs
And flows of state.
    Per. Believe it, sir, I hold
Myself in no small tie unto my fortunes,
For casting me thus luckily upon you,
Whose knowledge, if your bounty equal it,
May do me great assistance, in instruc-
    tion
For my behaviour, and my bearing, which
Is yet so rude and raw.
    Sir P. Why? came you forth
Empty of rules for travel ?
    Per. Faith, I had
Some common ones, from out that vulgar
    grammar,
Which he that cried *Italian to me, taught
    me.*[1]
    Sir P. Why, this it is that spoils all our
    brave bloods,
Trusting our hopeful gentry unto pedants,
Fellows of outside, and mere bark.[2]   You
    seem
To be a gentleman of ingenuous race :——
I not profess it, but my fate hath been
To be, where I have been consulted
    with,
In this high kind, touching some great
    men's-sons,
Persons of blood and honour.——

Enter Mosca *and* Nano *disguised, followed
by persons with materials for erecting a
Stage.*

    Per. Who be these, sir ?
    Mos. Under that window, there 't must
        be.   The same.
    Sir P. Fellows, to mount a bank.   Did
        your instructor
In the dear tongues, never discourse to you
Of the Italian mountebanks ?
    Per. Yes, sir.
    Sir P. Why,
Here you shall see one.
    Per. They are quacksalvers,
Fellows that live by venting oils and drugs.
    Sir P. Was that the character he gave
        you of them ?
    Per. As I remember.
    Sir P. Pity his ignorance.
They are the only knowing men of Europe !
Great general scholars, excellent physicians,
Most admired statesmen, profest favourites,
And cabinet counsellors to the greatest
    princes;
The only languaged men of all the world !
    Per. And, I have heard, they are most
        lewd impostors ;[3]
Made all of terms and shreds; no less be-
    liers
Of great men's favours, than their own vile
    med'cines ;
Which they will utter upon monstrous
    oaths :
Selling that drug for two-pence, ere they
    part,
Which they have valued at twelve crowns
    before.
    Sir P. Sir, calumnies are answered best
        with silence.

---

[1] *Which he that cried Italian to me, taught
me.*] "Some learned gentlemen," proposed (as
Mr. Whalley informs us) to "correct" the text
here, and alter *cried* to *read.* "If *chiamare*
(says one of these "learned gentlemen," who
appears to be poor Sympson) "had been used in
the sense of *indottrinare*, I should have liked it
much !" This is not a bad specimen of the
manner in which notes on our old poets are
sometimes composed. Utterly unacquainted
with the style and idiom of foreign languages,
the commentators run to their dictionaries, and
with great labour pick out just enough to expose
their own ignorance and mislead the unlearned
reader. Sympson knew that *clamare* was to
cry :—but he wanted the Italian synonym, he
therefore turns to *chiamare*, and boldly produces
it at once, as an equivalent to the English word
cry, though it merely means to call ! We have
too many Sympsons now-a-days. To return to

Jonson.   He had certainly heard enough of
Italian to be sensible that it was read with a
kind of musical intonation ; and this is just what
he means. Peregrine's language is purposely
affected to set off the simplicity of Sir Politick.

[2] *Fellows of outside, and mere bark.*] This,
as Upton observes, is a Greek phrase; φλοιωδης
ὁ ανηρ, *Long. sect.* 3.
    Daniel has the same expression in his *Hymen's
Triumph :*

   " And never let her think on me, who am
     But e'en the *bark* and *outside* of a man."

[3] *They are most* lewd *impostors* ;] i.e., ignorant, unlearned. The old and approved sense
of the word. Thus Chaucer :

   " And as *leude* pepill demith commonlie
     Of thingis, that ben made more subtilie
     Then thei can in ther *leudness* comprehend."
                          Squier's Tale, 241.

Yourself shall judge.—Who is it mounts,
    my friends?

Mos. Scoto of Mantua, sir.[1]

Sir P. Is't he? Nay, then
I'll proudly promise, sir, you shall behold
Another man than has been phant'sied to
    you.
I wonder yet, that he should mount his
    bank,
Here in this nook, that has been wont t'
    appear
In face of the Piazza!—Here he comes.

Enter Volpone, *disguised as a mountebank
    Doctor, and followed by a crowd of
    people.*

Volp. Mount, zany. [*To* Nano.]

Mob. Follow, follow, follow, follow!

Sir P. See how the people follow him!
    he's a man
May write ten thousand crowns in bank
    here. Note,

                [Volpone *mounts the stage.*
Mark but his gesture:—I do use to observe
The state he keeps in getting up.

Per. 'Tis worth it, sir.

Volp. "Most noble gentlemen, and my
worthy patrons! It may seem strange that
I, your Scoto Mantuano, who was ever
wont to fix my bank in face of the public
Piazza, near the shelter of the Portico to
the Procuratia, should now, after eight
months' absence from this illustrious city

of Venice, humbly retire myself into an
obscure nook of the Piazza."

Sir P. Did not I now object the same?

Per. Peace, sir.

Volp. "Let me tell you: I am not, as
your Lombard proverb saith, cold on my
feet; or content to part with my commodities at a cheaper rate, than I accustomed:
look not for it. Nor that the calumnious
reports of that impudent detractor, and
shame to our profession (Alessandro But-
tone, I mean,) who gave out, in public, I
was condemned a *sforzato* to the galleys,
for poisoning the Cardinal Bembo's—cook,
hath at all attached, much less dejected
me. No, no, worthy gentlemen; to tell
you true, I cannot endure to see the rabble
of these ground ciarlitani,[2] that spread their
cloaks on the pavement, as if they meant
to do feats of activity, and then come in
lamely, with their mouldy tales out of
Boccacio, like stale Tabarine, the fabulist:[3]
some of them discoursing their travels, and
of their tedious captivity in the Turk's
galleys, when, indeed, were the truth
known, they were the Christian's gallies,
where very temperately they eat bread, and
drunk water, as a wholesome penance, enjoined them by their confessors, for base
pilferies."

Sir P. Note but his bearing, and con-
    tempt of these.

Volp. "These turdy-facy-nasty-paty-

---

[1] *Scoto of Mantua, sir.*] I know not whether
Jonson had any contemporary quack in view here.
The name he has taken from an Italian juggler
who was in England about this time, and exhibited
petty feats of legerdemain. See the *Epigrams.*
Our poet was a great reader and admirer of the
facetious fopperies of a former age; and I am
strongly inclined to think that he intended to
imitate Andrew Borde, a physician of reputation
in Henry VIII.'s time, who used to frequent
fairs and markets, and there address himself to
the people. Here is an evident imitation of his
language. "He would make," Hearne says,
"humourous speeches, couched in such language
as caused mirth, and wonderfully propagated his
fame." But Borde was a man of learning, and
knew how to deal with the vulgar. He travelled
much to perfect himself in physic.

Antony Wood says that Borde was esteemed
"a noted poet, a witty and ingeniose person,
and an excellent physician of his time."—*Ath.
Ox.* v. i. 74. Having a rambling head and an
inconstant mind, he travelled over a great part
of Christendom, and finally concluded his vagaries and his life, as many other "ingeniose persons" have done, in the Fleet, in 1549.

[2] *These ground ciarlitani, &c.*] These ground
ciarlitani (petty charlatans, impostors, babblers)

are to be found in Italy at this hour, occupied
precisely as they were in the days of Scoto
Mantuano. Coryat gives a similar account of
them: "I have seen," he says, "some of them
stand *upon the ground* when they tell their tales,
which are such as they commonly call ciarata-
noes, or ciarlatans. The principal place where
they act is the first part of St. Mark's-street."
These tales or recitations, it should be observed,
are merely to draw the people together; and
always terminate with the production of some
trumpery articles for sale.

[3] *Like stale* Tabarine, *the fabulist:*] This
Tabarin, who is mentioned by Boileau, in his
Art of Poetry,

    "*Apollon travesti devint un Tabarin,*"

and again in his *Critical Reflections,* was, as
his annotators inform us, a celebrated jack-
pudding in the service of one Mondor: "*Ce
Mondor étoit un charlatan, ou vendeur du
beaume, qui établissoit son théâtre dans la
Place Dauphine, vers le commencement du
xvii siècle. Il rouloit aussi dans les autres
villes du roïaume avec Tabarin, le bouffon de
sa troupe. Les plaisanteries de Tabarin ont
été imprimées plusieurs fois à Paris et à Lyons.
Elles ne peuvent plaire qu'à la canaille.*"

lousy-fartical rogues, with one poor groat's-worth of unprepared antimony, finely wrapt up in several scartoccios,[1] are able, very well, to kill their twenty a week, and play; yet these meagre, starved spirits, who have half stopt the organs of their minds with earthy oppilations, want not their favourers among your shrivelled sallad-eating arti-zans, who are overjoyed that they may have their half-pe'rth of physic; though it purge them into another world, it makes no matter."

Sir P. Excellent! have you heard better language, sir.

Volp. "Well, let them go. And, gen-tlemen, honourable gentlemen, know, that for this time, our bank, being thus removed from the clamours of the canaglia, shall be the scene of pleasure and delight; for I have nothing to sell, little or nothing to sell."

Sir P. I told you, sir, his end.

Per. You did so, sir.

Volp. " I protest, I, and my six servants, are not able to make of this precious liquor, so fast as it is fetched away from my lodg-ing by gentlemen of your city; strangers of the Terra-firma;[2] worshipful merchants; ay, and senators too: who, ever since my arrival, have detained me to their uses, by their splendidous liberalities. And wor-thily; for, what avails your rich man to have his magazines stuft with moscadelli, or of the purest grape, when his physicians prescribe him, on pain of death, to drink nothing but water cocted with aniseeds? O, health! health! the blessing of the rich! the riches of the poor! who can buy thee at too dear a rate, since there is no enjoying this world without thee? Be not then so sparing of your purses, honourable gentlemen, as to abridge the natural course of life——"

Per. You see his end.

Sir P. Ay, is 't not good?

Volp. "For when a humid flux, or catarrh, by the mutability of air, falls from your head into an arm or shoulder, or any other part; take you a ducket, or your chequin of gold, and apply to the place affected: see what good effect it can work. No, no, 'tis this blessed unguento, this rare extraction, that hath only power to disperse all malignant humours, that proceed either of hot, cold, moist, or windy causes"——

Per. I would he had put in dry too.

Sir P. Pray you observe.

Volp. " To fortify the most indigest and crude stomach, ay, were it of one that, through extreme weakness, vomited blood, applying only a warm napkin to the place, after the unction and fricace;—for the ver-tigine in the head, putting but a drop into your nostrils, likewise behind the ears; a most sovereign and approved remedy; the mal caduco, cramps, convulsions, paralysies, epilepsies, tremor-cordia, retired nerves, ill vapours of the spleen, stopping of the liver, the stone, the strangury, hernia ventosa, iliaca passio; stops a dysenteria imme-diately; easeth the torsion of the small guts; and cures melancholia hypondriaca, being taken and applied, according to my printed receipt. [*pointing to his bill and his vial.*] For this is the physician, this the medicine; this counsels, this cures; this gives the direction, this works the effect; and, in sum, both together may be termed an abstract of the theorick and practick in the Æsculapian art. 'Twill cost you eight crowns. And,—Zan Fritada, prithee sing a verse extempore in honour of it."

Sir P. How do you like him, sir?

Per. Most strangely, I!

Sir P. Is not his language rare?

Per. But alchemy,
I never heard the like; or Broughton's books.[3]

Nano *sings.*

Had old Hippocrates, or Galen,
That to their books put med'cines all in,
But known this secret, they had never
(Of which they will be guilty ever)
Been murderers of so much paper,
Or wasted many a hurtless taper;
No Indian drug had e'er been famed,
Tobacco, sassafras not named;

---

[1] *Scartoccios,*] i.e., covers, folds of paper; whence our *cartouch.*

[2] *Terra-firma;*] It may be just worth while to notice that the Venetians distinguish their continental possessious by this expression.

[3] But *alchemy,*
I never heard the like; or Broughton's books, &c.] i.e., except alchemy, &c. The reader will understand the force of this when he comes to *The Alchemist.* Broughton was a man of very considerable learning, particularly in the He-brew; but disputatious, scurrilous, extravagant, and incomprehensible. He was engaged in con-troversy during the greatest part of his life. So common a circumstance scarcely deserved notice; yet there was this peculiarity in Broughton's case, namely, that he should find people to con-test what must have been equally unintelligible to all parties. See the *Alchemist.*

Ne yet of guacum one small stick, sir,
Nor Raymund Lully's great elixir.[1]
Ne had been known the Danish Gonswart,[2]
Or Paracelsus, with his long sword.[3]

Per. All this, yet, will not do; eight crowns is high.

Volp. "No more.—Gentlemen, if I had but time to discourse to you the miraculous effects of this my oil, surnamed Oglio del Scoto; with the countless catalogue of those I have cured of the aforesaid, and many more diseases; the patents and privileges of all the princes and commonwealths of Christendom; or but the depositions of those that appeared on my part, before the signiory of the Sanità and most learned College of Physicians; where I was authorized, upon notice taken of the admirable virtues of my medicaments, and mine own excellency in matter of rare and unknown secrets, not only to disperse them publicly in this famous city, but in all the territories, that happily joy under the government of the most pious and magnificent states of Italy. But may some other gallant fellow say, O, there be divers that make profession to have as good, and as experimented receipts as yours: indeed, very many have assayed, like apes, in imitation of that, which is really and essentially in me, to make of this oil; bestowed great cost in furnaces, stills, alembecks, continual fires, and preparation of the ingredients (as indeed there goes to it six hundred several simples, besides some quantity of human fat, for the conglutination, which we buy of the anatomists), but when these practitioners come to the last decoction, blow, blow, puff, puff, and all flies in fumo: ha, ha, ha! Poor wretches! I rather pity their folly and indiscretion, than their loss of time and money; for these may be recovered by industry: but to be a fool born, is a disease incurable.

For myself, I always from my youth have endeavoured to get the rarest secrets, and book them, either in exchange, or for money: I spared nor cost nor labour, where anything was worthy to be learned. And, gentlemen, honourable gentlemen, I will undertake, by virtue of chemical art, out of the honourable hat that covers your head, to extract the four elements; that is to say, the fire, air, water, and earth, and return you your felt without burn or stain. For, whilst others have been at the Balloo,[4] I have been at my book; and am now past the craggy paths of study, and come to the flowery plains of honour and reputation."

Sir P. I do assure you, sir, that is his aim.

Volp. "But to our price——"

Per. And that withal, Sir Pol.

Volp. "You all know, honourable gentlemen, I never valued this ampulla, or vial, at less than eight crowns; but for this time, I am content to be deprived of it for six: six crowns is the price, and less in courtesy I know you cannot offer me; take

---

[1] *Nor Raymund Lully's* great elixir.] Lully was a celebrated character of the fourteenth century. He was born in Majorca, and studied what was then termed natural philosophy, i.e., the transmutation of metals, &c. In this he was very successful; having, as every one knows, discovered the philosopher's stone, and above all, the *great elixir*, or drink of immortality. Thus secured against poverty and death, he turned beggar, hermit, missionary, and finally lost his life by an unlucky blow while preaching to the wild inhabitants of Mount Atlas. In a credulous age, and while men obstinately shut their eyes to conviction, Lully enjoyed an extraordinary degree of reputation. He is now deservedly forgotten. The following distich on him is as old as Zan Fritada's song:

" *Qui Lulli* lapidem *quærit, quem quærere nulli Profuit; haud Lullus, sed mihi Nullus erit.*"

[2] *The Danish Gonswart,*] Having no acquaintance with the Danish Gonswart, I cannot give the reader his history.—WHAL.

I regret to say, that I am equally unable to assist him: though my researches have been pretty extensive.

[3] *Or Paracelsus, with* his long sword.] For Paracelsus see the *Alchemist.* I cannot account for the introduction of the *long sword,* which yet must have been popular; for it is mentioned also by Fletcher: "Were Paracelsus the German now living, he (Forobosco) would take up his single rapier against his *horrible long sword.*"— *Fair Maid of the Inn,* act iv. Perhaps the allusion is to some print of Paracelsus, who, as he was certainly present at many sieges and battles, might choose to be represented with this formidable appendage to his physician's cloak. It must not be forgotten that Paracelsus always carried a familiar or demon in the hilt of this celebrated *long sword;* so that it was not without its use. [See Dyce's *Beaumont and Fletcher,* x. 69.—F. C.]

[4] *At the Balloo,*] This play, in which a huge ball is driven forward by a flat piece of wood fastened to the arm, is still much practised on the continent. It is mentioned in *Eastward Hoe:* "We had a match at *baloon* too, with my Lord Whackum, for four crowns."—Act i. The Mall takes its name from this game (*pasle maile,* Fr.), which was often played there by the cavaliers who returned with Charles II. from France.

it or leave it, howsoever, both it and I am at your service. I ask you not as the value of the thing, for then I should demand of you a thousand crowns, so the cardinals Montalto, Fernese, the great Duke of Tuscany, my gossip,[1] with divers other princes, have given me; but I despise money. Only to shew my affection to you, honourable gentlemen, and your illustrious State here, I have neglected the messages of these princes, mine own offices, framed my journey hither, only to present you with the fruits of my travels.—Tune your voices once more to the touch of your instruments, and give the honourable assembly some delightful recreation."

Per. What monstrous and most painful circumstance
Is here, to get some three or four gazettes,[2]
Some threepence in the whole! for that 'twill come to.

Nano *sings.*

You that would last long, list to my song,
Make no more coil, but buy of this oil.
Would you be ever fair and young?
Stout of teeth, and strong of tongue?
Tart of palate? quick of ear?
Sharp of sight? of nostril clear?

Moist of hand? and light of foot?
Or, I will come nearer to't,
Would you live free from all diseases?
Do the act your mistress pleases,
Yet fright all aches from your bones?
Here's a med'cine for the nones.[3]

Volp. "Well, I am in a humour at this time to make a present of the small quantity my coffer contains; to the rich in courtesy, and to the poor for God's sake. Wherefore now mark: I asked you six crowns; and six crowns, at other times, you have paid me; you shall not give me six crowns, nor five, nor four, nor three, nor two, nor one; nor half a ducat; no, nor a moccinigo.[4] Sixpence it will cost you, or six hundred pound—expect no lower price, for, by the banner of my front, I will not bate a bagatine,[5]—that I will have, only, a pledge of your loves, to carry something from amongst you, to shew I am not contemned by you. Therefore, now, toss your handkerchiefs, cheerfully, cheerfully; and be advertised, that the first heroic spirit that deigns to grace me with a handkerchief, I will give it a little remembrance of something, beside, shall please it better than if I had presented it with a double pistolet."

---

[1] *The great Duke of Tuscany, my* gossip,] i.e., my godfather. "*Godsib,* now pronounced *gossip.* Our Christian ancestors understanding a spirituall affinitie to grow between the parents and such as undertook for the chyld at baptisme, called each other by the name of *godsib,* which is as much as to say, as that they were *sib* together, that is, of kin together through God. And the chyld in like manner called such his godfathers or godmothers," &c.—*Verstegan, Restitution of Decayed Intelligence, &c.* p. 223.

[2] *What painful circumstance*
Is here, to get some three or four gazettes?] Peregrine is not in the secret: Volpone spins out his harangue in order to increase the chance of getting a sight of Celia. A *gazette* is a small Venetian coin, worth about three farthings; and as this was the usual price given for the newspapers, the name of the coin was afterwards transferred to be the name of the newspaper itself.—WHAL.
These *newspapers,* as Whalley calls them, were merely loose slips of paper, on which the occurrences of the day were written. There were no printed gazettes, as he seems to think.

[3] *Here's a med'cine* for the nones,] i.e., for the present occasion; for the immediate purpose. It is impossible to reflect without scorn on the elaborate attempts to explain the origin of this most simple and common expression. To say nothing of the *Dii minores,* even Tyrwhitt, who when he mixes with the commentators on Shak-

speare is no longer recognisable, gravely tells us that the phrase "was originally a corruption of corrupt Latin." Thus, says he, from *pro nunc* came *for the nunc,* and so for the nonce; just as from *ad nunc* came anon! This, it must be confessed, is sufficiently foolish: but by what term shall we characterize the stupendous absurdity of Mr. Chalmers? "The expression (he says) is local." It is as universal as the language. "This word (he continues) is probably derived from the Fr. *nonce,* a nuncio, the prelate whom the pope used to send for his special purposes." —*Glossary to Lyndsay.* For the nonce is simply *for the once,* for the *one thing* in question, whatever it be. This is invariably its meaning. The aptitude of many of our monosyllables beginning with a vowel to assume the *n* is well known; but the progress of this expression is distinctly marked in our early writers, "a ones," "an anes," "for the ones," "for the nanes," "for the nones," "for the nonce." Shall we have any more repetitions of "*pro nunc,*" and "*pro nuntio,* the prelate?" I am not without my fears; for, as I lately had occasion to observe, the race of Ding-dong's sheep is far from being extinct.

[4] *No, nor a* moccinigo,] A moccinigo, as Florio informs us in his *Worlde of Wordes,* is "a kinde of small coyne used in Venice." It is worth about ninepence.

[5] *A bagatine.*] A bagatine, he says, is "a little coyne used in Italie." It is about the third part of a farthing.

Per. Will you be that *heroic spark*, Sir
Pol?
  [*Celia, at a window above, throws
       down her handkerchief.*
O, see! the window has prevented you.

Volp. "Lady, I kiss your bounty; and
for this timely grace you have done your
poor Scoto of Mantua, I will return you,
over and above my oil, a secret of that
high and inestimable nature, shall make
you for ever enamoured on that minute,
wherein your eye first descended on so
mean, yet not altogether to be despised, an
object. Here is a powder concealed in
this paper, of which, if I should speak to
the worth, nine thousand volumes were
but as one page, that page as a line, that
line as a word; so short is this pilgrimage
of man (which some call life) to the expressing of it. Would I reflect on the
price? why, the whole world is but as an
empire, that empire as a province, that
province as a bank, that bank as a private
purse to the purchase of it. I will only
tell you; it is the powder that made Venus
a goddess (given her by Apollo), that kept
her perpetually young, cleared her wrinkles,
firmed her gums, filled her skin, coloured
her hair; from her derived to Helen, and
at the sack of Troy unfortunately lost: till
now, in this our age, it was as happily recovered, by a studious antiquary, out of
some ruins of Asia, who sent a moiety of
it to the court of France (but much sophis-
ticated), wherewith the ladies there now
colour their hair. The rest, at this present, remains with me; extracted to a
quintessence: so that, wherever it but
touches, in youth it perpetually preserves,
in age restores the complexion; seats your
teeth, did they dance like virginal jacks,
firm as a wall; makes them white as ivory,
that were black as——"

Enter Corvino.

Cor. Spight o' the devil, and my shame!
come down, here;
Come down;—No house but mine to make
your scene?
Signior Flaminio, will you down, sir?
down?
What, is my wife your Franciscina, sir?

No windows on the whole Piazza, here,
To make your properties, but mine? but
mine?
  [*Beats away* Volpone, Nano, &c.
Heart! ere to-morrow I shall be new-
christened,
And called the Pantalone di Besogniosi,[1]
About the town.
Per. What should this mean, Sir Pol?
Sir P. Some trick of state, believe it; I
will home.
Per. It may be some design on you.
Sir P. I know not.
I'll stand upon my guard.
Per. It is your best, sir.
Sir P. This three weeks, all my ad-
vices, all my letters,
They have been intercepted.
Per. Indeed, sir!
Best have a care.
Sir P. Nay, so I will.
Per. This knight,
I may not lose him, for my mirth, till night.
  [*Exeunt.*

SCENE II.—*A Room in* Volpone's
House.

Enter Volpone *and* Mosca.

Volp. O, I am wounded!
Mos. Where, sir?
Volp. Not without;
Those blows were nothing: I could bear
them ever.
But angry Cupid,[2] bolting from her eyes,
Hath shot himself into me like a flame;
Where now he flings about his burning heat,
As in a furnace an ambitious fire,
Whose vent is stopt. The fight is all
within me.
I cannot live, except thou help me, Mosca;
My liver melts, and I, without the hope
Of some soft air, from her refreshing
breath,
Am but a heap of cinders.
Mos. 'Las, good sir,
Would you had never seen her!
Volp. Nay, would thou
Hadst never told me of her!
Mos. Sir, 'tis true;
I do confess I was unfortunate,
And you unhappy; but I'm bound in con-
science,

---

[1]   *I shall be new christened,
And called the* Pantalone di Besogniosi,] i.e.,
the zany or fool of the beggars. Such at least is
the vulgar import of the words; but Jonson
probably affixed a more opprobrious sense to
them.
[2] *But angry Cupid, &c.*] This is prettily
imitated from the concluding lines of the 14th
Ode of Anacreon.

No less than duty, to effect my best
To your release of torment, and I will, sir.
  Volp. Dear Mosca, shall I hope?
  Mos. Sir, more than dear,
I will not bid you to despair of aught
Within a human compass.
  Volp. O, there spoke
My better angel. Mosca, take my keys,
Gold, plate, and jewels, all's at thy devotion ;
Employ them how thou wilt : nay, coin me too :
So thou in this but crown my longings, Mosca.
  Mos. Use but your patience.
  Volp. So I have.
  Mos. I doubt not
To bring success to your desires.
  Volp. Nay, then,
I not repent me of my late disguise.
  Mos. If you can horn him, sir, you need not.
  Volp. True :
Besides, I never meant him for my heir.
Is not the colour of my beard and eyebrows
To make me known ?
  Mos. No jot.
  Volp. I did it well.
  Mos. So well, would I could follow you in mine,
With half the happiness ! and yet I would
Escape your epilogue.[1]   [*Aside.*
  Volp. But were they gulled
With a belief that I was Scoto?
  Mos. Sir,
Scoto himself could hardly have distinguished !
I have not time to flatter you now, we'll part :
And as I prosper, so applaud my art.
          [*Exeunt.*

SCENE III.—*A Room in* Corvino's *House.*

Enter Corvino, *with his sword in his hand, dragging in* Celia.

  Corv. Death of mine honour, with the city's fool !

A juggling, tooth-drawing, prating mountebank !
And at a public window ! where, whilst he,
With his strained action, and his dole of faces,[2]
To his drug-lecture draws your itching ears,
A crew of old, unmarried, noted letchers,
Stood leering up like satyrs : and you smile
Most graciously, and fan your favours forth,
To give your hot spectators satisfaction !
What, was your mountebank their call?
their whistle?
Or were you enamoured on his copper rings,
His saffron jewel, with the toad-stone in 't,
Or his embroidered suit, with the copestitch,
Made of a herse cloth? or his old tilt-feather?
Or his starched beard? Well ! you shall have him, yes !
He shall come home, and minister unto you
The fricace for the mother. Or, let me see,
I think you'd rather mount ; would you not mount ?
Why, if you'll mount, you may ; yes, truly, you may !
And so you may be seen, down to the foot,
Get you a cittern, Lady Vanity,
And be a dealer with the virtuous man ;
Make one : I'll but protest myself a cuckold,
And save your dowry. I'm a Dutchman, I !
For if you thought me an Italian,
You would be damned ere you did this, you whore !
Thou'dst tremble, to imagine, that the murder
Of father, mother, brother, all thy race,
Should follow, as the subject of my justice.
  Cel. Good sir, have patience.
  Corv. What couldst thou propose[3]
Less to thyself, than in this heat of wrath,
And stung with my dishonour, I should strike
This steel into thee, with as many stabs
As thou wert gazed upon with goatish eyes?

---

[1]   *And yet I would*
Escape your epilogue.] i.e., the beating which Volpone had received from Corvino.

[2]   *Whilst he,*
With his strained action, and his dole of faces,] *Dole of faces* is the grimace, or change of features, which accompanied Volpone's action.

We have a parallel expression in the beginning of *Sejanus:*

  "We have no shift of faces."—WHAL.

[3] *What couldst thou propose, &c.*] This outragous respect for his honour is an admirable preparation for his conduct in the ensuing conversation with Mosca.

Cel. Alas, sir, be appeased! I could not think

My being at the window should more now

Move your impatience than at other times.

Corv. No! not to seek and entertain a parley

With a known knave, before a multitude!

You were an actor with your handkerchief,

Which he most sweetly kist in the receipt,

And might, no doubt, return it with a letter,

And point the place where you might meet; your sister's,

Your mother's, or your aunt's might serve the turn.

Cel. Why, dear sir, when do I make these excuses,

Or ever stir abroad, but to the church?

And that so seldom——

Corv. Well, it shall be less;

And thy restraint before was liberty,

To what I now decree: and therefore mark me.

First, I will have this bawdy light dammed up;

And till't be done, some two or three yards off,

I'll chalk a line; o'er which if thou but chance

To set thy desperate foot, more hell, more horror,

More wild remorseless rage shall seize on thee,

Than on a conjurer that had heedless left

His circle's safety ere his devil was laid.

Then here's a lock which I will hang upon thee,

And, now I think on't, I will keep thee backwards;

Thy lodging shall be backwards; thy walks backwards;

Thy prospect, all be backwards; and no pleasure,

That thou shalt know but backwards: nay, since you force

My honest nature, know, it is your own,

Being too open, makes me use you thus:

Since you will not contain your subtle nostrils

In a sweet room, but they must snuff the air

Of rank and sweaty passengers. [*Knocking within.*] One knocks.

Away, and be not seen, pain of thy life;

Nor look toward the window: if thou dost—

Nay, stay, hear this—let me not prosper, whore,

But I will make thee an anatomy,

Dissect thee mine own self, and read a lecture

Upon thee to the city, and in public.

Away!—   [*Exit* Celia.

Enter Servant.

Who's there?

Ser. 'Tis Signior Mosca, sir.

Corv. Let him come in. [*Exit* Serv.] His master's dead: there's yet

Some good to help the bad.

Enter Mosca.

                    My Mosca, welcome!

I guess your news.

Mos. I fear you cannot, sir.

Corv. Is't not his death?

Mos. Rather the contrary.

Corv. Not his recovery?

Mos. Yes, sir.

Corv. I am cursed,

I am bewitched, my crosses meet to vex me.

How? how? how? how?

Mos. Why, sir, with Scoto's oil;

Corbaccio and Voltore brought of it,

Whilst I was busy in an inner room——

Corv. Death! that damned mountebank! but for the law

Now, I could kill the rascal: it cannot be

His oil should have that virtue. Have not I

Known him a common rogue, come fiddling in

To the osteria,[1] with a tumbling whore,

And, when he has done all his forced tricks, been glad

Of a poor spoonful of dead wine, with flies in't?

It cannot be.   All his ingredients

Are a sheep's gall, a roasted bitch's marrow,

Some few sod earwigs, pounded caterpillars,

A little capon's grease, and fasting spittle:

I know them to a dram.

Mos. I know not, sir;

But some on't, there, they poured into his ears,

Some in his nostrils, and recovered him;

Applying but the fricace.

Corv. Pox o' that fricace!

Mos. And since, to seem the more officious

———————————————

[1] *To the* osteria,] The inn or hotel.   So Fletcher:

    " *Host.* Thy master

   That lodges here in my *osteria.*"

          Fair Maid of the Inn.—WHAL.

And flatt'ring of his health, there, they
　　have had,
At extreme fees, the college of physicians
Consulting on him, how they might restore
　　him ;
Where one would have a cataplasm of
　　spices,
Another a flayed ape clapped to his breast,
A third would have it a dog, a fourth an
　　oil,
With wild cats' skins : at last, they all re-
　　solved
That to preserve him, was no other means
But some young woman must be straight
　　sought out,
Lusty, and full of juice, to sleep by him ;
And to this service most unhappily,
And most unwillingly, am I now employed,
Which here I thought to pre-acquaint you
　　with,
For your advice, since it concerns you
　　most ;
Because I would not do that thing might
　　cross
Your ends, on whom I have my whole de-
　　pendence, sir ;
Yet, if I do it not, they may delate[1]
My slackness to my patron, work me out
Of his opinion ; and there all your hopes,
Ventures, or whatsoever, are all frustrate !
I do but tell you, sir. Besides, they are all
Now striving who shall first present him ;
　　therefore—
I could entreat you, briefly conclude some-
　　what ;
Prevent them if you can.
　　Corv. Death to my hopes,
This is my villainous fortune ! Best to hire
Some common courtezan.
　　Mos. Ay, I thought on that, sir ;
But they are all so subtle, full of art—
And age again doting and flexible,
So as—I cannot tell—we may, perchance,
Light on a quean may cheat us all.
　　Corv. 'Tis true.

　　Mos. No, no : it must be one that has no
　　tricks, sir,
Some simple thing, a creature made unto
　　it ;[2]
Some wench you may command. Have
　　you no kinswoman ?
Odso—Think, think, think, think, think,
　　think, think, sir.
One o' the doctors offered there his daugh-
　　ter.
　　Corv. How !
　　Mos. Yes, Signior Lupo, the physician.
　　Corv. His daughter !
　　Mos. And a virgin, sir. Why, alas,
He knows the state of's body, what it is ;
That nought can warm his blood, sir, but
　　a fever ;[3]
Nor any incantation raise his spirit :
A long forgetfulness hath seized that part.
Besides, sir, who shall know it ? some one
　　or two—
　　Corv. I pray thee give me leave. [*Walks
　　aside.*] If any man
But I had had this luck—The thing in't
　　self,
I know, is nothing—Wherefore should not I
As well command my blood and my affec-
　　tions
As this dull doctor? In the point of honour,
The cases are all one of wife and daughter.
　　Mos. I hear him coming.[4]　　　[*Aside.*
　　Corv. She shall do't : 'tis done.
Slight ! if this doctor, who is not engaged,
Unless 't be for his counsel, which is no-
　　thing,
Offer his daughter, what should I, that am
So deeply in ? I will prevent him: Wretch !
Covetous wretch ![5]—Mosca, I have deter-
　　mined.
　　Mos. How, sir?
　　Corv. We'll make all sure. The party
　　you wot of
Shall be mine own wife, Mosca.
　　Mos. Sir, the thing,
But that I would not seem to counsel you,

---

[1]　　　　　*They may* delate
My slackness to my patron,] i.e., accuse, or
complain of: a vile Latinism. "*Prevent* them,"
just below, is anticipate them.
　　[2] *A creature* made *unto it.*] See p. 287 *a.*
　　[3] *That nought can warm his blood, sir, but
a fever ;*]

" *Præterea minimus gelido jam corpore sanguis
Febre calet sola.*"—Juv. Sat.

What follows is from the same satire.

　　[4] *I hear him* coming.] Mosca, who overhears
Corvino's last words, speaks this aside ; and he
means that he is yielding, *or coming* into the

plot he had laid, to procure his wife for Volpone
So in *Eastward Hoe!* act v.: "No more ; I
am *coming* already : if I should give any further
ear, I were taken."—Whal.
　　[5]　　　　　*Wretch !*
　　Covetous wretch !] "How finely," says Upton, "is it imagined by our poet, to make
Corvino see the basely covetous character of the
physician, and yet be so strangely ignorant of his
own ! This is an instance of our comedian's great
insight into the characters of mankind."
　　This is one of ten thousand: but, indeed, no
language can do full justice to the various excellencies of this truly attic drama.

I should have motioned to you, at the first:
And make your count, you have cut all their
　throats.
Why, 'tis directly taking a possession !
And in his next fit, we may let him go.
'Tis but to pull the pillow from his head,
And he is throttled : it had been done be-
　fore
But for your scrupulous doubts.
　Corv. Ay, a plague on't,
My conscience fools my wit ! Well, I'll be
　brief,
And so be thou, lest they should be before
　us :
Go home, prepare him, tell him with what
　zeal
And willingness I do it ; swear it was
On the first hearing, as thou mayst do,
　truly,
Mine own free motion.
　Mos. Sir, I warrant you,
I'll so possess him with it, that the rest
Of his starved clients shall be banished all ;
And only you received.　But come not, sir,
Until I send, for I have something else
To ripen for your good, you must not
　know't.
　Corv. But do not you forget to send now.
　Mos. Fear not.　　　　　　　[*Exit.*
　Corv. Where are you, wife? my Celia !
　wife !
　　　Re-enter Celia.
　—What, blubbering ?
Come, dry those tears.　I think thou
　thought'st me in earnest ;
Ha ! by this light I talked so but to try
　thee :
Methinks, the lightness of the occasion
Should have confirmed thee.　Come, I am
　not jealous.
　Cel. No !
　Corv. Faith I am not, I, nor never was ;
It is a poor unprofitable humour.
Do not I know, if women have a will,
They'll do 'gainst all the watches of the
　world,
And that the fiercest spies are tamed with
　gold ?

Tut, I am confident in thee, thou shalt
　see't ;
And see I'll give thee cause too, to believe it.
Come kiss me.　Go, and make thee ready
　straight,
In all thy best attire, thy choicest jewels,
Put them all on, and, with them, thy best
　looks:
We are invited to a solemn feast,
At old Volpone's, where it shall appear
How far I am free from jealousy or fear.
　　　　　　　　　　　　　[*Exeunt.*

ACT III.

SCENE I.—*A Street.*

Enter Mosca.

　Mos. I fear I shall begin to grow in love
With my dear self, and my most prosperous
　parts,
They do so spring and burgeon ; I can feel
A whimsy in my blood : I know not how,
Success hath made me wanton.　I could
　skip
Out of my skin now, like a subtle snake,
I am so limber.　O ! your parasite
Is a most precious thing, dropt from above,
Not bred 'mongst clods and clodpoles,
　here on earth.
I muse, the mystery was not made a
　science,
It is so liberally profest ! Almost
All the wise world is little else, in nature,
But parasites or sub-parasites.　And yet
I mean not those that have your bare
　town-art,
To know who's fit to feed them ; have no
　house,
No family, no care, and therefore mould
Tales for men's ears, to bait that sense ;
　or get
Kitchen-invention, and some stale receipts
To please the belly, and the groin ; nor those,
With their court dog-tricks, that can fawn
　and fleer,
Make their revenue out of legs and faces,[1]
Echo my lord, and lick away a moth :[2]

---

[1] *Make their revenue out of* legs and faces,]
i.e., out of bows and smiles, or rather perhaps, as
Juvenal expresses it, moulding their faces to suit
the humour of their patron's—*alienum sumere
vultum, &c.*
[2] *Echo my lord, and* lick away a moth :]
This, as Upton affectedly observes, is an allusion " to such officious kind of parasites as are
called in Low Dutch *pluyme-strācker, qui
plumas pilosque ex vestibus assentatorie legit.*"
All this learning is from Minsheu : Jonson,

however, did not go to Holland for his flatterer,
but to Attica, a country with which he was much
better acquainted : Απο του ιματιου αφελειν
κροκιδα και εαν τι προς το τριχωμα της κεφαλης
απο πνευματος προσενεχθη αχυρον καρφελογησαι.
Theophras. περι κολακειας.
Hall has the same allusion :
" But some one, like a claw-backe parasite,
　Picked *mothes from his patron's* cloake in
　　sight."—*Sat.* lib. 6.

But your fine elegant rascal, that can rise
And stoop, almost together, like an arrow ;
Shoot through the air as nimbly as a star ;
Turn short as doth a swallow ; and be here,
And there, and here, and yonder, all at once ;
Present to any humour, all occasion ;
And change a visor swifter than a thought !
This is the creature had the art born with
 him ;
Toils not to learn it, but doth practise it
Out of most excellent nature : and such
 sparks
Are the true parasites, others but their
 zanis.[1]

Enter Bonario.

Who's this ? Bonario, old Corbaccio's
 son ?
The person I was bound to seek. Fair
 sir,
You are happily met.
 Bon. That cannot be by thee.
 Mos. Why, sir ?
 Bon. Nay, pray thee know thy way,
 and leave me :
I would be loth to interchange discourse
With such a mate as thou art.
 Mos. Courteous sir,
Scorn not my poverty.
 Bon. Not I, by heaven ;
But thou shalt give me leave to hate thy
 baseness.
 Mos. Baseness !
 Bon. Ay ; answer me, is not thy sloth
Sufficient argument ? thy flattery ?
Thy means of feeding ?
 Mos. Heaven be good to me !
These imputations are too common, sir,
And easily stuck on virtue when she's poor.
You are unequal to me,[2] and however
Your sentence may be righteous, yet you
 are not,
That, ere you know me, thus proceed in
 censure :
St. Mark bear witness 'gainst you, 'tis
 inhuman.   [*Weeps.*

 Bon. What ! does he weep ? the sign is
 soft and good :
I do repent me that I was so harsh.
                    [*Aside.*
 Mos. 'Tis true, that, swayed by strong
 necessity,
I am enforced to eat my careful bread
With too much obsequy ; 'tis true, beside,
That I am fain to spin mine own poor
 raiment
Out of my mere observance, being not born
To a free fortune : but that I have done
Base offices, in rending friends asunder,
Dividing families, betraying counsels,
Whispering false lies, or mining men with
 praises,
Trained their credulity with perjuries,
Corrupted chastity, or am in love
With mine own tender ease, but would not
 rather
Prove the most rugged and laborious
 course,
That might redeem my present estimation,
Let me here perish, in all hope of good-
 ness.
 Bon. This cannot be a personated
 passion.   [*Aside.*
I was to blame, so to mistake thy nature ;
Prithee forgive me : and speak out thy
 business.
 Mos. Sir, it concerns you ; and though
 I may seem
At first to make a main offence in manners,
And in my gratitude unto my master ;
Yet for the pure love which I bear all
 right,
And hatred of the wrong, I must reveal it.
This very hour your father is in purpose
To disinherit you——
 Bon. How !
 Mos. And thrust you forth,
As a mere stranger to his blood : 'tis true,
 sir.
The work no way engageth me, but, as
I claim an interest in the general state
Of goodness and true virtue, which I hear

---

[1] Mr. Cumberland parallels this exquisite speech with that of a parasite, preserved to us in a fragment of Eupolis. The advantage, however, is on the side of Jonson. His

 " Fine elegant rascal, that can rise
 And stoop, almost together, like an arrow ;
 Shoot through the air as nimbly as a star ;
 Turn short as doth a swallow," &c.

Is much superior to the parasite of the Greek dramatist, whom our poet undoubtedly had in view, and over whom he manifestly triumphs in the conclusion of his speech.

Lucian's parasite, who is here brought forward by Upton, is, it must be confessed, a sprightly, impudent, pleasant fellow ; from him, however, Jonson has taken nothing but the idea that "the mystery should be made a science," &c. Indeed the two characters are perfectly distinct.

[2] *You are* unequal *to me, &c.*] i.e., unjust ; you do not judge equitably. The sentiment itself is from the *Medea* of Seneca :

 " *Qui statuit aliquid, parte inauditâ alterâ,
 Æquum licet statuerit, haud æquus fuit.*"
                              WHAL.

To abound in you ; and for which mere respect,
Without a second aim, sir, I have done it.
　Bon. This tale hath lost thee much of the late trust
Thou hadst with me ; it is impossible :
I know not how to lend it any thought,
My father should be so unnatural.
　Mos. It is a confidence that well becomes
Your piety ; and formed, no doubt, it is
From your own simple innocence : which makes
Your wrong more monstrous and abhorred. But, sir,
I now will tell you more.　This very minute,
It is, or will be doing ; and if you
Shall be but pleased to go with me, I'll bring you,
I dare not say where you shall see, but where
Your ear shall be a witness of the deed ;
Hear yourself written bastard, and profest
The common issue of the earth.
　Bon. I am mazed !
　Mos. Sir, if I do it not, draw your just sword,
And score your vengeance on my front and face ;
Mark me your villain : you have too much wrong,
And I do suffer for you, sir.　My heart
Weeps blood in anguish——
　Bon. Lead ; I follow thee.　　[*Exeunt.*

SCENE II.—*A Room in* Volpone's *House.*

　　　　Enter Volpone.

　Volp. Mosca stays long, methinks.—
　Bring forth your sports,
And help to make the wretched time more sweet.

Enter Nano, Androgyno, *and* Castrone.

　Nan. "Dwarf, fool, and eunuch, well met here we be.
A question it were now, whether of us three,
Being all the known delicates of a rich man,
In pleasing him, claim the precedency can?"
　Cas. "I claim for myself."
　And. "And so doth the fool."
　Nan. "'Tis foolish indeed : let me set you both to school.

First for your dwarf, he's little and witty,
And everything, as it is little, is pretty ;
Else why do men say to a creature of my shape,
So soon as they see him, It's a pretty little ape?
And why a pretty ape, but for pleasing imitation
Of greater men's actions, in a ridiculous fashion?
Beside, this feat body of mine doth not crave
Half the meat, drink, and cloth, one of your bulks will have.
Admit your fool's face be the mother of laughter,
Yet, for his brain, it must always come after :
And though that do feed him, it's a pitiful case,
His body is beholding to such a bad face."
　　　　　　　　　　[*Knocking within.*
　Volp. Who's there ? my couch ; away !
look ! Nano, see :
　　　　　　　　[*Exeunt* And. *and* Cas.
Give me my caps first — go, enquire.
　　　　　　[*Exit* Nano.] Now, Cupid
Send it be Mosca, and with fair return !
　Nan. [*within.*] It is the beauteous madam—
　Volp. Would-be—is it ?
　Nan. The same.
　Volp. Now torment on me ! Squire her in ;
For she will enter, or dwell here for ever :
Nay, quickly. [*Retires to his couch.*] That my fit were past ! I fear
A second hell too, that my loathing this
Will quite expel my appetite to the other :
Would she were taking now her tedious leave.
Lord, how it threats me what I am to suffer !

　　Re-enter Nano *with* Lady Politick Would-be.

　Lady P. I thank you, good sir.　Pray you signify
Unto your patron I am here.—This band
Shews not my neck enough.—I trouble you, sir ;
Let me request you bid one of my women
Come hither to me. In good faith, I am drest
Most favourably[1] to-day ! It is no matter :
'Tis well enough.

　　　Enter 1 Waiting-woman.

　　　　Look, see these petulant things,
How they have done this !

---

[1] [Jonson could not have written "favourably." The word perhaps was "carelessly" or "shamefully."—F. C.]

Volp. I do feel the fever
Entering in at mine ears ; O, for a charm,
To fright it hence !   [*Aside.*
Lady P. Come nearer : is this curl
In his right place, or this? Why is this
higher
Than all the rest? You have not washed
your eyes yet !
Or do they not stand even in your head?
Where is your fellow ? call her.
                                          [*Exit* 1 Woman.
Nan. Now, St. Mark
Deliver us ! anon she'll beat her women,
Because her nose is red.

Re-enter 1 *with* 2 Woman.

Lady P. I pray you view
This tire, forsooth : are all things apt,
or no?
  1 *Wom.* One hair a little **here** sticks
  out, forsooth.
Lady P. Does't so, forsooth ! and where
was your dear sight,
When it did so, forsooth ! What now !
bird-eyed ?[1]
And you, too? Pray you, both approach
and mend it.
Now, by that light I muse you are not
ashamed !
I, that have preached these things so oft
unto you,
Read you the principles, argued all the
grounds,
Disputed every fitness, every grace,
Called you to counsel of so frequent
dressings.
  Nan. More carefully than of your fame
  or honour.   [*Aside.*
Lady P. Made you acquainted what an
ample dowry
The knowledge of these things would be
unto you,

Able alone to get you noble husbands
At your return : and you thus to neglect it !
Besides, you seeing what a curious nation
The Italians are, what will they say of me ?
The English lady cannot dress herself.
Here's a fine imputation to our country !
Well, go your ways, and stay in the next
room.
This fucus was too coarse too ; it's no
matter.—
Good sir, you'll give them entertainment ?
              [*Exeunt* Nano *and* Waiting-women.
Volp. The storm comes toward me.
Lady P. [*goes to the couch.*] How does
my Volpone?
Volp. Troubled with noise, I cannot
sleep ; I dreamt
That a strange fury entered now my house,
And, with the dreadful tempest of her
breath,
Did cleave my roof asunder.
  La.y P. Believe me, and I
Had the most fearful dream, could I re-
member 't——
Volp. Out on my fate! I have given her
the occasion
How to torment me : she will tell me hers.
                                          [*Aside.*
  Lady P. Methought the golden medio-
  crity,
Polite, and delicate——
  Volp. O, if you do love me,
No more : I sweat, and suffer, at the men-
tion
Of any dream ; feel how I tremble yet.
  Lady P. Alas, good soul ! the passion of
the heart.
Seed-pearl were good now, boiled with
syrup of apples,
Tincture of gold, and coral, citron-pills,
Your elicampane root, myrobalanes——
  Volp. Ah me, I have ta'en a grasshopper
by the wing ![2]   [*Aside.*

---

[1] *What now !* bird-eyed ?] What particular
defect is here meant I know not ; unless it be
near-sightedness. We had the expression in
Cynthia's Revels, p. 189 *b* : "'Tis the horse-
start out of a brown study. *Amor.* Rather the
bird-eyed stroke." It is also in Bulleyn's *Dialogue,* republished by Mr. Waldron ; where the
citizen says to his wife, whose horse had just
started : "He is a *bird-eyed* jade, I warrant
you." Perhaps the allusion is to the askaunt or
side view which birds appear to take of every
object.
  Upton has noticed various imitations of Juvenal's sixth Satire in Lady Would-be's colloqy
with her maids : they are all, however, so obvious as scarcely to require pointing out, though
Whalley copied most of them.

[2] *Ah me, I have ta'en a* grasshopper *by the
wing !*] "This," says Upton, who merely
copies Erasmus (*in Adag.*) "was a proverb of
the poet Archilochus, as Lucian tells us in the
beginning of his *Pseudologista* : Τα δε του Αρχι-
λοχου εκεινο ηδη σοι λεγω, ότι τεττιγα του πτερου
συνειληφας. For the faster you hold them by
the wings the louder they scream. But is this
true of grasshoppers ? *Cicada* and Τεττιξ is not
a grasshopper, for the poets describe it as sitting
and singing on trees : however, the common
translations must excuse our poet."
  This is certainly not our grasshopper, which is
the locust. It is to be wished that we could
adopt some other name for the foreign insect to
prevent confusion : *cigale* or *chicale* would serve;
though indeed, *tettix* is as good as either. Both

Lady P. Burnt silk and amber. You
　have muscadel
Good in the house——
　Volp. You will not drink, and part?
　Lady P. No, fear not that. I doubt we
　shall not get
Some English saffron, half a dram would
　serve;
Your sixteen cloves, a little musk, dried mints;
Bugloss, and barley-meal——
　Volp. She's in again!
Before I feigned diseases, now I have one.
　　　　　　　　　　　[Aside.
　Lady P. And these applied with a right
　scarlet cloth.[1]
　Volp. Another flood of words! a very
　torrent!　　　　　　　　*[Aside.*
　Lady P. Shall I, sir, make you a poultice?
　Volp. No, no, no,
I'm very well, you need prescribe no more.
　Lady P. I have a little studied physic;
　but now
I'm all for music, save, in the forenoons,
An hour or two for painting. I would have
A lady, indeed, to have all letters and arts,
Be able to discourse, to write, to paint,
But principal, as Plato holds, your music,
And so does wise Pythagoras, I take it,
Is your true rapture: when there is concent[2]
In face, in voice, and clothes: and is, indeed,
Our sex's chiefest ornament.

Volp. The poet
As old in time as Plato, and as knowing,
Says that your highest female grace is
　silence.[3]
　Lady P. Which of your poets? Petrarch,
　or Tasso, or Dante?
Guarini? Ariosto? Aretine?
Cieco di Hadria? I have read them all.
　Volp. Is everything a cause to my de-
　struction?　　　　　　　*[Aside.*
　Lady P. I think I have two or three of
　them about me.
　Volp. The sun, the sea, will sooner both
　stand still
Than her eternal tongue! nothing can
　scape it.　　　　　　　*[Aside.*
　Lady P. Here's Pastor Fido——
　Volp. Profess obstinate silence;
That's now my safest.　　　　*[Aside.*
　Lady P. All our English writers,
I mean such as are happy in the Italian,
Will deign to steal out of this author,
　mainly;
Almost as much as from Montagnié:
He has so modern and facile a vein,
Fitting the time, and catching the court-
　ear!
Your Petrarch is more passionate, yet he,
In days of sonnetting, trusted them with
　much:[4]
Dante is hard, and few can understand him.

Ray and Chandler witnessed the *singing* of the
cicada, the one in Italy, and the other in Greece:
they do not speak of it with much rapture; and
to say the truth, a more tiresome, annoying
sound cannot well be heard. See the *Poetaster*,
p. 266 a.
　[1] *And these applied with a right scarlet cloth.*]
The virtues of a *right scarlet cloth* were once
held so extraordinary, that Dr. John Gaddesden,
by wrapping a patient in scarlet, cured him of
the small-pox, without losing so much as one
mark in his face: and he commends it for an
excellent method of cure: *Capiatur scarletum,
et involvatur variolosus totaliter, sicut ego feci,
et est bona cura.*—WHAL.
　[2] *When there is concent*] i.e., agreement or
harmony, a Platonic expression.
　[3]　　　　　*The poet
As old in time as Plato, and as knowing,
Says that your highest female grace is silence.*]
The poet perhaps is Sophocles:

Γυναιξι κοσμον ἡ σιγη φερει.

Or Euripides, whom the Oracle pronounced
the wiser:

Γυναικι γαρ σιγη τε, και το σωφρονειν
Καλλιστον.

This is Upton's note, though fathered as usual
by Whalley. Jonson, however, whose reading
was far more extensive than Upton suspected,
alludes to a passage in Libanius. (*Declam.* vi.)

Συ δε, ει μη εμε, αλλα κ'αν τον σοφωτατον ποιητην
αισχυνθητι, λεγοντα,

Γυναι, γυναιξι κοσμον ἡ σιγη φερει. κ. τ. λ.

As what follows in the rhetorician sufficiently
demonstrates.
　[4] *Your Petrarch is more passionate, yet he,
In days of sonnetting, trusted them with
much;*] Lady Would-be is perfectly correct,
both in what she says here of Petrarch and
above of Guarini. The *Pastor Fido* was plun-
dered without mercy or judgment: yet the
theft was not unhappy; for though much poor
conceit and unnatural passion was thus introduced among us, many graces of expression and
delicacies of feeling accompanied them, which in
the gradual improvement of taste now first become an object of concern, enriched the language
with beauties which have not yet lost their
power to charm. To Petrarch we are still more
indebted—though the coarse and wholesale
manner in which he was at first copied gave
occasion to the well-merited reproofs of our
early satirists. Thus Hall:

" Or filch whole pages at a clap for need,
　From honest Petrarch, clad in English weed."

Again:

" Or an '*hos ego*' from old Petrarch's spright,
　Unto a plagiary sonnet-wight," &c.

But for a desperate wit, there's Aretine;
Only his pictures are a little obscene——
You mark me not.
    Volp. Alas, my mind's perturbed.
    Lady P. Why, in such cases, we must
      cure ourselves,
Make use of our philosophy——
    Volp. Oh me!
    Lady P. And as we find our passions do
      rebel,
Encounter them with reason, or divert
    them,
By giving scope unto some other humour
Of lesser danger: as, in politic bodies,
There's nothing more doth overwhelm the
    judgment,
And cloud the understanding, than too much
Settling and fixing, and, as 'twere, sub-
    siding
Upon one object.   For the incorporating
Of these same outward things, into that
    part,
Which we call mental, leaves some certain
    fæces
That stop the organs, and, as Plato says,
Assassinate our knowledge.
    Volp. Now, the spirit
Of patience help me!   [*Aside.*
    Lady P. Come, in faith, I must
Visit you more a days; and make you well:
Laugh and be lusty.
    Volp. My good angel save me!   [*Aside.*
    Lady P. There was but one sole man in
    all the world
With whom I e'er could sympathize; and
    he
Would lie you, often, three, four hours to-
    gether
To hear me speak; and be sometime so
    rapt,
As he would answer me quite from the
    purpose,
Like you, and you are like him, just.   I'll
    discourse,
An't be but only, sir, to bring you asleep,

How we did spend our time and loves to-
    gether,
For some six years.
    Volp. Oh, oh, oh, oh, oh, oh!
    Lady P. For we were cœtanei, and
    brought up——
    Volp. Some power, some fate, some for-
    tune rescue me!

          Enter Mosca.

    Mos. God save you, madam!
    Lady P. Good sir.
    Volp. Mosca! welcome,
Welcome to my redemption.
    Mos. Why, sir?
    Volp. Oh,
Rid me of this my torture, quickly, there;
My madam with the everlasting voice:
The bells, in time of pestilence, ne'er made
Like noise, or were in that perpetual motion!
The Cock-pit comes not near it.[1]   All my
    house,
But now, steamed like a bath with her
    thick breath,
A lawyer could not have been heard; nor
    scarce
Another woman, such a hail of words
She has let fall.   For hell's sake, rid her
    hence.
    Mos. Has she presented?
    Volp. O, I do not care;
I'll take her absence upon any price,
With any loss.
    Mos. Madam——
    Lady P. I have brought your patron
A toy, a cap here, of mine own work.
    Mos. 'Tis well,
I had forgot to tell you I saw your knight,
Where you would little think it,——
    Lady P. Where?
    Mos. Marry,
Where yet, if you make haste, you may
    apprehend him,
Rowing upon the water in a gondole,
With the most cunning courtezan of Venice.[2]

---

[1] *The Cock-pit comes not near it.*] The *Cock-pit!* Had Jonson forgot that he was now in Venice?—But perhaps he saw no impropriety in given this name to a theatre there.   The Cock-pit was one of our earliest theatres, and from the allusion in the text, as well as from many others which occur in our old dramatists, it may be collected that it was frequented by the lowest and most disorderly of the people.   After all, Venice was not much injured:—for Coryat, who was there about this time, says, "I was at one of their play-houses, where I saw a comedie acted.   The house is very beggarly and base in comparison of our stately play-houses in England: neither can the actors compare with us

for apparel, shewes, and musicke."—P. 247 The conclusion of this speech is from Juvenal. *Sat.* vi.

[2] *With the* most cunning courtezan *of Venice.*] Venice succeeded, and not unjustly, to all the celebrity of Corinth for rapacious, subtle, and accomplished wantons.   Shakspeare notices this circumstance; as, indeed, do all the writers of his age, who have occasion to mention the city. The "leg-stretcher of Odcombe," (as Coryat aptly calls himself,) whose simple love of novelty involved him in the most ridiculous adventures, has a great deal of curious matter on this subject.

Lady P. Is't true?

Mos. Pursue them, and believe your eyes: Leave me to make your gift.

[*Exit* Lady P. *hastily.*

I knew 'twould take:
For, lightly, they that use themselves most licence,[1]
Are still most jealous.

Volp. Mosca, hearty thanks,
For thy quick fiction, and delivery of me.
Now to my hopes, what sayst thou?

Re-enter Lady P. Would-be.

Lady P. But do you hear, sir?——

Volp. Again! I fear a paroxysm.

Lady P. Which way
Rowed they together?

Mos. Toward the Rialto.

Lady P. I pray you lend me your dwarf.

Mos. I pray you take him.

[*Exit* Lady P.

Your hopes, sir, are like happy blossoms, fair,
And promise timely fruit, if you will stay
But the maturing; keep you at your couch,
Corbaccio will arrive straight, with the Will;
When he is gone, I'll tell you more.

[*Exit.*

Volp. My blood,
My spirits are returned; I am alive:
And, like your wanton gamester at primero,[2]
Whose thought had whispered to him, not go less,
Methinks I lie, and draw——for an encounter.

[*The scene closes upon* Volpone.

SCENE III.—*The Passage leading to* Volpone's *Chamber.*

Enter Mosca *and* Bonario.

Mos. Sir, here concealed [*shews him a closet,*] you may hear all. But, pray you,
Have patience, sir [*knocking within.*]—the same's your father knocks:
I am compelled to leave you.   [*Exit.*

Bon. Do so.—Yet
Cannot my thought imagine this a truth.

[*Goes into the closet.*

SCENE IV.—*Another part of the Same.*

Enter Mosca *and* Corvino, Celia *following.*

Mos. Death on me! you are come too soon, what meant you?
Did not I say I would send?

Corv. Yes, but I feared
You might forget it, and then they prevent us.

Mos. Prevent! did e'er man haste so for his horns?
A courtier would not ply it so for a place.

[*Aside.*

Well, now there is no helping it, stay here;
I'll presently return.   [*Exit.*

Corv. Where are you, Celia?
You know not wherefore I have brought you hither?

Cel. Not well, except you told me.

Corv. Now I will:
Hark hither.   [*Exeunt.*

SCENE V.—*A Closet opening into a Gallery.*

Enter Mosca *and* Bonario.

Mos. Sir, your father hath sent word,
It will be half an hour ere he come;
And therefore, if you please to walk the while
Into that gallery—at the upper end,
There are some books to entertain the time:
And I'll take care no man shall come unto you, sir.

Bon. Yes, I will stay there.—I do doubt this fellow.   [*Aside, and exit.*

Mos. [*Looking after him.*] There; he is far enough; he can hear nothing:
And for his father, I can keep him off.

[*Exit.*

SCENE VI.—Volpone's *Chamber.* Volpone *on his couch.* Mosca *sitting by him.*

Enter Corvino *forcing in* Celia.

Corv. Nay, now, there is no starting back, and therefore,

---

[1] *For, lightly,*] i.e., usually, or in common course.—WHAL. See p. 157 a.

[2] *And like your wanton gamester at primero,* &c.] Jonson has adopted the terms of this game as they appear in what Sir John Harington is pleased to call an *Epigram* upon "The story of Marcus' life at Primero."

" Our Marcus never can *encounter* right,
Yet *drew* two aces, and, for further spight,
Had colour for it with a hopeful *draught*,
But not *encountered* it availed him naught."

Not *to go less*, as I have already observed,— is not to adventure a smaller sum.

Resolve upon it: I have so decreed.
It must be done.   Nor would I move't
  afore,
Because I would avoid all shifts and tricks,
That might deny me.
   Cel. Sir, let me beseech you,
Affect not these strange trials; if you
  doubt
My chastity, why, lock me up for ever;
Make me the heir of darkness.   Let me
  live
Where I may please your fears, if not your
  trust.
   Corv. Believe it, I have no such humour, I.
All that I speak I mean; yet I'm not mad;
Not horn-mad, see you? Go to, shew your-
  self
Obedient, and a wife.
   Cel. O heaven!
   Corv. I say it,
Do so.
   Cel. Was this the train?
   Corv. I've told you reasons;
What the physicians have set down; how
  much
It may concern me; what my engagements
  are;
My means; and the necessity of those
  means
For my recovery: wherefore, if you be
Loyal, and mine, be won, respect my
  venture.
   Cel. Before your honour?
   Corv. Honour! tut, a breath:[1]
There's no such thing in nature: a mere
  term
Invented to awe fools.   What is my gold
The worse for touching, clothes for being
  looked on?
Why, this 's no more.   An old decrepit
  wretch,
That has no sense, no sinew; takes his
  meat
With others' fingers; only knows to gape
When you do scald his gums; a voice, a
  shadow;
And what can this man hurt you?
   Cel. Lord! what spirit
Is this hath entered him?   [*Aside.*

---

[1] *Honour! tut, a breath,* &c.] This is excellent after what we had from him, p. 358. The
genius and skill with which Jonson has conceived
and conducted this extraordinary vicious character are altogether surprising. The conclusion
of this speech is from Juvenal:
         "*Hujus*
Pallida labra cibum capiunt digitis alienis:
Ipse ad conspectum cœnæ diducere rictum
Suetus, hiat tantum," &c.—Sat. x.

   Corv. And for your fame,
That's such a jig; as if I would go tell it,
Cry it on the Piazza! who shall know it
But he that cannot speak it, and this
  fellow,
Whose lips are in my pocket? Save your-
  self,
(If you'll proclaim't, you may,) I know no
  other
Should come to know it.
   Cel. Are heaven and saints then no-
  thing?
Will they be blind or stupid?
   Corv. How!
   Cel. Good sir,
Be jealous still, emulate them; and think
What hate they burn with toward every
  sin.
   Corv. I grant you: if I thought it were
  a sin
I would not urge you.   Should I offer this
To some young Frenchman, or hot Tuscan
  blood
That had read Aretine, conned all his
  prints,
Knew every quirk within lust's labyrinth,
And were profest critic in lechery;
And I would look upon him, and applaud
  him,
This were a sin: but here, 'tis contrary,
A pious work, mere charity for physic,
And honest polity, to assure mine own.
   Cel. O heaven! canst thou suffer such a
  change?
   Volp. Thou art mine honour, Mosca,
  and my pride,
My joy, my tickling, my delight! Go
  bring them.
   Mos. [*advancing.*] Please you draw near,
  sir.
   Corv. Come on, what——
You will not be rebellious? by that
  light——
   Mos. Sir,
Signior Corvino, here, is come to see
  you.
   Volp. Oh!
   Mos. And hearing of the consultation
  had,
So lately, for your health, is come to offer,
Or rather, sir, to prostitute——
   Corv. Thanks, sweet Mosca.
   Mos. Freely, unasked, or unintreated——
   Corv. Well.
   Mos. As the true fervent instance of his
  love,
His own most fair and proper wife; the
  beauty
Only of price in Venice——

Corv. 'Tis well urged.

Mos. To be your comfortress, and to preserve you.

Volp. Alas, I am past, already! Pray you, thank him
For his good care and promptness; but for that,
'Tis a vain labour e'en to fight 'gainst heaven;
Applying fire to stone—uh, uh, uh, uh! [*coughing.*]
Making a dead leaf grow again. I take
His wishes gently, though; and you may tell him
What I have done for him: marry, my state is hopeless.
Will him to pray for me; and to use his fortune
With reverence when he comes to 't.

Mos. Do you hear, sir?
Go to him with your wife.

Corv. Heart of my father!
Wilt thou persist thus? come, I pray thee, come.
Thou seest 'tis nothing, Celia. By this hand,
I shall grow violent. Come, do 't, I say.

Cel. Sir, kill me, rather: I will take down poison,
Eat burning coals, do anything—

Corv. Be damned!
Heart, I will drag thee hence home by the hair;
Cry thee a strumpet through the streets; rip up
Thy mouth unto thine ears; and slit thy nose,
Like a raw rochet![1]—Do not tempt me; come,
Yield, I am loth—Death! I will buy some slave
Whom I will kill, and bind thee to him alive;
And at my window hang you forth, devising
Some monstrous crime, which I, in capital letters,
Will eat into thy flesh with aquafortis,
And burning corsives, on this stubborn breast.
Now, by the blood thou hast incensed, I'll do it!

Cel. Sir, what you please, you may, I am your martyr.

Corv. Be not thus obstinate, I have not deserved it:
Think who it is intreats you.   Prithee, sweet;—
Good faith, thou shalt have jewels, gowns, attires,
What thou wilt think, and ask. Do but go kiss him.
Or touch him but. For my sake. At my suit—
This once. No! not! I shall remember this.
Will you disgrace me thus? Do you thirst my undoing?

Mos. Nay, gentle lady, be advised.

Corv. No, no.
She has watched her time. Ods pr tus, this is scurvy,
'Tis very scurvy; and you are——

Mos. Nay, good sir.

Corv. An arrant locust—by hea *v*en, a locust!—
Whore, crocodile, that hast thy tears prepared,
Expecting how thou'lt bid them flow[2]——

Mos. Nay, pray you, sir!
She will consider.

Cel. Would my life would serve
To satisfy——

Corv. 'Sdeath! if she would but speak to him,
And save my reputation, it were somewhat;
But spightfully to affect my utter ruin!

Mos. Ay, now you have put your fortune in her hands.
Why i' faith, it is her modesty, I must quit her.
If you were absent, she would be more coming;
I know it: and dare undertake for her.
What woman can before her husband? pray you,
Let us depart, and leave her here.

Corv. Sweet Celia,
Thou mayst redeem all yet; I'll say no more:
If not, esteem yourself as lost. Nay, stay there.
[*Shuts the door, and exit with* Mosca.

Cel. O God, and his good angels! whither, whither,
Is shame fled human breasts? that with such ease,

---

¹ *Like a* raw rochet!] A *rochet* or *rouget*, so named from its *red colour*, is a fish of the gurnet kind, but not so large.—WHAL.

² *That hast thy tears prepared,*
Expecting how thou'lt bid them flow.]

" Plorat
Uberibus semper lacrymis, semperque paratis
In statione suâ, atque expectantibus illam,
Quo jubeat manare modo."—Juv. *Sat.* vi.

Men dare put off your honours, and their
　own?
Is that, which ever was a cause of life,
Now placed beneath the basest circum-
　stance,
And modesty an exile made, for money?
　Volp. Ay, in Corvino, and such earth-fed
　minds,
　　　　　　　　　[Leaping from his couch.
That never tasted the true heaven of love.
Assure thee, Celia, he that would sell thee,
Only for hope of gain, and that uncertain,
He would have sold his part of Paradise
For ready money, had he met a cope-man. [1]
Why art thou mazed to see me thus re-
　vived?
Rather applaud thy beauty's miracle;
'Tis thy great work: that hath, not now
　alone,
But sundry times raised me, in several
　shapes,
And, but this morning, like a mountebank,
To see thee at thy window: ay, before
I would have left my practice, for thy love,
In varying figures, I would have contended

With the blue Proteus, or the horned flood. [2]
Now art thou welcome.
　Cel. Sir!
　Volp. Nay, fly me not.
Nor let thy false imagination
That I was bed-rid, make thee think I am
　so:
Thou shalt not find it. I am now as fresh,
As hot, as high, and in as jovial plight,
As when, in that so celebrated scene,
At recitation of our comedy,
For entertainment of the great Valois, [3]
I acted young Antinous; and attracted
The eyes and ears of all the ladies present,
To admire each graceful gesture, note, and
　footing.   *[Sings.*

Come, my Celia, [4] let us prove,
While we can, the sports of love,
Time will not be ours for ever,
He, at length, our good will sever;
Spend not then his gifts in vain:
Suns that set may rise again;
But if once we lose this light,
'Tis with us perpetual night.

---

[1] *Had he met a* cope-man.] "For this we now
say chapman: which is as much as to say a
merchant, or *cope-man.*" Verstegan on the
word *ceapman.*—WHAL.
　Is it not rather pure Dutch, *koopman,* or *coop-
man?*
[2] *Or the horned flood.*] I should have passed
this, had I not observed a query as to "the pagan
deity" here meant, in the margin of Mr. Whalley's copy. It is Acheloüs, of whose "contention" there is a pretty story in Ovid.
[3] *For entertainment of the great Valois,*] He
probably alludes to the magnificent spectacles
which were exhibited for the amusement of
Henry III., in 1574, when he passed through
Venice, in his return from Poland, to take possession of the crown of France, vacant by the
death of his brother Charles, of infamous
memory.
[4] *Come, my Celia, &c.*] This song, as
Upton says, is imitated from Catullus.
　　　　　　　　　　　　　　　WHAL.
　As the original is not long, it is subjoined, that
the extent of Jonson's obligation to it may be
seen at once:

" *Vivamus, mea Lesbia, atque amemus,*
　Rumoresque senum seviorum
　Omnes unius æstimemus assis.
　Soles occidere et redire possunt;
　Nobis, cum semel occidit brevis lux,
　Nox est perpetua una dormiunda.
　Da me basia mille, deinde centum,
　Dein mille altera, dein secunda centum;
　Dein usque altera mille, deinde centum.
　Dein, cum millia multa fecerimus,
　Conturbabimus illa, ne sciamus,
　Aut ne quis malus invidere possit,
　Cum tantum sciat esse basiorum. "

Here is nothing similar to the concluding lines
of this beautiful little poem, which seem to bear
an ingenious reference to the well-known Insti-
tutes of Sparta respecting theft. The praise,
however, which is bestowed on Jonson's genius,
can scarcely be extended to his judgment in
this instance. The song is evidently introduced
somewhat too much in the style of that in the
Rovers, where the conspirators join in chorus
" to conceal their purpose." This impropriety
has not escaped the critics. "Celia," says one
of them, "is surprised, and would fain fly: but
being seized and forced to stay, she quietly
listens to *an entertainment of music.* Methinks
she should have rent, torn, and cried out for
help, as she does afterwards:—but that would
have spoiled the song." From the words in
italics, it might be supposed that Volpone had
called in a band of musicians to amuse Celia,
instead of endeavouring to captivate her by
a few of the "graceful notes" which had
"attracted the ears of the ladies" at the Doge's
palace.
　Nor is it clear that she "ought to have rent,
torn," &c. She had hitherto sustained no actual violence, nor seemed to be in immediate
danger of any. Her husband, for aught she
knew, was in the plot against her: and having
delivered her up to prostitution, was not likely
to be recalled by her complaints. Afterwards,
indeed, when she is seized by Volpone, her innate horror of impurity prevails over every other
consideration, and her cries are just and natural.
I have said thus much, to moderate, if possible,
the indiscriminate levity with which the faults of
this great man are censured; and not to defend
the introduction of the song itself, which is confessedly ill-timed.

Why should we defer our joys?
Fame and rumour are but toys.
Cannot we delude the eyes
Of a few poor household spies?
Or his easier ears beguile,
Thus removed by our wile?
'Tis no sin love's fruits to steal;
But the sweet thefts to reveal:
To be taken, to be seen,
These have crimes accounted been.

Cel. Some serene blast me,[1] or dire
　lightning strike
This my offending face!
Volp. Why droops my Celia?
Thou hast, in place of a base husband
　found
A worthy lover: use thy fortune well,
With secrecy and pleasure. See, behold,
What thou art queen of; not in expecta-
　tion,
As I feed others: but possessed and
　crowned.
See, here, a rope of pearl; and each more
　orient
Than that the brave Ægyptian queen ca-
　roused:
Dissolve and drink them. See, a car-
　buncle,

May put out both the eyes of our St.
　Mark;
A diamond would have bought Lollia
　Paulina,
When she came in like star-light, hid with
　jewels,
That were the spoils of provinces;[2] take
　these,
And wear, and lose them; yet remains an
　earring
To purchase them again, and this whole
　state.
A gem but worth a private patrimony,
Is nothing: we will eat such at a meal.
The heads of parrots, tongues of nightin-
　gales,
The brains of peacocks, and of estriches,
Shall be our food:[3] and, could we get the
　phœnix,
Though nature lost her kind, she were our
　dish.
Cel. Good sir, these things might move
　a mind affected
With such delights; but I, whose inno-
　cence
Is all I can think wealthy, or worth th' en-
　joying,
And which, once lost, I have nought to
　lose beyond it,

---

[1] *Some* serene *blast me*,] "I found," says Upton, "this passage thus printed, in a modern edition, ' Some *siren* blast me': and the editor hugged himself, I dare say, with the thought of this emendation: but the poet alludes to a disease in the eye, called by physicians *gutta serena*," p. 44. O Nemesis, how watchful art thou!—and Upton, " I dare say, hugged himself;" although his explanation is just as little to the purpose as the emendation of his prede-cessor. A *serene*, as Whalley discovered in Cotgrave, while his work was in the press (for the word is pure French), is " a mildew, or that harmful dew of moist summer evenings, which occasions blights." Jonson uses it again in his *Epigrams*:

" Wherever death doth please t' appear,
Seas, *serenes*, swords, shot, sickness, all are
　there."—Epig. 32.

And it is used also by Daniel, in the same sense:

" The fogs and the *serene* offend us more,
　Or we may think so, than they did before."
　　　　Queen's Arcadia, act i. sc. 1.—WHAL.

[2] *A diamond would have bought Lollia
Paulina,
When she came in, like star-light, hid with
　jewels,
That were the spoils of provinces:*] Lolliam Paulinam, quæ fuit Caii principis matrona, ne serio quidem, aut solemni cærimoniarum aliquo apparatu, sed mediocrium etiam sponsalium

canâ, vidi smaragdis margaritisque opertam, alterno textu fulgentibus, toto capite, crinibus, spira, auribus, collo, monilibus, digitisque. Nec dona prodigi principis fuerant, sed avitæ opes, provinciarum scilicet spoliis partæ.
　　　　　　　　Plin. L. 9. 3. 58.
This extract Whalley found in Upton, who refers to Tacitus and Suetonius for further proofs of the extravagance of this lady: which, indeed, is frequently noticed by our old dramatists. Thus Machin:

　　" And for thee, not
Lollia Paulina, nor those blazing stars
Which make the world the apes of Italy,
Shall match thyself in *sun-bright* splendancy."
　　　　　　　Dumb Knight.

Milton applies this epithet (sun-bright) to the chariot of Satan, and is complimented for it by one of his editors, as having "beautifully im-proved" the *light-bright* of old Joshua Sylvester! Milton has a thousand claims to our admiration: but that of introducing beautiful epithets into our language is not one of them. He found them formed to his hands.

[3] *The heads of parrots, tongues of nightin-
gales,
The brains of peacocks, and of estriches
Shall be our food:*] This is a strain of luxury taken from the Emperor Heliogabalus. Comedit, says Ælius Lampridius, *linguas pavonum et lusciniarum:* and he had the brains of 500 ostriches to furnish out a single dish.
　　　　　　　　　　　　WHAL.

Cannot be taken with these sensual baits:
If you have conscience——
  Volp. 'Tis the beggar's virtue ;
If thou hast wisdom, hear me, Celia.
Thy baths shall be the juice of July-flowers,
Spirit of roses, and of violets,
The milk of unicorns, and panthers' breath[1]
Gathered in bags, and mixed with Cretan
  wines.
Our drink shall be prepared gold and am-
  ber ;
Which we will take until my roof whirl
  round
With the vertigo : and my dwarf shall dance,
My eunuch sing, my fool make up the
  antic,
Whilst we, in changed shapes, act Ovid's
  tales,
Thou, like Europa now, and I like Jove,
Then I like Mars, and thou like Erycine:
So of the rest, till we have quite run
  through,
And wearied all the fables of the gods.
Then will I have thee in more modern
  forms,
Attired like some sprightly dame of France,
Brave Tuscan lady, or proud Spanish
  beauty ;
Sometimes unto the Persian sophy's wife ;
Or the grand signior's mistress ; and for
  change,
To one of our most artful courtezans,

Or some quick Negro, or cold Russian ;
And I will meet thee in as many shapes:
Where we may so transfuse our wandering
  souls   )
Out at our lips, and score up sums of plea-
  sures,   *[Sings.*

  That the curious[2] shall not know
  How to tell them as they flow ;
  And the envious, when they find
  What their number is, be pined. '

  Cel. If you have ears that will be pierced
    —or eyes
That can be opened —a heart that may be
  touched—
Or any part that yet sounds man about
  you—
If you have touch of holy saints—or hea-
  ven—
Do me the grace to let me 'scape—if not,
Be bountiful and kill me. You do know,
I am a creature, hither ill betrayed,
By one whose shame I would forget it
  were :
If you will deign me neither of these graces,
Yet feed your wrath, sir, rather than your
  lust,
(It is a vice comes nearer manliness,)
And punish that unhappy crime of nature,
Which you miscall my beauty : flay my
  face,
Or poison it with ointments for seducing

---

[1] *The* milk of unicorns, *and* panthers' breath]
I know not for what particular quality the milk
of unicorns is celebrated, the animal being confined to the terra incognita of Africa, where
few can go to suck it. Pliny, indeed, observes
that "the milk of camels is extremely sweet ;"
and this may have been in Jonson's mind :—
but his knowledge was so universal, that it is
very hazardous, at least in one so little read as
myself, to decide upon his authorities. The
sweetness of the panther's breath, or rather body,
is sufficiently notorious. It is remarked by Pliny,
Lib. xxi. c. 7 : "*Animalium nullum odora-
tum nisi de pantheris quod dictum est, credi-
mus.*" Ælian also mentions it ; but the passage
which our author had in view was probably the
following : Εκ του στοματος αυτου ευωδια τις
εξεισιν αρωματικη δι' ης τα αλλα ζωα θελγομενα
τα εγγυς και τα πορρωθεν εγγιζουσιν αυτω και
επουται. Eustat. *Comment.* in *Hexaëmeron,*
4to, p. 38. Frequent allusions to this circumstance occur in our old poets. Thus Shirley :

  " Your Grace is bound
To hunt this spotted *panther* to his ruin,
Whose *breath is only sweet* to poison virtue."
      The Royal Master.
And Glapthorne :

  " The panther so,
Breathes odours precious as the fragrant gums

Of eastern groves, but the delicious scent,
Not taken in at distance, chokes the sense
With the too muskie savour."
      The Hollander.

And Randolph, in some pretty stanzas to a
"very deformed gentlewoman, but of a voice in-
comparably sweet :"

" Say, monster strange, what mayst thou be ?
  Whence shall I fetch thy pedigree ?
  What but a panther could beget,
  A beast so foul, a breath so sweet ?"

[I know a case in India of hyena's blood being
given to an English lady in a consumption.—
F. C.]

[2] *That the curious, &c.*] These lines form
an elegant imitation of the concluding hendeca-
syllables from Catullus, (p. 370), and are reprinted, together with the rest, in *The Forest,*
a collection of the author's smaller poems.
  It would scarcely be just to Jonson's merits to
pass over this admirable scene without remarking on the boundless fertility of his mind. Temptations are heaped upon temptations with a
rapidity which almost outstrips the imagination ;
and a richness, variety, and beauty, which render mean and base all the allurements that preceding poets have invented and combined, to
facilitate the overthrow of purity and virtue.

Your blood to this rebellion. Rub these
    hands
With what may cause an eating leprosy,
E'en to my bones and marrow: anything
That may disfavour me, save in my ho-
    nour—
And I will kneel to you, pray for you, pay
    down
A thousand hourly vows, sir, for your
    health ;
Report, and think you virtuous——
    Volp. Think me cold,
Frozen, and impotent, and so report me?
That I had Nestor's hernia, thou wouldst
    think.
I do degenerate, and abuse my nation,
To play with opportunity thus long ;
I should have done the act, and then have
    parleyed.
Yield, or I'll force thee.   [*Seizes her.*
    Cel. O! just God!
    Volp. In vain——
    Bon. [*rushing in.*] Forbear, foul ravisher!
        libidinous swine !
Free the forced lady, or thou diest, impos-
    tor.
But that I'm loth to snatch thy punish-
    ment
Out of the hand of justice, thou shouldst
    yet
Be made the timely sacrifice of vengeance,
Before this altar and this dross, thy idol.——
Lady, let's quit the place, it is the den
Of villainy ; fear nought, you have a guard :
And he ere long shall meet his just reward.
                    [*Exeunt* Bon. *and* Cel.

Volp. Fall on me, roof, and bury me in
    ruin !
Become my grave, that wert my shelter ! O !
I am unmasked, unspirited, undone,
Betrayed to beggary, to infamy——

Enter Mosca, *wounded and bleeding.*

Mos. Where shall I run, most wretched
    shame of men,
To beat out my unlucky brains ?
    Volp. Here, here.
What ! dost thou bleed ?
    Mos. O, that his well-driven sword
Had been so courteous to have cleft me
    down
Unto the navel, ere I lived to see
My life, my hopes, my spirits, my patron, all
Thus desperately engaged by my error !
    Volp. Woe on thy fortune !
    Mos. And my follies, sir.
    Volp. Thou hast made me miserable.
    Mos. And myself, sir.
Who would have thought he would have
    hearkened so ?
    Volp. What shall we do ?
    Mos. I know not ; if my heart
Could expiate the mischance, I'd pluck it
    out.
Will you be pleased to hang me, or cut my
    throat ?
And I'll requite you, sir. Let's die like
    Romans,[1]
Since we have lived like Grecians.
                    [*Knocking within.*
    Volp. Hark! who's there?
I hear some footing ; officers, the saffi,[2]

---

[1] *Let's* die like Romans,] i.e., by our own
hands, fearlessly. *Since we have lived like
Grecians;* like debauchees: *pergræcari,* as Upton
observes, from Plautus, is "to spend the hours
in mirth, wine, and banquets." All this is very
well ; but when he adds, "Hence the proverb,
as merry as a Greek ;" and "hence too Sebastian
in *Twelfth-Night,* calls the clown *foolish
Greek,* for his unseasonable *mirth ;*" he talks as
idly, as the *commentators* on Shakspeare usually
do, on this subject. How often will it be necessary to observe, that our old dramatists affixed
no appropriate idea to these patronymic appellations; which were used merely as augmentatives,
and must be understood from the context? To
be as mad or as merry, as foolish or as wise, as
Greeks, Trojans, Lacedemonians, &c. (for all
these terms were indiscriminately used) was
simply to be *very* mad, merry, foolish, &c., and
nothing can be more absurd than the attempts
to fasten upon such expressions a constant and
determinate sense. One happy specimen of this
is before me. In the *Lover's Melancholy,* Cu-
culus, a foolish courtier, says : "I come to speak
with a young lady, the old *Trojan's* daughter of

this house." To explain this obscure speech,
the editor musters up all his wisdom. "The
popularity," he says, "of the achievements of
the Greeks and Trojans led to an application of
their names not very honourable to them" (Mr.
Weber wanted Partridge at his elbow), "the
former being used for cheats, and the latter for
thieves." So that "old Trojan," in the text,
means old *thief;* and being applied to the general of the Famagostan armies, and the most respectable character in the drama, does as much
credit to the judgment of Ford, as to the
sagacity of Mr. Weber. It would be a pity to
withhold the grave conclusion of this note from
the reader : "It is difficult to conceive a greater
degradation, if we except the common misap-
plication of the venerable names of Hector,
Cæsar, Pompey, &c. to dogs." *Venerable !*—but
let it go : it is some praise to be uniform, even
in folly.
    [2] *The* saffi,] "These," says Whalley, "as
we learn from Coryat, are officers subordinate to
the Podestaes and Prætors ; of whom some have
authority only by land, and some by sea. Their
habit is a red camlet gown with long sleeves." It

Come to apprehend us ! I do feel the brand
Hissing already at my forehead ; now
Mine ears are boring.
   Mos. To your couch, sir, you,
Make that place good, however. [*Volpone
lies down as before.*]—Guilty men
Suspect what they deserve still.[1]

       Enter Corbaccio.

Signior Corbaccio !
   Corb. Why, how now, Mosca?
   Mos. O, undone, amazed, sir.
Your son, I know not by what accident,
Acquainted with your purpose to my patron,
Touching your Will, and making him your
   heir,
Entered our house with violence, his sword
   drawn,
Sought for you, called you wretch, un-
   natural,
Vowed he would kill you.
   Corb. Me !
   Mos. Yes, and my patron.
   Corb. This act shall disinherit him in-
   deed :
Here is the Will.
   Mos. 'Tis well, sir.
   Corb. Right and well :
Be you as careful now for me.

       Enter Voltore *behind.*

   Mos. My life, sir,
Is not more tendered ; I am only yours.
   Corb. How does he? will he die shortly,
   think'st thou?
   Mos. I fear
He'll outlast May.
   Corb. To-day?
   Mos. No, last out May, sir.
   Corb. Couldst thou not give him a dram?

   Mos. O, by no means, sir.
   Corb. Nay, I'll not bid you.
   Volt. [*coming forward.*] This is a knave,
   I see.
   Mos. [*seeing* Volt.] How ! Signior Vol-
   tore ! did he hear me ?   [*Aside.*
   Volt. Parasite !
   Mos. Who's that?—O, sir, most timely
   welcome——
   Volt. Scarce,
To the discovery of your tricks, I fear.
You are his, *only ?* and mine also, are you
   not ?
   Mos. Who? I, sir !
   Volt. You, sir. What device is this
About a Will?
   Mos. A plot for you, sir.
   Volt. Come,
Put not your foists[2] upon me ; I shall scent
   them.
   Mos. Did you not hear it?
   Volt. Yes, I hear Corbaccio
Hath made your patron there his heir.
   Mos. 'Tis true,
By my device, drawn to it by my plot,
With hope——
   Volt. Your patron should reciprocate?
And you have promised?
   Mos. For your good I did, sir.
Nay, more, I told his son, brought, hid
   him here,
Where he might hear his father pass the
   deed ;
Being persuaded to it by this thought, sir,
That the unnaturalness, first, of the act,
And then his father's oft disclaiming in him,[3]
(Which I did mean t' help on), would sure
   enrage him
To do some violence upon his parent,
On which the law should take sufficient
   hold,
And you be stated in a double hope :

---

is impossible that Coryat could say this ; for
the *saffi* are mere bailiffs' followers, and subordinate to the commandadori. Whalley probably mistook *savi* for *saffi*. The *savi*, indeed,
wear a red gown, as doctors of law ; but they
rank *above* the Podestaes and Prætors, not below
them, as he says. In short, his whole note is a
blunder.
  [1] *Guilty men,* &c.] The occasional qualms of
these two knaves, who pass with the rapidity of
Falstaff "from praying to purse-taking," are
marked throughout this scene with admirable
truth and humour.
  [2] *Put not,* &c.] Foists are juggling tricks,
frauds ; but the line contains also a punning
allusion to a meaning which our delicate ancestors affixed to the word when they gave the name
of foisting-hounds to the ladies' favourites, the
small chamber-dogs of those days.

  [3] *And then his father's* oft disclaiming in
him,] i.e., disclaiming him. Our poet's contemporaries use the same diction: so Fletcher:

     "Thou *disclaim'st in me ;*
    Tell me thy name."—*Philaster,* act ii.
                    WHAL.

And Shakspeare :

" Cowardly rascal ! Nature *disclaims in thee.*"
                Lear, act ii. sc. 2.

  The expression is very common in our old
writers : it seems, however, to have been wearing
out about this time, since it is found far less frequently in the second than in the first impressions of these plays. Two instances of *disclaim
in* occur in the quarto edition of *Every Man in
his Humour;* both of which, in the folio, are
simplified into *disclaim.*

Truth be my comfort, and my conscience,
My only aim was to dig you a fortune
Out of these two old rotten sepulchres——[1]
  Volt. I cry thee mercy, Mosca.
  Mos. Worth your patience,
And your great merit, sir. And see the
  change!
  Volt. Why, what success?
  Mos. Most hapless! you must help, sir.
Whilst we expected the old raven,[2] in comes
Corvino's wife, sent hither by her hus-
  band——
  Volt. What, with a present?
  Mos. No, sir, on visitation;
(I'll tell you how anon;) and staying long,
The youth he grows impatient, rushes forth,
Seizeth the lady, wounds me, makes her
  swear
(Or he would murder her, that was his
  vow)
To affirm my patron to have done her
  rape:
Which how unlike it is, you see! and
  hence,
With that pretext he's gone, to accuse his
  father,
Defame my patron, defeat you——
  Volt. Where is her husband?
Let him be sent for straight.
  Mos. Sir, I'll go fetch him.
  Volt. Bring him to the Scrutineo.
  Mos. Sir, I will.
  Volt. This must be stopt.
  Mos. O you do nobly, sir.
Alas, 'twas laboured all, sir, for your good;
Nor was there want of counsel in the plot:
But fortune can, at any time, o'erthrow
The projects of a hundred learned clerks,
  sir.
  Corb. [*listening.*] What's that?
  Volt. Wilt please you, sir, to go along?
    [*Exit* Corbaccio, *followed by* Voltore.
  Mos. Patron, go in, and pray for our
  success.
  Volp. [*rising from his couch.*] Need
makes devotion: heaven your labour
  bless!   [*Exeunt.*

ACT IV.

SCENE I.—*A Street.*

Enter Sir Politick Would-be *and* Peregrine.

  Sir P. I told you, sir, it was a plot; you
  see
What observation is! You mentioned me
For some instructions: I will tell you, sir,
(Since we are met here in this height of
  Venice,)
Some few particulars I have set down,
Only for this meridian, fit to be known
Of your crude traveller; and they are these.
I will not touch, sir, at your phrase, or
  clothes,
For they are old.[3]
  Per. Sir, I have better.
  Sir P. Pardon,
I meant, as they are themes.
  Per. O, sir, proceed:
I'll slander you no more of wit, good sir.
  Sir P. First, for your garb, it must be
  grave and serious,[4]
Very reserved and locked; not tell a secret
On any terms, not to your father; scarce
A fable, but with caution: make sure choice
Both of your company and discourse; be-
  ware
You never speak a truth——
  Per. How!
  Sir P. Not to strangers,
For those be they you must converse with
  most;
Others I would not know, sir, but at dis-
  tance,
So as I still might be a saver in them:
You shall have tricks else past upon you
  hourly.
And then, for your religion, profess none,
But wonder at the diversity of all;
And, for your part, protest, were there no
  other
But simply the laws o' th' land, you could
  content you.
Nic Machiavel and Monsieur Bodin,[5] both

---

[1] *My only aim was to dig you a fortune*
  Out of these two old rotten sepulchres—]
The expression is as natural as the image is just;
treasure has been often found in ancient monuments and sepulchres.—WHAL.
  [2] *Whilst we expected the old raven,*] i.e.,
Corbaccio.—WHAL.
  [3] Sir P. *I will not touch, sir, at your phrase,*
    or clothes,
  For they are old.
Per. *Sir, I have better.*] This captious kind
of wit (such as it is) occurs in Donne:

    " Your *only* wearing is your grogram.
    Not so, sir, I have more."—*Sat.* iv.

  [4] *First, for your garb, it must be grave and
serious,* &c.] Jonson with much humour ridicules the stale counsel and advice, which at this
time, when travelling in Italy was so much in
vogue, were retailed by every pretender to a
knowledge of the world.—WHAL.
  [5] Monsieur Bodin was a French lawyer of
eminence, and a very voluminous writer. Not
being so well acquainted with his works as Sir

Were of this mind. Then must you learn
    the use
And handling of your silver fork at meals, [1]
The metal of your glass ; (these are main
    matters
With your Italian ;) and to know the hour
When you must eat your melons and your
    figs.
    Per. Is that a point of state too?
    Sir P. Here it is:
For your Venetian, if he see a man
Preposterous in the least, he has him straight;
He has; he strips him. I'll acquaint you, sir,
I now have lived here 'tis some fourteen
    months :
Within the first week of my landing here,
All took me for a citizen of Venice,
I knew the forms so well——
    Per. And nothing else.   [*Aside.*
    Sir P. I had read Contarene, [2] took me
    a house,
Dealt with my Jews to furnish it with
    moveables——
Well, if I could but find one man, one man
To mine own heart, whom I durst trust, I
    would——
    Per. What, what, sir?
    Sir P. Make him rich; make him a
    fortune :
He should not think again. I would com-
    mand it.
    Per. As how?
    Sir P. With certain projects that I have;
Which I may not discover.
    Per. If I had
But one to wager with, I would lay odds
    now,
He tells me instantly.   [*Aside.*

    Sir P. One is, and that
I care not greatly who knows, to serve the
    state
Of Venice with red herrings for three years,
And at a certain rate, from Rotterdam,
Where I have correspondence. There's a
    letter,
Sent me from one o' the states, and to that
    purpose :
He cannot write his name, but that's his
    mark.
    Per. He is a chandler?
    Sir P. No, a cheesemonger.
There are some others too with whom I
    treat
About the same negociation ;
And I will undertake it : for 'tis thus.
I'll do't with ease, I have cast it all. Your
    hoy
Carries but three men in her, and a boy ;
And she shall make me three returns a
    year :
So if there come but one of three, I save ;
If two, I can defalk :—but this is now,
If my main project fail.
    Per. Then you have others?
    Sir P. I should be loth to draw the
    subtle air
Of such a place, without my thousand aims.
I'll not dissemble, sir : where'er I come,
I love to be considerative ; and 'tis true,
I have at my free hours thought upon
Some certain goods unto the state of
    Venice,
Which I do call *my Cautions ;* and, sir,
    which
I mean, in hope of pension, to propound
To the Great Council, then unto the Forty,

Pol, I cannot tell to which of them he alludes,
unless it be to his "Republics," which was
once read at our Universities, and about the
time when this play appeared, translated into
English, by Richard Knolles. Bodin died in
1596.
    [1] *Then must you learn the use
    And handling of your silver* fork *at meals,*]
See *Devil's an Ass.*
    [2] *I had read* Contarene,] A treatise *della re-
publica et magistrati di Venetia, di Gasp. Con-
tarini.—*WHAL.
    It was translated in 1599, by Lewis Lewkenor,
Esq. Coryat speaks of this work as very elegantly rendered into English ; though somewhat deficient in the description of sign-posts,
grave-stones, &c., matters in which Tom greatly
delighted. But a more valuable testimony to
its merits is the approbation of Spenser, who
accompanied the publication (as the manner then
was) with a commendatory sonnet, now become
not a little interesting from the fallen estate of
this "flower of the last world's delight." Rome,

in defiance of Spenser's prophecy, may yet rise
from her ashes ; but Venice, like Babylon, is
sunk for ever.

" The antique *Babel,* Empresse of the East,
    Upreard her buildinges to the threatned
    skie :
And Second *Babel,* tyrant of the West,
    Her ayry towers upraised much more high.
But with the weight of their own surquedrie
    They both are fallen, that all the earth did
    feare,
And buried now in their own ashes lye ;
    Yet shewing by their heapes how great they
    were.
But in their place doth now a third appeare,
    Fayre Venice, flower of the last world's
    delight,
And next to them in beauty draweth neare,
    But farre exceeds in policie of right.
Yet not so fayre her buildinges to behold,
    As Lewkenor's stile that hath her beautie
    told."

So to the Ten.   My means are made already——
Per. By whom?
Sir P. Sir, one that though his place be obscure,
Yet he can sway, and they will hear him. He's
A commandador.
Per. What! a common serjeant?
Sir P. Sir, such as they are, put it in their mouths,
What they should say, sometimes; as well as greater:
I think I have my notes to shew you——
                    [*Searching his pockets.*
Per. Good sir.
Sir P. But you shall swear unto me, on your gentry,
Not to anticipate——
Per. I, sir!
Sir P. Nor reveal
A circumstance——My paper is not with me.
Per. O, but you can remember, sir.
Sir P. My first is
Concerning tinder-boxes.[1] You must know,
No family is here without its box.
Now, sir, it being so portable a thing,
Put case, that you or I were ill affected
Unto the state, sir; with it in our pockets,
Might not I go into the Arsenal,
Or you come out again, and none the wiser?
Per. Except yourself, sir.
Sir P. Go to, then.   I therefore
Advertise to the state, how fit it were
That none but such as were known patriots,
Sound lovers of their country, should be suffered
To enjoy them in their houses; and even those
Sealed at some office, and at such a bigness
As might not lurk in pockets.
Per. Admirable!
Sir P. My next is, how to enquire, and be resolved,

By present demonstration, whether a ship,
Newly arrived from Soria,[2] or from
Any suspected part of all the Levant,
Be guilty of the plague: and where they use
To lie out forty, fifty days, sometimes,
About the Lazaretto, for their trial;
I'll save that charge and loss unto the merchant,
And in an hour clear the doubt.
Per. Indeed, sir!
Sir P. Or——I will lose my labour.
Per. My faith, that's much.
Sir P. Nay, sir, conceive me.   It will cost me in onions,
Some thirty livres——
Per. Which is one pound sterling.
Sir P. Beside my waterworks: for this I do, sir.
First, I bring in your ship 'twixt two brick walls;
But those the state shall venture.   On the one
I strain me a fair tarpauling, and in that
I stick my onions, cut in halves; the other
Is full of loopholes, out at which I thrust
The noses of my bellows; and those bellows
I keep, with waterworks, in perpetual motion,
Which is the easiest matter of a hundred.
Now, sir, your onion, which doth naturally
Attract the infection, and your bellows blowing
The air upon him, will shew instantly,
By his changed colour, if there be contagion;
Or else remain as fair as at the first.
Now it is known, 'tis nothing.
Per. You are right, sir.
Sir P. I would I had my note.
Per. Faith, so would I:
But you have done well for once, sir.
Sir P. Were I false,

---

[1] *My first is*
Concerning tinder-boxes, &c.] Surely Jack the Painter had stumbled upon Sir Pol's memorandums; for this was precisely the mode which he pursued in firing the naval arsenal at Portsmouth.   It would not be much amiss if men in trust would sometimes turn over the pages of our crack-brained projectors; for though their schemes are, as Milton says, "slothful to good," yet a knowledge of them may occasionally furnish a hint for obviating the effects of any partial and mischievous adoption of them.   The whole of this scene is a most ingenious satire on the extravagant passion for monopolies, which prevailed at this time; and which was encouraged by the greedy favourites of the court, who were allowed to receive large sums for procuring the patents.   Many of these monopolies were for objects altogether as absurd as this of Sir Politick.   The subject is resumed with great pleasantry and effect in the *Devil's an Ass.*

[2]   *Whether a ship*
Newly arrived from Soria,] i.e. *Syria.*
The city Tyre, from whence the whole country had its name, was anciently called *Zur* or *Zor*; since the Arabs erected their empire in the East it has been again called *Sor*, and is at this day known by no other name in those parts.   Hence the Italians formed their *Soria.*—WHAL.

Or would be made so, I could shew you
  reasons
How I could sell this state now to the
  Turk,
Spite of their gallies, or their——
              [*Examining his papers.*
Per. Pray you, Sir Pol.
Sir P. I have them not about me.
Per. That I feared:
They are there, sir.
Sir P. No, this is my diary,
Wherein I note my actions of the day.
Per. Pray you let's see, sir. What is
  here? *Notandum*,   [*Reads.*

"A rat had gnawn my spur-leathers;[1]
  notwithstanding,
I put on new, and did go forth; but first
I threw three beans over the threshold.
  Item,
I went and bought two toothpicks, whereof
  one
I burst immediately, in a discourse
With a Dutch merchant, 'bout ragion del
  stato.
From him I went and paid a moccinigo
For piecing my silk stockings; by the way
I cheapened sprats; and at St. Mark's I
  urined."

'Faith these are politic notes!
Sir P. Sir, I do slip
No action of my life, but thus I quote it.
Per. Believe me, it is wise!
Sir P. Nay, sir, read forth.

Enter, at a distance, Lady Politick Would-
  be, Nano, *and two* Waiting-women.

  Lady P. Where should this loose knight
  be, trow? sure he's housed.
Nan. Why, then he's fast.
Lady P. Ay, he plays both with me.[2]
I pray you stay. This heat will do more
  harm
To my complexion than his heart is worth.
(I do not care to hinder, but to take him.)
How it comes off!   [*Rubbing her cheeks.*

1 *Wom.* My master's yonder.
Lady P. Where?
2 *Wom.* With a young gentleman.
Lady P. That same's the party;
In man's apparel! Pray you, sir, jog my
  knight:
I will be tender to his reputation,
However he demerit.
Sir P. [*seeing her.*] My lady!
Per. Where?
Sir P. 'Tis she indeed, sir; you shall
  know her. She is,
Were she not mine, a lady of that merit,
For fashion and behaviour; and for beauty
I durst compare——
Per. It seems you are not jealous,
That dare commend her.
Sir P. Nay, and for discourse——
Per. Being your wife, she cannot miss
  that.
Sir P. [*introducing* Per.] Madam,
Here is a gentleman, pray you, use him
  fairly;
He seems a youth, but he is——
Lady P. None.
Sir P. Yes one
Has put his face as soon into the world——
Lady P. You mean, as early? but to-
  day?
Sir P. How's this?
Lady P. Why, in this habit, sir; you
  apprehend me:
Well, Master Would-be, this doth not
  become you;
I had thought the odour, sir, of your good
  name
Had been more precious to you; that you
  would not
Have done this dire massacre on your
  honour;
One of your gravity, and rank besides!
But knights, I see, care little for the
  oath
They make to ladies; chiefly their own
  ladies.
Sir P. Now, by my spurs, the symbol of
  my knighthood——

---

1 *A rat had gnawn my spur-leathers; &c.*]
This is from Theophrastus; and if superstition
were not of all ages and countries, might be
thought somewhat too recondite for Sir Pol. The
expiatory virtues of the bean have been acknowledged since the days of Pythagoras, by every
dealer in old wives' fables. *In faba*, says Pliny,
with great gravity, *peculiaris religio;* especially,
I presume, when administered by "*threes*," the
sacred number. Smollett has made good use of
this speech in his *Peregrine Pickle.*

2 *Ay, he plays* both *with me.*] i.e., *both* fast
and loose.—WHAL.
This game, to which our old dramatists are
fond of alluding, is now better known by the
vulgar appellation of "pricking i' the garter."
There is both truth and humour in the following
reference to it by Butler:

  " For when he'd got himself a name
    For fraud and tricks, he spoil'd his game;
    And forced his neck into a noose,
  To shew his play at *fast and loose.*"
               Hud. Pt. iii. l. 2.

Per. Lord, how his brain is humbled
　　for an oath ！[1]　　　　　[*Aside.*
Sir P. I reach you not.
Lady P. Right, sir, your policy
May bear it through thus. Sir, a word
　　with you.　　　　　[*To* Per.
I would be loth to contest publicly
With any gentlewoman, or to seem
Froward, or violent, as the courtier says ;
It comes too near rusticity in a lady,
Which I would shun by all means : and
　　however
I may deserve from Master Would-be, yet
T' have one fair gentlewoman thus be made
The unkind instrument to wrong another,
And one she knows not, ay, and to
　　perséver ;
In my poor judgment, is not warranted
From being a solecism in our sex,
If not in manners.
Per. How is this !
Sir P. Sweet madam,
Come nearer to your aim.
Lady P. Marry, and will, sir.
Since you provoke me with your im-
　　pudence,
And laughter of your light land-syren here,
Your Sporus, your hermaphrodite——
Per. What's here ?
Poetic fury and historic storms !
Sir P. The gentleman, believe it, is of
　　worth,
And of our nation.
Lady P. Ay, your Whitefriars nation.[2]
Come, I blush for you, Master Would-be, I;
And am ashamed you should have no
　　more forehead,
Than thus to be the patron, or St. George,
To a lewd harlot, a base fricatrice,
A female devil, in a male outside.

Sir P. Nay,
An you be such a one, I must bid adieu
To your delights. The case appears too
　　liquid.　　　　　[*Exit.*
Lady P. Ay, you may carry't clear, with
　　your state-face !
But for your carnival concupiscence,
Who here is fled for liberty of conscience,
From furious persecution of the marshal,
Her will I dis'ple.[3]
Per. This is fine, i' faith !
And do you use this often? Is this part
Of your wit's exercise, 'gainst you have
　　occasion ?
Madam——
Lady P. Go to, sir.
Per. Do you hear me, lady ?
Why, if your knight have set you to beg
　　shirts,
Or to invite me home, you might have done it
A nearer way by far.
Lady P. This cannot work you
Out of my snare.
Per. Why, am I in it, then ?
Indeed your husband told me you were fair,
And so you are ; only your nose inclines,[4]
That side that's next the sun, to the queen-
　　apple.
Lady P. This cannot be endured by any
　　patience.

　　　　　Enter Mosca.

Mos. What is the matter, madam ?
Lady P. If the senate
Right not my quest in this, I will protest
　　them
To all the world no aristocracy.
Mos. What is the injury, lady ?
Lady P. Why, the callet[5]
You told me of, here I have ta'en disguised.

---

[1] *Lord, how his brain is* humbled *for an
oath !*] How so? Surely Peregrine forgets that
the *spurs* are the most honourable part of a
knight's dress.
[2] *Ay, your Whitefriars nation.*] Whitefriars was at this time a privileged spot, in which
fraudulent debtors, gamblers, prostitutes, and
other outcasts of society usually resided. They
formed a community, adopted the cant language
of pickpockets, and openly resisted the execution of every legal process upon any of their members. To the disgrace of the civil powers, this
atrocious combination was not broken up till
the commencement of the last century.
[3] *Her will I* dis'ple.] i.e., teach by the whip :
disciple, or discipline. The word is thus used
by Spenser, and others of our old writers :

" And bitter pennance with an iron whip
　　Was wont him once to *disple* every day."
　　　　　F. Q. B. I. c. x. S. 27.

[4]　　　*Only your nose inclines,*
*That side that's next the sun, to the queen-
apple.*] This burlesque similitude seems to
have furnished Sir John Suckling with a very
pretty allusion, in his description of the rural
bride :

" For streaks of red were mingled there,
　　Such as are on a catharin-pear,
　　The side that's next the sun."—WHAL.

[5] *Why, the* callet, *&c.*] *Callet, callat,* or
calot, is used by all our old writers for a strumpet
of the basest kind. It is derived, as Urry observes, from *calote,* Fr. a sort of cap once worn
by country girls ; and, like a hundred other
terms of this nature, from designating poverty or
meanness, finally came, by no unnatural progress, to denote depravity and vice.

Mos. Who? this! what means your ladyship? the creature
I mentioned to you is apprehended now,
Before the senate; you shall see her——
Lady P. Where?
Mos. I'll bring you to her. This young gentleman,
I saw him land this morning at the port.
Lady P. Is't possible! how has my judgment wandered?
Sir, I must, blushing, say to you, I have erred;
And plead your pardon.
Per. What, more changes yet!
Lady P. I hope you have not the malice to remember
A gentlewoman's passion. If you stay
In Venice here, please you to use me, sir——
Mos. Will you go, madam?
Lady P. Pray you, sir, use me; in faith,
The more you see me the more I shall conceive
You have forgot our quarrel.
[*Exeunt* Lady Would-be, Mosca, Nano, *and* Waiting-women.
Per. This is rare!
Sir Politick Would-be? no, Sir Politick Bawd,
To bring me thus acquainted with his wife!
Well, wise Sir Pol, since you have practised thus
Upon my freshman-ship, I'll try your salt-head,
What proof it is against a counter-plot.
[*Exit.*

SCENE II.—*The Scrutineo, or Senate House.*

Enter Voltore, Corbaccio, Corvino, *and* Mosca.

Volt. Well, now you know the carriage of the business,
Your constancy is all that is required
Unto the safety of it.

Mos. Is the lie
Safely conveyed amongst us? is that sure?
Knows every man his burden?
Corv. Yes.
Mos. Then shrink not.
Corv. But knows the advocate the truth?
Mos. O, sir,
By no means; I devised a formal tale,
That salved your reputation. But be valiant, sir.
Corv. I fear no one but him that this his pleading
Should make him stand for a co-heir——
Mos. Co-halter!
Hang him; we will but use his tongue, his noise,
As we do croaker's here.[1]
Corv. Ay, what shall he do?
Mos. When we have done, you mean?
Corv. Yes.
Mos. Why, we'll think:
Sell him for mummia; he's half dust already.
Do you not smile, [*to* Voltore.] to see this buffalo,
How he doth sport it with his head? I should,
If all were well and past. [*Aside.*] Sir, [*to* Corbaccio.] only you
Are he that shall enjoy the crop of all,
And these not know for whom they toil.
Corb. Ay, peace.
Mos. [*turning to* Corvino.] But you shall eat it. Much![2] [*Aside.*] Worshipful sir, [*to* Voltore.]
Mercury sit upon your thundering tongue,
Or the French Hercules,[3] and make your language
As conquering as his club, to beat along,
As with a tempest, flat, our adversaries;
But much more yours, sir.
Volt. Here they come, have done.
Mos. I have another witness, if you need, sir, I can produce.
Volt. Who is it?
Mos. Sir, I have her.

---

[1]   *We will but use his tongue,
As we* croaker's, *here.*] i.e., the old raven's, Corbaccio's: this word would not have required a note, had not its meaning been overlooked by Upton, who wishes to read *"crackers,* that is, squibs"!

[2] *But you shall eat it. Much!*] Upton and Whalley constantly mistake the sense of this interjection: they will have it to be elliptical, for "*Much* good may it do you!" whereas it is merely ironical, as I have already observed, and means, *Not at all.*

[3] *Or the* French Hercules,] "The *Gallic* or *Celtic Hercules* (says Upton) was the symbol of eloquence. Lucian has a treatise on this *French Hercules,* surnamed *Ogmius;* he was pictured drest in a lion's skin; in his right hand he held his club; in his left his bow: several very small chains were figured reaching from his tongue to the ears of crowds of men at some distance."

Enter Avocatori, *and take their seats,*
Bonario, Celia, Notario, Commandadori, Saffi, *and other* Officers of Justice.

1 *Avoc.* The like of this the senate never
heard of.

2 *Avoc.* 'Twill come most strange to
them when we report it.

4 *Avoc.* The gentlewoman has been ever
held

Of unreproved name.

3 *Avoc.* So has the youth.

4 *Avoc.* The more unnatural part that
of his father.

2 *Avoc.* More of the husband.

1 *Avoc.* I not know to give

His act a name, it is so monstrous!

4 *Avoc.* But the impostor, he's a thing
created

To exceed example!

1 *Avoc.* And all after-times!

2 *Avoc.* I never heard a true voluptuary

Described but him.

3 *Avoc.* Appear yet those were cited?

Not. All but the old magnifico, Volpone.

1 *Avoc.* Why is not he here?

Mos. Please your fatherhoods,

Here is his advocate: himself so weak,

So feeble——

4 *Avoc.* What are you?

Bon. His parasite,

His knave, his pandar. I beseech the
court

He may be forced to come, that your grave
eyes

May bear strong witness of his strange impostures.

Volt. Upon my faith and credit with
your virtues,

He is not able to endure the air.

2 *Avoc.* Bring him, however.

3 *Avoc.* We will see him.

4 *Avoc.* Fetch him.

Volt. Your fatherhoods fit pleasures be
obeyed;   [*Exeunt* Officers.

But sure, the sight will rather move your
pities

Than indignation.   May it please the
court,

In the mean time, he may be heard in me:

I know this place most void of prejudice,

And therefore crave it, since we have no
reason

To fear our truth should hurt our cause.

3 *Avoc.* Speak free.

Volt. Then know, most honoured fathers,
I must now

Discover to your strangely abused ears,

The most prodigious and most frontless
piece

Of solid impudence, and treachery,

That ever vicious nature yet brought forth

To shame the state of Venice.   This lewd
woman,

That wants no artificial looks or tears

To help the vizor she has now put on,

Hath long been known a close adulteress

To that lascivious youth there; not suspected,

I say, but known, and taken in the act

With him; and by this man, the easy
husband,

Pardoned; whose timeless bounty makes
him now

Stand here, the most unhappy, innocent
person,

That ever man's own goodness made accused.

For these not knowing how to owe a gift

Of that dear grace, but with their shame;
being placed

So above all powers of their gratitude,

Began to hate the benefit; and in place

Of thanks, devise to extirpe the memory

Of such an act: wherein I pray your fatherhoods

To observe the malice, yea, the rage of
creatures

Discovered in their evils: and what heart

Such take, even from their crimes:—but
that anon

Will more appear.—This gentleman, the
father,

Hearing of this foul fact, with many
others,

Which daily struck at his too tender ears,

And grieved in nothing more than that he
could not

Preserve himself a parent (his son's ills

Growing to that strange flood), at last decreed

To disinherit him.

1 *Avoc.* These be strange turns!

2 *Avoc.* The young man's fame was ever
fair and honest.

Volt. So much more full of danger is
his vice,

That can beguile so under shade of virtue.

But, as I said, my honoured sires, his
father

Having this settled purpose, by what
means

To him betrayed, we know not, and this
day

Appointed for the deed; that parricide,

I cannot style him better, by confederacy

Preparing this his paramour to be there,

Entered Volpone's house (who was the man,
Your fatherhoods must understand, designed
For the inheritance), there sought his father:—
But with what purpose sought he him, my lords?
I tremble to pronounce it, that a son
Unto a father, and to such a father,
Should have so foul, felonious intent!
It was to murder him: when being prevented
By his more happy absence, what then did he?
Not check his wicked thoughts; no, now new deeds;
(Mischief doth never end where it begins)[1]
An act of horror, fathers! he dragged forth
The aged gentleman that had there lain bed-rid
Three years and more, out of his innocent couch,
Naked upon the floor, there left him; wounded
His servant in the face; and with this strumpet,
The stale to his forged practice, who was glad
To be so active,—(I shall here desire
Your fatherhoods to note but my collections,
As most remarkable,—) thought at once to stop
His father's ends, discredit his free choice
In the old gentleman, redeem themselves,
By laying infamy upon this man,
To whom, with blushing, they should owe their lives.
    1 *Avoc.* What proofs have you of this?
    Bon. Most honoured fathers,
I humbly crave there be no credit given
To this man's mercenary tongue.
    2 *Avoc.* Forbear.
    Bon. His soul moves in his fee.
    3 *Avoc.* O, sir.
    Bon. This fellow,
For six sols more would plead against his Maker.

    1 *Avoc.* You do forget yourself.
    Volt. Nay, nay, grave fathers,
Let him have scope: can any man imagine
That he will spare his accuser, that would not
Have spared his parent?
    1 *Avoc.* Well, produce your proofs.
    Cel. I would I could forget I were a creature.
    Volt. Signior Corbaccio!
            [*Corbaccio comes forward.*
    4 *Avoc.* What is he?
    Volt. The father.
    2 *Avoc.* Has he had an oath?
    Not. Yes.
    Corb. What must I do now?
    Not. Your testimony's craved.
    Corb. Speak to the knave?
I'll have my mouth first stopt with earth;
    my heart
Abhors his knowledge: I disclaim in him.
    1 *Avoc.* But for what cause?
    Corb. The mere portent of nature!
He is an utter stranger to my loins.
    Bon. Have they made you to this?[2]
    Corb. I will not hear thee,
Monster of men, swine, goat, wolf, parricide!
Speak not, thou viper.
    Bon. Sir, I will sit down,
And rather wish my innocence should suffer
Than I resist the authority of a father.
    Volt. Signior Corvino!
            [*Corvino comes forward.*
    2 *Avoc.* This is strange.
    1 *Avoc.* Who's this?
    Not. The husband.
    4 *Avoc.* Is he sworn?
    Not. He is.
    3 *Avoc.* Speak then.
    Corv. This woman, please your fatherhoods, is a whore,
Of most hot exercise, more than a partrich,[3]
Upon record——
    1 *Avoc.* No more.
    Corv. Neighs like a jennet.
    Not. Preserve the honour of the court.

---

[1] (*Mischief doth* ever *end where it begins*)] But the reverse of this seems the truer remark, and what he intended to say—namely, that mischief does not stop where it first began, or set out. So that, notwithstanding the authority of the old copies, it is probable we should read:

"*Mischief doth* never *end where it begins.*"
                                        WHAL.

[2] *Have they* made *you to this?*] Wrought you by previous instruction, &c. See p. 287 *a*.

[3] *More than a* partrich,] The salacious nature of this bird is taken notice of by all the ancient writers of natural history. Thus Ælian, L. iii. c. 5. Περδικες δε ακρατορες εισιν αφροδιτης. And again, Λαγνιστατον δε ὁ περδιξ και μοιχικον. Ibid. L. vii. c. 19. And Pliny, *Nat. Hist.* L. x. c. 33: *Neque in alio animali par opus libidini, &c.*—WHAL.

Corv. I shall,
And modesty of your most reverend ears.
And yet I hope that I may say, these eyes
Have seen her glued unto that piece of
　cedar,
That fine well timbered gallant : and that
　here[1]
The letters may be read, thorough the
　horn,
That make the story perfect.
　Mos. Excellent ! sir.
　Corv. There is no shame in this now, is
　there?　　　　　　　[*Aside to* Mosca.
Mos. None.
　Corv. Or if I said, I hoped that she
　were onward
To her damnation, if there be a hell
Greater than whore and woman ; a good
　Catholic
May make the doubt.
　3 *Avoc.* His grief hath made him frantic.
　1 *Avoc.* Remove him hence.
　2 *Avoc.* Look to the woman.
　　　　　　　　　　　[*Celia swoons.*
Corv. Rare !
Prettily feigned again !
　4 *Avoc.* Stand from about her.
　1 *Avoc.* Give her the air.
　3 *Avoc.* What can you say ?
　　　　　　　　　　　　[*To* Mosca.
Mos. My wound,
May it please your wisdoms, speaks for
　me, received
In aid of my good patron, when he mist
His sought-for father, when that well-
　taught dame
Had her cue given her to cry out, A rape !
　Bon. O most laid impudence ![2] Fathers—
　3 *Avoc.* Sir, be silent ;
You had your hearing free, so must they
　theirs.
　2 *Avoc.* I do begin to doubt the im-
　posture here.
　4 *Avoc.* This woman has too many
　moods.
Volt. Grave fathers,
She is a creature of a most profest
And prostituted lewdness.
　Corv. Most impetuous,
Unsatisfied, grave fathers !
　Volt. May her feignings

Not take your wisdoms : but this day she
　baited
A stranger, a grave knight, with her loose
　eyes,
And more lascivious kisses. This man saw
　them,
Together on the water, in a gondola.
　Mos. Here is the lady herself, that saw
　them too,
Without ; who then had in the open streets
Pursued them, but for saving her knight's
　honour.
　1 *Avoc.* Produce that lady.
　2 *Avoc.* Let her come.　　[*Exit* Mosca.
　4 *Avoc.* These things,
They strike with wonder.
　3 *Avoc.* I am turned a stone.

Re-enter Mosca *with* Lady Would-be.

　Mos. Be resolute, madam.
　Lady P. Ay, this same is she.
　　　　　　　　　　　[*Pointing to* Celia.
Out, thou camelion harlot ! now thine eyes
Vie tears with the hyæna. Dar'st thou
　look
Upon my wronged face? I cry your
　pardons,
I fear I have forgettingly transgrest
Against the dignity of the court——
　2 *Avoc.* No, madam.
　Lady P. And been exorbitant——
　2 *Avoc.* You have not, lady.
　4 *Avoc.* These proofs are strong.
　Lady P. Surely, I had no purpose
To scandalize your honours, or my sex's.
　3 *Avoc.* We do believe it.
　Lady P. Surely you may believe it.
　2 *Avoc.* Madam, we do.
　Lady P. Indeed you may ; my breeding
Is not so coarse——
　4 *Avoc.* We know it.
　Lady P. To offend
With pertinacy——
　3 *Avoc.* Lady——
　Lady P. Such a presence !
No surely.
　1 *Avoc.* We well think it.
　Lady P. You may think it.
　1 *Avoc.* Let her o'ercome.[3] What wit-
　nesses have you,
To make good your report?

---

[1] *And that,* here, *&c.*] Δεικτικως, pointing
to his forehead : the allusion, in the next line, is
to the *horn-book* of children. Our old writers
are never weary of their ridiculous jests on the
transparency of these badges of cuckoldom :
Thus Shakspeare : " He hath the *horn* of abundance, and the lightness of his wife shines through
it.'—*Henry IV.* Pt. 2, act i. sc. 2.

[2] *O most laid impudence !*] i.e., plotted, designed, well contrived.—WHAL.
[3] 1 Avoc. *Let her o'ercome.*] There never
was a character supported with more propriety
than this of Lady Would-be. She comes into
the court in all the violence of passion, and having vented her rage in a hasty epithet or two, re-
lapses into her usual formality, and begins to

Bon. Our consciences.
Cel. And heaven, that never fails the
   innocent.
4 *Avoc.* These are no testimonies.
Bon. Not in your courts,
Where multitude and clamour overcomes.
  1 *Avoc.* Nay, then you do wax insolent.

Re-enter Officers, *bearing* Volpone
on a couch.

Volt. Here, here,
The testimony comes that will convince,
And put to utter dumbness their bold
   tongues!
See here, grave fathers, here's the ravisher,
The rider on men's wives, the great
   impostor,
The grand voluptuary! Do you not think
These limbs should affect venery? or these
   eyes
Covet a concubine? pray you mark these
   hands;
Are they not fit to stroke a lady's breasts?
Perhaps he doth dissemble!
Bon. So he does.
Volt. Would you have him tortured?
Bon. I would have him proved.
Volt. Best try him then with goads, or
   burning irons;
Put him to the strappado: I have heard
The rack hath cured the gout; faith, give
   it him,
And help him of a malady; be courteous.
I'll undertake, before these honoured
   fathers,
He shall have yet as many left diseases,
As she has known adulterers, or thou
   strumpets.
O, my most equal hearers, if these deeds,
Acts of this bold and most exorbitant
   strain,
May pass with sufferance, what one
   citizen
But owes the forfeit of his life, yea, fame,
To him that dares traduce him? which of
   you
Are safe, my honoured fathers? I would ask,
With leave of your grave fatherhoods, if
   their plot
Have any face or colour like to truth?
Or if, unto the dullest nostril here,
It smell not rank, and most abhorred
   slander?

---

compliment the judges. Tired with her breeding
and eloquence, they cease to notice her, and
proceed to the examination of the other parties.
                  WHAL.

I crave your care of this good gentleman,
Whose life is much endangered by their
   fable;
And as for them, I will conclude with this,
That vicious persons, when they're hot,
   and fleshed
In impious acts, their constancy abounds:
Damned deeds are done with greatest confidence.
  1 *Avoc.* Take them to custody, and
   sever them.
  2 *Avoc.* 'Tis pity two such prodigies
   should live.
  1 *Avoc.* Let the old gentleman be
   returned with care.
      [*Exeunt* Officers *with* Volpone.
I'm sorry our credulity hath wronged him.
  4 *Avoc.* These are two creatures!
  3 *Avoc.* I've an earthquake in me.
  2 *Avoc.* Their shame, even in their
   cradles, fled their faces.
  4 *Avoc.* You have done a worthy service
   to the state, sir,
In their discovery.   [*To* Volt.
  1 *Avoc.* You shall hear, ere night,
What punishment the court decrees upon
   them.
    [*Exeunt* Avocat. Not. *and* Officers
      with Bonario *and* Celia.
  Volt. We thank your fatherhoods. How
   like you it?
  Mos. Rare.
I'd have your tongue, sir, tipt with gold
   for this;
I'd have you be the heir to the whole city;
The earth I'd have want men ere you
   want living:
They're bound to erect your statue in St.
   Mark's.
Signior Corvino, I would have you go
And shew yourself that you have con-
   quered.
  Corv. Yes.
  Mos. It was much better that you should
   profess
Yourself a cuckold thus, than that the
   other
Should have been proved.
  Corv. Nay, I considered that:
Now it is her fault.
  Mos. Then it had been yours.
  Corv. True; I do doubt this advocate
   still.
  Mos. I' faith,
You need not, I dare ease you of that
   care.
  Corv. I trust thee, Mosca.   [*Exit.*
  Mos. As your own soul, sir.
  Corb. Mosca!

Mos. Now for your business, sir.

Corb. How I have you business?

Mos. Yes, yours, sir.

Corb. O, none else.

Mos. None else, not I.

Corb. Be careful then.

Mos. Rest you with both your eyes, sir.

Corb. Dispatch it.

Mos. Instantly.

Corb. And look that all,
Whatever, be put in, jewels, plate, moneys,
Household stuff, bedding, curtains.

Mos. Curtain-rings, sir :
Only the advocate's fee must be deducted.

Corb. I'll pay him now ; you'll be too
prodigal.

Mos. Sir, I must tender it.

Corb. Two chequines is well.

Mos. No, six, sir.

Corb. 'Tis too much.

Mos. He talked a great while ;
You must consider that, sir.

Corb. Well, there's three——

Mos. I'll give it him.

Corb. Do so, and there's for thee.
                                            [*Exit.*

Mos. Bountiful bones! What horrid
strange offence
Did he commit 'gainst nature,[1] in his
youth,
Worthy this age? [*Aside.*] You see, sir,
[*to* Volt.] how I work
Unto your ends ; take you no notice.

Volt. No,
I'll leave you.   [*Exit.*

Mos. All is yours, the devil and all:
Good advocate!—Madam, I'll bring you
home.

Lady P. No, I'll go see your patron.

Mos. That you shall not:
I'll tell you why. My purpose is to urge
My patron to reform his will ; and for

The zeal you have shewn to-day, whereas
before
You were but third or fourth, you shall be
now
Put in the first ; which would appear as
begged
If you were present. Therefore——

Lady P. You shall sway me. [*Exeunt.*

ACT V.

SCENE I.—*A Room in* Volpone's House.
Enter Volpone.

Volp. Well, I am here, and all this brunt
is past.
I ne'er was in dislike with my disguise
Till this fled moment: here 'twas good, in
private ;
But in your public,—*cave* whilst I breathe.
'Fore God, my left leg 'gan to have the
cramp,
And I apprehended straight some power
had struck me
With a dead palsy.[2] Well! I must be
merry,
And shake it off. A many of these fears
Would put me into some villainous disease,
Should they come thick upon me: I'll pre-
vent 'em.
Give me a bowl of lusty wine, to fright
This humour from my heart. [*Drinks.*]
Hum, hum, hum !
'Tis almost gone already ; I shall conquer.
Any device now of rare ingenious knavery,
That would possess me with a violent
laughter,
Would make me up again. [*Drinks again.*]
So, so, so, so !
This heat is life ; 'tis blood by this time:—
Mosca !

---

[1]   *What strange offence
Did he commit 'gainst nature, &c.*]

    " *Cur hæc in tempore duret ?
Quod facinus dignum tam longo admiserit
ævo.*"—Juv. Sat. 10.

There are other imitations of Juvenal in this
scene, which, like this, are all sufficiently
obvious.

[2] *'Fore God, my left leg 'gan to have the*
    cramp,
*And I apprehended straight some power had
    struck me
With a dead palsy.*] Alluding to a piece of
ancient superstition, that all sudden conster-
nation of mind, and sudden pains of the body,
such as cramps, palpitations of the heart, &c.,
were ominous, and presages of evil. Hence we

may explain, as Mr. Upton remarks, a passage
in Plautus's *Miles Gloriosus:*

   " *Schel. Timeo quod rerum gesserim hic, ita
        dorsus totus prurit.*"

And in his *Bacchides,* Nicobulus says, " *Caput
prurit, perii.*"—WHAL.

   This note, the whole of which Whalley took
from Upton, is carefully retained in his corrected
copy. That two men of learning (for Whalley
was also a scholar) should fall into such absurdities, is truly pitiable. Volpone, by lying so long
immovable in his constrained situation, naturally
begins to feel the cramp : this, his fears, magni-
fied by his guilt, represent as the commencement
of a divine punishment. Such is the plain sense
of the passage.

Enter Mosca.

Mos. How now, sir? does the day look
    clear again?
Are we recovered, and wrought out of
    error,
Into our way, to see our path before us?
Is our trade free once more?
    Volp. Exquisite Mosca!
    Mos. Was it not carried learnedly?
    Volp. And stoutly:
Good wits are greatest in extremities.
    Mos. It were a folly beyond thought to
    trust
Any grand act unto a cowardly spirit:
You are not taken with it enough, me-
    thinks.
    Volp. O, more than if I had enjoyed the
    wench.
The pleasure of all woman-kind's not like it.
    Mos. Why, now you speak, sir. We must
    here be fixed;
Here we must rest; this is our master-
    piece;
We cannot think to go beyond this.
    Volp. True,
Thou hast played thy prize, my precious
    Mosca.
    Mos. Nay, sir,
To guil the court——
    Volp. And quite divert the torrent
Upon the innocent.
    Mos. Yes, and to make
So rare a music out of discords——
    Volp. Right.
That yet to me's the strangest, how thou
    hast borne it!
That these, being so divided 'mongst them-
    selves,
Should not scent somewhat, or in me or
    thee,
Or doubt their own side.
    Mos. True, they will not see't.
Too much light blinds them, I think. Each
    of them
Is so possest[1] and stuft with his own
    hopes

That anything unto the contrary,
Never so true, or never so apparent,
Never so palpable, they will resist it——
    Volp. Like a temptation of the devil.
    Mos. Right, sir.
Merchants may talk of trade, and your
    great signiors
Of land that yields well; but if Italy
Have any glebe more fruitful than these
    fellows,
I am deceived. Did not your advocate
    rare?
    Volp. O—"My most honoured fathers,
    my grave fathers,
Under correction of your fatherhoods,
What face of truth is here? If these strange
    deeds
May pass, most honoured fathers"—I had
    much ado
To forbear laughing.
    Mos. It seemed to me, you sweat, sir.
    Volp. In troth, I did a little.
    Mos. But confess, sir,
Were you not daunted?
    Volp. In good faith, I was
A little in a mist, but not dejected;
Never but still myself.
    Mos. I think it, sir.
Now, so truth help me, I must needs say
    this, sir,
And out of conscience for your advocate,
He has taken pains, in faith, sir, and de-
    served,
In my poor judgment, I speak it under
    favour,
Not to contrary you, sir, very richly—
Well—to be cozened.
    Volp. Troth, and I think so too,
By that I heard him in the latter end.
    Mos. O, but before, sir: had you heard
    him first
Draw it to certain heads, then aggravate,
Then use his vehement figures—I looked
    still
When he would shift a shirt;[2] and doing
    this
Out of pure love, no hope of gain——

---

[1]   *Each of them*
Is so possest, &c.] These touches are skilful
in the extreme. They are natural in the speaker,
and at the same time the best explanation and
defence of the plot of the drama.
[2]   *I looked still*
When he would shift a shirt;] Through the
violence of action accompanying his eloquence.
The modern Italian preachers are known to use
great vehemence of gesture in their declamatory
harangues; and perhaps it may be equally so
with the advocates at the bar. Nor was it
otherwise with the advocates of old; the death

of the great orator Hortensius was occasioned
by a cold he got, after pleading with his usual
energy and warmth in behalf of a client.—
WHAL.
    Could Whalley have heard the Neapolitan
"advocates" of the present day plead the cause
of an ass-driver or a basket-woman, where the
value of the whole matter in dispute (grapes or
apples) frequently falls short of threepence, he
would have found his conjecture amply verified.
The fees which stimulate the supernatural exertions of these "poor rags" of the law are not
unworthy of the magnificent questions agi-

Volp. 'Tis right.
I cannot answer him Mosca, as I would,
Not yet ; but for thy sake, at thy entreaty,
I will begin, even now—to vex them all,
This very instant.
   Mos. Good sir.
   Volp. Call the dwarf
And eunuch forth.
   Mos. Castrone, Nano !

     Enter Castrone *and* Nano.

   Nano. Here.
   Volp. Shall we have a jig now ?[1]
   Mos. What you please, sir.
   Volp. Go,
Straight give out about the streets, you
   two,
That I am dead ; do it with constancy,
Sadly, do you hear ?[2] impute it to the grief
Of this late slander.
        [*Exeunt* Cast. *and* Nano.
   Mos. What do you mean, sir ?
   Volp. O,
I shall have instantly my Vulture, Crow,
Raven, come flying hither, on the news,
To peck for carrion, my she-wolf, and all,
Greedy, and full of expectation——
   Mos. And then to have it ravished from
   their mouths !
   Volp. 'Tis true. I will have thee put on
   a gown,
And take upon thee, as thou wert mine
   heir ;
Shew them a Will. Open that chest, and
   reach
Forth one of those that has the blanks ; I'll
   straight
Put in thy name.
   Mos. It will be rare, sir.
          [*Gives him a paper.*
   Volp. Ay,
When they ev'n gape, and find themselves
   deluded——
   Mos. Yes.
   Volp. And thou use them scurvily !
Dispatch, get on thy gown.
   Mos. [*putting on a gown.*] But what,
   sir, if they ask
After the body ?

   Volp. Say, it was corrupted.
   Mos. I'll say it stunk, sir ; and was fain
   to have it
Coffined up instantly, and sent away.
   Volp. Anything ; what thou wilt. Hold,
   here's my Will.
Get thee a cap, a count-book, pen and ink,
Papers afore thee ; sit as thou wert taking
An inventory of parcels : I'll get up
Behind the curtain, on a stool, and hearken :
Sometime peep over, see how they do look,
With what degrees their blood doth leave
   their faces.
O, 'twill afford me a rare meal of laughter!
   Mos. [*putting on a cap, and setting out
   the table, &c.*] Your advocate will turn
   stark dull upon it.
   Volp. It will take off his oratory's edge.
   Mos. But your clarissimo, old round-
   back, he
Will crump you like a hog-louse, with the
   touch.
   Volp. And what Corvino ?
   Mos. O, sir, look for him,
To-morrow morning, with a rope and dag-
   ger,
To visit all the streets ; he must run mad,
My lady too, that came into the court,
To bear false witness for your worship——
   Volp. Yes,
And kissed me 'fore the fathers, when my
   face
Flowed all with oils—
   Mos. And sweat, sir. Why, your gold
Is such another med'cine, it dries up
All those offensive savours : it transforms
The most deformed, and restores them
   lovely,
As 'twere the strange poetical girdle.[3] Jove
Could not invent t' himself a shroud more
   subtle
To pass Acrisius' guards. It is the thing
Makes all the world her grace, her youth,
   her beauty.
   Volp. I think she loves me.
   Mos. Who ? the lady, sir ?
She's jealous of you.
   Volp. Dost thou say so ?
             [*Knocking within.*

---

tated. The *siccus petasunculus et vas Pelami-dum*, which, in Juvenal's days, rewarded the toil and skill of their learned predecessors, are now seldom heard of. The joint labours of the whole fraternity would scarce'y be estimated at the price of the humblest of such dainties.

  [1] *Shall we have a jig now ?*] A piece of low humour, a farce : such as that which he immediately proposes.

  [2] Sadly, *ao you hear ?*] Not scrrowfully ; but

with a confirmed and *serious* countenance. See p. 236 *a*.

  [3]   *It transforms
  The most deformed, and restores them lovely,
  As 'twere the strange poetical girdle.*] This is from the dialogue of Lucian, already quoted : Μεταποιει τους αμορφοτερους ωσπερ ὁ ποιητικος εκεινος κεστος.—WHAL.
  The allusion in the next line is to the well-known fable of Danaé, the daughter of Acrisius.

Mos. Hark,
There's some already.
Volp. Look.
Mos. It is the Vulture;
He has the quickest scent.
Volp. I'll to my place,
Thou to thy posture.
           [Goes behind the curtain.
Mos. I am set.
Volp. But, Mosca,
Play the artificer now, torture them rarely.

      Enter Voltore.

Volt. How now, my Mosca?
Mos. [*writing.*] "Turkey carpets,
nine——"

Volt. Taking an inventory! that is well.

Mos. "Two suits of bedding, tissue——"

Volt. Where's the Will.
Let me read that the while.

Enter Servants *with* Corbaccio *in a chair.*

Corb. So, set me down,
And get you home.   [*Exeunt* Servants.
Volt. Is he come now, to trouble us!

Mos. "Of cloth of gold, two more——"

Corb. Is it done, Mosca?

Mos. "Of several velvets, eight——"

Volt. I like his care.
Corb. Dost thou not hear?

      Enter Corvino.

Corv. Ha! is the hour come, Mosca?
Volp. [*peeping over the curtain.*] Ay,
now they muster.
Corv. What does the advocate here,
Or this Corbaccio?
Corb. What do these here?

    Enter Lady Pol. Would-be.

Lady P. Mosca!
Is his thread spun?

Mos. "Eight chests of linen——"

Volp. O,
My fine Dame Would-be, too!
Corv. Mosca, the Will,
That I may shew it these, and rid them
hence.

Mos. "Six chests of diaper, four of
damask."—There.
     *[Gives them the Will carelessly,
      over his shoulder.*

Corb. Is that the Will?
Mos. "Down-beds, and bolsters——"

Volp. Rare!
Be busy still. Now they begin to flutter:
They never think of me. Look, see, see,
    see!
How their swift eyes run over the long
    deed,
Unto the name, and to the legacies,
What is bequeathed them there——

Mos. "Ten suits of hangings——"

Volp. Ay, in their garters, Mosca. Now
    their hopes
Are at the gasp.
Volt. Mosca the heir!
Corb. What's that?
Volp. My advocate is dumb; look to
    my merchant,
He has heard of some strange storm, a
    ship is lost,
He faints; my lady will swoon. Old
    glazen-eyes,
He hath not reached his despair yet.
Corb. All these
Are out of hope; I am, sure, the man.
            [Takes the Will.

Corv. But, Mosca——

Mos. "Two cabinets——"

Corv. Is this in earnest?

Mos. "One
Of ebony——"

Corv. Or do you but delude me?

Mos. "The other, mother of pearl"—
I am very busy.
Good faith, it is a fortune thrown upon
    me——
"Item, one salt of agate"—not my seek-
    ing.

Lady P. Do you hear, sir?

Mos. "A perfumed box"—Pray you
    forbear,
You see I'm troubled—"made of an
    onyx——"

Lady P. How!
Mos. To-morrow or next day, I shall be
    at leisure
To talk with you all.
Corv. Is this my large hope's issue?
Lady P. Sir, I must have a fairer answer.
Mos. Madam!
Marry, and shall: pray you, fairly quit my
    house.
Nay, raise no tempest with your looks;
    but hark you,

Remember what your ladyship offered me
To put you in an heir; go to, think on it:
And what you said e'en your best madams
  did
For maintenance; and why not you?
  Enough.
Go home, and use the poor Sir Pol, your
  knight, well,
For fear I tell some riddles; go, be melan-
  choly.
          [*Exit* Lady Would-be.
Volp. O, my fine devil!
Corv. Mosca, pray you a word.
Mos. Lord! will not you take your dis-
  patch hence yet?
Methinks, of all, you should have been the
  example.
Why should you stay here? with what
  thought, what promise?
Hear you; do you not know, I know you
  an ass,
And that you would have most fain have been a
  wittol
If fortune would have let you? that you are
A declared cuckold, on good terms? This
  pearl,
You'll say, was yours? right: this diamond?
I'll not deny 't, but thank you. Much here
  else?
It may be so. Why, think that these good
  works
May help to hide your bad. I'll not be-
  tray you;
Although you be but extraordinary,
And have it only in title, it sufficeth:
Go home, be melancholy too, or mad.
          [*Exit* Corvino.
Volp. Rare Mosca! how his villainy be-
  comes him!
Volt. Certain he doth delude all these
  for me.
Corb. Mosca the heir!
Volp. O, his four eyes have found it.
Corb. I am cozened, cheated, by a para-
  site slave;
Harlot, thou hast gulled me.
Mos. Yes, sir. Stop your mouth,
Or I shall draw the only tooth is left.
Are not you he, that filthy covetous wretch,
With the three legs, that here, in hope of prey,
Have, any time this three years, snuffed
  about,
With your most grovelling nose, and would
  have hired
Me to the poisoning of my patron, sir:
Are not you he that have to-day in court
Professed the disinheriting of your son?
Perjured yourself? Go home, and die, and
  stink;

If you but croak a syllable, all comes out:
Away, and call your porters! [*Exit* Cor-
  baccio.] Go, go, stink.
Volp. Excellent varlet!
Volt. Now, my faithful Mosca,
I find thy constancy—
Mos. Sir!
Volt. Sincere.
Mos. [*writing.*] "A table
Of porphyry"—I marle you'll be thus
  troublesome.
Volt. Nay, leave off now, they are gone.
Mos. Why, who are you?
What! who did send for you? O, cry you
  mercy,
Reverend sir! Good faith, I am grieved
  for you,
That any chance of mine should thus de-
  feat
Your (I must needs say) most deserving
  travails:
But I protest, sir, it was cast upon me,
And I could almost wish to be without it,
But that the will o' the dead must be ob-
  served.
Marry, my joy is that you need it not;
You have a gift, sir (thank your education),
Will never let you want, while there are
  men,
And malice, to breed causes. Would I
  had
But half the like, for all my fortune, sir!
If I have any suits, as I do hope,
Things being so easy and direct, I shall
  not,
I will make bold with your obstreperous
  aid,
Conceive me,—for your fee, sir. In mean
  time,
You that have so much law, I know have
  the conscience
Not to be covetous of what is mine.
Good sir, I thank you for my plate; 'twill
  help
To set up a young man. Good faith, you
  look
As you were costive; best go home and
  purge, sir.   [*Exit* Voltore.
Volp. [*comes from behind the curtain.*]
  Bid him eat lettuce well.[1] My witty
  mischief,

---

[1] *Bid him eat lettuce well.*]—as a soporific.
"Did I eat any *lettuce* to supper last night,
that I am so *sleepy!*"—*Green's Tu Quoque.*
And Pope:
          "If your point be *rest,*
Lettuce, and cowslip-wine; probatum est."

Let me embrace thee. O that I could now
Transform thee to a Venus!—Mosca, go,
Straight take my habit of clarissimo,
And walk the streets; be seen, torment
    them more:
We must pursue, as well as plot. Who
    would
Have lost this feast?
    Mos. I doubt it will lose them.
    Volp. O, my recovery shall recover all.
That I could now but think on some dis-
    guise
To meet them in, and ask them questions:
How I would vex them still at every turn!
    Mos. Sir, I can fit you.
    Volp. Canst thou?
    Mos. Yes, I know
One o' the commandadori, sir, so like you;
Him will I straight make drunk, and bring
    you his habit.
    Volp. A rare disguise, and answering
    thy brain!
O, I will be a sharp disease unto them.
    Mos. Sir, you must look for curses——
    Volp. Till they burst;
The Fox fares ever best when he is curst.
                            [*Exeunt.*

SCENE II.—*A Hall in* Sir Politick's
            House.

Enter Peregrine *disguised, and three*
            Merchants.

    Per. Am I enough disguised?
    1 Mer. I warrant you.
    Per. All my ambition is to fright him
    only.
    2 Mer. If you could ship him away,
    'twere excellent.
    3 Mer. To Zant, or to Aleppo!
    Per. Yes, and have his
Adventures put i' the Book of Voyages,[1]
And his gulled story registered for truth.
Well, gentlemen, when I am in a while,
And that you think us warm in our dis-
    course,
Know your approaches.
    1 Mer. Trust it to our care.
                    [*Exeunt Merchants.*

Enter Waiting-woman.

    Per. Save you, fair lady! Is Sir Pol
    within?
    Wom. I do not know, sir.
    Per. Pray you say unto him
Here is a merchant, upon earnest business,
Desires to speak with him.
    Wom. I will see, sir.   [*Exit.*
    Per. Pray you.
I see the family is all female here.

Re-enter Waiting-woman.

    Wom. He says, sir, he has weighty
    affairs of state,
That now require him whole; some other
    time
You may possess him.
    Per. Pray you say again,
If those require him whole, these will exact
    him,
Whereof I bring him tidings.   [*Exit
    Woman.*]   What might be
His grave affair of state now! how to
    make
Bolognian sausages here in Venice, sparing
One o' the ingredients?

Re-enter Waiting-woman.

    Wom. Sir, he says, he knows
By your word *tidings*,[2] that you are no
    statesman,
And therefore wills you stay.
    Per. Sweet, pray you return him;
I have not read so many proclamations,
And studied them for words, as he has
    done——
But—here he deigns to come.
                        [*Exit* Woman.

Enter Sir Politick.

    Sir P. Sir, I must crave
Your courteous pardon.   There hath
    chanced to-day
Unkind disaster 'twixt my lady and me;
And I was penning my apology,
To give her satisfaction, as you came now.
    Per. Sir, I am grieved I bring you worse
    disaster:

---

[1] *In the Book of Voyages,*] I know not what
particular book Jonson had in view here, unless
he may be thought to allude to the early volumes
of Hakluyt, a man never to be mentioned without
praise and veneration. Collections of voyages,
however, were sufficiently numerous in the poet's
time, when they formed the delight of all classes
of people; many of them too contained "stories"
not only "registered" but received "for truth,"
altogether as extravagant as this ridiculous adventure of Sir Politick's, which had nothing in
it to shock the taste, or even to tax the credulity
of our forefathers.

[2] *By your word* tidings,] The state term, I
presume, was *intelligence*. Tidings, Sir Pol
seems to consider as a mercantile or city phrase.

The gentleman you met at the port to-
day,
That told you he was newly arrived——
　Sir P. Ay, was
A fugitive punk ?
　Per. No, sir, a spy set on you :
And he has made relation to the senate,
That you profest to him to have a plot
To sell the State of Venice to the Turk.
　Sir P. O me !
　Per. For which warrants are signed by
　this time,
To apprehend you, and to search your
　study
For papers——
　Sir P. Alas, sir, I have none, but notes
Drawn out of play-books——
　Per. All the better, sir.
　Sir P. And some essays.　What shall
I do ?
　Per. Sir, best
Convey yourself into a sugar-chest :
Or, if you could lie round, a frail were
　rare.[1]
And I could send you aboard.
　Sir P. Sir, I but talked so,
For discourse sake merely.
　　　　　　　　　　　[*Knocking within.*
　Per. Hark ! they are there.
　Sir P. I am a wretch, a wretch !
　Per. What will you do, sir ?
Have you ne'er a currant-butt to leap
　into ?
They'll put you to the rack ; you must be
　sudden.
　Sir P. Sir, I have an ingine——
　3 *Mer.* [*within.*] Sir Politick Would-be !
　2 *Mer.* [*within.*] Where is he ?
　Sir P. That I have thought upon before
　time.
　Per. What is it ?
　Sir P. I shall ne'er endure the torture.
Marry, it is, sir, of a tortoise-shell,
Fitted for these extremities : pray you, sir,
　help me.
Here I've a place, sir, to put back my legs,
Please you to lay it on, sir, [*Lies down
　while* Per. *places the shell upon him.*]
—with this cap,
And my black gloves.　I'll lie, sir, like a
　tortoise,
Till they are gone.
　Per. And call you this an ingine ?

　Sir P. Mine own device——Good sir,
　bid my wife's women
To burn my papers.　　　　　[*Exit* Per.

　　The three Merchants *rush in.*

　1 *Mer.* Where is he hid ?
　3 *Mer.* We must,
And will sure find him.
　2 *Mer.* Which is his study ?

　　　Re-enter Peregrine.

　1 *Mer.* What
Are you, sir ?
　Per. I am a merchant, that came here
To look upon this tortoise ?
　3 *Mer.* How !
　1 *Mer.* St. Mark !
What beast is this ?
　Per. It is a fish.
　2 *Mer.* Come out here !
　Per. Nay, you may strike him, sir, and
　tread upon him :
He'll bear a cart.
　1 *Mer.* What, to run over him ?
　Per. Yes, sir.
　3 *Mer.* Let's jump upon him.
　2 *Mer.* Can he not go ?
　Per. He creeps, sir.
　1 *Mer.* Let's see him creep.
　Per. No, good sir, you will hurt him.
　2 *Mer.* Heart, I will see him creep, or
　prick his guts.
　3 *Mer.* Come out here !
　Per. Pray you, sir.—Creep a little.
　　　　　　　　　[*Aside to* Sir Pol.
　1 *Mer.* Forth.
　2 *Mer.* Yet farther.
　Per. Good sir !—Creep.
　2 *Mer.* We'll see his legs.
　　[*They pull off the shell and discover
　　him.*
　3 *Mer.* Ods so, he has garters !
　1 *Mer.* Ay, and gloves !
　2 *Mer.* Is this
Your fearful tortoise ?
　Per. [*discovering himself.*] Now, Sir Pol,
we are even ;
For your next project I shall be prepared :
I am sorry for the funeral of your notes, sir.
　1 *Mer.* 'Twere a rare motion to be seen
　in Fleet-street.[2]
　2 *Mer.* Ay, in the Term.

---

[1] *A frail were rare,*] A rush-basket in which
raisins and figs are usually packed.—WHAL.
[2] '*Twere a rare motion to be seen in Fleet-
street.*] Where exhibitions of this nature were
usually made (see p. 87 *a*), and where not
improbably some such "fearful tortoise," half
natural and half artificial, was at this very instant
abusing the credulous curiosity of the worthy
citizens and their wives.　There is a pleasant incident of this kind in *The City Match.*

1 *Mer.* Or Smithfield, in the fair.
3 *Mer.* Methinks 'tis but a melancholy
    sight.
Per. Farewell, most politic tortoise !
        [*Exeunt* Per. *and* Merchants.

Re-enter Waiting-woman.

Sir P. Where's my lady ?
Knows she of this ?
  Wom. I know not, sir.
  Sir P. Enquire.—
O, I shall be the fable of all feasts,
The freight of the gazetti,[1] ship-boys' tale ;
And, which is worst, even talk for ordinaries.
  Wom. My lady's come most melancholy
    home,
And says, sir, she will straight to sea, for
    physic.
  Sir P. And I, to shun this place and
    clime for ever,
Creeping with house on back, and think it
    well
To shrink my poor head in my politic shell.
                  [*Exeunt.*

SCENE III.—*A Room in* Volpone's
House.

Enter Mosca *in the habit of a clarissimo,
and* Volpone *in that of a commandadore.*

Volp. Am I then like him ?
Mos. O, sir, you are he :
No man can sever you.
  Volp. Good.
  Mos. But what am I ?
  Volp. 'Fore heaven, a brave clarissimo ;
    thou becom'st it !
Pity thou wert not born one.
  Mos. If I hold
My made one, 'twill be well.   [*Aside.*
  Volp. I'll go and see
What news first at the court.   [*Exit.*
  Mos. Do so. My Fox
Is out of his hole, and ere he shall re-enter,
I'll make him languish in his borrowed case,

Except he come to composition with me.—
Androgyno, Castrone, Nano !

Enter Androgyno, Castrone, *and* Nano.

All. Here.
Mos. Go, recreate yourselves abroad ;
  go, sport.—   [*Exeunt.*
So, now I have the keys, and am possest.
Since he will needs be dead afore his time,
I'll bury him, or gain by him : I am his heir,
And so will keep me, till he share at least.
To cozen him of all, were but a cheat
Well placed ; no man would construe it a
  sin :
Let his sport pay for 't. This is called the
  Fox-trap.   [*Exit.*

SCENE IV.—*A Street.*

Enter Corbaccio *and* Corvino.

Corb. They say the court is set.
Corv. We must maintain
Our first tale good, for both our reputations.
  Corb. Why, mine's no tale : my son
    would there have killed me.
  Corv. That's true, I had forgot :—mine
    is, I'm sure.   [*Aside.*
But for your Will, sir.
  Corb. Ay, I'll come upon him
For that hereafter, now his patron's dead.

Enter Volpone.

Volp. Signior Corvino ! and Corbaccio !
  sir,
Much joy unto you.
  Corv. Of what ?
  Volp. The sudden good
Dropt down upon you——
  Corb. Where ?
  Volp. And none knows how,
From old Volpone, sir.
  Corb. Out, arrant knave !
  Volp. Let not your too much wealth, sir,
    make you furious.
  Corb. Away, thou varlet.[2]

---

[1] *The freight of the gazetti,*] i.e., the subject
of the newspapers. This whole scene, says
Upton, seems to be impertinent ; and to interrupt the story. It is not indeed very intimately
connected with the main plot ; yet it is not altogether without its use. Jonson wanted time for
Mosca to make "the commandadore drunk,"
and "procure his habit" for Volpone ; and it
does not appear that he could have filled up the
interval more pleasantly in any other manner.
For the rest, this little interlude (it is no more) is
entitled to a considerable degree of praise. The

satire is strong and well directed. Sir Politick
is a very amusing piece of importance, and may
be styled the prototype of all our travelled poli-
ticians : and it would be an absolute defect of
understanding, to place any of the *précieuses
ridicules* of our own stage, or even that of
France (more happy in such characters), by the
side of the "Fine Lady Would-be."
  [2] *Away, thou varlet.*] This term in Jonson's
time was commonly applied to serjeants at mace.
(It should be recollected that Volpone is disguised like an officer of the court.) Originally

Volp. Why, sir?

Corb. Dost thou mock me?

Volp. You mock the world, sir; did you not change Wills?

Corb. Out, harlot!

Volp. O! belike you are the man, Signior Corvino? faith, you carry it well; You grow not mad withal; I love your spirit:

You are not over-leavened with your fortune.

You should have some would swell now, like a wine-fat,

With such an autumn—Did he give you all, sir?

Corv. Avoid, you rascal!

Volp. Troth, your wife has shown Herself a very woman; but you are well, You need not care, you have a good estate, To bear it out, sir, better by this chance: Except Corbaccio have a share.

Corb. Hence, varlet.

Volp. You will not be acknown, sir; why, 'tis wise.

Thus do all gamesters, at all games, dissemble:

No man will seem to win. [*Exeunt* Corvino *and* Corbaccio.] Here comes my vulture,

Heaving his beak up in the air, and snuffing.

Enter Voltore.

Volt. Outstript thus, by a parasite! a slave,

Would run on errands, and make legs for crumbs

Well, what I'll do——

Volp. The court stays for your worship. I e'en rejoice, sir, at your worship's happiness,

And that it fell into so learned hands, That understand the fingering——

Volt. What do you mean?

Volp. I mean to be a suitor to your worship,

For the small tenement, out of reparations, That, at the end of your long row of houses, By the Piscaria: it was, in Volpone's time, Your predecessor, ere he grew diseased, A handsome, pretty, customed bawdy-house As any was in Venice, none dispraised;

But fell with him: his body and that house Decayed together.

Volt. Come, sir, leave your prating.

Volp. Why, if your worship give me but your hand,

That I may have the refusal, I have done. 'Tis a mere toy to you, sir; candle-rents; As your learned worship knows——

Volt. What do I know?

Volp. Marry, no end of your wealth, sir; God decrease it!

Volt. Mistaking knave! what, mock'st thou my misfortune? [*Exit.*

Volp. His blessing on your heart, sir; would 'twere more!——

Now to my first again, at the next corner. [*Exit.*

SCENE V.—*Another part of the Street.*

Enter Corbaccio *and* Corvino ;—Mosca *passes over the Stage, before them.*

Corb. See, in our habit! see the impudent varlet!

Corv. That I could shoot mine eyes at him, like gun-stones!

Enter Volpone.

Volp. But is this true, sir, of the parasite?

Corb. Again, to afflict us! monster!

Volp. In good faith, sir, I'm heartily grieved, a beard of your grave length

Should be so over-reached. I never brooked That parasite's hair; methought his nose should cozen;

There still was somewhat in his look, did promise

The bane of a clarissimo.

Corb. Knave——

Volp. Methinks Yet you, that are so traded in the world, A witty merchant, the fine bird, Corvino, That have such moral emblems on your name,

Should not have sung your shame, and dropt your cheese,

To let the Fox laugh at your emptiness.

Corv. Sirrah, you think the privilege of the place,

---

it signified a knight's follower, or personal attendant. Harlot, which occurs just after, had probably once the same meaning. When the word first became (like *knave*) a term of reproach, it was appropriated solely to males: in Jonson's days it was applied indiscriminately to both sexes; though without any determinate import; and it was not till long afterwards that it was restricted to females, and to the sense which it now bears. To derive harlot from Arlotta, the mistress of the Duke of Normandy, is ridiculous. If it be not the same word as varlet, its most likely derivation is from *carl*, or *churl*, of which it appears to be a diminutive.

And your red saucy cap, that seems to me
Nailed to your jolt-head with those two
  chequines,[1]
Can warrant your abuses; come you hither:
You shall perceive, sir, I dare beat you;
  approach.
  Volp. No haste, sir, I do know your
  valour well,
Since you durst publish what you are, sir.
  Corv. Tarry,
I'd speak with you.
  Volp. Sir, sir, another time——
  Corv. Nay, now.
  Volp. O lord, sir! I were a wise man,
Would stand the fury of a distracted
  cuckold.
  [*As he is running off, re-enter* Mosca.
  Corb. What, come again!
  Volp. Upon 'em, Mosca; save me.
  Corb. The air's infected where he
  breathes.
  Corv. Let's fly him.
          [*Exeunt* Corv. *and* Corb.
  Volp. Excellent basilisk! turn upon the
  vulture.

              Enter Voltore.

  Volt. Well, flesh-fly, it is summer with
  you now;
Your winter will come on.
  Mos. Good advocate,
Prithee not rail, nor threaten out of place
  thus;
Thou'lt make a solecism, as madam says.[2]
Get you a biggin more;[3] your brain breaks
  loose.   [*Exit.*
  Volt. Well, sir.
  Volp. Would you have me beat the in-
  solent slave,
Throw dirt upon his first good clothes?
  Volt. This same
Is doubtless some familiar.
  Volp. Sir, the court,
In troth, stays for you.   I am mad, a mule
That never read Justinian, should get up,
And ride an advocate.   Had you no quirk
To avoid gullage, sir, by such a creature?
I hope you do but jest; he has not done it:

'Tis but confederacy to blind the rest.
You are the heir.
  Volt. A strange, officious,
Troublesome knave! thou dost torment me.
  Volp. I know——
It cannot be, sir, that you should be
  cozened;
'Tis not within the wit of man to do it;
You are so wise, so prudent; and 'tis fit
That wealth and wisdom still should go
  together.   [*Exeunt.*

SCENE VI.—*The Scrutineo or Senate
                House.*

Enter Avocatori, Notario, Bonario, Celia,
  Corbaccio, Corvino, Commandadori,
  Saffi, &c.

  1 *Avoc.* Are all the parties here?
  Not. All but the advocate.
  2 *Avoc.* And here he comes.

        Enter Voltore *and* Volpone.

  1 *Avoc.* Then bring them forth to sen-
  tence.
  Volt. O, my most honoured fathers, let
  your mercy
Once win upon your justice, to forgive——
I am distracted——
  Volp. What will he do now?   [*Aside.*
  Volt. O,
I know not which to address myself to
  first;
Whether your fatherhoods, or these inno-
  cents——
  Corv. Will he betray himself? [*Aside.*
  Volt. Whom equally
I have abused, out of most covetous
  ends——
  Corv. The man is mad!
  Corb. What's that?
  Corv. He is possest.
  Volt. For which, now struck in con-
  science, here I prostrate
Myself at your offended feet, for pardon.
  1, 2 *Avoc.* Arise.
  Cel. O heaven, how just thou art!

---

1 *With those* two chequines,] The dress of a
commandadore (officer of justice), in which Volpone was now disguised, consisted of a black stuff
gown and a red cap with two *gilt buttons* in front.
2 *Thou'lt make a* solecism, *as madam says.*]
Referring to what Lady Would-be had said just
before:
              "To perséver,
In my poor judgment, is not warranted
From being a *solecism* in our sex,
If not in manners."

3 *Get you a* biggin *more;*] A kind of *coif,* or
nightcap. Our old dramatists usually connect
it with infancy or old age; though the allusion
in this place seems to be to the law, the profession of Voltore. Thus Mayne:

" One, whom the good old man, his uncle,
Kept to the Inns of Court, and would in time
Have made him barrister, and raised him to
The satin cap and *biggin.*"—*City Match.*

Volp. I am caught
In mine own noose—— 　　　　[*Aside.*
　Corv. [*to* Corbaccio.] Be constant, sir ;
　　nought now
Can help but impudence.
　1 *Avoc.* Speak forward.
　Com. Silence !
　Volt. It is not passion in me, reverend
　　fathers,
But only conscience, conscience, my good
　si.:s,
That makes me now tell truth. That pa-
　rasite,
That knave, hath been the instrument of
　all.
　1 *Avoc.* Where is that knave ? fetch him.
　Volp. I go. 　　　　　　　. [*Exit.*
　Corv. Grave fathers,
This man's distracted ; he confest it now :
For, hoping to be old Volpone's heir,
Who now is dead——
　3 *Avoc.* How !
　2 *Avoc.* Is Volpone dead?
　Corv. Dead since, grave fathers.
　Bon. O sure vengeance !
　1 *Avoc.* Stay,
Then he was no deceiver.
　Volt. O no, none :
The parasite, grave fathers.
　Corv. He does speak
Out of mere envy, 'cause the servant's made
The thing he gaped for : please your father-
　hoods,
This is the truth, though I'll not justify
The other, but he may be some-deal faulty.
　Volt. Ay, to your hopes, as well as mine,
　Corvino :
But I'll use modesty. Pleaseth your wis-
　doms,
To view these certain notes, and but con-
　fer them ;
As I hope favour, they shall speak clear
　truth.
　Corv. The devil has entered him !
　Bon. Or bides in you.
　4 *Avoc.* We have done ill, by a public
　　officer
To send for him, if he be heir.
　2 *Avoc.* For whom?
　4 *Avoc.* Him that they call the parasite.
　3 *Avoc.* 'Tis true,
He is a man of great estate, now left.
　4 *Avoc.* Go you, and learn his name, and
　　say the court
Entreats his presence here, but to the
　clearing
Of some few doubts. 　　　[*Exit* Notary.
　2 *Avoc.* This same's a labyrinth !
　1 *Avoc.* Stand you unto your first report ?

　Corv. My state,
My life, my fame——
　Bon. Where is it ?
　Corv. Are at the stake.
　1 *Avoc.* Is yours so too ?
　Corb. The advocate's a knave,
And has a forked tongue——
　2 *Avoc.* Speak to the point.
　Corb. So is the parasite too.
　1 *Avoc.* This is confusion.
　Volt. I do beseech your fatherhoods,
　read but those—
　　　　　　　　[*Giving them papers.*
　Corv. And credit nothing the false spirit
　hath writ :
It cannot be but he's possest, grave
　fathers. 　　　　　[*The scene closes.*

SCENE VII.—*A Street.*

Enter Volpone.

　Volp. To make a snare for mine own
　neck ! and run
My head into it, wilfully ! with laughter !
When I had newly scaped, was free and
　clear,
Out of mere wantonness ! O, the dull devil
Was in this brain of mine when I devised it,
And Mosca gave it second ; he must now
Help to sear up this vein, or we bleed dead.

Enter Nano, Androgyno, *and* Castrone.

How now ! who let you loose? whither go
　you now?
What, to buy gingerbread, or to drown kit-
　lings ?
　Nan. Sir, Master Mosca called us out of
　doors,
And bid us all go play, and took the keys.
　And. Yes.
　Volp. Did Master Mosca take the keys ?
　why, so !
I'm farther in. These are my fine con-
　ceits !
I must be merry, with a mischief to me !
What a vile wretch was I, that could not
　bear
My fortune soberly? I must have my
　crotchets,
And my conundrums ! Well, go you, and
　seek him:
His meaning may be truer than my fear.
Bid him, he straight come to me to the
　court ;
Thither will I, and, if't be possible,
Unscrew my advocate, upon new hopes:
When I provoked him, then I lost myself.
　　　　　　　　　　　　　[*Exeunt*

SCENE VIII.—*The Scrutineo, or Senate House.*

Avocatori, Bonario, Celia, Corbaccio, Corvino, Commandadori, Saffi, &c., as before.

1 *Avoc.* These things can ne'er be reconciled. He here
                        [*Shewing the papers.*
Professeth that the gentleman was wronged,
And that the gentlewoman was brought thither,
Forced by her husband, and there left.
Volt. Most true.
Cel. How ready is heaven to those that pray!
1 *Avoc.* But that
Volpone would have ravished her, he holds
Utterly false, knowing his impotence.
Corv. Grave fathers, he's possest; again, I say,
Possest: nay, if there be possession, and
Obsession, he has both.[1]
3 *Avoc.* Here comes our officer.

Enter Volpone.

Volp. The parasite will straight be here, grave fathers.
4 *Avoc.* You might invent some other name, sir varlet.
3 *Avoc.* Did not the notary meet him?
Volp. Not that I know.
4 *Avoc.* His coming will clear all.
2 *Avoc.* Yet it is misty.
Volt. May't please your fatherhoods——
Volp. [*whispers* Volt.] Sir, the parasite
Willed me to tell you that his master lives;
That you are still the man; your hopes the same;
And this was only a jest——
Volt. How?
Volp. Sir, to try
If you were firm, and how you stood affected.
Volt. Art sure he lives?
Volp. Do I live, sir?

Volt. O me!
I was too violent.
Volp. Sir, you may redeem it.
They said you were possest; fall down, and seem so:
I'll help to make it good. [Voltore *falls.*]
        God bless the man!——
Stop your wind hard, and swell—See, see, see, see!
He vomits crooked pins [2] his eyes are set,
Like a dead hare's hung in a poulter's shop!
His mouth's running away! Do you see, signior?
Now it is in his belly.
Corv. Ay, the devil!
Volp. Now in his throat.
Corv. Ay, I perceive it plain.
Volp. 'Twill out, 'twill out! stand clear.
        See where it flies,
In shape of a blue toad, with a bat's wings!
Do you not see it, sir?
Corb. What? I think I do.
Corv. 'Tis too manifest.
Volp. Look! he comes to himself!
Volt. Where am I?
Volp. Take good heart, the worst is past, sir.
You are dispossest.
1 *Avoc.* What accident is this!
2 *Avoc.* Sudden, and full of wonder!
3 *Avoc.* If he were
Possest, as it appears, all this is nothing.
Corv. He has been often subject to these fits.
1 *Avoc.* Shew him that writing:—do you know it, sir?
Volp. [*Whispers* Volt.] Deny it, sir, forswear it; know it not.
Volt. Yes, I do know it well, it is my hand;
But all that it contains is false.
Bon. O practice![3]
2 *Avoc.* What maze is this!
1 *Avoc.* Is he not guilty then,
Whom you there name the parasite?
Volt. Grave fathers,
No more than his good patron, old Volpone.

---

[1]   *If there be* possession, *and*
Obsession, *he has both.*] In *possession*, the evil spirit was supposed to enter the body of the demoniac; in *obsession* he was thought to besiege and torment him from without.
[2] *He vomits crooked pins!* &c.] This, with what follows, as every one knows, always took place when a person chose to appear bewitched. It is to the praise of Jonson that he lets slip no opportunity of shewing his contempt for the popular opinions on this head; opinions which in his days indeed were manifested to the destruction of many innocent persons; but which operated, as Puritanism increased in influence and power, with a virulence that took away all security from age and infirmity; and crowded the prisons with bedridden old women, and the courts of justice with victims of ignorance, imposture, and blind and bloody superstition.

[3] *O practice!*] i.e., confederacy, concerted fraud. The word is very common in this sense.

4 *Avoc.* Why, he is dead.
Volt. O no, my honoured fathers,
He lives——
　1 *Avoc.* How ! lives ?
Volt. Lives.
2 *Avoc.* This is subtler yet !
3 *Avoc.* You said he was dead.
Volt. Never.
3 *Avoc.* You said so.
Corv. I heard so.
4 *Avoc.* Here comes the gentleman ;
　make him way.

　　　Enter Mosca.

3 *Avoc.* A stool.
4 *Avoc.* A proper man ; and were Vol-
　pone dead,
A fit match for my daughter.　　[*Aside.*
3 *Avoc.* Give him way.
Volp. Mosca, I was almost lost ; the ad-
　vocate
Had betrayed all ; but now it is recovered;
All's on the hinge again——Say I am
　living.　　　　　　[*Aside to* Mos.
Mos. What busy knave is this !—Most
　reverend fathers,
I sooner had attended your grave plea-
　sures,
But that my order for the funeral
Of my dear patron did require me——
　Volp. Mosca !　　　　　　[*Aside.*
Mos. Whom I intend to bury like a gen-
　tleman.
Volp. Ay, quick, and cozen me of all.
　　　　　　　　　　　　[*Aside.*
2 *Avoc.* Still stranger !
More intricate !
　1 *Avoc.* And come about again !
4 *Avoc.* It is a match, my daughter is
　bestowed.　　　　　　　[*Aside.*
Mos. Will you give me half ?
　　　　　　　　　[*Aside to* Volp.
Volp. First I'll be hanged.
Mos. I know
Your voice is good, cry not so loud.[1]
　1 *Avoc.* Demand
The advocate.—Sir, did you not affirm
Volpone was alive?
Volp. Yes, and he is ;
This gentleman told me so.—Thou shalt
　have half.　　　　　　[*Aside to* Mos.
Mos. Whose drunkard is this same?
　speak, some that know him :

----

[1]　　　　　*I know*
Your voice is good, cry not so loud.] From
the *Mostellaria* of Plautus, as Upton remarks :
"Tr. *Scio te bonâ esse voce, ne clama nimis.*"

I never saw his face.—I cannot now
Afford it you so cheap.　　[*Aside to* Volp.
　Volp. No !
　1 *Avoc.* What say you ?
Volt. The officer told me.
Volp. I did, grave fathers,
And will maintain he lives, with mine own
　life,
And that this creature [*points to* Mosca]
　told me.—I was born
With all good stars my enemies.　[*Aside.*
　Mos. Most grave fathers,
If such an insolence as this must pass
Upon me, I am silent : 'twas not this
For which you sent, I hope.
　2 *Avoc.* Take him away.
Volp. Mosca !
3 *Avoc.* Let him be whipt.
Volp. Wilt thou betray me ?
Cozen me ?
3 *Avoc.* And taught to bear himself
Toward a person of his rank.
　4 *Avoc.* Away.
　　　　　　[*The* Officers *seize* Volpone.
Mos. I humbly thank your fatherhoods.
Volp. Soft, soft ! Whipt !
And lose all that I have ! If I confess,
It cannot be much more.　　[*Aside.*
4 *Avoc.* Sir, are you married?
Volp. They'll be allied anon ; I must be
　resolute :
The Fox shall here uncase.
　　　　　　[*Throws off his disguise.*
Mos. Patron !
Volp. Nay, now
My ruin shall not come alone ; your match
I'll hinder sure : my substance shall not
　glue you,
Nor screw you into a family.
Mos. Why, patron !
Volp. I am Volpone, and this is my
　knave ;　　　　[*Pointing to* Mosca.
This [*to* Volt.], his own knave ; this [*to*
　Corb.], avarice's fool ;
This [*to* Corv.], a chimera of wittol, fool,
　and knave :
And, reverend fathers, since we all can
　hope
Nought but a sentence, let's not now de-
　spair it.
You hear me brief.
　Corv. May it please your fatherhoods——
　Com. Silence.
　1 *Avoc.* The knot is now undone by
　miracle.
2 *Avoc.* Nothing can be more clear.
3 *Avoc.* Or can more prove
These innocent.
　1 *Avoc.* Give them their liberty.

Bon. Heaven could not long let such gross crimes be hid.

2 Avoc. If this be held the highway to get riches,
May I be poor !

3 Avoc. This is not the gain, but torment.

1 Avoc. These possess wealth, as sick men possess fevers,
Which trulier may be said to possess them.

2 Avoc. Disrobe that parasite.

Corv. Mos. Most honoured fathers !——

1 Avoc. Can you plead aught to stay the course of justice?
If you can, speak.

Corv. Volt. We beg favour.

Cel. And mercy.

1 Avoc. You hurt your innocence, suing for the guilty.
Stand forth ; and first the parasite. You appear
T'have been the chiefest minister, if not plotter,
In all these lewd impostures, and now, lastly,
Have with your impudence abused the court,
And habit of a gentleman of Venice,
Being a fellow of no birth or blood :
For which our sentence is, first, thou be whipt ;
Then live perpetual prisoner in our gallies.

Volp. I thank you for him.

Mos. Bane to thy wolfish nature !

1 Avoc. Deliver him to the saffi. [*Mosca is carried out.*] Thou, Volpone,
By blood and rank a gentleman, canst not fall
Under like censure ; but our judgment on thee
Is, that thy substance all be straight confiscate
To the hospital of the Incurabili :
And since the most was gotten by imposture,
By feigning lame, gout, palsy, and such diseases,
Thou art to lie in prison, cramp'd with irons,
Till thou be'st sick and lame indeed.
Remove him.
          [*He is taken from the Bar.*

Volp. This is called mortifying of a Fox.

1 Avoc. Thou, Voltore, to take away the scandal
Thou hast given all worthy men of thy profession,
Art banished from their fellowship, and our state.
Corbaccio !—bring him near. We here possess
Thy son of all thy state, and confine thee
To the monastery of San Spirito ;
Where, since thou knewest not how to live well here,
Thou shalt be learned to die well.

Corb. Ha ! what said he ?

Com. You shall know anon, sir.

1 Avoc. Thou, Corvino, shalt
Be straight embarked from thine own house, and rowed
Round about Venice, through the grand canale,
Wearing a cap, with fair long ass's ears,
Instead of horns ! and so to mount, a paper
Pinned on thy breast, to the Berlina[1]——

Corv. Yes,
And have mine eyes beat out with stinking fish,
Bruised fruit, and rotten eggs—'tis well.
    I am glad
I shall not see my shame yet.

1 Avoc. And to expiate
Thy wrongs done to thy wife, thou art to send her
Home to her father, with her dowry trebled ;
And these are all your judgments.

All. Honoured fathers—

1 Avoc. Which may not be revoked. Now you begin,
When crimes are done, and past, and to be punished,
To think what your crimes are : away with them.
Let all that see these vices thus rewarded,
Take heart, and love to study 'em ! Mischiefs feed
Like beasts, till they be fat, and then they bleed.
        [*Exeunt.*

Volpone *comes forward.*

"The seasoning of a play is the applause.
Now, though the Fox be punished by the laws,

           And so to mount
To the Berlina—] A *pillory*, or cucking-stool, as Florio says. I doubt whether John understood what the latter really was. Berlina

is always used for a raised stage on which malefactors are exposed to public view, and answers with sufficient accuracy to our pillory.

He yet doth hope, there is no suffering
　　due,
For any fact which he hath done 'gainst
　　you ;

If there be, censure him ; here he doubtful
　　stands :[1]
If not, fare jovially, and clap your hands."
　　　　　　　　　　　　　　　　　[*Exit.*[2]

[1] *Here he doubtful stands : &c.*] This modest
Epilogue to the *Fox*, a play which holds so conspicuous a station among the noblest exertions
of human wit, forms a singular contrast to the
audacious vouching for the merits of *Cynthia's
Revels*, p. 204 *b*.

[2] "*The Fox* is indubitably the best production
of its author, and in some points of substantial
merit yields to nothing which the English stage
can oppose to it ; there is a bold and happy
spirit in the fable, it is of moral tendency, female
chastity and honour are beautifully displayed,
and punishment is inflicted on the delinquents of
the drama with strict and exemplary justice.
The characters of the *Hæredipetæ*, depicted
under the titles of birds of prey, *Voltore, Corbaccio*, and *Corvino*, are warmly coloured, happily contrasted, and faithfully supported from
the outset to the end : *Volpone*, who gives his
name to the piece, with a fox-like craftiness
deludes and gulls their hopes by the agency of
his inimitable Parasite, or (as the Greek and
Roman authors expressed it) by his *Fly*, his
Mosca ; and in this finished portrait Jonson may
throw the gauntlet to the greatest masters of
antiquity ; the character is of classic origin ; it
is found with the contemporaries of Aristophanes,
though not in any comedy of his now existing ;
the Middle Dramatists seem to have handled it
very frequently, and in the New Comedy it
rarely failed to find a place ; Plautus has it
again and again, but the aggregate merit of all
his Parasites will not weigh in the scale against
this single *Fly* of our poet. The incident of his
concealing *Bonario* in the gallery, from whence
he breaks in upon the scene to the rescue of
Celia and the detection of *Volpone*, is one of the
happiest contrivances which could possibly be
devised, because at the same time that it produces the catastrophe, it does not sacrifice
Mosca's character in the manner most villains
are sacrificed in comedy, by making them
commit blunders, which do not correspond with
the address their first representation exhibits,
and which the audience has a right to expect
from them throughout, of which the *Double
Dealer* is amongst others a notable instance.
But this incident of *Bonario's* interference does
not only not impeach the adroitness of the Parasite, but it furnishes a very brilliant occasion for
setting off his ready invention and presence of
mind in a new and superior light, and serves to
introduce the whole machinery of the trial and
condemnation of the innocent persons before the
court of *Advocates*. In this part of the fable
the contrivance is inimitable, and here the poet's
art is a study, which every votarist of the
dramatic Muses ought to pay attention and
respect to : had the same address been exerted
throughout, the construction would have been
a matchless piece of art, but here we are to
lament the haste of which he boasts in his pro-

logue ; and that rapidity of composition which
he appeals to as a mark of genius, is to be
lamented as the probable cause of incorrectness,
or at least the best and most candid plea in
excuse of it. For who can deny that nature
is violated by the absurdity of *Volpone's* unseasonable insults to the very persons who had
witnessed falsely in his defence, and even to the
very *Advocate*, who had so successfully defended him ? Is it in character for a man of his
deep cunning and long reach of thought to
provoke those on whom his all depended to
retaliate upon him, and this for the poor triumph
of a silly jest ? Certainly this is a glaring defect,
which everybody must lament and which can
escape nobody. The poet himself knew the
weak part of his plot, and vainly strives to
bolster it up by making *Volpone* exclaim against
his own folly—

'　I am caught in mine own noose—'　.

"And again :

' To make a snare for mine own neck ! and run
My head into it, wilfully ! with laughter !
When I had newly scaped, was free and clear,
Out of mere wantonness ! O, the dull devil
Was in this brain of mine when I devised it,
And Mosca gave it second———
———These are my fine conceits !
I must be merry, with a mischief to me !
What a vile wretch was I, that could not bear
My fortune soberly ? I must have my crotchets,
And my conundrums !'

"It is with regret I feel myself compelled to
protest against so pleasant an episode as that
which is carried on by *Sir Politick Would-be*
and *Peregrine*, which in fact produces a kind of
double plot and catastrophe ; this is an imperfection in the fable which criticism cannot overlook ; but *Sir Politick* is altogether so delightful
a fellow, that it is impossible to give a vote for
his exclusion ; the most that can be done against
him is to lament that he has not more relation to
the main business of the fable.

"The judgment pronounced upon the criminals
in the conclusion of the play is so just and solemn
that I must think the poet has made a wanton
breach of character, and gained but a sorry jest
by the bargain, when he violates the dignity of
his court of judges by making one of them so
abject in his flattery to the Parasite upon the
idea of matching him with his daughter, when
he hears that Volpone has made him his heir ;
but this is an objection that lies within the
compass of two short lines, spoken aside from
the bench, and may easily be remedied by their
omission in representation : it is one only, and
that a very slight one, amongst those venial
blemishes—

　　　　　quas incuria fudit.

"It does not occur to me that any other

remark is left for me to make upon this celebrated drama that could convey the slightest censure; but very many might be made in the highest strain of commendation, if there was need of any more than general testimony to such acknowledged merit. *The Fox* is a drama of so peculiar a species, that it cannot be dragged into a comparison with the production of any other modern poet whatsoever; its construction is so dissimilar from anything of Shakspeare's writing, that it would be going greatly out of our way, and a very gross abuse of criticism, to attempt to settle the relative degrees of merit where the characters of the writers are so widely opposite. In one we may respect the profundity of learning, in the other we must admire the sublimity of genius; to one we pay the tribute of understanding, to the other we surrender up the possession of our hearts; Shakspeare with ten thousand spots about him dazzles us with so bright a lustre, that we either cannot or will not see his faults; he gleams and flashes like a meteor, which shoots out of our sight before the eye can measure its proportions, or analyse its properties—but Jonson stands still to be surveyed, and presents so bold a front, and levels it so fully to our view, as seems to challenge the compass and the rule of the critic, and defy him to find out an error in the scale and composition of his structure.

"Putting aside therefore any further mention of Shakspeare, who was a poet out of all rule, and beyond all compass of criticism, one whose excellencies are above comparison, and his errors beyond number, I will venture an opinion that this drama of *The Fox* is, critically speaking, the nearest to perfection of any one drama, comic or tragic, which the English stage is at this day in possession of."—*Observer*, vol. iii. p. 170-176.

This excellent analysis of *The Fox* was written by Mr. Cumberland, a man peculiarly fitted by nature for dramatic criticism; but who wasted his ingenuity and his talents in an eager and excessive chase after general notoriety, which frequently led him beyond the sphere of his knowledge. With a respectable portion of ancient literature, a style at once elegant and impressive; with an archness that formed a pleasing substitute for wit, and enough of taste to give zest and currency to his opinions, he wanted little but a distrust of his own powers to render him at once the delight and ornament of the age. How much he fell short of this cannot be remembered without sorrow. His fate, however, may "point a moral," and teach that overweening confidence and negligence (inseparable companions), though they cannot wholly destroy, may yet debase the noblest gifts of nature, and the most valuable acquirements of art. But ingenious and liberal as these strictures confessedly are (for though an idolater of Shakspeare, Mr. Cumberland could be just to Jonson), they yet seem capable of some degree of modification. The point on which Mr. Cumberland chiefly rests is the injury done to the unity of the plot by the disguise of Volpone in the last act, which he terms a violation of nature. Now

it is evident, I think, that this forms the great moral of the play, and that Jonson had it in view from the beginning. "Is it in character," Mr. Cumberland asks, "for a man of Volpone's deep cunning and long reach of thought to provoke those on whom his all depended, to retaliate upon him, and this for the poor triumph of a silly jest?" Mr. Cumberland shall answer his own question. In his review of the *Double Dealer* (*Ibid.* p. 244), he finds Maskwell, like Volpone, losing his caution in the exultation of success; upon which he observes: "I allow that it is in character for him to grow wanton in success; there is *a moral in a villain outwitting himself.*" This appear a singular change of opinion in the course of a few pages: but whatever may be Mr. Cumberland's versatility, Jonson is consistent with himself and with the invariable experience of mankind. "See," says Falstaff, "how wit may be made a jackanapes when 'tis upon an ill employ!" The same sentiment is to be found in Beaumont and Fletcher:

" Hell gives us *art* to reach the depths of sin,
But leaves us *wretched fools* when we are in."
Queen of Corinth.

This, too, is the moral of the *New Way to Pay Old Debts*, so strikingly pointed out by Massinger:

" Here is a precedent to teach wicked men,
That when they quit religion and turn atheists,
Their own abilities leave them."

And finally, this is inculcated by Butler in the quatrain already given, and which its shrewdness and applicability will justify me in giving once more:

" But when he'd got himself a name
For frauds and tricks, he spoiled his game;
And forced his neck into a noose,
To shew his play at Fast-and-Loose."

Mr. Cumberland allows Sir Politick to be "a delightful fellow," and will not therefore hear of his exclusion. But could he find nothing to say for his lady, the most finished and amusing female pedant which the stage ever produced? Through her Sir Politick is in some measure connected with the plot; and both are occasionally subservient to the poet's main design. With regard to "the breach of character in making one of the judges conceive the idea of matching his daughter with Mosca," Mr. Cumberland himself admits that the objection is confined to the "compass of two lines spoken aside." But in justice to this learned personage, let it be further remarked that his determination is founded upon the actual demise of Volpone, in which case, as he justly concludes, the parasite is freed from all suspicions of fraud and imposture. It seems to have escaped Mr. Cumberland's recollection that Mosca is not the servant, but the humble friend of Volpone; and it is quite certain that he has not penetrated into the author's views in this part of the scene.

Mr. Cumberland pronounces the *Fox* "indubitably the best production of *its* author," and this appears to be the prevailing opinion. I venture, however, to declare my dissent, and to place that prodigy of human intellect, the ALCHEMIST, at the head of Jonson's labours. The opinion of Mr. Cumberland may be candidly accounted for, from his more intimate acquaintance with the illustrious originals which furnished much of the strength and beauty of the *Fox*, than with the obscure and humble sources from which this mighty genius derived the rude materials of the *Alchemist*. With respect to the popular decision on this subject, it has no better foundation perhaps than the accidental collocation of his plays in the homely couplet so often repeated:

" The *Fox*, the *Alchemist*, and *Silent Woman*,
 Done by Ben Jonson, and outdone by no man."

But it is time to draw to a conclusion. I shall therefore only subjoin a few lines from Hurd (a man seldom just to Jonson, never friendly), and leave the reader to wonder at the perversity which could maintain that the author of the FOX had "stalked for two centuries on the *stilts of artificial* reputation."

"Later writer for the stage have no doubt avoided these defects (the sporting with Corbaccio's deafness, &c. p. 346 *a*) of the exactest of our old dramatists. But do they reach his excellencies? Posterity, I am afraid, will judge otherwise, whatever may be now thought of some fashionable comedies. And if they do not,—neither the state of general manners, nor the turn of public taste appears to be such as countenances the expectation of greater improvements."—Μαντι κακων !—"To those who are not over sanguine in their hopes, our forefathers will perhaps be thought to have furnished (what in nature seemed linked together) the fairest example of dramatic as of real manners."—*Hor.* vol. ii. p. 244.

Epicœne; or, The Silent Woman.

———

EPICŒNE.] This Comedy was first acted in 1609, not, as Mr. Whalley says, "by the King's Majesty's servants," but by "the children of her Majesty's Revels." It would seem from the list of performers that a great change had taken place among the "children" since the appearance of the *Poetaster*, for, with the exception of Field, the names are altogether different from those subjoined to that drama. Salathiel Pavy, the poet's favourite, was dead; of the rest, some perhaps had ripened into men, and joined other companies, and some left the "quality" altogether. "Barksted," better known as a poet than an actor, "Carie, Attawel, and Pen," are among the principal performers in Beaumout and Fletcher's plays, and were undoubtedly of some eminence in their profession. Of "Smith, Allin, and Blaney," who complete the list, I can say nothing. The *Silent Woman* was printed in quarto with this motto :—

Ut sis tu similis Cœli, Byrrhique latronum,
Non ego sim Capri, neque Sulci.   Cur metuas me?

and went through several editions. I have one dated 1620. The *Companion to the Playhouse* mentions another, printed in 1609, (as does Whalley, in the margin of his copy,) which I have not been able to discover; the earliest which has fallen in my way, bearing date 1612. All these are exclusive of the folio, 1616. In a word, this has always been the most popular of Jonson's dramas. It was revived immediately after the Restoration, with great applause, and continued on the stage to the middle of the last century. Notwithstanding the current opinion in its favour, Mr. Malone has discovered that the *Silent Woman* was "unfavourably received," "for"—I entreat the reader's attention—"for Mr. Drummond of Hawthornden, Jonson's *friend*, informs us, that when it was first acted there were found verses on the stage, concluding that that play was well named the Silent *Woman*, BECAUSE there was never one *man* to say *plaudite* to it !"[1] The story is highly worthy of the hypocrite who picked it up ; and not at all discreditable to the loads of malignant trash which the reporter has so industriously heaped together to fling at Jonson.

After Cibber's retirement, and the death of Wilks, Booth, Mills, Jonson, &c., who often delighted the town in this comedy, it was laid aside till 1776, when it was revived, with a few unimportant alterations, by Mr. Colman. It failed of success from a singular circumstance : the managers most injudiciously gave the part of Epicœne to a woman ; so that when she threw off her female attire in the last act, and appeared as a boy, the whole cunning of the scene was lost, and the audience felt themselves rather trifled with than surprised. Garrick was immediately sensible of his error, and attempted to remedy it by a different cast of the parts; but it was too late. In 1798 an edition of this play appeared by Mr. Penn. He arranged the scenes according to the French model ; but whether with a view to exemplify his own ideas of dramatic writing, or to its being again brought on the stage, I know not.

The Portuguese have a translation of this Comedy, which I never saw. Mr. Twiss tells us in the appendix to his *Travels*, that it was sometimes "performed at Lisbon." It has also been translated into French ; but very imperfectly.

---

[1] [Drummond's words are, "When his play of a Silent Woman was first acted, ther was found verses after on the stage against him, concluding that that play was well named the Silent Woman ; ther was never one man to say Plaudite to it."—*F. C.*]

TO THE TRULY NOBLE BY ALL TITLES,

SIR FRANCIS STUART.[1]

" SIR,—My hope is not so nourished by example, as it will conclude this dumb piece should please you, because it hath pleased others before : but by trust, that when you have read it, you will find it worthy to have displeased none.   This makes that I now number you, not only in the names of favour, but the names of justice to what I write ; and do presently call you to the exercise of that noblest and manliest virtue : as coveting rather to be freed in my fame, by the authority of a judge, than the credit of an undertaker.[2]   Read therefore, I pray you, and censure.   There is not a line, or syllable in it changed from the simplicity of the first copy.   And when you shall consider, through the certain hatred of some, how much a man's innocency may be endangered by an uncertain accusation ; you will, I doubt not, so begin to hate the iniquity of such natures, as I shall love the contumely done me, whose end was so honourable as to be wiped off by your sentence.

" Your unprofitable, but true Lover,   BEN. JONSON."

〜〜〜〜〜〜〜〜〜〜〜〜〜

DRAMATIS PERSONÆ.

Morose, *a gentleman that loves no noise.*	Page to Clerimont.
Sir Dauphine Eugenie, *a knight, his nephew.*	Epicœne, *supposed the* SILENT WOMAN.
Ned Clerimont, *a gentleman, his friend.*	Lady Haughty,
Truewit, *another friend.*	Lady Centaure, } *ladies collegiates.*
Sir John Daw, *a knight.*	Mistress Dol. Mavis, }
Sir Amorous La-Foole, *a knight also.*	Mistress Otter, *the Captain's wife,* }
Thomas Otter, *a land and sea captain.*	Mistress Trusty, *Lady* } *pretenders.*
Cutbeard, *a barber.*	Haughty's woman, }
Mute, *one of Morose's servants.*	Pages, Servants, &c.
Parson.	

The SCENE,—London.

---

[1] *To the truly noble by all titles, Sir* Francis Stuart.] Of whom Antony Wood gives us the following character : "He was a learned gentleman, was one of Sir Walter Raleigh's club at the Mermaid-tavern in Friday-street, London, and much venerated by Ben Jonson, who dedicated to him his comedy called *The Silent Woman:* he was a person also well seen in marine affairs, was a captain of a ship, and bore the office for some time of a vice or rear-admiral."—*Athen. Oxon. Fast.* vol. i. p. 203.   WHAL.

This dedication is from the folio, 1616.

[2] *An undertaker.*]   "An *undertaker* was at this time a very offensive character ; and given to certain persons who *undertook* through their influence in the House of Commons, in the Parliament of 1614, to carry things agreeably to His Majesty's wishes."—WHAL.

To prevent any of Jonson's enemies from wresting this Dedication into a confession that the *Silent Woman* was "ill-received," it is necessary to observe that the objection of which the author speaks was similar to that brought long before against the *Poetaster*, a charge of personality (probably towards some captious member of the law), and which was "honourably wiped off" by his present patron.

Epicœne; or, The Silent Woman.

PROLOGUE.

Truth says, of old the art of making plays
Was to content the people ;[1] and their
    praise
Was to the poet money, wine, and bays.

But in this age a sect of writers are,
That only for particular likings care,
And will taste nothing that is popular.

With such we mingle neither brains nor
    breasts ;
Our wishes, like to those make public
    feasts,
Are not to please the cook's taste but the
    guests.

Yet if those cunning palates hither come,
They shall find guests' entreaty, and good
    room ;
And though all relish not, sure there will
    be some,

That when they leave their seats shall
    make them say,
Who wrote that piece, could so have wrote
    a play ;
But that he knew this was the better way.

For, to present all custard or all tart,
And have no other meats to bear a part,
Or to want bread and salt, were but coarse
    art.

The poet prays you then, with better
    thought
To sit ; and when his cates are all in
    brought,
Though there be none far-fet, there will
    dear-bought,

Be fit for ladies : some for lords, knights,
    squires ;
Some for your waiting-wench, and city-
    wires ;[2]
Some for your men, and daughters of
    Whitefriars.

Nor is it only while you keep your seat
Here that his feast will last ; but you shall
    eat
A week at ord'naries on his broken meat :
    If his muse be true,
    Who commends her to you.

ANOTHER.

The ends of all, who for the scene do
    write,
Are, or should be, to profit and delight.
And still 't hath been the praise of all best
    times,
So persons were not touched to tax the
    crimes.
Then in this play, which we present to-
    night,
And make the object of your ear and
    sight,
On forfeit of yourselves, think nothing
    true :
Lest so you make the maker to judge you.
For he knows, poet never credit gained
By writing truths, but things, like truths,
    well feigned.
If any yet will, with particular sleight
Of application,[3] wrest what he doth write ;
And that he meant, or him, or her, will
    say :
They make a libel, which he made a play.

[1] *Truth says, of old the art of making plays*
Was to content the people ;] From the Prologue to the *Andria ;* as Upton observes :

" *Id sibi negoti credidit solum dari,*
  Populo ut placerent, quas fecisset fabulas."

[2] *City-wires ;*] This term, which seems to
designate the matrons of the city in opposition
to the "Whitefriars nation," (see p. 379 *a*), is
new to me. In the stiff and formal dresses of
those days wire indeed was much used ; but I
know not that it was peculiar to the city dames.
Perhaps I have missed the sense.

[3] " Occasioned by some person's impertinent
exceptions." This marginal note of the author
confirms what is said in the Dedication :—that
some particular person was supposed to be
aimed at in one of the characters. As the
opinion was unfounded, it is needless to pursue
the inquiry.

ACT I.

SCENE I.—*A Room in* Clerimont's *House.*

Enter Clerimont *making himself ready, followed by his* Page.

Cler. Have you got the song yet perfect I gave you, boy?

Page. Yes, sir.

Cler. Let me hear it.

Page. You shall, sir; but i' faith let nobody else.

Cler. Why, I pray?

Page. It will get you the dangerous name of a poet in town, sir; besides me a perfect deal of ill-will at the mansion you wot of, whose lady is the argument of it; where now I am the welcomest thing under a man that comes there.

Cler. I think; and above a man too, if the truth were racked out of you.

Page. No, faith, I'll confess before, sir. The gentlewomen play with me, and throw me on the bed, and carry me in to my lady; and she kisses me with her oiled face, and puts a peruke on my head; and asks me an I will wear her gown? and I say no: and then she hits me a blow o' the ear, and calls me Innocent !¹ and lets me go.

Cler. No marvel if the door be kept shut against your master, when the entrance is so easy to you——Well, sir, you shall go there no more, lest I be fain to seek your voice in my lady's rushes a fortnight hence. Sing, sir. [*Page sings.*

　　Still to be neat, still to be drest—

Enter Truewit.

True. Why, here's the man that can melt away his time, and never feels it! What between his mistress abroad and his ingle² at home, high fare, soft lodging, fine clothes, and his fiddle; he thinks the hours have no wings, or the day no post-horse. Well, sir gallant, were you struck with the plague this minute,³ or condemned to any capital punishment to-morrow, you would begin then to think, and value every article of your time, esteem it at the true rate, and give all for it.

Cler. Why, what should a man do?

True. Why, nothing; or that which, when 'tis done, is as idle. Hearken after the next horserace, or hunting-match, lay wagers, praise Puppy, or Peppercorn, White-foot, Franklin;⁴ swear upon Whitemane's party; speak aloud, that my lords may hear you; visit my ladies at night, and be able to give them the character of every bowler or better on the green. These be the things wherein your fashionable men exercise themselves, and I for company.

Cler. Nay, if I have thy authority, I'll not leave yet. Come, the other are considerations, when we come to have gray heads and weak hams, moist eyes and shrunk members. We'll think on 'em then; then we'll pray and fast.

True. Ay, and destine only that time of age to goodness, which our want of ability will not let us employ in evil !

Cler. Why, then 'tis time enough.

True. Yes; as if a man should sleep all

---

¹ *And calls me* Innocent !] i.e., fool or simpleton. See p. 410 *a*, and act iii. sc. 2.

² *And his* ingle *at home*,] This word is invariably confounded by the commentators with enghle, though perfectly distinct in its meaning. Enghle, as I have already observed, p. 222 *a*, is either a gull, a simpleton, or a bait to decoy this description of persons: whereas engle or *ingle* is a familiar, a bosom friend. It is loosely used also by our old writers in an opprobrious sense for catamite, &c. I know not whence it crept into our language. If it be the Spanish word *ingle* (a groin), its acceptation in the latter sense is accounted for: but it is more probably corrupted from *ignicule*, a little fire; whence perhaps it came to signify a chimney-companion, an inmate of the same house. Ingle is still used for fire in many parts of the country.

³ *Well, sir gallant, were you struck with the* plague *this minute*,] There had been no *plague* in London since the dreadful one of 1603-4: but as Jonson usually brings up his action as closely as possible to the period of writing, it is not unlikely that he alludes to a dangerous contagious distemper which broke out in 1607, and of which some remains might still linger about the city when *Epicœne* was produced. Of this disease, which seems to have escaped the notice of our historians, the following account occurs in a book called the *City Remembrancer*: "In 1607 was a pestilential distemper at London; and the time so sickly in general, that sailors did not escape at great distance from land: as may be seen in some diaries in Purchas's Pilgrim."—Vol. i. p. 266.

⁴ *Puppy, or Peppercorn, White-foot, Franklin*:] Horses of the time, as Jonson tells us. Three of them are mentioned in *Ignoramus*; but a much more copious list may be found in Shirley's *Hyde-Parke. Whitemane* was a very noted racer. In some MS. memoirs of Sir H. Fynes the following passage occurs: "Alsoe in these my trobles with my wife, I was forced to give my Lord of Holdernes my grey running horse called *Whitmayne* for a gratuity, for which I might have had £100."

the term, and think to effect his business the last day. O, Clerimont, this time,[1] because it is an incorporeal thing, and not subject to sense, we mock ourselves the fineliest out of it, with vanity and misery indeed! not seeking an end of wretchedness, but only changing the matter still.

Cler. Nay, thou'lt not leave now——

True. See but our common disease! with what justice can we complain, that great men will not look upon us, nor be at leisure to give our affairs such dispatch as we expect, when we will never do it to ourselves? nor hear, nor regard ourselves?

Cler. Foh! thou hast read Plutarch's Morals, now, or some such tedious fellow; and it shows so vilely with thee! 'fore God, 'twill spoil thy wit utterly. Talk to me of pins, and feathers, and ladies, and rushes, and such things: and leave this Stoicity alone till thou mak'st sermons.

True. Well, sir; if it will not take, I have learned to lose as little of my kindness as I can; I'll do good to no man against his will, certainly. When were you at the college?

Cler. What college?

True. As if you knew not!

Cler. No, faith, I came but from court yesterday.

True. Why, is it not arrived there yet, the news? A new foundation, sir, here in the town, of ladies, that call themselves the collegiates, an order between courtiers and country-madams, that live from their husbands; and give entertainment to all the wits, and braveries of the time, as they call them: cry down, or up, what they like or dislike in a brain or a fashion, with most masculine, or rather hermaphroditical authority; and every day gain to their college some new probationer.

Cler. Who is the president?

True. The grave and youthful matron, the Lady Haughty.

Cler. A pox of her autumnal face, her pieced beauty! there's no man can be admitted till she be ready now-a-days, till she has painted, and perfumed, and washed, and scoured, but the boy here; and him she wipes her oiled lips upon, like a sponge. I have made a song (I pray thee hear it) on the subject.   [Page *sings.*

> Still to be neat, still to be drest,[2]
> As you were going to a feast;

---

[1] *O, Clerimont, this time, &c.*] There is something uncommonly striking in this part of the dialogue. Truewit assumes a lofty tone of morality, and his language is solemn and impressive. Jonson's mind was deeply imbued with a sense of what the comic Muse might fitly inculcate in her "higher mood;" and he has interspersed in all his works maxims and sentences of singular importance in the economy of human life. Much of his contempt for the "hocus-pocus" tricks of the stage, which has been unjustly attributed to personal enmity, clearly originated from the strong dislike of what he conceived to be a violation of its dignity and decorum.

[2] "This song," says Upton, "is very happily imitated from the following poem, which I found at the end of an edition of Petronius: the verses there printed are known to the learned by the title of Priapeia Carmina:"—rather, of Errones Venerei.

> " *Semper munditias, semper, Basilissa, decores,*
>   *Semper compositas arte recente comas,*
> *Et comptos semper cultus, unguentaque*
>   *semper,*
> *Omnia sollicitâ compta videre, manu,*
> *Non amo.   Neglectim mihi se quæ comit*
>   *amica*
> *Se det; et ornatus simplicitate valet.*
> *Vincula ne cures capitis discussa soluti,*
>   *Nec ceram in faciem; mel habet illa suum.*
> *Fingere se semper, non est confidere amori;*
>   *Quid quod sæpe decor, cum prohibetur,*
>   *adest?*"

It seems from this that Upton was ignorant of the author of these verses. They were written by Jean Bonnefons (Bonnefonius), and make part of what he calls his *Pancharis.* Bonnefons was born about the middle of the 16th century, at Clermont in Auvergne, where he cultivated Latin poetry with considerable success. He affected to imitate Catullus: there was one, however, whom he followed more closely, though he made "no boast of it;" this was Johannes Secundus. Bonnefons died in 1614.

Jonson's version, which with equal elegance possesses rather more smoothness than the original, has produced a number of imitators. Herrick has founded two or three little poems upon it, of more than usual sweetness; and, what the reader will be less prepared to hear, Flecknoe, the mythological father of Shadwell, has caught a gleam of common sense and poetry from it. The following is the conclusion of his "Address to the Duchess of Richmond:"

> " Poor beauties! whom a look, a glance,
>   May sometimes make seem fair by chance;
>   Or curious dress, or artful care,
>   Cause to look fairer than they are!—
>   Give me the eyes, give me the face,
>   To which no art can add a grace;
>   And me the looks, no garb nor dress,
>   Can ever make more fair, or less."

To return to Jonson. His little madrigal appears to have altogether astonished the modern critics. "This," says Dr. Aikin, (*Essay on Song Writing*, p. 168), "is one of the *very few*

Still to be powdered, still perfumed :
Lady, it is to be presumed,
Though art's hid causes are not found,
All is not sweet, all is not sound.

Give me a look, give me a face,
That makes simplicity a grace :
Robes loosely flowing, hair as free :
Such sweet neglect more taketh me,
Than all the adulteries of art ;
They strike mine eyes, but not my heart.

True. And I am clearly on the other side : I love a good dressing before any beauty o' the world. O, a woman is then like a delicate garden ; nor is there one kind of it ;[1] she may vary every hour ; take often counsel of her glass, and choose the best. If she have good ears, show them ; good hair, lay it out ; good legs, wear short clothes ; a good hand, discover it often : practise any art to mend breath, cleanse teeth, repair eyebrows ; paint and profess it.

Cler. How ! publicly ?

True. The doing of it, not the manner :

that must be private.[2] Many things that seem foul in the doing, do please done. A lady should, indeed, study her face, when we think she sleeps ; nor, when the doors are shut, should men be enquiring ; all is sacred within then. Is it for us to see their perukes put on, their false teeth, their complexion, their eyebrows, their nails ? You see gilders will not work, but inclosed. They must not discover how little serves, with the help of art, to adorn a great deal. How long did the canvas hang afore Aldgate? Were the people[3] suffered to see the city's Love and Charity, while they were rude stone, before they were painted and burnished? No; no more should servants approach their mistresses, but when they are complete and finished.

Cler. Well said, my Truewit.

True. And a wise lady will keep a guard always upon the place, that she may do things securely. I once followed a rude fellow into a chamber, where the poor madam, for haste, and troubled, snatched at her peruke to cover her baldness ; and put it on the wrong way.[4]

productions of this *once* celebrated author, which by their singular elegance and neatness, form a striking contrast to the prevalent coarseness of his tedious effusions." I believe that no great injustice will be done to Dr. Aikin's patience by supposing it to be utterly exhausted before he had actually read a page of Jonson. The song he might have found in a hundred other places ; but he could not look into the poet and have thus written. There are *very many* "productions of this *once* celebrated author," equal, if not superior to the present, which persons of more perseverance and less delicacy than the doctor may easily discover among his "tedious effusions."

[1] *Nor is there one kind of it ;* &c.]

" *Nec genus ornatûs unum est ; quod quamque decebit,*
  Eligat ; et speculum consulat ante suum,
Longa probat facies capitis discrimina puri :
  Sic erat ornatis Laodomia comis.
i xiguum summâ nodum sibi fronte relinqui
Ut pateant aures, ora rotunda volunt."
                       Art. Amand. lib. iii. v. 140.

Upton, who gives these lines, observes that we should read *Ne pateant* in the last of them. The text, however, is right as it stands. In those matters Ovid's opinion will always outweigh the critics'.

[2] *That must be private*, &c.] All from Ovid. *Art. Amand.* lib. iii. v. 216, *et seq.* :

" *Ista dabunt faciem ; sed erunt deformia visu.*
  Multaque, dum fiunt turpia, facta placent.—
Tu quoque dum coleris, nos te dormire putemus ;
Aptius a summâ conspiciare manu.

Cur mihi nota tuo causa est candoris in ore?
  Claude forem thalami, quid rude prodis opus ?—
Aurea quæ pendent ornato signa theatro ;
  Inspice, quam tenuis bractea ligna tegat ;
Sed neque ad illa licet populo, nisi facta, venire ;
  Nec nisi submotis forma paranda viris,"&c.

[3] *How long did the canvas hang before Aldgate? Were the people,* &c.] *Aldgate,* as Stow informs us, "began to be taken down in 1606, and was very worthily and famously finished in 1609 ;" so that the *canvas hung before it* about two years. The good old annalist's description of the "city's Love and Charity," is amusing : " To grace each side of the gate are set two feminine personages, the one southward appearing to be Peace, with a silver dove upon one hand, and a guilded wreath or garland in the other. On the north side standeth Charity, with a child at her breast, and another led in her hand : implying (as I conceive) that where Peace and love, or Charity, do prosper, and are truly embraced, that city shall be for ever blessed."

[4] *I once followed a rude fellow into a chamber, where the poor madam, for haste, snatched at her peruke, and put it on the wrong way.*] Improved, as Upton observes, with comic humour, from the following :

" *Quæ male crinita est, custodem in limine ponat,*
  Ornetur ve Bonæ semper in æde Deæ :
Dictus eram cuidam subito venisse puellæ,
  Turbida perversas induit illa comas."
                       Ibid. v. 243.

Cler. O prodigy !

True. And the unconscionable knave held her in compliment an hour with that reverst face, when I still looked when she should talk from the t'other side.

Cler. Why, thou shouldst have relieved her.

True. No, faith, I let her alone, as we'll let this argument, if you please, and pass to another. When saw you Dauphine Eugenie ?

Cler. Not these three days. Shall we go to him this morning ? he is very melancholy, I hear.

True. Sick of the uncle, is he ? I met that stiff piece of formality, his uncle, yesterday,[1] with a huge turban of nightcaps on his head, buckled over his ears.

Cler. O, that's his custom when he walks abroad. He can endure no noise, man.

True. So I have heard. But is the disease so ridiculous in him as it is made ? They say he has been upon divers treaties with the fish-wives and orange-women ; and articles propounded between them : marry, the chimney-sweepers will not be drawn in.

Cler. No, nor the broom-men : they stand out stiffly. He cannot endure a costard-monger, he swoons if he hear one.

True. Methinks a smith should be ominous.

Cler. Or any hammer man.[2] A brasier is not suffered to dwell in the parish, nor an armourer. He would have hanged a pewterer's prentice once upon a Shrove-Tuesday's riot,[3] for being of that trade, when the rest were quit.

True. A trumpet should fright him terribly, or the hautboys.

Cler. Out of his senses. The waights of the city have a pension of him not to come near that ward. This youth practised on him one night like the bell-man ; and never left till he had brought him down to the door with a long sword ; and there left him flourishing with the air.

Page. Why, sir, he hath chosen a street to lie in so narrow at both ends, that it will receive no coaches, nor carts, nor any of these common noises : and therefore we that love him devise to bring him in such as we may, now and then, for his exercise, to breathe him. He would grow resty else in his ease : his virtue would rust without action. I entreated a bearward one day to come down with the dogs of some four parishes that way, and I thank him he did ; and cried his games under Master Morose's window : till he was sent crying away with his head made a most bleeding spectacle to the multitude. And another time, a fencer marching to his prize had his drum most tragically run through, for taking that street in his way at my request.

True. A good wag ! How does he for the bells ?

Cler. O, in the Queen's time,[4] he was wont to go out of town every Saturday at ten o'clock, or on holy day eves. But now,

---

[1] *I met that stiff piece of formality, his uncle, yesterday,* &c.] Theobald, who at one period of his life seems to have had an idea of republishing Jonson's works, wrote a few short memorandums, or rather references, on the margin of his copy (the 8vo of 1715). These fell into the hands of Mr. Whalley, and subsequently of Mr. Waldron, who with his usual frankness communicated them to me. They are utterly insignificant, with the exception of the following *N.B.* "*Libanii Declamatio lepidissima de Moroso, qui cum uxorem loquacem duxisset, se ipsum accusat.* Probably Jonson borrowed the character and marriage of Morose from this declamation." Theobald must have been furnished with this information by a friend, for as Whalley observes it does not appear that he was at all acquainted with the work. His correspondent, however, was right in his conjecture ; for not only the name and character of Morose, but several of his shorter speeches are copied, or imitated from Libanius. The declamation in question forms the sixth of what the Sophist calls his Μελεται Πραγματικαι, and is labelled Δυσκολος γημας λαλον γυναικα, ἑαυτον προσαγγελλει.

[2] *Methinks a smith should be ominous—Or*

any hammer-man, &c.] Και μην των γε εργαστηριων, ὁσα μεν ακμονα και σφυραν εχει και τυπους, φυγη φευγω, τα αργυροκοπεια, τα χαλκεια· πολλα ἑτερα. τας δε δια σιγης γιγνομενας ασπαζομαι των τεχνων. και τοι και ζωγραφους ειδον ηδη μετ' ωδης γραφοντας· ὑτως ἡδυ τι τοις πολλοις λαλειν, και κατεχειν ἑαυτους ου δυνανται· *Liban. Edit. Paris.* fol. 1606, p. 302. Jonson's conversion of the ζωγραφοι into "chimney-sweepers and broom-men" is humourous.

[3] *Upon a Shrove-Tuesday's riot,* &c.] The turbulent and disorderly conduct of the apprentices on Shrove-Tuesday, which in Jonson's time was a day of general festivity for them, is noticed by most of our old writers. Thus Decker, in the *Seven Deadly Sins of London*: "They presently, like prentises upon Shrove-Tuesday, take the law into their hands, and do what they list."—*Quit,* as Whalley observes, means discharged from work, and should not, as in his edition, have been altered to *quiet*. [Does it not rather mean *acquitted* ?—F. C.]

[4] *O, in the Queen's time,* &c.] This seems to be an indirect satire on the growing laxity of attendance on public worship. Elizabeth was very strict in this matter.

by reason of the sickness,[1] the perpetuity of ringing has made him devise a room, with double walls and treble ceilings ; the windows close shut and caulked ; and there he lives by candlelight. He turned away a man last week, for having a pair of new shoes that creaked. And this fellow waits on him now in tennis court socks, or slippers soled with wool : and they talk each to other in a trunk.[2] See, who comes here?

Enter Sir Dauphine Eugenie.

Daup. How now ! what ail you, sirs? dumb?

True. Struck into stone, almost, I am here, with tales o' thine uncle. There was never such a prodigy heard of.

Daup. I would you would once lose this subject, my masters, for my sake. They are such as you are, that have brought me into that predicament I am with him.

True. How is that ?

Daup. Marry, that he will disinherit me ; no more. He thinks I and my company are authors of all the ridiculous Acts and Monuments are told of him.[3]

True. 'Slid, I would be the author of more to vex him ; that purpose deserves it : it gives thee law of plaguing him. I'll tell thee what I would do. I would make a false almanack, get it printed ; and then have him drawn out on a coronation day to the Tower-wharf, and kill him with the noise of the ordnance. Disinherit thee ! he cannot, man. Art not thou next of blood, and his sister's son?

Daup. Ay, but he will thrust me out of it, he vows, and marry.

Truc. How ! that's a more portent. Can he endure no noise, and will venture on a wife?

Cler. Yes : why, thou art a stranger, it seems, to his best trick yet. He has employed a fellow this half-year all over England to hearken him out a dumb woman ; be she of any form, or any quality, so she be able to bear children : her silence is dowry enough, he says.

True. But I trust to God he has found none.

Cler. No : but he has heard of one that's lodged in the next street to him, who is exceedingly soft-spoken : thrifty of her speech ; that spends but six words a day. And her he's about now, and shall have her.

True. Is't possible ! who is his agent in the business ?

Cler. Marry, a barber, one Cutbeard ; an honest fellow, one that tells Dauphine all here.

True. Why, you oppress me with wonder ; a woman, and a barber, and love no noise !

Cler. Yes, faith. The fellow trims him silently, and has not the knack with his sheers or his fingers ;[4] and that continence in a barber he thinks so eminent a virtue, as it has made him chief of his counsel.

True. Is the barber to be seen, or the wench ?

Cler. Yes, that they are.

True. I prithee, Dauphine, let's go thither.

Daup. I have some business now, I cannot, i' faith.

True. You shall have no business shall make you neglect this, sir ; we'll make her talk, believe it ; or, if she will not, we can give out at least so much as shall interrupt the treaty ; we will break it. Thou art bound in conscience, when he suspects thee without cause, to torment him.

Daup. Not I, by any means. I'll give

---

[1] *By reason of the* sickness,] See p. 405 *a.*

[2] *And they talk each to other in a trunk.*] i.e., a tube. "There are a people (says Montaigne), where no one speaks to the king except his wife and children, but through a *trunk.*" All our old writers have the word in this sense. [Hence the *trunk* of an elephant.—F. C.]

[3] *He thinks I and my company are authors of all the ridiculous Acts and Monuments are told of him.*] Perhaps here, Upton says, but doubtless in a former play (p. 107 *a*), "he hints at Fox's book." Jonson was at this period a Catholic, and might therefore perhaps think himself justified in indulging a little spleen against the man whom the professors of that religion justly considered as the most formidable of their opponents :—but this is conjecture. "The audience," Upton continues, "by these

descriptions of Morose, are well prepared for him when he makes his entrance : and as we love to know something of a man before we get into his company, so the poet has taken pains to bring us acquainted with his principal characters before they make their appearance in person."

[4] *And has not the* knack *with his sheers or his fingers :*] This was and perhaps may still be a very common practice : thus Motto, the barber in Lilly's *Midas :* "Thou knowest, boy, I have taught thee the *knacking of the hands.*" And Cooke, in *Green's Tu Quoque :* "Amongst the rest, let not the barber be forgotten : and look that he be an excellent fellow, and one that can *snap his fingers* with dexterity." The want of this quality sufficiently accounts for Morose's selection of Cutbeard.

no suffrage to't. He shall never have that plea against me, that I opposed the least phant'sy of his. Let it lie upon my stars to be guilty, I'll be innocent.

True. Yes, and be poor, and beg; do, innocent: when some groom of his has got him an heir, or this barber, if he himself cannot. *Innocent!* I prithee, Ned, where lies she? Let him be innocent still.

Cler. Why, right over against the barber's; in the house where Sir John Daw lies.

True. You do not mean to confound me!

Cler. Why?

True. Does he that would marry her know so much?

Cler. I cannot tell.

True. 'Twere enough of imputation to her with him.

Cler. Why?

True. The only talking Sir in the town! Jack Daw! and he teach her not to speak! God be wi' you. I have some business too.

Cler. Will you not go thither, then?

True. Not with the danger to meet Daw, for mine ears.

Cler. Why, I thought you two had been upon very good terms.

True. Yes, of keeping distance.

Cler. They say he is a very good scholar.

True. Ay, and he says it first. A pox on him, a fellow that pretends only to learning, buys titles, and nothing else of books in him!

Cler. The world reports him to be very learned.

True. I am sorry the world should so conspire to belie him.

Cler. Good faith, I have heard very good things come from him.

True. You may; there's none so desperately ignorant to deny that; would they were his own! God be wi' you, gentlemen. [*Exit hastily.*

Cler. This is very abrupt!

Daup. Come, you are a strange open man, to tell everything thus.

Cler. Why, believe it, Dauphine, Truewit's a very honest fellow.

Daup. I think no other; but this frank nature of his is not for secrets.

Cler. Nay then, you are mistaken, Dauphine: I know where he has been well trusted, and discharged the trust very truly, and heartily.

Daup. I contend not, Ned; but with the fewer a business is carried, it is ever the safer. Now we are alone, if you'll go thither, I am for you.

Cler. When were you there?

Daup. Last night: and such a Decameron of sport fallen out! Boccace never thought of the like. Daw does nothing but court her; and the wrong way. He would lie with her, and praises her modesty; desires that she would talk and be free, and commends her silence in verses; which he reads, and swears are the best that ever man made. Then rails at his fortunes, stamps, and mutines, why he is not made a councillor, and called to affairs of state.

Cler. I prithee, let's go. I would fain partake this.—Some water, boy.
[*Exit* Page.

Daup. We are invited to dinner together, he and I, by one that came thither to him, Sir La-Foole.

Cler. O, that's a precious mannikin!

Daup. Do you know him?

Cler. Ay, and he will know you too, if e'er he saw you but once, though you should meet him at church in the midst of prayers. He is one of the braveries, though he be none of the wits.[1] He will salute a judge upon the bench, and a bishop in the pulpit, a lawyer when he is pleading at the bar, and a lady when she is dancing in a masque, and put her out. He does give plays and suppers, and invites his guests to them, aloud, out of his window, as they ride by in coaches. He has a lodging in the Strand for the purpose: or to watch when ladies are gone to the china-houses, or the Exchange, that he may meet them by chance, and give them presents, some two or three hundred pounds worth of toys, to be laughed at. He is never without a spare banquet, or sweetmeats in his chamber, for their women to alight at, and come up to for a bait.

Daup. Excellent! he was a fine youth last night; but now he is much finer! what is his Christian name? I have forgot.

---

[1] *He is one of the* braveries, *though he be none of the* wits.] This alludes to Truewit's description of the collegiate ladies, p. 406:—"they give entertainment to all the wits and braveries of the time." *Braveries* were the beaus of the age; men distinguished by the splendour and fashion of their apparel. The *Exchange* mentioned just below was the New Exchange, built in 1608. "It had rows of shops (Pennant says) over the walk, filled chiefly with milliners, sempstresses, &c. This was a place of fashionable resort." See *Massinger*, vol. iv. p. 50.

Re-enter Page.

Cler. Sir Amorous La-Foole.

Page. The gentleman is here below that owns that name.

Cler. 'Heart, he's come to invite me to dinner, I hold my life.

Daup. Like enough : prithee, let's have him up.

Cler. Boy, marshal him.

Page. With a truncheon, sir ?

Cler. Away, I beseech you. [*Exit* Page.] —I'll make him tell us his pedigree now ; and what meat he has to dinner ; and who are his guests ; and the whole course of his fortunes ; with a breath.

Enter Sir Amorous La-Foole.

La-F. Save, dear Sir Dauphine ! honoured Master Clerimont !

Cler. Sir Amorous ! you have very much honested my lodging with your presence.

La-F. Good faith, it is a fine lodging : almost as delicate a lodging as mine.

Cler. Not so, sir.

La-F. Excuse me, sir, if it were in the Strand, I assure you. I am come, Master Clerimont, to entreat you to wait upon two or three ladies, to dinner, to-day.

Cler. How, sir! wait upon them? did you ever see me carry dishes?

La-F. No, sir, dispense with me ; I meant, to bear them company.

Cler. O, that I will, sir : the doubtfulness of your phrase, believe it, sir, would breed you a quarrel once an hour with the terrible boys,[1] if you should but keep them fellowship a day.

La-F. It should be extremely against my will, sir, if I contested with any man.

Cler. I believe it, sir. Where hold you your feast ?

La-F. At Tom Otter's, sir.

Daup. Tom Otter ! What's he?

La-F. Captain Otter, sir ; he is a kind of gamester, but he has had command both by sea and by land.

Daup. O, then he is *animal amphibium ?*

La-F. Ay, sir : his wife was the rich china-woman, that the courtiers visited so often ;[2] that gave the rare entertainment. She commands all at home.

Cler. Then she is Captain Otter.

La-F. You say very well, sir ; she is my kinswoman, a La-Foole by the mother-side, and will invite any great ladies for my sake.

Daup. Not of the La-Fooles of Essex ?

La-F. No, sir ; the La-Fooles of London.

Cler. Now he's in.   [*Aside.*

La-F. They all come out of our house, the La-Fooles of the north, the La-Fooles of the west, the La-Fooles of the east and south—we are as ancient a family as any is in Europe—but I myself am descended lineally of the French La-Fooles—and, we do bear for our coat yellow,[3] or *or*, checkered *azure*, and *gules*, and some three or four colours more, which is a very noted coat, and has sometimes been solemnly worn by divers nobility of our house—but let that go, antiquity is not respected now. —I had a brace of fat does sent me, gentlemen, and half a dozen of pheasants, a dozen or two of godwits, and some other fowl, which I would have eaten, while they are good, and in good company :—there will be a great lady or two, my Lady Haughty, my Lady Centaure, Mistress Dol Mavis—and they come o' purpose to see

[1] *The* terrible boys,] These *terrible boys* are mentioned in the *Alchemist*, act iii. sc. 3.

"*Kast.* Sir, not so young, but I have heard
    some speech
Of the *angry boys*, and seen 'em take tobacco."

A citation from Wilson's *Life of King James* will make the allusion still more manifest: "The king minding his sports, many riotous demeanours crept into the kingdom ; divers sects of vicious persons, going under the title of *roaring boys, bravadoes, roysters, &c.*, commit many insolencies ; the streets swarm, night and day, with bloody quarrels, private duels fomented," &c.—UPTON.

These pestilent miscreants continued under various names to disturb the peace of the capital down to the accession of the present royal family.

[2] *His wife was the rich china-woman, that*

the courtiers visited so often ;] In Jonson's days the trade with the East had not been long opened ; and the china and lacquered ware which we derived either directly or through the medium of the Dutch from China and the Japanese islands, were objects of very general curiosity in both sexes. Enough remains in our old dramatists to show that advantage was taken of this to convert the places of exhibition (almost always private houses) into a kind of bagnios, of which the owners were the most convenient of procuresses. If we may trust the poets and essayists of Queen Anne's days, matters were not much mended when they wrote ; as no place of assignation is more frequently mentioned than a "china-house." [*India*-house rather.—F. C.]

[3] *And we do bear for our coat* yellow, *&c.*] This is a humourous allusion to the parti-coloured dress of the domestic fool of our ancestors, which is still retained on the stage.

the silent gentlewoman, Mistress Epicœne, that honest Sir John Daw has promised to bring thither—and then, Mistress Trusty, my lady's woman, will be there too, and this honourable knight, Sir Dauphine, with yourself, Master Clerimont—and we'll be very merry, and have fiddlers, and dance. —I have been a mad wag in my time, and have spent some crowns since I was a page in court, to my Lord Lofty, and after, my Lady's gentleman-usher, who got me knighted in Ireland, since it pleased my elder brother to die.—I had as fair a gold jerkin on that day as any worn in the island voyage, or at Cadiz, none dispraised;[1] and I came over in it hither, shewed myself to my friends in court, and after went down to my tenants in the country, and surveyed my lands, let new leases, took their money, spent it in the eye o' the land here, upon ladies:—and now I can take up at my pleasure.

Daup. Can you take up ladies, sir?

Cler. O, let him breathe, he has not recovered.

Daup. Would I were your half in that commodity!

La-F. No, sir, excuse me: I meant money, which can take up anything. I have another guest or two to invite, and say as much to, gentlemen. I'll take my leave abruptly, in hope you will not fail—— Your servant. [*Exit.*

Daup. We will not fail you, sir precious La-Foole; but she shall, that your ladies come to see, if I have credit afore Sir Daw.

Cler. Did you ever hear such a windsucker[2] as this?

Daup. Or such a rook as the other, that will betray his mistress to be seen! Come, 'tis time we prevented it.

Cler. Go. [*Exeunt.*

ACT II.

SCENE I.—*A Room in* Morose's *House.*

Enter Morose *with a tube in his hand, followed by* Mute.

Mor. Cannot I yet find out a more compendious method, than by this trunk, to save my servants the labour of speech, and mine ears the discords of sounds? Let me see: all discourses but my own afflict me;[3] they seem harsh, impertinent, and irksome. Is it not possible that thou shouldst answer me by signs, and I apprehend thee, fellow? Speak not, though I question you. You have taken the ring off from the street door, as I bade you? answer me not by speech, but by silence; unless it be otherwise. [*Mute makes a leg.*]—very good. And you have fastened on a thick quilt, or flock-bed, on the outside of the door; that if they knock with their daggers, or with brickbats, they can make no noise?—But with your leg, your answer, unless it be otherwise. [*makes a leg.*]—Very good. This is not only fit modesty in a servant, but good state and discretion in a master. And you have been with Cutbeard the barber, to have him come to me? [*makes a leg.*]— Good. And, he will come presently? Answer me not but with your leg, unless it be otherwise: if it be otherwise, shake your head, or shrug. [*Makes a leg.*] So! Your Italian and Spaniard are wise in these: and it is a frugal and comely gravity. How long will it be ere Cutbeard come? Stay; if an hour, hold up your whole hand; if half an hour, two fingers; if a quarter, one. [*Holds up a finger bent.*] —Good: half a quarter? 'tis well. And have you given him a key, to come in without knocking? [*Makes a leg.*]—good.

---

[1] *I had as fair a gold jerkin on that day as any was worn in the* island voyage, *or at* Cadiz, *none dispraised;*] "This *island voyage* (as Upton observes) was undertaken 1585, Sir Francis Drake being admiral, with a fleet of one and twenty sail, and with above two thousand volunteers aboard: they went to Hispaniola, and there made themselves masters of the town of St. Domingo. The other adventure here mentioned was undertaken in 1596, when the Earl of Essex and Sir Walter Raleigh burnt the Indian fleet at *Cadiz*, consisting of forty sail, and brought home immense treasures. Shakspeare alludes to this finery of dressing, when our youth went abroad, in *King John:*

"And some
Have sold their fortunes at their native homes,
Bearing their birthright proudly on their backs,
To make a hazard of new fortunes here."
Act ii. sc. 1.—WHAL.

[2] *Did you ever hear such a* wind-sucker,] A kind of kite that supports itself for a considerable time in the air with little or no motion, its beak being turned towards the wind, which it seems to suck.—WHAL. [Had Gifford known anything about *horses* he would have shouted at Whalley for this note. Wind-suckers, crib-biters, roarers, must have been in existence before —as they are after—this peculiar kind of kite.—F. C.]

[3] *All discourses but my own afflict me:*] This is well observed; for Morose, like his namesake in *Libanus*, is extremely delighted with the sound of his own voice. This, however, is a trait of nature, and must have been taken from actual observation.

And is the lock oiled, and the hinges, to-day? [*Makes a leg.*]—Good. And the quilting of the stairs nowhere worn out and bare? [*Makes a leg.*]—Very good. I see, by much doctrine, and impulsion, it may be effected; stand by. The Turk, in this divine discipline, is admirable, exceeding all the potentates of the earth; still waited on by mutes; and all his commands so executed; yea, even in the war, as I have heard, and in his marches, most of his charges and directions given by signs, and with silence:[1] an exquisite art! and I am heartily ashamed, and angry oftentimes, that the princes of Christendom should suffer a barbarian to transcend them in so high a point of felicity. I will practise it hereafter. [*A horn winded within.*]—How now? oh! oh! what villain, what prodigy of mankind is that? Look. [*Exit* Mute.] —[*Horn again.*] Oh! cut his throat, cut his throat! what murderer, hell-hound, devil can this be?

Re-enter Mute.

Mute. It is a post from the court——
Mor. Out, rogue! and must thou blow thy horn too?
Mute. Alas, it is a post from the court, sir, that says he must speak with you, pain of death——
Mor. Pain of thy life, be silent!

Enter Truewit *with a post-horn, and a halter in his hand.*

True. By your leave, sir;—I am a stranger here :—Is your name Master Morose? is your name Master Morose? Fishes! Pythagoreans all! This is strange. What say you, sir? nothing! Has Harpocrates been here with his club,[2] among you? Well, sir, I will believe you to be the man at this time: I will venture upon you, sir. Your friends at court commend them to you, sir——
Mor. O men! O manners! was there ever such an impudence?
True. And are extremely solicitous for you, sir.
Mor. Whose knave are you?
True. Mine own knave, and your compeer, sir.
Mor. Fetch me my sword——
True. You shall taste the one half of my dagger, if you do, groom; and you the other, if you stir, sir. Be patient, I charge you, in the king's name, and hear me without insurrection. They say you are to marry; to marry! do you mark, sir?
Mor. How then, rude companion!
True. Marry, your friends do wonder, sir, the Thames being so near,[3] wherein you may drown so handsomely; or London Bridge, at a low fall, with a fine leap, to hurry you down the stream; or, such a delicate steeple in the town, as Bow, to vault from; or, a braver height, as Paul's. Or, if you affected to do it nearer home, and a shorter way, an excellent garret-window into the street; or, a beam in the said garret, with this halter—[*shews him the halter*]—which they have sent, and

---

[1] *Yea, even in the war, as I have heard, and in his marches, most of his charges and directions given by signs, and with silence.*] A little enlargement perhaps of the reports of travellers: but the exact discipline and order observed in the Turkish army, is remarked by Busbequius: "*Videbam summo ordine cujusque corporis milites suis locis distributos, et (quod vix credat, qui nostratis militiæ consuetudinem novit) summum erat silentium, summa quies, rixa nulla, nullum cujusquam insolens factum, sed ne vox quidem aut vitulatio per lasciviam aut ebrietatem emissa.*"—WHAL.
　　The Turks have long lost this *divine discipline*, as far at least as war is concerned. Nothing on earth can be more noisy and tumultuous than the marches and encampments of a Turkish army at present.
[2] *Has Harpocrates been here with his club,*] Harpocrates, as every one knows, is the god of silence : but he is usually described with a finger on his lip, and a cornucopia, instead of a club, in his hand. Æsculapius, indeed, is thus represented on many antique gems; and perhaps Jonson may have confounded the two

deities : but I desire to be understood as speaking with great deference, whenever I venture to question the accuracy of so universal a scholar. In terming them *Pythagoreans*, he alludes to the long probationary *silence* imposed by Pythagoras on his followers.
[3] *Marry, your friends do wonder, sir, the Thames being so near, &c.*] Here begins Jonson's imitations of the sixth *Satire* of Juvenal, which are scattered profusely through the remainder of this scene. They are adapted to the manners of the poet's time with sufficient ingenuity; but appear almost too obvious to be pointed out. If the reader will compare the opening of this speech with the original, he will be enabled to judge of the general resemblance :

"*Ferre potes dominam salvis tot reetibus*
　　ullam,
Cum pateant altæ caligantesque fenestræ,
Et tibi vicinum se præbeat Æmilius pons?"

Upton has transcribed all the passages imitated; but apparently more for the purpose of showing his dexterity in correcting Juvenal than illustrating Jonson. See his *Remarks*, p. 65 *et seq.*

desire, that you would sooner commit your grave head to this knot, than to the wedlock noose; or, take a little sublime, and go out of the world like a rat; or, a fly, as one said, with a straw in your arse: any way rather than follow this goblin Matrimony. Alas, sir, do you ever think to find a chaste wife in these times? now? when there are so many masques, plays, Puritan preachings, mad folks, and other strange sights to be seen daily, private and public? If you had lived in King Etheldred's time, sir, or Edward the Confessor, you might, perhaps, have found one in some cold country hamlet, then, a dull frosty wench, would have been contented with one man: now, they will as soon be pleased with one leg or one eye. I'll tell you, sir, the monstrous hazards you shall run with a wife.

Mor. Good sir, have I ever cozened any friends of yours of their land? bought their possessions? taken forfeit of their mortgage? begged a reversion from them? bastarded their issue? What have I done that may deserve this?

True. Nothing, sir, that I know, but your itch of marriage.

Mor. Why, if I had made an assassinate upon your father, vitiated your mother, ravished your sisters——

True. I would kill you, sir, I would kill you, if you had.

Mor. Why, you do more in this, sir: it were a vengeance centuple, for all facinorous acts that could be named, to do that you do.

True. Alas, sir, I am but a messenger: I but tell you, what you must hear. It seems, your friends are careful after your soul's health, and would have you know the danger (but you may do your pleasure for all them, I persuade not, sir.) If, after you are married, your wife do run away with a vaulter, or the Frenchman that walks upon ropes, or him that dances the jig, or a fencer for his skill at his weapon; why, it is not their fault, they have discharged their consciences; when you know what may happen. Nay, suffer valiantly, sir, for I must tell you all the perils that you are obnoxious to. If she be fair, young and vegetous, no sweetmeats ever drew more flies; all the yellow doublets and great roses[1] in the town will be there. If foul and crooked, she'll be with them, and buy those doublets and roses, sir. If rich, and that you marry her dowry, not her, she'll reign in your house as imperious as a widow. If noble, all her kindred will be your tyrants. If fruitful, as proud as May, and humorous as April; she must have her doctors, her midwives, her nurses, her longings every hour; though it be for the dearest morsel of man. If learned, there was never such a parrot; all your patrimony will be too little for the guests that must be invited, to hear her speak Latin and Greek; and you must lie with her in those languages too, if you will please her. If precise,[2] you must feast all the silenced brethren, once in three days; salute the sisters; entertain the whole family, or wood of them;[3] and hear long-winded exercises, singings and catechisings, which you are not given to, and yet must give for; to please the zealous matron your wife, who, for the holy cause, will cozen you over and above. You begin to sweat, sir!—but this is not half, i' faith: you may do your pleasure, notwithstanding, as I said before; I come not to persuade you. [*Mute is stealing away.*]—Upon my faith, master serving-man, if you do stir, I will beat you.

Mor. O, what is my sin! what is my sin!

True. Then, if you love your wife, or rather dote on her, sir; O, how she'll torture you, and take pleasure in your torments! you shall lie with her but when she lists; she will not hurt her beauty, her complexion; or it must be for that jewel or that pearl when she does; every halfhour's pleasure must be bought anew, and with the same pain and charge you wooed

---

[1] *All the* yellow *doublets and great roses.*] Yellow doublets appear to have been fashionable about this time, as they are mentioned by several of our poet's contemporaries. He had already noticed them in *Every Man out of his Humour:* "O, he looked like a sponge in that pinked *yellow* doublet." *Roses* were ribands gathered into a knot in the form of those flowers, and fastened on the instep. They were sometimes of an enormous size. See Mass. vol. iv. p. 11. They are thus noticed in one of Beedome's little poems:

" He's a neat foot as ever kist the ground,
His shoes and *roses cost at least five pound.*"

But this was no unusual price for this favourite article of finery; which formed an indispensable part of the dress of the fashionable world in James's days, and even in those of his immediate successor.

[2] *If precise*,] i.e., a Precisian, a Puritan.—Whal.

[3] *The whole family, or* wood *of them*;] See the *Alchemist.*

her at first. Then you must keep what servants she please ; what company she will ; that friend must not visit you without her licence ; and him she loves most, she will seem to hate eagerliest, to decline your jealousy ; or, feign to be jealous of you first ; and for that cause go live with her she-friend, or cousin at the college, that can instruct her in all the mysteries of writing letters, corrupting servants, taming spies ; where she must have that rich gown for such a great day ; a new one for the next ; a richer for the third ; be served in silver ; have the chamber filled with a succession of grooms, footmen, ushers, and other messengers ; besides embroiderers, jewellers, tire-women, sempsters, feathermen, perfumers ; whilst she feels not how the land drops away, nor the acres melt ; nor foresees the change, when the mercer has your woods for her velvets ; never weighs what her pride costs, sir ; so she may kiss a page, or a smooth chin, that has the despair of a beard ; be a

stateswoman, know all the news, what was done at Salisbury, what at the Bath, what at court, what in progress ;[1] or so she may censure poets, and authors, and styles, and compare them ; Daniel with Spenser, Jonson with the t'other youth, and so forth :[2] or be thought cunning in controversies, or the very knots of divinity ; and have often in her mouth the state of the question ; and then skip to the mathematics and demonstration ; and answer, in religion to one, in state to another, in bawdry to a third.

Mor. O, O !

True. All this is very true, sir. And then her going in disguise to that conjurer, and this cunning woman : where the first question is, how soon you shall die ? next, if her present servant love her ? next, if she shall have a new servant ? and how many ? which of her family would make the best bawd, male or female ? what precedence she shall have by her next match ? and sets down the answers, and believes

[1] *What was done at* Salisbury, *what in* progress ;] *At Salisbury,* "that is," says Upton, "at the time of the races there : *in progress—*when the king went to Scotland," or rather, when he visited the nobility at their country residences.

[2] *She may censure poets, and authors, and styles, and compare them ;* Daniel *with* Spenser, Jonson *with the* t'other youth, *and so forth :*] "This is artful," says Upton, and "an ingenious ridicule on the bad taste of women : for *Daniel* was no more to be compared with *Spenser* than *Decker,* as our poet thought, was to be brought into a comparison with himself : for 'tis Decker he hints at by the *t'other youth.*"

Mr. Malone, who is worse haunted by the "envy and jealousy of Jonson" than ever Cæsar was by the victories of Alexander, differs from Upton on this point. He produces this unfortunate passage as "an instance of the clumsy sarcasms and malevolent reflections with which Jonson persecuted Shakspeare during his life, and for many years afterwards." "In the *Silent Woman,* (he says,) the author perhaps pointed at Shakspeare, as one whom he viewed with fearful, yet with jealous eyes—So they may censure poets—*and compare Jonson with the t'other youth.*" I am sorry to be obliged to remark here, that "lust" is not the only passion which will "prey on garbage." A more improbable conceit than the above has rarely been hazarded. With what propriety could Shakspeare be called the t'other *youth ?* He was now in his 46th year, a time of life to which such an expression can scarcely be applied. Having vented a part of his spleen, Mr. Malone recurs to Upton's discovery, and adds, as a salvo to his former conjecture, "Decker, however, might be meant !"—But neither was Decker meant : for, however

meanly Mr. Malone may think of Jonson, his contemporaries, who were somewhat better acquainted with his talents, would have been very far indeed from *comparing* Decker with him. For Upton's mistake, an excuse may readily be found. He was not acquainted with the dramatic history of that age ; and probably had no better reason for his assertion than the knowledge that Decker had attacked Jonson in the *Satiromastix.* Upton, however, had sufficient judgment to comprehend that when a man of 35 speaks of a competitor of 46, he does not usually call him the *t'other* youth.

It is more easy to say who is not meant than who is. To judge from the date of Marston's various publications, he must have been about Jonson's age ; and from his learning, austerity, &c., might perhaps, by some of the collegiates, great affecters of the abstract sciences, be opposed to him. Others might be named ; but I forbear to pursue an uncertain inquiry.

Whalley adds, that the comparison of "Daniel with Spenser" was *really* made by those who complimented him on the facility of his genius : and he produces the following epigram from Fitz Geoffrey (*Oxon.* 8vo, 1601) to prove it. If it does this, it is well.

" *Spenserum si quis nostrum velit esse Maro-*
      nem,
   Tu, Daniele, mihi Naso Britaunus eris :
Sin illum potius Phœbum velit esse Britan-
      num,
   Tum, Daniele, mihi tu Maro noster eris.
Nil Phœbo ulterius ; si quid foret, illud as-
      beret
   Spenserus, Phœbus tu, Daniele, fores.
Quippe loqui Phœbus cuperet si more &c's
      tanno,
   Haud scio quo poterat, ni velit ore tuo."

them above the scriptures. Nay, perhaps
she'll study the art.

Mor. Gentle sir, have you done? have
you had your pleasure of me? I'll think of
these things.

True. Yes, sir; and then comes reeking
home of vapour and sweat, with going a
foot, and lies in a month of a new face, all
oil and birdlime; and rises in asses' milk,
and is cleansed with a new fucus. God be
wi' you, sir. One thing more, which I had
almost forgot. This too, with whom you
are to marry, may have made a conveyance
of her virginity aforehand, as your wise
widows do of their states, before they
marry, in trust to some friend, sir. Who
can tell? Or if she have not done it yet,
she may do, upon the wedding-day, or the
night before, and antedate you cuckold.
The like has been heard of in nature.
'Tis no devised, impossible thing, sir.
God be wi' you: I'll be bold to leave this
rope with you, sir, for a remembrance.
Farewell, Mute!   [*Exit.*

Mor. Come, have me to my chamber;
but first shut the door. [Truewit *winds the
horn without.*] O, shut the door, shut the
door! is he come again?

Enter Cutbeard.

Cut. 'Tis I, sir, your barber.

Mor. O Cutbeard, Cutbeard, Cutbeard!
here has been a cut-throat with me: help
me in to my bed, and give me physic with
thy counsel.   [*Exeunt.*

SCENE II.—*A Room in* Sir John
Daw's *House.*

Enter Daw, Clerimont, Dauphine, *and*
Epicœne.

Daw. Nay, an she will, let her refuse at
her own charges; 'tis nothing to me, gentlemen; but she will not be invited to the
like feasts or guests every day.

Cler. O, by no means, she may not refuse——to stay at home, if you love your
reputation. 'Slight, you are invited thither
o' purpose to be seen, and laughed at by
the lady of the college, and her shadows.
This trumpeter hath proclaimed you.
                              [*Aside to* Epi.

Daup. You shall not go; let him be
laughed at in your stead, for not bringing
you: and put him to his extemporal
faculty of fooling and talking loud, to
satisfy the company.   [*Aside to* Epi.

Cler. He will suspect us; talk aloud.

Pray, Mistress Epicœne, let's see your
verses; we have Sir John Daw's leave; do
not conceal your servant's merit, and your
own glories.

Epi. They'll prove my servant's glories,
if you have his leave so soon.

Daup. His vainglories, lady!

Daw. Shew them, shew them, mistress;
I dare own them.

Epi. Judge you, what glories.

Daw. Nay, I'll read them myself, too:
an author must recite his own works. It
is a madrigal of Modesty.

  " Modest and fair, for fair and good
      are near
              Neighbours, howe'er."

Daup. Very good.
Cler. Ay, is't not?

Daw. " No noble virtue ever was alone,
              But two in one."

Daup. Excellent!
Cler. That again, I pray, Sir John.
Daup. It has something in't like rare
wit and sense.
Cler. Peace.

Daw.
  " No noble virtue ever was alone,
              But two in one.
    Then, when I praise sweet modesty,
      I praise
              Bright beauty's rays:
    And having praised both beauty and
      modesty,
              I have praised thee."

Daup. Admirable!
Cler. How it chimes, and cries tink in
the close, divinely!
Daup. Ay, 'tis Seneca.
Cler. No, I think 'tis Plutarch.
Daw. The dor on Plutarch and Seneca!
I hate it: they are mine own imaginations,
by that light. I wonder those fellows have
such credit with gentlemen.
Cler. They are very grave authors.
Daw. Grave asses! mere essayists: a
few loose sentences, and that's all. A
man would talk so his whole age. I do
utter as good things every hour, if they were
collected and observed, as either of them.
Daup. Indeed, Sir John!
Cler. He must needs; living among the
wits and braveries too.
Daup. Ay, and being president of them,
as he is.
Daw. There's Aristotle, a mere common-place fellow; Plato, a discourser;

Thucydides and Livy, tedious and dry; Tacitus an entire knot: sometimes worth the untying, very seldom.

Cler. What do you think of the poets, Sir John?

Daw. Not worthy to be named for authors. Homer, an old tedious, prolix ass,[1] talks of curriers, and chines of beef; Virgil, of dunging of land and bees; Horace, of I know not what.

Cler. I think so.

Daw. And so Pindarus, Lycophron, Anacreon, Catullus, Seneca the tragedian, Lucan, Propertius, Tibullus, Martial, Juvenal, Ausonius, Statius, Politian, Valerius Flaccus, and the rest——

Cler. What a sack full of their names he has got!

Daup. And how he pours them out! Politian with Valerius Flaccus!

Cler. Was not the character right of him?

Daup. As could be made, i' faith.

Daw. And Persius, a crabbed coxcomb, not to be endured.

Daup. Why, whom do you account for authors, Sir John Daw?

Daw. Syntagma juris civilis; Corpus juris civilis; Corpus juris canonici; the King of Spain's bible——

Daup. Is the King of Spain's bible an author?

Cler. Yes, and Syntagma.

Daup. What was that Syntagma, sir?

Daw. A civil lawyer, a Spaniard.

Daup. Sure, Corpus was a Dutchman.

Cler. Ay, both the Corpuses, I knew 'em: they were very corpulent authors.

Daw. And then there's Vatablus, Pomponatius, Symancha: the other are not to be received within the thought of a scholar.

Daup. 'Fore God, you have a simple learned servant, lady—in titles. [*Aside.*

Cler. I wonder that he is not called to the helm, and made a counsellor.

Daup. He is one extraordinary.

Cler. Nay, but in ordinary: to say truth, the state wants such.

Daup. Why, that will follow.

Cler. I muse a mistress can be so silent to the dotes of such a servant.[2]

Daw. 'Tis her virtue, sir. I have written somewhat of her silence too.

Daup. In verse, Sir John?

Cler. What else?

Daup. Why, how can you justify your own being of a poet, that so slight all the old poets?

Daw. Why, every man that writes in verse is not a poet; you have of the wits that write verses, and yet are no poets: they are poets that live by it, the poor fellows that live by it.

Daup. Why, would not you live by your verses, Sir John?

Cler. No, 'twere pity he should. A knight live by his verses! he did not make them to that end, I hope.

Daup. And yet the noble Sidney lives by his, and the noble family not ashamed.

Cler. Ay, he profest himself; but Sir John Daw has more caution: he'll not hinder his own rising in the state so much. Do you think he will? Your verses, good Sir John, and no poems.

Daw. "Silence in woman, is like speech
      in man;
                    Deny 't who can."

Daup. Not I, believe it: your reason, sir.

Daw.   "Nor is 't a tale,
   That female vice should be a virtue
      male,
   Or masculine vice a female virtue be:
                You shall it see
                   Proved with increase;
   I know to speak, and she to hold her
      peace."
Do you conceive me, gentlemen?

Daup. No, faith; how mean you *with increase*, Sir John?

Daw. Why, with increase is, when I court her for the common cause of mankind, and she says nothing, but *consentire videtur;* and in time is *gravida.*

<hr />

[1] *Homer, an old tedious, prolix ass,* &c.] Those brief and sententious criticisms on the principal writers of antiquity, which do so much honour to Sir John's taste and judgment, have been recently repeated with great applause. The author, however, has been unfairly dealt with by his copyists, who have illiberally conspired to suppress his name. Indeed, impudence and ingratitude go together in this prodigious age. Our new critics and philosophers steal the absurdities of their forefathers without measure, and appropriate them without shame, or acknowledgment.

[2] *I muse a mistress can be so silent to the dotes of such a servant.*] To the endowments, or good qualities; the word is pure Latin.——WHAL.

It is not, however, peculiar to Jonson; nor was it first introduced into the language by him. I find it in many writers before his time.

Daup. Then this is a ballad of procreation?

Cler. A madrigal of procreation; you mistake.

Epi. Pray give me my verses again, servant.

Daw. If you'll ask them aloud, you shall.   [*Walks aside with the papers.*

Enter Truewit *with his horn.*

Cler. See, here's Truewit again! Where hast thou been, in the name of madness, thus accoutred with thy horn?

True. Where the sound of it might have pierced your senses with gladness, had you been in ear-reach of it. Dauphine, fall down and worship me; I have forbid the bans, lad: I have been with thy virtuous uncle, and have broke the match.

Daup. You have not, I hope.

True. Yes, faith; an thou shouldst hope otherwise, I should repent me: this horn got me entrance; kiss it. I had no other way to get in, but by feigning to be a post; but when I got in once, I proved none, but rather the contrary, turned him into a post, or a stone, or what is stiffer, with thundering into him the incommodities of a wife, and the miseries of marriage. If ever Gorgon were seen in the shape of a woman, he hath seen her in my description: I have put him off o' that scent for ever. Why do you not applaud and adore me, sirs? why stand you mute? are you stupid? You are not worthy of the benefit.

Daup. Did not I tell you? Mischief!

Cler. I would you had placed this benefit somewhere else.

True. Why so?

Cler. 'Slight, you have done the most inconsiderate, rash, weak thing, that ever man did to his friend.

Daup. Friend! if the most malicious enemy I have, had studied to inflict an injury upon me, it could not be greater.

True. Wherein, for God's sake? Gentlemen, come to yourselves again.

Daup. But I presaged thus much afore to you.

Cler. Would my lips had been soldered when I spake on't! Slight, what moved you to be thus impertinent?

True. My masters, do not put on this strange face to pay my courtesy; off with this vizor. Have good turns done you, and thank 'em this way!

Daup. 'Fore heaven, you have undone me. That which I have plotted for, and been maturing now these four months, you have blasted in a minute. Now I am lost, I may speak. This gentlewoman was lodged here by me o' purpose, and, to be put upon my uncle, hath profest this obstinate silence for my sake: being my entire friend, and one that for the requital of such a fortune as to marry him, would have made me very ample conditions; where now all my hopes are utterly miscarried by this unlucky accident.

Cler. Thus 'tis when a man will be ignorantly officious, do services, and not know his why. I wonder what courteous itch possest you. You never did absurder part in your life, nor a greater trespass to friendship or humanity.

Daup. Faith, you may forgive it best; 'twas your cause principally.

Cler. I know it; would it had not.

Enter Cutbeard.

Daup. How now, Cutbeard! what news?

Cut. The best, the happiest that ever was, sir. There has been a mad gentleman with your uncle this morning, [*seeing* Truewit.]—I think this be the gentleman—that has almost talked him out of his wits, with threatening him from marriage——

Daup. On, I prithee.

Cut. And your uncle, sir, he thinks 'twas done by your procurement; therefore he will see the party you wot of presently; and if he like her, he says, and that she be so inclining to dumb as I have told him, he swears he will marry her to-day, instantly, and not defer it a minute longer.

Daup. Excellent! beyond our expectation!

True. Beyond our expectation! By this light I knew it would be thus.

Daup. Nay, sweet Truewit, forgive me.

True. No, I was *ignorantly officious, impertinent;* this was the *absurd, weak part.*

Cler. Wilt thou ascribe that to merit now, was mere fortune?

True. Fortune! mere providence. Fortune had not a finger in't. I saw it must necessarily in nature fall out so: my genius is never false to me in these things. Shew me how it could be otherwise.

Daup. Nay, gentlemen, contend not; 'tis well now.

True. Alas, I let him go on with *inconsiderate,* and *rash,* and what he pleased.

Cler. Away, thou strange justifier of thyself, to be wiser than thou wert, by the event !

True. Event ! by this light, thou shalt never persuade me but I foresaw it as well as the stars themselves.

Daup. Nay, gentlemen, 'tis well now. Do you two entertain Sir John Daw with discourse, while I send her away with instructions.

True. I'll be acquainted with her first, by your favour.

Cler. Master Truewit, lady, a friend of ours.

True. I am sorry I have not known you sooner, lady, to celebrate this rare virtue of your silence.

[*Exeunt* Daup. Epi. *and* Cutbeard.

Cler. Faith, an you had come sooner, you should have seen and heard her well celebrated in Sir John Daw's madrigals.

True. [*advances to* Daw.] Jack Daw, God save you ! when saw you La-Foole ?

Daw. Not since last night, Master Truewit.

True. That's a miracle ! I thought you two had been inseparable.

Daw. He's gone to invite his guests.

True. 'Odso ! 'tis true ! What a false memory have I towards that man ! I am one.[1] I met him even now, upon that he calls his delicate fine black horse, rid into foam, with posting from place to place, and person to person, to give them the cue——

Cler. Lest they should forget ?

True. Yes : there was never poor captain took more pains at a muster to shew men, than he at this meal to shew friends.

Daw. It is his quarter-feast, sir.

Cler. What ! do you say so, Sir John ?

True. Nay, Jack Daw will not be out, at the best friends he has, to the talent of his wit. Where's his mistress, to hear and applaud him ? is she gone ?

Daw. Is Mistress Epicœne gone ?

Cler. Gone afore, with Sir Dauphine, I warrant, to the place.

True. Gone afore ! that were a manifest injury, a disgrace and a half ; to refuse him at such a festival-time as this, being a bravery, and a wit too !

Cler. Tut, he'll swallow it like cream : he's better read in Jure civili, than to esteem anything a disgrace is offered him from a mistress.

Daw. Nay, let her e'en go ; she shall sit alone, and be dumb in her chamber a week together, for John Daw, I warrant her. Does she refuse me ?

Cler. No, sir, do not take it so to heart ; she does not refuse you, but a little neglects you. Good faith, Truewit, you were to blame, to put it into his head, that she does refuse him.

True. Sir, she does refuse him palpably, however you mince it. An I were as he, I would swear to speak ne'er a word to her to-day for 't.

Daw. By this light, no more I will not.

True. Nor to anybody else, sir.

Daw. Nay, I will not say so, gentlemen.

Cler. It had been an excellent happy condition for the company, if you could have drawn him to it.   [*Aside.*

Daw. I'll be very melancholy, i' faith.

Cler. As a dog, if I were as you, Sir John.

True. Or a snail, or a hog-louse. I would roll myself up for this day ; in troth, they should not unwind me.

Daw. By this picktooth, so I will.

Cler. 'Tis well done : he begins already to be angry with his teeth.

Daw. Will you go, gentlemen ?

Cler. Nay, you must walk alone if you be right melancholy, Sir John.

True. Yes, sir, we'll dog you, we'll follow you afar off.

[*Exit* Daw.

Cler. Was there ever such a two yards of knighthood measured out by time, to be sold to laughter ?

True. A mere talking mole, hang him ! no mushroom was ever so fresh.[2] A fellow so utterly nothing, as he knows not what he would be.

Cler. Let's follow him : but first let's go to Dauphine, he's hovering about the house to hear what news.

True. Content.   [*Exeunt.*

---

[1] *I am one.*] i.e., one of the guests. Whalley has strangely mistaken the sense of this simple passage ; *I am one*, he says, is "elliptical for, I am such a one ! and is used when a person forgets what he ought to remember."

[2] *No* mushroom *was ever so* fresh.] Taken, as Upton observes, from Plautus :

" *Jam nihil sapit,*
Nec sentit ; tanti 'st, quanti est fungus pu-
tidus."

Mole, Upton "corrects" (why, it is impossible to guess) into *mule.* Animal for animal, the former was surely best adapted to represent the imbecility of this purblind knight.

SCENE III.—*A Room in* Morose's
House.

Enter Morose *and* Mute, *followed by*
Cutbeard *with* Epicœne.

Mor. Welcome, Cutbeard! draw near
with your fair charge: and in her ear softly
entreat her to unmask [Epi. *takes off her
mask.*] So! Is the door shut? [Mute *makes
a leg.*] Enough. Now, Cutbeard, with
the same discipline I use to my family, I
will question you. As I conceive, Cutbeard, this gentlewoman is she you have
provided, and brought, in hope she will
fit me in the place and person of a wife?
Answer me not but with your leg, unless it
be otherwise. [Cut. *makes a leg.*] Very
well done, Cutbeard. I conceive besides,
Cutbeard, you have been pre-acquainted
with her birth, education, and qualities, or
else you would not prefer her to my acceptance, in the weighty consequence of
marriage. [*makes a leg.*] This I conceive,
Cutbeard. Answer me not but with your
leg, unless it be otherwise. [*bows again.*]
Very well done, Cutbeard. Give aside now
a little, and leave me to examine her condition and aptitude to my affection. [*goes
about her and views her.*] She is exceeding fair, and of a special good favour; a
sweet composition or harmony of limbs;
her temper of beauty has the true height of
my blood. The knave hath exceedingly
well fitted me without: I will now try her
within.—Come near, fair gentlewoman; let
not my behaviour seem rude, though unto
you, being rare, it may haply appear
strange. [Epicœne *curtsies.*] Nay, lady,
you may speak, though Cutbeard and my
man might not; for of all sounds, only the
sweet voice of a fair lady has the just
length of mine ears. I beseech you, say,
lady; out of the first fire of meeting eyes,
they say, love is stricken: do you feel any

such motion suddenly shot into you, from
any part you see in me? ha, lady? [Epi.
curtsies.] Alas, lady, these answers by
silent curtsies from you are too courtless
and simple. I have ever had my breeding
in court; and she that shall be my wife,
must be accomplished with courtly and
audacious ornaments.[1] Can you speak,
lady?
Epi. [*softly.*] Judge you, forsooth.
Mor. What say you, lady? Speak out,
I beseech you.
Epi. Judge you, forsooth.
Mor. On my judgment, a divine softness! But can you naturally, lady, as I
enjoin these by doctrine and industry, refer
yourself to the search of my judgment, and,
not taking pleasure in your tongue, which
is a woman's chiefest pleasure, think it
plausible to answer me by silent gestures,
so long as my speeches jump right with
what you conceive? [Epi. *curtsies.*] Excellent! divine! if it were possible she
should hold out thus! Peace, Cutbeard,
thou art made for ever, as thou hast made
me, if this felicity have lasting: but I will
try her further. Dear lady, I am courtly,
I tell you, and I must have mine ears banquetted with pleasant and witty conferences,
pretty girds, scoffs, and dalliance in her
that I mean to choose for my bed-phere.[2]
The ladies in court think it a most desperate impair to their quickness of wit, and
good carriage, if they cannot give occasion
for a man to court 'em; and when an amorous discourse is set on foot, minister as
good matter to continue it as himself. And
do you alone so much differ from all them,
that what they, with so much circumstance,
affect and toil for, to seem learned, to seem
judicious, to seem sharp and conceited, you
can bury in yourself with silence, and rather
trust your graces to the fair conscience of
virtue, than to the world's or your own
proclamation?

---

[1] *With courtly and* audacious *ornaments.*]
i.e., liberal, spirited. Audacious was not always
used by our old writers in a bad sense. In *Love's
Labour Lost,* we have, "Witty without affectation, *audacious without impudency.*" One of
the characters in the *Utopia* is, I think, named
Eutolmos.

[2] *I must have mine ears banquetted with
pleasant and witty conferences, pretty girds,
scoffs, and dalliance in her I choose for my* bed-
phere.] "Very elegantly expressed from Plato,
de repub. ἐστιασας λογων καλων. Hence Cicero,
Cogitationum bonarum epulæ—Discendi epulas.
For *bed-phere,* we must read bedfere, i.e., bed-

companion. So *fere* is used in our old poets:
the word we had from the Danes."
These are Upton's remarks, on which it is only
necessary to say that *phere* is quite as common
in our old poets as *fere,* and that it comes to us
from the Saxons. "Gird," he adds, "is derived from the Greek γυρος; and, indeed, it has
one resemblance which our etymologists sometimes overlook, it begins with the same letter:
but *gird* (and I mention it for the sake of the
commentators) is a mere metathesis of *gride,* and
means a thrust, a blow; the metaphorical use of
the word for a smart stroke of wit, taunt, reproachful retort, &c., is justified by a similar
application of kindred terms in all languages.

Epi. [*softly.*] I should be sorry else.

Mor. What say you, lady ? good lady, speak out.

Epi. I should be sorry else.

Mor. That sorrow doth fill me with gladness. O Morose, thou art happy above mankind ! pray that thou mayst contain thyself. I will only put her to it once more, and it shall be with the utmost touch and test of their sex. But hear me, fair lady ; I do also love to see her whom I shall choose for my heifer,[1] to be the first and principal in all fashions, precede all the dames at court by a fortnight, have council of tailors, lineners, lace-women, embroiderers ; and sit with them sometimes twice a day upon French intelligences, and then come forth varied like nature, or oftener than she, and better by the help of art, her emulous servant. This do I affect : and how will you be able, lady, with this frugality of speech, to give the manifold but necessary instructions, for that bodice, these sleeves, those skirts, this cut, that stitch, this embroidery, that lace, this wire, those knots, that ruff, those roses, this girdle, that fan, the t'other scarf, these gloves ? Ha ! what say you, lady ?

Epi. [*softly.*] I'll leave it to you, sir.

Mor. How, lady ? Pray you rise a note.

Epi. I leave it to wisdom and you, sir.

Mor. Admirable creature ! I will trouble you no more. I will not sin against so sweet a simplicity. Let me now be bold to print on those divine lips the seal of being mine. Cutbeard, I give thee the lease of thy house free ; thank me not but with thy leg. [*Cutbeard shakes his head.*] I know what thou wouldst say,[2] she's poor and her friends deceased. She has brought a wealthy dowry in her silence, Cutbeard ;

and in respect of her poverty, Cutbeard, I shall have her more loving and obedient, Cutbeard. Go thy ways, and get me a minister presently, with a soft low voice, to marry us ; and pray him he will not be impertinent, but brief as he can ; away : softly, Cutbeard. [*Exit.* Cut.] Sirrah, conduct your mistress into the dining-room, your now mistress. [*Exit* Mute, *followed by* Epi.] O, my felicity ! how shall I be revenged on my insolent kinsman, and his plots to fright me from marrying ! This night I will get an heir, and thrust him out of my blood like a stranger. He would be knighted, forsooth, and thought by that means to reign over me ; his title must do it. No, kinsman, I will now make you bring me the tenth lord's and the sixteenth lady's letter, kinsman ; and it shall do you no good, kinsman. Your knighthood itself shall come on its knees, and it shall be rejected ; it shall be sued for its fees to execution, and not be redeemed ; it shall cheat at the twelve-penny ordinary, it knighthood, for its diet, all the term time, and tell tales for it in the vacation to the hostess ; or it knighthood shall do worse, take sanctuary in Cole-harbour,[3] and fast. It shall fright all it friends with borrowing letters ; and when one of the fourscore hath brought it knighthood ten shillings, it knighthood shall go to the Cranes, or the Bear at the Bridge-foot, and be drunk in fear ; it shall not have money to discharge one tavern-reckoning, to invite the old creditors to forbear it knighthood, or the new, that should be, to trust it knighthood. It shall be the tenth name in the bond to take up the commodity of pipkins and stone-jugs : and the part thereof shall not furnish it knighthood forth for the attempting of a

---

[1] *My* heifer,] My yoke-mate. Morose is not over-delicate in his choice of terms for a wife: perhaps, he alludes to the proverbial expression, *Judges* c. xiv. v. 18.

[2] *I know what thou wouldst say, &c.*] This, as Upton observes, is taken from the *Aulularia* of Plautus:

" Me.   *Ejus cupio filiam*
Virginem mihi desponderi—Verba ne facias,
    soror :
Scio quid dictura es, hanc esse pauperem.
Hæc pauper placet."

At the break Eunomia (like Cutbeard) shakes her head, which Megadorus interprets as a sign of disapprobation, and proceeds to obviate. The passage is thus translated by Thornton :

" *Meg.* His daughter I would marry—Nay, nay, sister,

Speak not a word : I know what you would say, She has no fortune. What of that ? I like her."

[3] *Take sanctuary in* Cole-harbour,] Cole, or more commonly Cold-harbour, was a very ancient building in the parish of Allhallows the Less, near the Thames. Stow gives a long account of the various hands through which it passed, till it came to the Earl of Shrewsbury, who, about the end of the sixteenth century, "took it down, and in place thereof builded a number of small tenements, now letten out for great rents to *people of all sorts.*" It seems, at this time, to have been a place of retreat for debtors, gamesters, &c. There is considerable humour in this long monologue of Morose ; but his ungenerous triumph over the imaginary distresses of his nephew cannot be justified ; and fully warrants the plot meditated against him in return. This might possibly be what the poet intended by it.

baker's widow, a brown baker's widow. It shall give it knighthood's name for a stallion, to all gamesome citizens' wives, and be refused, when the master of a dancing-school, or how,[1] do you call him, the worst reveller in the town, is taken : it shall want clothes, and by reason of that, wit, to fool to lawyers. It shall not have hope to repair itself by Constantinople, Ireland, or Virginia ;[2] but the best and last fortune to it knighthood, shall be to make Dol Tear-sheet or Kate Common a lady, and so it knighthood may eat.   [*Exit.*

SCENE IV.—*A Lane near* Morose's *House.*

Enter Truewit, Dauphine, *and* Clerimont.

True. Are you sure he has not gone by?
Daup. No, I staid in the shop ever since.
Cler. But he may take the other end of the lane.
Daup. No, I told him I would be here at this end : I appointed him hither.
True. What a barbarian it is to stay then !
Daup. Yonder he comes.
Cler. And his charge left behind him, which is a very good sign, Dauphine.

Enter Cutbeard.

Daup. How now, Cutbeard ! succeeds it or no?

Cut. Past imagination, sir, *omnia secunda;* you could not have prayed to have had it so well. *Saltat senex,* as it is in the proverb ; he does triumph in his felicity, admires the party ! he has given me the lease of my house too ! and I am now going for a silent minister to marry them, and away.
True. 'Slight ! get one of the silenced ministers ;[3] a zealous brother would torment him purely.
Cut. Cum privilegio, sir.
Daup. O, by no means ; let's do nothing to hinder it now : when 'tis done and finished, I am for you, for any device of vexation.
Cut. And that shall be within this half hour, upon my dexterity, gentlemen. Contrive what you can in the mean time, *bonis avibus.*   [*Exit.*
Cler. How the slave doth Latin it ![4]
True. It would be made a jest to posterity, sirs, this day's mirth, if ye will.
Cler. Beshrew his heart that will not, I pronounce.
Daup. And for my part. What is it?
True. To translate all La-Foole's company and his feast thither to-day, to celebrate this bride-ale.[5]
Daup. Ay, marry ; but how will't be done ?
True. I'll undertake the directing of all the lady-guests thither, and then the meat must follow.

---

[1] *Or how, do you call him, &c.*] From the manner in which this is printed in the old copies, I should take it to be personal, and one *Howe* to be pointed at as the "worst reveller," &c.

[2] *To repair itself by Constantinople,* Ireland, *or* Virginia :] This alludes probably to James's schemes for establishing order in *Ireland,* one of which was the grant of lands about this time to English settlers in the province of Ulster ; and to the revival of the colonies in *Virginia,* whither two bodies of planters had just been sent, one in 1608, the other in 1609. What is meant by *Constantinople* is not so easy to guess. Sir Puntarvolo, we know, (*Every Man out of his Humour,*) took five to one upon the return of himself, his dog, and cat, from thence ; but it is more likely that the poet refers to some circumstances respecting the Turkey company, established in the preceding reign.

[3] *'Slight ! get one of the* silenced ministers :] Alluding, says Grey, to the nonconformist clergy *silenced* in the year 1604, after the Hampton Court conference. Calderwood observes, "That in the second year of King James, three hundred ministers were either silenced, or deprived of their benefices, or excommunicated, or cast into prison, or forced to leave their own country." But Dr. Heylin and Mr. Foulis, in answer, tell

us, "that only forty-nine were deprived upon all occasions, as appears by the rolls brought in to Archbishop Bancroft before his death ; which in a realm containing nine thousand parishes, was no great matter."
This statement, which is abridged from a former note, though imperfect, and, I suspect, inaccurate, may yet suffice for a general view of Jonson's meaning. It may perhaps be added, that however great the number of silenced nonconformists might be, it was surpassed in a tenfold degree by that of the deprived ministers of the Church during the puritanical persecution which followed. Dissenters (of whatever denomination) have seldom "borne their faculties meekly" in the day of success, or thought it necessary to copy the moderation and forbearance which they experienced while yet the feebler party.

[4] *How the slave doth* Latin *it !*] This is an artful preparation for the part which Cutbeard is destined to play in the last act. See also what is said of Captain Otter below.

[5] *To celebrate this bride-ale.*] This marriage festival. Our old writers frequently use *ale,* in composition, for a merry-meeting. Separately, it commonly stands for an *ale-house.*

Cler. For God's sake, let's effect it ; it will be an excellent comedy of affliction, so many several noises.

Daup. But are they not at the other place already, think you ?

True. I'll warrant you for the college-honours : one of their faces has not the priming colour laid on yet, nor the other her smock sleeked.

Cler. O, but they'll rise earlier than ordinary to a feast.

True. Best go see, and assure ourselves.

Cler. Who knows the house ?

True. I'll lead you.   Were you never there yet ?

Daup. Not I.

Cler. Nor I.

True. Where have you lived then ? not know Tom Otter !

Cler. No : for God's sake, what is he ?

True. An excellent animal, equal with your Daw or La-Foole, if not transcendent ; and does Latin it as much as your barber. He is his wife's subject ; he calls her princess, and at such times as these follows her up and down the house like a page, with his hat off, partly for heat, partly for reverence.   At this instant he is marshalling of his bull, bear, and horse.

Daup. What be those, in the name of Sphinx ?[1]

True. Why, sir, he has been a great man at the Bear-garden in his time ; and from that subtle sport has ta'en the witty denomination of his chief carousing cups.   One he calls his bull, another his bear, another his horse.   And then he has his lesser glasses, that he calls his deer and his ape ; and several degrees of them too ; and never is well, nor thinks any entertainment perfect till these be brought out, and set on the cupboard.

Cler. For God's love !—we should miss this if we should not go.

True. Nay, he has a thousand things as good, that will speak him all day.   He will rail on his wife, with certain commonplaces, behind her back, and to her face——

Daup. No more of him.   Let's go see him, I petition you.   [*Exeunt.*

ACT III.

SCENE I.—*A Room in* Otter's *House.*

Enter Captain Otter *with his cups, and* Mistress Otter.

Ott. Nay, good princess, hear me *pauca verba.*

Mrs. Ott. By that light, I'll have you chained up, with your bull-dogs and bear-dogs, if you be not civil the sooner.   I'll send you to kennel, i' faith.   You were best bait me with your bull, bear, and horse. Never a time that the courtiers or collegiates come to the house, but you make it a Shrove Tuesday !   I would have you get your Whitsuntide velvet cap, and your staff in your hand, to entertain them : yes, in troth, do.

Ott. Not so, princess, neither ; but under correction, sweet princess, give me leave. These things I am known to the courtiers by.   It is reported to them for my humour, and they receive it so, and do expect it. Tom Otter's bull, bear, and horse is known all over England, *in rerum natura.*

Mrs. Ott. 'Fore me, I will *na-ture* them over to Paris-garden, and *na-ture* you thither too if you pronounce them again. Is a bear a fit beast, or a bull, to mix in society with great ladies ? think in your discretion, in any good policy.

Ott. The horse then, good princess.

Mrs. Ott. Well, I am contented for the horse ; they love to be well horsed, I know : I love it myself.

Ott. And it is a delicate fine horse this : *Poetarum Pegasus.*   Under correction, princess, Jupiter did turn himself into a— *taurus,* or bull, under correction, good princess.

Enter Truewit, Clerimont, *and* Dauphine, *behind.*

Mrs. Ott. By my integrity, I'll send you over to the Bank-side ; I'll commit you to the master of the Garden, if I hear but a syllable more.   Must my house or my roof be polluted with the scent of bears and bulls, when it is perfumed for great ladies ? Is this according to the instrument when I

1 *What be those in the name of* Sphinx ?] In the name of *ignorance*, says Upton, who is followed, as usual, by Whalley. This is another instance of the inutility of learning without judgment   That Sphinx is sometimes typical of ignorance is certain, as Jonson himself has shown

in one of his Masques ; but she is here introduced in the character by which she is vulgarly known, as a dealer in riddles, merely.   Why should Dauphine invoke ignorance, when he was in quest of information ?

married you? that I would be princess, and reign in mine own house; and you would be my subject, and obey me? What did you bring me, should make you thus peremptory? do I allow you your half-crown a day, to spend where you will, among your gamesters, to vex and torment me at such times as these? Who gives you your maintenance, I pray you? who allows you your horse-meat and man's-meat? your three suits of apparel a year? your four pair of stockings, one silk, three worsted? your clean linen, your bands and cuffs, when I can get you to wear them?—'tis marle you have them on now. Who graces you with courtiers or great personages, to speak to you out of their coaches, and come home to your house? Were you ever so much as looked upon by a lord or a lady before I married you, but on the Easter or Whit-sun-holidays? and then out at the banquet-ing-house window, when Ned Whiting or George Stone were at the stake?[1]

True. For God's sake, let's go stave her off him.

Mrs. Ott. Answer me to that. And did not I take you up from thence, in an old greasy buff-doublet, with points, and green velvet sleeves, out at the elbows? you for-get this.

True. She'll worry him, if we help not in time.   [*They come forward.*

Mrs. Ott. O, here are some of the gal-lants. Go to, behave yourself distinctly, and with good morality; or, I protest, I'll take away your exhibition.[2]

True. By your leave, fair Mistress Otter, I'll be bold to enter these gentlemen in your acquaintance.

Mrs. Ott. It shall not be obnoxious, or difficil, sir.

True. How does my noble captain? is the bull, bear, and horse in *rerum natura* still?

Ott. Sir, *sic visum superis.*

Mrs. Ott. I would you would but inti-mate them, do. Go your ways in, and get toasts and butter made for the woodcocks: that's a fit province for you.

                   [*Drives him off.*

Cler. Alas, what a tyranny is this poor fellow married to.

True. O, but the sport will be anon, when we get him loose.

Daup. Dares he ever speak?

True. No Anabaptist ever railed[3] with the like licence: but mark her language in the meantime, I beseech you.

Mrs. Ott. Gentlemen, you are very aptly come. My cousin, Sir Amorous, will be here briefly.

True. In good time, lady. Was not Sir John Daw here, to ask for him, and the company?

Mrs. Ott. I cannot assure you, Master Truewit. Here was a very melancholy knight in a ruff, that demanded my sub-ject for somebody, a gentleman, I think.

Cler. Ay, that was he, lady.

Mrs. Ott. But he departed straight, I can resolve you.

Daup. What an excellent choice phrase this lady expresses in!

True. O, sir, she is the only authentical courtier, that is not naturally bred one, in the city.

Mrs. Ott. You have taken that report upon trust, gentlemen.

True. No, I assure you, the court governs it so, lady, in your behalf.

Mrs. Ott. I am the servant of the court and courtiers, sir.

True. They are rather your idolaters.

Mrs. Ott. Not so, sir.

Enter Cutbeard.

Daup. How now, Cutbeard! any cross?

Cut. O no, sir, *omnia bene.* 'Twas never better on the hinges; all's sure. I have so pleased him with a curate, that he's gone to't almost with the delight he hopes for soon.

Daup. What is he for a vicar?[4]

---

[1] *When* Ned Whiting *or* George Stone *were at the stake?*] Two noted bears of that age, who went by the names of their owners. So in the *Widow of Watling Street,* act iii., a fellow who has just escaped from the hands of the bailiffs, says, "How many dogs do you think I had upon me? almost as many as *George Stone* the bear."—WHAL.

Poor George! the dogs were too many for him at last. "A goodly bear" he is called by his keepers, who feelingly lament his loss, in their petition to the court for a renewal of their licence.

[2] *I'll take away your* exhibition.] i.e., your allowance for pocket-money; the "half-crown a day" mentioned above.

[3] *No Anabaptist ever railed,* &c.] It may be just worth observing that this sect, which has now been so long noted for its mild and decorous conduct, was, at its original formation, turbu-lent, frantic, and mischievous, above all others.

[4] *What is he for a vicar?*] What vicar is he? This is pure German, or, as the authorized phrase seems to be, Saxon in its idiom, and is very common in our old writers. *Was ist das für ein.*—It is somewhat singular that E. K. the

Cut. One that has catched a cold, sir, and can scarce be heard six inches off; as if he spoke out of a bulrush that were not picked, or his throat were full of pith : a fine quick fellow, and an excellent barber of prayers.[1] I came to tell you, sir, that you might *omnem movere lapidem*, as they say, be ready with your vexation.

Daup. Gramercy, honest Cutbeard ! be thereabouts with thy key, to let us in.

Cut. I will not fail you, sir ; *ad manum.*
                                        [*Exit.*

True. Well, I'll go watch my coaches.

Cler. Do ; and we'll send Daw to you, if you meet him not.   [*Exit* Truewit.

Mrs. Ott. Is Master Truewit gone ?

Daup. Yes, lady, there is some unfortunate business fallen out.

Mrs. Ott. So I adjudged by the physiognomy of the fellow that came in ; and I had a dream last night too of the new pageant, and my lady mayoress, which is always very ominous to me. I told it my Lady Haughty t'other day, when her honour came hither to see some China stuffs ; and she expounded it out of Artemidorus, and I have found it since very true. It has done me many affronts.

Cler. Your dream, lady ?

Mrs. Ott. Yes, sir, anything I do but dream of the city. It stained me a damask tablecloth, cost me eighteen pound, at one time ; and burnt me a black satin gown, as I stood by the fire at my Lady Centaure's chamber in the college, another time. A third time, at the lords' masque, it dropt all my wire and my ruff with wax candle, that I could not go up to the banquet. A fourth time, as I was taking coach to go to Ware, to meet a friend, it dashed me a new suit all over (a crimson satin doublet and black velvet skirts) with a brewer's horse, that I was fain to go in and shift me, and kept my chamber a leash of days for the anguish of it.

Daup. These were dire mischances, lady.

Cler. I would not dwell in the city an 'twere so fatal to me.

Mrs. Ott. Yes, sir : but I do take advice of my doctor to dream of it as little as I can.

Daup. You do well, Mistress Otter.

Enter Sir John Daw, *and is taken aside by* Clerimont.

Mrs. Ott. Will it please you to enter the house farther, gentlemen ?

Daup. And your favour, lady : but we stay to speak with a knight, Sir John Daw, who is here come. We shall follow you, lady.

Mrs. Ott. At your own time, sir. It is my cousin Sir Amorous his feast——

Daup. I know it, lady.

Mrs. Ott. And mine together. But it is for his honour, and therefore I take no name of it, more than of the place.

Daup. You are a bounteous kinswoman.

Mrs. Ott. Your servant, sir.   [*Exit.*

Cler. [*coming forward with* Daw.] Why, do not you know it, Sir John Daw ?

Daw. No, I am a rook if I do.

Cler. I'll tell you then ; she's married by this time. And whereas you were put in the head, that she was gone with Sir Dauphine, I assure you Sir Dauphine has been the noblest, honestest friend to you, that ever gentleman of your quality could boast of. He has discovered the whole plot, and made your mistress so acknowledging, and indeed so ashamed of her injury to you, that she desires you to forgive her, and but grace her wedding with your presence to-day. She is to be married to a very good fortune, she says, his uncle, old Morose ; and she willed me in private to tell you, that she shall be able to do you more favours, and with more security now than before.

Daw. Did she say so, i' faith ?

Cler. Why, what do you think of me, Sir John ! ask Sir Dauphine.

Daw. Nay, I believe you. Good Sir Dauphine, did she desire me to forgive her ?

Daup. I assure you, Sir John, she did.

Daw. Nay, then, I do with all my heart, and I'll be jovial.

Cler. Yes, for look you, sir, this was the injury to you. La-Foole intended this feast to honour her bridal day, and made you the property to invite the college ladies, and promise to bring her ; and then at the time she would have appeared,

---

commentator on Spenser's *Pastorals*, should think it necessary to explain the expression in his time. On the line "What is he for a lad ?" he subjoins, "a strange manner of speaking, q. d. What manner of lad is he ?" What is he

for a creature, occurs in *Every Man out of his Humour.*

[1] *An excellent* barber *of prayers.*[1] i.e., one who cuts them short, &c. Rabelais calls Friar John an excellent *estropier des Heures ;* and the author perhaps had this expression in view.

as his friend, to have given you the dor.[1] Whereas now, Sir Dauphine has brought her to a feeling of it, with this kind of satisfaction, that you shall bring all the ladies to the place where she is, and be very jovial; and there she will have a dinner, which shall be in your name; and so disappoint La-Foole, to make you good again, and, as it were, a saver in the main.

Daw. As I am a knight, I honour her; and forgive her heartily.

Cler. About it then presently. Truewit is gone before to confront the coaches, and to acquaint you with so much, if he meet you. Join with him, and 'tis well.—

Enter Sir Amorous La-Foole.

See; here comes your antagonist; but take you no notice, but be very jovial.

La-F. Are the ladies come, Sir John Daw, and your mistress? [*Exit* Daw.] Sir Dauphine! you are exceeding welcome, and honest Master Clerimont. Where's my cousin? did you see no collegiates, gentlemen?

Daup. Collegiates! do you not hear, Sir Amorous, how you are abused?

La-F. How, sir!

Cler. Will you speak so kindly to Sir John Daw, that has done you such an affront?

La-F. Wherein, gentlemen? let me be a suitor to you to know, I beseech you.

Cler. Why, sir, his mistress is married to-day to Sir Dauphine's uncle, your cousin's neighbour, and he has diverted all the ladies, and all your company thither, to frustrate your provision, and stick a disgrace upon you. He was here now to have enticed us away from you too: but we told him his own, I think.

La-F. Has Sir John Daw wronged me so inhumanly?

Daup. He has done it, Sir Amorous, most maliciously and treacherously: but if

you'll be ruled by us, you shall quit him, i' faith.

La-F. Good gentlemen, I'll make one, believe it. How, I pray?

Daup. Marry, sir, get me your pheasants, and your godwits, and your best meat, and dish it in silver dishes of your cousin's presently; and say nothing, but clap me a clean towel about you, like a sewer; and, bareheaded, march afore it with a good confidence ('tis but over the way, hard by,) and we'll second you, where you shall set it on the board, and bid them welcome to 't, which shall show 'tis yours, and disgrace his preparation utterly: and for your cousin, whereas she should be troubled here at home with care of making and giving welcome, she shall transfer all that labour thither, and be a principal guest herself; sit ranked with the college honours, and be honoured, and have her health drunk as often, as bare, and as loud as the best of them.

La-F. I'll go tell her presently. It shall be done, that's resolved. [*Exit.*

Cler. I thought he would not hear it out but 'twould take him.

Daup. Well, there be guests and meat now; how shall we do for music?

Cler. The smell of the venison, going through the street, will invite one noise of fiddlers or other.[2]

Daup. I would it would call the trumpeters thither!

Cler. Faith, there is hope; they have intelligence of all feasts. There's good correspondence betwixt them and the London cooks: 'tis twenty to one but we have them.

Daup. 'Twill be a most solemn day for my uncle, and an excellent fit of mirth for us.

Cler. Ay, if we can hold up the emulation betwixt Foole and Daw, and never bring them to expostulate.

Daup. Tut, flatter them both, as Truewit says, and you may take their understandings in a purse-net.[3] They'll believe

---

[1] *To have given you the* dor.] See p. 184 *b.*

[2] *One noise of fiddlers or other.*] This term, which occurs perpetually in our old dramatists, means a *company* or *concert*. In Jonson's days they sedulously attended taverns, ordinaries, &c., and seem to have been very importunate for admission to the guests. They usually consisted of three, and took their name from the leader of their little band. Thus we hear of "Mr. Sneak's *noise*," "Mr. Creak's *noise*," and, in Cartwright, of "Mr. Spindle's *noise*." These

names are probably the invention of Shakspeare, and the rest; but they prove the existence of the custom. When this term went out of use I cannot tell; but it was familiar in Dryden's time, who has it in his *Wild Gallant*, and elsewhere: "I hear him coming, and a whole *noise* of fiddlers at his heels."—*Maiden Queen.*

[3] *In a* purse-net.] A net, Johnson says, of which the mouth is drawn together by a string. It is mentioned by Decker: "These two conies will we ferret into our purse-net."—*Honest Whore.*

themselves to be just such men as we make them, neither more nor less. They have nothing, not the use of their senses, but by tradition.

Re-enter La-Foole, *like a sewer.*

Cler. See! Sir Amorous has his towel on already. Have you persuaded your cousin?

La-F. Yes, 'tis very feasible: she'll do anything, she says, rather than the La-Fooles shall be disgraced.

Daup. She is a noble kinswoman. It will be such a pestling device,[1] Sir Amorous; it will pound all your enemy's practices to powder, and blow him up with his own mine, his own train.

La-F. Nay, we'll give fire, I warrant you.

Cler. But you must carry it privately, without any noise, and take no notice by any means——

Re-enter Captain Otter.

Ott. Gentlemen, my princess says you shall have all her silver dishes, *festinate:* and she's gone to alter her tire a little, and go with you——

Cler. And yourself too, Captain Otter?

Daup. By any means, sir.

Ott. Yes, sir, I do mean it: but I would entreat my cousin Sir Amorous, and you, gentlemen, to be suitors to my princess, that I may carry my bull and my bear, as well as my horse.

Cler. That you shall do, Captain Otter.

La-F. My cousin will never consent, gentlemen.

Daup. She must consent, Sir Amorous, to reason.

La-F. Why, she says they are no decorum among ladies.

Ott. But they are *decora,* and that's better, sir.

Cler. Ay, she must hear argument. Did not Pasiphae, who was a queen, love

a bull? and was not Calisto, the mother of Arcas, turned into a bear, and made a star, Mistress Ursula, in the heavens?

Ott. O lord! that I could have said as much! I will have these stories painted in the Bear-garden, *ex Ovidii metamorphosi.*

Daup. Where is your princess, Captain? pray be our leader.

Ott. That I shall, sir.

Cler. Make haste, good Sir Amorous.
　　　　　　　　　　　　　　　　　[*Exeunt.*

SCENE II.—*A Room in* Morose's
House.

Enter Morose, Epicœne, Parson, *and*
Cutbeard.

Mor. Sir, there's an angel for yourself, and a brace of angels for your cold. Muse not at this manage of my bounty. It is fit we should thank fortune, double to nature, for any benefit she confers upon us; besides, it is your imperfection, but my solace.

Par. [*speaks as having a cold.*] I thank your worship; so it is mine now.

Mor. What says he, Cutbeard?

Cut. He says *præsto,* sir, whensoever your worship needs him, he can be ready with the like. He got this cold with sitting up late, and singing catches with cloth-workers.[2]

Mor. No more. I thank him.

Par. God keep your worship, and give you much joy with your fair spouse!—uh! uh! uh!

Mor. O, O! stay, Cutbeard! let him give me five shillings of my money back. As it is bounty to reward benefits, so it is equity to mulct injuries. I will have it. What says he?

Cler. He cannot change it, sir.

Mor. It must be changed.

Cut. Cough again. [*Aside to* Parson.

Mor. What says he?

Cut. He will cough out the rest, sir.

Par. Uh, uh, uh!

---

[1] *It will be such a* pestling *device,* &c.] Whalley has a portentous note here. "*Pestling* is a colloquial corruption of pestilence, or pestilent, used by our old writers for a sign of the superlative degree." It is certain, as he says, that pestilent is frequently used as an augmentative; but if he had only read to the end of the line, before he undertook to comment on the beginning of it, he would have seen that *pestling* meant simply pounding with a *pestle.*

This over haste is a sore evil with the commentators.

[2] *He got this cold with sitting up late, and singing catches with* cloth-workers.] The Protestants, who came from Flanders, and brought with them the woollen manufactory, were much given to singing at their work. To this Falstaff alludes. "I would I were a *weaver;* I could sing all manner of songs." These are the people whom our author here calls *cloth-workers,*— WHAL.

Mor. Away, away with him! stop his mouth! away! I forgive it.——
[*Exit* Cut. *thrusting out the* Par.

Epi. Fie, Master Morose, that you will use this violence to a man of the church.

Mor. How!

Epi. It does not become your gravity or breeding, as you pretend, in court, to have offered this outrage on a waterman, or any more boisterous creature, much less on a man of his civil coat.

Mor. You can speak then!

Epi. Yes, sir.

Mor. Speak out, I mean.

Epi. Ay, sir. Why, did you think you had married a statue, or a motion only? one of the French puppets, with the eyes turned with a wire? or some innocent out of the hospital,[1] that would stand with her hands thus, and a plaise mouth,[2] and look upon you?

Mor. O immodesty! a manifest woman! What, Cutbeard!

Epi. Nay, never quarrel with Cutbeard, sir; it is too late now. I confess it doth bate somewhat of the modesty I had, when I writ simply maid: but I hope I shall make it a stock still competent to the estate and dignity of your wife.

Mor. She can talk!

Epi. Yes, indeed, sir.

Enter Mute.

Mor. What, sirrah! None of my knaves there? where is this impostor Cutbeard?
[Mute *makes signs.*

Epi. Speak to him, fellow, speak to him! I'll have none of this coacted, unnatural dumbness in my house, in a family where I govern. [*Exit* Mute.

Mor. She is my regent already! I have married a Penthesilea, a Semiramis; sold my liberty to a distaff.

Enter Truewit.

True. Where's Master Morose?

Mor. Is he come again! Lord have mercy upon me!

True. I wish you all joy, Mistress Epicœne, with your grave and honourable match.

Epi. I return you the thanks, Master Truewit, so friendly a wish deserves.

Mor. She has acquaintance too!

True. God save you, sir, and give you all contentment in your fair choice, here! Before, I was the bird of night to you, the owl; but now I am the messenger of peace, a dove, and bring you the glad wishes of many friends to the celebration of this good hour.

Mor. What hour, sir?

True. Your marriage hour, sir. I commend your resolution, that, notwithstanding all the dangers I laid afore you, in the voice of a night-crow, would yet go on, and be yourself. It shews you are a man constant to your own ends, and upright to your purposes, that would not be put off with left-handed cries.[3]

Mor. How should you arrive at the knowledge of so much?

---

[1] *Or some* innocent *out of the hospital*,] i.e., some natural fool. In the margin of Whalley's copy I find this extract from the register of some parish church, probably his own: "Thomas Sole, an *innocent*, about the age of fifty years and upward, buried 19th September, 1605." Enough has now been said of this very common expression.

[2] *A plaise mouth*,] A mouth drawn all on one side.—WHAL.

So in a satire by T. Lodge, reprinted in Beloe's *Anecdotes*, vol. ii. p. 115:

"This makes Amphidius welcome to good cheer,
And spend his master fortie pounds a yeere,
And keep his *pleise-mouthed* wife in welts and gardes."

"Plaise-mouthed, I presume," the editor says, "means *foul-mouthed*, or rather, perhaps, with a mouth as *large* as that of the plaise." But the plaise has a small mouth: and plaise-mouthed is used by our old writers for primness, affected prudery, or contempt. Thus Decker: "I should have made a *wry mouth* at the world like a playse."—*Honest Whore.* And Nashe, in his

Lenten Stuff, "None woone the day but the Herring, whom all their clamorous suffrages saluted with *Vive le roy*, save only the *playse* and the butte, that made *wry mouthes* at him, and for their mocking have *wry* mouths ever since." The editor is not more fortunate in his explanation of *welts and gardes* in the same line. "Welts and gardes," he says, "are gowns and petticoats." Welts, it is well known, are broad hems, or facings; gardes are borderings of lace, fur, &c. It is better to leave our old terms alone, than to explain them at random.

[3] *That would not be put off with* left-handed cries.] Inauspicious or unlucky cries; alluding to Virgil:

"*Sæpe* sinistra *cavâ prædixit ab ilice cornix;*"

as he had called himself the *night-crow* before.—WHAL.

This is Upton's note, with the exception of the conclusion, which seems incorrect. Whatever the *night-crow* may be, it is not the *cornix* of Virgil. Jonson literally translates the Greek word νυκτικοραξ, a species of owl, with which we are not acquainted.

True. Why, did you ever hope, sir, committing the secrecy of it to a barber, that less than the whole town should know it? you might as well have told it the conduit, or the bake-house, or the infantry that follow the court,[1] and with more security. Could your gravity forget so old and noted a remnant as, *Lippis et tonsoribus notum?* Well, sir, forgive it yourself now, the fault, and be communicable with your friends. Here will be three or four fashionable ladies from the college to visit you presently, and their train of minions and followers.

Mor. Bar my doors! bar my doors! Where are all my eaters?[2] my mouths, now?——

Enter Servants.

Bar up my doors, you varlets!

Epi. He is a varlet that stirs to such an office. Let them stand open. I would see him that dares move his eyes toward it. Shall I have a barricado made against my friends, to be barred of any pleasure they can bring in to me with their honourable visitation?

[*Exeunt* Ser.

Mor. O Amazonian impudence!

'*True.* Nay, faith, in this, sir, she speaks but reason; and, methinks, is more continent than you. Would you go to bed so presently, sir, afore noon? a man of your head and hair should owe more to that reverend ceremony, and not mount the marriage-bed like a town-bull, or a mountain-goat; but stay the due season; and ascend it then with religion and fear. Those delights are to be steeped in the humour and silence of the night; and give the day to

---

[1] *The infantry that follow the court,*] Meaning perhaps the idle train that attended the Progresses, and found accommodation as they could. One of this description is mentioned by Webster: "A lousy knave, that within this twenty years rode with the *blackguards,* p. 125 *b,* in the duke's carriages, amongst spits and dripping-pans."—*White Devil.*

[2] *Where are all my* eaters?] Eaters, as I have already observed, p. 124 *b,* are servants. In *Antony and Cleopatra* a similar expression occurs—"by one that looks on feeders," i.e., says Dr. Johnson, "by one that looks on while others are eating." That Dr. Johnson should give a wrong interpretation of the word is not extraordinary, as he totally mistakes the whole drift of the passage. He is followed by Steevens, who, in a few plain words, sets everything right; and quotes the expression in the text, to justify his sense of the term. Mr. Malone throws aside the judicious interpretation of Steevens, and brings back the egregious blunder of Dr. Johnson. The opportunity of insulting the memory of our poet was not to be lost.—"So *fantastick* and *pedantick* a writer," he says, "as Ben Jonson, having *in one passage* made *one* of his characters call his attendants *eaters,* appears to *me* a very slender ground for supposing *feeders* and *servants* to be synonymous." There can be no doubt of it; but Mr. Malone is so imperfectly acquainted with "Ben Jonson," that he constantly hazards his own character for accuracy, (to say nothing more,) whenever he attempts to speak of him on any specific grounds. Eaters, and its synonyms, are used in *more than one place,* and by more than *one character,* in Jonson, for servants. Nor does this sense of the word rest on his authority, as Mr. Malone supposes. I can produce him twenty instances of the same expressions, used in the same sense. Sir W. Davenant was not a *pedantic* writer, yet he has (*The Wits,* act iii.) " tall *eaters* in *blue coats,*" the livery of *servants,* as Mr. Malone

well knows; nor was Fletcher a *fantastic* one, yet we find in the *Nice Valour,* act iii. sc. 1, "*servants* he has, lusty tall feeders." And again—but these are so direct to the purpose, that more is unnecessary.

The passage in *Antony and Cleopatra,* which gave rise to these remarks, is contained in the last scene of the third act. Antony enters unexpectedly, and finds Thyreus (Cæsar's messenger) kissing Cleopatra's hand — upon which, after treating Thyreus with the utmost contempt, and ordering him to be whipt, like a slave—he exclaims,

"Ha!
Have I my pillow left unpressed in Rome,
Forborne the getting of a lawful race,
And by a gem of women, to be abused
By one that looks on feeders!"

Both Dr. Johnson and Mr. Malone take the person by whom Antony is *abused* to be Thyreus. A stranger idea was never conceived. It is Cleopatra. To ask Thyreus, who, by the bye, is out of hearing, whether he had left his wife, &c., to be abused by him, would be an absurdity without a name; but to put the same question to Cleopatra, was perfectly just and natural. Have I abandoned Octavia, "a gem of women," to be abused by a woman so base as to look on servants!—and accordingly he harps on nothing through several speeches but the indiscriminate lewdness of Cleopatra, and the low and servile occupation of Thyreus.

It was not without surprise that I read Mr. Pye's criticism on this passage: " I think Malone and Johnson right," he says; "I do not see how it can be a reproach to look on servants."—*Comm. on Shak.* p. 268. Surely it cannot be necessary to remind Mr. Pye that to *look on* means to affect, to regard with kindness; and if he thinks this no reproach to a queen, and a declared mistress of "the triple pillar of the world," I can only say that he differs much from Shakspeare and Mark Antony.

other open pleasures,[1] and jollities of feasting, of music, of revels, of discourse : we'll
have all, sir, that may make your Hymen
high and happy.

Mor. O my torment, my torment !

True. Nay, if you endure the first half
hour, sir, so tediously, and with this irksomeness ; what comfort or hope can this fair
gentlewoman make to herself hereafter, in
the consideration of so many years as are
to come——

Mor. Of my affliction. Good sir, depart,
and let her do it alone.

True. I have done, sir.

Mor. That cursed barber !

True. Yes, faith, a cursed wretch indeed,
sir.

Mor. I have married his cittern, that's
common to all men.[2] Some plague above
the plague——

True. All Egypt's ten plagues.

Mor. Revenge me on him !

True. 'Tis very well, sir. If you laid on
a curse or two more, I'll assure you he'll
bear them. As, that he may get the pox
with seeking to cure it, sir ; or, that while
he is curling another man's hair, his own
may drop off ; or, for burning some male-
bawd's lock, he may have his brain beat
out with the curling-iron.

Mor. No, let the wretch live wretched.
May he get the itch, and his shop so lousy,
as no man dare come at him, nor he come
at no man !

True. Ay, and if he would swallow all
his balls for pills, let not them purge him.

Mor. Let his warming-pan be ever cold.

True. A perpetual frost underneath it,
sir.

Mor. Let him never hope to see fire
again.

True. But in hell, sir.

Mor. His chairs be always empty, his
scissors rust, and his combs mould in their
cases.

True. Very dreadful that ! And may he
lose the invention, sir, of carving lanterns
in paper.

Mor. Let there be no bawd carted that
year, to employ a bason of his :[3] but let him
be glad to eat his sponge for bread.

True. And drink lotium to it, and much
good do him.

Mor. Or, for want of bread——

True. Eat ear-wax, sir. I'll help you.
Or draw his own teeth, and add them to
the lute-string.

Mor. No, beat the old ones to powder,
and make bread of them.

True. Yes, make meal of the mill-
stones.

Mor. May all the botches and burns
that he has cured on others break out upon
him.

---

[1] *Give the day to open pleasures,* &c.] These
are the precise delights which attended the nuptials of poor Morose, in Libanius : ην μεν γαρ
ουδ' εκεινα μετρια, κροτος πολυς, γελως σφοδρος,
ορχησις ασχημων, ὑμεναιος νουν ουκ εχων· κ. τ. λ.
p. 303.

[2] *I have married his* cittern, *that's* common
to all men.] On this expression much has been
written which might easily be spared. It appears from innumerable passages in our old
writers, that barbers' shops were furnished with
some musical instrument, (commonly a cittern,* or
guitar,) for the amusement of such customers as
chose to strum upon it while waiting for their
turn to be shaved, &c. : and this point once established, no farther difficulty remains. It should
be recollected that the patience of the customers,
if the shop was at all popular, must, in those
tedious days of lovelocks and beards of the
most fantastic cuts, have been frequently put to
very severe trials. Some kind of amusement,
therefore, was necessary to beguile the time,
and as newspapers had not then descended to
the lower classes, a more innocent or effectual
one than an instrument, in pretty general use,
could not readily be found. However this may
be, the practice is certain. Thus Middleton :
"I gave that *barber* a fustian suit, and twice redeemed his *cittern.*"—*Mayor of Quinborough,*

act iii. sc. 3. And Decker, "A barber's *cittern*
for *every serving-man to play upon.*"—*Honest
Whore.* Again : in the first edition of *Every
Man in his Humour :* "I can compare him to
nothing more happily than a *barber's virginals,*†
for *every* man may play upon him," act iii. sc. 2.
And finally, for enough perhaps has already
been said on the subject, in a *Defence of the Female Sex,* published at a subsequent period, the
writer observes of a virtuoso, that "his inventory
can be no more compleat without two or three
remarkable signatures, than an apothecarie's
shop without a tortoise and a crocodile, or a
barber's without a *battered cittern.*"

[3] *Let there be no bawd carted, to employ a*
bason *of his :*] To make the punishment of these
and inferior characters more notorious, beadles,
and sometimes volunteers among the rabble,
attended the progress of the cart, beating
basons, brass kettles, &c. To this practice there
are numerous allusions in our old writers. See
the *New Inn.*

---

* The cittern of Jonson's days differed little
from the guitar, as to form. It was strung with
wire instead of catgut, like the guitar, and seems
to have been in great vogue.

† In the subsequent edition this is altered to
"a drum."

True. And he now forget the cure of them in himself, sir; or, if he do remember it, let him have scraped all his linen into lint for 't, and have not a rag left him for to set up with.

Mor. Let him never set up again, but have the gout in his hands for ever! Now, no more, sir.

True. O, that last was too high set; you might go less with him, i' faith, and be revenged enough: as, that he be never able to new-paint his pole——

Mor. Good sir, no more, I forgot myself.[1]

True. Or, want credit to take up with a combmaker——

Mor. No more, sir.

True. Or, having broken his glass in a former despair, fall now into a much greater, of ever getting another——

Mor. I beseech you, no more.

True. Or, that he never be trusted with trimming of any but chimney-sweepers——

Mor. Sir——

True. Or, may he cut a collier's throat with his razor, by chance-medley, and yet be hanged for 't.

Mor. I will forgive him rather than hear any more. I beseech you, sir.

Enter Daw, *introducing* Lady Haughty, Centaure, Mavis, *and* Trusty.

Daw. This way, madam.

Mor. O, the sea breaks in upon me! another flood! an inundation! I shall be overwhelmed with noise. It beats already at my shores. I feel an earthquake in myself for 't.

Daw. 'Give you joy, mistress.

Mor. Has she servants too![2]

Daw. I have brought some ladies here to see and know you. My Lady Haughty [*as he presents them severally,* Epi. *kisses them.*]—this my Lady Centaure—Mistress Dol Mavis — Mistress Trusty, my Lady Haughty's woman. Where's your husband? let's see him: can he endure no noise? let me come to him.

Mor. What nomenclator is this!

True. Sir John Daw, sir, your wife's servant, this.

Mor. A Daw, and her servant! O, 'tis decreed, 'tis decreed of me, an she have such servants. [*Going.*

True. Nay, sir, you must kiss the ladies; you must not go away now; they come toward you to seek you out.

Hau. I' faith, Master Morose, would you steal a marriage thus, in the midst of so many friends, and not acquaint us? Well, I'll kiss you, notwithstanding the justice of my quarrel: you shall give me leave, mistress, to use a becoming familiarity with your husband.

Epi. Your ladyship does me an honour in it, to let me know he is so worthy your favour: as you have done both him and me grace to visit so unprepared a pair to entertain you.

Mor. Compliment! compliment!

Epi. But I must lay the burden of that upon my servant here.

Hau. It shall not need, Mistress Morose; we will all bear rather than one shall be opprest.

Mor. I know it: and you will teach her the faculty, if she be to learn it.

[*Walks aside while the rest talk apart.*

Hau. Is this the Silent Woman?

Cen. Nay, she has found her tongue since she was married, Master Truewit says.

Hau. O, Master Truewit! 'save you. What kind of creature is your bride here? she speaks, methinks!

True. Yes, madam, believe it, she is a gentlewoman of very absolute behaviour, and of a good race.

Hau. And Jack Daw told us she could not speak!

True. So it was carried in plot, madam, to put her upon this old fellow, by Sir Dauphine, his nephew, and one or two more of us: but she is a woman of an excellent assurance, and an extraordinary happy wit and tongue. You shall see her make rare sport with Daw ere night.

---

[1] *Good sir, no more, I forgot myself.*] "This (as Upton observes) is a very fine instance of the suspense of character. Morose, through the impetuous desire of revenge, for a while acts out of his real character."—WHAL.

Notwithstanding this note is quoted by Whalley with approbation, it does not altogether satisfy me. "Suspense of character" is very fine, and has probably some meaning or other, though I am unable to discover it. I can see, however, that both Upton and Whalley have mistaken the character of Morose: they suppose it to be a dislike of noise; whereas this is an accidental quality altogether dependent upon the master-passion, or "humour," a most inveterate and odious self-love. This will explain his conduct in many places where it has been taxed with inconsistency, and vindicate the deep discernment of the poet.

[2] *Has she servants too!*] Authorised admirers; see p. 38 b.

Hau. And he brought us to laugh at her!

True. That falls out often, madam, that he that thinks himself the master-wit, is the master-fool. I assure your ladyship, ye cannot laugh at her.

Hau. No, we'll have her to the college. An she have wit, she shall be one of us, shall she not, Centaure? we'll make her a collegiate.

Cen. Yes, faith, madam, and Mavis and she will set up a side.[1]

True. Believe it, madam, and Mistress Mavis she will sustain her part.

Mav. I'll tell you that, when I have talked with her, and tried her.

Hau. Use her very civilly, Mavis.

Mav. So I will, madam.
                              [*Whispers her.*

Mor. Blessed minute! that they would whisper thus ever!   [*Aside.*

True. In the mean time, madam, would but your ladyship help to vex him a little; you know his disease, talk to him about the wedding ceremonies, or call for your gloves, or——

Hau. Let me alone. Centaure, help me. Master bridegroom, where are you?

Mor. O, it was too miraculously good to last!   [*Aside.*

Hau. We see no ensigns of a wedding here; no character of a bride-ale: where be our scarves and our gloves? I pray you, give them us. Let us know your bride's colours, and yours at least.

Cen. Alas, madam, he has provided none.

Mor. Had I known your ladyship's painter, I would.

Hau. He has given it you, Centaure, i' faith. But do you hear, Master Morose? a jest will not absolve you in this manner. You that have sucked the milk of the court, and from thence have been brought up to the very strong meats and wine of it; been a courtier from the biggen to the night-cap,[2] as we may say, and you to offend in such a high point of ceremony as this, and let your nuptials want all marks of solemnity! How much plate have you lost to-day (if you had but regarded your profit), what gifts, what friends, through your mere rusticity!

Mor. Madam——

Hau. Pardon me, sir, I must insinuate your errors to you ; no gloves? no garters? no scarves? no epithalamium? no masque?

Daw. Yes, madam, I'll make an epithalamium, I promise my mistress; I have begun it already: will your ladyship hear it?

Hau. Ay, good Jack Daw.

Mor. Will it please your ladyship command a chamber, and be private with your friend? you shall have your choice of rooms to retire to after: my whole house is yours. I know it hath been your ladyship's errand into the city at other times, however now you have been unhappily diverted upon me; but I shall be loth to break any honourable custom of your ladyship's. And therefore, good madam——

Epi. Come, you are a rude bridegroom, to entertain ladies of honour in this fashion.

Cen. He is a rude groom indeed.

True. By that light you deserve to be grafted, and have your horns reach from one side of the island to the other. Do not mistake me, sir; I but speak this to give the ladies some heart again, not for any malice to you.

Mor. Is this your bravo, ladies?

True. As God [shall] help me, if you utter such another word, I'll take mistress bride in, and begin to you in a very sad cup; do you see? Go to, know your friends, and such as love you.

Enter Clerimont, *followed by a number of musicians.*

Cler. By your leave, ladies. Do you want any music? I have brought you variety of noises.[3] Play, sirs, all of you.
               [*Aside to the musicians, who strike up all together.*

Mor. O, a plot, a plot, a plot, a plot upon me! this day I shall be their anvil to work on, they will grate me asunder. 'Tis worse than the noise of a saw.

Cler. No, they are hair, rosin, and guts: I can give you the receipt.

True. Peace, boys!

Cler. Play! I say.

---

[1] *Cen. Yes, faith, madam, and Mavis and she will* set up a side.] Alluding to parties at cards. To *set up a side* was to become partners in the game. See Massinger, vol. i. p. 150, where several examples of this familiar expression will be found.

[2] *From the biggen to the* night-cap, *as we may say,*] i.e., from infancy to age. See p. 394.

[3] *I have brought you variety of* noises] i.e. several little bands of musicians. See above, p. 426.

True. Peace, rascals! You see who's your friend now, sir: take courage, put on a martyr's resolution. Mock down all their attemptings with patience: 'tis but a day, and I would suffer heroically. Should an ass exceed me in fortitude? no. You betray your infirmity with your hanging dull ears, and make them insult: bear up bravely, and constantly. [*La Foole passes over the stage as a sewer, followed by servants carrying dishes, and* Mistress Otter.] Look you here, sir, what honour is done you unexpected, by your nephew; a wedding-dinner come, and a knight-sewer before it, for the more reputation: and fine Mistress Otter, your neighbour, in the rump or tail of it.

Mor. Is that Gorgon, that Medusa come! hide me, hide me.

True. I warrant you, sir, she will not transform you. Look upon her with a good courage. Pray you entertain her, and conduct your guests in. No!—Mistress bride, will you entreat in the ladies? your bridegroom is so shamefaced here.

Epi. Will it please your ladyship, madam?

Hau. With the benefit of your company, mistress.

Epi. Servant, pray you perform your duties.

Daw. And glad to be commanded, mistress.

Cen. How like you her wit, Mavis?

Mav. Very prettily, absolutely well.

Mrs. Ott. 'Tis my place.

Mav. You shall pardon me, Mistress Otter.

Mrs. Ott. Why, I am a collegiate.

Mav. But not in ordinary.

Mrs. Ott. But I am.

Mav. We'll dispute that within.
　　　　　　　　[*Exeunt* Ladies.

Cler. Would this had lasted a little longer.

True. And that they had sent for the heralds.

Enter Captain Otter.

—Captain Otter! what news?

Ott. I have brought my bull, bear, and horse, in private, and yonder are the trumpeters without, and the drum, gentlemen. [*The drum and trumpets sound within.*

Mor. O, O, O!

Ott. And we will have a rouse in each of them,[1] anon, for bold Britons, i' faith.
　　　　　　　　[*They sound again.*

Mor. O, O, O!　　　　　[*Exit hastily.*

Omnes. Follow, follow, follow!
　　　　　　　　[*Exeunt.*

ACT IV.

SCENE I.—*A Room in* Morose's *House.*

Enter Truewit *and* Clerimont.

True. Was there ever poor bridegroom so tormented? or man, indeed?

Cler. I have not read of the like in the chronicles of the land.

True. Sure, he cannot but go to a place of rest, after all this purgatory.

Cler. He may presume it, I think.

True. The spitting, the coughing, the laughter, the neezing, the farting, dancing, noise of the music, and her masculine and loud commanding, and urging the whole family, makes him think he has married a fury.[2]

Cler. And she carries it up bravely.

True. Ay, she takes any occasion to speak: that's the height on't.

Cler. And how soberly Dauphine labours to satisfy him, that it was none of his plot!

True. And has almost brought him to the faith, in the article. Here he comes.——

Enter Sir Dauphine.

Where is he now? what's become of him, Dauphine?

Daup. O, hold me up a little, I shall go away in the jest else.[3] He has got on his

---

[1] *And we will have a* rouse *in each of them,*] A *rouse,* it may be just necessary to observe, is a full glass, a bumper, and was usually drank to some toast. See more of this in *Massinger,* vol. i. 237. Whalley justly observes that this scene is conducted with consummate art and judgment: the gradual accumulation and swell of the several noises, from the speaking of Epiœne to the grand finale, or chorus of boisterous shouts, drums, and trumpets, which drives

Morose off the stage, is highly comic, and in action must be singularly amusing.

[2] *He has married a fury.*] This, with what precedes it, is from Libanius: ἅπαντα πανταχόθεν, ἡνίκα ἡγούμην ταύτην τὴν ἐρινννυν, κ. τ. λ. See p. 303.

[3] Daup. *O, hold me up a little, I shall go away in the jest else.*] I shall faint, or fall down with laughing.—WHAL.
Is it not rather, I shall expire in my fit, i.e., die with laughing?

whole nest of nightcaps, and locked himself up in the top of the house, as high as
ever he can climb from the noise. I peeped
in at a cranny, and saw him sitting over a
cross-beam of the roof, like him on the
saddler's horse in Fleet-street, upright : and
he will sleep there.

Cler. But where are your collegiates ?

Daup. Withdrawn with the bride in
private.

True. O, they are instructing her in the
college-grammar. If she have grace with
them, she knows all their secrets instantly.

Cler. Methinks the Lady Haughty looks
well to-day, for all my dispraise of her in
the morning. I think I shall come about
to thee again, Truewit.

True. Believe it, I told you right.
Women ought to repair the losses time and
years have made in their features, with
dressings.[1] And an intelligent woman, if
she know by herself the least defect, will
be most curious to hide it : and it becomes
her. If she be short,[2] let her sit much,
lest, when she stands, she be thought to
sit. If she have an ill foot, let her wear
her gown the longer, and her shoe the
thinner. If a fat hand and scald nails, let

her carve the less, and act in gloves. If a
sour breath, let her never discourse fasting,
and always talk at her distance. If she
have black and rugged teeth, let her offer
the less at laughter, especially if she laugh
wide and open.

Cler. O, you shall have some women,[3]
when they laugh, you would think they
brayed, it is so rude and——

True. Ay, and others, that will stalk in
their gait like an estrich, and take huge
strides.[4] I cannot endure such a sight. I
love measure in the feet, and number in
the voice : they are gentlenesses that oftentimes draw no less than the face.

Daup. How camest thou to study these
creatures so exactly ? I would thou wouldst
make me a proficient.

True. Yes, but you must leave to live in
your chamber, then, a month together upon
Amadis de Gaul, or Don Quixote, as you
are wont ; and come abroad where the
matter is frequent, to court, to tiltings,
public shows and feasts, to plays, and
church sometimes : thither they come to
shew their new tires too, to see, and to be
seen.[5] In these places a man shall find
whom to love, whom to play with, whom

---

[1] *True. Believe it, I told you right. Women
ought to repair the losses time and years have
made in their features, with dressings.*] Truewit, as Upton observes, here resumes the subject
of ladies' dressings, &c. into which he had entered
on his first meeting with Clerimont (p.407 *a*), and
which he continues to illustrate from Ovid. He
certainly could not easily have had recourse to
better authority ; but the reader perhaps will be
inclined to think that he has availed himself of
it too freely. All that can be said is, that in
Jonson's days the original was less familiarly
known than at present ; that it is copied with
elegance and spirit, and adapted to the language
and manners of the age with no inconsiderable
degree of ingenuity. Upton (for Whalley, who
merely copies him, is out of the question) has
produced a few of the passages imitated, to
which I have added such as readily occurred to
me. More might unquestionably be found ; but
the subject is not of sufficient importance to
justify a laborious research.

[2] *If she be short, &c.*]

" *Rara tamen mendo facies caret ; occule
mendas,
Quamque potes, vitium corporis abde tui.
Si brevis es, sedeas, ne stans videare sedere,
Inque tuo jaceas quantulacunque toro——
Pes malus in nivea semper celetur aluta
Arida nec vinclis crura resolve suis.—
Exiguo signet gestu quodcunque loquetur,
Cui digiti pingues, et scaber unguis erunt.
Cui gravis oris odor, nunquam jejuna lo-
quatur,*

*Et semper spatio distet ab ore viri.
Si niger, aut ingens, aut non erit ordine
natus
Dens tibi, ridendo maxima damna feres.*"
Art. Amand. lib. iii. 260.

[3] *O, you shall have some women, &c.*]

" *Illa sonat raucam, quiddam inamabile
stridet,
Ut rudit ad scabram turpis asella molam.*"
Ibid.

[4] *Ay, and others that will take huge strides,
&c.*]

" *Est et in incessu pars non temnenda decoris :
Allicit ignotos ille fugatque viros,
Hæc movet arte latus, tunicisque fluentibus
auras
Excipit ; extensos fertque refertque pedes,
&c.*—Ibid. v. 300.

[5] Thither they come to shew their new tires,
to see and be seen, &c.]

" *Sic ruit ad celebres cultissima fæmina ludos,
Copia judicium sæpe morata meum :
Spectatum veniunt, veniunt spectentur ut
ipsæ ;
Ille locus casti damna pudoris habet.—
Sed tu præcipue curvis venare theatris ;
Hæc loca sunt voto fertiliora tuo.
Illic invenies quod ames, quod ludere possis,
Quodque semel tangas, quodque tenere
velis.*"—Lib. i. 90.

to touch once, whom to hold ever. The variety arrests his judgment. A wench to please a man comes not down dropping from the ceiling, as he lies on his back droning a tobacco-pipe.[1] He must go where she is.

Daup. Yes, and be never the nearer.

True. Out, heretic! That diffidence makes thee worthy it should be so.

Cler. He says true to you, Dauphine.

Daup. Why?

True. A man should not doubt to overcome any woman. Think he can vanquish them, and he shall: for though they deny, their desire is to be tempted. Penelope herself cannot hold out long. Ostend, you saw, was taken at last.[2] You must perséver, and hold to your purpose. They would solicit us, but that they are afraid. Howsoever, they wish in their hearts we should solicit them. Praise them, flatter them, you shall never want eloquence or trust: even the chastest delight to feel themselves that way rubbed. With praises you must mix kisses too : if they take them they'll take more—though they strive, they would be overcome.

Cler. O, but a man must beware of force.

True. It is to them an acceptable violence,[3] and has oft-times the place of the greatest courtesy. She that might have been forced, and you let her go free without touching, though then she seem to thank you, will ever hate you after; and glad in the face, is assuredly sad at the heart.

Cler. But all women are not to be taken all ways.[4]

True. 'Tis true; no more than all birds, or all fishes. If you appear learned to an ignorant wench, or jocund to a sad, or witty to a foolish, why, she presently begins

---

[1] *A wench to please a man comes not down dropping from the ceiling, as he lies on his back* droning a tobacco-pipe.] When I first observed this passage quoted by Upton, I turned to it with some curiosity, in the hope of discovering the meaning of *droning a tobacco-pipe*, an expression which had puzzled me in a former play, p. 114 *a*, and was not a little confounded at meeting with the following note, which may perhaps amuse the reader : "A *wench, ôuella*: so the word was used formerly." Shakspeare is then quoted for the fact—and the critic proceeds: "The etymology of the word seems to me to come from *juvenca, juvencula, ôer aphæresin; uti* uncle *ab avunculus*, belly *ab umbilicus, pars pro toto*" ! (p. 81). There was not a person in the kingdom who wanted any information concerning the meaning of *wench*; (which, by the way, is not given, after all) ; whereas many perhaps would have thanked him for an explanation of "droning a tobacco-pipe." Whether this alludes to inhaling the smoke with a monotonous sound, imitative of the sleepy hum of a drone ; or simply to using the pipe with the characteristic indolence of this insect, or to both, as I have never met with the expression in any other writer, I cannot tell ; but think the last not improbable. As to Upton's ridiculous derivation of wench, it is kept in excellent countenance by Horne Tooke, who brings it from the Saxon pincian, to *wink*: i.e., "one who may be had by a nod or *wink!*" To conclude a note already too long, *wench* (*wensch*) was used by the Saxons, as it is by their descendants at this day, for a young woman (generally for a domestic, or one of inferior degree), and the context, as in all similar cases, determines whether it means anything more. The idea is from Ovid :

" *Elige cui dicas, Tu mihi sola places;
Hæc tibi non tenues veniet delapsa per auras ;
Quærenda est oculis apta puella tuis.*"
Ib. v. 678.

[Jonson was evidently thinking of the *drone* of a *bagpipe*—its largest tube.—F. C.]

[2] Penelope *herself cannot hold out long.* Ostend, *you saw, was taken at last.*]

"*Penelopen ipsam, persta modo, tempore vinces,
Capta vides sero Pergama, capta tamen,
&c.*—Ibid. v. 477.

"*Ostend*," Upton says, "was taken in 1604, by the Marquis Spinola, after a siege of three years, and the slaughter of a hundred and twenty thousand men on both sides."

[3] *It is to them an acceptable violence, &c.*]

" *Vim licet apelles, grata est vis ipsa puellis,
Quod juvat, invitæ sæpe dedisse volunt,
Quæcunque est subitæ Veneris violata rapina,
Gaudet, et improbitas muneris instar habet.
At quæ cum cogi posset, non tacta recessit,
Ut simulet vultu gaudia, tristis erit.*"
Ibid. v. 678.

[4] *But all women are not to be taken all ways.*]

" *Finiturus eram—sed svnt diversa puellis
Pectora; mille animos excipe mille modis.*"

What follows is from the same source :

" *Hi jaculo pisces, illi capiuntur ab hamis ;
Hos cava contento retia fune trahunt:
Nec tibi conveniat cunctos modus unus ad annos ;
Longius insidias cauta videbit anus.
Si doctus videare rudi, petulansve pudenti ;
Diffidet miseræ protinus illa sibi :
Inde fit, ut, quæ se timuit committere honesto,
Vilis in amplexus inferioris eat.*"
Ibid. i. 770.

The remainder is copied with somewhat more freedom ; but the reader perhaps is already more than satisfied.

to mistrust herself. You must approach them in their own height, their own line; for the contrary makes many that fear to commit themselves to noble and worthy fellows, run into the embraces of a rascal. If she love wit, give verses, though you borrow them of a friend, or buy them, to have good. If valour, talk of your sword, and be frequent in the mention of quarrels, though you be staunch in fighting.[1] If activity, be seen on your barbary often, or leaping over stools, for the credit of your back. If she love good clothes or dressing, have your learned council about you every morning, your French tailor, barber, linener, &c. Let your powder, your glass, and your comb be your dearest acquaintance. Take more care for the ornament of your head, than the safety; and wish the commonwealth rather troubled, than a hair about you. That will take her. Then, if she be covetous and craving, do you promise anything, and perform sparingly; so shall you keep her in appetite still. Seem as you would give, but be like a barren field that yields little; or unlucky dice to foolish and hoping gamesters. Let your gifts be slight and dainty, rather than precious. Let cunning be above cost. Give cherries at time of year, or apricots; and say, they were sent you out of the country, though you bought them in Cheapside. Admire her tires; like her in all fashions; compare her in every habit to some deity; invent excellent dreams to flatter her, and riddles; or, if she be a great one, perform always the second parts to her: like what she likes, praise whom she praises, and fail not to make the household and servants yours, yea, the whole family, and salute

them by their names ('tis but light cost, if you can purchase them so), and make her physician your pensioner, and her chief woman. Nor will it be out of your gain to make love to her too, so she follow, not usher her lady's pleasure. All blabbing is taken away, when she comes to be a part of the crime.

Daup. On what courtly lap hast thou late slept, to come forth so sudden and absolute a courtling?

True. Good faith, I should rather question you, that are so hearkening after these mysteries. I begin to suspect your diligence, Dauphine. Speak, art thou in love in earnest?

Daup. Yes, by my troth, am I; 'twere ill dissembling before thee.

True. With which of them, I prithee?

Daup. With all the collegiates.

Cler. Out on thee! We'll keep you at home, believe it, in the stable, an you be such a stallion.

True. No; I like him well. Men should love wisely, and all women; some one for the face, and let her please the eye; another for the skin, and let her please the touch; a third for the voice, and let her please the ear; and where the objects mix, let the senses so too. Thou wouldst think it strange if I should make them all in love with thee afore night!

Daup. I would say, thou hadst the best philtre in the world, and couldst do more than Madam Medea, or Doctor Foreman.[2]

True. If I do not, let me play the mountebank for my meat while I live, and the bawd for my drink.

Daup. So be it I say.

---

[1] *Be frequent in the mention of quarrels, though you be* staunch *in fighting.*] The sense seems to be:—Though you should really be a brave man, and therefore not naturally inclined to boast of your valour; yet, to please your mistress, you may often make it the subject of your discourse.

[2] *Doctor Foreman.*] This was a poor stupid wretch who pretended to deal with spirits for the recovery of lost spoons, &c. Stupid as he was, however, he found employment in his profession, and had credit enough to be implicated in the infamous business of Sir Thomas Overbury. Luckily he died before the transaction became public, and thus escaped the halter. "He lived in Lambeth" (says Lilly, almost as great a knave as himself) "with a very good report of the neighbourhood, especially of the poor, unto whom he was charitable. He was a person that in horary questions, especially thefts,

was very judicious and fortunate, so also in sicknesses, which indeed was his masterpiece. In resolving questions about marriage he had good success; in other questions very moderate."—Lilly's *Hist.* p. 17. One of his books, written by the devil, fell into the historian's hands. Such things were then too common to excite any astonishment: and therefore Lilly contents himself with copying the doctor's memorandum, "This I made the devil write with his own hand" (should it not be claw?) "in Lambeth Fields, 1596, in June or July, as I now remember." This "worthy person" foretold his own death; and continued in good health so near the appointed period, that his wife became very uneasy, and "twitted him in the teeth." He saved his time, however, and died with more honesty than he had lived, according to his promise: "a most sad storm of wind immediately following."—*Ibid.* p. 23.

Enter Otter, *with his three cups,* Daw, *and* La-Foole.

Ott. O lord, gentlemen, how my knights and I have mist you here !

Cler. Why, Captain, what service, what service ?

Ott. To see me bring up my bull, bear, and horse to fight.

Daw. Yes, faith, the Captain says we shall be his dogs to bait them.

Daup. A good employment.

True. Come on, let's see your course, then.

La-F. I am afraid my cousin will be offended, if she come.

Ott. Be afraid of nothing.—Gentlemen, I have placed the drum and the trumpets, and one to give them the sign when you are ready. Here's my bull for myself,[1] and my bear for Sir John Daw, and my horse for Sir Amorous. Now set your foot to mine, and yours to his, and——

La-F. Pray God my cousin come not.

Ott. St. George and St. Andrew, fear no cousins. Come, sound, sound! [*Drum and trumpets sound.*] *Et rauco strepuerunt cornua cantu.*   [*They drink.*

True. Well said, Captain, i' faith; well fought at the bull.

Cler. Well held at the bear.

True. Low, low! Captain.

Daup. O, the horse has kicked off his dog already.

La-F. I cannot drink it, as I am a knight.

True. Ods so ! off with his spurs, somebody.

La-F. It goes against my conscience. My cousin will be angry with it.

Daw. I have done mine.

True. You fought high and fair, Sir John.

Cler. At the head.

Daup. Like an excellent bear-dog.

Cler. You take no notice of the business, I hope ?

Daw. Not a word, sir; you see we are jovial.

Ott. Sir Amorous, you must not equivocate. It must be pulled down, for all my cousin.

Cler. 'Sfoot, if you take not your drink they'll think you are discontented with something ; you'll betray all, if you take the least notice.

La-F. Not I; I'll both drink and talk then.

Ott. You must pull the horse on his knees, Sir Amorous ; fear no cousins. *Jacta est alea.*

True. O, now he's in his vein, and bold. The least hint given him of his wife now will make him rail desperately.

Cler. Speak to him of her.

True. Do you, and I'll fetch her to the hearing of it.   [*Exit.*

Daup. Captain He-Otter, your She-Otter is coming, your wife.

Ott. Wife ! buz ! *titivilitium ?*[2] There's no such thing in nature. I confess, gentlemen, I have a cook, a laundress, a house-drudge, that serves my necessary turns, and goes under that title; but he's an ass that will be so uxorious to tie his affections to one circle. Come, the name dulls appetite. Here, replenish again ; another bout. [*Fills the cups again.*] Wives are nasty, sluttish animals.

Daup. O, Captain.

Ott. As ever the earth bare, *tribus verbis.* Where's Master Truewit.

Daw. He's slipt aside, sir.

Cler. But you must drink and be jovial.

Daw. Yes, give it me.

La-F. And me too.

Daw. Let's be jovial.

La-F. As jovial as you will.

Ott. Agreed. Now you shall have the bear, cousin, and Sir John Daw the horse, and I'll have the bull still. Sound, Tritons of the Thames ! [*Drum and trumpets sound again.*] *Nunc est bibendum, nunc pede libero——*

Mor. [*above.*] Villains, murderers, sons of the earth, and traitors, what do you there?

Cler. O, now the trumpets have waked him, we shall have his company.

Ott. A wife is a scurvy clogdogdo, an unlucky thing, a very foresaid bear-whelp, without any good fashion or breeding, *mala bestia.*

---

[1] *Here's my bull for myself, &c.*] These cups probably were distinguished, not only by their sizes and forms, but by some kind of representation of the different animals, on their covers. The *bull* was undoubtedly the largest, and therefore appropriated by the Captain to his own use.

[2] *Titivilitium !*] Not a " word of *no signifi-*

cation," as Whalley repeats from Upton, but a term strongly expressive of contempt :—"paltry, good for nothing," as Ainsworth says. It is used by Plautus, in a passage which Jonson evidently had in view :

" *Non ego istud verbum emissim titivilitio.*"
                                Cas. act ii. sc. 5

Re-enter Truewit *behind, with* Mistress
Otter.

Daup. Why did you marry one then,
Captain?
Ott. A pox! I married with six thou-
sand pound, I. I was in love with that.
I have not kissed my Fury these forty
weeks.
Cler. The more to blame you, Captain.
True. Nay, Mistress Otter, hear him a
little first.
Ott. She has a breath worse than my
grandmother's, *profecto.*
Mrs. Ott. O treacherous liar! kiss me,
sweet Master Truewit, and prove him a
slandering knave.
True. I'll rather believe you, lady.
Ott. And she has a peruke that's like
a pound of hemp, made up in shoe-
threads.
Mrs. Ott. O viper, mandrake!
Ott. A most vile face! and yet she spends
me forty pound a year in mercury and
hogs'-bones. All her teeth were made in
the Blackfriars, both her eyebrows in the
Strand, and her hair in Silver-street.
Every part of the town owns a piece of
her.
Mrs. Ott. [*comes forward.*] I cannot
hold.
Ott. She takes herself asunder still when
she goes to bed, into some twenty boxes;
and about next day noon is put together
again, like a great German clock :[1] and so
comes forth, and rings a tedious larum to
the whole house, and then is quiet again
for an hour, but for her quarters.—Have you
done me right, gentlemen?
Mrs. Ott. [*Falls upon him and beats
him.*] No, sir, I'll do you right with my
quarters, with my quarters!

Ott. O, hold, good princess.
True. Sound, sound!
[*Drum and trumpets sound.*
Cler. A battle, a battle!
Mrs. Ott. You notorious stinkardly bear-
ward, does my breath smell?
Ott. Under correction, dear princess.
Look to my bear and my horse, gentlemen.
Mrs. Ott. Do I want teeth and eyebrows,
thou bull-dog?
True. Sound, sound still.
[*They sound again.*
Ott. No, I protest, under correction——
Mrs. Ott. Ay, now you are under cor-
rection, you protest : but you did not pro-
test before correction, sir. Thou Judas,
to offer to betray thy princess! I'll make
thee an example——   [*Beats him.*

Enter Morose *with his long sword.*

Mor. I will have no such examples in
my house, Lady Otter.
Mrs. Ott. Ah!——
[*Mrs. Otter, Daw, and La-Foole
run off.*
Mor. Mistress Mary Ambree,[2] your examples are dangerous. Rogues, hell-
hounds, Stentors! out of my doors, you
sons of noise and tumult, begot on an ill
May-day, or when the galley-foist is afloat
to Westminster![3] [*Drives out the* Musicians.] A trumpeter could not be conceived but then.
Daup. What ails you, sir?
Mor. They have rent my roof, walls,
and all my windows asunder, with their
brazen throats.   [*Exit.*
True. Best follow him, Dauphine.
Daup. So I will.   [*Exit.*
Cler. Where's Daw and La-Foole?
Ott. They are both run away, sir.

---

[1] *Like a great German clock :*] These and
similar allusions to the cumbrous and complicated machinery of the first clocks (which we
received from Germany), are very frequent in our
old dramatists. Thus Middleton :

"What is she took asunder from her clothes?
Being ready, she consists of hundred pieces,
Much like a *German* clock, and near allyed."
        A Mad World my Masters.
And Shakspeare :

"A woman that is like a *German clock,*
Still a repairing, ever out of frame!"
        Love's Labour Lost.

[2] *Mistress Mary Ambree,*] Of this celebrated
Amazon, who "fought at the siege of Ghent,"
1584, Jonson makes frequent mention. In the

second vol. of Percy's *Antient Poetry* there is a
ballad of her achievements, which must have
been very popular, as it is often quoted by our
old writers, who, like Jonson, "call any remarkable virago by her name." See the *Fortunate Isle.*

[3] *Sons of noise and tumult, begot on an* ill
May-day, *or when the* galley-foist *is afloat to
Westminster!*] Alluding to the sports which
were anciently used on May-day : and particularly to the insurrection of the apprentices in
London against foreigners and aliens upon May-
day 1517; which on that account was afterwards
called *Evil May-day.* The *galley-foist* is the
city-barge, which was used upon the lord
mayor's day, when he was sworn into his office
at Westminster.—WHAL.

Good gentlemen, help to pacify my princess, and speak to the great ladies for me. Now must I go lie with the bears this fortnight, and keep out of the way, till my peace be made, for this scandal she has taken. Did you not see my bull-head, gentlemen?[1]

Cler. Is't not on, Captain?

True. No ; but he may make a new one, by that is on.

Ott. O, here it is. An you come over, gentlemen, and ask for Tom Otter, we'll go down to Ratcliff, and have a course i' faith, for all these disasters. There is *bona spes* left.

True. Away, Captain, get off while you are well. [*Exit* Otter.

Cler. I am glad we are rid of him.

True. You had never been unless we had put his wife upon him. His humour is as tedious at last as it was ridiculous at first. [*Exeunt.*

SCENE II.—*A long open Gallery in the same.*

Enter Lady Haughty, Mistress Otter, Mavis, Daw, La-Foole, Centaure, *and* Epicœne.

Hau. We wondered why you shrieked so, Mistress Otter.

Mrs. Ott. O lord, madam, he came down with a huge long naked weapon in both his hands, and looked so dreadfully ! sure he's beside himself.

Mav. Why, what made you there, Mistress Otter ?

Mrs. Ott. Alas, Mistress Mavis, I was chastising my subject, and thought nothing of him.

Daw. Faith, mistress, you must do so too : learn to chastise. Mistress Otter corrects her husband so he dares not speak, but under correction.

La-F. And with his hat off to her : 'twould do you good to see.

Hau. In sadness, 'tis good and mature counsel ; practise it, Morose. I'll call you Morose still now, as I call Centaure and Mavis ; we four will be all one.

Cen. And you'll come to the college, and live with us ?

Hau. Make him give milk and honey.

Mav. Look how you manage him at first, you shall have him ever after.

Cen. Let him allow you your coach and four horses, your woman, your chambermaid, your page, your gentleman-usher, your French cook, and four grooms.

Hau. And go with us to Bedlam, to the china-houses, and to the Exchange.

Cen. It will open the gate to your fame.

Hau. Here's Centaure has immortalized herself with taming of her wild male.

Mav. Ay, she has done the miracle of the kingdom.

Enter Clerimont *and* Truewit.

Epi. But, ladies, do you count it lawful to have such plurality of servants, and do them all graces ?

Hau. Why not? why should women deny their favours to men ? are they the poorer or the worse?

Daw. Is the Thames the less for the dyers' water, mistress?

La-F. Or a torch for lighting many torches ?[2]

True. Well said, La-Foole ; what a new one he has got !

Cen. They are empty losses women fear in this kind.

Hau. Besides, ladies should be mindful of the approach of age, and let no time want his due use. The best of our days pass first.[3]

---

[1] *Did you not see my bull-head, gentlemen ?*] This seems to confirm the conjecture (p. 437), that the animals which gave name to the Captain's cups were described on the respective covers. The answer of Clerimont evidently alludes to the bull's *horns*.

[2] *Is the Thames the less for the dyers' water, mistress?*

La-F. *Or a torch for lighting many torches ?*] The poet, as Upton says (for Whalley merely copies him), seems desirous of introducing the whole of Ovid's *Art of Love* :

" *Quid vetet adposito lumen de lumine sumi,*
Quisve cavo vastas in mare servet aquas ?
Det tamen ulla viro mulier non expedit,
inquis ;

Quid, nisi quam sumes, dic mihi, perdis aquam ?"—Lib. iii. v. 96.

And again :

" *Tempus erit, quo tu, quæ nunc excludis amantes,*
Frigida desertâ nocte jacebis anus."

[3] *The best of our days pass first.*] This is humorously applied, or rather misapplied, from Virgil :

" *Optima quæque dies miseris mortalibus ævi*
Prima fugit."—*Geor.* lib. iii. v. 66.

The lady president's next speech (but one) is from Ovid.

Mav. We are rivers that cannot be called back, madam : she that now excludes her lovers may live to lie a forsaken beldam in a frozen bed.

Cen. 'Tis true, Mavis ; and who will wait on us to coach then? or write, or tell us the news then, make anagrams of our names, and invite us to the Cockpit, and kiss our hands all the play-time, and draw their weapons for our honours?

Hau. Not one.

Daw. Nay, my mistress is not altogether unintelligent of these things ; here be in presence have tasted of her favours.

Cler. What a neighing hobby-horse is this !

Epi. But not with intent to boast them again, servant. And have you those excellent receipts, madam, to keep yourselves from bearing of children?

Hau. O yes, Morose : how should we maintain our youth and beauty else? Many births of a woman make her old, as many crops make the earth barren.

Enter Morose *and* Dauphine.

Mor. O my cursed angel, that instructed me to this fate !¹

Daup. Why, sir?

Mor. That I should be seduced by so foolish a devil as a barber will make !

Daup. I would I had been worthy, sir, to have partaken your counsel ; you should never have trusted it to such a minister.

Mor. Would I could redeem it with the loss of an eye, nephew, a hand, or any other member.

Daup. Marry, God forbid, sir, that you should geld yourself, to anger your wife.

Mor. So it would rid me of her ! and that I did supererogatory penance in a belfry, at Westminster-hall, in the Cockpit, at the fall of a stag, the Tower-wharf—what place is there else?—London-bridge, Paris-garden, Billinsgate, when the noises are at their height, and loudest. Nay, I would sit out a play,² that were nothing

---

¹ *O my cursed angel, that* instructed *me to this fate* [] i.e., designed, appointed me, &c. This harsh Latinism occurs also in *Sejanus.*

² *Nay, I would sit out a play,* &c.] This is the passage which has furnished the commentators with such abundant materials for convicting Jonson of "the most inveterate malignity to Shakspeare ;" it may not therefore be improper to examine it. After recapitulating a variety of tumultuous noises, the poet adds— "Nay, I would sit out a play that were NOTHING *but fights at sea :*"—evidently meaning one of which these should form the principal or characteristic incidents.

It affords a melancholy picture of human nature to look upon the base drudgery to which men will stoop for the gratification of any vile propensity. After toiling to no purpose through nine huge volumes of the *Variorum Shakspeare,* the commentators fortunately stumble about the middle of the tenth on a *stage direction,* "Firing heard at sea."³ There is not a syllable more on the subject ; for the dialogue immediately commences with a description of night ! and thus it is fully proved that Jonson made it the chief business of his life "to tear the wreath from the brow of Shakspeare." It turns out, however, that the play in which these words appear was not written by Shakspeare, but by Christopher Marlowe : this untoward circumstance (which is prudently overlooked by Mr. Steevens) forces Mr. Malone, who had previously admitted the fact, to go further a-field for the object of Jonson's "malignity," which is now found to be *Antony and Cleopatra.* Here, as before, the attack is confined to a simple stage direction : "Alarum *afar off,* as at a sea-fight :"—and on this admirable foundation is the poet accused—not in one or two—but in a hundred places, of "calumniating ALL the historic plays of Shak-

speare." No :— I am wrong : there is yet another word produced to substantiate the charge—namely, *target :* "fights at sea," it seems (which were merely made known to the audience by letting off a cracker behind the scenes), being solely carried on by this defensive implement.

Long before the *Silent Woman* was written, nay, before Shakspeare was known to the stage, the theatres were in possession of many rude pieces founded on the remarkable events of our history, of which battles, &c. always formed a prominent feature. The miserable attempts to represent these favourite scenes were often made a subject of mirth by succeeding writers ; and it is not easy to discover why Jonson might not allude to them as freely as Sir Philip Sidney, Nash, Greene, and almost every author of the times ; unless it be that the commentators are determined to accumulate upon Shakspeare's head every possible absurdity, for the mere gratification of venting their spleen on Jonson for exposing them.

I shall, as usual, be reprehended for enlarging too frequently on the subject : assuredly, I should not have entered upon the task of reprinting Jonson, unless I had been prepared for this and more. I know how much pleasanter it is for the gentle reader to listen to calumny than to a laborious investigation of facts ; but I shall nevertheless pursue my course on every fitting occasion. If I cannot silence malice, I will at least shame it : if I cannot disencumber the pages of Shakspeare from the scurrility and falsehood with which they are disgraced, I will at all events show that nothing but the grossest stupidity can in future attend to them with decency or credit.

---

³ *Henry VI. Second Part,* act iv sc. 1.

but fights at sea, drum, trumpet, and target.

Daup. I hope there shall be no such need, sir. Take patience, good uncle. This is but a day, and 'tis well worn too now.

Mor. O, 'twill be so for ever, nephew, I foresee it, for ever. Strife and tumult are the dowry that comes with a wife.[1]

True. I told you so, sir, and you would not believe me.

Mor. Alas, do not rub those wounds, Master Truewit, to blood again; 'twas my negligence. Add not affliction to affliction. I have perceived the effect of it too late in Madam Otter.

Epi. How do you, sir?

Mor. Did you ever hear a more unnecessary question? as if she did not see! Why, I do as you see, empress, empress.

Epi. You are not well, sir; you look very ill: something has distempered you.

Mor. O horrible, monstrous impertinencies! would not one of these have served, do you think, sir? would not one of these have served?

True. Yes, sir; but these are but notes of female kindness, sir;[2] certain tokens that she has a voice, sir.

Mor. O, is it so! Come, an't be no otherwise——What say you?

Epi. How do you feel yourself, sir?

Mor. Again that!

True. Nay, look you, sir, you would be friends with your wife upon unconscionable terms; her silence.

Epi. They say you are run mad, sir.

Mor. Not for love, I assure you, of you; do you see?

Epi. O lord, gentlemen! lay hold on him, for God's sake. What shall I do? who's his physician, can you tell, that knows the state of his body best, that I might send for him? Good sir, speak; I'll send for one of my doctors else.

Mor. What, to poison me, that I might die intestate, and leave you possest of all!

Epi. Lord, how idly he talks, and how his eyes sparkle! he looks green about the temples! do you see what blue spots he has![3]

Cler. Ay, 'tis melancholy.

Epi. Gentlemen, for heaven's sake, counsel me. Ladies—servant, you have read Pliny and Paracelsus; ne'er a word now to comfort a poor gentlewoman? Ah me, what fortune had I to marry a distracted man!

Daw. I'll tell you, mistress——

True. How rarely she holds it up!
                              [*Aside to* Cler.

Mor. What mean you, gentlemen?

Epi. What will you tell me, servant?

Daw. The disease in Greek is called μανια, in Latin *insania, furor, vel ecstasis melancholica*, that is, *egressio*, when a man *ex melancholico evadit fanaticus.*

Mor. Shall I have a lecture read upon me alive?

Daw. But he may be but *phreneticus* yet, mistress; and *phrenetis* is only *delirium*, or so.

Epi. Ay, that is for the disease, servant; but what is this to the cure? We are sure enough of the disease.

Mor. Let me go.

True. Why, we'll entreat her to hold her peace, sir.

Mor. O no, labour not to stop her. She is like a conduit-pipe,[4] that will gush out with more force when she opens again.

Hau. I'll tell you, Morose, you must talk divinity to him altogether, or moral philosophy.

---

[1] *Strife and tumult are the dowry that comes with a wife.*]

" *Hoc decet uxores: dos est uxoria lites.*"
                              Ibid. l. ii. v. 155.

[2] *These are but notes of female kindness, sir,* &c.] This is the consolation which Morose receives in Libanius: αναστας απειμι παρα την προμνηστριαν, και τι τουτο εστιν ερωτων· νυμφη ρηματα αφιησιν· ναι φησι, φιλτρου σημειον τουτο εστι, και αμα της φωνης επιδειξις.—*Ibid.* p. 303.

[3] *He looks green about the temples! do you see what blue spots he has!*] " A plain imitation (as Upton remarks) of the *Menæchmi* of Plautus:"

" *Mul. Viden' tu illi oculos virere! ut viridis exoritur color Ex temporibus atque fronte, ut oculi scintillant, vide!*"

A passage, he adds, which Shakspeare had also in view in the *Comedy of Errors;* "though the imitation lies more concealed:"

" Alas, how fiery and how sharp he looks!"

Concealed indeed! The commentators surely imagine that Shakspeare was born without eyes.

[4] *She is like a conduit-pipe,* &c.] This is improved from Libanius: ωσπερ γαρ οι τους κρουνους επισχοντες, ειτ' αφελοντες το κωλυον, σφοδροτεραν ειργασαντο την φοραν· ουτως εγω μικρον αναστειλας την φωνην μειζον επισπασαμην το ρειθρον.—*Ibid.* p. 111.

La-F. Ay, and there's an excellent book[1] of moral philosophy, madam, of Reynard the Fox, and all the beasts, called Doni's Philosophy.

Cen. There is indeed, Sir Amorous La-Foole.

Mor. O misery!

La-F. I have read it, my Lady Centaure, all over, to my cousin here.

Mrs. Ott. Ay, and 'tis a very good book as any is, of the moderns.

Daw. Tut, he must have Seneca read to him, and Plutarch, and the ancients; the moderns are not for this disease.

Cler. Why, you discommended them too to-day, Sir John.

Daw. Ay, in some cases: but in these they are best, and Aristotle's ethics.

Mav. Say you so, Sir John? I think you are deceived: you took it upon trust.

Hau. Where's Trusty, my woman? I'll end this difference. I prithee, Otter, call her. Her father and mother were both mad, when they put her to me.

Mor. I think so. Nay, gentlemen, I am tame. This is but an exercise, I know, a marriage ceremony, which I must endure.

Hau. And one of them, I know not which, was cured with the Sick Man's Salve,[2] and the other with Green's Groat's-worth of Wit.[3]

True. A very cheap cure, madam.

Enter Trusty.

Hau. Ay, 'tis very feasible.

Mrs. Ott. My lady called for you, Mistress Trusty: you must decide a controversy.

Hau. O, Trusty, which was it you said, your father, or your mother, that was cured with the Sick Man's Salve?

Trus. My mother, madam, with the Salve.

True. Then it was the sick woman's salve?

Trus. And my father with the Groat's-worth of Wit. But there was other means used: we had a preacher that would preach folk asleep still; and so they were prescribed to go to church by an old woman that was their physician, thrice a week——

Epi. To sleep!

Trus. Yes, forsooth: and every night they read themselves asleep on those books.

Epi. Good faith, it stands with great reason. I would I knew where to procure those books.

Mor. Oh!

La-F. I can help you with one of them, Mistress Morose, the Groat's-worth of Wit.

Epi. But I shall disfurnish you, Sir Amorous: can you spare it?

La-F. O yes, for a week or so; I'll read it myself to him.

---

[1] *There's an excellent book*, &c.] There was a very old collection of Oriental apologues, called *Calilah u Dumnah* (better known as the *Fables of Pilpay*), which was translated about the middle of the 11th century out of the Persian or Arabic into Greek by Simeon Seth: it was afterwards turned into Latin, and subsequently into Italian, by one Doni. This last was rendered into English by Sir Thomas North, 1605, under the title of *Doni's Moral Philosophy*: and to this Sir Amorous alludes, though he ignorantly confounds it with the popular history of *Reynard the Fox*. We have now the good fortune to possess a very complete and elegant translation of this curious work from the original language, by Sir William Jones.

[2] *One was cured with the* Sick Man's Salve,] This was a devotional tract, written by Thomas Becon, an old Calvinistical divine, and published about 1591. From the quaintness of its title (which yet was not uncommon), or some other cause, it was a frequent subject of ridicule with the wits of those days. The repentant Quicksilver, in *Eastward Hoe*, could "speak it all without book;" as could many others. The *Sick Man's Salve* is in the list of suspected

books found in the library of Lord Cobham; which, if it does nothing else, will at least prove that our old dramatists were not apt to be turned out of their way by an anachronism more or less. In this catalogue the *Bible* is with some humour set down as "a book of heresie." *First Part of Sir John Oldcastle*, act iv. sc. 2.

[3] *And the other with Green's Groat's-worth of Wit.*] This was one of the last works of this popular writer; and was published after his death under the title of Robert Greene's *Groat's-worth of witte, bought with a million of repentance.* To judge from some of the titles of his numerous works, Greene must have experienced many checks of conscience in his profligate career. He has the *Repentance*, the *Last Vision*, the *Farewell to Folie*, &c. &c. His "witte" was indeed dearly bought, for Greene served a hard taskmaster. Health, credit, and excellent talents were miserably prostituted to purchase nothing but beggary, contempt, and an early grave. His contrition, however, was very bitter; and his last moments, it is just to hope, were neither unprofitable to himself nor others.

Epi. No, I must do that, sir ; that must be my office.

Mor. Oh, oh.

Epi. Sure he would do well enough if he could sleep.

Mor. No, I should do well enough if you could sleep. Have I no friend that will make her drunk,[1] or give her a little laudanum, or opium ?

True. Why, sir, she talks ten times worse in her sleep.

Mor. How !

Cler. Do you not know that, sir ? Never ceases all night.

True. And snores like a porpoise.

Mor. O redeem me, fate ; redeem me, fate ! For how many causes may a man be divorced, nephew?

Daup. I know not, truly, sir.

True. Some divine must resolve you in that, sir, or canon lawyer.

Mor. I will not rest, I will not think of any other hope or comfort, till I know.

[*Exit with* Dauphine.

Cler. Alas, poor man !

True. You'll make him mad indeed, ladies, if you pursue this.

Hau. No, we'll let him breathe now, a quarter of an hour, or so.

Cler. By my faith, a large truce !

Hau. Is that his keeper, that is gone with him ?

Daw. It is his nephew, madam.

La-F. Sir Dauphine Eugenie.

Cen. He looks like a very pitiful knight——

Daw. As can be. This marriage has put him out of all.

La-F. He has not a penny in his purse, madam.

Daw. He is ready to cry all this day.

La-F. A very shark ; he set me in the nick t'other night at Primero.

True. How these swabbers talk !

Cler. Ay, Otter's wine has swelled their humours above a spring-tide.

Hau. Good Morose, let's go in again. I like your couches exceeding well ; we'll go lie and talk there.

[*Exeunt* Hau. Cen. Mav. Trus. La-
Foole, *and* Daw.

Epi. [*following them.*] I wait on you, madam.

True. [*stopping her.*] 'Slight, I will have them as silent as signs, and their post too, ere I have done. Do you hear, lady-bride? I pray thee now, as thou art a noble wench, continue this discourse of Dauphine within ; but praise him exceedingly : magnify him with all the height of affection thou canst ;—I have some purpose in't :—and but beat off these two rooks, Jack Daw and his fellow, with any discontentment, hither, and I'll honour thee for ever.

Epi. I was about it here. It angered me to the soul, to hear them begin to talk so malepert.

True. Pray thee perform it, and thou winn'st me an idolater to thee everlasting.

Epi. Will you go in and hear me do't ?

True. No, I'll stay here. Drive them out of your company, 'tis all I ask ; which cannot be any way better done than by extolling Dauphine, whom they have so slighted.

Epi. I warrant you ; you shall expect one of them presently. [*Exit.*

Cler. What a cast of kestrils are these,[2] to hawk after ladies, thus !

True. Ay, and strike at such an eagle as Dauphine.

Cler. He will be mad when we tell him. Here he comes.

Re-enter Dauphine.

Cler. O, sir, you are welcome.

True. Where's thine uncle?

Daup. Run out of doors in his night-caps, to talk with a casuist about his divorce. It works admirably.

True. Thou wouldst have said so, an thou hadst been here ! The ladies have laughed at thee most comically, since thou went'st, Dauphine.

Cler. And asked if thou wert thine uncle's keeper.

True. And the brace of baboons answered, Yes ; and said thou wert a pitiful poor fellow, and didst live upon posts, and hadst nothing but three suits of apparel, and some few benevolences that the lords gave thee to fool to them, and swagger.

Daup. Let me not live, I'll beat them : I'll bind them both to grand-madam's bed-posts, and have them baited with monkies.

---

[1] *Have I no friend that will make her drunk,* &c.] From Libanius : ουκ εστιν η γυνη μοι μεθυσος· τουτο γαρ εστι το δεινον ; ει γαρ μεθυσεν, εκαθευδεν· ει δε εκαθευδεν, ισως εσιγα. *Ibid.* 308.

[2] *What a cast of* kestrils *are these,* &c.] A kestril (see p. 41 *b,* is a base, degenerate hawk. It occurs in all our old writers as an expression of strong contempt. *Cast,* I scarcely need inform the reader is the fowler's term for a couple.

True. Thou shalt not need, they shall be beaten to thy hand, Dauphine. I have an execution to serve upon them, I warrant thee, shall serve ; trust my plot.

Daup. Ay, you have many plots ! so you had one to make all the wenches in love with me.

True. Why, if I do it not yet afore night, as near as 'tis, and that they do not every one invite thee, and be ready to scratch for thee, take the mortgage of my wit.

Cler. 'Fore God, I'll be his witness thou shalt have it, Dauphine : thou shalt be his fool for ever, if thou dost not.

True. Agreed. Perhaps 'twill be the better estate. Do you observe this gallery, or rather lobby indeed? Here are a couple of studies, at each end one : here will I act such a tragi-comedy between the Guelphs and the Ghibellines,[1] Daw and La-Foole ——which of them comes out first, will I seize on ;—you two shall be the chorus behind the arras,[2] and whip out between the acts and speak—If I do not make them keep the peace for this remnant of the day, if not of the year, I have failed once——I hear Daw coming : hide [*they withdraw*], and do not laugh, for God's sake.

Re-enter Daw.

Daw. Which is the way into the garden, trow ?

True. O, Jack Daw ! I am glad I have met with you. In good faith, I must have this matter go no further between you : I must have it taken up.

Daw. What matter, sir? between whom ?

True. Come, you disguise it : Sir Amorous and you. If you love me, Jack, you shall make use of your philosophy now, for this once, and deliver me your sword. This is not the wedding the Centaurs were at, though there be a she one here. [*takes his sword.*] The bride has entreated me I will see no blood shed at her bridal : you saw her whisper me erewhile.

Daw. As I hope to finish Tacitus, I intend no murder.

True. Do you not wait for Sir Amorous ?

Daw. Not I, by my knighthood.

True. And your scholarship too ?

Daw. And my scholarship too.

True. Go to, then I return you your sword, and ask your mercy ; but put it not up, for you will be assaulted. I understood that you had apprehended it, and walked here to brave him ; and that you had held your life contemptible in regard of your honour.[3]

Daw. No, no ; no such thing, I assure you. He and I parted now as good friends as could be.

True. Trust not you to that visor. I saw him since dinner with another face : I have known many men in my time vexed with losses, with deaths, and with abuses ; but so offended a wight as Sir Amorous did I never see or read of. For taking away his guests, sir, to-day, that's the cause ; and he declares it behind your back with such threatenings and contempts—— He said to Dauphine you were the arrant'st ass——

---

[1] *The Guelphs and the Ghibellines,*] Two factions that, in the twelfth and thirteenth centuries, harassed Italy with great animosity and violence ; the former taking part with the Pope, and the latter with the Emperor. The origin of their names is uncertain.—Whal.

[2] *You two shall be the chorus behind the arras, and whip out between the acts, and speak.*] This passage also is brought forward with great exultation by the commentators on Shakspeare, as a manifest sneer at two of his best plays, and by Mr. Malone, in particular, to show that Jonson viewed "our great poet with *scornful yet with* jealous eyes." The fact itself is proved in the established mode, wherever our author is concerned. There is a piece of *arras* in *Hamlet*, and there is a *chorus* in *Henry V.* Can anything be plainer? But the arras in *Hamlet* is without a chorus, and the chorus in *Henry V.* is without an arras. No matter: if, as Lord Peter says, the accusation cannot be proved *totidem verbis*, it must be made out *totidem literis;* and so the reputation of Jonson is juggled away! How long will the reader's good sense

be imposed upon by such deplorable stupidity ? How long will his candour be warped by such grovelling malice? What is there in the use of these words that can lead to a suspicion of a sneer at anything? *Arras* was then the constant furniture of the stage, and formed a screen or hiding-place in almost every drama in existence. A *chorus* was by no means unfrequent : and, indeed, appears in the greater number of Jonson's own plays. Did he ridicule himself; or was he debarred the use of the words because they were found in Shakspeare? Had the expression in the text been used by any one but Jonson, it would be termed, as it really is, an application of a familiar phrase, with the speaker's characteristic sprightliness and good humour.

[3] *That you had held your life contemptible in regard of your honour.*] This application of Virgil's fine lines to poor Sir John is highly humorous :

"*Est hic, est animus lucis contemptor, et istum*
Qui vita bene credat emi, quo tendis, honorem !"

Daw. Ay, he may say his pleasure.

True. And swears you are so protested a coward, that he knows you will never do him any manly or single right; and therefore he will take his course.

Daw. I'll give him any satisfaction, sir—but fighting—

True. Ay, sir : but who knows what satisfaction he'll take : blood he thirsts for, and blood he will have; and whereabouts on you he will have it, who knows but himself?

Daw. I pray you, Master Truewit, be you a mediator.

True Well, sir, conceal yourself then in this study till I return. [*Puts him into the study.*] Nay, you must be content to be locked in; for, for mine own reputation, I would not have you seen to receive a public disgrace, while I have the matter in managing. Ods so, here he comes; keep your breath close, that he do not hear you sigh.—In good faith, Sir Amorous, he is not this way; I pray you be merciful, do not murder him; he is a Christian, as good as you : you are armed as if you sought revenge on all his race. Good Dauphine, get him away from this place. I never knew a man's choler so high, but he would speak to his friends, he would hear reason. —Jack Daw, Jack! asleep!

Daw. [*within.*] Is he gone, Master Truewit?

True. Ay; did you hear him?

Daw. O lord! yes.

True. What a quick ear fear has!

Daw. [*Comes out of the closet.*] But is he so armed as you say?

True. Armed! did you ever see a fellow set out to take possession?[1]

Daw. Ay, sir.

True. That may give you some light to conceive of him; but 'tis nothing to the principal. Some false brother in the house has furnished him strangely; or, if it were out of the house, it was Tom Otter.

Daw. Indeed he's a captain, and his wife is his kinswoman.

True. He has got somebody's old two-hand sword, to mow you off at the knees : and that sword hath spawned such a dagger! —But then he is so hung with pikes, halberds, petronels, calivers,[2] and muskets, that he looks like a justice-of-peace's hall : a man of two thousand a year is not cessed at so many weapons as he has on. There was never fencer challenged at so many several foils. You would think he meant to murder all St. Pulchre's parish. If he could but victual himself for half a year in his breeches,[3] he is sufficiently armed to overrun a country.

Daw. Good lord! what means he, sir? I pray you, Master Truewit, be you a mediator.

True. Well, I'll try if he will be appeased with a leg or an arm; if not—you must die once.

Daw. I would be loth to lose my right arm, for writing madrigals.

True. Why, if he will be satisfied with a

---

[1] *Did you ever see a fellow set out to take possession?*] When estates were litigated, or, as was too frequently the case formerly, transferred to a hungry favourite, this was a service of some danger; and the new owner set forth with his attendants and friends well armed. This is not an uncommon case in Ireland at this day; in this country the practice has happily been long obsolete.

[2] *Petronels and calivers.*] These weapons seem to answer to our blunderbusses or horse pistols, and fowling-pieces respectively. Whalley says that the caliver was a larger kind of musquet; but this is contrary to the description given of it in the *Soldier's Accidence*, and other books of the time.

[3] *If he could but victual himself for half a year in his breeches*, &c.] Thus Butler :

"With a huge pair of round trunk hose,
In which he carried as much meat
As he and all his knights could eat."

This is not the only idea which the author of Hudibras has taken from this play. What is more to Jonson's honour, Shakspeare himself has condescended to be obliged to it; for there can be no doubt but that the attempt of Sir Toby and Fabian to bring on a quarrel between Aguecheek and Viola, is imitated from this scene. It is really edifying to see the complacency with which Mr. Malone resigns his best arguments to his *friend*. He first proves, beyond the reach of cavil, that *Twelfth Night* could not be written before 1614; yet because Steevens, with equal folly and malignity, asserts that Jonson "took every opportunity to find fault with Shakspeare, and ridiculed the conduct of that comedy in *Every Man out of his Humour*," which, as I have already shown, p. 104 *b*, preceded it by a dozen years or more, Mr. Malone calmly subjoins to this contemptible trash, "I *had* supposed this play (*Twelfth Night*) to be written in 1614, if, however, the foregoing passage from *Every Man, &c.*, *be* levelled at it, my speculation falls to the ground." Condescension worthy of all praise. To renounce a rational certainty—to embrace a senseless impossibility—and for what?—for nothing higher or better than the hopeless chance of heaping another absurd calumny on the memory of Jonson. So much can prejudice do—

"*Tantum potuit suadere malorum!*"

thumb or a little finger, all's one to me.
You must think, I'll do my best.

[*Shuts him up again.*

Daw. Good sir, do.

[*Clerimont and* Dauphine *come forward.*

Cler. What hast thou done?

True. He will let me do nothing; he does all afore; he offers his left arm.

Cler. His left wing, for a Jack Daw.

Daup. Take it by all means.

True. How! maim a man for ever, for a jest? What a conscience hast thou!

Daup. 'Tis no loss to him; he has no employment for his arms but to eat spoon-meat. Beside, as good maim his body as his reputation.

True. He is a scholar and a wit, and yet he does not think so. But he loses no reputation with us; for we all resolved him an ass before. To your places again.

Cler. I pray thee, let me be in at the other a little.

True. Look, you'll spoil all; these be ever your tricks.

Cler. No, but I could hit of some things that thou wilt miss, and thou wilt say are good ones.

True. I warrant you. I pray, forbear, I'll leave it off else.

Daup. Come away, Clerimont.

[Daup. *and* Cler. *withdraw as before.*

Enter La-Foole.

True. Sir Amorous!

La-F. Master Truewit.

True. Whither were you going?

La-F. Down into the court to make water.

True. By no means, sir; you shall rather tempt your breeches.

La-F. Why, sir?

True. Enter here, if you love your life.

[*Opening the door of the other study.*

La-F. Why?—why?

True. Question till your throat be cut, do: dally till the enraged soul find you.

La-F. Who is that?

True. Daw it is: will you in?

La-F. Ay, ay, I'll in: what's the matter?

True. Nay, if he had been cool enough to tell us that, there had been some hope to atone you;[1] but he seems so implacably enraged!

La-F. 'Slight, let him rage! I'll hide myself.

True. Do, good sir. But what have you done to him within that should provoke him thus? You have broke some jest upon him afore the ladies.

La-F. Not I, never in my life broke jest upon any man. The bride was praising Sir Dauphine, and he went away in snuff,[2] and I followed him; unless he took offence at me in his drink erewhile, that I would not pledge all the horse full.

True. By my faith, and that may be; you remember well: but he walks the round up and down,[3] through every room o' the house, with a towel in his hand, crying, *Where's La-Foole? Who saw La-Foole?* And when Dauphine and I demanded the cause, we can force no answer from him, but—*O revenge, how sweet art thou! I will strangle him in this towel*—which leads us to conjecture that the main cause of his fury is for bringing your meat to-day with a towel about you, to his discredit.

La-F. Like enough. Why, an he be angry for that I'll stay here till his anger be blown over.

True. A good becoming resolution, sir; if you can put it on o' the sudden.

La-F. Yes, I can put it on: or, I'll away into the country presently.

True. How will you go out of the house, sir? He knows you are in the house, and he'll watch this se'ennight but he'll have you: he'll outwait a serjeant for you.[4]

La-F. Why, then I'll stay here.

True. You must think how to victual yourself in time then.

La-F. Why, sweet Master Truewit, will you entreat my cousin Otter to send me a cold venison pasty, a bottle or two of wine, and a chamber-pot.

---

[1] *There had been some hope to* atone *you.*] To make you friends, to set you *at one* again.—WHAL.

[2] *Went away in snuff,*] i.e., in anger: alluding, I presume, to the offensive manner in which a candle goes out. The word is frequent in our old writers, and furnishes Shakspeare with many playful opportunities of confounding it with the dust of tobacco.

[3] *But he walks the* round *up and down.*] A

phrase taken from the army; where it was the business of certain inferior officers to go round to the sentinels and outguards, who from thence were called *gentlemen of the round.*—WHAL.
To watch, in short. See p. 32 *a.*

[4] *He'll outwait a* serjeant *for you.*] The perseverance of *serjeants* (sheriffs' officers) in watching their prey, is well known. Our old poets, who had but too many proofs of it, mention it, either in mirth or anger, upon all occasions.

True. A stool were better, sir, of Sir
Ajax his invention.[1]

La-F. Ay, that will be better indeed ;
and a pallet to lie on.

True. O, I would not advise you to sleep
by any means.

La-F. Would you not, sir? Why, then
I will not.

True. Yet there's another fear——

La-F. Is there ! What is't?

True. No, he cannot break open this
door with his foot, sure.

La-F. I'll set my back against it, sir. I
have a good back.

True. But then if he should batter.

La-F. Batter ! if he dare, I'll have an
action of battery against him.

True. Cast you the worst. He has sent
for powder already, and what he will do
with it no man knows : perhaps blow up
the corner of the house where he suspects
you are. Here he comes ; in quickly.
[*Thrusts in* La-Foole *and shuts the door.*]
—I protest, Sir John Daw, he is not this
way : what will you do? Before God, you
shall hang no petard here : I'll die rather.
Will you not take my word? I never knew
one but would be satisfied.—Sir Amorous,
[*speaks through the key-hole,*] there's no
standing out : he has made a petard of an
old brass pot, to force your door. Think
upon some satisfaction, or terms to offer
him.

La-F. [*within.*] Sir, I'll give him any
satisfaction : I dare give any terms.

True. You'll leave it to me then?

La-F. Ay, sir : I'll stand to any conditions.

True. [*beckoning forward* Cler. *and*
Dauph.] How now—what think you, sirs ?
Were't not a difficult thing to determine
which of these two feared most?

Cler. Yes, but this extreme fears the bravest :
the other a whiniling dastard, Jack Daw !
But La-Foole, a brave heroic coward ! and
is afraid in a great look and a stout accent ;
I like him rarely.

True. Had it not been pity these two
should have been concealed ?

Cler. Shall I make a motion ?

True. Briefly : for I must strike while
'tis hot.

Cler. Shall I go fetch the ladies to the
catastrophe?

True. Umph ! ay, by my troth.

Daup. By no mortal means. Let them
continue in the state of ignorance, and err
still ; think them wits and fine fellows, as
they have done. 'Twere sin to reform them.

True. Well, I will have them fetched,
now I think on't, for a private purpose of
mine : do, Clerimont, fetch them, and discourse to them all that's past, and bring
them into the gallery here.

Daup. This is thy extreme vanity, now !
thou think'st thou wert undone if every
jest thou mak'st were not published.

True. Thou shalt see how unjust thou
art presently. Clerimont, say it was Dauphine's plot. [*Exit* Clerimont.] Trust me
not if the whole drift be not for thy good.
There is a carpet[2] in the next room, put it
on, with this scarf over thy face, and a
cushion on thy head, and be ready when I
call Amorous. Away ! [*Exit* Daup.]—
John Daw ! [*Goes to* Daw's *closet, and
brings him out.*]

Daw. What good news, sir ?

True. Faith, I have followed and argued
with him hard for you. I told him you
were a knight, and a scholar, and that you
knew fortitude did consist *magis patiendo
quam faciendo, magis ferendo quam fe-
riendo.*

---

[1] *A stool were better, sir, of Sir* Ajax *his invention.*] Sir Ajax seems to have been a title
familiarly imposed on Sir John Harrington, for
a very meritorious attempt to introduce clean-
liness into our dwellings, at a period when the
sweetest of them would have offended the dullest
nose of modern times. In 1596 he published,
under the name of Misacmos, a little treatise
called, *A New Discourse of a Stale Subject, or
the Metamorphosis of Ajax*, of which the object
was to point out the propriety of adopting something like the water-closets of the present day,
in the place of the wretched utensils which were
then common in every house. As the nature of
his subject led him to lay open the interior
of our palaces and great houses, offence was
taken at his freedom : he lost, at least for a time,
the favour of Elizabeth (his godmother,) and

was banished from court. His gains, from his
well-timed labours, were apparently confined to
the honour of contributing to the merriment of
the wits, Shakspeare, Jonson, Nabbes, and many
others, who took advantage of his own pun,
(a-jakes,) and dubbed him a knight of the stool ;
under which title he frequently appears in their
pages. Even the grave Camden condescends to
be facetious at his expense—but enough on the
subject.

[2] *There is a* carpet, &c.] i.e., a table-cover.
Formerly these ornamental pieces of tapestry
furnished employment for the ladies in the long
nights of winter. I have seen several of them in
our old mansion-houses. Carpets were not at
this period laid on the floor ; except occasionally to kneel on, or for purposes of state.

Daw. It doth so indeed, sir.

True. And that you would suffer, I told him : so at first he demanded by my troth, in my conceit, too much.

Daw. What was it, sir ?

True. Your upper lip and six of your fore-teeth.

Daw. 'Twas unreasonable.

True. Nay, I told him plainly, you could not spare them all. So after long argument *pro et con*, as you know, I brought him down to your two butter-teeth, and them he would have.

Daw. O, did you so? Why, he shall have them.

True. But he shall not, sir, by your leave. The conclusion is this, sir : because you shall be very good friends hereafter, and this never to be remembered or upbraided ; besides, that he may not boast he has done any such thing to you in his own person ; he is to come here in disguise, give you five kicks in private, sir, take your sword from you, and lock you up in that study during pleasure : which will be but a little while, we'll get it released presently.

Daw. Five kicks ! he shall have six, sir, to be friends.

True. Believe me, you shall not overshoot yourself, to send him that word by me.

Daw. Deliver it, sir ; he shall have it with all my heart, to be friends.

True. Friends ! Nay, an he should not be so, and heartily too, upon these terms, he shall have me to enemy while I live. Come, sir, bear it bravely.

Daw. O lord, sir, 'tis nothing.

True. True ! what's six kicks to a man that reads Seneca ?

Daw. I have had a hundred, sir.

True. Sir Amorous !

Re-enter Dauphine, *disguised.*

No speaking one to another, or rehearsing old matters.

Daw. [*as Daup. kicks him.*] One, two, three, four, five. I protest, Sir Amorous, you shall have six.

True. Nay, I told you you should not talk. Come, give him six, an he will needs. [*Dauphine kicks him again.*] Your sword [*takes his sword.*] Now return to your safe custody ; you shall presently meet afore the ladies, and be the dearest friends one to another. [*Puts Daw into the study.*] Give me the scarf now, thou shalt beat the other barefaced. Stand by :

[*Dauphine retires, and* Truewit *goes to the other closet, and releases* La-Foole.] Sir Amorous !

La-F. What's here ! A sword?

True. I cannot help it, without I should take the quarrel upon myself. Here he has sent you his sword——

La-F. I'll receive none on't.

True. And he wills you to fasten it against a wall, and break your head in some few several places against the hilts.

La-F. I will not : tell him roundly. I cannot endure to shed my own blood.

True. Will you not ?

La-F. No. I'll beat it against a fair flat wall, if that will satisfy him : if not, he shall beat it himself, for Amorous.

True. Why, this is strange starting off, when a man undertakes for you ! I offered him another condition ; will you stand to that ?

La-F. Ay, what is't ?

True. That you will be beaten in private.

La-F. Yes, I am content, at the blunt.[1]

Enter, above, Haughty, Centaure, Mavis, Mistress Otter, Epicœne, *and* Trusty.

True. Then you must submit yourself to be hoodwinked in this scarf, and be led to him, where he will take your sword from you, and make you bear a blow over the mouth *gules*, and tweaks by the nose *sans nombre.*

La-F. I am content. But why must I be blinded ?

True. That's for your good, sir ; because if he should grow insolent upon this, and publish it hereafter to your disgrace (which I hope he will not do), you might swear safely, and protest he never beat you to your knowledge.

La-F. O, I conceive.

True. I do not doubt but you'll be perfect good friends upon't, and not dare to utter an ill thought one of another in future.

La-F. Not I, as God help me, of him.

True. Nor he of you, sir. If he should, [*binds his eyes.*]—Come, sir. [*leads him forward.*] All hid, Sir John !

Enter Dauphine, *and tweaks him by the nose.*

La-F. Oh, Sir John, Sir John ! Oh, o-o-o-o-o-Oh——

---

[1] *At the blunt,*] i.e., with the flat side of the sword.

True. Good Sir John, leave tweaking, you'll blow his nose off. 'Tis Sir John's pleasure you should retire into the study. [*Puts him up again.*] Why, now you are friends. All bitterness between you I hope is buried ; you shall come forth by and by Damon and Pythias upon 't, and embrace with all the rankness of friendship that can be. I trust we shall have them tamer in their language hereafter. Dauphine, I worship thee. God's will, the ladies have surprised us !

Enter Haughty, Centaure, Mavis, Mistress Otter, Epicœne, *and* Trusty *behind.*

Hau. Centaure, how our judgments were imposed on by these adulterate knights !

Cen. Nay, madam, Mavis was more deceived than we ; 'twas her commendation uttered them in the college.

Mav. I commended but their wits, madam, and their braveries. I never looked toward their valours.

Hau. Sir Dauphine is valiant, and a wit too, it seems.

Mav. And a bravery too.

Hau. Was this his project ?

Mrs. Ott. So Master Clerimont intimates, madam.

Hau. Good Morose, when you come to the college, will you bring him with you ? he seems a very perfect gentleman.

Epi. He is so, madam, believe it.

Cen. But when will you come, Morose?

Epi. Three or four days hence, madam, when I have got me a coach and horses.

Hau. No, to-morrow, good Morose ; Centaure shall send you her coach.

Mav. Yes, faith, do, and bring Sir Dauphine with you.

Hau. She has promised that, Mavis.

Mav. He is a very worthy gentleman in his exteriors, madam.

Hau. Ay, he shews he is judicial in his clothes.

Cen. And yet not so superlatively neat as some, madam, that have their faces set in a brake.[1]

Hau. Ay, and have every hair in form.

Mav. That wear purer linen than ourselves, and profess more neatness than the French hermaphrodite.

Epi. Ay, ladies, they, what they tell one of us, have told a thousand ; and are the only thieves of our fame, that think to take us with that perfume, or with that lace, and laugh at us unconscionably when they have done.

Hau. But Sir Dauphine's carelessness becomes him.

Cen. I could love a man for such a nose.

Mav. Or such a leg.

Cen. He has an exceeding good eye, madam.

Mav. And a very good lock.[2]

---

[1] *Not so superlatively neat as some that have their faces set in a* brake.] A *brake*, amongst other acceptations, is a sort of bridle, which they made use of to young horses, in order to make them carry their heads steady, and in a proper place.—WHAL.
A *brake* is a powerful iron curb, by which the tongue and jaws of restive horses are so compressed as to prevent their *taking the bit*: but the *brake* which seems to be meant here is a strong wooden frame in which the feet of young and vicious horses are frequently confined by farriers, preparatory to their being shod. Jonson uses the word again in his beautiful poem to Charis, and in a similar sense :

"Drest, you still for man should take him ;
    And not think he'd eat a stake,
    Or were set up in a *brake*."

[2] *A very good* lock.] A favourite *lock* of hair, which it was the fashion of those times to nourish. —WHAL.
To make it more conspicuous, a rose or knot of ribands was sometimes attached to it. Thus Shirley :

"Who knows but he
May lose the riband by it, in his *lock* ?"
                            Coronation.

And Davenant :

"A *lock* on the left side, so rarely hung
    With ribanding."—*Love and Honour.*

This practice was so rooted, that it flourished for near a century, in spite of all the ridicule of the stage, and all the thunder of the press. From the following curious passage in *Mydas*, it appears that the form of these love-locks was as various and capricious as that of the beards, already noticed : "How will you be trimmed, sir ? Will you have your beard like a spade or a bodkin ? A penthouse on your upper lip or an alley on your chin ? A low curle on your heade like a ball, or dangling locks like a spaniell ? Your mustachoes sharp at the ends like shoemakers' aules, or hanging downe to your mouth like goates' flakes ? Your *love*-locks wreathed with a silken twist, or shaggie to fall on your shoulders ?" act iii. sc. 2. Certainly an assemblage of "braveries" at this time must have presented a very amusing spectacle, as far as the head was concerned. From the prints of the unfortunate Charles, it appears that he and his courtiers wore love-locks. The king, it is said, cut off his in 1646. His favourites probably followed his example. Business of higher import than considering whether their "*locks*

Cen. Good Morose, bring him to my chamber first.

Mrs. Ott. Please your honours to meet at my house, madam.

True. See how they eye thee, man! they are taken, I warrant thee.

[*Haughty comes forward.*

Hau. You have unbraced our brace of knights here, Master Truewit.

True. Not I, madam; it was Sir Dauphine's ingine: who, if he have disfurnished your ladyship of any guard or service by it, is able to make the place good again in himself.

Hau. There is no suspicion of that, sir.

Cen. God so, Mavis, Haughty is kissing.

Mav. Let us go too, and take part.

[*They come forward.*

Hau. But I am glad of the fortune (beside the discovery of two such empty caskets) to gain the knowledge of so rich a mine of virtue as Sir Dauphine.

Cen. We would be all glad to style him of our friendship, and see him at the college.

Mav. He cannot mix with a sweeter society, I'll prophesy; and I hope he himself will think so.

Daup. I should be rude to imagine otherwise, lady.

True. Did not I tell thee, Dauphine! Why, all their actions are governed by crude opinion, without reason or cause; they know not why they do anything; but as they are informed, believe, judge, praise, condemn, love, hate, and in emulation one of another, do all these things alike. Only they have a natural inclination sways them generally to the worst, when they are left to themselves. But pursue it, now thou hast them.

Hau. Shall we go in again, Morose?

Epi. Yes, madam.

Cen. We'll entreat Sir Dauphine's company.

True. Stay, good madam, the interview of the two friends, Pylades and Orestes: I'll fetch them out to you straight.

Hau. Will you, Master Truewit?

Daup. Ay; but, noble ladies, do not confess in your countenance, or outward bearing to them, any discovery of their follies,

that we may see how they will bear up again, with what assurance and erection.

Hau. We will not, Sir Dauphine.

Cen. Mav. Upon our honours, Sir Dauphine.

True. [*goes to the first closet.*] Sir Amorous, Sir Amorous! The ladies are here.

La-F. [*within.*] Are they?

True. Yes; but slip out by and by, as their backs are turned, and meet Sir John here, as by chance when I call you. [*Goes to the other.*]—Jack Daw!

Daw. [*within.*] What say you, sir?

True. Whip out behind me suddenly, and no anger in your looks to your adversary. Now, now!

[*La-Foole and Daw slip out of their respective closets, and salute each other.*

La-F. Noble Sir John Daw! where have you been?

Daw. To seek you, Sir Amorous.

La-F. Me! I honour you.

Daw. I prevent you, sir.

Cler. They have forgot their rapiers.

True. O, they meet in peace, man.

Daup. Where's your sword, Sir John?

Cler. And yours, Sir Amorous?

Daw. Mine! my boy had it forth to mend the handle, e'en now.

La-F. And my gold handle was broke too, and my boy had it forth.

Daup. Indeed, sir!—How their excuses meet!

Cler. What a consent there is in the handles!

True. Nay, there is so in the points too, I warrant you.

Enter Morose, *with the two swords, drawn, in his hands.*

Mrs. Ott. O me! madam, he comes again, the madman! Away!

[*Ladies, Daw, and La-Foole run off.*

Mor. What make these naked weapons here, gentlemen?

True. O, sir! here hath like to have been murder since you went; a couple of knights fallen out about the bride's favours! We were fain to take away their weapons; your house had been begged by this time else.[1]

---

should be wreathed with silk, or left shaggie to fall on the shoulders," now occupied their attention; and in the hateful times which immediately succeeded, the fashion went to decay with a thousand better things.

[1] *Your house had been begged by this time*

else.] For a riot, &c., for which it would have fallen, as a deodand, to the crown. The quick-scented rapacity of James's courtiers is well marked by this expression, which, though used in jest, contains little more than the simple fact.

Mor. For what?

Cler. For manslaughter, sir, as being accessary.

Mor. And for her favours?

True. Ay, sir, heretofore, not present.— Clerimont, carry them their swords now. They have done all the hurt they will do.

　　　[*Exit* Cler. *with the two swords.*

Daup. Have you spoke with the lawyer, sir?

Mor. O no! there is such a noise in the court,[1] that they have frighted me home with more violence than I went! such speaking and counter-speaking, with their several voices of citations, appellations, allegations, certificates, attachments, interrogatories, references, convictions, and afflictions indeed, among the doctors and proctors, that the noise here is silence to't, a kind of calm midnight!

True. Why, sir, if you would be resolved indeed, I can bring you hither a very sufficient lawyer, and a learned divine, that shall enquire into every least scruple for you.

Mor. Can you, Master Truewit?

True. Yes, and are very sober, grave persons, that will dispatch it in a chamber, with a whisper or two.

Mor. Good sir, shall I hope this benefit from you, and trust myself into your hands?

True. Alas, sir! your nephew and I have been ashamed and oft-times mad, since you went, to think how you are abused. Go in, good sir, and lock yourself up till we call you; we'll tell you more anon, sir.

Mor. Do your pleasure with me, gentlemen. I believe in you, and that deserves no delusion.　　　　　　[*Exit.*

True. You shall find none, sir;—but heaped, heaped plenty of vexation.

Daup. What wilt thou do now, Wit?

True. Recover me hither Otter and the barber, if you can, by any means, presently.

Daup. Why? to what purpose?

True. O, I'll make the deepest divine and gravest lawyer out of them two, for him——

Daup. Thou canst not, man; these are waking dreams.

True. Do not fear me. Clap but a civil gown with a welt[2] on the one, and a canonical cloke with sleeves on the other, and give them a few terms in their mouths, if there come not forth as able a doctor and complete a parson, for this turn, as may be wished, trust not my election: and I hope, without wronging the dignity of either profession, since they are but persons put on, and for mirth's sake, to torment him. The barber smatters Latin, I remember.

Daup. Yes, and Otter too.

True. Well then, if I make them not wrangle out this case to his no comfort, let me be thought a Jack Daw or La-Foole, or anything worse. Go you to your ladies, but first send for them.

Daup. I will.　　　　　　　[*Exeunt.*

　　　　　———

ACT V.

SCENE I.—*A Room in* Morose's *House.*

Enter La-Foole, Clerimont, *and* Daw.

La-F. Where had you our swords, Master Clerimont?

Cler. Why, Dauphine took them from the madman.

La-F. And he took them from our boys, I warrant you.

Cler. Very like, sir.

La-F. Thank you, good Master Clerimont. Sir John Daw and I are both beholden to you.

Cler. Would I knew how to make you so, gentlemen!

Daw. Sir Amorous and I are your servants, sir.

Enter Mavis.

Mav. Gentlemen, have any of you a pen and ink? I would fain write out a riddle in Italian, for Sir Dauphine to translate.

Cler. Not I, in troth, lady; I am no scrivener.

Daw. I can furnish you, I think, lady.

　　　　　[*Exeunt* Daw and Mavis.

---

[1] *O no! there is such a noise in the court, &c.*] This, with the legal terms which follow, is adapted, with considerable humour, from Libanius: των εκκλησιων ου μαλα κοινωνων, ου δια το των κοινη συμφεροντων αμελειν, αλλα δια τας των ου δυναμενων σιγησαι βοας ρητορων. εις αγοραν ου σφοδρα εμβαλλων, δια τα πολλα ταυτα των δικων ονοματα, φασις, ενδειξις, απαγωγη, διαδικασια, παραγραφη, ἀ και οἱς ουδεν εστι πραγμα φιλουσιν ονομασειν. Ibid. p. 301-2.

[2] *Clap but a civil gown with a welt, &c.*] A *civil* gown is the gown of a civilian: a *welt*, as I have already observed, is a hem or border of fur, &c. In the conclusion of this speech, Jonson shews himself yet sore of the censure passed on him for his alleged reflection on the law, in the *Poetaster.*

Cler. He has it in the haft of a knife, I believe.

La-F. No, he has his box of instruments.

Cler. Like a surgeon !

La-F. For the mathematics : his square, his compasses, his brass pens, and blacklead, to draw maps of every place and person where he comes.

Cler. How, maps of persons !

La-F. Yes, sir, of Nomentack, when he was here,[1] and of the Prince of Moldavia, and of his mistress, Mistress Epicœne.

Re-enter Daw.

Cler. Away ! he hath not found out her latitude, I hope.

La-F. You are a pleasant gentleman, sir.

Cler. Faith, now we are in private, let's wanton it a little, and talk waggishly.— Sir John, I am telling Sir Amorous here that you two govern the ladies wherever you come ; you carry the feminine gender afore you.

Daw. They shall rather carry us afore them, if they will, sir.

Cler. Nay, I believe that they do withal[2] —but that you are the prime men in their affections, and direct all their actions——

Daw. Not I ; Sir Amorous is.

La-F. I protest Sir John is.

Daw. As I hope to rise in the state, Sir Amorous, you have the person.

La-F. Sir John, you have the person, and the discourse too.

Daw. Not I, sir. I have no discourse— and then you have activity beside.

La-F. I protest, Sir John, you come as high from Tripoly as I do, every whit :[3]

---

[1] *Yes, sir, of Nomentack, when he was here,* &c.] Nomentack was an Indian chief, from Virginia, who was brought to England some years before this was written. Of the Prince of Moldavia, I can give no account.

[2] *Nay, I believe that they do withal*—] I quote these words, merely because the collocation of them recalls to my mind an expression in Shakspeare, on which I have something to say. In one of the prettiest speeches surely that ever was penned, that of Portia (*Merchant of Venice*, act iii. sc. 4), to Nerissa, she describes the appearance she shall make, and the language she shall hold when "accoutred like a man :"

　　　　" I'll speak of frays
Like a fine bragging youth, and tell quaint lies,
How *honourable ladies* sought my love,
Which I denying, they fell sick, and died ;
I could not do withal ?'

The last line, or rather a corruption of it, the commentators, who are always routing in the mire of impurity, explain in the most indecent manner. I will not say of Portia, as of Desdemona, that her " motion blushed at herself," yet she was assuredly a woman of modesty, and therefore little likely to use the language of a brothel, or to attribute the manners of one to the "*honourable ladies* who sought her love." The fact is, that the phrase so shamelessly misinterpreted is in itself perfectly innocent, and means neither more nor less than I COULD NOT HELP IT. In *Morte Arthur*—where Guinever is accused of poisoning one of the knights of the round table, the king says to her, " None of them will say well of you, nor none of them will doe battle for you, and that shall be great slaunder for you in this court. Alas ! said the queen, *I cannot doe withall*," (I cannot help it,) " and now I miss Sir Launcelot," part iii. c. 108. In the trial of Udall, Lord Anderson says : " You had as good say you were the author." *Udall.* "That will not follow, my lord : but if you think so, *I cannot do withal,*" (I cannot help it.)—

State Trials, fol. vol. i. p. 162. And in that excellent old play, the *Little French Lawyer,* Dinant, who is reproached by Clerimont for not silencing the music, which endangered his safety, replies :

" *I cannot do withal ;* (I cannot help it ;)
I have spoke and spoke : I am betrayed and lost too."

I make no apology for this long note, irrelevant as it will perhaps be thought. Shakspeare is in every hand ; and it is therefore incumbent on all those who feel a due respect for youth and innocence, to take every opportunity of removing the impurities with which his pages are wantonly overcharged. As the sense of the words is now fully ascertained, we have a right to expect that the stupid and indecent comments of Collins and others on it shall be henceforth omitted. " *Withal,* the reading of the old copies," Mr. Malone tells us, " was *corrected* (corrected, with a vengeance !) "to *with all,* (as it stands in his and Steevens' editions) by Mr. Pope." Notwithstanding this cheering assurance, the future editors of Shakspeare will do well to let him speak his own language, and to print the line as it stands above, and as it ought always to have stood : " I could not do withal." *Withal* in Jonson, is a mere expletive.

[3] *I protest, Sir John, you* come *as high* from Tripoly *as I do, every whit :*] " A phrase, (Upton says), to signify feats of activity, vaulting, leaping, &c. Jonson has it again in his Epigrams, (cxv.)

" Can come from *Tripoly,* leap stools, and wink."

And so likewise his contemporaries :

" Get up to the window there, and presently,
Like a most compleat gentleman come from
　Tripoly."—*Monsieur Thomas,* act iv. sc. 2.

Tripoly, Whalley subjoins, " was famous for the justs and tournaments held there in the days of

and lift as many joined stools, and leap over them, if you would use it.

Cler. Well, agree on't together, knights; for between you, you divide the kingdom or commonwealth of ladies' affections. I see it, and can perceive a little how they observe you, and fear you indeed. You could tell strange stories, my masters, if you would, I know.

Daw. Faith, we have seen somewhat, sir.

La-F. That we have—velvet petticoats, and wrought smocks, or so.

Daw. Ay, and——

Cler. Nay, out with it, Sir John; do not envy your friend the pleasure of hearing, when you have had the delight of tasting.

Daw. Why—a—Do you speak, Sir Amorous.

La-F. No, do you, Sir John Daw.

Daw. I' faith, you shall.

La-F. I' faith, you shall.

Daw. Why, we have been——

La-F. In the great bed at Ware together in our time. On, Sir John.

Daw. Nay, do you, Sir Amorous.

Cler. And these ladies with you, knights?

La-F. No, excuse us, sir.

Daw. We must not wound reputation.

La-F. No matter—they were these, or others. Our bath cost us fifteen pound when we came home.

Cler. Do you hear, Sir John? You shall tell me but one thing truly, as you love me.

Daw. If I can, I will, sir.

Cler. You lay in the same house with the bride here?

Daw. Yes, and conversed with her hourly, sir.

Cler. And what humour is she of? Is she coming and open, free?

Daw. O, exceeding open, sir. I was her servant, and Sir Amorous was to be.

Cler. Come, you have both had favours from her: I know, and have heard so much.

Daw. O no, sir.

La-F. You shall excuse us, sir; we must not wound reputation.

Cler. Tut, she is married now, and you cannot hurt her with any report; and there-fore speak plainly: how many times, i' faith? which of you led first? ha!

La-F. Sir John had her maidenhead, indeed.

Daw. O, it pleases him to say so, sir; but Sir Amorous knows what's what as well.

Cler. Dost thou, i' faith, Amorous?

La-F. In a manner, sir.

Cler. Why, I commend you, lads. Little knows Don Bridegroom of this; nor shall he for me.

Daw. Hang him, mad ox!

Cler. Speak softly; here comes his nephew, with the Lady Haughty: he'll get the ladies from you, sirs, if you look not to him in time.

La-F. Why, if he do, we'll fetch them home again, I warrant you.

[*Exit with* Daw.   Cler. *walks aside.*

Enter Dauphine *and* Haughty.

Hau. I assure you, Sir Dauphine, it is the price and estimation of your virtue only that hath embarked me to this adventure; and I could not but make out to tell you so: nor can I repent me of the act, since it is always an argument of some virtue in ourselves, that we love and affect it so in others.

Daup. Your ladyship sets too high a price on my weakness.

Hau. Sir, I can distinguish gems from pebbles——

Daup. Are you so skilful in stones?
[*Aside.*

Hau. And howsoever I may suffer in such a judgment as yours, by admitting equality of rank or society with Centaure or Mavis——

Daup. You do not, madam; I perceive they are your mere foils.

Hau. Then are you a friend to truth, sir; it makes me love you the more. It is not the outward but the inward man that I affect. They are not apprehensive of an eminent perfection, but love flat and dully.

Cen. [*within.*] Where are you, my Lady Haughty?

Hau. I come presently, Centaure.—My chamber, sir, my page shall shew you; and

---

chivalry, and from those feats perhaps the phrase was derived." I think not: "justs and tournaments," wherever held, were grave and serious amusements, and could scarcely give name to such apish tricks as leaping over sticks, &c. It seems far more probable that the phrase grew out of one of those *jests nominal,* (as Owen Feltham calls them,) of which our ancestors were so fond; and that the sole claim which Tripoly has to the honour conferred upon it, lies in the first part of its name.

Trusty, my woman, shall be ever awake for you: you need not fear to communicate anything with her, for she is a Fidelia. I pray you wear this jewel for my sake, Sir Dauphine.—

Enter Centaure.

Where's Mavis, Centaure?
Cen. Within, madam, a writing. I'll follow you presently. [*Exit* Hau.] I'll but speak a word with Sir Dauphine.
Daup. With me, madam?
Cen. Good Sir Dauphine, do not trust Haughty, nor make any credit to her[1] whatever you do besides. Sir Dauphine, I give you this caution, she is a perfect courtier, and loves nobody but for her uses; and for her uses she loves all. Besides, her physicians give her out to be none o' the clearest, whether she pay them or no, heaven knows; and she's above fifty too, and pargets![2] See her in a forenoon. Here comes Mavis, a worse face than she! you would not like this by candle-light.

Re-enter Mavis.

If you'll come to my chamber one o' these mornings early, or late in an evening, I'll tell you more. Where's Haughty, Mavis?
Mav. Within, Centaure.
Cen. What have you there?
Mav. An Italian riddle for Sir Dauphine, —you shall not see it, i' faith, Centaure.— [*Exit* Cen.] Good Sir Dauphine, solve it for me: I'll call for it anon.   [*Exit.*
Cler. [*coming forward.*] How now, Dauphine! how dost thou quit thy self of these females?
Daup. 'Slight, they haunt me like fairies, and give me jewels here; I cannot be rid of them.
Cler. O, you must not tell though.[3]

Daup. Mass, I forgot that: I was never so assaulted. One loves for virtue, and bribes me with this [*shews the jewel*]— another loves me with caution, and so would possess me; a third brings me a riddle here: and all are jealous, and rail each at other.
Cler. A riddle! pray let me see it. [*Reads.*

"Sir Dauphine, I chose this way of intimation for privacy. The ladies here, I know, have both hope and purpose to make a collegiate and servant of you. If I might be so honoured as to appear at any end of so noble a work, I would enter into a fame of taking physic to-morrow, and continue it four or five days, or longer, for your visitation.   MAVIS."

By my faith, a subtle one! Call you this a riddle? what's their plain-dealing, trow?
Daup. We lack Truewit to tell us that.
Cler. We lack him for somewhat else too: his knights reformadoes are wound up as high and insolent as ever they were.
Daup. You jest.
Cler. No drunkards, either with wine or vanity, ever confessed such stories of themselves. I would not give a fly's leg in balance against all the women's reputations here, if they could be but thought to speak truth; and for the bride, they have made their affidavit against her directly——
Daup. What, that they have lain with her?
Cler. Yes; and tell times and circumstances, with the cause why, and the place where. I had almost brought them to affirm that they had done it to-day.
Daup. Not both of them?
Cler. Yes, faith; with a sooth or two more I had effected it. They would have set it down under their hands.

---

[1] *Do not trust* Haughty, *nor make any credit to her.*] i.e., nor give her any credit; from the Latin idiom, *fidem facere.* Jonson is too bold in introducing phrases from the learned languages.—WHAL.
It was the vice, or rather the fashion of the times. Shakspeare has as many words, if not phrases, as Jonson. I do not recollect to have yet marked a Latinism in him which is not to be found in his contemporaries, except perhaps in *Sejanus.*
[2] *She's above fifty too, and* pargets !] i.e., daubs, or plasters her face: see p. 204 *b.*
[3] *O, you must not tell, though.*] It was the received opinion, that it was extremely dangerous to betray the confidence of the fairies : the loss of all future favour from them was the least

part of the evil; personal or family misfortune usually followed the indiscretion. To this the old Clown in the *Winter's Tale* cunningly alludes: "'Tis *fairy gold,* boy, and will prove so. Up with it ; *keep it close.*" And so in the *Honest Man's Fortune* :

" *Mont.* Your ladyship cannot tell me when I
      kissed her.
Lady. But *she* can, sir.
Mont. But she will not, madam ;
For when they talk once, 'tis *like fairy money,*
They get no more close kisses."

And again :

" A prince's secrets are like fairy favours ;
  Wholesome if kept ; but poison if discovered."

Daup. Why, they will be our sport, I see, still, whether we will or no.

Enter Truewit.

True. O, are you here? Come, Dauphine; go call your uncle presently: I have fitted my divine and my canonist, dyed their beards and all. The knaves do not know themselves, they are so exalted and altered. Preferment changes any man. Thou shalt keep one door and I another, and then Clerimont in the midst, that he may have no means of escape from their cavilling, when they grow hot once again. And then the women, as I have given the bride her instructions, to break in upon him in the l'envoy.[1] O, 'twill be full and twanging! Away! fetch him.

[*Exit* Dauphine.

Enter Otter, *disguised as a divine, and* Cutbeard *as a canon lawyer.*

Come, master doctor, and master parson, look to your parts now, and discharge them bravely; you are well set forth, perform it as well. If you chance to be out, do not confess it with standing still, or humming, or gaping one at another; but go on, and talk aloud and eagerly; use vehement action, and only remember your terms, and you are safe. Let the matter go where it will: you have many will do so. But at first be very solemn and grave, like your garments, though you loose yourselves after, and skip out like a brace of jugglers on a table. Here he comes: set your faces, and look superciliously while I present you.

Re-enter Dauphine *with* Morose.

Mor. Are these the two learned men?
True. Yes, sir; please you salute them.
Mor. Salute them! I had rather do anything than wear out time so unfruitfully, sir. I wonder how these common forms,[2] as *God save you,* and *You are welcome,* are come to be a habit in our lives: or, *I am*

glad to see you! When I cannot see what the profit can be of these words, so long as it is no whit better with him whose affairs are sad and grievous, that he hears this salutation.

True. 'Tis true, sir; we'll go to the matter then.—Gentlemen, master doctor, and master parson, I have acquainted you sufficiently with the business for which you are come hither; and you are not now to inform yourselves in the state of the question, I know. This is the gentleman who expects your resolution, and therefore, when you please, begin.

Ott. Please you, master doctor.
Cut. Please you, good master parson.
Ott. I would hear the canon-law speak first.
Cut. It must give place to positive divinity, sir.

Mor. Nay, good gentlemen, do not throw me into circumstances. Let your comforts arrive quickly at me, those that are. Be swift in affording me my peace, if so I shall hope any. I love not your disputations, or your court-tumults. And that it be not strange to you, I will tell you: My father, in my education, was wont to advise me,[3] that I should always collect and contain my mind, not suffering it to flow loosely; that I should look to what things were necessary to the carriage of my life, and what not; embracing the one and eschewing the other: in short, that I should endear myself to rest, and avoid turmoil; which now is grown to be another nature to me. So that I come not to your public pleadings, or your places of noise; not that I neglect those things that make for the dignity of the commonwealth; but for the mere avoiding of clamours and impertinences of orators, that know not how to be silent. And for the cause of noise, am I now a suitor to you. You do not know in what a misery I have been exercised this day, what a torrent of evil! my very house turns round with the tumult! I dwell in a windmill: the perpetual motion is here, and not at Eltham.[4]

---

[1] *In the l'envoy.*] i.e., in the conclusion. See Massinger, vol. iv. p. 417.

[2] *I wonder how these common forms,* &c.] From Libanius: Και μην εκεινο δειν εξελασαι της αγορας, το της προσρησεως, ουκ οιδ' οθεν εις τον βιον επελθον, τον δεινα χαιρειν· ου γαρ εγωγε μα τους θεους ορω του ρηματος το κερδος· ου γαρ ψγε λυπης αξιως εχει τα πραγματα, βελτιω παρα το χαιρειν ακουσαι γιγνεται. *Ibid.* p. 302.

[3] *My father, in my education, was wont to advise me,* &c.] This also is from Libanius.

Εμοι δ' ὁ πατηρ, ω βουλη, παρηνει, τον νουν αει συναγειν και συνεχειν, και μη συγχωρειν διαχεισθαι· διοραν των εν τω βιω τα τε αναγκαια και τα μη, και των μεν εχεσθαι, των δ' απεχεσθαι· τιμαν την ησυχιαν, φευγειν τας ταραχας· ἁ και ποιων, ω βουλη, διατελω· των εκκλησιων ου μαλα κοινωνων, ου δια το των κοινη συμφεροντων αμελειν, αλλα δια τας των ου δυναμενων σιγησαι βοας ῥητορων.—*Ibid.* p. 301.

[4] *The perpetual motion is here, and not at Eltham.*] Here was a puppet-show of great

True. Well, good master doctor, will you break the ice? master parson will wade after.

Cut. Sir, though unworthy, and the weaker, I will presume.

Ott. 'Tis no presumption, *domine* doctor.

Mor. Yet again!

Cut. Your question is, For how many causes a man may have *divortium legitimum,* a lawful divorce? First, you must understand the nature of the word, divorce, *à divertendo*——

Mor. No excursions upon words, good doctor; to the question briefly.

Cut. I answer then, the canon-law affords divorce but in few cases; and the principal is in the common case, the adulterous case. But there are *duodecim impedimenta,* twelve impediments, as we call them, all which do not *dirimere contractum,* but *irritum reddere matrimonium,* as we say in the canon law, *not take away the bond, but cause a nullity therein.*

Mor. I understood you before: good sir, avoid your impertinency of translation.

Ott. He cannot open this too much, sir, by your favour.

Mor. Yet more!

True. O, you must give the learned men leave, sir.—To your impediments, master doctor.

Cut. The first is *impedimentum erroris.*

Ott. Of which there are several species.

Cut. Ay, as *error personæ.*

Ott. If you contract yourself to one person, thinking her another.

Cut. Then, *error fortunæ.*

Ott. If she be a beggar, and you thought her rich.

Cut. Then, *error qualitatis.*

Ott. If she prove stubborn or headstrong, that you thought obedient.

Mor. How! is that, sir, a lawful impediment? One at once, I pray you, gentlemen.

Ott. Ay, *ante copulam,* but not *post copulam,* sir.

Cut. Master parson says right. *Nec post nuptiarum benedictionem.* It doth indeed but *irrita reddere sponsalia,* annul

the contract; after marriage it is of no obstancy.

True. Alas, sir, what a hope are we fallen from[1] by this time!

Cut. The next is *conditio:* if you thought her free born and she prove a bond-woman, there is impediment of estate and condition.

Ott. Ay, but, master doctor, those servitudes are *sublatæ* now, among us Christians.

Cut. By your favour, master parson——

Ott. You shall give me leave, master doctor.

Mor. Nay, gentlemen, quarrel not in that question; it concerns not my case: pass to the third.

Cut. Well then, the third is *votum:* if either party have made a vow of chastity. But that practice, as master parson said of the other, is taken away among us, thanks be to discipline.[2] The fourth is *cognatio;* if the persons be of kin within the degrees.

Ott. Ay: do you know what the degrees are, sir?

Mor. No, nor I care not, sir; they offer me no comfort in the question, I am sure.

Cut. But there is a branch of this impediment may, which is *cognatio spiritualis:* if you were her godfather, sir, then the marriage is incestuous.

Ott. That comment is absurd and superstitious, master doctor: I cannot endure it. Are we not all brothers and sisters, and as much akin in that as godfathers and god-daughters?

Mor. O me! to end the controversy, I never was a godfather, I never was a godfather in my life, sir. Pass to the next.

Cut. The fifth is *crimen adulterii;* the known case. The sixth, *cultus disparitas,* difference of religion. Have you ever examined her, what religion she is of?

Mor. No, I would rather she were of none than be put to the trouble of it.

Ott. You may have it done for you, sir.

Mor. By no means, good sir; on to the rest: shall you ever come to an end, think you?

---

celebrity in our author's time. It is called, in Peacham's verses to Coryat, "that *divine motion* at Eltham;" so that it was probably some piece of scripture history. Jonson introduces it again in his Epigrams, and in very bad company:

"See you yon motion? not the old Fa-ding,
  Nor Captain Pod, nor yet the *Eltham* thing,"
    &c.

[1] *What a hope are we fallen from!*] Literally from Terence: *Quanta de spe decidi!*—WHAL.

[2] *Thanks be to* discipline.] This was a term much affected by the Puritans, when they spoke of the reformation of the Church. In *Bartholomew Fair* it is termed the *beauteous discipline.*

True. Yes, he has done half, sir. On to the rest.—Be patient, and expect, sir.

Cut. The seventh is, *vis:* if it were upon compulsion or force.

Mor. O no, it was too voluntary, mine; too voluntary.

Cut. The eighth is, *ordo;* if ever she have taken holy orders.

Ott. That's superstitious too.

Mor. No matter, master parson; would she would go into a nunnery yet.

Cut. The ninth is, *ligamen;* if you were bound, sir, to any other before.

Mor. I thrust myself too soon into these fetters.

Cut. The tenth is, *publica honestas;* which is *inchoata quædam affinitas.*

Ott. Ay, or *affinitas orta ex sponsalibus;* and is but *leve impedimentum.*

Mor. I feel no air of comfort blowing to me in all this.

Cut. The eleventh is, *affinitas ex fornicatione.*

Ott. Which is no less *vera affinitas* than the other, master doctor.

Cut. True, *quæ oritur ex legitimo matrimonio.*

Ott. You say right, venerable doctor; and, *nascitur ex eo, quod per conjugium duæ personæ efficiuntur una caro—*

True. Hey-day, now they begin!

Cut. I conceive you, master parson: *Ita per fornicationem æque est verus pater, qui sic generat—*

Ott. *Et vere filius qui sic generatur—*

Mor. What's all this to me?

Cler. Now it grows warm.

Cut. The twelfth and last is, *si forte coire nequibis.*

Ott. Ay, that is *impedimentum gravissimum:* it doth utterly annul and annihilate,

that. If you have *manifestam frigiditatem,* you are well, sir.

True. Why, there is comfort come at length, sir. Confess yourself but a man unable, and she will sue to be divorced first.

Ott. Ay, or if there be *morbus perpetuus, et insanabilis;* as *paralysis, elephantiasis,* or so—

Daup. O, but *frigiditas* is the fairer way, gentlemen.

Ott. You say troth, sir, and as it is in the canon, master doctor——

Cut. I conceive you, sir.

Cler. Before he speaks!

Ott. That a boy, or child, under years, is not fit for marriage, because he cannot *reddere debitum.* So your *omnipotentes*——

True. Your *impotentes,* you whoreson lobster!   [*Aside to* Ott.

Ott. You *impotentes,* I should say, are *minime apti ad contrahenda matrimonium.*

True. *Matrimonium!* we shall have most unmatrimonial Latin with you: *matrimonia,* and be hanged.

Daup. You put them out, man.

Cut. But then there will arise a doubt, master parson, in our case, *post matrimonium:* that *frigiditate præditus*—do you conceive me, sir?

Ott. Very well, sir.

Cut. Who cannot *uti uxore pro uxore,* may *habere eam pro sorore.*

Ott. Absurd, absurd, absurd, and merely apostatical!

Cut. You shall pardon me, master parson, I can prove it.

Ott. You can prove a will, master doctor, you can prove nothing else. Does not the verse of your own canon say:

Hæc socianda vetant connubia, facta
        retractant?[1]

---

[1] *Does not the verse of your own canon say,*
" *Hæc socianda vetant connubia, facta retractant?*"]

"The following (as Upton observes) are the verses alluded to:

   1   2   3   4   5
' *Error, conditio, votum, cognatio, crimen,*
       6   7   8   9
 Cultûs disparitas, vis, ordo, ligamen,
    TO
  honestas,
    11   12
Si sis affinis, si forte coire nequibis;
Si parochi et duplicis desit præsentia testis,
Raptave sit mulier, nec parti reddita tutæ.
Hæc facienda vetant connubia, facta retractant.'

The canon law allows fourteen impediments, which are comprehended in the verses above, though only twelve of them are enumerated by our author's casuists."

It is scarcely possible to read this humorous discussion without adverting to one of a serious kind, which took place on the divorce of Lord Essex. If it were not ascertained beyond a doubt that the *Silent Woman* appeared on the stage in 1609, four years at least prior to the date of that most infamous transaction, it would be difficult to persuade the reader that a strong burlesque of it was not here intended. The bishops Neal and Andrews are the very counterparts of Otter and Cutbeard; nor does Morose himself display more anxiety for the fortunate termination of his extraordinary suit than the credulous and ever-meddling James exhibited on that occasion for the success of his unworthy favourite.

Cut. I grant you; but how do they *retractare*, master parson?

Mor. O, this was it I feared.

Ott. In æternum, sir.

Cut. That's false in divinity, by your favour.

Ott. 'Tis false in humanity to say so. Is he not *prorsus inutilis ad thorum?* Can he *præstare fidem datam?* I would fain know.

Cut. Yes; how if he do *convalere?*

Ott. He cannot *convalere*, it is impossible.

True. Nay; good sir, attend the learned men; they'll think you neglect them else.

Cut. Or if he do *simulare* himself *frigidum, odio uxoris*, or so?

Ott. I say he is *adulter manifestus* then.

Daup. They dispute it very learnedly, i' faith.

Ott. And *prostitutor uxoris;* and this is positive.

Mor. Good sir, let me escape.

True. You will not do me that wrong, sir?

Ott. And, therefore, if he be *manifeste frigidus*, sir——

Cut. Ay, if he be *manifeste frigidus*, I grant you——

Ott. Why, that was my conclusion.

Cut. And mine too.

True. Nay, hear the conclusion, sir.

Ott. Then, *frigiditatis causa*——

Cut. Yes, *causa frigiditatis*——

Mor. O, mine ears!

Ott. She may have *libellum divortii* against you.

Cut. Ay, *divortii libellum* she will sure have.

Mor. Good echoes, forbear.

Ott. If you confess it.——

Cut. Which I would do, sir——

Mor. I will do anything.

Ott. And clear myself in *foro conscientiæ*——

Cut. Because you want indeed——

Mor. Yet more!

Ott. Exercendi potestate.

Epicœne rushes in, followed by Haughty, Centaure, Mavis, Mistress Otter, Daw, *and* La-Foole.

Epi. I will not endure it any longer. Ladies, I beseech you help me. This is such a wrong as never was offered to poor bride before: upon her marriage-day to have her husband conspire against her, and a couple of mercenary companions to be brought in for form's sake, to persuade a separation! If you had blood or virtue in you, gentlemen, you would not suffer such earwigs about a husband, or scorpions to creep between man and wife.

Mor. O the variety and changes of my torment!

Hau. Let them be cudgelled out of doors by our grooms.

Cen. I'll lend you my footman.

Mav. We'll have our men blanket them in the hall.

Mrs. Ott. As there was one at our house, madam, for peeping in at the door.

Daw. Content, i' faith.

True. Stay, ladies and gentlemen; you'll hear before you proceed?

Mav. I'd have the bridegroom blanketted too.

Cen. Begin with him first.

Hau. Yes, by my troth.

Mor. O mankind generation![1]

Daup. Ladies, for my sake forbear.

Hau. Yes, for Sir Dauphine's sake.

Cen. He shall command us.

La-F. He is as fine a gentleman of his inches, madam, as any is about the town, and wears as good colours when he lists.

True. Be brief, sir, and confess your infirmity; she'll be a-fire to be quit of you, if she but hear that named once, you shall not entreat her to stay: she'll fly you like one that had the marks upon him.[2]

Mor. Ladies, I must crave all your pardons——

True. Silence, ladies.

Mor. For a wrong I have done to your whole sex, in marrying this fair and virtuous gentlewoman——

Cler. Hear him, good ladies.

Mor. Being guilty of an infirmity which,

---

[1] *O* mankind *generation!*] i.e., simply masculine, always a term of reproach, when applied to a female. Upton quotes several passages to prove that it means *wicked*, in every one of which it means *mannish.* That the word, however, is sometimes used in an ill sense as an augmentative, for violent, outrageous, &c., is certain:

Cotgrave calls some fierce animal "a *mankind* wild beast;" and Hall (Mass. vol. iv. p. 53) speaks of "stripes for the correction of a *mankind* ass."

[2] *She'll fly you like one that had the* marks *upon him.*] Of the plague or some contagious distemper.—WHAL.

before I conferred with these learned men, I thought I might have concealed——

True. But now being better informed in his conscience by them, he is to declare it, and give satisfaction by asking your public forgiveness.

Mor. I am no man, ladies.

All. How!

Mor. Utterly unabled in nature, by reason of frigidity, to perform the duties or any the least office of a husband.

Mav. Now out upon him, prodigious creature !

Cen. Bridegroom uncarnate !

Hau. And would you offer it to a young gentlewoman?

Mrs. Ott. A lady of her longings?

Epi. Tut, a device, a device, this ! it smells rankly, ladies. A mere comment of his own.

True. Why, if you suspect that, ladies, you may have him searched——

Daw. As the custom is, by a jury of physicians.

La-F. Yes, faith, 'twill be brave.

Mor. O me, must I undergo that?

Mrs. Ott. No, let women search him, madam: we can do it ourselves.

Mor. Out on me ! worse.

Epi. No, ladies, you shall not need, I'll take him with all his faults.

Mor. Worst of all !

Cler. Why then, 'tis no divorce, doctor, if she consent not?

Cut. No, if the man be *frigidus*, it is *de parte uxoris*, that we grant *libellum divortii*, in the law.

Ott. Ay, it is the same in theology.

Mor. Worse, worse than worst !

True. Nay, sir, be not utterly disheartened; we have yet a small relick of hope left, as near as our comfort is blown out. Clerimont, produce your brace of knights. What was that, master parson, you told me *in errore qualitatis*, e'en now? —Dauphine, whisper the bride, that she carry it as if she were guilty and ashamed. [*Aside.*

Ott. Marry, sir, *in errore qualitatis* (which master doctor did forbear to urge), if she be found *corrupta*, that is, vitiated or broken up, that was *pro virgine desponsa*, espoused for a maid——

Mor. What then, sir?

Ott. It doth *dirimere contractum*, and *irritum reddere* too.

True. If this be true, we are happy again, sir, once more. Here are an

honourable brace of knights that shall affirm so much.

Daw. Pardon us, good MasterClerimont.

La-F. You shall excuse us, Master Clerimont.

Cler. Nay, you must make it good now, knights, there is no remedy; I'll eat no words for you, nor no men : you know you spoke it to me.

Daw. Is this gentleman-like, sir?

True. Jack Daw, he's worse than Sir Amorous; fiercer a great deal. [*Aside to Daw.*]—Sir Amorous, beware, there be ten Daws in this Clerimont. [*Aside to* La-Foole.

La-F. I'll confess it, sir.

Daw. Will you, Sir Amorous, will you wound reputation?

La-F. I am resolved.

True. So should you be too, Jack Daw : what should keep you off? she's but a woman, and in disgrace : he'll be glad on't.

Daw. Will he? I thought he would have been angry.

Cler. You will dispatch, knights; it must be done, i' faith.

True. Why, an it must, it shall, sir, they say : they'll ne'er go back.—Do not tempt his patience. [*Aside to them.*

Daw. It is true indeed, sir.

La-F. Yes, I assure you, sir.

Mor. What is true, gentlemen? what do you assure me?

Daw. That we have known your bride, sir——

La-F. In good fashion. She was our mistress, or so——

Cler. Nay, you must be plain, knights, as you were to me.

Ott. Ay, the question is, if you have *carnaliter*, or no?

La-F. *Carnaliter !* what else, sir?

Ott. It is enough; a plain nullity.

Epi. I am undone, I am undone !

Mor. O let me worship and adore you, gentlemen !

Epi. I am undone ! [*Weeps.*

Mor. Yes, to my hand, I thank these knights. Master parson, let me thank you otherwise. [*Gives him money.*

Cen. And have they confessed?

Mav. Now out upon them, informers !

True. You see what creatures you may bestow your favours on, madams.

Hau. I would except[1] against them as

---

[1] *I would except against them as beaten knights, wench, and not good witnesses in law.*]

beaten knights, wench, and not good witnesses in law.

Mrs. Ott. Poor gentlewoman, how she
takes it !

Hau. Be comforted, Morose, I love you
the better for 't.

Cen. So do I, I protest.

Cut. But, gentlemen, you have not known
her since *matrimonium ?*

Daw. Not to-day, master doctor.

La-F. No, sir, not to-day.

Cut. Why, then I say, for any act before,
the *matrimonium* is good and perfect ; unless the worshipful bridegroom did precisely, before witness, demand, if she were
virgo ante nuptias.

Epi. No, that he did not, I assure you,
master doctor.

Cut. If he cannot prove that, it is *ratum
conjugium,* notwithstanding the premisses ;
and they do no way *impedire.* And this is
my sentence, this I pronounce.

Ott. I am of master doctor's resolution
too, sir ; if you made not that demand *ante
nuptias.*

Mor. O my heart ! wilt thou break ? wilt
thou break ? this is worst of all worst worsts
that hell could have devised ! Marry a
whore, and so much noise !

Daup. Come, I see now plain confederacy in this doctor and this parson, to
abuse a gentleman. You study his affliction. I pray be gone, companions.—And,
gentlemen, I begin to suspect you for having
parts with them.—Sir, will it please you
hear me ?

Mor. O do not talk to me ; take not
from me the pleasure of dying in silence,
nephew.[1]

Daup. Sir, I must speak to you. I have
been long your poor despised kinsman, and
many a hard thought has strengthened
you against me : but now it shall appear

if either I love you or your peace, and
prefer them to all the world beside. I
will not be long or grievous to you, sir. If
I free you of this unhappy match absolutely and instantly, after all this trouble,
and almost in your despair, now——

Mor. It cannot be.

Daup. Sir, that you be never troubled
with a murmur of it more, what shall I
hope for, or deserve of you?

Mor. O, what thou wilt, nephew ! thou
shalt deserve me, and have me.

Daup. Shall I have your favour perfect
to me, and love hereafter?

Mor. That, and anything beside. Make
thine own conditions. My whole estate is
thine ; manage it, I will become thy ward.

Daup. Nay, sir, I will not be so unreasonable.

Epi. Will Sir Dauphine be mine enemy
too ?

Daup. You know I have been long a
suitor to you, uncle, that out of your estate,
which is fifteen hundred a year, you would
allow me but five hundred during life, and
assure the rest upon me after ; to which I
have often, by myself and friends, tendered you a writing to sign, which you
would never consent or incline to. If you
please but to effect it now——

Mor. Thou shalt have it, nephew ; I
will do it, and more.

Daup. If I quit you not presently, and
for ever, of this cumber, you shall have
power instantly, afore all these, to revoke
your act, and I will become whose slave
you will give me to for ever.

Mor. Where is the writing? I will seal
to it, that, or to a blank, and write thine
own conditions.

Epi. O me, most unfortunate, wretched
gentlewoman !

Hau. Will Sir Dauphine do this ?

When the method of determining causes by *wager,*
or *trial* of battle, subsisted, either on a writ of
right, or in an appeal, or an approvement, if
either of the combatants, and particularly the
appellant, became *recreant,* and pronounced
the horrible word *craven,* he became infamous,
and was no longer accounted *liber et legalis
homo ;* and being by the event supposed to be
forsworn, he was never put upon a jury, or admitted as a witness in any cause. It is to this
custom that our poet alludes. See *Blackstone's
Commentaries,* vol. iii. p. 337, and vol. iv. p. 340,
with Mr. Reed's note on Ford's *'Tis Pity she's a
Whore,* act i.—WHAL.

[1] *Take not from me the pleasure of dying in
silence, nephew.*] Thus Morose in Libanius:

Δοτε δη, δοτε την χαριν, ω βουλη, πεμψατε
με ταχεως εις την τελειαν ἡσυχιαν. Ibid. 312.
In conclusion he meditates an escape from
the loquacity of his wife by a dose of hemlock, though somewhat alarmed at the tales
which he has heard of law suits, and other
clamorous affairs among the ghosts. Upon the
whole, however, he resolves, in opposition to
Hamlet, that it is better to venture on an uncertain evil than to bear a certain one ; and he
winds up his long harangue with a supplication
which, for a sophist, must be allowed to possess
a considerable degree of humour: Ω θεοι παντες
και πασαι, ει λογου μετεστι τοι; απελθουσι,
δοιητε τη γυναικι προς εσχατον γηρως ελθειν, ως
τε με τυχειν εν ᾁδου τελειονος αναπαυσεως. Ibid.
p. 314.

Epi. Good sir, have some compassion on me.

Mor. O, my nephew knows you, belike; away, crocodile !

Cen. He does it not sure without good ground.

Daup. Here, sir.

[*Gives him the parchments.*

Mor. Come, nephew, give me the pen ; I will subscribe to anything, and seal to what thou wilt for my deliverance. Thou art my restorer. Here, I deliver it thee as my deed. If there be a word in it lacking, or writ with false orthography, I protest before [heaven] I will not take the advantage. [*Returns the writings.*

Daup. Then here is your release, sir. [*Takes off* Epicœne's *peruke and other disguises.*] You have married a boy, a gentleman's son that I have brought up this half year at my great charges, and for this composition which I have now made with you. What say you, master doctor? This is *justum impedimentum* I hope, *error personæ* ?

Ott. Yes, sir, *in primo gradu.*

Cut. *In primo gradu.*

Daup. I thank you, good doctor Cutbeard, and parson Otter. [*Pulls their false beards and gowns off.*] You are beholden to them, sir, that have taken this pains for you; and my friend, Master Truewit, who enabled them for the business. Now you may go in and rest ; be as private as you will, sir. [*Exit* Morose.] I'll not trouble you till you trouble me with your funeral, which I care not how

soon it come.—Cutbeard, I'll make your lease good. *Thank me not, but with your leg, Cutbeard.* And Tom Otter, your princess shall be reconciled to you.—How now, gentlemen, do you look at me ?

Cler. A boy !

Daup. Yes, Mistress Epicœne.

True. Well, Dauphine, you have lurched your friends of the better half of the garland, by concealing this part of the plot :[1] but much good do it thee, thou deserv'st it, lad. And, Clerimont, for thy unexpected bringing these two to confession, wear my part of it freely. Nay, Sir Daw and Sir La-Foole, you see the gentlewoman that has done you the favours ! we are all thankful to you, and so should the woman-kind here, specially for lying on her, though not with her ! you meant so, I am sure. But that we have stuck it upon you to-day, in your own imagined persons, and so lately, this Amazon, the champion of the sex, should beat you now thriftily, for the common slanders which ladies receive from such cuckoos as you are. You are they that,[2] when no merit or fortune can make you hope to enjoy their bodies, will yet lie with their reputations, and make their fame suffer. Away, you common moths of these, and all ladies' honours. Go, travel to make legs and faces, and come home with some new matter to be laughed at : you deserve to live in an air as corrupted as that wherewith you feed rumour. [*Exeunt* Daw *and* La-Foole.] Madams, you are mute upon this new metamorphosis ! But here stands

---

[1] True. *Well, Dauphine, you have lurched your friends of the better half of the garland,* &c.] "I formerly" (says Mr. Malone) "thought this a *sneer* at Shakspeare, but have lately met with nearly the same phrase in a pamphlet written by Nashe, and suppose it to have been a common phrase of the time." A better specimen of the manner with which Jonson is commonly criticised, or, more properly calumniated, cannot be desired. If Mr. Malone, whose reading is not universal, had not fortunately met with another example of this expression, he would, it seems, have continued to think (i.e., to call) it a *sneer* at Shakspeare ! I can furnish Mr. Malone with several examples of it: but—suppose none had existed, why must it be a "*sneer*?" It is not an inelegant phrase ; it is used in the text with perfect sincerity, and with a degree of taste and propriety which admits of no dispute. The words, if really taken from Shakspeare, might indeed be construed into a compliment to our great bard ; but could appear only to a jaundiced eye, and perverted mind, as a designed ridicule upon him. They were, however, public property, and as

free for Jonson as for any of his contemporaries. Much more might be said on the subject ; but I gladly turn from such splenetic revilings to the just and liberal observation with which Upton concludes his strictures on this play. "Hardly, I believe, can be given a better instance of a happy discovery, and unravelling of the whole plot than we have now before us. The persons of the play are all met together, and all in the highest suspense of the catastrophe: by concealing this part of the plot, Dauphine has lurched his friends of the better half of the garland. And let this praise which Truewit gives to his friend, be returned back again to our poet."

[2] *You are they,* &c.]

"*Parva queror: fingunt quidam, quæ vera negarent,*
  Et nulli non se concubuisse ferunt.
Corpora si nequeant, quæ possint nomina tractant,
  Famæque, non tacto corpore, crimen habet."
      Art. Aman. ii. v. 633.

she that has vindicated your fames. Take heed of such insectæ hereafter. And let it not trouble you, that you have discovered any mysteries to this young gentleman : he is almost of years, and will make a good visitant within this twelvemonth. In the mean time, we'll all un-dertake for his secrecy, that can speak so well of his silence. [*Coming forward.*] *Spectators, if you like this comedy, rise cheerfully, and now Morose is gone in, clap your hands. It may be that noise will cure him, at least please him.*

[*Exeunt.*[1]

[1] Now we have gone through this celebrated poem of our author, it would be unjust not to take notice of the judgment passed upon it by a greater genius than Jonson, and one who fell very little short of him, or who was perhaps his equal, in critical abilities and learning. The genius I mean is Mr. Dryden ; whose just and great commendations of this play are such as the poet would have thought himself honoured in receiving, had he been then alive.—WHAL.

With all my respect for Dryden, whose critical examination of the *Silent Woman* is undoubtedly creditable to his talents, I cannot subscribe to this extravagant encomium. I do not believe that he was "a greater genius than Jonson ;" and I am quite sure that in "learning and critical abilities" he was not to be compared with him. Jonson was a most profound scholar, fixed in his sentiments, and uniform in his principles of criticism, which were drawn from the ancient masters. Dryden had merely the Greek and Latin of a clever schoolboy, derived his critical notions (principles he never possessed) from the French writers, and shifted them without care, as flattery or resentment occupied his mind. But to what he calls his "*Examen of the Silent Woman :*"

"To begin first with the length of the action ; it is so far from exceeding the compass of a natural day, that it takes not up an artificial one. It is all included in the limits of three hours and an half, which is no more than is required for the presentment on the stage : a beauty perhaps not much observed ; if it had we should not have looked on the Spanish translation of *Five Hours* with so much wonder. The scene of it is laid in London ; the latitude of place is almost as little as you can imagine ; for it lies all within the compass of two houses, and after the first act in one. The continuity of scenes is observed more than in any of our plays, except his own *Fox* and *Alchemist*. They are not broken above twice or thrice at most in the whole comedy ; and in the two best of Corneille's plays, the *Cid* and *Cinna*, they are interrupted once. The action of the play is entirely one ; the end or aim of which is the settling of Morose's estate on Dauphine. The intrigue of it is the greatest and most noble of any pure unmixed comedy in any language : you see in it many persons of various characters and humours, and all delightful. As first, Morose, or an old man, to whom all noise but his own talking is offensive. Some who would be thought critics say this humour of his is forced ; but to remove that objection, we may consider him first to be naturally of a delicate hearing, as many are to whom all sharp sounds are un-pleasant ; and secondly, we may attribute much of it to the peevishness of his age, or the wayward authority of an old man in his own house, where he may make himself obeyed ; and to this the poet seems to allude in his name Morose. Besides this, I am assured from divers persons, that Ben Jonson was actually acquainted with such a man, one altogether as ridiculous as he is here represented.

"Besides Morose, there are at least nine or ten different characters and humours in the *Silent Woman ;* all which persons have several concernments of their own, yet are all used by the poet to the conducting of the main design to perfection. I shall not waste time in commending the writing of this play ; but I will give you my opinion, that there is more wit and acuteness of fancy in it than in any of Ben Jonson's. Besides, that he has here described the conversation of gentlemen in the persons of Truewit and his friends with more gaiety, air, and freedom than in the rest of his comedies. For the contrivance of the plot, 'tis extreme elaborate, and yet withal easy ; for the λύσις, or untying of it, 'tis so admirable that when it is done no one of the audience would think the poet could have missed it ; and yet it was concealed so much before the last scene, that any other way would sooner have entered into your thoughts. But I dare not take upon me to commend the fabric of it, because it is altogether so full of art, that I must unravel every scene in it to commend it as I ought. And this excellent contrivance is still the more to be admired, because 'tis comedy where the persons are only of common rank and their business private, not elevated by passions or high concernments, as in serious plays. Here every one is a proper judge of all he sees ; nothing is represented but that with which he daily converses : so that by consequence all faults lie open to discovery, and few are pardonable. 'Tis this which Horace has judiciously observed :

Creditur, ex medio quia res arcessit, habere
Sudoris minimum ; sed habet Comedia tanto
Plus oneris, quanto veniæ minus.

"But our poet, who was not ignorant of these difficulties, has made use of all advantages ; as he who designs a large leap, takes his rise from the highest ground. One of these advantages is that which Corneille has laid down as the greatest which can arrive to any poem, and which he himself could never compass above thrice in all his plays ; viz., the making choice of some signal and long-expected day, whereon the action of the play is to depend. This day was that designed by Dauphine for the settling of his uncle's estate upon him : which to compass, he contrives to marry him. That the marriage had been plotted by him long before-hand, is made evident by what he tells Truewit in the second act, that in one moment he had destroyed what he had been raising many months.

"There is another artifice of the poet, which I cannot here omit, because by the frequent practice of it in his comedies he has left it to us almost as a rule; that is, when he has any character or humour wherein he would show a *coup de maître*, or his highest skill, he recommends it to your observation by a pleasant description of it before the person first appears. Thus in *Bartholomew Fair* he gives you the pictures of Numps and Cokes, and in this those of Daw, La-Foole, Morose, and the Collegiate Ladies; all which you hear described before you see them. So that before they come upon the stage you have a longing expectation of them, which prepares you to receive them favourably; and when they are there, even from their first appearance, you are so far acquainted with them, that nothing of their humour is lost to you.

"I will observe yet one thing further of this admirable plot; the business of it rises in every act. The second is greater than the first; the third than the second; and so forward to the fifth. There too you see, till the very last scene, new difficulties arising to obstruct the action of the play; and when the audience is brought into despair that the business can naturally be effected, then, and not before, the discovery is made. But that the poet might entertain you with more variety all this while, he reserves some new characters to show you, which he opens not till the second and third act. In the second, Morose, Daw, the Barber, and Otter; in the third, the Collegiate Ladies; all which he moves afterwards in bye-walks, or under-plots, as diversions to the main design, lest it should grow tedious, though they are still naturally joined with it, and somewhere or other subservient to it. Thus, like a skilful chess-player, by little and little he draws out his men, and makes his pawns of use to his greater persons."—*Essay on Dramatic Poesy;* Dryden's *Works,* vol. xv. p. 354.

It appears that Dryden, as well as the modern critics who have favoured us with their remarks on this play, was utterly ignorant of the source from which the character of Morose was derived. The poet's "actual acquaintance with such a man" is now placed upon certain grounds:—and those who accuse him of dealing in illiberal personalities, or extravagancies peculiar to himself, may if they please derive a lesson of forbearance from the instance in the text, and not eagerly press, as they always do, to decide every point against Jonson before the smallest part of the question has been examined. Not only the name of *Morose* (which Dryden seems to think so happily allusive), but the whole frame and contexture of his character, our poet found in Libanius. He has, however, rendered him far more natural and interesting than he appears in the sophist of Antioch, and thrown him into situations calculated, with admirable address, to place the peculiarities of his humour in the strongest light, and render them at once instructive and amusing.

It is somewhat singular that Dryden should dismiss the Collegiates with a bare mention. They merited more of his care. The comic stage cannot boast of more legitimate objects of satire: and while their profligacy is treated with unmixed severity, their absurd pretensions to literature are advanced with such serious mockery, ridiculed with such natural and easy dexterity, and exposed with such sarcastic and overwhelming contempt, that though we hear of some combinations of this kind about the period of the *Silent Woman's* appearance, no traces of them as here drawn are afterwards discoverable. "They vanished at the crowing of the cock."— Our days have witnessed an attempt to revive the Collegiates—but this was a water-suchy club, merely ridiculous; and so unsubstantial as not to require the clarion of the cock; but to "melt into thin air" at the twittering of a wren.

END OF VOL. I.

PRINTED BY
BALLANTYNE & COMPANY LTD
AT THE BALLANTYNE PRESS
TAVISTOCK STREET COVENT GARDEN
LONDON